Schroeder's Collectible TOYS Antique to Modern Price Guide

2008
ELEVENTH EDITION

Identification & Values
of Over 20,000
Collectible Toys

COLLECTOR BOOKS
A Division of Schroeder Publishing Co., Inc.

Front cover: Toonerville Trolley wind-up toy, 7½" tall, $485.00 (photo couresy James D. Julia). Erector set, MIB, $160.00. Partridge Family lunch box, $40.00 – $80.00, bottle, $15.00 – $30.00. Barbie, Goddess of the Sun (Bob Mackie series), 1995, from $135.00 to $150.00 (photo courtesy Lee Garmon). Snow White giant sand pail, 1930s Ohio Art, 10" tall, NM, $300.00 (photo courtesy David Longest and Michael Stern). Mohair bear on wooden wheeled bicycle pull toy, jointed, E, $2,750.00 (photo courtesy Morphy Auction). City Cab, Marx, friction, 7", EX+, $175.00. Flash Gordon Click Ray Pistol, Marx, 1930s $350.00. Star Wars Power of the Force Darth Vader with coin, 1984, MIB, $295.00.

Back cover: Marx Johnny Tremain Revolutionary War playset, $935.00. Rin Tin Tin Fort Apache playset, $5,500.00. Marx Wagon Train playset, $1,650.00. Fort Apache playset, $3,025.00. Marx The Alamo playset, $4,400.00.

Cover design by Beth Summers
Book design by Heather Carvell & Allan Ramsey
Editors: Donna Newnum and Loretta Suiters
Contributing Editor: Sharon Huxford
Editorial Assistant: Kimberly Vincent

Collector Books
P.O. Box 3009
Paducah, Kentucky 42002-3009

www.collectorbooks.com

The current values of this book should be used only as a guide. They are not intended to set prices, which vary from one section of the country to another. Auction prices as well as dealer prices vary greatly and are affected by condition as well as demand. Neither the editors nor the publisher assumes responsibility for any losses that might be incurred as a result of consulting this guide.

Searching for a Publisher?

We are always looking for knowledgeable people considered to be experts within their fields. If you feel that there is a real need for a book on your collectible subject and have a large comprehensive collection, contact Collector Books.

Introduction

#733 Mickey Mouse Safety Patrol, Fisher-Price, VG, $175.00. (Photo courtesy Serious Toyz)

The big news this year is that our book is in color! And we've added even more photographs than ever before! Toys themselves are all about color, and now we can show you just how beautiful some of the vintage lithographed tin toys can be, especially the battery-ops and windups made in Germany, Japan, and the United States from the 1930s through the 1950s and beyond. Many photos are of the spectacular higher-end toys that some of us seldom see. We're keeping up with today's trends and preferences, so you'll note that some categories where there is little interest have been omitted, while information on topics that today's collectors focus on the most have been expanded. With the help of our advisors, toy dealers, and many major auction houses, our goal is to provide our readers with fresh information issue after issue. The few categories that remain unchanged year after year are those that are as complete as we can make them, and the values are checked and rechecked for every new edition to make sure that all of our information is current. We've dropped the dealer codes that were used in past editions, since few if any toy dealers still put out catalogs. (Many of the country's top dealers are referenced in the Directory.) We hope you will enjoy our new look.

How the market has changed since our first edition! It continues to evolve as technological advances give both buyers and sellers more flexibility. Auction houses are now combining live auctions with the Internet. Some of the major auction houses have set up their own websites and are utilizing online auction sites such as eBay and LiveAuctioneers. This results in high prices for good toys, simply because these auctions have worldwide exposure. (If you opt to do your buying in this venue, it is important to note that depending on which auction site you deal with, from 15% to 25% will be added to the 'hammer' price.)

On the other hand, standard Internet auctions such as those on eBay are resulting in such a high volume of sales (many by sellers who have neglected to do even basic research), the market is literally flooded with toys. This is a venue that favors the buyer, and very often the one who exercises patience and diligence will be rewarded by winning a desirable item at a much lower price than usual. But there are still high shipping charges to reckon with, and condition, being relative, is sometimes hard to convey or grasp from a word description, as standards of the buyer compared to the seller often differ.

Shows are rebounding, not only here but abroad as well. 'European toy shows are picking up in both number and quality as evidenced in the twice-annual Paris Toy Show and numerous shows in England and Italy,' to quote our advisor Scott Smiles. Cindy Sabulis (our doll advisor and author of several books on dolls) reports that doll shows are picking up, 'as some collectors, including those who have previously been burnt by online purchases prefer to hold a doll in their hands before they buy it, rather than purchase one from online sources.' She goes on to say that 'there are some newer collectors who are just learning that there is such a thing as a doll show. At every show we do we meet new collectors attending for the first time who are discovering the joy of on-the-spot buying after learning of a show from an ad or an online listing.' This observation can apply not only to dolls but to any field. As prices began to sag from their high in the nineties, the number of toy shows declined. With that trend starting to reverse itsef, today's younger collectors are rediscovering the thrill a big toy show has to offer. The downside is that very often the dealers who sell directly may have higher prices on their merchandise, and in this transitional time frame (traditional selling vs. Interent) may be more attuned to the past rather than the present. Today, more than ever, the selling price of any toy in question is simply determined through bartering between buyer and seller.

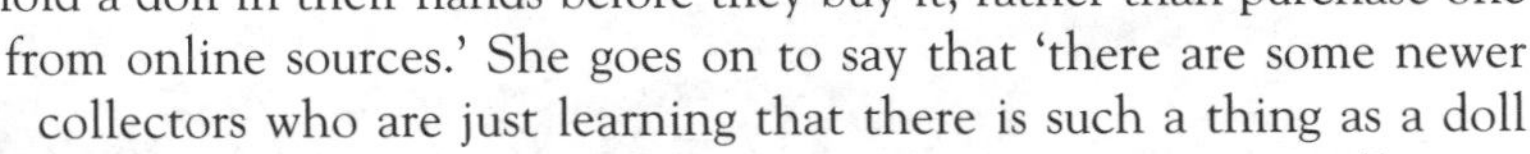

Yogi Bear, 1970s, from $75.00 to $125.00. (Photo courtesy Carole Bess White and L.M. White)

Tin toy mechanicals, in general, seem to be holding their own in value. The exception would be character toys such as Disney, Popeye, and comic characters, which continue to appreciate in value over time. Another area that continues to show price increases is toys from quality manufacturers, especially Lehmann, Martin, Marx, and Unique Art. Quoting Scott Smiles again, 'More and more collectors...indicate a willingness to purchase toys from these manufacturers because of *who* made them.' Themes that continue to be popular are space, robots, Western or cowboy/Indian, clowns, and amusement park or circus tin toys. Smiles notes that tin toys are 'becoming more of a newspaper item' in publications with sections on antiques that feature articles on special interests with photos and pricing.

Mystery Car, pressed steel, 10", EX, A, $800.00.
(Photo courtesy Morphy Auctions)

It goes without saying that it's the rare and excellent condition toys that continue to fetch the higher prices. Evenyone wants to own the best, and many are willing to pay well for the privilege. Because of the volume of merchandise that passes through Internet auctions on any given day, condition has become an even weightier worth-assessing factor than ever before. Dealers report that toys in played-with condition are slow to sell as collectors can locate better examples in a relatively short period of time. Unless priced reasonably, 'played-with' toys are passed by more often than not.

Banded Opaque, black with green bands, two pontils, gold mica center band, ¾", NM+, A, $250.00.
(Photo courtesy Morphy Auctions)

Looking ahead, our board of advisors agrees that the soft end of the market will firm up when the abundance of the more contemporary toys eventually diminishes. As new collectors seek the toys of their youth, many will gravitate to older or newer toys, expanding their collections in both directions outside the parameters of their memories. This folible of human nature will assure the future value of collectible toys.

Our advice: Continue to add high quality toys to your collection. There are some real bargains out there right now. Future values are impossible to predict, but if you buy what you like in the best condition you can afford, your collections will continue to appreciate over the long term.

Our suggested values in most cases are prices realized at auction (buyer's premium included; postage if it is charged) and should be regarded simply as a starting point for the transaction. There are two main factors determining selling price: the attitude of the individual collector (how strongly he desires to own) and the motivation of the dealer (does he need to turn over his merchandise quickly to replenish and freshen his stock, or can

Dracula Mystery Game, Hasbro, 1962, EXIB, A, $75.00.
(Photo courtesy serioustoyz.com)

he wait for the most opportune time to turn it over for maximum profit). Where you buy affects prices as well. One of our advisors used this simple analogy: while a soda might cost you $2.50 at the ball park, you can buy the same thing for 39¢ at the corner 711. So all we (or anyone) can offer is whatever facts and information we can compile, and ask simply that you arrive at your own evaluations based on the data we've provided, adapted to your personal buying/selling arena.

We hope you enjoy our book and that you'll be able to learn by using it. We don't presume to present it as the last word on toys or their values — there are many specialized books by authors who are able to devote an entire publication to one subject, covering it from 'A' to 'Z,' and when we're aware that such a book exists, we'll recommend it in our narratives.

Pals and Pets, Saalfield #2612, 1952, $35.00.
(Photo courtesy Mary Young)

How to Use This Book

Concept. This book is a market report compiled from many sources, meant to be studied and digested by our readers, who can then better arrive at their own conclusion regarding prices. Were you to ask 10 active toy dealers for their opinion as to the value of a specific toy, you would no doubt get 10 different answers, and who's to say which is correct? Quite simply, there are too many variables to consider. Where you buy is critical. Condition is certainly subjective, prices vary from one area of the country to another, and probably the most important factor is how badly you want to add the item in question to your collection or at what price you're willing to sell. So use this as a guide along with your own observations.

The Directory contains names and addresses of our advisors; feel free to contact them. If you're looking for an appraisal, some may charge a fee. Be sure to ask. If you would like a reply, be sure to send an SASE with your mailing. There is also a section on Clubs, Newsletters, and Other Publications devoted to specific areas of toy collecting.

Toys are listed by name. Every effort has been made to list a toy by the name as it appears on the toy itself or on the original box. There have been very few exceptions made, and then only if the collector-given name is more recognizable. For instance, if we listed 'To-Night Amos 'n' Andy in Person' (as the name appears on the box), few would recognize the toy as the Amos 'n' Andy Walkers. But these exceptions are few. Sizes may have been rounded off to the next inch on some of the larger items.

Source of our suggested values. An 'A' at the end of the line description indicates a price realized at auction. Some categories, such as Cast Iron, will include pre-auction estimates in parenthesis after the 'A.' If our advisor determines that an auction value is out of line (due to 'auction fever,' etc.), he may change the price. If this is the case, the 'A' and the estimate will have been removed. Our advisors as well as most collectors have various viewpoints regarding auction results. Some feel they're too high to be used to establish prices while others prefer them to 'asking' prices that can sometimes be speculative. You'll have to make that call yourself. Because the average auction-consigned toy is in especially good condition and many times even retains its original box, it will naturally bring higher prices than the norm. And auctions often offer the harder-to-find, more unusual items. Unless you take these factors into consideration, prices may seem high, when in fact, they may not be at all. Some fear that prices may be driven up by high reserves, but not all galleries have reserves. For the most part, we find auction prices to be farily stable from year to year, allowing for natural appreciation and fluxation in the marketplace.

Categories that have priority. Obviously there are thousands of toys that would work as well in one category as they would in another, depending on the preference of the collector. For instance, a Mary Poppins game would appeal to a games collector just as readily as it would to someone who bought character-related toys of all kinds. The same would be true of many other types of toys. We tried to make our decisions sensibly and keep our sorts simple. We'll guide you to those specialized categories with cross-references and 'see alsos.' If all else fails, refer to the index. It's as detailed as we know how to make it.

Price ranges. Once in awhile, you'll find a listing that gives a price range. These result from our having found varying prices for the same item. We've taken a mid-range — less than the highest, a little over the lowest, if the actual difference in the selling prices was too wide to really be helpful. If the range is still coded 'A' for auction, all that were averaged were auction prices.

Condition – how it affects value, how to judge it. The importance of condition can't be stressed enough. Unless a toy is exceptionally rare, it must be excellent or better to really have much collector value. But here's where the problem comes in: though each step downward on the grading scale drastically decreases a toy's value, as the old saying goes, 'beauty is in the eye of the beholder.' What is acceptable wear and damage to one individual may be regarded by another as entirely too degrading. Criteria used to judge condition even varies from one auction company to the next, so we had to attempt to sort them all out and arrive at some sort of standardization. Please be sure to read and comprehend what our description is telling you about condition; otherwise you can easily be mislead. Auction galleries often describe missing parts, repairs, and paint touch-ups, summing up overall appearance in the condition code. Remember that a toy, even in mint restored condition, still isn't worth as much as one in mint original condition. And even though a toy may be rated 'otherwise EX' after losses and repairs are noted, it won't be worth as much as one with original paint and parts in excellent condition. Keep this in mind when you use our listings.

These are the conditions codes we have used throughout the book and their definitions as we have applied them:

M — mint. Unplayed with, brand new, flawless.
NM — near mint. Appears brand new except on very close inspection.
EX — excellent. Has minimal wear, very minor chips and rubs, a few light scratches.
VG — very good. Played with, loss of gloss, noticeable problems, several scratches.
G — good. Some rust, considerable wear and paint loss, well used.
P — poor. Generally unacceptable except for a filler.

Because we do not use a three-level pricing structure as many of you are used to and may prefer, we offer this table to help you arrive at values for toys in conditions other than those that we give you. If you know the value of a toy in excellent condition and would like to find an approximate value for it in near mint condition, for instance, just run your finger down the column under 'EX' until you find the approximate price we've listed (or one that easily factors into it), then over to the column headed 'NM.' We'll just go to $100.00, but other values will be easy to figure by addition or multiplication.

G	VG	EX	NM	M
40/50%	55/65%	70/80%	85/90%	100%
5.00	6.00	7.50	9.00	10.00
7.50	9.00	11.00	12.50	15.00
10.00	12.00	15.00	18.00	20.00
12.00	15.00	18.00	22.00	25.00
14.00	18.00	22.50	26.00	30.00
18.00	25.00	30.00	35.00	40.00
22.50	30.00	37.50	45.00	50.00
27.00	35.00	45.00	52.00	60.00
32.00	42.00	52.00	62.00	70.00
34.00	45.00	55.00	65.00	75.00
35.00	48.00	60.00	70.00	80.00
40.00	55.00	68.00	80.00	90.00
45.00	60.00	75.00	90.00	100.00

Condition and value of original boxes and packaging. When no box or packaging is referred to in the line or in the narrative, assume that the quoted price is for the toy only. Please read the narratives! In some categories (Corgi, for instance), all values are given for items mint and in original boxes. When the box is present, condition codes (for example: 'EXIB' or 'MIB') will be relevant to both toy and box. If a box is less than excellent, the condition of the box alone will be in parenthesis immediately following the condition code for the toy itself. Collector interest in original boxes, cards, and packaging began several years ago, and today many people will pay very high prices for them, depending on scarcity, desirability, and condition. The more colorful, graphically pleasing boxes are favored, and those with images of well-known characters are especially sought after. Just how valuable is a box? Again, this is very subjective to the individual. We posed the question to several top collectors around the country, and the answers they gave ranged from 20% to 100% above mint-no-box prices.

Tarzan A Game by Edgar Rice Burroughs, Parker Brothers, EXIB, A, $450.00. (Photo courtesy Morphy Auctions)

Listing of Standard Abbreviations

These abbreviations have been used throughout this book in order to provide you with the most detailed descriptions possible in our limited space. No periods are used after initials or abbreviations. When two dimensions are given, height is noted first. When only one measurement is given, it will be the greater — height if the toy is vertical, length if it is horizontal. (Remember that in the case of duplicate listings representing various conditions, we found that sizes often varied as much as an inch or more.)

att .... attributed to
bkgrd .... background
bl .... blue
blk .... black
b/o .... battery-operated
brn .... brown
BRT .... black rubber tires
c .... copyright
ca .... circa
cb .... cardboard
CI .... cast iron
compo .... composition
dbl .... double
dk .... dark
emb .... embossed
EX .... excellent
EXIB .... excellent in box
EXIC .... excellent in container
EXIP .... excellent in package
ft, ftd .... feet, foot, footed
G .... good
GIB .... good in box
gr .... green
hdl .... handle, handled
illus .... illustrated, illustration
inscr .... inscribed
jtd .... jointed
L .... long, length
litho .... lithographed
lt .... light, lightly
M .... mint
MB .... minimum bid
MBP .... mint in bubble pack
mc .... multicolored
MDW .... metal disk wheels
Mfg .... Manufacturing
MIB .... mint in box
MIP .... mint in package
mk .... marked
MOC .... mint on card
MOT .... mint on tree
MSW .... metal spoke wheels
NM .... near mint
NOS .... new old stock
NP .... nickel plated
NPDW .... nickel-plated disk wheels
NPP .... National Periodicals Publications
NPSW .... nickel-plated spoke wheels
NRFB .... never removed from box
NRFP .... never removed from package
orig .... original
o/w .... otherwise
P .... poor
pk .... pink
pkg .... package
PMDW .... painted metal disk wheels
pnt .... paint, painted
pr .... pair
Prod .... Products, Productions
prof .... professional
PS .... pressed steel
r/c .... remote control
rnd .... round
rpl .... replaced
rpr .... repaired
rpt .... repainted
rstr .... restored
sgn .... signed
sz .... size
turq .... turquoise
unmk .... unmarked
unpt .... unpainted
VG .... very good
VGIB .... very good in box
W .... width
WDE .... Walt Disney Enterprises
WDP .... Walt Disney Productions
wht .... white
WRT .... white rubber tires
WS .... wingspan
WWT .... whitewall tires
w/ .... with
w/up .... windup
yel .... yellow

A.C. Gilbert

The A.C. Gilbert Company, best known for the Erector set, also marketed various types of scientific activity sets, magic sets, and games. Gilbert started producing the Erector set in 1913. Over the years, collectors have divided the sets into three basic categories: Type I sets include the years 1913 to 1923, Type II from 1924 to 1962, and Type III from 1963 to 1988. Each type consists of a major revamping of parts. Although the A.C. Gilbert Company was sold in 1961 to the Jack Wrather Group, the Gilbert name was used until 1976.

The following listings are auction results with estimates given for comparison.

For more information, refer to Clubs, Newsletters, and Other Publications in the back of this guide.

Air-Kraft Set, #A103, 1919, complete, cb box, VG, A (Est: $2,000-$4,000) $1,800.00

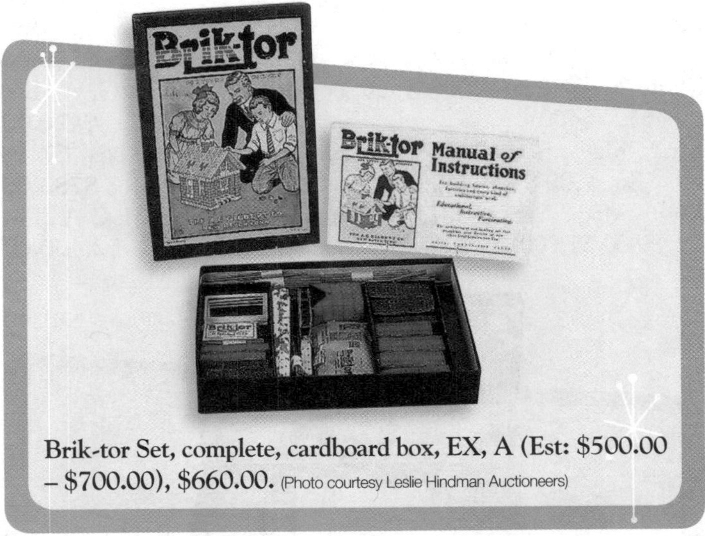

Brik-tor Set, complete, cardboard box, EX, A (Est: $500.00 – $700.00), $660.00. (Photo courtesy Leslie Hindman Auctioneers)

Carpenter's Outfit, #6325, complete, cb box, VG, A (Est: $300-$500) $180.00

Carpentry Set, #780, 1920s, complete, wood box, EX, A (Est: $500-$700) $1,020.00

Chemical Magic Set, #2022, 1922, complete, VG, A (Est: $200-$400) $2,280.00

Chemistry Set, #12065, complete & unused, folding cb box w/cb shipping carton, VG, A (Est: $500-$700) $360.00

Designer & Toy Maker Set, 1920s, incomplete, cb box, VG, A (Est: $200-$400) $132.00

Electric Toys & Tricks Set, #3003, complete, cb box, EX, A (Est: $400-$600) $540.00

Electrical Set, #3002, 1920s, complete, cb box, EX, A (Est: $500-$700) $480.00

Electrical Set, #3003, 1916, complete, cb box w/orig insert, EX, A (Est: $400-$600) $1,320.00

Electrical Set, #3005, 1920s, New Erector..., complete, cb box, EX, A (Est: $350-$450) $420.00

Erector Set, #A, 1927, complete, cb box w/cb insert, EX, A (Est: $1,200-$1,800) $1,400.00

Erector Set, #A, 1931, Locomotive, complete, red wood box, orig wood dividers & insert, VG+, A (Est: $3,000-$5,000). $2,400.00

Erector Set, #B, 1929, Accessory Set, complete, red wood box, 3 repro wood insert boxes, VG+, A (Est: $700-$900) . $900.00

Erector Set, #S, 1935, Skyscraper Set, complete, red cb box w/orig inserts, VG+, A (Est: $1,000-$1,500) $1,140.00

Erector Set, #2 A, 1918, complete, cb box w/orig cb insert, EX, A (Est: $100-$200) $120.00

Erector Set, #4, 1922, complete, blk wood box w/cb top, red cb tray, EX, A (Est: $500-$700) $360.00

Erector Set, #4, 1924-33, complete, red cb box w/cb inserts, VG, A (Est: $250-$350) $156.00

Erector Set, #4½, 1938, complete & unused, red cb box w/orig insert, EX, A (Est: $400-$600) $480.00

Erector Set, #4½, 1941-42, complete & unused, red cb box w/ inserts, VG, A (Est: $200-$400) $120.00

Erector Set, #6, 1914, Mysto, complete, wood box, EX, A (Est: $500-$700) $1,020.00

Erector Set, #6, 1915, complete, wood box, wood dividers, EX, A (Est: $300-$500) $215.00

Erector Set, #6, 1933, complete, gr metal box w/orig cb insert, VG, A (Est: $300-$500) $180.00

Erector Set, #6, 1950, Whistle Kit, complete, red cb box, EX, A (Est: $300-$400) $228.00

Erector Set, #7, 1915, complete, wood box, wood dividers, VG, A (Est: $600-$800) $840.00

Erector Set, #7, 1923, complete, stained wood box w/red cb insert, VG+, A (Est: $700-$900) $1,440.00

Erector Set, #7, 1928, Steam Shovel, complete, wood box w/ repro cb inserts, VG, A (Est: $150-$250) $108.00

Erector Set, #7, 1931, Steam Shovel, complete, red wood box, G+, A (Est: $250-$350) $330.00

Erector Set, #7, 1934, complete, red metal box w/orig cb inserts, VG+, A (Est: $700-$900) $780.00

Erector Set, #7½, 1926, complete, wood box, orig wood dividers, VG+, A (Est: $5,000-$7,000) $4,320.00

Erector Set, #7½, 1929, White Truck Set, complete, red wood box, repro cb inserts, VG+, A (Est: $350-$450) $450.00

Erector Set, #7½, 1934, complete, bl-gr metal box, VG, A (Est: $600-$800) $575.00

Erector Set, #7½, 1946, complete, bl cb w/orig cb inserts & trays, EX, A (Est: $300-$500) $240.00

Erector Set, #8, 1915, complete, stained wood box w/wood inserts, VG+, A (Est: $1,000-$2,000) $960.00

Erector Set, #8, 1925, complete, wood box w/repro wood dividers, cb display insert, VG+, A (Est: $2,000-$4,000) $1,560.00

Erector Set, #8, 1925, near complete, wood box, VG+, A (Est: $2,000-$4,000) $1,560.00

Erector Set, #8, 1929, Zeppelin (Trail Blazing), complete, red wood box w/blk cb insert, EX, A (Est: $2,500-$3,500) $3,120.00

Erector Set, #8½, 1935, Automotive, complete, bl metal box, EX, A (Est: $600-$800) $720.00

Erector Set, #10, Junior Erector, complete, unused, yel cb box, EX, A (Est: $300-$500) $270.00

Erector Set, #10½, 1937, complete, bl-gr metal, EX, A (Est: $2,500-$3,500) $2,880.00

Erector Set, #10½, 1941, Electric Train Set, complete, bl metal box, perforated insert, VG, A (Est: $1,000-$1,500) $1,440.00

Erector Set, #10 ½, 1951, Amusement Park, complete, red metal box, repro cb inserts, EX, A (Est: $250-$350)........... $300.00

Erector Set, #12 ½, 1949, Walking Giant, Remote Control, complete, red metal box, VG+, A (Est: $1,500-$2,500)....$1,152.00

Erector Set, #15, Senior Wheels Machineray, incomplete, cb box, G, A (Est: $900-$1,200)................................ $540.00

Erector Set, #44, 1918-19, Master Engineer's set, complete, wood box w/orig cb, very rare, EX, A (Est: $800-$1,200)...........$1,200.00

Erector Set, #77, 1928, Steam Shovel, complete, red wood box, VG, A (Est: $250-$350).. $156.00

Erector Set, #10021, Young Builders, complete, cb tube container, EX, A (Est: $80-$120)................................ $108.00

Erector Set, #10032, 1960, Engineer's Set, complete, cb tube container, VG, A (Est: $80-$120)..............................$50.00

Erector Set, #10053, 1959, 50th Anniversary, complete, cb box, EX, A (Est: $50-$75)..$50.00

Erector Set, #10072, 1958, Musical Ferris Wheel, complete & unused, red cb box, EX, A (Est: $600-$800)........... $360.00

Erector Set, #10083, 1959, Amusement Park, complete, red metal box, VG+, A (Est: $900-$1,200) $672.00

Erector Set, #10092, 1958, Walking Robot, complete, red metal box, cardboard insert, EX, A (Est: $1,500.00 – $2,500.00), $2,280.00. (Photo courtesy Leslie Hindman Auctioneers)

Glass Blowing Set, #2, complete, cb box, EX, A (Est: $400-$600).. $420.00

Kaster Kit Jr Set, #3, 1933, complete, red cb box, EX, A (Est: $250-$350) $390.00

Light Experiments, 1920s, incomplete, blk cb box, VG, A (Est: $250-$350) $780.00

Light Experiments Set, ca 1915, complete, wood box, EX, A (Est: $1,200-$1,800).. $2,880.00

Magnetic Fun & Facts Set, #2, complete, cb box, EX, A (Est: $80-$120) $240.00

Magnetic Fun & Facts Set, #5606, complete, cb box, VG+, A, (Est: $100-$150).. $270.00

Magnetic Fun & Facts Set, #6507, 1920s, complete, wood box, VG+, A (Est: $1,000-$1,500) $2,040.00

Meteor Game, #1053, 1920, complete, cb box w/inserts, EX, A (Est: $80-$120)..$96.00

Microscope Set, #8, complete, cb box, orig tissue paper, EX, A (Est: $300-$500).. $180.00

Mineralogy Set, #2, 1920s, complete & unused, cb box, VG+, A (Est: $300-$500)... $510.00

Mysto Magic Set, #2½, complete, cb box, EX, A (Est: $100-$200).. $180.00

Mysto Magic Set, #3, 1938, complete, cb box, EX, A (Est: $300-$400).. $300.00

Mysto Magic Set, #3 A, 1933, complete, cb box, VG, A (Est: $300-$400) $480.00

Mysto Magic Set, #5, 1933, complete, red metal box, EX, A (Est: $600-$800) $720.00

Mysto Magic Set, #6, 1952, complete, cb box, EX, A (Est: $1,000-$1,500) $840.00

Mysto Magic Set, #20, 1950, complete, cb box, EX, A (Est: $2,000-$3,000) $2,280.00

Mysto Magic Set, #25, complete, red fabric-covered hinged box, EX, A (Est: $2,000-$3,000)..................................$2,640.00

Mysto Magic Set, #2002, 1917, complete, cb box, VG, A (Est: $75-$125) $84.00

Mysto Magic Set, #2003, 1920, complete, cb box, EX, A (Est: $100-$200) $300.00

Mysto Magic Set, #2006, 1923, complete, wood box, EX, A (Est: $600-$800) $540.00

Mysto Magic Set, #2006, 1925, complete, cb box, VG, A (Est: $300-$500) $420.00

Mysto Magic Set, #2007, 1929, complete, red wood box, EX, A (Est: $200-$400).. $780.00

Mysto Magic Set, #2007, 1932, complete, cb box, EX, A (Est: $800-$1,200) $2,400.00

Nurse's Outfit for Girls, 1918, complete, black cardboard box with labels, VG+, A (Est: $1,000.00 – $1,500.00), $1,920.00. (Photo courtesy Leslie Hindman Auctioneers)

Opto Kit, #6, complete & unused, red cb box w/inserts, EX, A (Est: $400-$600).. $420.00

Pak O' Fun Moovy Sho, complete, cb box, VG, A (Est: $300-$500).. $570.00

Phono Set, #3505, 1918-1921, complete, cb box, VG+, A (Est: $500-$700) $1,680.00

Problem Puzzles, #1034, complete, cb box, VG, A (Est: $30-$50)..$60.00

Puzzles Set, #1033, complete & unused, cb box, EX, A (Est: $60-$80)..$84.00

Ring Toss Set, 1930s, complete, cb box, EX, A (Est: $50-$75) $200.00

Swinging Aeroplane Set C, 1919, complete, cb box, VG+, A (Est: $2,000-$4,000) $2,640.00
Swinging Clown, #B677, 1920s, complete, cb box, VG, A (Est: $200-$400), A $300.00
Tele-Set, #3502, 1922, complete, cb box, EX, A (Est: $350-$450) $240.00

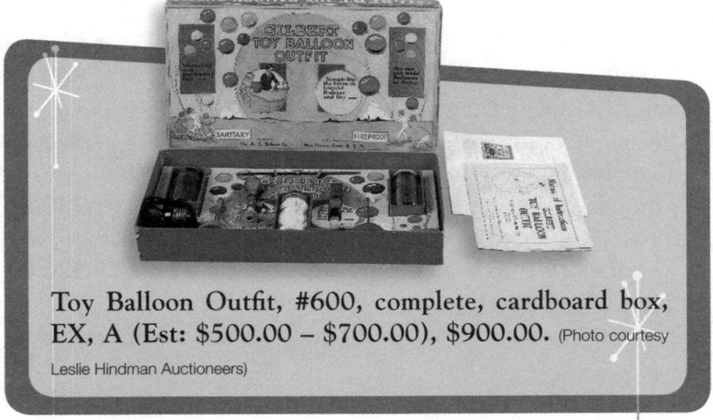

Toy Balloon Outfit, #600, complete, cardboard box, EX, A (Est: $500.00 – $700.00), $900.00. (Photo courtesy Leslie Hindman Auctioneers)

Tubular Toy Set, 1937-38, complete, EX, A (Est: $250-$350) $192.00
Weather Bureau Set, #6533, 1920, complete, cb box, VG+, A (Est: $1,500-$2,500) $3,120.00
Wireless Telegraph Outfit, 1920, complete, cb box, G+, A (Est: $300-$400) $840.00

Action Figures

You will find a wide range of asking prices from dealer to dealer, and under the influence of the Internet, prices fluctuate greatly. Be critical of condition! Original packaging is extremely important. In fact, when it comes to recent issues, loose, played-with examples are seldom worth more than a few dollars. When no size is given, assume figures are 3¾" or standard size for that line. Listings for 'loose' figures that come with accessories are complete unless noted otherwise.

See also Character, TV, and Movie Collectibles; Dolls, Celebrity; GI Joe; Star Trek; Star Wars.

A-Team, accessory, Combat Headquarters (w/4 figures), Galoob, MIB, from $70 to $80.00
A-Team, accessory, Command Chopper & Enforcer Van, MIP, from $20 to $25.00
A-Team, accessory, Corvette (w/Face figure), Galoob, M, from $30 to $35.00
A-Team, accessory, Interceptor Jet Bomber (w/Murdock figure), Galoob, MIP, from $50 to $55.00
A-Team, accessory, Off Road Attack Cycle, Galoob, MIP, from $20 to $25.00
A-Team, accessory, Patrol Boat (w/Hannibal figure), Galoob, MIB, from $25 to $30.00
A-Team, accessory, van w/removable roof, Galoob, M, from $35 to $45.00
A-Team, figure, 3¾", Bad Guys, set of 4 (Cobra, Python, Rattler & Viper), Galoob, MOC (all on 1 card), from $50 to $60.00
A-Team, figure, 3¾", Soldiers of Fortune, set of 4, Galoob, MOC (all on 1 card), from $50..........$60.00
A-Team, figure, 6½", Amy Allen, MOC, from $55 to $65.00
A-Team, figure, 6½", Bad Guys, any character, Galoob, MOC, ea from $18.00 to $26.00
A-Team, figure, 6½", Soldiers of Fortune, any character, Galoob, MOC, ea from $28 to $38.00
A-Team, figure, 12", Mr T, nontalking, Galoob, MIB, from $50 to $60.00
A-Team, figure, 12", Mr T, talking, Galoob, MIB, from $65 to.$75.00
Action Jackson, accessory, Campmobile, Mego, MIB..........$75.00
Action Jackson, accessory, Fire Rescue Pack or Parachute Plunge, Mego, MIB, ea from $12 to $18.00
Action Jackson, accessory, Jungle House, Mego, MIB..........$75.00
Action Jackson, accessory, Scramble Cycle, Mego, MIB...$45.00
Action Jackson, accessory, Strap-On Helicopter, Mego, MIB, from $12 to $18.00
Action Jackson, accessory, Water Skooter, Mego, NRFB, from $12 to..........$18.00
Action Jackson, figure, any color hair or beard except blk figure, Mego, MIB, ea from $25 to $30.00
Action Jackson, figure, blk, Mego, MIB, from $35 to $40.00
Action Jackson, outfit, any, Mego, MIP, ea from $8 to $12.00
Adventures of Indiana Jones, see Indiana Jones (Adventures of)
Alien, figure, Alien, 18", Kenner, M, from $175 to $200.00
Alien, figure, Alien, 18", Kenner, MIB, from $475 to..... $500.00
Aliens, accessory, Evac Fighter or Hovertread, Kenner, MIP, from $15 to..........$20.00
Aliens, accessory, Power Loader or Stinger XT-37, Kenner, MIP, ea from $15 to..........$20.00

Aliens, figure, Ripley, Kenner, MOC, from $15.00 to $20.00.

Aliens, figure, Series 1, Apone, Bishop, Bull Alien, Drake, Gorilla Alien or Hicks, Kenner, MOC, ea from $8 to..........$10.00
Aliens, figure, Series 1, Queen Alien, Ripley or Scorpion Alien, Kenner, MOC, ea from $15 to $20.00

Aliens, figure, Series 2, Flying Queen Alien, Queen Face Hugger or Snake Alien, Kenner, MOC, ea from $12 to..........$16.00
Aliens, figure, Series 3, Arachnid Alien, Clan Leader Predator, King Alien or Swarm Alien, Kenner, MOC, ea from $18 to $22.00
Aliens, figure, Series 3, Atax, Cracked Tusk Predator, Kill Krab or Lava Predator, Kenner, MOC, ea from $10 to........$15.00
Aliens, figure, Series 3, Mantis Alien, Night Cougar Alien or Night Storm Predator, Kenner, MOC, ea from $10 to..$15.00
Aliens, figure, Series 3, Panther, Rhino, Spiked Tail, Stalker or Wild Boar, Kenner, MOC, ea from $10 to..........$15.00
Aliens, figure set, Series 2, Alien vs Predator, Kenner, MOC, from $28 to $32.00
American West, figure, Buffalo Bill Cody or Cochise, Mego, MIB, ea from $65 to..........$75.00
American West, figure, Buffalo Bill Cody or Cochise, Mego, MOC, from $80 to..........$90.00
American West, figure, Davy Crockett, Mego, MIB, from $90 to $100.00
American West, figure, Davy Crockett, Mego, MOC, from $125 to..........$135.00
American West, figure, Shadow (horse), Mego, MIB, from $125 to..........$135.00
American West, figure, Sitting Bull, Wild Bill Hickok or Wyatt Earp, Mego, MIB, ea from $70 to..........$80.00
American West, figure, Sitting Bull, Wild Bill Hickok or Wyatt Earp, Mego, MOC, ea from $100 to..........$125.00
American West, figure, Wild Bill Hickok or Wyatt Earp, Mego, MIB, ea from $65 to..........$75.00
American West, playset, Dodge City, Mego, MIB, from $150 to $175.00

ANTZ, figure, Colonel Cutter, Playmates, 1998, MOC, from $3.00 to $5.00.

ANTZ, figure, any, Playmates, 1998, MOC, ea from $3 to..$5.00
Archies, figure, any, Marx, 1975, MOC, ea from $65 to....$75.00
Avengers, figure gift sets, Ant-Man/Giant Man, Hulk, Iron Man, The Wasp, Toy Biz, MOC, ea from $18 to..........$22.00
Avengers, figures, any character from any series, Toy Biz, MOC, from $6 to $10.00
Banana Splits, figure, any, Sutton, 1970s, MIP, ea from $120 to..........$130.00

Batgirl, figure, 8", Batgirl, Mego, MOC, from $290 to.... $310.00
Batman, see also Captain Action, Comic Action Heroes, Pocket Super Heroes, Super Heroes or Super Powers
Batman (Animated), accessory, Aero Boat, BATV Vehicle, Batcycle or Bat-Signal Jet, Kenner, 1992-95, MIP, ea from $18 to..........$32.00
Batman (Animated), accessory, Batcave, Kenner, MIP, from $100 to..........$130.00
Batman (Animated), accessory, Batmobile, Kenner, MIP, from $50 to..........$60.00
Batman (Animated), accessory, Crime Stalker, Hoverboat, Ice Hammer or Joker Mobile, Kenner, MIP, ea from $12 to.$18.00
Batman (Animated), accessory, Robin's Dragster, Kenner, MIP, from $200 to $230.00
Batman (Animated), accessory, Street Jet or Turbo Batplane, Kenner, MIP, ea from $18 to..........$26.00
Batman (Animated), figure, Anti-Freeze, Bane, Bruce Wayne, Ground Assault or Infrared Batman, Kenner, MOC, ea from $8 to..........$12.00
Batman (Animated), figure, Battle Helmet Batman, High-Wire Batman or Poison Ivy, Kenner, MOC, ea from $28 to.$35.00
Batman (Animated), figure, Bola Trap Robin or Sky Dive Batman, Kenner, MOC, ea from $8 to..........$12.00
Batman (Animated), figure, Catwoman, Radar Scope Batman or Rapid Attack Batman, Kenner, MOC, ea from $22 to.$26.00
Batman (Animated), figure, Combat Belt Batman, Kenner, MOC, from $28 to..........$35.00
Batman (Animated), figure, Knight Star Batman, Lightning Strike Batman or Mech-Wing Batman, Kenner, MOC, ea from $8 to $12.00
Batman (Animated), figure, Man-Bat, Kenner, MOC, from $12 to..........$16.00
Batman (Animated), figure, Penguin, Kenner, MOC, from $45 to..........$50.00
Batman (Animated), figure, Riddler, Tornado Batman or Two Face, Kenner, MOC, ea from $22 to..........$26.00
Batman (Animated), figure set, Ninja Batman & Robin, Kenner, MOC, from $18 to..........$22.00
Batman (Crime Squad), accessory, Attack Jet, Kenner, MOC, from $18 to $22.00

Batman (Crime Squad), figure, Ski Blast Robin, Kenner, MOC, each from $8.00 to $12.00.

Batman (Crime Squad), figure, any character, Kenner, MOC, ea from $8 to $12.00
Batman (Dark Knight), accessory, Batcycle, Kenner, MIP, ea from $35 to $45.00
Batman (Dark Knight), accessory, Batjet, Kenner, MIP, from $45 to $50.00
Batman (Dark Knight), accessory, Batmobile, Kenner, MIP, from $75 to $85.00
Batman (Dark Knight), accessory, Batwing, Kenner, MIP, from $50 to $60.00
Batman (Dark Knight), accessory, Bola Bullet, Kenner, MIP, from $30 to $40.00
Batman (Dark Knight), accessory, Joker Cycle, Kenner, MIP, from $12 to $18.00
Batman (Dark Knight), figure, Blast Shield, Claw Climber, Power Wing, Thunder Whip, Kenner, MOC, ea from $20 to $30.00
Batman (Dark Knight), figure, Bruce Wayne, Kenner, MOC, from $18 to $22.00
Batman (Dark Knight), figure, Crime Attack, Iron Winch, Shadow Wing or Wall Scaler, Kenner, MOC, ea from $18 to $22.00
Batman (Dark Knight), figure, Knockout Joker, Kenner, MOC, from $45 to $55.00
Batman (Dark Knight), figure, Night Glider, Kenner, MOC, from $30 to $40.00
Batman (Dark Knight), figure, Sky Escape Joker, Kenner, MOC, from $22 to $28.00
Batman (Movie), accessory, Batcave Master Playset, Toy Biz, MIB, from $65 to $75.00
Batman (Movie), accessory, Batmobile (Turbine Sound), Toy Biz, MIB, from $25 to $30.00
Batman (Movie), accessory, Joker Cycle (Detachable Launching Sidecar), Toy Biz, MIB, from $20 to....$25.00
Batman (Movie), figure, Batman (any except sq jaw), Toy Biz, MOC, ea from $10 to $15.00
Batman (Movie), figure, Batman (sq jaw), Toy Biz, MOC, from $18 to $22.00
Batman (Movie), figure, Bob (Joker's Goon), Toy Biz, MOC, from $20 to $25.00
Batman (Movie), figure, Joker (hair curl), Toy Biz, MOC, from $20 to $25.00
Batman (Movie), figure, Joker (Squirting Orchid), Toy Biz, MOC, from $18 to....$22.00
Batman & Robin, accessory, Batgirl's Icestrike Cycle, Kenner, MIP, from $15 to....$20.00
Batman & Robin, accessory, Batmobile, Batmobile (Sonic) or Ice Hammer, Kenner, MIP, ea from $18 to....$22.00
Batman & Robin, accessory, Ice Fortress, Kenner, MIP, from $8 to $12.00
Batman & Robin, accessory, Ieeglow Bathammer, Kenner, MIP, from $45 to $55.00
Batman & Robin, accessory, Jet Blade, Kenner, MIP, from $18 to $22.00
Batman & Robin, accessory, Nightsphere, Kenner, MIP, from $20 to....$30.00
Batman & Robin, accessory, Wayne Manor Batcave, Kenner, MIP, from $45 to....$55.00
Batman & Robin, figure, 5", Bane, Batman (Ambush Attack or Batman (Battle Board w/Ring), Kenner, ea from $6 to..$10.00
Batman & Robin, figure, 5", Batgirl, Kenner, MIP, from $4 to $6.00
Batman & Robin, figure, 5", Batgirl w/Icestrike Cycle, Kenner, Deluxe, MIP, from $18 to $22.00
Batman & Robin, figure, 5", Batman, Kenner, Deluxe, MIP, from $10 to $12.00
Batman & Robin, figure, 5", Batman (Aerial Combat), Kenner, Series 1, MIP, from $18 to $22.00
Batman & Robin, figure, 5", Batman (Blast Wing), Batman (Rooftop Pursuit), Kenner, Deluxe, MIP, ea from $8 to....$10.00
Batman & Robin, figure, 5", Batman (Heat Scan), Batman (Hover Attack), Batman (Ice Blade), Kenner, MIP, ea from $6 to $10.00
Batman & Robin, figure, 5", Batman (Ice Blade & Ring), Kenner, MIB, from $6 to....$10.00
Batman & Robin, figure, 5", Batman (Laser Cape & Ring), Kenner, MIP, from $6 to....$10.00
Batman & Robin, figure, 5", Batman (Neon Armor & Ring), Batman (Rotoblade & Ring), Kenner, MIP, ea from $6 to $10.00
Batman & Robin, figure, 5", Batman (Neon Armor), Batman (Snow Tracker), Kenner, MIP, ea from $6 to $10.00
Batman & Robin, figure, 5", Batman (Sky Assault & Ring), Batman (Thermal Shield & Ring), Kenner, MIP, ea from $10 to $12.00
Batman & Robin, figure, 5", Batman (Snow Tracker), Batman (Wing Blast), Kenner, MIP, ea from $6 to $10.00
Batman & Robin, figure, 5", Bruce Wayne (Battle Gear) or Frostbite, Kenner, MIP, ea from $6 to $10.00
Batman & Robin, figure, 5", Jungle Venom Poison Ivy, Robin (Iceboard), Robin (Razor Skate), Kenner, MIP, ea from $4 to $6.00
Batman & Robin, figure, 5", Mr Freeze (Ice Terror) or Robin, Kenner, Deluxe, MIP, ea from $6 to....$10.00
Batman & Robin, figure, 5", Mr Freeze (Iceblast), Kenner, series 1, MIP, from $8 to....$12.00
Batman & Robin, figure, 5", Mr Freeze (Jet Wing w/Ring), Kenner, series 2, MIP, ea from $18 to....$22.00
Batman & Robin, figure, 5", Mr Freeze (Ultimate Armor w/ Ring), Kenner, MIP, ea from $10 to $12.00
Batman & Robin, figure, 5", Robin, Kenner, Deluxe, MIP, from $10 to....$12.00
Batman & Robin, figure, 5", Robin (Gacier Battle), Kenner, Deluxe, MIP, from $12 to $15.00
Batman & Robin, figure, 5", Robin (Talon Strike) or Robin (Triple Strike), Kenner, MIP, ea from $4 to $6.00
Batman & Robin, figure, 12", Batgirl, Kenner, MIB, from $30 to $36.00
Batman & Robin, figure, 12", Batman, Kenner, MIB, from $20 ....$28.00
Batman & Robin, figure, 12", Batman & Poison Ivy (set), Kenner, MIP, from $35 to....$45.00
Batman & Robin, figure, 12", Ice Battle Batman, Mister Freeze or Robin, Kenner, MIB, ea from $20 to....$25.00
Batman & Robin, figure, 12", Ultimate Batman or Ultimate Robin, Kenner, MIB, ea from $18 to....$22.00

Batman & Robin, figure set, 5", Batman vs Poison Ivy, Kenner, MIP, from $35 to $45.00
Batman & Robin, figure set, 5", Challengers of the Night, Kenner, MIP, from $12 to $18.00
Batman & Robin, figure set, 5", Cold Night at Gotham, Brain vs Brawn or Guardians of Gotham, Kenner, MIP, ea from $8 ....$12.00
Batman & Robin (Adventures of), accessory, Nightsphere w/Batman figure, series 1, Kenner, MIP, from $35 to $45.00
Batman & Robin (Adventures of), figure, any character from any series, Kenner, MOC, from, $8 to $12.00

Batman & Robin (Adventures of), figure, series 2, Harley Quinn, Kenner, 1997, MOC, from $8.00 to $12.00.

Batman & Robin (Adventures of), figure set, Rogues Gallery, series 2, Kenner, 1997, MIP, from $45 to $50.00
Batman Forever, accessory, Batboat or Batwing, Kenner, MIB, ea from $22 to $28.00
Batman Forever, accessory, Batcave, Batmobile or Triple Action Vehicle Set, Kenner, MIB, ea from $35 to $45.00
Batman Forever, accessory, Robin Cycle, Kenner, MIB, from $10 to $15.00
Batman Forever, accessory, Wayne Manor, Kenner, MIB, from $45 to $55.00
Batman Forever, figure, Attack Wing Batman, Laser Disc Batman or Lightwing Batman, Kenner, MOC, ea from $20 to $28.00
Batman Forever, figure, Batarang Batman or Ice Blade Batman, Kenner, MOC, ea from $10 to $15.00
Batman Forever, figure, Blast Cape Batman, Fireguard Batman, Hydro Claw Robin, Kenner, MOC, ea from $10 to....$15.00
Batman Forever, figure, Bruce Wayne or The Riddler, Kenner, MOC, ea from $40 to $45.00
Batman Forever, figure, Manta Ray Batman, Martial Arts Robin or Neon Armor Batman, Kenner, MOC, ea from $12 to..$16.00
Batman Forever, figure, Night Hunter Batman, Power Beacon Batman or Recon Hunter Batman, Kenner, MOC, ea from $12 to $16.00
Batman Forever, figure, Riddle (w/Bazooka) or Triple Strike Robin, Kenner, MOC, ea from $10 to $12.00
Batman Forever, figure, Skyboard Robin, Solar Shield Batman or Sonar Sensor Batman, Kenner, MOC, ea from $12 to $16.00
Batman Forever, figure, Street Biker Robin, Street Racer Batman or Transforming Bruce Wayne, Kenner, MOC, ea from $12 to $16.00
Batman Forever, figure, Talking Riddler, Tide Racer Robin, Kenner, MOC, ea from $18 to $22.00
Batman Forever, figure, Transforming Bruce Wayne or Transforming Grayson, MOC, ea from $12 to $16.00
Batman Forever, figure, Two-Face or Wing Blast Batman, Kenner, MOC, ea from $12 to $16.00
Batman Forever, figure set, any, Kenner, MOC, ea from $38 to $42.00
Batman Returns, accessory, All-Terrain Batskiboat, Kenner, MIP, from $40 to $45.00
Batman Returns, accessory, Bat Cave Command Center, Kenner, MIB, from $55 to $65.00
Batman Returns, accessory, Bat Cycle, Kenner, MIP, from $20 to $25.00
Batman Returns, accessory, Batmissle Batmobile, Kenner, MIB, from $60 to $70.00
Batman Returns, accessory, Batmobile, Kenner, MIP, from $50 to $60.00
Batman Returns, accessory, Bruce Wayne Custom Coupe (w/figure), Kenner, MIB, from $25 to $30.00
Batman Returns, accessory, Camo Attack Batmobile, Kenner, MIP, from $50 to $60.00
Batman Returns, accessory, Robin Jetfoil, Kenner, MIP, from $15 to $20.00
Batman Returns, accessory, Sky Blade, Kenner, 1992, MIP, from $30 to $35.00
Batman Returns, accessory, Sky Drop, Kenner, MIP, from $25 to $30.00
Batman Returns, figure, Aerostrike Batman, Air Attack Batman or Arctic Batman, Kenner, MOC, ea from $10 to $12.00
Batman Returns, figure, Bola Strike Batman, Bruce Wayne or Catwoman, Kenner, MOC, ea from $12 to $16.00
Batman Returns, figure, Claw Climber Batman, Crime Attack Batman or Deep Dive Batman, Kenner, MOC, ea from $10 to $12.00
Batman Returns, figure, Firebolt Batman or Rocket Blast Batman, Kenner, MOC, ea from $20 to $25.00
Batman Returns, figure, Glider Batman, High Wire Batman or Hydro Charge Batman, Kenner, MOC, ea from $10 to..$12.00
Batman Returns, figure, Jungle Tracker Batman, Laser Batman or Night Climber Batman, Kenner, MOC, ea from $10 to $12.00
Batman Returns, figure, Penguin Commandos or Robin, Kenner, MOC, ea from $12 to $16.00
Batman Returns, figure, Polar Blast Batman, Powerwing Batman or Shadow Wing Batman, Kenner, MOC, ea from $10 to..$12.00
Batman Returns, figure, 16", Batman, Kenner, MIB, from $60 to $65.00
Battlestar Galactica, figure, 3¾", Cylon Commander or Lucifer, series 1, MOC, ea from $105 to.................... $115.00
Battlestar Galactica, accessory, Colonial Scarab, Mattel, MIB, from $65 to $70.00

Battlestar Galactica, accessory, Colonial Steller Probe, Colonial Viper or Cylon Raider, Mattel, MIB, ea from $65 to..$75.00
Battlestar Galactica, figure, 3¾", Baltar or Boray, series 2, Mattel, MOC, ea from $75 to $80.00
Battlestar Galactica, figure, 3¾", Commander Adama or Cylon Centurian, 1st series, Mattel, MOC, ea from $38 to $42.00
Battlestar Galactica, figure, 3¾", Daggit, Imperious Leader, series 1, Mattel, MOC, ea from $28 to $32.00
Battlestar Galactica, figure, 12", Colonial Warrior or Cylon Centurian, Mattel, MIB, ea from $80 to $90.00
Beetlejuice, accessory, any, Kenner, 1989-90, MIP, ea from $10 to $20.00

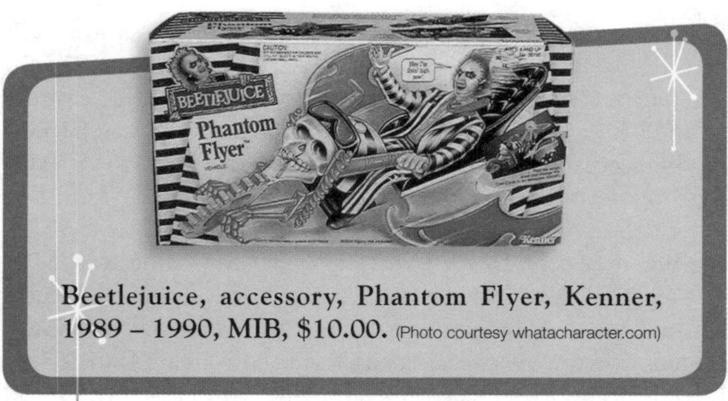

Beetlejuice, accessory, Phantom Flyer, Kenner, 1989 – 1990, MIB, $10.00. (Photo courtesy whatacharacter.com)

Beetlejuice, figure, Adam Maitland, Kenner, 1989-90, MOC, from $8 to $12.00
Beetlejuice, figure, Exploding Beetljuice, Kenner, 1989-90, MOC, from $4 to..$6.00
Beetlejuice, figure, Harry the Haunted Hunter, Old Buzzard, Kenner, 1989-90, MOC, ea from $8 to $12.00

Beetlejuice, figure, Showtime Beetlejuice and Shipwreck Beetljuice, Kenner, 1989 – 1990, MOC, each from $8.00 to $10.00.

Beetlejuice, figure, Street Rat, Teacher Creature, Kenner, 1989-90, MOC, ea from $10 to $12.00
Beetljuice, figure, Talking Beetlejuice, Kenner, 1989-90, MIP, from $35 to $40.00
Best of the West, accessory, Buckboard w/Horse & Harness, Marx, MIB, from $175 to $200.00
Best of the West, accessory, Circle X Ranch, Marx, MIB, from $275 to $300.00
Best of the West, accessory, Covered Wagon, Marx, MIB, from $200 to $235.00
Best of the West, accessory, Fort Apache Playset, Marx, MIB, from $350 to $375.00
Best of the West, accessory, Jeep & Horse Trailer, Marx, MIB, from $125 to $150.00

Best of the West, accessory, Travel Case, Marx, unused, M, from $50.00 to $75.00. (Photo courtesy Paris and Susan Manos)

Best of the West, figure, Bill Buck, Marx, 1967, EX (w/some or all accessories), from $200 to.................................. $250.00
Best of the West, figure, Bill Buck, Marx, 1967, NMIB (w/some or all accessories), from $300 to $350.00
Best of the West, figure, Captain Maddox, bl body, Marx, 1967, EX (w/some or all accessories), from $50 to...............$75.00
Best of the West, figure, Captain Maddox, bl body, Marx, 1967, NMIB (w/some or all accessories), from $100 to $125.00
Best of the West, figure, Chief Cherokee, Marx, 1965, EX (w/some or all accessories), from $50 to $75.00
Best of the West, figure, Chief Cherokee, Marx, 1965, NMIB (w/some or all accessories), from $125 to $150.00
Best of the West, figure, Daniel Boone, Marx, 1965, EX (w/some or all accessories), from $100 to $125.00
Best of the West, figure, Daniel Boone, Marx, 1965, NMIB (w/some or all accessories), from $150 to $250.00
Best of the West, figure, Davy Crockett, Marx, 1965, EX (w/some or all accessories), from $75 to $100.00
Best of the West, figure, Davy Crockett, Marx, 1965, MIB (w/some or all accessories), from $225 to $250.00
Best of the West, figure, Fighting Eagle, Marx, 1967, EX (w/some or all accessories), from $50 to $100.00
Best of the West, figure, Fighting Eagle, Marx, 1967, MIB (w/some or all accessories), from $200 to $250.00
Best of the West, figure, General Custer, Marx, 1967, EX (w/some or all accessories), from $50 to $75.00
Best of the West, figure, General Custer, Marx, 1967, NMIB (w/some or all accessories), from $100 to $150.00
Best of the West, figure, Geronimo, Marx, 1967, EX (w/some or all accessories), from $50 to.......................................$75.00

Best of the West, figure, Geronimo, Marx, 1967, MIB (w/some or all accessories), from $90 to....................................... $125.00
Best of the West, figure, Jamie West, Marx, 1967, EX (w/some or all accessories), from $25 to...$50.00
Best of the West, figure, Jamie West, Marx, 1967, NMIB (w/some or all accessories), from $75 to $100.00
Best of the West, figure, Jane West, Marx, 1966, EX (w/some or all accessories), from $35 to...$50.00
Best of the West, figure, Jane West, Marx, 1966, NMIB (w/some or all accessories), from $75 to $100.00
Best of the West, figure, Jane West w/Flame, Marx, 1966, NMIB (w/some or all accessories), from $85 to.................... $125.00
Best of the West, figure, Janice West, Marx, 1967, EX (w/some or all accessories), from $20 to...$30.00
Best of the West, figure, Janice West, Marx, 1967, NMIB (w/ some or all accessories), from $50 to $75.00
Best of the West, figure, Jay West, Marx, 1967, EX (w/some or all accessories), from, $20 to...$30.00
Best of the West, figure, Jay West, Marx, 1967, NMIB (w/some or all accessories), from $50 to $75.00
Best of the West, figure, Jed Gibson, bl body, Marx, 1967, NMIB (w/some or all accessories), from $600 to................. $800.00
Best of the West, figure, Jed Gibson, blk body, Marx, 1967, M (w/some or all accessories), from $300 to................. $400.00
Best of the West, figure, Johnny West, Marx, 1965, EX (w/some or all accessories), from $25 to $50.00
Best of the West, figure, Johnny West, Marx, 1965, MIB (w/some or all accessories), from $75 to $100.00
Best of the West, figure, Johnny West w/Thunderbolt, Marx, 1967, NMIB (w/some or all accessories), from $100 to........ $150.00
Best of the West, figure, Josie West, Marx, 1967, EX (w/some or all accessories), from $15 to...$30.00
Best of the West, figure, Josie West, Marx, 1967, NMIB (w/some or all accessories), from $50 to $75.00
Best of the West, figure, Princess Wildflower, Marx, 1974, EX (w/some or all accessories), from $30 to.......................$50.00
Best of the West, figure, Princess Wildflower, Marx, 1974, NMIB (w/some or all accessories), from, $75 to.................. $100.00
Best of the West, figure, Sam Cobra, Marx, 1972, EX (w/some or all accessories), from $25 to...$35.00
Best of the West, figure, Sam Cobra, Marx, 1972, NMIB (w/some or all accessories), from $50 to $75.00
Best of the West, figure, Sam Cobra (quick-draw grip), Marx, EX (w/some or all accessories), from $25 to......................$35.00
Best of the West, figure, Sam Cobra (quick-draw grip), Marx, MIB (w/some or all accessories), from $50 to $75.00
Best of the West, figure, Sam Cobra w/Thunderbolt, Marx, 1975, NMIB (w/some or all accessories), from $50 to $75.00
Best of the West, figure, Sheriff Garrett, Marx, 1973, NM (w/ some or all accessories), from $40 to $60.00
Best of the West, figure, Sheriff Garrett, Marx, 1973, NMIB (w/ some or all accessories), from $125 to $150.00
Best of the West, figure, Sheriff Garrett w/Horse, Marx, mail-in figure set, NM (w/mailer), from $175 to $200.00
Best of the West, figure, Zeb Zachary, Marx, 1967-69, NM (w/ some or all accessories), from $125 to $150.00
Best of the West, figure, Zeb Zachary, Marx, 1967-69, NMIB (w/ some or all accessories), from $200 to $250.00
Best of the West, horse, Comanche (palomino w/tack), Marx, NM, from $35 to $45.00
Best of the West, horse, Comanche (palomino), Marx, NMIB, from $50 to $75.00
Best of the West, horse, Flame (palomino w/tack), NM, from $35 to $45.00
Best of the West, horse, Pancho (palomino w/tack), Marx, NM, from $35 to $45.00
Best of the West, horse, Poncho, NMIB, from $50 to........$75.00
Best of the West, horse, Thunderbolt (bay w/tack), Marx, NM, from $25 to $35.00
Best of the West, horse, Thunderbolt (bay), Marx, NMIB, from $50 to $60.00
Big Jim, accessory, Action Sets, any, Mattel, MIB, ea from $12 to $15.00
Big Jim, accessory, Adventure Gear, any, Mattel, MIB, ea from $12 to $15.00
Big Jim, accessory, Baja Beast, Mattel, MIB, from $60 to ..$70.00
Big Jim, accessory, Boat & Buggy Set, Mattel, MIB, from $45 to $55.00
Big Jim, accessory, Devil River Trip (w/figure & alligator), Mattel, MIB, from $45 to $55.00
Big Jim, accessory, Jungle Truck, Mattel, MIB, from $45 to.$55.00
Big Jim, accessory, Motorcross Honda, Mattel, MIB, from $45 to.$55.00
Big Jim, accessory, Rescue Rig, Mattel, MIB, from $45 to .$55.00
Big Jim, accessory, Safari Hut, Mattel, M, from $30 to $40.00
Big Jim, accessory, Sky Commander, Mattel, MIB, from $60 to $70.00
Big Jim, accessory, Sport Camper w/Boat, Mattel, MIB, from $35 to $45.00
Big Jim, figure, Big Jack, Big Jeff, Big Josh, Dr Alec or Dr Steel, Mattel, MIB, ea from $45 to..$55.00
Big Jim, figure, Big Jack (Gold Medal), Mattel, MIB, from $70 to $80.00
Big Jim, figure, Big Jim, Mattel, MIB, from $75 to............$85.00
Big Jim, figure, Big Jim (Gold Medal Olympic Boxing Match), Mattel, MIB, from $75 to $85.00

Big Jim, figure, Dr. Alec, Mattel, MIB, from $45.00 to $55.00.

Big Jim's PACK, accessory, Beast, Mattel, MIB, from $85 to.. $110.00
Big Jim's PACK, accessory, Frogman, Mattel, MIP, from $40 to .. $50.00
Big Jim's PACK, accessory, Howler, Mattel, MIB, from $55 to .$65.00
Big Jim's PACK, accessory, LazerVette, Mattel, MIP, from $80 to $90.00

Big Jim's PACK, accessory, Martial Arts, Mattel, MIP, from $10 to $15.00
Big Jim's PACK, accessory, Secret Spy, Mattel, MIP, from $55 to $65.00
Big Jim's PACK, figure, Big Jim (Commander), gold pants, Mattel, MIB, from $175 to $225.00
Big Jim's PACK, figure, Big Jim (Commander), wht pants, Mattel, MIB, from $120 to $130.00
Big Jim's PACK, figure, Big Jim (Double Trouble), Mattel, MIB, from $185 to $200.00
Big Jim's PACK, figure, Dr Steel, Mattel, MIB, from $100 to $115.00
Big Jim's PACK, figure, Torpedo Fist, Mattel, MIB, from $125 to $135.00
Big Jim's PACK, figure, Warpath or The Whip, Mattel, MIB, ea from $125 to $135.00
Big Jim's PACK, figure, Zorack the Enemy, Mattel, MIB, from $125 to $135.00
Bionic Woman, accessory, Beauty Salon, Kenner, MIB, from $65 to $75.00
Bionic Woman, accessory, Bubblin' Bath 'n Shower, Kenner, MIB, from $50 to $75.00
Bionic Woman, accessory, House Playset, Kenner, MIP, from $25 to $50.00
Bionic Woman, accessory, Spots Car, Kenner, MIB, from $90 to $110.00
Bionic Woman, figure, Fembot, Kenner, MIB, from $200 to $225.00

Bionic Woman, figure, Jaime Sommers, Kenner, MIB, from $125.00 to $150.00. (Photo courtesy Paris and Susan Manos)

Bionic Woman, figure, Jaime Sommers (w/Mission Purse), Kenner, MIB, from $160 to $180.00
Bionic Woman, outfits, any, Kenner, MOC, ea from $25 to $35.00
Black Hole, figure, 3¾", Captain Holland, Dr Alex Durant or Dr Hans Reinhardt, Mego, MIB, from $22 to $28.00
Black Hole, figure, 3¾", Harry Booth or Kate McCrae, Mego, MOC, from $22 to $28.00
Black Hole, figure, 3¾", Humanoid, Mego, MOC, from $675 to $700.00
Black Hole, figure, 3¾", Maximillian, Mego, MOC, from $70 to $80.00
Black Hole, figure, 3¾", Old BOB, Mego, MOC, from $1 to $175.00
Black Hole, figure, 3¾", Pizer, Mego, MOC, from $45 to $55.00

Black Hole, figure, Sentry Robot, Mego, MOC, from $70.00 to $80.00.
(Photo courtesy Wallace M. Chrouch)

Black Hole, figure, 3¾", STAR, Mego, MOC, from $275 to $325.00
Black Hole, figure, 3¾", VINcent, Mego, MOC, from $65 to $75.00
Black Hole, figure, 12", Captain Holland or Dr Alex Durant, Mego, MIB, ea from $70 to $80.00
Black Hole, figure, 12", Dr Hans Reinhardt, Mego, MIB, from $70 to $80.00
Black Hole, figure, 12", Harry Booth, Mego, MIB, from $85 to $90.00
Black Hole, figure, 12", Kate McCrae, Mego, MIB, from $95 to $100.00
Blackstar, accessory, Battle Wagon, Galoob, MIB, from $70 to $80.00
Blackstar, accessory, Ice Castle, Galoob, MIB, from $70 to $80.00
Blackstar, accessory, Triton, Galoob, MIB, from $45 to $55.00
Blackstar, accessory, Warlock, Galoob, MIB, from $50 to $60.00
Blackstar, accessory, Wind Machine w/2 Trobbits, Galoob, MIB, from $55 to $65.00
Blackstar, figure, Blackstar, Galoob, MIB, from $20 to $30.00
Blackstar, figure, Blackstar (w/Laser Light), Galoob, 1983, MOC, from $40 to $45.00
Blackstar, figure, Devil Knight (w/Laser Light), Galoob, 1983, MOC, from $50 to $55.00
Blackstar, figure, Gargo, Galoob, 1983, MOC, from $30 to $40.00
Blackstar, figure, Gargo (w/Laser Light), Galoob, 1983, MOC, from $40 to $45.00
Blackstar, figure, Kadray, Galoob, 1983, MOC, from $40 to $45.00
Blackstar, figure, Kadray (w/Laser Light), Galoob, 1983, MOC, from $40 to $45.00
Blackstar, figure, Klone (w/Laser Light), Galoob, 1983, MOC, from $50 to $55.00
Blackstar, figure, Lava Loc (w/Laser Light), Galoob, 1983, MOC, from $45 to $50.00
Blackstar, figure, Mara, Galoob, 1983, MOC, from $60 to $65.00
Blackstar, figure, Meuton, Galoob, 1983, MOC, from $40 to $45.00
Blackstar, figure, Neptul (w/Laser Light), Galoob, 1983, MOC, from $55 to $60.00

Blackstar, figure, Overlord, Galoob, 1984, MOC, from $25 to .$30.00
Blackstar, figure, Overlord (w/Laser Light), Galoob, 1984, MOC, from $45 to ...$50.00
Blackstar, figure, Palace Guard, Galoob, 1984, MOC, from $30 to...$35.00
Blackstar, figure, Palace Guard (w/Laser Light), Galoob, 1984, MOC, from $35 to...$40.00
Blackstar, figure, Tongo, Galoob, 1983, MOC, from $35 to.$40.00
Blackstar, figure, Tongo (w/Laser Light), Galoob, 1983, MOC, from $35 to ...$40.00
Blackstar, figure, Vizar (w/Laser Light), Galoob, 1983, MOC, from $40 to ...$45.00
Blackstar, figure, White Knight (w/Laser Light), Galoob, 1983, MOC, from $45 to...$50.00
Bonanza, accessory, wagon (4-in-1), American Character, M, from $45 to ...$50.00
Bonanza, accessory, wagon (4-in-1), American Character, MIB, from $75 to ... $100.00
Bonanza, figure, Ben, Little Joe, Hoss or Outlaw, American Character, M, ea from $50 to ...$60.00
Bonanza, figure, Ben, Little Joe or Outlaw, American Character, MIB, ea from $125 to... $175.00

Bonanza, figure, Hoss, American Character, MIB, from $125.00 to $175.00. (Photo courtesy serioustoyz.com)

Bonanza, figure w/horse, any, American Character, M, ea from $75 to...$85.00
Bonanza, figure w/horse, any, American Character, MIB, ea from $175 to ... $225.00
Bonanza, horse, any, American Character, M, ea from $25 to..$30.00
Bonanza, horse, any, American Character, MIB, ea from $65 to ...$75.00
Buck Rogers, accessory, Draconian Marauder, Mego, MIP, from $45 to...$50.00
Buck Rogers, accessory, Land Rover, Mego, NMIB, from $40 to ...$45.00
Buck Rogers, accessory, Laserscope Fighter, Mego, MIB, from $40 to...$45.00
Buck Rogers, accessory, Star Fighter, Mego, MIB, from $50 to... $55.00
Buck Rogers, accessory, Star Fighter Command Center, Mego, MIB, from $100 to ... $125.00
Buck Rogers, accessory, Star Seeker, Mego, MIP, from $60 to. $65.00
Buck Rogers, figure, 3¾", Adrella, Mego, MOC, from $15 to.... $18.00
Buck Rogers, figure, 3¾", Buck Rogers, Mego, MOC, from $60 to ...$65.00
Buck Rogers, figure, 3¾", Dr Huer, Mego, MOC, ea from $18 to ... $22.00

Buck Rogers, figure, Draco and Killer Kane, Mego, MOC, each from $18.00 to $22.00. (Photo courtesy Wallace M. Chrouch)

Buck Rogers, figure, 3¾", Draconian Guard, Mego, MOC, from $18 to...$22.00
Buck Rogers, figure, 3¾", Tiger Man or Wilma Deering, Mego, MOC, from $24 to...$28.00
Buck Rogers, figure, 3¾", Twiki, Mego, MOC, from $40 to ... $50.00
Buck Rogers, figure, 12", any accept Tiger Man, Mego, MIB, ea from $65 to ...$75.00
Buck Rogers, figure, 12", Tiger Man, Mego, MIB, from $125 to... $130.00
Bug's Life, figure, any character, Mattel, 1998, MOC, ea from $4 to...$6.00
Captain Action, accessory, Action Cave, Ideal, MIB, from $600 to... $675.00
Captain Action, accessory, Anti-Gravitational Power Pack, Ideal, MIB, from $200 to ... $275.00
Captain Action, accessory, Directional Communicator, Ideal, MIB, from $275 to ... $325.00
Captain Action, accessory, Headquarters, Ideal, MIB, from $450 to... $550.00
Captain Action, accessory, Inter-Galactic Jet Mortar, Ideal, MIB, from $275 to ... $325.00
Captain Action, accessory, Parachute Pack, Ideal, MIB, from $200 to ... $230.00
Captain Action, accessory, Silver Streak Amphibian Car, Ideal, MIB, from $1,000 to ...$1,500.00
Captain Action, accessory, Silver Streak Garage, Ideal, MIB, from $1,800 to ...$2,000.00
Captain Action, accessory, Survival Kit, Ideal, MIB, from $225 to... $250.00
Captain Action, accessory, Weapons Arsenal, Ideal, MIB, from $175 to ... $200.00
Captain Action, figure, Action Boy, Ideal, MIB, from $850 to... $875.00

Captain Action, figure, Action Boy, Ideal, NM, from $225 to $250.00
Captain Action, figure, Action Boy (space suit), Ideal, MIB, from $900 to $1,000.00
Captain Action, figure, Captain Action, Ideal (Lone Ranger box), MIB, from $525 to $550.00
Captain Action, figure, Captain Action, Ideal (Lone Ranger box), NM, from $200 to $225.00

Captain Action, figure, Captain Action, Ideal (parachute offer), MIB, from $675.00 to $700.00. (Photo courtesy Paris and Susan Manos)

Captain Action, figure, Captain Action, Ideal (parachute offer box), NM, from $250 to $275.00
Captain Action, figure, Captain Action, Ideal (photo box), MIB, from $875 to $900.00
Captain Action, figure, Captain Action, Ideal (photo box), NM, from $275 to $300.00
Captain Action, figure, Dr Evil, Ideal, MIB (photo box), from $450 to $475.00
Captain Action, figure, Dr Evil, Ideal, NM (photo box), from $250 to $265.00
Captain Action, outfit, Aquaman, Ideal, MIB, from $600 to $625.00
Captain Action, outfit, Aquaman, Ideal, NM, from $150 to $200.00
Captain Action, outfit, Aquaman (w/ring), Ideal, MIB, from $900 to $950.00
Captain Action, outfit, Aquaman (w/ring), Ideal, NM, from $200 to $225.00
Captain Action, outfit, Batman, Ideal, MIB, from $700 to $725.00
Captain Action, outfit, Batman, Ideal, NM, from $175 to $225.00
Captain Action, outfit, Batman (w/ring), Ideal, MIB, from $1,000 to $1,200.00
Captain Action, outfit, Buck Rogers (w/ring), Ideal, MIB, from $2,000 to $2,500.00
Captain Action, outfit, Buck Rogers (w/ring), Ideal, NM, from $425 to $500.00
Captain Action, outfit, Captain America, Ideal, MIB, from $825 to $875.00
Captain Action, outfit, Captain America, Ideal, NM, from $200 to $250.00
Captain Action, outfit, Captain America (w/ring), Ideal, MIB, from $950 to $1,100.00
Captain Action, outfit, Flash Gordon, Ideal, MIB, from $525 to $550.00
Captain Action, outfit, Flash Gordon, Ideal, NM, from $225 to $250.00
Captain Action, outfit, Flash Gordon (w/ring), Ideal, MIB, from $750 to $775.00
Captain Action, outfit, Flash Gordon (w/ring), Ideal, NM, from $200 to $250.00
Captain Action, outfit, Green Hornet (w/ring), Ideal, MIB, from $6,500 to $7,000.00
Captain Action, outfit, Green Hornet (w/ring), Ideal, NM, from $2,000 to $2,500.00
Captain Action, outfit, Lone Ranger, Ideal, MIB, from $650 to $675.00
Captain Action, outfit, Lone Ranger, Ideal, NM, from $175 to $225.00
Captain Action, outfit, Lone Ranger (w/ring), Ideal, MIB, from $900 to $950.00
Captain Action, outfit, Phantom, Ideal, complete, NM, from $200 to $250.00
Captain Action, outfit, Phantom (w/ring), Ideal, MIB, from $850 to $875.00
Captain Action, outfit, Robin, Ideal, MIB, from $1,000 to $1,250.00
Captain Action, outfit, Robin, Ideal, NM, from $300 to $350.00

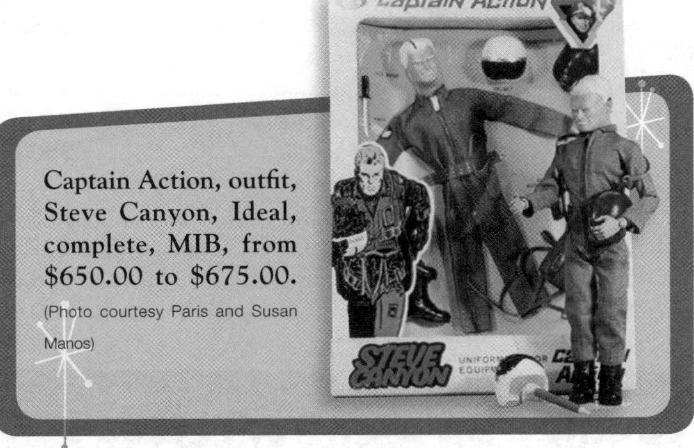

Captain Action, outfit, Steve Canyon, Ideal, complete, MIB, from $650.00 to $675.00. (Photo courtesy Paris and Susan Manos)

Captain Action, outfit, Steve Canyon, Ideal, NM, from $200 to $250.00
Captain Action, outfit, Steve Canyon (w/ring), Ideal, MIB, from $775 to $800.00
Captain Action, outfit, Steve Canyon (w/ring), Ideal, NM, from $175 to $225.00
Captain Action, outfit, Superboy, Ideal, MIB, from $900 to $1,000.00
Captain Action, outfit, Superboy, Ideal, NM, from $300 to $350.00
Captain Action, outfit, Superman, w/accessories & Krypto the dog, Ideal, NM, from $200 to $250.00
Captain Action, outfit, Superman (w/Krypto the dog), Ideal, MIB, from $650 to $750.00
Captain Action, outfit, Tonto (w/ring), Ideal, MIB, from $900 to $1,000.00
Captain America, see also Marvel Super Heroes

Charlie's Angels (Movie), figure, any, Jakks Pacific, MIB, ea from $20 to $25.00
Charlie's Angels (TV Series), accessory, Adventure Van, Hasbro, MIB, from $70 to $80.00

Charlie's Angels (TV Series), figures, any character, Hasbro, MOC, each from $75.00 to $85.00. (Photo courtesy Morphy Auctions)

Charlie's Angels (TV Series), figure gift set, Kelly, Kris & Sabrina, MIP, from $175 to $200.00
CHiPs, accessory, motorcycle & ramp for 3¾" figures, Mego, MIP, from $45 to $55.00
CHiPs, accessory, motorcycle for 3¾" figures, Mego, MIP, from $25 to $35.00
CHiPs, accessory, motorcycle for 8" figures, Mego, MIP, from $75 to $80.00
CHiPs, figure, 3¾", Jimmy Squeaks or Wheels Willie, Mego, MOC, ea from $15 to $18.00
CHiPs, figure, 3¾", Jon or Ponch, Mego, MOC, ea from $18 to. $22.00
CHiPs, figure, 3¾", Sarge, Mego, MOC, from $22 to $28.00
CHiPs, figure, 8", Sarge, Mego, MOC, from $28 to $30.00

CHiPs, figures, 8", Jon and Ponch, Mego, MOC, each from $40.00 to $45.00. (Photo courtesy Morphy Auctions)

Clash of the Titans, figure, Calibas, Mattel, MOC, from $40 to $45.00
Clash of the Titans, figure, Charon, Mattel, MOC, from $60 to $65.00
Clash of the Titans, figure, Kraken, Mattel, rare, MOC, from $250 to $275.00
Clash of the Titans, figure, Perseus, Mattel, MOC, from $50 to $55.00
Clash of the Titans, figure, Thallo, Mattel, MOC, from $40 to $45.00
Clash of the Titans, figure set, Pegasus & Perseus, Mattel, MIP, from $75 to $100.00
Clash of the Titans, horse, Pegasus, Mattel, MOC, from $65 to $70.00
Clash of the Titans, horse & figure set, Pegasus & Perseus, Mattel, MIB, from $75 to $100.00
Comic Action Heroes, accessory, Batcopter, w/Batman figure, Mego, MIP, from $90 to $110.00
Comic Action Heroes, accessory, Batmobile, w/Batman figure, Mego, MIP, from $145 to $155.00
Comic Action Heroes, accessory, Collapsing Tower w/Wonder Woman figure & Invisible Plane, Mego, MIP, from $200 to $225.00
Comic Action Heroes, accessory, Exploding Bridge w/Batmobile, Mego, MIP, from $175 to $225.00
Comic Action Heroes, accessory, Fortress of Solitude w/Superman figure, Mego, MIP, from $200 to $225.00
Comic Action Heroes, accessory, Spider-Car w/Spider-Man & Green Goblin figures, Mego, MIP, from $250 to...... $275.00
Comic Action Heroes, accessory, The Mangler, Mego, MIP, from $250 to $275.00
Comic Action Heroes, figure, Aquaman, Batman, Captain America or Joker, Mego, MOC, ea from $70 to..........$75.00
Comic Action Heroes, figure, Aquaman, Batman, Captain America or Joker, Mego, NM, ea from $25 to............$30.00
Comic Action Heroes, figure, Green Goblin, Mego, MOC, from $120 to $130.00
Comic Action Heroes, figure, Green Goblin, Mego, NM, from $25 to $30.00
Comic Action Heroes, figure, Hulk, Mego, MOC, from $50 to $55.00
Comic Action Heroes, figure, Hulk, Mego, NM, from $18 to ..$22.00
Comic Action Heroes, figure, Penguin, Shazam or Spider-Man, Mego, MOC, ea from $70 to $80.00
Comic Action Heroes, figure, Penguin, Shazam or Spider-Man, Mego, NM, ea from $20 to $25.00
Comic Action Heroes, figure, Robin, Superman or Wonder Woman, Mego, MOC, ea from $60 to $65.00
Comic Action Heroes, figure, Robin, Superman or Wonder Woman, Mego, NM, ea from $60 to $70.00
Commando (Schwarzenegger), figure, 3¾", any except Matrix, Diamond Toymakers, MOC, ea from $24 to..............$28.00
Commando (Schwarzenegger), figure, 3¾", any except Matrix, Diamond Toymakers, NM to M, ea from $8 to..........$12.00
Commando (Schwarzenegger), figure, 3¾", Matrix, Diamond Toymakers, MOC, from $120 to $128.00
Commando (Schwarzenegger), figure, 3¾", Matrix, Diamond Toymakers, NM, from $35 to $45.00
Commando (Schwarzenegger), figure, 6", any except Matrix, Diamond Toymakers, M, ea from $12 to....................$18.00

Commando (Schwarzenegger), figure, 6", any except Matrix, MIP, from $28 to....................$32.00
Commando (Schwarzenegger), figure, 6", Matrix, Diamond Toymakers, MIP, from $65 to....................$70.00
Commando (Schwarzenegger), figure, 6", Matrix, Diamond Toymakers, NM to M, from $24 to....................$28.00
Commando (Schwarzenegger), figure, 18", Matrix, Diamond Toumakers, MIB (red box), from $265 to $280.00
Commando (Schwarzenegger), figure, 18", Matrix, Diamond Toymakers, MIB (blk box), from $165 to................ $180.00
Commando (Schwarzenegger), figure, 18", Matrix, Diamond Toymakers, NM to M, from $65 to....................$75.00
DC Comics Super Heroes, see also Super Heroes
DC Comics Super Heroes, figure, Aquaman, Batman or Bob the Goon, Toy Biz, MOC, ea from $12 to....................$14.00
DC Comics Super Heroes, figure, Flash, Flash II, Jorker or Mr Freeze, Toy Biz, MOC, ea from $10 to $12.00
DC Comics Super Heroes, figure, Green Lantern, Hawkman, Two Face, Toy Boz, MOC, ea from $18 to $22.00
DC Comics Super Heroes, figure, Lex Luther or Riddler, Toy Biz, MOC, ea from $8 to $12.00

DC Comics Super Heroes, figure, Mr. Freeze, MOC, from $10.00 to $12.00.

DC Comics Super Heroes, figure, Penguin, missile firing (short or long), Toy Biz, MOC, ea from $24 to....................$28.00
DC Comics Super Heroes, figure, Penguin, umbrella-firing, Toy Biz, MOC, from $8 to $12.00
DC Comics Super Heroes, figure, Superman, Toy Biz, MOC, from $24 to $28.00

DC Comics Super Heroes, figure, Wonder Woman, MOC, from $15.00 to $18.00.

Dukes of Hazzard, accessory, 3¾", Cadillac w/Boss Hogg or Police Car w/Sheriff Rosco figure, MIP, ea from $75 to $85.00
Dukes of Hazzard, accessory, 3¾", Cadillac w/Boss Hogg or Police Car w/Sheriff w/Rosco, Mego, M, ea from $35 to $45.00
Dukes of Hazzard, accessory, 3¾", Daisy's Jeep or General Lee w/Bo & Luke figures, Mego, M, ea from $25 to $30.00
Dukes of Hazzard, accessory, 3¾", Daisy's Jeep w/figure or General Lee w/Bo & Luke figures, Mego, MIP, from $60 to $65.00
Dukes of Hazzard, figure, 3¾", Bo or Luke, Mego, 1981-82, MOC, ea from $18 to $22.00
Dukes of Hazzard, figure, 3¾", Boss Hogg or Daisy, Mego, MOC, ea from $24 to....................$26.00
Dukes of Hazzard, figure, 3¾", Cletus, Cooter, Coy, Rosco, Jesse or Vance, Mego, MOC, ea from $28 to....................$32.00
Dukes of Hazzard, figure, 8", Bo or Luke, Mego, MOC, from $28 to $32.00
Dukes of Hazzard, figure, 8", Boss Hogg, Mego, MOC, from $24 to $26.00
Dukes of Hazzard, figure, 8", Coy (Bo) or Vance (Luke), Mego, MOC, ea from $48 to $52.00
Dukes of Hazzard, figure, 8", Daisy, Mego, MOC, from $48 to..$52.00
Emergency, accessory, Fire House, LJN, MIP, from $200 to...$225.00
Emergency, accessory, Rescue Truck, LJN, MIP, from $250 to .$275.00
Emergency, figure, John or Roy, LJN, MOC, ea from $75 to.$85.00
Fantastic Four, see also Marvel Super Heroes and Super Heroes (8" Mego)
Fantastic Four, accessory, Fantasticar, Toy Biz, 1995, MIB, from $35 to....................$40.00
Fantastic Four, accessory, Mr Fantastic Sky Shuttle, Toy Biz, 1995, MIB, from $18 to $22.00
Fantastic Four, accessory, The Thing's Sky Cycle, Toy Biz, 1995, MIP, from $18 to....................$22.00
Fantastic Four, figure, 5", any character, Toy Biz, 1995, MIB, ea from $10 to $15.00
Fantastic Four, figure, 10", any character, MIB, from $10 to ..$15.00
Fantastic Four, figure, 14", electronic, Galactus, Toy Biz, 1995, MIP, from $35 to....................$45.00
Fantastic Four, figure, 14", electronic, Talking Thing, Toy Biz, 1995, MIP, from $18 to....................$22.00
Flash Gordon, figure, Dale Arden, Mego, MOC, from $80 to ..$90.00
Flash Gordon, figure, Dr Zarkov, Mego, MOC, from $100 to $115.00
Flash Gordon, figure, Flash Gordon, Mego, MOC, from $100 to $115.00
Flash Gordon, figure, Ming the Merciless, Mego, MOC, from $80 to....................$90.00
Ghostbusters, accessory, Firehouse Headquarters, Kenner, 1986, MIP, from $75 to $100.00
Ghostbusters, figure, Ecto-Glow characters, Kenner, 1991, MIP, ea from $24 to....................$28.00
Happy Days, accessory, Fonz's Garage, Mego, MIB, from $150 to $175.00
Happy Days, accessory, Fonz's Jalopy or Motorcycle, Mego, MIB, ea from $70 to....................$80.00
Happy Days, figure, any, Mego, MOC, ea from $75 to.......$85.00
Hercules (The Legend Continues), accessory, Hercules Tower of Power, Toy Biz, 1995-97, MIP, from $8 to....................$10.00
Hercules (The Legend Continues), figure, 5", any character, Toy Biz, 1995-97, MOC, ea from $4 to $6.00

Hercules (The Legend Continues), figure, 10", any character, Toy Biz, 1995-97, MIP, ea from $30 to $35.00
Hercules (The Legend Continues), Monsters, any character, Toy Biz, 1995-97, MOC, ea from $8 to $10.00
Hercules (The Legendary Journeys), figure, 10", any character, MIP, ea from $18 to $20.00
Hercules (The Legendary Journeys), figure, 5", any character, Marvel/Toy Biz, 1995-97, MOC, from $8 to $10.00
Hercules (The Legendary Journeys), figure set, 5", Hercules & Iolaus or Hercules & Xena, Toy Biz, 1997, MOC, from $18 to $22.00
Hercules (The Legendary Journeys), figure set, 5", Xena & Gabrielle, Toy Biz, 1997, MOC, from $30 to $35.00
Incredible Hulk, figure, 6", any character, Toy Biz, 1996-97, MOC, from $8 to $10.00
Incredible Hulk (Outcasts), figure, 5", any character, Marvel/Toy Biz, 1997, MOC, ea from $6 to $8.00
Incredible Hulk (Smash & Crash), figure, 5", any character, Marvel/Toy Biz, 1996-97, MOC, ea from $8 to $10.00
Incredible Hulk (Transformations), figure, 6", any character, MOC, ea from $8 to $10.00
Indiana Jones & the Temple of Doom, figure, Giant Thuggee or Mola Ram, LJN, MOC, ea from $70 to $80.00
Indiana Jones & the Temple of Doom, figure, Indiana, LJN, MOC, from $140 to $150.00
Indiana Jones in Raiders of the Lost Ark, accessory, Arabian Horse, Kenner, MIB, from $200 to $225.00
Indiana Jones in Raiders of the Lost Ark, accessory, Convoy Truck, Kenner, MIB, from $100 to $125.00
Indiana Jones in Raiders of the Lost Ark, accessory, Map Room, Kenner, MIB, from $75 to $85.00
Indiana Jones in Raiders of the Lost Ark, accessory, Streets of Cairo, Kenner, MIB, from $65 to $75.00
Indiana Jones in Raiders of the Lost Ark, accessory, Well of the Souls Action Playset, MIB (sealed), from $100 to... $125.00
Indiana Jones in Raiders of the Lost Ark, figure, Belloq, Kenner, MOC, from $55 to $60.00
Indiana Jones in Raiders of the Lost Ark, figure, Belloq (Ceremonial Robe), M (mailing bag), from $25 to $30.00
Indiana Jones in Raiders of the Lost Ark, figure, Belloq (Ceremonial Robe), MOC from $725 to $750.00

Indiana Jones in Raiders of the Lost Ark, figure, Cairo Swordsman, Kenner, MOC, from $30.00 to $35.00.

Indiana Jones in Raiders of the Lost Ark, figure, German Mechanic, Kenner, MOC, from $55 to $60.00
Indiana Jones in Raiders of the Lost Ark, figure, Indiana, 12", Kenner, MIB, from $200 to $225.00
Indiana Jones in Raiders of the Lost Ark, figure, Indiana (German Uniform), Kenner, MOC, from $70 to $75.00
Indiana Jones in Raiders of the Lost Ark, figure, Indiana w/whip, Kenner, MOC, from $200 to $225.00
Indiana Jones in Raiders of the Lost Ark, figure, Marion Ravenwood, Kenner, MOC, from $250 to $275.00
Indiana Jones in Raiders of the Lost Ark, figure, Sallah, Kenner, MOC, from $70 to $75.00
Indiana Jones in Raiders of the Lost Ark, figure, Toht, Kenner, MOC, from $25 to $30.00
Inspector Gadget, accessory, Gadgetmobile, Tiger Toys, 1992, MIP, from $24 to $28.00
Inspector Gadget, figure, any character, Tiger Toys, 1992, MOC, ea from $12 to $18.00
Inspector Gadget, figure, 11", complete, Galoob, 1983, MIB, from $75 to $100.00
James Bond, figure, Bond (Pierce Brosnan), 12", Medicom, MIB, from $75 to $85.00
James Bond (Moonraker), figure, Bond, 12", Mego, MIB, from $140 to $160.00
James Bond (Moonraker), figure, Bond, 12", w/suit & accessories, Mego, MIB, from $450 to $475.00
James Bond (Moonraker), figure, Drax or Holly, 12", Mego, MIB, from $150 to $175.00
James Bond (Moonraker), figure, Jaws, 12", Mego, MIB, from $450 to $475.00
James Bond (Secret Agent 007), accessory, Aston Martin car, w/ ejecting passenger, b/o, bump-&-go action, 12" L, NM. $300.00
James Bond (Secret Agent 007), accessory, Dr No's Dragon Tank & Largo's Hydrofoil Yacht, Gilbert, 1965, MOC, from $25 to $30.00
James Bond (Secret Agent 007), figure, 4", 'M', Moneypenny or Odd Job, Gilbert, 1965, MIP, from $18 to $22.00
James Bond (Secret Agent 007), figure, 4", Domino, Dr Noor Largo, Gilbert, 1965, MIP, from $18 to $22.00
James Bond (Secret Agent 007), figure, 4", Goldfinger, Gilbert, 1965, MIP, from $24 to $28.00
James Bond (Secret Agent 007), figure, 12", Bond, wht shirt & swim trunks, snorkling, Gilbert, 1965, MIB, from $325 to $350.00
James Bond (Secret Agent 007), figure, 12", Odd Job, wht judo outfit, Gilbert, 1965, MIB, from $250 to $275.00
James Bond (Spy Who Loved Me), figure, Bond (Roger Moore) in ski gear, 12", Hasbro, 1999, MIB $55.00
James Bond (Thunderball), accessory, Disguise Kit #16255, Gilbert, MIB $345.00
Johnny Apollo (Astronaut), figure, Jane Apollo, Marx, MIB, from $100 to $125.00
Johnny Apollo (Astronaut), figure, Johnny Apollo, Marx, MIB, $150 to $175.00
Johnny Apollo (Astronaut), figure, Kennedy Space Center Astronaut, Marx, MIB, from $130 to $150.00
Jurassic Park, dinosaur, any, Kenner, 1993, MOC, ea from $6 to $12.00

Jurassic Park, figure, any character, Kenner, 1993, MOC, ea from $6 to $12.00
Knight Rider, accessory, Knight 2000 Voice Car w/Michael figure, Kenner, MIB, from $45 to $50.00
Knight Rider, figure, Michael Knight, Kenner, MOC, from $18 to $20.00
Legend of the Lone Ranger, accessory, Western Town, Gabriel, MIB, $75 to....$100.00
Legend of the Lone Ranger, figure, Buffalo Bill Cody, Gabriel, MOC, from $24 to....$28.00
Legend of the Lone Ranger, figure, Butch Cavendish, Gabriel, MOC, from $24 to....$28.00
Legend of the Lone Ranger, figure, Lone Ranger, Gabriel, MOC, from $24 to $28.00
Legend of the Lone Ranger, figure, Tonto, Gabriel, MOC, from $14 to....$18.00
Legend of the Lone Ranger, figure w/horse, any set, Gabriel, MOC, ea from $45 to $55.00
Legend of the Lone Ranger, horse, Scout, Gabriel, MOC, from $18 to....$22.00
Legend of the Lone Ranger, horse, Silver, Gabriel, MOC, from $28 to....$32.00
Legend of the Lone Ranger, horse, Smoke, Gabriel, MOC, from $24 to....$26.00
Lone Ranger, see also Captain Action
Lone Ranger Rides Again, accessory, Blizzard Adventure, Gabriel, MIB, from $25 to....$30.00
Lone Ranger Rides Again, accessory, Carson City Bank Robbery, Gabriel, MIB, from $45 to....$50.00

Lone Ranger Rides Again, accessory, Hidden Rattler Adventure, Gabriel, MIB, from $25.00 to $30.00.

(Photo courtesy whatacharacter.com)

Lone Ranger Rides Again, accessory, Landslide Adventure, Gabriel, MIB, from $25 to....$30.00
Lone Ranger Rides Again, accessory, Mysterious Prospector, Gabriel, MIB, from $70 to....$75.00
Lone Ranger Rides Again, accessory, Red River Flood Waters, MIB, from $25 to $30.00
Lone Ranger Rides Again, accessory, Tribal Teepee, Gabriel, MIB, from $25 to $30.00
Lone Ranger Rides Again, figure, any, Gabriel, MIB, ea from $65 to $75.00
Lone Ranger Rides Again, figure & horse sets, any, Gabriel, MIB, ea from $65 to....$75.00
Lord of the Rings, creature, Charger of the Ringwraith, Knickerbocker, 1979, MIP, from $140 to $150.00
Lord of the Rings, creature, Frodo's Horse, Knickerbocker, 1979, MIP, from $90 to.... $100.00
Lord of the Rings, creature, Ringwraith, Knickerbocker, 1979, MIP, from $250 to.... $275.00
Lord of the Rings, figure, any, Knickerbocker, 1979, MIP, from $90 to $100.00
Lord of the Rings, figure, any, Toy Vault, 1998-99, MOC, ea from $12 to $18.00
Love Boat, figure, any 4" character, Mego, 1982, MOC, ea from $18 to....$22.00
M*A*S*H, accessory, 3¾", Ambulance (w/Hawkeye figure), Tri-Star, MIP, from $40 to $45.00
M*A*S*H, accessory, 3¾", Helicopter (w/Hawkeye figure), Tri-Star, MIP, from $40 to $45.00
M*A*S*H, accessory, 3¾", Jeep (w/Hawkeye figure), Tri-Star, MIB, from $35 to $40.00
M*A*S*H, accessory, 3¾", Military Base, Tri-Star, MIB, from $75 to.... $100.00
M*A*S*H, figure, 3¾", BJ, Col Potter, Father Mulcahy, Hawkeye, Klinger, or Winchester, Tri-Star, MOC, ea from $15 to..$20.00
M*A*S*H, figure, 3¾", Hot Lips, Tri-Star, MOC, from $20 to....$25.00
M*A*S*H, figure, 3¾", Klinger (in dress), Tri-Star, MOC, from $30 to....$35.00
Mad Monster Series, accessory, Mad Monster Castle, Mego, 1974, MIB, from $550 to $600.00
Mad Monster Series, figure, Dreadful Dracula, 8", Mego, 1974, MIB, from $150 to.... $175.00
Mad Monster Series, figure, Frankenstein, 8", Mego, 1974, MIB, from $175 to $200.00
Mad Monster Series, figure, Horrible Mummy, 8", Mego, 1974, MIB, from $80 to.... $100.00
Mad Monster Series, figure, Human Wolfman, 8", Mego, 1974, MIB, from $125 to.... $150.00
Major Matt Mason, accessory, Astro Trac, Mattel, MIB, from $100 to.... $125.00
Major Matt Mason, accessory, Fireball Space Cannon, Mattel, MIB, from $75 to.... $100.00
Major Matt Mason, accessory, Gamma Ray Guard, Mattel, MIB, from $75 to $100.00
Major Matt Mason, accessory, Moon Suit Pak, Mattel, MIB, from $75 to.... $100.00
Major Matt Mason, accessory, Rocket Launch, Mattel, MIB, from $70 to $80.00
Major Matt Mason, accessory, Satellite Locker, Mattel, MIB, from $65 to $75.00
Major Matt Mason, accessory, Space Crawler Action Set (w/figure), Mattel, MIB, from $100 to.... $125.00
Major Matt Mason, accessory, Space Probe, Mattel, MIB, from $70 to....$80.00
Major Matt Mason, accessory, Space Station, Mattel, MIB, from $300 to.... $325.00
Major Matt Mason, accessory, Uni-Tred & Space Bubble, Mattel, MIB, from $125 to.... $150.00

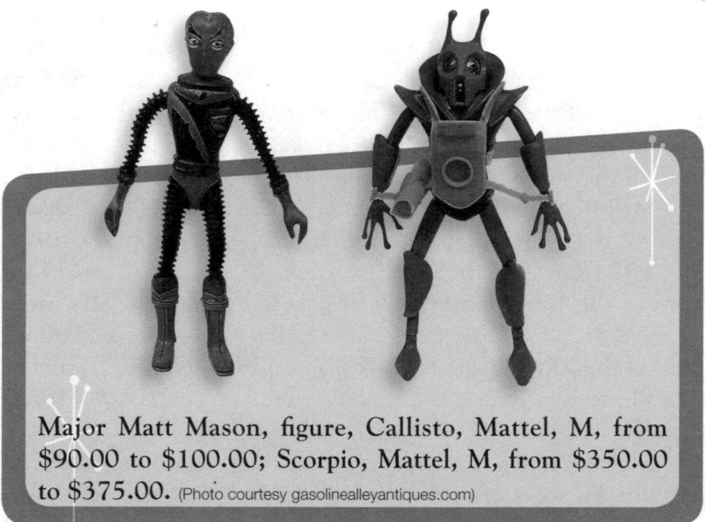

Major Matt Mason, figure, Callisto, Mattel, M, from $90.00 to $100.00; Scorpio, Mattel, M, from $350.00 to $375.00. (Photo courtesy gasolinealleyantiques.com)

Major Matt Mason, figure, Callisto, Mattel, MOC, from $225 to $250.00
Major Matt Mason, figure, Captain Lazer, Mattel, M, from $130 to $140.00
Major Matt Mason, figure, Captain Lazer, Mattel, MOC, from $275 to $325.00
Major Matt Mason, figure, Doug Davis (w/helmet), Mattel, M, from $115 to $125.00
Major Matt Mason, figure, Doug Davis (w/helmet), Mattel, MOC, from $275 to $300.00
Major Matt Mason, figure, Jeff Long, Mattel, M, from $170 to $180.00
Major Matt Mason, figure, Jeff Long (w/helmet), Mattel, MOC, from $500 to $550.00
Major Matt Mason, figure, Major Matt Mason, Mattel, M, from $75 to $85.00
Major Matt Mason, figure, Major Matt Mason, Mattel, MOC, from $175 to $200.00
Major Matt Mason, figure, Scorpio, Mattel, MOC, from $800 to $850.00
Major Matt Mason, figure, Sgt Storm, Mattel, MOC, from $375 to $400.00
Major Matt Mason, figure, Sgt Storm (w/helmet), Mattel, M, from $100 to $115.00
Man From UNCLE, accessory, Arsenal Set #1 or #2, Gilbert, MIP, from $35 to $45.00
Man From UNCLE, accessory, Jumpsuit Set, Gilbert, MIP, from $40 to $50.00
Man From UNCLE, accessory, Scuba Set, Gilbert, MIP, from $50 to $75.00
Man From UNCLE, figure, Illya Kuryakin or Napoleon Solo, Gilbert, M, ea from $175 to $200.00
Man From UNCLE, figure, Illya Kuryakin or Napoleon Solo, Gilbert, MIB, ea from $325 to $375.00
Marvel Super Heroes, accessory, Training Center, Toy Biz, MIB, from $25 to $35.00
Marvel Super Heroes, figure, Annihilus, Deathlok, Hulk, Human Torch, Mr Fantastic or Thing, Toy Biz, MOC, ea from $15 to $18.00
Marvel Super Heroes, figure, Captain America, Toy Biz, MOC, from $18 to $22.00
Marvel Super Heroes, figure, Daredevil, Toy Biz, MOC, from $34 to $38.00

Marvel Super Heroes, figure, Dr. Doom (Power Driven Weapons), Toy Biz, MOC, from $24.00 to $28.00. (Photo courtesy Morphy Auctions)

Marvel Super Heroes, figure, Dr Doom or Dr Octopus, Toy Biz, MOC, ea from $24 to $28.00
Marvel Super Heroes, figure, Green Goblin (back lever) or Thor (back lever), Toy Biz, MOC, ea from $38 to....................$42.00
Marvel Super Heroes, figure, Green Goblin (no lever) or Thor (no lever), Toy Boz, MOC, ea from $24 to $28.00
Marvel Super Heroes, figure, Human Torch (fireball flinging action), Toy Biz, MOC, from $15 to $18.00
Marvel Super Heroes, figure, Invisible Woman (catapult), Toy Biz, MOC, from $15 to $18.00
Marvel Super Heroes, figure, Invisible Woman (vanishing), Toy Biz, MOC, from $140 to $160.00
Marvel Super Heroes, figure, Mr Fantastic (5-way stretch), Toy Biz, MOC, from $18 to $20.00
Marvel Super Heroes, figure, Punisher (cap-firing or machine gun sound), Silver Surfer (chrome), Toy Biz, MOC, ea $15 to. $18.00
Marvel Super Heroes, figure, Spider-Man (ball joints or web tracer), Toy Biz, MOC, ea from $15 to $18.00
Marvel Super Heroes, figure, Spider-Man (web climbing or web-shooting), Toy Biz, MOC, ea from $30 to....................$35.00

Marvel Super Heroes, figure, Venom (Living Skin Slime Pores), MOC, from $18.00 to $22.00.

Marvel Super Heroes (Secret Wars), accessory, Doom Copter, Mattel, MOC, from $30 to....$35.00
Marvel Super Heroes (Secret Wars), accessory, Doom Copter (w/Dr Doom figure), Mattel, MOC, from $45 to....$50.00
Marvel Super Heroes (Secret Wars), accessory, Doom Cycle, Mattel, MOC, from $18 to....$22.00
Marvel Super Heroes (Secret Wars), accessory, Doom Cycle (w/ Dr Doom figure), Mattel, MOC, from $30 to....$35.00
Marvel Super Heroes (Secret Wars), accessory, Doom Roller, Mattel, MOC, from $18 to....$22.00
Marvel Super Heroes (Secret Wars), accessory, Freedom Fighter, Mattel, MOC, from $25 to....$30.00
Marvel Super Heroes (Secret Wars), accessory, Tower of Doom, Mattel, MOC, from $30 to....$40.00
Marvel Super Heroes (Secret Wars), accessory, Training Center, Mattel, MOC, from $20 to....$25.00
Marvel Super Heroes (Secret Wars), figure, Baron Zemo, Mattel, MOC, from $24 to....$28.00
Marvel Super Heroes (Secret Wars), figure, Captain America, Mattel, MOC, from $24 to....$28.00
Marvel Super Heroes (Secret Wars), figure, Daredevil, Mattel, MOC, from $30 to....$35.00
Marvel Super Heroes (Secret Wars), figure, Dr Doom, Dr Octopus, Kang or Magento, Mattel, MOC, ea from $18 to....$22.00
Marvel Super Heroes (Secret Wars), figure, Falcon, Mattel, MOC, from $40 to....$45.00
Marvel Super Heroes (Secret Wars), figure, Hobgoblin, Mattel, MOC, from $55 to....$60.00
Marvel Super Heroes (Secret Wars), figure, Iron Man, Mattel, MOC, from $24 to....$28.00
Marvel Super Heroes (Secret Wars), figure, Spider-Man (blk outfit), Mattel, MOC, from $40 to....$45.00
Marvel Super Heroes (Secret Wars), figure, Spider-Man (red & bl outfit), Mattel, MOC, from $28 to....$32.00
Marvel Super Heroes (Secret Wars), figure, Wolverine (blk claws), Mattel, MOC, from $110 to....$115.00
Marvel Super Heroes (Secret Wars), figure, Wolverine (silver claws), Mattel, MOC, from $38 to....$42.00
Marvel Super Heroes (Talking), figure, any, Toy Biz, MIP, ea from $20 to....$25.00

Masters of the Universe, accessory, Battlecat, Mattel, MIB, from $45.00 to $55.00. (Photo courtesy Morphy Auctions)

Masters of the Universe, accessory, He-Man & Wind Raider, Mattel, MIP, from $80 to....$90.00
Masters of the Universe, accessory, Jet Sled, Mattel, MIP, from $12 to....$18.00
Masters of the Universe, accessory, Mantisaur, Mattel, MIP, from $24 to....$28.00
Masters of the Universe, accessory, Monstroid, Mattel, MIP, from $40 to....$45.00
Masters of the Universe, accessory, Night Stalker, Mattel, MIP, from $25 to....$35.00
Masters of the Universe, accessory, Panthor, MIP, from $40 to....$50.00
Masters of the Universe, accessory, Screech, Mattel, MIP, from $35 to....$45.00
Masters of the Universe, accessory, Stilt Stalker, Mattel, MIP, from $18 to....$22.00
Masters of the Universe, accessory, Weapons Pak, Mattel, MIP, from $12 to....$18.00
Masters of the Universe, accessory, Zoar, Mattel, MIP, from $28 to....$32.00
Masters of the Universe, figure, Battle Armor He-Man, Mattel, MOC, from $50 to....$55.00

Masters of the Universe, figure, Battle Armor Skeletor, Mattel, MOC, from $40.00 to $50.00; Beast Man, Mattel, MOC, from $85.00 to $95.00. (Photo courtesy Morphy Auctions)

Masters of the Universe, figure, Blade, Mattel, MOC, from $65 to....$75.00
Masters of the Universe, figure, Blast Attack, Mattel, MOC, from $52 to....$58.00
Masters of the Universe, figure, Buzz-Off, Buzz-Off Hordak or Clawful, MOC, ea from $38 to....$42.00
Masters of the Universe, figure, Clamp Champ, Mattel, MOC, from $68 to....$72.00
Masters of the Universe, figure, Dragstor the Evil Horde, Mattel, MOC, from $55 to....$65.00
Masters of the Universe, figure, Evil-Lyn, Mattel, MOC, from $100 to....$115.00
Masters of the Universe, figure, Extender, Mattel, MOC, from $40 to....$50.00
Masters of the Universe, figure, Faker, Mattel, MOC, from $200 to....$225.00
Masters of the Universe, figure, Faker II, Mattel, MOC, from $65 to....$75.00

Masters of the Universe, figure, Fisto or Grizzlor, Mattel, MOC, ea from $38 to....................$42.00

Masters of the Universe, figure, Grizzlor (blk), Mattel, MOC, from $120 to....................$130.00

Masters of the Universe, figure, Gwilder, Mattel, MOC, from $40 to....................$50.00

Masters of the Universe, figure, He-Man, Mattel, MOC, from $200 to....................$210.00

Masters of the Universe, figure, He-Man (Thunder Punch), Mattel, MOC, from $40 to....................$50.00

Masters of the Universe, figure, Hordak, Mattel, MOC, from $60 to....................$70.00

Masters of the Universe, figure, Horde Trooper, Mattel, MOC, from $138 to....................$142.00

Masters of the Universe, figure, Jitsu or King Hiss, Mattel, MOC, ea from $38 to....................$42.00

Masters of the Universe, figure, King Randor, Mattel, MOC, from $80 to....................$85.00

Masters of the Universe, figure, Leech, Mattel, MOC, from $38 to....................$42.00

Masters of the Universe, figure, Man-At-Arms, Mattel, MOC (unpunched), from $105.00 to $115.00. (Photo courtesy Morphy Auctions)

Masters of the Universe, figure, Man-E-Faces, Mattel, MOC, from $60 to....................$70.00

Masters of the Universe, figure, Mantenna, Mattel, MOC, from $38 to....................$42.00

Masters of the Universe, figure, Mekaneck, Mattel, MOC, from $58 to....................$62.00

Masters of the Universe, figure, Mer-Man, Mattel, MOC, from $108 to....................$115.00

Masters of the Universe, figure, Modulok, Mattel, MOC, from $38 to....................$42.00

Masters of the Universe, figure, Moss Man or Multi-Bot, Mattel, MOC, ea from $38 to....................$42.00

Masters of the Universe, figure, Ninjor, Mattel, MOC, from $75 to....................$85.00

Masters of the Universe, figure, Orko, Mattel, MOC, from $45 to....................$55.00

Masters of the Universe, figure, Prince Adam, Mattel, MOC, from $60 to....................$70.00

Masters of the Universe, figure, Ram-Man, Mattel, MOC, from $60 to....................$70.00

Masters of the Universe, figure, Rattlor, Mattel, MOC, from $38 to....................$42.00

Masters of the Universe, figure, Rio Blast, Mattel, MOC, from $45 to....................$55.00

Masters of the Universe, figure, Roboto, Mattel, MOC, from $38 to....................$42.00

Masters of the Universe, figure, Rokkon, Mattel, MOC, from $30 to....................$35.00

Masters of the Universe, figure, Rotar, Mattel, MOC, from $65 to....................$75.00

Masters of the Universe, figure, Saurod, Mattel, MOC, from $40 to....................$50.00

Masters of the Universe, figure, Scare Glow Spector, Mattel, MOC, from $120 to....................$130.00

Masters of the Universe, figure, Skeletor, Mattel, MOC, from $175 to....................$200.00

Masters of the Universe, figure, Snake Face, Mattel, MOC, from $65 to....................$75.00

Masters of the Universe, figure, Snout Spout, Mattel, MOC, from $50 to....................$60.00

Masters of the Universe, figure, Sorceress, Mattel, MOC, from $80 to....................$90.00

Masters of the Universe, figure, Spikor, Mattel, MOC, from $38 to....................$42.00

Masters of the Universe, figure, Sssqueeze, Mattel, MOC, from $60 to....................$70.00

Masters of the Universe, figure, Stratos, Mattel, MOC, from $115 to....................$125.00

Masters of the Universe, figure, Sy-Klone, Mattel, MOC, from $35 to....................$45.00

Masters of the Universe, figure, Teela, Mattel, MOC (unpunched), from $110.00 to $120.00. (Photo courtesy Morphy Auctions)

Masters of the Universe, figure, Trapjaw, Mattel, MOC, from $65 to....................$75.00

Masters of the Universe, figure, Tri Klops, Mattel, MOC, from $55 to....................$65.00

Masters of the Universe, figure, Tung Lasher, Mattel, MOC, from $40 to....................$50.00

Masters of the Universe, figure, Twistoid, Mattel, MOC, from $70 to....................$80.00

Masters of the Universe, figure, Two-Bad, Mattel, MOC, from $35 to $45.00
Masters of the Universe, figure, Webstor, Mattel, MOC, from $35 to $45.00
Masters of the Universe, figure, Whiplash, Mattel, MOC, from $30 to $40.00
Masters of the Universe, figure, Zodac, Mattel, MOC, from $125 to $135.00
Micronauts, accessory, Astro Station, Mego, MIP, from $20 to $25.00
Micronauts, accessory, Battle Cruiser, Mego, MIP, from $65 to $75.00
Micronauts, accessory, Galactic Command Center, MIP, from $40 to $50.00
Micronauts, accessory, Hornetroid, Mego, MIP, from $45 to . $50.00
Micronauts, accessory, Hydro Copter, Mego, MIP, from $30 to $40.00
Micronauts, accessory, Mega City, Mego, MIP, from $35 to.. $35.00
Micronauts, accessory, Microrail City, Mego, MIP, from $40 to $45.00
Micronauts, accessory, Mobile Exploration Lab, Mego, MIP, from $30 to $40.00
Micronauts, accessory, Neon Orbiter, Mego, MIP, from $20 to $25.00
Micronauts, accessory, Photon Sled w/Figure, Mego, 1976, unused & unassembled, MIP, from $50 to $75.00
Micronauts, accessory, Rocket Tubes, Mego, MIP, from $45 to $55.00
Micronauts, accessory, Star Searcher, Mego, MIP, from $35 to $45.00
Micronauts, accessory, Stratastation, Mego, MIP, from $30 to $40.00
Micronauts, figure, Andromeda, Mego, MIP, from $20 to . $30.00
Micronauts, figure, Antron, Mego, MIP, from $90 to $100.00
Micronauts, figure, Baron Karza, Mego, MIP, from $25 to . $35.00
Micronauts, figure, Biotron, Mego, MIP, from $20 to $30.00
Micronauts, figure, Centaurus, Mego, MIP, from $200 to . $210.00
Micronauts, figure, Force Commander, Mego, MIP, from $20 to $30.00
Micronauts, figure, Galactic Defender or Galactic Warrior, Mego, MIP, ea from $20 to $30.00
Micronauts, figure, Giant Acroyear, Mego, MIP, from $20 to . $30.00
Micronauts, figure, Kronos, Mego, MIP, from $200 to $210.00
Micronauts, figure, Lobros, Mego, MIP, from $200 to..... $210.00
Micronauts, figure, Membros, Mego, MIP, from $90 to... $100.00
Micronauts, figure, Microtron, Mego, MIP, from $40 to $50.00
Micronauts, figure, Nemesis Robot, Mego, unused, MIP, from $25 to $30.00
Micronauts, figure, Oberon, Mego, unassembled, MIP, from $30 to $40.00
Micronauts, figure, Pharoid w/Time Chamber, Mego, MIP (unpunched), from $30 to $40.00
Micronauts, figure, Phobos Robot, Mego, MIP, from $20 to .. $30.00
Micronauts, figure, Repto, Mego, MIP, from $90 to $100.00
Micronauts, figure, Time Traveler, Mego, MIP, from $25 to.. $35.00
Official World's Greatest Super Heroes, see Super Heroes
One Million BC, accessory, Tribal Lair, Mego, MIB, from $200 to $210.00
One Million BC, accessory, Tribal Lair Gift Set (w/5 figures), MIB, from $350 to $375.00
One Million BC, creature, Dimetrodon, Mego, MIB, from $200 to $225.00
One Million BC, creature, Hairy Rhino, Mego, MIB, from $250 to $275.00
One Million BC, creature, Tyrannosaur, Mego, MIB, from $250 to $275.00
One Million BC, figure, Grok, Mada, Orm, Trag or Zon, Mego, MOC, ea from $45 to $55.00
Planet of the Apes, accessory, Action Stallion, r/c, Mego, 1970s, MIB, from $75 to $110.00
Planet of the Apes, accessory, Battering Ram, Jail, or Dr Zaius' Throne, Mego, 1970s, MIB, ea from $35 to $45.00
Planet of the Apes, accessory, Catapult & Wagon, Mego, 1970s, MIB, from $155 to $165.00
Planet of the Apes, accessory, Forbidden Zone Trap or Treehouse (w/5 figures), Mego, 1970s, MIB, ea $175 to $225.00

Planet of the Apes, accessory, Fortress, Mego, 1970s, MIB, from $175.00 to $225.00. (Photo courtesy Morphy Auctions)

Planet of the Apes, accessory, Village, Mego, 1970s, MIB, from $175 to $225.00
Planet of the Apes, figure, 5", any Bend 'n Flex, Mego, MOC, ea from $20 to $25.00
Planet of the Apes, figure, 7", any, Hasbro, 1999, MIP, ea from $5 to $8.00
Planet of the Apes, figure, 8", Astronaut, any, Mego, 1970s, MIB, from $225 to $275.00
Planet of the Apes, figure, 8", Astronaut, any, Mego, 1970s, MOC, ea from $100 to $130.00
Planet of the Apes, figure, 8", Cornelius, Dr Zaius, Galen or Zira, Mego, 1970s, MIB, ea from $175 to $225.00
Planet of the Apes, figure, 8", Cornelius, Dr Zaius, Galen or Zira, Mego, 1970s, MOC, ea from $120 to $130.00
Planet of the Apes, figure, 8", General Urko, General Ursus or Soldier Ape, Mego, 1970s, MIB, ea from $240 to.... $260.00
Planet of the Apes, figure, 8", General Urko, General Ursus or Soldier Ape, Mego, 1970s, MOC, ea from $200 to . $225.00
Planet of the Apes, figure, 12", any, Hasbro, 1999, MIP, from $20 to $30.00

Pocket Super Heroes, accessory, Batcave, Mego, MIB, from $275 to $325.00
Pocket Super Heroes, accessory, Batmachine, Mego, MIB, from $100 to $125.00
Pocket Super Heroes, accessory, Batmobile (w/Batman & Robin), Mego, MIB, from $175 to $225.00
Pocket Super Heroes, accessory, Spider-Car (w/Spider-Man & the Hulk), Mego, MIB, from $70 to $80.00
Pocket Super Heroes, accessory, Spider-Machine, Mego, MIB, from $75 to $125.00
Pocket Super Heroes, figure, Aquaman, Captain America or Green Goblin, Mego, MOC (wht card), ea from $90 to $110.00
Pocket Super Heroes, figure, Batman, Mego, MOC (red card), from $65 to $75.00
Pocket Super Heroes, figure, Batman, Mego, MOC (wht card), from $120 to $130.00
Pocket Super Heroes, figure, Gen Zod, Mego, MOC (red card), from $20 to $30.00
Pocket Super Heroes, figure, Incredible Hulk, Mego, MOC (red card), from $28 to $32.00
Pocket Super Heroes, figure, Incredible Hulk, Mego, MOC (wht card), from $38 to $42.00
Pocket Super Heroes, figure, Jor-El or Lex Luthor, MOC (red card), from $18 to $22.00
Pocket Super Heroes, figure, Robin, Mego, MOC (red card), from $55 to $65.00
Pocket Super Heroes, figure, Robin, Mego, MOC (wht card), from $90 to $110.00
Pocket Super Heroes, figure, Spider-Man, Mego, MOC (red card), from $45 to $55.00
Pocket Super Heroes, figure, Spider-Man, Mego, MOC (wht card), from $90 to $110.00
Pocket Super Heroes, figure, Superman, Mego, MOC (red card), from $35 to $45.00
Pocket Super Heroes, figure, Superman, Mego, MOC (wht card), from $70 to $80.00
Pocket Super Heroes, figure, Wonder Woman, Mego, MOC (wht card), from $70 to $80.00
Power Lords, figure, any, MOC, ea from $20 to $30.00
Rambo, accessory, .50 Caliber Anti-Aircraft Gun or .50 Caliber Machine Gun, Coleco, MIP, ea from $10 to $15.00
Rambo, accessory, Defender 6x6 Assault Vehicle, Coleco, MIB, from $28 to $32.00
Rambo, accessory, SAVAGE Strike Cycle, Coleco, MIB, from $18 to $22.00
Rambo, accessory, SAVAGE Strike Headquarters, Coleco, MIB, from $50 to $60.00
Rambo, accessory, Skywolf Assault Jet, Coleco, MIB, from $25 to $30.00
Rambo, accessory, Swamp Dog, Coleco, MIB, from $18 to $22.00
Rambo, accessory, 106 Recoilless Anti-Tank Gun or 81mm Motar, Coleco, MIP, ea from $10 to $15.00
Rambo, figure, Black Dragon, Chief, Colonel Troutman, General Warhawk or Gripper, Coleco, MOC, ea from $8 to $12.00
Rambo, figure, Dr Hyde, Snakebite, TD Jackson or X-ray, Coleco, MOC, ea from $18 to $22.00
Rambo, figure, KAT, Mad Dog, Nomad, Rambo or Rambo w/Fire Power, Coleco, MOC, ea from $8 to $15.00
Rambo, figure, Sgt Havoc, Turbo or White Dragon, Coleco, MOC, ea from $8 to $15.00
Rambo, Skyfire Assault Copter, Coleco, MIB, from $28 to $32.00
Robin Hood & His Merry Men, figure, Friar Tuck, Mego, MIB, from $60 to $70.00
Robin Hood & His Merry Men, figure, Little John, Mego, MIB, from $150 to $160.00
Robin Hood & His Merry Men, figure, Robin Hood, Mego, MIB, from $275 to $300.00
Robin Hood & His Merry Men, figure, Will Scarlet, Mego, MIB, from $250 to $275.00
Robin Hood Prince of Thieves, accessory, Battle Wagon, Kenner, 1991, MIP, from $25 to $35.00
Robin Hood Prince of Thieves, accessory, Bola Bomber, Kenner, 1991, MIP, from $8 to $12.00
Robin Hood Prince of Thieves, accessory, Net Launcher, Kenner, 1991, MIP, from $10 to $15.00
Robin Hood Prince of Thieves, accessory, Sherwood Forest Playset, Kenner, 1991, MIP, from $55 to $65.00
Robin Hood Prince of Thieves, figure, Azeem, Little John or Sheriff of Nottingham, Kenner, 1991, MOC, ea from $12 to $18.00

Robin Hood Prince of Thieves, figure, Friar Tuck, Kenner, MOC, from $15.00 to $25.00

Robin Hood Prince of Thieves, figure, Robin Hood (either head) w/Cross Bow, Kenner, 1991, MOC, ea from $12 to $18.00
Robin Hood Prince of Thieves, figure, Robin Hood w/Long Bow, Kenner, 1991, MOC, from $12 to $18.00
Robin Hood Prince of Thieves, figure, The Dark Warrior or Will Scarlet, Kenner, 1991, MOC, from $12 to $18.00
Robocop (Ultra Police), accessory, Robo-Command vehicle w/ figure, Kenner, MIB, from $25 to $35.00
Robocop (Ultra Police), accessory, Robo-Jailer vehicle, Kenner, MIB, from $38 to $42.00
Robocop (Ultra Police), figure, any, Kenner, 1988-90, MOC, ea, from $15 to $25.00
Robotech, accessory, Armoured Cyclone, Matchbox, MIB, from $35 to $45.00
Robotech, accessory, Bioroid Hover Craft, Matchbox, MIB, from $20 to $30.00

Robotech, accessory, Bioroid Invid Fighter, Dana's Hover Cycle, or Excaliber MkVI, Matchbox, MIB, ea from $35 to..$45.00
Robotech, accessory, Gladiator, Invid Scout Ship, Invid Shock Trooper or Raider X, Matchbox, MIB, ea from $35 to..$45.00
Robotech, accessory, SDF-1 Playset, Matchbox, MIB, from $425 to............ $475.00
Robotech, accessory, Spartan, Tactical Battle Pod or Veritech Fighter, Matchbox, MIB, ea from $35 to............$45.00
Robotech, accessory, Veritech Hover Tank or Zentraedi Officer's Battle Pod, Matchbox, MIB, ea from $30 to............$45.00
Robotech, accessory, Zentraedi Powered Armor, Matchbox, MIB, from $40 to............$50.00
Robotech, figure, 3¾", Bioroid Terminator, Lisa Hayes or Micronized Zentraedi, Matchbox, MOC, ea from $12 to.........$18.00
Robotech, figure, 3¾", Corg, Lunk, Max Sterling, Miriya (red) or Rick Hunter, Matchbox, MOC, ea from $20 to $25.00
Robotech, figure, 3¾", Dana Sterling or Roy Fokker, MOC, ea from $28 to............$32.00
Robotech, figure, 3¾", Miriya (blk), Matchbox, MOC, from $60 to............$70.00
Robotech, figure, 3¾", Miriya (red), Matchbox, MOC, from $18 to............$22.00
Robotech, figure, 3¾", Rand, Robotech Master or Zor Prime, Matchbox, MOC, ea from $10 to............$18.00
Robotech, figure, 3¾", Scott Bernard, MOC, from $40 to....$45.00
Robotech, figure, 6", any character, Matchbox, MOC, ea from $18 to............$22.00
Robotech, figure, 8", Armoured Zentraedi, Matchbox, MIP, from $20 to............$25.00
Robotech, figure, 12", Dana Sterling, Lisa Hayes, Lynn Minmei or Rick Hunter, Matchbox, MIB, ea from $45 to $55.00
Schwarzenegger Commando, see Commando (Schwarzenegger)
She-Ra Princess of Power, accessory, Crystal Castle or Crystal Falls, Mattel, 1984-86, MIP, ea from $55 to............$65.00
She-Ra Princess of Power, figure, Angella, Bow, Castaspella or Double Trouble, Mattel, 1984-86, MOC, ea from $12 to............$18.00
She-Ra Princess of Power, figure, any creature, Mattel, 1984-86, MIP, ea from $35 to............$45.00
She-Ra Princess of Power, figure, Castaspella, She-Ra or Shower Power Catra, Mattel, 1984-86, MOC, ea from $35 to .$45.00
She-Ra Princess of Power, figure, Catra, Mattel, 1984-86, MOC, from $40 to............$50.00
She-Ra Princess of Power, figure, Entrapta, Flutterina, Frosta, Glimmer or Kowl, Mattel, 1984-86, MOC, ea from $18 to............$22.00
She-Ra Princess of Power, figure, Loo-Kee, Mermista, Peekablue, Perfuma or Spinerella, Mattel, 1984-86, MOC, ea from $18............$22.00
She-Ra Princess of Power, figure, Netossa, Mattel, 1984-86, MOC, from $20 to............$30.00
She-Ra Princess of Power, figure, Starburst She-Ra or Sweet Bee, Mattel, 1984-86, MOC, ea from $35 to............$45.00
She-Ra Princess of Power, outfit, any, Mattel, 1984-86, MIP, ea from $10 to............$15.00
Six Million Dollar Man, accessory, Backpack Radio, Bionic Cycle or Bionic Mission Vehicle, Kenner, MIP, ea from $20 to............$30.00
Six Million Dollar Man, accessory, Bionic Transport & Repair Station, Kenner, MIB, from $40 to............$50.00
Six Million Dollar Man, accessory, Mission Control Center, Kenner, MIB, from $75 to............$85.00
Six Million Dollar Man, accessory, OSI Headquarters, Kenner, MIB, from $65 to............$75.00
Six Million Dollar Man, accessory, Venus Space Probe, Kenner, MIB, from $250 to............$300.00
Six Million Dollar Man, figure, Bionic Bigfoot, Kenner, MIB, from $175 to............$200.00
Six Million Dollar Man, figure, Maskatron, Kenner, MIB, from $145 to............$155.00
Six Million Dollar Man, figure, Oscar Goldman, Kenner, MIB, from $90 to............$110.00
Six Million Dollar Man, figure, Steve Austin, Kenner, MIB, from $100 to............$125.00
Six Million Dollar Man, figure, Steve Austin (Biosonic Arm), Kenner, MIB, from $300 to............$325.00
Six Million Dollar Man, figure, Steve Austin (w/engine block or girder), Kenner, MIB, from $145 to............$155.00
Space: 1999, accessory, Moonbase Alpha, Mattel, MIB, from $150 to............$175.00
Space: 1999, figure, any except Zython Alien, Mattel, MOC, ea from $60 to............$70.00
Space: 1999, figure, Zython Alien, Mattel, MOC, from $270 to............$280.00
Spider-Man (New Animated Series), accessory, 5", Daily Bugle Play Set, Toy Biz, 1994-96, MIP, from $15 to............$25.00
Spider-Man (New Animated Series), figure, 5", any except Rhino or S-M w/Web Cannon, Toy Biz, 1994-96, MOC, ea $10 to............$15.00

Spider-Man (New Animated Series), figure, Rhino, Toy Biz, 1994 – 1996, MOC, from $18.00 to $22.00.

Spider-Man (New Animated Series), figure, 5", Spider-Man (w/ cannon), Toy Biz, 1994-96, MOC, from $18 to..........$22.00
Spider-Man (New Animated Series), figure, 10", any character, Mattel, 1994-96, MIP, ea from $25 to............$35.00
Spider-Man (New Animated Series), Projectors, any, Toy Biz, 1994-96, MIP, ea from $12 to............$18.00
Starsky & Hutch, accessory, car, Mego, MIB, from $150 to .$175.00

Starsky & Hutch, figure, any character, Mego, MOC, ea from $35 to $45.00

Super Heroes, see also DC Comics Super Heroes and Pocket Super Heroes

Super Heroes, accessory, Batcave, Mego, 1974, NMIB, from $350 to $375.00

Super Heroes, figure, 8", see also Super Heroes (Fantastic Four) and Super Heroes (Fist Fighting)

Super Heroes, figure, 8", Aquaman, Mego, MIB (solid box), from $800 to $1,000.00

Super Heroes, figure, 8", Aquaman, Mego, MIB (window box) or MOC, ea from $150 to $200.00

Super Heroes, figure, 8", Aquaman, Mego, MOC, from $300 to $400.00

Super Heroes, figure, 8", Batgirl, Mego, MIB, from $300.00 to $325.00; Batman (removable mask), MIB (window box), from $750.00 to $850.00. (Photo courtesy Morphy Auctions)

Super Heroes, figure, 8", Batman (pnt cowl), Mego, MIB or MOC, from $150 to $175.00

Super Heroes, figure, 8", Batman (removable cowl), Mego, MIB (solid box), from $1,000 to $1,100.00

Super Heroes, figure, 8", Batman (removable cowl), Mego, MOC, from $300 to $350.00

Super Heroes, figure, 8", Captain America, Mego, MIB, from $400 to $425.00

Super Heroes, figure, 8", Captain America, Mego, MOC, from $145 to $155.00

Super Heroes, figure, 8", Catwoman, Mego, MIB, from $300 to $350.00

Super Heroes, figure, 8", Catwoman, Mego, MOC, from $1,500 to $1,750.00

Super Heroes, figure, 8", Clark Kent, Mego, MIB, from $1,500 to $1,750.00

Super Heroes, figure, 8", Conan, Mego, MIB, from $350 to.... $375.00

Super Heroes, figure, 8", Conan, Mego, MOC, from $450 to $475.00

Super Heroes, figure, 8", Falcon, Mego, MIB, from $150 to.... $175.00

Super Heroes, figure, 8", Falcon, Mego, MOC, from $1,200 to $1,600.00

Super Heroes, figure, 8", Green Arrow, Mego, MIB, from $400 to $450.00

Super Heroes, figure, 8", Green Arrow, Mego, MOC, from $1,500 to $1,750.00

Super Heroes, figure, 8", Green Goblin, Mego, MIB, from $200 to $250.00

Super Heroes, figure, 8", Green Goblin, Mego, MOC, from $1,500 to $1,750.00

Super Heroes, figure, 8", Incredible Hulk, Mego, MIB, from $50 to $60.00

Super Heroes, figure, 8", Incredible Hulk, Mego, MOC, from $100 to $125.00

Super Heroes, figure, 8", Iron Man, Mego, MIB, from $100 to $125.00

Super Heroes, figure, 8", Iron Man, Mego, MOC, from $425 to $450.00

Super Heroes, figure, 8", Isis, Mego, MIB, from $200 to .. $250.00

Super Heroes, figure, 8", Isis, Mego, MOC, from $100 to . $125.00

Super Heroes, figure, 8", Joker, Mego, MIB, from $150.00 to $175.00. (Photo courtesy Morphy Auctions)

Super Heroes, figure, 8", Lizard, Mego, MIB, from $175 to ..$250.00

Super Heroes, figure, 8", Lizard, Mego, MOC, from $1,500 to ..$1,750.00

Super Heroes, figure, 8", Mr Mxyzptlk (open mouth), Mego, MIB, from $70 to $80.00

Super Heroes, figure, 8", Mr Mxyzptlk (open mouth), Mego, MOC, from $155 to $165.00

Super Heroes, figure, 8", Mr Mxyzptlk (smirk), Mego, MIB, from $145 to $155.00

Super Heroes, figure, 8", Penguin, Mego, MIB, from $155 to ..$165.00

Super Heroes, figure, 8", Penguin, Mego, MOC, from $150 to $200.00

Super Heroes, figure, 8", Riddler, Mego, MIB, from $275 to $325.00

Super Heroes, figure, 8", Riddler, Mego, MOC, from $1,500 to $1,750.00

Super Heroes, figure, 8", Robin (pnt mask), Mego, MIB, from $145 to $155.00

Super Heroes, figure, 8", Robin (pnt mask), Mego, MOC, from $90 to $110.00

Super Heroes, figure, 8", Robin (removable mask), Mego, MIB (window box), from $700 to $725.00

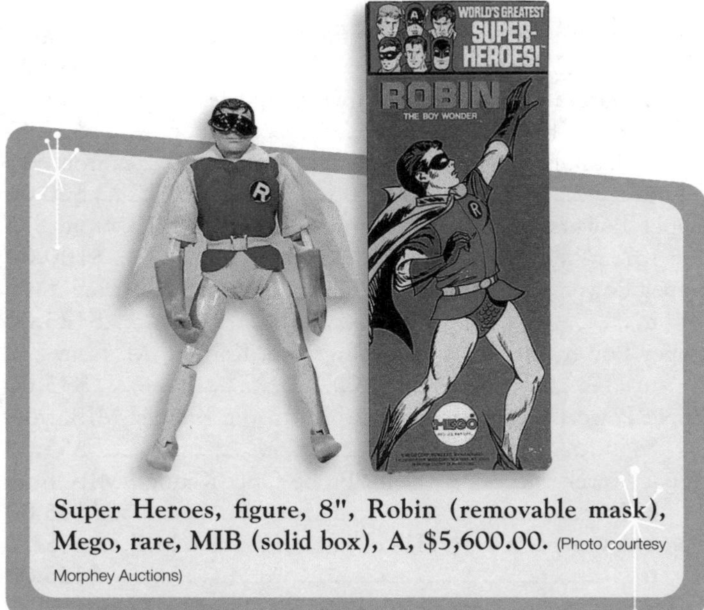

Super Heroes, figure, 8", Robin (removable mask), Mego, rare, MIB (solid box), A, $5,600.00. (Photo courtesy Morphey Auctions)

Super Heroes, figure, 8", Shazam, Mego, MIB, from $175 to . $200.00
Super Heroes, figure, 8", Shazam, Mego, MOC, from $140 to $160.00
Super Heroes, figure, 8", Spider-Man, Mego, MIB, from $75 to $100.00
Super Heroes, figure, 8", Spider-Man, Mego, MOC, from $50 to $60.00
Super Heroes, figure, 8", Supergirl, Mego, MIB, from $450 to . $500.00
Super Heroes, figure, 8", Supergirl, Mego, MOC, A $2,700.00
Super Heroes, figure, 8", Superman, Mego, MIB (solid box), from $725 to $775.00
Super Heroes, figure, 8", Superman, Mego, MIB (window box), from $200 to $300.00
Super Heroes, figure, 8", Superman, Mego, MOC, A .. $1,750.00
Super Heroes, figure, 8", Tarzan, Mego, MIB, from $150 to . $175.00
Super Heroes, figure, 8", Tarzan, Mego, MOC, from $220 to $230.00
Super Heroes, figure, 8", Thor, Mego, MIB, from $400 to. $425.00
Super Heroes, figure, 8", Thor, Mego, MOC, from $450 to .. $475.00
Super Heroes, figure, 8", Wonder Woman, Mego, MIB, from $350 to $375.00
Super Heroes, figure, 8", Wonder Woman, Mego, MOC, from $475 to $525.00
Super Heroes, figure, 12½", see also Super Heroes (Fly-Away Action)
Super Heroes, figure, 12½", Batman, Mego, MIB, from $125 to $150.00
Super Heroes, figure, 12½", Captain America, Mego, MIB, from $175 to $200.00
Super Heroes, figure, 12½", General Jod, Mego, MIB, from $100 to $150.00
Super Heroes, figure, 12½", Incredible Hulk, Mego, MIB, from $100 to $150.00
Super Heroes, figure, 12½", Jor-El (Superman's father), Mego, MIB, from $100 to $150.00
Super Heroes, figure, 12½", Lex Luthor, Mego, MIB, from $100 to $150.00
Super Heroes, figure, 12½", Spider-Man, Mego, MIB, from $100 to $150.00
Super Heroes, figure, 12½", Superman, Mego, MIB, from $100 to $150.00
Super Heroes (Bend 'n Flex), figure, Aquaman, 5", Mego, MOC, from $125 to $150.00
Super Heroes (Bend 'n Flex), figure, Batgirl, 5", Mego, MOC, from $125 to $150.00
Super Heroes (Bend 'n Flex), figure, Batman, 5", Mego, MOC, from $75 to $100.00
Super Heroes (Bend 'n Flex), figure, Captain America, 5", Mego, MOC, from $75 to $100.00
Super Heroes (Bend 'n Flex), figure, Catwoman, 5", Mego, MOC, from $175 to $200.00
Super Heroes (Bend 'n Flex), figure, Joker, 5", Mego, MOC, from $150 to $175.00
Super Heroes (Bend 'n Flex), figure, Mr Mxyzptlk, 5", Mego, MOC, from $125 to $150.00
Super Heroes (Bend 'n Flex), figure, Penguin, 5", Mego, MOC, from $150 to $175.00
Super Heroes (Bend 'n Flex), figure, Riddler, 5", Mego, MOC, from $150 to $175.00
Super Heroes (Bend 'n Flex), figure, Robin, 5", Mego, MOC, from $75 to $100.00
Super Heroes (Bend 'n Flex), figure, Shazam, 5", Mego, MOC, $125 to $150.00
Super Heroes (Bend 'n Flex), figure, Spider-Man, 5", Mego, MOC, from $125 to $150.00
Super Heroes (Bend 'n Flex), figure, Supergirl, 5", Mego, MOC, from $175 to $200.00
Super Heroes (Bend 'n Flex), figure, Superman, 5", Mego, MOC, from $75 to $100.00
Super Heroes (Bend 'n Flex), figure, Tarzan, 5", Mego, MOC, from $50 to $75.00
Super Heroes (Bend 'n Flex), figure, Wonder Woman, 5", Mego, MOC, from $100 to $125.00

Super Heroes (Fantastic Four), figure, 8", Human Torch, Mego, MIB, from $75.00 to $85.00; Invisible Girl, 8", MOC, from $140.00 to $150.00. (Photo courtesy Morphy Auctions)

Super Heroes (Fantastic Four), figure, Human Torch, 8", Mego, MOC, from $45 to....................$55.00

Super Heroes (Fantastic Four), figure, Invisible Girl, 8", Mego, MOC, from $55 to....................$65.00

Super Heroes (Fantastic Four), figure, Mr Fantastic, 8", Mego, MIB, from $140 to....................$150.00

Super Heroes (Fantastic Four), figure, Mr Fantastic, 8", Mego, MOC, from $55 to....................$65.00

Super Heroes (Fantastic Four), figure, Thing, 8", Mego, MIB, from $145 to....................$155.00

Super Heroes (Fantastic Four), figure, Thing, 8", Mego, MOC, from $55 to....................$65.00

Super Heroes (Fist Fighting), figure, Batman, 8", Mego, MIB, from $400 to....................$425.00

Super Heroes (Fist Fighting), figure, Robin, 8", Mego, MIB, from $375 to....................$425.00

Super Heroes (Fist-Fighting), figure, Joker, 8", Mego, MIB, from $550 to....................$575.00

Super Heroes (Fist-Fighting), figure, Riddler, 8", Mego, MIB, from $550 to....................$575.00

Super Heroes (Fly-Away Action), figure, Batman, 12½", Mego, from $120 to....................$130.00

Super Heroes (Fly-Away Action), figure, Batman, 12½", (Magnetic), Mego, MIB, from $200 to....................$250.00

Super Heroes (Fly-Away Action), figure, Captain America, 12½", Mego, MIB, from $175 to....................$200.00

Super Heroes (Fly-Away Action), figure, Incredible Hulk, 12½", Mego, MIB, from $100 to....................$150.00

Super Heroes (Fly-Away Action), figure, Robin, 12½", Mego, MIB, from $200 to....................$250.00

Super Heroes (Fly-Away Action), figure, Robin, 12½", (Magnetic), Mego, MOC, from $225 to....................$275.00

Super Heroes (Fly-Away Action), figure, Spider-Man, 12½", Mego, from $150 to....................$175.00

Super Heroes (Fly-Away Action), figure, Superman, 12½", Mego, MIB, from $130 to....................$140.00

Super Monsters, figure, Count Dracula, Ahi, 1960s, MOC, from $150.00 to $175.00. (Photo courtesy Morphy Auctions)

Super Monsters, figure, Frankenstein, The Mummy or Wolfman, Ahi, 1960s, MOC, ea from $150 to....................$175.00

Super Naturals, accessory, Ghost Finder, Tonka, 1986, MIB, from $25 to....................$30.00

Super Naturals, accessory, Lionwings Battle Creature, Tonka, 1986, MIB, from $20 to....................$25.00

Super Naturals, figure, any character, Tonka, MOC, ea from $15 to....................$20.00

Super Powers, accessory, Batcopter, Kenner, MIB, from $75 to....................$100.00

Super Powers, accessory, Batmobile, Kenner, MIB, from $100 to....................$125.00

Super Powers, accessory, carrying case, Kenner, M, from $30 to....................$35.00

Super Powers, accessory, Darkseid Destroyer, Kenner, MIB, from $45 to....................$55.00

Super Powers, accessory, Delta Probe One, Kenner, MIB, from $30 to....................$35.00

Super Powers, accessory, Hall of Justice, Kenner, MIB, from $200 to....................$225.00

Super Powers, accessory, Kalibak Boulder Bomber, Kenner, MIB, from $20 to....................$30.00

Super Powers, accessory, Lex-Sor 7, Kenner, MIB, from $20 to....................$30.00

Super Powers, accessory, Supermobile, Kenner, MIB, from $25 to....................$35.00

Super Powers, figure, Aquaman, Kenner, MOC, from $40 to....................$50.00

Super Powers, figure, Batman, Kenner, MOC, from $70 to....................$80.00

Super Powers, figure, Brainiac, Kenner, MOC, from $25 to....................$35.00

Super Powers, figure, Clark Kent, Kenner, MOC (mail-in), from $50 to....................$60.00

Super Powers, figure, Cyborg, Kenner, MOC, from $270 to....................$280.00

Super Powers, figure, Cyclotron, Kenner, MOC, from $45 to....................$55.00

Super Powers, figure, Darkseid, Kenner, MOC, from $15 to....................$20.00

Super Powers, figure, DeSaad, Kenner, MOC, from $25.00 to $35.00. (Photo courtesy serioustoyz.com)

Super Powers, figure, Dr Fate, Kenner, MOC, from $55 to....................$65.00

Super Powers, figure, Firestorm, Kenner, MOC, from $30 to....................$40.00

Super Powers, figure, Flash, Kenner, MOC, from $20 to....................$25.00

Super Powers, figure, Golden Pharaoh, Kenner, MOC, from $75 to...$85.00
Super Powers, figure, Green Arrow, Kenner, MOC, from $45 to...$55.00
Super Powers, figure, Green Lantern, Kenner, MOC, from $55 to...$65.00
Super Powers, figure, Hawkman, Kenner, MOC, from, $55 to...$65.00

Super Powers, figure, Joker, Kenner, MOC, from $25.00 to $35.00. (Photo courtesy serioustoyz.com)

Super Powers, figure, Kalibak, Kenner, MOC, from $20 to...$30.00
Super Powers, figure, Lex Luthor, Kenner, MOC, from $15 to...$20.00
Super Powers, figure, Mantis, Kenner, MOC, from $20 to...$30.00
Super Powers, figure, Martian Manhunter, Kenner, MOC, from $40 to...$50.00
Super Powers, figure, Mister Freeze, Kenner, MOC, from $60 to...$70.00
Super Powers, figure, Mister Miracle, Kenner, MOC, from $125 to...$135.00
Super Powers, figure, Orion, Kenner, MOC, from $30 to...$40.00
Super Powers, figure, Parademon, Kenner, MOC, from $25 to...$35.00
Super Powers, figure, Penguin, Kenner, MOC, from $45 to...$55.00
Super Powers, figure, Plastic Man, Kenner, MOC, from $100 to...$115.00
Super Powers, figure, Red Tornado, Kenner, MOC, from $45 to...$55.00
Super Powers, figure, Samurai, Kenner, MOC, from $90 to...$100.00
Super Powers, figure, Shazam, Kenner, MOC, from $65 to...$75.00
Super Powers, figure, Steppenwolf, Kenner, MIP (mail-in), from $15 to...$20.00
Super Powers, figure, Steppenwolf, Kenner, MOC, from $65 to...$75.00
Super Powers, figure, Superman, Kenner, MOC (unpunched), from $90 to...$100.00
Super Powers, figure, Tyr, Kenner, MOC, from $45 to...$55.00
Super Powers, figure, Wonder Woman, Kenner, MOC, from $55 to...$65.00
Superman (Animated), figure, Anti-Kryptonite Superman or Brainiac, Kenner, 1995, MOC, ea from $8 to...$12.00
Superman (Animated), figure, Capture Claw Superman, Electro Energy Superman, Kenner, 1995, MOC, ea from $15 to. $20.00
Superman (Animated), figure, Capture Net Superman, City Camp Superman, Kenner, 1995, MOC, ea from $8 to...$12.00
Superman (Animated), figure, Cyber Crunch Superman, Fortress of Solitude Superman, Kenner, 1995, MOC, ea from $18 to...$22.00
Superman (Animated), figure, Darkseid or Evil Bizarro, Kenner, 1995, MOC, ea from $25 to...$30.00
Superman (Animated), figure, Deep Dive Superman, Electro Energy Superman, Kenner, 1995, MOC, ea from $8 to...$12.00
Superman (Animated), figure, Flying Superman, Fortress of Solitude Superman, Kenner, 1995, MOC, ea from $8 to...$12.00
Superman (Animated), figure, Kryptonite Escape Superman, Kenner, 1995, MOC, from $15 to...$20.00
Superman (Animated), figure, Lex Luthor, Neutron Star Superman, Kenner, 1995, MOC, ea from $8 to...$12.00
Superman (Animated), figure, Metallo, Kenner, 1995, MOC, from $18 to...$22.00

Superman (Animated Series), figure, Neutron Star Superman, Kenner, 1995, MOC, from $8.00 to $12.00.

Superman (Animated), figure, Power Swing Superman, Supergirl, Kenner, 1995, MOC, ea from $15 to...$20.00
Superman (Animated), figure, Quick Change Superman, Strong Arm Superman, Kenner, 1995, MOC, ea from $8 to...$12.00
Superman (Animated), figure, Tornado Force Superman, Vision Blast Superman, Kenner, 1995, MOC, ea from $15 to...$20.00
Superman (Animated), figure, Ultra Shield Superman, X-Ray Vision Superman, Kenner, 1995, MOC, ea from $8 to...$12.00
Superman (Man of Steel), figure, Blast Hammer Steel (Deluxe), Kenner, 1995-96, MOC, from $8 to...$12.00
Superman (Man of Steel), figure, Conduit, Laser Superman, Kenner, 1995-96, MOC, ea from $8 to...$12.00
Superman (Man of Steel), figure, Lex Luthor, Kenner, 1995-96, MOC, from $18 to...$22.00

Superman (Man of Steel), figure, Power Flight Superman, Solar Suit Superman, Steel, Kenner, 1995-96, MOC, ea from $8 to $12.00
Superman (Man of Steel), figure, Street Guardian Superman or Superboy, Kenner, 1995-96, MOC, ea from $8 to $12.00
Superman (Man of Steel), figure, Ultra Heat Vision Superman, Ultra Shield Superman, Kenner, 1995-96, MOC, ea from $8 to $12.00
Superman (Man of Steel), figure set, Cyber-Link Superman & Cyber-Link Batman, Kenner, 1995, MOC, from $18 to $22.00
Superman (Man of Steel), figure set, Hunter-Prey Superman & Doomsday, Kenner, 1995, MOC, from $12 to $15.00
Teen Titans, figure, Aqualad, Mego, MOC, from $350 to.. $375.00
Teen Titans, figure, Aqualad, Mego, NM, from $175 to . $200.00
Teen Titans, figure, Kid Flash, Mego, MOC, from $450 to ..$475.00
Teen Titans, figure, Kid Flash, Mego, NM, from $150 to . $175.00
Teen Titans, figure, Speedy, Mego, MOC, from $525 to. $550.00
Teen Titans, figure, Speedy, Mego, NM, from $300 to.......... $325.00

Teen Titans, figure, Wondergirl, MOC, from $500.00 to $525.00. (Photo courtesy Morphy Auctions)

Teen Titans, figure, Wondergirl, Mego, NM, from $200 to ..$225.00
Teenage Mutant Ninja Turtles, figure, Donatello or Leonardo, Playmates, 1988, 1st series, from $15 to $20.00
Teenage Mutant Ninja Turtles, figure, Michelangelo or Raphael, Playmates, 1988, 1st series, MOC, ea from $15 to......$20.00
Terminator 2, figure, any character, Kenner, 1992, MOC, ea from $10 to $20.00
Universal Monsters, figure, 8", Creature From the Black Lagoon, Remco, 1979, MIP, from $175 to........................... $225.00
Universal Monsters, figure, 8", Dracula, Remco, 1979, MIP, from $75 to $125.00
Universal Monsters, figure, 8", Frankenstein, Remco, 1979, MIP, from $30 to $50.00
Universal Monsters, figure, 8", Mummy, Remco, 1979, MIP, from $30 to $50.00
Universal Monsters, figure, 8", Phantom of the Opera, Remco, 1979, MIP, from $225 to $275.00
Universal Monsters, figure, 8", Wolfman, Remco, 1979, MIP, from $125 to $150.00
Waltons, accessory, barn or country store, Mego, MIB, ea from $140 to $160.00
Waltons, accessory, farm house only, Mego, M, from $75 to ..$85.00
Waltons, accessory, farm house w/6 figures, Mego, MIB, from $400 to $425.00
Waltons, accessory, truck, Mego, MIB, from $65 to..........$75.00
Waltons, figure set, John Boy & Mary Ellen, Mom & Pop or Grandma & Grandpa, Mego, MIB, ea set from $65 to ..$75.00
Welcome Back Kotter, figure, Barbarino, 9", Mattel, 1976, MOC, from $65 to $75.00
Welcome Back Kotter, figure, Epstein, Horshack, Mr Kotter or Washington, 9", Mattel, 1976, MOC, ea from $45 to ..$55.00
Wizard of Oz, accessory, Emerald City (w/7 8" figures), Mego, MIB, from $350 to $375.00
Wizard of Oz, accessory, Wizard of Oz & His Emerald City (w/8" Wizard figure only), Mego, MIB, from $100 to $125.00
Wizard of Oz, figure, 4", Munchkins, any, Mego, MIB, ea from $150 to $160.00
Wizard of Oz, figure, 8", any except the Wicked Witch or the Wizard, MIB, ea from $40 to $50.00
Wizard of Oz, figure, 8", Wicked Witch, Mego, MIB, from $90 to $115.00
Wizard of Oz, figure, 8", Wizard, Mego, MIB, from $250 to .$275.00
Wonder Woman (TV Series), figure, Nubia or Queen Hippolyte, Mego, M, ea from $100 to $125.00
Wonder Woman, (TV Series) figure, Steve Trevor, Mego, NRFB, A $100.00

Wonder Woman (TV Series), figure, Wonder Woman, with Diana Prince outfit, Mego, M, from $100.00 to $125.00. (Photo courtesy Wallace M. Chrouch)

World's Greatest Super Heroes, or Official World's Greatest Super Heroes, see Super Heroes or Pocket Super Heroes
World's Greatest Super Knights, figure, Black Knight, Mego, MIB, from $325 to $375.00
World's Greatest Super Knights, figure, Ivanhoe, Mego, MIB, from $225 to $275.00

World's Greatest Super Knights, figure, King Arthur, Mego, MIB, from $175 to $225.00
World's Greatest Super Knights, figure, Sir Galahad, Mego, MIB, from $275 to $325.00
World's Greatest Super Knights, figure, Sir Lancelot, Mego, MIB, from $275 to $325.00
WWF, accessory, Official WWF Monster Ring (Get Ready to Rumble), Jakks, 1996, MIB (sealed), from $35 to . $45.00
WWF, accessory, Raw is War Monster Ring, Jakks, MIB (sealed), from $60 to $70.00
WWF, accessory, Titan Sports Wrestling Stars Sling 'Em Fling 'Em Wrestling Ring, LJN, 1986, EX (Poor box), from $30 to $40.00
WWF, figure, Adam Bomb, Hasbro, 1994, MOC, from $25 to $35.00
WWF, figure, Akeem, Hasbro, MOC, from $35 to $40.00
WWF, figure, All Star Wrestlers Tag Team w/Jimmy Garvin, Precious & Steven Regal, Remco, MOC, from $40 to $50.00
WWF, figure, All Star Wrestlers Tag Team w/The Long Riders (Wild Bill Irwin & Scott Hog Irwin), Remco, MOC, from $30 to $40.00
WWF, figure, Bart 'Smoking Gunns' Gunn, Hasbro, 1994, MOC, from $30 to $40.00
WWF, figure, Big John Studd, wht skin, LJN, MOC, from $175 to $200.00

WWF, figure, Billy Jack Haynes, LJN, 1985, MOC, from $30.00 to $40.00; Jesse 'The Body' Ventura, LJN, 1985, MOC, from $20.00 to $25.00.

WWF, figure, Billy 'Smoking Gunns' Gunn, Hasbro, 1994, MOC, from $30 to $40.00
WWF, figure, Bret Hart (Superstars #1), Jakks, MOC, from $20 to $25.00
WWF, figure, Capt Lou Albano (red lapel), LJN, Series 3, MOC, from $25 to $30.00
WWF, figure, Classy Freddie Blassie, LJN, Series 3, MOC, from $25 to $30.00
WWF, figure, Crush, Hasbro, 1993, MOC (yel card), from $20 .... $25.00
WWF, figure, Crush, Hasbro, 1994, MOC (gr card), from $45 to $50.00
WWF, figure, Diesel (Superstars #3 reissue), Jakks, MOC, from $15 to $20.00
WWF, figure, Doink the Clown, Hasbro, 1993, MOC, from $20 to $25.00
WWF, figure, Doink the Clown, Jakks, Series 6, MOC, from $20 to $25.00
WWF, figure, Dusty Rhodes, Hasbro, MOC (bl card), from $140 to $160.00
WWF, figure, Greg 'The Hammer' Valentine, Hasbro, 1992, MOC, from $15 to $20.00
WWF, figure, Hacksaw Jim Duggan, Hasbro, 1990, MOC (bl card), from $25 to $30.00
WWF, figure, Hacksaw Jim Duggan, Hasbro, 1993, MOC (purple card), from $40 to $45.00
WWF, figure, Hacksaw Jim Duggan, LJN, 1989, MOC (blk card), from $60 to $65.00
WWF, figure, Harley Race, LJN, 1985, MOC, from $75 to . $80.00
WWF, figure, Honky Tonk Man, Hasbro, MOC, from $20 to $25.00
WWF, figure, Hulk Hogan, any except mail-in, Hasbro, MOC, from $15 to $25.00
WWF, figure, Hulk Hogan, mail-in, Hasbro, MIP, from $45 to $55.00
WWF, figure, Hulk Hogan, wht shirt, knee pads & shoes, red shorts, LJN, MOC (bl card), from $350 to $375.00
WWF, figure, Hulk Hogan, wht shirt, knee pads & shoes, red trunks, LJN, MOC (blk card), from $300 to $325.00
WWF, figure, Hulk Hogan, yel trunks, no shirt, LJN, 1984, MOC (bl card), from $75 to $85.00
WWF, figure, Hulk Hogan as Thunderclips, Appleworks, 1985, MOC, from $25 to $30.00
WWF, figure, Hulk Hogan vs Big John Studd, 2-pack, LJN, 1985, MOC, from $25 to $30.00
WWF, figure, Hulk Hogan vs Iron Sheik Thumb Wrestlers, LJN, 1985, MOC, from $25 to $30.00
WWF, figure, Iron Sheik, LJN, 1985, MOC, from $30 to .. $40.00
WWF, figure, Jake 'The Snake' Roberts, Hasbro, MOC, from $10 to $15.00
WWF, figure, Jim 'The Anvil' Neidhart, Hasbro, MOC, from $10 to $15.00
WWF, figure, Jimmy 'Superfly' Snuka, Hasbro, 1990, MOC, from $30 to $35.00
WWF, figure, Jimmy 'Superfly' Snuka, LJN, 1984, MOC, from $80 to $90.00
WWF, figure, Jimmy 'Superfly' Snuka, Rock 'n' Wrestling, LJN, 1985, MOC, from $30 to $35.00
WWF, figure, Jimmy Hart (w/no hearts on megaphone), LJN, Series 3, MOC, from $25 to $30.00
WWF, figure, King Kong Bundy, LJN, 1985, MOC, from $35 to $45.00
WWF, figure, Legion of Doom w/Animal & Hawk, Hasbro, 1990, MOC, from $40 to $50.00
WWF, figure, Lex Lugar, Hasbro, MOC, from $15 to $20.00
WWF, figure, Ludvig Borga, Hasbro, 1994, MOC, from $35 to $45.00
WWF, figure, Luscious Johnny Valiant, LJN, 1985, MOC, from $30 to $40.00
WWF, figure, Macho Man, Hasbro, 1990, MOC, $25 to... $30.00

WWF, figure, Macho Man Randy Savage, Elbow Smash!, Hasbro, 1990, MOC, from $70 to $80.00
WWF, figure, Macho Man Randy Savage, w/Macho Masher, Hasbro, MOC, from $40 to $50.00
WWF, figure, Macho Man Randy Savage, yel skin, LJN, MOC, from $175 to $200.00
WWF, figure, Magnificent Maraco, LJN, Series 3, MOC, from $25 to $30.00
WWF, figure, Mean Gene Okerlund, LJN, 1985, MOC, from $25 to $35.00
WWF, figure, Mr Perfect (w/Perfect Plex), Hasbro, MOC, from $20 to $25.00
WWF, figure, New Age Outlaws (2-Tuff #2), Jakks, MOC, from $10 to $15.00
WWF, figure, Nikolai Volkoff, LJN, 1985, MOC, from $25 to .$35.00
WWF, figure, Ravishing Rick Rude, 'Rude Awakening Headlock' pose, Hasbro, 1990, MOC, from $35 to $40.00
WWF, figure, Razor Ramon, Hasbro, MOC (yel or red card), ea from $20 to $25.00
WWF, figure, Razor Ramon, Hasbro, 1994, MOC (bl card), from $30 to $35.00
WWF, figure, Ricky 'The Dragon' Steamboat, LJN, 1985, MOC, from $30 to $40.00
WWF, figure, Rowdy Roddy Piper, Hasbro, MOC, from $25 to $35.00
WWF, figure, Shawn Michaels, Hasbro, 1994, MOC, from $35 to $40.00
WWF, figure, Sid Justice, Hasbro, MOC, from $15 to $20.00
WWF, figure, Tatanka, Hasbro, MOC, from $25 to $30.00
WWF, figure, Ted Arcidi, LJN, 1985, MOC, from $30 to..$40.00
WWF, figure, Ted Dibiase, blk tux w/purple lapels & cummerbun, LJN, 1985, MOC, from $50 to $55.00
WWF, figure, Ted Dibiase (Million Dollar Man), in blk tux w/ gold lapels & cummerbun, Hasbro, 1990, MOC, from $20 to $25.00
WWF, figure, Ted Dibiase (Million Dollar Man), in blk wrestling trunks & boots, Hasbro, 1994, MOC, from $45 to $50.00
WWF, figure, The Rockers w/Marty Jannetty & Shawn Michaels, Hasbro, 1990, MOC, from $25 to $30.00
WWF, figure, The 1-2-3 Kid, Hasbro, 1994, MOC, from $60 to $70.00
WWF, figure, Typhone w/Tidal Wave, Hasbro, MOC, from $30 to $35.00
WWF, figure, Undertaker (mail-in), Hasbro, MOC, from $45 to $55.00
WWF, figure, Undertaker & Kane (2-Tuff #4), Jakks, MOC, from $15 to $20.00
WWF, figure, Undertaker Warrior, w/Warrior Wham, Hasbro, 1992, MOC, from $40 to $45.00
WWF, figure, Undertaker Warrior w/Graveyard Smash, Hasbro, 1992, MOC, from $15 to $20.00
WWF, figure, Vince McMann, LJN, Series 5, MOC, from $50 to $60.00
WWF, figure, Warlord, Hasbro, MOC, from $15 to..........$20.00
WWF, figure, WWF Referee, LJN, 1987, MOC, from $35 to $45.00
WWF, figure, Yokozuna, Hasbro, 1994, MOC, from $30 to $35.00

X-Files, figure, Agent Scully or any character except Fireman With Cryolitter, McFarlane, 1997, MOC, each from $8.00 to $12.00.

X-Files, figure, Fireman w/Cryolitter, McFarlane, 1997, MOC, from $15 to $20.00
X-Men/X-Force, figure, Arctic Armor Cable, Avalanche, or Cable Cyborg, Toy Biz, MOC, ea from $5 to $10.00
X-Men/X-Force, figure, Black Tom, Blob or Bonebraker, Toy Biz, MOC, from $10 to $15.00
X-Men/X-Force, figure, Bridge or Brood, Toy Biz, MOC, ea from $5 to $10.00
X-Men/X-Force, figure, Cable I, Cable II or Cable III, Toy Biz, MOC, ea from $10 to $15.00
X-Men/X-Force, figure, Cable V, Toy Biz, MOC, from $10 to $15.00
X-Men/X-Force, figure, Cannonball (pk), Toy Biz, MOC, from $$10 to $15.00
X-Men/X-Force, figure, Cannonball (purple), Toy Biz, MOC, from $5 to $10.00
X-Men/X-Force, figure, Commando, Toy Biz, MOC, from $5 to $10.00
X-Men/X-Force, figure, Deadpool (1992), Toy Biz, MOC, from $5 to $10.00
X-men/X-Force, figure, Deadpool (1995) or Domino, Toy Biz, MOC, ea from $5 to $10.00
X-Men/X-Force, figure, Forearm, Genesis, Gideon or Grizzly, Toy Biz, MOC, ea from $5 to $10.00

X-Men/X-Force, figure, Kane (I or II), Toy Biz, MOC, each from $5.00 to $10.00.

X-Men/X-Force, figure, Killspree or Killspree II, Toy Biz, MOC, ea from $5 to....................$10.00
X-Men/X-Force, figure, Krule or Kylun, Toy Biz, MOC, from $5 to....................$10.00
X-Men/X-Force, figure, Longshot, Mojo, Nimrod, Pyro, Quark, Random, Rictor or Rogue, Toy Biz, MOC, ea from $5 to....... $10.00
X-Men/X-Force, figure, Rogue, Toy Biz, MOC, from $24 to..$28.00
X-Men/X-Force, figure, Sabretooth I or Sabretooth II, Toy Biz, MOC, ea from $5 to....................$10.00
X-Men/X-Force, figure, Shatterstar I, Shatterstar II or Shatterstar III, Toy Biz, MOC, ea from $5 to....................$10.00
X-Men/X-Force, figure, Silver Samurai, Slayback, Stryfe or Sunspot, Toy Biz, MOC, ea from $5 to....................$10.00
X-Men/X-Force, figure, Urban Assault, Warpath I, Warpath II, or X-Treme, Toy Biz, MOC, ea from $5 to....................$10.00

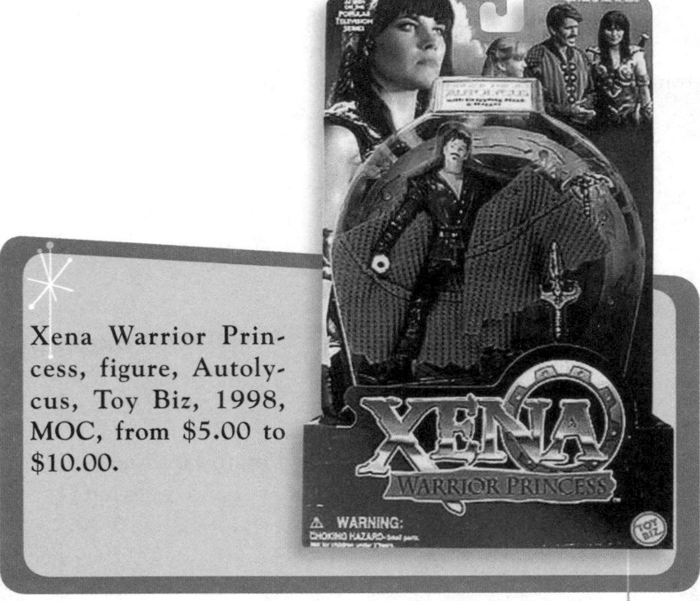

Xena Warrior Princess, figure, Autolycus, Toy Biz, 1998, MOC, from $5.00 to $10.00.

Xena Warrior Princess, figure, Harem Xena, Velasca, Toy Biz, 1998, MOC, ea from $5 to....................$10.00
Xena Warrior Princess, figure, Callisto, Gabrielle (Orphan of War), Toy Biz, 1998, MOC, ea from $12 to....................$18.00
Zorro (Cartoon Series), figure, Captain Ramon or Sgt Gonzoles, Gabriel, MOC, ea from $20 to....................$25.00
Zorro (Cartoon Series), figure, Tempest or Picaro, Gabriel, MOC, ea from $50 to....................$50.00
Zorro (Cartoon Series), figure, Zorro or Amigo, Gabriel, MOC, ea from $25 to....................$35.00

Activity Sets

Activity sets that were once enjoyed by so many children are finding their way back to some of those same kids, now grown up. The earlier editions, especially, are carrying a pretty respectable price when they can be found complete or near complete.

The following listings are complete unless noted otherwise.

See also Character, TV, and Movie Collectibles; Coloring, Activity, and Paint Books; Disney; Playsets; and other specific categories.

Barney's Auto Factory Motorized Assembly Line, Remco, 1961, NMIB, A....................$175.00

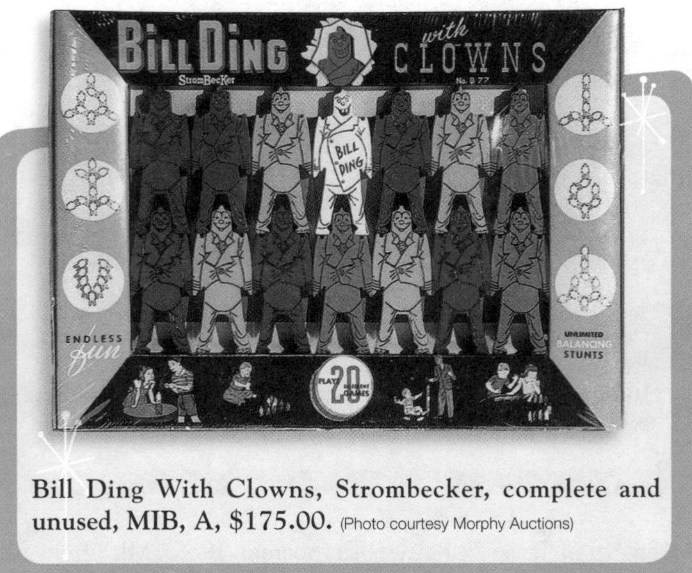

Bill Ding With Clowns, Strombecker, complete and unused, MIB, A, $175.00. (Photo courtesy Morphy Auctions)

Colorforms My House Printer Kit, 1962, EXIB, from $20 to .$25.00
Colorforms Totem Pole Kit, 1958, NMIB, from $30 to $40.00
Creepy Crawlers, see Thingmaker
Crime Lab, Amsco, 1976, unused, MIB, from $40 to $50.00
David Berglas Conjouring Tricks Magic Set, Kay Ltd/London, EXIB, from $75 to....................$100.00
Design-O-Marx Set, 1960s, scarce, unused, MIB, from $40 to .$50.00
Etch-A-Sketch, Ohio Art, 1960, 1st issue, unused, MIB, A .$155.00
Famous Monsters Plaster Casting Kit, Rapco, 1974, complete & unused, MIB, from $75 to....................$100.00

Fist Faces, Remco, 1966, NMIB, from $25.00 to $30.00.

Hocus-Pocus Magic Set, Adams, 1962, unused, MIB, from $65 to....................$75.00

Hocus-Pocus Magic Set, Adams, 1976, NMIB, from $40 to .$50.00
Jerry the Magician's Complete Magic Act, 1940s-50s, unused, EX (in photo envelope)....$50.00
Johnny Toymaker Car Molding Set, EXIB, from $40 to $50.00

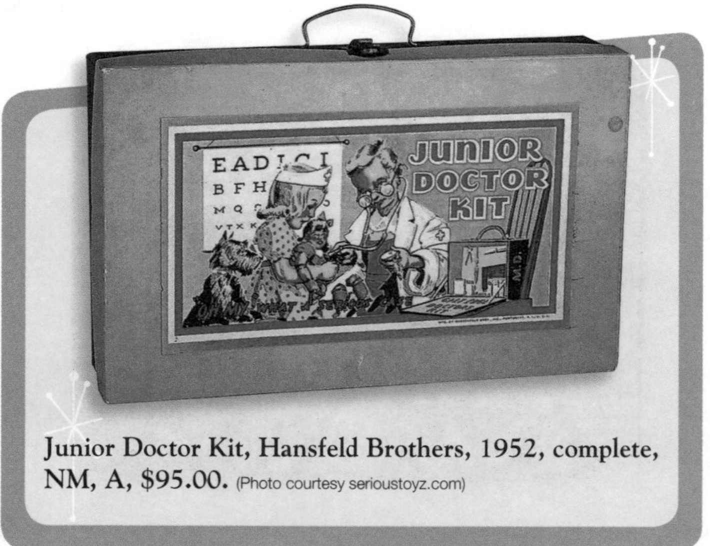

Junior Doctor Kit, Hansfeld Brothers, 1952, complete, NM, A, $95.00. (Photo courtesy serioustoyz.com)

Magic Kit of Tricks & Puzzles, Transogram, 1960s, MIB, from $65 to....$75.00
Magic Set, w/10 tricks, Redhill, 1930s-40s, MIB $50.00
Magician Magic Set, features Bill Bixby, 1974, NMIB $70.00
Mandrake the Magician Kit, briefcase-style box w/clasp, 1950s, complete, NMIB....$75.00
Mandrake the Magician Magic Tricks, KFS, 1949, w/6 complete tricks, VG+IB....$35.00
Master Magic, Sherms S set, 1930s-40s, EXIB $100.00
Meccano Foundry Kit, 1930s, EX (EX wood box), A $420.00
Mighty Men & Monster Maker Set, 1978, EXIB....$30.00
Mister Funny Face Clay & Plastic, 1953, EXIB $100.00
Monster Machine, Gabriel, MIB....$25.00
Motorized Monster Maker, Topper, 1960s, EXIB, A $95.00
Mr Magic Art, Adams 1960s, NMIB....$50.00
Mr Potato Head & Pete the Pepper Set, Hasbro, 1960s, MIB ..$30.00
Mr Potato Head In the Parade Set, Hasbro, 1960s, MIB ...$35.00
Picture Maker Hot Birds Skyway Scene, Mattel, 1970s, MIB. $75.00
Play-Doh Fun Factory, 1960s, rare, MIB $50.00
Playstone Funnies Kasting Kit w/11 Extra Molds, Allied Mfg, 1930s, EX+IB, A....$225.00
Power Mite Work Shop, Ideal, 1969, EXIB....$130.00
Power Shop, Mattel, 1960s, NMIB $50.00
Pre-Flight Training Cockpit, Einson, 1942, NMIB....$50.00
Shrunken Head Apple Sculpture, Milton Bradley, 1975, MIB $75.00
Sneaky Pete's Magic Show, Remco #702, 1950s-60s, VG+IB ..$85.00
Space Faces, Pressman 1950s, unused, NMIB $175.00
Space Scientist Drafting Set, 1950s, EXIB....$65.00
Specks & Things Molding Set, MIB $50.00
Spirograph, Kenner, 1967, unused, MIB (sealed) $110.00
Starmaster Astromony Set, Reed, 1950s, EXIB $50.00
Tasket Basket Shape Sorter, Holgate, 1953, NM $35.00
Thingmaker (Triple), Mattel, EXIB $125.00
Thingmaker Creeple Peeple, Mattel, 1965, MIB.... $100.00
Thingmaker Creepy Crawlers, 1st issue, Mattel, 1964, EXIB.. $75.00
Thingmaker Creepy Crawlers II, Mattel, 1978, NMIB......$50.00
Thingmaker Fright Factory, Mattel, MIB (sealed) $150.00
Thingmaker Fun Flowers Maker Pak, Mattel, 1966, EXIB ..$30.00
Thingmaker Giant Creepy Crawlers Maker Pak #2, Mattel, 1965, EXIB....$75.00
Thingmaker Men Set, Mattel, 1965, EXIB $75.00
Thingmaker Mini Dragon Maker Pack, Mattel, 1967, MIB (sealed) $150.00
Tinker Fish, Toy Tinkers, 1927, EXIB $50.00
Tinker Spots, Toy Tinkers, 1930s, EXIB....$50.00
Tinkerbeads No 4, Toy Tinkers, 1928, EX (in tin container). $75.00
Trix Stix, Harry Dearly, 1952, MIP $50.00
Vac-U-Form Playset, Mattel, 1962, NMIB.... $100.00
Voodini Magic Set, Transogram, 1960, NMIB....$50.00
Winky Dink Paint Set, Pressman, 1950s, EX $75.00
Wood Doh Modeling Compound, 1959, 'Recommended By Captain Kangaroo' on display box w/3 cans, unused, MIB, A $40.00
Young Magicians Box of Tricks, Saalfield, 1958, NMIB $50.00

Mr Potato Head and His Tooty Frooty Friends, Hasbro, 1950, $50.00.

Advertising

The assortment of advertising memorabilia geared toward children is vast — plush and cloth dolls, banks, games, puzzles, trucks, radios, watches, and much, much more. And considering the popularity of advertising memorabilia in general, when you add to it the crossover interest from the realm of toys, you have a real winning combination! Just remember to check for condition very carefully. Signs of play wear are common. You need to think twice about investing much money in soiled items like cloth or plush dolls since stains are often impossible to remove.

For more information we recommend *B.J. Summers' Guide to Coca-Cola*, *Collectible Soda Pop Memorabilia*, and *Antique and Contemporary Advertising Memorabilia*, all by B.J. Summers; *Cracker Jack Toys* and *Cracker Jack, the Unauthorized Guide to Advertising* both by Larry White; *Pepsi-Cola Collectibles, Vols I, II,* and *III*, by Bill Vehling and Michael Hunt.

See also Buddy L (and other vehicle categories); Character, TV, and Movie Collectibles; Disney; Pin-Back Buttons; Premiums; other specific categories.

A&W Root Beer, bears, bean-stuffed plush, 2 different, 1997-98, ea from $15 to $20.00
AC Spark Plugs, figure, AC man w/1 arm extended & other on hip, wht & gr w/AC on chest, gr hat, 6", EXIB $160.00
AC Spark Plugs, figure, Sparky the Horse, inflatable vinyl w/logo, 24x15" L, Ideal, 1960s, EX $100.00
Alka-Seltzer, figure, Speedy, vinyl, 5½", 1960s, EX, from $250 to $275.00
Allied Van Lines, doll, gr uniform & hat, Lion Uniform Inc, 14", MIB $1,200.00
Alpo, w/up figure, Dan the Dog, walks on his front paws, 3", 1970s, EX+ $12.00

American Stores Co., puzzle titled 'Pride of the Plantation,' framed, 15x12", VG, A, $50.00. (Photo courtesy Morphy Auctions)

Arco, premium, Noah figure, brn & wht plastic, ca 1971, EX ..$20.00
Arco, premium, Noah's ark, brn & wht plastic, ca 1971, EX .$80.00

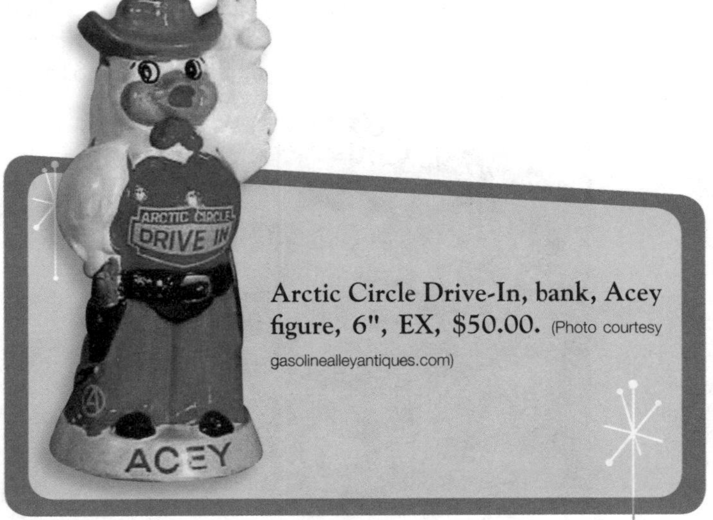

Arctic Circle Drive-In, bank, Acey figure, 6", EX, $50.00. (Photo courtesy gasolinealleyantiques.com)

Atlas Van-Lines Inc, tractor-trailer truck, Buddy L, 29", EXIB, A $1,725.00
Aunt Jemima, Breakfast Bear, plush, 13", M $175.00
Aunt Jemima, dolls, Aunt Jemima, Diana, Mose & Wade, stuffed & printed oilcloth, 9" to 12", 1950s, NM, ea from $40 to $50.00
Aunt Jemima, Jr Chef Pancake Set, Argo Industries, 1949, EX $150.00
Baskin-Robins, figure, Pinky the Spoon, bendable vinyl, 5", 1990, MIP $10.00
Bazooka Bubble Gum, doll, Bazooka Joe, stuffed print cloth, 19", 1970s, NM, from $25 to $30.00
Betty Crocker, Doll & Bake Set, stuffed print cloth doll w/baking kit, Kenner, 1970s, unused, MIB $25.00
Big Boy, bank, plastic figure wearing red & wht checked overalls, 9", 1970s, NM, from $12 to $18.00
Big Boy, comic book, Adventures of Big Boy #1, NM $250.00
Big Boy, comic book, Adventures of Big Boy #2-#5, NM, ea $50.00
Big Boy, comic book, Adventures of Big Boy #6-#10, NM, ea $35.00
Big Boy, comic book, Adventures of Big Boy #11-#100, NM, ea....$25.00
Big Boy, comic book, Adventures of Big Boy #101-#250, NM, ea....$10.00
Big Boy, doll, stuffed cloth w/Big Boy on wht T-shirt, red & wht overalls, 15", MIP ('Yes, I'm Your Pal' on header) $25.00
Big Boy, figure on surfboard w/wave, PVC, 3", 1990, EX $5.00
Big Boy, kite, paper w/Big Boy logo, 1960s, M $100.00
Big Boy, kite, paper w/Big Boy logo, 1960s, unused, MIP.. $250.00
Big Boy, nodder figure, 1960s, NM, from $20 to $25.00
Big Boy, yo-yo, wood w/die-stamp seal, 1960s, M $10.00
Blue Bonnet Margarine, doll, Blue Bonnet Sue, stuffed cloth w/yel yarn hair, 1980s, NM $5.00
Borden, baby rattle, Baby Beauregard figure standing in diaper sucking on bottle, hard plastic, 5", 1950s, VG....$125.00
Borden, bank, Beauregard, red plastic figure, 5", Irwin, 1950s, EX....$65.00
Borden, Elsie's Funbook Cut-Out Toys & Games, 1940s, EX . $65.00
Borden, Elsie's Good Food Line punch-out train, cb, 25x37", 1940s, unpunched, M (EX envelope)....$150.00
Borden, figure, Elsie, plush w/vinyl head, has 'moo' sound, 12", 1950s, EX $50.00
Borden, figure, Elsie, vinyl, aqua dress w/striped skirt, wht apron, gold felt shoes & bib, 22", EX+ $100.00
Borden, game, Elsie the Cow, Jr Edition, EXIB....$125.00
Borden, milk truck, Keystone #D402, PS, wht w/red Borden's decal, 9", EXIB....$375.00
Borden, night light, Elsie the Cow head figure, rubber-type compo, 9", NM $180.00
Borden, pull toy, Elsie ('The Cow That Jumped Over the Moon'), wood, 1940s, EX+ $35.00
Borden, push-button puppet, Elsie the Cow, wood, EX+, A . $165.00
Borden figure, Elsie, PVC, 3½", M, from $10 to....$20.00
Bosco Chocolate, doll, Bosco the Clown, vinyl, EX+....$50.00
Bradford House Restaurants, figure, Bucky Bradford standing on base reading 'It's Yum Yum Time,' vinyl, 1976, 9", EX $35.00
Burger Chef, hand puppet, Burger Chef, cloth body & hat w/ vinyl head, 1970s, EX $10.00

Burger Chef, pillow figure, Burger Chef, stuffed printed cloth, 1970s, EX....$12.00

Burger King, doll, Burger King, stuffed cloth, 16" (1973 or 1977) or 18" (1980), NM, ea....$10.00

Burger King, doll, Magic King, 20", Knickerbocker, 1980, MIB....$20.00

Burger King, Home of the Whopper Cheeseburger Set, plastic, Multi Toys, 1987, unused, MIB, $15.00. (Photo courtesy gasolinealleyantiques.com)

Burlington Northern Air Freight, w/up figure carrying box marked People Not Planes Deliver, MIB....$75.00

Buster Brown, hobby horse, wood w/pnt advertising as saddle, 28x36", very rare, VG....$300.00

Buster Brown, kite, 1940s, NM....$40.00

Buster Brown Shoes, bank, molded plastic ball shape w/busts of Buster Brown & Tige on top, 1960s, 3½" dia....$25.00

Buster Brown Shoes, booklet, Playing Movies w/Buster Brown, 1910s-20s, 20 pgs, EX+....$75.00

Buster Brown Shoes, clicker, tin shoe-sole form, bl (Blue Ribbon) lettering on yel, VG....$20.00

Buster Brown Shoes, clicker, tin w/head image of Buster & Tige, VG....$20.00

Buster Brown Shoes, paddle ball toy, Froggy the Gremlin graphics on die-cut cb, Ed McConnel, 1940s, EX+....$75.00

Buster Brown Shoes, shoe box w/Treasure Hunt Game on side, 1930s, unused, from $50 to....$75.00

Butterfinger Candy Bar, Butterfinger Bear, plush, 15", 1987, M....$25.00

Campbell's Soup, coloring book, 'A Story of Soup,' 1977, EX....$25.00

Campbell's Soup, comic book, 'Captain America & Campbell Kids,' 1980s promo, EX+....$25.00

Campbell's Soup, doll, boy, pirate, 10", Home Shopper, 1995, EX (in soup can box)....$80.00

Campbell's Soup, doll, boy & girl, beanbag type in Alphabet Soup outfits, 8", 2001, MIP, ea....$12.00

Campbell's Soup, doll, boy & girl, compo w/molded hair in chef outfits, pnt shoes & socks, 12", Horsman, MIB, pr....$250.00

Campbell's Soup, doll, boy & girl, farm kids dressed in denim, 7", 2000, MIB, ea....$12.00

Campbell's Soup, doll, boy & girl, Paul Revere & Betsy Ross attire, 10", 1976, M, ea....$50.00

Campbell's Soup, doll, boy & girl, pnt vinyl w/movable heads, 7", Product People, 1970s, NM, pr....$50.00

Campbell's Soup, doll, boy & girl, stuffed cloth, 1970s, MIB, pr....$75.00

Campbell's Soup, doll, boy or girl, vinyl w/rooted hair, red & wht checked outfits, 1988 special edition, MIP, ea....$20.00

Campbell's Soup, doll, chef, 12", M, $50.00. (Photo courtesy gasolinealleyantiques.com)

Campbell's Soup, doll, girl, cheerleader, vinyl, 1967, 8", EX.$75.00

Campbell's Soup, doll, girl, compo w/cloth bow atop molded hair, cloth dress, pnt shoes & socks, 12", G, A....$200.00

Campbell's Soup, doll, girl, rubber & vinyl w/cloth outfit, 8", Ideal, 1955, NM, minimum value....$125.00

Campbell's Soup, game, Campbell Kids Shopping Game, Parker Bros, 1955, scarce, NMIB....$65.00

Campbell's Soup, kaleidoscope, replica of soup can, 1981, EX..$40.00

Campbell's Soup, mug, molded plastic Campbell's Kid head, 1960s premium, unused, MIB (plain mailer box)....$15.00

Campbell's Soup, playset, Campbell Kids Chuck Wagon Set, Amsco Toys, NMIB, $100.00. (Photo courtesy Morphy Auctions)

Campbell's Soup, semi truck, diecast metal, 'M'm M'm Good!' & Kids perched on crescent moon in trailer, 12½", MIB ..$50.00
Campbell's Soup, wristwatch, 4 different, 1980s, MIB, ea ..$50.00
Castile Soap, Paul's Soap Circus ark, paper on wood, hinged roof, 15 prs of animals, 3 figures, 5 singles, 10", EX, A..... $165.00
Castoria, doll, uncut front/back image of 'Mammy Castoria' on 11x14" oil cloth, EX, A $85.00
Cheer, doll, Cheer Girl, plastic w/cloth clothes, 10", Proctor & Gamble, 1960, NM..........$20.00
Cheetos, doll, Chester Cheetah, 18", NM $40.00

Chevron, The Chevron Cars, Freddy 4-Wheeler, unused, MIB (sealed), $6.00. (Photo courtesy gasolinealleyantiques.com)

Chiquita Bananas, doll, stuffed printed cloth, 16", M $30.00
Chiquita Bananas, doll, uncut printed cloth, framed, NM ..$50.00
Chuck-E-Cheese, bank, vinyl figure, 7", EX..........$10.00
Chuck-E-Cheese, doll, plush, 'Show Biz Pizza Time,' 10", 1996, M $10.00
Chuck-E-Cheese, hand puppet, plush, 9", 1992, EX..........$12.00
Coca-Cola, ball & cup, wooden ball on string attached to cup on hdl w/Coke advertising, 1960s, NM..........$45.00
Coca-Cola, bang gun, 'G Man'/'It's the Real Thing,' M $20.00
Coca-Cola, bank, can shape w/repeated red & wht diamond design, NM $85.00
Coca-Cola, bank, pig wearing hat, red plastic w/wht 'Drink Coca-Cola'/'Sold Everywhere' on sides, EX $35.00
Coca-Cola, bank, vending machine, curved top, red w/wht lettering, 'Work Refreshed,' 5½", complete, EX, A...... $110.00
Coca-Cola, bank, vending machine, sq top, red w/wht lettering, 'Drink...Ice Cold 5¢,' MSR #1234, 7", MIB, A........ $110.00
Coca-Cola, book, 'Freckles & His Friends,' Whitman Better Little Book, 1927 premium, VG+ $35.00
Coca-Cola, carousel, metal w/mc Coca-Cola graphics, EX..$50.00
Coca-Cola, dispenser, red, w/set-of-4 glasses, 1950s, NMIB..$75.00
Coca-Cola, doll, Buddy Lee dressed as Coca-Cola route driver, 13", 2nd limited ed, 1997-98, M $350.00
Coca-Cola, figure, bear holding Coke bottle, wht plush, 1990s, MIB $15.00
Coca-Cola, figure, Frozen Coca-Cola mascot, stuffed cloth, 1960s, NM $150.00
Coca-Cola, game, Broadsides, Milton Bradley, 1940s-50s, VG+ $150.00
Coca-Cola, game, checkers, metal pegs fit in holes on board w/ wave logo, 1970s, NM+ $75.00
Coca-Cola, game, Double-Six Dominos, brn vinyl case w/Sprite Boy logo, 1970s, EX $40.00
Coca-Cola, jigsaw puzzle, Teenage Party, NMIB.......... $100.00

Coca-Cola, playset, Playtown Luncheonette with the 'Drink Coca-Cola' logo, Playtown Products #800, 1940s, unused, NMIB, A, $295.00. (Photo courtesy serioustoyz.com)

Coca-Cola, vehicle, A-frame delivery truck, Buddy L, yellow, screened sides, with two cases and metal card, 12", VG, A, $100.00. (Photo courtesy Morphy Auctions)

Coca-Cola, vehicle, A-frame delivery truck, Metalcraft, 1930s, PS, orange & yel, electric lights, 10 bottles, 12", EX+ ..$1,325.00
Coca-Cola, vehicle, A-frame delivery truck, Metalcraft, 1930s, PS, orange & yel, simulated lights, 10 bottles, 12", VG $450.00
Coca-Cola, vehicle, delivery truck, Buddy L #5426, yel w/chrome grille, WRT, w/plastic cases & bottles, 15", 1EX...... $300.00
Coca-Cola, vehicle, delivery truck, Marusan, 1950s, tin, friction, yel w/bl, center ad divider, 4-wheeled, 8", EXIB, A . $1,150.00
Coca-Cola, vehicle, delivery truck, Marx, plastic, 2-tiered, yel w/red detail, w/cases, 11", NMIB.......... $275.00
Coca-Cola, vehicle, delivery truck, Sanyo, litho tin, wht, yel & red, BRT, 13", NMIB $375.00
Coca-Cola, vehicle, Ford cabover A-frame delivery truck, Smith-Miller, 1940s, PS & wood, red, wooden cases, 14", VG+ $2,400.00

Coca-Cola, vehicle, Ford Taxi, Taiyo, litho tin, friction, 9", MIB $400.00
Coca-Cola, vehicle, GMC delivery truck, Smith-Miller, 1950s, PS, 2-tiered bed, red, cases w/glass bottles, BRT, 14", NOS $1,500.00
Coca-Cola, vehicle, Mac delivery truck, Les-Paul, yel w/red, ad header on 2-tier bed, 22½", NM $400.00
Coca-Cola, vehicle, pickup truck, Buddy L, PS, friction, w/red 'Sign of Good Taste' logo over 2 white stripes, 8", VG $175.00
Coca-Cola, vehicle, sedan, Taiyo, tin, friction, red & wht, 10½", NMIB, A $125.00
Coca-Cola, vehicle, stake truck, Marx #0991, PS, yel, Sprite Boy sign, covered wheels, 20", VG $250.00
Coca-Cola, vehicle, stake truck, Marx #1088, litho tin, red, yel & bl, 'Take Some Home Today' sign, 18", VG+, A. $510.00
Coca-Cola, vehicle, Volkswagen delivery truck, Tipp, 1950s, tin, friction, open bay, center ad panel, cases/bottles, 9". $675.00
Coca-Cola, vehicle, VW van bus, Taiyo, 1950s, litho tin.. $225.00
Coca-Cola, vehicle, 1936 Ford pickup truck, Solido, diecast, 1.18 scale, NM $35.00
Cocomalt, jigsaw puzzle, 'The Flying Family,' 6½x10", 1932, complete, EX (w/orig envelope) $35.00
Cracker Jack, Angelus Marshmallow horse wagon, litho tin, 2", EX+, A $50.00
Cracker Jack, Angelus Marsmallow truck, litho tin, 2", EX, A $88.00

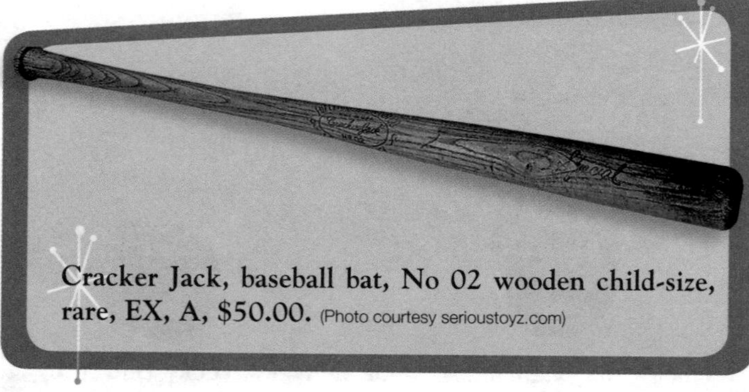

Cracker Jack, baseball bat, No 02 wooden child-size, rare, EX, A, $50.00. (Photo courtesy serioustoyz.com)

Cracker Jack, book, Animated Jungle Book, paper, NM ...$90.00
Cracker Jack, Checkers goat wagon, 1½", EX+, A $88.00
Cracker Jack, chicken figure, chenile, NM $7.50
Cracker Jack, figure, man made of wooden beads & wire, NM.. $27.50
Cracker Jack, Flip-Action Movie, various subjects, paper, NM $11.50
Cracker Jack, fortune teller, Cracker Jack, paper, NM $95.00
Cracker Jack, game, Drawing Made Easy, paper, NM $35.00
Cracker Jack, Handy Andy, paper, any of 12, NM, ea $65.00
Cracker Jack, rickshaw, tin & wood, 2-wheeled, yel & gr w/ Cracker Jack lettered on back, 4½", EX+, A $32.00
Cracker Jack, slide card, Animal, any of 26, NM, ea $9.50
Cracker Jack, spinner, 'Keep 'Em Flying,' metal, NM $55.00
Cracker Jack, Squeeze Faces, paper, any of 9, NM, ea $15.00
Cracker Jack, stand-up, Skeezix, metal, 2", EX+, A $32.00
Cracker Jack, stand-up, Smitty, metal, 2", EX+, A $40.00
Cracker Jack, Tele-Viz, paper, any of 10, NM, ea $65.00
Cracker Jack, Toonerville Trolley, Nifty, tin, 2", EX, A.. $450.00

Crayola, figure, Crayola Ballerina, plush, 14", Gund, M....$10.00
Crayola, figure, Crayola Bear, plush, 7½", EX $15.00
Cream of Wheat, doll, stuffed blk chef holding printed image of 'Cream of Wheat' bowl, w/apron & hat, 16", 1949, G, A $1,000.00
Curèl Lotion, doll, Curèl Baby, plastic w/jtd arms & legs, 6", 1980, EX $20.00
Curad, bank, The Taped Crusader, plastic, 8", NM $6.00
Curity, doll, Miss Curity, dressed in nurse's uniform, 17", NM (Fair mailing box) $110.00

Dairy Queen, figure, Chips Ahoy Blizzard boy, bendable vinyl, 4¼", M, $8.50. (Photo courtesy gasolinealleyantiques.com)

Dairy Queen, figure, Dairy Queen Kid, stuffed cloth, 1974, EX $20.00
Dairy Queen, figure, Marsh Mallo, plush moose, 7", 1980s, scarce, EX $12.00
Dairy Queen, figure, Sweet Nell, plush, 12", 1974, EX $20.00
Dairy Queen, hand puppet, Curly, wht cloth body w/pk hands & chest logo, vinyl head, 1950s, NM $175.00
Dairy Queen, whistle, plastic ice-cream cone shape, 2", NM $5.00
Del Monte, figures, Fluffy Lamb, Lushie Peach or Reddie Tomato, plush, 1980s, EX, ea $20.00
Domino's Pizza, figure, Noid, bendable rubber, 7", 1986, NM+ .$6.00
Domino's Pizza, figure, Noid, plush, 16", Matchbox Toys, 1987, EX $12.00
Domino's Pizza, figure, Noid, plush, 19", 1988, MIP $20.00
Domino's Pizza, figure, Noid as boxer, PVC, 2¾", 1988, NM+ ..$5.00
Domino's Pizza, figure, Noid as sorcerer, PVC, 2½", 1980s, MIP $6.00
Domino's Pizza, Noid Ring Toss Game, Larami, 1989, NRFC (12x6") $10.00
Domino's Pizza, yo-yo, 'Nobody Delivers Faster,' plastic, Humphery, NM+ $5.00
Dots Candy, doll, Dots Candy Baby, beanbag type w/vinyl face & hands, Hasbro, 1970s, MIB $15.00
Dubble Bubble Bubble Gum, beanie, mc suede w/metal top button, rnd 'Fleers...' logo on front, 1930s, rare, EX+ ... $100.00

Dunkin' Donuts, figures, koala bears, plush, 2 different, 4½", EX+, ea $6.00
Eli's Cheesecake, doll, cloth, holding lg wht cloth fork, 6", EX $8.00
Energizer Batteries, figure, Energizer Bunny, beanbag type, 7", Creata, 1999, MIP $15.00
Energizer Batteries, figure, Energizer Bunny, plush, flip-flop shoes, 25", MIP $85.00
Energizer Batteries, flashlight, Energizer Bunny w/movable arms & head, 4", MIP $8.00
Eskimo Pie, doll, stuffed cloth, 15", 1964-74, EX, from $15 to .. $20.00
Eveready Batteries, bank, Black Cat, plastic, 1980s, EX+ . $12.00
Fanny Farmer Candies, delivery truck, tin, friction, red & wht, 8", Japan, 1950s, G $50.00
Fig Newtons, doll, balancing cookie on her head & holding lg cookie in her hand, 4½", Nabisco, 1980s, NM $15.00
Flintstones Vitamins, doll, Fred Flintstone, inflatable vinyl w/removable plastic cloths, 1970s, M $12.00
Fould's Macaroni, figurine, Tarzan w/chimp at his feet, plaster, 5", 1939, issued in Midwest only, NM+ $175.00
Franco-American Spaghetti, hand puppet, King Sauce, cloth body w/vinyl head, 1966, NM $120.00
Fruit Stripe Gum, figure, Yipes, plush, 15", EX $50.00
Fruit Stripe Gum, figure shaped like pack of gum riding motorcycle, bendable vinyl, 7½", 1967, EX+ $175.00

Funny-Face Drink, book, 'How Freckle Face Strawberry Got His Freckles,' Pillsbury, 1965, EX, $28.00. (Photo courtesy gasolinealleyantiques.com)

Funny Face Drink, masks, die-cut paper images of 6 different characters, Pillsbury, 1960s, unused, M, ea from $250 to .. $275.00
Funny Face Drink, mugs, various character faces pnt on plastic, 3", Pillsbury, M (in mailer box), ea $30.00
Funny Face Drink, pitcher, Goofy Grape, molded plastic, Pillsbury, 10", EX, from $65 to $85.00
General Mills, bank, Twinkles, the Elephant, Trix cereal premium, 1965, MIP $50.00
General Mills, Cocoa Puffs Train, litho tin, w/up, premium, 1959, 12" L, NM $110.00
General Mills, Cocoa Puffs Train Station Tent, premium, 1961, EX $100.00
General Mills, hand puppet, Champy the Lion, cloth body w/vinyl head, Wheaties, premium, 1957, EX+ $75.00
General Mills, mask, Count Chocula, plastic, premium, 1970s, NM+ $35.00
General Mills, pencil topper, Frankenberry, premium, 1½", NM $15.00
General Mills, Pokemon 'Gotta Catch 'Em All!' pocket camera, Cap'n Crunch premium, 1999, MIP, from $6 to $8.00
General Mills, ring, Rocket to the Moon, brass w/spring-loaded launcher, glow-in-the-dark plastic rockets, Kix, 1951, VG $225.00
General Mills, Wacky Racer, any, 1969, NM, ea. $50.00
General Mills, Walky Squawky Talkies, Trix cereal, 1965, MIP $50.00
Goodrich Silvertown Tires, wrecker, Metalcraft, 1930s, orange & wht, w/visor, BRT, 3 extra tires, 12", VG $250.00
Green Giant, bank, Little Sprout figure, compo, plays 'Valley of the Green Giant' song, 8½", EX $50.00
Green Giant, doll, girl, vinyl w/rooted hair, yel & gr dress & hat, corn motif on purse, 17", 1950s, M $40.00

Green Giant, figure, vinyl, 9", M, $125.00. (Photo courtesy gasolinealleyantiques.com)

Green Giant, figure, Little Sprout, talker, MIP $55.00
Green Giant, flashlight, Little Sprout figural handle, gr, M $50.00
Green Giant, jump rope, Little Sprout hdls, MIP $20.00
Hamburger Helper, Helping Hand figure, plush, 14", M $10.00
Hardee's, doll, Gilbert Giddyup, doll, stuffed printed cloth, 1971, EX $25.00
Harley-Davidson, Harley Hog figure, 9", M $25.00
Hawaiian Punch, doll, Punchy, beanbag type, 10", 1997, MIP $15.00
Hawaiian Punch, doll, Punchy, stuffed cloth, 20", NM $65.00
Hawaiian Punch, game, Mattel, 1978, NMIB $50.00
Heinz, delivery truck, PS, electric lights, wht w/ad decals, BRT, 12", Metalcraft, 1930s, VG, A $300.00
Heinz, doll, Heinz Baby Doll, squeeze vinyl, 9", Hungerford, 1950s, NRFP (poly bag w/header card) $175.00
Heinz, H-57 Rocket Blaster, w/instructions, MIB $15.00

Heinz, talking alarm clock, plastic, round base, 10x6", 1980s, NM....... $125.00

Hershey's, Hershey Bar Bank, red plastic candy bar vending machine, 6", Felsenthal & Sons, EX+IB, A, $75.00. (Photo courtesy Randy Inman Auctions)

Hershey's, figure, Hershey's Bear, plush, in sweater, 7", NM .. $8.00
Hess, semi, Hess Gasoline, w/3 oil drums, b/o, Hong Kong, 1976, unused, M (NM box), A....... $275.00
Hess, Tank Trailer, M Mack cab, Hong Kong, 1964, w/funnel, 12½", NM (EX+ box), A....... $995.00
Hess, Voyager Tanker Ship, 17½", 1966, MIB, A $1,452.00
Hobo Joe Restaurants, bank, Hobo Joe figure on rnd base w/ name, NM+ $75.00

Hobo Joe Restaurants, figure, Hobo Joe, vinyl with cloth outfit, complete with dog and newspaper, 9", Dakin, NM+, 150.00. (Photo courtesy gasolinealleyantiques.com)

Hoover, coloring book, clown w/sweeper pictured on cover, 1960s, partially colored, EX....... $25.00
Hot Point, hand puppet, cloth body w/logo on chest, vinyl head, 1950s, EX+....... $250.00
Hush Puppies, plush dog, 10", Presents, 1980s, EX+....... $14.00
Icee, bank, Icee Bear figure, vinyl, 8", 1970s, VG....... $20.00
Jell-O, puppet, Mr Wiggle, red vinyl, 1966, M $125.00
Jet Ball Sneakers, Super Space Ring, plastic, 1950s, unassembled, MIP $75.00

Jewel Tea, delivery truck, PS, brn w/gold advertising, 10", 1940s, EX $350.00

KC Pistons, nodder figure, plastic, NM, A $215.00. (Photo courtesy Morphy Auctions)

Kebbler, mug, plastic figural Ernie mug, 3", NM $10.00
Keebler, bank, Ernie the Keebler Elf, ceramic, 10", M....... $50.00
Keebler, doll, Ernie, cloth beanbag type, 5", EX+ $6.00
Keebler, doll, Ernie, vinyl, 1970s, 7", NM....... $25.00
Kellogg's, Battery Powered Electric Train, premium, 1957-58, MIP $100.00
Kellogg's, canteen, yel plastic w/Pop! decal, 5½" dia, Rice Krispies premium, 1973, NM $12.00
Kellogg's, Color Magic Cards, Rice Krispies premium, 1930s, complete & unused, EX+ (EX+ envelope) $65.00
Kellogg's, Crater Critters, 8 different figures, premiums, 1968-1972, M, ea $35.00
Kellogg's, hand puppets, Snap!, Crackle! & Pop!, cloth bodies w/ vinyl heads, Rice Krispies premiums, 1940s, EX, ea....... $75.00
Kellogg's, jigsaw puzzle, 'Keep Going With...,' shows child throwing baseball, 8x6", premium, 1930s, NM $65.00
Kellogg's, Pep Model Warplane Series, any in series, unpunched, premium, 1940s, M, ea $30.00
Kellogg's, Story Book of Games #1, features, Sambo, Cinderella, 3 Little Pigs, etc, premium, 1950s, VG $55.00
Kellogg's, Superman Satellite Launcher, premium, 1956, M $40.00
Kentucky Fried Chicken, bank, Colonel Sanders figure w/cane on sm round base, 12½", Starling Plastics, 1965, EX+ $30.00
Kentucky Fried Chicken, coloring book, Favorite Chicken Stores, 1960s, EX $25.00
Kentucky Fried Chicken, hand puppet, Colonel Sanders, plastic, 1960s, EX $20.00
Kentucky Fried Chicken, mask, Colonel Sanders face, molded plastic, 1960s, NM $55.00
Kentucky Fried Chicken, nodder, Colonel Sanders, 'Kentucky Fried Chicken' on base, 7½", pnt compo, 1980s, EX ... $65.00
Kentucky Fried Chicken, nodder, Colonel Sanders figure holding a bucket of chicken & cane, plastic, 7", NM $12.00
Kentucky Fried Chicken, Wacky Wobbler, PVC Colonel Sanders figure, MIB $20.00

Knoor Soup, doll set, hard plastic, dressed in costumes from various countries, Best Foods, 1963-64, M, pr....................$15.00
Kool-Aid, bank, mascot pitcher standing on base, hard plastic, mechanical actions, 7", 1970s, NM..............................$50.00
Kool-Aid, figure, Kool-Aid man w/barbells, PVC, 2", EX ...$4.00
Kraft, figures, Cheesasaurus Rex in various sporting poses, PVC, 1990s premiums, M, ea $10.00
Kraft, pull toy, Kraft TV Theater cameraman seated on rolling camera base, plastic, 1950s, Velveeta premium, EX. $100.00
Kraft, truck, GMC cab w/box van, PS, yel, 14", Smith-Miller, 1950s, EX, A $230.00
Kraft, wristwatch, Macaroni & Cheese, 1980s, M $10.00
Lee Jeans, doll, Buddy Lee as train engineer in Lee overalls, bl shirt & bl & wht striped hat, 13", EX $150.00
Lee Jeans, doll, girl, stuffed denim w/various yarn hair styles, EX+ $40.00
Lifesavers, bank, cb & metal cylinder w/Lifesavers graphics, 12", 1960s, EX $20.00
Little Caesar's Pizza, doll, Pizza Pizza Man holding slice of pizza, plush, 1990, EX..$5.00
Little Debbie, doll, vinyl w/cloth dress & straw hat, 1980s, 11", NM...$85.00

Log Cabin Syrup, Log Cabin Express pull toy, NMIB, A, $900.00. (Photo courtesy Wm Morford)

M&M Candy, figure, peanut golfer or witch, cloth beanbag type, 6", M, ea...$10.00
M&M Candy, figure, peanut shape w/bendable arms & legs, 7", M, ea $15.00
M&M Candy, figure, plain shape, cloth beanbag type, various colors, M, ea..$5.00
M&M Candy, figure, plain shape, plush, 4½", M $5.00
M&M Candy, figure, plain shape, plush, 8", M.....................$8.00
M&M Candy, figure, plain shape, plush, 12", M $10.00
M&M Candy, figure, plain shape, plush, 48" from fingertip to fingertip, NM $75.00
M&M Candy, figure, plain shape dressed as bride, 36", EX..$40.00
Maypo Oat Cereal, bank, Marky Maypo figure, plastic, 1960s, EX... $100.00
McDonald's, action figures, several different, Remco, 1976, NM, ea..$25.00
McDonald's, bank, Grimace, ceramic, purple w/pnt features, 9", 1985, NM...$20.00
McDonald's, bank, Grimace, compo, 1985, NM................$15.00
McDonald's, bank, Ronald McDonald bust, plastic, Taiwan, 1993, EX $40.00
McDonald's, bop bag, Grimace, inflatable vinyl, name in blk across front, 9", 1978, MIP $12.00

McDonald's, dish set, Plastic Manufacturing, 1991, NM+, $25.00. (Photo courtesy gasolinealleyantiques.com)

McDonald's, doll, Fry Girl, stuffed cloth, 4", 1987, M $5.00
McDonald's, doll, Fry Girl, stuffed cloth, 12", 1987, NM..$10.00
McDonald's, doll, Fry Guy, stuffed cloth, 12", 1987, NM..$12.00
McDonald's, doll, Grimace, plush w/plastic eyes, 8", M $10.00
McDonald's, doll, Hamburgler, cloth w/purple stripes, 15", early 1970s, NM $20.00
McDonald's, doll, Hamburgler, cloth w/vinyl head head & hat, cloth cape, blk stripes, 11", 1980s, NM+ $20.00
McDonald's, doll, Ronald McDonald, cloth, raised arm, 13", 1987, NM...$20.00
McDonald's, doll, Ronald McDonald, cloth w/plastic head, yarn hair, real lace shoes, 15", Dakin, 1991, M...................$15.00
McDonald's, doll, Ronald McDonald, stuffed body w/plastic head, hands & shoes, yarn hair, sm Grimace in pocket, 20", M...$50.00
McDonald's, doll, Ronald McDonald, stuffed printed cloth, 2 different versions, 17", Chase Bag Co, 1970s, EX, ea......$20.00
McDonald's, doll, Ronald McDonald, vinyl w/cloth costume, 7", Remco, 1976, MIB...$30.00
McDonald's, game, McDonald's, Milton Bradley, 1975, MIB. $25.00
McDonald's, game, Playland Funburst, Parker Bros, 1984, MIB $20.00
McDonald's, hand puppet, Ronald, Grimace or Hamburgler, cloth bodies w/vinyl heads, 1993, MIB, ea.................$35.00
McDonald's, playset, McDonaldland, Remco, 1976, MIB ...$125.00
McDonalds, puzzle, fr-tray; shows Ronald performing magic tricks in front of audience, Golden #4552A, 1984, NM+ $30.00
Michelin Tires, figure, Mr Bib, cloth, 21", Chase Bag Co, 1967, EX $40.00
Michelin Tires, figure, Mr Bib holding baby, rubber, 7", NM ...$125.00
Michelin Tires, puzzle, put together to form figure of Mr Bib on motorcycle, MIP $55.00
Michelin Tires, ramp walker, w/up Mr Bib figure, MIB... $125.00
Michelin Tires, yo-yo, Mr Bib in blk outline on wht, EX ..$10.00
Mobil Oil/Detroit Tigers, bank, milk glass baseball shape on blk base, red Pegasus on 1 side & Tigers on other, EX+, A .$100.00

Mobilgas, tanker truck #163, Japan, 1960s, tin, friction, 8", VG, A $32.00
Mr Clean, figure w/arms crossed, pnt vinyl, 8", Proctor & Gamble, 1961, EX....$65.00
Nabisco, Breakfast Buddies, 7-pc set of colorful Winnie the Pooh characters, 2" to 2½", Rice Honeys, 1965, M $80.00
Nabisco, Dinosaur Set, set of 5 in ea series A or B w/Dinosaur Guide, 1950s, NM (w/mailer box), ea set $85 to..... $110.00
Nabisco, doll, Mr Salty, stuffed cloth, 1983, NM, minimum value....$25.00

Nabisco, doll, Nabisco boy in rain gear w/product box, composition, 16", EX, A, $525.00. (Photo courtesy Wm Morford)

Nabisco, Prehistoric Beasts figures, gray plastic, 8 different, 1957, NM, ea from $18 to $20.00
Nabisco, Spoonmen, plastic, 3 different, Shreaded Wheat Junior, 1959, ea from $20 to....$25.00
Nestlé, book, Magic Tricks, 1970s, NM $8.00
Nestlé, doll, P Nutty as Morsal Family Clown, Trudy Co, 1984, 10", EX+....$18.00
Nestlé, figure, Quik Bunny, bendable, 6", EX....$6.00
Nestlé, figure, Quik Bunny, plush, w/'Q' necklace, 1980s, 21", EX....$25.00
Oreo Cookies, figure, Oreo Cookie w/bendable arms & legs, 4½", M....$6.00
Oreo Cookies, Oreo Cookie Box Wind-Up Walker, plastic, 2½", 1984, NRFC....$45.00
Orkin, coloring book, 'Otto' the Orkin Man, 1966, VG+..$20.00
Oscar Mayer, puppet, Little Oscar, plastic w/printed image, EX+ $6.00
Oscar Mayer, whistle, plastic Wienermobile, 2x1", NM....$15.00
Oscar Mayer, Wienermobile, plastic, Little Oscar pops up when wheels move, earliest version, 1950s, 10" L, EX $100.00
Pepsi-Cola, dispenser/bank, b/o, 10", Linemar, 1950s, unused, EXIB.... $350.00
Pepsi-Cola, pull toy, puppy w/hot dog wagon, wood, 10", EX.... $250.00
Pepsi-Cola, truck, Buddy L, 1970s, metal, 2-tier open bay w/ 'Enjoy Pepsi' ad panel, bl & wht, w/cases, 16", EXIB $100.00

Pepsi-Cola, truck, Buddy L, wood, Railway Express, 16", 1940s, VG, A, $500.00. (Photo courtesy Morphy Auctions)

Pepsi-Cola, truck, Marx, 1940s-50s, tin, wht w/plastic cases on open bay, P=C cap logos on doors & back, 7", NM. $100.00
Pepsi-Cola, truck, Ny-Lint, metal, 3-part open-sided bays w/Pepsi ads on inside walls, 16", no accessories o/w VG....... $100.00
Pepsi-Cola, truck, Ny-Lint, metal, 3-part open-sided bays w/Pepsi ads on inside walls, 16", w/accessories, VGIB.......... $175.00
Pepsi-Cola, truck, Smith-Miller, GMC cabover, PS w/wooden open box bay & cases, metal divider, 13", NM........ $165.00
Pepsi-Cola, truck, Solido, Chevy pickup (1946), diecast, 9½", M, from $15 to $25.00
Peters Weatherbird Shoes for Girls, figure, porc, Germany imprinted across back, red, wht & bl pnt, w/tag, 3½", EX, A....$110.00
Phillips 66, doll, Buddy Lee dressed as service man in lt brn hat, shirt & pants w/orange logos, 13", VG, A................ $400.00
Pillsbury, figure, Poppin' Fresh, talker, Mattel, 16", NM. $100.00
Pillsbury, figure, Poppin' Fresh, vinyl, standing w/arms open on sq plastic base w/emb name, 7½", 1971, EX+.............$30.00
Pillsbury, finger puppet, Biscuit (cat) or Flapjack (dog), vinyl, 1974, ea....$35.00
Pillsbury, finger puppet, Poppin' Fresh, Poppie Fresh, Bun Bun (girl) or Popper (boy), vinyl, 1974, ea....$25.00
Pillsbury, hand puppet, Poppin' Fresh, plastic w/vinyl head, 1971, EX $25.00
Pizza Hut, bank, Pizza Hut Pete, plastic, 1969, 8", EX+.....$25.00
Pizza Hut, kite, Garfield, MIP....$5.00
Planters, beachball, yel w/image of Mr Peanut in bl, 13½" dia, 1970s, EX $10.00
Planters, belt buckle, plastic emb w/crossed pistols above Mr Peanut logo, rope border, 2x4", Pyro, 1960s, M...............$45.00
Planters, coloring book, 'America an Ecology Coloring Book,' 1970s, unused, M $15.00
Planters, coloring book, '12 Months,' 1970s, unused, M ...$12.00
Planters, coloring book, '50 States,' 1970s, unused, M $15.00
Planters, figure, Mr Peanut, cloth, 18", Chase Bag Co, 1970, NM....$25.00
Planters, figure, Mr Peanut, cloth, 21", Chase Bag Co, 1967, EX....$40.00
Planters, figure, Mr Peanut, pnt wood bead-type, 8½", VG $125.00
Planters, frisbee, wht plastic w/Heritage logo, M $15.00
Planters, game, Planters Peanut Party, lg premium version, 1930s, unused, NM $100.00

Planters, hand puppet, Mr Peanut, rubber, 1942, EX, from $750 to $1,000.00
Planters, iron-on transfer, Mr Peanut image in famous pose & Planters name, 9", 1970s, unused, NM........ $12.00
Planters, mug, Mr Peanut figural head, plastic, name emb on hat band, 1960s mail-in premium, M........ $18.00
Planters, nodder, Mr Peanut figure, pnt compo, 1960s, 7", VG........ $80.00
Planters, top, pnt wood w/ad label, 1940s, 2½", EX........ $150.00
Planters, whistle, plastic Mr Peanut figure, 1970s, NM........ $6.00
Planters, yo-yo, Mr Peanut image, Humphery, 1976, NM. $12.00
Popsicle, Music Maker Truck, plastic, 11", Mattel, VG.. $150.00
Post Cereal Co, Sugar Bear doll, stuffed cloth, 5", Sugar Crisp cereal premium, EX+........ $8.00
Pure Oil Co, tank truck, PS, electric lights, PS, bl w/wht lettering, BRT, 15", VG, A........ $825.00
Quaker Oats Co, bank, Cap'n Crunch figure, molded vinyl, 7", Cap'n Crunch cereal premium, 1960s or 1970s, EX+. $35.00
Quaker Oats Co, Cavern Helmet, w/headlight, plastic, cereal premium, 1967, NM........ $225.00
Raid, figure, Raid Bug, plush, 1980, EX+........ $25.00
Raid, figure, Raid Bug, w/up, mean expression, 4", NM..... $50.00

Ralston Purina, chuck wagon squeeze toy, vinyl, 8", 1975, M, $40.00. (Photo courtesy gasolinealleyantiques.com)

RCA, figure, Radiotron Man, pnt beaded wood w/chest banner, 16", Maxfield Parrish design, 1920s, A........ $690.00
Red Goose Shoes, bank, Red Goose figure, CI, red w/gold emb advertising on both sides, 3½", EX+, A........ $550.00
Red Goose Shoes, doll, stuffed girl figure w/compo head, orig outfit w/ad tag on chest, socks & shoes, 24", early, EX, A........ $240.00
Reddy Whip, hand puppet, Reddy Whip Boy, cloth body w/vinyl head, 1960s, EX+........ $75.00
Rival Dog Food, delivery van & can bank, Buddy L, PS, rear doors open, 14½", NMIB........ $600.00
Roi-Tan Cigars, toy car promoting the 1939 Roi-Tan Cigar Chevy give-way on the Sophie Tucker CBS radio show, 5", NMIB, A........ $675.00
Sambo's Restaurants, Family Funbook, Fun Games & Puzzles Featuring JT & the Tiger Kids, 1978 premium, some use, VG........ $28.00
Sambo's Restaurants, figure, Sambo's Tiger, plush, Dakin, MIB (cb cage box)........ $75.00
Sealtest Ice Cream, hand puppet, Mr Cool, cloth body w/vinyl head, 1950s, VG........ $50.00

Seven-Up, figure, Fresh-Up Freddie, squeeze vinyl, 9", 1959, NM+, $250.00. (Photo courtesy gasolinealleyantiques.com)

Seven-Up, figure, Fresh-Up Freddie, stuffed cloth w/rubber head, 15", Canada, EX........ $75.00
Seven-Up, figure, Spot, bendable, 3", NM........ $5.00
Seven-Up, figure, Spot, folds away into cloth bag shaped like 7-Up can, premium time, 12", EX+........ $15.00
Seven-Up, figure, Spot w/suction-cup hands, Commonwealth, 6", 1980s, NM+........ $8.00
Sheffield Farms Company, pull toy, horse-drawn delivery wagon, pnt wood, w/glass bottles, 9" L, EX+, A........ $800.00
Shell, bank, litho tin service station shape, 6", EX+, A. $220.00
Shell, tank truck, Minic/Tri-ang, tin, w/up, gr cab w/gold Shell decal on red tank, 5½", EX, A........ $110.00
Shell BP, tank truck, Minic/Tri-ang, wht cab w/Shell BP on red tank, 6-wheeled, 24", G+, A........ $185.00
Shell Motor Oil, stake truck, Metalcraft, 1930s, PS, red & yel, w/oil cans, 12", VG, A........ $385.00
Shell Oil, tanker truck, SK, yel tin w/lithoed graphics, friction, 13", NM (EX Shell Gasoline Hauler box), A........ $475.00
Shoney's, bank, Shoney's Bear, vinyl, 1990s, 8", NM........ $15.00
Snickers Candy Bar, doll, fits into bag resembling Snickers bar, 12", Mars, 1990s, EX........ $12.00
Snow Crop Frozen Foods, bear, Teddy Show Crop, wht plush w/molded vinyl face, rnd red cloth label, 9", 1950s, EX.. $50.00
Snow Crop Frozen Foods, hand puppet, Teddy Snow Crop, wht plush w/molded vinyl face, red cloth label, 1950s, EX........ $25.00
Snow Crop Frozen Foods, toy van, litho tin, friction, BRT, 8½", H/Japan, 1960s, EX+........ $100.00
Snuggle Fabric Softener, figure, Snuggles the bear, 6", plush, Lever Bros, 1983, NM........ $15.00
Snuggle Fabric Softener, figure, Snuggles the bear, 8", plush beanbag type, Lever Bros, 1999, NM........ $15.00
Snuggle Fabric Softener, figure, Snuggles the bear, 14", Lever Bros, 1986, NM+........ $30.00
Snuggle Fabric Softener, hand puppet, Snuggles the bear (full body), 15", Lever Bros, 1990s, EX+........ $15.00

Spaghetti-Os, bowl, ceramic w/image of Spaghetti-O kid skateboarding in center, 8½" dia, MIB (plain mailer box)..$25.00
Squirt, doll, Squirt Boy, vinyl w/cloth outfit, yel molded hair, jtd limbs, 1961, EX...$150.00
Star Brand Shoes, racer, die-cut tin litho, 'The Winner' on rear, 8½" L, unused, M, A...$3,900.00
Star-Kist, bank, Charlie the Tuna figure standing on tuna can, 9½", 1988, NM...$20.00
Star-Kist, figure, Charlie the Tuna 'Talkin' Patter Pillow,' stuffed print cloth, 15", Mattel, 1950s, NM+........................$25.00
Star-Kist, lamp base, Charlie the Tuna figure, pnt plaster, 12½", 1970s, EX+...$65.00

Star-Kist, pencil toppers, Charlie Tuna figures in various colors, 2", M, $8.00 each. (Photo courtesy gasolinealleyantiques.com)

Star-Kist, truck, PS, red cab w/bl box van, opening rear doors, ads on cab & van, 14½", 1950s, VG $500.00
Star-Kist, Wack Wobbler, Charlie the Tuna figure, PCV, M.$15.00
Sunbeam Bread, doll, Little Miss Sunbeam, stuffed cloth, 17", NM...$35.00
Sunshine Biscuits, truck, Metalcraft, 1930s, PS, w/NP van top, electric lights, BRT, 12", VG+ $300.00
Taco Bell, dog, beanbag type, w/tags, 1999, M...................$12.00
Texaco, boat, Toy Tanker 'North Dakota,' 28", AMF/Wen-Mac, 1960s mail-in premium, 28", unused, MIB, A.......... $850.00
Texaco, fire chief's hat, red plastic w/wht shield, 1960s, G+, A.. $55.00
Texaco, fire engine, Fire Chief, Buddy L American La France Pumper, 1962, PS, gas station promo, 25", MIB, A . $550.00
Texaco, tanker truck, Buddy L, modern sq wht cab & red sq tank, plastic windows, 24", VG+...$65.00
Texaco, tanker truck, Park Plastics, 1960s, PS & plastic, red cab w/silver tank, 24", unused, MIB $250.00
Toys R Us, roly poly figure, Baby Gee, orange plastic w/name on wht bib, 9", Arco, 1980s, NM $15.00
U-Haul, truck, U-Haul Maxi-Mover #8411, Ny-Lint, PS, 20", unused, NRFB, A...$75.00
US Postal Service, figure, mailbox w/arms & legs, vinyl, 7½", scarce, EX.. $125.00
USDA Forest Service, bank, Smokey standing w/legs together & holding shovel upright, vinyl, 14", Play Pal, 1970s, EX..$35.00
USDA Forest Service, bank, Woodsy Owl standing on rnd base, marked Give A Hoot..., ceramic, 8½", 1970s, EX.......$50.00
USDA Forest Service, book, 'Smokey Bear's Story of the Forest,' 1968, softcover, 16 pgs, VG..$18.00
USDA Forest Service, figure, Smokey Bear, inflatable vinyl, 20", Ideal, 1960s, EX $40.00
USDA Forest Service, figure, Smokey Bear, plush w/cloth bl jeans, yel hat, w/belt & badge, 22", Knickerbocker, VG.........$50.00
USDA Forest Service, figure, Smokey Bear, stuffed brn felt w/cloth pants, printed face, 6½", Knickerbocker, 1972, MIB......$55.00
USDA Forest Service, figure, Smokey Bear, stuffed plush, denim jeans w/wht stitching, felt hat, 9", Bon Ton Toys, NM+.. $10.00
USDA Forest Service, figure, Smokey Bear, vinyl w/cloth pants, holding shovel, 8", Dakin, 1970s, NM+.....................$30.00
USDA Forest Service, figure, Woodsy Owl, 7", Knickerbocker, 1972, NMIB, A...$30.00
USDA Forest Service, hand puppet, Smokey Bear, printed cloth body w/vinyl head, Ideal, 1959, scarce, NM+.......... $175.00
USDA Forest Service, mug, ceramic w/emb image of Smokey Bear w/shovel, w/phrase, 3½", NM.............................$28.00

USDA Forest Service, playset, Smokey Bear & His Friends Forest patrol Helicopter, Multiple Toymakers, 1969, MIB, $55.00. (Photo courtesy whatacharacter.com)

USDA Forest Service, ruler, Smokey Bear, die-cut paper image of Smokey behind log wall w/sign, 6" ruler, 1962, EX.....$18.00
Visking, Willie the Wizard Magic Tricks premium, uncut, M (w/mailer).. $125.00
Vlasic Pickles, figure, Vlasic Stork, fluffy wht fur w/glasses & bow tie, 22", Trudy Toys, 1989, NM $40.00
Wool Soap, block set, stenciled wood alphabet blocks w/soap ad graphics, Swift & Co, EXIB (7x9" box), A $165.00
Wrigley's Chewing Gum, Mother Goose Booklet, Introducing the Sprightly Spearman (illus throughout), 1915, 28 pgs, EX...$60.00
WT Grand Five & Dime, bank, Jo Joy jack-in-the-box figure, chalkware, 1947, NM $175.00

Advertising Signs, Ads, and Displays

With the intense passion toy buffs pour into their collections, searching for advertising items to complement those collections is a natural extension of their enthusiasm, adding even more diversity to an already multifaceted collecting field.

Arcade Cast Iron Toys, wood billboard display, 'They look real...'/ 'Arcade Mfg Co Freeport Ill,' 14½" L, EX+, A........... $385.00

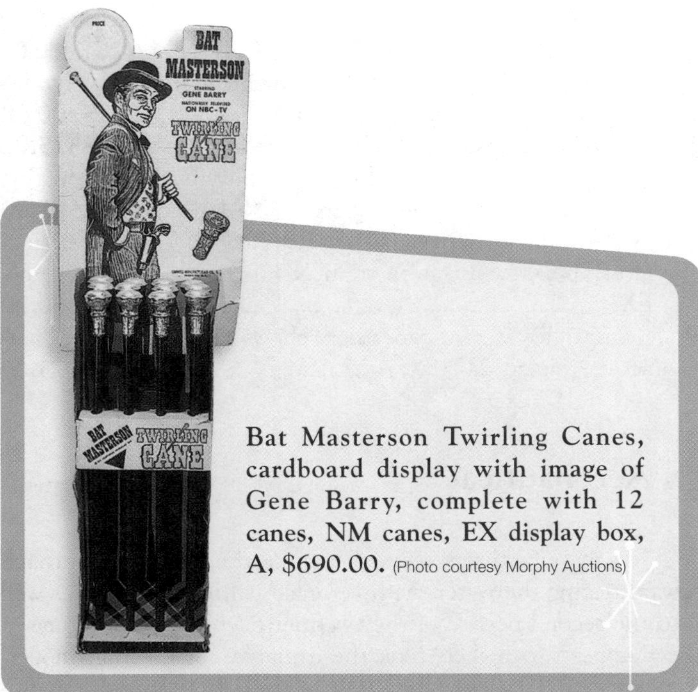

Bat Masterson Twirling Canes, cardboard display with image of Gene Barry, complete with 12 canes, NM canes, EX display box, A, $690.00. (Photo courtesy Morphy Auctions)

Batman Wallets, die-cut cb sign w/lettering over oval logo, Standard Plastic/Mattel/NPP, 1960s, fits on rack, 6x16", EX.......... $75.00

Buck Rogers on the Air This Summer for Creamsicle, paper sign, 'Save Bags'/'Swell Gifts'/'Ask Here For...,' 1939, 8x20", EX, A $1,265.00

Captain Kangaroo T-Shirts Only 50¢, Durkee's fold-out recipe brochure w/premium T-shirt offer, 1960, NM............$22.00

Casper Spinning Ghost Tops, counter display box w/12 tops, box marked $1.00, EX $250.00

Crystal White Soap, die-cut cb Mickey Mouse figure touting a 'FREE' Mickey Mouse Balloon, 30", 1936, VG, A .. $165.00

Davy Crocket Badges, display card w/12 diecast badges, orange cb w/red lettering, 11x10", G+, A.......................... $100.00

Dennis the Menace Flashlights, cb display card w/10 of 12 'key chain' flashlights, shows Dennis shining light, NM, A .$500.00

Disneykings, stepped cb display w/3 rows of 20 character figures, complete, EX, A $550.00

Donald Duck Bread, sign, cb, Donald's head & bread loaf on yel, 'Oven Fresh Flavor' on blk bottom band, 11x25", 1950s, NM...$50.00

Donald Duck Bread, 3 die-cut cb dwarfs (Snow White) ea holding a loaf of bread, 12" to 13", VG, A..................... $130.00

Donald Duck Icy-Frost Twins, die-cut cb display w/image of Donald & product, 8", EX, A $75.00

Duncan Jeweled Professional Yo-Yo Tops 69¢, display box w/die-cut header, complete w/12 yo-yos, NM, A........... $2,250.00

Gabby Hayes Prospector's Hat Only 75¢/Quaker Puffed Wheat Puffed Rice, store sign, 1950s, NM.......................... $200.00

Gabby Hayes Western Gun Collection, cb folder display w/ complete set of 6 guns, premiums for Quaker, 1951, 7x12", EX..$125.00

Gene Autry World's Greatest Cowboy & Champion World's Wonder Horse, die-cut cb stand-up, 59x31", EX, A .. $400.00

Hep Magic String Balls 49¢, cb display box w/12 plastic Hep baseballs, NM, A $650.00

Howdy Doody Doll Promotion ('Presenting Welch's Sentational...'), fold-out brochure, from 9x12" to 18x24", VG, A..$150.00

Howdy Doody Keychain Puzzles, display card w/11 plastic Howdy keychain puzzle figures, 12x8", NM, A.................... $100.00

Howdy Doody Likes Nabisco Cereals, cb figural stand-up, 24", VG, A $1,250.00

Howdy Doody Sale/Welch's, paper sign w/Howdy head image & price dot for grape jelly, 13x10", 1951, VG, A......... $225.00

Howdy Doody Says 'M-M-M! Royal's My Favorite Dessert!,' cb stand-up of Howdy holding sign & product box, 20", VG, A... $1,200.00

Ingersoll Sterling Silver Rings $1.50, die-cut cardboard display card with 10 adjustable rings, early post WWII, EX, A, $715.00. (Photo courtesy Randy Inman Auctions)

Ingersoll Walt Disney Watches, display w/all 10 boxed '1948 Mickey Mouse 20th Anniversary' watches w/in lg box, EX+, A $4,400.00

Krazy Kat Balloons, cb trifold display w/assortment of balloons featuring Krazy Kat, Ashland Rubber, 1950s, 14" T, EX....$50.00

Lionel Commando Assault Train, cb display, tan 'windshield' shape w/battlefield graphics & closeup insets, EX, A...$30.00

Lionel Trains, die-cut fold-out display shaped like flashing signal, 'Hey Kids Win A Free Lionel Train...,' 9x22", NM, A..$275.00

Lone Ranger Badges, red cb display card w/11 badges, 11", NM+, A $250.00

Marx Toys Advertising Figure, plastic 1" figure on sq base w/his body as rnd Marx logo, scarce, M..............................$48.50

Matchbox, display set, w/5 cars & boxes, NM, A $225.00

Mickey Mouse, display figure, stuffed plush w/red velvet shorts, gold velvet shoes & 5-fingered hands, Deans Rag, VG, A $560.00

Mickey Mouse Anklets/Roy Rogers Socks, yel tin sign w/Socks labels above/below head images of Mickey & Roy, 30"x11", EX $150.00

Mickey Mouse Pocket Watch Display, 6 Bradley watches on board at $7.95, w/6 individual boxes, EX, A............ $660.00

Mickey Mouse/Donald Duck Cereal Bowl, sign, cb, 'Free While They Last...' Post's 40% Bran/Grape=Nuts, 1930s, 14x10", VG $1,600.00

New Haven Animated Character Watches, die-cut cb stand-up, A Oakley/D Tracy/G Aurty images, 12x9", 1950s, no watches, VG $125.00
Pinocchio, mechanical display figure promoting the 1940 film release, compo, cloth outfit, 40", VG, A........ $1,100.00
Pinocchio Chewing Gum, display box, cb w/image of Pinocchio & birds in nest, 1940s, 8½", VG, A $300.00
Popeye Flashlite, die-cut cb stand-up w/fold-out 3-D effect, shows Popeye in crow's nest, Bantamlite, 1950s, EX ..$65.00
Quiz Kids CBS TV Show, cb stand-up, 'Blackie the Famous Cat-Tex Puppet!,' 'Send Coupon & 35¢ Today!,' 1955, NM........ $150.00
Red Ryder 1000 Shot Carbine, die-cut cb sign, red, wht & blk image of RR w/hat in hand by Christmas tree, 22x21", VG, A $690.00
Rin-Tin-Tin Cavalry Rifle Pen, full-color newspaper ad from Nabisco Shredded Wheat, 6½x13", 1956, EX........$25.00

Roy Rogers Cowboy Flashlights, die-cut cardboard display with five flashlights, EX, A, $800.00. (Photo courtesy Morphy Auctions)

Roy Rogers Straight Shooter Gun Puzzle Key Chains, cb display card w/2 gun key chains, EX........$75.00
Roy Rogers Wagon Train of Bargains, brn & yel litho cb display, folds for standing up, 8x13", 1950s, unused, NM..... $150.00
Roy Rogers Wild West Action Toy, sign, paper, 'Free!...w/Every Box of...Roy Rogers Cookies,' 13x17", 1950s, NM, A........ $345.00
Saturday Night Fever Bubble Gum & Cards, display box w/36 sealed gum packs, Donruss, 1977, NM, A........$95.00
Sgt Preston's 10 in 1 Trail Kit, full color newspaper ad promoting Quaker cereal premium, 1958, NM+ $25.00
Snow White & the Seven Dwarfs, die-cut cb display promoting the 1940s Walt Disney movie, VG, A $75.00
Space: 1999 Gum Cards, display box, complete w/24 sealed packs, Donruss, 1976, EX+, A........$85.00
Squirt, paper litho sign, '18" Squirt Doll for $2.95...$5.95 Value!,' 10x21", 1962, M $50.00
Star Wars Get a Free Bobba Fett Action Figure!....cb display header, 2 slots for attachment, blk, 13x24", 1979, EX, A $115.00

Steiff, peacock store display, 35" L, EX, A $275.00
Tasty Food Limited, cb store sign w/example of free toy train, 'Every Child Will Want...Ask Us About It,' 1920s, VG, A $630.00
Tobor-1 Robot, fiberglass light-up display figure, 60", EX, A..$1,680.00
Tom Mix Records 'Now Available'/'Straightshooters'... Everyone's Favorite!, red, wht & bl paper banner, M $200.00
Tonka, oval porc dealer sign, 11x23", 1968, MIB $325.00
Tootsietoy, cb w/up display w/Lincoln Zephyr & trailer, 'Be Sure It's a Toosietoy' on marquee, 9x12", NM, A $3,575.00
Tyco's Petticoat Junction HO Scale Electric Train Set, sign, glossy paper w/image of train & CBS logo, 11x20", 1966, EX........ $260.00
Welcome to Toy Town, paper sign, shows Santa w/Disney characters, framed, 21", EX, A $175.00

Aeronautical

Toy manufacturers seemed to take the cautious approach toward testing the waters with aeronautical toys, and it was well into the second decade of the twentieth century before some of the European toymakers took the initiative. The earlier models were bulky and basically inert, but by the 1950s, Japanese manufacturers were turning out battery-operated replicas with wonderful details that advanced with whirling motors and flashing lights. For more information we recommend *Big Book of Toy Airplanes* by W. Tom Miller, Ph.D. (Collector Books).

See also Battery-Operated Toys; Cast Iron, Airplanes; Gasoline-Powered Toys; Model Kits; Pull Toys; Robots and Space Toys; Windup, Friction, and Other Mechanical Toys.

Aero Circus, Newton, ca 1931, complete, NMIB, A...... $750.00
Air Control Tower, Bandai, r/c, w/USAF helicopter & plane, 11" tower, NM+IB, A $400.00
Air France F-Anny, tin, w/up, 4-props, VG, A $350.00
Air France F-PA-N-AM, France, tin, w/up, 24" WS, rpnt, A..$600.00
Airliner, France, tin, w/up, early 4-prop w/F on tail, 23½" WS, VG, A $500.00
Airways Express Trimotor, Girard, tin w/celluloid props, w/up, 13", VG+, A $385.00
Amphibian Plane, Bing, tin, w/up, pontoons under top wing, simulated wood & silver, 16" WS, EX, A........ $880.00

American Airlines DC-7C Passenger Plane, Y, 1950s, lithographed tin, battery-operated, 24" wingspan, EX, $1,265.00. (Photo courtesy serioustoyz.com)

Army Scout Plane, Steelcraft, PS, gr w/yel top wing, tail, prop & wheels, 22½" WS, VG+ $725.00
Biplane, France, tin, rubber-band driven, b/o lights, 2-tone gr w/red prop, 20" WS, EX, A $1,430.00
Biplane, Germany, tin, w/up, electric light, orange, wht & bl, 20" WS, EX, A $1,650.00
Biplane, Kingsbury, PS, 12" WS, G, A $250.00
Biplane (4-Motor), Marx, tin w/celluloid props, w/up, red & wht, 18" WS, EXIB, A $450.00
Bomber, Japan, tin, w/up, camouflage detail, 4 NP props, 12" W, EX, A $385.00
Capital Airlines Viscount Airliner, Linemar, tin, r/c, 14" WS, EXIB, A $200.00
Catapult Airplane & Hangar, Buddy L, plane catapults out of hangar, PS, 10" WS/8x12" hangar, EX, A $2,800.00
Catapult Hangar w/Monocoupe, Buddy L, 1930s, 12x8" hangar, G+, A $660.00
Cessna Skymaster NI705Z, Cragstan, 1950s, friciton, front/rear single props, dbl tail, 11½" WS, NMIB, A $150.00
China Clipper, Wyandotte, pnt PS, wooden wheels, 13" WS, EX+, A $175.00
Cragstan Jet (Smoking Jet Plane), Nomura, 1950s, b/o, litho tin, 11½" L, EX+IB, A $200.00
Curtiss Jenny Trainer (Biplane), S&E, tin, friction, 11" WS, EX+IB, A $190.00
D-A LBA Monoplane, Marklin, tin, wht w/lt gr & blk trim, 21" W, VG, A $500.00
Disney Airliner, Linemar, tin, friction, 7" WS, EX, A $600.00
Douglas Sky Rocket/Navy B-335, Japan, tin, friction, 18" L, VGIB, A $150.00

Early Flapping-Wing Airplane, Gunthermann, tin with cardboard propellers, windup, 12", EX, A, $1,200.00. (Photo courtesy Morphy Auctions)

F-ABX Cargo Plane, France, tin, w/up, red, wht & bl, lithoed pilots, 3 props, 20" WS, EX, A $500.00
Fighter Plane, Germany, tin w/celluloid fins, w/up, Mickey Mouse decal, 14" WS, EX, A $1,320.00
Graf LZ 127 Zeppelin, Tipco/Germany, silver tin, w/up, 10", EX, A $700.00
Graf Zeppelin, Steelcraft, PS, 26", EX, A $1,100.00
Graf Zeppelin CZ2017, Strauss, tin, w/up, silver, 16", VG, A $360.00
Graf Zeppelin D-LZ 130, Germany, tin w/celluloid props, w/up, silver, 10½" L, EX, A $880.00
Graf Zeppelin GZ 2017, Strauss, aluminum w/metal prop, w/up, 18", VG+IB, A $935.00
Graf Zeppelin Jr LA 1016, Strauss, aluminum w/metal prop, w/up, 10", VG+IB, A $410.00

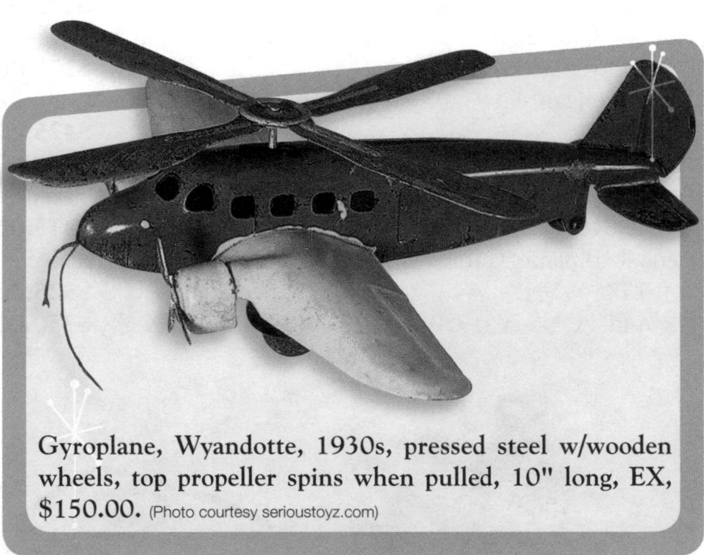

Gyroplane, Wyandotte, 1930s, pressed steel w/wooden wheels, top propeller spins when pulled, 10" long, EX, $150.00. (Photo courtesy serioustoyz.com)

Helicopter w/Whirling Lighted Blades, Hong Kong, 1960s, plastic, b/o, 11½", unused, NMIB, A $50.00
HUKI 10-3 Stratoliner, Huki/Germany, tin, friction, 8", MIB, A $950.00
Interceptor, S&E, b/o, litho tin, front part of plane on tripod shoots rockets from hand-op lever, 14" W, EXIB, A $110.00
JD 2755/D-19 Biplane, Distler, tin, w/up, red w/wht & yel details, 16½" L, some rstr, A $475.00
Lockheed Coupe, Buddy L, PS, b/o, open dbl cockpits, low wing, 1 prop, covered wheels, 22" WS, VG, A $1,100.00
Los Angeles Zeppelin, German, silver tin w/red cb props, w/up, 7" L, EX, A $350.00
Macon Zeppelin, Steelcraft, PS, electric headlight, wht, 25", VG, A $1,200.00
Mailplane, Strauss, tin, w/up, 8" WS, VG (VG box), A... $330.00
Meteor HWN-XL7 Fighter Jet, tin, friction, 13" L, EX, A. $195.00
ML 5 Plane, France, tin, w/up, 3-prop, yel, wht & bl w/red, wht & bl tailfin, 20" WS, A $650.00
N-X-4542 Ford Trimotor (Top Wing), Nomura, tin, friction, 15" WS, NM+IB, A (MB: $275) $1,350.00
NASA 905 Space Shuttle Challenger & Flying Jet Plane, Taiwan, b/o, tin & plastic, NMIB, A $110.00
Navy Fighter Bomber, Hubley, diecast metal, folding wings, 11" WS, unused, MIB, A $125.00
Navy Panther Jet, Y, tin, r/c, fold-up wings, 12½", VGIB, A.... $190.00
Navy 126 A Sparking Panther Jet Fighter, Masudaya, tin, friction, 6½" WS, EX+IB, A $150.00
Nifty Top Wing, Nifty, tin, wht w/red trim, 7" WS, VG+, A .. $250.00
NX 130 Top Wing, Steelcraft, 22" L, G+ $500.00
NX130 Top Wing, Steelcraft, PS, BRT, 22" WS, rstr, A.. $350.00
N35IR Fighter Plane, Japan, tin, friction, red, wht & bl design, 14" WS, EX, A $475.00

P-47 Thunderbolt Cap Firing Fighter Plane, Frankonia/Japan, tin, friction, 5½" L, EXIB, A $65.00
PAA N888861 Airliner, PS, 4-prop, silver, 22" WS, NM, A..$150.00
Pan Am Clipper, Marx, PS, wht w/bl wings & details, 4 NP props, 26" WS, rpnt, A $225.00
Pan Am Clipper, Wyandotte, PS, wht w/bl top wing, 4 NP props, 13" WS, rstr, A $275.00
Pan American Airways System China Clipper, Chein, w/up, tin, 11" WS, VG+, A $425.00
Pathfinder No 107, Katz, tin, red & yel, 22" WS, VG, A .. $750.00
Red Arrow, Katz, tin, makes clicking noise when pushed, red & yel, 18" W, VG+, A $415.00
Renault Biplane, Carl Rossignol/France, tin, w/up, bl, red & yel, 13½" WS, EX, A $525.00
Right Plane No 20, 1920s, PS, 27" WS & 30" L, EX, A.. $350.00

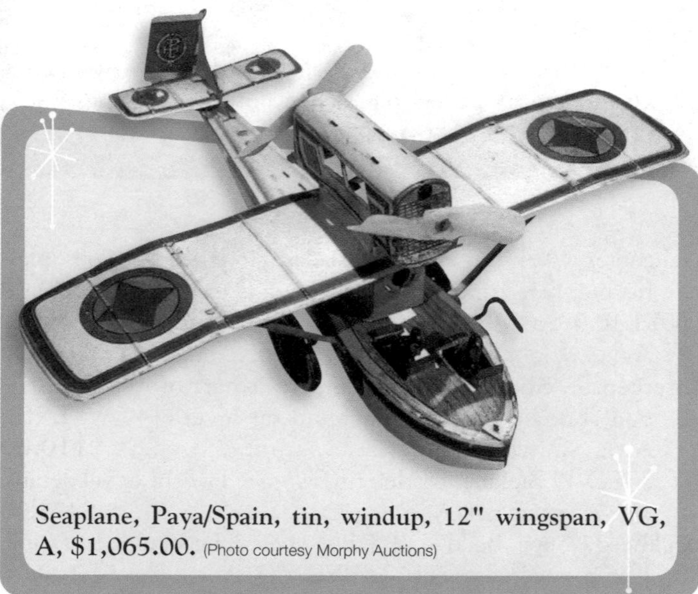

Seaplane, Paya/Spain, tin, windup, 12" wingspan, VG, A, $1,065.00. (Photo courtesy Morphy Auctions)

Silver Eagle, Strauss, emb aluminum, w/up, 12" L, VG+IB, A $935.00
Skycruiser NC 10 5034 (Two-Motored Transport Plane), Marx, tin, friction, 18" WS, EXIB, A $385.00
Super Sonic Jetplane MF-103, China, friction, litho tin, 10", NMIB, A...$65.00
TC 1029 Bomber, Tipp, ca 1930, tin w/celluloid tailfin, compo figure, w/up, 14½" L, EX, A $1,550.00
Tiger X-15, Japan, 1950s, tin, friction, 7½" WS, MIB, A ..$95.00
Tippco Airlines Single Prop, tin, w/up, 10" WS, VG, A... $400.00
Top Wing, Chein, tin, w/up, red, wht & bl star emblems on wings, 7" WS, VG+, A $175.00
Top Wing, France, tin, w/up, cream w/red bird insignias & red, wht & bl trim, 13½" WS, EX, A $375.00
Top Wing, Girard, tin, w/up, gray w/red detail, pilot in open cockpit, 10" WS, VG+, A $400.00
Top Wing, Marx, 1930s, PS, 4 props, Deco-style skirted wooden wheels, 6½" L, EX, A $75.00
Top Wing, Steelcraft, PS, articulated prop, yel & red, 22½" WS, early rpnt, A.. $150.00
Top Wing, Wyandotte, PS, trimotor, wooden wheels, 18" WS, VG, A $350.00
Top Wing & Hangar, Schiebles, PS, orange & lt bl, fold-up wings, 22", VG, A... $390.00
Toy Town Airways Helicopter, Chein, tin w/plastic blades, w/up, 13" L, VGIB, A... $225.00
Trans-Atlantic Zeppelin, Marx, tin, w/up, silver, 9½", EX, A ..$330.00
Transport Plane, Buddy L #603, PS, 4-prop, red & yel, 26" WS, VGIB, A $450.00
Transport Plane (Four-Motor), Marx, tin, friction, camouflage detail, 4 props, 17" WS, EXIB, A $400.00
Trimotor, Buddy L, PS, wooden wheels, 27" WS, EX+, A ...$275.00
US Air Force FW-996 (Lighted Jet Plane), Nomura, b/o, litho tin, 13" L, EX+IB, A... $350.00
US Air Force Jet Fighter 7452, Marx, 1950s, tin, r/c, 7", EX, A $50.00
US Air Force Jet Plane Base w/FW 707 Jet, Yonezawa, b/o, litho tin, 9" L plane, EXIB, A $475.00
US Army N 41312 Battle Helicopter, Alps, tin & plastic, w/up, 13½", NM+IB, A $185.00
US Army PBY Catalina Flying Boat, Chein, tin, w/up, 11" WS, EX, A $925.00
US Mail Plane, Steelcraft, trimotor, silver w/red tail, 26", G, A...$500.00
US Mail 990-5 Plane, Marx, tin, w/up, twin props, orange & yel w/gr details, 18" WS, EX, A $350.00
USAF BK-250 Bomber, Yonezawa, tin, friction, 4 props, 2 machine gun turrets, 18½" WS, VG+, A................ $425.00
USAF C-120 Pack Plane, Japan, tin, 2" Jeep & tank fit in plastic nose of plane, 11", NMIB, A $1,500.00
USAF Military Air Transport Service Plane, Wyandotte, #219, steel, 13" WS, NMIB, A.. $250.00
Winnie Mae, Wyandotte, PS, wooden wheels, 10" WS, VG, A $110.00
Zeppelin, Marklin, ca 1910, pnt tin w/celluloid props, w/up, 12", EX, A $4,125.00

Animation Cels

Some toy enthusiasts enjoy collecting character animation cels to complement their collections. Prior to the 1950s, these works of art were made of a celluloid material, thus the name 'cel.' Along with the original production cels, we have included some of the more recent sericels and limited editions, which are highly collectible in their own right. Although only animation cels are listed, background sketches, model sheets, storyboards, and preliminary sketches are also sought after by collectors. The following listings are from recent auctions.

Aladdin, Disney, sericel/no bkgrd, ed of 5,000, 'The Royal Embrace,' Aladdin & Jasmine embracing, 11x8", EX+, A $175.00
Aladdin, Disney, sericel/no bkgrd, Genie gives cast members a big hug, 7½x10½", EX+, A $250.00
Bambi, Disney, cel/bkgrd, ed of 500, Bambi & friend in deep forest, 8½x9½", EX+, A $600.00

Bambi, Disney, 1995, cel/bkgrd, ed of 350, Bambi, Faline & mothers in glow of light in forest, 11x19", EX+, A.. $750.00

Bugs Bunny, WB, 1948, prod cel/bkgrd, 'Hare Splitter,' Bugs as Cupid at side of house & wht fence, 8x11", EX+, A. $3,250.00

Bugs Bunny, WB, 1950s, prod cels/bkgrd, 'Lumberjack Rabbit' (?), Bugs & Elmer Fudd w/axe in landscape, 8x10", EX+, A, set $1,200.00

Bugs Bunny, Warner Brothers, 1953, production cel and background, 'Robot Rabbit,' shows Bugs & Elmer Fudd shaking hands in farm scene, 8½x12", EX, A, $1,100.00. (Photo courtesy Morphy Auctoins)

Bugs Bunny, WB, 1970s, prod cel, Bugs on stage in dressing robe, sgn Chuck Jones, 9x12", EX+, A............ $225.00

Bugs Bunny, WB, 1980, prod cel/bkgrd, 'Spaced Out,' Marvin the Martain & bugs atop spaceship, 8x25", EX+, A..... $2,000.00

Bugs Bunny, WB, 1980s, prod cel, Bugs on stage in bl tux w/purple curtain behind, sgn Friz Freleng, 9x12", EX+, A........ $175.00

Bugs Bunny/Daffy Duck, WB, 1980s, prod cel, Daffy tries to stuff Bugs back into hole, sgn Friz Freleng, 13x16", EX+, A.. $225.00

Daffy Duck/Porky Pig, WB, 1987, cel/bkgrd, ed of 200, Chuck Jones, flying around futuristic interstate, 9x12", EX+, A $350.00

Donald Duck, Disney, 1942, prod cel/Courvoisier bkgrd, Donald as soldier w/rifle over shoulder in landscape, 8x8, EX+, A............ $1,100.00

Donald Duck, Disney, 1950s, prod cel, frontal image standing w/mouth open & pointing finger, 5½x3", EX+, A $50.00

Donald Duck, Disney, 1950s, prod cel/no bkgrd, Donald standing w/feet & hands apart looking sideways, 5x5½", VG, A $75.00

Dudley Do-Right of the Mounties, sericel, Jay Ward, 1960s, Nell, Dudley & horse singing, sgn Jay Ward, 9x12", EX+, A . $400.00

Fantasia, Disney, 1940, prod cel/Courvoisier bkgrd, Mickey as Sorcerer commanding broom in corner, 9x12", rare, EX+, A............ $11,000.00

Fox & the Hound, Disney, cel, ed of 500, Tod & Copper at play in landscape, 5½x5½", EX+, A............ $250.00

Fox & the Hound, Disney, 1981, prod cel/no bkgrd, half-image of Tod the fox cub lying on his back, 7x8½", EX+, A.... $150.00

Great Mouse Detective, Disney, 1986, prod cel/no bkgrd, Basil gets Toby (bloodhound) to tract Fidget, 12 field, EX+, A.. $250.00

Great Mouse Detective, Disney, 1986, prod cel/no bkgrd, Dr Dawson doing the cancan with 2 cat girls, 12 field, EX+, A............ $500.00

Great Mouse Detective, Disney, 1986, prod cel/no bkgrd, Ratigan holds Figet's face in his hands, 10x12", EX+, A $300.00

Jiminy Cricket, Disney, 1950s, prod cel/no bkgrd, Jiminy making a soft landing w/open umbrella, 7x3", EX+, A......... $225.00

Lion King, Disney, cel, ed of 500, parent lions watching 2 cubs play, 7x14½", EX+, A $500.00

Lion King, Disney, sericel, ed of 500, Simba & Nala snuggling in forest, 11x12½", EX+, A............ $450.00

Lion King, Disney, sericel, ed of 5,000, Simba & Nala as cubs walking & conversing, 5½x9", EX+, A $150.00

Lion King, Disney, sericel/no bkgrd, ed of 5,000, image of Rafiki & adult Simba, 8x11", EX+, A............ $200.00

Lion King, Disney, sericel/no bkgrd, ed of 5,000, image of the 12 main characters in a line, 6x29", EX+, A $400.00

Lion King, Disney, sericel/no bkgrd, ed of 5,000, Simba wearing mane of leaves, 7½x8", EX+, A............$50.00

Marvin the Martain/Bugs Bunny, WB, 1988, w/bkgrd, ed of 300, Bugs tries to blow out match Marvin the Martian is using to light fuse, EX+............ $500.00

Mickey Mouse, Disney, 1935, prod cel/repro bkgrd, 'Band Concert,' Mickey conducting in oversized outfit, 10x12", EX+, A $6,500.00

Mickey Mouse, Disney, 1940, production cel with background, 'Mr. Mouse Takes a Vacation,' Mickey, Pluto, and Pete in a train car, EX, A, $13,000.00. (Photo courtesy Morphy Auctions)

Mickey's Christmas Carol, Disney, 1983, prod cel/no bkgrd, Willie the Giant holding up bunch of grapes, 12x16", EX+, A............ $150.00

101 Dalmatians, Disney, 1961, prod cel/bkgrd, 'Sgt Tibbs,' the tabby cat in snowy street scene, 4x7", EX+, A......... $650.00

Peter Pan, Disney, 1953, prod cel/bkgrd, Tiger Lily dances atop drum in village of tepees, 3½x6½", EX+, A $300.00

Peter Pan, Disney, 1953, prod cel/no bkgrd, St Bernard Dog 'Nana prancing in a nanny's hat, 8x6", EX+, A....... $450.00

Pistol Pete, Disney, 1952, prod cel/no bkgrd, 'Two-Gun Goofy,' PP holding dynamite, trimmed, framed, 5" dia, EX+, A $75.00

Pluto, Disney, ca 1940, prod cel/repro bkgrd, Pluto appears to be snoring on porch stoop at night, 8x11", EX+, A $550.00

Practical Pig, Disney, 1939, prod cels/Courvoisier bkgrd, wolf & 3 sons ready to 'butcher' 2 pigs, EX+, A................ $2,750.00

Ralph Wolf, WB, 1960s, prod cel/hand-prep bkgrd, Ralph Wolf w/stick of dynamite in landscape, 9x12", EX+, A.... $900.00

Rescuers, Disney, ltd cel/bkgrd, Bernard & Bianca riding in sardine can on Albatross' back, 12x16", EX+, A.......... $250.00

Rescuers, Disney, 1977, prod cel/no bkgrd, half-image of Madame Medusa holding on to rope, 8½x12", EX+, A $75.00

Robin Hood, Disney, 1973, prod cel/bkgrd, Robin & rhino guard having confrontation in landscape, 12x15", EX+, A ..$2,750.00

Sleeping Beauty, Disney, 1959, prod cel/bkgrd, Maleficent as fire-breathing dragon to stop Prince Phillip, 11x30", EX+ $12,000.00

Sleeping Beauty, Disney, 1959, prod cel/no bkgrd, 3 good fairies, 3¼x3", EX+, A.. $250.00

Snow White, Disney, cel/bkgrd, ltd ed, 'Off to Bed,' Snow White getting dwarfs off to bed, 7x15", EX+, A.............. $1,100.00

Sylvester the Cat and Pepe Le Pew, Warner Brothers, 1954, production cels with background, shows Pepe giving Sylvester a big bear hug, 8½x12", EX, A, $1,300.00. (Photo courtesy Morphy Auctions)

Uncle Scrooge, Disney, cel, ed of 313, 'Sport of Tycoons,' US diving into treasure, sgn Carl Banks, 18x24", EX+, A ... $700.00

Winnie the Pooh & the Blustery Day, Disney, 1968, prod cel, 4 separate character cels on snowy background, EX+, A $450.00

Wyle E Coyote, Warner Bros, prod cel/bkgrd, Wyle E Cyote ready to serve box of tennis balls in desert, 9x12", EX+, A . $650.00

Banks

The impact of condition on the value of a bank cannot be overrated. Cast-iron banks in near-mint condition with very little paint wear and all original parts are seldom found and might bring twice as much (if the bank is especially rare, up to five times as much) as one in average, very good original condition with no restoration and no repairs. Overpainting and replacement parts (even screws) have a very negative effect on value. Mechanicals dominate the market, and some of the hard-to-find banks in outstanding, near-mint condition may exceed $20,000.00! (Here's a few examples: Girl Skipping Rope, Calamity, and Mikado.) Modern mechanical banks are also emerging on the collectibles market, including Book of Knowledge and James D. Capron, which are reproductions with full inscriptions stating that the piece is a replica of the original. Still banks are widely collected as well, with more than 3,000 varieties having been documented. Beware of unmarked modern reproductions. All of the banks listed are cast iron unless noted otherwise.

The following listings were compiled from various auction sources with the estimates given in parenthesis. Dan Iannotti provided the listings for the modern mechanical banks. He is listed in the Categories of Special Interest under Banks.

For more information we recommend *The Dictionary of Still Banks* by Long and Pitman; *The Penny Bank Book* by Moore; *The Bank Book* by Norman; and *Penny Lane* by Davidson.

See also Advertising; Battery-Operated Toys; Character, TV, and Movie Collectibles; Chein; Disney; other specific categories.

Key:
B of K — Book of Knowledge
J&ES — J&E Stevens
JH — John Harper
K&R — Kyser & Rex
SH — Sherard Hardware

MECHANICAL BANKS

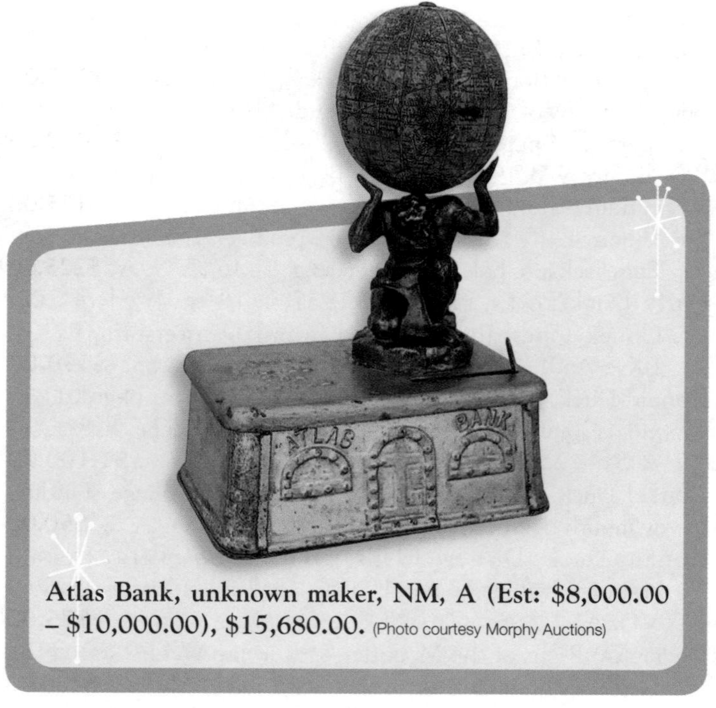

Atlas Bank, unknown maker, NM, A (Est: $8,000.00 – $10,000.00), $15,680.00. (Photo courtesy Morphy Auctions)

Acrobat, J&ES, VG, A (Est: $200-$300).................... $1,045.00

Always Did 'Spise a Mule, B of K, NM $175.00

Always Did 'Spise a Mule (Boy on Bench), J&ES, NM+, A (Est: $4,000-$6,000) $4,600.00

Always Did 'Spise a Mule (Boy on Bench), J&ES, VG, A (Est: $800-$1,000) $1,320.00

Always Did 'Spise a Mule (Jockey), J&ES, NM, A (Est: $3,000-$4,000) $3,080.00
Always Did 'Spise a Mule (Jockey), J&ES, VG, A (Est: $800-$1,200) $1,980.00
Archie Andrews, Starkie's, aluminum, VG, A (Est: $300-$500) $450.00
Artillery Bank, B of K, NM $150.00
Artillery Bank, SH, NP, EX, A (Est: $500-$700) $1,345.00
Bad Accident, J&ES, EX+, A (Est: $2,000-$4,000) $3,190.00
Bobby Riggs & Billy Jean King, John Wright, limited ed of 250, scarce, M $800.00
Boy & Bulldog, Judd, NM+, A (Est: $3,000-$5,000) $7,840.00
Boy on Trapeze, B of K, NM $150.00
Boy on Trapeze, J Barton Smith, G, A (Est: $1,000-$1,200) $1,100.00
Boy on Trapeze, J Barton Smith, NM+, A (Est: $7,000-$10,000) $19,040.00

Boy Robbing Bird's Nest, J&E Stevens, NM+, A (Est: $15,000.00 – $20.000.00), $25,200.00. (Photo courtesy Morphy Auctions)

Boy Scout Camp, J&ES, NM, A (Est: $20,000-$30,000) $24,150.00
Boy Scout Camp, J&ES, VG, A (Est: $5,000-$7,000) $8,400.00
Bread Winner's Bank, J&ES, EX+, A (Est: $30,000-$45,000) $33,350.00
Bull Dog Bank, J&ES, EX, A (Est: $300-$500) $440.00
Bull Dog Savings Bank, Ives Blakeslee & Williams, NM, A (Est: $15,000-$20,000) $15,680.00
Butting Buffalo, B of K, M $135.00
Cabin, J&ES, NM+, A (Est: $1,500-$2,000) $2,800.00
Cabin, J&ES, VG, A (Est: $300-$500) $500.00
Calamity, J&ES, NM, A (Est: $30,000-$50,000) $40,025.00
Cat & Mouse, B of K, NM $150.00
Cat & Mouse (Cat Balancing), J&ES, G, A (Est: $800-$1,000) $1,100.00
Cat & Mouse (Cat Balancing), J&ES, NM, A (Est: $5,000-$7,000) $13,440.00
Chief Big Moon, J&ES, EX, A (Est: $2,750-$3,500) $4,312.00
Circus Bank, SH, G, A (Est: $3,500-$4,500) $5,750.00
Clown on Globe (Funny Clown), J&ES, NM+, A (Est: $10,000-$20,000) $11,500.00
Clown on Globe (Funny Clown), J&ES, VG+, A (Est: $5,000-$7,000) $5,040.00
Clown on Globe (Funny Clown), James Capron, NM $450.00
Creedmoor, B of K, M $195.00
Creedmoor, J&ES, NM, A (Est: $1,000-$1,500) $1,350.00
Creedmoor, Starkie's, aluminum, VG, A (Est: $100-$200) $195.00
Cupola, J&ES, EX, A (Est: $4,000-$5,000) $4,480.00
Darktown Battery, J&ES, EX, A (Est: $4,000-$5,000) $5,040.00
Darktown Battery, J&ES, G, A (Est: $1,200-$1,500) $1,760.00
Dentist, B of K, EX $125.00
Dentist, J&ES, NM, A (Est: $20,000-$25,000) $20,875.00
Dentist, J&ES, VG, A (Est: $4,000-$5,000) $7,840.00

Dinah (Long Arm), John Harper, EX, A (Est: $500.00 – $700.00) $895.00. (Photo courtesy Morphy Auctions)

Dinah (Short Arm), JH, EX, A (Est: $300-$500) $560.00
Dog on Turntable, Judd, G, A (Est: $100-$200) $220.00
Dog on Turntable, Judd, NM+, A (Est: $2,000-$3,000) $4,200.00
Dog Tray Bank 1880, K&R, NM, A (Est: $5,000-$7,000) $13,440.00
Eagle & Eaglets, B of K, M $195.00
Eagle & Eaglets, J&ES, EX+, A (Est: $800-$1,200) $1,200.00
Eagle & Eaglets, J&ES, VG, A (Est: $500-$700) $575.00
Elephant & Three Clowns, J&ES, EX, A (Est: $2,000-$3,000) $3,080.00
Elephant w/Howdah (Pull Tail), Hubley, EX, A (Est: $300-$500) $660.00
Football Bank, JH, NM, A (Est: $10,000-$15,000) $11,200.00
Frog Bank (Two Frogs), J&ES, EX, A (Est: $1,000-$1,500) $1,540.00

Frog on Base (Lattice), J&E Stevens, NM, A (Est: $3,000.00 – $4,000.00), $2,240.00. (Photo courtesy Morphy Auctions)

Frog on Rock, Kilgore, NM+, A (Est: $2,000-$3,000) $1,456.00

Giant in Tower, JH, NM, A (Est: $10,000-$15,000) .$42,000.00
Girl Skipping Rope, J&ES, VG, A (Est: $12,000-$15,000).$15,400.00
Hall's Excelsior, J&ES, G+, A (Est: $200-$400) $225.00
Hall's Excelsior, J&ES, NM, A (Est: $2,000-$3,000)... $3,080.00
Hall's Liliput Bank, J&ES, NM+, A (Est: $3,000-$4,000) .$6,160.00
Hen & Chick, J&ES, NM, A (Est: $6,000-$8,000)..... $6,160.00
Home Bank, J&E, EX, A (Est: $100-$200)................... $415.00
Hoopla Bank, JH, VG, A (Est: $1,500-$2,000) $1,345.00
Horse Race (Straight Base), J&ES, VG, A (Est: $1,800-$2,200)..$3,025.00
Humpty Dumpty, B of K, M... $150.00
Humpty Dumpty, SH, EX, A (Est: $1,000-$1,500)...... $1,000.00
Humpty Dumpty, SH, G, A (Est: $300-$400)................ $415.00

Independence Hall Tower, Enterprising Manufacturing, NM, A, (Est: $2,000.00 – $3,000.00), $5,600.00. (Photo courtesy Morphy Auctions)

Indian Shooting Bear, B of K, M $195.00
Indian Shooting Bear, J&ES, EX, A (Est: $3,000-$4,000) .$3,920.00
Initiating First Degree, Mechanical Novelty Works, NM, A (Est: $20,000-$30,000) $42,000.00
Initiating Second Degree, Mechanical Novelty Works, NM+, A (Est: $15,000-$20,000).......................................$12,320.00
Jolly N, JH, moving eyes, fixed ears, red shirt w/wht collar, dk bl bow tie, EX, A (Est: $200-$300) $225.00
Jolly N, JH, moving eyes, fixed ears, red shirt w/wht collar, lt bl bow tie, pk lips, NM, A (Est: $700-$1,000)............ $725.00
Jolly N, JH, moving eyes, fixed ears, wht top hat, VG, A (Est: $300-$500) $670.00
Jolly N, SH, moving eyes, fixed ears, gr shirt, yel bow tie, NM+, A (Est: $4,000-$5,000).......................................$10,640.00
Jolly N, Starkie's, aluminum, moving eyes & ears, rpnt, A (Est: $100-$200) $45.00
Jolly N (Full Figure), aluminum, blk skin, bl coat w/yel buttons & pants, rnd base, 13", G+, A (Est: $2,000-$3,000)..$2,860.00
Jolly N (Little Joe), JH, moving eyes, fixed ears, red shirt w/wht collar, dk bl bow tie, EX, A (Est: $500-$700) $335.00
Jonah & the Whale, B of K, M...................................... $150.00
Jonah & the Whale, SH, NM, A (Est: $12,000-$18,000) ...$10,935.00
Jonah & the Whale, SH, VG, A (Est: $800-$1,200)... $1,200.00
Leap Frog, B of K, NM... $175.00
Leap Frog, SH, EX, A (Est: $1,500-$2,000)................$1,955.00
Lion & Two Monkeys, James Capron, NM.................... $550.00
Lion & Two Monkeys, K&R, VG, A (Est: $1,200-$1,400)... $1,200.00
Lucky Wheel, W&R Jacob & Co, litho tin, VG, A (Est: $300-$500)... $280.00
Magician Bank, B of K, MIB $150.00
Magician Bank, J&ES, G+, A (Est: $2,500-$3,000).... $2,700.00
Magician Bank, J&ES, NM, A (Est: $14,000-$18,000) .. $18,400.00
Magician Bank, James Capron, M................................ $450.00
Mama Katzenjammer, Kenton, NM, A (Est: $30,000-$40,000) $67,200.00

Mammy and Child, Kyser and Rex, EX, A (Est: $3,000.00 – $5,000.00), $4,200.00. (Photo courtesy Morphy Auctions)

Mason Bank, SH, EX, A (Est: $2,000-$2,500)............$3,160.00
Memorial Money Bank, Enterprise Mfg, NM+, (Est: $2,000-$3,000)..$8,960.00
Mikado, K&R, rare, VG, A (Est: $15,000-$20,000)..$16,500.00
Monkey & Coconut, J&ES, NM+, A (Est: $7,000-$10,000)... $10,640.00
Monkey Bank, Hubley, EX, A (Est: $700-$1,000) $895.00
Monkey Bank, Hubley, G+, A (Est: $200-$400) $250.00
Mosque, Judd, NM+, A (Est: $5,000-$7,000) $12,320.00
Mule Entering Barn, J&ES, G+, A (Est: $500-$700) $770.00
Mule Entering Barn, J&ES, NM+, A (Est: $2,000-$3,000) $2,240.00
Multiplying Bank, J&ES, NM, A (Est: $3,000-$4,000) . $2,800.00
National Bank, J&ES, NM, A (Est: $15,000-$20,000) .. $17,920.00
Novelty Bank, J&ES, EX, A (Est: $1,200-$1,500).......$1,760.00
Novelty Bank, J&ES, G, A (Est: $200-$300) $450.00
Novelty Bank, J&ES, NM, A (Est: $2,000-$3,000).....$2,520.00
Organ Bank (Boy & Girl), B of K, NM.......................... $150.00
Organ Bank (Cat & Dog), K&R, EX, A (Est: $1,200-$1,600) $1,650.00
Organ Bank (Cat & Dog), K&R, G, A (Est: $200-$400). $350.00
Organ Bank (Medium w/Monkey), K&R, NM+, A (Est: $3,000-$5,000)...$2,015.00
Organ Bank (Miniature w/Monkey), K&R, NM, A (Est: $4,000-$5,000)...$2,800.00

Organ Grinder & Performing Bear, K&R, some rpnt, A (Est: $1,500-$1,800) $2,160.00
Owl (Turns Head), B of K, NM $150.00
Owl (Turns Head), J&ES, VG, A (Est: $400-$600) $460.00
Paddy & the Pig, B of K, NM $175.00
Paddy & the Pig, J&ES, NM+, A (Est: $15,000-$20,000) .$9,520.00
Paddy & the Pig, J&ES, VG, A (Est: $1,100-$1,300) . $1,980.00
Panorama Bank, J&ES, EX, A (Est: $3,000-$5,000) ... $4,255.00
Patronize the Blind Man & His Dog, J&ES, VG, A (Est: $2,400-$2,500) $2,875.00
Peg-Leg Begger, Judd, NM, A (Est: $3,000-$4,000)...$10,080.00
Pelican (Man Thumbs Nose), J&ES, VG+, A (Est: $1,500-$2,500) $2,125.00

Picture Gallery Bank, Shepard Hardware, NM, A (Est: $30,000.00 – $40,000.00), $67,200.00. (Photo courtesy Morphy Auctions)

Pig in Highchair, J&ES, VG, A (Est: $300-$400) $770.00
Pistol, Richard Elliot Co, NM+, A (Est: $2,000-$3,000) . $4,200.00
Plantation Bank, Weeden, pnt tin, VG, A (Est: $1,000-$1,200). $1,200.00
Popeye Knockout Bank, Straits Mfg, litho tin, EX+IB, A (Est: $1,200-$1,500) $1,540.00
Presto Bank, K&R, VG, A (Est: $200-$300) $275.00
Professor Pug Frog's Great Bicycle Feat, J&ES, NM, A (Est: $25,000-$45,000) $51,750.00
Punch & Judy, B of K, NM $150.00
Punch & Judy (Large Letters), SH, VG+, A (Est: $800-$1,000)..$1,100.00
Punch & Judy (Medium Letters), SH, NM, A (Est: $7,000-$10,000) $9,520.00
Punch & Judy (Medium Letters), SH, VG, A (Est: $1,000-$1,200) $1,045.00
Rabbit Standing (Small), NM+, A (Est: $1,000-$1,500). $1,790.00
Reclining Chinaman, J&ES, G+, A (Est: $2,000-$3,000) .$2,300.00
Reclining Chinaman, J&ES, NM+, A (Est: $10,000-$15,000) ... $28,000.00
Rooster, K&R, NM, A (Est: $2,000-$3,000)................$1,900.00
Santa Claus at Chimney, SH, VG, A (Est: $400-$500) . $720.00
Savings Bank (Fortune Horse Race), Norton Bros, litho tin box, EX, A (Est: $2,000-$3,000) $8,800.00
Speaking Dog, SH, EX+, A (Est: $1,500-$2,000) $1,680.00
Speaking Dog, SH, VG, A (Est: $500-$700) $600.00

Stump Speaker, SH, VG, A ($1,500-$2,500) $2,815.00
Symphonion Musical Savings, Lochmann, NM, A (Est: $10,000-$15,000) $28,000.00
Tammany Bank, B of K, NMIB $200.00
Tammany Bank, J&ES, VG, A (Est: $300-$500)............ $500.00
Tank & Cannon Bank, Starkie's, VG, A (Est: $700-$1,000). $560.00
Teddy & the Bear, B of K, NM $135.00
Teddy & the Bear, J&ES, EX, A (Est: $1,400-$1,800) .. $1,650.00
Toad on Stump, J&ES, NM+, A (Est: $2,000-$3,000) ... $952.00
Trick Dog, Hubley, solid base, NM+, A (Est: $1,000-$1,500) .$1,792.00
Trick Dog, Hubley, 6-part base, EX, A (Est: $1,500-$2,000) $1,065.00
Trick Pony, B of K, NM $350.00
Trick Pony, SH, NM+, A (Est: $3,000-$5,000) $7,840.00
Trick Pony, SH, VG, A (Est: $800-$1,000) $1,100.00
Uncle Remus, B of K, M $150.00
Uncle Sam, SH, EX, A (Est: $3,000-$5,000)............... $3,920.00
Uncle Tom (Lapels & One Star), K&R, VG+, A (Est: $800-$1,200) $660.00
US & Spain, B of K, M... $150.00
US & Spain, J&ES, NM+, A (Est: $10,000-$15,000) .$30,800.00
US & Spain, J&ES, VG, A (Est: $900-$1,200) $1,725.00
Watchdog Safe, J&E Stevens, NM, A (Est: $1,500-$2,000) . $3,360.00
Weeden's Plantation Darkie Bank, VG+, A (Est: $800-$1,200) $2,860.00
William Tell, B of K, M $200.00
William Tell, J&ES, G, A (Est: $400-$800) $690.00
Wimbledon, JH, NM, A (Est: $10,000-$15,000).......$30,800.00
World's Fair Bank, J&ES, NM+, A (Est: $3,000-$4,000). $4,200.00

Zoo Bank, Kyser and Rex, NM, A (Est: $4,000.00 – $5,000.00), $7,840.00. (Photo courtesy Morphy Auctions)

Registering Banks

Ben Franklin Thrift Bank, Marx, litho tin, 4", VG+, A (Est: $25-$50) $25.00
Captain Marvel Magic Dime Saver, litho tin, 2½" sq, VG, A . $140.00

Codey Magic Money Box, litho tin, 5", VG, A (Est: $50-$100). $65.00

Commonwealth Three Coin Bank (Cash Register), 5", EX, A (Est: $50-$100) $32.00

Davy Crockett Frontier Dime Bank, litho tin, 2½" sq, EX, A.. $140.00

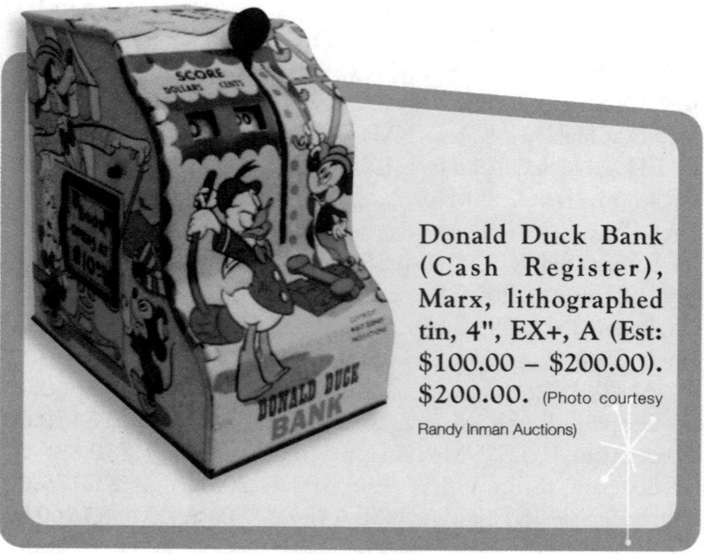

Donald Duck Bank (Cash Register), Marx, lithographed tin, 4", EX+, A (Est: $100.00 – $200.00). $200.00. (Photo courtesy Randy Inman Auctions)

Donald Duck Dime Register Bank, litho tin, 2½" sq, EX+, A . $440.00

Dopey Dime Register, litho tin octagonal box, 2½" sq, VG, A (Est: $100-$200) $150.00

Five Coin Security Bank (Cash Register), Shonk, 7½", EX.. $55.00

Get Rich Quick Bank, Marx, litho tin, 3½", VG+, A ($25-$50) $40.00

Home Five-Coin Savings Bank (Cash Register), American Can Co, 7", VG, A (Est: $50-$100).................... $55.00

Keep 'Em Flying Dime Register Bank, litho tin, 2½" sq, G+, A (Est: $175-$225) $165.00

Keep 'Em Rolling Dime Register Bank, litho tin, 2½" sq, VG, A (Est: $250-$350) $330.00

Keep 'Em Sailing Dime Register Bank, litho tin, 2½" sq, G+, A (Est: $125-$175) $190.00

Little Orphan Annie 10¢ Register Bank, litho tin, rnd w/flat tip, 3" W, ca 1936, VG, A (Est: $150-$250) $225.00

Mickey Mouse Dime Register, litho tin, 2½" sq, 1950s, VG . $440.00

Mickey Mouse Dime Register, litho tin octagonal box, 2½", EX, A (Est: $100-$200) $385.00

Nickel Register (Cauldron/Bean Pot), bail handle, red, 3½", EX, A (Est: $100-$200) $155.00

Penny Register (Bucket), K&R, 3", VG, A (Est: $50-$100) $125.00

Popeye Daily Quarter Bank, Kalon Mfg, litho tin, 5", EX+IB, A (Est: $200-$400) $300.00

Prince Valient Dime Bank, litho tin, 2½" sq, 1950s, VG, A.. $88.00

Recording Dime Bank (Building), NP, 6½", VG, A (Est: $100-$200) $120.00

Truck Dime Register, w/emb detail, curved top, 4½", G+, A (Est: $100-$200) $65.00

Uncle Sam's Dime Register, Durable Toy & Novelty Co, VG, A (Est: $50-$100) $40.00

Uncle Sam's 3-Coin Register Bank, Durable Toy & Novelty Toy Co, 6¼", VG, A (Est: $50-$100) $32.00

Watch Your Savings Grow, English, litho tin box w/circus graphics, 5½", VG+, A (Est: $50-$100) $100.00

Registering Dime Savings, NM+, A (Est: $3,000.00 – $4,000.00), $5,600.00. (Photo courtesy Morphy Auctions)

Still Banks

Andy Gump Seated on Stump, Arcade, EX, A (Est: $1,500-$1,750) $1,320.00

Apple on Two-Leaf Branch, Kyser and Rex, 3x5x5", NM, A (Est: $1,000.00 – $1,500.00), $2,125.00. (Photo courtesy Morphy Auctions)

Aunt Jemima w/Spoon, AC Williams, blk skin & dress w/wht apron, red head scarf, 6", NM, A (Est: $100-$200). $1,100.00

Auto (4-Passenger), AC Williams, spoke wheels, red, 6¾", VG, A (Est: $150-$250) $355.00

Baseball on Three Bats (Stand), Hubley, 5¼", EX, A (Est: $200-$400) $1,870.00

Bear Standing on Hind Legs Looking Up, japanned, 6", EX, A (Est: $100-$200) $165.00

Billikin, AC Williams, gold-pnt w/red topknot, 4", G+, A (Est: $50-$100) $32.00

Bull Dog Seated on Hind Legs, ceramic, blk & wht airbrushing, collar w/padlock & key, 7", EX+, A (Est: $50-$100) .. $50.00

Buster Brown & Tige Good Luck Bank, Arcade, gold Buster, Tige & horseshoe surround blk horse, 5", NM, A (Est: $300-$500) $300.00
Cadet Marching w/Rife, Hubley, bl w/gold trim, 5", EX, A (Est: $200-$300) $825.00
Castle (2 Towers), JH, japanned, 7", EX, A (Est: $700-$900) . $880.00
Castle (4 Towers), JH, 3¾", VG+, A (Est: $100-$200) .. $1,650.00
Clown in Pointed Hat Standing, AC Williams, gold pnt w/red trim, 6", VG, A (Est: $100-$150) $165.00
Cottage w/Couple on Front Porch Steps, Gray Iron, NP version, 3¾", EX, A (Est: $200-$400) $360.00
Deposit (Bank Building), japanned, 4", VG+, A (Est: $100-$200) $110.00
Donkey w/Saddle, Arcade, various colors, 4½", VG, A (Est: $50-$100) $50.00
Double Head, see Two-Faced
Elephant on Wheels, AC Williams, gold pnt w/red trim, wht rubber wheels, 4½", EX, A (Est: $100-$200) $600.00

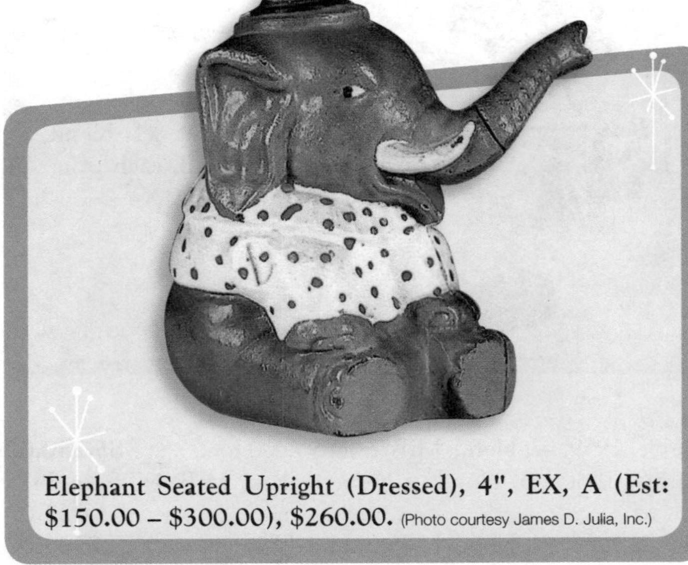

Elephant Seated Upright (Dressed), 4", EX, A (Est: $150.00 – $300.00), $260.00. (Photo courtesy James D. Julia, Inc.)

Elephant w/Howdah, AC Williams, various colors, 4", EX, A (Est: $50-$100) $85.00
Fido Seated on Pillow Looking Up, 7½" L, NM, A (Est: $500-$700) $785.00
Foxy Grandpa Standing w/Hands in Pockets, Hubley, 5½", EX, A (Est: $200-$300) $350.00
General Butler, J&ES, pnt CI, 7", VG, A (Est: $1,300-$1,500) $1,495.00
Gingerbread House, Denmark, silver-plated, emb detail, 3¾", VG+, A (Est: $100-$200) $200.00
Give Me a Penny (Sharecropper), Wing/Hubley, toes not showing, 5½", NM, A (Est: $300-$500) $450.00
Give Me a Penny (Sharecropper), Wing/Hubley, toes showing, 5½", NM, A (Est: $300-$500) $450.00
Graf Zeppelin, 6¾", EX, A (Est: $100-$200) $120.00
Half-Pint Coin Bank, glass milk bottle w/metal lid locked w/padlock & key, 4½", VG, A (Est: $40-$60) $40.00
Home Savings Bank, J&ES, VG, A (Est: $100-$200) $120.00
Horse Rearing on Platform, AC Williams, blk w/silver hooves, 7½", VG, A (Est: $75 to $125) $110.00
House (2-Story Colonial), AC Williams, 4", G+, A (Est: $75-$125) $40.00
Humpty Dumpty, seated on 'brick' wall, brass-colored, 5½", A (Est: $25-$50) $55.00

Indian Scout With Tomahawk, Hubley, 6", NM+, A (Est: $500.00 – $700.00). $950.00.
(Photo courtesy Morphy Auctions)

Junior Cash Register, J&ES, 4¼", EX+, A (Est: $100-$200) .. $125.00
Key, WJ Somerville, brass tone, 5½", EX, A (Est: $300-$500) $385.00
Little Miss Muffet (Box), litho tin, 4" sq, VG+, A (Est: $50-$100) $65.00
Log Cabin, end chimney, thatched roof, beveled base, 3½", EX, A (Est: $100-$200) $250.00
Mammy w/Hands on Hips, Hubley, red & wht w/bl head scarf, 5¼", MIB, A (Est: $300-$500) $335.00
Mammy w/Spoon in Hand, see Aunt Jemima
Marietta Silo, electroplated, 5½", VG, A (Est: $300-$500) .. $385.00
Money Saver (Clock), Arcade, blk w/gold detail, 3½", VG, A (Est: $75-$125) $165.00
Mulligan the Cop, Hubley, w/baton & hand on hip, 5¾", VG, A (Est: $100-$200) $300.00
New Deal FD Roosevelt, Kenton, pnt version, gr base, 5", VG, A (Est: $200-$400) $275.00
North Pole Bank (Ice Cream Freezer), Gray Iron, 4", VG, A (Est: $100-$200) $150.00
Oregon (Boat), J&ES, japanned, 5", EX, A (Est: $200-$400) . $330.00
Palace, Ives, ca 1885, japanned building w/gold trim, 2-sided stairway, center tower, 8" L, NM+, A (Est: $3,000-$5,000) $8,960.00
Policeman, see Mulligan the Cop
Ranch Style (Old Fashioned) Telephone Bank, Linemar, tin & plastic, crank rings bells, 8", NM (EX+ box), A (MB: $125) $235.00
Safe (Home Savings), Kenton, NP knob, 5¼", VG, A (Est: $100-$200) $65.00
Safe (Jewell), J&ES, NP, barred gate on front, w/key, 5½", G+, A (Est: $100-$200) $110.00
Safe (Security Safe Deposit), K&R, window-pane sides w/emblems, emblem on front, 4", G+, A (Est: $50-$100) $65.00

Safe (Thrift Dial Bank), tin w/wooden wheels, 4¾", VG, A (Est: $50-$100) $30.00
Safe (Tiny Mite Bank-Safe), w/3 combination dials, 3½", VG+, A (Est: $50-$100) $32.00
Santa w/Tree, Hubley, 6", NM, A (Est: $700-$1,000) . $1,120.00
Save For a Rainy Day, Hubley, wht duck in blk top hat & umbrella under wing on red tub, 6", EX, A (Est: $200-$400) $130.00
Scotty Dog Seated, Hubley, blk w/red collar, 6", EX, A (Est: $100-$200) $100.00
Soldier w/Gun Across Chest, Hubley, brn w/gold trim, 6", EX, A $600.00
St Bernard w/Pack, AC Williams, 5½", G+, A (Est: $75-$125) $55.00
State Bank, Kenton, 8", NM+, A, (Est: $1,500-$2,000) . $1,000.00
Suitcase, Marx, litho tin, 4", EX, A (Est: $50-$100) $75.00
Three Wise Monkeys, 3½", VG, A (Est: $100-$200) $125.00
Top Hat, blk, 3", EX, A ($100-$200) $75.00
Treasure Chest (Musical), OH Braiser, 4½" H, EX, A (Est: $400-$600) $275.00
Turkey, AC Williams, 3½", EX, A (Est: $100-$200) $165.00
Two-Faced (Double Head) Black Boy, AC Williams, blk skin, gold hat, 4", VG, A (Est: $100-$200) $110.00
US Air Mail Mailbox, Dent, pedestal type, painted CI, red w/ wht & bl trim, 6½", VG+, A (Est: $400-$600) $630.00
Watch Me Grow w/Coins Large & Small, tin canister w/various character graphics, hats/feet, EX+, A (Est: $50-$100) ..$75.00
Welback Hot Zone Water Heater, 4½", VG, A (Est: $100-$200) $55.00
Westinghouse Automeal (Roaster), National Products, metal, 4", VG, A (Est: $100-$200) $50.00
Wise Pig/Thrifty, Hubley, 6½", VG, A (Est: $100-$200) .. $130.00
Young N (Bust), 4½", VG, A (Est: $150-$200) $200.00

Barbie Doll and Friends

Barbie doll was first introduced in 1959, and since then her face has changed three times. She's been blond and brunette. Her hair has been restyled over and over, and it's varied in length from above her shoulders to the tips of her toes. She's worn high-fashion designer clothing and pedal pushers. She's been everything from an astronaut to a veterinarian, and no matter what her changing lifestyle required, Mattel (her 'maker') has provided it for her.

Though Barbie doll items from recent years are bought and sold with fervor, those made before 1970 are the most sought after. You'll need to do a lot of studying and comparisons to learn to distinguish one Barbie doll from another, but it will pay off in terms of making wise investments. There are several books available; we recommend them all: *Barbie® Doll Fashion, Vol.1, 1959 – 1967, Vol. II, 1968 – 1974, Vol. III, 1975 – 1979,* by Sarah Sink Eames; *Barbie®, The First 30 Years, 1959 Through 1989, 2nd Edition,* by Stefanie Deutsch; *Collector's Encyclopedia of Barbie® Doll Exclusives, Barbie® Doll Around the World,* and *Barbie® Doll Collector's Edition* by J. Michael Augustyniak; and *The Barbie Doll Years,* by Patrick C. and Joyce L. Olds (all published by Collector Books).

As a general rule, a mint-in-box doll is worth about twice as much as a mint doll with no box. A doll that has been played with, and shows some use, is worth half as much as the mint doll with no box (or even less). Never-removed-from-box examples sell at a premium.

Dolls

Allan, 1964, straight legs, red-pnt hair, MIB $100.00
Allan, 1965, bendable legs, MIB $300.00

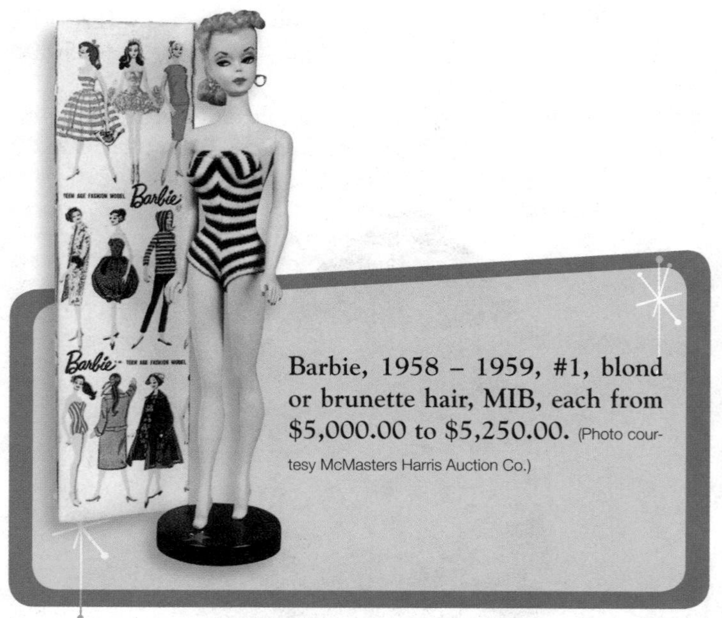

Barbie, 1958 – 1959, #1, blond or brunette hair, MIB, each from $5,000.00 to $5,250.00. (Photo courtesy McMasters Harris Auction Co.)

Barbie, 1959, #2, blond, MIB, from $5,000 to............. $5,250.00
Barbie, 1960, #3, blond or brunette hair, MIB, ea, from $925 to $1,025.00
Barbie, 1960, #4, blond, MIB, from $475 to................... $525.00
Barbie, 1961, #5, blond, MIB, from $325 to................... $350.00
Barbie, 1962, #5, redhead, MIB, from $475 to............... $500.00
Barbie, 1962, #6, any color hair, MIB, ea from $375 to ... $425.00
Barbie, 2001, blk or wht, NRFB $45.00
Barbie, 2002, blk, NRFB....................$35.00
Barbie, 2002, wht, NRFB....................$40.00
Barbie, 2003, blk or wht, NRFB, ea....................$50.00
Barbie, 2003, redhead, NRFB $100.00
Barbie, American Beauty Queen, 1991, blk or wht, MIB..$25.00
Barbie, American Girl, 1965, blond, brn, brunette, NRFB, ea $1,500.00
Barbie, American Girl, 1965, redhead, MIB............... $2,000.00
Barbie, American Girl, 1965, redhead, NRFB $2,500.00
Barbie, American Girl, 1966, Color-Magic, NRFB $3,000.00
Barbie, American Girl, 1966, side-part, blond, NRFB. $3,000.00
Barbie, Angel Face, 1982, MIB, from $25 to....................$30.00
Barbie, Angel of Peace, 1999, Timeless Sentiments, blk or wht, NRFB $40.00
Barbie, Antique Rose, 1996, NRFB.................... $190.00
Barbie, Aquarius, blk or wht, NRFB....................$20.00

Barbie, Arctic, 1996, Dolls of the World, NRFB $25.00
Barbie, Army Desert Storm, 1993, Stars & Stipes, blk or wht, NRFB $25.00
Barbie, Astronaut, 1985, blk or wht, NRFB..............$25.00
Barbie, Autumn in London, 1999, City Season Collection, NRFB $30.00
Barbie, Avon Representative, 1999, wht or Hispanic, NRFB. $40.00
Barbie, Ballerina Barbie on Tour, 1976, #1, NRFB $75.00
Barbie, Barbie Celebration, 1987, NRFB $30.00
Barbie, Barbie Sign Language, 1999, blk or wht, NRFB $20.00
Barbie, Bath Magic, 1992, NRFB..............$15.00
Barbie, Baywatch, 1995, blk or wht, NRFB $20.00
Barbie, Beach Blast, 1989, NRFB..............$15.00
Barbie, Benefit Ball, 1992, NRFB..............$45.00
Barbie, Bicyclin', 1994, NRFB..............$25.00
Barbie, Birthday Party, 1993, NRFB..............$30.00
Barbie, Birthday Wishes, 1999, blk, NRFB $25.00
Barbie, Blossom Beautiful, 1992, NRFB.............. $225.00
Barbie, Brazilian, 1990, Dolls of the World, NRFB..............$25.00
Barbie, Bridesmaid, 1991, NRFB..............$30.00
Barbie, Bubble-Cut, 1961-62, redhead, MIB.............. $350.00

Barbie, Bubble-Cut, 1962, blond or brunette hair, MIB, each from $175.00 to $200.00. (Photo courtesy McMasters Harris Auction Co.)

Barbie, Bubble-Cut, 1965, side part, any hair color, MIB.. $875.00
Barbie, Busy Talking, 1972, MIB $200.00
Barbie, Butterfly Princess, 1995, any, NRFB $25.00
Barbie, California Dream, 1988, MIB $15.00
Barbie, Calvin Klein, 1996, Bloomingdale's, NRFB $40.00
Barbie, Camp, 1994, NRFB $25.00
Barbie, Career Girl, 1964, MIB $750.00
Barbie, Carnival Cruise Lines, 1997, NRFB..............$30.00
Barbie, Carolina Fun, 1995, NRFB $20.00
Barbie, Catwoman, 2004, NRFB $20.00
Barbie, Celebration, 1986, NRFB..............$65.00
Barbie, Celebration Cake, 1999, any, NRFB..............$20.00
Barbie, Charity Ball, 1998, blk or wht, NRFB $30.00
Barbie, Chataine, 2003, NRFB.............. $425.00
Barbie, Children's Doctor, 2000, NRFB $20.00
Barbie, Chinese, 1993, Dolls of the World, NRFB $20.00
Barbie, Cinderella, 1996, NRFB..............$25.00
Barbie, Circus Star, 1995, NRFB..............$70.00
Barbie, City Sophisticate, 1994, NRFB..............$50.00
Barbie, Color Magic, 1966, blond, MIB (plastic box)..$1,800.00
Barbie, Color Magic, 1966, midnight blk, MIB (plastic box) ..$3,000.00

Barbie, Color Magic, 1967, blond hair, MIB (cardboard box), $3,000.00. (Photo courtesy Masters Harris Auction Co.)

Barbie, Color Magic, 1967, midnight blk, MIB (cb box) . $4,000.00
Barbie, Color Magic, 2004, blond, NRFB $175.00
Barbie, Color Magic, 2004, brunette, NRFB..............$40.00
Barbie, Color Magic, 2004, redhead, NRFB.............. $200.00
Barbie, Color Me, 1998, NRFB $15.00
Barbie, Cool & Sassy, 1992, NRFB $25.00
Barbie, Cool Times, 1989, NRFB $20.00
Barbie, Country Rose, 1997, NRFB..............$50.00
Barbie, Cut & Style, 1995, any, NRFB..............$20.00
Barbie, Dance 'N Twirl, 1994, NRFB $35.00
Barbie, Dance Magic, 1990, NRFB $20.00
Barbie, Day-to-Night, 1985, NRFB..............$45.00
Barbie, Dazzlin' Date, 1992, NRFB $25.00
Barbie, Dinner Date, 1998, redhead, NRFB..............$20.00
Barbie, Disney Fun, 1992, NRFB..............$35.00
Barbie, Doctor, 1988, NRFB..............$55.00
Barbie, Dorothy (Wizard of Oz), 1994, Hollywood Legends Series, NRFB..............$75.00
Barbie, Dramatic New Living, 1970, MIB.............. $225.00
Barbie, Dream Date, 1983, NRFB $40.00
Barbie, Dream Glow, 1986, blk, MIB $25.00
Barbie, Dream Glow, 1986, Hispanic, MIB..............$45.00
Barbie, Dream Glow, 1986, wht, MIB $35.00
Barbie, Dream Time, 1988, NRFB..............$35.00
Barbie, Dress 'N Fun, 1994, any, NRFB..............$15.00
Barbie, Dutch, 1994, Dolls of the World, MIB $25.00
Barbie, Earring Magic, 1993, blk or wht (blond), NRFB...$15.00

Barbie, Earring Magic, 1993, brunette, NRFB $20.00
Barbie, Easter, 1997, NRFB $15.00
Barbie, Easter Party, 1995, NRFB $20.00
Barbie, Eliza Dolittle (My Fair Lady), 1995, Hollywood Legends, NRFB $75.00
Barbie, Elizabethan, 1994, Great Eras, MIB $50.00
Barbie, Enchanted Evening, 1991, JC Penney, NRFB $50.00
Barbie, Enchanted Princess, 1993, Sears, NRFB $75.00
Barbie, Eskimo, 1982, Dolls of the World, NRFB $400.00
Barbie, Evening Sparkle, 1990, Hill's, NRFB $35.00
Barbie, Fabulous Fur, 1986, NRFB $65.00
Barbie, Fantastica, 1992, MIB $55.00
Barbie, Fantasy Goddess of Asia, 1998, Bob Mackie, NRFB. $150.00
Barbie, Feelin' Groovy, 1987, NRFB $175.00
Barbie, Fire Fighter, 1995, blk or wht, Toys R Us, NRFB ..$30.00
Barbie, Fountain Mermaid, 1993, blk or wht, NRFB, ea $20.00
Barbie, French Lady, 1997, Great Eras Collection, NRFB.$50.00
Barbie, Gap Barbie, 1996, blk or wht, NRFB $65.00
Barbie, Glinda (Wizard of Oz), 2000, NRFB $40.00
Barbie, Goddess of the Sun, 1995, Bob Mackie, NRFB $75.00

Barbie, Gold & Lace, 1989, MIB, $35.00. (Photo courtesy Margo Rana)

Barbie, Gold Medal Skater or Skier, 1975, NRFB $75.00
Barbie, Great Shapes, 1984, blk or wht, NRFB $15.00
Barbie, Great Shapes, 1984, w/Walkman, NRFB $20.00
Barbie, Growin' Pretty Hair, 1971, NRFB $325.00
Barbie, Hawaiian Superstar, 1977, MIB $75.00
Barbie, Holiday, 1988, NRFB $325.00
Barbie, Holiday, 1989, NRFB $150.00
Barbie, Holiday, 1990, NRFB $75.00
Barbie, Holiday, 1991, NRFB $75.00
Barbie, Holiday, 1992, NRFB $50.00
Barbie, Holiday, 1993, NRFB $50.00
Barbie, Holiday, 1994, NRFB $65.00
Barbie, Holiday, 1995, NRFB $45.00
Barbie, Holiday, 1996, NRFB $35.00
Barbie, Holiday, 1997, NRFB $35.00
Barbie, Holiday, 1998, NRFB $20.00
Barbie, Island Fun, 1988, NRFB $15.00

Barbie, Jamaican, 1992, Dolls of the World, NRFB $25.00
Barbie, Jewel Essence, 1996, Bob Mackie, NRFB $125.00
Barbie, Kenyan, 1994, Dolls of the World, NRFB $25.00
Barbie, Knitting Pretty, 1964, pk, NRFB $1,265.00
Barbie, Knitting Pretty, 1965, royal bl, NRFB $635.00
Barbie, Lights 'N Lace, 1991, NRFB $15.00
Barbie, Lily, 1997, FAO Schwarz, NRFB $150.00
Barbie, Live Action on Stage, 1970, NRFB $275.00
Barbie, Malibu, 1971, MIB $55.00
Barbie, Malibu (Sunset), 1975, MIB $35.00
Barbie, Malt Shop, 1993, Toys R Us, NRFB $30.00
Barbie, Medieval Lady, 1995, Great Eras Collection, NRFB.. $60.00
Barbie, Miss America, 1972, Kellogg Co, NRFB $175.00
Barbie, Moon Goddess, 1996, Bob Mackie, NRFB $75.00
Barbie, Moonlight Magic, 1993, Toys R Us, NRFB $60.00
Barbie, My First Barbie, 1981, NRFB $20.00
Barbie, NASCAR 50th Anniversary, 1998, NRFB $25.00
Barbie, Native American #1, 1993, Dolls of the World, NRFB $35.00
Barbie, Nifty Fifties, 2000, Great Fashions of the 20th Century, NRFB $50.00
Barbie, Opening Night, 1993, Classique Collection, NRFB.. $50.00
Barbie, Oreo Fun, 1997, Toys R Us, NRFB $20.00
Barbie, Paleontologist, 1997, Toys R Us, NRFB $25.00
Barbie, Party in Pink, 1991, Ames, NRFB $20.00
Barbie, Peach Blossom, 1992, NRFB $40.00
Barbie, Peach Pretty, 1989, K-Mart, MIB $35.00
Barbie, Peaches 'N Cream, 1984, blk or wht, MIB $40.00
Barbie, Pen Friend, 1996, NRFB $20.00
Barbie, Pepsi Spirit, 1989, Toys R Us, NRFB $75.00
Barbie, Perfume Pretty, 1988, blk or wht, NRFB $20.00
Barbie, Pet Doctor, 1996, brunette, NRFB $25.00
Barbie, Phantom of the Opera, 1998, FAO Schwarz, NRFB $90.00

Barbie, Picnic Pretty, 1992, MIB, $35.00. (Photo courtesy Margo Rana)

Barbie, Picnic Pretty, 1992, Osco, NRFB $30.00
Barbie, Pilgrim, 1995, American Stories Collection, NRFB.. $15.00
Barbie, Pink & Pretty, 1982, MIB $50.00

Barbie, Pink Sensation, 1990, Winn Dixie, NRFB............$25.00
Barbie, Pioneer, 1995 or 1996, American Stories Collection, NRFB, ea..........$15.00
Barbie, Police Officer, 1993, blk or wht, Toys R Us, NRFB ..$75.00
Barbie, Polly Pockets, 1994, Hill's, NRFB..........$25.00
Barbie, Portrait in Blue, 1998, blk or wht, Wal-Mart, NRFB.. $20.00
Barbie, Queen of Hearts, 1994, Bob Mackie, NRFB....... $175.00
Barbie, Queen of Sapphires, 2000, Royal Jewels, NRFB. $115.00

Barbie, Quick Curl, 1972, MIB, $75.00. (Photo courtesy Sarah Sink Eames)

Barbie, Quick Curl, 1974, Miss America, blond, NRFB....$80.00
Barbie, Quick Curl, 1974, Miss America, brunette, NRFB..$130.00
Barbie, Quick Curl, 1976, Deluxe, NRFB..........$80.00
Barbie, Rappin' Rock, 1992, NRFB..........$25.00
Barbie, Rendezvous, 1998, NRFB..........$50.00
Barbie, Rising Star Barbie, 1998, Grand Old Opry, NRFB ..$75.00
Barbie, Rockettes, 1993, FAO Schwarz, NRFB $100.00
Barbie, Romantic Wedding 2001, 2000, Bridal Collection, NRFB..........$50.00
Barbie, Russian, 1988, Dolls of the World, NRFB $25.00
Barbie, Safari, 1983, Disney, MIB..........$25.00
Barbie, Sapphire Sophisticate, 1997, Toys R Us, NRFB....$30.00
Barbie, Savvy Shopper, 1994, Bloomingdale's, NRFB $40.00
Barbie, School Spirit, 1993, blk or wht, Toys R Us, NRFB..$30.00
Barbie, Scottish, 1981, Dolls of the World, NRFB $75.00
Barbie, Sea Princess, 1996, Service Merchandise, NRFB ..$25.00
Barbie, Sentimental Valentine, 1997, Hallmark, NRFB....$25.00
Barbie, Serenade in Satin, 1997, Barbie Couture Collection, MIB..........$80.00
Barbie, Shampoo Magic, 1996, NRFB..........$15.00
Barbie, Snow Princess, 1994, blond, Enchanted Seasons, NRFB..........$80.00
Barbie, Snow Princess, 1994, brunette, Mattel Festival, NRFB $1,100.00
Barbie, Snow White, 1999, Children's Collector Series, NRFB.......... $25.00
Barbie, Something Extra, 1992, Meijer, NRFB..........$25.00

Barbie, Southern Beauty, 1991, Winn Dixie, NRFB..........$30.00
Barbie, Southern Belle, 1994, Great Eras Collection, NRFB.. $50.00
Barbie, Sports Star, 1979, NRFB..........$25.00
Barbie, Spring Parade, 1992, blk or wht, NRFB..........$35.00
Barbie, Standard, 1967, any hair color, MIB.......... $425.00
Barbie, Starlight Dance, 1996, Classique Collection, NRFB .. $30.00
Barbie, Steppin' Out Barbie 1930s, 1999, Great Fashions of the 20th Century, NRFB..........$45.00
Barbie, Strawberry Sorbet, 1999, Avon, NRFB..........$20.00
Barbie, Sugar Plum Fairy, 1997, Classic Ballet Series, NRFB.. $30.00
Barbie, Sun Gold Malibu, 1984-85, any, NRFB..........$20.00
Barbie, Sun Lovin' Malibu, 1979, NRFB $25.00
Barbie, Sun Valley, 1973, NRFB.......... $125.00
Barbie, Sunsational Malibu, 1981, wht or Hispanic, NRFB..$30.00
Barbie, Super Hair, 1987, blk or wht, NRFB..........$20.00
Barbie, Super Size, 1977-79, NRFB.......... $130.00
Barbie, Super Size Bride, 1977-79, NRFB $225.00
Barbie, Swan Lake Ballerina, 1998, blk or wht, Classic Ballet, NRFB..........$30.00
Barbie, Swirl Ponytail, 1964, blond or brunette, NRFB . $625.00

Barbie, Swirl Ponytail, 1964, brunette hair, MIB, $625.00. (Photo courtesy McMasters Harris Auction Co.)

Barbie, Swirl Ponytail, 1964, platinum, NRFB $1,300.00
Barbie, Swirl Ponytail, 1964, redhead, NRFB $625.00
Barbie, Talking, 1968, blond, brunette or redhead, NRFB...$400.00
Barbie, Talking, 1970, blond, brunette or redhead, NRFB...$475.00
Barbie, Ten Speeder, 1973, NRFB..........$30.00
Barbie, Thailand, 1998, Dolls of the World, NRFB..........$25.00
Barbie, That Girl, 2003, Pop Culture Collection, NRFB ..$35.00
Barbie, Twirly Curls, 1982, wht or Hispanic, MIB, ea $25.00
Barbie, Twist 'N Turn, 1967, long straight red hair w/bangs, MIB $575.00
Barbie, Twist 'N Turn, 1969, flipped hairdo, blond or brunette, NRFB $475.00

Barbie, Twist 'N Turn, 1971, any color hair, eyes centered, MIB.......$575.00
Barbie, Unicef, 1989, NRFB.......$20.00
Barbie, University Barbie (Indiana), 1998, NRFB.......$15.00
Barbie, University Barbie (Xavier), 1999, NRFB.......$15.00
Barbie, Winter Fantasy, 1990, FAO Schwarz, NRFB.......$75.00
Barbie, Wonder Woman, 2000, Pop Culture Collection, NRFB.......$45.00
Barbie, Working Woman, 1999, blk or wht, NRFB.......$25.00
Barbie, Yuletide Romance, 1996, Hallmark, NRFB.......$25.00
Barbie, 1959, #2, brunette, MIB, from $6,000 to.......$6,250.00
Barbie, 1960, #4, brunette, MIB, from $375 to.......$425.00
Barbie, 1961, #5, brunette, MIB, from $375 to.......$400.00
Brad, Talking, 1970, NRFB.......$225.00
Brad, 1970, darker skin, bendable legs, NRFB.......$200.00
Cara, Free Moving, 1974, MIB.......$115.00
Casey, Twist 'N Turn, 1968, blond or brunette, NRFB.......$300.00
Chris, 1967, any hair color, MIB.......$200.00
Christie, Beauty Secrets, 1980, MIB.......$50.00
Christie, Fashion Photo, 1978, MIB.......$60.00
Christie, Golden Dream, 1980, MIB.......$40.00
Christie, Kissing, 1979, MIB.......$50.00
Christie, Pink & Pretty, 1982, NRFB.......$40.00
Christie, Pretty Reflections, 1979, NRFB.......$75.00
Christie, Sunsational Malibu, 1982, NRFB.......$55.00
Christie, Superstar, 1977, MIB.......$80.00

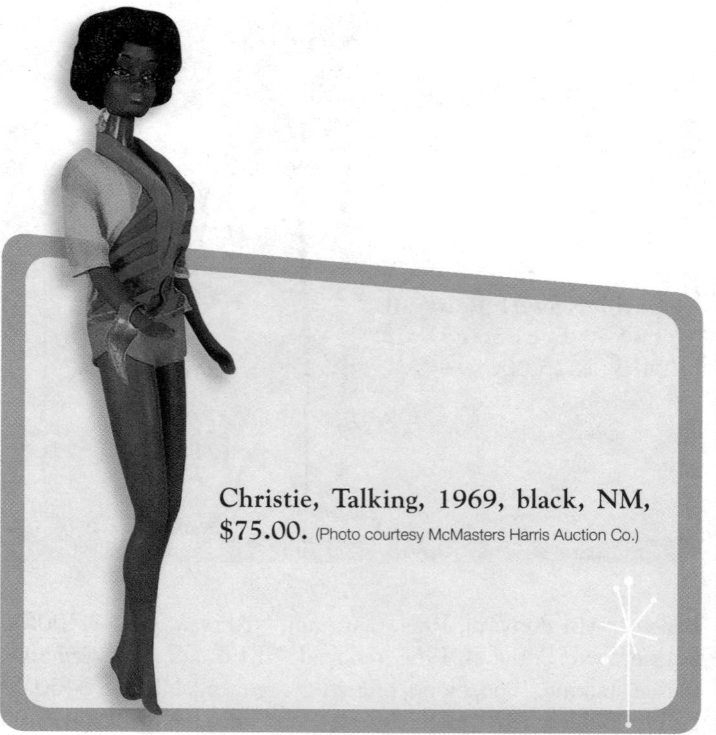

Christie, Talking, 1969, black, NM, $75.00. (Photo courtesy McMasters Harris Auction Co.)

Christie, Talking, 1970, MIB.......$250.00
Christie, Talking, 1970, NRFB.......$300.00
Christie, Twist 'N Turn, 1968, redhead, MIB.......$300.00
Francie, 1966, bendable legs, brunette, MIB.......$375.00
Francie, Busy, 1971, NRFB.......$325.00
Francie, Growin' Pretty Hair, 1971, MIB.......$150.00
Francie, Malibu, 1971, NRFB.......$50.00
Francie, Twist 'N Turn, 1967, blk or wht (blond or brunette), MIB.......$1,200.00
Francie, Twist 'N Turn, 1969, blond or brunette, long or short hair, MIB.......$425.00
Francie, 1966, straight leg, blond or brunette, MIB.......$325.00
Francie, 30th Anniversary, 1996, NRFB.......$50.00
Ginger, Growing Up, 1977, MIB.......$115.00
Jamie, New & Wonderful Walking, 1970, blond hair, MIB.......$200.00
Kelley, Quick Curl, 1972, NRFB.......$80.00
Kelley, Yellowstone, 1974, NRFB.......$300.00
Ken, 1961, flocked hair, blond or brunette, NRFB.......$150.00
Ken, 1962, pnt hair, blond or brunette, NRFB.......$100.00
Ken, 1963, pnt hair, ¾" shorter, NRFB.......$125.00
Ken, 1965, bendable legs, blond or brunette, NRFB.......$325.00
Ken, Air Force, 1994, Stars 'N Stripes, NRFB.......$30.00
Ken, Arabian Nights, 1964, NRFB.......$400.00
Ken, Army, 1993, blk, NRFB.......$35.00
Ken, Beach Blast, 1989, NRFB.......$15.00
Ken, Busy Talking, 1972, NRFB.......$150.00
Ken, California Dream, 1988, NRFB.......$15.00
Ken, Crystal, 1984, blk, NRFB.......$20.00
Ken, Dream Date, 1983, NRFB.......$30.00
Ken, Fashion Jeans, 1982, NRFB.......$25.00
Ken, Flight Time, 1990, NRFB.......$25.00
Ken, Fraternity Meeting, 1964, NRFB.......$375.00
Ken, Free Moving, 1974, MIB.......$75.00
Ken, Funtime, 1975, NRFB.......$65.00
Ken, Gold Medal Skier, 1975, NRFB.......$75.00
Ken, Hawaiian, 1981, NRFB.......$40.00
Ken, Henry Higgins, 1996, Hollywood Legends Series, NRFB.......$35.00
Ken, Horse Lovin', 1983, NRFB.......$30.00
Ken, In-Line Skating, 1996, FAO Schwarz, NRFB.......$20.00
Ken, Jewel Secrets, 1987, NRFB.......$20.00
Ken, Live Action on Stage, 1971, NRFB.......$150.00
Ken, Malibu, 1976, NRFB.......$30.00
Ken, Marine Corps, 1992, Stars 'N Stripes, NRFB.......$25.00

Ken, Mod Hair, 1973, NRFB, $100.00. (Photo ourtesy Sarah Sink Eames)

Ken, Mod Hair, 1974, MIB.......$175.00

Ken, New Look, 1976, longer or shorter hair, NRFB, ea ...$75.00
Ken, Ocean Friends, 1996, NRFB $15.00
Ken, Rhett Butler, 1994, Hollywood Legend Series, NRFB..$35.00
Ken, Rocker, 1986, MIB $30.00
Ken, Sport & Shave, 1980, MIB $40.00
Ken, Sun Lovin' Malibu, 1979, NRFB $25.00
Ken, Sunset Malibu, 1971, NRFB $60.00
Ken, Super Sport, 1982, MIB $20.00
Ken, Superstar, 1977, MIB.................... $100.00
Ken, Talking, 1970, NRFB $115.00
Ken, Walk Lively, 1972, MIB $150.00
Ken, Western, 1982, MIB....................$20.00
Midge, 1963, straight legs, brunette hair, MIB.............. $130.00
Midge, 1965, bendable legs, any color hair, MIB $450.00

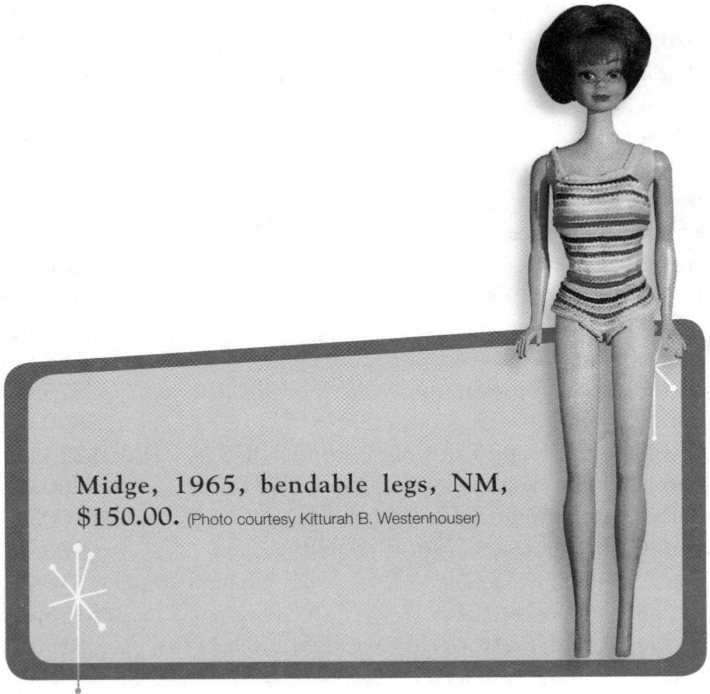

Midge, 1965, bendable legs, NM, $150.00. (Photo courtesy Kitturah B. Westenhouser)

Midge, Cool Times, 1989, NRFB $15.00
Midge, Earring Magic, 1993, NRFB $20.00
Midge, Ski Fun, 1991, MIB $30.00
Midge, 30th Anniversary, 1992, porcelain, MIB..............$60.00
Nikki, Animal Lovin', 1989, NRFB $15.00
PJ, Deluxe Quick Curl, 1976, MIB....................$55.00
PJ, Fashion Photo, 1978, MIB $75.00
PJ, Free Moving, 1974, MIB $75.00
PJ, Free Moving, 1976, MIB $85.00
PJ, Gold Medal Gymnast, 1975, MIB....................$80.00
PJ, Live Action, 1971, MIB $225.00
PJ, Malibu, 1978, MIB $55.00
PJ, Malibu (Sun Lovin'), 1979, MIB $50.00
PJ, Malibu (Sunsational), 1982, MIB $30.00
PJ, Malibu (The Sun Set), 1971, blond hair, MIB $55.00
PJ, New & Groovy Talking, 1969, orig swimsuit, beads & glasses, NM.................... $150.00
Ricky, 1965, MIB $130.00
Scott, 1979, MIB....................$55.00
Skipper, 1964, straight legs, any hair color, MIB............ $130.00
Skipper, 1965, bendable legs, any hair color, MIB $150.00

Skipper, 1965, red hair, Me 'N My Doll outfit, mint doll is $75.00 and mint outfit is $75.00. (Photo courtesy Kitturah B. Westenhouser)

Skipper, Deluxe Quick Curl, 1975, NRFB $65.00
Skipper, Dramatic New Living, 1970, MIB.................... $130.00
Skipper, Growing Up, 1976, MIB.................... $100.00
Skipper, Hollywood Hair, 1993, NRFB $25.00
Skipper, Homecoming Queen, 1989, NRFB $20.00
Skipper, Malibu, 1977, MIB $50.00
Skipper, Malibu (Sunsational), 1982, MIB $40.00
Skipper, Music Lovin', 1985, NRFB....................$25.00
Skipper, Super Teen, 1980, NRFB....................$20.00
Skipper, Totally Hair, 1991, NRFB....................$25.00
Skipper, Twist 'N Turn, 1969, any hair style or color, MIB.... $230.00
Skipper, Western, 1982, NRFB....................$40.00
Skipper, Workout Teen Fun, 1988, NRFB $25.00
Skooter, 1966, bendable legs, any color hair, MIB.......... $275.00
Skooter, 1965, straight leg, any hair color, MIB............. $130.00
Stacey, Talking, any hair color, MIB $430.00
Stacey, Twist 'N Turn, 1969, any hair color, NRFB $450.00
Teresa, All American, 1991, MIB $25.00
Teresa, Country Western Star, 1994, NRFB....................$25.00
Teresa, Rappin' Rockin', 1992, NRFB....................$30.00
Tutti, 1967, any hair color, MIB.................... $175.00
Whitney, Style Magic, 1989, NRFB $15.00

Cases

Barbie, All That Jazz outfit, 1967, NM....................$40.00
Barbie, Circus Star, FAO Schwarz, 1995, M $25.00
Barbie, Easter Parade, 1961, EX+ $20.00
Barbie, Fashion Queen, 1963, red vinyl, w/mirror & wig stand, EX $100.00
Barbie, Goes Travelin', 1965, EX+ $75.00
Barbie, Madison Avenue, blk w/pk hdl, FAO Schwarz, 1992, M $35.00

Barbie & Ken, Barbie in Party Date & Ken in Sat Night Date, blk vinyl, 1963, EX $50.00

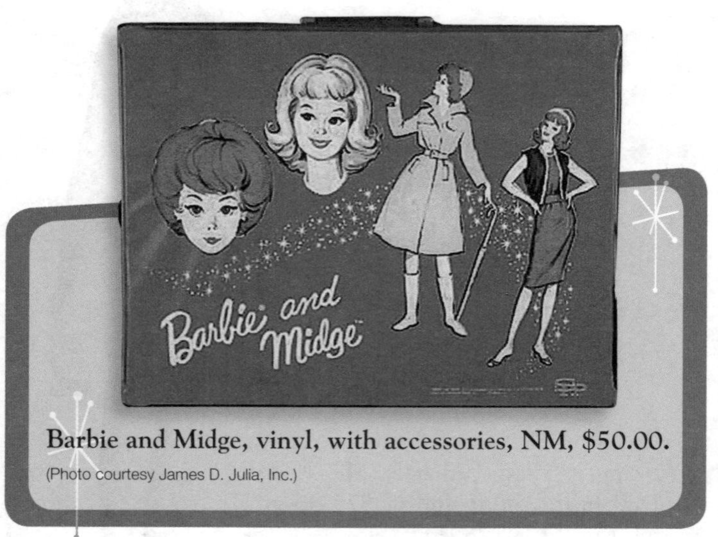

Barbie and Midge, vinyl, with accessories, NM, $50.00. (Photo courtesy James D. Julia, Inc.)

Barbie & Stacey, Sleep 'N Keep, 1960s, NM $75.00
Francie & Casey, Francie in Groovy Get-Up & Casey in Iced Blue, rare, NM+ $75.00
Ken, gold vinyl w/blk plastic handle, metal clasp, w/hang tag, 1962, NM $35.00
Ken, w/3 smaller images of Barbie in casual wear, gr, 1961, NM..$35.00
Midge, Movie Date, 1964, NM $35.00
Miss Barbie, blk patent, 1963, NM+ $150.00
Miss Barbie, wht vinyl, w/orig wig, wig stand & mirror, rare, EX $75.00
Skipper, School Days, 1964, NM $65.00
Skipper & Scooter, 1965, NM $150.00
Skooter, in Country Picnic outfit chasing butterflies, 1965, rare, NM $125.00
Tutti, Play Case, bl or pk vinyl w/various scenes, EX $30.00

Clothing and Accessories

Barbie, Busy Morning, #956, 1963, MIP, $230.00; M, $100.00. (Photo courtesy Sarah Sink Eames)

Barbie, After Five, #934, 1962, NRFP $150.00
Barbie, All That Jazz, #1848, 1968, NRFP $150.00
Barbie, All Turned Out, #4822, 1984, NRFP $20.00
Barbie, American Airlines Stewardess, #984, 1961, NRFP..$175.00
Barbie, Baby Doll Pinks, #3403, 1971, NRFP $100.00
Barbie, Backyard Barbecue, #5719, 1983, NRFP $20.00
Barbie, Balleria, #989, 1961, NRFP $175.00
Barbie, Beach Dazzler, #1939, 1981, NRFP $10.00
Barbie, Beach Party, #5541, 1983, NRFP $20.00
Barbie, Best Bow, Pak, 1967, NRFP $175.00
Barbie, Bouncy Flouncy, #1805, 1967, NRFP $300.00
Barbie, Bridal Brocade, #3471, 1971, NRFP $250.00
Barbie, Bride's Dream, #947, 1963, NRFP $225.00
Barbie, Brunch Time, #1628, 1965, NRFP $375.00
Barbie, Camping, #7702, 1973, NRFP $45.00
Barbie, Caribbean Cruise, #1687, 1967, NRFP $230.00
Barbie, Change Abouts, Pak, 1968, NRFP $150.00
Barbie, Cheerleader, #876, 1964, NRFP $175.00
Barbie, Cinderella, #872, 1964, NRFP $450.00
Barbie, City Sparklers, #1457, 1970, NRFP $125.00
Barbie, Close-Ups, #1864, 1969, NRFP $125.00
Barbie, Club Meeting, #1672, 1966, NRFP $400.00
Barbie, Cruise Stripes, #918, 1959, NRFP $175.00
Barbie, Disco Dazzle, #1011, 1979, NRFP $15.00
Barbie, Dream Wraps, #1476, 1969, NRFP $80.00
Barbie, Drizzle Dash, #1808, 1967, NRFP $200.00
Barbie, Drum Majorette, #875, 1964, NRFP $225.00
Barbie, Enchanted Evening, #983, 1960, NRFP $325.00
Barbie, Evening Gala, #1660, 1966, NRFP $400.00
Barbie, Evening Outfit, #2221, 1978, NRFP $30.00
Barbie, Eye Popper, #1937, 1981, NRFP $10.00
Barbie, Fancy Free, #943, 1963, NRFP $75.00
Barbie, Floral Petticoat, #921, 1959, NRFP $75.00
Barbie, Fraternity Dance, #1638, NRFP $600.00
Barbie, Friday Night Date, #979, 1960, NRFP $225.00
Barbie, Fringe Benefits, #1701, 1965, NRFP $60.00
Barbie, Fun Fakes, #3412, 1971, NRFP $100.00
Barbie, Fur Sighted, #1796, 1970, NRFP $20.00
Barbie, Galaxy A Go-Go, #2742, 1986, NRFP $30.00
Barbie, Garden Party, #0931, 1962, NRFP $175.00
Barbie, Garden Party, #5701 or #5835, 1983, NRFP, ea $10.00
Barbie, Glamour Group, #1510, 1970, NRFP $350.00
Barbie, Gold 'N Glamour, #1647, NRFP $1,500.00
Barbie, Graduation, #945, 1963, NRFP $75.00
Barbie, Great Coat, #1459, 1970, NRFP $90.00
Barbie, Happy Go Pink, #1868, 1969, NRFP $200.00
Barbie, Have Fun, Pak, 1966, NRFP $325.00
Barbie, Holiday Dance, #1639, 1965, NRFP $550.00
Barbie, Homecoming, #16076, 1996, NRFP $30.00
Barbie, In Blooms, #3424, 1971, NRFB $90.00
Barbie, Indian Print Separates, #7241, 1975, NRFP $35.00
Barbie, Invitation to Tea, #1632, 1965, NRFP $550.00
Barbie, Jumpin' Jeans, Pak, 1964, NRFP $85.00
Barbie, Lady in Blue, #2303, 1978, NRFP $15.00
Barbie, Little Red Riding Hood & the Wolf, #880, 1964, NRFP $550.00
Barbie, Madras Mad, #3485, 1972, NRFP $120.00
Barbie, Masquerade, #944, 1963, NRFP $200.00
Barbie, Midi-Marvelous, #1870, 1969, NRFP $160.00
Barbie, Movie Groovie, #1866, 1969, NRFP $125.00
Barbie, Now Knit, #1452, 1970, NRFP $100.00
Barbie, Overall Denim, #3488, 1972, NRFP $110.00
Barbie, Patio Party, #1708, 1965, NRFP $50.00

Barbie, Pedal Pushers, Pak, 1968, NRFP........................ $120.00
Barbie, Perfect Beginnings, #60, 1970, NRFP...................$90.00
Barbie, Perfectly Pink, #4805, 1984, NRFP $10.00
Barbie, Plush Pony, #1873, 1969, NRFP $175.00
Barbie, Rain or Shine, #2788, 1979, NRFP $15.00
Barbie, Raincoat, #949, 1963, NRFP $100.00
Barbie, Rare Pair, #1462, 1970, NRFP $125.00
Barbie, Reception Line, #1654, 1966, NRFP $600.00
Barbie, Red Flair, #939, 1962, NRFP............................ $175.00
Barbie, Royal Ball, #2668, 1979, NRFP $15.00
Barbie, Scene-Stealers, #1845, 1968, NRFP $240.00
Barbie, Scuba Do's, #1788, 1970, NRFP $65.00
Barbie, Sea-Worthy, #1872, 1969, NRFP........................ $225.00
Barbie, Shape-Ups, #1782, 1970-71, NRFP $200.00
Barbie, Sharp Shift, #20, 1970, NRFP............................ $110.00
Barbie, Sheath Sensation, #986, 1961, NRFP................ $150.00
Barbie, Silken Flame, #977, 1960, NRFP $175.00
Barbie, Silver Serenade, #3419, 1971-72, NRFP $350.00
Barbie, Ski Party Pink, #5608, 1983, NRFP......................$10.00
Barbie, Slip On Wrap 'n Tie, #1910, 1981, NRFP $10.00
Barbie, Snap Dash, #1824, 1968, NRFP......................... $140.00
Barbie, Star of the Snow in Golden Glow, #9741, 1977, NRFP $15.00
Barbie, Sugar Plum Fairy, #9326, 1976, NRFP.................$40.00
Barbie, Swingin' Easy, #955, 1963, NRFP $225.00
Barbie, Topsy Twosider, #4826, 1984, NRFP.....................$10.00
Barbie, Trail Blazer, #1846, 1968, NRFP $250.00
Barbie, Two-Way Tiger, #3402, 1971, NRFP.................. $110.00
Barbie, Velvet Touch, #2789, 1979, NRFP $15.00
Barbie, Walking Pretty Pak, 1971, NRFP........................ $130.00
Barbie, Wild 'N Wonderful, #1856, 1968-69, NRFB $200.00
Barbie, Yellow Go, #1816, 1967, NRFP $800.00
Barbie & Stacey, All the Trimmings Fashion Pak, #0050, 1970, MOC..$75.00
Francie, Cheerleading Outfit, #7711, 1973, NRFP...........$80.00
Francie, Dancing Party, #1257, NRFP........................... $275.00
Francie, Furry-Go-Round, #1294, Sears Exclusive, 1967, NRFP $500.00
Francie, Hip Knits, #1265, 1966, NRFB $225.00
Francie, Little Knits, #3275, 1972, NRFP...................... $125.00
Francie, Merry-Go-Rounders, #1230, NRFB $375.00
Francie, Peach Plush, #3461, 1971, NRFP..................... $250.00
Francie, Quick Shift, #1266, 1966, NRFP...................... $200.00
Francie, Slightly Summery Fashion Pak, 1968, NRFP.......$95.00
Francie, Summer Number, #3454, 1971-72 & 1974, MIP . $175.00
Francie, Totally Terrific, #3280, 1972, MIP................... $225.00
Francie, Wedding Whirl, #1244, 1970-71 & 1974, complete, M $275.00
Francie & Casey, Cool It! Fashion Pak, 1968, MIP $50.00
Francie & Stacey, Culotte-Wot?, #1214, 1968-69, MIB. $300.00
Francie & Stacey, Tennis Time, #1221, 1969-70, MIP ... $150.00
Fun at McDonald's, #4276, 1983, NRFP..........................$15.00
Jazzie, Mini Dress, #3781 or #3783, 1989, NRFP, ea..........$10.00
Ken, Army & Air Force, #797, 1963, NRFP.................... $250.00
Ken, Beach Beat, #3384, 1972, NRFP.............................$80.00
Ken, Big Business #1434, 1970, NRFP $75.00
Ken, Blazer, Pak, 1962, NRFP $25.00
Ken, Breakfast at 7, #1428, 1969, NRFP $70.00
Ken, Campus Corduroys, #1410, 1964, NRFP..................$75.00
Ken, Casual All-Stars, #1436, 1970, NRFP $50.00
Ken, Casual Suit, #9167, 1976, NFRB..............................$70.00
Ken, Cool 'N Casual, #3379, 1972, NRFP........................$70.00
Ken, Country Clubbin', #1400, 1964, NRFP $100.00
Ken, Date Night, #5651, 1983, NRFP...............................$10.00
Ken, Date w/Barbie, #5824, 1983, NRFP.........................$10.00
Ken, Denims for Fun, #3376, 1972, NRFP........................$70.00
Ken, Doctor, #7705, 1973, NRFP.....................................$80.00
Ken, Double Play, #4886, 1984, NRFP.............................$10.00
Ken, Fountain Boy, #1407, 1964, NRFP $250.00
Ken, Fraternity Meeting, #1408, 1964, NRFP $75.00
Ken, Fun on Ice, #791, 1963, NRFP.............................. $125.00
Ken, Goin' Huntin', #1409, 1964, NRFP......................... $125.00
Ken, Going Bowling, #1403, 1964, NRFP $50.00
Ken, Graduation, #795, 1963, NRFP $65.00
Ken, Groom, #9596, 1976, NRFP $15.00
Ken, Gym Shorts & Hooded Jacket, #2795, 1979, NRFP ..$60.00
Ken, Hiking Holiday, #1412, 1965, NMIP...................... $225.00
Ken, In the Limelight, #2802, 1979, NRFP $20.00
Ken, Jazz Concert, #1420, 1966, NRFP.......................... $275.00
Ken, Midnight Blues, #1719, 1972, NRFP....................... $115.00
Ken, Mod Madras, #1828, 1972, NRFP........................... $115.00
Ken, Night Scene, #1496, 1971, NRFP........................... $100.00
Ken, Olympic Hockey, #7247, 1975, NRFP.......................$70.00
Ken, Pepsi Outfit, #7761, 1974, NRFP.............................$40.00
Ken, Play Ball, #792, 1963, NRFP.................................. $120.00
Ken, Rally Day, #788, 1962, NRFP $90.00
Ken, Roller Skate Date, #1405, 1964, NRFP $130.00
Ken, Running Start, #1404, 1981, NRFP..........................$10.00
Ken, Safari, #7706, 1973, NRFP......................................$70.00
Ken, Sea Scene, #1449, 1971, NRFP $60.00
Ken, Ship-Shape, #4885, 1984, NRFP $10.00
Ken, Sportsman, Pak, 1964, NRFP..................................$90.00
Ken, Suede Scene, #1439, 1971, NRFP $60.00
Ken, Summer Job, #1422, 1966, NRFP $450.00
Ken, United Airlines Pilot Uniform, #7707, 1973, NRFP. $100.00
Ken, Vest Dressed, #2799, 1979, NRFP $15.00
Ken, Victory Dance, #1411, 1964, NRFP $155.00
Ken, Way-Out West, #1720, 1972, NRFP..........................$65.00
Ken, Well Suited, #1407, 1980, NRFP.............................$10.00
Ken, Western Winner, #3378, 1972, NRFP $60.00
Ken, White Is Right Fashion Pak, 1964, NRFP $40.00
Ken & Brad, Sun Fun Fashion Pak, 1971, MIP.................$75.00
Midge, Orange Blossom, #987, 1962, NRFP $75.00
Skipper, All Over Felt, #3476, NRFP............................. $150.00
Skipper, All Spruced Up!, #1941, 1967, NRFP $145.00
Skipper, Ballerina, #3471, 1971, NRFP............................$75.00
Skipper, Beach, #7848, 1974, NRFP $50.00
Skipper, Beach Party, #1409, 1980, NRFP $10.00
Skipper, Bicentennial Fashions, #9165, 1976, NRFP $70.00
Skipper, Budding Beauty, #1731, 1970, NRFP...................$75.00
Skipper, Check the Suit, Pak, 1971, NRFP.......................$45.00
Skipper, Chill Chasers, #1926, 1966, NRFP $75.00
Skipper, Chilly Chums, #1973, 1969, NRFP.................. $125.00
Skipper, City Shopping, #2809, 1979, NRFP.....................$15.00
Skipper, Cookie Time, #1912, 1965, NRFP $125.00
Skipper, Dressed in Velvet, #3477, 1971, NRFP $125.00

Skipper, Get-Ups 'N Go Flower Girl, #7847, 1974-76, MIP. $100.00
Skipper, Hearts 'N Flowers, #1945, 1967, NRFB $300.00
Skipper, Ice Skatin', #3470, 1971-72, MIP $150.00
Skipper, Jeepers Creepers, #1966, 1969, NRFP............... $125.00
Skipper, Lacey Charmer & Partytimer, #9746, 1977, NRFP.. $15.00
Skipper, Masquerade, #1903, 1964, NRFP $160.00
Skipper, Nifty Knickers, #3291, 1972, NRFP..................... $85.00
Skipper, Olympic Skating, #7251, 1975, NRFP $70.00
Skipper, Party Pair, #3297, 1972, NRFP.............................. $90.00
Skipper, Platter Party, #1914, 1965, NRFP $125.00
Skipper, Popover, #1943, 1967, NRFP $175.00
Skipper, Rain or Shine, #1916, 1965, NRFP....................... $95.00
Skipper, Real Sporty, #1961, 1968, NRFP....................... $200.00
Skipper, School's Cool, #1976, 1969-70, MIP................. $200.00
Skipper, Shoe Parade Fashion Pak, 1965, NRFP................ $45.00
Skipper, Skimmy Stripes, #1956, 1968, MIP.................. $200.00
Skipper, Tea Party, #1924, 1966, NRFP $325.00
Skipper & Fluff, Fun Runners, #3372, 1972, MIP............. $50.00
Skipper & Fluff, Some Shoes Fashion Pak, 1971, MIP $65.00
Skipper & Fluff, Super Snoozers, #3371, 1972, NRFB....... $55.00
Tutti, Birthday Beauties, #3617, 1968, NRFP $160.00
Tutti, Pink PJs, #3616, 1968-69, MIP............................. $150.00

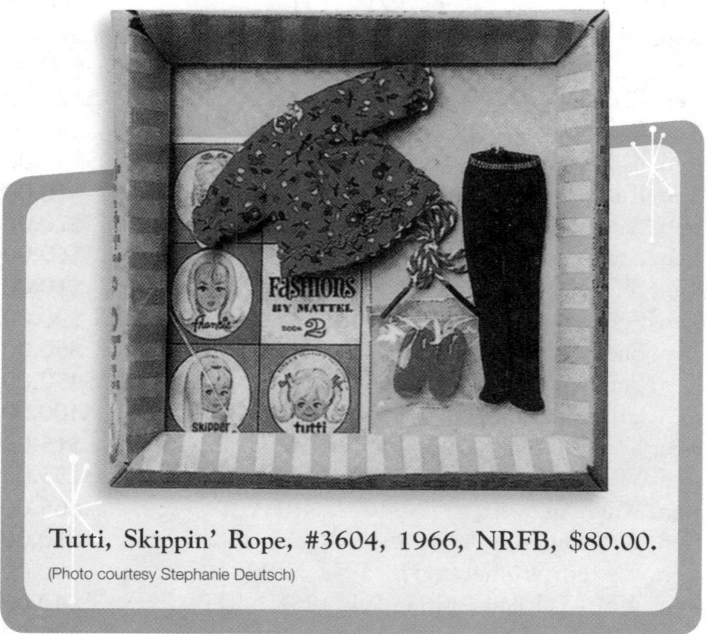

Tutti, Skippin' Rope, #3604, 1966, NRFB, $80.00. (Photo courtesy Stephanie Deutsch)

Twiggy, Twiggy Turnouts, #1726, 1968, NRFP $250.00

Furniture, Rooms, Houses, and Shops

Action Sewing Center, 1972, MIB.................................... $50.00
Barbie & Midge Queen Size Chifferobe (Susy Goose), NM. $100.00
Barbie & Skipper Deluxe Dream House, Sears Exclusive, 1965, MIB, minimum value... $175.00
Barbie & The Beat Dance Cafe, 1990, MIB $35.00
Barbie & the Rockers Hot Rockin' Stage, 1987, MIB $40.00
Barbie Beauty Boutique, 1976, MIB $40.00
Barbie Cafe Today, 1971, MIB... $400.00
Barbie Cookin' Fun Kitchen, MIB $100.00
Barbie Dream Armoire, 1980, NRFB $35.00
Barbie Dream Bed & Nightstand, 1984, pk, MIB $25.00
Barbie Dream Glow Vanity, 1986, MIB $20.00
Barbie Dream House Bedroom, 1981, MIB $6.00
Barbie Dream Kitch-Dinette, #4095, 1964, MIB $600.00
Barbie Dream Store Makeup Department, 1983, MIB....... $40.00

Barbie Fashion Living Room Set, #7404, 1984, NRFB, $30.00. (Photo courtesy Stephanie Deutsch)

Barbie Fashion Wraps Boutique, 1989, MIB $35.00
Barbie Lively Livin' Room, MIB $50.00
Barbie Playhouse Pavilion, Europe, MIB........................... $75.00
Barbie's Apartment, 1975, MIB..................................... $140.00
Barbie's Room-Fulls Firelight Living Room, 1974, MIB . $100.00
Barbie Unique Boutique, Sears Exclusive, 1971, MIB $185.00
Coot Tops Skipper T-Shirt Shop, 1989, complete, MIB.... $25.00
Francie House, 1966, complete, M $150.00
Go-Together Chaise Lounge, MIB $75.00
Go-Together Dining Room, Barbie & Skipper, 1965, MIB... $50.00
Go-Together Lawn Swing & Planter, 1964, complete, MIB. $150.00
Ice Capades Skating Rink, 1989, MIB $70.00

Ken Wardrobe (Susy Goose), 1963, NM+, $50.00 (without Ken doll or clothing and accessories). (Photo courtesy Paris and Susan Manos)

Living Pretty Cooking Center, 1988, MIB......................... $25.00
Magical Mansion, 1989, MIB $125.00

Party Garden Playhouse, 1994, MIB $275.00
Pink Sparkles Armoire, 1990, NRFB $25.00
Pink Sparkles Starlight Bed, 1990, MIB......................... $300.00
Skipper Dream Room, 1964, MIB $300.00
Skipper's Jeweled Vanity (Susy Goose), Sears Exclusive, 1965, NRFP $100.00
Superstar Barbie Beauty Salon, 1977, MIB $55.00
Surprise House, 1972, MIB.. $100.00
Susy Goose Canopy Bed, 1962, MIB............................. $150.00
Susy Goose Four Poster Bed Outfit, M $35.00
Susy Goose Mod-A-Go-Go Bedroom, 1966, NRFB $2,300.00
Susy Goose Wardrobe, 1962, EX $35.00
Tutti Playhouse, 1966, M... $100.00
World of Barbie House, 1966, MIB $175.00

Gift Sets

Ballerina Barbie on Tour, 1976, MIB.............................. $175.00
Barbie & Ken Campin' Out, 1983, MIB $75.00
Barbie Dance Club & Tape Player Set, #4217, 1989, MIB ..$75.00

Barbie Fashion Gift Set, Wholesale Clubs, 1996, NRFB, $25.00.

Barbie's Olympic Ski Village, MIB $75.00
Barbie's Wedding Party, 1964, MIB $700.00
Barbie Snap 'N Play Deluxe Gift Set, JC Penney Exclusive, 1992, MIB $40.00
Barbie 35th Anniversary Gift Set, 1994, NRFP............. $150.00
Birthday Fun at McDonald's, 1994, NRFB........................$75.00
Cinderella, 1992, NRFB $125.00
Dance Sensation Barbie, 1985, MIB $35.00
Dramatic New Living Skipper Very Best Velvet, Sears Exclusive, 1970-71, NRFB.. $1,500.00
Golden Dreams Glamorous Nights, 1980, NRFB $100.00
Halloween Party Barbie & Ken, Target, 1998, NRFB........$65.00
Happy Meal Stacie & Whitney, JC Penney Exclusive, 1994, MIB $30.00
Ken Red, White & Wild, Sears Exclusive, 1970, NRFB. $525.00
Living Barbie Action Accents, Sears Exclusive, 1970, MIB . $450.00
Malibu Barbie Beach Party, M (M case)............................$75.00
Malibu Ken Surfs Up, Sears Exclusive, 1971, MIB $350.00
New 'N Groovy PJ Swingin' in Silver, MIB, A $770.00
Night Night Sleep Tight Tutti, NRFB............................ $300.00

Barbie Paint 'N Dazzle, #10924, 1993, MIB, $35.00.
(Photo courtesy Margo Rana)

Pretty Pairs Nan 'N Fran, 1970, NRFB $250.00
Skipper Party Time, 1964, NRFB $500.00
Stacey Nite Lighting, Sears Exclusive, 1969, NRFB.... $2,000.00
Sun Sensation Barbie Spray & Play Fun, Wholesale Clubs, 1992, MIB $60.00
Superstar Barbie Fashion Change-Abouts, 1978, NRFB.. $100.00
Talking Barbie Golden Groove Set, Sears Exclusive, 1969, MIB...$1,500.00
Talking Barbie Perfectly Plaid, Sears Exclusive, 1971, MIB .. $500.00
Tutti & Todd Sundae Treat, 1966, NRFB $500.00
Wedding Party Midge, 1990, NRFB $150.00

Vehicles

Barbie Star Cycle, MIB, $20.00; Barbie Motor Bike, MIB, $25.00. (Photo courtesy Paris and Susan Manos)

Allan's Roadster, 1964, aqua, MIB $500.00
ATC Cycle, Sears Exclusive, 1972, MIB..........................$65.00
Austin Healy, Irwin, 1962, red & wht, very rare, NRFB .. $3,500.00
Barbie & Ken Dune Buggy, Irwin, 1970, pk, MIB........... $250.00
Barbie & the Rockers Hot Rockin' Van, 1987, MIB..........$60.00
Barbie's Own Sports Car, NMIB.................................... $150.00
Barbie Silver 'Vette, MIB...$30.00

Barbie Travelin' Trailer, MIB $40.00
Beach Buggy for Skipper, Irwin, 1964, rare, MIB, minimum value $500.00
Beach Bus, 1974, MIB $45.00
California Dream Beach Taxi, 1988, MIB $35.00
Ken's Classy Corvette, 1976, yel, MIB $75.00
Ken's Dream 'Vette, 1981, dk bl, MIB $100.00
Ken's Hot Rod, Sears Exclusive, 1964, red, MIB $900.00
Snowmobile, Montgomery Ward, 1972, MIB $65.00
Sports Plane, Sears Exclusive, 1964, MIB $3,600.00
Star 'Vette, 1977, red, MIB $100.00
Starlight Motorhome, 1994, MIB $45.00
Sunsailer, 1975, NRFB $55.00
Western Star Traveler Motorhome, 1982, MIB $50.00
1957 Belair Chevy, 1989, 1st edition, aqua, MIB $150.00
1957 Belair Chevy, 1990, 2nd edition, pk, MIB $125.00

Miscellaneous

Barbie & the Rockers, purse, vinyl, w/comb & cologne, M .$15.00

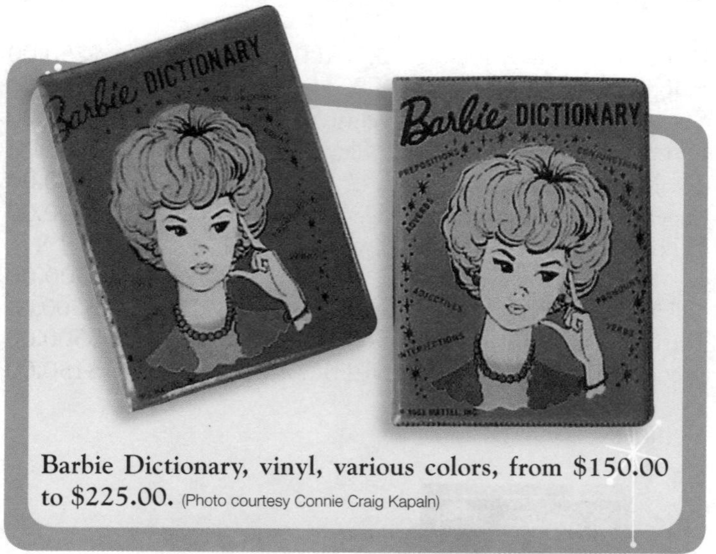

Barbie Dictionary, vinyl, various colors, from $150.00 to $225.00. (Photo courtesy Connie Craig Kapaln)

Barbie Dictionary, vinyl w/head image of Bubble-Cut Barbie encircled by lettering & stars graphics, 1963, G, A $20.00
Barbie Ge-Tar, 1965, M $325.00
Barbie Pretty-Up Time Perfume Pretty Bath, 1964, complete, M $150.00
Barbie Shrinky Dinks, 1979, MIB $30.00
Book, Barbie's Fashion Success, Random House, 1962, hardcover, EX $20.00
Carrying Case, cloth w/vinyl trim, Barbie's name & allover flower design, grip hdl, zipper, VG, A $75.00
Coloring Book, Barbie & Ken, 1963, unused, NM $50.00
Embroidery Set, Barbie & Ken, 1962, complete, rare, NMIB, D2 ....$150.00
Game, Barbie 35th Anniversary, Golden, 1994, MIB $60.00
Knitting for Barbie, cb canister w/metal ends, complete contents, VG, A $30.00
Ornament, Holiday Barbie, Hallmark, 1993, 1st edition, MIB $75.00
Paper Dolls, Barbie, Whitman #4601, 1963, uncut, M $85.00
Paper Dolls, Midge Cut-Outs, Whitman #1962, 1963, uncut, NM $150.00
Party Set, 31-pc pk & wht plastic set w/graphics, cups, plates, silverware, pots & pans, 1983, MIB (sealed) $35.00
Puzzle, jigsaw; Barbie & Ken, Whitman, 1963, 100 pcs, MIB. $40.00
Quick Curl Miss America Beauty Center, Sears Exclusive, 1975, MIB $75.00

Record Totes, vinyl with plastic handles, $150.00 each. (Photo courtesy Connie Craig Kaplan)

Sweet Sixteen Promotional Set, 1974, M $70.00
Tea Set, Barbie 25th Anniversary, 1984, complete, M ... $150.00
Wagon, Camp Barbie, 1995, 34", EX $50.00
Wallet, 1962, vinyl w/graphics, VG $25.00
Yo-yo, Spectra Star, plastic w/paper sticker, MIP $5.00

Battery-Operated Toys

From the standpoint of being visually entertaining, nothing can compare with the battery-opetated toy. Most (probably as much as 95%) were made in Japan from the 1940s through the 1960s, though some were distributed by American companies, such as Marx, Ideal, and Daisy, for instance, who often sold them under their own names. So even if they're marked, sometimes it's just about impossible to identify the manufacturer. Though batteries had been used to power trains and provide simple illumination in earlier toys, the Japanese toys could smoke, walk, talk, drink, play instruments, blow soap bubbles, and do just about anything else humanly possible to dream up and engineer. Generally, the more actions the toy performs, the more collectible it is. Rarity is important as well, but first and foremost to consider is condition. Because of their complex mechanisms, many will no longer work. Children often stopped them in mid-cycle, rubber hoses and bellows aged and cracked, and leaking batteries caused them to corrode, so very few have survived to the present intact and in good enough condition to interest a collector. Although it is sometimes possible to have them repaired, it is probably better to wait on a better example. Original boxes are a definite plus in assessing the value of a battery-op and can sometimes be counted on to add from 30% to 50% (and up), depending on the box's condition, of course, as well as the toy's age and rarity.

If the name of the toy is on the toy, that name will be listed first with the box name (if different) listed in parenthesis. If there is no name on the toy, then the name on the box will be listed first. Some cross referencing has been used to help identify toys without boxes. For more information we recommend *Collecting Toys* by Richard O'Brien (Books Americana).

Note: The following listings are for toys in working order, and boxes are in excellent condition or better unless noted otherwise.

Advisor: Tom Lastrapes

See also Aeronautical; Boats; Games; Guns; Japanese and Other Tin Replica Vehicles; Marx; Robots and Space Toys; Santa; Tin Vehicles.

ABC Toyland Express, MT, 1950s, 14½", NM................ $125.00
Accordion Bear, Alps, 1950s, r/c microphone, 10½", NMIB. $725.00
Accordion Player Hobo (w/Monkey), Alps, 1950s, NMIB... $350.00
Acro-Chimp Porter, YM, 1960s, 9", NMIB.................... $100.00
Acrobatic Umbrella, lady in cloth outfit holding litho tin umbrella, 10", GIB... $110.00
Air Control Tower (w/Airplane & Helicopter), Bandai, 1960s, 10½", EXIB.. $250.00
All Stars Mr Baseball Jr, K, 1950s, 8", EXIB $825.00

Animal Yacker/Crackers the Talking Plush Parrot, MIB, $450.00. (Photo courtesy Don and Kathy Lewis)

Animated Squirrel, S&E, 1950s, 9", MIB $150.00
Annie Tugboat, Y, 1950s, 12½", NM $140.00
Answer Game Machine (Robot), Ichida, 1960s, 15", NMIB.. $450.00
Antique Fire Car, TN, 1950s, 10", EXIB........................ $175.00
Antique Gooney Car, Alps, 1960s, 9", EX+......................$75.00
Arthur A-Go-Go, Alps, 1960s, 10", NM+IB................. $450.00
Arthur A-Go-Go, Alps, 1960s, 10", VG......................... $250.00
Aston Martin Secret Ejector Car, #M101, r/c, 11", EX... $250.00
Astro Dog, Y, 1960s, r/c, 11", EXIB............................... $125.00
Auto-Matic (Rock 'N Roll Monkey), see Rock 'N Roll Monkey
Automatic Train Station & Rubber Track, Tomiyama/Yonezawa, 8½" L, NMIB, A $190.00
B-Z Porter (Baggage Truck), MT, 1950s, 8" L, EXIB....... $125.00
B-Z Rabbit, MT, 1950s, 7" L, EX.................................. $100.00
Baby & Carriage Pony Tail Girl, Rosko/S&E, 1950s, 8" H, EXIB $175.00
Baby Bertha the Watering Elephant, Mego, 1960s, 9" L, MIB..$475.00
Baby Carriage, TN, 1950s, 13", EXIB............................ $120.00
Baggage Porter, Cragstan, plush dog pulling 2-wheeled stake cart, 12", EXIB $125.00
Ball Blowing Clown (w/Mystery Action), TN, 1950s, cloth costume, 11", EXIB... $175.00
Ball Playing Bear, 1940s, bear, goose, umbrella & celluloid balls in spiral wire on tin base, 11", EXIB....................... $900.00
Balloon Blowing Monkey w/Lighted Eyes, Alps, 1950s, plush w/cloth overalls, 12", EXIB.................................... $130.00
Balloon Vendor, Y, 1960s, tin w/cloth outfit, 11", GIB... $165.00
Barber Bear, TN, 1950s, plush, tin base, 10", EXIB $400.00
Barky Puppy, Alps, r/c, plush, 9" H, EXIB.........................$50.00
Barney Bear the Drumming Boy, Alps, 1950s, r/c, 11", NM+IB.. $200.00
Bartender, TN, 1960s, wht-haired gent in red jacket standing behind tin bar, 12", EXIB $30.00
Bartender w/Revolving Eyes TN, 1950s, 11½", NMIB... $250.00
Batman & Robin Batcycle, Hong Kong, NMIB, A $615.00
Batman Flying Batplane, Remco, 1966, r/c, plastic, performs aerial stunts, 12", EXIB... $125.00
Batman Zoomcycle, DC Comics, 1977, unused, MIB........$85.00
Batmobile, Taiwan, tin & plastic, w/Batman & Robin figures, 12", EX+ (VG box), A $250.00
Batmobile (Mystery Action/Blinking Warning Light/Engine Noise), Ahi, 1970s, blk w/red trim, Batman figure, 12", EX $225.00
Bear Target Game, MT, 1950s, tin, 9", NMIB................. $300.00
Bear the Cashier, MT, 1950s, plush, 8" H, EXIB............. $250.00
Bear the Shoe Maker, TN, 1950s, 8½", EX+................... $200.00

Bear the Shoe Maker, TN, 1950s, 8½", EXIB, $300.00. (Photo courtesy Don Hultzman)

Bear the Xylophone Player, Y, 1950s, r/c, plush & tin, 10", EX...$275.00
Beauty Parlor, S&E, 1950s, 9½" H, EX $525.00
Beethoven the Piano Playing Dog, see Pianist (Jolly Pianist)
Big Dipper, Technofix, 1960s, 3 cars on track, 21" L, EX.. $150.00
Big John the Chimpee Chief, Alps, 1960s, chimp in Indian headdress seated at drum, 13", EXIB...........................$80.00
Big Ring Circus (Circus Parade), MT, 1950s, truck, 13", EXIB.. $200.00
Big Top Champ Circus Clown, Alps, 1960s, 14", NMIB. $150.00
Big Wheel Ice Cream Truck, Taiyo, 1970s, 10", EX..........$75.00

Bimbo the Drumming Clown, Cragstan, 1950s, r/c, 11", EXIB...$225.00
Birdwatcher Bear, MT, plush, seated w/bird on paw, 10", VG..$440.00
Black Smithy Bear, TN, 1950s, plush bear seated at anvil, 10", EXIB....$325.00
Black Tap Dancer, Japan, litho tin, figure in straw hat, plaid jacket & striped pants on round base, 11", VG+, A....$300.00
Blacksmith Bear, A-1, 1950s, plush bear standing at anvil & fire pit, 9", EXIB....$375.00
Blinky the Clown, Amico Toy/Japan, r/c, EX+IB, A....$250.00
Blushing Frankenstein, Nomura, tin & vinyl, 13", NMIB, A....$175.00
Blushing Gunfighter, Y, 1960s, tin w/cloth shirt, 11", NMIB. $125.00
Blushing Willie, Y, 1960s, wht-haired gent pouring himself a drink, 10", EXIB....$75.00
Bobby Drinking Bear, Y, 1950s, r/c, plush, 10", VGIB....$425.00
Bongo Monkey (w/Bongo Drums & Lited Eyes), Alps, 1960s, plastic hat, 10", EXIB....$175.00
Bowling Bank, ASC/Daniel Imports, 1960s, 10", unused, MIB, A....$100.00
Brave Eagle (Beating Drum & Raising War-Hoop), TN, 1950s, cloth outfit, 13", MIB, A....$125.00
Bruin the Bear & His Ball Playing Act, Cragstan, tin & celluloid, 10", NMIB....$500.00

Bruno Accordion Bear, Y, 1950s, remote control, 10", EXIB, $350.00. (Photo courtesy Don Hultzman)

Bubble Bear, MT, 1950s, blows bubbles, 9½", EXIB....$325.00
Bubble Blowing Boy, Y, 1950s, 8", NMIB....$225.00
Bubble Blowing Monkey, Alps, 1950s, 11", EXIB....$125.00
Bubble Blowing Musician, Y, 1950s, 10", NMIB....$225.00
Bubble Blowing Popeye, Linemar, 1950s, 12", EXIB....$1,400.00
Bubble Blowing Popeye, Linemar, 1950s, 12", VG....$475.00
Bubble Blowing Washing Bear, Y, 1950s, 8", EXIB....$375.00
Bubble Kangaroo, MT, 1950s, 9", NM+IB....$300.00
Bubble Lion, MT, 1950s, 7", EXIB....$125.00
Bubbling Bull, see Wild West Rodeo
Bump Bump Cars, Datsun, 1960s, plastic, unused, 12", MIB, A..$40.00
Bumper Automatic Control Bus, Bandai, 15", EXIB....$225.00
Bunny the Busy Secretary, MT, plush & tin, 7½", NMIB. $600.00
Bunny the Magician, Alps, 1950s, plush, 14", VG+IB....$325.00
Burger Chef, Y, 1950s, plush & tin, 9", EXIB....$175.00
Busy Housekeeper (Bear), Alps, 1950s, pushing sweeper, plush w/cloth dress, 9", EXIB....$200.00
Busy Housekeeper (Rabbit), Alps, 1950s, pushing sweeper, plush w/cloth dress, 10", EXIB....$200.00
Busy Secretary, Linemar, 1950s, 7½" H, EXIB....$250.00
Cadillac (Musical Open Car), Yoshiya, w/cowboy driver, 9", NMIB....$450.00
Calypso Joe, Linemar, 1950s, r/c, 10", EX....$300.00
Cappy the Happy Baggage Porter, Alps, 1960s, 12", MIB. $275.00
Captain Blushwell, Yone, 1960s, 11", nonworking o/w NMIB, A....$65.00
Captain Hook, Marusan, 1950s, 11", rare, EX, minimum value....$750.00
Captain Kidd Pirate Ship, Y, 1960s, 13", rare, MIB....$275.00
Champion Weight Lifter, TM, 1960s, plush dressed monkey w/lg barbell, 10", EXIB....$175.00
Chap the Obedient Dog, Rosko, 1960s, MIB....$150.00
Charlie the Drumming Clown, see Cragston Melody Band (Charlie the Drumming Clown)
Charlie the Funny Clown, Alps, 1960s, clown in cloth outfit on circus car, 10" L, EXIB....$220.00
Charlie Weaver Bartender, TN, 1960s, NMIB....$125.00
Chee Chee Chihauhua, Mego, 1960s, 8", EX....$50.00
Cheerful Dachshund, Y, 1960s, r/c, plush, 9", EXIB....$50.00
Chef Cook, Y, 1960s, 9", EXIB....$125.00
Chimpy the Jolly Drummer, Alps, plush monkey seated at drum w/cymbals, 9", EXIB....$50.00
Chippy the Chipmunk, Alps, 1950s, 12", MIB....$125.00
Cindy the Meowing Cat, Tomiyama, 1950s, 12", EX....$35.00

Circus Lion, Rock Valley, 1950s, with whip and carpet, 10", EXIB, $425.00. (Photo courtesy Smith House Toy & Auction Co.)

Circus Fire Engine, MT, 1960s, tin & plastic, 11", EX....$200.00
Circus Parade, see Big Ring Circus
Circus Queen (Seal), Kosuge, 1950s, 11", rare, MIB....$375.00
Clancy the Great, Ideal, 1960s, MIB....$275.00
Climbing Linesman (Clown), TPS, 1950s, clown climbing metal rod atop vehicle, 24" (assembled), EXIB....$675.00
Clown & Lion, MT, 1960s, clown spins up & down pole as lion roars, tin base 13", NMIB....$325.00
Clown the Magician, Cragstan, #40244, 1950s, cloth costume, 11", VGIB....$200.00
Clucking Clara, CK, 1950s, NM....$50.00
Coffeetime Bear, TN, 1960s, plush & tin, 10", EXIB....$250.00
College Jalopy, Linemar, 10", NMIB....$375.00

Collie, Alps, 1950s, r/c, plush, barks & begs, eyes light up, EXIB $75.00
Comic Choo Choo, Cragstan, 1960s, 10", EX $65.00
Comic Hungry Bug (Volkswagen Beetle), Tora, 1960s, 8", NMIB, A $80.00

Coney Island Penny Machine, Remco, NMIB, $100.00. (Photo courtesy Morphy Auctions)

Coney Island Rocket Ride, Remco, 1950s, 14", EXIB $950.00
Cragstan Crapshooter, Y, 1950s, 9½", NMIB, A $150.00
Cragstan Dog Shuttling Train, Yonezawa, 38" L, NMIB. $125.00
Cragstan Melody Band (Charlie the Drumming Clown), Alps, 1960s, 10", MIB $200.00
Cragstan Melody Band (Daisy the Jolly Drummer Duck), Alps, 1950s, plush & tin, eyes light up, 9", EXIB $200.00
Cragstan Melody Band (Mambo the Jolly Drumming Elephant), 9", EXIB $200.00
Cragstan Overland Stage, Ichida, 1950s, 18", NMIB $175.00
Cragstan Playboy, 1960s, 13", EXIB $125.00
Cragstan Remote Driving-Dashboard Control Car (1959 Buick), Normura, 11½", NMIB $425.00
Cragstan Roulette Man, Y, 1960s, 9", unused, MIB $250.00
Cragstan Telly Bear, S&E, 1950s, plush, tin desk, 9", EXIB .. $275.00
Cragstan Tootin'-Chuggin' Locomotive w/Mystery Action (Santa Fe), tin, 24", EXIB $65.00
Crowing Rooster, Y, 1950s, plush, wht, yel & orange, 9", EXIB $75.00
Cycling Daddy, Bandai, 1960s, 10", EXIB $125.00
Cymbal Playin' Monkey, r/c, lt brn plush w/pointed hat, metal cymbals, 12", VGIB $40.00
Daisy the Jolly Drumming Duck, see Cragstan Melody Band
Dalmatian (The Jolly Drumming Dog), Cragstan, plush, 9", EXIB $150.00
Dancing Dan (w/His Mystery Mike), Bell, 1950s, 16", EXIB. $175.00
Dancing Merry Chimp, Kuramochi, 1960s, 11", NM $150.00
Dancing Sam, litho tin, 11", EX, A $200.00
Dandy the Happy Drumming Pup, Cragstan, 1950s, 9", EXIB $150.00
Dandy Turtle, DSK, 1950s, 8", M $150.00
Dashee the Derby Hat Dachshund, Mego, 1970s, r/c, plush w/ plsatic hat, MIB $80.00
Dennis the Menace (Playing Xylophone), TN, 1950s, 8", EXIB $300.00
Dentist Bear, S&E, 1950s, plush & tin, 10", MIB $150.00
Dilly Dalmatian, Cragstan, 1950s, r/c, plush, 8", VGIB.. $100.00
Dip-ie the Whale, SH, 1960s, 13", M $275.00
Disney Acrobat (Donald Duck), Linemar, celluloid figure on wire apparatus, EXIB, A $450.00
Disney Acrobat (Mickey Mouse), Linemar, celluloid figure on wire apparatus, 9", EXIB $450.00
Disney Piston Race Car, Masudaya, Mickey driver, 9", NMIB .. $200.00
Distant Early Warning Radar Station, see Radar N Scope
Dixie the Dog (Dachshund), Linemar, r/c, 10", EXIB $75.00
Dolly Dressmaker (Seamstress), TN, 1950s, 6", NMIB... $300.00
Donald Duck Locomotive, MT, 1970, tin & plastic, 9", M.. $125.00
Dozo the Steaming Clown, Rosko, 1960s, 14", VGIB $275.00
Dream Boat (Rock 'N Roll Hot Rod), TN, tin, 7", EX... $175.00
Dream Boat (Rock 'N Roll Hot Rod), TN, tin, 7", NMIB. $400.00
Drinking Captain, S&E, cloth outfit, 12", EXIB $125.00
Drinking Dog, Y, plush & tin, NMIB $100.00
Drinking Licking Cat, TN, 1950s, tin & plush, NMIB .. $250.00
Drumming Mickey Mouse (Lighted Eyes), Linemar, r/c, 11", EXIB $925.00
Dune Buggy (w/Surf Board), TPS, w/driver, 10", EXIB .. $100.00
El Toro, TN, 1950s, tin, NMIB $225.00
Electronic Periscope-Firing Range, Cragstan, 1950s, VGIB.. $150.00
Emergency Service Truck, Nomura, tin, AAA on vehicle & driver's back, 9½", NMIB, A $575.00
Expert Motor Cyclist, MT, 1950s, tin, 12", EX $375.00
Father Bear, MT, 1950s, plush, in rocking chair reading & drinking, EXIB $175.00
FBI Godfather Car, Bandai, 1970s, 10", MIB $125.00
Feeding Bird Watcher, Linemar, 1950s, 7", EX+IB $450.00
Fido the Xylophone Player, Alps, 1950s, plush, 9", EXIB . $150.00
Fighter F-50 Jet Plane, KO, 'chunky' plastic plane w/pilot under clear dome, 9", VG+IB $150.00
Fighting Bull, Alps, 1950s, 15", MIB $175.00
Fire Boat, MT, 1950s, 15", MIB $350.00
Fire Tricycle, TN, tin, w/driver, 10", EXIB $650.00

Fishing Bear (Lighted Eyes), Alps, 11", EXIB, $225.00. (Photo courtesy Don Hultzman)

Fishing Panda Bear (Lighted Eyes), Alps, 1950s, plush & tin, 11", EX+IB $275.00
Flexi the Pocket Monkey, ALps, 1960s, 12", MIB $200.00

Flintstone Yacht, Remco, 1960s, 17", NM+ $175.00
Flying Circus, Tomiyco, 14" H, EXIB $650.00
Ford Mustang Fastback 2x2, plastic, lt bl, 16", EXIB (box mk 2x2 Cool & 'Pow!') $150.00
Frankenstein, Poynter, 1970s, mostly plastic, standing on 'rock' base, red & wht striped suit, belly showing, 13", VGIB $100.00
Frankenstein (Mod Monster — Blushing Frankenstein), TN, 1960s, standing on litho tin base w/name, 13", EXIB. $175.00
Frankie the Roller Skating Monkey, Alps, 1950s, r/c, plush w/ cloth outfit, 12", VGIB $115.00
Fred Flintstone's Bedrock Band, Alps, 1960s, 10", MIB.. $750.00
Fred Flintstone's Bedrock Band, Alps, 1960s, 10", VGIB.. $350.00
French Cat, Alps, 1950s, 10" L, MIB $125.00
Friendly Joco My Favorite Pet, Alps, 1950s, r/c, dressed monkey, 10", EXIB $125.00
Funland Cup Ride, Kanto, 7" wide, NMIB $250.00
Galloping Horse & Rider, Cragstan, 12", EXIB $225.00
Gino Neapolitan Balloon Blower, Rosko, 1960s, 11", EX+IB. $175.00
Godzilla Monster, Marusan, 1970s, 12", NMIB $300.00

Good Time Charlie, MT, 1960s, 13", EXIB, $150.00.
(Photo courtesy Don Hultzman)

Gorilla, see also Roaring Gorilla Shooting Gallery, Shooting Gorilla or Walking Gorilla
Gorilla, TN, 1950s, r/c, wht or brn plush, 10", EXIB, ea. $300.00
Grand-Pa Panda Bear, MT, 1950s, plush, in rocker, 9", NMIB..$200.00
Grandpa Bear (Smoking & Rocking w/Lighted Pipe), Alps, plush, 9", EXIB $225.00
Grasshopper, MT, 1950s, 6", M $350.00
Green Caterpillar, Daiya, tin & fabric, 10", NMIB $200.00
Green Hornet Secret Service Car, ASC, 1960s, 11", EX+. $700.00
Gypsy Fortune Teller, Ichida, 1950s, 10", EXIB $1,250.00
Hamburger Chef, K, 1960s, 8", MIB $250.00
Handy-Hank Mystery Tractor w/Light, TN, 1950s, 11", NMIB.. $125.00
Happy 'N Sad Magic Face Clown, Y, 1960s, r/c, 11", EXIB.. $200.00
Happy Band Trio, MT, 1970s, 11", NMIB $500.00
Happy Drive Car, see Speed Star 3
Happy Fiddler Clown, Cragstan, 1950s, cloth outfit, 10", MIB...$500.00
Happy Naughty Chimp, Daishin, 1960s, 10", EXIB $100.00
Happy Santa, Alps, 1950s, r/c, plush, walking w/drum, 11", VGIB $150.00
Happy Singing Bird, MT, 1950s, 3" L, M $75.00
Happy the Clown Puppet Show, Y, 1960s, 10", EXIB $275.00
Hasty Chimp, Y, 1960s, 9", MIB, from $100 to $125.00
High Jinks at the Circus, TN, 1950s, 10", NMIB $225.00
Hobo Accordion Player w/Monkey, Alps/Cragstan, 11", NMIB. $200.00
Hoop Zing Girl, Linemar, 1950s, 12", MIB $365.00
Hoopy the Fishing Duck, Alps, 1950s, 10", NMIB $375.00
Hooty the Happy Owl, Alps, 1960s, 9", EXIB $300.00
Hot Rod #158 (Dream Boat), TN, 1950s, teen driver, 10", NM. $275.00
Hovercraft (Brace), TPS, 1950s, r/c, 8", NMIB $225.00
Hungry Baby Bear, Y, 1950s, plush momma & baby, 9", EXIB..$150.00
Hungry Cat, Linemar, 1960s, cat swipes at fishbowl, 9", EXIB..$500.00
Hungry Hound Dog, Y, 1950s, 10", NMIB $300.00
Hungry Sheep, MT, 1950s, r/c, plush, 8" H, EXIB $200.00
Hy-Que the Amazing Monkey, TN, 1960s, plush, 17", EXIB.. $225.00
I May Look Busy/I'm the Boss (Telephone Bear), see Telephone Bear (I May Look Busy/I'm the Boss)
Ice Cream Baby Bear, MT, 1950s, 10", rare, NM $475.00
Indian Joe, Alps, 1960s, beats drum between legs, 12", VG..$50.00
Indian Signal Choo-Choo, Kanto Toys, 1960s, 10", EXIB...$50.00
Jig-Saw Magic, Z Co, 1950s, 7x7x9", MIB $100.00
Joco the Drinking Monkey, Linemar, 1950s, plush w/plastic face, in tux & top hat, 10", EXIB $115.00
Johnny Speed Mobile, Remco, 1960s, 15", MIB $175.00
Jolly Bambino, Alps, 1950s, plush monkey in highchair, 9", MIB $550.00
Jolly Daddy the Smoking Elephant, Marusan, 1950s, r/c, plush in cloth outfit, 9", VGIB $150.00
Jolly Peanut Vendor, Cragston, plush bear, 9", EXIB $325.00
Jolly Pianist, see Pianist (Jolly Pianist)
Journey Pup, S&E, 1950s, 8" L, M $50.00
Jumbo (the Elephant), Alps, 1960s, r/c, plush w/circus blanket & headdress, picks up pole w/trunk, 10" H, VGIB $175.00
Jumbo the Bubble Blowing Elephant, Y, 1950s, 7", NMIB...$125.00
Jumping Rabbit (Light-Up Eyes), Japan, 1950s, 10", NMIB, A.. $95.00
Jungle Jumbo, BN-C Toy, 1950s, hunter on elephant, 10", EXIB $125.00

Jungle Trio, Linemar, 8", NMIB, $750.00. (Photo courtesy Morphy Auctions)

King Zor, Ideal, 1961, 26" L, very rare, M $500.00
Kissing Couple, Ichido, 1950s, 11", MIB $350.00

Knight in Armor Target Game, 1950s, 12" figure, NMIB . $500.00
Knitting Grandma (Lighted Eyes), TN, 1950s, plush bear, 9", VGIB........ $175.00
Lady Pup Tending Her Garden, Cragstan, 1950s, cloth outfit, 9", EXIB........ $250.00
Laughing Clown (Robot), Waco, mc plastic, 14", NMIB . $200.00
Leo the Growling Pet Lion (w/Magic Face-Change Action), Tomiyama, 1970s, 9", MIB $275.00
Light-A-Wheel Lincoln, Rosko, 1950s, bump-&-go action, 11", NM........ $150.00
Linemar Music Hall, 6", EXIB........ $150.00
Lite-O-Wheel Go-Kart, Rosko, 1950s, 11", EXIB $175.00
Little Indian, TN, 1960s, 9", rare, NM........ $175.00
Little Poochie in Coffee Cup, Alps, 1960s, 9", M........ $75.00
Loop the Loop Clown, TN, 1960s, 12", EXIB........ $75.00
Lucky Cement Mixer Truck, MT, 1960s, 12", M $125.00
Mac the Turtle w/The (Whiskey) Barrel, Y, 1960s, 9", EXIB. $175.00
Magic Action Bulldozer, TN, 1950s, 10", MIB $150.00
Magic Beetle, Linemar, 7", EXIB........ $55.00
Magic Man (Clown), Marusan, 1950s, r/c, puffs smoke, 12", EXIB........ $250.00
Magic Snow Man, MT, 1950s, w/broom, 11", EXIB $150.00
Main Street, Linemar 1950s, 20", rare, MIB $1,200.00
Major Tooty (Drum Major), Alps, tin, 11", NM+IB........ $175.00
Mambo the Jolly Drumming Elephant, see Cragstan Melody Band
Man From UNCLE Headquarters Transmitter, NMIB ... $200.00
Marching Bear, Alps, 1960s, plush, drums/cymbals, 10", EXIB ...$125.00
Marshal Wild Bill, Y, 1950s, r/c, cloth outfit, 11", VGIB.. $150.00
Marvelous Locomotive, 1950s, TN, 10", M $50.00
Maxwell Coffee-Loving Bear, TN, 1960s, plush & tin, 10", EXIB........ $250.00
McGregor, TN/Rosko import/Japan, 1960s, tin figure seated on trunk holding cane, cloth outfit, 12", MIB, A $275.00
Mechanical Toy, Santa in Reindeer Sleigh (Mystery Action), b/o, 17", MT, 1950s, EXIB........ $300.00
Melody Camping Car, Y, 1970s, 10", NM $150.00
Mew-Mew the Walking Cat, MT, 1950s, r/c, plush, 7", VGIB.. $85.00
Mexicali Pete the Drum Player, Alps, 1960s, 10", EXIB. $175.00
Mickey Mouse & Donald Duck Fire Truck, MT, 1960s, 16", EXIB........ $325.00
Mickey Mouse Locomotive, MT, 1960s, 9", NM $175.00
Mickey the Magician, Linemar, 1960s, 10", NMIB...... $1,750.00
Mickey the Magician, Linemar, 1960s, 10", VG........ $650.00
Mini Poodle w/Bone, TN/Rosko, 1950s, r/c, plush, 11" L, NMIB........ $75.00
Mischief (Mischievous Monkey), MT, 1950s, 13", EXIB. $250.00
Miss Friday the Typist, TN, 1950s, 8" H, EXIB........ $225.00
Monkee Mobile, ASC, 1960s, 12", EX........ $325.00
Monkee Mobile, ASC, 1960s, 12", EXIB........ $575.00
Monkey on a Picnic, Cragstan, plush, 10", EXIB........ $200.00
Monkey the Shoe Maker, TN, 1950s, 9", rare, NMIB $500.00
Monorail Set, Haji, 1950s, complete, EXIB $175.00
Mother Bear (Sitting & Knitting in Her Old Rocking Chair), MT, 1950s, plush, 10", EXIB $200.00
Mother Duck & Baby, see Worried Mother Duck & Baby
Mother Goose, Cragstan, plush, 10", VGIB........ $75.00
Mr Al-E-Gator (Amazing) Alps, 1950s, 12", unused, MIB, A....$215.00
Mr Baseball, see All Stars Mr Baseball Jr

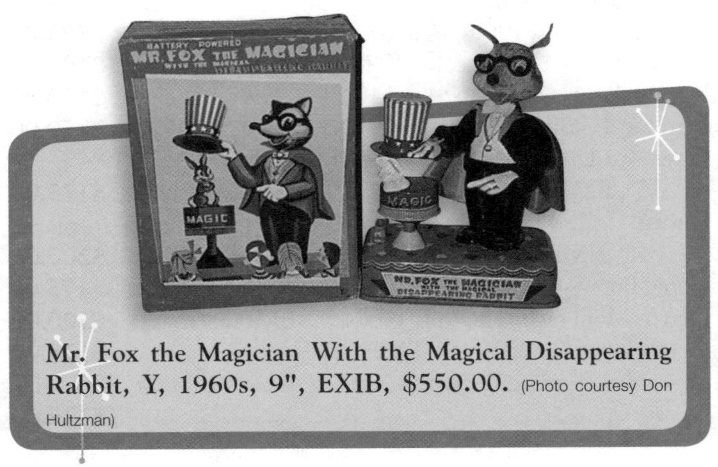

Mr. Fox the Magician With the Magical Disappearing Rabbit, Y, 1960s, 9", EXIB, $550.00. (Photo courtesy Don Hultzman)

Mr Fox the Magician (w/The Magical Disappearing Rabbit), Y, 1960s, 9", NM........ $325.00
Mr Magoo Car, Hubley, 1960s, 9", EXIB........ $275.00
Mr McPooch Taking a Walk & Smoking His Pipe, SAN, 1950s, r/c, EXIB $175.00
Mumbo Jumbo Hawaiian Dancer, Alps, 1960s, 10", MIB. $275.00
Mumbo Jumbo Hawaiian Drummer, Alps, 1960s, 10", VG .$125.00
Musical Comic Jumping Jeep, Alps, 12", M........ $175.00
Musical Ice Cream Truck, Bandai, 1960s, 11", NM........ $150.00
Musical Jackal, Linemar, 1950s, 10", very rare, MIB....... $750.00

Musical Jolly Chimp, C-K, 1960s, 10", EXIB, $80.00.

Musical Marching Bear, Alps, 1950s, r/c, 10", NMIB..... $400.00
Musical Melody Mixer, Taiyo, 1970s, 11", M........ $100.00
Mystery Action Tractor, Japan, 1950s, 7", MIB $150.00
Mystery Plane, TN, 1950s, 10", EXIB $250.00
Mystery Police Car, TN, 1960s, 10", NM........ $150.00
Naughty Dog & Busy Bee, MT, plush, 10", EXIB $65.00
NBC Television/RCA Victor Truck, Linemar, 9", VG+, A .$500.00
Nutty Nibbs, Linemar, 12", EXIB........ $950.00
O-Mar-X (Western Style Music Box), Linemar, 5", NMIB, A..$250.00
Ol' Sleepy Head RIP, Y/Toy-A-Joy Spesco import, 1950s, 9", NM........ $300.00
Overland Staqe Coach, MT, 1950s, 15", EXIB $175.00
Pa Pa Bear, Marusan, r/c, standing smoking pipe, 9", MIB. $100.00

Peppermint Twist Doll, Haji, 1950s, 12", EXIB $250.00
Peppy Puppy w/Bone, Y, 1950s, 7", M $75.00
Perky Pup, Alps, 1960s, r/c, plush, 8½", MIB, A................$75.00
Pesky Pup the Shoe Steeler, Y, 1950s, 8", M $100.00
Pet Turtle, Alps, 1960s, 8", NMIB.................................... $150.00
Pete the Talking Parrot, TN, 1950s, 18", M.................... $250.00
Peter the Drumming Rabbit (Lighting Eyes), Alps, 1950s, r/c, 12", EXIB $175.00
Pianist (Jolly Pianist), Marusan, 1950s, plush dog at tin piano, 8½", NMIB.. $200.00
Picnic Bunny (It Drinks), Alps, 1950s, plush, 10", NMIB. $175.00
Pierrot Monkey Cycle, MT, 1950s, 9", EXIB.................. $300.00
Piggy Cook, Y, 1950s, 10", EXIB $175.00
Pinky the Juggling Clown, Japan, 1950s, cloth outfit, 19", MIB, A $275.00

Pinocchio Playing Xylophone, Rosco, 9½", EXIB, $225.00. (Photo courtesy Bertoia Auctions)

Pioneer Covered Wagon, Ichida, 1960s, 15", EXIB........ $125.00
Pipie the Whale, Alps, 1950s, 12", NM $200.00
Pistol Pete, Marusan, 1950s, 10", EXIB.......................... $350.00
Playful Puppy w/Caterpillar, MT, 8" H, EXIB $125.00
Playing Monkey, S&E, 10", NMIB................................... $150.00
Pluto, Illco/WDP, 1960s or 1970s, r/c plastic, 5x10", MIB. $150.00
Pluto, Linemar, 1960s, r/c, plush, 10", EXIB $65.00
Pluto Lantern, Linemar, tin figure w/glass middle, 7", EX+IB.. $250.00
Police Car, Japan, 1950s, policeman in wht open car w/siren on hood, bump-&-go action, 10" L, NM, A $85.00
Popcorn Eating Bear, MT, 1950s, EX $150.00
Popeye & Olive Oyl Tumbling Buggy, Hong Kong, 1981, 7", NMIB..$60.00
Popeye Lantern, Linemar, litho tin figure w/glass middle, 7½", EXIB.. $550.00
Pretty Peggy Parrot, Rosko, plush, 11", NMIB............... $275.00
Professor Owl, Y, 1950s, 8", NMIB................................ $425.00
Puffy Morris (Cigarette Smoker), Rosko, Y, 1960s, uses real cigarettes, 11", NMIB... $275.00
Quick Draw McGraw Target Car w/Baba Looie, EXIB... $200.00
Rabbits & the Carriage, S&E, 1950s, 9", NMIB............ $275.00
Rambling Ladybug, MT, 1960s, 8", EX.............................$75.00
Red Gulch Bar (Western Bad Man), MT, 1960s, 10", VGIB. $450.00
Rembrandt the Monkey Artist, Alps, 1950s, 8", rare, NMIB .. $350.00

Rex Doghouse, Tel-E-Toy, 1950s, 5", M $125.00
River Steam Boat (w/Whistle & Smoke), MT, 14", VGIB..$75.00
Roaring Gorilla Shooting Gallery, MT, 1950s, 9", NMIB. $225.00
Robo Tank TR2, TN, 1960s, 6", NM+........................... $175.00
Rock 'N Roll Monkey (Auto-Matic), Alps, 1950s, 12", EXIB....$250.00
Rocky (Fred Flintstone look-alike), Japan, tin, 4", NMIB, A .. $100.00

Root Beer Stand, K, 1960s, 8x8", NM, $150.00. (Photo courtesy Don Hultzman)

Sam the Shaving Man, Plaything Toy Co, 1960s, 12", EXIB... $175.00
Sammy Wong the Tea Totaler, Rosko/TN, 1950s, 10", EXIB.. $200.00
Sea Hawk Future Car, Japan, 1964, driver seated under plastic dome, 12", EX, A $385.00
Shark U-Control Race Car, Remco #610, 1961, 10", unused, MIB, A $165.00
Shoe Shine Bear (Lighted Pipe), TN, 1950s, 9", EXIB .. $200.00
Shooting Bear, Marusan, 1950s, r/c, plush, 10", EXIB $275.00
Shutter Bug, TN, 1950s, 9", EX, A................................. $275.00
Shutter Bug, TN, 1950s, 9", NMIB $800.00
Shuttling Train & Freight Yard, Alps, 1950s, 16", EXIB.. $100.00
Skating Circus Clown, TPS, 1950s, r/c, 6", VGIB....... $1,500.00
Skipping Monkey, TN, 1960s, jumps rope, 10", EXIB $65.00
Sleeping Baby Bear, Linemar, 10", VGIB....................... $225.00
Smokey Bill on Old-Fashioned Car, TN, 1960s, 9", MIB . $250.00
Smoking & Shoe Shining Panda Bear, Alps, 1950s, 10", EXIB..$250.00
Smoking Bunny, Cragstan, r/c, plush, NMIB $200.00
Smoking Grandpa (in Rocker), SAN, 1950s, 9", NMIB . $350.00
Smoking Pa Pa Bear, SAN, r/c, 8", EXIB $100.00
Smoking Popeye, Linemar, 1950s, 9", NM.................. $1,500.00
Smoky Bear, SAN, 1950s, r/c, EXIB.............................. $350.00
Smurf Choo Choo w/Headlight, Durham Industries, 1980s, unused, MIB...$40.00
Snake Charmer, Linemar, 1950s, 8", NMIB................... $575.00
Snappy Puppy, Alps, 1960s, plush, 9", VGIB....................$50.00
Sneezing Bear (Lighted Eyes), Linemar, 1950s, 9", EXIB.. $200.00
Space Patrol (Snoopy), MT, 1960s, 12", EXIB............... $200.00
Space Traveling Monkey, Yanoman, 1960s, 9", EXIB..... $125.00
Spanking Bear, Linemar, 1950s, 10", EXIB $200.00
Sparky the Seal, TN, 1950s, 7" L, NMIB, A $72.00
Speed Star 3 (Happy Drive Car), Nomura, litho tin w/vinyl driver, 8", NMIB, A $160.00

Squirmy Hermy the Snake, HTC, r/c, 12", NMIB.......... $225.00
Strange Explorer, DSK, 1960s, 8", EXIB........................ $275.00
Strutting My Fair Dancer, Haji, 1950s, 9", EXIB............ $275.00
Super Susie, Linemar, 1950s, 8x6", EXIB........................ $500.00
Superman (Army) Tank, Linemar, 8½", EXIB, A........$1,650.00
Suzette the Eating Monkey, Linemar, 1950s, 9", EXIB... $475.00
Suzette the Eating Monkey, Linemar, 1950s, 9", G......... $150.00
Swimming Duck, Bandai, 1950s, 8", rare, NM..................$75.00
Swimming Fish, Koshibe, 1950s, 11", NM..................... $125.00
Switchboard Operator, Linemar, 1950s, 7", EXIB........... $500.00
Talking Batmobile, Palitoy (Hong Kong)/DC Comics, 1977, 10", NM+IB, A.. $175.00
Tarzan, Marusan, 1966, 13", NMIB (Japanese box)........ $975.00
Taxi Cab, Y, 1970s, rear side door opens, bump-&-go, blinking lights, turning meter, 9", MIB, A...............................$80.00
Teddy Balloon Blowing Bear, Alps, 1950s, 11", EXIB..... $125.00
Teddy Bear Swing, TN, 1950s, bear on trapeze, 14", NMIB..$550.00
Teddy Go-Kart, Alps, 1960s, 10", EXIB......................... $175.00
Teddy the Artist, Electro Toy/Y, 1950s, 10", EXIB.......... $425.00
Teddy the Champ Boxer, Y, 1950s, 10", EXIB............... $175.00
Telephone Bear, Linemar, 1950s, 9", EXIB.................... $250.00
Telephone Bear (I May Look Busy/I'm the Boss), Linemar, 1950s, bear at desk, 8", EXIB.. $275.00
Telephone Bear (Ringing & Talking in His Old Rocking Chair), MT, 1950s, 10", EXIB... $275.00
Telephone Rabbit (Ringing & Talking in Her Old Rocking Chair), MT, 1950s, 10", EXIB................................ $275.00
Tin Man Robot (The Wizard of Oz), Remco, 1969, plastic, 21", MIB.. $200.00
Tom & Jerry Car, Rico/Spain, 13", NMIB....................... $575.00

Tom and Jerry Comic Car, MT, 11", EX+IB, A, $250.00. (Photo courtesy Smith House Toy & Auction Co.)

Tom Tom Indian, Y, 1960s, 11", NMIB.......................... $125.00
Topo Gigio Xylophone Player, TN, 1960s, 11", rare, MIB. $750.00
Tractor (Robot Driver/Visible Lighted Piston Movement), Linemar, 1950s, 10", MIB.. $425.00
Traveler Bear, K, 1950s, r/c, 8", NMIB.......................... $250.00
Traveler Bear, K, 1950s, r/c, 8", VG $100.00
Tric-Cycling Clown, MT, 1960s, 12", EX+IB................. $300.00
Trik-Trak Cross Country Road Rally, Transogram, 1966, complete, NMIB, A..$50.00
Trumpet Monkey, Alps, 1950s, 10", EXIB...................... $225.00
Tugboat (w/Realistic Noises & Puffs of Real Smoke...), SAN/Cragstan, 1950s, 13", EXIB..................................... $175.00
Tumbles the Bear, YM, 1960s, 9", NMIB....................... $150.00
Tumbling Bozo the Clown, Sonsco, 1970s, 8", M.............$75.00
Twirly Whirly Rocket Ride, Alps, 1950s, 13", EXIB....... $500.00
Two-Gun Sheriff, Cragstan, r/c, 10", EXIB.................... $200.00
Union Mountain Monorail, TN, 1950s, MIB................. $225.00
US Air Force F-105, lg-figured pilot in open cockpit, 11" L, EX, A.. $275.00
US Army Light Bulldog Tank, Remco, 1960s, plastic, 9" (15" w/gun barrel), fires plastic shells, MIB, A............... $275.00
VIP the Busy Boss, S&E, 1950s, 8", EXIB...................... $200.00
V8 Roadster, Daiya, vinyl-headed driver, 11", VG+, A.. $190.00
Waddles Family Car, Y, 1960s, MIB.............................. $100.00
Wagon Master, MT, 1960s, 18", NM.............................. $150.00
Wal-Boot Hobo, Tomy, 1960s, 20", NM $100.00
Walking Bear w/Xylophone, Linemar, 1950s, 10", EXIB. $350.00
Walking Donkey, Linemar, 1950s, r/c, 9", VGIB............ $150.00
Walking Elephant, Linemar, 1950s, r/c, 9" H, VGIB.........$75.00
Walking Elephant (Carrying Free Flying Ball), MT, 1950s, r/c, 9", EXIB... $100.00
Walking Gorilla, Linemar, r/c, 7", NMIB....................... $275.00
Walking Horse (Cowboy Rider), Linemar, 1950s, r/c, 7", EXIB.. $350.00
Wee Little Baby Bear (Reading Bear/Lighted Eyes), Alps, 10", EXIB.. $375.00
Western Bad Man, see Red Gulch Bar
Western Style Music Box, see O-Mar-X
Whistling Hobo, Waco, 1960s, 13", EXIB...................... $100.00
Windy the Juggling Elephant, TN, 1950s, 10", EX+IB... $200.00
Worried Mother Duck & Baby, TN, 1950s, 7", MIB...... $150.00
Xylophone Ace, 1950s, 6" L, NM $50.00
Yo-yo Clown, S&E, 1960s, 10", rare, MIB...................... $425.00

Bicycles and Tricycles

The most interesting of the vintage bicycles are those made from the 1920s into the 1960s, though a few later models are collectible as well. Some of the '50s models were very futuristic and styled with sweeping Art Deco lines; others had wonderful features such as built-in radios and brake lights, and some were decked out with saddlebags and holsters to appeal to fans of Hoppy, Gene, and other western heroes. Watch for reproductions.

Condition is everything when evaluating bicycles, and one worth $2,500.00 in excellent or better condition might be worth as little as $50.00 in unrestored, poor condition. But here are a few values to suggest a range.

Note: A girl's bicycle does not command the price as a boy's bicycle in the same model. The value could be from ⅓ to ½ less than a boy's.

Advisor: Richard Trautwein

AMF Spiderman Jr Roadmaster, boy's, 1978, EX........... $100.00
Cleveland Deluxe Roadmaster, boy's, prewar, light on front fender, horn on tank, rear carrier, 24", EX.............. $375.00
Colson Bullnose, boy's, 1939, light on front fender, EX rstr . $1,800.00
Columbia Airrider, boy's, 1940-42, EX.......................... $800.00

Columbia Superb, boy's, 1941, VG, from $300 to.......... $525.00
Columbia 3-Speed Playbike, boy's, 1970s-80s, VG...........$75.00
Elgin Blackhawk, boy's, 1934, rstr $2,000.00
Elgin Bluebird, boy's, 1936, VG.................................. $7,000.00
Elgin Deluxe, girl's, 1940, G, from $350 to $550.00
Elgin Robin, boy's, 1937, G $1,600.00
Elgin Sport Model, girl's, 1940s, G, from $350 to $550.00
Evans, boy's, 1960s, middleweight truss frame, G $75.00
Hawthorn Comet, boy's, Montgomery Ward, 1938, EX, from $600 to $800.00

Hawthorn Zep, boy's, 1939, with dual Silver Ray lights, leather seat, Riverside white-wall tires, VG, from $2,500.00 to $3,000.00. (Photo courtesy Copake Auction, Inc.)

Huffy American Thunderbird, boy's, 1960s, G, from $75 to. $100.00
Huffy BMX, boy's, 1970s, VG, from $100 to.................. $150.00
Huffy Radio, boy's, 1955, orig pnt & graphics, EX....... $2,900.00
Humber Sports Classic English 3-Speed, boy's, 1960s, Strumy Archer gears & handbreaks, rear book rack, EX...... $100.00
JC Higgins, boy's, Winderide Spring Fork, EX, from $800 to. $900.00
JC Higgins Flow Motion, girl's, 1948, G, from $100 to... $150.00
JC Higgins Murray, boy's, 1948, rstr, from $150 to.......... $200.00
Monarch Firestone Pilot, boy's, 1941, chrome headlight & rear rack, VG $400.00
Monarch Silver King Model M1, boy's, 1938, EX........... $900.00
Monarch Silver King Wingbar, girl's, 1939, EX $600.00
Moulton Mark III, boy's, 1970, G................................... $325.00
Murray Fire Cat, boy's, 1977, VG.................................. $250.00
Raleigh Chopper, boy's, 1970s, EX, from $150 to $250.00
Raleigh Space Rider 3-Speed, boy's, 1968, EX............... $150.00
Raleigh Superb 3-Speed, girl's, Brooks saddle, G, from $75 to. $100.00
Roadmaster Luxury Liner, girl's, 26", EX, from $500 to .. $700.00
Schwinn American Bendix 2-Speed, boy's, 1960, w/Cadet speedometer, G, from $75 to $100.00
Schwinn Bantam, girl's, 1960, G.......................................$75.00
Schwinn Black Phantom, girl's, 1950s, balloon tires, rstr.. $800.00
Schwinn Fair Lady, 1960s, VG $125.00
Schwinn Green Phantom, boy's, 1951, 26", EX............. $700.00
Schwinn Grey Ghost Sting Ray 5-Speed, boy's, 1971, rstr. $650.00
Schwinn Lady's Standard Model BC308, VG, from $100 to. $200.00
Schwinn Mark IV Jaguar, boy's, 1960s, West Wind tires, VG. $800.00
Schwinn Model B, girl's, spring fork & fender headlight, VG. $250.00
Schwinn Red Phantom, boy's, 1950s, rstr $1,000.00
Schwinn Sting Ray, girl's, 1970s, G....................................$55.00
Sears Free Spirit, boy's, 1960s, EX, from $100 to $150.00
Sears Spaceliner, boy's, 1960s, G, from $100 to $150.00
Shelby Donald Duck, boy's, yel w/bl trim, Donald Duck head mounted under handlebars, NM+ (NOS) $5,500.00
Shelby Donald Duck, girl's, bl w/yel trim, Donald Duck head mounted under handlebars, NM+ (NOS), A $4,000.00
Shelby Traveler, boy's, 1938, G $175.00
Swiss Army, boy's, 1941, VG, from $700 to $1,000.00
Vista Banana 3-Speed, boy's, 1970s, 20", M, from $200 to. $550.00
Western Flyer Buzz Bike 2+1, boy's, 1960-70, G............ $300.00

Tricycles

AMF Junior Tow-Trike, w/Delta front light, cleated tires, rear boom w/crank & chain pulley, NM......................... $350.00
Art Deco, airflow-type wheel covers on all 3 wheels, bell on handlebars, padded seat, 30" L, EX rstr $350.00
Art Deco, back airflow-type rear wheel covers on 2 back wheels, straight handlebars, 26" L, EX rstr.......................... $425.00
Bell Car, name stenciled on paddle-formed seat, 27" L, VG. $230.00
Boycraft Handcar, 32½" L, G, A $230.00
Colson Fairy, 1920s, chain drive, EX rstr $375.00
Early American, CI w/wooden seat & handlebars, VG .. $575.00
Gendron Pioneer, no fenders, 19½", G $375.00
Jaxon, 1950s, w/unusual rear 3 wheels, hard tires, G $350.00
Mattel V-Room! Trike, w/plastic engine, 35", EX.............$60.00
Monark Silver King, 1939, extremely rare, VG $5,250.00
Murray Airflow Jr, 17½", G... $200.00
Pony Tricycle, hide-covered pony w/leather trappings, sulky seat w/metal trim, 3 spoke wheels, 39" L, VG, A........... $180.00

Steelcraft Streamline, red and white, 28", M restoration, A, from $500.00 to $800.00. (Photo courtesy Morphy Auctions)

Sterling Speedway Racer, w/chain gears, flat wooden seat & handlebars, 46" L, VG, A $600.00

Black Americana

Black subjects were commonly depicted in children's toys as long ago as the late 1870s. Among the most widely collected today are the fine windup toys made both here and in Germany. Early cloth and later composition and vinyl dolls are favorites of many; others enjoy ceramic figurines. Many factors enter into evaluating Black Americana, especially in regard to the handmade dolls and toys, since quality is subjective to individual standards. Because of this, you may find wide ranges in asking prices.

Advisor: Judy Posner

See also Banks; Battery-Operated Toys; Schoenhut; Windup, Friction, and Other Mechanical Toys.

Banjo, plastic w/image of various figures around steamboat spewing musical notes from 2 stacks, 22", EX $250.00

Bank, lithographed tin cabin with image of girl dancing to banjo player's tune, Chein, 3", EX, A, $400.00.

(Photo courtesy James D. Julia, Inc.)

Bank, litho tin clown bust sticks out tongue to receive coin, 5½", VG, A $360.00

Bank, litho tin cylindrical man figure in straw hat playing banjo, figure gets taller as money is added, 6", VG+, A...... $220.00

Book, Little Colored Boy & Other Stories, Abingdon Press, undated but from 1800s, hardback, EX $125.00

Book, Treasury of Steven Foster, Random House, 1st ed, 1946, hardback, EX...$55.00

Book, Uncle Tom's Cabin, Harriet Beecher Stowe, John P Jewett & Co, Boston, 1853, 36 pgs, softcover, G $400.00

Candy Container, molded cb watermelon shape w/smiling face, opens to reveal celluloid doll, 4" L, G+ $175.00

Doll, Baby Grumpy, Effanbee, compo head, arms & legs, molded hair, pnt features, cloth dress, 12", EX, A $375.00

Doll, girl, Armand Marseille, ca 1920s, wood & compo body w/ bisque head, wig, re-dressed, 18", EX, A $175.00

Doll, girl, Bebe Bru Jne 5, kid body w/bisque head, shoulders, arms & legs, 16½", VG+, A................................$52,250.00

Doll, girl, Simon & Halbig #0949, compo body w/brn bisque socket head, wig, glass eyes, jtd, red dress, 20", VG+, A $2,750.00

Doll, girl, Simon & Halbig #1039, compo jtd body w/bisque head, orig dress & shoes, 19", EX, A $2,475.00

Doll, Golliwog, handcrafted, knitted, yarn hair, red coat w/tails, bl pants, turq shoes, wht bow tie, 1950s-60s, 13", EX..$38.00

Doll, Kewpie, Rose O'Neill, blk bisque w/red shield logo on chest, jtd arms, 8½", EXIB, A $2,200.00

Doll, Leslie, Madame Alexander, 1960s, vinyl w/long brn hair, jtd shoulders & hips, orig dress, 17", EXIB, A.......... $250.00

Doll, Leslie Bride, Madame Alexander, 1966-71, rooted hair, complete orig bridal outfit w/bouquet, 17", EXIB, A $150.00

Doll, Miss Golli, R John Wright, stuffed felt w/mohair wig, felt outfit, leather shoes, glancing eyes, 11", MIB, A $300.00

Doll, toddler, Heubeck Koppelsdorf #444, brn-pnt bisque body, blk wig, sleep eyes, closed red mouth, 12", VG, A... $330.00

Game, Bean-Em, All Fair, 1930s, EX+IB $275.00

Game, Chuckler's Game, USA, 1930s, EXIB $100.00

Game, Comic Conversation Cards, Ottman, complete, EXIB..$135.00

Game, Five Little 'N' Boys (Target), Chad Valley, w/rubber band gun, VGIB, A $220.00

Game, Jolly Darky Target Game, McLoughlin Bros, EXIB, A.$385.00

Game, Little Black Sambo, Cadaco-Ellis, 1940s, complete, EXIB.. $100.00

Game, Poosh-M-Up Senior Bagatelle, Northwestern Prod, 1933, 24x14", EX, A...$75.00

Game, Snake Eyes, Selchow & Richter, 1940s, EXIB........$85.00

Game, Watch On De Rind, All Fair, 1931, NMIB......... $675.00

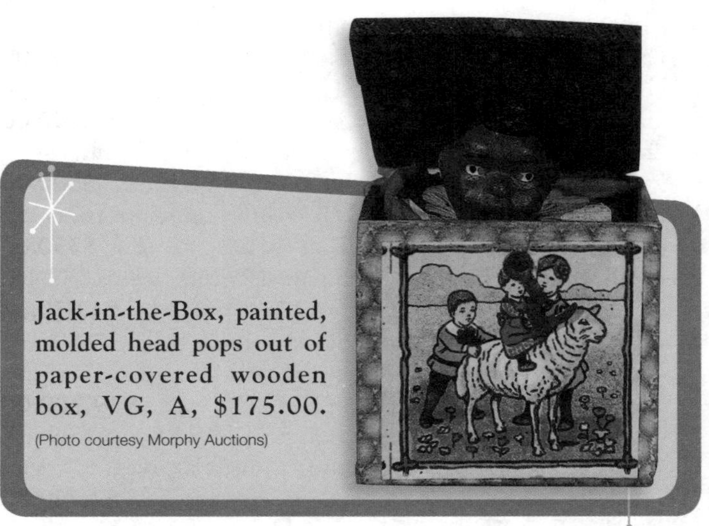

Jack-in-the-Box, painted, molded head pops out of paper-covered wooden box, VG, A, $175.00.

(Photo courtesy Morphy Auctions)

Jack-in-the-Box, man in top hat pops up in wood box w/paper images on sides, 7" H, VG, A $500.00

Marionette, banjo player, wood, cloth outfit, 13", Pelham, MIB... $200.00

Mechanical Toy, Bones Player, Jerome Secor, 1870s, w/up, seated cloth-dressed figure on wooden base, 11", NM+, A...$42,000.00

Mechanical Toy, Boxers on Wooden Box, Ives, Pat 1876, cloth-dressed figures, 8¼" L, EX, A $4,950.00

Mechanical Toy, Boy Drummer, celluloid, 8", NM, A $125.00

Mechanical Toy, Colored Dancer, Ives, 1875, w/up, articulated cloth-dressed figure on litho tin drum, 10", VG, A . $935.00

Mechanical Toy, Dancers (Sam & Bess) on Wooden Box, Ives, 1854 MO, hand-crank, VG, A $825.00

Mechanical Toy, Dancers (2 Ladies) on Wooden Box, Ives, 1880, cloth dress, decal of woman's profile on box, 7x11", EX...$990.00

Mechanical Toy, Dancing Dan, b/o, plastic, 13½", NMIB, A..$100.00

Mechanical Toy, Dancing Man at Street Sign (Lenox Ave/125 St), celluloid w/cloth outfit, 8", VG, A.................. $275.00
Mechanical Toy, Elderly Lady in Headscarf Standing w/ Cane & Holding Basket, w/up, pnt tin, 7", German, EX, A $950.00
Mechanical Toy, Gely, German, litho tin w/up, 6", VG, A..$450.00
Mechanical Toy, Greyhound/World Bus, Marusan, 1930s, tin, friction, blk lady in rear w/all-wht passengers, 13", EX, A.. $900.00
Mechanical Toy, Hot Mammy, Fisher-Price #810, w/up, wooden head & lead feet, cloth dress, 6", EXIB, A $800.00
Mechanical Toy, Jigger, polychromed carved wood, jtd, stick in back operates movements, 12", EX, A $715.00
Mechanical Toy, Jolly Sambo, litho tin head talker in top hat atop box mechanisim, 7", VG+, A.......................... $300.00
Mechanical Toy, Mammy Standing Holding Basket, German, w/up, pnt tin, pk dress w/wht apron, 7", VG, A....... $350.00
Mechanical Toy, man w/backside molded to horn playing cymbols atop drum when string is pulled, litho tin, 5", EX, A....$75.00
Mechanical Toy, Minstrel Seated Playing Accordion, Gunthermann, litho tin body w/pnt face, paper bellows, 7", VG+, A..$1,760.00
Mechanical Toy, Old Aunt Chloe (Washerwoman), Ives, ca 1880, w/up, cloth-dressed figure at washtub on wooden base, NM+ $11,200.00
Mechanical Toy, Old Kentucky Home, crank-op, 6 paper litho figures dance in 10x15" wooden box, EX, A $2,250.00
Mechanical Toy, Poor Pete, w/up, celluloid w/cloth outfit, eating watermelon while dog bites his rear, 5½" H, EX+.... $500.00
Mechanical Toy, Roller Skater w/Tray, litho tin, cloth pants, 6", VG, A $350.00
Mechanical Toy, Shoo-Fly Champion Dancers, w/up, 2 cloth-dressed figures on wooden stage, 10½", VG, A $1,050.00
Mechanical Toy, Tambourine Player, Jerome Secor, 1870s, w/up, seated cloth-dressed figure on wooden base, 11", NM, A $39,200.00
Mechanical Toy, The Advocate (Governor Add Ryman/Subject School Question...San Francisco Minstrels), Ives, 10", VG, A $2,750.00
Mechanical Toy, Washer Woman (Old Aunt Cloe), Ives, 1890, w/up, cloth-dressed figure at washtub on box, 10" H, VG, A.. $5,225.00
Noisemaker, litho tin w/imge of dancing minstrel & party highlights on gr, US Metal Toy Mfg Co, 5x3", EX............$22.00
Premium, Sambo's Restaurant Family Fun Book, Fun Games & Puzzles Featuring JT & the Tiger Kids, 1978, EX........$28.00
Puppet, boy or girl, flannel cloth bodies w/vinyl heads, pnt features, Hazelle, 1950s, MIP, ea $60.00
Puppet Set, grandparents, parents & 3 children, pnt rubber, 8½", Child Craft, 1965, EX+ $60.00
Puppet Set, Multicultural Family, set of 5, cloth bodies w/vinyl heads, Learning Rescources, 1990s, unused, MIB.......$25.00
Puzzle, fr-tray, Little Black Sambo giving jacket to tiger, 1930s, VG $35.00
Record, Brave Little Sambo, 78 rpm, Peter Pan, 1950s, red vinyl, G (G sleeve w/8 color pictures).................................$50.00
Squeeze Toy, golliwog figure, pnt rubber, 4", Robertson's Marmalade premium, 1950s, EX+...................................... $100.00
Tea Set, matt porc w/golliwog graphics by Florence Upton, 5 pcs, 1904, M.. $250.00
Turtle, yel & gr cloth body w/blk & wht circles on back, gr vinyl head w/lg molded 'bug' eyes, Hazelle, 1960s, MIP $45.00

Roly Poly, clown, molded and painted composition, VG, A, $225.00. (Photo courtesy Morphy Auctions)

Boats

Though some commercially made boats date as far back as the late 1800s, they were produced on a much larger scale during WWI and the decade that followed and again during the years that spanned WWII. Some were scaled-down models of battleships measuring nearly three feet in length. While a few were actually seaworthy, many were designed with small wheels to be pulled along the floor or out of doors on dry land. Some were steam powered while others were windups or even battery-operated. Some of the larger manufacturers were Bing (Germany), Dent (Pennsylvania), Orkin Craft (California), Liberty Playthings (New York), and Arnold (West Germany).

Advisor: Richard Trautwein

See also Battery-Operated Toys; Cast Iron, Boats; Paper-Lithographed Toys; Tootsietoys; Windup, Friction, and Other Mechanical Toys; other specific categories or manufacturers.

Aircraft Carrier CVA56, Nomura, friction, lithographed tin, 12", NM+IB, A, $735.00. (Photo courtesy Smith House Toy & Auction Co.)

Aircraft Carrier, Marx, litho tin, 20", b/o, many accessories, EXIB, A....... $355.00
Armada (Battleship w/5 Smaller Cruisers), Hess, litho tin, 8" battleship & 5" cruisers, EX, A....... $880.00
Atomic Submarine 571, Linemar, litho tin, 14½", r/c, fires missiles, M (EX+ box), A....... $345.00
Atomic Warship, Marx, 26", needs assembly, unused, M (VG box)....... $200.00
Battleship, Bing, pnt tin, 20", w/up, 2-tone gray, 2 stacks & fire towers, EX, A....... $2,475.00
Battleship, Bing, pnt tin, 31", w/up, gray w/red bottom, 4 stacks & 2 masts, multiple turrets, rstr, A....... $3,025.00
Battleship, Carette, pnt tin, 23", w/up, 2-tone gray w/red trim, 3 stacks, rstr, A....... $1,650.00
Battleship, Dayton Hill Climber, PS, 13", w/up, 2 wooden masts, 2 stacks & lifeboats, EX, A....... $700.00
Battleship, Fleischmann, pnt tin, 17", w/up, wht & bl w/red deck, 2 stacks, turrets & masts, rstr, A....... $1,430.00
Battleship, Fleischmann, pnt tin, 18", w/up, gray & wht w/blk & red trim, 3 stacks, 2 turrets & masts, rstr, A....... $1,870.00
Battleship, Fleischmann, pnt tin, 21", w/up, gr w/maroon stripe, wht deck, EX, from $825 to....... $1,200.00
Battleship, Radiguet, zinc hull w/wooden deck, 22", steam-powered, British flag on stern, VG, A....... $8,800.00
Battleship, Schiebles, WWI, PS, 15", counterweight-driven push action, VG, A....... $450.00

Battleship (Missouri), Marklin, 1930s, windup, painted tin, 36", VG+, A, $20,900.00. (Photo courtesy Noel Barrett Antiques & Auctions Ltd.)

Battleship (New York), Orkin, PS, 25", w/up, gray w/dk gr hull, VG+, A....... $2,200.00
Battleship (Nurnberg), Carette, pnt tin, 24", w/up, wht & red, 2 gr masts, rstr, A....... $3,850.00
Battleship (Oregon), Converse, ca 1910, litho tin & wood, 17½", wht w/red & bl, EX+, A....... $870.00
Battleship (Pennsylvania), Orkin, PS, 30", w/up, wooden turrets, 2 fire control towers, EX, A....... $2,750.00
Boat Carriage, Marklin, pnt tin, 16½", 4-wheeled, G, A.. $2,750.00
Cabin Cruiser, Boucher, pnt wood, 49", live steam, gr & wht, 2 removable cabin sections, VG, A....... $3,575.00
Cabin Cruiser, Chein, #60, litho tin, 15", w/up, EXIB, A....$125.00
Cabin Cruiser, Orkin, pnt wood w/metal, 28", nonworking o/w VG, A....... $750.00
Cabin Cruiser (Marlin), Fleet Line, wood, 16", b/o, w/Atwater motor, EXIB, A....... $400.00
Cabin Cruiser (Vacationer), Linemar, litho tin, 12½", w/motor, unused, MIB, A....... $300.00
Cruiser, Bing, pnt tin, 19", live steam, wht w/gray bottom & rudder, red & gold trim, G, A....... $2,530.00
Cruiser, Bing, pnt tin, 28", gray w/blk bottom, 4 stacks, completely railed, some rpnt, A....... $3,300.00
Cruiser, Keystone, pnt wood, 23", w/up, cream decks w/wht & lt bl hull, 2 stacks & masts, VGIB, A....... $630.00
Destroyer, Fleischmann, 1950s, 15", w/up, gray & brn, 2 stacks & masts, some rstr, A....... $990.00
Destroyer, wood, 32", b/o, bl w/red bottom, blk stripe, gold trim, VG, A....... $225.00
Destroyer (K-55), Nomura, litho tin, 8½" L, friction, A ...$85.00
F-570 Zoom Boat, 1960s, litho tin, 12", r/c, w/driver in front seat, G+, A....... $50.00
Ferryboat (Union), Bing, pnt tin, 16", w/up, wht w/wood-tone open ended railed deck, rstr, A....... $825.00
Ferryboat w/Side Wheel, Bing, pnt tin, 21", cream w/brn deck, blk stack, 2-story cabin, railed ends, G+, A....... $3,160.00
Freighter (Eggo), Fleischmann, pnt tin, 21", w/up, wht deck w/ blk & red hull, some rpnt, A....... $825.00
Gunboat, Bing, pnt tin, 25", w/up, gray w/red trim, 3 stacks, 2 masts, VG, A....... $3,850.00
Gunboat, Carette, litho tin, 9½", inertia-powered, VG, A....... $250.00

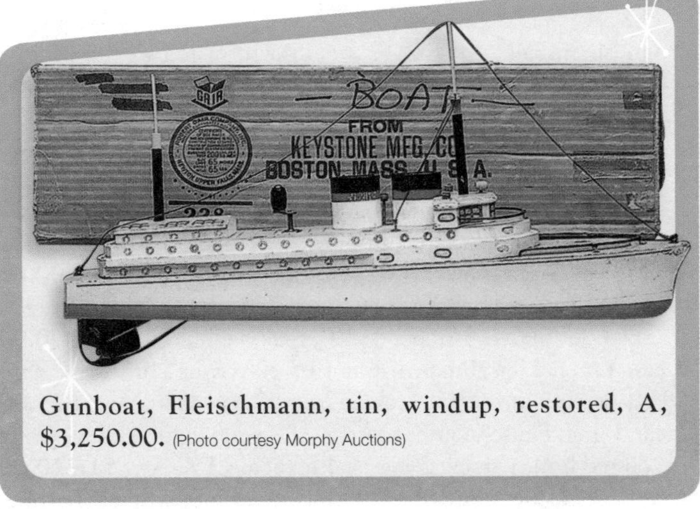

Gunboat, Fleischmann, tin, windup, restored, A, $3,250.00. (Photo courtesy Morphy Auctions)

Gunboat, Orobr, pnt tin, 10", wht w/red trim, EX....... $800.00
Gunboat (Chanzy), Bing, pnt tin, 21", wht w/red trim, gold deck, rail & trim, 2 stacks & masts, rstr, A....... $2,750.00
Harbour Patrol Boat #117, Japan, litho tin, 10", friction/crank-op, NMIB, A....... $80.00
Hawk Speed Boat, Sutcliff, tin, 13", w/up, 13", NMIB... $180.00
Hornby Speed Boat (Venture), Meccano #4, EXIB, A... $550.00
Keystone Boat, wood, 10", b/o, brn w/yel deck, red & wht flag, NOS, A....... $100.00
Keystone Boat, wood, 13", b/o, natural w/blk K & stripes on deck w/cut-out seat, red & wht flag, G, A....... $75.00
Luxury Liner, Marx, litho tin, 15", friction, EXIB, A..... $125.00
Motor Boat, Lang Craft, plastic, 11", b/o, w/outboard motor (in own box), 11", EXIB, A....... $140.00

Motor Boat, Linemar, wood, 11", b/o, natural deck w/pnt sides, MIB, A $110.00
Motor Boat, Rico, wood, 10", b/o, 3-color pnt, w/motor (in own box), EXIB, A $100.00
Motor Boat, Schilling, plastic, 14", b/o, EXIB, A $85.00
Motor Boat (Diamond D-63), Yonezawa, litho tin, 8", b/o, NMIB, A $100.00
Motor Boat (Thunderbolt), Fleet Line, 13", unused, MIB, A.. $100.00
Motor Boat (Viking), Fleetline, plastic, 10", b/o, w/Johnson motor (in own box), NMIB $250.00
Motor Boat (Zephyr), Fleetline, plastic, 10", b/o, w/Mercury motor (in own box), NMIB $250.00
Nautilus (Walt Disney's '20,000 Leagues Under the Sea'), Sutcliffe, 1950s, tin, 10", w/up, MIB, A $345.00
Ocean Liner, Bing, pnt tin, 16", w/up, wht & red w/red & blk trim, 3 stacks, 2 masts, EXIB, A $2,750.00
Ocean Liner, Bing, pnt tin, 27", w/up, wht deck, red hull & trim, 4 stacks, 2 masts, 10 lifeboats, railed, rpnt, A $4,950.00
Ocean Liner, Bing, pnt tin, 30", steam-powered, wht & gray w/red trim, 2 stacks, 3 masts, rstr, A $6,050.00
Ocean Liner, Bing, pnt tin, 33", w/up, wht, blk & red, 3 stacks & masts, VG, A $6,050.00
Ocean Liner, Carette, pnt tin, 11½", w/up, red, wht & bl, 3 stacks, 2 masts, railed bow & stern, rstr, A $385.00
Ocean Liner, Carette, pnt tin, 11½", w/up, wht, blk & red, 3 stacks, 1 mast, railed bow & stern, EX, A $465.00
Ocean Liner, Carette, pnt tin, 18", wht & red, 3 decks, 2 stacks, EX, A $1,400.00
Ocean Liner, Falk, pnt tin, 17", w/up, wht & red w/gold deck, 3 blk stacks w/gold & red, 2 masts, rstr, A $500.00
Ocean Liner, Fleischmann, pnt tin, 12½", wht, blk & red, 2 stacks, masts & lifeboats, NMIB, A $1,800.00
Ocean Liner, Fleischmann, pnt tin, 13", w/up, wht w/bl stripe, red trim, 2 stacks & masts, VG $700.00
Ocean Liner, Fleischmann, pnt tin, 14", w/up, wht, blk & red w/2 yel & red stacks, NM $700.00
Ocean Liner, Fleischmann, pnt tin, 19", w/up, wht, blk & red, 2 stacks & masts, 4 lifeboats, 19", rstr $1,200.00
Ocean Liner, Fleischmann, pnt tin, 20", w/up, brn deck w/bl stripe on wht hull, 1 stack & 2 masts, some rstr, A.. $825.00
Ocean Liner, Fleischmann, pnt tin, 20", w/up, wht deck, gr stripe on red hull, 1 stack, 2 masts, 4 lifeboats, EX, A.... $1,320.00
Ocean Liner, Fleischmann, pnt tin, 20", w/up, wht w/bl stripe, red trim, 1 stack, 2 masts, VG, A $825.00
Ocean Liner, Fleischmann, pnt tin, 20", wht w/bl side stripe, 1 bl stack, 4 lifeboats, NM+IB, A $2,750.00
Ocean Liner, Fleischmann, tin, 20", w/up, wht w/bl trim, 1 stack, 2 masts, EX+ $1,400.00
Ocean Liner, Fleischmann, pnt tin, 21", w/up, wht w/red & bl trim, 1 stack, 2 masts, rstr, A $935.00
Ocean Liner, Fleischmann, pnt tin, 21", wht w/bl & red trim, 1 stack, 2 masts, NM, A $1,300.00
Ocean Liner, G&K/German, pnt tin, 12", w/up, bl w/wht trim, EX, A $750.00
Ocean Liner, Marklin, pnt tin, 15½", w/up, wht, blk & red w/brn deck, 2 stacks, 1 mast, rpnt, A $1,320.00
Ocean Liner (Albert Ballin), Fleischmann, pnt tin, 20", w/up, wht w/bl trim, 2 stacks & masts, rstr, A $1,870.00
Ocean Liner (Bremen), Marklin, pnt tin, 3 stacks & 2 masts, wht, blk & red, 28½", prof rstr, A $11,000.00
Ocean Liner (Columbus), Fleischmann, pnt tin, 19", w/up, wht, blk & red, rstr, A $1,320.00
Ocean Liner (Leviathan), Bing, pnt tin, 29", w/up, wht, blk & red, 3 stacks & masts, 12 lifeboats, some rstr, A ... $6,050.00
Ocean Liner (Leviathon), Bing, pnt tin, 14½", w/up, wht, blk & red, some rpnt, A $1,430.00
Ocean Liner (Robert Fulton), Marklin, pnt tin, 14", red & wht, 1 stack, 3 levels, old rstr, A $1,980.00
Ocean Liner (Sea Queen), Masuya, litho tin, 11½", friction, NMIB, A $300.00
Ocean Liner (United States), Japan, litho tin, 15", w/up, wht, blk & red, 2 stacks, EX+IB, A $525.00
Oil Tanker, Fleischmann, pnt tin, 21", w/up, wht & red, 1 stack, on 4-wheeled platform, EX, A $525.00
Oil Tanker (Esso), Fleischmann, pnt tin, 20", wht/red/blk, VG, A $550.00
Patrol Boat, Radiguet, pnt tin, 22", w/up, brn & cream, some rpnt, A $2,750.00
Patrol Boat (Kasuga), Bing, pnt tin, 20", w/up, wht & red, 2 blk stacks w/red trim, lg turret on bow, rpnt, A $935.00

Phantom Raider, Ideal, 1960s, plastic, 30", EXIB, A, $250.00. (Photo courtesy Morphy Auctions)

Pilot Boat (B-168 Harbour Department), Bandai, litho tin, 10½", crank-op, w/driver, NMIB, A $200.00
Pioneer M-1023 Boat, Mitsuhashi, litho tin, 10½", crank-op, NMIB, A $85.00
Pond Boat, Kellerman, wood, 26", w/up, NMIB, A $990.00
PT-49-LST Boat, Buddy L, PS, 14", gray, complete w/tank, cargo hauler & soldiers, EX+, A $245.00
Racing Boat, Ideal, plastic, 13", crank-op, integral figure, NOS (in orig box), A $110.00
Racing Boat (Tempo-VI), Sankei, litho tin, r/c, EX+IB, A $65.00
River Boat, Bing, pnt tin, 19½", w/up, wht over red, full canopy, railed deck, w/windows, some rpnt, VG, A $2,090.00
River Boat, Carette, pnt tin, 16½", w/up, wht, blk & red, red & wht canopy over cabin, rpnt, A $1,430.00
River Boat, Carette, pnt tin, 21", w/up, red & wht, canopied & railed bow w/diners, cabin on stern, some rstr, A . $2,200.00

River Boat, German, pnt tin, 15", live steam, yel & blk w/wht cabin & canopy, rstr, A.. $800.00
River Boat (Sally), Ives, pnt tin, 10", w/up, wht & red w/red stack & lifeboat, canopied stern, rstr, A.................. $300.00
River Boat (St Louis), Marklin, pnt tin, 26½", w/up, red & wht w/brass trim, VG, A..$11,500.00
Rowboat, Arnold, pnt tin, 8", w/up, wht w/bl band, compo oarsman, NM.. $800.00
Rowboat, Ives, pnt tin, 11", w/up, clothed oarsman, G, A.$1,208.00
Runabout, IMP, wood, 16", b/o, blk & wht w/natural deck, chrome detail, VG, A... $275.00
Runabout, Liberty, wood & tin, 15", w/up, G+, A.............$88.00
Runabout, TMY, pnt wood, 14", w/up, w/windshield & deck detail, American flag, EX, A $200.00
Sailboat, Keystone, wood, 42", 2 cloth sails, EX, A $150.00
Sailboat (Peggy Ann), Chein, tin w/cloth sails, 12", steerable rudder, VG+, A... $135.00
Sailboat (Racing), Keystone, wood, 17", 2 cloth sails, VGIB, A.. $125.00
Sailboat (Resolute), pnt tin, 14", wooden mast w/cloth sails, EX, A $100.00
Sailboat (1045), Hess, litho tin, 12", litho cb sails, EX, A..$1,000.00
Schooner (Sachem), Bliss, 1880s, wood w/paper litho & cb accents, 42½", 3 sails, EX, A $3,025.00
Schuco Boat No 1015, litho tin, 5", w/up, w/driver, NM+. $250.00
Sea Wolf Atomic Submarine, Sutcliffe, w/up, tin, yel & red, 10", MIB, A.. $185.00
Side-Wheeler, Carette, pnt tin, 15", w/up, cream w/red bottom, cream canopy, center stack, rstr, A....................... $1,000.00
Side-wheeler, Orbr, tin, w/up, wht w/red trim, 9", EX, A.. $300.00
Side-Wheeler (Lorelei), Marklin, pnt tin, 13½", wht w/brn bottom, prof rstr, A $9,900.00
Side-Wheeler (New York), Marklin, pnt tin, 19", wht & red w/gold details, NM $7,000.00
Side-Wheeler (Water Witch), Weeden, pnt tin, 12", VG (w/wooden box), A..$6,095.00
Speed Boat (Flying Yankee), Sea Worthy, 1930s, wood, 20", w/up, dk brn tones, EX $700.00
Speedboat, German, pnt tin, 8", w/up, w/driver, VG...... $300.00
Speedboat, German, tin w/wooden deck, 29", G, A....... $600.00

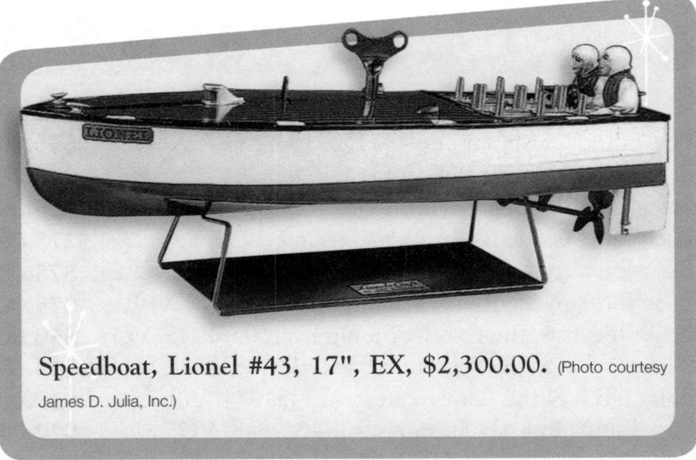

Speedboat, Lionel #43, 17", EX, $2,300.00. (Photo courtesy James D. Julia, Inc.)

Speedboat, Lionel-Craft Model MB, PS, 18", w/up, wht & red, 2 figures, EXIB, A $1,035.00
Speedboat, Nikko Toy, litho tin, 7", r/c, w/driver, NMIB.. $100.00
Speedboat (Corvette), Wen-Mac, 1954, celluloid w/gas-powered PS motor, 19", wht, MIB $225.00
Speedboat (Hornby), Meccano, wood & tin, 17½", w/up, VG..$225.00
Speedboat (NIXE), wood, 25", b/o, long pointed nose w/rear steering wheel in opening, VG+, A $660.00
Speedboat (Orcan), Calwis Industries, pnt tin, 27", wht & red w/red trim, VG, A $1,800.00
Speedboat (Racer-1), Sutcliff, pnt steel, 10", crank-op, MIB. $150.00
Speedboat (Ruban Bleu), Zep, 1930, pnt tin, 20", wht w/red trim, NMIB... $950.00
SSN-58 Nautilus, Marusan, 1950s, w/up, litho tin, unused, M (partially restored box), A $305.00
Steam Launch, Carette, pnt tin, 18", wht & red w/blk metal filigree-edge canopy, G, A..$1,760.00
Steam Launch (Miss Liberty), tin, 14", silver & red, American Flag, EX... $400.00
Structo I, Structo, wood, 12", b/o, red & wht, w/motor, EXIB. $300.00
Structo II, Structo, wood, 9", w/motor, VGIB, A $110.00
Submarine, Marklin, pnt tin, 31", w/up, army gr, VG+, A.$9,900.00
Torpedo Boat, Bing, pnt tin, 21", w/up, 2-tone gray w/bl deck, 2 masts, G, A $880.00
Torpedo Boat (PT 107), Linemar, litho tin, 11", r/c, NMIB, A $125.00
Torpedo Boat (Sparkling), Ideal, plastic, 11", gray & wht, NMIB, A $85.00
Tugboat, Marusan, litho tin, 12½", b/o, NM+IB, A........ $150.00
Tugboat (Annie), Japan, litho tin, 13", b/o, EXIB $100.00
US Destroyer, Ideal, plastic, 15", red, wht & bl, NMIB, A...$100.00
Warship (Phantom Raider) Ideal, 1960s, plastic, 30", EX (G box), A... $150.00
Water Ski Boat, Haji, tin & plastic, 14", w/motor & skiing figure, MIB, A $245.00
Wooden Model, Union or MHM, various types from 12½" to 13½", NOS, A, ea from $65 to $110.00
Yacht, Ideal, plastic, 15", w/up, G+, A $40.00
Yacht, Tri-Ang, PS, 18", red w/blk trim, 2 cloth sails, NMIB. $180.00
Yacht, wood, 18", b/o, wht deck & cabin w/black sides & red bottom, detail on cabin roof, NM, A $385.00
Yacht (Phillips 66), plastic, 15", w/marina accessory, MIB, A.. $110.00

Yacht (Jolanda), Marklin, painted tin, windup, some restoration, A, $14,300.00. (Photo courtesy Beretoia Auctions)

Outboard Motors

Allyn Seafury, 5½", EX+ $250.00
Chester A Pimmer, 7", VG, A $175.00
Evinrude, early, 2-tone bl w/wht trim, 6", NOS (box bottom only), A $300.00
Johnson Sea Horse, 5", NOS (in orig box), A $300.00
K&O, 5", NM $195.00
NBK No 0-4, orange & wht, 4", NOS (in orig box) $185.00

Books

Books have always captured and fired the imagination of children, and today books from every era are being collected. No longer is it just the beautifully illustrated Victorian examples or first editions of books written by well-known children's authors, but more modern books as well.

One of the first classics to achieve unprecedented success was *The Wizard of Oz* by author L. Frank Baum — such success, in fact, that far from his original intentions, it became a series. Even after Baum's death, other authors wrote Oz books until the decade of the 1960s, for a total of more than 40 different titles. Other early authors were Beatrix Potter, Kate Greenaway, Palmer Cox (who invented the Brownies), and Johnny Gruelle (creator of Raggedy Ann and Andy). All were accomplished illustrators as well.

Everyone remembers a special series of books they grew up with, the Hardy Boys, Nancy Drew Mysteries, Tarzan — there were countless others. And though these are becoming very collectible today, there were many editions of each, and most are very easy to find. Generally the last few in any series will be most difficult to locate, since fewer were printed than the earlier stories which were likely to have been reprinted many times. As is true of any type of book, first editions or the earliest printing will have more collector value.

Big Little Books came along in 1933, and until edged out by the comic-book format in the mid-1950s, sold in huge volumes. They were printed by Whitman, Saalfield, Goldsmith, Van Wiseman, Lynn, and World Syndicate and all stuck to the thick hand-sized sagas of adventure. The first hero to be immortalized in this arena was Dick Tracy, but many more were to follow. Some of today's more collectible feature well-known characters like G-Men, Tarzan, Flash Gordon, Little Orphan Annie, Mickey Mouse, and Western Heroes by the dozen.

Little Golden Books were first published in 1942 by Western Publishing Co. Inc. The earliest had spines of blue paper that were later replaced with gold foil. Until the 1970s, the books were numbered from 1 to 600, while later books had no numerical order. The most valuable are those with dust jackets from the early 1940s or books with paper dolls and activities. The three primary series of books are Regular (1 – 600), Disney (1 – 140), and Activity (1 – 52). Books with the blue or gold paper spine (not foil) often sell at $8.00 to $15.00. Dust jackets alone are worth $20.00 and up in good condition. Paper doll books are generally valued at about $30.00 to $35.00, and stories about TV Western heroes at $12.00 to $18.00. First editions of the 25¢ and 29¢ cover-price books can be identified by a code (either on the title page or the last page); '1/A' indicates a first edition while a 'number/Z' will refer to the twenty-sixth printing. Condition is important but subjective to personal standards.

See also Black Americana; Coloring, Activity, and Paint Books; and other specific categories.

Big Little Books

Ace Drummond, #1177, 1935, EX $30.00
Alice in Wonderland Featuring Charlotte Henry as Alice, #759, 1933, VG $35.00
Ally Oop & Dinny, #763, 1935, VG $30.00
Andy Panda in the City of Ice, #1441, 1948, VG $25.00
Apple Mary & Dennie's Luck Apples, #1403, 1939, VG $20.00
Arizona Kid on the Bandit Trail, #1192, 1936, EX+ $35.00
Beasts of Tarzan, #1410, 1937, EX+ $75.00
Betty Boop in Snow White, #1119, 1934, VG $75.00
Big Chief Wahoo & the Magic Lamp, #1432, 1942, VG $20.00
Billy the Kid, #773, 1935, VG $20.00
Black Beauty, #1057, 1934, VG $18.00
Blaze Brandon With the Foreign Legion, #1447, 1938, EX $35.00
Blondie & Dagwood in Hot Water, #1410, 1946, EX $25.00
Blondie & Dagwood in Some Fun!, #703-10, 1949, EX+ $35.00

***Blondie in Cookie and Daisy's Pups*, #1491, 1943, EX+, $48.00.** (Photo courtesy gasolinealleyantiques.com)

Boss of the Chisholm Trail, #1153, 1939, EX+ $35.00
Brer Rabbit, #1426, 1947, VG+ $40.00
Broncho Bill, #1181, 1940, VG+ $25.00
Buck Jones & the Night Riders, #4069, 1937, EX $275.00
Buck Jones in Ride 'Em Cowboy, #116, 1937, EX+ $75.00
Buck Jones in the Roaring West, #1174, 1935, EX+ $75.00
Buck Rogers & the Depth of Jupiter, #1169, 1935, VG+ $50.00
Buck Rogers & the Planetoid Plot, #1197, EX+ $125.00
Buffalo Bill & the Pony Express, #713, 1934, VG $20.00
Bugs Bunny in Risky Business, #1440, 1948, VG $20.00
Bullet Benton, #1169, 1939, NM+ $55.00
Captain Easy Soldier of Fortune, #1128, 1934, EX $45.00
Captain Midnight & the Secret Squadron, #1488, 1941, NM $125.00
Charlie Chan Solves a Mystery, #1459, 1940, VG $22.00

Chester Gump in the Pole Flight, #1402, 1937, EX+ $50.00
Corley of the Wilderness Trails, #1607, 1937, EX+ $35.00
Cowboy Maloy, #1171, 1940, VG $20.00
Crimson Cloak, #1161, 1939, EX+ $35.00
Dan Dunn on the Trail of Wu Fang, #1454, 1938, VG $25.00
David Copperfield, #1148, 1934, VG $30.00
Desert Eagle Rides Again, #1458, 1939, EX+ $35.00
Detective Dick Tracy & the Spider Gang, #1446, 1937, VG+.$40.00
Dick Tracy & the Stolen Bonds, #1105, 1934, VG...........$35.00
Dick Tracy Detective & Federal Agent, #6833, 1936, VG+.$75.00
Dick Tracy in Chains of Crime, #1185, 1936, VG.............$35.00
Dick Tracy Special FBI Operative, #1449, 1943, EX $75.00
Don Winslow & the Giant Girl Spy, #1408, 1946, EX+ ...$50.00
Don Winslow Navy Intelligence Ace, #1418, 1946, VG+ ..$30.00
Don Winslow USN, #1107, 1935, EX+ $45.00
Donald Duck & the Green Serpent, #1432, 1947, EX+. $100.00
Donald Duck Hunting for Trouble, #1478, 1938, VG $45.00
Donald Duck Lays Down the Law, #1449, 1948, VG+......$50.00

***Donald Duck Up in the Air*, #1486, 1945, $35.00.** (Photo courtesy gasolinealleyantiques.com)

Dumbo — Only His Ears Grew, #1400, 1942, scarce, VG.$50.00
Eddie Cantor in an Hour With You, 1934, EX+ $65.00
Ella Cinders Plays Duchess, 1938, EX $50.00
Ellery Queen the Master Detective, #1472, 1942, EX+.....$50.00
Fighting Heroes Battle for Freedom, 1943, VG $18.00
Flame Boy & the Indians' Secret, #1464, 1938, EX+ $30.00
Flash Gordon & the Tournaments of Mongo, #1171, 1935, VG $65.00
Flash Gordon in the Forest Kindom of Mongo, 1938, EX. $135.00
Flash Gordon in the Water World of Mongo, 1937, VG...$50.00
Frank Merriwell at Yale, #1121, 1935, EX........................$35.00
Frankenstein Jr in the Menace of the Heartless Monster, 1968, NM...$25.00
G-Man & the Gun Runners, #1469, EX+..........................$35.00
G-Man in Action, #1173, 1940, EX+ $35.00
G-Man on the Trail, #1157, 1938, VG+ $20.00
Gang Busters in Action, #1451, 1938, NM.......................$65.00
Gene Autry & Raiders of the Range, #1409, 1946, EX $40.00
Gene Autry & the Gun-Smoke Reckoning, #1434, 1943, EX+ $50.00
Gene Autry & the Hawk of the Hills, #1493, 1942, VG+...$35.00
George O'Brien & the Hooded Riders, #1457, NM $50.00
Ghost Avenger, #1462, 1943, EX+...................................$35.00
Goofy in Giant Trouble, 1968 (reprint), NM+ $10.00
Green Hornet Returns, #1496, 1941, VG+ $100.00
Gulliver's Travels, #1172, 1939, VG $65.00

***Gulliver's Travels*, #1172, 1939, VG+, $45.00.** (Photo courtesy gasolinealleyantiques.com)

Gunsmoke, #1647, 1958, EX+...$35.00
Hal Hardy in the Lost Land of Giants, #1413, 1938, VG+..$25.00
Houdini's Big Little Book of Magic, #715, 1927, VG+......$35.00
In the Name of the Law, #1125, VG $20.00
Inspector Charlie Chan in Villany on the High Seas, #1424, EX...$45.00
Invisible Scarlet O'Neil, #1403, 1942, EX $35.00
It Happened One Night, #1098 or #1578, 1935, VG, ea...$35.00
Jack Swift & His Rocket Ship, #1102, 1934, VG+............$40.00
Jackie Cooper in Peck's Bad Boy, #1314, 1934, VG+ $35.00
Jane Withers in Keep Smiling, #1463, EX $40.00
Jim Hardy Ace Reporter, #1180, 1940, VG+ $25.00
Joe Palooka the Heavyweight Boxing Champ, #1123, 1934, VG+ $50.00
John Carter of Mars, #1402, 1940, NM.......................... $400.00
Jungle Jim & the Vampire Woman, #1139, NM............. $100.00
Junior G-Men, #1442, 1937, EX.......................................$30.00
Just Kids & Deep-Sea Dan, #1184, 1940, EX+ $50.00
Kayo & Moon Mullins & the One Man Gang, #1415, 1939, EX+ $40.00
Kayo in the Land of Sunshine, #1180, EX $35.00
Ken Maynard in Western Justice, 1430, EX.......................$35.00
Laurel & Hardy, #1086 or #1316, 1934, EX+, ea $75.00
Lee Brady Range Detective, #1149, 1938, EX+ $35.00
Li'l Abner Among the Millionaires, #1401, 1939, EX+ $75.00
Little Lord Fauntleroy, #1598, 1936, EX $35.00
Little Orphan Annie, #708, 1933, VG.......................... $100.00
Little Orphan Annie & the Ghost Gang, #1154, 1935, EX+. $75.00
Little Women, #757, 1934, VG+ $40.00
Lone Ranger & the Black Shirt Highwayman, #1450, 1939, EX+ $75.00
Lone Ranger & the Great Western Span w/Tonto & Silver, #1477, 1942, EX, A $25.00
Lost Patrol, #753, 1934, VG+ $30.00
Mandrake the Magician & the Flame Pearls, #1418, 1946, EX+...$65.00

Maximo the Amazing Superman, EX+ $50.00
Mickey Mouse & Bobo the Elephant, #1160, 1935, VG ...$45.00
Mickey Mouse & the Bat Bandit, #1153, 1935, G............$25.00
Mickey Mouse Bell Boy Detective, #1483, 1945, EX+ $85.00
Mickey Mouse in the Foreign Legion, #1428, 1940, EX+ . $100.00
Mickey Mouse Sails for Treasure Island, #750, 1933, VG+..$75.00
Mickey Mouse the Detective, #1139, 1934, G..................$25.00
Moon Mullins & the Pushbottom Twins, #1134, 1935, VG..$35.00
New Adventures of Tarzan, #1180, 1935, EX+ $100.00
Phantom & the Girl of Mystery, #1416, 1947, VG...........$30.00
Phantom & the Sky Pirates, #1468, 1945, EX $50.00
Popeye & the Quest for the Rainbird, #1459, 1943, EX+...$50.00
Popeye the Spinach Eater, #1480, 1945, EX+...................$60.00
Radio Patrol & Big Dan's Mobsters, #1498, 1937, EX $35.00
Red Death on the Range, #1449, 1940, VG $20.00
Red Ryder & the Squaw-Tooth Rustlers, #1414, 1946, VG..$20.00
Red Ryder Acting Sheriff, #702-10, 1949, NM $45.00
Robinson Crusoe, #719, EX+ $55.00
Roy Rogers & the Mystery of the Howking Mesa, #1448, 1948, EX+ $60.00
Roy Rogers King of the Cowboys, #1476, 1943, VG $35.00
Scrappy, #112, 1934, very scarce, VG+ $55.00
Secret Agent X-9 & the Mad Assassin, #1472, 1938, EX+..$50.00
Shirley Temple in the Littlest Rebel, #115, 1935, VG $35.00
Skippy, #761, 1934, VG..$25.00

Smilin' Jack and the Stratosphere Ascent, #1152, 1937, VG+, **$30.00.** (Photo courtesy gasolinealleyantiques.com)

Smilin' Jack in Wings Over the Pacific, #1416, 1939, EX+ ..$50.00
Smokey Stover Firefighter of Foo, #1010, 1937, VG $20.00
Spike Kelly of the Commandos, #1467, 1943, EX+...........$30.00
Spook Riders on the Overland, #1144, 1938, VG+...........$18.00
Superman in the Phantom Zone Connection, #5780-2, 1980, EX+ $10.00
Tailspin Tommy & the Last Transport, #1423, 1939, NM ..$50.00
Tailspin Tommy in the Great Air Mystery, #1184, 1936, VG+. $30.00
Tarzan & the Golden Lion, #1448, 1943, VG $35.00
Tarzan & the Jewels of Opar, #1495, 1941, VG $30.00
Tarzan & the Tarzan Twins w/Jad-Dal-Ja the Golden Lion, #4056, 1936, EX+ $50.00
Tarzan Lord of the Jungle, #1407, VG..............................$35.00
Tarzan's Revenge, #1488, 1938, G+, A $55.00
Terry & the Pirates in the Mountain Stronghold, #1499, 1941, VG $25.00
Terry Lee Flight Officer USA, #1492, 1944, EX+ $40.00
Texas Kid, #1429, 1937, VG...$20.00
Tim McCoy in the Westerner, #1193, 1938, EX $50.00
Tim McCoy on the Tomahawk Trail, #1436, 1937, VG $20.00
Tom Mix & the Scrouge of Paradise Valley, #4068, 1937, G+..$75.00
Tom Mix Plays a Lone Hand, #1173, 1935, EX $35.00
Uncle Wiggily's Adventures, #1405, 1946, VG $30.00
Walt Disney's Cinderella, #711-10, 1950, VG $20.00
Walt Disney's Minnie Mouse & the Antique Chair, #845, VG $20.00
Wimpy the Hamburger Eater, #1458, 1938, EX $50.00
Wings of the USA, #1407, 1940, EX $30.00
Zane Grey's King of the Royal Mounted, #1103, 1936, VG..$22.00

Little Golden Books

Aladdin & His Magic Lamp, #371, A ed, 1959, VG $12.00
All Aboard!, #152, A ed, 1952, VG+ $15.00
Animals of Farmer Jones, #282, H ed, VG...........................$8.00
Annie Oakley & the Rustlers, #221-25, A ed, NM $22.00
Baby Animals, #274, B ed, 1956, EX................................$12.00
Barbie, #125, 1st ed, 1954, EX+ $10.00

The Brave Little Tailor, A edition, EX+, **$15.00.** (Photo courtesy gasolinealleyantiques.com)

Broken Arrow, A ed, 1957, EX...$12.00
Buffalo Bill Jr, #254, A ed, 1956, VG $18.00
Busy Timmy, F ed, 1948, EX+...$18.00
Cave Kids, #539, A ed, 1963, EX $18.00
Children's Garden Verses, #493, B ed, 1962, EX $12.00
Chitty Chitty Bang Bang, #581, 1968, EX.........................$12.00
Colors Are Nice, #207-1, L ed, 1979, EX+ $3.50
Counting Rhymes, #361, A ed, 1960, EX $10.00
Dale Evans & the Lost Gold Mine, #213, A ed, 1954, NM..$25.00
Danny Beaver's Secret, #160, A ed, 1953, VG+ $12.00
Disneyland on the Air, #D43, C ed, 1955, EX $12.00
Doctor Dan the Bandage Man, #111, A ed, 1950, VG......$10.00
Emerald City of Oz, #151, A ed, 1952, EX.........................$40.00

Friendly Book, #199, A ed, 1954, VG $12.00
Gay Purr-ee, #488, 1962, VG $20.00
Gene Autry, #230, A ed, 1955, EX+ $25.00
Golden Book of Fairy Tales, #9, 1st ed, 1942, EX+ $42.00
Golden Book of Words, #45, D ed, 1948, VG $18.00
Guess Who Lives Here, #60, B ed, 1949, G $12.00
Hansel & Gretel, #17, 1st ed, 1943, EX $25.00
Happy Birthday, #123, A ed, 1952, EX $20.00
Here Comes the Parade, #143, A ed, 1950, VG+ $15.00

***Heroes of the Bible*, #236, 1955, VG+, $20.00.** (Photo courtesy gasolinealleyantiques.com)

Hokey Wolf & Ding-A-Ling Featuring Huckleberry Hound, A ed, 1961, EX+ $28.00
Howdy Doody & Clarabell, A ed, 1951, EX+ $35.00
Howdy Doody & Santa Claus, A ed, #237, EX+ $35.00
Howdy Doody in Funland, A ed, 1953, EX+ $35.00
I'm an Indian Today, #425, A ed, 1961, EX+ $20.00
Indian Indian, #149, A ed, 1952, VG+ $15.00
Jungle Book, #D120, A ed, 1967, EX $12.00
Kitten's Surprise, A ed, 1951, EX+ $15.00
Land of the Surprise Guest, #136, 1st ed, 1975, EX+ $12.00
Lippy the Lion & Hardy Har Har, A ed, 1963, NM $35.00
Little Golden Holiday Book, #109, A ed, 1951, VG $35.00
Little Lively Rabbit, #15, 2nd ed, 1944, VG $16.00
Little Red Caboose, #306-22, 1981, EX $8.00
Little Red Hen, #438, 2nd ed, 1974, EX $9.50
Littlest Raccoon, #459, A ed, 1961, NM $18.00
Lively Little Rabbit, L ed, 1943, VG $18.00
Lone Ranger & Tonto, #297, A ed, 1957, VG $18.00
Maverick, #354, A ed, 1959, EX+ $20.00
Merry Shipwreck, #170, A ed, 1953, EX $12.00
Mr Rogers' Neighborhood — Henrietta Meets Someone New, #133, 1st ed, 1974, NM $8.00
Night Before Christmas, L ed, 1949, 3rd cover variation w/Santa stepping out of fireplace, EX+ $12.00
Open Up My Suitcase, #207, A ed, 1954, VG $18.00
Pebbles Flintstone, A ed, #531, 1963, EX $20.00
Puss in Boots, #137, A ed, 1952, EX+ $12.00
Riddles Riddles From A to Z, #490, F ed, 1974, NM $4.00
Rootie Kazootie Detective, #150, A ed, 1953, VG $25.00
Roy Rogers & the New Cowboy, #177, A ed, 1953, VG $20.00
Steve Canyon, #356, A ed, 1959, EX+ $20.00
Three Little Kittens, #1, O ed, 1942, VG $15.00
Tom & Jerry Meet Little Quack, #181, A ed, 1953, VG $8.00
Uncle Wiggily, #148, A ed, 1953, VG+ $18.00

***We Help Daddy*, #468, A edition, 1962, NM, $20.00.** (Photo courtesy gasolinealleyantiques.com)

Where Jesus Lived, #147, 1st ed, 1977, NM+ $8.00
Wild Kingdom, #151, 1st ed, 1976, NM+ $8.00
Woody Woodpecker at the Circus, #149, 1st ed, 1976, NM $80.00

Pop-Up & Movable Books

***Buck Rogers — Strange Adventures in the Spider-Ship*, 1935, three pop-ups, VG+, A, $175.00.** (Photo courtesy Morphy Auctions)

America in Action On Land at Sea In the Air, Action Playbooks Inc, 1942, EX $125.00
Animal's Merry Christmas, by Kathryn Jackson, Press, 1950, w/ pop-up tree, EX $125.00
Benny Beaver & Fuzzy Bear, Fawcett/John Martin's House, 1945, 1st ed, EX $35.00
Buck Rogers — Strange Adventures in the Spider-Ship, Pleasure Books, 1935, 3 pop-ups, EX $75.00

Christmas Tale, Bancroft, 1960, VG $100.00
Christmas Treasure Book, Simon & Shuster, 1950, 37 pgs, 1 pop-up, EX $45.00
Cinderella A Peepshow Book, Brett Lithographing Co, 1950, G.. $50.00
Dick Tracy — The Capture of Boris Arson, by Chester Gould, Blue Robbon Books, 1935, 3 pop-ups, EX............... $125.00
Goldilocks & the Three Bears, Bancroft, 1961, 7 pop-ups, G. $25.00
Goldilocks & the Three Bears, Blue Ribbon, 1934, 3 pop-ups, NM.. $200.00
Hansel & Gretel, Bancroft, 1961, 7 pop-ups, EX.............. $20.00
Jack & the Beanstalk/Hop O'My Thumb, Bancroft & Co, 1962, EX $50.00
Little Orphan Annie & Jumbo the Circus Elephant, Blue Ribbon Books, 3 pop-ups, NM+... $250.00
Mickey Mouse in King Arthur's Court, Blue Ribbon Books, 1933, 4 pop-ups, VG... $250.00
Mickey Mouse Presents Silly Symphonies/Babes in the Woods/King Neptune, Dean & Son Ltd, 1st ed, 4 pop-ups, G $50.00
New Adventures of Tarzan, 1935, G $50.00
Peter Rabbit the Magician, Strathmore, 1942, spiralbound, VG $35.00
Picture Show, New York EP Dutton & Co, printed in Bavaria, late 1800s or early 1900s, 8x10", VG $275.00
Pinocchio, by Marion Merrill, Cima Publishing, 1945, spiral-bound, w/dust jacket, VG $32.00

***Pinocchio*, Harold Lentz, copyright 1932, VG, A, $100.00.** (Photo courtesy Morphy Auctions)

Pop-Goes-The-Joke Book, Hallmark, VG.......................... $35.00
Pop-up Minnie Mouse, Blue Ribbon Books, 1933, 3 pop-ups, EX... $175.00
Pop-Up Popeye w/The Hag of the Seven Seas, by EC Segar, 1935, 3 pop-ups, EX.. $125.00
Santa's Circus, White Plains Greeting Card Corp, 1952, 3 pop-ups, spiralbound, EX $40.00
Tarzan (New Adventures of) 'Pop-Up,' 3 pop-ups, EX, A.. $100.00
Terry & the Pirates in Shipwrecked, by Milton Caniff, Blue Ribbon/Pleasure Books, 1935, 3 pop-ups, EX $75.00
Tim Tyler in the Jungle, by Lyman Young, King Features, 1933, 3 pop-ups, VG... $225.00
Winnie the Pooh & the Bees, by AA Milne, Metheun & Co, 1952, 1st ed, spiralbound, 4 pop-ups, VG $50.00
Wizard of Oz, Random House, 1960s or 1970s, VG.......... $50.00

TELL-A-TALE BY WHITMAN

A Special Pet, 1968, EX $8.00
Aristocats, 1970, EX $9.00
Bugs Bunny Party Best, 1976, EX+...................................... $6.00
Bugs Bunny's Big Invitation, 1953, G $10.00
Captain Kangaroo & the Too-Small House, 1958, EX+.... $14.00
Donald Duck — The New Birdhouse, VG $6.50
Donald Duck on Tom Sawyer's Island, 1978, EX $6.00
Eloise & the Old Blue Truck, 1971, EX+ $8.00
Flintstones at the B Bar B, 1966, NM $28.00
Flintstones at the Circus, 1963, EX+................................. $25.00

***The Gingerbread Man*, 1953, VG, $12.00.** (Photo courtesy gasolinealleyantiques.com)

House That Jack Built, 1960, EX+ $15.00
Hungry Lion, 1960, VG+ $12.00
I Love My Grandma, 1960, VG.. $10.00
Jim Jump, 1954, EX+ $10.00
Let's Play, 1952, EX... $15.00
Little Red Bicycle, 1953, EX+ $10.00
Loppy de Loop Odd Jobber, 1964, EX+ $28.00
My Little Book About Flying, 1978, NM+ $5.00
My Little Book of Big Machines, 1975, EX........................... $8.00
Nancy & Sluggo in The Big Surprise, 1974, VG $6.00
Nursery Rhymes, 1945, VG $10.00
Once Upon a Windy Day, 1947, VG+ $12.00
Pebbles Flintstone Daddy's Little Helper, 1964, NM+....... $28.00
Pebbles Flintstone Runaway, 1964, NM............................. $28.00
Pink Panther, 1976, VG $8.00

Raggedy Andy's Treasure Hunt, 1973, EX............................$9.00
Roy Rogers at the Lane Ranch, #811-15, 1950, EX...........$25.00
Snooty, 1944, VG...$12.00
Swiss Family Duck, 1964, EX...$9.00
Sylvester & Tweety Bird in A Visit to the Vet, EX.............$5.00
Three Bears, 1955, VG...$8.00
Tom & Jerry in Model Mice, 1951, VG...............................$8.00
Under Dog, 1966, VG+...$8.00
Very Best Friends, 1963, VG...$7.50
Wally Gator in Guess What's Hiding at the Zoo, 1963, VG..$6.00
Walt Disney's Bear Country, 1954, G.................................$7.00
Walt Disney's Beaver Valley, 1954, VG...............................$9.00
Yogi Bear Helps Santa, 1962, EX+....................................$25.00
Yogi Bear No Picnic, 1963, EX..$20.00

Yogi Bear Takes a Vacation, $35.00. (Photo courtesy gasolinealleyantiques.com)

WHITMAN

Annette in Sierra Summer, 1960, EX..............................$15.00

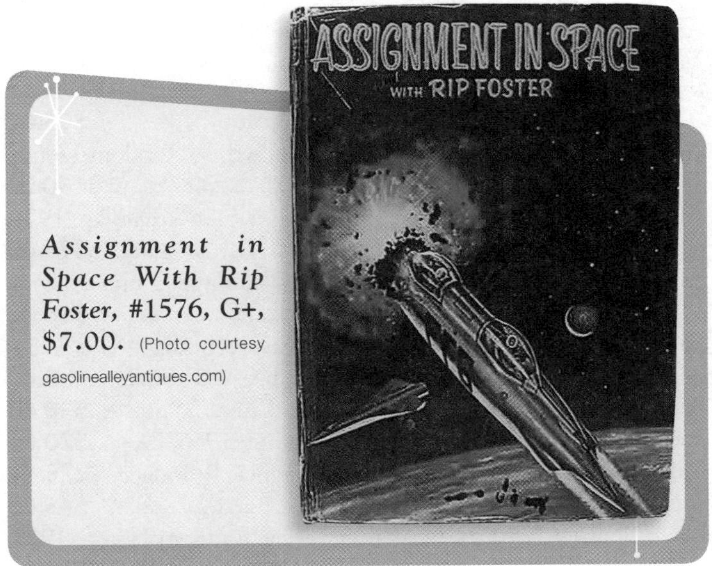

Assignment in Space With Rip Foster, #1576, G+, $7.00. (Photo courtesy gasolinealleyantiques.com)

Bedtime Stories Book (365), 1955, G..............................$32.00
Beverly Hillbillies in The Saga of Wildcat Creek, 1963, NM. $15.00
Big Valley, 1966, EX...$20.00
Black Beauty, #1604, 1955, NM...$12.00
Bugs Bunny's Big Invitation, 1953, EX.................................$10.00
Champions All the Way, 1960, EX+.....................................$10.00
Cheyenne & the Lost Gold of Lion Park, 1958, Authorized TV Edition, EX...$18.00
Crusader Rabbit in Bubble Trouble, 1960, NM...................$20.00
Dick Tracy the Detective, Penny Book, 1938, EX+...........$50.00
Donald Duck in Bringing Up the Boys, EX..........................$15.00
Farmer in the Dell, 1939, G..$15.00
Flipper in the Mystery of the Black Shadow, 1966, NM+....$10.00
Gene Autry & the Golden Ladder Gang, 1950, EX..........$18.00
Gene Autry in the Ghost Riders, 1955, NM.......................$20.00
Have Gun Will Travel, 1959, EX...$15.00
Indian Mummy Mystery, 1964, EX.......................................$10.00
John Paul Jones Boy Sailor, 1946, EX................................$15.00
Lassie & the Blackberry Bog, 1956, EX..............................$25.00
Little Black Sambo, 1950, G+..$75.00
Magic Train, 1959, EX..$25.00
Maverick, 1959, EX..$25.00
Mickey Mouse & His Friends, #904, 1936, EX.............. $150.00
Mickey Mouse the Big Big Book, 1935, EX.........................$65.00
Munsters & the Great Camera Caper, #1510, 1965, NM..$20.00
National Velvet, 1962, M...$10.00
On a Torn-Away World, #2348, 1930s, EX+ (w/dust jacket) . $25.00
Patty Duke & Mystery Mansion, 1964, NM+......................$10.00
Pinocchio, 1940, EX...$50.00
Quick Draw McGraw Badman Beware, 1960, EX+...........$10.00
Rifleman, 1959, EX..$25.00

***Rocky and Bullwinkle Go to Hollywood*, Top-Top Tales #2494, 1961, EX+, $32.00.** (Photo courtesy gasolinealleyantiqus.com)

Roy Rogers & the Raiders of Sawtooth Ridge, #2329, EX..$25.00
Sally Squirrel's Wish, #2952, 1950, VG............................$12.00
Son of the Phantom, 1946, VG..$15.00
Thimble Theatre Starring Popeye, Big Big Book, 1935, EX...$50.00
Tom Sawyer, #1603, 1955, NM..$12.00

Tom Stetson & the Giant Ants, 1948, EX $18.00
Tortoise & the Hare, 1935, EX $60.00
Wagon Train Authorized TV Edition, 1959, EX $15.00
Yogi Bear, 1962, EX+ $15.00
Zorro, 1958, EX $20.00

Wonder Books

Peter Rabbit and Reddy Fox, #611, 1954, NM, $25.00. (Photo courtesy gasolinealleyantiqes.com)

A Child's Garden of Verses, 1958, VG $10.00
ABC & Counting Rhymes, #823, NM+ $8.00
Animal's Playground, #825, 1964, EX $10.00
Babar the King, #602, 1953, VG+ $16.00
Baby Elephant, #541, 1950, VG $8.00
Baby Racoon, #797, 1963, EX+ $10.00
Baby's Day, #663, VG $15.00
Bedtime Stories, #507, 1946, VG $10.00
Billy & His Steam Roller, #557, 1951, EX+ $14.00
Black Beauty, #595, 1952, EX $8.00
Blowaway Hat, #554, 1946, EX $17.00
Busy Baby Lion, #737, 1959, EX $12.00
Casper & Wendy Adventures, #855, 1969, VG $10.00
Choo Choo Train, #718, 1958, EX+ $12.00
Christmas Favorites, 1974, EX $8.00
Churkendoose, #832, 1974, rare, VG $35.00
Cow in the Silo, VG+ $35.00
December Is for Christmas, #776, 1961, EX $12.00
Deputy Dawg, 1961, VG $11.00
Doll Family, #802, 1962, EX $25.00
Farmer Al Falfa, #736, 1959, VG $12.00
Fluffy Little Lamb, 1962, VG+ $10.00
Gandy Goose, #695, 1957, EX $15.00
How the Clown Got His Smile, #566, 1951, VG+ $8.00
Jetsons in the Great Pizza Hunt, 1976, EX+ $8.00
Kittens Who Hid From Their Mother, 1950, EX+ $18.00
Little Dog Who Forgot How to Bark, #504, 1946, VG $12.00
Little Peter Cottontail, #641, 1956, VG $10.00
Little Schoolhouse, 1958, VG $8.00
Littlest Christmas Tree, #525, 1954, VG $12.00
Merry Christmas Book, #820, 1953, VG $8.00
Mighty Mouse, #662, 1955, VG+ $15.00
Mighty Mouse — Dinky Learns to Fly, 1953, G+ $10.00
Minute-And-A-Half Man, 1960, VG $15.00
Mr Bear Squash-You-All-Flat, #523, 1950, very scarce, VG+ $95.00
Nine Rabbits & Another, #845, 1957, VG $12.00
Nonsense Alphabet, #725, 1959 .... $10.00
Once There Was a House, #842, 1965, EX+ $10.00
Peter Pan, #597, 1952, EX+ $14.00
Pinocchio, #615, 1954, VG $8.00
Popeye's Big Surprise, #791, VG $12.00
Raggedy Ann's Tea Part, spiral-bound, VG+ $15.00

Rolling Wheels, #762, 1950, EX+, $20.00. (Photo courtesy gasolinealleyantiques.com)

Snowman's Christmas Present, 1951, NM $20.00
Sonny the Lucky Bunny, VG, A $6.00
Surprise For Felix, 1959, NM $15.00
There Was Once a Little Boy, VG $8.00
Three Mice & a Kitten, #533, 1950, VG $20.00
Too Little Fire Engine, 1950, VG+ $7.00
Visit to the Hospital, #690, EX+ $8.00
What Am I?, #832, 1946, VG $40.00
Who Goes There?, #779, 1961, EX+ $25.00

Miscellaneous

Adventures of Andy Panda, Dell Fast-Action, NM $75.00
Adventures of Superman, by George Lowther, Random House, 1942, hardback, EX+ $150.00
Alice in Wonderland (Movie Edition), Grosset & Dunlap, 1934, hardback w/Charlotte Henry illus, EX $75.00
American Indian Tales & Legends, by Vladimir Hulpach, Paul Hamlyn CO, 1966, hardback, VG $18.00
Baby's Day, by Annette Edwards, Treasure Books #859, 1953, illus by Priscilla Pointer, hardback, EX+ $8.00
Bambi, Grosset & Dunlap, 1942, EX+ $30.00
Batman — Three Villains of Doom, Signet, 1966, EX+ $20.00
Billy Wisker's Treasure Hunt, illus by Francis Brundage, Saalfield, 1928, EX $45.00
Black Stallion Returns, by Walter Farley, Random House, 1983, hardback, EX $15.00
Blondie's Family, Treasure Book #887, King Features Syndicate, 1954, hardback, EX $20.00

Building a Skyscraper, by Louise L Kozak, Rand McNally, 1973, Start Right series, illus by Paul Frame, hardback, EX ...$6.00
Captain Marvel in the Return of the Scorpion, Dell Fast-Action, NM.......... $225.00
Cave of the Lost Fraggle, by M Teitelbaum, Weekly Reader Books, 1984, EX..........$8.00
Charlie Brown's All-Stars, Charles M Schulz, Signet Books, 1966, EX $5.00
Chuck Squirrel, Goldsmith Publishing, 1922, die-cut cover of lg squirrel, EX $30.00
Crocks of Gold, by Carol Ryie Brink, Saalfield #4110, 1940, VG+ $15.00
Dale Evans Prayer Book for Children, Big Golden Book, 1956, hardback, VG+ $10.00
Dilly the Dinosaur, by Tony Bradman, Weekly Reader Books, 1987, hardback, VG+ $10.00

***Donald Duck and His Friends*, by Jean Ater, 1939, NM, $45.00.**

Donald Duck Takes It on the Chin, Dell Fast-Action, 1941, soft-cover, EX..........$75.00
Early One Morning, Elf Tip-Top #8656, 1963, hardback, G..$8.00
Emerald City of Oz, by Frank Baum, 1st ed, 1st printing, 1910, hardback, VG, A $100.00
Fantasia (Stories From Walt Disney's), Random House/WDP, 1940, hardback, EX+ $100.00
Fire House, by Leo Manso, World Publishing, 1949, Rainbow Playbook, spiral-bound, hardback, EX $25.00
First Book of the Antarctic, by JB Icenhower, F Watts Co, 1956, 7th printing, hardback, EX+ $18.00
First Circus, Platt & Munk #3100-C, 1932, hardback, EX...$12.00
Flash Gordon, Treasure Books #906, 1956, illus by Alex Berger, hardback, NM..........$30.00
Fonzie Drops In, by Johnston, #2, 1974, paperback, EX $10.00
Gingerbread Boy, Platt & Munk, 1932, paperback, EX $18.00
Gnome King of Oz, Reilly & Lee, by Ruth Plumly Thompson, 1st edition, 1st state, 12-color plated, EX, A $50.00
God's Plan for Growing Things, by Mary Alice Jones, Rand McNally Junior Elf Book #8112, hardcover, 1964, EX+ ..$8.00
Happy Birthday to You by Dr Seuss, Random House, 1959, early reprint, hardback, EX $25.00
Henny Penny (Story of), See & Say Storybook/Read Along With Me, Samuel Lowe, 1962, EX..........$10.00
Here's to You Charlie Brown, by Charles Schulz, 1970, hardback, EX+ $8.00
Here We Go!, John Martin's House, 1950, hardback, G ...$12.00
Huckleberry Hound & the Dream Pirates, by H Elias, Modern Promotions, 1972, booklet, EX..........$6.00
Jasper & the Watermelons, Diamond Publishing, 1945, hard-back, scarce, VG $12.00
Knight Rider, by G Larson & R Hill, Pinnacle Books, 1983, paperback, EX+..........$10.00
Land of Surprise, by Gladys & Corianne Malvern, McLoughlin Bros, 1938, hardback, VG $45.00
Land of the Giants — The Hot Spot, #2, by M Leinster, 1969, Pyramid, 1st ed, paperback, VG $5.00
Let's Have a Farm, by Jeffery Victor, Capitol Publishing, 1940s, landscape scene changes w/ea turn of the pg, EX+ $65.00
Little Brown Bear, by Alice E Radford, illus by Clayton Rawson, Rand McNally, 1934, hardback, EX..........$35.00
Little Deer, by Naomi Zimmerman, Rand McNally, 1956, Jr Elf series, illus by Marge Opitz, hardback, EX+ $15.00
Little Dorothy & Toto of Oz, Rand McNalley, 1939, hardback, EX+ $75.00
Little Red Riding Hood, Rand McNally, 1958, Tip Top Elf series, illus by Anne Sellers Leaf, hardback, NM $15.00
Little Toot, by Hardie Gramatky, Weekly Reader Book Club, 1960s (?), hardback, VG..........$12.00
Masters of the Universe — The Trap, Golden Storybook, 1983, EX $6.00
Meet the Care Bears, Random House, mini, EX..........$8.00
Monkey Shines, by Elinor Andrews, Platt & Munk #520, 1st ed, 1940, hardback, EX..........$32.00
My Little Book of Prayers, John Martin's House, 1948, hardback, VG $10.00
My Picture Story Book, Platt & Munk, 1941, hardback, EX .. $40.00
Night Before Christmas, by Clement C Moore, Random House, 1975, EX $10.00
Noah's Ark, Rand McNally Giant Book, 1961, hardback, EX .. $12.00
Once Upon a Time — Story of the Frog Prince, Rand McNally Jr Elf #8068:15, 1960, hardback, VG $10.00
Pandora Story Book, Pied Piper Books, 1946, hardback, EX..$28.00
Partridge Family in The Haunted Hall, by M Avalone, Curtis Books, 1970, paperback, EX $8.00
Pastoral, Harper & Bros/WDP, 1940, hardback, EX $50.00
Peter Rabbit, by Phoebe Erickson, Children's Press, 1947, hard-back, VG..........$15.00
Peter Rabbit in the Tale of the Flopsy Bunnies, by B Potter, McDonald's ed, 1988, paperback, EX..........$10.00
Pinocchio, Grosset & Dunlap, 1939, EX+ $50.00
Play It Again Charlie Brown, Charles M Schulz, Times Mirror/World Publising, 1st edition, 1971, hardback, EX+......$5.00
Popeye Puppet Show, Pleasure Books, 1936, EX+ $75.00
Poppyseed, Top Tales #2475, 1954, hardcover, EX $18.00
Raggedy Ann & Andy & the Camel With the Wrinkled Knees, by Johnny Gruelle, Bobbs-Merrill, 1960, hardback, EX+..........$14.00
Raggedy Ann in the Deep Woods, by Johnny Gruelle, MA Donohue, 1930, hardback, G $15.00

Raggedy Ann Stories, by Johnny Gruelle, Bobbs-Merrill, 1960, hardback, EX....$12.00
Raggedy Ann Stories, by Johnny Gruelle, MA Donohue, 1920, hardback, VG....$20.00
Road Runner in A Very Scary Lesson, by Schroeder, Merrigold Press, hardback, NM+....$8.00
Road to Oz, by L Frank Baum, 1st ed, 1st state, 1909, EX, A. $175.00
Rocket Away!, by Francis Frost, 1953, hardback, EX....$35.00
Scalawag the Monkey, by Ruth Dixon, Rand McNally, 1952, photographs by Rie Gaddis, hardback, EX....$15.00
Scalawagons of Oz, Reilly & Lee, by John R Neill, 1st ed, VG, A....$100.00
Sgt Preston & Yukon King, by MH Comfort, Rand McNally, 1955, NM+....$10.00
Stories From Fantasia, Random House/WDP, 1940, hardback, EX....$50.00
Story of Jesus, by Gloria Diener Glover, Rand McNally, 1949, Junior Elf series, illus by Priscilla Pointer, hardback, NM....$14.00
Storyland, Samuel Lowe, 1947 reprint, VG....$10.00

***The Three Little Pigs*, Rand McNally, Jr. Elf edition, by Ruth Bendel, NM, $15.00.** (Photo courtesy gasolinealleyantiques.com)

Thunder Cats in Quest for the Magic Crystal, Random House, 1985, booklet, EX....$6.00
Time for Everything, Elf Book #8562, Rand McNally, 1972, EX....$8.00
Tinder Box, Stephen Daye Inc, c 1945, 5 mechanical pgs animated by Julian Wehr, EX....$85.00
Treasure Island, by Robert Louis Stevenson, John C Winston Co, 1924, hardback, EX+....$30.00
Ugly Duckling & Other Stories, Tower Books, NY, 1930, EX+....$28.00
Uncle Wiggly & the Apple Dumpling, by Howard R Gais, Platt & Munk #3600A, 1939, illus by George Carlson, EX+....$18.00
Wizard of Oz, by Frank Baum, 5th edition, 2nd state, 1903, VG+ (w/jacket), A....$125.00
Yip & Yap, by Ruth Dixon, Rand McNally #8690, 1958, Tip-Top Elf series, photos by Harry W Frees, hardback, VG+....$15.00
Your Friend the Policeman, Ding Dong School Book, by Miss Frances, Rand McNally, 1953, illus by William Neebe, EX+....$8.00

Breyer

Breyer collecting seems to be growing in popularity, and though the horses dominate the market, the company also made dogs, cats, farm animals, wildlife figures, dolls, and tack and accessories such as barns for their models. They've been in continuous production since the 1950s, all strikingly beautiful and lifelike in both modeling and color. Earlier models were glossy, but since 1968 a matt finish has been used, though glossy and semiglossy colors are now being reintroduced, especially in special runs. (A special run of Family Arabians was done in the glossy finish in 1988.)

One of the hardest things for any model collector is to determine the value of his or her collection. The values listed below are for models in excellent to near mint condition. This means no rubs, no scratches, no chipped paint, and no breaks — nothing that cannot be cleaned off with a rag and little effort. A model which has been altered in any way, including having the paint touched up, is considered a customized model and has an altogether different set of values than one in the original finish. The models listed herein are completely original. For More information we recommend *Breyer Animal Collector's Guide*, by Felicia Browell, Kelly Korber-Weimer, and Kelly Kesicki.

Classic Scale

Cutting Horse, bay with black points, 1997, $31.00. (Photo courtesy Felicia Browell)

Andalusian Foal (#3060FO), Precious Beauty & Foal Gift Set, bay blanket appaloosa w/blk points, socks, 1996-97....$6.00
Andalusian Mare (#3060MA), Classic Andalusian Family, dapple gray w/darker points, socks, 1979-93....$11.00
Andalusian Stallion (#3030ST), Classic Andalusian Family, alabaster w/gray-shaded points, gray or pk hooves, 1979-93....$11.00
Arabian Foal (#3055FO), Drinkers of the Wind, rose gray w/darker gray points, right hind sock, Toys R Us, 1993....$10.00
Arabian Mare (#3055MA), Arabian Mare & Foal Set, lt bay w/blk points, dappling, front socks/hind stockings, 1997-98....$11.00
Arabian Stallion (#3055ST), Classic Arabian Family, lt brn bay w/blk points, diamond star, socks, Sears Book, 1984-85....$18.00

Black Beauty (#3040BB), Quarter Horse, sorrel w/lighter mane & tail, gray hooves, 2002 ....$13.00

Black Stallion (#3030BS), Arabian, seal bay w/blk points, star, socks, 2002 ....$12.00

Bucking Bronco (#190), gray w/darker mane & tail, bald face, stockings, 1961-67 ....$43.00

Charging Mesteño (#4812ME), Grulla Charging Mustang & Dun Foal Set, grulla w/brn points, Wal-Mart, 1995....$12.00

Cutting Horse (#491), Cutting Horse & Calf Set, chestnut w/ darker mane & tail, hind socks, 2004....................$31.00

Fighting Mesteño (#4811ME), Rufo & Diablo, bay roan w/blk points, shading, blaze, front Stockings, Wal-Mart, 2001.. $13.00

Ginger (#3040GI), Black Beauty Family, chestnut w/darker mane, tail & hooves, strip & snip, 1980-93 ....$12.00

Ginger (#3040GI), Pinto Family, grulla pinto w/blk points & bald face $20.00

Hobo (#625), Hobo the Mustang of Lazy Heart Ranch, buckskin w/blk mane & tail, shading, 1975-80 ....$32.00

Jet Run (#3035JR), Pinto Sporthorse, blk pinto w/blk & wht mane, wht tail & legs, blk head w/star, 2001-current .$12.00

Johar (#3030JO), Dapple Gray Mare & Bat Foal, dapple gray w/wht mane & tail, shaded leg joints, Wal-Mart, 2002-current. $15.00

Keen (#3035KE), Liver Chestnut Appaloosa Sporthorse, liver chestnut blanket appaloosa w/darker points, socks, 1998......... $11.00

Kelso (#601), Ladies of the Bluegrass, red chestnut w/blaze, left front sock, QVC, 2002 ....$20.00

Lipizzan Stallion (#620), Pegasus, alabaster w/pk hooves, wings fit in slots on back, 1984-87 ....$29.00

Man O' War (#602), War Admiral, blk bay, Wal-Mart, 2003-current....................$24.00

Merrylegs (#3040ML), Black Beauty Family, dapple gray w/wht mane & tail, lighter face & lower legs, 1980-83 ....$12.00

Mesteño (#480), Spirit (Spirit Kiger Mustang Family), buckskin w/blk points, Wal-Mart, 2002 ....$13.00

Mesteño Foal (#4810FO), Rojo (Nekana Rojo), red dun w/chestnut points, shaded, leg bars, Wal-Mart, 2001...............$7.00

Mesteño's Mother (#4810MO), Cloud's Legacy, bl roan w/blk points & head, narrow star/strip/snip, 2003-current...$28.00

Might Tango, palomino with white mane and tail, strip and snip, right hind sock, $13.00. (Photo courtesy Felicia Browell)

Might Tango (#3035MT), US Olympic Team Set, bay w/blk points, hind socks, Sears Wish Book, 1987 ....$15.00

Mustang Foal (#3065FO), Cloud's Legacy, grulla w/blk mane & tail, star, shaded leg joints w/bars, 2004-current $28.00

Mustang Mare (#3065MA), Mustang Family, chestnut pinto w/ chestnut mane & tail, gray hooves, Sears Wish Book, 1976-90 ....$12.00

Mustang Stallion (#3065ST), Mustang Family, buckskin w/blk points, knee stripes, no dorsel stripe, Sears Wish Book, 1985....................$15.00

Polo Pony (#626), bay w/blk points, early ones w/socks, molded woodgrain base, 1976-82 ....$29.00

Quarter Horse Foal (#3045FO), palamino w/wht mane & tail, socks, gray hooves, 1975-82....................$11.00

Quarter Horse Mare (#3045MA), Quarter Horse Family, dk chestnut w/darker or blk points, hind socks, JC Penney, 1991 ....$15.00

Quarter Horse Stallion (#3045ST), Quarter Horse Family, dk chestnut/bay w/darker points, hind sock, JC Penney, 1991..... $16.00

Rearing Stallion (#180), bay w/blk mane & tail, bald face, stockings, hooves, 1965-80 ....$17.00

Reflections Mesteño (#481), buckskin w/blk points, leg bars, 1996 ....$16.00

Rojo (#4812RO), Roano (Sdriano & Roano Set), chestnut blanket appaloosa, shaded, front socks, Wal-Mart, 2001...$10.00

Ruffian (#606), dark bay w/blk points, star, left hind sock, 1977-90 ....$16.00

Sagr (#3030SA), Arabian Stallion, blk w/high stockings, 2003-current....................$12.00

Shire A (#627A), dapple gray w/shaded knees, hocks & muzzle, half blaze, high stockings, bl & wht ribbons, 2002-current.... $14.00

Silky Sullivan (#603), T Bone, blk roan w/blk points, gray speckles, 1991-92....................$13.00

Sombra, grulla, J.C. Penney, 1994, $25.00; cocoa dunn, B.L.M. Adopt-A-Horse, 1997, $21.00. (Photo courtesy Felicia Browell)

Swaps (#604), chestnut w/darker mane & tail, star, hind socks & lt hoof w/3 dk hooves, 1975-90 ....$17.00

Terrang (#605), dk brn w/darker mane & tail, lighter hind leg, 1975-90....................$17.00

Wagoo King (#466), Roping Horse & Calf Set, bay w/blk points, hind socks, 2000 ....$16.00

Paddock Pals Scale

American Saddlebred (#9030), bay w/blk points, wht w/5-point star, 1985-88 ......$7.00
American Saddlebred (#9030), English Show Horse & Rider Set, blk w/3 stockings, star & stripe, w/rider figure, 2003 ....$9.00
Arabian Stallion (#9001), bay w/blk points, 1984-88 ....$8.00
Arabian Stallion (#9001), Half-Arabian, bay pinto w/bicolor mane & gray striped tail & hooves, narrow blaze, 1999-2000 ......$6.00
Clydesdale (#9025), chestnut w/blk mane & tail, bald or solid face, stockings, gray hooves, 1984-88 ......$9.00
Clydesdale (#9025), red bay w/blk points, broad wht blaze, stockings, 1999-2003 ......$6.00
Morgan Stallion (#9005), buckskin w/blk points, socks, pk/natural hooves, 1999-2000 ......$6.00
Morgan Stallion (#9005), seal brn w/blk points, 1984-88 ...$8.00
Quarter Horse Stallion (#9015), Breyer Parade of Breeds, smoke gray w/blk points, socks, JC Penney, 1988 ......$8.00
Quarter Horse Stallion (#9015), liver chestnut blanket appaloosa w/lighter tail, darker lower legs, shaded face, 2001-03..$6.00
Thoroughbred Stallion (#9010), dk gray w/blk points, hind socks, 1989-94 ......$7.00
Throughbread Stallion (#9010), Breyer Parade of Breeds, dk bay w/blk points, bald face, hind sock, JC Penney, 1988.. $100.00
Unicorn (#9020), wht w/gray shading on mane, tail & hooves, wht & gold horn, 1999, 2003 ......$6.00
Unicorn (#9020), wht w/powder bl mane, tail, beard & feathers, gold horn, Montgomery Ward, 1985 ......$31.00

Stablemate Scale

American Saddlebred (#5608), Just About Horses Special Edition Stablemates Gift Set, blk w/star & snip, hind socks, 1998 ......$9.00
Andalusian (#5606), Just About Horses Special Edition Stablemates Set, dk dapple gray w/blk points, snip, socks, 1998 ...... $9.00
Appaloosa (#5601), Silver Cup Series/First Collection 2002, glossy bay pinto w/blk points, hind sock, QVC $12.00
Arabian Mare (#5011), dapple gray w/darker mane & tail, stockings, gray hooves, 1975-76......$22.00
Arabian Rearing (#5603), Just About Horses Special Edition Gift Set, chestnut w/lighter mane & tail, blaze, socks, 1998 ...... $9.00
Arabian Stallion (#5010), dapple gray w/darker mane & tail, stockings, 1975-76 ......$32.00
Cantering Foal (#5614), Flocky Set II, flocked buckskin appaloosa w/blk mane & tail, hind stockings, BreyerFest, 2001 ......$12.00
Citation (#5020), bay w/dk points, left hind sock, 1975-90 .. $8.00
Clydesdale (#5604), Just About Horses Special Edition Gift Set, bl roan w/blk points, bald face, stockings, 1998 ....$9.00
Draft Horse (#5055), dk chestnut w/darker mane & tail, socks, gray hooves, Riegseckers, 1985 ......$33.00
Morgan Mare (#5038), chestnut w/darker mane & tail, hind stockings, lighter lower forelegs, gray hooves, 1976 ...... $24.00
Morgan Prancing (#5612), Silver Cup Series/Second Collection 2002, glossy seal bay w/blk mane & tail, shading, QVC $13.00
Morgan Stallion (#5035), bay w/blk mane, tail, knees & socks, left hind sock, 1976-88 ......$13.00
Mule (#5609), blk leopard appaloosa w/blk tail & face, gray shading, blk splash spots, 1998-2002 ......$4.00
Native Dancer (#5023), blood bay w/blk points, Sears Wish Book, 1989 ......$8.00
Paso Fino (#5610), Just About Horses Special Edition Gift Set, smutty buckskin w/blk points, shaded back, 1998 ....$9.00
Quarter Horse Mare (#5048), buckskin w/blk points, no dorsal stripe, socks, gray hooves, 1976-88 ......$11.00
Quarter Horse Stallion (#5045), matt/semigloss chestnut w/darker mane & tail, socks/stocking, gray hooves, 1976 ....$25.00

Quarter Horse Stallion, Paint, grulla pinto, gray body with darker points, 1998, from $4.00 to $6.00. (Photo courtesy Felicia Browell)

Saddlebred (#5002), dapple gray w/darker points, bald face, gray hooves, 1975-76......$33.00
Scrambling Foal (#5613), Fun Foals Gift Pack, mostly wht bay pinto w/blk mane on upper neck, shaded muzzle, 2002 .. $9.00
Shetland Pony (#5605), Just About Horses Special Edition Gift Set, brn/chestnut w/silver dapple, wht mane & tail, 1998 .... $9.00
Silky Sullivan (#5022), chestnut w/darker mane & tail, right hind stocking, 1976-94 ......$7.00
Standard Bred (#5611), Just About Horses Special Edition Gift Set, med chestnut, right front & left rear socks, 1998 .. $9.00
Swaps (#5021), blk leopard appaloosa w/blk points, sm spots, Sears Wish Book, 1989 ......$8.00
Thoroughbred (#5602), dappled gray w/blk mane & tail, star/stripe/snip, hind sock, from Reflections Set, Toys R Us, 2002......$10.00
Thoroughbred Lying Foal (#5700LF), Lying & Standing Foals bay w/darker mane & tail, w/ or w/o hind stockings, 1975-76......$12.00
Thoroughbred Mare (#5026), matt/semigloss blk, front socks & hind stockings, gray hooves, 1975-88......$8.00
Thoroughbred Standing Foal (#5700SF), Stable Set, dk bay w/darker mane, tail, legs & stockings, 1976-80 ....$11.00
Warmblood (#5607), Double Exposure, glossy grulla w/darker points, star/stripe, right socks, Just Ahead Horses, 2003.............. $13.00

Traditional Scale

Action Stock Foal (#235), appaloosa w/blk points & hooves, blanket over hind quarters, 1984-88 ....$13.00
Adios (#50), Clayton Quarter Horse, dapple palomino w/wht mane & tale, resist dappling, stackings, 1995-96........$24.00
Adios (#50), Vales of Phoenix, buckskin w/blk points, 1978. $232.00
Amber (#488), Twin Appaloosa Foals, bay blanket appaloosa w/blk mane & tail, wht blaze, 2 socks, Sears, 1998.....$17.00
American Saddlebred Stallion (#571), Blue Note, glossy bay w/ shading, blk mane, tail & above socks, QVC, 2002 ...$66.00
Appaloosa Performance Horse (#99), Appaloosa Stallion, gray w/blk points, hind blanket pattern, JC Penney, 1984.$44.00
Ashley (#489), Great Spirit Mare & Foal, bay pinto w/blk tail & top of mane, wht legs & rear, bay head, JC Penney, 2001..... $19.00
Balking Mule (#207), bay/chestnut w/darker mane & tail, gray hooves, brn or dk red bridle, 1968-73 ....$74.00
Belgian (#92), Buddy, glossy liver chestnut w/reddish mane & tail, bald face, socks, 1998 ....$48.00
Big Ben (#483), Hickstead, glossy red bay w/shading, blk points, broad blaze, hind striped hooves & socks, QVC, 2002..$57.00
Black Beauty (#89), Donovan Running Appaloosa Stallion, gray w/blanket pattern & chestnut spots, 3 socks, 1995-97 ....$24.00
Black Stallion (#401), Majestic Arabian Stallion, leopard appaloosa w/blk points, brn & blk splash spots, 1989-90...$26.00
Brown Sunshine (#484), sorrel w/wht mane & tail, lighter lower legs, gray hooves, 1996-97 ....$23.00
Buckshot (#415), Spanish Barb, chestnut pinto w/darker mane, tail & lower front legs, 1988-89 ....$26.00
Cantering Welsh Pony (#104), bay w/blk points, yel or bl ribbons, 1971-73 ....$74.00
Cedarfarm Wixom (#573), matt blk w/slight dappling, gray chestnuts, bl tail bow, 2001-03 ....$34.00
Clydesdale Foal (#84), dapple gray (sm dapples), darker gray mane & tail, socks, Horses Int'l, 1988.........................$46.00
Clydesdale Mare (#83), Clydesdale Family Set, red bay w/blk mane & tail, wht legs & belly, bald face, JC Penney, 1982-84 ....$46.00
Clydesdale Stallion (#80), muscle version, bay w/blk mane & tail, bald face, stockings, red bobs, JC Penney, 1982-84......$46.00
Cody (#471), Buster, buckskin pinto w/blk & wht mane & tail w/blk points, blk spot on muzzle, 1999-2001 ....$27.00
Donkey (#81), gray w/stockings, dk mane & tail, pale muzzle or bay variation, 1958-74, ea $22.00
El Pastor (#61), bay w/blk points, solid face, left socks, 1987.. $124.00
Family Arabian Foal (#9), lt chestnut w/flaxen mane & tail, narrow blaze, JC Penney, 1983 ....$17.00
Family Arabian Mare (#8), Dickory, charcoal w/wht mane & tail, bald face, socks, gray hooves, 1967-73................$21.00
Family Arabian Stallion (#7), matt or semigloss blk, no markings, Model Congress, Bently Sales Co, 1978.............$63.00
Fighting Stallion (#31), King, woodgrain, narrow blaze, socks, blk hooves, 1963-73... $109.00
Five Gaiter (#52), American Saddlebred, dapple gray w/wht mane & tail, bald face, socks, pk hooves, ribbons, 1987-88 .... $39.00
Foundation Stallion (#64), American Indian Pony, fleabit, gray w/reddish gray points, fine speckles, 1988-91.............$26.00
Friesian (#485), Jack Frost, speckled gray w/darker points, 1999 .... $60.00
Fury Prancer (#P45), woodgrain, may or may not have hat reins, 1960 .... $211.00
Galiceno (#100), Crillo Pony, yel dun w/darker points, dorsal stripe, blaze, shaded muzzle, right hind sock, 1998-99 .... $23.00
Gem Twist (#495), Champion Show Jumper, alabaster w/gray-shaded tail, knees & socks, natural hooves, 1993-95..$28.00
Grazing Foal, (#151), bald face, stockings, 1964-70 ....$32.00
Grazing Mare (#141), Grazing Mare & Foal, matt or semigloss mahogany bay w/blk points, 2 socks, 1998-99 ....$24.00
Halla (#63), Nobel Jumper, dapple gray w/blk points, hind socks, 1990-91 ....$29.00
Hanoverian (#58), dk bay w/blk points, 1980-84 ....$29.00
Hatflinger (#156), sorrel w/flaxen mane & tail, faint socks, gray hooves, Horses Int'l, 1984-85...................................$27.00
Huckleberry Bey, (#472), Paradign, glossy dapple gray w/blk points, dk shading w/some peach on head & mane, QVC, 2001 ....$71.00
Ideal American Quarter Horse (#497), Offspring of Go Man Go, red roan w/solid points, coon tail, 'J bar' brand, 1998... $31.00
Indian Pony (#175), Black Horse Ranch, blk leopard appaloosa w/gray points, blk spots, stockings, 1987....................$89.00
Iron Metal Chief (#486), Fanfare, glossy Gold Charm w/wht mane & tail, bald face, stockings, Breyer 50 Years, 2000 ...... $119.00
John Henry (#445), Western Horse, dk chestnut w/darker mane & tail, star & stripe, socks, JC Penney, 1994 ....$28.00
Jumping Horse (#300), bay w/blk mane & tail, bald face, front socks, 1965-88...$27.00
Justin Morgan (#65), lt chestnut w/darker mane & tail, shaded knees & hocks, left hind sock, JC Penney, 1988.........$28.00
Lady Phase (#40), Family Appaloosa Mare, blk leopard appaloosa, gray points, stenciled spots, 1992-94................$33.00
Lady Roxanna (#425), Prancing Arabian Mare, chestnut w/ flaxen mane & tail, 3 socks, gray hooves, 1988-89 .....$22.00
Le Fire (#581), chestnut w/lt front sock & 3 stockings, natural hooves, star & odd-shaped blaze w/snip, 2002-current... $35.00
Legionario (#68), Stardust, dapple gray w/wht mane & tail, lt wht dapples, socks, Toys R Us, 1997 ....$26.00
Llanarth True Briton (#494), Sunny Boy, Welsh Cob, shaded palomino w/wht mane & tail, shaded knees, socks, 1997.....$28.00
Lonesome Glory (#572), Mosaic, bay pinto w/blk points, wht left hind leg, half-apron face, glossy version, 2001......... $700.00
Lying Down Foal (#245), blk appaloosa w/bald face, rear blanket, 1969-84 ....$19.00
Man O' War (#47), Traveler (Gen Lee's Horse), lt shaded gray w/blk mane & tail, Horses in American History, 1998-99........ $41.00
Marabella (#487), Morgan Mare, liver chestnut w/flaxen mane & tail, stripe/snip, lighter lower legs, 1999-2000 ....$27.00
Midnight Sun (#60), Tennessee Walking Horse, red bay w/blk points, red & wht braids, gray hooves, 1988-89..........$30.00
Misty (#20), Marguerite Henry's Misty, palomino pinto w/dbl eye circles, old Misty pinto pattern, 1972 ....$80.00

Misty's Twilight (#470), Romanesque, lt dapple gray w/shaded muzzle, hocks, knees & hooves, 1999-2000 ....$26.00

Morgan (#48), blk bald face, front socks, back stockings, 1965-87 ....$38.00

Morgan, Stonington, seal brown with darker mane and tail, shadowed, star, strip, and left front stocking, Mid-States Distributing, 1998, from $27.00 to $50.00. (Photo courtesy Felicia Browell)

Morganglanz (#59), chestnut w/flaxen mane & tail, stripe, stockings, gray hooves, 1980-87................$21.00

Mustang (#87), Diablo, glossy alabaster w/lt gray mane, tail & hooves, blk eyes, 1961-66................ $129.00

Mustang (#87), Gray Hawk, bl roan pinto, w/Indian markings, QVC, 2002 ....$50.00

Nursing Foal (#3155FO), Thoroughbred Mare & Foal Gift Set, lt chestnut w/darker mane & tail, 1973-84................$14.00

Old Timer (#200), buckskin w/blk points, bald face, socks, blk harness w/gold band, bl hat, 1998-99................$26.00

Pacer (#46), liver chestnut w/slightly darker mane & tail, socks, halter & gold trim, 1967-87 ....$27.00

Peruvian Paso (#576), dapple gray w/darker points, shaded, 2002-current $31.00

Phantom Wings (#18), Three Generations Appaloosa Set, bay appaloosa w/darker points, 3 socks, JC Penney, 1993 .$16.00

Phar Lap (#90), Phar Lap Famous Race Horse, red chestnut w/reverse C-shaped star, hind legs, 1985-88 ....$29.00

Pluto (#475), Embajador XI, Andalusian, med dapple gray w/lighter face, flank & tail, darker legs, 1996-97................$24.00

Pony of the Americas (#155), Just Justin Quarter Pony, coffee dun w/blk points, blaze, 1993-95................$20.00

Proud Arabian Foal (#218), Joy, glossy alabaster w/blk & dk gray mane, tail & hooves, 1956-60 ....$31.00

Proud Arabian Mare (#215), matt/semigloss mahogany bay w/blk points, socks, 1972-80................$30.00

Proud Arabian Stallion (#211), Black Horse Ranch, red bay w/blk points, pk nose, 1987 ....$65.00

Quarter Horse Gelding (#97), Traditional Horse Set, palomino w/wht man & tail, stockings, brn halter, JC Penney, 1990.. $29.00

Quarter Horse Yearling (#101), liver chestnut, crooked blaze, hind socks, gray hooves, 1970-80................$29.00

Racehorse (#36), glossy chestnut w/bald face, stockings, blk hooves & halter, 1956-67 ....$71.00

Rejoice (#479), Charisma, palomino pinto w/wht mane & tail, shaded muzzle, front stockings, hind stockings, QVC, 2001 ....$57.00

Roemer (#465), Quiet Fox Hunters Set, seal bay/brn w/blk points, diamond star, 3 socks, Sears Wish Book, 1992 ....$30.00

Roy the Belgian (#455), Belgian Brabant, gray dun w/darker points, chestnut shading, 1991-93................$26.00

Roy the Belgian (#455), Legacy Gift Set II, lt gray w/shadedmuzzle knees, hocks & hooves, Sears Wish Book, 1999 ....$29.00

Running Foal (#130), bay chestnut w/blk mane, tail & hooves, bald face, stockings, 1963-87................$13.00

Running Mare (#120), chestnut pinto, flaxen mane & tail w/chestnut tip, blaze on lower face, 3 stockings, 1991-93 ....$25.00

Running Stallion, glossy charcoal w/wht points, bald face, 1968-71 .... $164.00

Saddlebred Weanling (#62), chestnut w/slighty darker mane & tail, 3 socks, 1984................ $134.00

San Domingo (#67), chestnut pinto (mostly wht), chestnut medicine hat, natural hooves, 1978-87................$28.00

Scratching Foal (#168), liver chestnut w/darker mane & tail, stockings, 1970-71 ....$64.00

Sham (#410), Rana, dk grayish tan mane & tail, stockings, 1992-93 ....$27.00

Sherman Morgan (#430), chestnut w/darker mane & tail & hooves, stripes, right hind sock, 1987-90................$47.00

Shetland Pony (#23), bay pinto w/blk mane & tail, blaze, natural hooves, 1989-91................$19.00

Shire (#95), shaded lt bay w/blk points, 1998-99 ....$28.00

Silver (#574), Hidalgo, chestnut pinto w/lighter tail, 2-colors mane, intricate pattern, 2004-current................$31.00

Smoky (#69), Remington, Pinto, bay pinto w/blk points, apron face, socks, natural hooves, 1997................$24.00

Stock Horse Foal (#228), American Quarter Horse Foal, bay w/blk points, shading, star/stripe/snip, socks, 1999-2001 ....$15.00

Stock Horse Foal (#228), Palomino Horse & Foal Set, wht w/mane & tail, bald face, stockings, Montgomery Ward, 1983 ....$44.00

Stock Horse Mare (#227), Sorrel Quarter Horse Stock Mare, flaxen mane & tail, stripe, right hind sock, 1982................$26.00

Stock Horse Stallion (#226), Bay Quarter Stock Stallion, bay w/blk points, 1981-88 ....$25.00

Stock Horse Stallion (#226), Brown & White Pinto Stock Horse, bay pinto w/blk points, stockings, JC Penney, 1984 ....$31.00

Strapless (#583), dk bay w/tiny star, 2003................$35.00

Stud Spider (#66), blk appaloosa w/stenciled blanket pattern over back half, thin star, front sock, 1978-89................$28.00

Thoroughbred Mare (#3155MA), Pinto Mare & Suckling Foal Set, bay pinto w/blk points, Sears Wish Book, 1982-83 ....$38.00

Touch of Class (#420), Selle Francais, dk chestnut w/darker mane & tail, blaze, stockings, gray hooves, 1991-92...$25.00

Trakehner (#54), Spotted Trakehner Warmblood, blk pinto w/wht hind legs, wht over rump, stripe, 1998-99................$26.00

Western Horse (#57), glossy blk, gold hooves, complete w/saddle, 1956-60 .... $73.00
Western Horse (#57), palomino, complete w/saddle, QVC, 1995 .... $26.00
Western Prancing Horse (#110), Cheyenne, glossy blk pinto w/ bald face, socks, complete w/saddle, 1961-66 .... $69.00
Zippo Pine Bar (#466), chestnut w/star & stripe, right hind stocking, 1999-current $28.00

Other

Australian Shepherd (#1515), bl merle w/wht ruff & feet, wht spot in muzzle, 2000-current $6.00
Bear Cub (#308), dk brn w/lighter head, horns & lower legs, darker hooves, 1997-current $25.00

Benji, tan matt/semigloss with shading, 1978 – 1979, from $24.00 to $56.00. (Photo courtesy Felicia Browell)

Black Angus Bull (#365), no markings, 1978-current $25.00
Border Collie (#1518), blk & wht, 2000-current $5.00
Boxer (#1), semigloss woodgrain w/wht face stripe, blk muzzle, 1959-65 .... $242.00
Buffalo (#76), med brn w/dk brn head & mane, wht horns w/dk tips, 1965-91 .... $30.00
Calf (#347), Brown Swiss, cocoa brn, 1972-73 .... $31.00
Calico Cat (#1517), wht, brn & blk, 2000-current $3.00
Charolais Bull (#360), alabaster, 1975-95 .... $21.00
Collie (#2), Lassie, semigloss chestnut & wht, gold or blk eyes, 1958-65 .... $45.00
Cougar (#822), Rufo & Diablo, tan & wht w/blk muzzle, from American Wild Mustangs, Wal-Mart, 2001 .... $7.00
Cow (#341), Cow Family, blk & wht pinto pattern, horns point forward & slighty down, 1974-89 .... $27.00
Cow (#341), Holstein, blk & wht, 2001-current $24.00
Cutting Calf (#492), Cutting Horse & Calf set, lt tan w/shading, gray ears & hooves, pk nose, 2000-01 .... $10.00
Deer (#301BU), Buck, tan w/blk nose & hooves, w/bl ribbon, 1965-73 .... $12.00
Elephant Trumpeting (#91), solid gray, 1958-60 .... $145.00
English Foxhound (#1519), Fox Hunting Gift Shop, brn & wht, 2001-2003 .... $7.00
German Shepard (#327), Rin Tin Tin, matt/semigloss brn w/ darker back, lighter face & legs, 1958-66 .... $44.00

Great Dane (#1520), brindle w/blk muzzle, tiger-striped, blk paws, 2001-2002 .... $8.00
Irish Setter, red w/shaded muzzle, 2004-current $6.00
Kitten (#335), Siamese Kitten, gray or seal point, bl or gr eyes, 1966-71 .... $64.00

Kitten, Socks, black and white matt/semigloss, 1995 – 1996, from $16.00 to $24.00. (Photo courtesy Felicia Browell)

Montana Mountain Goat (#312), alabaster w/shading, blk horns, 1973-76 (1989 reissue w/gray horns is same price) $37.00
Polled Hereford Bull (#74), red-brn & wht, 1968-current $26.00
Poodle (#67), silver-gray, 1968-73 .... $43.00

Pronghorn Antelope, brown and white with white sides, white throat with brown bars, 1971 – 1976, from $40.00 to $105.00; chestnut and white, red-gold body color including legs, white belly, 1997, from $20.00 to $24.00. (Photo courtesy Felicia Browell)

Red Fox (#820), Fox Hunting Gift Set, glossy red chestnut w/blk points, wht throat trail tip & inner ears, 2001-03 .... $6.00
Shetland Sheepdog (#1504), Popular Small Dog 3-Piece Gift Set, bl merle, grayer back, 2004-current $11.00
Spanish Fighting Bull (#73), blk, wht horns w/dk tips, 1970-85 .... $57.00
Walking Hereford Bull, glossy, semigloss or matt dk brn to red, brn & wht, 1958-81 .... $37.00

Welsh Corgi (#1506), golden brn & wht, 1999-current......$4.00
Wolf (#821), Tipi Set, gray w/wht on face & throat, 2001-03 .... $10.00

Buddy L

Buddy L vehicles were produced by Fred Lundahl, founder of Moline Pressed Steel Co. Mr. Lundahl first designed the toys for his young son, Buddy. They were advertised as being 'Guaranteed Indestructible,' and indeed they were sturdy and well built pressed-steel toys. Wartime brought on a shortage of the heavy-gauge pressed steel, at which time wood was used to make some of the vehicles. Many were based on actual models and some were hydraulically activated. The ride-ons were capable of supporting a grownup's weight.

Condition is everything. Remember that unless the work is done by a professional restorer, overpainting and amateur repairs do nothing to enhance the value of a toy in poor condition.

See also Advertising; Aeronautical; Boats; Catalogs.

Cars and Buses

Ambulance, 1950s, wht w/red cross and 'Ambulance' on cloth canopy, 15", EX+ $75.00
Army Staff Car, 1960s, army gr, 16", EX+............ $125.00
Colt Sportsliner, 1960s, NM+............$50.00
Convertible Coupe, 1949, retractable top, 19", EX+...... $375.00
Flivver Coupe, 1920s, blk, MSW, 11", EX $850.00

Flivver Coupe, 1920s, 11", NM, $1,200.00. (Photo courtesy James D. Julia, Inc.)

Flivver Roadster, simulated cloth top, blk w/red spokes, MSW, 12", VG............ $750.00
Jr Camaro, 1960s, 9", EX+............$20.00
Scarab, w/up, #711, 10", VG $150.00
Station Wagon, 1960s, 16", EX $85.00
Station Wagon w/Travel Trailer, 1960s, 28" overall, EXIB...$200.00

Construction

Cement Mixer, 1920s, rubber treads, EX............$3,500.00
Cement Mixer, 1940s, #832, VG+ $250.00
Cement Mixer, 1950s, makes motor sound, 10" L, EX+ .. $100.00
Cement Truck, 1960s, red w/wht revolving cement drum, 8-wheeled, 15", NM+ $225.00
Construction Crane, 1950s, 20" H, VG $125.00
Construction Derrick, 1950s, VG $175.00
Dandy Digger, 1920s, #33, 28", EX............ $150.00
Derrick, 1920s, 24" H, VG $500.00
Giant Digger, 44", G............ $150.00
Hoisting Tower, 1920s, #350, VG+............ $850.00
Mobile Power Digger, 1950s, 32", EX+ $175.00
Pile Driver, 1920s, #260, 23" H, EX+............ $900.00
Road Grader, 1970s, yel, 7" L, EX+............$15.00
Sand Loader, 1920s, 18" H, EX+ $200.00
Steam Shovel, 1920s, blk & red, VG $200.00

Steam Shovel, 1920s, black and red, VG+, $250.00. (Photo courtesy Morphy Auctions)

Steam Shovel Truck, International, 2-color, BRT, 30", VG+ .. $500.00

Firefighting

Aerial Ladder Truck, 1926 – 1930, open seat, nickel-plated ladders and disk wheels, 39", VG+, $1,375.00. (Photo courtesy James D. Julia, Inc.)

American La France Pumper Truck, 1960s, 25½", EX+.....$75.00
Extension Ladder Truck, 1941-42, #801, unused, NM+IB............ $1,000.00
Fire Hose & Water Pumper, 1950s, 12", NMIB (NOS).. $300.00

Hook & Ladder Truck, 1924-31, #205, open seat, red ladders, NPDW, 27", EX $2,200.00
Hose Truck, 1933, electric lights, 22", EX........ $500.00
Husky Dumper, 1960s, yel, 14½", EX+........ $35.00
Hydraulic Aeriel Ladder Truck, 1931-32, open seat, NP ladders, headlights & bumper, 42", VG........ $2,500.00
Hydraulic Snorkel Fire Pumper, 1960s, red w/2 wht ladders, 21", EX+........ $125.00
Hydraulic Water Tower Truck, 1930s, diagonal red & yel pnt, electric headlights, 45", EX+........ $750.00
Ladder Truck, 1930s, #W36, International cab, red w/wht ladders, 22", EX+........ $500.00
Ladder Truck, 1930s, sq cab w/visor, chrome radiator, red w/yel ladders, 23", VG........ $175.00
Ladder Truck, 1940s, diagonal red & wht pnt, wht ladders, chrome grille, 18", EX........ $250.00
Ladder Truck, 1940s, red w/chrome trim, blk wooden wheels, 12", EX+........ $150.00
Pumper Truck, 1925-30, #205A, open seat, chrome boiler, NPDW, 27", EX........ $1,100.00
Suburban Pumper, 1960s, red station wagon w/wht plastic bumpers, 15", EX+........ $125.00
Water Tower Truck, 1920s, open bench seat, MDW, separate headlights & cowl light, 38½", G w/some overpnt . $1,950.00

Ride-On Toys

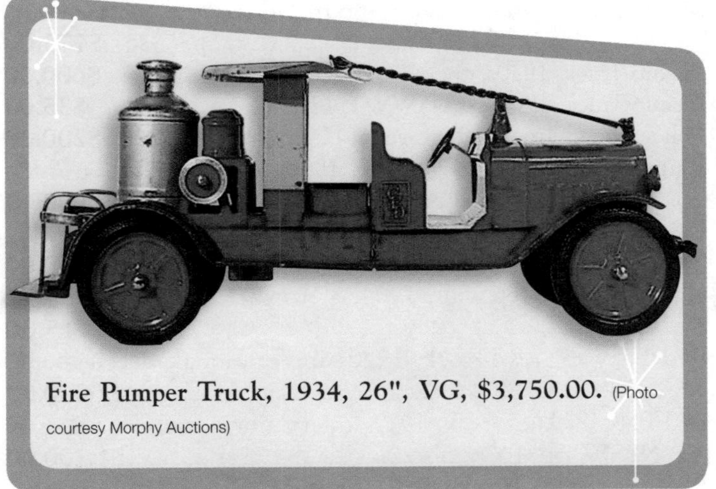

Fire Pumper Truck, 1934, 26", VG, $3,750.00. (Photo courtesy Morphy Auctions)

Baggage Truck, 1950s, 2-color, BRT, 6-wheeled, w/seat & hdl, 25", VG........ $300.00
Delivery Truck, 1920s International, 2-color horizontal pnt, w/seat & hdl, 24", VG........ $450.00
Delivery Truck, 1930s International, stake bed, diagonal 2-color pnt, w/seat & hdl, 25", EX+IB........ $2,500.00
Delivery Truck, 1930s International, stake bed, horizontal 2-color pnt, w/seat & hdl, 23", VG+........ $600.00
Dump Truck, 1930s International, curved cab, w/seat & hdl, 25", G........ $1,000.00
Dump Truck, 1930s International, sq cab w/visor, w/seat & hdl, 20", G+........ $250.00
Dump Truck, 1930s International, working headlights, w/seat & hdl, 24", G........ $550.00
Dump Truck, 1950s, 20", w/seat, no hdl, G........ $100.00
Fire Pumper Truck, 1934, red w/yel seat, BRT, hdl, 26", EX........ $3,500.00
Fire Water Tower Truck, BRT, removable seat, w/hdl, 27", 42", VG........ $2,500.00
Hydraulic Dump Truck, International, 2-color, BRT, w/seat & hdl, 27", NMIB........ $3,000.00
Sand & Gravel Truck, opening lift gate, diagonal 2-color pnt, w/seat & hdl, 21", EX........ $500.00
Wrecker, 1938 International, 28", no seat or hdl o/w VG........ $2,000.00

Trains

Industrial Balliste Car, opening side doors, 8", NMIB . $2,000.00
Industrial Roundhouse, w/round table, 2 switches & 14-pc track, VG........ $700.00
Industrial Set, locomotive & 4 cars w/2 sections of track, VG........ $1,200.00
Outdoor Boxcar, 20", EX+........ $900.00
Outdoor Caboose, 18", EX........ $950.00
Outdoor Coal Car, 22", EX+........ $1,050.00
Outdoor Dredger on Flatcar, 30", EX........ $1,300.00
Outdoor Flatcar, stake & chain sides, 20", VG........ $650.00
Outdoor Gondola, 20", NM+........ $2,250.00
Outdoor Locomotive (4-6-2 1927), Tender, Stock Car (1927), Caboose (#3017), 4-pc track, 78", VG........ $1,550.00
Outdoor Locomotive & Tender, 3-pc track, brass railing trim, bell, rpnt........ $800.00
Outdoor Pile Driver, 23x22", partial rpnt........ $800.00
Outdoor Tank Car, red & blk, 19", G........ $1,200.00
Zephyr, 1-car, #121, 30", VGIB, A........ $1,900.00
Zephyr, 2-car, #221, 50", NMIB........ $3,960.00
Zephyr, 3-car, #20-21, EXIB, A........ $3,300.00

Trucks, Buses, and Vans

Air Force Searchlight Truck, 1950s, plastic searchlight, BRT, 4-wheeled, 15", G........ $50.00
Air Force Supply Transport Truck, 1950s, bl w/bl cloth canopy, 15", EX........ $125.00
Airway Delivery Truck, 1950s, GMC cab w/box van, gr, 4-wheeled, VG........ $250.00
Allied Van Lines Semi, removable van roof, blk & orange, BRT, 6-wheeled, 29", G........ $300.00
Anti-Aircraft Unit w/Electric Searchlight Trailer, 1950s, GMC cab, bl, 24", EX+........ $400.00
Army Supply Truck, 1956, canvas cover, 14½", NM........ $75.00
Army Transport, 1940s, gr w/US Army on cloth cover, BRT, 21", G+........ $175.00
Army Transport w/Tank, 1950s, 26½" overall, EX........ $125.00
Atlas Van Lines Semi, gr & wht w/red lettering, silver van top, BRT, logo on doors, 29", VG........ $550.00
Auto Transport, 1980s, #001, 55", EX, A........ $1,500.00
Baggage Stake Truck, 1920s, blk cab w/yel bed, MDW w/red hubs, 27", EX+........ $1,500.00
Camper Truck, 1960s, WWT, 15", VG........ $65.00
City Dray, 1930s, electric lights, 20", EX........ $450.00

Coal Truck, 1920s, doorless cab, V-shaped bed, blk w/red chassis & hubs, MDW, 25", G $2,000.00
Dump Truck, 1920s, doorless cab, blk, NPDW w/red hubs, 6-wheeled, VG, A $600.00
Dump Truck, 1920s, enclosed cab, electric lights, blk & red, BRT, 4-wheeled, 20", G $300.00
Dump Truck, 1920s, open seat, chain lift bed, blk, MDW w/red hubs, 4-wheeled, 25", VG+ $1,050.00

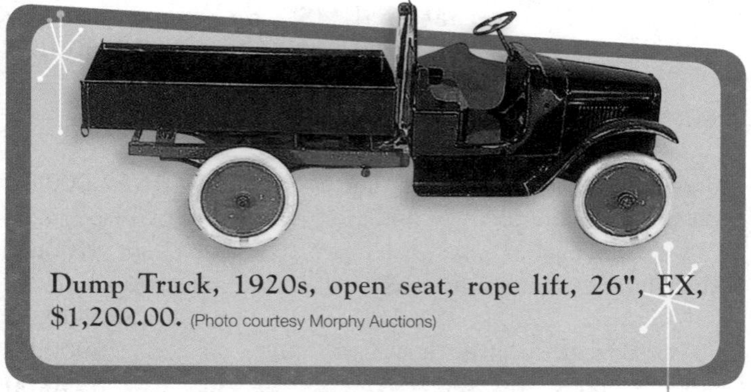

Dump Truck, 1920s, open seat, rope lift, 26", EX, $1,200.00. (Photo courtesy Morphy Auctions)

Dump Truck, 1930s, enclosed cab, curved dump bed, BRT, 4-wheeled, 24", G $200.00
Dump Truck, 1940s, enclosed cab, curved dump bed, blk wooden wheels, 4-wheeled, 17", VG $100.00
Dump Truck, 1960s, enclosed cab, side-crank dump bed, BRT, 6-wheeled, 14", VG $50.00
Electric Emergency Unit, 1950s, yel, 14½", rstr $55.00
Emergency Auto Wrecker, 1940s, NP grille, 15", EX $225.00
Emergency Auto Wrecker, 1950s, BRT, 17", VG $125.00
Express Line Tandem Truck, early cab w/2 trailers, electric lights, 3-color, BRT, 40" overall, EX+ $925.00
Express Line Tractor-Trailer, 1930s, box van w/removable roof, 25", G+ $300.00
Express Line Van, roof over open seat, enclosed sides, 25", VG+ $2,000.00
Express Line Van, roof over open seat, screened sides, 25", VG $1,700.00
Farm Supplies Dump Truck, 1940s, 2-color, 20", VG+IB . $450.00
Fast Freight Semi, 1950s, open U-shaped trailer w/chain across open back, 6-wheeled, 20", NMIB $650.00
Fast Freight Semi, 1950s, open U-shaped trailer w/chain across open back, 6-wheeled, 20", VG $100.00
Firestone Tire Service Truck, 1940s, bl, orange & wht, 24", VG $600.00
Flivver Dump Cart, 1926-30, 12½", VG+ $1,500.00
Flivver Huckster Truck, 1920s, 14", G $2,475.00
Flivver Pickup Truck, 1920s, ragtop, blk, MSW, 12", VG $650.00
Freight Hauler, 1950s, GMC cab, orange, 8-wheeled, 22", G+ $150.00
Greyhound Lines Bus, 1938, #755, bl & wht, opening door, electric brake lights, 16", EX $300.00
Greyhound Lines Bus, 1938, #755, bl & wht, opening door, electric brake lights, 16", EX+IB $650.00
Hi-Lift Scoop & Dump, #3322, 17" (w/scoop extended), VG+ $150.00
Highway Maintenance Dump Truck & Sand Hopper, 1950s, orange, 14" ea, G $100.00
Horse Van, 1960s, red w/wht van, BRT, 18", GIB $175.00
Hydraulic Dumper, 1920s, open seat, VG+ $600.00
Hydraulic Dumper, 1930s, 25", VG+ $500.00
Hydraulic Dumper, 1950s, 10-wheeled, 20", VG $225.00
Hydraulic Dumper, 1960s, turq, BRT, 6-wheeled, 20", VG .. $150.00
Hydraulic Heavy Hauling Dumper, 1950s, 4-wheeled, 21", Fair, ... $65.00
Ice Truck, 1920s, doorless cab, railed bed, blk & yel w/red hubs, 26", complete, EX+ $1,200.00
Ice Truck, 1940s, stake bed, 22½", VG+ $500.00
Jr Air-Mail Truck, blk & red, 22", G $2,100.00
Jr Dump Truck, 1930s, rear dual wheels, BRT, G, A (Est: $700-$900) $660.00
Jr Milk Delivery Truck, 1930s, stepped stake bed, w/milk cans, 24", G $1,300.00
Jr Tanker Truck, 25", VG+ $1,750.00
Lumber Truck, 1920s, blk w/red stake sides & hubs, crank bed, NPDW, w/lumber, 25", EX $3,000.00
Machinery Truck, 1950s, 6-wheeled, 23", VG+ $250.00
Merry-Go-Round Truck, 1960s, 13", NM $150.00
Mobile Repair-It Unit Tow Truck, 1950s, complete, 21", EXIB $400.00
Motor Coach, 1920s, opening door, MDW, side spares, 26", VG+ $5,500.00
Motor Market Truck, 20", G $225.00
Moving Van, 1920s, roof extends over open front seat, blk, VG+ $775.00
Pickup Truck, 1920s, open bench seat, MSW, 24", VG.. $600.00
Pickup Truck, 1960s, lt bl, WWT, 12", VG $35.00
Police Squad Truck, 1940s, yel & bl-gr, 21½", EX+ $200.00
Railway Express Agency Truck, 1930s, Wrigley's ads on sides, electric lights, 6-wheeled, 23", EX $2,000.00
Railway Express Agency Truck, 1950s, ice cream ad on sides, BRT, 6-wheeled, 22", G+ $450.00
REA Express Step Van, 1964, gr w/wht trim, WWT, 11½", EX $115.00
Red Baby Express Truck, 1920s International, doorless cab, NPSW, 24", EX $1,000.00
Red Baby Pickup Truck, 1920s International, tall doorless cab, NPSW, 24", EX+ $1,200.00
Robotoy Dump Truck, 1930s, electric lights, red & gr, 21½", VG+ $1,100.00
Rockin' Giraffes Truck, 1960s, WWT, complete w/2 giraffes, 13½", NM $250.00
Sand & Gravel Truck, 1920s, doorless cab, blk, MDW w/red hubs, 24", EX $1,000.00
Sand & Gravel Truck, 1940s, gr w/wht bumpers, 13½", EX+ .. $125.00
Scoop & Dump Truck, 1950s, 4-wheeled, 18", G $75.00
Scoop & Dump Truck, 1950s, 6-wheeled, 18", G $75.00
Scoop & Dump Truck, 1950s, 10-wheeled, 22", G $100.00
Tank Line Truck, 1920s, w/sprinkler, 26", EX+ $1,800.00
US Mail Truck 2592, 1940s, Buy Defense Bonds, gr, BRT, 6-wheeled, 25", EX+ $325.00
Utilities Service Truck, 1950s, GMC, 15", EX $350.00
Van Freight Carriers, #3413, 20", unused, NMIB $400.00
Wild Animal Circus Truck, 1960s, 26", complete, M $400.00

Wrecker, 1926-27, #209, open bench seat, NPDW, 25", VG..$1,850.00
Wrecker, 1941-42, #503, 19", VG $400.00
Wrigley's Van, see Express Agency Van (Wrigley's)
Zoo Truck, red & yel, WWT, 13", EX+ $100.00

WOODEN VEHICLES

Army Supply Truck, 1940s, 16", no canvas cover o/w VG...$75.00
Army Tank, 11½", VG..................$75.00
Buick Convertible, 1940s, electric lights, 18", NMIB..$5,500.00

Buick Station Wagon, electric headlights, folding rear gate, 18", VG, $1,150.00. (Photo courtesy Randy Inman Auctions)

Fire Aerial Hook & Ladder Truck, 1940s, 33", EX+ $1,750.00
Fire Ladder Truck, 22½", G $75.00
Greyhound Bus, 1940s, bl & wht w/red hubs, 18", VG .. $400.00
Long Distance Moving Van, orange & blk w/yel hubs, 27", EX+..................$400.00
Milk Farms Truck, wht w/blk top, sliding door, 13", EX . $400.00
Pontoon Boat, 1940s, w/up motor, 16", NM $2,800.00
Railway Express Van, #480, gr w/silver-tone roof, sliding side door, rear doors open, 16", NMIB $1,200.00
Railway Express Van, #480, gr w/silver-tone roof, sliding side door, rear doors open, 16", VG+ $500.00
Timber Truck, 27", G+.................. $250.00
Woody Station Wagon, maroon, WWT, chrome hubs, 19", VG $175.00
Wrecking Truck, 18", G+ $175.00

MISCELLANEOUS

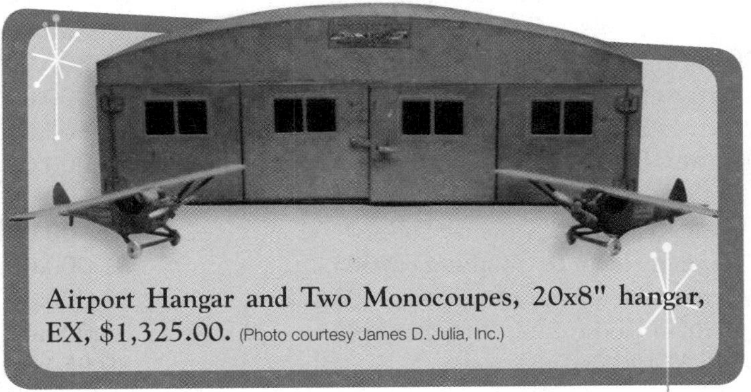
Airport Hangar and Two Monocoupes, 20x8" hangar, EX, $1,325.00. (Photo courtesy James D. Julia, Inc.)

Buddy L Savings & Recording Bank, litho tin, lever action, 6½", EX $185.00
Fire Station, 1940s, pnt wood, 16x16", EX $500.00
Gas Pump, plastic pump w/magnetic nozzle, 7", EXIB.... $125.00
Tool Box, blk & red wooden box w/metal corners, 11x23", box only, VG+ $50.00

Building Blocks and Construction Toys

Toy building sets were popular with children well before television worked its mesmerizing influence on young minds; in fact, some were made as early as the end of the eighteenth century. Important manufacturers include Milton Bradley, Joel Ellis, Charles M. Crandall, William S. Tower, W.S. Read, Ives Manufacturing Corporation, S.L. Hill, Frank Hornby (Meccano), A.C. Gilbert, The Toy Tinkers, Gebruder Bing, R. Bliss, S.F. Fischer, Carl Brandt Jr., and F. Ad. Richter (see Anchor Stone Building Sets by Richter). Whether made of wood, paper, metal, glass, or 'stone,' these toys are highly prized today for their profusion of historical, educational, artistic, and creative features.

Richter's Anchor (Union) Stone Building Blocks were the most popular building toy at the beginning of the twentieth century. As early as 1880, they were patented in both Germany and the USA. Though the company produced more than 600 different sets, only their New Series is commonly found today (these are listed below). Their blocks remained popular until WWI, and Anchor sets were one of the first toys to achieve international 'brand name' acceptance. They were produced both as basic sets and supplement sets (identified by letters A, B, C, or D) which increased a basic set to a higher level. There were dozens of stone block competitors, though none were very successful. During WWI the trade name Anchor was lost to A.C. Gilbert (Connecticut) who produced Anchor blocks for a short time. Richter responded by using the new trade name 'Union' or 'Stone Building Blocks,' sets considered today to be Anchor blocks despite the lack of the Richter's Anchor trademark. The A.C. Gilbert Company also produced the famous Erector sets which were made from about 1913 through the early 1960s.

Note: Values for Richter's blocks are for sets in very good condition; (+) at the end of the line indicates these sets are being reproduced today.

Advisor: George Hardy, Anchor Stone Building Sets by Richter.

American Model Builder Set, EXIB (wood box), A $1,020.00
Ges Gesch, Wood Architectural Building Set, Germany, prewar, wooden blocks in various shapes & sizes, EXIB (wood box), A $127.00
Ideal, Super City Heliport Building Set, 1968, EX (EX vinyl case) $50.00
Ideal, Super City Skyscraper Building Set, 1960s, EXIB....$75.00
Kelmet Steel Engineering Set, #1, complete, EXIB, A ... $180.00
Kelmet Steel Engineering Set, #10, 1923, complete, VGIB (wood box), A $360.00
Kenner Girder & Panel Constructioneer Set #8, EXIB.. $100.00

Kenner Girder & Panel Hydro-Dynamic Double Set #18, VGIB........$200.00
Kenner Girder & Panel Hydro-Dynamic Single Set #17, VGIB........$175.00
Kenner Girder & Panel International Airport, 1977, EXIB...$40.00
Kenner Girder & Panel Skyscraper w/Working Elevator Set #72050, NMIB, A........$65.00
Kenner Mold Master Road Builder, 1964, NMIB........$125.00
Lionel Construction Set #222, unused, NMIB........$100.00
Marklin #2, 1940s, appears unused, VG+IB (cb box), A. $240.00
Marklin Auto-Baukasten, contemporary reissue of the 1930s race car, MIB........$185.00
Meccano Accessory Outfit #4A, EXIB, A........$90.00
Meccano Aeroplane Constructor #0, EXIB........$375.00
Meccano Aeroplane Constructor #1, VGIB........$325.00
Meccano Aeroplane Constructor #2, EX+IB........$450.00
Meccano Roadster Constructor, EXIB........$500.00
Meccano Truck & Ship Set, 1930-31, EXIB, A........$1,080.00
Meccano Truck & Ship Set, 1930-36, w/P56 motor, VG+IB, A........$3,240.00
Meccano Truck Set #110, 1930-31, VGIB, A........$480.00
Metalcraft Spirit of St Louis Airplane Kit, complete, VGIB,...$145.00
Pyro Design-A-Car...Automobile Designing-Construction Set, 1950s, complete, NMIB, A........$75.00
Questor Big Tinkertoy Construction Set for Little hands, 1976, EXIB........$25.00
Questor Tinkertoy Design Blocks EXIC........$30.00
Questor Tinkertoy Giant Engineer, EXIC........$25.00
Questor Tinkertoy Junior Architect, EXIC........$25.00
Questor Tinkertoy Little Designer, EXIC........$25.00
Questor Tinkertoy Locomotive & Driver, EXIC........$15.00
Questor Tinkertoy Master Builder, EXIC........$25.00
Renwal Busy Mechanic Construction Kit #375-198, EXIB..$30.00

Structo Tractor-Builder, #11, early 1900s, VGIB, A, $600.00. (Photo courtesy Randy Inman Auctions)

Schoenhut Aeroplane Builder, unfinished wood, EXIB.. $200.00
Schoenhut Hollywood Home Builder, wood, EXIB........$200.00
Schoenhut Toy Train to Build, makes 5-pc wooden train set, 11" L, VG+IB, A........$300.00
Schuco Elektro Champion Deluxe Set, VGIB........$325.00
Schuco Montage-Mercedes 190SL Kit, #2097, EX+IB... $165.00
Schuco-Studio Steerable Driving School Car, unused, NMIB, A........$200.00
Spalding Big Toy Tinkertoy, 1950s-60s, EXIB........$50.00
Spalding Curtain Wall Builder No 640, 1959-64, EXIC....$40.00
Spalding Executive Tinkertoy Set, 1966, EXIC........$35.00
Spalding Major Tinkertoy, 1964, EXIC........$25.00
Spalding Motorized Tinkertoy, EXIC........$60.00
Spalding Teck Tinkertoy, 1963, EXIC........$25.00
Spalding Tinker Zoo No 717, 1970, EXIC........$15.00
Spalding Tinker Zoo No 737, 1962-70, EXIC........$25.00
Spalding Tinkertoy Panel Builder #600, 1958, EXIC........$30.00
Spalding Tinkertoy Panel Builder #800, 1958, EXIC........$40.00
Spalding Tinkertoy Wonder Builder, 1954-54, EXIC........$30.00
Spaulding Junior Tinkertoy, 1963, EXIC........$25.00

Anchor Stone Building Sets by Richter

American House & Country Set #206........$600.00
American House & Country Set #208........$600.00
American House & Country Set #210........$700.00
DS Set #E3, w/metal parts & roof stones........$80.00
DS Set #03A, w/metal parts & roof stones........$80.00
DS Set #05, w/metal parts & roof stones........$150.00
DS Set #05A, w/metal parts & roof stones........$150.00
DS Set #07, w/metal parts & roof stones........$270.00
DS Set #07A, w/metal parts & roof stones........$200.00
DS Set #09A, w/metal parts & roof stones........$250.00
DS Set #11, w/metal parts & roof stones........$675.00
DS Set #11A, w/metal parts & roof stones........$300.00
DS Set #13A, w/metal parts & roof stones........$325.00
DS Set #15, w/metal parts & roof stones........$1,500.00
DS Set #15A, w/metal parts & roof stones........$475.00
DS Set #19A, w/metal parts & roof stones........$475.00
DS Set #21A, w/metal parts & roof stones........$975.00
DS Set #23A, w/metal parts & Roof stones........$750.00
DS Set #25A, w/metal parts & roof stones........$1,500.00
DS Set #27, w/metal parts & roof stones........$6,000.00
DS Set #27B, w/metal parts & roof stones........$2,000.00
Fortress Set #402........$100.00
Fortress Set #402A........$130.00
Fortress Set #404........$250.00
Fortress Set #404A........$275.00
Fortress Set #406........$500.00
Fortress Set #406A........$400.00
Fortress Set #408........$1,000.00
Fortress Set #408A........$800.00
Fortress Set #410........$1,800.00
Fortress Set #410A........$1,000.00
Fortress Set #412A........$1,500.00
Fortress Set #414........$5,000.00
German House & Country Set #301........$500.00
German House & Country Set #301A........$500.00
German House & Country Set #303........$1,000.00
German House & Country Set #303A........$2,000.00
German House & Country Set #305........$3,000.00
GK-AF Great-Castle Set........$9,950.00

GK-NF Set #06 (+) $140.00
GK-NF Set #06A (+) $160.00
GK-NF Set #08 .... $300.00
GK-NF Set #08A (+) $180.00
GK-NF Set #10 .... $480.00
GK-NF Set #10A (+) $200.00
GK-NF Set #12 .... $680.00
GK-NF Set #12A (+) $250.00
GK-NF Set #14A $250.00
GK-NF Set #16 .... $1,180.00
GK-NF Set #16A $300.00
GK-NF Set #18A $400.00
GK-NF Set #20 .... $2,000.00
GK-NF Set #20A $500.00
GK-NF Set #22A $500.00
GK-NF Set #24A $600.00
GK-NF Set #26A $1,000.00
GK-NF Set #28 .... $4,000.00
GK-NF Set #28A $1,200.00
GK-NF Set #30A $1,200.00
GK-NF Set #30A $1,200.00
GK-NF Set #32B $1,600.00
GK-NF Set #34 .... $7,000.00
KK-NF Set #05 .... $110.00
KK-NF Set #05A $100.00
KK-NF Set #07 .... $200.00
KK-NF Set #07A $115.00
KK-NF Set #09A $120.00
KK-NF Set #11 .... $315.00
KK-NF Set #11A $275.00
KK-NF Set #13A $300.00
KK-NF Set #15A $450.00
KK-NF Set #17A $750.00
KK-NF Set #19A $2,500.00
KK-NF Set #21 .... $4,500.00
Neue Reihe Set #102 .... $100.00
Neue Reihe Set #104 .... $150.00
Neue Reihe Set #106 .... $200.00
Neue Reihe Set #108 .... $300.00
Neue Reihe Set #110 .... $600.00
Neue Reihe Set #112 .... $1,000.00
Neue Reihe Set #114 .... $1,500.00
Neue Reihe Set #116 .... $2,000.00

Candy Containers

As early as 1876, candy manufacturers used figural glass containers to package their candy. They found the idea so successful that they continued to use them until the 1960s. The major producers of these glass containers were Westmoreland, West Bros., Victory Glass, J.H. Millstein, J.C. Crosetti, L.E. Smith, and Jack and T.H. Stough. Some of the most collectible and sought after today are the character-related figures such as Amos 'N Andy, Barney Google, Santa Claus, and Jackie Coogan, to name a few.

There are many reproductions; know your dealer. For a listing of these reproductioins, refer to *Schroeder's Antiques Price Guide*.

In the early 1900s, Germany produced candy containers made of composition. Many were of famous advertising and cartoon characters of the time.

For other types of candy containers, see Halloween; Pez Dispensers; Santa.

Alphonse Emerging From Eggshell w/Feet Showing, pnt compo, 5", Germany, VG $175.00
Amos & Andy Car, clear glass w/pnt figures, tires & bumper, 4½", EX+ $375.00
Barney Google on Pedestal, glass, 3¾", 1920s, EX $150.00
Baseball Player Standing on Square Base, glass, 5", 1916, EX+ $800.00
Bear on Circus Tub Holding Fan, glass, blow through tube to turn fan, 4", TG Stough, ca 1916, VG $175.00
Black & White Taxi, glass w/blk & wht checked tin tip, tin spoke wheels, 4" L, Westmoreland Specialty Co, EX $650.00
Black Cat for Luck, glass, 4¼", VG+ $1,250.00
Bobby Blake Holding Rabbit in Arm, pnt compo, red outfit w/lg yel hat, 6", VG $100.00
Brownie Standing w/Hands on Round Tummy, pnt compo, gr sailor suit, pointed hat, rnd base, 6", Germany, VG.. $150.00

Buddy, lithographed tin figure with glass candy/coin jar, serves as bank when empty, 4¼", Marx, EX, A $300.00. (Photo courtesy James D. Julia Inc.)

Buster Brown Seated on Tige, pnt compo, 6", Germany, NM $1,425.00
Buster Brown Standing, pnt compo, lg rnd eyes, red pnts, bl top hat, 4½", EX+ $200.00
Camera on Tripod, glass w/pnt trim, lens cover on cord, 5", EX, A $650.00
Campbell Kid, pnt compo, bl hat, red coat & yel pants, rnd base, 4½", EX+ $150.00
Campbell Kids, pnt compo, boy in wht w/bl plaid, blk shoes, girl in wht w/pk stripes, red shoes, 4", EX, pr $200.00
Charlie Chaplin Standing Next to Barrel, glass w/pnt figure, tin lid, 3¾", EX, A $150.00
Donald Duck in Airplane, pnt compo w/glittery detail, 8" L, EX $400.00
Donald Duck in Barrel, celluloid figure in cb barrel, 5½", Japan, 1930s, EX, A $400.00
Felix the Cat, pnt compo roly-poly figure, 5", Germany, EX.. $1,568.00
Felix the Cat Standing Next to Barrel, glass w/pnt figure, tin lid, 1920s, EX $425.00

Flossie Fisher's Funnies Bed, gold & blk litho tin w/glass panel, 3¾" L, G+ $700.00
Flossie Fisher's Funnies Chair, gold & blk litho tin w/glass panel, 3", G+ $250.00
Flossie Fisher's Funnies China Closet, gold & blk litho tin w/ front glass panel, 4", G $400.00
Foxy Grandpa Seated on Egg, pnt compo, 5", Germany, VG .. $150.00
Foxy Grandpa Seated Sideways on Chicken, pnt compo, 7", Germany, EX, A $275.00
Happy Fat Standing on Drum, 4¾", Borgfeldt, ca 1915, G .. $100.00
Happy Hooligan & Policeman, pnt compo, policeman straddles Happy Hooligan's head that is bursting egg, 5" H, VG $400.00

Happy Hooligan Head, painted composition, jiggly eyes, 5", EX+, $350.00. (Photo courtesy Morphy Auctions)

Happy Hooligan Seated Sideways on Chick, pnt compo, 5", Germany, EX $150.00
Independence Hall (Building), clear glass w/blk base, 7½", Kirchner, EX+, A $275.00
Jackie Coogan Standing on Round Base, glass, 15", 1920s, EX+ $500.00
Katzenjammer Kid (Fritz) Emerging From Eggshell w/Feet Showing, pnt compo, 5", Germany, EX $125.00
Katzenjammer Kid (Hanz) Riding Rooster, pnt compo, 7", Germany, VG $300.00
Los Angeles Dirigible, silver-pnt glass, mk VG Co Jenet PA USA, 1920s, 6" L, EX $450.00
Mama Katzenjammer Holding 'Nodding' Fritz & Hanz, 6", pnt compo, 6", Germany, EX $1,300.00
Mama Katzenjammer Standing Holding Switch, pnt compo, w/ eye glasses, Germany, 6", EX $400.00
Papa Katzenjammer Standing w/Hands on Round Tummy, pnt compo, rnd base, 4½", Germany, EX $200.00
Rabbit Banjo Player w/Cup on Round Base, papier-machè, metal glasses, metal coiled neck/ears/1 arm, musical, 14", German $200.00
Rabbit Family, glass, mk VG Co Jeannette PA Avor Oz, 1920s, mama, papa & baby rabbit on base, 5x4", VG $485.00
Rabbits (Mama & Daughter) Standing Upright in Dresses, glass, mk w/VG log/USA Avor, 5¼", G $175.00

Snookums Playing w/Roller Devil's Toy, pnt compo on wood base, Germany, EX $250.00
Spirit of St Louis Airplane, glass fuselage w/name on tin wings, 6" WS, Westmoreland, 1920s, EX+ $650.00

Toonerville Trolley, glass, 3½" high, ca 1922, VG, $375.00.

Uncle Sam Standing on Barrel, glass, 4", ca 1918, EX+ $65.00
Veggie Man Riding Rooster, pnt compo w/spring legs, 6", VG, A $990.00
Yellow Kid Emerging From Eggshell, pnt compo, 2¾", Germany, EX $300.00

Cast Iron

Realistically modeled and carefully detailed cast-iron toys enjoyed their heyday from about the turn of the century (some companies began production a little earlier) until about the 1940s when they were gradually edged out by lighter-weight toys that were less costly to produce and to ship. Some of the cast irons were more than 20" in length and very heavy. Many were vehicles faithfully patterned after actual models seen on city streets at the time. Horse-drawn carriages were phased out when motorized vehicles came into use.

Some of the larger manufacturers were Arcade (Illinois), who by the 1920s was recognized as a leader in the industry; Dent (Pennsylvania); Hubley (Pennsylvania); and Kenton (Ohio). In the 1940s Kenton came out with a few horse-drawn toys which are collectible in their own right but naturally much less valuable than the older ones. In addition to those already noted, there were many minor makers; you will see them mentioned in the listings. For more detailed information on these companies, we recommend *Collecting Toys* by Richard O'Brien (Books Americana).

The following listings have been compiled from major toy auctions. The estimates have been added at the end of each listing for comparison. You will see that some toys have sold for way over or way under the estimate, and some have sold within range. This is a new feature that we are sure will facilitate the use of this guide.

See also Banks; Dollhouse Furniture; Guns; Pull and Push Toys.

Airplanes

Air Mail Plane, Kenton, 9" L, VG, A (Est: $500-$700).. **$1,230.00**

Airplane, Arcade, 1941, 10" WS, wooden wheels, VG+, A (Est: $250-$350) **$300.00**

America, Hubley, 17" WS, NM, A (Est: $5,000-$7,000). **$4,480.00**

America, Hubley, 17" WS, VG, A (Est: $1,800-$2,200).. **$2,070.00**

Bremen, Hubley, 7" L, 2 NP pilots, NM, A (Est: $1,000-$1,500) **$1,120.00**

Bremen Junker D1167, Hubley, 10 L", G+, A (Est: $2,500-$3,500) **$1,760.00**

DO-X Top-Wing, Hubley, 3½" WS, G+, A (Est: $250-$350). **$230.00**

Do-X Top-Wing, Hubley, 3½" WS, VG, A (Est: $400-$500).. **$465.00**

Ford #1417 Top Wing, Dent, 1920s, 10", NM, A (Est: $5,000.00 – $7,000.00), $5,600.00. (Photo courtesy Morphy Auctions)

Friendship Seaplane, Hubley, 13" WS, VG, A (Est: $2,000-$2,500) **$3,220.00**

Giro Plane, Hubley, 4½" L, NM+, A (Est: $200-$300) .. **$500.00**

Lindy, Hubley, 11" L, EX, A (Est: $1,000-$1,500) **$2,128.00**

Lockheed, Vindex, 10" WS, silver w/NP prop, EX, A (Est: $4,000-$5,000) **$8,250.00**

Lucky Boy, 12½" WS, NPDW, EX+, A (Est: $2,500-$3,000) . **$2,200.00**

Mighty Minder, Hubley, 1930s, NM, A (Est: $10,000.00 – $12,000.00), $8,960.00. (Photo courtesy Morphy Auctions)

Monocoupe, Arcade, 7" WS, NP wheels, G+, A (Est: $400-$600) **$500.00**

Monocoupe, Arcade, 10½" WS, WRT, VG, A (Est: $600-$800), A **$825.00**

Question Mark, Dent, 12" WS, EX, A (Est: $2,000-$3,000)... **$4,480.00**

Question Mark, Dent, 12" WS, rpnt, A (Est: $1,250-$2,250) **$1,840.00**

Sea Gull, Kilgore, 8" L, VG, A (Est: $700-$1,000)......... **$560.00**

Seaplane, Arcade, 1939, 4" WS, EX, A (Est: $250-$300).... **$440.00**

TAT Top Wing Trimotor, Kilgore, 13" WS, EX, A (Est: $2,000-$3,000) **$3,920.00**

Travel Air Mystery, Kilgore, 6" L, NM, A (Est: $700-$1,000) ... **$390.00**

Bell Toys

Acrobats (2) Balancing 2 Bells Each on Spinning Star on 4-Wheeled Platform, 6", G, A (Est: $600-$800)......... **$935.00**

Alligator & Boy on 4-Wheeled Base (Gator Baiter), NN Hill Brass Co, 9", some rpnt, VG, A (Est: $1,200-$1,500)...... **$1,200.00**

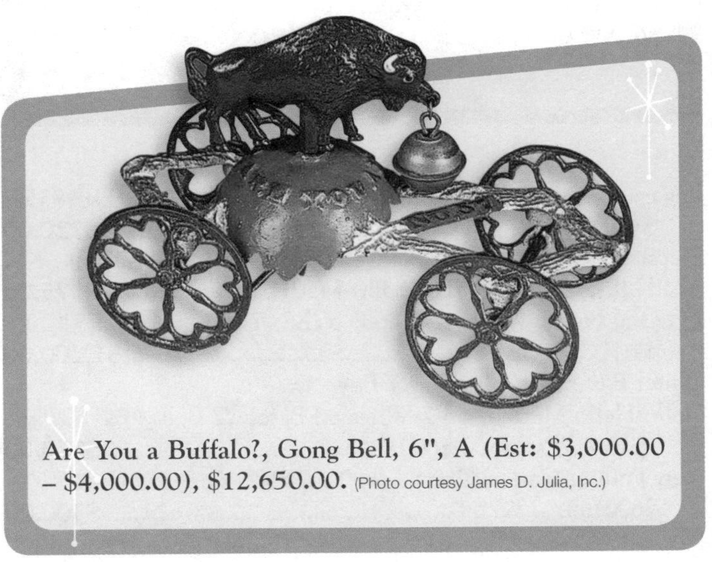

Are You a Buffalo?, Gong Bell, 6", A (Est: $3,000.00 – $4,000.00), $12,650.00. (Photo courtesy James D. Julia, Inc.)

Bell w/Eagle Finial on 4-Wheeled Platform w/Cloth US Flag (Independence 1776-1876), 8", VG, A (Est: $1,200-$1,500). **$770.00**

Boy Fishing on 4-Wheeled Platform, NN Hill, 8", EX, A (Est: $1,000-$1,200) **$3,300.00**

Buster Brown & Tige on 4-Wheeled Base, 7", EX, A (Est: $2,000-$3,000) **$1,080.00**

Cat Luring Dog Out of Doghouse on 3-Wheeled Base, Gong Bell, 9", bell under base, some overpnt, A (Est: $1,000-$1,200) **$935.00**

Clown in Pig Cart, Gong Bell, 6¼" L, EX, A (Est: $300-$400) **$500.00**

Clown in Pony Cart Fanning Himself, Gong Bell, 7¼", Fair, A (Est: $500-$700) **$330.00**

Clown Riding Pig While Holding His Ear, Gong Bell, 6" L, 2 lg wheels, VG, A (Est: $300-$400) **$275.00**

Clown w/Poodle Jumping Hoop on 4-Wheeled Base, Gong Bell, 13", 2 bells, flower-petal spokes, G, A (Est: $1,500-$2,000).... **$2,160.00**

Columbia (Figure Standing w/Flag in Leaf-Shaped Seat w/4 Wheels & Bell), Gong Bell, 7½", G, A (Est: $1,200-$1,500) **$1,650.00**

Couple on Teeter-Totter w/Center Bell on 4-Wheeled Platform, 7" L, Fair+, A (Est: $1,200-$1,500)......................... $880.00
Daisy (4-Wheeled Horse Sleigh), Gong Bell, 8½" L, Fair, A ($800-$1,200)... $275.00
Darky & Alligator, see Alligator & Boy
Ding Dong Bell Pussy's Not in the Well, Gong Bell, 9¼" L, some rpnt, A (Est: $1,200-$1,500)................................... $770.00

Double Ripper Sled, N.N. Hill, 8½" long, VG, A (Est: $6,000.00 – $8,000.00), $5,175.00. (Photo courtesy James D. Julia, Inc.)

Eagle on Rocker, lg bell in mouth, 4¾" L, VG, A (Est: $350-$450)... $220.00
Elephant on 4-Wheeled Platform w/Bell at End of Trunk, NN Hill, 6½", Fair, A (Est: $350-$450) $275.00
Evening News w/Baby Quieter, J&ES, 7½" L, A (Est: $1,200-$1,500).. $1,200.00
Gaiter Baiter, see Alligator & Boy
Hello-Hello Monkey on 2-Wheeled Base w/2 Bells, 8½" L, some rpnt, A (Est: $500-$600).. $770.00
Hen Pulling Cart w/Chicks on Top, 8¼", Fair+, A (Est: $400-$600)... $300.00
Horse (Sm) on 2 Lg Rockers w/Bell Underneath, Gong Bell, 4½", US flag pnt on rocker platform, VG, A (Est: $300-$400)... $300.00
Horses (2) Prancing Side by Side on 4-Wheeled Platform, 6½" L, G, A (Est: $600-$800)... $385.00
Jonah & the Whale on 4-Wheeled Platform, NN Hill, 5½", G, A (Est: $400-$500).. $825.00
Lady Driving Pony Cart, Gong Bell, 6¼", G, A (Est: $300-$400) $220.00
Landing of Columbus, Gong Bell, 7", VG, A (Est: $400-$500).. $385.00
Men (2) Sawing Watermelons on 4-Wheeled Platform, Gong Bell, 9", VG, A (Est: $1,500-$2,000)................... $2,475.00
Monkey in Bell Cart w/4 Wheels (Jim Along Jose), K&R, 7" L, rpnt, A (Est: $2,000-$3,000)............................... $465.00
Monkey on Velocipede, J&ES, 8" L, some rpnt, A (Est: $2,000-$2,500).. $1,100.00
Monkey w/Coconut on 4-Wheeled Platform, NN Hill, 6" L, rpnt, A (Est: $600-$800).................................... $3,300.00
No 49 Monkey (Monkey Running w/Bell in Hand on 4-Wheeled Platform), Gong Bell, 6" L, VG+, A (Est: $700-$900).$880.00
Raccoon & Hunter Facing Off Inside of Log, Gong Bell, 8½" L, some rpnt, A (Est: $1,500-$2,000)...................... $3,025.00

Swan Chariot w/Girl Driver, J&ES, 10" L, some rpnt, A (Est: $2,000-$2,500) $990.00
Teddy Bear Between 2 Bells On 4 Spoke Wheels, Gong Bell, 6½", VG, A (Est: $400-$500)................................ $825.00
Teddy Bear Standing on 4-Wheeled Platform w/2 Bells, Gong Bell, 6½", VG, A (Est: $400-$500) $600.00
Tramp No 4, Gong Bell, 6" L, A (Est: $600-$800) $385.00
Trick Mule Bell Ringer, Gong Bell, 7¾" L, VG, A (Est: $800-$1,000)...$1,540.00
Uncle Sam & the Don Dueling on 4-Wheeled Platform w/US Flag, Gong Bell, 7½", some rpnt, A (Est: $1,200-$1,500) ...$1,200.00

Whoa Dar Ceaser, attributed to Ives, 5½", G, A (Est: $400.00 – $600.00), $515.00. (Photo courtesy James D. Julia, Inc.)

Boats

Showboat, Arcade, 11", VG, A (Est: $600.00 – $1.000.00), $1,725.00.

Battleship Kentucky, J&ES, 10", some rpnt, A (Est: $800-$1,000)... $990.00
Battleship Maine, 8½", VG, A (Est: $2,000-$2,500)... $3,850.00
Battleship New York, Dent, 20", EX, A (Est: $3,000-$4,000) $2,875.00
Battleship New York, Dent, 20", rstr, A (Est: $1,000-$2,000) $1,265.00

Motorboat, Freidag, 1920s, 10", EX+, A (Est: $1,200-$1,500) $5,500.00
Racing Skull w/Pace Man & 8 Rowers, Union, 14½", EX, A (Est: $2,500-$3,500) $8,280.00
Sailboat, Kilgore, 3½", VG+, A (Est: $300-$400) $1,540.00
Side-Wheeler Adirondack, Dent, 15", NM, A (Est: $2,000-$2,500) $5,175.00
Side-Wheeler City of Chicago, Wilkens, 16", NM, A (Est: $800-$1,200) $1,100.00
Side-Wheeler City of New York, Wilkins, 15", EX+, A (Est: $1,500-$2,000) $5,865.00
Side-Wheeler New Orleans, Wilkins/Harris, 10½", EX, A (Est: $1,000-$1,200) $975.00
Side-Wheeler Priscilla, Dent, 10½", EX, A (Est: $700-$900) $800.00
Speedboat, Hubley, 4", cast figure & motor, G rpnt, A (Est: $50-$100) $100.00
Speedboat Static, Hubley, 10", no driver, G, A (Est: $500-$700) $840.00

Character

Alfonse Nodder in Horse Cart, Kenton, 10", 1 horse, 2 MSW, seated figure, G, A (Est: $400-$600) $360.00
Alfonse Nodder in Mule Cart, Hubley, 6½", 1 mule, 2 MSW, VG, A (Est: $300-$400) $140.00

Andy Gump Car #348, Arcade, 7", EX, A (Est: $1,000.00 – $1,500.00), $950.00. (Photo courtesy Morphy Auctions)

Andy Gump Car #348, Arcade, 7", G, A (Est: $500-$700) $460.00
Chester Gump Cart, Arcade, 7", horse-drawn, 2 MSW, figure standing in 'basket,' VG, A (Est: $400-$500) $275.00
Cupid in Horse-Drawn Shoe, Kenton, 8½", VG, A (Est: $400-$600) $300.00
Foxy Grandpa Nodder in Horse Cart, Kenton, 10½", 1 horse, 2 MSW, seated figure, G, A (Est: $350-$550) $200.00
Gloomy Gus in Mule Cart, Harris, 7", bed w/slant front, 2 MSW, standing figure, G, A (Est: $225-$275) $225.00
Gloomy Gus in Mule Stake Wagon w/Driver, Harris, 13", 2 sm & 2 lg MSW, G+, A (Est: $250-$300) $415.00
Goofy & Mickey in Motorcycle w/Sidecar, Pride Lines, 1970s, 8½", BRT w/spokes, M, A (MB $125) $2,207.00
Happy Hooligan Comical Racer, NN Hill Brass & Watrous Mfg, 6", MSW, VG, A (Est: $400-$600) $470.00
Happy Hooligan Goat Cart, Kenton, 7½", 2 MSW, standing figure, G cart/P figure, A (Est: $200-$300) $110.00
Happy Hooligan Nodder in Horse-Drawn Cart, Kenton, 10", 1 horse, 2 MSW, G, A (Est: $400-$600) $415.00
Happy Hooligan Police Patrol, Kenton, 18", 2 horses, Gloomy Gus driver, cop hitting HH, VG, A (Est: $2,000-$2,400) ... $2,530.00
Mama Katzenjammer Spanking Baby on Mule Cart, Kenton, 11½", 1 mule, 2 MSW, 3 figures, G, A (Est: $600-$800) $1,100.00
Popeye Patrol Motorcycle, Hubley, 1938, 9", BRT, spoke wheels, no pull string, VG, A (Est: $2,000-$2,500) $2,280.00

Popeye Patrol Motorcycle, Hubley, 1938, 9", NM+, A (Est: $7,000.00 – $10,000.00), $17,920.00. (Photo courtesy Morphy Auctions)

Popeye Spinach Cycle, Hubley, 1938, 5½", M, A (Est: $1,500-$2,000) $3,360.00
Santa Sleigh, Hubley, 16", 1 reindeer, EX, A ($650-$850) . $1,200.00
Santa Sleigh, Hubley, 17", 2 reindeer, VG, A (Est: $750-$950) $1,540.00
Santa Sleigh, Kyser & Rex, 13", 2 reindeer, red boxy-type sleigh, EX+, A (Est: $4,000-$5,000) $7,280.00
Uncle Sam in Horse-Drawn Eagle Chariot, Hubley, 10", VG, A (Est: $1,500-$2,000) $1,980.00
Yellow Kid Goat Cart, Kenton, 7½", 2 MSW, standing figure, G, A (Est: $200-$250) $225.00

Circus

Bandwagon, Hubley, 30", 4 wht horses, 8 musicians, driver, EX+, A (Est: $12,000-$16,000) $20,700.00
Clown in Camel Chariot, Kenton, 10", VG, A (Est: $1,500-$2,000) $1,100.00
Clown in Chariot, Kenton, 7½", horse-drawn, standing driver, G, A (Est: $250-$300) $250.00
Clown in Elephant Chariot, Kenton, 9", VG, A (Est: $700-$1,000) $550.00
Elephant on 4-Wheeled Platform w/Clown Rider, Shimer, 5", NP, VG, A (Est: $350-$450) $250.00
Greatest Show on Earth Cage Wagon w/Elephant, Ives, no horses or driver, G, A (Est: $2,000-$3,000) $1,320.00

Lion Cage Wagon, Arcade, 14", driver, 2 horses, VG, A (Est: $700-$1,000) $450.00

Overland Circus Band Wagon, Kenton, 14", 2 wht horses (1 rider), 6 musicians, driver, red/yel, VG+, A (Est: $400-$500) $600.00

Overland Circus Band Wagon, Kenton, 16", 2 horses, 6 musicians, driver, wht, orange, red & gold, G+, A (Est: $200-$300) $240.00

Overland Circus Cage Truck, Kenton, 9", w/bear, MDW, G, A (Est: $500-$700) $880.00

Overland Circus Cage Wagon, Kenton, 14", wht bear, 2 horses, driver, VG+, A (Est: $250-$500) $315.00

Overland Circus Cage Wagon, Kenton, 14", wht bear, 2 horses w/riders, driver, NM, A (MB: $495) $600.00

Overland Circus Calliope Truck, Kenton, 7", EX, A (Est: $700.00 – $1,000.00), $1,760.00. (Photo courtesy James D. Julia)

Royal Circus Band Wagon, Hubley, 16", 2 horses, 6 musicians, driver, VG, A (Est: $1,000-$1,200) $770.00

Royal Circus Band Wagon, Hubley, 28", 4 horses, 6 musicians, driver, rpnt, A (Est: $1,000-$1,200) $1,320.00

Royal Circus Cage Wagon, Hubley, 9½", empty, 2 horses, driver, some rpr & rpnt, A (Est: $1,000-$1,200) $880.00

Royal Circus Cage Wagon, Hubley, 15½", empty, 2 horses, driver, VG, A (Est: $700-$900) $1,540.00

Royal Circus Calliope Wagon, Hubley, 2 horses, driver, VG+, A (Est: $1,500-$1,750) $1,540.00

Royal Circus Giraffe Cage Wagon, Hubley, 23", giraffe w/baby, 4 wht horses, , driver, EX, A (Est: $5,000-$7,000) .. $10,450.00

Royal Circus Rhino Wagon w/Farmer's Head, Hubley, 16", 2 horses, driver, head pops out of top, VG, A (no estimate) ... $4,400.00

Royal Circus Wagon w/Trapeze Apparatus, Hubley, 16", EX, A (Est: $3,000-$4,000) $5,225.00

Tom Mix Circus & Wild West, Arcade, 14", wood wagon w/CI driver & 2 horses, metal spoke wheels, EX, A (Est: $700-$1,000) $1,870.00

Construction

Austin Roller-A-Plane, Arcade, 7½", no driver, G, A (Est: $150-$250) $410.00

Avery Tractor, Arcade, 1920s, 4½", roadwork vehicle w/roof over driver's seat, 4 MSW, VG, A (Est: $400-$500) $135.00

Bates 40 Steel Mule Tractor, Vinxex, 1929, cast treads, NP driver, EX, A (Est: $8,000-$10,000) $11,000.00

Buckeye Ditcher, Hubley, 9½", VG, A (Est: $300-$500) . $785.00

Buckeye Ditcher, Kenton, 12" L, chain treads, EX+, A (Est: $1,200-$1,500) $1,650.00

Caterpillar Tractor, Arcade, 8", enclosed engine, metal treads, NP driver, EX, A (Est: $2,000-$2,500) $1,750.00

Caterpillar Tractor, Arcade, 8", exposed engine, metal treads, NP driver, some rpnt, A (Est: $500-$700) $990.00

Contractors Dump Truck, Kenton, 10", EX+, A (Est: $2,000-$2,500) $2,090.00

Contractors Dump Wagon (Motorized), Kenton, 9", w/3 dump buckets, NPDW, EX, A (Est: $400-$500) $990.00

Diesel Tractor, Arcade, 1937, 8", NP treads & driver, VG (Est: $500-$700) $935.00

Fordson Tractor w/Front Pully & Scoop, Hubley, 9", rear metal traction wheels, NP driver, VG, A (Est: $800-$1,000) $880.00

Gallion Master Road Roller, Kenton, 7", cast driver, NM, A (Est: $700-$900) $515.00

General (Mack) Digger, Hubley, 5", gray & red, WRT, integral driver, no standing figure in crane, VG, A (Est: $300-$500) $315.00

General (Mack) Digger, Hubley, 8", gr & red, WRT, integral driver & figure standing in crane, VG, A (Est: $300-$500) $350.00

General (Mack) Digger, Hubley, 11", gr & red, WRT, integral drive & figure standing in crane, VG, A (Est: $500-$700) $450.00

Huber Road Roller, Hubley, 8", gr, w/driver, VG, A (Est: $400-$500) $450.00

Huber Road Roller, Hubley, 14", NM with EX+ rollers, A (Est: $5,000.00 – $7,000.00), $5,320.00. (Photo courtesy Morphy Auctions)

Ingersoll-Rand Air-Compressor Truck, Hubley, 1933, 8", Mack cab w/integral driver, MSW, VG+, A ($6,000-$7,000) .. $9,350.00

International Diesal TracTracTor, Arcade, 1940s, 7½", blk rubber treads, NP driver, EX, A (Est: $2,500-$3,000) $3,300.00

Jaeger Mixer (Cement) Truck, Kenton, 1940, 9½", WRT, red w/NP barrel mixer, WRT, NM, A (Est: $1,000-$1,200) $1,210.00

Lansing Cement Cart, Vindex, 6½", rnd-bottom bucket w/metal spoke wheels, gr & red, EX, A (Est: $2,000-$2,500) . $1,980.00

Machine Hauler, AC Williams, 28½", truck pulling 3 trailers w/ construction vehicles, EX, A (Est: $3,000-$4,000) . $4,950.00

Mack Hoist Truck, Arcade, 1932, 7", NM winch, WRT, integral driver, VG, A (Est: $1,200-$1,500)........................$1,540.00

Morgan Crane, Kenton, 9x16x12", EX, A (Est: $2,500-$3,500)..$2,200.00

Oh Boy Tractor, Kilgore, 1930s, 6", rubber treads, cast driver, EX, A (Est: $1,200-$1,500).......................................$3,025.00

P&H Excavator, Vindex, 12" L, crank-op, EX, A (Est: $2,000-$2,500)..$2,300.00

P&H Steam Shovel, Vindex, 8½x6" L, integral treads, gr & red w/gold trim, NM, A (Est: $6,000-$8,000)..........$12,100.00

Panama Steam Shovel (Mack) Truck, Hubley, 12", WRT, 10-wheeled, cast driver & 2 operators, NM, A (Est: $2,000-$2,500)..$2,585.00

Sand Loading Shovel, Arcade, 8½", side lever lifts shovelk, integral driver, A (Est: $1,000-$1,200).......................$1,320.00

Steam Shovel, 3", NM shovel & axles, wht rubber treads, VG+, A (Est: $75-$150)..$115.00

Tractor, Arcade, 1929, 5½", NP chain treads, NP driver operating dual controls, G, A (Est: $300-$400)................$715.00

Jaeger Cement Mixer, Kenton, 6x6½", EX, A (Est: $400.00 – $700.00), $400.00.

(Photo courtesy James D. Julia, Inc.)

Farm Toys

See also Horse-Drawn.

Allis-Chalmers Tractor (WC), Arcade, 7", BRT, NP driver, VG, A (Est: $200-$300)..$275.00

Allis-Chalmers Tractor & Dump Trailer, Arcade, 8", WRT, integral driver, EX, A (Est: $400-$500).........................$165.00

Allis-Chalmers Tractor & Dump Trailer, Arcade, 12½", BRT, integral driver, VG, A (Est: $300-$400).................$165.00

Case Combine, Vindex, 13", silver w/red trim, EX+, A (Est: $3,000-$3,500)..$6,600.00

Case Hay Loader, Vindex, 9½", EX, A (Est: $2,500-$3,000)..$4,180.00

Case Manure Spreader, Vindex, 11½", EX, A (Est: $1,500-$2,000)..$1,870.00

Case Tractor (L), Vindex, 7", rear metal traction wheels, NP driver, NM, A (Est: $2,000-$2,500)......................$3,575.00

Case Tractor (L), Vindex, 7", rear metal traction wheels, NP driver, VG, A (Est: $1,200-$1,500).......................$1,100.00

Case 3-Bottom Plow, Vindex, 10", EX+, A (Est: $1,000-$1,200)..$1,980.00

Case 3-Bottom Plow, Vindex, 10", some rpr, A (Est: $800-$1,000)..$600.00

Cultivision Tractor (A), Arcade, 7", BRT, NP driver, VG, A (Est: $400-$500)..$300.00

Farmall Tractor (M), Arcade, 7", BRT, NP driver, G, A (Est: $250-$350)..$300.00

Farmall Tractor (Regular), Arcade, 6", WRT, driver, G, A (Est: $400-$500)..$415.00

Ford Tractor (9N), Arcade, 9", BRT, integral driver, Fair+, A (Est: $300-$400)..$250.00

Ford Tractor (9N), Arcade, 9", BRT, integral driver & 2-bottom plow, VG, A (Est: $500-$700)...............................$880.00

Ford Tractor w/Dump Trailer, Arcade, 14", BRT, integral driver, A (Est: $300-$400)..$140.00

Fordson Tractor, Arcade, 6", metal traction wheels, NP driver, VG, A (Est: $250-$350)..$110.00

Fordson Tractor & Scraper, Arcade, 12", MSW, integral driver, VG, A (Est: $300-$400)..$360.00

Fordson Tractor & Wagon, Skogland & Olson, 14", NP driver, simulated stake bed, G, A (Est: $1,000-$1,200)...$1,540.00

John Deere Combine, Vindex, 13½", figure on platform, EX, A (Est: $3,000.00 – $4,000.00). $4,125.00.

(Photo courtesy Bertoia Auctions)

John Deere Farm Wagon w/2 Horses, Vindex, 13", open box-type w/high seat, 4 MSW, NM, A (Est: $1,500-$2,000)..$3,300.00

John Deere Gas Engine, Vindex, 3½", EX+, A (Est: $700-$900)..$1,320.00

John Deere Hay Loader, Vindex, 9", EX, A (Est: $2,500-$3,000)..$2,750.00

John Deere Manure Spreader, Vindex, NM, A (Est: $2,500-$3,000)..$2,200.00

John Deere Thresher, Vindex, 15", NM, A (Est: $2,500-$3,000)..$3,575.00

John Deere Thresher, Vindex, 15", some rpr, A (Est: $1,500-$2,000)..$1,045.00

John Deere Tractor (A), Arcade, 8", gr w/yel hubs, BRT, NP driver & steering wheel, EXIB, A (Est: $800-$1,200).......$1,840.00

John Deere Tractor (A), Arcade, 8", gr w/yel hubs, BRT, NP driver & steering wheel, VG, A (Est: $400-$500)... $300.00

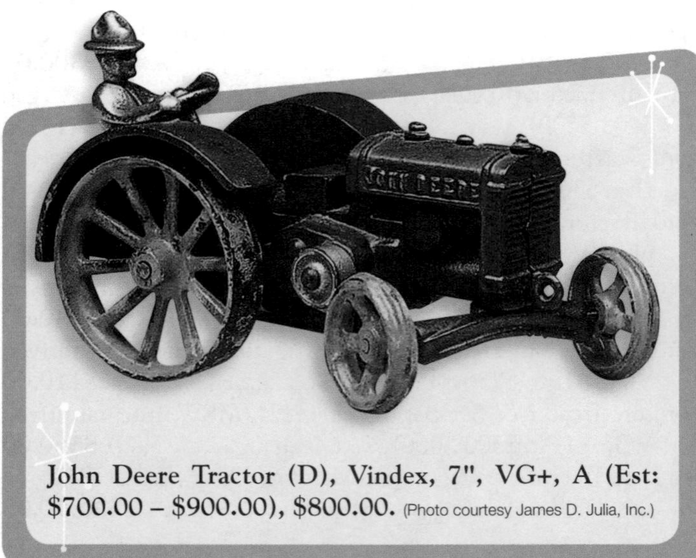

John Deere Tractor (D), Vindex, 7", VG+, A (Est: $700.00 – $900.00), $800.00. (Photo courtesy James D. Julia, Inc.)

John Deere Van Brunt Drill, Vindex, 9½", VG, A (Est: $1,200-$1,500) $1,540.00

John Deere 3-Bottom Plow, Vindex, 9½", EX, A (Est: $800-$1,000) $1,540.00

McCormick-Deering Buckboard, Arcade, 11½", NP yoke, 2 horses, no driver, rstr, A (Est: $200-$400) $330.00

McCormick-Deering Farmall Tractor, Arcade, driver, VG, A (Est: $500-$600) $415.00

McCormick-Deering Manure Spreader, Arcade, 14", 2 horses, VG, A (Est: $300-$500) $670.00

McCormick-Deering Thresher, Arcade, 10", MSW, VG, A (Est: $400-$800) $385.00

McCormick-Deering Thresher, Arcade, 10", MSW, rpnt, A ($200-$300) $140.00

McCormick-Deering Tractor, Arcade, 7", BRT, disk wheels, NP driver, G, A (Est: $150-$200) $220.00

McCormick-Deering Tractor (10-20), Kilgore, 6", rear metal traction wheels, NP driver, G, A (Est: $400-$500) . $440.00

McCormick-Deering Tractor (10-20) w/2-Bottom Plow, Arcade, 14", VG, A (Est: $300-$400) $300.00

McCormick-Deering Weber Wagon, Arcade, 12", 2 sm/2 lg MSW, 2 horses, no driver, VG, A (Est: $600-$800) . $330.00

Oliver Superior Spreader, Arcade, VG, A (Est: $250-$500) $250.00

Oliver Tractor (Orchard), Hubley, 5", BRT, driver, EX, A (Est: $300-$400) $470.00

Oliver Tractor (70-Row Crop), Arcade, 7", BRT, NP driver, VG, A (Est: $400-$500) $715.00

Oliver Tractor & Row Corn Picker, Arcade, 10" overall, BRT, cast driver, VG, A (Est: $400-$500) $250.00

Oliver 2-Bottom Plow, Arcade, 6", VG, A (Est: $200-$250).. $80.00

Wallis Tractor, Freidag, 5", rear metal traction wheels, integral driver, EX+, A (Est: $3,000-$3,500) $4,125.00

Wallis Tractor, Friedag, 5", rear metal traction wheels, integral driver, VG, A (Est: $1,200-$1,500) $1,200.00

Whitehead & Kales Tractor & Stake Wagon, Arcade, 12½", tractor w/BRT, wagon w/MDW, NP driver, G, A (Est: $400-$600) $220.00

FIREFIGHTING

Accessory, Engine House, Carpenter #58, 26½" L, CI sides w/ cloth canopy top, VG+, A (Est: $6,000-$7,500) .. $9,775.00

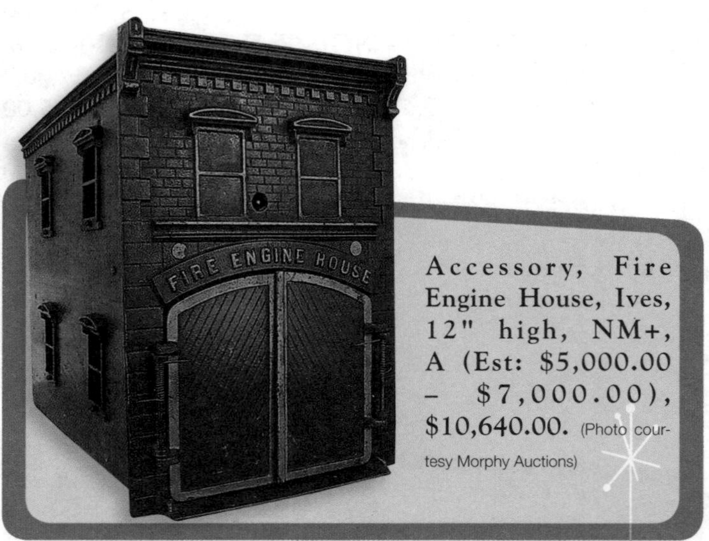

Accessory, Fire Engine House, Ives, 12" high, NM+, A (Est: $5,000.00 – $7,000.00), $10,640.00. (Photo courtesy Morphy Auctions)

Accessory, Fire Station & Fire Pumper, 20" L, arched gated door, 3 side windows, w/figure, EX, A (Est: $1,200-$1,800).... $1,050.00

Aerial Ladder Truck, Kenton, 12", open, red, NP ladders & driver, MDW, yel hubs, side levers, G, A (Est: $700-$900).... $1,650.00

Aherns-Fox Fire Engine, Hubley, 11", WRT, 2 NP ladders & driver, EX, A (Est: $800-$1,200) $1,380.00

Aherns-Fox Pumper Truck, Hubley, 11½", open, red, NP details, ladders & driver, NM, A (Est: $4,000-$5,000) $1,565.00

Fire Chief Car, Arcade, 6", BRT, G, A (Est: $75-$150) $75.00

Fire Chief Car, Dent, 5", slanted windshield, bell cast on hood & driver in window, NPDW, VG, A (Est: $400-$500). $600.00

Fire Chief Car, Kenton, 5½", bell cast on hood, driver cast in window, NPDW, VG, A (Est: $400-$500) $660.00

Fire Engine, Arcade, 14", open, red & silver, BRT, 2 figures in front/1 on ea side/2 in back VG, A (Est: $700-$1,000) $775.00

HFD Fire Truck, Hubley, 14½", NPDW, front & rear figures, license plate #7292, NM+, A (Est: $3,000-$5,000) $7,840.00

Hook & Ladder Truck, Arcade, 16", open, red w/yel ladders, 3 integral figures, 6-wheeled, G, A (Est: $300-$400) . $440.00

Hook & Ladder Truck, Dent, 19", open, red w/yel ladders, 2 figures, NPDW, yel hubs, 4-wheeled, EX+ (Est: $1,800-$2,200) $3,160.00

Horse-Drawn Aerial Hook & Ladder Wagon, Wilkins, 23", 2 horses, front & rear drivers, EX+, A (Est: $2,000-$2,500).... $6,325.00

Horse-Drawn Chemical Wagon, Wilkins, 19½", 2 horses, driver, VG+, A (Est: $4,500-$5,500) $12,075.00

Horse-Drawn Chief's Cart, Shimer, 15", 1 horse, driver, w/sledge-hammer & axe, VG, A (Est: $1,500-$2,000) $1,950.00

Horse-Drawn Chief's Cart, Wilkins, 11½", 12 horses, driver, EX, A (Est: $1,500-$2,000) $2,875.00

Horse-Drawn FD Chief Wagon, Hubley, 15", 1 horse, driver, EX, A (Est: $300-$400) ... $245.00
Horse-Drawn Fire Patrol #55, Carpenter, 16", MSW, 2 horses, driver & 2 seated figures, EX, A (Est: $2,500-$3,500) ... $4,885.00
Horse-Drawn Fire Patrol Wagon, Hubley, 15½", 2 horses, driver & 3 passengers, EX+, A (Est: $2,000-$3,000) ... $4,200.00
Horse-Drawn Fire Pumper, Wilkins, 21", 3 horses, driver, VG, A ($1,000-$1,200) ... $900.00
Horse-Drawn Hook & Ladder Wagon, Wilkins, 21", 3 horses, front & rear drivers, VG+, A (Est: $300-$500) ... $575.00
Horse-Drawn Hose Cart, Carpenter, 14½", 1 horse, 2 lg/2sm MSW, driver & rear figure, G+, A (Est: $1,000-$1,500) ... $1,600.00
Horse-Drawn Hose Cart, Hubley, 16½", 1 horse, 2 lg/2 sm MSW, driver on high bench seat, VG, A ($1,000-$1,500) .. $630.00
Horse-Drawn Hose Cart, Ives, 15½", 1 horse, driver, G, A (Est: $500-$700) ... $840.00
Horse-Drawn Hose Cart, Kenton, 14", 3 horses, driver, VG, A (Est: $500-$700) ... $725.00
Horse-Drawn Hose Cart, Pratt & Letchworth, 14", 1 horse, 2 lg/2 sm MSW, driver on high seat, EX, A (Est: $1,000-$1,500) . $1,500.00
Horse-Drawn Hose Cart, Shimer, 10", 1 horse, 2 MSW, NP, pnt driver, G, A (Est: $350-$450) ... $500.00
Horse-Drawn Ladder Wagon, Carpenter 25½", 2 horses, front & rear drivers, VG, A (Est: $700-$1,000) ... $1,680.00
Horse-Drawn Ladder Wagon, Hubley, 27", 3 horses, front & rear drivers, NM, A (Est: $3,000-$4,000) ... $2,240.00
Horse-Drawn Ladder Wagon, Kenton, 27", 3 horses, driver, rear seated figure, VG, A (Est: $700-$1,000) ... $1,010.00
Horse-Drawn Ladder Wagon, Wilkins, 23", 2 horses, front & rear drivers, VG, A (Est: $1,900-$2,300) ... $2,530.00
Horse-Drawn Patrol Wagon, Dent, 21½", 3 horses, driver & 5 firemen passengers, VG, A (Est: $700-$1,000) ... $785.00
Horse-Drawn Phoenix Pumper, Ives, 18", 2 horses, driver, VG, A (Est: $700-$900) ... $575.00
Horse-Drawn Pumper Cart, Carpenter, 18", 2 horses, 2 lg/2 sm MSW, front & rear figures, VG+, A (Est: $500-$700)..$745.00
Horse-Drawn Pumper Cart, Ives, 19½", 2 horses, 2 lg/2 sm MSW, eagle finial, driver, VG+, A (Est: $1,000-$1,500). $1,840.00
Horse-Drawn Pumper Wagon, Hubley, 21", NP boiler, lg/sm wheels, 2 horses, driver & rear figure, G, A (Est: $700-$1,000) ... $1,120.00
Horse-Drawn Pumper Wagon, Kenton, 26½", 2 horses, driver, EX, A (Est: $2,250-$2,750) ... $3,735.00
Horse-Drawn Pumper Wagon, Wilkins, 14", 2 horses, driver, G, A (Est: $400-$500) ... $400.00
Horse-Drawn Water Tower Wagon, Dent, 26", 3 horses, driver, G, A (Est: $800-$1,000) ... $1,200.00
Horse-Drawn Water Tower Wagon, Wilkins, 43", 3 horses, no driver, G+, A (Est: $4,000-$6,000) ... $3,450.00
Hose Truck, Kenton, 6½", very early open model w/lantern rack on railed bed, MDW, driver, G+, A (Est: $250-$350) ... $330.00
Hose Truck, Kenton, 8½", yel, w/driver, EX, A (Est: $1,000-$1,500) ... $690.00
Ladder Truck, AC Williams, 7", open, take-apart, red w/silver hood bell & grille, WRT, VG, A (Est: $400-$500) . $440.00
Ladder Truck, Arcade, 12", open, red w/yel ladders, NPDW, driver & 1 standing figure by driver, rstr, A (Est: $200-$400) ... $275.00
Ladder Truck, Arcade, 20", open 4-wheeled vehicle w/ladder trailer, red w/yel ladders, 3 figures, VG, A (Est: $500-$700) .. $440.00
Ladder Truck, Hubley, 6", red & NP take-apart body w/2 figures cast in open seat, 2 NP ladders, WRT, NM, A (MB: $150) ... $150.00
Mack Ladder Truck, Arcade, 18" (22" w/ladders), open cab, NP driver, yel ladders, EX, A (Est: $700-$1,000) ... $1,065.00

Patrol (Chemical) Truck, Hubley, 12½", NM+, A (Est: $5,000.00 – $7,000.00), $10,080.00. (Photo courtesy Morphy Auctions)

Pumper Truck, Dent, 12½", open, red w/gold trim, NPDW, w/driver & rear fireman standing, EX, A (Est: $750-$850) ... $1,210.00
Pumper Truck, Hubley, 5", red & NP take-apart body w/2 figures cast in open seat, WRT, NM, A (MB: $150) ... $150.00
Pumper Truck, Hubley, 11½", open, BRT w/spoke wheels, red w/silver trim, NP driver, EX, A (Est: $500-$700) ... $460.00
Pumper Truck, Hubley, 14½", early auto, red/NP, 2 lg/2sm MSW, driver & rear figure, EX, A (Est: $3,000-$4,000) .. $4,600.00
Pumper Truck, Kenton, 11½", early, red w/wht boiler, yel MSW, driver, EX, A (Est: $1,000-$1,500) ... $920.00

Pumper Truck, Kenton, 14½", open, with driver and rear standing figure, EX, A (Est: $700.00 – $1,000.00), $840.00. (Photo courtesy Morphy Auctions)

Horse-Drawn (and Other Animals)

See also Farm (Horse-Drawn John Deere and Horse-Drawn McCormick Deering); Firefighting.

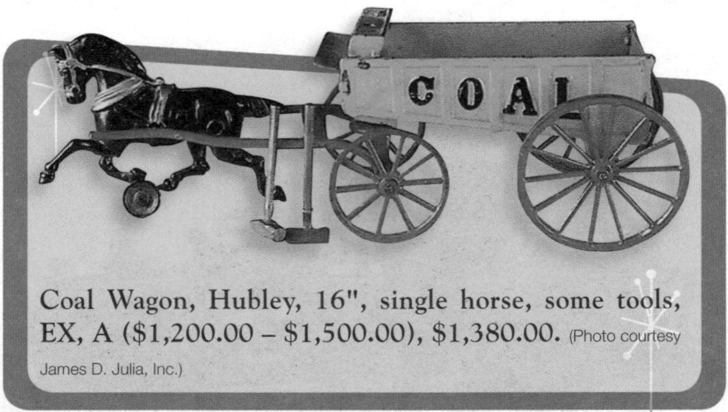

Coal Wagon, Hubley, 16", single horse, some tools, EX, A ($1,200.00 – $1,500.00), $1,380.00. (Photo courtesy James D. Julia, Inc.)

Adams Express Wagon, Ives, 18½", box bed w/bench seat, 2 sm/2 lg MSW, 1 horse, driver, VG, A (Est: $1,200-$1,500).... **$770.00**
Ambulance (2nd Regiment) Wagon, Kenton, rear roof over drivers seat, 2 horses, w/driver, VG, A (Est: $800-$1,200) .. **$1,550.00**
Bakery Wagon, Kenton, 12½", 1 horse, VG, A (Est: $300-$400)..**$220.00**
Brake (2-Seat), Hubley, 17", 2 horses, 4 figures, EX, A (Est: $6,000-$10,000) **$7,590.00**
Brake (3-Seat), Hubley, 18", 2 horses, 6 figures, VG, A (Est: $4,500-$6,000) **$8,625.00**
Brake (4-Seat), Hubley, 29", 4 horses, 8 figures, VG, A (Est: $8,000-$12,000) **$11,500.00**
Break (4-Seat), Hubley, 29", 4 horses, 8 figures, EX+, A (Est: $15,000-$20,000) **$21,280.00**
Broadway Car Line 72 Trolly, Wilkins, 5½", 1 horse, driver, red & yel, VG+, A (Est: $1,200-$1,500)..... **$1,400.00**
Buckboard, Harris, 13", 1 horse, male driver, G, A (Est: $250-$350)..... **$330.00**
Buckboard, Harris, 13", 2 goats, lady driver, G+, A (Est: $350-$450)..... **$825.00**
Buckboard, Hubley, 13½", 1 horse, driver, G, A (Est: $1,000-$1,500)..... **$1,495.00**
Butcher Stake Cart, Welker Crosby, 11", 2 MSW, 1 horse, no driver, some rpr & rpnt, A (Est: $600-$800) **$525.00**
Cairo Express, Kenton, 9½", 2 MSW, elephant, NP driver, VG, A (Est: $300-$400)..... **$275.00**
Carriage, Hubley, 11½", 2-wheeled, folded roof, 1 horse, female driver, VG, A (Est: $300-$500)..... **$345.00**
Cement Wagon, Kenton, 14", 1 horse, driver, EX, A (Est: $500-$700)..... **$2,415.00**
Chariot w/Roman Driver, Hubley, 11", w/up, 3 horses, VG+, A (Est: $2,000-$2,500)..... **$2,090.00**
City Delivery, Harris, 16", 1 horse, no driver, G, A (Est: $1,000-$1,200)..... **$990.00**
City Delivery, Harris, 16", 2 horses, driver, EX, A (Est: $1,750-$2,250)..... **$2,475.00**
City Sprinkler, Hubley, 8", 1 horse, seated driver, VG, A (Est: $300-$400) **$220.00**

Coal & Wood Wagon, Harris, 12", 2 sm/2 lg MSW, 1 horse, seated driver, VG, A (Est: $600-$800)..... **$770.00**
Coal Cart, Ives, 10", dump bed w/slant back, 2 MSW, 1 horse, seated driver, EX, A (Est: $400-500)..... **$220.00**
Coal Cart, Ives, 10", dump bed w/slant back, 2 MSW, 1 mule, standing driver, VG, A (Est: $250 -$350)..... **$150.00**
Coal Cart, Ives, 14", dump bed w/slant back, 2 MSW, 1 mule, standing driver, G+, A (Est: $500-$700) **$220.00**
Coal Wagon, Hubley, 13", open box bed w/slant sides, high seat, 2 sm/2 lg MSW, 1 horse, driver, EX, A (Est: $300-$500).. **$450.00**
Coal Wagon, Hubley, 18", open box bed w/high seat, 2 sm/2 lg MSW, 2 horses, driver, VG, A (Est: $600-$800) **$715.00**
Consolidated Street RR #372 (Trolley), Wilkins, 13", 1 horse, driver, EX, A (Est: $1,400-$1,800)..... **$3,100.00**
Contractor's Dump Wagon, Arcade, 14", shallow bottom, 2 horses, driver, VG, A (Est: $300-$500)..... **$280.00**
Contractor's Dump Wagon, Arcade, 15", deep bottom, 1 horse, driver, G, A (Est: $200-$300) **$115.00**
Doctor's Cart, Carpenter, 10½", 1 horse, standing figure, G, A (Est: $500-$700) **$280.00**
Doctor's Cart, Wilkins, 10", 1 horse, driver, VG, A (Est: $500-$700)..... **$165.00**
Dog Cart, Pratt & Letchworth, 13", 1 horse, 2 MSW, seated driver, EX, A (Est: $1,500-$1,750)..... **$2,750.00**
Dog-Drawn Cart, Harris, 7", 2 MSW, seated driver, VG, A (Est: $225-$275) **$300.00**
Donkey Cart, Harris, 9", blk boy standing in 2-wheeled cart, NPSW, VG, A (Est: $300-$500)..... **$400.00**

Dray Cart, Pratt and Letchworth, 10½", single horse and stand-up driver, NM, A (Est: $800.00 – $1,000.00), $2,645.00. (Photo courtesy James D. Julia, Inc.)

Dray Wagon, Hubley, 31", stake sides w/openings, high bench seat, 2 sm/2 lg MSW, 4 horses, driver, G, A ($900-$1,000)..... **$935.00**
Dray Wagon, Kenton 14½", 2 horses, driver, G, A (Est: $300-$500)..... **$165.00**
Dray Wagon, Wilkens, 21", flat bed w/posts & chains, 2 sm/2 lg MSW (wheel covers), 2 horses, VG, A (Est: $600-$800) **$550.00**
Dray Wagon, Wilkins, 21", slanted tin bed, 2 sm/2 lg MSW, 2 horses, driver on high bench, G, A (Est: $500-$700)..... **$450.00**

Dump Rake, Arcade, 1 horse, no driver, VG, A (Est: $400-$600) $500.00

Eagle Milk Wagon, Hubley, 13", 1 horse, VG, A (Est: $700-$900) $770.00

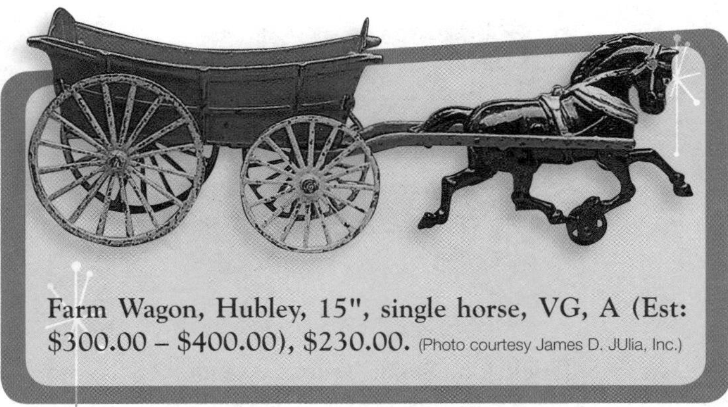

Farm Wagon, Hubley, 15", single horse, VG, A (Est: $300.00 – $400.00), $230.00. (Photo courtesy James D. JUlia, Inc.)

Farm Wagon, Kenton, 14", open box bed w/high bench seat, 4 MSW, 1 horse, driver, VG, A (Est: $400-$500) $275.00

Farm Wagon, Shimer, 12", bed w/curved & railed sides, 2 sm/2 lg MSW, 1 horse, standing driver, VG, A (Est: $350-$450) $110.00

Flying Artillery Caisson, Ives, 32", 4 horses (2 w/riders), caisson driver, VG, A (Est: $1,500-$2,000) $3,160.00

Gig, Shimer, 10", NP, 2 lg MSW, 1 horse, gentleman driver, G, A (Est: $250-$350) $225.00

Gig, Shimer, 10", NP, 2 lg MSW, 1 horse, lady driver, VG, A (Est: $350-$450) $385.00

Hansom Cab, Pratt & Letchworth, 11", 2-wheeled, 1 horse, driver, G, A (Est: $500-$700) $615.00

Hay Mower, Wilkins, 10½", operating cycle bar, 2 MSW w/rubber treads, 2 horses, driver, EX, A (Est: $800-$1,000)... $1,870.00

Hay Wagon, Hubley, 14½", stake sides w/curved edge, 4 MSW, yoke of oxen, standing driver, VG, A (Est: $300-$400) $250.00

Hay Wagon, Shimer, 16", NP, stake sides, high bench seat, 2 sm/2 lg MSW, 1 horse, driver, VG, A (Est: $800-$1,000) $440.00

Hay Wagon, Vindex, 8", open flat bed w/stake ends, 4 MSW, horses, VG, A (Est: $1,000-$1,200) $990.00

Hay Wagon, Vindex, 14½", open sides w/stake ends, MSW, 2 horses, no driver, VG+, A (Est: $1,200-$1,400) ... $1,200.00

Horse Cart, J&E Stevens, 9", 2 flower-petal spoke wheels, 1 horse, articulated driver, VG, A (Est: $500-$700)... $250.00

Ice Wagon, Hubley, 8", 1 horse, G, A (Est: $200-$300). $110.00

Ice Wagon, Ives, 11", 1 horse, NP driver, VG, A (Est: $600-$800) $360.00

Log Wagon, Hubley, 15", plantation worker seated atop log, yoke of oxen, EX, A (Est: $600-$800) $935.00

Log Wagon, Kenton, 15", plantation worker seated atop log, 2 horses, VG, A (Est: $600-$750) $770.00

Milk Wagon, Kenton, 14", 1 horse, VG, A (Est: $300-$400).. $200.00

Mule Stake Cart, Welker Crosby, 11½", vertical stakes, 2 MSW, 1 mule, no driver, G+, A (Est: $600-$800) $360.00

Ox Cart, Welker, 11", 2 oxen, VG+, A (Est: $500-$700). $575.00

Oxford Trap, Kenton, 15", 2 lg/2 sm MSW, 2 horses, 3 seated figures, G, A (Est: $1,200-$1,500) $2,200.00

Panama Dump Wagon, Wilkens, 20", dump bed w/slant back, 2 horses, driver seated on high seat, VG, A (Est: $500-$600) $470.00

Phaeton, Kenton, 14½", 2 lg/2 sm MSW, 2 horses, driver & lady passenger, EX, A (Est: $500-$700) $600.00

Plantation Cart, Hubley, 10½", stake bed, 1 mule, driver, VG, A (Est: $300-$500) $165.00

Plantation Cart, Hubley, 13½", enclosed sides, 1 horse, standing driver, G, A (Est: $300-$500) $140.00

Plantation Cart, Shimer, 12", NP, 2 MSW, seated driver, VG, A (Est: $300-$500) $225.00

Plantation Stake Wagon, Hubley, 15", yoke of oxen, standing driver, G, A (Est: $700.00 – $900.00), $920.00. (Photo courtesy James D. Julia)

Police Patrol Wagon, Hubley, 17", 3 horses, driver, 4 police passengers, G, A (Est: $500-$700) $500.00

Police Patrol Wagon, Kenton, 19", 2 horses, driver, 4 police passengers, VG, A (Est: $700-$1,000) $1,000.00

Pony Cart, Welker Crosby, 10", 2 MSW, 1 pony, no driver, VG (wooden box w/no lid), A (Est: $600-$800) $1,540.00

Rabbit Cart, Kenton, 5", pulled by rabbit & w/rabbit driver, G, A (Est: $200-$300) $275.00

Sleigh, see also Santa Sleigh in Character sub-category

Sleigh, Dent, 16", single horse, driver, EX, A (Est: $1,200-$1,400) $1,870.00

Sleigh, Hubley, no size given, swan-head design, gold trim, 2 horses, lady driver, VG, A (Est: $400-$500) $525.00

Sleigh, Hubley, 15", curved body, ornate curved runners, 1 horse, w/lady driver, VG, A (Est: $500-$700) $275.00

Stake Wagon, Hubley, 15", 2 sm/2 lg wheels, 1 horse, seated driver, VG, A (Est: $500-$700) $310.00

Stake Wagon, Ives, 15", 2 sm/2 lg wheel MSW, 1 horse, rpl driver, VG, A (Est: $700-$1,000) $225.00

Stake Wagon, Kenton, 14½", 2 sm/2 lg MSW, 2 horses, driver, VG, A (Est: $200-$300) $120.00

Surrey, Hubley, 14", 2 sm/2 lg MSW, 1 horse, driver, G, A (Est: $400-$500) $220.00

Surrey, Ideal, 12½", 2 sm/2 lg MSW, 1 horse, 2 seats, NP, pnt driver, EX, A (Est: $400-$600) $200.00

Surrey, Pratt & Letchworth, 15", tin body w/CI wheels & horse, no figure, G, A (Est: $500-$700) $330.00

Surrey, Shimer, 12", 2 sm/2 lg MSW, driver & passenger, VG, A (Est: $300-$350) ... $200.00

Tally-Ho, Carpenter, 28", 1 gray/1 blk/2 wht horses, 7 figures on coach, VG, A (Est: $20,000-$40,000) ... $31,625.00

Transfer Wagon, Dent, 19", 2 horses, driver, G, A (Est: $500-$700) ... $200.00

Transfer Wagon, Kenton, 10", paper litho on tin covered wagon top, 2 horses, seated driver, G, A (Est: $1,500-$2,000) ... $1,570.00

Trap, Dent, 13", railed sides, 2 sm/2 lg MSW, 2 horses, driver & 3 passengers, G, A (Est: $800-$1,000) ... $990.00

Trilby Horse Cart, Wilkins, 12", dbl seat, 2 sm/2 lg MSW, 1 horse, seated driver, G, A (Est: $275-$350) ... $165.00

US Mail Cart, 6¼", box cart w/roof & windows, 2 MSW, 1 horse, VG, A (Est: $200-$300) ... $110.00

Victor Cart, Ives, 9½", articulated horse, EX, A (Est: $1,000.00 – $1,500.00), $3,450.00. (Photo courtesy James D. Julia, Inc.)

Weber Wagon, Arcade, 11", high bench seat, 2 sm/2 lg BRT, 2 horses, driver, EX, A (Est: $700-$900) ... $385.00

White Water Wagon, Vindex, 12", MSW, 2 horses, no driver, G, A (Est: $1,200-$1,500) ... $660.00

Wild Boar Cart w/Egyptian Driver, Kenton, 8", 2 MSW, seated driver, VG, A (Est: $400-$500) ... $385.00

World's Fair Car Line 712 Trolley, Wilkins, 19", 2 horses, red & yel, NP figure, VG, A (Est: $1,000-$1,200) ... $300.00

Motor Vehicles

Note: Description lines for generic vehicles may simply begin with 'Bus,' 'Coupe,' or 'Motorcycle,' for example. But more buses will be listed as 'Coach Bus,' 'Coast-To-Coast,' 'Greyhound,' 'Interurban,' 'Mack,' or 'Public Service' (and there are other instances); coupes may be listed under 'Ford,' 'Packard,' or some other specific car company; and lines describing motorcycles might be also start 'Armored,' 'Excelsior-Henderson,' 'Delivery,' 'Policeman,' 'Harley-Davidson,' and so on. Look under 'Yellow Cab' or 'Checker Cab' and other cab companies for additional 'Taxi Cab' descriptions. We have given any lettering or logo on the vehicle priority when entering descriptions, so with this in mind, you should have a good idea where to look for your particular toy. Body styles (Double-Decker Bus, etc.) have also been given priority.

Ambulance, Arcade, 6", wht w/red cross on door & back lattice windows, EX, A (Est: $250-$350) ... $415.00

Ambulance, Kenton, 10", MSW, driver, VG, A (Est: $800-$1,000) ... $1,100.00

American Oil Co Tank Truck, see Mack American Oil Tank Truck

Anchor Truck Co. Stake Truck, Arcade, 10", with driver, VG, A (Est: $500.00 – $700.00), $560.00. (Photo courtesy Morphy Auctions)

Anthony Dump Truck, Arcade, 8", NPSW, G+, A (Est: $400-$500) ... $660.00

Auto Carrier, Arcade, 24", Ford Model A cab w/4 Model A cars on flatbed trailer, NPSW, G+, A (Est: $1,200-$1,500) . $1,980.00

Auto Carrier, Hubley, 10", w/4 vehicles, WRT, VG+, A (Est: $300-$400) ... $430.00

Auto Express 546 Truck, Kenton, 7", open bench seat, MSW, VG, A (Est: $250-$350) ... $360.00

Aviation Gas Tank Truck, Kilgore, 12", EX, A (Est: $1,200.00 – $1,600.00), $1,955.00. (Photo courtesy James D. Julia, Inc.)

Bell Telephone Truck, Hubley, 4", red, WRT, EX, A (Est: $175-$225) ... $350.00

Bell Telephone Truck, Hubley, 5", gr, WRT, VG, A (Est: $150-$200) ... $275.00

Bell Telephone Truck, Hubley, 8", gr, NPSW, NP ladder & tools, VG, A (Est: $400-$500) ... $500.00

Bell Telephone Truck, Hubley, 9", gr, WRT, w/pole trailer, pully & NP ladders, EX+, A (Est: $1,200-$1,500) ... $935.00

Bell Telephone Truck, Hubley, 10", gr, MSW, no accessories, G, A (Est: $200-$300) ... $350.00

Bell Telephone Truck, Hubley, 10", red, WRT, w/boom & pole trailer, integral driver VG, A (Est: $700-$1,000) ... $500.00

Bell Telephone Truck, Hubley, 11", gr, MSW, w/ladder, auger & trailer, EX, A (Est: $500-$1,000) $1,380.00
Borden's Milk Bottle Truck, Arcade, 6", WRT, G+, A (Est: $300-$500) $1,100.00
Borden's Milk Truck, Hubley, 6", wht, WRT, pnt grille, VG, A (Est: $500-$800) $1,100.00
Buick Coupe, Arcade, 8½", WRT, spoke wheels, rear spare, no driver, Fair+, A (Est: $600-$800) $2,200.00
Buick Sedan, Arcade, 8", 1927 model, NPDW w/spokes, rear spare, NP driver, G+, A (Est: $600-$800) $1,320.00
Buick Sedan, Arcade, 8", 1927 model, WRT w/spokes, rear spare, NP driver, VG+, A (Est: $1,500-$1,800) $3,300.00
Bus, see also Double-Decker Bus, Greyhound, etc.
Bus, Hubley, 8", Deco style short rounded nose, WRT, silver w/red fenders, rear fin & hums, EX+, A (Est: $100-$200) ... $470.00
Bus, Skoglund & Olson, 10½", long nose, open windows, WRT, w/driver, VG, A (Est: $400-$600) $500.00

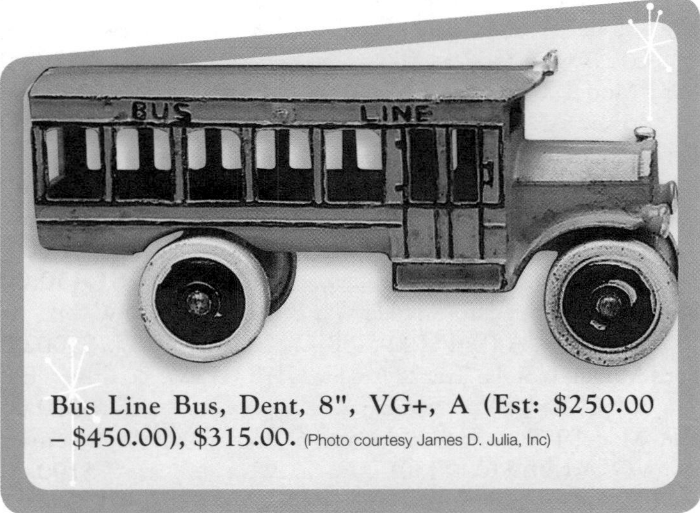

Bus Line Bus, Dent, 8", VG+, A (Est: $250.00 – $450.00), $315.00. (Photo courtesy James D. Julia, Inc)

Central Garaget (Garage) Wrecker, Skoglund & Olsen, wht w/red trim, VG, A (Est: $1,200-$1,500) $440.00
Century of Progress, see also Greyhound Lines
Century of Progress Chicago 1933 World's Fair Sedan, Arcade, 6", NP grille, WRT (rpl), Fair+, A (Est: $300-$400) $300.00
Champion Gas & Motor Oil Tanker Truck, 8", NPDW, no driver, VG, A (Est: $200-$300) $250.00
Champion Panel Truck, 8", WRT, emb side spares, no driver, G, A (Est: $300-$400) $355.00
Champion Police Motorcycle, 7", WRT, integral driver, Fair+, A (Est: $100-$150) $135.00
Champion Police Motorcycle, 7", 2-cylinder, WRT w/red hubs, integral driver, VG+, A (Est: $150-$250) $300.00
Champion Police Motorcycle w/Side Car, 9", WRT, integral passenger & driver, VG, A (Est: $250-$350) $330.00
Champion Police Motorcycle w/Sidecar, 6", WRT, integral passenger, no driver, G, A (Est: $200-$300) $135.00
Checker Cab, Arcade, 1923, 9", tan over blk, WRT, NP driver, NM, A (Est: $2,000-$3,000) $8,400.00
Chevy Coupe, Arcade, 6½", blk, WRT w/blk spokes, blk rear spare, NP driver, VG, A (Est: $200-$250) $360.00
Chevy Coupe, Arcade, 8", blk & gray, NPW w/blk hubs, NP rear spare & door knobs, VG+, A (Est: $700-$900) $865.00
Chevy Coupe, Arcade, 8", blk & gray, WRT (w/tread), blk hubs, NP rear spare, no driver, NM+, A (Est: $4,000-$5,000) $2,240.00
Chevy Sedan, Arcade, 8", NPSW, rear spare, no driver, G+, A (Est: $400-$500) $800.00
Chrysler Airflow, Hubley, 6", NP trim, WRT & rear spare, G+, A (Est: $150-$200) $190.00
Chrysler Airflow, Hubley, 8", electric lights, WRT, NP trim, NM+, A (Est: $3,000-$4,000) $5,600.00
Chrysler Airflow, Hubley, 8", electric lights, WRT, NP trim, VG, A (Est: $300-$400) $430.00
Civilian Motorcycle, see also Champion, Harley-Davidson or Indian
Civilian Motorcycle, Hubley, 6", WRT w/spokes, integral driver, EX, A (Est: $300-$500) $450.00
Civilian Motorcycle, Hubley, 9", BRT w/spokes, driver w/movable arms & head, VG, A (Est: $1,200-$1,500).... $2,090.00
Coast to Coast Bus, Hubley, 7", MDW, integral driver, older rstr, A (Est: $150-$250) $85.00
Coast to Coast Stake Truck, AC Williams, 7", 6-wheeled, MSW, EX, A (Est: $300-$400) $990.00
Coupe, see also Geneva Coupe
Coupe, AC Williams, 6", functional rumble seat, MSW, Fair, A (Est: $50-$100) $75.00
Coupe, Champion, 7", long nose, opening rear rumble seat, WRT, rear spare, rstr, A ($150-$250) $165.00
Coupe, Champion, 7½", long nose, curved back, WRT, cast side spares, G+, A (Est: $250-$350) $360.00
Coupe, Freidag, 6", 1924 model, MSW, integral driver, VG+, A (Est: $200-$250) $275.00
Coupe, Hubley, 6", long low Deco body w/sm low top, fin down back, WRT, NM, A (Est: $400-$600) $285.00
Coupe, Hubley, 7", MDW, rear spare, integral driver, G+, A ($300-$350) $300.00

Coupe, Kenton, 10", Stop — 1926 on rear spare, EX, A (Est: $1,500.00 – $2,000.00), $1,100.00. (Photo courtesy Bertoia Auctions)

Crash Car, Hubley, 5", WRT, disk wheels, integral driver, NM, A (Est: $200-$300) $165.00
Crash Car, Hubley, 6½", WRT, spoke wheels, integral police driver, NM+, A (Est: $1,000-$2,000) $2,240.00

Crash Car, Hubley, 9½", 'Indian' emb on tank, WRT w/spokes, integral driver, accessories, EX, A (Est: $2,000-$2,500) .. **$4,125.00**

Crash Car, Hubley, 11", BRT, 'Indian' decal on tank, BRT w/spokes, removable driver, EX+, A (Est: $3,500-$5,000) **$3,300.00**

Crash Car, Hubley, 11", BRT w/spokes, removable driver, VG, A (Est: $500-$2,500) **$1,800.00**

DeSoto Sedan, Hubley, 4", 1934 model, electric lights, NM, A (Est: $5,000.00 – $7,000.00), $6,720.00. (Photo courtesy Morphy Auctions)

Dodge Coupe, Arcade, 1926 model, gr w/blk roof, wht-pnt MDW & rear spare, some rpnt, A (Est: $250-$350) **$360.00**

Double-Decker Bus, Kenton, 10", WRT, no driver, 4 orig passengers, EX, A (Est: $700-$900) **$770.00**

Double-Decker Bus, Kenton, 12", WRT, w/driver, no passengers, VG, A (Est: $500-$700) **$500.00**

Double-Decker Bus, Kenton, 1927, 12", with original figures, NM, A (Est: $2,000.00 – $3,000.00), $3,360.00. (Photo courtesy Morphy Auctions)

Dump Truck, Arcade, 8", cabover, 6-wheeled, WRT, rstr, A (Est: $200-$400) **$165.00**

Dump Truck, Arcade, 11", 1940s model, CI cab w/tin crank-op bed, gr, yel & red, BRT, EX, A (Est: $500-$700) **$300.00**

Dump Truck, Freidag, 7½", doorless cab, fixed bed, NPSW, NP driver, G+, A (Est: $100-$150) **$1,430.00**

Dump Truck, Kilgore, 8", early model w/curved-back dump bed, NPDW, w/pick & shovel, VG, A (Est: $500-$700) **$500.00**

Elgin Street Sweeper, Hubley, 9", NP driver, G+, A (Est: $1,800-$2,500) **$2,300.00**

Elgin Street Sweeper, Hubley, 9", pnt driver, NM+, A (Est: $7,000-$10,000) **$8,400.00**

Fageol Safety Coach, Arcade, 12", BRT, NP driver, G, A (Est: $300-$500) **$150.00**

Five (5) Ton Truck, Hubley, 16½", MSW, w/driver, G, A (Est: $500-$800) **$400.00**

Flowers 3-Wheeled Cycle, Hubley, 1933, 3¼", WRT, integral driver, NM, A (Est: $1,500-$2,000) **$1,565.00**

Ford Coupe, Arcade, 1924 model, 5", NPSW, VG, A (Est: $100-$200) **$200.00**

Ford Dump Truck, Arcade, 7½", 1929 model, NPSW, EX, A (Est: $200-$400) **$525.00**

Ford Model A Auto Carrier, see Auto Carrier, Arcade

Ford Model A Coupe, Arcade, 7", working rumble seat, NPDW w/spokes, no rear spare, A (Est: $300-$400) **$260.00**

Ford Model A Sedan, Arcade, 7", MSW, no driver, G+, A (Est: $250-$350) **$385.00**

Ford Model A Stake Truck, AC Williams, 7", NPSW, VG+, A (Est: $100.00-$150.00) **$300.00**

Ford Model A Stake Truck, Arcade, 7½", WRT, spoke wheels, G+, A (Est: $200-$300) **$250.00**

Ford Model T Coupe, Arcade, 7", NPSW, no rear spare, no driver, VG+, A (Est: $150-$200) **$275.00**

Ford Model T Sedan, Arcade, 7", 'cloth' top up, WRT, spoke wheels, no driver, EX+, A (Est: $200-$300) **$715.00**

Ford Model T Sedan, Arcade, 7", bank, 'cloth' top up, WRT, spoke wheels, NP driver, EX+, A (Est: $1,000-$1,500) **$1,430.00**

Ford Model T Sedan, Arcade, 7", center door, MSW, blk, no driver, G+, A (Est: $100-$150) **$300.00**

Ford Model T Stake Truck, Arcade, 7½", NPSW, no driver, EX, A ($200-$400) **$200.00**

Ford Model T Touring Car, Arcade, 6", top up, NPSW, no driver, VG, A (Est: $100-$150) **$190.00**

Ford Sedan, Arcade, 6½", long nose w/NP grille, WRT, G, A (Est: $200-$250) **$385.00**

Ford Sedan w/Trailer, Arcade, 5½" 1937 model, 5½" car & 6" trailer, rstr, A (Est: $300-$400) **$990.00**

Ford Truck w/Dump Trailer, Arcade, 13½", 1931 model, gr & red, NPSW & driver, G, A (Est: $400-$600) **$600.00**

Ford Wrecker, Arcade, 6", NPSW, no driver, EX (Est: $500-$700) **$1,760.00**

Ford Wrecker, Vindex, 7", opening tailgate, MDW, NM, A (Est: $3,000-$4,000) **$7,150.00**

Ford Wrecker, 11", red w/gr Weaver boom, NPSW, NM driver, VG+, A (Est: $500-$800) **$660.00**

Freeman's Dairy Truck, Dent, 8", red w/blk roof, WRT, G+, A (Est: $350-$450) **$715.00**

Gas Truck (Diamond T), Hubley, 7", silver w/red separately cast grille, WRT w/red hubs, red trim, NM, A (Est: $200-$300) **$465.00**

Gasoline Tank Truck, AC Williams, 7", Gasoline emb on sides, WRT, VG, A (Est: $300-$500) **$120.00**

Gasoline/Motor Oil Tank Truck, AC Williams, 10", gr cab w/red tank trailer, NPSW, 6-wheeled, VG, A (Est: $300-500) **$385.00**

Geneva Coupe, Champion, 7½", NPSW, G, A (Est: $200-$400) **$185.00**

Greyhound Lines Bus, Arcade, 9", bl & wht w/NP front, WRT, VG, A (Est: $300-$400) $275.00
Greyhound Lines Century of Progress Chicago 1933 GMC Tandem Bus, Arcade, 10", EX+, A (Est: $300-$400) $385.00
Greyhound Lines Century of Progress Chicago 1933 GMC Tandem Bus, Arcade, 14½", WRT, EX, A (Est: $300-$500) $400.00
Greyhound Lines Century of Progress Chicago 1934 GMC Tandem Bus, Arcade, 7½", WRT, VG, A (Est: $100-$200) $185.00
Greyhound Lines Century of Progress Chicago 1934 GMC Tandem Bus, Arcade, 10½", WRT, G, A (Est: $100-$200) $130.00
Greyhound Lines Coast to Coast, Arcade, 7½", BRT, lt bl w/wht stripe & Greyhound dog on sides, EX ($200-$300). $310.00
Greyhound Lines GMC Tandem Bus, Arcade, 5½", WRT, EX, A (Est: $100-$200) $140.00
Greyhound Lines GMC Tandem Bus, Arcade, 7", WRT, NM, A (MB: $295) $350.00
Greyhound Lines Great Lakes Exposition 1935 Tandem Bus, Arcade, 11", WRT, G, A (Est: $250-$350) $190.00
Greyhound Lines Great Lakes Exposition 1937 Bus, Arcade, 7", WRT, VG+, A (Est: $350-$450) $250.00
Greyhound Lines New York World's Fair Bus, Arcade, 11", flat roof, 3 open doors ea side, NP trim, VG, A (Est: $500-$600) $275.00
Greyhound Lines New York World's Fair Tractor Train, Arcade, 8", tin canopy, NP driver, EX, A (Est: $300-400) $385.00
Harley-Davidson Civilian Motorcycle, Hubley, 6", WRT, integral driver, VG, A (Est: $200-$300) $310.00
Harley-Davidson Civilian Motorcycle, Hubley, 6", WRT, integral driver, EX, A (Est: $350-$450) $525.00

Harley-Davidson Civilian Motorcycle With Sidecar, Hubley, 6", NM+, A (Est: $1,500.00 – $2,000.00), $4,200.00. (Photo courtesy Morphy Auctions)

Harley-Davidson Civilian Motorcycle w/Sidecar, Hubley, 6", NPSW, integral driver, G, A (Est: $500-$800) $770.00
Harley-Davidson Hill Climber Motorcycle #2, Hubley, 7", WRT, spoke wheels, swivel-head driver, rpnt, A (Est: $150-$200) $390.00
Harley-Davidson Hill Climber Motorcycle #2, Hubley, 7", WRT, spoke wheels, swivel-head driver, VG, A (Est: $300-$600) $840.00

Harley-Davidson Parcel Post Cycle, Hubley, 9", BRT, removable driver, pull string, NM+, A ($5,000-$7,000) $30,800.00
Harley-Davidson Parcel Post Cycle, Hubley, 9", BRT, spoke wheels, removable driver, G, A (Est: $1,500-$2,000) $2,300.00
Harley-Davidson Police Motorcycle, Hubley, 6", WRT w/red hubs, integral driver, VG+, A (Est: $300-$400) $465.00
Harley-Davidson Police Motorcycle, Hubley, 9", BRT w/spokes, w/driver, G, A (Est: $400-$500) $660.00
Harley-Davidson Police Motorcycle w/Sidecar, Hubley, 5", WRT w/spokes, integral driver, G+, A (Est: $200-$300) .. $220.00
Harley-Davidson Police Motorcycle w/Sidecar, Hubley, 5", WRT w/spokes, integral driver, NM, A (Est: $500-$700) . $575.00
Harley-Davidson Police Motorcycle w/Sidecar, Hubley, 9", BRT, spoke wheels, driver & passenger, VG, A (Est: $500-$700) $785.00
Hathaway's Bread/Cake Delivery Van, see International Delivery Van
Hill Climber HD-45 Motorcycle, Hubley, 6½", WRT w/spokes, integral driver w/#2 emb on back, G+, A (Est: $400-$600) $660.00
Huckster, AC Williams, 7", take-apart body, red & blk, WRT, G, A (Est: $300-$400) $385.00
Ice Truck, see also Mack Ice Truck
Ice Truck (1938 Studebaker), Arcade, 7", red w/NP grille, WRT w/bl hubs, integral driver, EX+, A (Est: $250-$350).. $355.00
Indian Crash Car, see Crash Car
Indian Police Armored Motorcycle w/Sidecar (Armored), Hubley, 9", BRT, spokes, driver/rider, EX, A (Est: $1,600-$2,000) $1,800.00
Indian Police Motorcycle, Hubley, 9", BRT, spoke wheels, removable driver, rare lime gr color, EX, (Est: $2,000-$3,000) $2,128.00
Indian Police Motorcycle, Hubley, 9", BRT, spoke wheels, removable driver, some rpnt, A (Est: $600-$800) $935.00
Indian Police Motorcycle w/Sidecar, Hubley, 9", BRT, spoke wheels, driver & rider, EX, A (Est: $1,500-$2,500) $1,050.00
Indian Traffic Car, see Traffic Car $1,265.00

International Delivery Van, Arcade, 1932, 9½", Hathaways, rear door opens, with driver, NM+, A (Est: $5,000.00 – $7,000.00), $6,160.00. (Photo courtesy Morphy Auctions)

International Dump Truck, Arcade, 9", cab-over w/U-shaped dump bed, BRT, VG+, A (Est: $300-$400) $770.00
International Dump Truck, Arcade, 11", high-sided dump bed, no tailgate, rear duals, BRT, rstr, A (Est: $300-$500) $190.00
International Dump Truck, Arcade, 11", low-sided bed w/tailgate, WRT, spoke wheels, NP driver, EX+, A (Est: $800-$1,200) $1,035.00

International Dump Truck, Arcade, 11", spring-loaded U-shaped dump bed w/open back, BRT, G, A (Est: $200-$300). $330.00

International Dump Truck (Red Baby), Arcade, 11", MDW, NP driver, VG, A (Est: $1,750-$2,750) $690.00

International Harvester Tow Truck, Arcade, 10", red w/gr wench, NPDW, NP driver, A (Est: $300-$500) $500.00

International Panel Truck, Arcade, 5½", w/visor, gr w/yel stripe, WRT w/yel hubs, G, A (Est: $400-$600)................ $465.00

International Panel Truck, Arcade, 9", no visor, red, NP grille, WRT, EX, A (Est: $1,750-$2,500) $1,560.00

International Panel Truck, Arcade, 9½", w/visor, gr w/yel stripe, WRT w/yel hubs, NP driver, G, A (Est: $400-$600).. $660.00

International Pickup Truck, Arcade, 9", 1941 model, VG, A (Est: $300-$500) $300.00

International Stake Truck, Arcade, 8", WRT, spoke wheels, driver, EX, A (Est: $1,500-$2,000)...................... $1,455.00

International Stake Truck, Arcade, 11½", WRT, NP driver, VG, A (Est: $600-$800).. $600.00

Lincoln Touring Car, AC Williams, 9", top up, NPSW, no driver, VG, A (Est: $300-$400)..................................... $1,430.00

Lincoln Zephyr Sedan, Hubley, 6", WRT, VG, A (Est: $100-$150).. $165.00

Mack American Oil Co Tank Truck, Arcade, 15", MSW, rpnt, A (Est: $600-$1,000) $780.00

Mack Coal Truck, Arcade, 10", BRT, NP driver, VG, A (Est: $700-$1,000) $750.00

Mack Dump Truck, Arcade, 9", NPWS, NP driver, G, A (Est: $200-$300) $275.00

Mack Dump Truck, Arcade, 12", T-bar bed, MSW w/rear duals, NP driver, VG+, A (Est: $400-$600)...................... $715.00

Mack Dump Truck, Champion, 8", WRT, VG, A (Est: $150-$200).. $220.00

Mack Dump Truck, Dent, 15½", opening tailgate, MSW, NP driver, VG, A (Est: $1,000-$1,200)..................... $1,045.00

Mack Dump Truck, Hubley, 7", NM+, A (Est: $1,500.00 – $2,000.00), $2,125.00. (Photo courtesy Morphy Auctions)

Mack Dump Truck, Kenton, 15", crank-action dump bed, MSW, driver, G, A (Est: $1,500-$2,000) $1,610.00

Mack Dump Truck, Kilgore, 8", slanted-back dump bed, WET, no driver, VG, A (Est: $200-$200) $112.00

Mack Gasoline Tank Truck, Arcade, 13", enclosed cab, bl, Gasoline emb on sides, NPSW, NP driver, VG+, A (Est: $700-$900)... $880.00

Mack Ice Truck, Arcade, 8", NPSW, Fair+, A (Est: $300-$400)... $330.00

Mack Junior Supply Co Delivery Truck, Dent, 15½", caged box van, MSW, NP driver, VG, A (Est: $1,000-$1,200) $2,750.00

Mack Stake Truck, Arcade, 11½", NPDW, NP driver, EX, A (Est: $500-$700) $715.00

Mack Stake Truck, Dent, 5", WRT, no driver, VG, A (Est: $100-$200)... $100.00

Mack Tank Truck, Arcade, 13", all CI, Lubrite Gasoline emb on sides of tank, WRT, NP driver, A (Est: $600-$800). $690.00

Mack Tank Truck, Arcade, 13", CI w/tin tank, gr w/Gasoline stenciled in wht, BRT, BP driver, EX, A (Est: $700-$900) $715.00

Mack Tank Truck, Champion, 8", WRT, rstr, A (Est: $250-$400) $715.00

Mack Tank Truck, Dent, 10½", American Oil Co emb on sides, red, gold trim, MDW, driver, VG, A (Est: $400-$500) $600.00

Mack Wrecker, Arcade, 11, enclosed cab, Wrecker stenciled on railed sides, NPSW, no driver, VG, A (Est: $800-$1,000)...$1,200.00

Mack Wrecker, Champion, 8", NP boom, WRT, no driver, G, A (Est: $150-$200) $110.00

Motor Express Truck, Hubley, 7½", WRT, no driver, VG, A (Est: $300-$400) $175.00

National Transit Co 15 Trolley, Kenton, 12", yel w/red lettering, VG, A (Est: $700-$1,000).. $560.00

Nucar Transport, Hubley, 16", BRT, w/2 vehicles (not take-apart), G, A (Est: $300-$400) $375.00

Nucar Transport, Hubley, 16", with four Champion take-apart vehicles, EX, A ($1,000.00 – $1,500.00), $1,120.00. (Photo courtesy Morphy Auctions)

Oldsmobile Coupe, Vindex, 8", functional rumble seat, NPSW, cast rear spare, 8", G+, A (Est: $1,500-$2,000) $1,540.00

Oldsmobile Sedan, Vindex, 6", 2-door, NPSW, cast rear spare, VG, A (Est: $1,200-$1,500) $2,750.00

Packard Sedan, Hubley, 12", bl & blk, PMDW, NP driver & grille, old prof rstr, A (Est: $8,000-$10,000) $12,075.00

Panel Truck, Arcade, 8", NPDW w/side spares, NP driver, EX, A (Est: $3,000-$4,000) $3,575.00

Parcel Post Cycle, see Harley-Davidson Parcel Post Cycle

Parmalee Systems Taxi, Arcade, 6½", Grant 8100 on blk roof, orange body, NP grille, WRT, VG, A (Est: $600-$900)............ $935.00

Parmalee Yellow Cab Co, Arcade, 8", blk & yel, NP grille, WRT, VG+, A (Est: $600-$800) $1,650.00

Patrol Motorcycle, Hubley, 6½", BRT, cast driver, EX, A . $385.00

Patrol Truck, Kenton (?), 6½", NPDW, integral driver w/3 riders in railed back, NM, A (Est: $350-$450) $400.00

Pickup Truck, Hubley, 6", take-apart body, EX, A (Est: $200.00 – $300.00), $450.00. (Photo courtesy Morphy Auctions)

Plymouth Coupe, Arcade, 5", cast rumble seat, WRT, G, A (Est: $100-$150) $135.00

Police Motorcycle, see also Champion, Harley-Davidson or Indian

Police Motorcycle, AC Williams, 5", 'fat cop' style rider, rubber tires w/wooden hubs, VG, A (Est: $150-$200)........ $165.00

Police Motorcycle, Hubley, 6", electric light, WRT, integral driver, VG, A (Est: $300-$400)............................. $350.00

Police Motorcycle, Hubley, 6½", integral light & driver, BRT, EX, A (Est: $200-$300)... $150.00

Police Motorcycle, Hubley, 9½", 4-cylinder, removable driver, orig pull string, NM, A (Est: $2,000-$3,000)........ $2,240.00

Police Motorcycle, Kilgore, 5½", WRT w/spokes, integral driver, VG+, A (Est: $400-$600) $650.00

Police Motorcycle, Kilgore, 6½", 2-pc casting w/separate handlebars, WRT, driver, rare, VG+, A (Est: $1,000-$1,200) $3,520.00

Police Motorcycle w/Sidecar, Hubley, 9", red, BRT w/spokes, removable driver, EX, A (Est: $800-$1,200)........... $920.00

Police Motorcycle w/Sidecar, Hubley, 9", red, BRT w/spokes, removable driver & passenger, rpnt, A (Est: $400-$600) $400.00

Police Motorcycle w/Sidecar, Kilgore, 5", all red, integral driver, NM, A (Est: $400-500) $450.00

Police Patrol Panel Truck, Dent, 8½", bl w/red trim, MDW, rpnt, A (Est: $400-$500).. $935.00

Pontiac Coupe, Vindex, 5½", NPDW, rstr, A (Est: $150-$250).. $465.00

Pontiac Sedan, Arcade, 6", NP grille & headlights, WRT, G, A (Est: $100-$150)... $165.00

Pontiac Sedan, Vindex, 6", 2-door, NPSW, cast rear spare, rpnt, A (Est: $1,200-$1,500)... $935.00

Public Service Bus, Dent, 13", NPDW, rpnt, A (Est: $300-$400)... $550.00

Racer, Champion, 8½", emb pistons, rear fin, WRT, NP driver, EX, A (Est: $500-$700)... $560.00

Racer, Hubley, 6½", pistons on hood, single electric lights, yel w/blk removable driver, WRT, G+, A (Est: $400-$600)....... $390.00

Racer, Hubley, 7", enclosed seat, raised pistons on hood, silver/red trim, WRT, w/driver, EX+, A (Est: $350-$450). $525.00

Racer, Hubley, 10½", 'flames' shoot out of exhaust holes on top of hood, NPDW, w/driver, rpnt, A (Est: $350-$450).... $385.00

Racer (Rocket), Kilgore, 6½", bl w/WRT, no driver, G+, A (Est: $150-$250) $165.00

Racer #3, Kenton, 7", boattail, MDW, w/driver, G, A (Est: $100-$150)... $135.00

Racer #5, Hubley, 10", hood opens to motor, 4 piston holes ea side, BRT, spokes, driver, VG, A (Est: $1,000-$2,000) ... $1,265.00

Racer #8, Hubley, 5½", red w/silver trim, WRT, integral driver, VG+, A (Est: $100-$150) $410.00

Racer #8, Hubley, 8", red w/silver trim, WRT, removable silver driver, EX+, A (Est: $200-$300) $440.00

Railway Express Truck, Hubley, 5", gr, WRT, no driver, VG, A (Est: $150-$250) $175.00

Red Baby, see International (Red Baby)

REO Coupe, Arcade, 9", VG, A (Est: $1,000.00 – $1,500.00), $2,250.00. (Photo courtesy Morphy Auctions)

Roadster, Kilgore, 6", open, orange w/NPDW, no driver, G, A (Est: $200-$400)... $165.00

Roadster, Kilgore, 8", open, red w/silver-pnt MDW, silver-pnt driver, VG, A (Est: $500-$700)............................... $500.00

Sedan, AC Williams, 5", take-apart body, curved back w/spare, electric lights, WRT, no driver, G, A (Est: $100-$200)... $145.00

Sedan, AC Williams, 6½", long nose w/cast side spares, WRT, VG, A (Est: $150-$250).. $210.00

Sedan, AC Williams, 7", take-apart body, long nose w/extended front bumper, WRT, no driver, VG+, A (Est: $350-$450) $660.00

Sedan, Arcade, 6", 1930s model, rear wheels covered, WRT, NP headlights & bumper, VG+, A (Est: $250-$300) $770.00

Sedan, Arcade, 6½", early model w/center door, blk w/grey-gr doors, wht-pnt MSW, NP driver, VG, A (Est: $200-$400)... $150.00

Sedan, Dent, 7", bl w/blk roof, NPDW, G, A (Est: $150-$200)... $385.00

Sedan, Hubley, 7", curved back w/rear wheels covered, lt bl w/NP grille & bumpers, no driver, NM, A (Est: $300-$400)... $570.00

Sedan, Kenton, 7½", sq back w/flat roof, long hood, gr w/blk top, NPDW & spare, EX, A (Est: $600-$800) $935.00
Sedan, Kenton, 10", slanted windshield, no visor, MDW w/ spokes, rear spare, VG+, A (Est: $1,200-$1,500) .. $1,100.00
Sedan, Skoglund & Olsen, 7½", gr w/WRT, rear spare, G+, A (Est: $500-$700) $440.00
Silver Arrow, Arcade, 7", NP grille, WRT, EX, A (Est: $200-$400) $385.00
Speed Motorcycle #5, Hubley, 4", integral driver hunched forward, Fair+, A (Est: $100-$175) $250.00
Speed Stake Truck, Kenton, 5½", open bench seat, MDW, EX, A (Est: $100-$150) $165.00

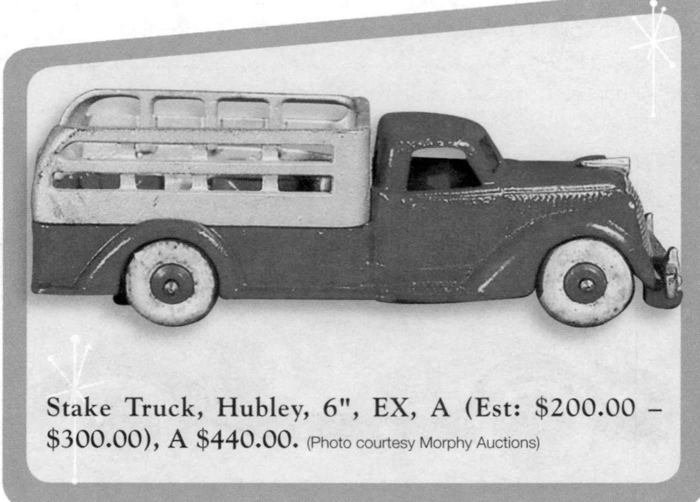

Stake Truck, Hubley, 6", EX, A (Est: $200.00 – $300.00), A $440.00. (Photo courtesy Morphy Auctions)

Studebaker Sedan, Hubley, 7", WRT, rear spare, G+, A (Est: $350-$400) $330.00
Studebaker Town Car, Hubley, 7", NP headlights grille & bumper, WRT, no driver, G+, A (Est: $150-$250) $285.00
Stutz Bearcat Open Roadster, Kilgore, 10", NP details, NPDW & spare, EX, A (Est: $1,000-$1,200) $3,025.00
Taxi, Hubley, 8", orange, blk pnt MDW w/orange hubs, VG, A (Est: $650-$850) $465.00
Texaco Tanker, Kenton, 9", Ford cab, red, WRT w/red hubs, 6-wheeled, EX (Est: $600-$800) $990.00
Touring Car, Dent, 9½", top down, MSW, gold trim, VG, A (Est: $300-$600) $285.00
Touring Car, Kenton, 8½", open w/2 high bench seats, MSW, NP driver, red w/gold trim, G+, A (Est: $200-$300) $250.00
Touring Car, Kenton, 9", simulated cloth top over 2 high bench seats, MSW, passenger/driver, VG, A (Est: $1,400-$1,600) $1,495.00
Traffic Car, Hubley, 5", WRT, integral driver, EX+, A (Est: $1,200-$1,500) $1,680.00
Traffic Car, Hubley, 9", NPSW, integral driver, VG, A (Est: $700-$1,000) $1,100.00
Traffic Car, Hubley, 9", WRT, integral police driver, NM+, A (Est: $3,000-$4,000) $3,360.00
Traffic Car, Hubley, 11½", Indian decal, BRT, spoke wheels, removable police driver, NM, A (Est: $4,000-$5,000) $5,600.00
Trolley, Harris, 7½", Trolley emb on sides, figures cast on front & rear platforms, red & bl, EX, A (Est: $600-$800) $360.00

US Air Mail Cycle, Hubley, 9", 'Indian' decal, hinged door, BRT, spoke wheels, driver, NM+, A (Est: $5,000-$7,000) . $8,400.00
Valley View Dairy Truck, Dent, 8", bl w/blk hood, WRT, EX, A (Est: $400-$500) $2,090.00
Weaver Wrecker, see Ford Wrecker
White Dump Truck, Arcade, 11½", WRT, NP driver, EX+, A (Est: $7,000-$10,000) $4,480.00
White Moving Van, Arcade, 13", MDW, NP driver, VG+, A (Est: $3,000-$4,000) $3,850.00
White Panel Truck, Arcade, 8½", WRT & side spares, NP driver, VG, A (Est: $2,500-$3,500) $4,675.00
Woody Station Wagon, Hubley, 6", take-apart body, WRT, EX, A (Est: $400-$500) $460.00
Wrecker, Hubley, 8", railed sides, NP grill, bumper & wench, WRT, VG, A (Est: $150-$250) $260.00
Wyman's Moving Van, Arcade, 8½", gr & blk w/NPDW & NP side spares, NP driver, VG+, A (Est: $2,500-$3,500) $4,400.00

Yellow Cab, Arcade, 8", marked 880, EX+, A (Est: $3,000.00 – $3,500.00), $3,160.00. (Photo courtesy James D. Julia, Inc.)

Yellow Cab, Arcade, 9", curved top, bank version, blk & yel, WRT, w/driver, EX, A (Est: $1,500-$2,500) $2,575.00
Yellow Cab, Arcade, 9", curved top, blk & yel, wht-pnt MDW w/yel hubs, w/driver, VG, A (Est: $300-400) $385.00
Yellow Cab, Freidag, 7½", blk & yel, NPDW, w/driver, P pnt, A (Est: $400-$600) $300.00
Yellow Cab, Hubley, 8", curved back w/rear luggage shelf, yel w/ blk trim, WRT, w/driver, VG, A (Est: $300-$500) .. $350.00
Yellow Cab Co, see also Parmalee Yellow Cab
Yellow Coach Double-Decker Bus, Arcade, 13½", WRT, NP driver, VG, A (Est: $1,500-$2,500) $1,725.00

Trains

Arcade, locomotive, tender, 2 boxcars, 2 coal trucks & caboose, 62" overall, NP, EX+, A (Est: $700-$900) $385.00
Arcade, locomotive, tender & 2 coaches (Michigan Central), 28", NP, EX+, A (Est: $250-$300) $145.00
Arcade, locomotive, tender & 2 gondolas, NP, 19½", EX+, A (Est: $150-$200) $165.00
Arcade, locomotive, tender & 3 coaches, 33", EX+, A (Est: $250-$300) $185.00
Arcade, locomotive, 2 coaches, 15½", NP, VG, A (Est: $200-$250) $110.00

Arcade, locomotive, 3 coaches, 25", NP, EX+, A (Est: $150-$250)........ $145.00
Arcade, pile driver, 11", EX, A (Est: $300-$500)........ $250.00
Arcade, Railplane, 5", EX+, A (Est: $150-$200)........ $85.00
Arcade, Railplane, 10", G, A (Est: $100-$150)........ $110.00
Arcade, Railplane/Pullman, 9", G, A (Est: $175-$250).. $120.00
Arcade, streamliner, 3-pc, 26", VG, A (Est: $400-$650) .. $360.00
Arcade, wrecker car, 10½", EX, A (Est: $300-$500)........ $300.00
Carpenter, locomotive (Pattened), 8", w/up, 2 sm front MSW w/2 lg back MSW, VG, A (Est: $300-$500)........ $390.00

Dent, locomotive, tender (PRR Co.), and four Coaches (Ivanhoe), 39", NM+, A (Est: $300.00 – $500.00), $1,065.00. (Photo courtesy Morphy Auctions)

Dent, locomotive, tender (1085) & 3 coaches, 22½" overall, VG+, A (Est: $200-$250)........ $250.00
Grey Iron, locomotive, tender & 3 coaches (300 & 301), NP, EX+, A (Est: $250-$350)........ $220.00
Hubley, locomotive, tender (PRR) & 2 coaches (America), 23" overall, EX, A (Est: $200-$300)........ $990.00
Hubley, locomotive, tender (PRR) & 2 coaches (Pennsylvania/Narcissus #44), NM, A (Est: $1,500-$2,000)........ $840.00
Hubley, locomotive, 8", w/up, VG, A (Est: $300-$500). $200.00
Hubley, locomotive (#7 Electric Outline), 2 coaches (1929), 17" overall, G, A (Est: $150-$200)........ $135.00
Hubley, locomotive (PRR NO 5), 2 Coaches (Pennsylvania RR/Washington (44/Narcissus 44), VG, A (Est: $500-$700)........ $615.00
Ives, locomotive, tender, coach (Limited Vestibule Express) & boxcar (Union Line), 55", VG, A ($2,000-$3,000)........ $1,455.00
Ives, locomotive, tender, coach (Queen), 20", w/up, VG, A (Est: $500-$700)........ $1,455.00
Ives, locomotive, tender, 10", w/up, VG, A (Est: $300-$500).. $840.00
Ives, locomotive, tender & 2 coaches, NP, 42", VG, A (Est: $400-$600)........ $250.00
Ives, locomotive, tender & 2 coaches (Fast Express), 28", VG, A (Est: $300-$500)........ $390.00
Ives, locomotive, tender & 2 gondolas (CP/RR), 23", standing figures in ea gondola, VG, A (Est: $500-$700)........ $500.00
Kenton, locomotive (600 Camel Back), tender (Erie) & 3 boxcars (yel stock), VG, A (Est: $500-$700)........ $1,230.00

Pratt & Letchworth, locomotive, tender (370), 4 sm front MDW w/4 lg back MSW on loco, EX, A (Est: $300-$500). $500.00
Pratt & Letchworth, locomotive, 8", w/up, VG, A (Est: $300-$500)........ $500.00
Pratt & Letchworth, locomotive, 10", w/up, VG, A (Est: $300-$500)........ $675.00
Secor, locomotive, 9", w/up, EX, A (Est: $500-$700).. $1,455.00
Welker & Crosby, locomotive, 12", w/up, 2 sm front MDW w/4 lg back MSW, EX, A (Est: $500-$700)........ $1,565.00
Welker & Crosby, locomotive (3-4-0), 11", 2 sm front MSW w/4 lg back MSW, train engineer, VG, A (Est: $500-$700).. $390.00
Wilkins, locomotive, tender & 2 gondolas (stake-sides), 33", EX, A (Est: $300-$500)........ $280.00

Ives, locomotive, tender, and coach (Limited Express), 27" overall, EX, A (Est: $500.00 – $700.00), $2,800.00. (Photo courtesy Morphy Auctions)

Miscellaneous

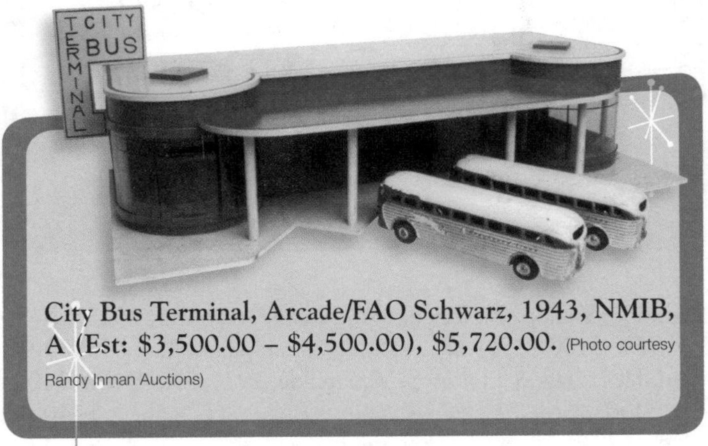

City Bus Terminal, Arcade/FAO Schwarz, 1943, NMIB, A (Est: $3,500.00 – $4,500.00), $5,720.00. (Photo courtesy Randy Inman Auctions)

Arcade Service, wood, wht w/name & windows stamped in gr, 3 center pumps, car lift, 13" L, VG+, A (Est: $400-$500)........ $525.00
Arcade Super Service, wood, wht w/red stamping, 12" L, NM, A (Est: $1,200-$1,500)........ $1,870.00
Arcadia Airport, Arcade, wood, wht w/blk & red trim, 2 CI planes w/7" WS, 12" L, EX, A (Est: $500-$700)........ $990.00
Engine Co No 99 Station, Arcade, wood, wht w/red trim, 12" L, EX, A (Est: $500-$600)........ $880.00

Fence Set, Hubley, 28-pc set, 13 w/reindeer & 15 w/dogs, 7" ea, EX, A (Est: $1,000-$1,500) $450.00
Filling Station (Gasoline-Motor Oils), Arcade, portico over 2 pumps, wood, wht & gr, 12" L, EX+, A (Est: $400-$600) $1,870.00
Fire Dept Alarm Box, free-standing, 4¾", VG+, A (Est: $75-$125) $250.00
Fire Hydrant, red-pnt CI, 2½", EX, A (Est: $50-$100) $90.00
Garage, Arcade, wood, wht & gr, dbl doors open from center, 15" L, VG, A (Est: $200-$250) $825.00
Garage, Arcade, wood, wht & gr, dbl doors open from 1 side, 13" L, G+, A (Est: $250-$300) $825.00
Garage, Arcade, wood, wht & gr, Garage stamped above 5 opening doors, 16" L, EX, A (Est: $200-$300) $1,980.00
Gas Pump, Gas emb on lollipop top, rnd gauge on body, 6¾", G, A (Est: $100-$200) $135.00
Jack Set, complete in burlap drawstring bag, Arcade, 1935, VG+ $75.00
Jack Set, complete in glass jar w/litho tin lid, Arcade, 1935, EX, A $165.00
Jax Set, complete on card, Arcade, 1935, M $150.00
Sign, Curve, diagonal lollipop, 5", Arcade, 1934, EX, A (Est: $100-$200) $550.00

Sign, Dont Park Here/Police Department, 4¾", EX, A (Est: $75.00 – $125.00). $250.00 (Photo courtesy Randy Inman Auctions)

Sign, Go, T-shaped lollipop, 5¼", Arcade, emb May 1925, EX, A (Est: $100-$150) $35.00
Sign, Hill, diagonal lollipop, 5", Arcade, 1934, EX, A (Est: $100-$150) $440.00
Sign, Hill, free-standing diamond shape, 4¾", VG, A (Est: $75-$125) $300.00
Water Hand Pump, 4½", VG+, A (Est: $75-$125) $75.00

Catalogs

In any area of collecting, old catalogs are a wonderful source for information. Toy collectors value buyers' catalogs, those from toy fairs, and Christmas 'wish books.' Montgomery Ward issued their first Christmas catalog in 1932, and Sears followed a year later. When they can be found, these 'first editions' in excellent condition are valued at a minimum of $200.00 each. Even later issues may sell for upwards of $75.00, since it's those from the '50s and '60s that contain the toys that are now so collectible.

Action Man, Palitoy, 1980, EX+ $20.00
Aurora, 1973, M $125.00
Breyer Animal Creations, 1976, EX $20.00
Buck Jones...Free Prizes for Members of M Club!, 1937 premiums, NM+ $75.00
Buddy 'L' Catalog of Steel Toys for 1935, EX $450.00
Buddy 'L' De Luxe Steel Playthings, 1940, EX $225.00
Buddy 'L' Line (The Complete), 1929, Make Your Toy Department More Profitable, EX $500.00
Buddy 'L' Toys (Happy Days w/), 1929, 6x8", EX $125.00
Capt Frank, Free Bikes & Other Free Prizes for Capt Frank's 'Air Hawks,' NM+ $75.00
Coleco Toys, 1972, EX $10.00
FAO Schwarz Fun in the Sun, 1935, girl standing in swing on cover, 16 pgs, NM $95.00
FAO Schwarz Spring 1946, girl seated in swing on cover, 16 pgs, EX $40.00
Fisher-Price Toys, 1950, EX $135.00
GI Joe America's Movable Fighting Man, 1965, 14 pags, NM+ $25.00
Hartland Creations/Plastics, sales brochure, 1950s, reference to 27 different figures, 16 pgs, 5½x2¾", EX $55.00
Hot Wheels International Collector's Catalog, 1968, M ... $20.00

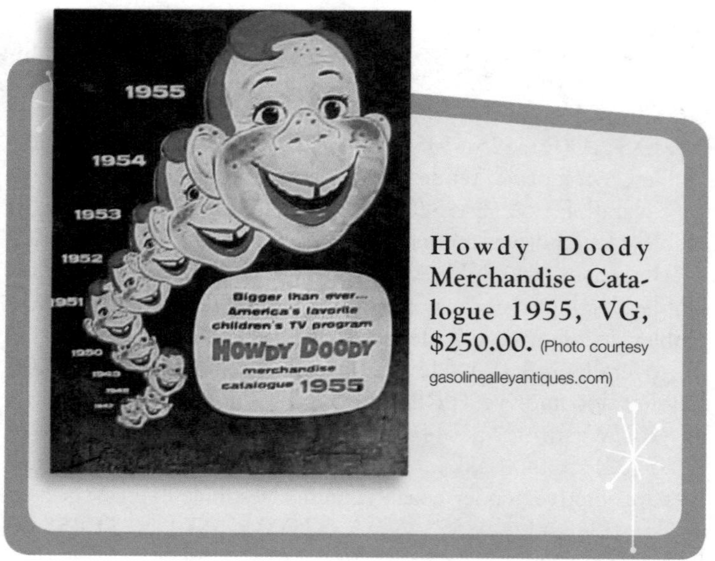

Howdy Doody Merchandise Catalogue 1955, VG, $250.00. (Photo courtesy gasolinealleyantiques.com)

Keystone Steam Shovels & Trucks, 1925, 6x4", G $130.00
Lionel Electric Trains & Multiple Transformers, Catalog of; 1917, EX $325.00
Lionel 1941 Price List, red, wht & bl cover, includes prices & photos of dealer displays, M $250.00
Marx, 1975, 48 pgs, EX $50.00
Marx Toyland, 1950, M $40.00
Mattel Toys, 1968, for distributors & stores only, EX+ ... $250.00
Meccano Instructions for No 3 Outfit, 1947, gr cover, NM .. $18.00

Mego Superstars, 1974, EX $250.00
Nylint, 1967, EX $35.00
Parker Brothers Games & Toys, 1976, EX $80.00
Playthings the Official Magazine of the Toy Trade, Toy Fair, 1950, EX, A $138.00
Railroading w/American Flyer, 1946, NM $150.00
Space Patrol Official Catalog, Ralston, 22 Space Patrol items pictured, scarce, EX $135.00
Steiff, 1957, features 150 animals, 15 pgs, M $35.00
Thingmaker, Mattel, 1967, EX $15.00
Tinkertoys, 1927, 1931 or 1935, EX, ea $50.00
Tom Mix Premiums Catalog, 1938, well illus, NM $50.00

Tomy Corporation Catalog 1981, for distributors and stores, M, $40.00. (Photo courtesy gasolinealleyantiques.com)

Transogram, 1969, EX $75.00
Weeden Toy Steam Engines, 1937, 20 pgs, EX $32.00
Wolverine Toys, 1973, EX $20.00

Character and Promotional Drinking Glasses

Once given away by fast-food chains and gas stations, a few years ago you could find these at garage sales everywhere for a dime or even less. Then, when it became obvious to collectors that these glass giveaways were being replaced by plastic, as is always the case when we realize no more (of anything) will be forthcoming, we all decided we wanted them. Since many were character-related and part of a series, we felt the need to begin to organize these garage-sale castaways, building sets and completing series. Out of the thousands available, the better ones are those with super heroes, sports stars, old movie stars, Star Trek, and Disney and Walter Lantz cartoon characters. Pass up those whose colors are worn and faded. Unless another condition or material is indicated in the description, values are for glass tumblers in mint condition. Cups are plastic unless noted otherwise.

There are some terms used in our listings that may be confusing if you're not familiar with this collecting field. 'Brockway' style tumblers are thick and heavy, and they taper at the bottom. 'Federal' is thinner, and top and diameters are equal. For more information we recommend *McDonald's Drinkware* by Michael J. Kelly (Collector Books) and *The Collector's Guide to Cartoon and Promotional Drinking Glasses* by John Hervey. See also Clubs, Newsletters, and Other Publications.

Harvey Cartoons, Pepsi, 1970s, static pose, Casper, from 12.00 to $15.00. (Photo courtesy whatacharacter.com)

Al Capp, Dogpatch USA, ruby glass, oval portraits of Daisy or Li'l Abner, ea from $15 to $20.00
Al Capp, Shmoos, USF, 1949, Federal, 3 different sizes (3½", 4¾", 5¼"), from $10 to $20.00
Al Capp, 1975, flat bottom, Daisy Mae, Li'l Abner, Mammy, Pappy, Sadie, ea from $35 to $50.00
Al Capp, 1975, flat bottom, Joe Btsfplk, from $35 to $50.00
Al Capp, 1975, ftd, Daisy Mae, Li'l Abner, Mammy, Pappy, Sadie, ea from $35 to $50.00
Al Capp, 1975, ftd, Joe Btsfplk, from $40 to $60.00
Animal Crackers, Chicago Tribune/NY News Syndicate, 1978, Eugene, Gnu, Lana, Lyle Dodo, ea from $7 to $10.00
Animal Crackers, Chicago Tribune/NY News Syndicate, 1978, Louis, scarce $25.00
Arby's, Actor Series, 1979, 6 different, smoked-colored glass w/blk & wht images, silver trim, numbered, ea from $3 to $5.00
Arby's, Bicentennial Cartoon Characters Series, 1976, 10 different, 5", ea from $8 to $15.00
Arby's, Bicentennial Cartoon Characters Series, 1976, 10 different, 6", ea from $10 to $20.00
Arby's, see also specific name or series
Archies, Welch's, 1971 & 1973, many variations in ea series, ea from $2 to $4.00
Baby Huey & Related Characters, see Harvey Cartoon Characters
Batman & Related Characters, see also Super Heroes
Batman Forever, McDonald's, 1995, various emb glass mugs, ea from $2 to $4.00
Battlestar Galactica, Universal Studios, 1979, 4 different, ea from $7 to $10.00
Beatles, Dairy Queen/Canada, group photos & signatures in wht starburst, gold trim, ea, from $95 to $125.00
Beverly Hillbillies, CBS promotion, 1963, rare, NM...... $200.00
Bozo the Clown, Capital Records, 1965, Bozo head image around top w/related character at bottom, ea from $10 to $15.00

Bozo the Clown, Capital Records, 1965, Bozo on 3 sides only, from $8 to $10.00
Buffalo Bill, see Western Heroes or Wild West Series
Bugs Bunny & Related Characters, see Warner Bros
Bullwinkle, Rocky & Related Characters, see Warner Bros or PAT Ward
Burger Chef, Friendly Monster Series, 1977, 6 different, ea from $15 to $25.00
Burger King, Collector Series, 1979, 5 different Burger King characters featuring Burger Thing, etc, ea from $3 to ..$5.00
Burger King, Put a Smile in Your Tummy, features Burger King mascot, from $5 to $6.00
Burger King, see also specific name or series
California Raisins, Applause, 1989, juice, 12-oz, 16-oz, ea from $4 to $6.00
California Raisins, Applause, 1989, 32-oz, from $6 to $8.00
Captain America, see Super Heroes
Casper the Friendly Ghost & Related Characters, see Arby's Bicentennial or Harvey Cartoon Characters
Charlie McCarthy & Edger Bergen, Libbey, 1930s, set of 8, M (EX illus display box).. $600.00
Children's Classics, Libbey Glass Co, Alice in Wonderland, Gulliver's Travels, Tom Sawyer, from $10 to..............$15.00
Children's Classics, Libbey Glass Co, Moby Dick, Robin Hood, Three Musketeers, Treasure Island, ea from $10 to.....$15.00
Children's Classics, Libbey Glass Co, The Wizard of Oz, from $25 to $30.00
Chilly Willy, see Walter Lantz
Chipmunks, Hardee's (no logo on glass), 1985, Alvin, Simon, Theodore, Chipettes, ea from $1 to $3.00
Cinderella, Disney/Libbey, 1950s-60s, set of 8 .... $120.00
Cinderella, see also Disney Collector Series or Disney Film Classics
Daffy Duck, see Warner Bros
Dick Tracy, Domino's Pizza, M, from $95 to................... $125.00
Dick Tracy, 1940s, frosted, 8 different characters, 3" or 5", ea from $50 to $75.00
Dilly Dally, see Howdy Doody
Disney, see also Wonderful World of Disney or specific characters
Disney Characters, 1936, Clarabelle, Donald, F Bunny, Horace, Mickey, Minnie, Pluto, 4¼" or 4¾", ea from $30 to....$50.00
Disney's All-Star Parade, 1939, 10 different, ea from $25 to $50.00
Donald Duck, Donald Duck Cola, 1960s-70s, from $10 to..$15.00
Donald Duck or Daisy, see also Disney or Mickey Mouse (Happy Birthday)
Dynomutt, see Hanna-Barbera
ET, Pepsi/MCA Home Video, 1988, 6 different, ea from $15 to.. $25.00
ET, Pizza Hut, 1982, ftd, 4 different, from $2 to.................$4.00
Fantasia, see Disney Film Classics or Mickey Mouse (Through the Years)
Flintstones, see also Hanna-Barbera
Ghostbusters II, Sunoco/Canada, 1989, 6 different, ea from $3 to $5.00
Goonies, Godfather's Pizza/Warner Bros, 1985, 4 different, ea from $3 to $5.00
Green Arrow or Green Lantern, see Super Heroes

Hanna-Barbera, Pepsi, 1977, Dynomutt, Flintstones, Josie & the Pussycats, Mumbly, Scooby, Yogi & Huck, ea from $10 to......... $20.00
Hanna-Barbera, Welch's, Flintstones, 1962 (6 different), 1963 (2 different), 1964 (6 different), ea from $4 to.................$6.00
Hanna-Barbera, 1960s, jam glasses featuring Cindy Bear, Flintstones, Huck, Quick Draw, Yogi Bear, rare, ea from $60 to......... $90.00
Happy Days, Dr Pepper, 1977, Fonzie, Joanie, Potsie, Ralph, Richie, from $6 to $10.00
Happy Days, Dr Pepper/Pizza Hut, 1977, any character, ea from $6 to $10.00
Harvey Cartoon Characters, Pepsi, 1970s, action pose, Baby Huey, Hot Stuff, Wendy, ea from $8 to $10.00
Harvey Cartoon Characters, Pepsi, 1970s, static pose, Baby Huey, Hot Stuff, Wendy, ea from $12 to $15.00
Harvey Cartoon Characters, Pepsi, 1970s, static pose, Richie Rich, from $15 to..$20.00
Harvey Cartoon Characters, Pepsi, 1970s, static pose, Sad Sack, scarce, from $25 to $30.00
Harvey Cartoon Characters, see also Arby's Bicentennial Series
He-Man & Related Characters, see Masters of the Universe
Honey, I Shrunk the Kids, McDonald's, 1989, plastic, 3 different, ea from $1 to $2.00
Hopalong Cassidy, milk glass w/black graphics, Breakfast Milk, Lunch Milk, Dinner Milk, ea from $15 to $20.00
Hopalong Cassidy, milk glass w/red & black graphics, 3 different, ea from $20 to $25.00
Hopalong Cassidy's Western Series, ea from $25 to $30.00
Hot Stuff, see Harvey Cartoon Characters or Arby's Bicentennial
Howard the Duck, see Super Heroes
Howdy Doody, Welch's/Kagran, 1950s, 6 different, emb bottom, ea from $10 to $15.00
Huckleberry Hound, see Hanna-Barbera
Incredible Hulk, see Super Heroes
Indiana Jones & the Temple of Doom, 7-Up (w/4 different sponsers), 1984, set of 4, from $8 to.................................$15.00
James Bond 007, 1985, 4 different, ea from $10 to $15.00
Joker, see Super Heroes
Jungle Book, Disney/Canada, 1966, 6 different, numbered, 5", ea from $30 to $65.00

Jungle Book, Disney/Canada, 1966, six different, numbered, 6½", each from $20.00 to $40.00. (Photo courtesy Mark Chase and Michael Kelly)

Jungle Book, Disney/Pepsi, 1970s, Bagheera or Shere Kahn, unmk, ea from $35 to...$60.00

Jungle Book, Disney/Pepsi, 1970s, Mowgli, unmk, from $15 to $20.00
Jungle Book, Disney/Pepsi, 1970s, Rama, unmk, from $25 to. $35.00
Laurel & Hardy, see Arby's Actor Series
Leonardo TTV, see also Arby's Bicentennial Series
Leonardo TTV Collector Series, Pepsi, Underdog, Go-Go Gophers, Simon Bar Sinister, Sweet Polly, 6", ea from $10 to $15.00
Leonardo TTV Collector Series, Pepsi, Underdog, Simon Bar Sinister, Sweet Polly, 5", ea from $6 to $10.00
Little Mermaid, 1991, 3 different sizes, ea from $6 to........$10.00
Masters of the Universe, Mattel, 1983, He-Man, Man-at-Arms, Skeletor, Teels, ea from $5 to $10.00
Masters of the Universe, Mattel, 1986, Battle Cat/He-Man, Man-at-Arms, Orko, Panthor/Sketetor, ea from $3 to...........$5.00
McDonald's, McDonaldland Action Series or Collector Series, 1970s, 6 different ea series, ea from $2 to....................$3.00
MGM Collector Series, Pepsi, 1975, Tom, Jerry, Barney, Droopy, Spike, Tuffy, ea from $5 to $10.00

MGM Collector Series, Pepsi, 1975, 5", Tom against yellow background, from $10.00 to $14.00. (Photo courtesy whatacharacter.com)

Mickey Mouse, Happy Birthday, Pepsi, 1978, Clarabelle & Horace or Daisy & Donald, ea from $5 to $10.00
Mickey Mouse, Happy Birthday, Pepsi, 1978, Donald, Goofy, Mickey, Minnie, Pluto, Uncle Scrooge, ea from $5 to..$7.00
Mickey Mouse, Mickey's Christmas Carol, Coca-Cola, 1982, 3 different, ea from $5 to $7.00
Mickey Mouse, Pizza Hut, 1980, milk glass mug, Fantasia, MM Club, Steamboat Willie, Today, ea from $2 to.............$5.00
Mickey Mouse, see also Disney Characters
Mickey Mouse, Through the Years, K-Mart, glass mugs w/4 different images (1928, 1937, 1940, 1955), ea from $3 to $5.00
Mickey Mouse Club, 4 different w/filmstrip bands top & bottom, ea from $10 to $20.00
Mickey Mouse Club, 6 different characters w/name & club logo on reverse, ea from $8 to $12.00
Mister Magoo, Polomar Jelly, many different variations & styles, ea from $25 to $35.00

Pac-Man, Arby's Collector Series, 1980, rocks glass, from $20 to $4.00
Pac-Man, Bally Midway MFG/AAFES/Libbey, 1980, Shadow (Blinky), Bashful (Inky), Pokey (Clyde), Speedy (Pinky), ea $4 to $6.00
Pac-Man, Bally Midway MFG/Libbey, 1982, 6" flare top, 5⅜" flare top or mug, from $2 to $4.00
PAT Ward, Collector Series, Holly Farms Restaurants, 1975, Boirs, Bullwinkle, Natasha, Rocky, ea from $20 to.....$40.00

PAT Ward, Pepsi, late 1970s, action pose, Dudley Do-Right in canoe, 5", from $5.00 to $10.00. (Photo courtesy whatacharacter.com)

PAT Ward, Pepsi, late 1970s, action pose, Bullwinkle w/balloons, Rocky in circus, 5", ea from $5 to....................$10.00
PAT Ward, Pepsi, late 1970s, static pose, Boris, Mr Peabody, Natasha, 5", ea from $10 to $15.00
PAT Ward, Pepsi, late 1970s, static pose, Boris & Natasha, 6", from $15 to $20.00
PAT Ward, Pepsi, late 1970s, static pose, Bullwinkle, 5", from $15 to $20.00
PAT Ward, Pepsi, late 1970s, static pose, Bullwinkle (brn lettering/no Pepsi logo), 6", from $15 to....................$20.00
PAT Ward, Pepsi, late 1970s, static pose, Bullwinkle (wht or blk lettering), 6", from $10 to....................$15.00
PAT Ward, Pepsi, late 1970s, static pose, Dudley Do-Right, 5", from $10 to $15.00
PAT Ward, Pepsi, late 1970s, static pose, Dudley Do-Right (blk lettering), 6", from $10 to....................$15.00
PAT Ward, Pepsi, late 1970s, static pose, Dudley Do-Right (red lettering/no Pepsi logo), 6", from $10 to....................$15.00
PAT Ward, Pepsi, late 1970s, static pose, Rocky, 5", from $15 to $20.00
PAT Ward, Pepsi, late 1970s, static pose, Rocky (brn lettering/no Pepsi logo), 6", from $10 to $15.00
PAT Ward, Pepsi, late 1970s, static pose, Rocky (wht or blk lettering), 6", from $10 to $15.00
PAT Ward, Pepsi, late 1970s, static pose, Snidley Whiplash, 5", from $8 to $10.00
PAT Ward, Pepsi, late 1970s, static pose, Snidley Whiplash (wht or blk lettering), 6", from $10 to $15.00
PAT Ward, see also Arby's Bicentennial Series
Peanuts Characters, Dolly Madison Bakery, Snoopy for President or Snoopy Sport Series, 4 different ea series, ea $3 to ..$5.00

Peanuts Characters, McDonald's, 1983, Camp Snoopy, wht plastic w/Lucy or Snoopy, ea from $5 to............................$8.00
Peanuts Characters, milk glass mug, Snoopy for President, 4 different, numbered & dated, ea from $5 to.....................$8.00
Peanuts Characters, milk glass mug, Snoopy in various poses, from $2 to $4.00
Penguin, see Super Heroes
Peter Pan, see Disney Film Classics
Pinocchio, Dairy Promo/Libbey, 1938-40, 12 different, ea from $15 to..$25.00
Pinocchio, see also Disney Collector's Series or Wonderful World of Disney
Pluto, see Disney Characters
Pocahontas, Burger King, 1995, 4 different, MIB, ea...........$3.00
Popeye, Coca-Cola, 1975, Kollect-A-Set, any character, ea from $3 to..$5.00
Popeye, Popeye's Famous Fried Chicken, 1978, Sports Scenes, Brutus, Olive Oyl, Swee' Pea, ea from $10 to $15.00
Popeye, Popeye's Famous Fried Chicken, 1978, Sports Scenes, Popeye, from $7 to..$10.00
Popeye, Popeye's Famous Fried Chicken, 1979, Pals, 4 different, ea from $10 to...$15.00
Popeye, Popeye's Famous Fried Chicken/Pepsi, 1982, 10th Anniversary Series, 4 different, ea from $7 to $10.00
Quick Draw, McGraw, see Hanna-Barbera
Raggedy Ann & Andy, going down slide, skipping rope, stacking blocks, riding in wagon, ea from $5 to $10.00
Rescuers, Pepsi, 1977, Brockway tumbler, Bernard, Bianca, Brutus & Nero, Evinrude, Orville, Penny, ea from $5 to..$10.00
Rescuers, Pepsi, 1977, Brockway tumbler, Madame Medusa or Rufus, ea from $15 to..$25.00
Richie Rich, see Harvey Cartoon Characters
Riddler or Robin, see Super Heroes
Road Runner & Related Characters, see Warner Bros
Rocky & Bullwinkle, see Arby's Bicentennial or PAT Ward
Roy Rogers Restaurant, 1883-1983 logo, from $3 to...........$5.00
Sad Sack, see Harvey Cartoon Characters
Scooby Doo, see Hanna-Barbera
Sleeping Beauty, American, late 1950s, 6 different, ea from $8 to...$15.00
Sleeping Beauty, Canadian, late 1950s, 12 different, ea from $10 to...$15.00
Smurf's, Hardee's, 1982 (8 different), 1983 (6 different), ea, from $1 to..$3.00
Snidley Whiplash, see PAT Ward
Snoopy & Related Characters, see Peanuts Characters
Snow White & the Seven Dwarfs, Bosco, 1938, ea from $20 to.. $30.00
Snow White & the Seven Dwarfs, Libbey, 1930s, verses on back, various colors, 8 different, ea from $15 to..................$25.00
Snow White & the Seven Dwarfs, see also Disney Collector's Series or Disney Film Classics
Star Trek, Dr Pepper, 1976, 4 different, ea from $15 to $20.00
Star Trek, Dr Pepper, 1978, 4 different, ea from $25 to $30.00
Star Trek II, The Search for Spock, Taco Bell, 1984, 4 different, ea from $3 to...$5.00
Star Trek: The Motion Picture, Coca-Cola, 1980, 3 different, ea from $10 to $15.00

Star Wars Trilogy: Empire Strikes Back, Burger King/Coca-Cola, 1980, four different, each from $5.00 to $7.00.

Star Wars Trilogy: Return of the Jedi, Burger King/Coca-Cola, 1983, 4 different, ea from $3 to $5.00
Star Wars Trilogy: Star Wars, Burger King/Coca-Cola, 1977, 4 different, ea from $8 to $10.00
Sunday Funnies, 1976, Brenda Star, Gasoline Alley, Moon Mullins, Orphan Annie, Smilin' Jack, Terry & the Pirates, $5 to $7.00
Sunday Funnies, 1976, Broom Hilda, from $90 to.......... $125.00
Super Heroes, Marvel, 1978, Federal, flat bottom, Captain America, Hulk, Spider-Man, Thor, ea from $40 to $75.00
Super Heroes, Marvel, 1978, Federal, flat bottom, Spider-Woman, from $100 to.. $150.00
Super Heroes, Marvel/7 Eleven, 1977, ftd, Amazing Spider-Man, from $25 to $30.00
Super Heroes, Marvel/7 Eleven, 1977, ftd, Captain America, Fantastic Four, Howard the Duck, Thor, ea from $10 to.....$15.00
Super Heroes, Marvel/7 Eleven, 1977, ftd, Incredible Hulk, from $10 to..$15.00
Super Heroes, Pepsi Super (Moon) Series/DC Comics or NPP, 1976, Aquaman, Flash, Supergirl, Superman, Wonder Woman, $10 ....$15.00

Super Heroes, Pepsi Super (Moon) Series/DC Comics or NPP, 1976, Robin, from $10.00 to $15.00.

(Photo courtesy gasolinealley.com)

Super Heroes, Pepsi Super (Moon) Series/DC Comics or NPP, 1976, Batgirl, Batman, Shazam!, ea from $10 to.......................$15.00

Super Heroes, Pepsi Super (Moon) Series/DC Comics or NPP, 1976, Green Arrow, from $15 to $20.00
Super Heroes, Pepsi Super (Moon) Series/DC Comics or NPP, 1976, Green Lantern, Joker, Penguin, Riddler, ea from $15 to $25.00
Super Heroes, Pepsi/DC Comics, 1978, Brockway, flat bottom, Aquaman, Shazam!, Superman, The Flash, ea from $8 to $10.00
Super Heroes, Pepsi/DC Comics, 1978, Brockway, flat bottom, Batman, Robin, Wonder Womany (red boots), ea from $8 to $15.00
Super Heroes, Pepsi/DC Comics, 1978, Brockway, rnd bottom, Batman, Robin, Shazam!, 5½", ea from $15 to $25.00
Super Heroes, Pepsi/DC Comics, 1978, Brockway, rnd bottom, Superman, The Flash, Wonder Woman, ea from $15 to $25.00
Superman, M Polanar & Son/NPP, 1964, 6 different, various colors, 4¼" or 5¾", ea from $20 to $25.00
Sylvester the Cat or Tasmanian Devil, see Warner Bros
Tom & Jerry & Related Characters, see MGM Collector Series
Underdog & Related Characters, see Arby's Bicentennial or Leonardo TTV
Universal Monsters, Universal Studio, 1980, ftd, Creature, Dracula, Frankenstein, Mummy, Mutant, Wolfman, ea $125 to..$150.00

Walter Lantz, Pepsi, 1970s, Chilly Willy, from $15.00 to $20.00. (Photo courtesy whatacharacter.com)

Walter Lantz, Pepsi, 1970s, Wally Walrus, ea, from $15 to..$20.00
Walter Lantz, Pepsi, 1970s, Cuddles, from $30 to $50.00
Walter Lantz, Pepsi, 1970s, Space Mouse, from $75 to .$150.00
Walter Lantz, Pepsi, 1970s, Woody Woodpecker, from $15 to $20.00
Walter Lantz, Pepsi, 1970s-80s, Anty/Miranda, Chilly/Smelley, Cuddles/Oswald, Wally/Homer, ea from $20 to $30.00
Walter Lantz, Pepsi, 1970s-80s, Buzz Buzzard/Space Mouse, from $15 to $20.00
Walter Lantz, Pepsi, 1970s-80s, Woody Woodpecker/Knothead & Splinter, from $15 to $20.00
Walter Lantz, see also Arby's Bicentennial Series
Warner Bros, Acme Cola, 1993, bell shape, Bugs, Sylvester, Taz, Tweety, ea from $4 to $8.00
Warner Bros, Arby's, 1988, Adventures Series, ftd, Bugs, Daffy, Porky, Sylvester & Tweety, ea from $25 to $30.00
Warner Bros, Marriott's Great America, 1975, 12-oz, 6 different (Bugs & related characters), ea from $20 to $30.00
Warner Bros, Marriott's Great America, 1989, Bugs, Porky, Sylvester, Taz, ea from $7 to $10.00
Warner Bros, Pepsi, 1973, Brockway 12-oz tumbler, Bugs, Porky, Road Runner, Sylvester, Tweety, ea, from $5 to $10.00
Warner Bros, Pepsi, 1973, Federal 16-oz tumbler, Bugs Bunny, wht lettering, from $5 to $10.00
Warner Bros, Pepsi, 1973, Federal 16-oz tumbler, Cool Cat, blk lettering, from $5 to $10.00
Warner Bros, Pepsi, 1973, Federal 16-oz tumbler, Elmer Fudd, wht lettering, from $5 to $8.00
Warner Bros, Pepsi, 1973, Federal 16-oz tumbler, Henry Hawk or Slow Poke Rodriquez, blk lettering, ea from $25 to....$40.00
Warner Bros, Pepsi, 1973, Federal 16-oz tumbler, Speedy Gonzales, blk lettering, from $6 to $10.00
Warner Bros, Pepsi, 1973, wht plastic, 6 different, Bugs, Daffy, Porky, Road Runner, Sylvester, Tweety, ea from $3 to..$5.00
Warner Bros, Pepsi, 1976, interaction, Beaky Buzzard & Cool Cat w/kite or Taz & Porky w/fishing pole, ea from $8 to......$10.00
Warner Bros, Pepsi, 1976, interaction, Bugs & Yosemite w/ cannon, Yosemite & Speedy Gonzales panning gold, ea $10 to $15.00
Warner Bros, Pepsi, 1976, interaction, Foghorn Leghorn & Henry Hawk, from $10 to $15.00
Warner Bros, Pepsi, 1976, interaction, others, ea from $5 to .. $10.00
Warner Bros, Pepsi, 1979, Collector Series, rnd bottom, Bugs, Daffy, Porky, Road Runner, Sylvester, Tweety, ea $7 to .$10.00
Warner Bros, Pepsi, 1980, Collector Series, Bugs, Daffy, Porky, Road Runner heads on star, names on band above, ea $6 to $10.00
Warner Bros, Six Flags, 1991, clear, Bugs, Daffy, Sylvester, Wile E Coyote, ea from $5 to $10.00
Warner Bros, Six Flags, 1991, clear, Yosemite Sam, from $10 to $15.00
Warner Bros, Welch's, 1974, action poses, 8 different, phrases around top, ea from $2 to $4.00
Warner Bros, Welch's, 1976-77, 8 different, names around bottom, ea from $5 to $7.00
Warner Bros, Zak Designs, 1991, 4 different tumblers, 4", ea..$5.00
Warner Bros, 1995, Taz's Root Beer/Serious Suds, clear glass mug, from $5 to $7.00
Warner Bros, 1996, 8 different w/ea character against busy background of repeated characters, names below, ea from $4 to $6.00
Warner Bros, 1998, 6 different w/characters against vertically striped background, ea from $4 to $6.00
WC Fields, see Arby's Actor Series
Western Heroes, Annie Oakley, Buffalo Bill, Wild Bill Hickok, Wyatt Earp, ea from $8 to $12.00
Western Heroes, Lone Ranger, from $10 to $15.00
Western Heroes, Wyatt Earp, fight scene or OK Corral gunfight, name at top, from $12 to $22.00

Wild West Series, Coca-Cola, Buffalo Bill, Calamity Jane, ea from $10 to $15.00
Wile E Coyote, see Warner Bros
Winnie the Pooh, Sears/WDP, 1970s, 4 different, ea from $7 to $10.00
Wizard of Oz, see also Children's Classics
Wizard of Oz, Coca-Cola/Krystal, 1989, 50th Anniversary Series, 6 different, ea from $7 to $10.00
Wizard of Oz, Swift's, 1950s-60s, fluted bottom, Emerald City or Flying Monkeys, ea from $8 to $15.00
Wizard of Oz, Swift's, 1950s-60s, fluted bottom, Glinda, from $15 to $25.00
Wizard of Oz, Swift's, 1950s-60s, fluted bottom, Wicked Witch, from $35 to $50.00
Wonder Woman, see Super Heroes
Wonderful World of Disney, Pepsi, 1980s, Alice, Bambi, Lady & the Tramp, Pinocchio, Snow White, 101 Dalmatians, $15 to $20.00
Woody Woodpecker & Related Characters, see Arby's Bicentennial or Walter Lantz
Yogi Bear or Yosimite Sam, see Hanna-Barbera
Ziggy, Number Series, 1-8, ea from $4 to....................$8.00
Ziggy, 7-Up Collector Series, 1977, Here's to Good Friends, 4 different, ea from $3 to $5.00

Character Clocks and Watches

Clocks and watches with dials depicting favorite characters have been manufactured with kids in mind since the 1930s, when Ingersoll made a wristwatch, a pocket watch, and a clock featuring Mickey Mouse. The #1 Mickey wristwatch came in the now-famous orange box commonly known as the 'critter box,' illustrated with a variety of Disney characters. There is also a blue display box from the same time period. The watch itself featured a second hand with three revolving Mickey figures. It was available with either a metal or leather band. Babe Ruth starred on an Exacta Time watch in 1949, and the original box contained not only the watch but a baseball with a facsimile signature.

Collectors prize the boxes about as highly as they do the watches. Many were well illustrated and colorful, but most were promptly thrown away, so they're hard to find today. Be sure you buy only watches in very good condition. Rust, fading, scratches, or other signs of wear sharply devaluate a clock or a watch. Hundreds have been produced, and if you're going to collect them, you'll need to study *Comic Character Clocks and Watches* by Howard S. Brenner (Books Americana) for more information.

Note: Our values are typical of high retail. A watch in exceptional condition, especially an earlier model, may bring even more. Dealers, who will generally pay about half of book when they buy for resale, many times offer discounts on the more pricey items, and package deals, involving more than one watch, may sometimes be made for as much as a 15% discount.

Advisor: Bill Campbell

See also Advertising.

CLOCKS

Batman & Robin Talking Alarm Clock, Janex, 1970s, molded plastic w/Batman running & Robin in car, EXIB, from $100 to $125.00
Bugs Bunny Alarm Clock, Ingraham, 1940s, Bugs resting w/carrot, 4x4" sq, EX, from $150 to $200.00

Bugs Bunny Alarm Clock, Seth Thomas, 1970, 4" plastic cube, $33.00. (Photo courtesy whatacharacter.com)

Bugs Bunny Talking Alarm Clock, Janex, 1970s, molded plastic, Bugs leaning on clock, MIB....................$75.00

Charlie McCarthy Alarm Clock, Gilbert, nonworking otherwise VG, A, $770.00. (Photo courtesy Morphy Auctions)

Cinderella Alarm Clock, Bradley/Japan, image of Cinderella leaving slipper on steps, 3" dia, scarce, MIB $125.00
Cinderella Wall Clock, Phinney-Walker, 1960s, sq plastic w/Cinderella on wht rnd scalloped center, electric, 8", NM...$32.00
Felix the Cat, Bright Ideas, 1989, MIB $65.00
Garfield Alarm Clock, Sunbeam, Garfield lying down on wht face, blk numbers, 2 bells, 6" dia, MIB....................$40.00
Garfield Alarm Clock, Sunbeam, 1990s, blk paw print & image of Garfield from the arms up on wht face, 2 bells, 7", MIB $40.00
Green Hornet Alarm Clock, Official Green Hornet Agent graphics on rnd face, w/up, NM, A $92.00
Hopalong Cassidy Alarm Clock, US Time, close-up of Hoppy on Topper on rnd face, name on base, EX....................$650.00
Hopalong Cassidy Alarm Clock, US Time, rnd blk case w/wht name on oblong base, blk & wht Hoppy/Topper, red numbers, NM $300.00
Howdy Doody Talking Alarm Clock, Janex, 'It's Howdy Doody Time,' plastic, w/Howdy & Clarabelle figures, 7" L, EXIB....................$150.00

James Bond 007 Wall Clock, 1981, Roger Moore image, NM+ $50.00
Looney Tunes Alarm Clock, Westclox, 1994, Daffy Duck lecturing Bugs on wht face, blk 12-3-6-9, rnd case, unused, MIP... $25.00

Mickey Mouse Alarm Clock, Bayard/France, 1930s, EXIB, from $950.00 to $1,200.00. (Photo courtesy David Longest)

Mickey Mouse Alarm Clock, Bradley, 1960s, lg blk ears atop rnd case w/lg face on front, footed, 3½" dia, EXIB $85.00
Mickey Mouse Alarm Clock, Ingersoll, 1930s, electric, sq metal case w/Mickey figure on face, 4", nonworking o/w M . $425.00
Mickey Mouse Alarm Clock, US Time, full-figure Mickey on rnd face w/arched case, arms are clock hands, 4½", VG, A..$65.00
Minnie Mouse Alarm Clock, Bradley, red rnd case w/2 yel bells atop, footed, image & name on face, EXIB.................$65.00
Miss Piggy Alarm Clock, Timex, 1982, plastic dome shape w/image of Miss Piggy admiring self in mirror, 4½", MIB $30.00
Peanuts Alarm Clock, Japan, 1988, silver metal case, character faces as numbers, 3½" dia, MIB $60.00
Pluto Wall Clock, Allied, plastic figure w/clock attached to his chest, hands shaped as dog bones, 8", EXIB............ $300.00
Popeye Alarm Clock, Smiths, Great Britain, 1960s, Popeye & Swee' Pea, head moves to count seconds on rnd face, 5", VG.................... $200.00
Roy Rogers & Trigger Alarm Clock, Ingraham, desert mountain scene, 4½" sq, VG+ $280.00
Sesame Street Clock, Fantasma, 1990s, 9" Elmo figure standing next to rnd clock on oblong base, b/o, EX $15.00
Sesame Street Players Clock, Bradley, 1981, b/o, plastic theater w/waving Ernie figure, 8", NM+....................$28.00
She-ra Princess of Power Wall Clock, rnd w/image of She-ra on Pegasus, b/o, 10" dia, unused, M....................$25.00
Shmoo Wall Clock, Lux, bl plastic flat figure w/blk features & numbers & hands, working pendulum, 6½", EX+IB. $400.00
Sleeping Beauty Alarm Clock, Phinney-Walker, 1950s, Sleeping Beauty petting rabbit & surrounded by 3 birds, 5", EX+.. $65.00
Snoopy, Pawpet, plush, 11", Determined, 1970s, MIP.......$28.00
Snoopy Alarm Clock, Blessing, 1970s, wht Snoopy w/ears Up & appears to be dancing & wht numbers on blk, 5½", EX+..$38.00
Snoopy Alarm Clock, Equity, 1970s, Snoopy as tennis player against tan grid-patterned face, ball as second hand, 5", NM....................$40.00
Snoopy Alarm Clock, Equity, 1970s, Snoopy w/checkered flag & wht numbers on red face, 5", NM+....................$40.00
Superman Wall Clock, New Haven, 1978, b/o, framed w/image of Superman confronting spaceship, EX+ $40.00

Who's Afraid of the Big Bad Wolf? Alarm Clock, Ingersoll, wolf's head bobs, EX, A, $825.00. (Photo courtesy Morphy Auctions)

Woody Wood Pecker Wall Clock, Model No 535, molded plastic figure of Woody on horse w/clock face, 9" H, NRFB, A..... $250.00

Pocket Watches

Boy Scouts, Ingersoll, 1937, 'Be Prepared'/'A Scout Is' on yel hands pointing to phrases encircling numbers, chrome case, 2".................... $230.00
Buck Rogers, Ingraham, 1935, 2½" dia, EX.................... $550.00
Captain Marvel, Fawcett, 1948, rnd chrome case, full figure image, plastic strap, EXIB.................... $750.00
Dan Dare, Imperial Limited/London, 1950s, 2" dia, EX . $500.00
Don Winslow of the Navy, New Haven, 1938-39, EX. $1,600.00

Donald Duck, Ingersoll, 1939, EXIB, A, $1,100.00. (Photo courtesy Morphy Auctions)

Lone Ranger, 1970, rnd chrome case, Lone Ranger & Silver, bl strap, silver chain, NM $100.00
Mary Marvel, Fawcett, 1948, rnd chrome case, full figure, red plastic strap, VG $125.00
Mickey Mouse, Ingersoll, 1930s, full-figure Mickey on wht face, moving arms, blk strap, EXIB, A.................... $825.00

Mickey Mouse, Ingersoll, 1930s, full-figure Mickey on wht face, moving arms, blk strap, Mickey image emb on rnd fob, EX $440.00
Popeye, New Haven, 1935, 1¾" dia, NM+, from $550 to .. $1,000.00
Roy Rogers, Bradley, lg image of Roy w/sm image of Roy & Trigger in background, w/stopwatch feature, EX $600.00
Roy Rogers & Trigger Stop Watch, Bradley, 1959, bust image of Roy & Roy on rearing Trigger, chrome case, 2" dia, NM, A $285.00
Superman, New Haven, rectangular chrome case, 3-quarter figure, w/stopwatch feature, EX $600.00

Superman, 2" dia, VG, A $175.00. (Photo courtesy Morphy Auctions)

Three Little Pigs, Ingersoll, image of 3 pigs & wolf on red, w/fob, NMIB, A $3,575.00
Wizard of Oz, Westclock, 1980s, 4 characters on dial, silver-tone case, unsued, MIB $75.00
Woody (Toy Story), Fossil, 1996, limited ed, M (M box & container) $125.00

Wristwatches

Alice in Wonderland, Ingersoll, image of Alice, fabric strap, EX (EX rnd pk box w/clear plastic teacup), A, from $250 to $350.00
Alice in Wonderland, New Haven, 1950s, Alice & Mad Hatter on rnd face, leather strap, nonworking o/w NM, A $75.00

Alice in Wonderland, 1950s, vinyl band, NMIB (with plastic figure), A, $440.00. (Photo courtesy Randy Inman Auctions)

Angelique (Dark Shadows), Abbelare, MIB (coffin box) . $100.00
Bambi, Ingersoll-US Time/WDP, 1949, Birthday Series, rnd chrome case, animated ears for hands, leather band, MIB $275.00
Barnabas Collins (Dark Shadows), Abbelare, MIB (coffin box) $100.00
Batman, Fossil, 1990, limited ed, complete w/pin, M (M litho box), from $150 to $200.00
Batman, 1966, batwings keep time on rnd face encased in blk plastic wings, NMIB $850.00
Bionic Woman, MX Berger, 1970s, image & lettering on face, vinyl band, NM, from $60 to $80.00
Blondie, Danbros, Watch Co/KFS, 1949, rnd chrome case, Blondie, Dagwood & pups on band, NM+IB $950.00
Bongo, Ingersoll/US Time/WDP, Birthday Series, EXIB... $325.00
Bozo the Clown, 1960s, image & name in red, vinyl band, EX $50.00
Buffy & Jody, Sheffield, 1969, image & names on face, visible gears, various bands, M, ea $125.00
Bugs Bunny, Rexall Drug Co/Warner Bros, 1950s, rnd chrome case, animated carrot hands, EX $400.00
Bugs Bunny, Rexall Drug Co/Warner Bros, 1950s, rnd chrome case, animated carrot hands, NM+IB $1,600.00
Buzz Lightyear, Fossil, 1996, complete w/Buzz lightyear plaque, M (M rnd tin box) $75.00
Captain Marvel, Fawcett, 1948, rnd chrome case, vinyl band, unused, NM+IB $500.00
Captain Marvel, Fawcett, 1948, rnd chrome case, vinyl band, VG $160.00
Catwoman, Quintel, 1991, digital, NM+ $25.00
Charlie Brown, Determind, 1970s, baseball scene on yel background, blk band, EXIB $175.00
Charlie Chaplin, Bradley, 1985, Oldies Series, MIB $50.00
Cinderella, Timex, 1950s, full figure on rnd face, MIB (watch dislayed in clear plastic slipper), A $300.00
Cinderella, 1950s, name on plain white rnd face, vinyl strap, MIB (w/plastic figure), A $300.00
Cool Cat, Sheffield, 1960s, full-figure image, VG $50.00
Daisy Duck, US Time, 1948, EXIB $300.00
Dale Evans, Bradley, 1950s, oblong chrome case, Dale & Buttercup on face, leather band, MIB $225.00
Dale Evans, Bradley, 1960s, rnd gold-tone case, image of Dale & Buttercup framed by horseshoe, vinyl band, VG $50.00
Davy Crockett, US Time, 1950s, gr plastic case, tooled leather band, unused, MIB (w/powder horn display) $450.00
Dick Tracy, New Haven/Chester Gould, 1951, rnd chrome case, leather band, NM+IB (wht box) $650.00
Dick Tracy Official Police Watch, Larami, 1973, silver-tone case w/plastic strap, unused, MOC $18.00
Dizzy Dean, Everbrite-Ingersoll, 1933, scarce, M $1,100.00
Donald Duck, Ingersoll, 1936, leather band w/little Donalds, Donald hands, EXIB, from $2,500 to $3,000.00
Donald Duck, 1940s, oblong face, leather band, NMIB (pop-up cb figure in lid), A $275.00
Dopey, Ingersoll-US Time/WDP, Birthday Series, EXIB. $250.00
Dr Seuss' Cat in the Hat, 1972, NM $150.00
Evel Knievel, Bradley, 1976, vinyl band, EX $150.00
Flipper, ITF/MGM, glow-in-the-dark image, M $125.00

Frankenstein (Universal Monsters), 1995, glow-in-the-dark, MOC....................$25.00

Gene Autry, New Haven, 1951, Six Shooter, brn leather band, unused, MIB.................... $650.00

Gene Autry, Wilane, 1948, Champion, NMIB.............. $400.00

Girl From UNCLE, 1960s, pk face w/blk line drawing & numbers, EX....................$65.00

Goofy, Helbros/WDP, 1972, runs backwards, rnd chrome case, animated hands, leather band, MIB.................... $675.00

Hopalong Cassidy, Anniversary, w/watch, neckerchief & steer slide, MIB.................... $150.00

Hopalong Cassidy, US Time/William Boyd, 1955, blk plastic case, decorated band, unused, MIB.................... $525.00

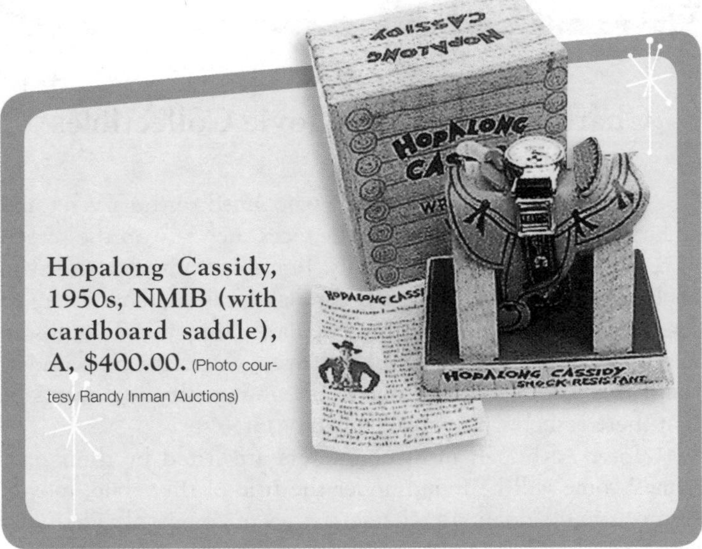

Hopalong Cassidy, 1950s, NMIB (with cardboard saddle), A, $400.00. (Photo courtesy Randy Inman Auctions)

Howdy Doody, Ideal/Kagran, 1950s, rnd chrome case, plastic band, MIB.................... $650.00

Howdy Doody, Patent Watch Co, 1954, head image w/movable eyes on rnd chrome case, vinyl strap, NMIB, A $250.00

Jetsons (Judy), Lewco, 1986, pk vinyl figure posing w/watch face in her hand, unused, MOC $18.00

Joe Carioca, Ingersoll-US Time/WDP, 1953, chrome case animated bands, EX+IB (20th birthday box)............... $250.00

Joe Paloka, New Haven/Ham Fisher, 1948, unused, NMIB.$950.00

Joker, Fossil, 1980s, NMIP....................$75.00

Josie & the Pussycats, Bradley, 1971, complete w/3 bands, MIB.$350.00

Kaptain Kool & the Kongs, 1977, Kaptain Kool on face, M.$100.00

Lahs LaRue, MIB....................$50.00

Li'l Abner Animated, New Haven, 1947, rare, MIB, from $600 to.................... $800.00

Lone Ranger, New Haven, 1939, MIB, from $500 to $800.00

Man From UNCLE, Bradley, 1960s, MIB (very rare w/box).$200.00

Mary Marvel, Marvel/Fawcett, 1948, rnd chrome case, vinyl band, NMIB (oblong cb box).................... $600.00

Mary Marvel, Marvel/Fawcett, 1948, rnd chrome case, vinyl band, unused, MIB (oblong plastic box)................ $650.00

Max Headroom, Chrysalis Visual Programming Ldt/Criterion Watch Co, 1986, Network 23 XXIII/C-C-C-Catch The Time, MOC....................$15.00

Mickey Mouse, Ingersoll, 1930s, oblong chrome case, metal bracelet band, VGIB (box w/Mickey in top hat)..$1,500.00

Mickey Mouse, Ingersoll, 1930s, oblong gold-tone case, leather band, nonworking o/w EXIB $1,600.00

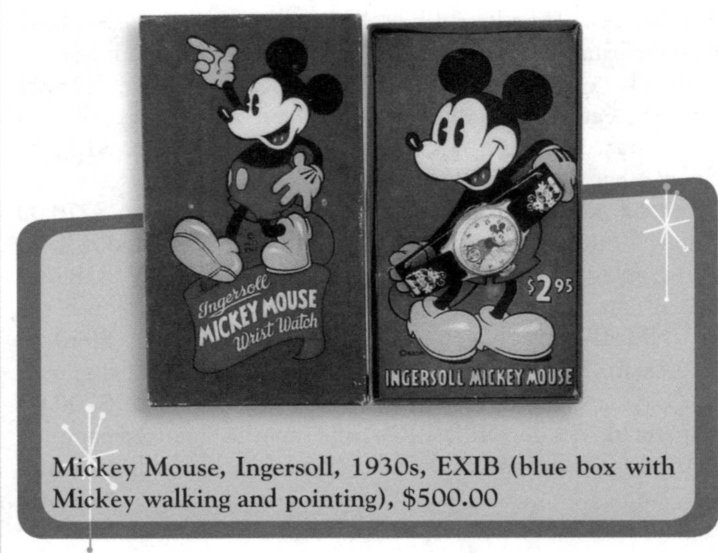

Mickey Mouse, Ingersoll, 1930s, EXIB (blue box with Mickey walking and pointing), $500.00

Mickey Mouse, Ingersoll, 1930s, rnd gold-tone case, vinyl band, VGIB.................... $150.00

Mickey Mouse, Ingersoll, 1940s, oblong chrome case, leather band, unused, MIB (yel Mickey box).................... $400.00

Mickey Mouse, Ingersoll, 1940s, rnd chrome case, vinyl band, NM+IB (yel Mickey box).................... $225.00

Mickey Mouse, Ingersoll, 1950s, rnd chrome case, full Mickey figure, leather band, MIB (plastic Mickey figure), A $385.00

Minnie Mouse, Timex, 1950s, Minnie on rnd face, w/emb celluloid plaque, MIB.................... $200.00

Orphan Annie Watch, oblong case w/image of Annie standing, leather band, VGIB, A $175.00

Partridge Family, 1970s, family image on face, NM, from $150 to $200.00

Pinocchio, Ingersoll-US Time/WDP, 1948, rnd chrome case, luminated face, leather band, MIB (20th birthday box) ... $450.00

Pluto, Ingersoll-US Time/WDP, 1948, rnd chrome case, luminated face, MIB (20th birthday box) $375.00

Pocahontas, Time Works/Disney, 1990s, leather strap, unused, MIB....................$75.00

Pokeman, General Mills premium, 1999, blk plastic band, MIP $12.00

Popeye, Bradley #308, 1964, gr case, EXIB $200.00

Popeye, New Haven/KFS, 1935, different Popeye characters on oblong face, leather band, NMIB....................$4,050.00

Popeye, Unique, 1987, digital, NMIB....................$50.00

Porky Pig, Ingraham/Warner Bros, 1949, MIB................ $880.00

Porky Pig, Sheffield, 1970s, rnd chrome case w/Porky tipping his hat on face, vinyl band, NMIB....................$75.00

Rocky Jones Space Ranger, Ingraham, 1950s, MIB......... $750.00

Roger Rabbit, Shiraka, 1980s, silhouette, gold case, blk band, unused, MIP.................... $150.00

Roy Rogers, Ingraham, 1960s, chrome case w/flickering image of Roy on Trigger, leather band, NM+ $150.00

Roy Rogers & Trigger, Bradley, 1960s, rnd chrome case w/close-up image of Roy holding Triggers bit, vinyl band, VG+ $50.00
Rudolph the Red Nosed Reindeer, Ingersoll, 1947, oblong chrome case, leather band, NM+IB $400.00
Smitty, New Haven, 1930s, VGIB $425.00
Smokey Bear, Hamilton, 1960s, MIB $150.00
Snoopy, Timex, 1970s, tennis theme w/articulated hands holding racket on denim background, denim band, NMIB $75.00
Snoopy, Determined, 1969, gold or silver case, dancing Snoopy on face, various bands, EX, ea $100.00
Snow White, Ingersoll, 1940s, 3-quarter figure on wht rnd face, leather band, NMIB (oval box w/flat scalloped bottom).............. $770.00
Snow White, name on plain wht rnd face, vinyl band, EX+IB (w/plastic figure), A $385.00
Space Patrol, US Time, 1950, chrome case w/expansion band, NM+IB $950.00
Superman, Bradley, 1959, chrome case w/Superman flying over cityscape, EXIB $700.00
Superman, Bradley/NPP, 1966, Superman in flight & name on yel face, chrome case & flex band, NM (cylindrical case), A...$280.00
Superman, Dabbs, NM $100.00

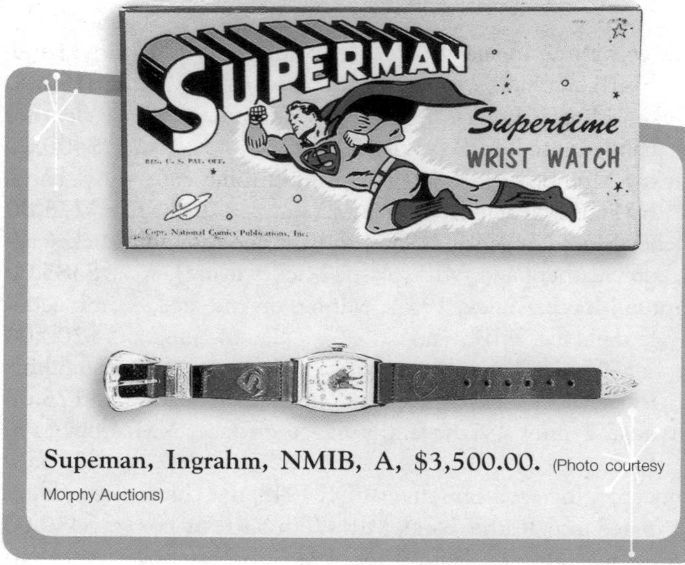

Supeman, Ingrahm, NMIB, A, $3,500.00. (Photo courtesy Morphy Auctions)

Superman, New Haven, 1939, Superman from the waist up on oval face, leather band, EXIB $1,000.00
Tarzan, Bradley, MIB...$60.00
Three Little Pigs, Ingersoll/WD, 1934, rnd case w/head image of BB Wolf, leather band, NMIB, A......................... $2,250.00
Three Little Pigs, Ingersoll/WD, 1934, rnd chrome case, metal bracelet band w/wolf & pigs, NM+ $950.00
Tim Holt, MIB $50.00
Tom Corbett Space Cadet, Ingraham, 1950s, rnd chrome case, leather band, NM+IB (w/rocket ship insert) $2,600.00
Tom Mix, 1983, 100th Anniversary, M......................... $275.00
Wizard of Oz, EKO, 1989, plastic band, unused, MIP........$50.00
Wonder Woman/Super Hero, Dabbs, 1970s, image on rnd face, leather band, NMIB.. $100.00
Woody (Toy Story), Fossil, 1996, w/Woody plaque, unused, M (M rnd tin box) $75.00

X-Files, Fossil, 2000, M (M see-through cylinder box)......$75.00

Zorro, U.S. Time, 1957, MIB (with hat display), A, $385.00. (Photo courtesy Randy Inman Auctions)

Character, TV, and Movie Collectibles

To the baby boomers who grew up glued to the TV set and addicted to Saturday matinees, the faces they saw on the screen were as familiar to them as family. Just about any character you could name has been promoted through retail merchandising to some extent; depending on the popularity they attain, exposure may continue for weeks, months, even years. It's no wonder, then, that the secondary market abounds with these items or that there is such wide-spread collector interest.

Note: Although most characters are listed by their own names, some will be found under the title of the group, movie, comic strip, or dominate character they're commonly identified with. The Joker, for instance, will be found in the Batman listings. They are also listed under the cartoon studio name from which they came, such as Hanna-Barbera, Harvey Cartoons, Looney Tunes, etc.

All items are complete unless noted otherwise.

See also Action Figures; Battery-Operated Toys; Books; Chein; Character and Promotional Drinking Glasses; Character Clocks and Watches; Coloring, Activity, and Paint Books: Disney; Dolls; Fisher-Price; Games; Guns; Halloween Costumes; Lunch Boxes; Marx; Model Kits; Paper Dolls; Pin-Back Buttons; Plastic Figures; Puzzles; Playsets; Ramp Walkers; Records; View-Master; Western; Windup, Friction, and Other Mechanical Toys.

A-Team, Blowgun Gliders, Arco, 1983, MOC $45.00
A-Team, Sliding Puzzle, Hong Kong, c 1983, NRFC (sealed)..$30.00
Addams Family, bank, The Thing, b/o, insert coin, box shakes & Thing grabs it, unused, MIB, A........................... $1,128.00
Addams Family, candy dispenser, Gomez figure in singing pose, plastic, 5", Bee Int'l, 1993, unused, MIP......................$8.00
Addams Family, figure, Gomez, stuffed cloth w/pk cloth outfit, plastic eyes, w/book, 13", Ace Novelty, 1992, NM+ ..$15.00
Addams Family, figure, Lurch, plastic, jtd head & arms, 5", Remco, 1960s, MIB $275.00
Addams Family, figure, Uncle Fester, vinyl, standing holding a frog in raised hand, 5", Remco, 1965, EX+ $125.00

Addams Family, hand puppet, Morticia, cloth body w/vinyl head, NM... $225.00
Alf, figure, stuffed plush, suction-cup hands, 7½", Coleco, 1988, MIB (box reads Stick Around Alf)..............................$15.00
Alf, figure, stuffed plush, 19", Coleco, 1986, NM+............$25.00
Alf, hand puppet, plush w/'Born to Rock' shirt, Alien Prod, NM..$20.00
Alvin & the Chipmunks, bank, Alvin figure holding harmonica, vinyl, 9", CBS Toys, 1984, NM..................................$20.00
Alvin & the Chipmunks, bubble bath container, any character, Colgate-Palmolive, 1960s, M, ea................................$15.00
Alvin & the Chipmunks, figure, Alvin, stuffed cloth, felt-like material, red 'A' on chest, 5", Christy Mfg, 1959, NM..$25.00
Alvin & the Chipmunks, figure, Alvin, stuffed plush, lg yel 'A' on red sweater, red hat, 12", CBS Toys, 1983, NM.....$15.00
Alvin & the Chipmunks, figure, Simon, stuffed cloth, musical, 13", Knickerbocker, 1963, EX....................................$75.00
Alvin & the Chipmunks, figure, Simon, stuffed plush, gym-shoe feet, wht 'S' on bl shirt, 8", Graphics Int'l, 1987, NM..$10.00
Alvin & the Chipmunks, figure, Simon, stuffed plush, gym-shoe feet, 13", CBS Toys, 1983, NM+, ea...........................$15.00
Alvin & the Chipmunks, figure, Simon, vinyl, jtd, bl shorts & wht tank top, gym shoes, bl glasses, 4", CBS, 1984, NM+.....$5.00
Alvin & the Chipmunks, figure, Theodore, plastic, gr 'T' on wht top, gr shorts & socks, gr & wht shoes, 3", CBS, NM...$5.00
Alvin & the Chipmunks, figure, Theodore, stuffed plush, pk 'T' on long gr shirt, 7", Graphics Int'l, 1980s, w/tag, NM+.....$10.00
Alvin & the Chipmunks, figure, Theodore, stuffed plush, talker, red 'T' on long gr shirt, 19", CBS Toys, 1983, NM+...$30.00
Alvin & the Chipmunks, hand puppet, Alvin, full cloth body w/vinyl head in red hat, Knickerbocker, 1960, EX+...$75.00
Alvin & the Chipmunks, harmonica, red plastic triangular shape w/Alvin decal, Dairy Queen, 1984, NM......................$8.00
Alvin & the Chipmunks, jack-in-the-box, plastic w/Alvin graphics & pop-up figure, 9", CBS Toys, 1983, NM............$35.00
Alvin & the Chipmunks, ornament, 3 on sled, emb resin, 4", Adler, MIP...$6.00

Amos N' Andy, figures, painted wood bead type with names on front, 6", EX+, pair, $350.00. (Photo courtesy Randy Inman Auctions)

Animal Crackers, bank, Grandpa Turtle, ceramic, 5", w/hang tag, NM+...$55.00
Animaniacs, figure set, Wakko, Dot & Yakko, PVC, standing w/arms raised, Dakin, 1990s, MIB..............................$15.00
Annie (Movie), wallet, wht vinyl w/name & image of Annie & Sandy, 3½", Henry Gordy Int'l, 1981, MIP (sealed)...$12.00
Archies, any character in car, Burger King, 1991, NM........$5.00

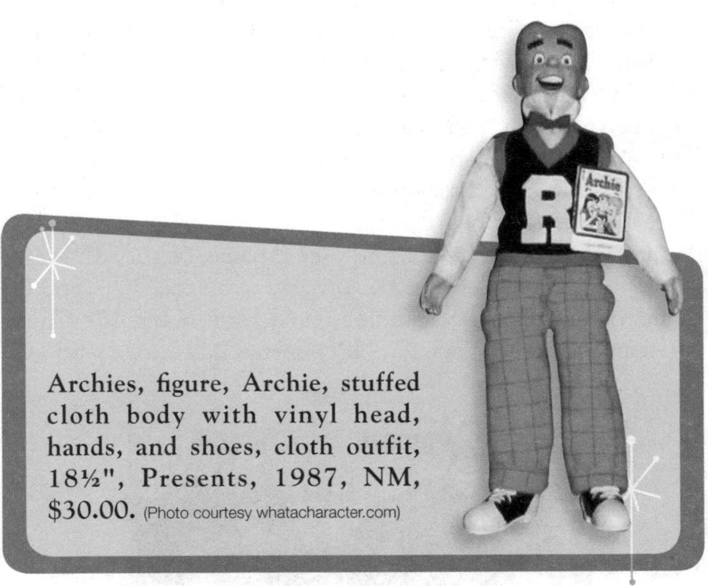
Archies, figure, Archie, stuffed cloth body with vinyl head, hands, and shoes, cloth outfit, 18½", Presents, 1987, NM, $30.00. (Photo courtesy whatacharacter.com)

Archies, figure, Reggie, bendable rubber, 6½", Jesco, 1989, NM+..$8.00
Archies, hand puppet, Archie, printed vinyl body w/vinyl head, Ideal, 1973, MIP (header reads TV Favorites)......... $125.00
Archies, Ring Toss, features Jughead stand-up figure, Ja-Ru, 1987, NRFC...$10.00
Atom Ant, see Hanna Barbera
Babar, fast-food toy, Arthur in car, plastic, 1¾x2¼", Arby's, 1992, M..$5.00
Babar, figure, Celeste, vinyl, 7", wht dress w/red dots, 1991, NM...$12.00
Babar, ornament, Babar the elephant driving car w/Christmas package, plastic/compo, 4" L, M.................................$6.00
Babar, squeeze toy, Arthur w/Zephir the monkey on his shoulder, vinyl, 3½", 1990, NM...$5.00
Babe, figure, stuffed plush, pk w/felt pouch holding 3 piglets, 1 gr foot pad & 1 red, 13", Equity Toys, 1998, NM...........$12.00
Baby Huey, see Harvey Cartoons
Banana Splits, see Hanna-Barbera
Barney, bank, Barney seated in chair w/mug, blanket & book, vinyl, 7", 1992, MIP...$10.00
Barney, figure, Barney, vinyl, baseball player catching ball in glove, 5¼", 1990s, NMIP...$10.00
Barney, night-light, plastic figure of Barney in hot-air balloon, 8½", Happiness Express, 1992, MIP $18.00
Barney, ornament, resin figure in Santa hat holding candy cane & gift, 4½", Kurt Adler, 2001, MIP.............................$6.00
Barney Bear, squeeze toy, bare-chested Barney w/arm raised, vinyl, 7", Alan Jay, 1950s, EX....................................$50.00
Barney Google & Spark Plug, bank, Spark Plug, pnt CI w/name emb on sides, 7½", EX, A $85.00
Barney Google & Spark Plug, drum, litho tin w/paper drumskins, 10" dia, 1920s, G, A $280.00

Barney Google & Spark Plug, figure, Spark Plug, wood, felt blanket, 10½", Schoenhut, EX $250.00

Barney Google & Spark Plug, figure set, Barney & Spark Plug, wood w/cloth outfits, 8" & 9", Schoenhut, EX+, A. $600.00

Barney Google & Spark Plug, figure set, stuffed cloth w/glass eyes, cloth dressed, 12" & 9", Knickerbocker, 1930, VG, A. $1,120.00

Barney Google & Spark Plug, hand puppet, Barney, printed cloth body w/name & vinyl head w/cigar, Gund, 1950s, NM+ $100.00

Barney Google & Spark Plug, pull toy, tin figures on 4-wheeled open platform, 8", Nifty, EX, A $2,125.00

Batman, bank, Batman, standing in wide stance, hands on hips on wht stepped base w/red name, ceramic, 7", Lego, 1966, NM.. $65.00

Batman, bank, Joker, bust figure w/emb name, plastic, 8", Mego, 1974, EX+ $60.00

Batman, bank, Batman standing on sq base w/ hands on hips, name on base, compo, 7", NPP/Japan, NM................. $80.00

Batman, Bat Grenade, shoots caps, Esquire Novelty, unused, M (VG card), $125.00. (Photo courtesy Morphy Auctions)

Batman, Batcopter Water Blaster, Blue Box Toy/Woolworth, 1989, unused, NRFB, A... $20.00

Batman, Batmobile, friction, blk w/red trim w/Batman & Robin figures, 7", NPP, 1960s, NMIB, A $450.00

Batman, Batmobile, plastic, Duncan, 1977, MOC (8x11" card), A $55.00

Batman, bubble bath container, Batman, bl & gray w/yel belt, Kid Care, 1995, unused, M $10.00

Batman, bubble bath container, Batman or Robin, Colgate-Palmolive, 1960s, NM, ea.. $30.00

Batman, Colorforms Adventure Set, 1989, NRFB, A $18.00

Batman, figure, Batman or Robin, Super Junior Squeak Toy, vinyl, 7", 1978, NM+, ea $20.00

Batman, figure, Joker, vinyl, cloth jacket & vest, jtd arms, 15", Presents, 1989, EX+.. $38.00

Batman, figure, Robin, vinyl w/yel cloth cape, jtd, 13", Presents, 1988, NM... $35.00

Batman, fork & spoon, name & emb images on hdls, Imperial, 1966, NM, A.. $30.00

Batman, hand puppet, Batman, blk cloth body, vinyl head w/flesh-tone face & blk mask, Punching Puppet, 1990, MIP $25.00

Batman, hand puppet, Batman, printed cloth body w/vinyl head, Ideal, 1966, NM+ $75.00

Batman, hand puppet, Batman, vinyl body w/name & molded vinyl head, Ideal, 1966, MIP $150.00

Batman, Helmet & Cape, bl plastic helmet w/blk face, Batman emblem, vinyl cape, Ideal, 1966, NMIB, A $450.00

Batman, mug, wht milk glass w/blk images of Batman front & back, Westfield, 1966, EX, A....................................... $45.00

Batman, Oil Painting by Numbers, NPP, 1965, unused, NMIB, A $140.00

Batman, Shooting Arcade, 8", Ahi/DC Comics, 1977, unused, NMIB, A.. $165.00

Batman, Utility Belt, complete w/accessories, Remco, unused, MIB, A $950.00

Batman & Robin, hand puppet set, all vinyl w/lithoed bodies, Ideal, 1966, MIB, A $1,090.00

Batman & Robin, scissors, Chemtoy, 1973, MOC............ $25.00

Batman and Robin, Stardust 'Touch of Velvet Art' by Numbers, Hasbro/NPP, 1966, unused, MIP (sealed), A, $150.00. (Photo courtesy Morphy Auctions)

Battlestar Galactica, Atomic Yo-Yo, plastic, Larami, 1978, MOC $35.00

Battlestar Galactica, Colorforms Adventure Set, Deluxe Edition #2359, 1978, MIB $75.00

Battlestar Galactica, ID Set, Larami, 1978, NRFC............ $18.00

Battlestar Galactica, Jet Discs, Larami, 1978, NRFC......... $20.00

Battlestar Galactica, Medical Kit, 12-pc set, Larami, 1978, NRFC.. $20.00

Battlestar Galactica, wallet, vinyl w/image of space cruiser & name, 1978, NRFC (unpunched) $20.00

Beany & Cecil, bubble bath container, Cecil, Purex, 1962, NM $20.00

Beany & Cecil, hand puppet, Beany, cloth body w/vinyl head, googley eyes, ca 1950, VG+ $75.00

Beany and Cecil, hand puppet, Dishonest John, talker, Mattel, 1962, NM, A, $175.00. (Photo courtesy serioustoyz.com)

Beetle Bailey, doll, Beetle Bailey, printed cloth body w/name, head, Gund, 1960, NM+ $150.00

Beetle Bailey, doll, General Halftrack, stuffed cloth body, vinyl head, hands & shoes, gr jumpsuit, 15", Toy Works, NM........... $20.00

Beetle Bailey, doll, Miss Buxley, stuffed cloth, vinyl head, red cloth dress, red shoes, 15", Sugar Loaf, 1990s, NM+ ..$20.00

Beetle Bailey, doll, Sgt Snorkel, stuffed body w/vinyl head, hands, flocked shoes, 15", Presents, 1985....................$30.00

Beetle Bailey, hand puppet, Beetle Bailey, printed cloth body w/name & vinyl head, Gund, 1960, EX.................. $100.00

Ben Casey MD, Paint-by-Number Water Color Set, Transogram #1825, 1962, unused, MIB (sealed)......................... $175.00

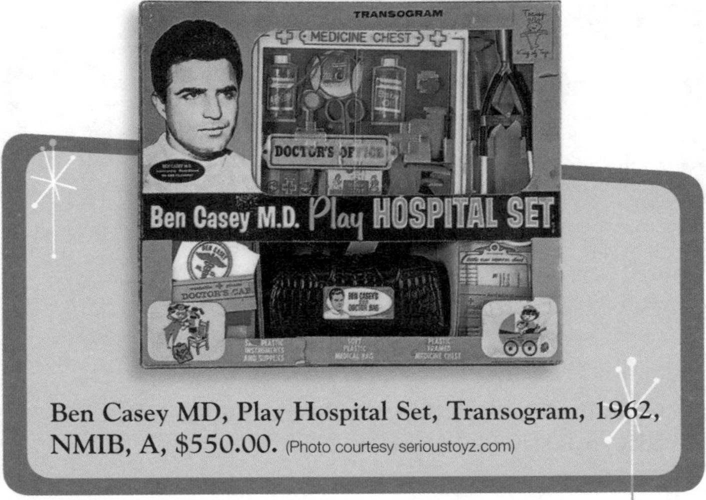

Ben Casey MD, Play Hospital Set, Transogram, 1962, NMIB, A, $550.00. (Photo courtesy serioustoyz.com)

Ben Casey MD, Sweater Guard, chain w/charms, Bing Crosby Products, 1962, NRFC...$45.00

Betty Boop, bank, red plastic coin sorter w/Betty Boop graphics, drop a coin & she winks, 8", Mag-Nif, 1986, MIB......$18.00

Betty Boop, doll, composition, cloth dress, shoes, and socks, 12", Cameo Doll Co, NMIB, A, $4,250.00. (Photo courtesy Morphy Auctions)

Betty Boop, Fancy Rings, set of 9, Ja-Ru, 1990s, unused, MOC. $8.00

Betty Boop, figure, Betty, stuffed cloth, in bathing suit w/chest banner, 13", Ace Novelty, 1989, NM.........................$15.00

Betty Boop, figure, Betty, stuffed cloth, w/guitar, faux red leather boots, zebra pants, 16", Good Stuff, 1999, NM...........$12.00

Betty Boop, figure, Betty, vinyl, jtd, short blk dress, looking up, 9½", M Shimmel Sons, unused, MIP (sealed)............$35.00

Betty Boop, mug, ceramic busty head figure w/eyes glancing up, 4" H, 1981, NM...$10.00

Betty Boop, nodder, celluloid, operates w/rubber band, 7", EX+IB $800.00

Betty Boop, nodder, celluloid, operates w/rubber band, 7", VG, A $300.00

Betty Boop, Play Set, includes watch, make-up case, lipstick, eye shadow kit, Ja-Ru, 1994, unused, MOC........................$8.00

Beverly Hillbillies, car w/Jed, Granny, Jethro, Ellie Mae & Duke (Jed's dog), plastic, crank-op, 23", Ideal, 1960s, NM . $485.00

Beverly Hillbillies, car w/Jed, Granny, Jethro, Ellie Mae & Duke (Jed's dog), plastic, crank-op, 23", Ideal, 1960s, NMIB.. $880.00

Beverly Hills 90210, frisbee, Wham-O, 1991, NRFP.........$22.00

Bimbo, figure, celluloid, blk & wht w/red shirt & shoes, pk & wht shorts, 6½", Japan, prewar, NM, A.................... $840.00

Bimbo, figure, stuffed cloth, blk & wht w/name on chest, side-glancing eyes, 12", French Novelty Co, EX, A $2,530.00

Bob Hope, hand puppet, cloth body w/vinyl head, Zany, 1940s, NM.. $125.00

Bonzo, figure, compo, standing upright, jtd arms & head, lg bl eyes, blk segmented tail, 13", 1920s, G, A $785.00

Bonzo, figure, stuffed velvet, stitched features, jtd, 22", Chad Valley, 1920s, EX..$1,000.00

Bonzo, figure, stuffed velvet, stitched features, orig suede collar, name on foot, jtd, 12", 1920s, VG, A $560.00

Bonzo, pull toy, Bonzo on scooter, litho tin, pushes & pulls on lever as scooter is pulled, 7" L, Chein, EX+, A........ $625.00

Boob McNutt, marionette, Schoenhut, 10½", EX, A $550.00
Boob McNutt, oilcloth, printed features, cloth outfit, 34", Averill, 1920s, EX, A $100.00
Bozo the Clown, bank, bust figure w/big smile, vinyl, 5", 1987, NM $20.00
Bozo the Clown, Bozo's Pocket Watch, plastic, 2", MIP.... $12.00

Bozo the Clown, bubble bath container, Colgate-Palmolive, 1960s, NM, A, $45.00. (Photo courtesy serioustoyz.com)

Bozo the Clown, Button Ball Game, yel plastic Bozo figure w/ball on string, 3½", MIP $12.00
Bozo the Clown, Circus Train, plastic, 3-pc w/Bozo in engine, Butchy & Belinda figures, Multiple Toymakers, 1970, MIB $35.00
Bozo the Clown, figure, stuffed cloth, fuzzy hair, plastic eyes, 7½", Ace Novelty, 1989, NM+ $15.00
Bozo the Clown, figure, stuffed cloth w/soft molded vinyl head, 12", 1972, NM $25.00
Bozo the Clown, figure, stuffed cloth w/vinyl face, pull-string talker, 21", Mattel, 1962, EX $35.00
Bozo the Clown, figure, vinyl, jtd, 7½", Dakin, 1974, NM .. $28.00
Bozo the Clown, gumball machine, plastic Bozo figure hugging clear gum globe on base & waving, 10", Leaf Inc, 1994, MIB $28.00
Bozo the Clown, hand puppet, cloth body, vinyl head w/open-mouth smile, Knickerbocker, 1962, EX+ $55.00
Bozo the Clown, puzzle blocks, paper-litho-on-wood, Bozo's portrait changes expressions, 7x7x1", Capitol, 1950s, EX+ $50.00
Bozo the Clown, Super Magnet, plastic horseshoe, 9½", Laurie Import Ltd, 1976, unused, MIP $15.00
Brady Bunch, Fishing Puzzle & Game, Larami, 1973, MOC .. $45.00
Brady Bunch, gum cards, complete set of 88 w/images on what appears to be a TV screen, 1969, rare set, EX to NM, A $600.00
Bringing Up Father, see Maggie & Jiggs
Broom-Hilda, bubble bath container, Lander, 1977, EX.... $20.00
Broom-Hilda, Spurt Stick, vinyl window stick-on reads Next Time Bring Your Wife, 14", Meyercord, 1975, unused, MIP $10.00
Buck Rogers, map of the solar system, 1933, 18x25", VG, A. $200.00
Buck Rogers, Twiki Robot Signal Flasher, b/o figure, 9½", MIB (worn box) $125.00

Bugs Bunny, see Looney Tunes
Bullwinkle, see Rocky & Friends

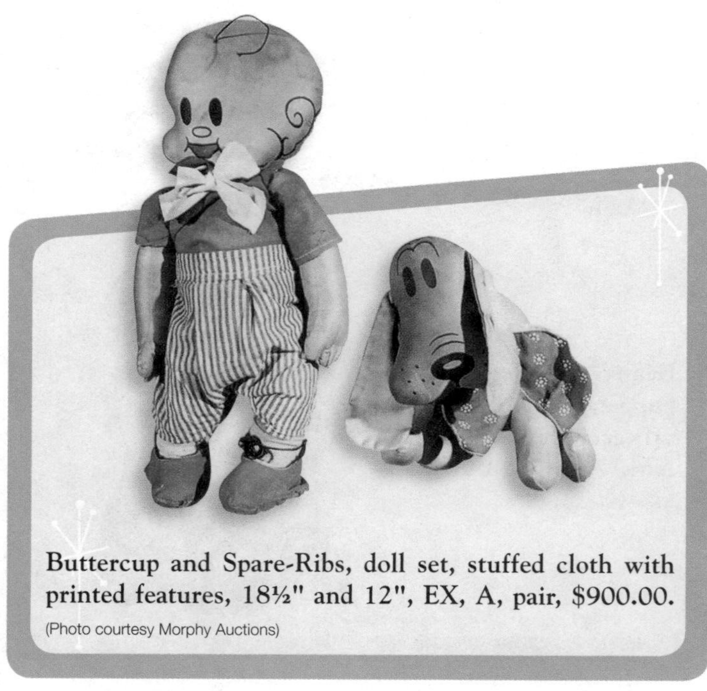
Buttercup and Spare-Ribs, doll set, stuffed cloth with printed features, 18½" and 12", EX, A, pair, $900.00. (Photo courtesy Morphy Auctions)

Buttercup & Spare-Ribs, pull toy, figures on 4-wheeled platform, tin, 4", Nifty/Chein, VG, A $725.00
Captain America, hand puppet, printed vinyl body w/molded vinyl head, Imperial, 1978, MIP $55.00
Captain America, Official Utility Belt, Remco, 1979, complete, NRFB, A $75.00

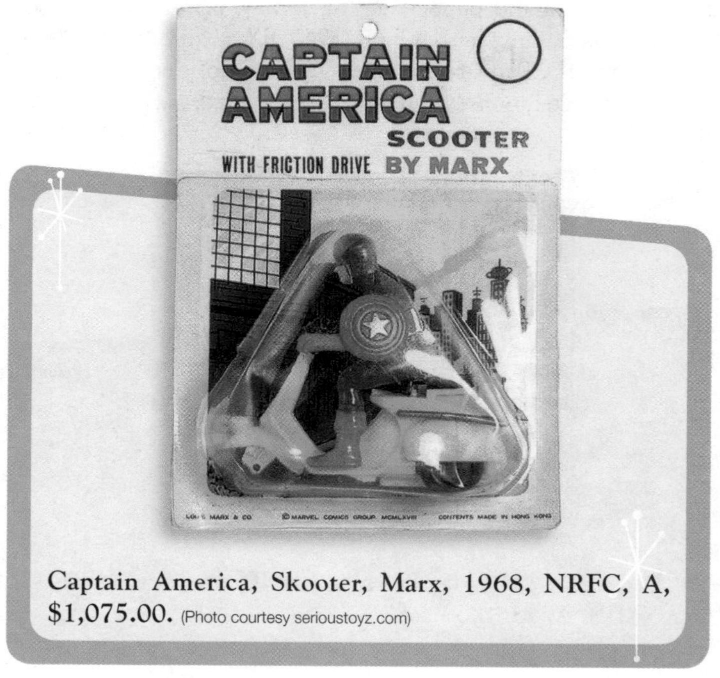

Captain America, Skooter, Marx, 1968, NRFC, A, $1,075.00. (Photo courtesy serioustoyz.com)

Captain Kangaroo, hand puppet, Captain Kangaroo, cloth body w/vinyl head, Rushton, 1950s, NM+ $75.00

Captain Kangaroo, mug, plastic figural Captain's head, googley-eyes, 4", 1950s premium, EX....................$15.00
Captain Kangaroo, table cover, character birthday graphics, 54x96" CA Reed, 1950s, unopened, NM+ $50.00
Captain Marvel, Flying Captain Marvel punch-out toy, 10x7", Reed & Associates, 1944, unused, MIP (envelope), A..$45.00
Captain Midnight, playsuit, US Flight Commander, army gr shirt & pants, w/Aviator Ace badge, Collegeville, EX, A.. $175.00
Car 54 Where Are You?, hand puppet, Patrolman Francis Muldon, cloth body w/vinyl head, 1961, NM $175.00
Carrot Top, hand puppet, cloth body w/vinyl head, goggle-eyed, Zany, 1940s, EX $125.00
Casper the Friendly Ghost, see Harvey Cartoons
Charlie McCarthy, doll, Eddie Bergen's Charlie McCarthy, comp head w/moving mouth, blk tux, 19", Effanbee, VGIB, A..........$465.00
Charlie McCarthy, doll, molded compo w/movable mouth, 12", EX, A $175.00
Combat, gum cards, full set of 66 cards w/blk & wht images, 1963, NM, A........................ $125.00
Crash Dummies, figure, stuffed cloth, plastic eyes, 14", Ace Novelty, 1992, NM+........................$12.00
Creature From the Black Lagoon, see, Universal Monsters
Curious George, figure, stuffed plush, name on red shirt, 8", Gund, 1990, M $10.00
Curious George, figure, stuffed plush, name on red shirt & hat, 10", Toy Network, 1990s, M........................$10.00
Curious George, jack-in-the-box, litho metal, Schylling, 1995, EX $25.00
Daisy Mae, see Li'l Abner

Dan Dare, 'Anatasia' Jet Plane, unused, NM, $50.00. (Photo courtesy Morphy Auctions)

Dennis the Menace, doll, Dennis, stuffed cloth, printed features & hair, cloth outfit, 8", Determined, 1976, NM+.......$15.00
Dennis the Menace, doll, Dennis, stuffed cloth, stitched nose & mouth, plastic eyes, cloth outfit, 11", Nanco, 1992, NM........................ $8.00
Dennis the Menace, doll, Dennis, stuffed cloth/vinyl, cloth outfit, 13", Mighty Star, MIB........................$38.00
Dennis the Menace, doll, Dennis, stuffed cloth/vinyl, cloth outfit, 9", Presents, 1987, w/hang tag, NM+ $30.00
Dennis the Menace, doll, Dennis, vinyl, walking pose, 8", Hall Syndicate, NM........................$40.00
Dennis the Menace, figure, Margaret, stuffed cloth & vinyl, synthetic hair, cloth outfit, 10", Presents, 1987, NM.......$30.00
Dennis the Menace, hand puppet, Alice (mother), cloth body w/vinyl head (open or closed mouth), EX+ $60.00
Dennis the Menace, hand puppet, Dennis, plain cloth body w/vinyl head, 1959, EX $60.00
Dennis the Menace, hand puppet, Dennis, striped cloth body w/vinyl head (lg or sm), Dennis Play Prod, NM $50.00
Dennis the Menace, hand puppet, Henry (father), printed cloth body w/vinyl head, w/glasses, EX+ $60.00
Dennis the Menace, hand puppet, Margaret, cloth body w/vinyl head, Hall Syndicate, 1959, NM........................ $100.00
Dennis the Menace, whistle, locomotive w/mouth piece, plastic, 5", Fortune, MIP (w/Dennis the Menace header card) $15.00
Deputy Dawg, bubble bath container, Colgate-Palmolive, 1960s, NM........................$25.00
Dick Dastardly, Flying Propeller, Larami, 1973, MOC $35.00
Dick Tracy, badge, Inspector General/Dick Tracy/Secret Service Patrol, brass, 2½", 1938, scarce, EX+, A $250.00
Dick Tracy, bank, Sparkle Plenty in highchair, ceramic, 'Sparkle Plenty Savings Bank'/'Dick Tracy God Father,' 13", EX $100.00
Dick Tracy, bank, Sparkle Plenty seated atop scale, ceramic, emb character images on sides of base, 12", VG, A $50.00
Dick Tracy, bubble bath container, Dicky Tracy, Colgate-Palmolive, 1965, NM........................$25.00

Dick Tracy, doll, Sparkle Plenty, composition with yellow yarn hair, 13", Ideal, NMIB, A, $350.00. (Photo courtesy Morphy Auctions)

Dick Tracy, hand puppet, Joe Jitsu, printed cloth w/vinyl head, 1960s, EX+........................$30.00
Dick Tracy, hand puppet, printed cloth body (blk suit & tie) w/vinyl head in blk vinyl hat, Ideal, 1961, EX $85.00
Dick Tracy, magnifying glass, plastic w/attached vinyl case, Larami, 1970s, unused, MOC........................$18.00
Dick Tracy, Talking Phone, Marx, 1967, nonworking o/w NMIB, A $92.00
Donkey Kong, figure, stuffed plush w/vinyl face, hands & feet, barrel applique on chest, Etone Int'l, 1982, NM $15.00
Dr Seuss, bookends, Cat in the Hat, emd red plastic figure, 14" H, M, pr $28.00
Dr Seuss, figure, Cat in the Hat, stuffed plush, 24", Eden, 1979, EX+ $45.00

Dr Seuss, figure, Cat in the Hat, stuffed plush, 25", Douglas Co, 1976, EX+ $45.00
Dr Seuss, figure, Cat in the Hat, stuffed plush, 28", Coleco, 1983, NM+ $50.00
Dr Seuss, figure, Grinch, stuffed plush, gr w/red collar, yel plastic eyes, 30", Macy's, 1997, EX+ $35.00
Dr Seuss, push-button puppet, Cat in the Hat, Little Kids Inc, 2003, MIP $10.00
Dracula, see Universal Monsters
Droopy Dog, hand puppet, cloth & plush body w/molded vinyl head, 12", Turner Ent/MGM, 1989, EX+ $12.00
Droopy Dog, hand puppet, cloth body w/vinyl head, Zany, 1950s, NM...$85.00
Dudley Do-Right, see Rocky & Friends
Dukes of Hazzard, paint set, Craft Master #N38001, 1980, unused, scarce, MIB (sealed) $75.00
Emmett Kelly, hand puppet, Willie the Clown character, blk & wht checked body w/vinyl head, Baby Barry, 1950, NM+ ...$100.00
ET, book, 'Fly Away With ET'/'A Shape Vinyl Book,' 6", Simon & Schuster, 1983, MIP $12.00

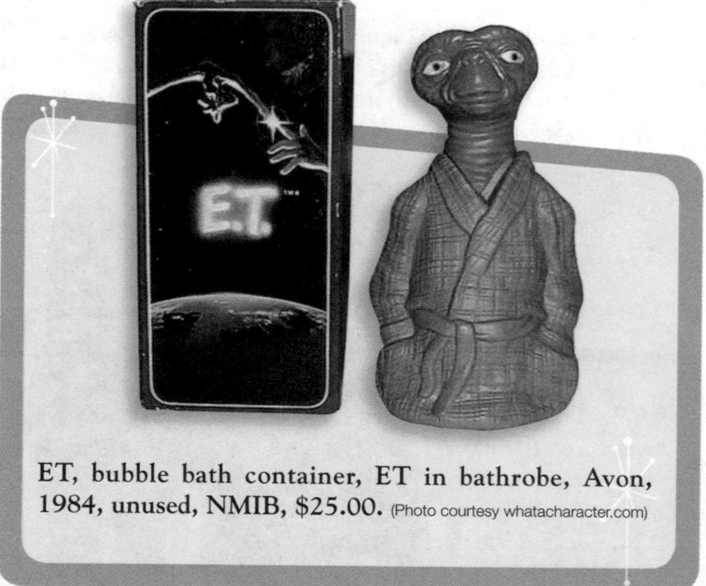

ET, bubble bath container, ET in bathrobe, Avon, 1984, unused, NMIB, $25.00. (Photo courtesy whatacharacter.com)

ET, charm bracelet, enameled metal, Aviva, 1982, MOC (Elliott & ET graphics) $6.00
ET, figure, ET, PVC, w/flower pot, The Original Collectibles, LJN, 1982, M (G card) $10.00
ET, Finger Light, vinyl finger shape, b/o, glows when pressed, 5", Knickerbocker, 1982, MOC $10.00
Fantastic Four, flicker ring, silver-tone plastic w/mc flicker image, vending machine itme, 1966, M $65.00
Fat Albert, doll, Fat Albert, stuffed cloth/vinyl, 'Hey Hey Hey I'm a Cosby Kid' on shirt, 22", Remco, 1985, MIB.....$90.00
Fat Albert, doll, Little Bill, stuffed cloth w/vinyl head, 'Hey Hey Hey! I'm a Cosby Kid,' 22", Remco, 1985, MIB $75.00
Fat Albert, figure, Russel on sled, PVC, 2½x3" L, WNK Ent, 1990, NM+ $8.00
Fat Albert, hand puppet, Fat Albert, printed vinyl body w/ molded vinyl head, Ideal, 1973, NM+ $150.00
Fat Albert, hand puppet, Weird Harold, all vinyl, Ideal, 1973, MIP (header card reads 'TV Favorites') $200.00
Felix the Cat, bubble bath container, color variations, Colgate-Palmolive, 1960s, NM $25.00
Felix the Cat, figure, compo, jtd arms, name in gold high on chest, gold neck bow, 13", c Pat Sullivan 1924, EX, A......$2,520.00
Felix the Cat, figure, squeeze-action w/cloth body, compo head & wooden hands & feet, squeeze legs and arms move, 8", EX..$1,455.00
Felix the Cat, figure, stuffed cloth, cowboy attire w/chaps, vest, gun & holster & hat, 24", Gund (?), 1930s, EX, A.$1,232.00

Felix the Cat, figure, stuffed orange cloth with papier-maché face, 24", 1930s, EX, A, $1,565.00. (Photo courtesy Morphy Auctions)

Felix the Cat, figure, stuffed plush, 'You're My CATnip' on red satin shirt, 16½", Applause, 1989, w/hang tag, NM ...$12.00

Felix the Cat, figure, stuffed plush, black with white face, shoe-button eyes, jointed limbs, 9½", Steiff, 1920s, A, $5,600.00. (Photo courtesy Morphy Auctions)

Felix the Cat, figure, stuffed plush, toothy grin, lg eyes, 23", Chad Valley (?), 1920s, VG, A $1,120.00
Felix the Cat, figure, stuffed velvet w/extra long arms, legs & tail, red neck ribbon, 29", 1920s, EX $450.00
Felix the Cat, figure, vinyl, standing w/legs together & arms down at sides, 6", Eastern Moulded Products, 1962, NM $45.00
Felix the Cat, figure, wood, blk & wht beaded type w/name on chest, 8", Schoenhut, EX (G box marked Felix the Movie Cat).. $560.00

Felix the Cat, figure, wood, flat-sided w/screwed-on jtd arms & legs, 7", ca 1930, EX, A $785.00
Felix the Cat, figure, Yes/No head movement when tail is moved, hard-stuffed blk body, 10", EX, A $1,120.00
Felix the Cat, figure, Yes/No head movement when tail is moved, hard-stuffed wht body, 13", 1920s, VG, A $560.00
Felix the Cat, hand puppet, plush body & head w/felt ears, EX, A $600.00
Felix the Cat, magic slate, red w/'Felix the Cat Slate' in outline lettering, mc image on header, Lowe #3068, 1950s, EX..... $50.00
Felix the Cat, push toy, blk pnt wood w/blk & wht features, jtd arms & legs, VG $250.00
Felix the Cat, sparkler, tin head w/'Copyright by Pat Sullivan'/ 'Felix' on lithoed tie, 5½", Chein/Borgfeldt, EXIB.. $1,230.00
Felix the Cat, tableware, 20-pc wht china w/Felix decals, red trim, Crown Pottery, EX, A $400.00
Felix the Cat, tea set, 14-pc tan lustre w/cups, saucers, plates, creamer & teapot, no sugar bowl, 1930s, EX, A $400.00
Felix the Cat, Walking Felix, papier-machè figure w/segmented wood tail, w/walking ramp, 5" figure & 20" ramp, EXIB, A $840.00
Felix the Movie Cat, pull toy, Felix chasing 2 mice on 4-wheeled platform, litho tin, Nifty/Chein, ca 1930, 8", VGIB, A $3,360.00
Flash Gordon, Strat-O-Wagon, PS w/wooden wheels & handle, 6" (w/o handle), Wyandotte, 1940s, VG+ $95.00
Flintstones, bank, Barney figure standing on 'rock' base, vinyl, 6", 1994, M $12.00
Flintstones, bank, Fred figure hugging golf club, vinyl, 7¾", NM $85.00
Flintstones, bank, Pebbles sleeping in chair, vinyl, Homecraft, 1970s, NM $30.00
Flintstones, bank, Wilma holding Pebbles on grassy base incised Wilma, 11", 1970s, NM+ $40.00
Flintstones, bubble bath container, any character, Purex, NM, ea $25.00
Flintstones, camera, Fred Flintstone Camera, Hong Kong/Hanna-Barbera, 1960s, MIB $35.00
Flintstones, figure, Baby Puss (sabor-tooth tiger) sitting upright, yel vinyl w/blk spots, gr belt, 10", 1960, rare, NM... $150.00
Flintstones, figure, Bamm-Bamm, squeeze vinyl, standing holding club down in front, 6", Sanitoy, 1979, EX+ $18.00
Flintstones, figure, Bamm-Bamm, stuffed cloth, felt hair, hat & outfit, 8", Knickerbocker, 1970s, MIB $45.00
Flintstones, figure, Bamm-Bamm, vinyl, standing, no club, jdt arms, swivel head, 6", Kenner, 1970s, M $15.00
Flintstones, figure, Bamm-Bamm, vinyl, standing holding club on gray rock base, 5½", 1994, NM $12.00
Flintstones, figure, Barney, stuffed cloth & vinyl, gr-pnt hair, brn fuzzy outfit w/2 patches, 12", Knickerbocker, EX $75.00
Flintstones, figure, Barney, vinyl, felt outfit, 7" or 8", Dakin, 1970, NM, ea $45.00
Flintstones, figure, Betty, plastic, standing w/arms behind head in gr dress, 3", Imperial, 1976, NM $10.00
Flintstones, figure, Betty, vinyl, standing w/1 arm in front, yel hair, bl dress, open-mouth smile, 12", 1960s, VG $50.00
Flintstones, figure, Dino, plush w/vinyl head, gr pants w/blk shirt, yel hands & feet, 10", Gund, 1960s, EX $75.00
Flintstones, figure, Dino, vinyl, swivel head, jtd arms, 6", Knixies/Knickerbocker, 1962, EX $55.00
Flintstones, figure, Fred, stuffed cloth w/vinyl head, bl fuzzy suit w/yel collar, red tie, 11", Knickerbocker, NM $125.00
Flintstones, figure, Hoppy, vinyl, jtd, Dakin, scarce, MIP ('The Flintstones' header card) $150.00
Flintstones, figure, Pebbles, squeeze vinyl, 6", Sanitoy, 1979, NM .. $25.00
Flintstones, figure, Pebbles, stuffed cloth, cloth outfit, brn felt hair, printed features, 7", Knickerbocker, 1970s, EX... $15.00
Flintstones, figure, Pebbles, vinyl w/cloth outfit, 4½", Knickerbocker, 1970s, EX $10.00
Flintstones, figure, Wilma, squeeze vinyl, seated talking on phone, 5½", Lanco, NM $45.00
Flintstones, figure, Wilma, squeeze vinyl, standing w/2-wheeled shopping cart, 9", 1960s (?), VG $60.00
Flintstones, figure, Wilma, stuffed cloth w/orange plush hair, wht dress & necklace, 17", Toy Works, 2000, w/tag, NM.. $10.00
Flintstones, hand puppet, Barney Rubble, stuffed cloth body w/ furry outfit, vinyl head, Knickerbocker, 1960s, NM.... $50.00
Flintstones, hand puppet, Pebbles, printed cloth body w/name & vinyl head, Ideal, 1966, NM $75.00
Flintstones, iron-on transfer, pictures Fred, Wilma & Pebbles on pk circle outline in yel, 7½x6", dated 1976, M $18.00
Flintstones, magnet, free-standing figures of any 6 characters w/ magnets on bottoms, MOC (sealed), ea $8.00
Flintstones, Magnetic Stickers, pkg of 3 featuring lg Barney, smaller Fred and Bamm-Bamm, c 1979, NRFP $20.00
Flintstones, marionette, Barney Rubble, stuffed cloth w/furry outfit, 12", Knicekrbocker, 1962, NM $35.00
Flintstones, mug, any character, molded plastic head, 3", F&F Mold Co, 1970s, NM $12.00
Flintstones, night-light, Barney figure, plastic, 4", Leviton, 1975, MOC $15.00
Flintstones, ornament, Bamm-Bamm figure, hollow plastic, 3¼", 1976, EX+ $6.00
Flintstones, pencil topper, any character, about 1½" ea, marked Hong Kong, 1970s, unused, M, ea $12.00
Flintstones, push-button puppet, any character, Kohner, 1960s, NM, ea $50.00
Flintstones, push-button puppet, Bamm-Bamm, Arco, 1976, EX+ $30.00

Flip the Frog, stuffed velvet, 6", Dean's Rag Book Co., EX, $400.00. (Photo courtesy Morphy Auctions)

Flipper, figure, plush, gray & wht w/lt bl sailor's vest & wht sailor's hat, 17", Knickerbocker, 1976, NM................$35.00

G-Men Fingerprint Set, New York Toy and Game Co., complete, EXIB, $300.00. (Photo courtesy Morphy Auctions)

G-Men, pencil box, blk & wht on red, about 5x8½", 1930s, EX $85.00

Garfield, aquarium, plastic figure w/clear plastic tummy bowl, 18", Hawkeye, 1980s-90s, EX $35.00

Garfield, bank, figure as basketball player, glossy ceramic, 5½", Enesco, 1980s, M $35.00

Garfield, bank, figure as hobo w/tooth missing & holding hat w/ slot, vinyl, 8", NM $20.00

Garfield, bank, figure sitting upright w/eyes half closed, vinyl, 6", Kat's Meow, 1980s, NM+ $15.00

Garfield, candy tin, rnd w/name above image of Garfield bursting through 'paper,' 3½" dia, Cheinco, 1980s, NM...........$10.00

Garfield, comb & brush set, orange plastic figural brush w/blk detail, orange comb w/blk printed detail, Avon, MIP..$12.00

Garfield, Ertl Die-Cast Metal Toy, Garfield in space shuttle, 1990, MOC (card reads Need a Lift?) $12.00

Garfield, figure, Arlene, stuffed plush, pk w/red felt lips, lg plastic eyes, 7", Dakin, 1974, NM..$10.00

Garfield, figure, Garfield, squeeze vinyl, 'Hug Me' nightshirt, bunny slippers, 4", Remco Baby, 1990, M $8.00

Garfield, figure, Garfield, stuffed plush, 'Mom Always Liked Me Best,' hugging-type hands/feet, 4", Dakin, 1980s, NM..$12.00

Garfield, figure, Garfield, stuffed plush, 'User Friendly,' 9", Dakin, 1980s, NM+ $12.00

Garfield, figure, Odie, stuffed plush, 7", Dakin, 1980s, NM+.. $8.00

Garfield, figure, Odie, stuffed plush, 10½", Dakin, 1983, NM. $12.00

Garfield, figure, Odie, stuffed plush, 14", Dakin/Fun Farm, 1983, NM+ $12.00

Garfield, figure, PVC, 'Eat Your Heart Out!' on red heart, 1½", Enesco, 1980s, NM (G 2x4" box) $15.00

Garfield, gumball machine, 'But It Will Cost You!' or 'Never Trust a Smiling Cat,' Superior Toy, 1970s-80s, NM, ea..........$35.00

Garfield, night-light, plastic blk-outlined image of Garfield resting on blk-outlined cloud, 2x3", Prestigeline, MOC..$10.00

Garfield, oranment, any, Dakin, 1990s, MIP, ea from $10 to . $12.00

Garfield, ornament, any, ceramic, 3", Enesco, 1980s, M, ea from $15 to $20.00

Garfield, snow dome, Garfield in Santa hat & ice skates, 'Happy Holidays' on base, 4½", Enesco, MIB $25.00

Garfield, squeeze toy, Odie hugging fire hydrant, vinyl, 4¼", Paws, 1990s, M $8.00

Garfield, wheeled toy, 'Racin' Garfield,' plastic Garfield w/bl blanket as cape & hat on backwards, Playmates, 1991, MOC $12.00

Garfield, yo-yo, plastic, emb figure encircled by name, 3½", Avon, 1990s, MOC (sealed) $8.00

Gasoline Alley, toothbrush holder, Uncle Walt & Skeezix figures holding hands, pnt bisque, 4", c FAS, G+..................$75.00

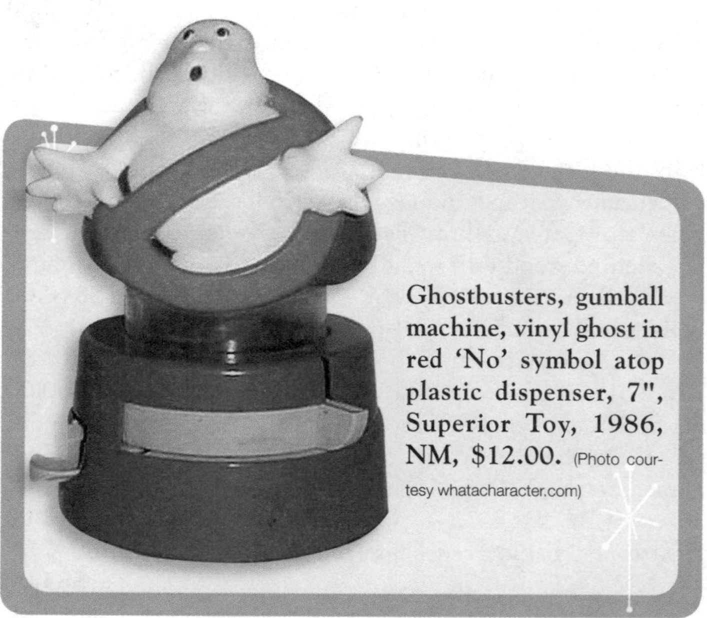

Ghostbusters, gumball machine, vinyl ghost in red 'No' symbol atop plastic dispenser, 7", Superior Toy, 1986, NM, $12.00. (Photo courtesy whatacharacter.com)

Ghostbusters, Streamer Kite, features the 'No Ghost' symbol & Slimer, Spectra Star, 1989, unused, MIP.....................$12.00

Ghostbusters (The Real Ghostbusters Cartoon Series), Pinball Game, plastic, Ja-Ru, 1986, unused, MOC.................$15.00

Gomer Pyle (TV Show), gum cards, complete set of 66 of blk & wht images, 1960s, all M, A $80.00

Good Times (TV Show), gum cards, complete set of 55, Topps, 1975, EX to NM (w/sealed wax pack), A...................$50.00

Green Hornet, Colorforms Cartoon Kit, Greenway Prod, 1966, unused, NM (VG box) $55.00

Green Hornet, flicker ring, silver base, 1966, EX, A..........$10.00

Green Hornet, Humming Bee, swing it around & it makes realistic buzzing noise, 5½", 1966 premium, NM $50.00

Green Hornet, playing cards, 'Official...52 Card Deck w/40 Official Action Photos,' 1966, unused, MIB, A $100.00

Green Hornet, Print Putty, Colorforms, 1966, MOC (sealed), A.. $80.00

Green Hornet, spoon, name & image on enamel oval inlayed on ornate hdl, 1966, 4½", M, A..$25.00

Gulliver's Travels, drum, litho tin, 3½x6" dia, Chein, 1939, EX+ . $75.00

Gulliver's Travels, figure, King Little, pnt compo bead type, 13", Ideal Novelty & Toy Co, 1930s, EX+, A $1,380.00

Gulliver's Travels, songbook, features 8 songs, Famous Music Corp, 1939, EX $40.00

Gulliver's Travels, top, litho tin, 8" dia, Chein, copyright 1939, EX, A $85.00

Gumby, Astronaut Adventure Costume, plastic playset, Lakeside, 1965, unused, MOC $22.00
Gumby, bubble bath container, Gumby, M&L Creative Packaging, 1987, NM..........$15.00
Gumby, figure, Gumby, bendable rubber, 6", Jesco, NM......$8.00
Gumby, figure, Gumby, cloth-covered wire upper body w/bean-stuffed lower body, 14", Sher-Stuff/Perma, 1982, EX..$15.00
Gumby, figure, Gumby, PVC, hand in pocket of brn bomber-type jacket w/wht collar, 3", Applause, 1989, NM+..........$6.00
Gumby, figure, Gumby, stuffed cloth or plush, any style, size or maker, 1980s-90s, NM+, ea from $10 to..........$15.00
Gumby, figure, Gumby, stuffed vinyl, pnt features, 17", Good Stuff, 1990s, EX+..........$12.00
Gumby, figure, Pokey, bendable rubber, red w/blk, 9½", Jesco, NM..........$12.00
Gumby, figure, Pokey, foam-stuffed bendy, red w/blk, 12", Sher Stuff, 1983, NM..........$22.00
Gumby, figure, Prickle, rubber, yel dinosaur figure, jtd, 1980s, NM..........$6.00
Gumby, paint set, 6 watercolors/pnt brush/plastic palette w/image of Gumby & Pokey, Henry Gordy Int'l, 1988, MOC...$13.00
Gumby, windup figures, Gumby or Pokey, vinyl, 4", Lakeside, 1966, EX, ea..........$45.00
Hair Bear, see Hanna-Barbera
Hanna-Barbera, see also Flintstones, Jetsons or Scooby Doo
Hanna-Barbera, bank, Baba Looey, vinyl, orange w/gr sombrero & blk neckerchief, 9", Roclar, 1976, NM..........$28.00
Hanna-Barbera, bank, Huckleberry Hound sitting upright w/arms crossed, lt bl w/pk bow tie, 5", 1980s, NM..........$22.00
Hanna-Barbera, bank, Huckleberry Hound standing, red w/blk hat, ears & nose, Knickerbocker, 1960s, NM+..........$28.00
Hanna-Barbera, bank, Yogi Bear standing on grassy base, vinyl, 6", 1980s, NM..........$22.00
Hanna-Barbera, bank, Yogi Bear standing w/1 hand on tie, other arm at side, 10", Knickerbocker, 1960s, VG+..........$30.00
Hanna-Barbera, bop bag, Pixie/Dixie reversable images on inflatable vinyl, 18", Kestral, M..........$50.00
Hanna-Barbera, bubble bath container, any character except Morocco Mole, Purex, 1960s, NM, ea from $20 to.....$25.00
Hanna-Barbera, bubble bath container, Morocco Mole, Purex, 1966, rare, NM+..........$65.00

Hanna-Barbera, bubble bath container, Yogi Bear, M (with neck tag), $35.00.

Hanna-Barbera, camera, Yogi Bear, blk plastic w/wht image of Yogi on side, 3x3½", Hong Kong, NM+IB..........$35.00
Hanna-Barbera, club membership kit, Banana Splits, 1968, NM (w/mailer)..........$100.00
Hanna-Barbera, figure, Augie Doggie, squeeze rubber, jtd, pale yel w/lt bl collar, 8", Bucky, 1970s, NM..........$75.00
Hanna-Barbera, figure, Baba Looey, stuffed plush/vinyl, 16", lt gr w/orange vinyl sombrero, Knickerbocker, 1959, EX...$50.00
Hanna-Barbera, figure, Boo Boo, stuffed cloth, printed face, felt hair & bow tie, 7", Knickerbocker, 1973, NRFB..........$50.00
Hanna-Barbera, figure, Cindy Bear, stuffed felt, printed features, felt hair, cloth skirt, 8", Knickerbocker, 1973, NRFB.$50.00
Hanna-Barbera, figure, Cindy Bear, stuffed plush w/vinyl face, 16", Knickerbocker, scarce, EX+..........$250.00
Hanna-Barbera, figure, Fleegle (Banana Splits), rubber, pk w/red hat & bow tie, 5", 1968, EX+..........$65.00
Hanna-Barbera, figure, Hair Bear, stuffed plush w/felt vest, belt & neck scarf, furry mop of hair, 8", Sutton & Sons, NM..$40.00
Hanna-Barbera, figure, Huckleberry Hound, inflatable vinyl, unused, MIP (pkg reads 'The Flintstone Inflatables') .$28.00

Hanna-Barbera, figure, Huckleberry Hound as policeman, squeeze vinyl, 10", Dell, EX+, $55.00. (Photo courtesy whatacharacter.com)

Hanna-Barbera, figure, Huckleberry Hound, squeeze vinyl, standing w/blk cane & top hat in hand, 6", Dell, NRFP.....$50.00
Hanna-Barbera, figure, Huckleberry Hound, squeeze vinyl, w/ice-cream cone, airbrushed details, 7", Elizabeth, MIP.....$75.00
Hanna-Barbera, figure, Huckleberry Hound, stuffed plush w/rubber face, red & wht, 18", Knickerbocker, 1959, EX+..$35.00
Hanna-Barbera, figure, Huckleberry Hound, vinyl, red w/bl top hat & tie, jtd arms, 6", Knickerbocker Knixies, NM..........$40.00
Hanna-Barbera, figure, Magilla Gorilla, squeeze rubber, brn w/red shorts & wht tie, blk cane, 6½", Bucky, 1974, EX+....$65.00
Hanna-Barbera, figure, Magilla Gorilla, stuffed felt w/vinyl head, 7½", Ideal, 1960s, EX+..........$55.00
Hanna-Barbera, figure, Magilla Gorilla, stuffed plush, 8½", Nanco, 1990, NM+..........$10.00
Hanna-Barbera, figure, Magilla Gorilla, stuffed ribbed cloth w/pk shorts, 7½", Playtime Toys, 1979, NM+..........$20.00
Hanna-Barbera, figure, Mr Jinks, soft rubber, standing w/hands on hips, 8½", Bucky, 1970s, EX+..........$75.00

Hanna-Barbera, figure, Mr Jinks, stuffed plush w/vinyl face, blk & wht, pk bow tie/buttons, 13", Knickerbocker, 1959, VG $50.00

Hanna-Barbera, figure, Mushmouse, stuffed felt w/vinyl head, red felt vest, 9", Ideal, 1960s, EX........ $75.00

Hanna-Barbera, figure, Pixie, vinyl, jtd head & arms, 6", Knixies/Knickerbocker, 1962, NM........ $40.00

Hanna-Barbera, figure, Quick Draw McGraw, stuffed plush, felt hands, feet, hat & gun holster, 13", Nanco, 1989, NM... $15.00

Hanna-Barbera, figure, Quick Draw McGraw, stuffed plush, felt hands, feet, hat & gun holster, 16", Presents, 1985, NM+ $20.00

Hanna-Barbera, figure, Snagglepuss, squeeze vinyl, jtd, standing w/feet together, dk pk w/blk trim, 9", Bucky, EX $75.00

Hanna-Barbera, figure, Snagglepuss, vinyl, pk, 7½", Dakin, 1971, MIP (clear plastic bag w/name & hdl) $65.00

Hanna-Barbera, figure, Top Cat, inflatable vinyl, unused, NRFP (pkg reads 'The Flintstones Inflatables') $25.00

Hanna-Barbera, figure, Top Cat, vinyl, seated upright w/legs spread, 1 hand on tummy & waving, 6", Bucky, EX+........ $35.00

Hanna-Barbera, figure, Wally Gator, stuffed cloth, standing upright, gr w/purple hat, 7", Playtime, 1979, NM........ $25.00

Hanna-Barbera, figure, Yogi Bear, plastic roly-poly body, chimes, 7", Sanitoy, 1979, NM $20.00

Hanna-Barbera, figure, Yogi Bear, squeeze vinyl, seated on log & tugging on tie, 6", Dell, 1960s, EX $35.00

Hanna-Barbera, figure, Yogi Bear, stuffed cloth pillow type w/ printed image, 17", 1977, NM+ $15.00

Hanna-Barbera, figure, Yogi Bear, stuffed felt, brn w/gr hat & tie, wht collar, 7½", Knickerbocker, 1973, NRFB $45.00

Hanna-Barbera, figure, Yogi Bear, stuffed plush w/vinyl face, gr felt hat & tie, 18½", Knickerbocker, 1959, EX+ $50.00

Hanna-Barbera, figure, Yogi Bear, vinyl, jtd arms & head, 6", Knixies/Knickerbocker, 1962, EX........ $35.00

Hanna-Barbera, flashlight, Huckleberry Hound, plastic w/molded face, 7", Laurie Import Ltd, 1976, unused, MIP $15.00

Hanna-Barbera, Flickers, Huckleberry Hound, Sonwell, 1960s, unused, NMIB........ $50.00

Hanna-Barbera, hand puppet, Droop-A-Long Coyote, cloth body w/vinyl head, Ideal, 1960s, NM........ $75.00

Hanna-Barbera, hand puppet, Magilla Gorilla, printed cloth body w/name, vinyl head, Ideal, 1960s, NM $75.00

Hanna-Barbera, hand puppet, Mr Jinks, plush body w/vinyl head, Knickerbocker, 1959, NM $75.00

Hanna-Barbera, hand puppet, Pixie & Dixie, plush bodies w/ vinyl heads, Knickerbocker, 1958, EX+, ea........ $50.00

Hanna-Barbera, hand puppet, Tweety Bird, cloth body w/vinyl head, Marriott's Great America, 1970s, EX+ $15.00

Hanna-Barbera, hand puppet, Yogi Bear, brn cloth body, vinyl head w/bl hat, EX+ $65.00

Hanna-Barbera, iron-on transfer, Yogi standing against bl circle outlined in yel & w/name, Holoubek Studios, 1976, M........ $18.00

Hanna-Barbera, Kite Fun Book, Top Cat, PG&E premium, 1963, Reddy Kilowatt on back cover, NM $35.00

Hanna-Barbera, Kut-Up Kit, Banna Splits, MOC $50.00

Hanna-Barbera, Modelcast 'N Color Kit, features Huckleberry Hound & Flintstones, Standard Toycraft, 1960, unused, MIB $100.00

Hanna-Barbera, Modelcast 'N Color Kit, Quick Draw McGraw, Standard Toycraft, 1960, complete, EX........ $50.00

Hanna-Barbera, mug, Fleegle (Banana Splits), plastic head shape, yel w/red tongue & bow tie, 3¼", 1960s, M $25.00

Hanna-Barbera, mug, Hair Bear, plastic, bl w/image, 4", 1970s, NM........ $10.00

Hanna-Barbera, night-light, Yogi Bear Nite Lite/Projects Yogi on Ceiling, plastic, 4", Hoyle Prod, 1980s, MIB $25.00

Hanna-Barbera, paste container, LePage's Yogi Bear...White Paste, brn vinyl head of Top Cat, 1965, unused, M w/cb header $20.00

Hanna-Barbera, Pile On Game, Whitman, 1962, complete w/ container, EX+........ $20.00

Hanna-Barbera, Play-Doh Playset, Yogi Bear, Kenner, 1980, unused, NRFB, $35.00. (Photo courtesy whatacharacter.com)

Hanna-Barbera, punch-out playset, Atom Ant, Whitman, 1960s, unused, EXIB $75.00

Hanna-Barbera, push-button puppet, any character, Kohner, 1960s, NM+, ea from $50 to $75.00

Hanna-Barbera, puzzle block w/sections of character images to mach up, 3", Arby's premium, 1996, NM+ $5.00

Hanna-Barbera, squeeze toy, see also figure

Hanna-Barbera, squeeze toy, Pixie & Dixie on cheese wedge, rubber, 5½", Dell, 1960s, EX+ $40.00

Hanna-Barbera, Stamp Set, Yogi Bear & Huckleberry Hound & Fred Flintstone 25 Piece..., 1975, unused, MOC $15.00

Hanna-Barbera, sticker, Huckleberry Hound, puffy vinyl figure standing w/arms at sides, 7", 1977, MIP $10.00

Hanna-Barbera, wall hook, Yogi & Ranger Smith, plastic, self-adhesive, Tiger Home Prod, 1978, unused, MOC $8.00

Hanna-Barbera, Wrist Glo Slate, Yo Yogi!, Ja-Rum 1991, unused, MOC........ $8.00

Hanna-Barbera, yo-yo, Yogi Bear, molded plastic head w/big smile, 3", Creativer Creations, MOC........ $22.00

Hansel & Gretel, marionette, Hansel, nonworking mouth, 14", Hazelle #813, NMIB $125.00

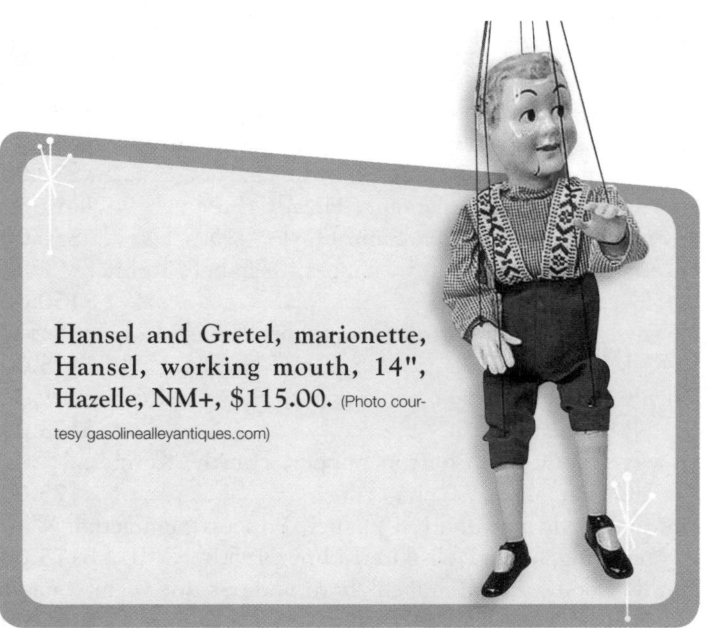

Hansel and Gretel, marionette, Hansel, working mouth, 14", Hazelle, NM+, $115.00. (Photo courtesy gasolinealleyantiques.com)

Hansel & Gretel, marionette, Hansel or Gretel, Pelham, NMIB, ea $100.00

Hansel & Gretel, marionette, Witch, working mouth, 14", Pelham, NM+IB $135.00

Happy Hooligan, doll, wood w/cloth outfit, 8½", Schoenhut, EX+IB, A $2,500.00

Happy Hooligan, marionette, wood w/cloth outfit, 10", Schoenhut, 1920s, EX+, A $450.00

Harvey Cartoons, bubble bath container, Casper the Friendly Ghost, Colgate-Palmolive, 1960s, NM+ $25.00

Harvey Cartoons, bubble bath container, Wendy, Colgate-Palmolive, 1960s, NM $20.00

Harvey Cartoons, figure, Wendy, stuffed plush w/vinyl head, 10", Gundikins/Gund, 1950s, EX $65.00

Harvey Cartoons, hand puppet, Baby Huey, cloth body w/vinyl head, Gund, 1950s, NM $75.00

Harvey Cartoons, hand puppet, Spooky, cloth body w/red trim, vinyl head w/blk hat, Gund, 1950s, NM+ $100.00

Harvey Cartoons, pull toy, Casper playing xylophone, wood, 9" long, 1960s, EX+, $320.00. (Photo courtesy whatacharacter.com)

Harvey Cartoons, squeeze toy, Casper figure w/'Casper the Friendly Ghost' on chest, 7", Sutton, 1972, EX+ $28.00

Heathcliff, bagatelle games, Heathcliff's Sports Board, 2-pc set w/ basketball & tennis, Smethport, 1983, unused, MOC $15.00

Heathcliff, figure, stuffed plush & cloth, printed cowboy outfit w/ hat red velvet vest, 12", Knickerbocker, 1981, EX+ $12.00

Heathcliff, friction toy, plastic, Heathcliff as football player, 8", Talbot Toys, 1982, NRFP $12.00

Heathcliff, stuffed plush & cloth, bl cloth bowler hat & vest, printed vest & tie, 12", Knickerbocker, 1981, NM+ $12.00

Heckle & Jeckle, bank, pnt wood figure, hang tag reads 'Famous Terry Toon Bank,' 8", VG+, A $150.00

Heckle & Jeckle, hand puppet, blk plush bodies w/yel hands & feet, Rusthon Creations, 1950s, ea $75.00

Henrietta Hippo (New Zoo Revue), 1970s, cloth body w/vinyl head, NM+ $100.00

Henry, doll, rubber with cloth outfit, 9½", Perfekta, 1940s, NM, $110.00. (Photo courtesy whatacharacter.com)

Henry, figure, pnt compo, workable mouth, red/blk striped cap, red jacket, yel pants, blk shoes, 12", EX $125.00

Henry, figure, rubber, jtd, wht plastic sailor's hat/shoes, wht cloth shorts/socks, red top w/M, 10", Perfecta, 1940s $100.00

Herman & Katnip, figure, Katnip, stuffed plush w/vinyl head, 10", Gundikins/Gund, 1950s, EX+ $55.00

Herman & Katnip, hand puppet, Katnip, cloth body w/vinyl head, Gund, 1950s, NM+ $75.00

Hi & Lois, figure, Hi, stuffed cloth w/vinyl head & hands, cloth outfit, brn flocked shoes, 16", Presents, 1985, NM+ $32.00

Homey the Clown, see In Living Color

Howdy Doody, bank, Clarabell, flocked plastic figure waving on base, 9", Straco, 1970s, NM $35.00

Howdy Doody, bank, Howdy in wide stance on base w/name on label, flocked plastic, 9", Straco, 1976, EX+ $35.00

Howdy Doody, bank, Mr Bluster Savings Bank, flock plastic figure, 9", Stauss, 1970s, EX+ $35.00

Howdy Doody, bath mitt, terry cloth w/printed image & name, 8", 1950s-60s, EX $15.00

Howdy Doody, bubble pipe, plastic Clarabell figure, 4½" L, Lido Toy, unused, NMOC, A $80.00

Howdy Doody, costume, Howdy Doody, Official Pl-A-Time Costume, shirt, pants & canvas mask, NMIB, A $110.00

Howdy Doody, doll, Howdy Doody, compo w/pnt hair, glass eyes, cloth outfit, 23", Effanbee, 1950s, EXIB.......... $345.00

Howdy Doody, doll, Howdy Doody, wood bead type w/compo head, cloth neckerchief, 13", Noma/Cameo, NM+IB, A..... $575.00

Howdy Doody, doll, Princess Summerfall-Winterspring, brn Indian outfit, blk pigtails, 7½", Beehler Arts, NM+IB, A...... $100.00

Howdy Doody, doll, stuffed body w/compo head & hands, red & wht checked shirt w/bl neckerchief, red pants, 19", G, A..........$250.00

Howdy Doody, Doodle Slate, Stickless Corp, EX+, A.......$65.00

Howdy Doody, figure, Howdy Doody, chalkware, standing on base w/name, hands at sides, 7", EX $20.00

Howdy Doody, figure set, 5 different characters, pnt hard plastic w/movable mouths, 4" ea, 1950s, EX to EX+, A...... $130.00

Howdy Doody, finger puppet, Howdy Doody, full-hand type, foam rubber & cb, 10½"x5", Bendy Toys, 1987, NM..$22.00

Howdy Doody, hand puppet, Buffalo Bob, cloth w/vinyl head, mouth open w/top teeth showing, red felt hands, EX+.......... $100.00

Howdy Doody, hand puppet, Clarabelle, cloth body w/felt hands, vinyl head, googley-eyed, EX+..........$75.00

Howdy Doody, hand puppet, Howdy Doody, full figure w/eyes & mouth operated from back, 13", Pride Prod, unused, MIB, A $125.00

Howdy Doody, hand puppet, Howdy Doody, plaid cloth body w/red neck scarf, vinyl head, goggle-eyed, 1950s, NM+ $100.00

Howdy Doody, hand puppet, Princess Summerfall Winterspring, cloth body, vinyl head, goggle-eyed, 1950s, NM.........$75.00

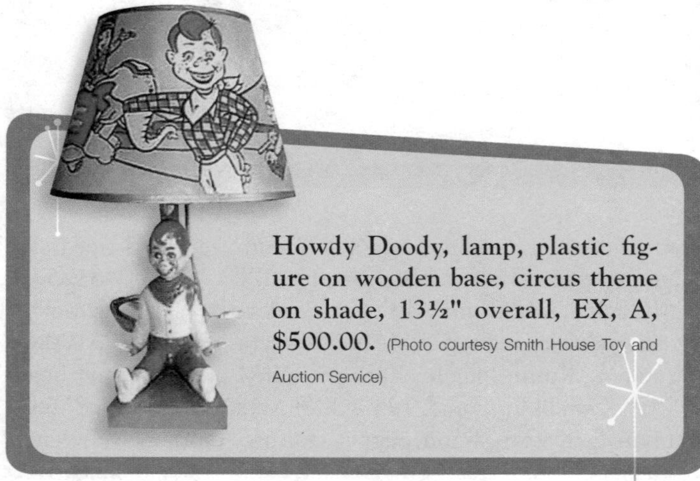

Howdy Doody, lamp, plastic figure on wooden base, circus theme on shade, 13½" overall, EX, A, $500.00. (Photo courtesy Smith House Toy and Auction Service)

Howdy Doody, marionette, Clarabelle, wood & compo w/ cloth outfit, 15", Peter Puppet Playthings, 1952, NMIB, A.......... $150.00

Howdy Doody, marionette, Flub-A-Dub, wood & compo w/cloth outfit, Peter Puppet Playthings, 1950s, EX+ $150.00

Howdy Doody, marionette, Howdy Doody, wood & compo w/ cloth outfit, 16½", Peter Puppet Playthings, 1952, NMIB, A..........$225.00

Howdy Doody, marionette, Mr Bluster, wood & compo w/cloth outfit, Peter Puppet Playthings, 1950s, EX.......... $200.00

Howdy Doody, marionette, Princess Summerfall-Winterspring, wood & compo w/cloth outfit, Peter Puppet, 1950s, NMIB.... $130.00

Howdy Doody, night light, Clarabell head figure, 2", Leco, NM+ (VG box), A $185.00

Howdy Doody, One Man Band, complete w/4 plastic instruments, Trophy Prod, EXIB.......... $150.00

Howdy Doody, pencil w/pencil topper, Howdy's head, pencil emb w/name, 1950s, NM..........$50.00

Howdy Doody, plate, ceramic, Howdy the cowboy w/lasso & name on wht, 8½" dia, Smith-Taylor, 1950s, EX+......$50.00

Howdy Doody, push-button puppet, Clarabell, Kohner, 1950s, EX, A $150.00

Howdy Doody, push-button puppet, Flub-A-Dub, Kohner, 1950s, NMIB.......... $175.00

Howdy Doody, push-button puppet, Howdy, Kohner, 1950s, NMIB.......... $175.00

Howdy Doody, push-button puppet, Howdy, Kohner, 1950s, VG+..........$75.00

Howdy Doody, push-button puppet, Princess Summerfall-Winterspring, fringed felt skirt, Kohner, 1950s, NMIB... $175.00

Howdy Doody, ring, Clarabell's horn on brass ring w/emb images of Howdy & Clarabell, horn works, EX, A $150.00

Howdy Doody, ring, flasher, Howdy appears to turn head, 1950s cereal premium, NM+ $50.00

Howdy Doody, sand bucket, plastic w/molded image on bottom, label on front, swing hdl, 5½", Ideal, scarce, EX, A....$85.00

Howdy Doody, squeeze toy, Clarabell, 7", Peter Puppet Playthings, MIB, A, $150.00. (Photo courtesy Smith House Toy and Auction Service)

Howdy Doody, squeeze toy, Howdy in airplane w/smiling face, yel rubber, 4½x5½", EX $175.00

Howdy Doody, straw holder, molded plastic head clips on side of glass, complete w/straws, Old Colony Paper Prod, NMIB, A $85.00

Howdy Doody, Sun-Ray Camera Outfit, complete, Silver Rich Corp, NMIB, A.......... $125.00

Howdy Doody, Television Set, complete w/5 rolls of film, All American Plastic Toy Co, MIB, A $150.00

Howdy Doody, ventriloquist doll, Howdy Doody, stuffed body w/ vinyl head & hands, 11", Goldberger, 1970s, NMIB $65.00

Howdy Doody, Wall Walking Wonder figure, plastic figure w/suction-cup wheel on back, 7", Tigrett, NMOC, A.........$85.00
HR Pufnstuf, figure, bean-stuffed plush, cloth outfit, 12", Street Players, 1999, NM+.........$10.00
HR Pufnstuf, figure, Cling, stuffed plush beanbag style w/red jacket & hat, 9", Living Toys, 1999, M.........$10.00

HR Pufnstuf, hand puppet, Dr. Blinky, Remco, 1970, EX, $100.00. (Photo courtesy gasolinealleyantiques.com)

HR Pufnstuf, hand puppet, Jimmy, printed vinyl body w/molded vinyl head, Remco, 1970, NM.........$150.00
HR Pufnstuf, hand puppet, Orson, cloth body w/vinyl head, Remco, 1970, NM.........$150.00
Hulk Hogan, hand puppet, red velvety cloth body w/mechanical blk vinyl boxing gloves, vinyl head w/headband, 1980s, NM+.........$25.00
Hunch Back of Notre Dame, figure, Glow-in-the-Dark Movie Monsters, plastic, 5½", Uncle Milton, 1990, MOC.....$12.00
I Dream of Jeannie, doll, posable vinyl w/rooted hair, cloth outfit, 6", Remco, 1966, NMIB, A.........$60.00
I Love Lucy, doll, any character, stuffed cloth w/vinyl head, hands & shoes, cloth outfit, 16", Presents, 1988, NM+, ea....$75.00
Ignatz Mouse, see Krazy Kat
In Living Color, figure, Homey D Clown, stuffed cloth w/satin-type costume, 24", Acme, 1992, NM+.........$25.00
Incredible Hulk, bank, Hulk breaking through wall, vinyl, 10", Renzi, 1977, EX+.........$25.00
Incredible Hulk, figure, bendable rubber, 6", Just Toys, 1989, EX+.........$8.00
Incredible Hulk, figure, rubber, 5½", 1970s, EX+.........$20.00
Incredible Hulk, figure, vinyl, jtd limbs, 14", Toy Biz, 1991, EX.........$25.00
Incredible Hulk, hand puppet, vinyl body w/gr molded vinyl head, blk-pnt hair, Imperial, 1978, EX.........$35.00
Incredible Hulk, playing cards, Nasta, 1979, complete deck, MIP (sealed).........$10.00
Inspector Gadget, squeeze toy, vinyl, figure in trench coat, 6½", Jugasa, 1983, MIP.........$50.00
Inspector Gadget, toy telephone, half-figure atop red & bl phone, 10", HG Toys, 1980s, NM.........$30.00

Iron Man, flicker ring, silver-tone plastic w/mc flicker image, vending machine item, 1966, NM.........$35.00
J Fred Muggs (Today Show), hand puppet, printed cloth body w/vinyl head, Imperial, 1954, NM.........$85.00
James Bond (Secret Agent), playset, Action Toy Set 5, Bond, Moneypenny & Bond's boss 'M', Gilbert, unused, NRFB......$55.00
Jerry Mahoney, hand puppet, printed vinyl body w/molded vinyl head, 1966, NM+.........$125.00
Jerry Mahoney, ventriloquist doll, 25", Juro Novelty, 1950s, EX+, A.........$150.00
Jetsons, Colorforms Cartoon Kit, 1963, NMIB, A.........$90.00
Jetsons, fast-food toy, Astro in space car & any other character in space vehicle, Wendy's, 1989, M, ea.........$6.00
Jetsons, figure, Astro, PVC, begging w/bone in mouth, 2¼", Applause, 1993, M.........$5.00
Jetsons, figure, Astro, stuffed plush, beige w/gr collar, felt tongue, plastic eyes, 10½", Nanco, 1989, M.........$10.00
Jetsons, figure, Astro, stuffed plush, gray w/gr collar, plastic eyes, 8", Applause, 1980s-90s, VG.........$10.00
Jetsons, figure, Elroy, stuffed cloth, printed features, fuzzy yel hair & beanie, 12", Dakin, 1986, EX+.........$12.00
Jetsons, figure, Elroy, stuffed cloth & vinyl, 5½", Applause, 1990, NM+.........$15.00
Jetsons, figure, Judy Jetson, vinyl, 2-tone pk cloth outfit, 10", Applause, 1990, NM+.........$15.00
Jetsons, figure, Rosie the Robot, 6", Applause, 1990s, NM..$12.00

Jetsons, game, The Jetsons Space Ball bagatelle game, Marx, VGIB, $150.00. (Photo courtesy Morphy Auctions)

Jetsons, figure, Rosie the Robot, 9", Applause, 1990s, NM..$15.00
Jetsons, hand puppet, any character, cloth body w/vinyl head, Knickerbocker, 1963, NM+, ea.........$75.00
Jetsons, night-light, Orbity, Elroy & Astro sleeping in bed, bisque, 6" L, Giftique, 1980s, M.........$35.00
Jetsons, ornament/clock, Astro Multi-Function Countdown Clock, vinyl, digital, 3¾", Radio Shack, 1999, MIB...$18.00
Jetsons, Star Scope, plastic, Ja-Ru, 1990, MOC (sealed)...$10.00
Jetsons, wheeled toy, Elroy waving on 4-wheeled skooter, plastic, 3", Applause, 1990, NM.........$5.00

Jiggs, see Maggie & Jiggs
Joe Palooka, bop bag, inflatable vinyl w/boxer image, Ideal, 1952, 44", NM, A $68.00
Jungle Book, bubble bath container, Baloo Bear, Colgate-Palmolive, 1966, NM $20.00
Katnip, see Herman & Katnip

Katzenjammer Kids, doll set, Mama, Captain, Hans, and Fritz, cloth with printed features, 16" to 20", Knickerbocker, 1925 – 1930, EX+ (with hang tags), $5,500.00. (Photo courtesy Morphy Auctions)

Kilo the Boxing Kangaroo, doll, blk & wht stuffed printed cloth w/pk rayon shorts, 16", EX, A $350.00
King Kong, bank, figure walking over building w/his name emb on front, vinyl, Relic Art Ltd, NM $150.00
King Kong, pennant, felt w/mc image of King Kong atop the World Trade Center, 'New York City' down side, 25", 1970s, NM....................$75.00
Koko the Klown ('Out of the Inkwell'), hand puppet, cloth body w/vinyl head, Gund, 1962, scarce, NM+ $200.00
Krazy Cat, figure, Ignatz Mouse, wood bead type w/bug-eyes, blk w/wht hands, feet, nose & chest, 5½", EX+, A........ $250.00
Krazy Kat, figure, Ignatz Mouse, wood, w/bendble limbs, blk w/wht face, Cameo Doll Co/Borgfeldt, ca 1930, VGIB $500.00
Krazy Kat, figure, Krazy Kat, wood bead type, blk, wht & yel w/ toothy grin, 7½", Chein, EX.................... $785.00
Krazy Kat, pull toy, Krazy Kat Chasing Ignatz Mouse (on 4-wheeled platform), EX (VG box), A.................... $3,080.00
Krazy Kat, pull toy, Krazy Kat Express (train engine), wood , 12", Int'l Feature Service, 1932, VG $675.00
Krazy Kat, tea set, litho tin, 16-pc set w/tray, teapot, creamer, sugar, 4 ea cups, saucers & plates, Chein, EX, A $125.00
Lamb Chop (Shari Lewis), bubble bath container, Lamb Chop holding duck, Kid Care, unused, w/tag, M $8.00
Lamp Chop, hand puppet, stocking body w/vinyl head, Tarcher Prod, 1960, NM $50.00
Laurel & Hardy, bank, either character, vinyl, 14", Play Pal Plastics, 1970s, NM, ea $45.00
Laurel & Hardy, figure, either character, bendable rubber, 6", Lakeside, 1967, EX+, ea $25.00
Laurel & Hardy, figure, either character, bendable vinyl w/cloth outfit, 8½", Knickerbocker, NM+, ea $40.00
Laurel & Hardy, figure, either character, squeeze vinyl, 5½", Dakin, 1970s, EX, ea....................$30.00
Laurel & Hardy, figure, either character, stuffed body w/vinyl head & hands, 12", Goldberger, 1986, NRFB, ea $35.00
Laurel & Hardy, figure, either character, vinyl w/cloth clothing, 8", Dakin, 1970s, w/hang tags, MIP, ea $50.00
Laurel & Hardy, hand puppet, Stan, cloth body w/vinyl head, Knickerbocker, 1965, NM $65.00
Laurel & Hardy, roly poly figure, Oliver Hardy, vinyl, red, wht & blk, chimes, 11", 1970s, VG+....................$30.00
Laverne & Shirley, doll set, Laverne & Shirley, 11½", Mego, 1977, no shoes o/w NM (VG+ box) $75.00
Laverne & Shirley, Paint-by-Numbers, acrylic paint set, Hasbro, 1981, unused, MIP (sealed) $20.00
Li'l Abner, bank, 'Can O' Coins,' company name on lid, 5", 1953 premium item, unused, M.................... $125.00
Li'l Abner, bank, Daisy Mae figure standing w/hands behind back on 'Dogpatch' base, compo, 8", 1975, NM....................$55.00
Li'l Abner, bank, Pappy Yokum standing atop base w/'Dogpatch USA' label on front, compo, 7", Al Capp Ent, 1970s, NM $55.00
Li'l Abner, bank, Shmoo figure, molded plastic, various colors, 7", WI Gould, 1940s, w/hang tag, EX $55.00

Krazy Kat, figure, Krazy Kat, hard-stuffed purple cloth, 18", Averill Mfg., 1930s, VG, $950.00. (Photo courtesy Morphy Auctions)

Li'l Abner, doll, vinyl with cloth outfit, 14", Baby Barry Toys, 1950s, NM, $100.00. (Photo courtesy whatacharacter.com)

Li'l Abner, doll, Mammy Yokum or Pappy Yokum, vinyl w/cloth outfit, 14", Baby Barry Toys, 1950s, NM, ea $100.00

Li'l Abner, hand puppet, any character, Ideal, 1960s, NM+, ea $75.00

Li'l Abner, w/up toy canoe, pnt plastic, w/Abner & Lonesome Polecat, w/up jug activates rowing, 12" L, 1940s, EX.. $100.00

Little Audrey, carrying case, 'Around the World With...'/graphics on wht vinyl hat-box shape w/handle, 1960s, EX.......$55.00

Little Audrey, doll, compo, blk synthetic hair in pigtails, cloth dress, felt hat, shoes & socks, 14", 1950s, EX, A...... $275.00

Little Audrey, doll, vinyl w/cloth dress & hair bow, wht vinyl shoes, 12½", Juro Novelty, 1950s, NM+ $175.00

Little Audrey, hand puppet, cloth body w/vinyl head, Gund, 1950s, NM $75.00

Little Iodine, hand puppet, cloth body w/vinyl head, Gund 1950s, MIP $100.00

Little King, walking spool toy, pnt wood figure, 4", Jaymar, 1939, VG+ (G box)...$50.00

Little Lulu, bank, Little Lulu standing beside blk fire hydrant, vinyl, 7½", Play Pal, 1970s, EX.................................$25.00

Little Lulu, bank, Little Lulu standing next to baby carriage, vinyl, 10", Play Pal Plastics, 1973, EX........................$55.00

Little Lulu, Cooking Set, plastic, Larami, 1974, unused, MOC (sealed) $15.00

Little Lulu, figure, inflatable vinyl, red dress w/name on breast pocket, 14", Sanitoy, 1973, M $30.00

Little Lulu, figure, stuffed cloth, red cloth dress w/wht collar & lace trim, 6½", Gund, 1972, MIB..............................$75.00

Little Lulu, squeeze toy, Little Lulu in red dress w/wht purse waving, 6", Romogosa Int'l, 1984, MIP $30.00

Little Orphan Annie, bubble bath container, Annie figure, Lander, 1977, NM..$15.00

Little Orphan Annie, figure set, Annie & Sandy, compo w/pnt features, cloth dress, 12" & 7", EXIB, A.................. $450.00

Little Orphan Annie, Jack Set, Arcade, 1935, NRFP, A, $175.00. (Photo courtesy Randy Inman Auctions)

Little Red Riding Hood, hand puppet, Big Bad Wolf, brn cloth body w/tie & collar, vinyl head, MPI Toys, 1960, NM...........$125.00

Little Red Riding Hood, hand puppet, Grandma, cloth body w/ vinyl head, MPI Toys, 1960, NM $85.00

Little Red Riding Hood, hand puppet, Little Red Riding Hood, cloth body w/vinyl head, MPI Toys, 1960, NM $85.00

Little Red Riding Hood, hand puppet, Little Red Riding Hood/Big Bad Wolf, dbl-sided vinyl head w/cloth body, NM $65.00

Little Red Riding Hood, marionette, Big Bad Wolf, nonmovable mouth, 15", Hazelle, NM.. $150.00

Little Red Riding Hood, marionette, Little Red Riding Hood, red & wht checked outfit, 15", Hazelle, EX+ $100.00

Looney Tunes, Bake A Craft Stained Glass Kit, Foghorn Leghorn, Road Champos, 1991, MOC (sealed) $12.00

Looney Tunes, bank, Bugs Bunny in basket of carrots labeled 'What's Up Doc,' NY Vinyl Products Corporation, 1972, 14", NM, $35.00. (Photo courtesy serioustoyz.com)

Looney Tunes, bank, Cool Cat image on yel on sq metal box, 4x4x1", Warner Bors, EX+ $22.00

Looney Tunes, bank, Daffy Duck hugging money bag emb w/the dollar symbol, ceramic, 6", Good Co, 1989, NM+ $40.00

Looney Tunes, bank, Porky Pig declaring 'That's All Folks!' on red LT logo, ceramic, 8", Good Co, 1989, NM $50.00

Looney Tunes, bank, Porky Pig standing w/arms behind back, bisque, 5", 1940s, G+...$75.00

Looney Tunes, bank, Porky Pig standing w/head turned looking up & arms behind back, ceramic, 10", 1990s, NM+ ...$15.00

Looney Tunes, bank, Porky standing w/1 arm bent up & 1 arm down, legs together, 6½", Dakin, NM $20.00

Looney Tunes, bank, Road Runner & Wile E Coyote figures emb on side of mountain, vinyl, 5", WB Stores, 1990s, NM $25.00

Looney Tunes, bank, Road Runner running on grassy base, pnt compo, 8", Holiday Fair, 1970s, NM $50.00

Looney Tunes, bank, Road Runner standing on dirt mound, plastic, 12", Dakin, 1971, EX...$45.00

Looney Tunes, bank, Speedy Gonzales standing on cheese wedge, vinyl w/cloth outfit, 9½", Dakin, MIP $75.00

Looney Tunes, bank, Tasmanain Devil as 'mean' football player, vinyl, 6½", HEI, 1994, M...$15.00

Looney Tunes, bank, Tasmanian Devil standing w/hands clasped in front, closed-mouth smile, vinyl, 5", Dakin, NM+ ...$75.00

Looney Tunes, bank, Tweety Bird atop birdhouse marked Tweety, compo, 9", Holiday Fair, 1971, NM+ $35.00

Looney Tunes, bank, Tweety Bird perched atop bird cage, vinyl, 10½", Dakin, 1971, NM+ $35.00

Looney Tunes, bank, Tweety Bird standing with hands on stomach, vinyl, Dakin, NM, $20.00. (Photo courtesy whatacharacter.com)

Looney Tunes, bank, Yosimite Sam w/'wooden' treasure chest, ceramic, 6", Applause, 1988, M..................................$40.00

Looney Tunes, bookends, big Bugs pushing little Bugs on a cart on hot pk base, 7" H, Holiday Fair, 1970, M, pr $50.00

Looney Tunes, bubble bath container, any character, Colgate-Palmoilve, 1960s, NM, ea from $20 to........................$25.00

Looney Tunes, bubble bath container, any character, Kid Care, 1992, NM+, ea...$8.00

Looney Tunes, Bugs Bunny Wonder Wiskers (Magnetic) Drawing Set, Henry Gordy Int'l, 1988, unused, MOC..........$8.00

Looney Tunes, candle, Tweety Bird figure w/'Happy Birthday' labeled on tummy, Wilton, 1979, unused, MIP $12.00

Looney Tunes, Cartoon-O-Graph Sketch Board, Moss Mfg, 1940s-50s, EXIB...$75.00

Looney Tunes, cookie cutter, Bugs Bunny, red plastic, 6", 1978, unused, NM+ $6.00

Looney Tunes, Ertl Die-Cast Metal Toy, Bugs Bunny standing w/arms crossed over chest, 1989, NRFC $8.00

Looney Tunes, Ertl Die-Cast Metal Toy, Foghorn Leghorn in Looney Tunes coal car, 3", 1989, MOC $15.00

Looney Tunes, Ertl Die-Cast Metal Toy, Road Runner in car, 1988, M (G+ card) $10.00

Looney Tunes, Ertl Die-Cast Metal Toy, Road Runner on scooter, 2½", 1989, MOC $12.00

Looney Tunes, Ertl Die-Cast Metal Toy, Tweety Bird perched on T-stand, 1989, MOC $8.00

Looney Tunes, figure, any character, PVC, Arby's, 1988-89, MIP, ea...$6.00

Looney Tunes, figure, Bugs Bunny, flocked plastic, gray & wht, 6", Lucky Bell, 1988, NRFC.......................................$10.00

Looney Tunes, figure, Bugs Bunny, plastic (hollow), gray & wht w/pk mouth, 5½", Dakin, 1960s-70s (?), NM $12.00

Looney Tunes, figure, Bugs Bunny, PVC, as magician pulling carrots out of hat, 4", Applause, 1990, NM $3.00

Looney Tunes, figure, Bugs Bunny, stuffed cloth, as 'Uncle Sam,' 11", Dakin, 1976, NM $25.00

Looney Tunes, figure, Bugs Bunny, stuffed cloth, lying down w/carrot, 8" L, Dakin (Fun Farm), 1978, NM................$25.00

Looney Tunes, figure, Bugs Bunny, stuffed plush & vinyl, w/toothy smile, 15", Mattel, 1960s, NM........................$25.00

Looney Tunes, figure, Bugs Bunny, vinyl, 'Happy Birthday,' 12", Dakin Goofy Gram, 1971, NM $38.00

Looney Tunes, figure, Bugs Bunny, vinyl, standing w/carrot, jtd, swivel head, 10", Dakin, 1960s-70s (?), NM $20.00

Looney Tunes, figure, Bugs Bunny, vinyl, standing w/legs apart/hand on hip w/carrot, solid orange, 6", Dakin, 1976, NM $20.00

Looney Tunes, figure, Bugs Bunny, vinyl (inflatable), gray & wht w/blk accents, 12", 1970s, NM $10.00

Looney Tunes, figure, Bugs Bunny figure w/snap-on Super Hero costume, 3½", McDonald's, 1991, NM.........................$4.00

Looney Tunes, figure, Daffy Duck, bisque, on flowery grassy base w/1 hand on head & 1 to mouth, 6", Price, 1979, M..$28.00

Looney Tunes, figure, Daffy Duck, PVC, as baseball player standing on base, 3", Applause, 1990, MIB ('Official' box)...$10.00

Looney Tunes, figure, Daffy Duck, stuffed cloth, pillow type w/printed image & name, 16", 1970s, NM $15.00

Looney Tunes, figure, Daffy Duck, stuffed plush, vinyl collar, 15", Mighty Star, 1971, NM $10.00

Looney Tunes, figure, Daffy Duck, vinyl, as part of barbershop quartet, jtd, 9", Applause, NM+ $15.00

Looney Tunes, figure, Daffy Duck, vinyl, standing w/legs together & feet spread, hand on hip, 9", Dakin, 1960s-70s, NM.......$20.00

Looney Tunes, figure, Elmer Fudd, vinyl, cloth hunting outfit & gun, vinyl boots, 7", Dakin, 1968, MIP......................$75.00

Looney Tunes, figure, Elmer Fudd, vinyl, jtd, blk cloth jacket, yel pants, red vinyl shoes & hat, 8", Dakin, NM+ $25.00

Looney Tunes, figure, Foghorn Leghorn, vinyl, jointed, Dakin, 1970, M, $55.00. (Photo courtesy whatacharacter.com)

Looney Tunes, figure, Henry Hawk, stuffed plush, stuffed felt feet & beak, lg plastic eyes, 18", 1990s, NM+....................$15.00
Looney Tunes, figure, Marvin Martian, vinyl, jtd arms, 8¼", 1990s, w/hang tag, NM+ $15.00
Looney Tunes, figure, Merlin the Mouse, vinyl, 'I'll Drink to That!' on rnd base, 7", Goofy Gram/Dakin, 1970s, EX............$25.00
Looney Tunes, figure, Pepe Le Pew, stuffed vinyl, 8", Ace Novelty, 1997, NM $8.00
Looney Tunes, figure, Pepe Le Pew, vinyl, on base marked 'You're A Real Stinker,' 9", Goofy Gram/Dakin, 1971, MIP ..$75.00
Looney Tunes, figure, Petunia Pig, squeeze vinyl, standing w/ hands on hips, 4¼", Spain, 1990s, NM $12.00
Looney Tunes, figure, Porky Pig, squeeze rubber, standing w/ head cocked & arms behind back, 7", Sun Rubber, 1940s, NM $50.00
Looney Tunes, figure, Porky Pig, squeeze vinyl, standing w/arms down & palms forward, blk jacket, 5", Dakin, 1960s, NM......... $20.00
Looney Tunes, figure, Porky Pig, squeeze vinyl, waving pose, turq jacket, orange bow tie, Reliance, 1978, NM+ $20.00
Looney Tunes, figure, Porky Pig, vinyl, blk cloth cape, wht bow tie, 8", Dakin, 1969, NRFP (Looney Tunes bag) $35.00
Looney Tunes, figure, Road Runner, PVC, 4½", Dakin, 1970s, EX $10.00
Looney Tunes, figure, Road Runner, vinyl, standing w/legs together, 9", Dakin, 1968, NM..................................$25.00
Looney Tunes, figure, Second Banana, vinyl, jtd, 6", Dakin, 1970, EX $25.00
Looney Tunes, figure, Tasmanian Devil, bendable foam rubber, 7½", Bendy Toys, 1988, MIP $25.00
Looney Tunes, figure, Tasmanian Devil, bendable vinyl, legs apart, arms up & mouth wide open, 6", Tyco, 1990, NM+ $6.00
Looney Tunes, figure, Tasmanian Devil, PVC, holding heart, 3", Tyco, 1994, MOC (card reads 'Heart Throbs Figurines').. $10.00
Looney Tunes, figure, Tasmanian Devil, rubber, arms over head & bent at elbows, tan & gray, 5", 1980, NM..............$10.00
Looney Tunes, figure, Tweety Bird, flat rubber, Tweety leaning to 1 side a bit, hand (wings) not seen, 4", EX $6.00
Looney Tunes, figure, Tweety Bird, flocked plastic, dressed as sheriff, 3", Lucky Bell, 1989, NM+...............................$8.00
Looney Tunes, figure, Tweety Bird, squeeze vinyl, standing w/ hands on tummy, 5", Dakin, 1970s, NM $20.00
Looney Tunes, figure, Tweety Bird, squeeze vinyl, standing wearing bl neck scarf & diaper, 6", Oak Rubber, 1940s, VG $25.00
Looney Tunes, figure, Tweety Bird, stuffed cloth, lt yel w/orange beak, seated, 18", Mighty Star, 1971, EX $12.00
Looney Tunes, figure, Tweety Bird, vinyl, swivel head & feet, 6", Dakin, 1969, NM...$25.00
Looney Tunes, figure, Wile E Coyote, plastic, standing w/legs apart, plastic, 5", Dakin, 1970s, EX $12.00
Looney Tunes, figure, Wile E Coyote, rubber, 3", Arby's, 1988, M $6.00
Looney Tunes, figure, Wile E Coyote, vinyl, jtd, 9½", Dakin, 1960s, MIP $45.00
Looney Tunes, figure, Yosemite Sam, vinyl, cloth outfit, red fuzzy beard, blk plastic hat, 7½", Dakin, 1968, NM............$20.00
Looney Tunes, figure, Yosimite Sam, PVC, standing w/legs apart & guns raised, 2¼", Applause, 1989, NM+ $5.00
Looney Tunes, figure Porky Pig, stuffed plush, felt hat, felt features, seated w/legs apart, 8", Dakin, 1975, EX+.........$15.00
Looney Tunes, finger puppet, any character, Starbuck's premium, 2004, M...$4.00
Looney Tunes, finger puppet, any character, vinyl, Dakin, 1970, MIP, ea $20.00
Looney Tunes, Flash Lite, Bugs Bunny figure, plastic, gray & wht, 5", 1940s, unused, M (VG box).................................$25.00
Looney Tunes, game, Dominoes, red plastic w/2 inset pics of LT characters on ea pc, Whitman, 1977, EXIB (Bugs on box) $15.00
Looney Tunes, gumball machine, Bugs Bunny, clear plastic head w/ wht teeth & gray ears, colored base, 10", Tarrson, EX+ ... $25.00
Looney Tunes, gumball machine, Bugs w/arms & legs crossed & carrot next to gum globe, Processed Plastic Co, 1988, EX+ $15.00
Looney Tunes, Gumball Pocket Pack Dispenser, any character, Processed Plastic Co, 1989, MOC, ea $10.00
Looney Tunes, hand puppet, any character, vinyl body & head, detergent premium, 1969, NM, ea from $20 to $25.00
Looney Tunes, hand puppet, Bugs Bunny, cloth body w/vinyl head, goggly-eyed, Zany, 1950s, EX+ $65.00

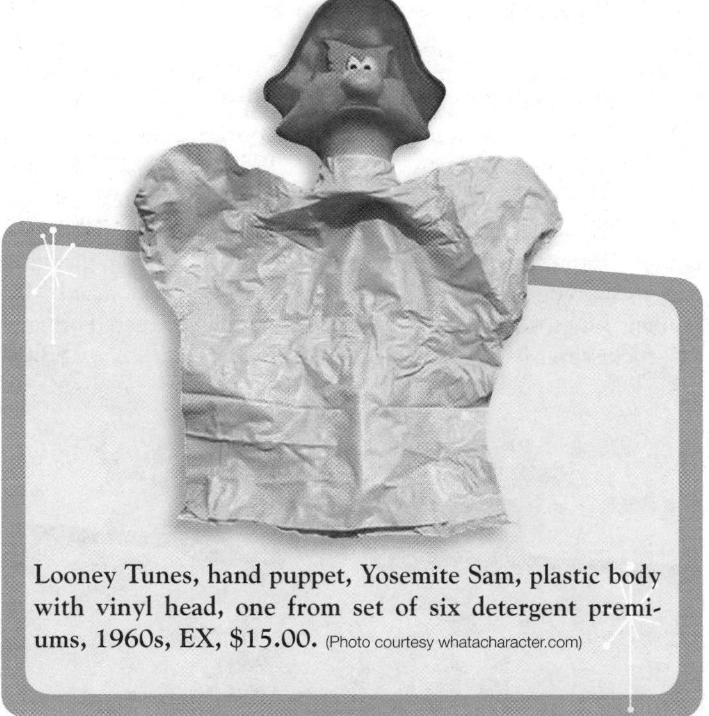

Looney Tunes, hand puppet, Yosemite Sam, plastic body with vinyl head, one from set of six detergent premiums, 1960s, EX, $15.00. (Photo courtesy whatacharacter.com)

Looney Tunes, Holiday Figurine Light, Bugs Bunny figure dressed as Santa waving, vinyl, 11", Minami, 1997, w/tag, M.. $12.00
Looney Tunes, ice machine, Marvin Martian, plastic, 12", Saltan, 1990s, NM+ $20.00
Looney Tunes, Looney Toonavision, makes different faces, litho cb w/control knobs, 1950s, VG $25.00
Looney Tunes, mug, any characher head, 4", Promotional Partners, 1992, M, ea...$6.00
Looney Tunes, mug, any character, ceramic, Applause, 1989-1990s, M, ea from $10 to $12.00

Looney Tunes, mug, any character, molded vinyl, Applause, 1995, M, ea ...$6.00
Looney Tunes, Music Maker, Bugs Bunny, litho tin, Mattel, 1963, working, VG ...$38.00
Looney Tunes, ornament, Tweety Bird, flocked plastic figure, w/ red (ribbon) scarf, 4", Liberty Bell, 1978, NM+...$8.00
Looney Tunes, pencil holder/sharpener, Bugs Bunny figure standing eating carrot, compo, 6", Holiday Fair, 1970, NM... $18.00
Looney Tunes, pencil topper, Marvin Martian on spacecraft, PVC, 2½", NM+ ...$5.00
Looney Tunes, pull toy, Porky Pig & Petunia on horses w/4 wheels & bell, paper-litho-on-wood, Brice Novelty #920, 8", EX ... $110.00
Looney Tunes, pull toy, Tweety Bird twirling figure atop wagon, 9½", Brice Novelty, 1950s, NM... $125.00
Looney Tunes, push-button puppet, any character, Kohner, 1960s, EX, ea...$30.00
Looney Tunes, snow dome, Bugs Bunny, 'A 24K Friend' on base, Bug's head & carrot in hand in plastic dome, 3", 1989, NM ...$10.00
Looney Tunes, snow dome, Bugs Bunny, musical, 'Singin' in the Rain,' glass globe w/wooden base, 6", Good Co, 1989, M ...$30.00
Looney Tunes, snow dome, Pepe Le Pew in clear plastic dome on red base marked 'Pour L'Amour,' 3", 1989, NM...$15.00
Looney Tunes, snow dome, Wile E Coyote in clear dome, 'Feel Better!' on orange base, 3", Acme, 1989, NM+...$12.00
Looney Tunes, Speedy Gonzales Turbine Tops, Larami, 1973, MOC...$30.00
Looney Tunes, squeeze toy, Bugs Bunny, vinyl, waving, glancing eyes, orange gloves, 7", Dakin, 1970s, NM+...$18.00
Looney Tunes, squeeze toy, Daffy Duck as cowboy seated on gray rock, vinyl, Vo-Toys, 1994, NM+...$8.00

Looney Tunes, squeeze toy, Pixie and Dixie, 5½", Dell, 1960s, EX+, $42.00. (Photo courtesy whatacharacter.com)

Looney Tunes, Stained Glass Kit, features Bugs Bunny, Road Chamos, 1991, unused, MOC...$10.00
Looney Tunes, stationery set, Fancy House Club, unused, MIP ...$6.00
Looney Tunes, wall plaque, Tasmanian Devil figure scowling, mc plastic popcorn-type material, 1973, M ...$12.00

Lucky Ducky, hand puppet, checked cloth body w/vinyl head, Zany, 1950s, NM...$50.00
Maggie & Jiggs, doll, Jiggs, stuffed cloth, cloth outfit, printed features, w/cigar, 18", Lars of Italy, 1920s, EX... $400.00

Maggie and Jiggs, doll set, wood with cloth outfits, 7" and 9", Schoenhut, NRFB ('Bringing Up Father'), A, $2,750.00. (Photo courtesy Morphy Auctions)

Magilla Gorilla, see Hanna-Barbera
Man From UNCLE, finger Puppets, set of 6, unused, NMIB. $325.00
Man From UNCLE, magic slate, Watkins-Strathmore, 1960s, unused, NM ...$75.00
Man From UNCLE, Secret Print Putty, USA, 1965, complete & unused, MOC ... $100.00
Man From UNCLE, Secret Weapon Set, Ideal, 1965, NMIB, ...$400.00
Man From UNCLE, Shooting Arcade, tin & plastic, Marx, 1960s, NMIB, A ... $200.00
Man From UNCLE, Target Game, plastic & cb, Ideal, MIB, A ... $200.00
Marvin the Martian, see Looney Tunes
Mary Hartline, Super Circus Puppet, punch-out cb pcs, Snickers Candy, 1950s, ununched, M... $130.00
Merlin the Mouse, see Looney Tunes
Mighty Mouse, bubble bath container, Colgate-Palmolive, 1960s, NM+ ...$25.00
Mighty Mouse, figure, Mighty Mouse, vinyl, Dakin, 1978, MIP ('Fun Farm') ... $125.00
Mighty Mouse, figure, Pearl Pureheart, stuffed cloth w/red cloth jacket, yel hair, 15", A&A Plush Inc, 1990s, NM+ ...$12.00
Mighty Mouse, flashlight, figural, 3½", 1970s, MIP ... $100.00
Mighty Mouse, Merry-Pack, complete collection of 20 games & toys, die-cut litho cb, CBS TV Ent, 1956, unused, EX+ ... $75.00
Mister Magoo, figure, stuffed cloth w/vinyl head, all yel w/shiny hat, shirt & feet, 13", Cuddle Wit, NM+...$18.00
Mister Magoo, figure, stuffed cloth w/vinyl head & hat, felt outfit w/3 plastic buttons, 16", Ideal, 1960s, NM ... $100.00
Mr Ed, hand puppet, plush body, vinyl head w/yarn mane, talker, Mattel, 1962, NM...$75.00
Mr Magoo, bubble bath container, Colgate-Palmolive, 1960s, EX...$15.00

Mr Rogers Neighborhood, hand puppet, King, full cloth body w/weighted base, vinyl head, Ideal, 1976, NM $60.00

Mr Rogers Neighborhood, hand puppet, X the Owl, full cloth body w/weighted base, Ideal, 1976, EX+ $60.00

Munchie Melon, hand puppet, brn cloth body w/pineapple detail on chest, vinyl pineapple head, Marx, 1967, EX $75.00

Munsters, Castex 5 Casting Set, Emenee, 1964, minimal use, EX+IB, A $288.00

Munsters, doll, any character, stuffed cloth w/vinyl head, cloth outfits, about 9", Presents/Hamilton Gifts, NM+, ea..$35.00

Munsters, doll, any character, stuffed cloth w/vinyl head, cloth outfits, about 14", Toy Works, unused, MIP, ea...........$20.00

Munsters, doll, Eddie Munster, vinyl, 8½", Ideal, 1965, NM+, $110.00. (Photo courtesy whatacharacter.com)

Munsters, hand puppet, any character, cloth body w/vinyl head & hands, 1960s, EX, ea...$50.00

Muppet Babies, hand puppet, Animal, plush w/plastic eyes, Dakin, 1988, NM..$10.00

Muppets, see also Sesame Street

Muppets, bank, Kermit seated on grassy base w/pk flowers, hand to cheek, 9", Applause, NM+....................................$15.00

Muppets, bubble bath container, any character, Calgon, 1996, M, ea $8.00

Muppets, figure, Gonzo, stuffed plush w/cloth outfit, plastic eyes, blk/wht plaid pants, chili-pepper tie, 14", Nanco, M..$10.00

Muppets, figure, Gonzo, vinyl, seated, yel bird on red outfit, 5", Hasbro, 1984, NM $8.00

Muppets, figure, Great Gonzo, Dress-up Muppet Doll, Fisher-Price #858, 1982-83, EX..$15.00

Muppets, figure, Kermit the Frog, Dress-Up Muppet Doll, Fisher-Price #857, EX $10.00

Muppets, figure, Kermit the Frog, stuffed plush, felt collar, 19", Hasbro, 1985, NM+...$22.00

Muppets, figure, Miss Piggy, stuffed cloth, vinyl head w/synthetic hair, purple gown, 14", Fisher-Price, 1980s, NMIB.....$25.00

Muppets, figure, Red (Fraggle Rock), plush w/stuffed arms & legs, red shirt, yarn hair, 16", Tommy, 1983, NM $25.00

Muppets, figure, Scooter, stuffed cloth, 17", 1978, EX.......$22.00

Muppets, hand puppet, Fozie Bear, plush, Fisher-Price, 1978, NM+, $15.00. (Photo courtesy whatacharacter.com)

Muppets, hand puppet, Miss Piggy, mouth moves, Fisher-Price #855, 1979-80, EX $8.00

Muppets, hand puppet, Rowlf, brn plush, Fisher-Price #852, 1977, EXIB...$35.00

Muppets, hand puppet, Scooter, plush, Fisher-Price #853, 1978-81, EX $10.00

Muppets, kaleidoscope, cb & metal w/lithoed Muppet characters, 9" L, Hallmark, 1981, EX+ $30.00

Muppets, mirror, Deco-style ceramic frame w/Miss Piggy figure admiring self in lower left corner, 9", Sigma, 1980s, M $75.00

Muppets, Muppet Show Players, Fisher-Price #846, 1979-83, MIB $30.00

Muppets, necklace, resin Kermit the Frog as hiker w/backpack, w/lt gr cord & bead, 3½" figure, Just Toys, NM+ $8.00

Muppets, Party Puzzlers, features Kermit the Frog, Hallmark, 1981, unused, MOC $10.00

Muppets, Stick Puppet, any character, Fisher-Price, 1970s-80s, NM, ea $10.00

Mutt & Jeff, drum, litho tin, 13" dia, Converse, EX $300.00

My Favorite Martian, Martian Magic Tricks set, Gilbert, 1964, complete & unused, NMIB, A $170.00

Nancy, figure, Nancy or Sluggo, stuffed cloth, 6½", Knickerbocker, 1970s, MIB (box reads Miniature Rag Doll), ea...........$40.00

Nancy, figure, Sluggo, squeeze rubber, standing w/boxing gloves on, 10", Dreamland Creations, 1955, EX....................$75.00

Nancy, figure, stuffed cloth, 6½", Knickerbocker, 1973, MIB (box reads 'Extra! U*Color*It Comic Strip on Back...').....$40.00

Natasha Fatale, see Rocky & Friends

New Zoo Revue, hand puppet, Henrietta Hippo, yel cloth body w/vinyl head, lg open mouth, 1970s, NM+.................$75.00

Nightmare on Elm Street, yo-yo, Freddie Kruger, Spectra Star, 1988, unused, MOC $20.00

Odie, see Garfield

Oswald the Rabbit, figure, squeeze rubber, 7½", Sun Rubber, 1940s, VG $50.00

Oswald the Rabbit, figure, stuffed plush w/name on chest banner, orange jacket, laced shoes, 17", Irwin, 1930s, EX $450.00

Our Miss Brooks, hand puppet, cloth body w/vinyl head, Zany, 1950S, NM $150.00

Out of the Ink Well, see Koko the Klown

Pac-Man, bank, plastic, marked 'Tomy Pac-Man' on front of base, 4½", 1980s, NM+ $15.00
Pac-Man, figure, stuffed plush, yel w/open red mouth, 17", 1980s, NM....$15.00
Pac-Man, gumball machine, clear plastic Pac-Man globe w/yel decal atop dk bl base, 6", Superior Toy, 1980s, EX......$25.00
Pac-Man, hand puppet, plush, Commonwealth Toy & Novelty, 1980s, EX $10.00
Paddington Bear, bank, Paddington seated, flocked plastic w/ cloth coat & hat, 6", Eden Toys, 1980s, EX+ $22.00
Paddington Bear, figure, stuffed cloth, lt bl cloth shirt w/name, blk printed features & ears, 13", Eden Toys, 1970s, NM.....$20.00
Peanuts, bank, Peppermint Patty standing in ball cap & leaning on baseball bat, compo, 7", Determined, 1972, NM+...$65.00
Peanuts, bank, Snoopy as Joe Cool on gr base, pnt compo, 6", 1970s, NM+ $35.00
Peanuts, bank, Snoopy Bank, globe w/flags of different countries & various Snoopy images, metal, 5", Ohio Art, 1970s, NM $40.00
Peanuts, bank, Snoopy in 'Racer,' pnt compo, 4x5", 1970s, EX $50.00
Peanuts, bank, Snoopy in 'The Express' truck, pnt compo, 4", 1970s, NM+ $55.00
Peanuts, bank, Snoopy in stocking cap & scarf standing holding pr of skis, vinyl, 6", Danara, 1970s, NM....$22.00
Peanuts, bank, Snoopy lying on back atop baseball, pnt compo, 5", 1970s, NM....$35.00
Peanuts, bank, Snoopy seated upright, clear glass, 6", Anchor Hocking, 1980s, M $22.00
Peanuts, bank, Woodstock standing, signed Schulz, 6", 1970s, NM+ $30.00
Peanuts, bicycle horn, plastic horn w/squeeze vinyl Snoopy head, 7", Hollywood Accessories, 1980s, MIP....$18.00

Peanuts, bubble bath container, Lucy, Avon, 1970, MIB, $15.00. (Photo courtesy whatacharacter.com)

Peanuts, bulletin board, cork, Snoopy sniffing 'love' note & 'Notes' lettered at bottom, 18x12", Butterfly, 1980s, MIP.........$18.00
Peanuts, bulletin board, cork w/images of Peanuts Gang amidst a musical staff, Schroeder playing piano, 18x23", NM+..$12.00
Peanuts, comb & brush set, Charlie Brown figural brush w/6" plastic comb, Avon, 1971, NM+IB $25.00

Peanuts, Cool Writer/Roly Poly Pen Holder, image of 'Joe Cool' on sides, plastic, 3", Butterfly Originals, 1980s, MIB $15.00
Peanuts, figure, Charlie Brown, bendable vinyl, arms stretched out w/ball glove, 6", 1960s, NM+ $20.00
Peanuts, figure, Charlie Brown, plastic w/cloth pants & shirt, jtd, 7", 1960s, NM $35.00
Peanuts, figure, Charlie Brown, squeeze vinyl, w/bowl of dog food, 5½", Con Agra, 1990s, NM+ $8.00
Peanuts, figure, Charlie Brown, stuffed cloth w/blk-printed face, orange cloth shirt, Rag Doll, Ideal, 1960s-70s, MIP ...$35.00
Peanuts, figure, Charlie Brown, stuffed felt pillow style w/printed image front & back, 7½x1", NM $8.00
Peanuts, figure, Charlie Brown, stuffed terrycloth pillow type w/ printed image, 8½", Determined, 1970s, unused, MIP..$35.00

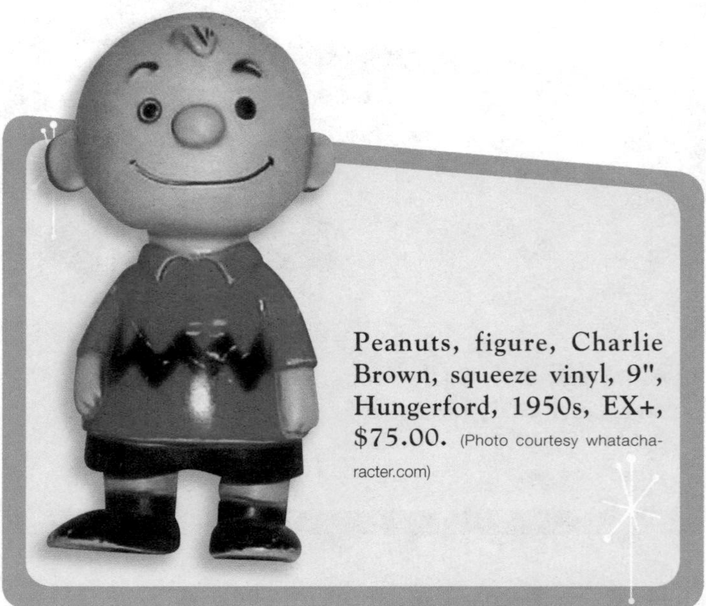

Peanuts, figure, Charlie Brown, squeeze vinyl, 9", Hungerford, 1950s, EX+, $75.00. (Photo courtesy whatacharacter.com)

Peanuts, figure, Charlie Brown, vinyl, red shirt w/blk zigzag design, blk shorts & shoes, 9", Hungerford, 1950s, MIP......... $100.00
Peanuts, figure, Linus, bendable vinyl, arms straight out, 5½", 1960s, NM $25.00
Peanuts, figure, Linus, squeeze vinyl, standing w/1 hand up by face & other on tummy, 7", Hungerford, 1950s, EX+...........$45.00
Peanuts, figure, Linus, squeeze vinyl, standing w/1 hand up by face & other on tummy, 9", Hungerford, 1950s, EX.$65.00
Peanuts, figure, Linus, stuffed cloth, printed features, cloth short, 8", Rag Doll, Ideal, 1960s, MIP (sealed) $40.00
Peanuts, figure, Linus, stuffed cloth, printed pillow type, 9", Determined, 1970s, MIP (sealed)....$35.00
Peanuts, figure, Linus, stuffed cloth body w/vinyl head, sucking thumb, w/blanket, 9", Determined, 1980s, EX............$25.00
Peanuts, figure, Lucy, bendable rubber, pk dress, 5¼", 1969, NM $25.00
Peanuts, figure, Lucy, squeeze vinyl, yel dress, 8", Hungerford, 1950s, NM $65.00
Peanuts, figure, Lucy, stuffed cloth, 'Director of Everything' printed on red shirt, 10", Determined, M....$18.00

Peanuts, figure, Lucy, stuffed cloth w/blk printed features & hair, red dress w/bl trim, 7½", Ideal, NRFP $40.00
Peanuts, figure, Lucy, stuffed print cloth, lg wht 'P' on red gym suit, red gym shoes, 6¼", Determined, EX+ $10.00
Peanuts, figure, Lucy, vinyl, yel dress, 9", Hungerford, 1950s, EX+ $75.00
Peanuts, figure, Peppermint Patty, foam-stuffed printed terry-cloth, 8½", Determined, 1970s, MIP (sealed) $35.00
Peanuts, figure, Peppermint Patty, stuffed cloth, cloth outfit, printed features, 7", MIP ('Peanuts Rag Doll' on header) $40.00
Peanuts, figure, Peppermint Patty, stuffed cloth, printed outfit & features, 6", Determined, NM $12.00
Peanuts, figure, Sally, squeeze vinyl, standing w/hands to mouth, 5½", Con Agra, 1990s, NM+......................................$8.00
Peanuts, figure, Schroeder, squeeze vinyl, seated as if playing piano, red-pnt outfit, 8", Hungerford, 1950s, EX..... $125.00

Peanuts, figure, Schroeder, vinyl with orange 'Beethoven' sweater, black trousers, 7½", Pocket Dolls, 1970s, EX+, $35.00. (Photo courtesy whatacharacter.com)

Peanuts, figure, Snoopy, foam-stuffed printed cloth, as train engineer, 8", Determined, 1970s, MIP $30.00
Peanuts, figure, Snoopy, squeeze vinyl, as sheriff, 6", Danara, 1970s, EX+..$12.00
Peanuts, figure, Snoopy, squeeze vinyl, asleep on tummy w/ rump in air, head stretched out, 7½" L, Con Agra, 1990s, NM $8.00
Peanuts, figure, Snoopy, squeeze vinyl, sitting upright holding yel flower, 4", Danara, 1970s, EX+.................................$12.00
Peanuts, figure, Snoopy, stuffed cloth w/jeans & name on red shirt, 8", Ideal, MIP (header reads 'Snoopy Rag Doll') $38.00
Peanuts, figure, Snoopy, stuffed plush, cloth sheriff's outfit, 12", Determined, NM $15.00
Peanuts, figure, Snoopy, vinyl, jtd, as astronaut, 9", Determined, 1969, G $100.00
Peanuts, figure, Snoopy, vinyl, jtd, cloth outfit w/'S' on red top, wearing roller skates, 10", Determined, 1980s, EX+ ...$28.00
Peanuts, figure, Woodstock, resin, standing w/eyes closed, 4", NM...$10.00
Peanuts, figure, Woodstock, stuffed body w/vinyl head & feet, cloth outfit w/name on top, 7", Applause, NM+ $15.00
Peanuts, figure, Woodstock, stuffed felt w/yarn hair, Determined, 1970s, EX $12.00
Peanuts, friction toy, Woodstock on ice-cream scooter, plastic, 6", Aviva, 1970s, EX $22.00
Peanuts, friction toy (Motorized Toy), Woodstock seat atop bird's nest, plastic, 3½", Aviva, 1970s, NRFP......................$35.00
Peanuts, Friction Wheelie, plastic, Snoopy seated on 3-wheeled scooter, 6", MIP $35.00
Peanuts, gyroscope, Charlie Brown sitting atop globe, 8½", Aviva, 1970s, MIB (box reads 'Snoopy Gyroscope')...$40.00
Peanuts, hand puppet, Lucy, cloth body w/vinyl head, red dress outlined in blk, Syncrgistics Research, NM+ $15.00
Peanuts, Jumbo Coloring Pencils, Empire, unused, MOC...$6.00
Peanuts, kaleidoscope, cb w/allover images of Snoopy laughing, 9", NM $30.00
Peanuts, magic slate, Top Dog, various images of Snoopy, Child Art Prod, 1970s, unused, M (sealed) $15.00
Peanuts, marionette, Charlie Brown, vinyl, jtd, 8", Pelham, 1980s, NRFB...$75.00
Peanuts, megaphone, litho tin w/images of Snoopy w/megaphone, Lucy & Charlie Brown, 6", Chein, 1970, EX..$25.00
Peanuts, night-light, plastic bulb w/image of Charlie Brown flying kite, 4", 1980s, NM...$10.00
Peanuts, oranment, Sally, wood w/various pnt images, 3" to 3½", 1970s, M, ea...$5.00
Peanuts, Pocket Bean Bags figure, Woodstock, printed image on bicycle, 4", Butterfly Originals, 1980s, NRFP $20.00
Peanuts, Pop-Up Toy, Snoopy doghouse w/Charlie Brown pop-up, plastic, 3", Aviva, 1970s, unused, MIB.................$35.00

Peanuts, push-button puppet, Charlie Brown, Ideal, 1960s, NM+, $35.00. (Photo courtesy whatacharacter.com)

Peanuts, push-button puppet, Snoopy as Joe Cool, Ideal, 1970, NM+ $75.00
Peanuts, push-button puppet, Woodstock Flying Trapeze Toy, Aviva, NM $25.00
Peanuts, Skediddler, Lucy, 4½", Mattel, 1969, M (Fair box) .$125.00
Peanuts, Snoopy Auto Refresheners, stuffed cloth Snoopy figure outline in blk, red collar, 3", Determined, MIP $12.00

Peanuts, Snoopy, Family Car, plastic, Snoopy driver w/3 passengers, 1970s, NMIB $75.00
Peanuts, Snoopy Fun Flashlight, plastic Snoopy figure as Flying Ace, squeeze to light, 4", Garrity, 1980s, MOC..........$15.00
Peanuts, Snoopy Mini Walker, plastic w/up figure, 3", Aviva, 1970s, MOC $10.00
Peanuts, Snoopy Photo Ornaments (Paint-by-Number), Craft House, unused, MOC $15.00
Peanuts, Snoopy's Pound-a-Ball, 17x13", Child Guidance, 1978, EX+IB $50.00
Peanuts, Snoopy Snippers Scissors, plastic, Mattel #7410, 1970s, NM+ $50.00
Peanuts, Snoopy Soaper, plastic, Kenner, 1975, MIB $45.00
Peanuts, snow dome/Snoopy Paperweight, Snoopy face up on house in dome on wht base, 3", Simple Simon Orig, 1968, NMIB $18.00
Peanuts, soap dish, Charlie Brown figure w/ball glove as soap dish, plastic, wall-mount, Avon, 1970s, NM+IB $25.00
Peanuts, squeeze toy, see also figure
Peanuts, squeeze toy, Snoopy as 'Flying Ace' in airplane, side emb 'Snoopy,' vinyl, 4x6" L, Danara, 1970s, NM $25.00
Peanuts, squeeze toy, Snoopy Dog Food Can, vinyl, 3½", Geisler, MIP $15.00
Peanuts, squeeze toy, Snoopy in stocking cap sitting upright leaning against gift box, vinyl, 5", Con Agra, EX+ $8.00
Peanuts, tea set, litho tin, Frieda & Schroeder portraits on plates, gang on tray, 7-pc, Chein, spoons missing, EXIB, A $100.00

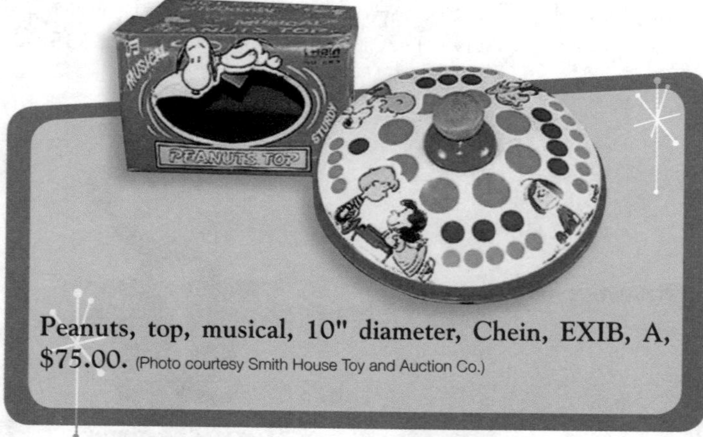

Peanuts, top, musical, 10" diameter, Chein, EXIB, A, $75.00. (Photo courtesy Smith House Toy and Auction Co.)

Peanuts, Woodstock Climbing String Action Toy, plastic, chirps, wings move, 5", Aviva, 1970s, NRFB....................$40.00
Pepe Le Pew, see Looney Tunes
Pink Panther, bank, bright pk & red PP golfer figure emb on yel container, plastic, 9x4x2½", 1970s, NM+ $50.00
Pink Panther, Chatter-Chum, Mattel, 1976, NM.............$50.00
Pink Panther, figure, bendable vinyl, skinny, 10", Amscan, 1970s, NM....................$18.00
Pink Panther, figure, stuffed pk plush in blk satin jacket, plastic eyes, 16", Mighty Star, 1987, NM $25.00
Pink Panther, figure, vinyl, jtd, legs apart, 2-tone tan, 8", Dakin, EX $25.00
Pink Panther, figure, vinyl, jtd arms only, legs together, 2-tone pk, 8", Dakin, 1971, NM $28.00
Pink Panther, gumball machine, transparent pk plastic head on yel base, 8", Tarrson Co, 1970s, NM $30.00
Pink Panther, marionette, compo w/cloth outfit, 12", JJK Assoc, 1960s-70s, MIP ('Want-Um Marionettes' on header card) $75.00
Pink Panther, mug, ceramic head form, pk w/dk pk nose, yel eyes, 4½", Royal Orleans, 1980s, NM+....................$50.00
Pink Panther, push-button puppet, atop cylindrical candy container, misspelling on label, Taiwan, 1970s, unused, M, A.................... $64.00
Pink Panther, windup swimming figure, plastic, Polly Gaz Int'l, 1979, MOC (sealed) $30.00
Pinky & Perky (1950s BBC TV Show), marionette, Pinky Pig, red pants & hat, bl & wht checked shirt, Pelham, NM+IB.$100.00
Planet of the Apes, bank, Galen figure standing, vinyl, 11", Play Pal Plastics, 1974, NM....................$35.00
Planet of the Apes, hand puppet, any character, plush, Commonwealth, 1960s, MIP, ea $150.00
Planet of the Apes, MB, 1974, NMIB....................$50.00
Planet of the Apes, Quick Draw Cartoons set, Pressman, 1967, complete, NMIB....................$15.00
Planet of the Apes, swimming pool, inflatable vinyl, colorful graphics around rim, 45" dia, Azrak-Hamway, 1970s, EX, A....................$175.00
Pogo, figure, Churchy La Femme, vinyl, jtd arms, swivel head, 5", detergent give-away, 1969, NM....................$18.00
Pogo, figure, Pogo, vinyl, blk & red striped top, 4¼", 1969 premium, NM $12.00
Pogo, figure, Porky Pine, vinyl, swivel head, standing holding stick, 5", 1969, NM....................$12.00
Pogo, mug, Churchy La Femme decal on wht plastic, cylindrical w/angled handle open at bottom, 4", 1970s, NM $10.00
Popeye, bath toy, vinyl, Popeye leaning forward in boat (soap dish), 5¼x6¼" L, Stahlwood, 1950s, VG $40.00
Popeye, bookmark, figural Olive Oyl w/tennis racket, plastic, 5", Durham Industries, 1980, NRFC (marked Popeye & Pals) ... $12.00

Popeye, bubble bath containers, Brutus, Colgate-Palmolive Soaky, 1960s, EX, $25.00; Popeye, Colgate-Palmolive Soaky, 1960s, NM, $30.00.

Popeye, Christmas Tree Set (Lights), set of 8 w/characters on ea Mazda lamp, Reliance, 1930s, NMIB.................... $175.00

Popeye, Colorforms Popeye the Weatherman, 1959, NMIB, A, $45.00. (Photo courtesy serioustoyz.com)

Popeye, dexterity game, Popeye the Juggler, tin w/glass top, 3½x5", Bar-Zim Toys, 1929, NM, A........................ $100.00

Popeye, figure, Brutus, stuffed body w/vinyl head & hands, flocked hair & beard, w/blk eye, 22", Presents, 1985, NM+ $28.00

Popeye, figure, Brutus, stuffed body w/vinyl head & hands, toothy grin, synthetic hair & beard, 13", Presents, 1985, NM+.$22.00

Popeye, figure, Olive Oyl, 'Push Me Down & I'll Pop Up,' compo head w/wire body, cloth outfit, umbrella, 7", EX+ ... $525.00

Popeye, figure, Olive Oyl, plush body w/vinyl head, red & wht, 9", Gundikins/Gund, 1950s, EX+..............................$50.00

Popeye, figure, Olive Oyl, stuffed cloth w/vinyl head, hands & shoes, cloth outfit, 12", Presents, 1985, w/tag, NM $20.00

Popeye, figure, Olive Oyl, stuffed printed foam, Olive holding flower bouquet, about 6", Cribmates, 1979, MIP........$22.00

Popeye, figure, Olive Oyl, vinyl, jtd, 7", Dakin, 1970s, NRFB ('Cartoon Theater' box)..$40.00

Popeye, figure, Olive Oyl, vinyl (hollow), swivel head & waist, arms & legs, 9", Multiple Toys, 1960s, NM................$55.00

Popeye, figure, Popeye, foam-stuffed print cloth, 6", Cribmates, 1979, NRFP ('Stuffed Foam Toy' on header).............$22.00

Popeye, figure, Popeye, squeeze vinyl, 4½", Playmakers, 1984, NRFP ('Vinyl Squeaker' on header card)...................$18.00

Popeye, figure, Popeye, squeeze vinyl, 9", Crib Mates, 1979, EX $25.00

Popeye, figure, Popeye, stuffed cloth, w/spinach can, 7", Dean's Rag, 1930s, G... $165.00

Popeye, figure, Popeye, stuffed cloth body w/vinyl head & arms, cloth shirt, 7", Uneeda, 1979, MIB..........................$35.00

Popeye, figure, Popeye, stuffed felt w/cloth outfit, printed face w/ plastic eyes, wooden pipe, can under arm, 11", VG, A.$150.00

Popeye, figure, Popeye, stuffed plush, vinyl head, lt gr & wht, 9½", Gundikins/Gund, 1950s, EX+..........................$50.00

Popeye, figure, Popeye, stuffed plush, vinyl head & arms, 10", Etone Int'l, 1984, NM $20.00

Popeye, figure, Popeye, stuffed plush, vinyl head winking & pipe in mouth, roly-poly body, chimes, 10", Gund, 1950s, EX..$50.00

Popeye, figure, Popeye, vinyl, cloth shirt, jtd head & arms, holding spinach can, 8½", Dakin, 1970s, NM+ $25.00

Popeye, figure, Popeye, vinyl, jtd, 13½", Cameo, 1950s, EX..$125.00

Popeye, figure, Popeye, w/up figure that grows taller while eating spinach, rubber & cloth over tin, 11", 1950s, NM, A. $220.00

Popeye, figure, Popeye, wood, painted bead type with pipe in mouth, 15", Ideal, VG+, A, $450.00. (Photo courtesy Morphy Auctions)

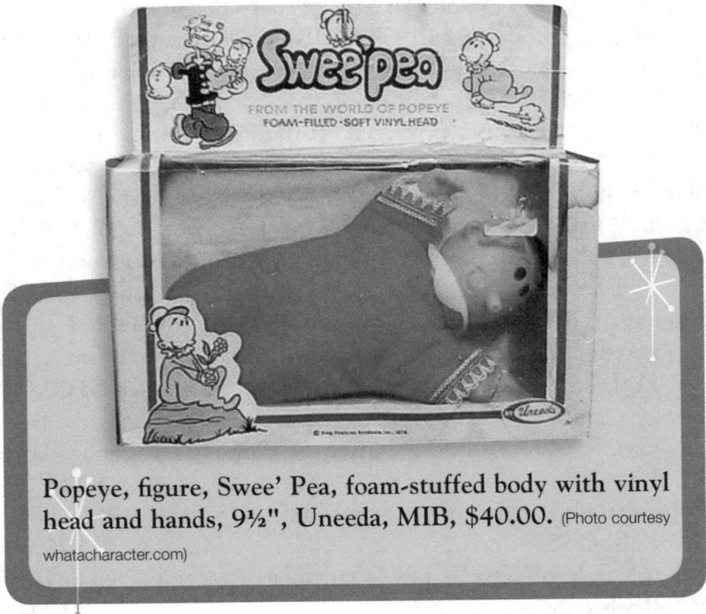

Popeye, figure, Swee' Pea, foam-stuffed body with vinyl head and hands, 9½", Uneeda, MIB, $40.00. (Photo courtesy whatacharacter.com)

Popeye, figure, Wimpy, stuffed cloth body w/vinyl head & hands, flocked shoes, cloth outfit, 12", Presents, 1985, M......$25.00

Popeye, game, Ring Toss, 1980, NRFC $12.00

Popeye, hand puppet, Olive Oyl, cloth body w/vinyl head, Gund, 1950s, EX $50.00

Popeye, Hip-Pop Ball, solid rubber, 2", Ja-Ru, 1981, NRFP..$10.00

Popeye, lamp, diecast metal boat w/'water' base & flag, Popeye figure in 'smokestack' light bulb, 7" H, G, A $230.00

Popeye, magic slate, lg head image of Popeye on header, Lowe, 1963, G $10.00

Popeye, marionette, cloth body w/vinyl head, plastic hands, cloth outfit, 12", Gund, 1950s, NM $75.00

Popeye, marionette, Popeye, compo w/cloth outfit, 12", NRFP ('Want-Up Marionettes' on header card) $75.00

Popeye, Paddle Ball, wooden paddle w/rubber ball attached, 9½", M Shimmel Sons Inc, NRFP....................................$15.00

Popeye, Pin Ball Game, plastic bagatelle, shows Popeye punching Brutus, 7½x4½", M Shimmel Sons Inc, MOC......$12.00

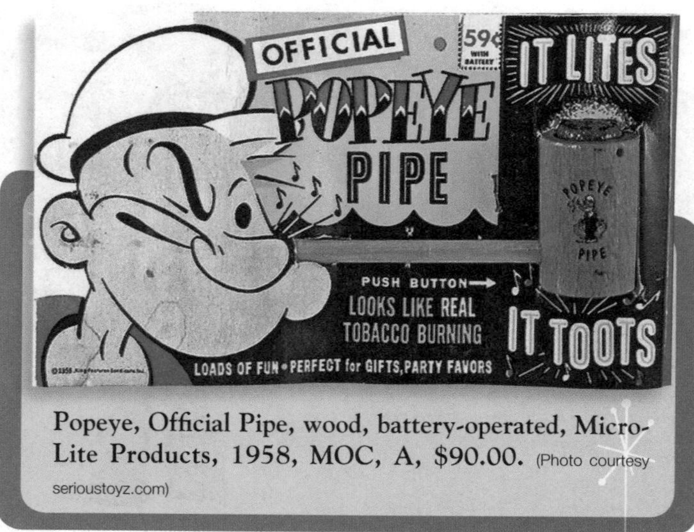

Popeye, Official Pipe, wood, battery-operated, Micro-Lite Products, 1958, MOC, A, $90.00. (Photo courtesy serioustoyz.com)

Popeye, playset, Thimble Theatre Mystery Playhouse, complete, Harding Products, ca 1959, EXIB, A........................ $990.00

Popeye, Pocket Puzzles, 4 dexterity puzzles on 1 card, Ja-Ru, 1989, NRFC...$12.00

Popeye, Popeye Music Box (jack-in-the box), litho tin, Mattel, 11", NM $650.00

Popeye, pull toy, Popeye & Olive Oyl Stretchy Hand Car, Linemar, litho tin, 6½" L, EX+ (VG box), A..............$2,200.00

Popeye, pull toy, Popeye Band Wagon, paper-litho-on-wood, 8½" H, EX $135.00

Popeye, pull toy, Popeye w/spinach can on wheeled surfboard (?), paper-litho-on-wood, articulated arms, 12" H, EX.. $100.00

Popeye, pull toy, SS Popeye, paper-litho-on-wood, Olive Oyl & Wimpy being pulled by Popeye's tugboat, 16", EX+ $225.00

Popeye, push-button puppet, any character, Kohner, 1960s, NM, ea from $50 to...$75.00

Popeye, slide-tile puzzle, blk & wht plastic, 4 character images, Roalex, unused, MOC..$50.00

Popeye, squeeze toy, Olive Oyl's head on squeeze hdl, vinyl, 5", Crib Mates, 1979, NRFP..$18.00

Popeye, squeeze toy, Popeye's head on squeeze hdl, vinyl, 6", Crib Mates, 1979, NRFP..$18.00

Popeye, stamp set, Popeye Comics Department, StamperKraft #4007, complete, used, EX $75.00

Popeye, Super Magnet, plastic horseshoe shape, 9½", Laurie Import Limited, 1976, NRFP...................................$15.00

Popeye, Telephone w/Bell, plastic w/Popeye image in center of rotary dial, Larami, 1970s, NRFC $15.00

Popeye, Wood Slate (chalkboard), Ja-Ru, 1983, NRFC....$12.00

Power Rangers, bubble bath container, any character, Kid Care, 1994, M...$6.00

Punch & Judy, hand puppet, cloth body w/vinyl head, Peter Puppet Playthings, 1949, MIB, ea $75.00

Punch & Judy, hand puppet set, 12 different, pnt wood w/cloth clothing, 13" Punch, German, EX, A...................... $700.00

Punch and Judy, hand puppet set of 13 different with hangman's gibbet, painted wood with cloth clothing, 18" Punch, EX+, A, $3,300.00. (Photo courtesy Noel Barrett Antiques & Auctions)

Raggedy Ann & Andy, Animal Friends, Larami, 1977, unused, MOC..$12.00

Raggedy Ann & Andy, baby rattle, plastic lollipop type w/Andy image on wht, 6", Stahlwood Toy, 1980s, MIP $20.00

Raggedy Ann and Andy, bank, Andy in 'Spirit of '76' outfit, vinyl and cloth, 9", Royalty, 1974, NM, $35.00. (Photo courtesy whatacharacter.com)

Raggedy Ann & Andy, bank, Andy sitting w/arms at sides, red shirt w/wht collar, vinyl, Imco, 1970s, NM.................$25.00

Raggedy Ann & Andy, bank, Andy standing w/ice-cream cone behind back on grassy base, compo, 7", Boudoir Pets, 1969, NM...$20.00

Raggedy Ann & Andy, bank, Ann & Andy seated leaning on each other, pnt compo, 6", Determined, 1971, EX+...$25.00

Raggedy Ann & Andy, bank, Ann seated, bl dress w/wht pinafore, ruffled collar/cuffs, blk shoes, 7", Play Pal, 1970s, EX $20.00
Raggedy Ann & Andy, bank, Ann standing w/arms at sides, ceramic, 8", Lefton, 1970s, NM........ $25.00
Raggedy Ann & Andy, bubble bath container, Ann, Lander, 1960s, NM $25.00
Raggedy Ann & Andy, figure, Ann or Andy, inflatable vinyl, 15", Ideal, NM, ea........ $15.00
Raggedy Ann & Andy, hand puppet, red/wht/bl cloth body, stuffed head, yarn hair, plastic eyes, Knickerbocker, 1960s, NM........ $50.00
Raggedy Ann & Andy, ornament, Andy figure w/arms at sides & legs spread, 4", pnt ceramic, 4", Duncan, 1970s, NM+ .. $10.00
Raggedy Ann & Andy, ornament, Ann standing w/hands together in front, hollow resin, 4", MacMillan Inc, 1992, NM........ $10.00

Raggedy Ann and Andy, pencil sharpener, 6", Janex, 1974, NM, $25.00. (Photo courtesy whatacharacter.com)

Raggedy Ann & Andy, rag doll, Andy, 5", plaid shirt, lt bl pants, sailor's hat, Knickerbocker, 1976, MIB $25.00
Raggedy Ann & Andy, rag doll, Andy, 6½", plaid shirt, bl pants, bl bow tie, Knickerbocker, 1970s, MIP $35.00
Raggedy Ann & Andy, rag doll, Andy, 6½", red & wht checked shirt, bl pants, bl bow tie, Knickerbocker, 1970s, NM........ $12.00
Raggedy Ann & Andy, rag doll, Andy, 13", red & wht checked shirt, bl pants, wht sailor's hat, Knickerbocker, 1979, MIB....... $75.00
Raggedy Ann & Andy, rag doll, Ann, 5", printed wht collar & apron straps outlined in blk, Knickerbocker, 1976, MIB........ $25.00
Raggedy Ann & Andy, rag doll, Ann, 6½", floral dress w/wht apron & collar, Knickerbocker, 1970s, MIP........ $35.00
Raggedy Ann & Andy, rag doll, Ann, 12", floral dress w/wht pinafore, Knickerbocker, 1979, NM+IB........ $75.00
Raggedy Ann & Andy, rag doll, Ann, 31", floral dress w/wht pinafore & bloomers, stenciled heart on chest, 1950s, EX $115.00
Raggedy Ann & Andy, squeeze toy, Ann seated w/hands on tummy in patched outfit, vinyl, 5", EX+ $15.00
Raggedy Ann & Andy, squeeze toy, Ann standing in pk dress w/wht apron & collar, 6", Regent Baby Prod, 1970s, MIP $22.00
Raggedy Ann & Andy, toothbrush, Andy, b/o, Janex, 1973, unused, MIB........ $45.00
Raggedy Ann & Andy, wall plaque, Ann figure standing holding coffeepot, cb, 14", Doll Toy Co, 1972, EX+ $10.00
Rainbow Brite, bubble bath container, Hallmark, 1995, NM .. $8.00
Ren & Stempy, figure, Ren, bendable stuffed cloth w/rubber face, bloodshot eyes, toothy frown, 12", Mattel, 1992, NM+........ $15.00
Ren & Stempy, figure, Ren, stuffed plush, fleshy pk, 17", Dakin, 1992, NM........ $15.00
Ren & Stempy, figure, Talking Ren Hoek, stuffed cloth w/vinyl head, 10", Mattel, 1992, unused, MIP........ $25.00
Ren & Stempy, Spitballs figure, soft rubber, Ren holding throat as if choking, eyes bulging, rubber, 5", Dakin, 1992, NM+ ... $12.00
Richie Rich, figure, Gloria Gad, PVC, 2½", Dimensions, 1981, MOC (sealed) $10.00
Ricochet Rabbit, hand puppet, printed cloth body as sheriff & name across bottom, vinyl head, Ideal, 1960s, NM . $100.00
Robocop, bubble bath container, Cosway, 1990, NM........ $10.00
Rocky & Friends, bank, Bullwinkle standing against tree trunk waving, brn vinyl, 12", Play Pal Plastics, 1973, EX+ $65.00

Rocky and Friends, bank, Bullwinkle standing with arms down and 'B' on green sweater, JM Co/Hong Kong, 1977, 10½", NM+, A, $100.00. (Photo courtesy serioustoyz.com)

Rocky & Friends, bank, Bullwinkle standing w/hands on hips on base, vinyl, 10", Imco, 1977, EX+ $50.00
Rocky & Friends, bank, Bullwinkle w/legs crossed leaning against tree trunk, brn vinyl, 11½", EX+ $65.00
Rocky & Friends, bank, rnd clock shape w/Bullwinkle on face w/arms as clock hands, plastic, 9x6", Larami Corp, 1969, MIP.... $75.00
Rocky & Friends, bank, Rocky, Bullwinkle, Sherman & Mr Peabody in band, figural ceramic, PAT Ward, c 1960, 5", EX, A .. $400.00
Rocky & Friends, bank, Rocky & His Friends Bank w/Rocky, Mr Peabody & Bullwinkle holding signs, ceramic, 5x7", 1960s, M. $175.00

Rocky & Friends, bop bag, Snidley Whiplash, inflatable vinyl, marked PAT Ward, 1982, M....................................$25.00

Rocky & Friends, bubble bath container, any character, Colgate-Palmolive, 1960s, NM, ea...$30.00

Rocky & Friends, Bullwinkle's Double Boomerang's, Larami #3804, 1969, MIP...$30.00

Rocky & Friends, Bullwinkle's Electric Quiz Game, Larami, 1971, unused, MIP..$20.00

Rocky & Friends, figure, Bullwinkle, bendable rubber, 'B' on gr sweater, 7", Jesco, 1991, MOC..................................$12.00

Rocky & Friends, figure, Bullwinkle, stuffed plush, 'B' on lt bl tank top, 12", Mighty Star, 1991, EX.........................$10.00

Rocky & Friends, figure, Bullwinkle, stuffed plush, 'B' on orange shirt, 16½", Wallace Berry, 1982, NM+......................$25.00

Rocky & Friends, figure, Bullwinkle, stuffed plush, 'B' on red sweater, felt antlers, 12", Dakin, 1978, w/tag, M.........$45.00

Rocky & Friends, figure, Bullwinkle, stuffed plush, gr scarf, red & wht striped cap, 24", Macy's Dept Store, 1996, NM+.$12.00

Rocky & Friends, figure, Dudley Do-Right, bendable vinyl, Wham-O, 1972, EX..$20.00

Rocky & Friends, figure, Natasha, bendable rubber, purple knee-length dress, Jesco, 1991, MOC...............................$10.00

Rocky & Friends, figure, Natasha, bendable rubber, purple knee-length dress, Wham-O, 1972, G...............................$15.00

Rocky & Friends, figure, Rocky, bendable rubber, 5", Jesco, 1991, MOC...$10.00

Rocky & Friends, figure, Rocky, stuffed plush, 12", Wallace Berrie, 1982, NM+...$20.00

Rocky & Friends, figure, Rocky, stuffed plush w/vinyl head, 9½", 1966, rare, VG..$150.00

Rocky & Friends, figure, Rocky, vinyl, jtd, 6½", Dakin, 1970s, MIB ('Cartoon Theater' box)....................................$75.00

Rocky & Friends, figure, Sherman, bendable rubber, 4", Wham-O, 1972, NM...$20.00

Rocky & Friends, figure, Snidley Whiplash, bendable rubber, blk & wht w/yel eyes, 5", Wham-O, 1970s, MOC............$28.00

Rocky & Friends, figure set, Bullwinkle & Rocky, plastic, jtd, 5" & 1½", Exclusive Toy Prod, 1998, unused, MIB.........$15.00

Rocky & Friends, pencil case, vinyl w/images of Rocky & Bullwinkle on trapeze bars, zippered, 4x8", 1962, scarce, NM+..$75.00

Rocky & Friends, wallet, Larami, MOC, $25.00. (Photo courtesy gasolinealleyantiques.com)

Rootie Kazootie, handkerchief, cloth w/Gala Poochie Pup in clubhouse, 9x9", RK Inc, 1950s, EX...........................$25.00

Rugrats, bubble bath container, Tommy, Kid Care, 1997, NM..$6.00

Rugrats, figure, Phil, vinyl w/cloth outfit, 4½", Mattel, 1998, NRFP..$10.00

Rugrats, hand puppet, Tommy, cloth body w/vinyl head & hands, Mattel, 1998, M...$8.00

Rugrats, oranment, Chuckie figure w/lg snowball, resin, 3½", Adler, M...$9.00

Rugrats (Movie), figure, Angelica, vinyl w/yarn hair & cloth outfit, 6", Mattel, 1998, NRFB.................................$10.00

Scooby Doo, bank, Scooby seated upright, vinyl, 6", 1980, EX. $18.00

Scooby Doo, figure, Scooby, stuffed plush, standing on all 4s, 7½", Sutton, 1970, NM.......................................$30.00

Scooby Doo, figure, Scooby, hard-stuffed ribbed cloth, 8", Dakin, 1979, NM, $15.00. (Photo courtesy whatacharacter.com)

Scooby Doo, figure, Scrappy, vinyl, 6½", Dakin, NM+, $75.00. (Photo courtesy whatacharacter.com)

Scooby Doo, figure, Scrappy, vinyl, standing upright, jtd, 6½", Dakin, 1982, NM+ $75.00
Scooby Doo, figure, Shaggy, bendable rubber, 5½", Equity Marketing, 1999, NM $5.00
Scooby Doo, night-light, Scooby, Scrappy & Ghost, bisque, 7", 1980s, NM $28.00
Scooby Soo, figure, Scooby, stuffed plush, felt tongue, seated, 8", Sutton, 1970, NM....................$28.00
Sesame Street, see also Muppets

Sesame Street, bank, Bert figure, vinyl, 13", New York Vinyl, 1971, EX+, $25.00.
(Photo courtesy whatacharacter.com)

Sesame Street, bank, Big Bird hugging lg egg while seated on nest w/'Sesame Street' sign, compo, 6", Gorham, 1978, NM+ .$20.00
Sesame Street, bank, Cookie Monster standing holding cookie jar, vinyl, 9½", Illco, 1980s, NM+ $15.00
Sesame Street, bath toy, bubble-blowing Elmo figure holding on to blanket, vinyl, 7", Kid Dimension, 1993, NM........$10.00
Sesame Street, bath toy, Cookie Monster eating cookie on innertube, vinyl, 4", Playskool, NM....................$6.00
Sesame Street, Bert Stacking Toy, figural, 10½", Child Guidance, 1975, NMIB....................$25.00
Sesame Street, bookends, plastic-framed photo images of characters, 7½", WPC Inc, 1980, NM, pr....................$20.00
Sesame Street, bubble bath container, Elmo, Kid Care, 1997, NM....................$6.00
Sesame Street, cake topper, Bert figure waving on oval base, plastic, 2½", Wilton, 1980s, M $5.00
Sesame Street, diecast metal toy, Grover in helicopter w/plastic propeller & plastic wheels, 2½", Hasbro, 1981, NM...$10.00
Sesame Street, figure, any character, PVC, 4", Jack-in-the-Box premium, MIP, ea....................$5.00
Sesame Street, figure, Bert, stuffed cloth, 8", Applause, 1980s-90s, NM+ $8.00
Sesame Street, figure, Bert, stuffed cloth, 10", Rag Doll #2601, Knickerbocker, 1975, MIB $35.00
Sesame Street, figure, Bert, stuffed cloth, 18", Applause, 1980s, NM+ $18.00
Sesame Street, figure, Big Bird, PVC, playing guitar, 3½", Tara, 1985, MOC....................$10.00
Sesame Street, figure, Big Bird, stuffed plush, stuffed cloth striped legs, bl felt shirt w/name, 10", Hasbro, NM+ $10.00
Sesame Street, figure, Big Bird, stuffed plush, 11" or 13" (fireman's hat), Knickerbocker, 1970s-80s, NM+, ea $15.00
Sesame Street, figure, Big Bird, stuffed plush, 12", Applause, 1993, NM....................$10.00
Sesame Street, figure, Big Bird, vinyl, jtd arms, swivel head & torso, 5", Tara Toy, 1985, NM+ $6.00
Sesame Street, figure, Cookie Monster, plastic (hollow), standing & waving, bright bl, 6½", CBS Inc, 1985, NM+ $10.00
Sesame Street, figure, Cookie Monster, stuffed plush, 'Cookies Make Me Happy' on apron, 12", Applause, NM.........$10.00
Sesame Street, figure, Cookie Monster, stuffed plush, lg plastic eyes, mouth wide open, 15", Applause, 1980s-90s, EX+ $10.00
Sesame Street, figure, Cookie Monster, stuffed plush, lg plastic eyes, 8", Nadel & Sons, 1980s, NM+ $12.00
Sesame Street, figure, Cookie Monster, stuffed plush, plastic eyes, musical, sings 'Sing,' 9", Knickerbocker, EX+ $18.00
Sesame Street, figure, Cookie Monster, stuffed plush, plastic eyes, 10", Knickerbocker, 1970s-80s, NM....................$12.00
Sesame Street, figure, Cookie Monster, stuffed plush, 5", Applause, 1980s, NM+ $8.00
Sesame Street, figure, Count, beanbag plush, gr cape, 8", Tyco Preschool, 1997, NM+ $12.00
Sesame Street, figure, Elmo, beanbag plush, plastic eyes, 9", Tyco, 1997, NM+ $8.00
Sesame Street, figure, Ernie, stuffed cloth, felt type w/flat felt hands, blk fuzzy hair, 6", Applause, NM+ $8.00
Sesame Street, figure, Ernie, stuffed cloth, orange parachute type, bl shirt w/yel dots, fuzzy hair, 12", Tyco, 1995, M $10.00
Sesame Street, figure, Ernie, stuffed cloth, pillow type w/printed image of Ernie waving, 17", NM+....................$15.00
Sesame Street, figure, Ernie, stuffed cloth, vinyl head/hands, striped sweater, print sneakers, 12", Applause, 1980s, NM....................$15.00
Sesame Street, figure, Grover, stuffed plush, bl w/lg pk nose, plastic eyes, 7", Applause, 1995, M $10.00
Sesame Street, figure, Grover, stuffed plush, bl w/lg pk nose, plastic eyes, 17", Nanco, 2000, NM+ $12.00
Sesame Street, figure, Grover, stuffed plush, bl w/lg pk nose, plastic eyes, 30", Nanco, 2003, M....................$20.00
Sesame Street, figure, Guy Smiley, stuffed cloth, felt-like w/blk fuzzy hair, 9", Tyco Preschool, 1997, M $10.00
Sesame Street, figure, Honker, beanbag plush, 9", Tyco Preschool, 1997, NM+....................$8.00
Sesame Street, figure, Oscar the Grouch, beanbag plush w/plastic eyes, 10", Knickerbocker, EX+ $12.00
Sesame Street, finger puppet, any character, vinyl, Applause, Dakin or Tara Toys, NM, ea from $5 to $8.00
Sesame Street, friction toy, any character, plastic, about 4x6", Illco, 1980s-90s, NM, ea from $8 to....................$10.00
Sesame Street, globe, w/removable base, 15" H, Rand McNally, 1985, NM....................$25.00

Sesame Street, hand puppet, Bert, stuffed cloth from head to feet, plastic eyes, Applause, EX $10.00
Sesame Street, hand puppet, Big Bird, plush w/felt hands & beak, yarn topknot, plastic eyes, Child Guidance, 1980, NM.$15.00
Sesame Street, hand puppet, Big Bird, plush w/stuffed felt hands, plastic eyes, Applause/Wallace Barry, NM....$10.00
Sesame Street, hand puppet, Cookie Monster, bright bl furry plush w/lg plastic eyeballs, Child Horizon, 1970s, NM....$20.00
Sesame Street, hand puppet, Oscar the Grouch, shaggy plush, Topper, 1970s, EX+....$20.00
Sesame Street, jack-in-the-box, Big Bird pops up w/guitar, plastic, 10", Playskool, 1986, NM+ $25.00
Sesame Street, lamp, Bert & Ernie w/instruments in wheeled washtub on rnd wooden base, graphical shade, 16", 1970s, NM....$35.00
Sesame Street, lamp, Big Bird figure in nest reading by lamppost on rnd wooden base w/ball feet, 20", NM $40.00
Sesame Street, magnet, Bert & Ernie figures holding 'Let's Be Friends!' sign, PVC, 3", 1980s, NM $5.00
Sesame Street, marionette, 'Make Your Own Big Bird Marionette,' Friends Industries, 1977, complete, unused, MIB....$40.00
Sesame Street, ornaments, any character, 1980s-90s, MIP, ea from $8 to $10.00
Sesame Street, Party Blowouts, features Big Bird, pkg of 8, Party Maker Beach Prod, 1990, unused, MIP....$8.00

Sesame Street, pull toy, Cookie Monster on tricycle, Hasbro, 1982, M, $20.00. (Photo courtesy whatacharacter.com)

Sesame Street, push-button puppet, Ernie standing on base w/ Sesame Street label, 8", Tara Toy Co, EX+ $20.00
Sesame Street, radio, w/up musical, plastic, shows emb Big Biord on front, 6", Illco, 1980s, NM+ $12.00
Sesame Street, squeeze toy, any character, Playskool, 1980s, NM+, ea....$8.00
Sesame Street, squeeze toy, Cookie Monster sitting holding cookie jar, vinyl, 4", Child Guidance, 1978, NM $12.00
Sesame Street, squeeze toy, Elmo on his knees w/toy cement truck, 5", Tyco Preschool, EX....$6.00
Sesame Street, TV set w/Big Bird figure, musical, plastic, 9x11", Illco, 1980s, EX+ $15.00
Sesame Street, windup toy, Big Bird on tricycle w/name on plaque, plastic, 7", Illco, 1980s, NM $12.00
Shazam, flowerpot, ceramic, wht w/Shazam in flight saying 'Super Plants,' 3", 1970s, M $15.00
Shmoo, see Li'l Abner
Simpsons, bank, any character, vinyl, Street Kids, 1990, NM+ $10.00

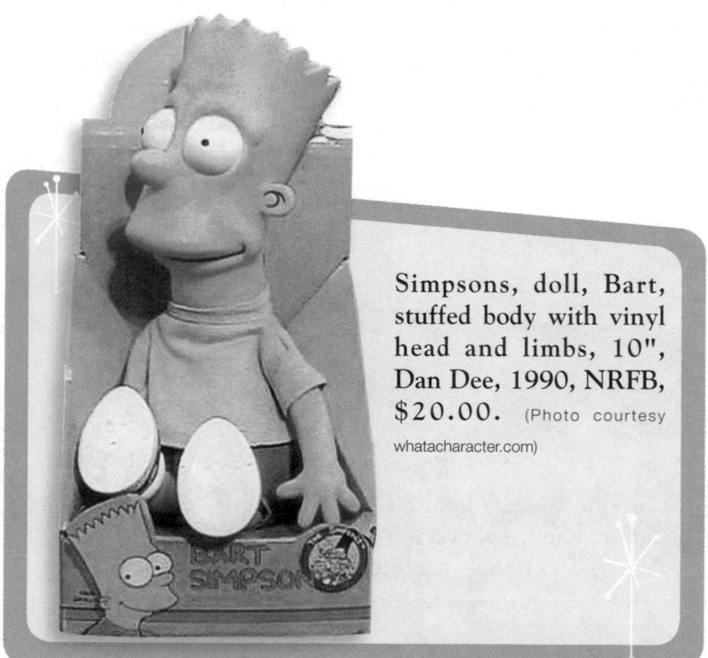

Simpsons, doll, Bart, stuffed body with vinyl head and limbs, 10", Dan Dee, 1990, NRFB, $20.00. (Photo courtesy whatacharacter.com)

Simpsons, doll, Bart, stuffed cloth w/plastic bug eyes, printed nose & mouth, cloth outfit, 18", Dan Dee, 1990, NM....$15.00
Simpsons, doll, Bart, stuffed cloth w/print face, bl cloth outfits & shoes, 11", Dan Dee, 1990, MOC $12.00
Simpsons, doll, Bart, stuffed cloth w/vinyl head & hands, knit top, bl felt pants & shoes, 5", Dan Dee, 1990, M....$8.00
Simpsons, doll, Bart, stuffed plush w/vinyl head, cloth outfit, 24", Acme, 1990, NM....$22.00
Simpsons, doll, Bart, vinyl, bl cloth shirt & shorts, bl shoes, holding slingshot, 9", Presents, 1990, M $15.00
Simpsons, doll, Cooties Man!, stuffed body w/vinyl head, arms & legs, 12", Dan Dee, 1990, NM....$15.00
Simpsons, doll, Homer, Talking & Dancing, dressed as Santa, b/o, Gemmy Industries, 2004, MIB $20.00
Simpsons, doll, Lisa, stuffed cloth, printed features & necklace, red felt dress & shoes, 11", Dan Dee, 1990, M....$12.00
Simpsons, doll, Maggie, stuffed cloth w/vinyl head & hands, bl night gown, 7½", Burger King, 1990, NM+ $10.00
Simpsons, eight ball, turn ball to reveal answers to questions in triangle, image of Bart, 1990s, NM+....$10.00
Simpsons, figure, any character, vinyl, 4" to 6", Jesco, 1990s, NM+, ea from to....$8.00
Simpsons, figure, any character figure, stuffed cloth w/vinyl head, cloth outfit, 12", Burger King, 1990, MIP, ea $10.00
Simpsons, gumball machine, plastic globe w/Lisa decal, front reads The Simpsons, 6", Rinco, 2000, NM+....$12.00
Simpsons, ornament, Bart figure w/hands at sides, PVC, 4", 1990, EX+ $6.00

Simpsons, soap figure, Bart, 5", Cosrich, 1990, unused, MIB (box reads 'Wash It, Dude!') $10.00
Skeezix, pull toy, die-cut pressed wood, Skeezix being pulled by Pal (dog), pnt detail, 6½" H, Trixie Toy, 1930s, G....$65.00
Skeezix, see Gasoline Alley
Skippy, figure, pnt bisque, standing on rnd base w/name, 5½", Percy L Crosby, 1930s, VG+ $50.00
Sluggo, see Nancy
Smokey Bear, see Advertising category under USDA Forest Service
Smurfs, bank, Smurf figure standing w/legs together holding wht heart in hand, plastic, bl & wht, 11", Renzi, 1980s, EX..$12.00
Smurfs, Chatter-Chum figure, any character, plastic, 7", Mattel, 1980s, EX $20.00
Smurfs, figure, baby Smurf on tummy, stuffed plush in pk PJ's, 6½" H, Applause, 1980s, NM....$10.00
Smurfs, figure, Brainy Smurf, bisque, standing holding book, 4", Wallace Barry, 1982, M $20.00

Smurfs, figure, Gargamel, stuffed cloth, 15", M, $15.00.
(Photo courtesy gasolinealleyantiques.com)

Smurfs, figure, Greedy Smurf, bisque, in chef's hat & carrying lg birthday cake, 4", Wallace Berrie, 1980s, M $22.00
Smurfs, figure, Hefty Smurf, bisque, using mallet to pound Smurf Village sign into ground, Wallace Berrie, 1980, NM+....$22.00
Smurfs, figure, Papa Smurf, stuffed red & bl plush w/wht shaggy beard, seated pose, 8", Wallace Berrie, 1980s, NM.....$10.00
Smurfs, figure, Papa Smurf, vinyl, jtd, 3¼", Irwin, 1996, MOC (sealed) $10.00
Smurfs, figure, Smurf kneeling looking up holding candle w/red flame, squeeze vinyl, 5", Danara, 1984, NM+ $12.00
Smurfs, figure, Smurf standing w/eyes closed, smiling & hand to chin, squeeze vinyl, bl & wht, 5", Haco, 1980s, NM..$12.00
Smurfs, ornament, satin ball, No 1 Teacher, Brainy & Papa Smurf at chalkboard, 3", Wallace Berrie, 1982, MIB..$10.00
Smurfs, push-button puppet, any character, Kohner, 1980s, NM, ea, from $20 to $25.00
Smurfs, top, litho tin w/rubber suction cup on bottom, Ohio Art, 1980s, 10x9" dia, EX+ $25.00
Smurfs, toy telephone, Smurf atop desk phone w/rotary dial, plastic, 10" H, HG Toys, 1980s, VG+ $28.00
Snuffy Smith, cloth body w/vinyl head, Gund, 1950s, NM .$100.00
Soupy Sales, hand puppet, yel cloth body w/red trim ('Soupy Sez Let's Do the Mouse'), vinyl head, Gund, 1965, NM+ $225.00
South Park, figure, Cartman, stuffed plush, 9", Fun 4 All Corp, 1998, NM....$10.00
South Park, figure, Cartman, vinyl, 6", Fun 4 All Corp, 1998, NM+ $10.00
South Park, figure, Kenny McCormick, stuffed plush, head hidden in orange parka, 7", Fun 4 All, 1998, NM+ $12.00
Speedy Gonzales, see Looney Tunes
Spider-Man, bank, bust figure w/arms crossed & blk spider logo on chest, plastic, Street Kids, 1991, NFRP $16.00
Spider-Man, Crazy Foam, unused, 1970s, MIP....$50.00
Spider-Man, figure, vinly, jtd arms, 13", Presents/Hamilton Gifts, 1990, M (w/hang tag), ...$45.00
Spider-Man, hand puppet, plastic body w/vinyl head, 1970s, NM+ $40.00

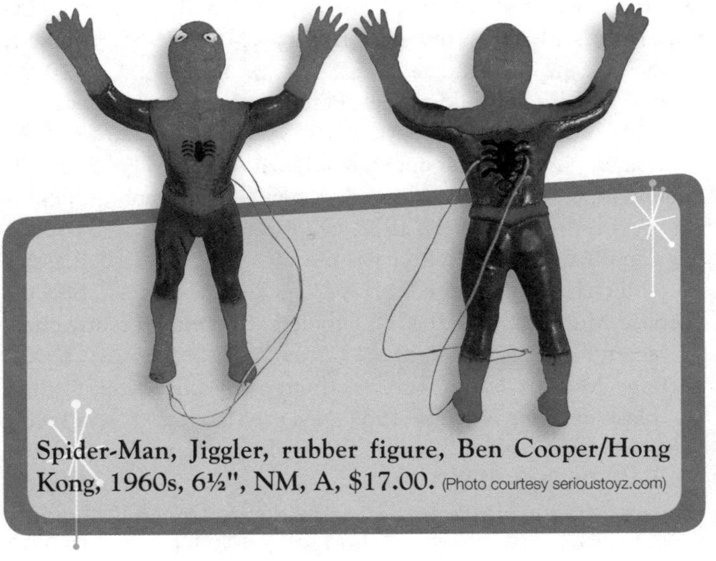
Spider-Man, Jiggler, rubber figure, Ben Cooper/Hong Kong, 1960s, 6½", NM, A, $17.00. (Photo courtesy serioustoyz.com)

Spider-Man, Kazoo, plastic head shape, Straco, MOC $50.00
Spider-Man, Official Big Buckle Secret Gumball Dispenser, Superior Toy, 1985, MOC (sealed) $35.00
Steve Canyon, Jet Helmet, Ideal, 1959, NMIB, A $75.00
Super Mario Bros, bank, Mario standing w/arms at sides, vinyl, 5½", Applause, 1989, EX $12.00
Super Mario Bros, figure, Mario, stuffed cloth & vinyl, 12", Applause, 1989, NM+ $20.00
Superboy, Oil Painting by Numbers, Hasbro/NNP, 1965, unused, NMIP (sealed), A $225.00
Superman, bubble bath container, Avon, 1978, unused, MIB $25.00
Superman, bubble bath container, Colgate-Palmolive, 1965, NM $25.00
Superman, flicker rings, gold-tone plastic w/various scenes, 1966, EX to NM, A, ea.... $150.00

Superman, hand puppet, printed cloth body w/name & molded vinyl head, Ideal, 1960s, NM $100.00

Superman, Kiddie Paddlers, Super-Swim, 1940s, NMIB, $150.00. (Photo courtesy serioustoyz.com)

Superman, Krypto-Raygun, flashes picture stories on the wall, plastic, b/o, complete, VGIB $750.00

Superman, Kryptonite Rock, Pro Arts, 1977, MIB $90.00

Superman, Movie Viewer, Chemtoy/NPP, 1965, unused, MOC.. $20.00

Superman, Muscle Building Set, Peter Puppet Playthings #1001, 1954, complete, EXIB, A....................................... $225.00

Superman, push-button puppet, Kohner, 1960s, NM+... $120.00

Superman, record player, suitcase style w/allover graphics including inside lid, 12x9½", 1978, EX, A $160.00

Superman, wallet, yel vinyl w/snap closure, Standard Plastics (Mattel), 1966, unused, M, A $88.00

Teenage Mutant Ninja Turtles, bubble bath container, any character, Kid Care, 1990, M $8.00

Teenage Mutant Ninja Turtles, figure, any character, stuffed plush, 8", Ace Novelty, 1989, NM+, ea $10.00

Teenage Mutant Ninja Turtles, Safety Target Set, Henry Gordy Int'l, 1990s, NRFP...$10.00

Teenage Mutant Ninja Turtles, snow dome, Donatello holding Christmas tree, plastic, 4", Int'l Silver Co, NM+ $10.00

Teenage Mutant Ninja Turtles, snow dome, Leonardo w/ Noel book, name on gr base, 4", Int'l Silver Co, 1990, NM+.. $10.00

Teenie Weenies, doll set, oil cloth w/printed features & detail, set of 3, 3" to 5¾", 1920s, rare, VG to EX, A.......... $150.00

Tennessee Tuxedo, bubble bath container, w/ice-cream cone, Colgate-Palmolive, 1960s, NM $20.00

Thor (Super Hero), hand puppet, printed vinyl body w/molded vinyl head, Imperial Toy, 1978, MIP..........................$45.00

Three Stooges, figure, any, stuffed cloth in blk & wht striped prisoner's suit, 15", Play-by-Play, 1999, NM+, ea $15.00

Three Stooges, figure, any, stuffed cloth in mismatched plaid outfits, 16", Play-by-Play, 1999, M, ea $15.00

Three Stooges, figure, any, stuffed cloth in skeleton's outfit, 16", Good Stuff, 2002, NM+ $12.00

Three Stooges, hand puppet, any character, printed cloth bodies w/names, molded vinyl heads, 1950s, EX+, ea......... $150.00

Tom & Jerry, bank, Jerry popping out of cheese wedge, ceramic, 4x5½" L, Gorham, 1981, M..$45.00

Tom & Jerry, bank, litho tin container w/Tom chasing Jerry carrying piggy bank, T&J Savings Bank, 5", Presents, 1989, NM..$12.00

Tom & Jerry, bank, Tom resting atop hamburger, ceramic, 5", Gorham, 1980s, M...$50.00

Tom & Jerry, bank, Tom seated w/legs crossed holding sleeping Jerry, ceramic, 6", Gorham, 1980s, M.........................$45.00

Tom & Jerry, bath toy, Jerry in duck intertube on seashell, hole in duck's mouth squirts water, 3", Turner, 1993, NM+........$5.00

Tom & Jerry, Fight the Friction Mouse, plastic mouse, 3", Larami, 1970s, MOC $12.00

Tom & Jerry, figure, bendable rubber, 7", Just Toys, 1989, NM..$8.00

Tom & Jerry, figure, Jerry, plastic, standing showing muscles on gr kidney-shaped base, Marx, 1973, EX+ $28.00

Tom & Jerry, figure, Tom, bendable rubber, 6", 1979, EX+..$8.00

Tom & Jerry, figure, Tom, plastic, standing w/hands on hips, lt bl & wht w/peachy ears, yel eyes, 6", Marx, 1973, EX+..$28.00

Tom & Jerry, figure, Tom, squeeze vinyl, yel & wht, standing rigidly w/fists clinched at sides, 1970, NM+....................$25.00

Tom and Jerry, figure, Tom with two small mice in creel, stuffed cloth with vinyl wading boots, 18", Italian, 1960s, EX, $725.00. (Photo courtesy Morphy Auctions)

Tom & Jerry, figure set, bendable vinyl, Amscan Inc, 1967, MOC, A..$25.00

Tom & Jerry, figure set, plastic, 6" lt bl Tom & 5" brn Jerry, Marx, 1973, MIB...$65.00

Tom & Jerry, hand puppet, Tom, plush body w/vinyl head, 1989, NM..$15.00

Tom & Jerry, hand puppet, Tom or Jerry, cloth body w/vinyl head, Zany, 1950s, EX, ea $75.00

Tom & Jerry, kaleidoscope, litho metal, Green Monk, 1970s, NM+ $28.00

Tom & Jerry, pull toy, all-in-one Tom & Jerry figure standing on 4-wheeled bl & pk plastic platform, 7", Combex, NM......$50.00

Tom & Jerry, soap figures, Tom or Jerry, unused, MIB (box reads Fine Quality Soap), ea $20.00
Tom & Jerry, squeeze toy, Tom leaning back w/legs crossed in life preserver, rubber, 4" L, Lanco, 1990s, M $12.00

Tom and Jerry, Water Gun, Marx, 1973, NMIB, $50.00. (Photo courtesy whatacharacter.com)

Tom Corbett Space Cadett, doll, compo w/cloth outfit, sleep eyes, 7½", EX, A $85.00
Toonerville Trolley, figure set, Mickey Maquire, Powerful Katrinka, Skipper & trolley, bisque, Borgfeldt, 1931, NMIB, A . $230.00
Top Cat, see Hanna-Barbera
Umbriago (Jimmy Durante's Friend), printed oilcloth body w/ compo head, American Merchandise, 1945, NM .$100.00
Underdog, bank, Underdog standing w/arms at sides, vinyl, 8", Play Pals, 1970s, NM $40.00

Underdog, bank, standing with elbows out, plastic, JM Co./Hong Kong, 10", NM, A, $40.00. (Photo courtesy serious-toyz.com)

Underdog, bank, Underdog standing w/hands on hips, vinyl, 11", Play Pals, 1973, NM+ $50.00
Underdog, playset, 'It's a boat — it's a plane — it's a car!, it's Underdog,' Playskool, 1974, NMIB, A $95.00
Universal Monsters, bubble bath container, any character, Colgate-Palmolive, 1960s, NM $50.00
Universal Monsters, Famous Monsters Plaster Casting Kit, Creature From the Black Lagoon, Rapco, 1974, unused, MIB, A $160.00
Universal Monsters, figure, any of 6 Glow-in-the-Dark Movie Monsters, about 5", Uncle Milton Industries, 1990, MOC, ea $12.00
Universal Monsters, figure, Creature From the Black Lagoon, glow-in-the-dark plastic, 6", Uncle Milton, 1990, MOC $12.00
Universal Monsters, figure, Dracula, bendable rubber, 6", JusToys, 1991, MOC $10.00
Universal Monsters, figure, Dracula, stuffed, printed features, satin cape, w/cb coffin, Commonwealth Toy & Novelty, EX+ $40.00
Universal Monsters, figure, Mummy, vinyl jtd, 7½", Imperial (card reads Universal Classic Movie Monster) $22.00
Universal Monsters, figure, vinyl, cloth cape, jtd, 13", Presents, 1991, M $30.00

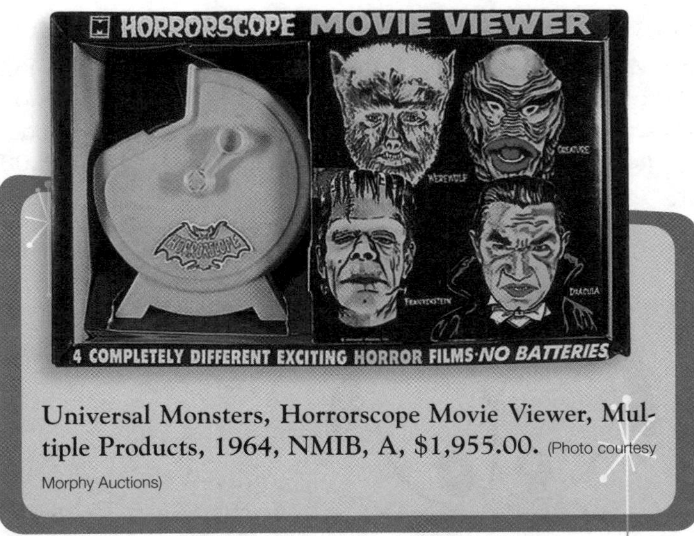

Universal Monsters, Horrorscope Movie Viewer, Multiple Products, 1964, NMIB, A, $1,955.00. (Photo courtesy Morphy Auctions)

Universal Monsters, Magnetic Disguise Set, Wolfman, Imperial, 1987, unused, MOC $10.00
Walter Lantz, bank, Chilly Willy on skis, vinyl w/cloth cap & scarf, 8½", Royalty Industries, 1970s, NM........$35.00
Walter Lantz, bank, Woody Woodpecker popping out of tree trunk, ceramic, 7", Applause, 1980s, MIB........$40.00
Walter Lantz, bank, Woody Woodpecker standing w/head turned, hand on hip & pointing up, plastic, 10", Imco, 1977, NM........$45.00
Walter Lantz, Bubb-A-Loons, Imperial Toy, 1970s, NRFP ..$15.00
Walter Lantz, bubble bath container, Woody Woodpecker, Colgate-Palmolive, 1960s, NM $20.00
Walter Lantz, figure, any character, plush & vinyl, California Stuffed Toys, 1980s, NM, ea from $20 to $25.00
Walter Lantz, figure, Woody Woodpecker, stuffed plush, 13½", Ace Novelty, 1985, NM $12.00

Walter Lantz, figure, Woody Woodpecker, stuffed plush, 19", Ace Novelty, 1989, w/tag, NM $18.00
Walter Lantz, hand puppet, Woody Woodpecker, bl & wht printed cloth body w/name & vinyl head, 1950s, EX ..$75.00

Walter Lantz, hand puppet, Woody Woodpecker, talker, Mattel, 1962, EX, A, $40.00. (Photo courtesy serioustoyz.com)

Walter Lantz, Magic Draw, featuring Woody Woodpecker, Ja-Ru, 1992, NRFC..$8.00
Walter Lantz, Motor Friend friction toy, featuring Woody Woodpecker, plastic, 5", Nasta, 1975, EX............................$18.00

Walter Lantz, mug, Chilly Willy head, 5 & Dime Inc., 1970s, 4½", NM, $20.00. (Photo courtesy serioustoyz.com)

Walter Lantz, w/up hopping figure, Woody w/plush body w/vinyl head, plastic hands & feet, 9", Illco, 1980s, NM $38.00
WC Fields, bank, standing, vinyl, 7½", Play Pal, 1970s, EX .$20.00
Welcome Back Kotter, gum card set, complete set of 53, Topps, 1976, NM to M, A..$46.00
Wendy the Good Little Witch, see Harvey Cartoons
Wizard of Oz, doll, any, 50th Anniversary edition, vinyl w /cloth outfits, about 11½", Multi Toys, MIB, ea......................$30.00
Wizard of Oz, hand puppet, any character, thin vinyl body w/ molded vinyl head, detergent premium, 1960s, EX, ea ..$18.00
Wonder Woman, figure, vinyl, jtd arms, standing w/legs together, golden whip, 15", Presents, 1988, NM+......................$55.00
Woodsy Owl, see Advertising Category under USDA Forest Service
Woody Woodpecker, see Walter Lantz
Ziggy, figure, stuffed cloth, 'I Love A Smile' on shirt w/name & 'smiling' heart, 8", Knickerbocker, 1978, NM+ $12.00
Ziggy, snow dome, 'Your're #1' on base, plastic, oval, 1980s, NM $10.00

Welcome Back Kotter, portable record player, Teletone, 1996, NM, $60.00. (Photo courtesy serioustoyz.com)

Chein

Although the company was founded shortly after the turn of the century, this New Jersey-based manufacturer is probably best known for the toys it made during the '30s and '40s. Wind-up merry-go-rounds and Ferris wheels as well as many other carnival type rides were made of beautifully lithographed tin even into the '50s, some in several variations. The company also made banks, a few of which were mechanical and some that were character related. Mechanical, sea-worthy cabin cruisers, space guns, sand toys, and some Disney toys as well were made by this giant company. They continued in production until 1979.

Advisor: Scott Smiles

See also Banks; Character, TV, and Movie Collectibles; Disney; Sand Toys.

Windup, Friction, and Other Mechanical Toys

Aero-Swing, 12", NMIB $800.00
Alligator w/Native Rider, 15", EX................................. $125.00
Aquaplane, 1930s version, 7½" WS, EX $150.00
Aquaplane, 1930s version, 7½" WS, EX+ (partial box) . $225.00
Aquaplane, 1950s version, 7½" WS, EX+ $150.00
Army Cannon Truck, Mack C-style cab, 8", EX............ $150.00
Army Truck, Mack C-style cab, gr, 8", VG+ $125.00
Barnacle Bill Floor Puncher, EX.................................... $400.00
Barnacle Bill in Barrel, 7", EX $350.00
Barnacle Bill Walker, 6", NM.. $225.00
Big Top Tent, 1961, 10", EXIB $225.00
Broadway 270 Trolley, 8", EX $150.00

Cabin Cruiser, 15", MIB $300.00
Cabin Cruiser, 15", VG........ $150.00
Cathredral Organ, #130, crank-op, 9½", NMIB........ $225.00
Chipper Chipmunk, 19½" L, EX (P box)........ $100.00
Clown Balancing Parasol on Nose, 1920s, 8", EX........ $225.00
Clown Floor Puncher, 8", EX $650.00
Clown Floor Puncher, 8", NM........ $850.00
Clown in Barrel, 7", VG+........ $400.00
Clown Walking on Hands, #158, patriotic detail, 5", EX . $150.00
Dan-Dee Dump Truck, 8½", VG+........ $300.00
Dan-Dee Oil Truck, 8½", EX+........ $425.00
Dan-Dee Roadster, 9", EXIB........ $1,000.00
Disneyland Ferris Wheel, #172, 17", EXIB $425.00
Disneyland Ferris Wheel, #172, 17", G $275.00
Disneyland Roller Coaster, 19" L, EXIB........ $500.00
Disneyland Roller Coaster, 19" L, NMIB........ $675.00
Doughboy, 6", EX+, A $200.00

Drum Major, No. 111, 9", EXIB, $1,000.00. (Photo courtesy Morphy Auctions)

Drummer, #109, 9", EX+IB........ $150.00
Duck, in bellhop's hat & jacket, 1930s, 4", EX+........ $100.00
Easter Bunny Delivery Cart, VG+........ $200.00
Easter Truck, 8½", EX+........ $450.00
Fancy Groceries/Centre Market Delivery Van, 6", EX ... $300.00
Fish (Mechanical), #55, 1940s, 11" L, NM........ $125.00
Greyhound Coast-to-Coast Bus, disk wheels, 9", VG..... $225.00
Happy Hooligan, no name on hat, 6", EX........ $400.00
Indian Chief Walker, 5", EX........ $175.00
Junior Bus #219, 9", EX+ $350.00
Junior Truck, 8½", EX........ $150.00
Krazy Kat Sparkler, 1932, 6", EX $525.00
Limousine, 6", EX $300.00
Log Truck, 8½", VG+ $150.00
Marine Sergeant, 1960s, 5", EX........ $260.00
Mickey Mouse Sparkler, die-cut tin head w/name on bow tie, 6", EX........ $225.00
Mono-Wing Plane, 16½", 1920s, gr or orange version, EX ..$200.00
Native on Alligator, 15" L, EX $175.00
Native on Turtle, 9", VG $150.00
Navy Frog Man, 12", NMOC........ $150.00

Noise Maker, 4 musical frogs lithoed on side, 3", EX........$50.00
Pan American Seaplane, 11" WS, EX........ $550.00
Peggy Jane Motor Boat, 14½", NM+IB $150.00
Pelican, #222, 5", NM $125.00
Penguin in Tuxedo, 1940, 4", EX+ $150.00
Playland Merry-Go-Round, #385, 10", NMIB........ $425.00
Playland Whip, #340, 20" L, EX+IB, A $950.00
Popeye Drummer, #252, 7", EX $1,750.00
Popeye Drummer, #252, 7", EX+IB........$5,000.00
Popeye Heavy Hitter, 12" H, EX $3,575.00
Popeye in Barrel, 7", EX+IB $3,300.00
Popeye in Barrel, 7", VG+ $475.00

Popeye Over-the-Head Bag Puncher, 9", NMIB, $10,000.00. (Photo courtesy Morphy Auctions)

Popeye Shadow Boxer, 7", EX $1,200.00
Popeye Shadow Boxer, 7", G $525.00
Popeye Sparkler, die-cut head, NM+IB........$6,500.00
Popeye Sparkler, head image lithoed on rnd yel background, 5", EX........ $325.00
Popeye the Heavy Hitter, 12", NMIB........$13,200.00
Popeye Walker, 6", EX+IB........$3,300.00
Popeye Walker, 6", VG $350.00
Public Service Trolley, #365, 7", EX........ $150.00
Rabbit, standing upright w/hands in pockets, 1938, 5", NM.. $75.00
Racer #5, boattail w/spare tire, yel & orange, w/driver, 9", VG, A $300.00
Ride-A-Rocket (Rocket Ride), #400, 18", EX+IB........ $700.00

Ride-A-Rocket (Rocket Ride), #400, 18", VG, $400.00. (Photo courtesy James D. Julia, Inc.)

Roller Coaster, 1930s version, #275, 19" L, NM+IB....... $375.00
Roller Coaster, 1950s version, 19" L, NMIB.................. $300.00
Santa Walker, 5½", EX $400.00
Seaplane, see Aquaplane
Space Ride, VGIB... $600.00
Surf's-Up, tin & plastic, 10" L, EX+OC......................... $200.00
Turtle w/Native, 8", VG+ $100.00
Wimpy in Barrel Walker, 8", EX................................ $1,100.00
Yellow Taxi (Main 6531), 8", EX $375.00
Yellow Taxi (Main 7570), 6", VG+ $175.00

Hercules Series

Army Truck, cloth cover, 29", G $300.00
Coal Truck, 20", G+ $250.00
Coupe, 18", NM.. $1,900.00
Dairy Products Truck, 19½", EX $1,300.00
Dump Truck, open bench seat, blk, 17", G $150.00
Dump Truck, open bench seat, blk, 17", VG+ $375.00
Ferris Wheel, 17", NM.. $275.00
Ferris Wheel, 17", VG $175.00
Fire Ladder Truck, 18", no ladders, G............................ $200.00

Fire Pumper Truck, 18", EX, $2,500.00. (Photo courtesy Morphy Auctions)

Ice Truck, 20", VG+, $825.00. (Photo courtesy Morphy Auctions)

Mobile Clam Truck, 27", VG+ $900.00
Motor Express Stake Truck No 112, 19½", EX................ $525.00
Railway Express Agency Truck, 20", G+ $425.00
Ready-Mixed Concrete Truck, 17", VG $2,750.00
Roadster, w/rumble seat & luggage rack, 17½", VG........ $400.00
Royal Blue Line Bus, 18", G+ $350.00
Royal Blue Line Bus, 18", NMIB................................ $4,675.00
Sailboat (Peggy Jane), 36", VG $150.00
Tanker Truck, 19", G $750.00

Tow Truck, 20", $775.00. (Photo courtesy Morphy Auctions)

Miscellaneous

Bank, Church, #29, 1950s, VG $75.00
Bank, clown head, mechanical, 1949, 5", EX................. $135.00
Bank, Elephant seated upright on drum, mechanical, 1950s, 5", NM.. $200.00
Bank, monkey tips hat when coin is inserted, 1950s, 5¼", M .. $200.00
Bank, Uncle Sam Bank, red, wht & bl litho tin top hat, 3", VG+ $75.00

Bank, Uncle Wiggily, 5", EX, $225.00. (Photo courtesy Smith House Toy and Auction Co.)

Broadway #270 Trolley, tin, 8" L, EX $150.00
Clown Musical Top, litho tin w/pnt wood clown hat, 7" dia, EXIB.. $100.00
Horse-Drawn DSC New York City Cart, tin, 12", VG+. $250.00
Roly Poly (Clown), 6½", VG... $125.00

Roly Poly, clown, bank, 6½", EX, $175.00. (Photo courtesy Smith House Toy and Auction Co.)

Roly Poly (Monkey), 6½", VG+ $150.00
Roly Poly (Rabbit), 6½", EX $175.00
Spirit of Saint Louis Transcontinental Game, 8" dia, EX+IB $325.00
Stop-Go Sign, 10½", EX $125.00
Top, Mickey Mouse, Donald Duck & Pluto playing musical instruments, #41, 9½", VG (partial box) $125.00
Top, Three Little Pigs, 9" dia, VG $74.00

Circus Toys

If you ever had the opportunity to go to one of the giant circuses as a child, no doubt you still have very vivid recollections of the huge elephants, the daring trapeze artists, the clowns and their trick dogs, and the booming voice of the ringmaster. What a thrill it was! The circus toys presented here evoke that excitement of the 'big top.' All are auction listings.

See also Battery-Operated Toys; Cast Iron, Chein, Marx, Pull and Push Toys; Windups, Friction, and Other Mechanicals; Wyandotte.

Big Top Toy Circus, Britains style w/17" horse-drawn cage wagon, tight rope apparatus, etc, EX, A (Est: $75-$100) $250.00
Britains Spectacular Circus, w/diorama & pnt metal figures, ca 1897, NMIB, A (Est: $75 to $100) $45.00
Britains Three-Ring Circus, 19 pnt-lead figures, w/accessories, EX, A (Est: $100-$150) $250.00
Cage Wagon, German, wood, felt-covered elephant, compo animals, multi openings, sm wheels, 14" L, EX, A (Est: $600-$800) $330.00
Crandall Acrobats, 3 clowns (take-apart) on base, paper on wood, incomplete set, G (10x6" box), A (Est: $100-$200) $200.00
Crandall Happy Family Circus Cage, wood/paper, 9 flat-sided animals, etc, 17" L, VG+, A (Est: $1,500-$1,800) $1,430.00
DP Clark Circus Cage Wagon, inertia drive, pnt wood, paper animals, driver, 15" L, EX restoration, A (Est: $300-$400) $220.00
French Cirque International, 2 cloth-dressed clowns (1 w/internal w/up), 2 wooden donkeys, etc, VG+, A (Est: $300-$500) ... $385.00

German Circus Set, painted composition figures with wooden accessories, EX (EX 12x12" box), A (Est: $300.00 – $500.00), $355.00. (Photo courtesy Noel Barrett Antiques and Auctions)

Hagenbeck's Menagerie Wagon, elephant-drawn, pnt wood/compo, 22" L wagon, VG+, A (Est: $1,500-$2,000) $1,200.00
Reed Gigantic Circus & Mammoth Hippodrome, litho wood, crank-op, complete, VG+ (in 15" L box), A (Est: $2,000-$3,000) $715.00
Reeve-Mitchell Pull-A-Part Circus, pnt wood, complete, VG to EX, A (Est: $300-$500) $880.00

Reed Polar Bear Cage wagon, paper lithograph on wood, two horses, driver, bear, and keeper, 26" long, EX, A (Est: $3,000.00 – $5,000.00), $5,500.00. (Photo courtesy Noel Barrett Antiques and Auctions)

Coloring, Activity, and Paint Books

Coloring and activity books from the early years of the twentieth century are scarce indeed and when found can be expensive if they are tied into another collectibles field such as Black Americana or advertising; but the ones most in demand are those that represent familiar movie and TV stars of the 1950s and 1960s. Condition plays a very important part in assessing worth, and though hard to find, unused examples are the ones that bring top dollar — in fact, as much as 50% to 75% more than one even partially used.

ABC 184 Animals to Color, Merrill, 1941, unused, EX, A..$20.00
Adventures of Batman, Whitman, 1966, some use, EX+ ..$25.00
Adventures of Mumbley Super Sleuth Coloring Book, Rand McNally #06440, 1977, some use, scarce, EX............$55.00
Alice in Wonderland Coloring Book, Whitman #1001-3, unused, EX, A $20.00
Amazing Spider-Man Coloring Book, 1981, unused, M....$12.50
Atom Ant Coloring Book, Watkins-Strathmore #1850-F, unused, EX, A $55.00
Atom Ant Play Fun, Whitman, some use, VG+IB...........$85.00
Augie Doggie Coloring Book, Whitman #1186, 1960, some use, EX $35.00
Barbie & Ken 192-Page Coloring Book, Whitman #1646-59, 1962, unused, EX, A $25.00
Batman Coloring Book, Whitman #1002, unused, M, A ..$25.00
Batman Press-Out Book, Whitman, 1966, unused, M, A..$80.00

Beverly Hillbillies Coloring Book, Whitman #1137, 1963, $25.00.
(Photo courtesy Greg Davis and Bill Morgan)

Bewitched Fun & Activity Book, Grossett & Dunlap Treasure Books #8908, 1965, unused, M............$30.00
Big Jim, Whitman, 1975, some use, EX+ $20.00
Bionic Woman Adventure Coloring Book, #15011, 1976, unused, NM, A $20.00
Blondie Paint Book, 1940, some use, VG $45.00
Buffalo Bill Jr, Whitman #1316, 1956, some use, NM.......$15.00
Bugs Bunny & Elmer Fudd Coloring Book, Watkins-Strathmore, 1963, Bugs w/carrots & EF w/stringer of fish, unused, EX, A............$25.00
Bugs Bunny Book to Color, 1951, some use, VG $20.00
Bugs Bunny Coloring Book, Whitman #1087, 1972, unused, EX, A $22.00
Calling Dr Kildare for Fun & Games, Lowe #3092, 1960s, unused, EX $50.00
Captain Gallant, Lowe #2505, 1956, unused, NM $85.00
Captain Kangaroo, 1960, some use, EX+ $30.00
Captain Marvel's Fun Book, Fawcett, 1944, unused, EX, A..$95.00
Chilly Willy Paint Book, Whitman #2946, 1960, some use, EX+ $35.00
Choo Choo Coloring Book, Watkins-Strathmore #1857, 1961, unused, EX, A $75.00
Crusader Rabbit A Story Coloring Book, Treasure Books #298, 1957, some use, EX $65.00
Davy Crockett Coloring Book, Whitman, 1955, Davy filling gun from powder horn on red cover, unused, G, A............$18.00
Davy Crockett Punch-Out Book, Whitman #1943, 1955, unused, M............$75.00

Dick Tracy Paint Book, some use, EX+, $50.00.

Disneyland Coloring Book, Whitman, 1959, snow fun scene on cover, unused, M, A............$25.00
Donald Duck Coloring Book, Dell #144, 1957, unused, EX ..$30.00
Donald Duck Coloring Book, Whitman #1183, 1960, unused, EX $30.00
Dukes of Hazzard New Adventure Coloring & Activity Book, Modern Promotions, 1981, unused, M............$35.00
Eve Arden's Coloring Book, Treasure Books, 1958, unused, EX, A $18.00
Family Affair Coloring Book, Whitman, 1968, unused, EX, A . $25.00
Fantasitc Four, Whitman, 1977, some use, EX............$20.00
Flintstones Coloring Book, Whitman #1170, 1961, unused, M............$50.00
Flintstones w/Pebbles & Bamm-Bamm Coloring Book, Whitman #1117, 1963, unused, NM+............$50.00
Flipper, Watkins-Strathmore #1851, 1965, some use, VG.$20.00
Frankenstein Jr Coloring Book, Whitman #1115, 1967, unused, NM+ $75.00
Gene Autry Coloring Book, Whitman #1124, 1950, some use, VG+ $15.00
Gene Autry Cowboy Paint Book, Merrill, 1940, unused, NM+ . $50.00
Goofy Dots, 1952, some use, EX+ $20.00
Green Acres Coloring Book, Whitman, 1967, unused, EX, A . $18.00
Green Hornet Coloring Book, Whitman, 1966, unused, NM+, A $55.00
Hanna-Barbera Fun Coloring Book, Watkins-Strathmore, 1963, unused, M, A $55.00

Have Gun Will Travel Coloring Book, Lowe, 1960, unused, NM, A $165.00

Hey There It's Yogi Bear! Sticker Fun, Whitman #2190, 1964, unused, NM+ $65.00

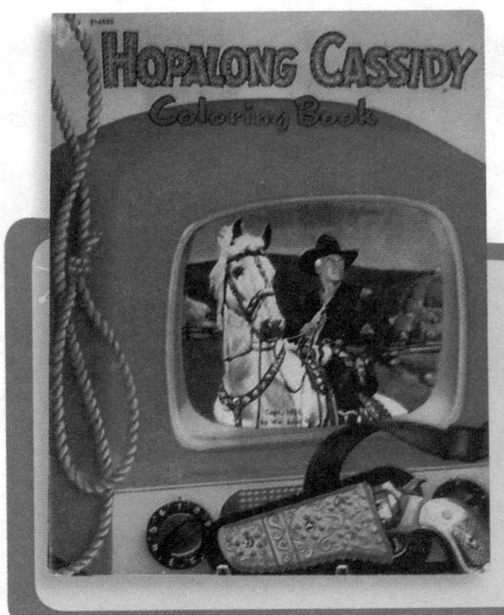

Hopalong Cassidy, #216525, 1951, some use, EX+, $40.00.

Howdy Doody Coloring Book, Whitman #1188, 1956, some use, VG $15.00

Howdy Doody Fun Book, Whitman #2187, 1950s, some use, VG $20.00

Incredible Hulk, Whitman, 1977, unused, M $25.00

Jerry Lewis Coloring Book, Treasure, 1959, unused, NM, A. $95.00

Jonny Quest Coloring Book, Whitman, 1965, unused, EX, A .. $115.00

Judy & Elroy Jetson Coloring Book, Watkins-Strathmore, 1963, unused, NM+, A $120.00

Leave It to Beaver Coloring Book, Saalfield #5338, 1958, unused, EX, A $125.00

Liddle Kiddles Coloring Book, Watkins-Strathmore, 1967, unused, M, A $25.00

Little Lulu, Whitman #1663, 1974, unused, M $45.00

Little Orphan Annie Coloring Book, #2437, 1943, some use, EX, $45.00.

Love Bug, Disney/Hunt's Ketchup promo, 1969, some use, EX. $22.00

Marvel Super Heroes Secret Wars Escape From Doom Coloring Activity Book, w/poster insert, unused, M $18.50

Marvel Super Heroes Secret Wars Secret of Spider-Man's Shield Sticker Adventures, 1984, unused, M $18.50

Marvel Super Heroes Secret Wars The Tower of Doom Sticker Adventures, 1984, unused, M $18.50

Masks of the Seven Dwarfs & Snow White Punch-Out Book, Whitman #990, 1938, unused, EX+, A $170.00

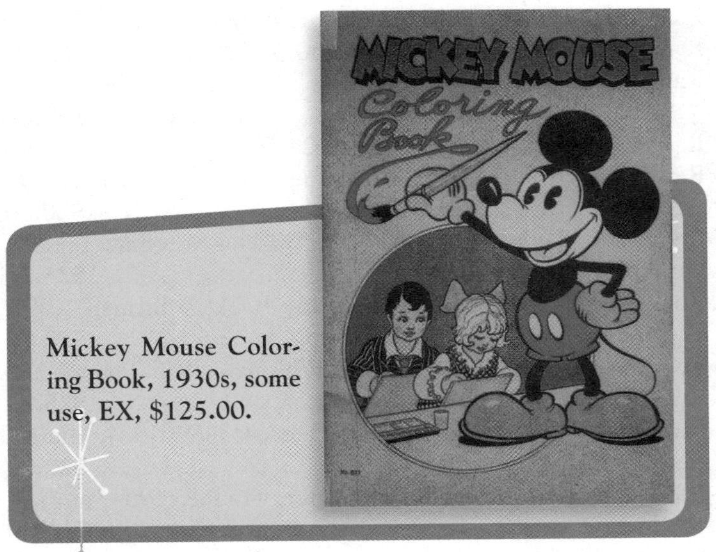

Mickey Mouse Coloring Book, 1930s, some use, EX, $125.00.

Munsters Coloring Book, Whitman, 1965, some use, G, A $32.00

My Little Margie, Saalfield, 1954, Gale Storm & Charles Farrell pictured on cover, unused, VG+, A $22.00

Partridge Family Coloring Book, 1971, standing in front of bus w/small kids in windows of bus, some use, EX, A $20.00

Peanuts Coloring Book Featuring Linus, Artcraft #4650, 1972, some use, VG+, $15.00. (Photo courtesy gasolinealleyantiques.com)

Peter Pan Animated Coloring Book, Derby Foods, 1950s, some use, NM $30.00

Planet of the Apes, 1974, cover shows Cornelius & Zira looking down at baby, some use, EX, A $50.00

Popeye & Krazy Kat (Connect the Dots) Secret Pictures Draw & Color, Lowe #3097, 1964, unused, EX $45.00
Popeye Coloring Book, Bonnie Books #2945, unused, NM+ . $65.00
Popeye Coloring Book, Lowe #2834, 1962, unused, EX+ ..$55.00
Pow! Robin Strikes for Batman Coloring Book, Watkins-Strathmore, 1966, unused, VG, A..$75.00
Prince Valiant Coloring Book, Saalfield #4611, 1957, unused, EX, A $50.00
QT Hush Private Eye & Shamus Private Nose — A Book to Color, Saalfield #9518-Q, 1962, unused, EX, A..........$25.00
Ramar of the Jungle, Saalfield #1029, 1955, unused, NM+ ..$65.00
Ranger Rider Coloring Book, Lowe #2506, 1950s, unused, M .. $40.00
Rango Texas Ranger Coloring Book, Artcraft #9675, unused, M $40.00
Ripcord Pictures to Color, Saalfield #9629, 1963, unused, NM. $38.00
Rita Hayworth Dancing Star Coloring Book, Merrill, 1942, EX, A $20.00
Rocky & Bullwinkle Coloring Book, Watkins-Strathmore #1803, 1962, unused, EX, A $25.00
Rocky Jones Space Ranger Coloring Book, Whitman, 1951, unused, VG, A $22.00
Roy Rogers Double-R-Bar Ranch, Whitman, 1955, unused, EX, A $25.00
Scooby-Doo Adventure Paint w/Water, #13369, 1984, unused, M...$22.00
Scooby-Doo Funtime Paint w/Water, #13368, 1984, unused, M... $22.00
Scooby-Doo Haunted House Paint w/Water, #13371, 1984, unused, M $22.00
Secret Squirrel Coloring Book, Watkins-Strathmore #1850-E, 1967, unused, EX, A $50.00
Sgt Preston Coloring Book, Whitman #2946, 1953, unused, EX $35.00
Shirley Temple Coloring Book, Saalfield #5353, 1959, unused, NM..$15.00
Six Million Dollar Man Dot-To-Dot, #C2412, 1977, unused, NM+ $35.00
Smokey Coloring Book, Abbott #320, 1950s, unused, M..$75.00

Snow White and the Seven Dwarfs Sticker Album, Panini, unused, M, $75.00.

Space Ghost Coloring Book, Whitman, 1968, unused, EX, A ...$130.00
Spike & Tyke Coloring Book, Whitman, 1957, unused, EX, A $18.00

Star Trek Punch-Out & Play Album, Saalfield #C2272, 1974, unused, NM $85.00

Super Friends Coloring Book, Whitman, NM+, some use, NM+, $15.00.

Superman Sticker Book, Whitman, 1977, unused, EX......$18.00

That Girl Coloring Book, Saalfield #4539, 1970, some use, EX+, $15.00.

Tom Corbett Space Cadet Coloring Book, Saalfield, 1950, Tom standing w/thumbs in belt befor spaceships, some use, VG, A $20.00
Tom Corbett Space Cadet Push-Outs, Saalfield, 1952, unused, NM, A.. $100.00
Tom Mix Draw & Paint, Whtiman, 1935, unused, G........$20.00
Toys to Color Coloring Book, 1958, sand pail, ball & boat on cover, unused, EX, A $22.00
Treasure Island Cut-Out Coloring Book, Whitman/Quaker Oats, 1968, unused, EX+...$20.00

TV Roundup of Western Heroes..., Saalfield Artcraft #7819, 1961, unused, NM $40.00
Wally Walrus Coloring Book, Saalfield #4547, 1962, unused, NM+ $55.00
Walt Disney's Big Coloring Book, Watkins-Strathmore #1871, 1959, unused, EX, A $60.00
Walter Lantz Woody Woodpecker Sticker Fun w/Activity Pages, Whitman #2180, 1964, some use, EX+ $25.00

We Land on the Moon Coloring Book, 1969, EX, $20.00.

Wonder Woman Homecoming High Jinks Coloring Book, Golden, 1979, w/paper doll & outfits in back, unused, M, A....................$20.00
Wonderbug, Whitman, 1978, unused, M $35.00

Comic Books

For more than a half a century, kids of America raced to the bookstand as soon as the new comics came in for the month and for 10¢ an issue kept up on the adventures of their favorite superheroes, cowboys, space explorers, and cartoon characters. By far, most were eventually discarded — after they were traded one friend to another, stacked on closet shelves, and finally confiscated by Mom. Discount the survivors that were torn or otherwise damaged over the years and those about the mundane, and of those remaining, some could be quite valuable. In fact, first editions of high-grade comic books, or those showcasing the first appearance of a major character, often bring $500.00 and more. Rarity, age, and quality of the artwork are prime factors in determining value, and condition is critical. If you want to seriously collect comic books, you'll need to refer to a good comic book price guide such as *The Official Overstreet Comic Book Price Guide*.

Abbott & Costello, #4, 1948, EX, from $250 to $350.00
Adventure Comics, #92, June/July, 1944, 'Last Manhunter Issue,' NM, A.................... $460.00
Air Fighters Comics Featuring the Black Commander, Hillman Publications #1, Nov 1941, NM, A $1,150.00
Amazing Fantasy (Introducing Spider-Man), #15, from $1,000 to $1,400.00
Amazing Spider-Man, Marvel, #1, EX, from $7,500 to.$8,000.00
America's Greatest, Fawcett #5, 1942, EX, from $700 to . $1,000.00
Andy Panda, Dell #280, 1950, EX, from $35 to....................$40.00
Annie Oakley, Dell #2, 1948, EX+, from $125 to.......... $150.00
Anthony & Cleopatra, Ideal #1, 1848, EX+, from $500 to..$850.00
Archie Comics, #32, 1948, VG, from $40 to $60.00
Atomic Thunderbolt, #1, 1946, EX, from $400 to.......... $500.00
Avengers, Marvel #100, EX, from $40 to $50.00
Batman, DC Comics #23, EX, from $1,200 to $1,500.00
Batman (Remarkable Ruse of the Riddler), DC Comics #171, 1965, VG, from $50 to $65.00
Beany & Cecil, Dell #2, 1962, rare, EX, from $35 to.........$40.00
Beatles Complete Life Stories, Dell Giant #1, 1964, EX+ ..$50.00
Black Cat Mystery, Harvey #41, VG+, from $40 to..........$50.00
Bouncer (The), Fox Features Syndicate #11, Sept 1944, NM+, A $690.00
Brady Bunch, Dell #2, 1970, NM, from $100 to $115.00
Buck Rogers (in the 25th Century), Toby Press #151, 1951, EX, from $65 to $75.00
Bugs Bunny Finds the Frozen Kingdom, Dell #164, 1947, EX+, from $50 to $70.00
Captain Marvel, Fawcett #38, Aug 1944, NM, A........... $575.00
Captain Marvel (New Adventures of)/Special Edition Comics, Fawcett #1, 1940, w/belt buckle, NM, from $9,000 to... $11,500.00
Captain Marvel Jr, Fawcett #26, Jan, 1945, NM, A........ $345.00
Captain Midnight, Fawcett #14, Nov 1944, NM, A....... $800.00
Casper the Friendly Ghost, #7, 1952, VG, from $50 to.....$65.00
Challengers of the Unknown, DC Comics #15, 1950s, G, from $40 to $50.00
Comics Parade (Li'l Abner in Tree), #21, Dec 1939, G+, from $45 to $45.00
Conan the Barbarian (Curse of the Golden Skull), Marvel #37, NM+, from $35 to $45.00

Crypt of Terror, E.C. Comics #19, August/September 1950, NM+, $2,300.00. (Photo courtesy Morphy Auctions)

Cyclone Comics, #1, June 1940, NM.................... $1,700.00
Daredevil, #27, 1944, NM, from $950 to $1,500.00
Daredevil (The Man Without Fear!), Marvel #1, EX+, from $550 to $650.00
Dennis the Menace, Marvel #1, 1981, NM+, from $12 to...$18.00

Detective Comics (New Feature The Boy Commandos), DC Comics #64, VG, from $550 to $750.00
Dick Tracy, Dell #13 (Series I), 1939, EX+, from $800 to ..$1,250.00
Doll Man Quarterly, #13, 1947, NM+, from $800 to... $1,250.00
Don Winslow of the Navy, Fawcett #2, 1943, NM+, from $700 to $1,000.00

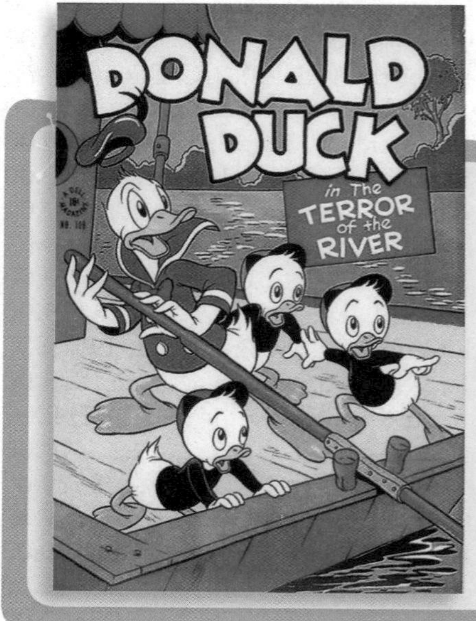

Donald Duck in the 'Terror of the River,' Dell #108, April 1946, EX+, A, $1,380.00. (Photo courtesy Morphy Auctions)

Famous Funnies (Fighting Buck Rogers), #211, 1954, EX+, from $800 to $1,100.00
Famous Gang Book of Comics, Firestone #nn, 1942, EX+, from $600 to $900.00
Fantastic Comics, #18, 1941, G+, from $65 to $85.00
Fantastic Four, Marvel #1, 1961, EX, from $2,500 to .. $3,000.00
Flintstones, Dell #2, NM, from $150 to $175.00
Flipper, Gold Key #1, 1966, EX+, from $50 to...................$60.00
Gene Autry, Dell #42, 1950, EX+, from $50 to $65.00
Green Hornet Fights Crime, Harvey #34, 1947, EX+, from $400 to $500.00

Green Lantern, Fall Issue, #1, 1941, EX, A, $11,500.00. (Photo courtesy Morphy Auctions)

Green Lantern Featuring 'Menace of the Giant Puppet,' DC Comics #1, Aug 1960, EX+, A............................$3,735.00
Hogan's Heroes, Dell #4, 1966, NM, from $50 to.............$60.00
Hopalong Cassidy, Fawcett #3, 1946, NM, from $350 to.. $550.00
I Dream of Jeannie, Dell #1, 1966, NM+, from $225 to . $250.00
I Love Lucy, Dell #10, 1956, EX, from $45 to $55.00
Incredible Hulk (& Now the Wolverine!), Marvel #181, NM, from $750 to $950.00
Incredible Hulk (Wolverine Cameo), Marvel #180, 1974, EX, from $35 to $45.00

Joker Comics, #10, July/August 1943, NM, A, $1,380.00. (Photo courtesy Morphy Auctions)

Justice League of America, DC #6, VG, from $55 to.........$65.00
Kay Keen Annual, Archie Giant Series #6, 1959-60, EX, from $75 to $85.00
Lassie, Dell #8, 1961, EX, from $35 to $45.00
Laurel & Hardy, #1, 1949, EX+, from $725 to $1,150.00
Lone Ranger, Dell #1, 1948, EX+, from $550 to............ $650.00

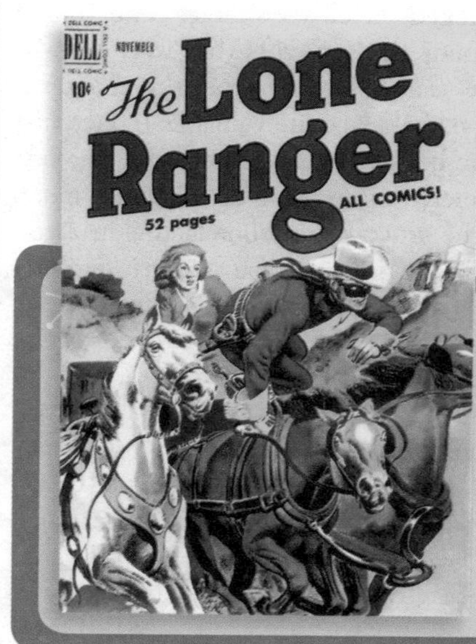

Lone Ranger, Dell #29, 1950, NM+, A, $345.00. (Photo courtesy Morphy Auctions)

Lone Ranger, Dell #125, 1946, EX+, from $40 to..............$50.00
Man From UNCLE, Gold Key #4, 1960s, EX+, from $40 to . $50.00
Marvel Tales, Dell #121, 1954, VG, from $65 to..............$75.00
Mickey Mouse, Dell #27, 1943, VG, from $165 to......... $175.00
Millie the Model, Marvel #3, 1946, NM+, from $550 to.. $750.00
New Funnies, Dell #87, 1940s, EX+, from $40 to.............$50.00
Partridge Family, Charlton #19, 1973, EX, from $15 to.....$20.00

Phantom, Gold Key 10015-502, Feb 1964, EX, from $25.00 to $30.00.

Planet of the Apes (w/Rod Serling Interview), Curtis #1, NM, from $35 to $45.00
Police Comics, Quality #75, 1948, VG+, from $40 to.......$60.00
Rawhide, Dell #1160, 1960, EX, from $45 to....................$50.00
Red Ryder, Dell #69, 1949, NM, from $45 to $50.00
Robin Hood, Dell #1, 1963, NM, from $85 to...................$95.00
Roy Rogers Comics, Dell #12, EX, from $35 to $45.00
Scooby-Doo, Marvel #1, 1977, NM+, from $30 to............$35.00
77 Sunset Strip, Dell #1159, EX+, from $65 to.................$75.00
Sheena Queen of the Jungle, Fiction House #14, 1951, NM+, from $600 to $800.00
Sick Cole, Vol 1 #4, June/July, NM+, A $690.00
Silver Surfer, Marvel, #1, G, from $40 to.........................$50.00
Six Million Dollar Man, Charlton #1, 1976, NM, from $20 to. $25.00
Smash Comics, #49, 1944, NM+, from $600 to........... $1,000.00
Smilin' Jack, Dell #4, 1942, EX+, from $525 to............. $825.00
Space Squadron, #3, VG, from $60 to.............................$70.00
Spotlight Comics, Chesler #1, 1944, NM, from $1,000 to.$2,000.00
Star Trek — To Err Is Vulcan!, Gold Key #59, 1978, NM+, from $40 to..$50.00
Star Wars, Marvel #1, NM $1,400.00
Superboy, DC Comics #1, EX, from $1,600 to............ $2,200.00
Superboy, DC Comics #2, May/June 1949, EX+, A..... $1,150.00
Superman, #3, DC Comics, 1943, EX, from $2,000 to.. $2,250.00
Superman's Girlfriend Lois Lane, Dell #13, EX+, from $125 to ..$135.00
Tales of Suspense (Guest-Starring the Angel), Marvel #49, G, from $45 to $55.00
Tarzan, Dell Vol 1 #52, Lex Barker cover, EX, from $55 to..$65.00
Tessie the Typist, #1, 1944, EX, from $450 to $650.00
Tex Ritter Western, Fawcett #2, 1954, VG, from $65 to...$75.00
Texan, Dell #1027, 1959, EX+, from $40 to $50.00
Tom & Jerry, Dell #115, EX, from $20 to..........................$25.00
Tomb of Dracula (Night of the Vampire), Marvel #1, EX+, from $45 to $65.00
Top Cat, Gold Key #5, 1963, EX, from $55 to..................$65.00
Uncanny X-Men (Wolverine vs Sabretooth), Marvel #213, 1987, NM+, from $40 to $50.00
Walt Disney's Snow White & the Seven Dwarfs, Dell #49, 1944, EX, A $350.00
Walt Disney's Uncle Scrooge in 'Only a Poor Old Man,' Dell #386, 1952, NM, A...$3,450.00
Wambi the Jungle Boy, Fiction House #10, 1950, EX, from $250 to $450.00
Werewolf (by Night), Marvel #32, EX, from $40 to $50.00
Western Tales, Harvey #32, 1950s, EX+, from $115 to .. $125.00
Wild Western, Atlas #3, Sept 1948, NM, A $750.00
Wolverine (Enemy of the State), Marvel #20, NM+, from $25 to $35.00
Wonder Woman in Shamrock Land, AA #14, 1945, G, from $50 to $75.00
Wyatt Earp, Dell #860, EX+, from $75 to $85.00
X-Men, #1, VG+, from $1,200 to............................... $1,500.00
Young Allies (Bucky & Toro in), Timely Comics #7, April 1943, EX, A $975.00
Zorro, Golden Key #4, 1966, NM, from $45 to.................$55.00

Special Edition Comics/New Adventures of Captain Marvel, Fawcett #1, August 1940, NM, A, $5,750.00. (Photo courtesy Morphy Auctions)

Corgi

The Corgi legacy is a rich one, beginning in 1934 with parent company Mettoy of Swansea, South Wales. In 1956, Mettoy merged with Playcraft Ltd. to form Mettoy Playcraft Ltd. and changed the brand name from Mettoy to Corgi, in honor of Queen Elizabeth's beloved Welsh Corgis, which she could regularly be seen taking for walks around Buckingham palace.

In 1993, Mattel bought the Corgi brand and attempted, for a short time, to maintain the tradition of producing Corgi quality collectible toys. Shortly afterward, employees of the Welsh manufacturing center purchased back the Corgi Collectibles line from Mattel. In July 1999, the brand was purchased again, this time by Zindart, an American-owned company based in Hong Kong, where the Corgi Classics line is now produced.

Some of the most highly prized Corgi toys in today's collectors' market are the character-related vehicles. The assortment includes the cars of secret agent James Bond, including several variations of his Aston-Martin, his lotus Esprit complete with underwater maneuvering fins, and other 007 vehicles. Batman's Batmobile and Batboat, and The Man From U.N.C.L.E.'s THRUSH-BUSTER are among the favorites as well.

Values represent models in new condition in their original package unless noted otherwise.

Adams Bros Probe 15, #384, from $60 to $75.00
Air France Concorde, #651, all others (no gold tail design), from $60 to $75.00
Airbourne Caravan, #420, from $80 to $110.00
Allis Chalmers Fork Lift, #409, from $35 to $50.00
AMC Pacer, #291, from $30 to $45.00
AMC Pacer Secours, #484, from $60 to $75.00
Aston Martin DB4, #309, from $100 to $125.00
Aston Martin DB4 Saloon, #218, from $100 to $125.00
Austin A-40, #216, 2-tone bl, from $115 to $140.00
Austin A-60, #236, right-hand drive, from $70 to $95.00
Austin A-60, #255, left-hand drive, from $225 to $250.00
Austin Cambridge, #201, from $175 to $200.00
Austin Cambridge, #201m, w/motor, from $200 to $225.00
Austin Healey, #300, red or cream, from $150 to $175.00
Austin Mini Van, #450, from $85 to $110.00
Austin Mini Van, #450, w/pnt grille, from $150 to $175.00
Austin Taxi, #418, w/whizzwheels, from $45 to $60.00
Austin 7, #225, red, from $100 to $125.00
Austin 7, #225, yel, from $300 to $325.00
Batboat & Trailer, #107, 1972-76, from $150 to $175.00
Batboat & Trailer, #107, 1976-80, from $90 to $110.00
Batcopter, #925, from $80 to $95.00
Batman's Bat Bike, #268, from $60 to $75.00
Batmobile, #267-A1, 1966, or #267-A2, 1967-72, from $500 to $550.00
Batmobile, #267-C1, 1973, from $400 to $450.00

Batmobile, #267, from $125.00 to $150.00.

Beast Carrier, #58, from $50 to $65.00

Beatle's Yellow Submarine, #802-A2, EX, from $150.00 to $200.00. (Photo courtesy serioustoyz.com)

Beatle's Yellow Submarine, #803, from $700 to $750.00
Bedford AA Road Service, #408, from $140 to $165.00
Bedford Ambulance, #412, split windscreen, from $125 to $150.00
Bedford Ambulance, #412, 1-pc windscreen, from $225 to $275.00
Bedford Dormobile, #404, cream, maroon & turq, from $100 to $125.00
Bedford Dormobile, #404, yel & 2-tone bl, from $215 to $240.00
Bedford Dormobile, #404m, w/motor, from $160 to $185.00
Bedford KLG Plugs, #403m, w/motor, from $250 to $275.00
Bedford Military Ambulance, #414, from $100 to $125.00
Bedford Tipper, #494, red & silver, from $175 to $200.00
Bedford Tipper, #494, red & yel, from $85 to $100.00
Bedford Utilicon Fire Department, #405, gr, from $160 to $185.00
Bedford Utilicon Fire Department, #405, red, from $200 to $250.00
Bedford Utilicon Fire Tender, #405m, w/motor, from $235 to $265.00
Bedford Van, Corgi Toys, #422, yel w/bl roof, from $200 to $250.00
Bell Helicopter, #920, from $35 to $45.00
Bentley Continental, #224, from $100 to $125.00
Bentley Mulliner, #274, from $80 to $100.00
Bermuda Taxi, #430, metallic bl & red, from $375 to $425.00
Bertone Runabout, #386, from $60 to $75.00
Bertone Shake Buggy, #392, from $45 to $60.00
Bluebird Record Car, #153, from $125 to $150.00
BMW M1 Racer, #308, gold plated, from $100 to $125.00
BMW M1 Racer, #308, yel, from $25 to $40.00
BOAC Concorde, #650, all others (no gold logo on tail), from $60 to $75.00
BOAC Concorde, #650, gold logo on tail, from $95 to $110.00
Breakdown Truck, #703, from $35 to $45.00
British Chieftain Tank, #903, from $60 to $75.00
BRM Racer, #152, from $85 to $100.00
Buck Rogers' Starfighter, #647, from $80 to $95.00
Buick Riviera, #245, from $85 to $100.00
Cadillac Ambulance, #437, from $95 to $120.00
Capt Marvel's Porsche, #262, from $60 to $75.00
Charlie's Angels Van, #434, from $60 to $75.00
Chevrolet Astro 1, #347, red hubs, from $100 to $125.00

Chevrolet Astro 1, #347, w/whizwheels, from $40 to $60.00
Chevrolet Caprice, #325, from $70 to $95.00
Chevrolet Caprice Cab, #327, from $45 to $65.00
Chevrolet Caprice Racer, #341, from $25 to $40.00
Chevrolet Corvair, #229, from $60 to $75.00
Chevrolet Corvette, #310, bronze, from $150 to $175.00
Chevrolet Corvette, #310, red or silver, from $70 to $95.00
Chevrolet Corvette Stingray, #300, from $100 to........... $125.00

Chevrolet Fire Chief Car, #439, from $100.00 to $125.00.

Chevrolet Impala, #248, from $80 to $95.00
Chevrolet Impala Taxi, #221, from $100 to $125.00
Chevrolet Kennel Service, #486, from $125 to $150.00
Chevrolet Police Car, #326, from $45 to $65.00
Chevrolet SS 350 Camaro, #338, from $70 to $95.00
Chevrolet Stingray, #337, from $60 to $80.00
Chevrolet Superior Ambulance, #405, from $35 to...........$50.00
Chipperfield's Circus Booking Office, #426, from $300 to . $350.00
Chipperfield's Circus Giraffe Transporter, #503, from $150 to .$175.00
Chipperfield's Circus Parade, #487, from $200 to $250.00
Chipperfield's Circus Poodle Pickup, #511, from $600 to . $675.00

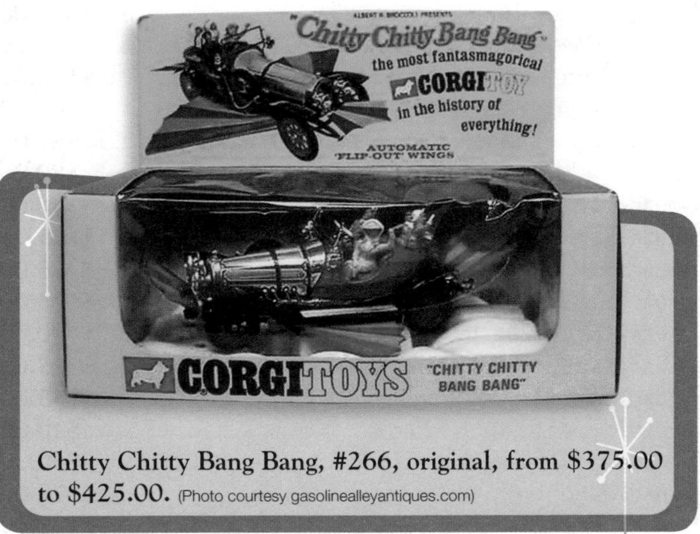

Chitty Chitty Bang Bang, #266, original, from $375.00 to $425.00. (Photo courtesy gasolinealleyantiques.com)

Chitty Chitty Bang Bang, #266, replica, from $125 to ... $150.00
Chrysler Ghia, #241, from $65 to...$80.00
Chrysler Imperial, #246, metallic turq, from $240 to...... $265.00
Chrysler Imperial, #246, red, from $100 to $125.00
Citroen DS19, #210, from $90 to $110.00
Citroen DS19 Monte Carlo, #323, from $140 to........... $170.00
Citroen Dyane, #287, from $30 to.......................................$45.00
Citroen Le Dandy, #259, bl, from $175 to....................... $200.00
Citroen Safari, #436, from $95 to................................... $120.00

Citreon Safari, #475, from $150.00 to $175.00. (Photo courtesy gasolinealleyantiques.com)

Citroen SM, #284, from $50 to $65.00
Citroen Tour De France, #510, from $125 to................. $150.00
Citroen 2 CV, #346, from $25 to $35.00
Coastguard Jaguar, #414, from $45 to..............................$60.00
Coca-Cola Van, #437, from $55 to.....................................$70.00
Commer Ambulance, #463, from $100 to....................... $125.00
Commer Army Field Kitchen, #359, from $150 to $175.00
Commer Lorry, #452, from $125 to $150.00
Commer Military Ambulance, #354, from $100 to $125.00
Commer Military Police, #355, from $110 to $135.00
Commer Milk Float, Co-Op, #466, from $170 to $200.00
Commer Pickup Truck, #465, from $65 to $80.00
Commer Platform Lorry, #454, from $125 to $150.00
Commer Police Van, #464, City Police, minimum value, from $350 to $400.00
Commer Police Van, #464, County Police, from $115 to. $140.00
Commer Police Van, #464, Police, bl, from $115 to....... $140.00
Commer Police Van, #464, Police, gr, from $750 to....... $800.00
Commer Police Van, #464, Rijks Politie, bl, minimum value, from $350 to $400.00
Commer Van, #462, Co-Op, from $150 to...................... $175.00
Commer Van, #462, Hammonds, from $175 to $200.00
Commer Walls Van, #453, from $175 to......................... $225.00
Conveyor on Jeep, #64, from $90 to............................. $120.00
DAF City Car, #283, from $30 to..$55.00
Daily Planet Helicopter, #929, from $80 to $95.00
Datsun 240Z, East African Safari, #394, from $55 to $70.00
Datsun 240Z, US Rally, #396, from $60 to $75.00

David Brown Tractor, #55, from $60 to....$75.00
Detomaso Mangusta, #203, from $40 to....$55.00
Dick Dastardly's Racer, #809, from $175 to....$200.00
Disneyland Bus, #470, from $45 to....$65.00
Dolphin Cabin Cruiser, #104, from $30 to....$45.00
Dougal's Car, #807, from $300 to....$350.00
DRAX Helicopter, #930, from $80 to....$95.00
Dropside Trailer, #100, from $25 to....$40.00
Elf-Tyrrell Project 34, #161, from $45 to....$60.00
ERF Cement Tipper, #460, from $40 to....$55.00
ERF Dropside Lorry, #456, from $115 to....$140.00
ERF Moorhouse Van, #459, from $350 to....$400.00
ERF Platform Lorry, #457, from $100 to....$125.00
ERF Tipper Dumper, #458, from $80 to....$100.00
Ferrari Berlinetta Le Mans, #314, from $55 to....$70.00
Ferrari Daytona 365 GTB4, #323, from $30 to....$45.00
Ferrari Formula I, #154, from $45 to....$60.00
Ferrari 206 Dino Sport, #344, from $75 to....$90.00
Fiat X1/9, #306, from $35 to....$50.00
Fiat 2100, #232, 1961, from $75 to....$90.00
Fiat 600 Jolly, #240, from $125 to....$150.00
Ford Capri, #311, orange, from $110 to....$135.00
Ford Capri, #311, red, from $70 to....$90.00
Ford Capri, #311, w/gold hubs, from $200 to....$250.00
Ford Capri S, #312, from $35 to....$50.00
Ford Cobra Mustang, #370, from $25 to....$40.00
Ford Consul, #200, dual colors, from $175 to....$200.00
Ford Consul, #200, solid colors, from $150 to....$175.00
Ford Consul, #200m, w/motor, from $175 to....$200.00
Ford Consul Classic, #234, from $85 to....$100.00

Ford Consul Cortina Estate Car, #491, 1966, from $120.00 to $145.00.

Ford Consul Cortina Super Estate Car, #444, w/golfer & caddy, from $150 to....$175.00
Ford Cortina, #313, bronze or bl, from $90 to....$120.00
Ford Cortina, #313, yel, from $275 to....$325.00
Ford Cortina GXL Police, #402, wht, from $60 to....$75.00
Ford Cortina GXL Polizei, #402, from $150 to....$175.00
Ford Escort, #334, from $30 to....$45.00
Ford GT 70, #316, from $40 to....$55.00
Ford Milk Float, #405, from $30 to....$45.00
Ford Mustang Competition, #325 from $75 to....$100.00
Ford Mustang Fastback 2x2 Stock Racing Car (Flower Power), #348, 1968, from $125 to....$150.00
Ford Mustang Organ Grinder Dragster, #166, from $35 to....$50.00
Ford Mustang Rally, #329, from $50 to....$70.00
Ford Sierra 2.3 Ghia, #299, from $25 to....$40.00
Ford Thunderbird, #214, no suspension, from $115 to....$140.00
Ford Thunderbird, #214m, w/motor, from $300 to....$325.00
Ford Thunderbird, #214s, w/suspension, from $95 to....$120.00
Ford Thunderbird, #801, from $40 to....$55.00
Ford Thunderbird Sport, #215, no suspension, from $115 to. $140.00
Ford Thunderbird Sport, #215s, w/suspension, from $100 to. $125.00
Ford Tipper Trailer, #62, from $25 to....$35.00
Ford Zephyr Estate Car, #424, from $80 to....$95.00
Ford Zephyr Politei, #419, from $300 to....$325.00
Ford 5000 Super Major Tractor, #67, from $80 to....$110.00
Ford 5000 Tractor & Scoop, #74, from $100 to....$125.00
Ford 5000 Tractor & Trencher, #72, from $110 to....$130.00
Fordson Disc Harrow, #71, from $25 to....$40.00
Fordson Half-Track Tractor, #54, from $150 to....$175.00
Fordson Power Major Tractor, #55, from $100 to....$125.00
Forward Control Jeep FC-150, #409, from $45 to....$60.00
Forward Control Jeep Tower Wagon, #478, from $100 to. $125.00
German Rocket Launcher, #907, from $80 to....$95.00
Ghia Mangusta De Tomaso, #271, from $65 to....$80.00

Green Hornet's Black Beauty, #268, 1967, from $350.00 to $400.00.

Hardy Boy's Rolls Royce, #805, from $300 to....$350.00
Heinkel Trojan, #233, from $75 to....$90.00
Hillman Hunter Rally, #302, kangaroo, from $125 to....$150.00
Hillman Husky, #206, metallic bl & silver, from $150 to..$175.00
Hillman Husky Estate, #206, solid colors, from $125 to. $150.00
Hillman Husky Estate, #206m, w/motor, from $150 to....$175.00
Hillman Imp Monte Carlo, #328, from $125 to....$150.00
Holiday Minibus, #508, from $115 to....$140.00
Honda Driving School, #273, from $50 to....$65.00
Incredible Hulk Mazda Pickup, #264, from $65 to....$80.00
Iso Grifo 7 Litre, #301, from $65 to....$80.00
Jaguar E Type, #307, from $125 to....$150.00
Jaguar E Type, #312, from $100 to....$125.00
Jaguar Fire Chief, #213, from $150 to....$175.00
Jaguar Fire Chief, #213s, w/suspension, from $200 to....$225.00
Jaguar MK10, #238, metallic gr or silver, from $165 to..$190.00
Jaguar MK10, #238, metallic red or bl, from $100 to....$125.00
Jaguar Police Car, #429, from $40 to....$55.00
Jaguar XJS, #319, from $25 to....$40.00
Jaguar XJ12C, #286, from $45 to....$60.00
Jaguar XK120 Rally, #804, w/spats, from $65 to....$75.00
Jaguar 2.4 Saloon, #208, no suspension, from $120 to....$140.00

Jaguar 2.4 Saloon, #208m, w/motor, from $155 to.......... $180.00
Jaguar 2.4 Saloon, #208s, w/suspension, from $140 to.... $165.00
Jaguar 4.2 Litre E Type, #335, from $140 to.................... $160.00
Jaguar 4.2 Litre E Type, #374, from $100 to.................... $125.00
James Bond's Aston Martin, #270, w/tire slashers, 1/43 scale, from $275 to $325.00
James Bond's Aston Martin, #270, w/whizzwheels, 1/43 scale, from $125 to $150.00
James Bond's Aston Martin, #271, from $100 to $125.00

James Bond's Aston Martin D.B.5, #261, from $250.00 to $275.00.

James Bond's Citroen 2CV, #272, from $50 to...................$65.00
James Bond's Ford Mustang, #391, from $250 to $275.00
James Bond's Lotus Esprit, #269, from $100 to $125.00
James Bond's Moon Buggy, #811, from $550 to $600.00

James Bond's Space Shuttle, #649, from $85.00 to $100.00. (Photo courtesy gasolinealleyantiques.com)

James Bond's Toyota 2000 GT, #336, from $375 to $400.00
Japan Air Line Concorde, #651, from $450 to................ $500.00
Jeep, #419, from $40 to...$50.00
Jet Police Helicopter, #931, from $55 to $65.00
John Wolfe's Dragster, #170, from $45 to...........................$60.00
Karrier Bantam Butcher Shop, #413, from $130 to $165.00
Karrier Bantam Butcher Shop, #413s, w/suspension, from $210 to $240.00
Karrier Bantam 2-Ton, #455, bl, from $115 to................ $140.00
Karrier Bantam 2-Ton, #455, red, from $300 to.............. $350.00
Karrier Dairy Van, #435, from $140 to........................... $165.00
Karrier Lucozade Van, #411, from $150 to...................... $175.00
Karrier Mobile Grocers, #407, from $150 to $175.00
Kojak's Buick, #290, w/hat, from $60 to.............................$90.00
Kojak's Buick, #290, no hat, from $125 to $150.00
Lamborghini P400 GT Miura, #342, from $70 to..............$90.00
Lancia Fulvia Sport, #332, red or bl, from $65 to $80.00
Lancia Fulvia Sport, #332, yel & blk, from $125 to........ $150.00
Land Rover Breakdown, #417, from $110 to $140.00
Land Rover Breakdown, #417s, w/spring suspension, from $75 to $100.00
Land Rover Breakdown, #477, w/whizzwheels, from $60 to..$75.00
Land Rover Lepra, #438, from $375 to............................ $425.00
Land Rover Pickup, #406, from $75 to...............................$95.00
Land Rover Weapons Carrier, #357, from $145 to $195.00
Lincoln Continental Limo, #262, bl, from $175 to $200.00
Lincoln Continental Limo, #262, gold, from $100 to..... $125.00
Livestock Transporter, #484, from $70 to...........................$85.00
London Routemaster Bus, #467, from $80 to.....................$95.00
London Transport Routemaster, Church's Shoes, #468, red, from $200 to $225.00
London Transport Routemaster, Corgi Toys, #468, brn, gr or cream, from $1,000 to..$1,250.00
London Transport Routemaster, Corgi Toys, #468, red, from $90 to $120.00
London Transport Routemaster, Design Centre, #468, red, from $250 to $275.00
London Transport Routemaster, Gamages, #468, red, from $200 to $225.00
London Transport Routemaster, Madame Tussand's, #468, red, from $200 to $250.00
London Transport Routemaster, Outspan, #468, red, from $60 to $75.00
Lotus Elan, #318, copper, from $275 to........................... $325.00
Lotus Elan, #318, metallic bl, from $100 to $125.00
Lotus Elan, #319, gr or yel, from $125 to $150.00

Lotus Elan, #319, red or blue, from $75.00 to $100.00.

Lotus Elan, #319, wht, from $125 to $175.00
Lotus Elite, #301, from $25 to $40.00

Lotus Elite, #382, from $30 to $45.00
Lotus John Player, #154, from $40 to $55.00
Lotus Texaco Special, #154, from $40 to $55.00
Lotus XI, #151, regular, from $90 to.............................. $110.00
Lotus-Climax F1 Racer, #155, from $60 to $75.00
Lunar Bug, #806, from $150 to.. $200.00
Magic Roundabout Carousel, #852, from $750 to $950.00
Magic Roundabout Playground, #853, from $1,500 to..$1,750.00
Magic Roundabout Train, #851, from $400 to $450.00
Magnum PI's Ferrari, #298, from $50 to...........................$65.00
Man From UNCLE, #497, wht, minimum value, from $650 to... $700.00
Man From UNCLE Gun Firing Thrush-Buster, #497, from $275 to.. $325.00
Marcos Mantis, #312, from $40 to.....................................$60.00
Marcos Volvo 1800 GT, #324, from $70 to.......................$95.00
Marcos 3 Litre, #377, wht & gray, from $100 to $125.00
Marcos 3 Litre, #377, yel or bl, from $70 to......................$95.00
Massey-Ferguson Tractor & Fork, #57, from $100 to...... $125.00
Massey-Ferguson Tractor Shovel, #53, from $100 to $125.00
Massey-Ferguson 165 Tractor, #66, from $75 to................$95.00
Massey-Ferguson 50B Tractor, #50, from $60 to $75.00
Massey-Ferguson 65 Tractor, #50, from $100 to............ $125.00
Mazda Camper, #415, from $45 to.....................................$60.00
Mazda Maintenence Truck, #413, from $50 to $65.00
Mazda Open Truck, #495, from $30 to..............................$45.00
Mazda Pickup, #440, from $30 to $45.00
Mazda Pickup, #493, from $45 to $60.00
McLaren Texaco-Marlboro, #191, from $60 to $75.00
Mercedes Benz C111, #388, from $50 to...........................$65.00
Mercedes Benz Unimog, #406, from $60 to $75.00
Mercedes Benz 220SE, #230, blk, from $120 to $140.00
Mercedes Benz 220SE, #230, red, from $75 to $90.00
Mercedes Benz 240 Rally, #291, from $35 to $50.00
Mercedes Benz 300SL, #303, from $100 to $125.00
Mercedes Benz 300SL, #303s, w/suspension, from $100 to ..$125.00
Mercedes Benz 300SL, #304, colors other than yel, from $100 to $125.00
Mercedes Benz 300SL, #304s, w/suspension, from $100 to $125.00
Mercedes Benz 350SL, #393, bl, from $50 to $65.00
Mercedes Benz 350SL, #393, metallic gr, from $100 to .. $125.00
Mercedes Benz 350SL, #393, wht, from $80 to $95.00
Mercedes Benz 600 Pullman, #247, from $75 to $90.00
Mercedes Police Car, #412, Police or Polizei, from $25 to ..$35.00
Mercedes 240D Taxi, #411, cream or blk, from $60 to $75.00
Mercedes 240D Taxi, #411, orange w/blk roof, from $45 to..$60.00
MGA Sports Car, #302, from $140 to........................... $155.00
MGB GT, #327, from $125 to $150.00
MGC GT, #345, orange, from $275 to........................... $325.00
MGC GT, #345, yel, from $125 to $150.00
MGC GT, #378, from $150 to.. $175.00
Mini BMC Police Van w/Tracker Dog, #448, 1964, from $215 to $260.00
Mini BMC 1000, #200, from $45 to $60.00
Mini Cooper Monte Carlo, #317, from $175 to............. $225.00
Mini Cooper Rally, #227, from $250 to.......................... $275.00
Mini Cooper Rally Car, #282, from $100 to $125.00
Mini Countryman Surfer, #484, w/silver grille, from $165 to. $190.00
Mini Countryman Surfer, #485, w/unpnt grille, from $250 to . $275.00
Mini Magnifique, #334, from $70 to $95.00
Mini Marcos GT850, #341, from $60 to $80.00
Mini Metro, #275, colors other than gold, from $25 to.....$40.00
Mini Metro, #275, gold, from $65 to................................$80.00

Mini Police Van With Dog and Handler, #448, 1964, from $215.00 to $260.00.

Mister Softee's Ice Cream Van, #428, from $225 to........ $250.00
Mobile Camera Van, #479, from $150 to........................ $175.00
Monkeemobile, #277, from $300 to $350.00
Monte Carlo (1967 Mini Cooper), #339, w/roof rack, from $275 to $325.00
Monte Carlo (1967 Sunbeam IMP), #340, from $125 to.. $150.00
Monte Carlo BMC Mini Cooper S, #308, from $100 to. $125.00
Monte Carlo Mini Cooper, #321, 1965, from $275 to.... $325.00
Monte Carlo Mini Cooper, #321, 1966, w/autographs, from $575 to $625.00
Morris Cowley, #202, from $125 to $150.00
Morris Cowley, #202m, w/motor, from $150 to............... $175.00
Morris Mini-Cooper, #249, wicker, from $120 to $135.00
Morris Mini-Minor, #204, bl, from $225 to..................... $250.00
Morris Mini-Minor, #226, from $100 to.......................... $125.00
Mr McHenry's Trike, #859, from $300 to........................ $350.00
Noddy's Car, #801, blk-face Noddy, from $650 to $700.00
Noddy's Car, #801, other than blk-face Noddy, from $350 to.. $400.00
Noddy's Car, #804, Noddy only, from $250 to $300.00
Noddy's Car, #804, w/Mr Tubby, from $325 to................ $375.00
NSU Sports Prinz, #316, from $75 to..................................$95.00
Oldsmobile Sheriff's Car, #237, from $95 to $120.00
Oldsmobile Staff Car, #358, from $125 to........................ $150.00

Oldsmobile Super 88, #235, 1962, from $70.00 to $100.00.

Oldsmobile Toronado, #264, from $100 to $125.00

Oldsmobile Toronado, #276, metallic gold, from $150 to. $200.00
Oldsmobile Toronado, #276, metallic red, from $75 to $90.00
Opel Senator, #329, bl or bronze, from $45 to $60.00
Opel Senator, #329, silver, from $50 to.............................$65.00

Penguinmobile, #259, from $60.00 to $75.00. (Photo courtesy gasolinealleyantiques.com)

Peugeot 505, #373, from $25 to..$40.00
Pinder's Circus Booking Office, #426, from $50 to $75.00
Platform Trailer, #101, from $25 to $40.00
Plymouth Sports Suburban, #219, from $90 to $110.00
Plymouth US Mail, #443, from $125 to $150.00
Police Range Rover, Belgian, #483, from $80 to............. $100.00
Police Vigilant Range Rover, Police, #461, from $40 to....$55.00
Pontiac Firebird, #343, red hubs, from $100 to............... $125.00
Pontiac Firebird, #343, w/whizwheels, from $60 to............$75.00
Pony Trailer, #102, from $25 to $40.00
Pop Art Morris Mini, #349, from $1,750 to.................$2,250.00
Pop Art Mustang Stock Car, #348, from $125 to............ $150.00
Popeye's Paddle Wagon, #802, from $600 to................... $650.00
Porsche Carrera 6, #330, wht & bl, from $120 to $145.00
Porsche Carrera 6, #330, wht & red, from $65 to $80.00
Porsche Police Car, Polizei, #509, from $85 to................ $100.00
Porsche Police Car, Ritjks Politie, #509, from $150 to... $175.00
Porsche 917, #385, from $35 to $50.00
Porsche 924, #303, from $25 to $40.00
Porsche 924, #321, metallic gr, from $60 to $75.00
Porsche 924, #321, red, from $40 to $55.00
Porsche 924 Polizei, #430, from $30 to $45.00
Professionals Ford Capri, #342, from $75 to.......................$95.00
Professionals Ford Capri, #342, w/chrome bumpers, from $100 to $125.00
Public Address Land Rover, #472, from $150 to............ $175.00
Quad Gun Tank, Trailer & Field Gun, #909, from $55 to ..$70.00
Radar Scanner, #353, from $65 to $80.00
Radio Rescue Rover, #416, bl, from $110 to $140.00
Radio Rescue Rover, #416, yel, from $380 to................. $415.00
Radio Rescue Rover, #416s, w/suspension, bl, from $110 to . $140.00
Radio Rescue Rover, #416s, w/suspension, yel, from $400 to. $450.00
RAF Land Rover, #351, from $95 to $120.00
RAF Vanguard Staff Car, #352, from $95 to $120.00
Rambler Marlin Sports Fastback, #263, from $75 to....... $100.00
Range Rover Ambulance, #482, from $55 to.....................$70.00
Reliant Bond Bug 700, #389, gr, from $120 to $140.00
Reliant Bond Bug 700 ES, #389, orange, from $65 to $80.00
Renault Alpine, #294, from $20 to $35.00
Renault Floride, #222, from $90 to $110.00
Renault R16, #260, from $60 to..$75.00
Renault Turbo, #381, from $25 to $40.00
Renault 11 GTL, #384, maroon, from $40 to $55.00
Renault 16TS, #202, from $45 to..$60.00
Renegade Jeep, #448, from $25 to $40.00
Riley Pathfinder, #205, bl, from $150 to $175.00
Riley Pathfinder, #205, red, from $100 to $125.00
Riley Pathfinder, #205m, w/motor, bl, from $150 to....... $175.00
Riley Pathfinder, #205m, w/motor, red, from $200 to..... $225.00
Riley Police Car, #209, from $100 to $125.00
Riot Police Wagon, #422, from $45 to...............................$60.00
Roger Clark's Ford Capri, #303, gold wheels w/red hubs, from $225 to $275.00
Roger Clark's Ford Capri, #303, w/whizwheels, from $75 to . $100.00
Rolls Royce Silver Shadow, #273, from $100 to $125.00
Rolls Royce Silver Shadow, #280, colors other than silver, from $50 to $65.00
Rolls Royce Silver Shadow, #280, silver, from $80 to..... $100.00
Rough Rider Van, #423, from $45 to..................................$60.00
Rover Monte Carlo, #322, from $150 to......................... $190.00
Rover Triplex, #340, from $25 to $40.00
Rover 2000, #252, metallic bl, from $80 to.........................$95.00
Rover 2000, #252, metallic maroon, from $175 to $200.00
Rover 2000 TC, #275, gr, from $75 to $90.00
Rover 2000 TC, #275, wht, from $150 to $200.00
Rover 2000 TC, #281, from $90 to $110.00
Rover 3500, #338, from $30 to...$45.00
Rover 3500 Police Car, #339, from $30 to $45.00
Rover 90, #204, other colors, from $175 to..................... $200.00
Rover 90, #204, wht & red, 2-tone, from $225 to........... $250.00
Rover 90, #204m, w/motor, from $200 to $225.00
Saint's Jaguar XJS, #320, from $80 to............................ $100.00
Saint's Volvo, #201, from $175 to $200.00
Saint's Volvo P1800, #258, red hood, from $250 to........ $275.00

Saint's Volvo P1800, #258, 1965, white hood, $175.00 to $200.00.

Santa Pod Commuter Dragster, #161, from $45 to $60.00
Santa Pod Dragster, #163, from $40 to..............................$55.00
Sikorsky Helicopter, #922, from $35 to.............................$45.00
Sikorsky Helicopter, #923, Military, from $35 to $45.00
Silver Jubilee Bus, #471, from $45 to $60.00

Simca Sports Car, #315, metallic bl, from $175 to $200.00
Simca Sports Car, #315, silver, from $55 to $70.00

Smith's-Karrier Mobile Canteen, #471, Joe's Diner, from $150.00 to $175.00.

Smith's-Karrier Mobile Canteen, #471, Potato Frittes, from $300 to $350.00
Space Shuttle (Moonraker), #649, from $45 to $60.00
Spider Van, #436, from $50 to...$70.00
Spiderbuggy, #261, from $100 to $125.00
Spidercopter, #928, from $85 to $100.00
Standard Vanguard, #207, from $125 to......................... $150.00
Standard Vanguard, #207m, w/motor, from $150 to $175.00
Starfighter Jet Dragster, #169, from $45 to.........................$60.00
Starsky & Hutch Ford Torino, #292, from $85 to........... $100.00
STP Patrick Eagle Racer, #159, from $45 to $60.00
Stromberg Helicopter, #926, from $85 to........................ $100.00
Studebaker Golden Hawk, #211, no suspension, from $125 to $150.00
Studebaker Golden Hawk, #211, w/suspension, from $150 to $175.00
Studebaker Golden Hawk, #211m, w/motor, from $150 to..$175.00
Studebaker Golden Hawk, #211s, gold-pnt, w/suspension, from $100 to $125.00
Stunt Bike, #681, from $250 to $275.00
Sunbeam Imp Police, #506, from $125 to $150.00
Superbike, #266, from $75 to $90.00
Superman Van, #435, from $50 to.....................................$75.00
Supermobile, #265, from $75 to $90.00
Surtees TS9, #150, from $45 to $60.00
SU100 Tank Destroyer, #905, from $60 to.........................$75.00
Talbot Matra Rancho, #457, gr or red, from $30 to $45.00
Talbot Matra Rancho, #457, wht or orange, from $45 to ..$60.00
Team Surtees, #153, from $45 to $60.00
Thunderbird Guided Missile, #350, from $100 to........... $125.00
Touring Caravan, #490, from $30 to $45.00
Toyota 2000 GT, #375, from $100 to $125.00
Triumph Acclaim, #276, from $25 to $40.00
Triumph Driving School, #277, from $30 to......................$45.00
Triumph Herald, #231, from $100 to.............................. $125.00
Triumph TR2 Sports Car, #301, from $150 to $175.00
Tyrell P34 Racer, #162, from $40 to $55.00
US Army Rover, #500, from $450 to $500.00
USA Racing Buggy, #167, from $30 to $45.00
Vantastic Van, #432, from $30 to.......................................$45.00
Vanwall, #150, regular, from $90 to................................ $110.00
Vauxhall Velox, #203, dual colors, from $175 to $200.00
Vauxhall Velox, #203, solid colors, from $150 to $175.00
Vauxhall Velox, #203, w/motor, dual colors, from $250 to...$275.00
Vauxhall Velox, #203, w/motor, red or yel, from $200 to.. $225.00
Vegas Ford Thunderbird, #348, from $85 to $105.00
Volvo P-1800, #228, from $75 to $90.00
VW Breakdown Truck, #490, from $100 to $125.00
VW Delivery Van, #433, from $100 to $125.00
VW Driving School, #400, bl, from $60 to.........................$75.00
VW Driving School, #400, red, from $150 to................ $175.00
VW Karman Ghia, #239, from $75 to.................................$90.00
VW Kombi, #434, from $100 to $125.00
VW Personnel Carrier, #356, from $125 to $150.00
VW Pickup, #431, metallic gold, from $300 to.............. $350.00
VW Pickup, #431, yel, from $100 to $125.00
VW Police Car, #489, from $45 to $60.00
VW Police Car, #492, w/gr mudguards, from $275 to..... $325.00
VW Police Car, Politie, #492, from $250 to $300.00
VW Police Car, Polizei, #73, from $150 to $175.00
VW Police Car, Polizei, #492, from $85 to $100.00
VW Polo, #289, from $25 to $40.00
VW Polo, #302, from $20 to $35.00
VW Polo Turbo, #309, from $25 to....................................$40.00
VW Toblerone Van, #441, from $125 to......................... $150.00
VW 1200, #383, red or orange, from $65 to $80.00
VW 1200, #383, yel ADAC, from $175 to $225.00
VW 1200, #401, from $60 to...$75.00
VW 1200, Swiss PTT, #383, from $125 to...................... $150.00
VW 1200 East Africa Safari, #256, from $225 to........... $250.00
VW 1200 Rally, #384, from $70 to.....................................$85.00
Walls Ice Cream Van, #447, from $300 to $350.00
Wild Honey Dragster, #164, from $40 to $55.00
Woolworth Silver Jubilee Bus, #471, from $50 to.............$65.00

Classics

Renault (1910) 12/16, #9032-A, M (no box), $50.00; MIB, from $75.00 to $85.00. (Photo courtesy gasolinealleyantiques)

Bentley (1927), #9001-A, from $70 to................................$80.00
Bentley (1927), #9002-A, from $75 to................................$85.00

Daimler 38 (1910), #9021-A, from $60 to $70.00
Ford Model T, #9013, any variation, from $60 to $70.00
Renault 12/16 (1910), #9031-A, from $75 to $85.00
Rolls-Royce Silver Ghost, #9041, from $50 to..................$60.00

Corgitronics

Chevrolet Fire Chief, #1008, from $50 to.........................$60.00
Corgitronics Beep Beep Bus, #1004, from $50 to..............$60.00
Corgitronics Firestreak, #1001, from $85 to.................. $100.00
Corgitronics Roadtrain, #1002, from $65 to $75.00
Firestreak, #1011, from $40 to..$50.00
Ford Torino, #1003, from $50 to $60.00
Land Rover & Compressor, #1007, from $60 to $70.00
Maestro MG1600, #10029, from $50 to...............................$60.00
Police Land Rover, #1005, from $50 to..............................$60.00
Roadshow, Radio, #1006, from $60 to.................................$70.00

Gift Sets

Agricultural Set, #5, from $275 to.................................. $325.00

Avengers John Steed's Vintage Bentley and Emma Peel's Lotus Elan, #40-A, 1966, from $750.00 to $800.00.

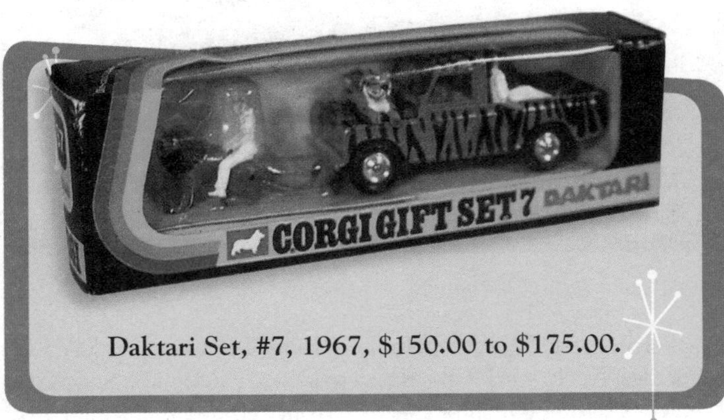

Daktari Set, #7, 1967, $150.00 to $175.00.

Batman Set, #40, from $250 to... $300.00
Batmobile & Batboat, #3, w/'Bat'-hubs, from $425 to $475.00
Batmobile & Batboat, #3, w/whizzwheels, from $225 to. $275.00
Buick Riviera & Boat, #31, from $250 to........................ $300.00
Car Transporter Set, #1, from $800 to..........................$1,000.00
Car Transporter Set, #20, minimum value from $1,000 to.$1,250.00
Centurion Tank & Transporter, #10, from $125 to......... $150.00
Chipperfield's Circus Crane Truck & Cage, #12, from $325 to...$350.00
Chopper Squad, #35, from $60 to $75.00
Combine Harvester Set, #8, from $375 to $425.00
Constructor Set, #24, from $150 to.................................. $175.00
Corporal Missile & Launcher, #9, from $575 to $625.00
Country Farm Set, #4, from $75 to......................................$90.00
Country Farm Set, #5, w/no hay, from $80 to $100.00
Ecurie Ecosse Set, #16, from $525 to............................. $600.00
Emergency Set, #80, from $80 to.......................................$95.00
ERF Milk Truck & Trailer, #21, from $350 to................. $375.00
ERF Truck & Trailer, #11, from $200 to......................... $225.00
Ferrari Racing Set, #29, from $75 to $90.00
Fiat & Boat, #37, from $60 to..$75.00
Ford Sierra & Caravan, #1, from $40 to.............................$50.00
Ford 500 Tractor & Beast Trailer, #1, from $150 to $175.00
Fordson Tractor & Plough, #13, from $150 to $175.00
Fordson Tractor & Plough, #18, from $125 to $140.00
Giant Daktari Set, #14, from $475 to............................. $525.00
Glider Set, #12, from $80 to $95.00
Golden Guinea Set, #20, from $275 to $325.00
Grand Prix Set, #12, from $425 to $500.00
Jaguar & Powerboat, #38, from $70 to $85.00
James Bond Set, #22, from $250 to $300.00
Jean Richards' Circus Set, #48, from $200 to................. $225.00
Jeep & Motorcycle Trailer, #10, from $30 to.....................$50.00
Land Rover & Horsebox, #15, from $95 to..................... $120.00
Land Rover & Pony Trailer, #2, from $175 to................. $200.00
Lions of Longleat, #8, from $175 to $225.00
London Set, #11, no Policeman, from $125 to $150.00
London Set, #11, w/Policeman, from $575 to................. $650.00
Lotus Racing Set, #32, from $100 to $125.00
Mantra Rancho & Trailer, #25, from $60 to $75.00
Matra Rancho & Racer, #26, from $70 to...........................$85.00
Mazda Pickup & Dinghy, #28, w/trailer, from $60 to.........$75.00
Military Set, #17, from $80 to $95.00
Monte Carlo Set, #38, from $575 to $650.00
Peugeot Tour De France, #13, from $80 to...................... $100.00
Pinder's Circus Rover & Trailer, #30, from $125 to $150.00
Pony Club Set, #47, from $45 to $60.00
Racing Car Set, #5, from $275 to $325.00
RAF Land Rover & Missile, #3, from $225 to $275.00
RAF Land Rover & Missile, #4, from $475 to $550.00
Rambler Marlin, #10, w/kayaks, from $200 to $225.00
Renault Tour De France, #13, from $150 to.................... $175.00
Rocket Age Set, #6, from $900 to $1,250.00
Royal Canadian Mounted Police, #45, from $80 to...........$95.00
Silo & Conveyor, #322, from $60 to $75.00
Silver Jubilee State Landau, #41, from $45 to....................$60.00
Silvertone Set, #15, from $1,750 to $2,000.00
Spider-Man Set, #23, from $225 to $250.00
Super Karts, #26, from $25 to $40.00
Tarzan Set, #36, from $250 to.. $275.00
Tower Wagon, #14, from $100 to $125.00
Tractor & Trailer, #7, from $125 to $150.00

Tractor & Trailer, #29, from $125 to $150.00
Tractor & Trailer, #32, from $175 to $200.00
Tractor w/Shovel & Trailer, #9, from $175 to $225.00
Unimog Dumper, #2, from $150 to $175.00
VW Transporter & Cooper Maserati, #6, from $175 to.. $200.00
VW Transporter & Cooper Masarati, #25, from $150 to. $175.00

Huskies

Huskies were marketed exclusively through the Woolworth stores from 1965 to 1969. In 1970, Corgi Juniors were introduced. Both lines were sold in blister packs. Listed below are some of the character-related examples.

Bat Boat, #1003A, Husky on base, from $125 to $150.00
Bat Boat, #1003B, Junior on base, from $80 to $95.00
Batmobile, #1002A, Husky on base, from $200 to.......... $225.00
Chitty Chitty Bang Bang, #1006A, Husky on base, from $200 to $225.00
Chitty Chitty Bang Bang, #1006B, Junior on base, from $175 to $200.00
Crime Busters Gift Set, #3008, scarce, from $825 to $900.00
Ironside Police Van, #1007, from $125 to $150.00
James Bond Aston Martin, #1001B, Junior on base, from $150 to $200.00
James Bond Bobsleigh, #1011, from $300 to.................. $325.00
James Bond's Aston Martin, #1001A, Husky on base, from $200 to $250.00
Jerry's Banger, #1014, from $70 to $85.00
Monkeemobile, #1004A, Husky on base, from $200 to.. $225.00
Monkeemobile, #1004B, Junior on base, from $175 to... $200.00
Popeye Paddle Wagon, #1008, from $200 to.................. $225.00
Spectre Bobsleigh, #1012, from $300 to......................... $325.00
Tom's Go-Kart, #1013, from $70 to $85.00
UNCLE Car, #1005A, Husky on base, from $175 to...... $200.00
UNCLE Car, #1005B, Junior on base, from $1,500 to. $1,750.00

Major Packs

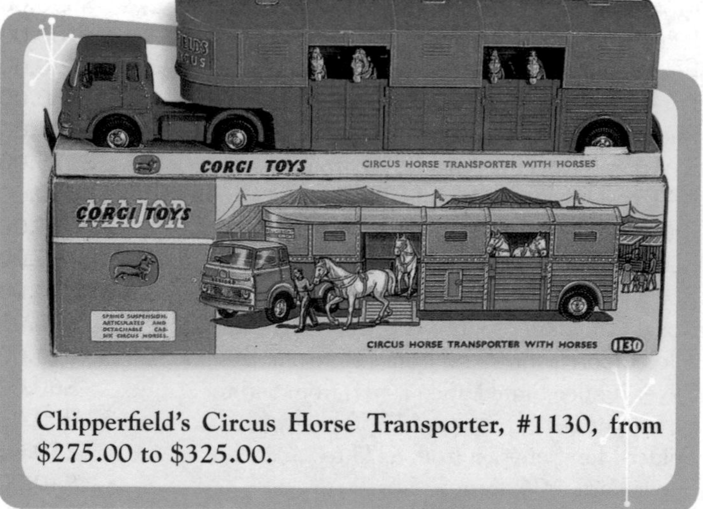

Chipperfield's Circus Horse Transporter, #1130, from $275.00 to $325.00.

Airport Crash Truck, #1103, from $100 to...................... $125.00
Airport Emergency Tender, #1118, from $80 to................$95.00
Berliet Container Truck, #1107, from $70 to....................$85.00
Berliet Racehorse Transporter, #1105, from $70 to...........$85.00
Berliet Wrecker, #1144, from $75 to $90.00
Bloodhound Missile Platform, #1116, from $100 to $125.00
Bloodhound Missile Trolley, #1117, from $70 to $85.00
Carrimore Car Transporter, #1001, bl cab, from $250 to . $300.00
Carrimore Car Transporter, #1138, from $150 to $200.00
Carrimore Low Loader, #1100, yel cab, from $250 to $275.00
Carrimore Low Loader, #1132, from $250 to $300.00
Carrimore Machinery Carrier, #1131, from $150 to $175.00
Chipperfield's Circus Animal Cage, #1123, from $150 to. $175.00
Chipperfield's Circus Crane, #1121, from $225 to $275.00
Corporal Erector & Missile, #1113, from $400 to........... $450.00
Corporal Missile on Launching Ramp, #1112, from $150 to . $200.00
Dolphinarium, #1164, from $150 to................................ $175.00
Ecurie Ecosse Transporter, #1126, from $200 to.............. $250.00
Euclid Tractor, #1102, gr, from $150 to $175.00
Euclid Tractor & Dozer, #1107, orange, from $300 to $350.00
Ferrymaster Truck, #1147, from $125 to $150.00
Ford Aral Tanker, #1161, from $90 to $110.00
Ford Car Transporter, #1159, from $100 to $125.00
Ford Car Transporter, #1170, from $90 to $110.00
Ford Esso Tanker, #1157, from $60 to $75.00
Ford Transit Wrecker, #1140, from $35 to $45.00
HDL Hovercraft, #1119, from $100 to............................ $125.00
Heavy Equipment Transporter, #1135, from $450 to...... $500.00
Holmes Wrecker, #1142, from $135 to............................ $180.00
Hydrolic Crane, #1101, from $60 to $75.00
Hyster Sealink, #1113, from $150 to.............................. $175.00
International Truck, #1118, gr, from $150 to $175.00
Machinery Carrier, #1104, from $150 to......................... $175.00

Mack-Priestman Crane Truck, #1154-A, 1972, from $100.00 to $125.00.

Mack Truck, #1152, Exxon Tanker, from $150 to........... $175.00
Mercedes Truck, #1129, from $35 to $50.00
Mercedes Unimog Dumper, #1145, from $60 to $75.00
Mercedes Unimog Snowplough, #1150, from $70 to.........$85.00
Michelin Container Truck, #1108, from $45 to.................$60.00
Michelin Truck, #1109, from $60 to $75.00
Mobilgas Tanker, #1110, from $275 to $325.00

Priestman Crane, #1154, from $125 to $150.00
Scammell Co-op Truck, #1151, from $250 to $300.00
Simon Snorkel Bedford Fire Engine, #1127, from $125 to. $150.00
Skyscraper Tower Crane, #1155, from $75 to $90.00
Troop Transporter, #1133, from $250 to......................... $300.00

Diecast

Diecast replicas of cars, trucks, planes, trains, etc., represent a huge corner of today's collector market, and their manufacturers see to it that there is no shortage. Back in the 1920s, Tootsietoy had the market virtually to themselves, but one by one, other companies had a go at it, some with more success than others. Among them were the American companies of Barclay, Hubley, and Manoil, all of whom are much better known for other types of toys. After the war, Metal Masters, Smith-Miller, and Doepke Ohlsson-Rice (among others) tried the market with varying degrees of success. Some companies were phased out over the years, while many more entered the market with fervor. Today it's those fondly remembered models from the 1950s and 1960s that many collectors yearn to own. Solido produced well-modeled, detailed little cars; some had dome lights that actually came on when the doors were opened. Politoy's were cleanly molded with good detailing and finishes. Mebetoys, an Italian company that has been bought out by Mattel, produced several; and some of the finest come from Brooklyn.

In 1968, the Topper Toy Company introduced its line of low-friction, high-speed Johnny Lightning cars to be in direct competition with Mattel's Hot Wheels. To gain attention, Topper sponsored Al Unser's winning race car, the 'Johnny Lightning,' in the 1970 Indianapolis 500. Despite the popularity of their cars, the Topper Toy Company went out of business in 1971. Today the Johnny Lightnings are highly sought after, and a new company, Playing Mantis, is reproducing many of the original designs as well as several models that never made it into regular production.

If you're interested in Majorette Toys, we recommend *Collecting Majorette Toys* by Dana Johnson; ordering information is given with Dana's listing under Diecast, in the section called Categories of Special Interest in the back of the book. Dana is also the author of *Toy Car Collector's Guide; Matchbox Toys, 1947 to 2003;* and *The Other Matchbox Toys, 1947 – 2004* (all published by Collector Books).

Values are for examples in mint condition and in the original packaging unless noted otherwise.

See also Corgi; Dinky; Farm Toys; Hot Wheels; Matchbox; Tekno; Tootsietoys.

Ahi, Buick, from $20 to..$25.00
Ahi, Darracq (1904) $15.00
Ahi, Dodge Military Ambulance..$15.00
Ahi, Dodge Military Lumber Truck...................................$15.00
Ahi, Dodge Military Searchlight Truck.............................$12.00
Ahi, Ford Model T (1915), from $15 to............................$20.00
Ahi, Mercedes-Benz 22OSE $16.00
Ahi, Midget Racer, from $20 to...$25.00
Ahi, Rambler (1903) $12.00
Ahi, Renault Floride...$16.00
Ahi, Rolls Royce Silver Wraith, from $25 to.....................$30.00
Ahi, Simca Aronde P60 ....$16.00
Ahi, Volvo PV 544 .... $160.00
Anker, Alfa Romeo 1300, from $20 to...............................$25.00
Anker, Audi 100 ....$18.00
Anker, Renault Rodeo Jeep $18.00
Asahi Model Pet, Nissan Silvia Coupe $75.00
Asahi Model Pet, Subary 360 .... $135.00
Ashai Model Pet, Datsun Bluebird UHT $50.00
Aurora Cigar Box, Buick Riviera..$35.00
Aurora Cigar Box, Ferrari Berlinetta.................................$35.00
Aurora Cigar Box, Ford J Car, yel, from $30 to.................$40.00
Aurora Cigar Box, Mercury Cougar $35.00
Auto Pilen, Ferrari 512 ....$60.00
Auto Pilen, Mercedes Taxi, from $40 to $50.00
Bandai, Hato Bus, bl & wht...$20.00
Bandai, Tank Lorry JAL...$6.00
Bandii, Mazda RX7 25i...$5.00
Bandii, Porsche 903, silver...$16.00
Bandii, Porsche 928, bl, from $16 to $20.00
Bang, Ford Mk II Le Mans, bl or blk, ea from $25 to.........$35.00
Barclay, Ambluance, #50, 5" $50.00
Barclay, Army Truck w/Gun, #151 ....$35.00
Barclay, Austin Coupe, 2"...$30.00
Barclay, Federal Truck (1937)...$25.00
Barclay, Renault Tank, #47..$40.00
Barclay, Searchlight Truck, from $145 to $160.00
Barclay, Streamline Car, #302, 3⅛" $35.00
Barlux, Ferarri B2...$12.00
Barlux, Fiat Ambulance, from $25 to..................................$35.00
Barlux, Road Roller $20.00
Barlux, Tyrell-Ford...$10.00
BBR, Ferrari 250 GTE (1959), from $150 to $180.00
BBR, Ferrari 275 GRB (1965) $175.00
BBR, Ferrari 308 GTB Coupe, red, from $165 to $185.00
Bburago, Bugatti Atlantic (1936), Bijoux series $25.00

Bburago, Chevrolet Corvette (1957), from $20.00 to $30.00. (Photo courtesy Dana Johnson)

Bburago, Dodge Viper GTS, metallic bl w/wht racing stripes, from $7 to $10.00
Bburago, Dump Truck, 1500 series, M, from $30 to...........$35.00
Bburago, Fiat Panda, 4000 series $12.00

Bburago, Fiat Tipo, from $12 to $15.00
Bburago, Jaguar SS 100, 1937 .... $30.00
BBurago, Lancia Stratos, 4000 series $12.00
Bburago, Porsche 911S $20.00
Benbros, AEC Box Van $30.00
Benbros, Armored Car (3¾") & Field Gun (4") $45.00
Benbros, Caterpillar Bulldozer, 4½" $55.00
Benbros, Lorry w/Searchlight $50.00
Benbros, Rolls Royce (1906), from $15 to $20.00
Bendros, Army Land Rover $25.00
Best Toys of Kansas, Pontiac Sedan, #100 .... $45.00
Best Toys of Kansas, Racer #76, 4", from $30 to $35.00
Best Toys of Kansas, Sedan, #87 .... $30.00
Best-Box of Holland, Ford Model T Coupe, from $24 to .. $27.00
Best-Box of Holland, Saloon, #501 DAF 1400 .... $27.00
Box Model, Ferrari 250 IM Street, red, #8434 .... $20.00
Brooklins, Rover 90 P4 Lansdowne (1957), from $45 to... $65.00
Brooklins (British Issues), Chevrolet El Camino (1959), from $60 to $75.00
Brooklins (Canadian Issues), Crysler Newport 4-Door (1940), from $175 to $225.00
Brooklins (Canadian Issues), Ford Victoria 2-Door (1930), from $100 to $250.00
Brooklins (Canadian Issues), Packard (1932) $225.00
Brooklins (Robeddie Models), Saab 99 (1969), from $60 to.. $85.00
Brookolins (British Issues), Buick Roadmaster Coupe (1949), from $65 to $150.00
Brumm, any model, ea $24.00
Brumm, Fiat S 61 (1903), from $18 to $24.00
Brumm, Limited Editions, any model, ea from $35 to $45.00

Brumm, Porsche 356 Speedster (1952), $15.00 to $20.00. (Photo courtesy Dana Johnson)

Buby, VW Buggy $5.00
Buccaneer, any model, ea from $20 to $25.00
Budgie, Coast to Coast Refrigeration Truck, #202, 1959, 6", EX, A $92.00
Budgie, Dump Truck $24.00
Budgie, Hansom Cab, #100, 1970s, 4½", MIB, A $45.00
Budgie, Horse Box, #294, 1960s, 4½", MIB, A $75.00
Budgie, London Taxi Cab, #101, 1970s, 4¼", MIB, A $50.00
Budgie, Pitt Alligator Low Loader, 1960s, 6½", NMIB, A.... $105.00
Budgie, Plateglass Transporter, #304, 1960s, 4¼", NMIB, A.. $83.00
Budgie, Rolls-Royce Silver Cloud, #102, from $30 to $40.00
Budgie, Routemaster Double-Decker Bus, #236, 1970s, Uniflow decals, 4¼", MIB, A $50.00
Budgie, Rover Squad Car $15.00
CD, Lelage Linousine $100.00
CD, MG Record Car $100.00
Chad Valley, Ambulance $35.00
Chad Valley, Commer Fire Engine, from $160 to $180.00
Chad Valley, Commer Flat Truck $175.00
Chad Valley, Guy Ice Cream Truck $250.00
Chad Valley, Post Office Van $35.00
Charbens, Alfa Romeo Racer $120.00
Charbens, Standard 6HP (1903), Old Crock series $18.00
Chrono, Porsche 550 RS (1953), silver, from $25 to $39.00
CIJ, Renault Floride, #3/58, 1960 .... $55.00

Clover, Melroe (Bobcat) M-200 Loader, from $15.00 to $20.00. (Photo courtesy Dana Johnson)

Con-Cor, Ferrari Testarossa $8.00
Conquest, Buick Super Hard Top (1955), 3-tone $225.00
Conrad, Magirus 4-Axle Dump Truck, #3274 .... $39.00
Conrad, Volkswagen Polo C $10.00
Conrad, Volvo Old Timer Fire Engine (1928) $59.00
Conrad, Volvo Titan L395 Flatbed Truck $48.00
Dalia, Vesper Scooter, gr $75.00
Dalia-Solido, Jaguar D Le Mans, bl, gr or red $100.00
Dalia-Solido, Porsche F2, silver & red $125.00
Dalia-Tekno, Monza GT Coupe $60.00
Danbury Mint, Ferrari 250 Testa Rossa, red, from $110 to... $135.00
Danbury Mint, Pierce Arrow (1933), silver, from $115 to ... $125.00
Diapet, Corvette, #G76, from $65 to $80.00
Diapet, Datsun 280Z Poice Car, #P53 .... $18.00
Diapet, Nissan Cedric Ultima Station Taxi, #P29 .... $39.00
Doepke, Unit Mobile Crane, 11½", MIB, from $300 to .. $400.00
Doepke, Victory 37 Bus (1972) $25.00
Dubuque, Greyhound Bus, 9½" $400.00
Dugu, Benz Victoria (1893), 1964 .... $40.00
Dugu, Fiat 500A Coupe (1936), 1966 .... $60.00
Dugu, OM Dump Truck, Sispla series $95.00
Durham Classics, Ford Pickup (1953), bl $120.00
Durham Classics, Lincoln Zephyr Coupe (1938) $100.00

Eagle's Race/Eagle Collectibles, Ford Hot Rod (1940), any color, from $30 to ...$35.00
Efsi, Commer Ambulance, from $12 to...$16.00

Eidai, Boom Truck, from $10.00 to $15.00. (Photo courtesy Dana Johnson)

Eligor, Chrysler New Yorker Convertible (1958)...$25.00
Eligor, Ford Police Sedan (1932), from $30 to...$35.00
Eligor, Ford Roadster Fire Chief (1932)...$25.00
Enchanted, Buick Riveria (1949)...$115.00
Enchanted, Chevy Nomad (1957), from $75 to...$100.00
Enchanted, Kaiser Manhattan (1953), from $75 to...$100.00
Enchanted, Packard Victoria (1937)...$85.00
Enchantment Land Coach Builders, Chevy Nomad Wagon (1957)...$125.00
Enchantment Land Coach Builders, Packard Victoria (1937)...$95.00
Ertl, Buick (1912), red & blk, 1:43 scale, 1985, from $20 to...$25.00
Ertl, Chevy Cameo Pickup (1955)...$8.00

Ertl, Chevrolet Stake Truck (1903), #2503, from $10.00 to $15.00. (Photo courtesy Dana Johnson)

Ertl, Corvette Coupe (1963), dk bl, 1:18 scale, from $30 to...$35.00
Ertl, Dodge Ram Truck (1995), blk or red...$25.00
Ertl, Dukes of Hazzard, 4-pc set, 1:64 scale, 1991, MIB (sealed), A...$125.00
Ertl, Hawkeye Flatbed (1931), True Value...$24.00
Ertl, John Deere 690C Excavator, MIB...$15.00
Ertl, Plymouth Hemi Roadrunner (1969), yel...$30.00
France Jouets, Ambulance (GMC Truck), 300 series, 1959...$80.00
France Jouets, Dump Truck (Berlier Straidair), 700 series, 1967...$80.00
France Jouets, Police Jeep, 1965, from $60 to...$75.00
Franklin Mint, Chevy Corvette (1953)...$95.00
Franklin Mint, Ford Model T (1913), 1:16 scale, from $120 to...$140.00
Franklin Mint, Ford Mustang (1964), 1:43 scale, from $65 to...$75.00
Franklin Mint, Ford Thunderbird (1962), from $55 to...$65.00
Fun Ho!, Land Rover, 1966-78, 1¾", from $40 to...$60.00
Gama, Ford Taunus 17M, #901, 1959, from $45 to...$55.00
Gama, Mercede-Benz 300CE, from $20 to...$30.00
Gama, Opel Rekord, 1978...$35.00
Goldvarg, Chevrolet Bel-Air 4-Door Sedan (1954)...$89.00
Goldvarg, Ford Deluxe Sedan (1946), from $85 to...$100.00
Goodee, GMC Pickup Truck (1953), 3"...$18.00
Goodee, GMC Pickup Truck (1953), 6"...$25.00
Goodee, Lincoln Capri Hardtop (1953), 3", from $16 to...$20.00
Goodee, Moving Van...$15.00
Guiloy, Harley-Davidson Custom Sport Motorcycle...$18.00
Guiloy, Indian Chief Motorcycle (1948), from $35 to...$45.00
Guisval, Chevy Camero (1979), from $16 to...$20.00
Guisval, Lincoln 4-Door Sedan (1928)...$15.00
Guisval, Porsche 959, from $16 to...$20.00
Hartoy, Wrigley's Mack Box Truck...$25.00
Hubley, Army Air Combat Squadron Hangar, 5-pc set, folding wings, unused, NMIB, A...$460.00
Hubley, Car Transport, w/4 plastic autos, 14", VG...$325.00
Hubley, Cement Mixing Truck, red cab w/NP drum on gr bed, BRT, 10", NMIB, A...$440.00
Hubley, Chrysler Airflow, 5", from $80 to...$95.00
Hubley, Hubley Transport #492, w/3 plastic cars, 14", EX (G+ box), A...$150.00
Hubley, Log Truck, 1960s, w/logs, 10", G, from $35 to...$45.00
Hubley, Poultry Truck, w/accessories, 10", from $265 to...$300.00
Hubley, School Bus, 9½", EX...$70.00

Hubley, School Bus, #493, 1950s, 9½", NMIB, A, $165.00. (Photo courtesy serioustoyz.com)

Hubley, Sedan, 1940s, BRT, 7", NM, A...$92.00
Hubley, Tractor, orange w/blk rubber tires, 7", from $150 to...$175.00
Hubley Kiddie Toy, Convertible, bl, 7", EXIB...$165.00
Hubley Kiddie Toy, Custom Sports Car, yel, 13", rare...$850.00
Hubley Kiddie Toy, De Luxe Sports Car...$250.00
Hubley Kiddie Toy, Dump Truck, #510, from $240 to...$265.00
Hubley Kiddie Toy, Sedan, #452, 7", from $30 to...$45.00
Hubley Kiddie Toy, Texaco Tanker Truck, all-in-one w/slanted back, 1940s, 5", EX+, A...$65.00

Hubley Mighty-Metal, Tow Truck, from $120 to........... $135.00
Husky, Man From UNCLE Gull Wing Car w/2 figures, 1968, 3" $60.00
Joal, Adams Probe 16, from $35 to.................................$45.00
Joal, Alfa Romeo Giulia 55 ....$25.00

Joal, CAT-920 Wheel Loader, from $12.00 to $16.00. (Photo courtesy Bertois Auctions)

Joal, Chrysler 150, from $35 to...$45.00
Joal, Ferrari 512S $40.00
Joal, Ford Fiesta..$25.00
Joal, Jaguar E-Type Roadster...$30.00
Johnny Lightning, Bug Bomb, M, from $25 to..................$35.00
Johnny Lightning, Custom El Camino, 1969, MIP...... $1,250.00
Johnny Lightning, Custom El Camino (1994), M..............$8.00
Johnny Lightning, Custom Eldorado, open doors, M $100.00
Johnny Lightning, Custom GTO, 1969, M.................... $250.00

Johnny Lightning, Custom Spoiler, 1970, MOC, A, $70.00. (Photo courtesy serioustoyz.com)

Johnny Lightning, Custom XKE, doors open, 1969, M .. $125.00
Johnny Lightning, Jet Powered Screamer, 1970, M...........$35.00
Johnny Lightning, Jumpin' Jag, MIP $35.00
Johnny Lightning, Jumpin' Jag, 1970, M, from $20 to.......$25.00
Johnny Lightning, Sand Stormer, 1970, M $30.00
Johnny Lightning, Vulture, MIP $70.00
Jouef, Honda Acura NSX, gray, from $25 to.....................$25.00
JRD, Unic Van Hafa, 1959 .... $195.00
Kansas Toy & Novelty, Army Truck, #74, 2¼", from $50 to.. $65.00
Kansas Toy & Novelty, Bearcat Racer, #26, 4" $90.00
Kansas Toy & Novelty, Convertible Coupoe, #35, 2¼".....$50.00
Kansas Toy & Novelty, Midget Racer w/Driver, 3"...........$40.00
Kemlows, Armored Car $55.00
Kenner Fast 111's, any model, ea from $4 to $6.00
Kenner Winner's Circle, Drag Racing models, 1:64 scale, ea from $4 to $5.00
Kiddie Car Classics, Ford Mustang (1964), 7" $55.00
Kiddie Car Classics, Garton Delivery Cycle (1950), 6¾" ...$45.00
Kirk, Chevrolet Monza GT, from $65 to...........................$75.00
Kirk, Chevy Monza Spider $60.00
Kyosho, MGB Mk-1 (1966), gr, red or wht, ea from $50 to..$65.00
Lansing Slik-Toys, Roadster, #9701, 3½", from $35 to.......$45.00
Lansing-Slik Toys, Fastback Sedan, #9600, 7" $40.00
Lansing-Slik Toys, Tanker Truck, #9705, 4".......................$30.00
Leslie-Henry, Cargo Comet Freight Train Set, complete, NMIB...$125.00
Lledo, Delivery Van, 1983, from $15 to $20.00
Lledo, Ford Model T Tanker, 1983, from $15 to...............$20.00
Lledo, Greyhound Scenicruiser, from $18 to......................$20.00
LLedo, Long Distance Coach, 1985 ....$10.00
Lledo, Packard Town Van, 1986, from $15 to $20.00
Lledo, Volkswagen Cabriolet, red.....................................$25.00
Londontoy, Chevy Master DeLuxe Coupe (1941), 6" $32.00
Londontoy, City Bus, 4", from $30 to..............................$35.00
Londontoy, Dump Truck, lg, from $110 to $125.00
Londontoy, Ford Pickup (1941), 4" $25.00
Londontoy, Ford Pickup (1941), 6", from $35 to $45.00
Lone Star, Chevy Corvette, coral......................................$65.00
Lone Star, Chevy Corvette, wht..$90.00
Lone Star, Dodge Dart Phoenix, metallic bl, from $80 to.. $100.00
Lone Star, Ford Mustang Fastback, Flyers #39, from $25 to..$40.00
Maisto, Bugatti EB110 (1992), bl or red, M......................$30.00
Maisto, Jaguar XK8, from $10 to $15.00
Maistro, Ferrari F50 Coupe, yel or red, ea from $25 to $35.00
Majorette, Bernard Circus Truck $18.00
Majorette, Citreon DS...$29.00
Majorette, Citreon Maserati SM, from $12 to $15.00

Majorette, Fiat Multi Benne Skip Truck, $18.00. (Photo courtesy Dana Johnson)

Majorette, Mercedes-Benz Stake Truck With Hay Load, $6.00. (Photo courtesy Dana Johnson)

Majorette, Toyota Truck & Trailer, from $12 to $15.00
Majorette, VW Golf, red, from $5 to $6.00
Majorette Sonic Flashers, Ambulance, from $8 to.............$12.00
Mandarin, Honda 9 Coupe, from $6 to..............................$8.00
Manoil, Bus, 1945-55, from $35 to...................................$50.00
Manoil, Fire Engine, 1945-55 ....$95.00
Manoil, Roadster, 1935-41, from $85 to.......................... $100.00
Master Caster, Yellow Cab (1947), 7" $225.00
Mebetoys, BMW 320 Rally, 1980, from $27 to.................$35.00
Mebetoys, Fiat 850 (1966), from $28 to............................$35.00
Mebetoys, Lotus JPS, 1973, from $65 to $90.00
Mebetoys, Pontiac Firebird (1983), from $28 to...............$35.00
Mebetoys, Porsche 912 Rally, 1974 ....$30.00
Mebetoys, Willys Fire Jeep (1974), from $35 to.................$40.00
Mercury, Alfa Romeo, 1951...$40.00
Mercury, Cadillac 62 Sedan (1949), from $140 to.......... $175.00
Mercury, Fiat 131 Fire Chief, 1971.....................................$25.00
Mercury, Fiat 131 Wagon & Trailer (1977), from $35 to...$45.00
Mercury, Jack's Demon Dragster, 1969 ....$29.00
Mercury, Sigma Grand Prix (1969) $35.00
Mercury, Stagecoach, from $80 to......................................$95.00
Midgetoy, American LeFrance Fire Pumper, 1957, A........$19.00
Midgetoy, Jeep, 1960s, red, from $8 to $12.00

Midgetoy, Playset, four vehicles, two boats, trailer, and two sets of gas pumps, 1974, MIB, A, 65.00. (Photo courtesy serioustoyz.com)

Milton, Ford Model T, from $27 to $30.00
Milton, Jaguar 3.8 Saloon...$49.00
Mira, Chevy Pickup (1953) $25.00
Mira, Ford Thunderbird (1956), from $30 to.....................$40.00
Mira, Renault Espace Ambulance $19.00
Morestone, Daimler Ambulance $120.00
Morestone, Mercedes-Benz Racer $40.00
Navy Fighter-Bomber Squadron, Hubley, #53, 1950s, set of 5, all w/folding wings, EX+IB, A $920.00
Nicky Toys, Daimler Jaguar 3.4 ....$29.00
Nostalgic, Chevy Corvette (1982) $79.00
Nostalgic, Ford Van (1936), maroon, from $55 to............$70.00
Nostalgic, LaSalle Roadster (1934)......................................$65.00
NZG, CAT 627 Scraper..$59.00
NZG, Kramer Tremo Utility Truck, from $25 to................$25.00
NZG, Scania City Bus CN112, from $45 to $55.00
Playart, Jeep, from $6 to $12.00
Playart, Man From UNCLE car, 2¾", 1960s, NM, A...... $109.00

Politoys, Samurai (1970), #580, $25.00. (Photo courtesy Dana Johnson)

Quiralu, Simca Marly Ambulance, 1957......................... $129.00
Racing Champions, any, ea from $6 to..............................$12.00
Ralstoy, Chevy Step Van (1982) $24.00
Ralstoy, Moving Van, any trade name, ea $39.00
Ralstoy, Safety-Kleen Van, M, from $30 to........................$45.00
Renwal, Pontiac Convertible, from $125 to $140.00
Rio, any, ea from $25 to...$35.00
Road Champs, Ford Woodie (1949), from $16 to..............$18.00
Road Champs, Grehound Eagle Coach.................................$5.00
Sakura, Toyota Land Cruiser, from $24 to..........................$27.00
Schabak, Audi 80 Sedan (1992), from $20 to....................$25.00
Schabak, Ford Transit Van (1986), 1987, from $32 to.......$36.00
Schabak, VW Jetta, 1984 ....$20.00
Schuco, Audi 80 LS, 1972, from $30 to.............................$35.00
Schuco, Krupp Cement Mixer, 3⅝", from $55 to...............$70.00
Schuco, MGA Coupe, 1958, 2", from $55 to.....................$75.00
Schuco, Volkswagen Polo, 1975 ....$25.00
Scottoys, Fiat 600 Saloon, from $30 to $35.00
Siku, Ford 12M, 1963, from $36 to $40.00
Siku, Jeep w/Trailer, 1964-72..$39.00

Siku, Police Bat Transporter, 1989 ....$25.00
Siku, Pontiac GTO (The Judge), 1972-74 ....$49.00
Siku, Porsche 901, 1964-69, from $45 to $60.00
Siku, Volkswagen Vanagon Bus (1973-74) $25.00
Solido, Alpine F3 (1965), 1996 reissue $24.00
Solido, Chrysler Windsor (1946), 1960s, from $30 to $40.00

Solido, Citroen ZX Aura, $15.00. (Photo courtesy Dana Johnson)

Solido, Ford Mustang (1965), 1994 ....$24.00
Solido, Ford Tanker (1936), 1994 ....$30.00
Solido, Jaguar XJ 12 (1978), from $12 to $16.00
Solido, Mack R 600 Fire Engine, from $30 to $35.00
Solido, Volkswagen Golf, 1981-82, from $20 to $36.00
Spot-On, Aston Martin DB3, from $225 to $250.00
Spot-On, Austin 1800 ....$120.00
Spot-On, Ford Consul Classic $165.00
Spot-On, Jaguar Mk 10, from $180 to $210.00
Sunnyside, BMW 728 Sedan, from $6 to $8.00
Tip Top Toy, Coupe, 3½" $39.00
Tip Top Toy, Stake Truck, 5", from $55 to $65.00

Tomica, BLMC Mini Cooper S Mark III, ca 1979, $8.00. (Photo courtesy Dana Johnson)

Tomica, Cadillac Ambulance, #F-2 ....$12.00
Tomica, Datsun Silva Coupe $20.00
Tomica, Datsun 200SX, #235-6, from $6 to $8.00
Tomica, Lotus Elite, #F47, from $6 to $8.00
Tomica, Volkswagen Microbus, #166-F29, from $18 to $24.00
Tomica Dandy, Nissan Skyline $18.00
Tomica Dandy, Toyota Landcruiser, from $22 to $27.00
Top Gear, Falcon XC Covra, from $32 to $39.00
Tri-Ang, Bentley Touring Car (1938), from $120 to $150.00
Tri-Ang, Rolls Royce Sedanca, 1937 ....$150.00
Tri-Ang, Town Coupe (1935), from $120 to $150.00
True Scale, Tru-Toy Truck Set, 4-pc, EXIB (NOS), A.... $375.00
Vitesse, any except Vitesse Victoria, ea $35.00
Vitesse Victoria, any, ea from $22 to $40.00
Western Models, Buick Riviera (1972) $175.00
Yat Ming, Ford Thunderbird (1955), from $25 to $35.00
Ziss, Chevrolet Phaeton (1916), 1969, from $24 to $32.00
Ziss, Ford Ranch Car (1909), 1966 ....$40.00
Ziss, Opel Commodore Coupe (1971), from $36 to $48.00

Dinky

Dinky diecasts were made by Meccano (Britain) as early as 1933, but high on the list of many of today's collectors are those from the decades of the 1950s and 1960s. They made commercial vehicles, firefighting equipment, farm toys, and heavy equipment as well as classic cars that were the epitome of high style, such as the #157 Jaguar XK120, produced from the mid-1950s through the early 1960s. Some Dinkys were made in France; since 1979 no toys have been produced in Great Britain. Values are for examples mint and in the original packaging unless noted otherwise.

Austin Van, #471, Nestlé's, #471, EX, $55.00. (Photo courtesy serioustoyz.com)

AA Motorcycle Patrol, #270, from $115 to $140.00
AC Acceca, #167, all cream, from $275 to $325.00
AC Acceca, #167, dual colors, from $200 to $240.00
AEC Articulated Lorry, #914, from $200 to $225.00
AEC Articulated Transporter & Helicopter, #618, from $170 to $195.00
AEC Articulated Transporter & Tank, #616, from $165 to $190.00
AEC Fuel Tanker, #945, Lucas, from $250 to $275.00
AEC Hoyner Transporter, #974, from $175 to $200.00
AEC Tanker, #991, Shell Chemicals, from $350 to $375.00
Airport Fire Rescue Tender, #263, from $120 to $145.00
Alfa Romeo Giulia, #514, from $175 to $200.00
Alfa Romeo Scarabo, #217, from $120 to $140.00
Alfa Romeo 33, #210, from $190 to $220.00
ANWB Motorcycle Patrol, #272, from $325 to $375.00
Armoured Command Car, #602, from $150 to $175.00

Armoured Command Vehicle, #677, from $175 to......... $200.00
Army Covered Wagon, #623, from $195 to.................... $220.00
Army Personnel, #603, box of 12, from $115 to $140.00
Army 1-Ton Cargo Truck, #641, from $165 to $190.00
Aston Martin, #506, from $200 to $225.00
Aston Martin DB6, #153, from $160 to......................... $195.00
Atlantean City Bus, #291, from $125 to........................ $150.00
Atlantean City Bus, #295, Yellow Pages, from $90 to $120.00
Atlas COPCO Compressor Lorry, #436, from $145 to ... $170.00
Austin Atlantic, #106, bl or blk, from $195 to $240.00
Austin Atlantic, #106, pk, from $385 to........................ $435.00
Austin A105, #176, cream or gray, from $170 to........... $220.00
Austin A105, #176, cream w/bl roof, or gray w/red roof, from $275 to... $325.00
Austin A105, #176, gray, from $170 to.......................... $220.00
Austin Champ, #674, olive drab, from $170 to $195.00
Austin Champ, #674, wht, UN version, from $525 to ... $540.00
Austin Countryman, #197, orange, from $300 to.......... $350.00
Austin Countryman, #199, bl, from $130 to.................. $170.00
Austin Covered Wagon, #413, lt & dk bl, or red & tan, from $675 to... $750.00
Austin Covered Wagon, #413, maroon & cream, or med & lt bl, from $220 to $250.00
Austin Covered Wagon, #413, red & gray, or bl or cream, from $450 to... $500.00
Austin Healey, #546, from $225 to................................ $250.00
Austin Healey Sprite, #112, from $110 to $135.00
Austin Somerset, #161, dual colors, from $275 to $325.00
Austin Somerset, #161, solid colors, from $175 to......... $225.00
Austin Taxi, #254, yel, from $170 to............................ $220.00
Austin 1800, #171, from $135 to.................................. $160.00
Aveling-Barford Dumper, #924, from $175 to................ $200.00
Beach Bunny, #227, from $115 to $130.00
Bedford Articulated Lorry, #409, from $275 to.............. $300.00
Bedford Articulated Lorry, #521, from $175 to.............. $200.00
Bedford Articulated Lorry, #921, from $325 to.............. $350.00
Bedford Fire Engine, #259, from $160 to $200.00
Bedford TK Box Van, #450, Castrol, from $270 to......... $295.00
Bedford TK Tipper, #435, gray or yel cab, from $170 to .. $210.00
Bedford TK Tipper, #435, silver & bl, from $250 to $275.00
Bedford Van, #410, MJ Hire, Marley or Collectors' Gazette, from $160 to... $195.00
Bedford Van, #410, Royal Mail, from $115 to................ $140.00
Bedford Van, #482, Dinky Toys, from $225 to $250.00
Beechcraft C-55 Baron, #715, from $170 to $195.00
Bell Police Helicopter, #732, M*A*S*H, from $100 to .. $125.00
Berliet Wrecker, #589, from $275 to $300.00
Big Bedford Lorry, #522, bl & yel, from $350 to $375.00
Big Bedford Lorry, #522, maroon & fawn, from $200 to .. $225.00
Big Bedford Van, #923, Heinz Ketchup bottle, from $2,000 to $2,250.00
Big Bedford Van, #923, Heinz 57 Varieties & Heinz Baked Beans can, from $750 to... $800.00
Big Ben Lorry, #408, bl & yel, or bl & orange, from $350 to.. $375.00
Big Ben Lorry, #408, maroon & fawn, from $300 to $325.00
Blaw-Knox Bulldozer, #561, from $125 to...................... $150.00
Blaw-Knox Bulldozer, #961, from $175 to...................... $200.00
Blaw-Knox Heavy Tractor, #563, from $120 to $145.00
Blaw-Knox Heavy Tractor, #963, from $175 to $200.00
BMW 1500, #534, from $200 to.................................... $225.00

Breakdown Lorry, #430 1954, M, from $145.00 to $160.00. (Photo courtesy Dana Johnson)

Brink's Armoured Car, #275, no bullion, from $110 to .. $140.00
Brink's Armoured Car, #275, w/gold bullion, from $175 to..$225.00
Brink's Armoured Car, #275, w/Mexican bullion, from $950 to...$1,250.00
BRM Racer, #243, from $145 to................................... $165.00
Buick Roadmaster, #538, from $350 to $375.00
Cadillac El Dorado, #131, from $195 to......................... $215.00
Cadillac El Dorado, #175, from $140 to......................... $195.00
Chevrolet Corvair, #552, from $230 to $255.00
Chevrolet El Camino Pickup, #449, from $145 to.......... $170.00
Chrysler New Yorker, #520, from $275 to...................... $325.00
Chrysler Saratoga, #550, from $350 to.......................... $375.00
Citroen Ambulance, #556, from $275 to $300.00
Citroen DS-19, #522, from $265 to............................... $290.00
Citroen ID-19, #539, from $225 to $250.00
Citroen Police Van, #556, from $205 to $230.00
Citroen 2-CV, #500, from $180 to $210.00
Coles Mobile Crane, #571, from $150 to $175.00
Coles Mobile Crane, #971, from $200 to $215.00
Coles 20-Ton Lorry, #972, mounted crane, yel & blk, from $225 to $250.00
Coles 20-Ton Lorry, #972, mounted crane, yel & orange, from $175 to $200.00
Commando Jeep, #612, from $95 to.............................. $120.00
Commer Breakdown Lorry, #430, all colors other than tan & gr, from $950 to $1,300.00
Commer Breakdown Lorry, #430, tan & gr, from $195 to.. $225.00
Connaught Racer, #236, from $170 to........................... $195.00
Continental Touring Coach, #953, from $475 to $525.00
Convoy Army Truck, #687, from $125 to $150.00
Convoy Dumper, #382, from $120 to............................ $145.00
Convoy Fire Rescue Truck, #384, from $115 to............. $140.00
Convoy Skip Truck, #380, from $120 to........................ $145.00
Corvette Stingray, #221, from $140 to.......................... $165.00
Cosmic Zygon Patroller, #363, for Marks & Spencer, from $230 to $255.00

Coventry-Climax Fork Lift, #401, orange, from $115 to .. $140.00
Coventry-Climax Fork Lift, #401, red, from $475 to...... $550.00
Covered Truck, #584, from $225 to.............................. $250.00
Customized Corvette Stingray, #206, from $130 to $160.00
Customized Land Rover, #202, from $110 to $140.00
Customized Range Rover, #203, from $110 to $130.00
Daimler V8, #146, from $160 to.................................. $185.00
David Brown Tractor, #305, from $125 to...................... $150.00
David Brown Tractor & Harrow, #325, from $160 to $185.00
De Soto Diplomat, #545, from $210 to $235.00
Desoto Fireflite, #192, from $210 to $240.00
Dinky Goods Train Set, #784, from $150 to $175.00
Dodge Royal Sedan, #191, cream w/bl flash, from $280 to ..$320.00
Dodge Royal Sedan, #191, cream w/brn flash, or gr w/blk flash, from $210 to $240.00
Dodge Tipper, #414, all colors other than royal bl, from $170 to $195.00
Dodge Tipper, #414, royal bl, from $190 to.................... $215.00
Dump Truck, #569, from $225 to $250.00
Dump Truck, #580, from $250 to $275.00
Dumper, #585, from $250 to.. $275.00
Duple Luxury Coach, #296, from $70 to..........................$90.00

Eagle Freighter, #359, 1975, MIB, A, $100.00. (Photo courtesy serioustoyz.com)

Eaton Yale Tractor Shovel, #973, from $600 to $650.00
Ed Straker's Car, #352, red, from $175 to....................... $205.00
Ed Straker's Car, #352, yel or gold-plated, from $225 to. $250.00
Electric Dairy Van, #490, Express Dairy, from $200 to ... $225.00
Electric Dairy Van, #491, NCB or Job Dairies, from $200 to. $225.00
Elevator Loader, #564, from $150 to $175.00
Elevator Loader, #964, from $175 to $200.00
ERF Fire Tender, #266, Falck, from $155 to................... $180.00
Estafette Pickup, #563, from $195 to............................ $220.00
Euclid Rear Dump Truck, #965, from $200 to................ $225.00
Farm Tractor & Trailer Set, #399, from $250 to $275.00
Ferrari, #204, from $115 to $135.00
Ferrari P5, #220, from $125 to...................................... $145.00
Ferrari 250 GT, #515, from $175 to............................... $200.00
Ferrari 312/B2, #226, from $125 to $140.00
Fiat 2300 Pathe News Camera Car, #281, from $175 to. $225.00
Fiat 2300 Station Wagon, #172, from $135 to............... $160.00
Fiat 850, #509, from $175 to $200.00
Fire Engine, #555, w/extension ladder, from $150 to...... $175.00
Fire Engine, #955, from $200 to $225.00
Fire Services Gift Set, #957, from $650 to $725.00
Fire Station, #954, from $425 to $450.00
Foden Army Truck, #668, from $125 to......................... $150.00
Foden Diesel 8-Wheel, #501, 2nd cab, from $625 to...... $675.00
Foden Dump Truck, #959, from $300 to $325.00

Foden Flat Truck, #502, first or second cab, from $1,000.00 to $1,250.00.

Foden Flat Truck, #503, 1st cab, from $1,250 to..........$1,500.00
Foden Flat Truck, #503, 2nd cab, bl & orange, from $400 to. $450.00
Foden Flat Truck, #503, 2nd cab, bl & yel, from $1,000 to.$1,500.00
Foden Flat Truck, #503, 2nd cab, 2-tone gr, from $2,750 to. $3,250.00
Foden Flat Truck, #902, from $450 to $475.00
Foden Flat Truck w/Chains, #505, 1st cab, from $3,000 to .. $3,250.00
Foden Flat Truck w/Chains, #505, 2nd cab, from $425 to.. $475.00
Foden Flat Truck w/Chains, #905, from $450 to............ $475.00
Foden Flat Truck w/Tailboard, #903, from $750 to......... $800.00
Foden S20 Fuel Tanker, #950, Burmah, from $200 to..... $225.00
Foden S20 Fuel Tanker, #950, Shell, from $200 to......... $225.00
Foden Tanker, #504, red, from $750 to $950.00
Foden Tanker, #504, 1st cab, 2-tone bl, from $475 to..... $525.00
Foden Tanker, #504, 2nd cab, red, from $600 to............ $650.00
Foden Tanker, #504, 2nd cab, 2-tone bl, from $3,500 to. $3,750.00
Foden Tipper, #432, from $115 to $140.00
Foden 8-Wheel Truck, #901, from $450 to $475.00

Foden 16-Ton Tanker, #942, Regent, MIB, $525.00.

Ford Berth Caravan, #188, from $135 to $175.00

Ford Capri, #143, from $130 to $155.00
Ford Capri, #165, from $160 to $195.00
Ford Corsair, #169, from $135 to...................................... $165.00
Ford Cortina, #139, from $140 to...................................... $165.00
Ford Cortina MKII, #159, from $125 to.......................... $175.00
Ford D 800 Tipper, #438, opening doors, from $120 to .. $145.00
Ford Escort, #168, from $135 to $165.00
Ford Fairlane, #148, gr, from $150 to $195.00
Ford Fairlane, #148, metallic gr, from $200 to $240.00
Ford Fordor, #170, dual colors, from $275 to $325.00
Ford Fordor, #170, solid colors, from $180 to................. $230.00
Ford Fordor US Army Staff Car, #170m, from $340 to... $365.00
Ford GT Racing Car, #215, from $120 to $140.00
Ford Model T, #475, from $170 to.................................... $195.00
Ford Model T w/Santa Claus, #485, from $225 to.......... $250.00
Ford Mustang, #161, from $165 to $200.00
Ford Panda Police Car, #270, from $120 to...................... $145.00
Ford Taunus, #261, Polizei, from $300 to $350.00
Ford Taunus, #551, Polizei, from $225 to $250.00
Ford Taunus, #559, from $225 to...................................... $250.00
Ford Taunus 17M, #154, from $160 to $195.00
Ford Thunderbird, #555, from $265 to............................. $280.00
Ford Transit, #407, from $115 to $140.00
Ford Transit Ambulance, #274, from $115 to $145.00
Ford Transit Ambulance, #276, from $120 to $145.00
Ford Transit Fire, #271, Appliance, from $115 to........... $140.00
Ford Transit Fire, #271, Falck, from $160 to $190.00
Ford Transit Fire, #286, Falck, from $145 to $170.00
Ford Transit Police Accident Unit, #269, Faulk Zonen, from $50 to $75.00
Ford Transit Police Accident Unit, #269, from $105 to . $135.00
Ford Transit Van, #416, 1,000,000 Transits, from $210 to . $240.00
Ford Transit Van, #416 or #417, ea from $115 to............ $140.00
Ford Zephyr, #162, from $185 to $210.00
Ford Zodiac MKIV, #164, bronze, from $175 to.............. $225.00
Ford Zodiac MKIV, #164, silver, from $150 to $185.00
Ford Zodiac Police Car, #255, from $100 to..................... $130.00
Ford 40-RV, #132, from $130 to $155.00
Fork Lift, #597, from $200 to... $225.00
Gabriel Model T Ford, #109, from $150 to $175.00
Glouster Javelin, #735, from $60 to $85.00
Goods Yard Crane, #752, from $75 to............................. $100.00
Goods Yard Crane, #973, from $200 to........................... $225.00
Guy Flat Truck, #512, all colors other than bl or red, from $750 to $900.00
Guy Flat Truck, #512, bl or red, from $400 to................. $450.00
Guy Flat Truck, #912, from $475 to $500.00
Guy Flat Truck w/Tailboard, #433, from $550 to $600.00
Guy Flat Truck w/Tailboard, #513, from $400 to $425.00
Guy Flat Truck w/Tailboard, #913, from $625 to $650.00
Guy Van, #514, Slumberland, from $650 to..................... $850.00
Guy Van, #514, Spratt's, from $650 to $850.00
Guy Van, #918, Ever Ready, from $800 to $950.00
Guy Van, #919, Golden Shred, from $2,000 to $2,250.00
Guy Warrior Flat Truck, #432, from $450 to.................... $525.00
Guy Warrior Van, #920, Heinz, from $3,000 to........... $3,250.00
Guy 4-Ton Lorry, #511, red, gr or brn, from $850 to.... $1,050.00
Guy 4-Ton Lorry, #511, 2-tone bl, from $350 to............ $400.00
Guy 4-Ton Lorry, #911, from $475 to............................. $500.00
Hawker Executive Jet, #723, from $55 to............................$80.00
Hawker Harrier, #722, from $75 to $95.00
Hawker Hunter, #736, from $60 to $85.00
Hawker Hurricane, #718, from $80 to...............................$95.00
Hesketh Racing Car, #222, dk bl, from $120 to............. $140.00
Hesketh Racing Car, #222, Olympus Camera, from $135 to... $160.00
Hillman Imp, #138, from $145 to..................................... $170.00
Hindle-Smart Electric Lorry, #421, from $170 to $195.00
Holden Special Sedan, #196, from $135 to..................... $160.00
Honest John Missile Erector, #655, from $275 to $300.00
Horse Box, Express Horse Van, #581, from $1,250 to.. $1,500.00
Howitzer & Tractor, #695, from $250 to $275.00
Hudson Commodore Sedan, #139a, dual colors, from $325 to $400.00
Hudson Commodore Sedan, #139a, solid colors, from $215 to $250.00
Humber Hawk, #165, from $195 to.................................. $240.00
Humber Hawk Police Car, #256, from $175 to............... $225.00
International Road Signs, #771, set of 12, from $150 to... $175.00
Jaguar E-Type, #120, from $160 to $185.00
Jaguar E-Type, 2+2, #131, from $135 to......................... $160.00
Jaguar Mark 10, #142, from $130 to $155.00
Jaguar Motorway Police Car, #269, from $165 to $195.00
Jaguar Type-D Racer, #238, from $160 to........................ $185.00

Jaguar XK 120, #157, VG, $45.00. (Photo courtesy serioustoyz.com)

Jaguar XJS Coupe, #219, from $120 to........................... $140.00
Johnson Dumper, #430, from $115 to $140.00
Johnson Road Sweeper, #449, from $120 to..................... $145.00
Klingon Battle Cruiser, #357, from $225 to $275.00
Klingon Battle Cruiser, #372, sm version, from $180 to .. $220.00
Ladder Truck, #568, from $225 to $250.00
Lady Penelope's Fab 1, #100, luminous pk, from $375 to.. $425.00
Lady Penelope's Fab 1, #100, pk, from $225 to $275.00
Lamborghini Marzal, #189, from $145 to........................ $185.00
Land Rover Bomb Disposal Unit, #604, from $135 to.... $160.00
Land Rover Breakdown Crane, Falck, #442, from $145 to ..$270.00
Land Rover Fire, #282, Appliance, from $110 to............ $135.00
Land Rover Fire, #282, Falck, from $110 to.................... $135.00
Land Rover Pickup, #344, from $130 to........................... $155.00

Lawn Mower, #386, from $115 to $140.00
Leopard Anti-Aircraft Tank, #696, from $175 to $200.00
Leopard Recovery Tank, #699, from $165 to $190.00
Leopard Tank, #692, from $170 to $195.00
Leyland Cement Truck, #933, from $300 to $325.00
Leyland Cement Wagon, #533, from $225 to $300.00
Leyland Comet Cement Lorry, #419, from $350 to $375.00
Leyland Comet Lorry, #417, from $170 to $295.00
Leyland Comet Lorry, #531, all colors other than bl or brn, from $275 to $300.00
Leyland Comet Lorry, #531, bl or brn, from $650 to $700.00

Leyland Comet Lorry, #531, from $275.00 to $300.00.

Leyland Comet Lorry, #931, all colors other than bl & brn, from $275 to $300.00
Leyland Comet Lorry, #931, bl & brn, from $525 to $550.00
Leyland Comet Wagon w/Tailboard, #932, from $275 to $300.00
Leyland Dump Truck, #925, from $250 to $275.00
Leyland Forward Control Lorry, #420, from $170 to $195.00
Leyland Octopus Tanker, Esso, #943, from $450 to $500.00
Leyland Octopus Wagon, #934, all colors other than bl & brn, from $650 to $700.00
Leyland Octopus Wagon, #934, bl & brn, from $2,000 to $2,250.00
Leyland 8-Wheel Test Chassis, #936, from $225 to $250.00
Lincoln Continental, #170, from $210 to $250.00
Lincoln Premiere, #532, from $275 to $300.00
Lockhead Shooting Star Fighter, #733, from $50 to $75.00
Lorry-Mounted Concrete Mixer, #960, from $200 to $225.00
Lotus Europa, #218, from $120 to $140.00
Lotus Formula 1 Racer, #225, from $110 to $135.00
Lotus Racer, #241, from $120 to $140.00
Loudspeaker Van, #492, from $180 to $200.00
Lunar Roving Vehicle, #355, from $180 to $215.00
Marrel Multi-Bucket Unit, #966, from $175 to $200.00
Maserati 2000, #505, from $200 to $225.00
Matra 630, #200, from $130 to $170.00
Med Artillery Tractor, #389, from $90 to $115.00
Mercedes Benz C111, #224, from $120 to $145.00
Mercedes Benz Racer, #237, from $160 to $185.00
Mercedes Benz Truck, #940, from $175 to $200.00
Mercedes Benz Truck & Trailer, #917, from $375 to $400.00
Mercedes Benz 190 SL, #526, from $200 to $225.00
Mercedes Benz 220 SE, #186, from $185 to $235.00
Mercedes Benz 250 SE, #160, from $150 to $185.00
Mercedes Benz 600, #128, from $170 to $195.00
Mercury Cougar, #174, from $140 to $195.00
Merryweather Fire Engine, #285, Falck, from $135 to $160.00
Merryweather Fire Engine, #285, from $130 to $155.00
Mersey Tunnel Police Van, #255, from $130 to $160.00
Messerschmitt, #726, desert camouflage, from $95 to $120.00
Messerschmitt, #726, gray & gr, from $190 to $215.00
MG Midget, #102, from $225 to $260.00
MG Midget, #108, from $200 to $250.00
MG Midget, #129, from $950 to $1,250.00
MGB, #113, from $135 to $160.00
Michigan Tractor Dozer, #976, from $275 to $300.00
Mighty Antar Low Loader w/Propeller, #986, from $500 to $525.00
Military Ambulance, #626, from $165 to $190.00
Mini Clubman, #178, from $120 to $145.00
Mini Klingon Cruiser, #802, from $120 to $160.00
Mini USS Enterprise, #801, from $120 to $160.00
Missile Erector Vehicle w/Corporal Missile & Launching, Platform, #666, from $525 to $550.00
MKI Corvette (boat), #671, from $125 to $150.00
Mobile Antiaircraft Gun, #690, from $170 to $195.00
Mobilgas Tanker, #440, from $170 to $195.00
Morris Mini Minor, #183, from $130 to $160.00
Morris Mini Traveller, #197, dk gr & brn, from $400 to $450.00
Morris Mini Traveller, #197, lime gr, from $250 to $325.00
Morris Oxford, #159, dual colors, from $275 to $325.00
Morris Oxford, #159, solid colors, from $175 to $225.00
Morris Oxford, #476, from $170 to $195.00
Morris Oxford, #486, Dinky Beats, from $170 to $195.00
Morris 1100, #140, from $130 to $155.00
Motor Patrol Boat, #675, from $150 to $175.00
Muir-Hill Dumper, #962, from $175 to $200.00
Muir-Hill Loader, #437, from $145 to $170.00
Muir-Hill Loader & Trencher, #967, from $150 to $175.00
NASA Space Shuttle, #364, w/booster, from $225 to $250.00
NASA Space Shuttle, #366, no booster, from $200 to $220.00

Nash Rambler, #173, EX+, $70.00. (Photo courtesy serioustoyz.com)

Nash Rambler, #173, from $175 to $225.00
NSU Rho, #176, metallic bl, from $160 to $195.00
NSU Rho, #176, metallic red, from $130 to $165.00
Opel Commodore, #179, from $175 to $210.00
Opel Kadett, #540, from $175 to $200.00
Opel Kapitan, #177, from $130 to $165.00

Packard Convertible, #132, from $195 to $220.00
Panhard Armoured Tank, #815, from $245 to $270.00
Paramedic Truck, #267, from $140 to $165.00
Parsley's Car, #477, from $170 to.................................. $195.00
Petrol Tanker, #441, Castrol, from $195 to..................... $220.00
Petrol Tanker, #442, Esso, from $170 to......................... $195.00
Petrol Tanker, #443, National Benzole, from $170 to..... $195.00
Peugeot, #533, from $225 to... $250.00
Peugeot Van, #570, from $200 to $225.00
Peugeot 204, #510, from $175 to..................................... $200.00
Peugeot 403-U, #525, from $225 to $250.00
Phantom II, #725, from $95 to $120.00
Pink Panther, #354, from $230 to $250.00
Plymouth Fury, #115, from $225 to $250.00
Plymouth Fury, #137, from $180 to $210.00

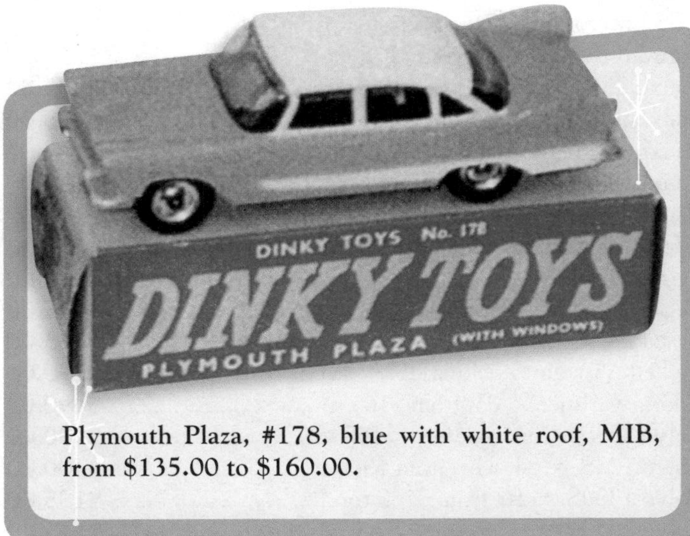

Plymouth Plaza, #178, blue with white roof, MIB, from $135.00 to $160.00.

Plymouth Plaza, #178, pk, gr or 2-tone bl, from $185 to... $220.00
Plymouth Police Racer, #244, from $125 to.................... $145.00
Plymouth Stock Car, #201, from $120 to........................ $135.00
Plymouth Taxi, #265, from $195 to................................ $225.00
Plymouth Yellow Cab, #278, from $125 to $150.00
Police Accident Unit, #272, from $120 to...................... $140.00
Police Accident Unit, #296, from $175 to...................... $200.00
Police Box, #752, from $50 to $65.00
Police Mini Clubman, #255, from $110 to...................... $135.00
Police Range Rover, #277 or #354, ea from $120 to....... $145.00
Pontiac Parisienne, #173, from $140 to $195.00
Porsche 356A Coupe, #182, cream, red or bl, from $230 to.. $260.00
Porsche 356A Coupe, #182, dual colors, from $315 to... $345.00
Prisoner Mini Moke, #106, from $375 to........................ $425.00
Pullman Car Transporter, #582, from $175 to................ $200.00
Pullman Car Transporter, #990, w/4 cars, from $2,500 to...$2,750.00
Pullmore Car Transporter, #982, from $100 to............... $200.00
Purdey's Triumph TR7, #112, from $110 to $135.00
RAC Patrol Mini Van, #273, from $175 to..................... $225.00
Racehorse Transporter, #979, from $625 to.................... $675.00
Racing Car Set, #201, from $750 to $1,000.00
RAF Avro Vulcan Bomber, #749, from $3,450 to........ $3,750.00

Rambler Station Wagon, #193, from $160 to $195.00
Range Rover, #192, from $110 to.................................... $130.00
Range Rover Ambulance, #268, from $105 to............... $135.00
Range Rover Fire Chief, #195, from $135 to $160.00
RCMP Patrol Car, #264, Cadillac or Fairlane, ea from $195 to $225.00
Renault Dauphine, #524, from $175 to........................... $200.00
Renault Dauphine Mini Cab, #268, rom $165 to $195.00
Renault Floride, #543, from $185 to $210.00
Renault Mail Car, #561, from $175 to $200.00
Renault R16, #166, from $135 to $170.00
Renault R8, #517, from $175 to $200.00
Renault 16-TX, #538, from $175 to $200.00
Renault 4L, #518, from $150 to...................................... $175.00
Riley, #158, from $175 to... $225.00
Road Grader, #963, from $150 to $175.00
Rolls Royce, #551, from $300 to $325.00
Rolls Royce Phantom V, #124, from $165 to $180.00
Rolls Royce Phantom V, #152, from $150 to $185.00
Rolls Royce Phantom V, #198, from $160 to $200.00
Rolls Royce Silver Shadow, #158, from $185 to $245.00
Rolls Royce Silver Wraith, #150, from $155 to $210.00
Routemaster Bus, #289, Esso, purple, from $775 to $850.00

Routemaster Bus, #289, Esso..., red, from $150.00 to $175.00.

Routemaster Bus, #289, Festival of London Stores, from $225 to $250.00
Routemaster Bus, #289, Madame Tussaud's, from $175 to ...$200.00
Routemaster Bus, #289, Silver Jubilee, from $125 to...... $150.00
Rover 3500 Sedan, #180, from $120 to........................... $145.00
Rover 75, #156, dual colors, from $275 to $325.00
Rover 75, #156, solid colors, from $175 to...................... $225.00
Saab 96, #156, from $150 to $200.00
Sam's Car, #108, gold, red or bl, from $150 to $175.00
Sam's Car, #108, silver, from $150 to $175.00
Scorpion Tank, #690, from $175 to................................ $200.00
SEPECAT Jaguar, #731, from $75 to.............................. $100.00

Service Station, #785, from $385 to $420.00
Shell-BP Fuel Tanker, #944, from $325 to $350.00
Shell-BP Fuel Tanker, #944, red wheels, from $675 to ... $725.00
Silver Jubilee Bus, #297, National or Woolworth, from $125 to.. $150.00
Simca Dump Truck, #578, from $250 to $275.00
Simca Taxi, #542, from $200 to...................................... $225.00
Simca Van, #577, Bailly, from $300 to $325.00
Simca Versailles, #541, from $200 to $225.00
Simca 100, #519, from $175 to...................................... $200.00
Simca 1500, #523, from $150 to.................................... $175.00
Singer Gazelle, #168, from $175 to $225.00
Single-Decker Bus, #283, from $120 to.......................... $145.00
Space Battle Cruiser, #367, from $210 to....................... $235.00
Spitfire MKII, #719, from $80 to $95.00
Spitfire MKII, #741, from $100 to $125.00
Spitfire MKII RAF Jubilee, #700, from $165 to $190.00
SRN-6 Hovercraft, #290, from $135 to.......................... $160.00
Standard Lamp, #755, single arm, from $25 to $40.00
Standard Lamp, #756, dbl arm, from $25 to.......................$40.00
Standard Vanguard-Spats, #153, from $175 to............... $225.00
Striker Antitank Vehicle, #691, from $175 to $200.00
Studebaker Golden Hawk, #169, from $190 to.............. $240.00
Studebaker Land Cruiser, #172, dual colors, from $300 to ...$350.00
Studebaker Land Cruiser, #172, solid colors, from $200 to ..$250.00
Sunbeam Alpine, #101, from $275 to $325.00
Sunbeam Alpine, #107, from $200 to $250.00
Sunbeam Rapier, #166, from $175 to $225.00
Superior Cadillac Ambulance, #267, from $150 to $180.00
Superior Cadillac Ambulance, #288, Falck, from $160 to ...$200.00
Superior Cadillac Ambulance, #288, from $150 to $175.00
Superior Criterion Ambulance, #263, from $180 to....... $210.00
Superior Criterion Ambulance, #277, from $150 to....... $200.00
Tank Transporter, #660, from $200 to $225.00
Tank Transporter & Tank, #698, from $335 to $360.00
Telephone Service Van, #261, from $150 to................... $200.00
Terex Dump Truck, #965, from $275 to $300.00
Thames Flat Truck, #422, bright gr, from $225 to........... $250.00
Thames Flat Truck, #422, dk gr or red, from $170 to...... $195.00
Thunderbird II & IV, #101, gr, from $275 to $325.00
Thunderbird II & IV, #101, metallic gr, from $375 to $425.00
Thunderbird II & IV, #106, from $200 to $250.00
Touring Gift Set, #122, from $2,000 to...................... $2,500.00
Tractor-Trailer, McLean, #948, from $400 to................. $425.00
Trailer, #428, lg, from $115 to $140.00
Trailer, #429, from $115 to $140.00
Trailer, #551, from $75 to $90.00
Trident Star Fighter, #362, from $230 to....................... $255.00
Triumph Spitfire, #114, gray, gold or red, from $135 to .. $160.00
Triumph Spitfire, #114, purple, from $155 to................. $180.00
Triumph TR2, #105, from $225 to $260.00
Triumph TR2, #111, from $150 to $180.00
Triumph TR7, #207, from $130 to $160.00
Triumph TR7, #211, from $110 to $140.00
Triumph Vitesse, #134, from $160 to $185.00
Triumph 1300, #162, from $160 to................................ $195.00
Triumph 1800 Saloon, #151, from $175 to $225.00
Triumph 2000, #135, from $140 to................................. $165.00
Trojan Van, #451, Dunlop, from $225 to $250.00
Trojan Van, #452, Chivers, from $250 to........................ $275.00
Turntable Fire Escape, #956, Bedford, from $200 to $225.00
Turntable Fire Escape, #956, Berliet, from $250 to......... $275.00
Twin-Engine Fighter, #731, from $50 to $75.00
UNIC Boilot Car Transporter, #894, from $400 to......... $425.00
UNIC Pipe-Line Transporter, #893, from $450 to.......... $475.00
Universal Jeep, #405, from $140 to $175.00
US Air Force F-4 Phantom II, #727, from $295 to $320.00
US Army Staff Car, #139a, from $345 to........................ $375.00
US Army T-42A, #712, from $120 to $145.00
US Jeep & 105mm Howitzer, #615, from $120 to $145.00
US Navy Phantom, #730, from $95 to............................ $120.00
USA Police Car, #251, Pontiac, from $145 to $180.00
USA Police Car, #258, Cadillac, Desoto, Dodge or Ford, ea from $175 to $225.00
USS Enterprise, #358, from $225 to............................. $250.00
USS Enterprise, #371, sm version, from $180 to $220.00
Vanwall Racer, #239, from $175 to $225.00
Vauxhall Cresta, #164, from $175 to............................. $225.00
Vauxhall Victor, #141, from $130 to $155.00
Vauxhall Victor Ambulance, #278, from $120 to $145.00
Vauxhall Victor 101, #151, from $150 to........................ $185.00
Vauxhall Viva, #136, from $140 to................................ $165.00
Vega Major Luxury Coach, #952, from $200 to $240.00
Vega Major Luxury Coach, #954, no lights, from $175 to....$200.00
Vega Major Luxury Coach, #961, from $350 to $375.00
Vespa 2-CV, #529, from $200 to.................................... $225.00
Vickers Viscount Airliner, BEA, #708, from $165 to...... $190.00
Viking Airliner, #705, from $165 to.............................. $190.00
Volvo 122S, #184, red, from $160 to............................. $190.00
Volvo 122S, #184, wht, from $360 to............................ $400.00
Volvo 1800S, #116, from $160 to $185.00
Volvo 265 Estate Car, #122, from $120 to $145.00
VW Porsche 914, #208, from $110 to $135.00
VW Swiss Post PTT Car, #262, casting #129, from $300 to .. $350.00
VW 1300 Sedan, #129, from $160 to............................. $175.00
VW 1500, #144, from $140 to.. $165.00
VW 1600 TL, #163, metallic bl, from $200 to................ $250.00
VW 1600 TL, #163, red, from $60 to...............................$80.00
Wayne School Bus, #949, from $400 to $425.00
Westland Sikorsky Helicopter, #716, from $85 to $110.00
Zero-Sen, #739, from $100 to.. $125.00
Zygon Marauder, #368, from $210 to $235.00

25-Pounder Gun Unit, #697, EXIB, A, $110.00. (Photo courtesy Lloyd Ralston Toys)

Disney

Through the magic of the silver screen, Walt Disney's characters have come to life, and it is virtually impossible to imagine a child growing up without the influence of his genius. As each classic film was introduced, toy manufacturers scurried to fill department store shelves with the dolls, games, battery-ops, and windups that carried the likeness of every member of its cast. Though today it is the toys of the 1930s and 1940s that are bringing top prices, later toys are certainly collectible as well, as you'll see in our listings. Even characters as recently introduced as Roger Rabbit already have their own cult following.

Since the advent of the Internet, condition and rarity are more important than ever when it comes to evaluation. Vintage items have done very well over the past several years, especially at auctions, and more recent items seem to be garnering decent prices.

For more information we recommend *Disneyana* by Cecil Munsey (Hawthorne Books, 1974); *Disneyana* by Robert Heide and John Gilman; *Walt Disney's Mickey Mouse Memorabilia* by Hillier and Shine (Abrams Inc., 1986); *Tomart's Disneyana Update Magazine;* and *Elmer's Price Guide to Toys* by Elmer Duellman (L-W Books); *Official Price Guide to Disney Collectibles* by Ted Hake (Random House Information Group).

Advisor: Joel J. Cohen

See also Battery-Operated; Books; Character and Promotional Drinking Glasses; Character Clocks and Watches; Coloring, Activity, and Paint Books; Comic Books; Fisher-Price; Games; Housewares; Lunch Boxes; Marx; Pin-Back Buttons; Plastic Figures; Puzzles; Ramp Walkers; Records; Sand Toys; View Master; Western; Windup, Friction, and Other Mechanical Toys.

Bank, Donald Duck Head, vinyl, 10", Play Pal Plastics, 1971, EX+, $28.00.
(Photo courtesy whatacharacter.com)

Bank, Aristocats kitten sitting on all fours, compo w/felt bow tie, Savings Bank sticker, 6", Enesco, 1960s, EX $40.00

Bank, Big Al (Song of the South) seated playing guitar, ceramic w/allover brn glaze, 8", WDP, NM+ $20.00

Bank, Dark Wing Duck holding onto safe, vinyl, 7", Happiness Express, 1990s, NM+ $10.00

Bank, Donald Duck looking up w/hand up in fist, compo, 7", NM...$22.00

Bank, Donald Duck resting on elbows on suitcase emb 'To Walt Disney World,' silver-plated metal, 6", Leonard, EX+ ..$35.00

Bank, Donald Duck standing, jtd right arm w/'thumbs-up' motion, vinyl, 5½", WDP, NM $12.00

Bank, Donald Duck tent shape w/emb Donald figure coming out of tent, Donald's name stenciled on side, compo, 5", WDP, NM...$20.00

Bank, Donald Duck w/mouth open & hands on hips, vinyl, 8", Play Pal Plastics, 1970s, EX $18.00

Bank, Dumbo seated upright, gray w/orange hat & gray, wht & red collar, hard vinyl, 8", Play Pal, 1970s, EX+...........$25.00

Bank, Dumbo seated upright w/trunk curled & looking upward, soft rubber, 7", Walter J Jamieson Inc, 1950s-60s, NM.........$28.00

Bank, Ferdinand the Bull sitting upright, chalkware, 8½" H, EX $50.00

Bank, Figment seated holding pot of coins marked Epcot Center, vinyl, 7½", 1982, NM+ $15.00

Bank, Ludwig Von Drake, hands clasped together as in deep thought, mc plastic, 10", 1961, VG...........................$35.00

Bank, Mickey Mouse figure w/legs crossed leaning on tree stump on grassy base, 8", EX+ $20.00

Bank, Mickey Mouse places coin into drum at his side, rnd gr base, vinyl, 9", Animal Plus Toys, 1970s, EX+............$12.00

Bank, Mickey Mouse seated on stool looking & pointing up, compo, 8", WDP, EX..$25.00

Bank, Mickey Mouse standing with hands on hips, shiny cast metal, 20", NM, A, $250.00.
(Photo courtesy Morphy Auctions)

Bank, Minnie Mouse holding broom emb on front of house w/mailbox, 5x3½x3½", UCGC, 1970s, G+............. $15.00

Bank, Mrs Potts (Beauty & the Beast) the teapot, vinyl, 7", 1990s, NM+ $15.00

Bank, Pinocchio bust, eyes looking up, lg bow tie, vinyl, 10", Play Pal, 1970s, NM $28.00

Bank, Pinocchio seated on stack of books, vinyl, 12", Play Pals, 1970s, EX+....$25.00
Bank, Pluto sitting upright looking up w/mouth open, thick bl collar, compo, 6½", WDP, NM....$25.00
Bank, Three Little Pigs Bank, tin building w/lithoed image of Wolf trying to blow it down, 3", Chein, 1930s, EX... $145.00
Bank, Winnie the Pooh seated licking his chops w/Pooh's Honey Bank between legs, ceramic, 5", Enesco/WDP, 1960, NM+....$30.00
Bank, 2nd National Duck Bank, litho tin building w/Donald as teller & Mickey & Minnie customers, 6½", VG+, A.... $200.00
Barrette, Snow White, Catalin plastic bow shape w/decaled bust image of Snow White flanked by 2 dwarfs, 2", EX+....$30.00
Birthday Party Kit, Donald Duck on box, Rendoll Paper Co, 1940s, some use, incomplete o/w VGIB....$55.00
Bop Bag, Donald Duck figure, ball shape w/name & charachter graphics, long neck & head, vinyl, 16", Ideal, 1960s, NM+.... $20.00
Bubble Bath Container, Anastasia, Kid Care, 1997, NM....$6.00
Bubble Bath Container, any character, Colgate-Palmolive, 1960s, NM....$15.00
Bubble Bath Container, any character, Avon, 1969, unused, MIB....$20.00
Bubble Bath Container, Three Little Pigs, any character, Tubby Times, 1960s, rare, M....$25.00
Camera, Mick-A-Matic, Child Guidance #880, 1960s, NMIB, A.... $125.00

Camera, Mickey Mouse Brownie Target Six-20, complete and unused, NMIB, A, $2,970.00. (Photo courtesy Randy Inman Auctions)

Camera Set, Mickey Mouse, w/camera, film, orig batteries, flashbulbs & pin, Ettleson Corp, unused, EXIB, A....$75.00
Celluloid Toy, Donald Duck figure standing on roly-poly base, 7", Japan, 1930s, EX, A.... $460.00
Celluloid Toy, Mickey Mouse & Donald Duck in rowboat, 6" L, NM, A.... $750.00
Chalkboard, Mickey Mouse, wood frame w/fold-out legs, top header w/Mickey graphics, 37x17", Falcon Toys, EX+.... $180.00
Color-By-Number Oil Set, Disneyland, Hasbro #2195, 1950s, unused, NMIB....$65.00
Colorforms Cartoon Kit, 101 Dalmatians, 1961, NMIB, A..$25.00
Colorforms Sew-Ons, 'Mickey & Minnie in lots of swell new cloths,' 6 unused cards, 1970s, EXIB....$30.00
Comb & Brush Set, Mickey Mouse, blk w/colorful figural decal of Mickey on brush, 4" brush w/6" comb, H Hughes Co, MIB, A....$65.00
Diecast Toy, Garden Set, Mickey & Donald figures w/wheelbarrow & garden tools, 3", Salco, EXIB, A.... $220.00
Diecast Toy, Mickey & Minnie on the River, wheeled boat w/Mickey & Minnie figures, 5½", Salco, VGIB... $300.00
Disneyland Blocks Set, 15 colorful wood blocks ea featuring 3 different characters, unused, MIB, A....$83.00
Disneyland Happy Birthday Carousel, litho tin, Mickey as Robin Hood & Minnie atop banner, 9", Ross Prod, EXIB, A..$110.00

Donald Race Car, tin with celluloid Donald head, 3", Occupied Japan, NMIB, A, $345.00. (Photo courtesy Morphy Auctions)

Drum, litho tin, Mickey, Minnie & Pluto on yel w/bl and top & bottom, 6½" dia, Ohio Art, EX, A.... $110.00
Drum, litho tin, Mickey in top hat leading parade of characters w/instruments on grass, 6½" dia, Ohio Art, VG, A....$85.00
Drum, Mickey Mouse parade graphics on cb w/tin top & bottom, 6" H, Happy Hak #601, England, EX, A.... $150.00
Drum, Snow White & the Seven Dwarfs, litho tin, w/drum sticks, 11" dia, Chein, VG+, A.... $125.00
Figure, Baloo (Jungle Book), stuffed, rusty-brn cloth w/beige felt chest, 2 bottom teeth, 6½", 1960s, NM....$30.00
Figure, Bambi, stuffed, tan w/brn spots on back, wht chest & tail plastic eyes, 8", Canada/WDP, 1970s-80s, NM....$15.00
Figure, Bambi, vinyl, brn w/wht chest & spots on back, blk hooves, jtd legs, 8", Dakin, 1970s, EX+....$25.00
Figure, Bashful (Snow White), stuffed, felt w/wht furry beard, eyes looking up, 7", 1960s-70s, NM....$25.00
Figure, Bashful (Snow White), stuffed, molded plastic face, furry beard, cloth outfit, 14", Knickerbocker, 1930s, EX.. $175.00
Figure, Brer Bear (Song of the South), ceramic, standing holding club, 8", WDP, M....$55.00
Figure, Captain Hook, vinyl, seated on gr base, cloth jacket, hat & & scarf, AD Sutton, 1960s, MIB (Small World Figures)....$75.00

Figure, Chip 'N Dale, plush, 16½", California Stuffed Toys, 8½", 1970s-80s, NM, ea....$18.00

Figure, Chip 'N Dale, rubber, bendable, 4½", Just Toys, 1980s, NM, ea....$10.00

Figure, Christopher Robin (Winnie the Pooh) PVC, seated w/legs crossed holding up a book, 3", NM+....$5.00

Figure, Cinderella, plush & vinyl, pk & wht, Gund, EX+..$50.00

Figure, Danny (lamb from 'So Dear to My Heart'), black plush with blue ribbon, button on chest, 1948, VG, A, $190.00. (Photo courtesy Randy Inman Auctions)

Figure, Daisy Duck, bisque, playing croquet, 4", WDP, 1970s, M....$28.00

Figure, Daisy Duck, bisque, seated in chair posing as glamour girl, 3", WDP, 1987, NM....$15.00

Figure, Dewey, see also Huey, Louie & Dewey

Figure, Dewey (Donald's Nephew), plush & vinyl, 'D' on bl sweater, 8", Applause, NM....$10.00

Figure, Dewey (Donald's Nephew), vinyl, jtd, Dakin, 1970s, NM....$22.00

Figure, Donald Duck, bisque, standing w/hands on hips & head turned, long-billed, 1¾", WDE, 1930s, EX....$65.00

Figure, Donald Duck, bisque, standing w/head turned, jtd limbs, bl jacket & hat, long-billed, 6", WDE, VG, A....$125.00

Figure, Donald Duck, bisque, strutting w/chest out & head upturned, 3½", WDE, 1940s, EX+....$65.00

Figure, Donald Duck, bisque, tangled in garden hose, 3", WDP, 1970s, NM+....$22.00

Figure, Donald Duck, celluloid, roly-poly type w/coiled neck, bottom bill & closed eyes move, EX, A....$715.00

Figure, Donald Duck, compo, in parade attire w/cape & blk fuzzy hat, 9", Knickerbocker/Cossack, ca 1935, NM....$1,065.00

Figure, Donald Duck, stuffed, Bavarian/Swiss outfit, 20", Lenci, 1950s, VG....$140.00

Figure, Donald Duck, stuffed, Boy Scout outfit, 30", Lenci, 1950s, NM....$670.00

Figure, Donald Duck, stuffed, plush, 12", Woolco/Woolikin, 1960s, G+ (w/pkg)....$22.00

Figure, Donald Duck, stuffed, plush & felt, 9", Character Novelty, EX....$200.00

Figure, Donald Duck, stuffed, plush w/vinyl face, open mouth, 9", Gund/Gundikins, 1950s, EX+....$45.00

Figure, Donald Duck, stuffed, plush w/vinyl face, stuffed felt feet, seated, 13", California Stuffed Toys/WDP, EX+....$25.00

Figure, Donald Duck, stuffed velvet in sailor suit with stern expression, 15", Kruegan, EX, A, $900.00. (Photo courtesy Morphy Auctions)

Figure, Donald Duck, stuffed, tam & jacket, red tie, long-billed, 18½", Knickerbocker, w/tag, VG, A....$500.00

Figure, Donald Duck, stuffed, wht hat & bl jacket, orange feet, long-billed, 5", Steiff (?), VG+, A....$200.00

Figure, Donald Duck, vinyl, cloth jacket & bow tie, 8", Dakin, EX+....$22.00

Figure, Donald Duck, wood, pnt bead type w/ball-shaped hands, 3", Fun-E-Flex, 1930s, EX, A....$375.00

Figure, Donald Duck, wood, pnt bead type w/fingered hands, 5", Fun-E-Flex, 1930s, EX+, A....$715.00

Figure, Dopey, bisque, high-stepping playing flute, 3", Sri Lanka, M....$15.00

Figure, Dumbo, inflatable vinyl, seated upright, 18", WDP, 1970s, MIP....$25.00

Figure, Dumbo, stuffed, gray plush w/pk felt ears & feet, orange felt hat & collar, applied eyes, 17", WDP, 1970s, NM....$18.00

Figure, Dumbo, stuffed, seated upright, tan & beige velvety material w/red hat, felt eyes, yel neck ribbon, 7", WDP, NM+....$20.00

Figure, Dumbo, vinyl, felt ears, goggly-eyed, 8½", Knickerbocker, 1941, EX....$150.00

Figure, Dumbo, vinyl, gray w/yel hat, pk ears, 6x7½", Dakin, 1970s, NM....$25.00

Figure, Eeyore, stuffed, gray corduroy w/blk felt features, 5", Gund, 1966, NM+....$35.00

Figure, Ferdinand the Bull, chalkware, sitting upright, lg head, 8½", EX....$50.00

Figure, Ferdinand the Bull, chalkware, standing w/head looking forward, flower in mouth, 7x11" L, EX....$75.00

Figure, Ferdinand the Bull, chalkware, standing w/head up & eyes glancing sideways, no flower, 8x9" L, VG....$65.00

Figure, Flip the Frog, composition, jointed arms, 7", Ub Iwerks, ca 1930, EX, A, $600.00. (Photo courtesy Bertoia Auctions)

Figure, Flower the Skunk (Bambi), plush, seated upright, plastic eyes, red neck ribbon, 8", Knickerbocker, 1970, NM...$15.00
Figure, Geppetto (Pinocchio), vinyl, bendable, cloth outfit, 6", Marx, NM+....$15.00
Figure, Geppetto (Pinocchio), wood fiber, sitting on box w/chin in hand, 5x3x3", Multi-Prod, 1940s, EX....$55.00
Figure, Goofy, stuffed, orange shirt & pk vest, gr hat, 17", Mattel, EX....$100.00
Figure, Goofy, stuffed, plush, wearing Santa suit w/blk vinyl belt, 10", Canasa Trading Corp, NM+....$15.00
Figure, Goofy, stuffed, plush w/cloth overalls & shirt, 14", Schuco, 1950s, 14", EX....$250.00
Figure, Grumpy (Snow White), stuffed, wht furry beard, felt features, vinyl belt, 7", 1960s-70s, EX+....$25.00
Figure, Gus (Cinderella), stuffed plush w/red felt top & gr felt shoes, 15", Gund, NM+....$250.00
Figure, Huey, Louie & Dewey, vinyl, standing, jtd limbs, 5", Dakin, 1970s, M, ea....$25.00
Figure, Jack Skellington (Nightmare Before Christmas), vinyl, 9", Hasbro, 1993, MOC (sealed)....$25.00
Figure, Jack Skellington (Nightmare Before Christmas), vinyl w/cloth outfit, jtd, w/coffin, 16", Jun Planning, NM. $100.00
Figure, Jessica Rabbit (Roger Rabbit), vinyl, bendable, w/cloth wrap skirt, 6½", LJN, 1987, NM+....$6.00
Figure, Jiminy Cricket, wood, pnt bead-type w/felt-brimmed hat & umbrella, 8½", Ideal, 1939, EX+, A....$550.00
Figure, Jiminy Cricket, wood compo, lt gr body w/blk felt hat & jacket, orange vest, 10", Knickerbocker, 1939, VG+, A....$650.00
Figure, Joe Carioca, stuffed, cloth eyes, stitched mouth, cloth outfit, hat & umbrella, 16", VG....$400.00
Figure, Lady (Lady & the Tramp), stuffed, WDP, seated upright, corduroy-type cloth w/felt ears, 7", NM....$75.00
Figure, Mary Poppins, plastic, synthetic hair, yel cloth dress, 12", Gund/WDP, 1960s, NM....$75.00
Figure, Mary Poppins, vinyl, jtd, purple dress, blk folded umbrella, 7", Multiple Toys/WDP, 1967, NM+IB....$75.00
Figure, Mickey Mouse, bisque, standing next to Pluto, 5½", Borgfelt, 1930s, EX, A....$465.00

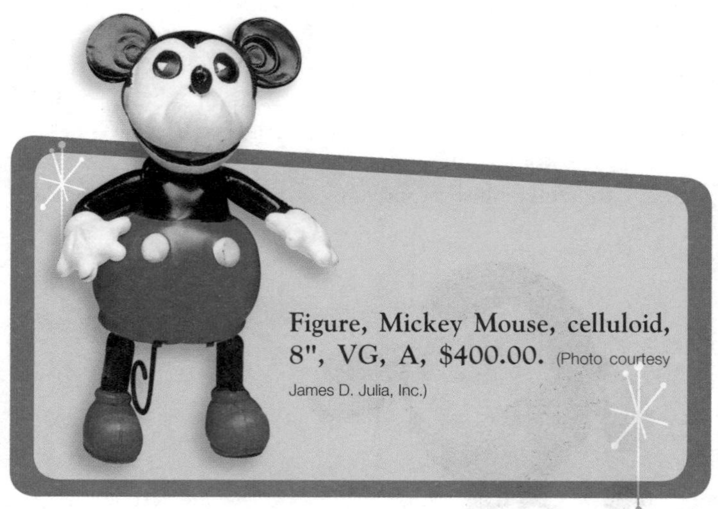

Figure, Mickey Mouse, celluloid, 8", VG, A, $400.00. (Photo courtesy James D. Julia, Inc.)

Figure, Mickey Mouse, composition, cowboy outfit with two guns in holster, 10", Knickerbocker, VG+, A, $750.00. (Photo courtesy James D. Julia, Inc.)

Figure, Mickey Mouse, compo, in parade attire w/cape & blk fuzzy hat, 9", Knickerbocker/Cossack, ca 1935, EX....$1,345.00
Figure, Mickey Mouse, stuffed, blk & wht w/yel hands, pie-eyed, 14", Lenci, EX....$225.00
Figure, Mickey Mouse, stuffed, cloth w/plastic shoes, 12", Knickerbocker/Charlotte Clark, 1935, EX....$625.00
Figure, Mickey Mouse, stuffed, cowboy outfit w/2 6-shooters, red plastic shoes, 10", Knickerbocker, EX....$500.00
Figure, Mickey Mouse, stuffed, felt w/printed toothy grin, red shorts, yel feet, 8½", Dean Rag/Borgfeldt, EX, A....$355.00
Figure, Mickey Mouse, stuffed, felt w/stuffed hands & feet, red shorts, 4½", Steiff, NOS, A....$2,860.00
Figure, Mickey Mouse, stuffed, red velvet shorts, orange plastic shoes, 12", Knickerbocker/Charlotte Clark, 1935, EX+....$750.00
Figure, Mickey Mouse, stuffed, red velvet shorts, orange velvet shoes, yel silk hands, 12", Knickerbocker/C Clark, EX, A....$1,050.00
Figure, Mickey Mouse, stuffed, velvet w/velvet shorts, 4-fingered, 20", Knickerbocker/Charlotte Clark, 1934, EX, A ... $100.00
Figure, Mickey Mouse, wood, bead-type body w/fingered hands, 7", Fun-E-Flex, 1930s, MIB, A....$3,190.00
Figure, Mickey Mouse, wood, bead-type body w/lollipop hands, blk, wht & yel, 9½", Cameo, VG, A....$1,065.00

Figure, Mickey Mouse, wood, bead-type body w/lollipop hands, 7", Fun-E-Flex, 1930s, NM, A $670.00

Figure, Mickey Mouse, wood, bead-type body w/lollipop hands, 7", Fun-E-Flex, 1930s, VG, A $350.00

Figure, Mickey Mouse, wood, bead-type body w/pancake hands, chest banner, 5", Fun-E-Flex, 1930s, EX, A $300.00

Figure, Minnie Mouse, celluloid, movable head & arms, 5½", Borgfeldt, 1930s, VG+ $275.00

Figure, Minnie Mouse, stuffed, felt w/cloth skirt, hat w/flower on long stem, 6", Steiff, no tags, VG, A $1,100.00

Figure, Minnie Mouse, stuffed, felt w/cloth skirt & bloomers, jtd arms, 14", Nifty, G+, A $350.00

Figure, Minnie Mouse, stuffed felt with printed toothy grin, black shoe-button eyes, cloth skirt, 8", Dean Rag/Borgfeldt, EX, A, $520.00. (Photo courtesy Randy Inman Auctions)

Figure, Minnie Mouse, stuffed, pk plush w/wht hands & bl feet, bl skirt w/wht dots, 13", Woolco, 1960s, G+ $25.00

Figure, Minnie Mouse, vinyl, cloth dress, jtd, 8", Dakin, 1970s, NM+ $25.00

Figure, Minnie Mouse, wood, bead-type w/fingered hands, 7", Fun-E-Flex, VG, A $175.00

Figure, Peter Pan, plastic, jtd, sleep eyes, cloth outfit & hat, 9", Dutchess, 1950s, NM $125.00

Figure, Piglet (Winnie the Pooh), stuffed, plush w/blk & red striped body, 7", 1966, EX+ $25.00

Figure, Pinocchio, compo, cloth outfit & hat, 20", Ideal, 1940s, EX+ $450.00

Figure, Pinocchio, compo, felt outfit & hat, 13", Ideal, EX .. $275.00

Figure, Pinocchio, rubber, standing w/school books & an apple for the teacher, 7", Dell, EX $30.00

Figure, Pinocchio, stuffed, plush roly-poly body w/vinyl face, cloth feet, 8", Gund, 1950s, EX $35.00

Figure, Pinocchio, stuffed, plush w/vinyl face, lime gr & wht, 12", Gund, 1950s, EX $50.00

Figure, Pinocchio, wood, bead-type w/name on tummy, felt collar & bow tie, 8", Ideal, 1930s-40, EX+, A $210.00

Figure, Pinocchio, wood, bead-type w/name on tummy, felt collar & bow tie, 11", Ideal, G+, A $150.00

Figure, Pinocchio, wood/compo, standing on sq base w/name, Multi Prod, EX+ $50.00

Figure, Pluto, rubber, bendable, on all fours, 3x5½" L, Lakeside/WDP, 1960s, EX $20.00

Figure, Pluto, stuffed blond fur with black ears, nose, tail, and collar, 12", VG, A, $110.00. (Photo courtesy Morphy Auctions)

Figure, Pluto, vinyl, standing on all fours, jtd, 8x9" L, Dakin, 1970s, EX+ $22.00

Figure, Rabbit (Winnie the Pooh), stuffed, corduroy-type cloth w/felt chest, 6½", Gund, 1960s, NM $35.00

Figure, Roger Rabbit, stuffed, plush w/cloth overalls, 14½", Applause, EX $8.00

Figure, Roo (Winnie the Pooh), stuffed, brn plush w/turq felt inner ears & shirt, 10½", Sears, 1970s, NM $18.00

Figure, Shere Khan (Jungle Book), stuffed, 4x6", Gund, 1966, EX $32.00

Figure, Snow White, chalk, standing looking sideways lifting skirt w/both hands, bl, yel & red, 9½", EX, A $110.00

Figure, Snow White, compo, pnt features, molded hair, cloth dress, 15", Knickerbocker, G, A $75.00

Figure, Tigger, stuffed, ribbed cloth w/felt features & stripes, long whiskers, 6" L, Sears, 1960s, NM+ $35.00

Figure, Timon (Lion King), stuffed, plush w/fuzzy topknot & elbows, 9½", Mattel, NM $12.00

Figure, Tinker Bell, plastic, jtd, synthetic hair, gr velvet dress & gold wings, 8", Dutchess, 1950s, EX+ $65.00

Figure, Tinker Bell, rubber & plastic, 7", Sutton, 1960s, EX+ ... $35.00

Figure, Tramp (Lady & the Tramp), stuffed, plush 2-color roly-poly body w/vinyl face, musical chimes, 9", Gund, EX+ $40.00

Figure, Winnie the Pooh, stuffed, standing waving, gold plush w/red cloth top, 6½", Gund, 1966, NM+ $35.00

Figure, Winnie the Pooh, vinyl, seated holding 'Hunny' pot, 7", Sears/WDP, 1970s, NM $25.00

Figure Set, Mickey & Minnie, bisque, Mickey & 2 Minnies playing musical instruments, 3½", Borgfeldt, 1933, EXIB, A .. $440.00

Figure Set, Mickey & Minnie, celluloid, string-jtd, Mickey in red shorts & Minnie in yel top hat, 5", EX+ $440.00

Figure Set, Mickey & Minnie, wood, Mickey & 2 Minnies, bead-type, 5", Nifty, EXIB (1 shared box), A $935.00

Figure Set, Seven Dwarfs, stuffed, cloth & vinyl, felt eyes, pnt mouths/cheeks, fur beards, 9", Gund, 1967, NM, ea... $32.00

Figure Set, Snow White & the Seven Dwarfs, bisque, 13" Snow White, Borgfeldt, 1938, EXIB, A $400.00

Figure Set, Snow White & the Seven Dwarfs, bisque, 2½" dwarfs & 3½" Snow White, Borgfeldt, 1938, EXIB $275.00

Figure Set, Snow White & the Seven Dwarfs, celluloid, mk Foreign, 6" ea, VGIB, A $600.00

Figure Set, Snow White & the Seven Dwarfs, compo, cloth outfits, 18" Snow White, Ideal, EX (in individual boxes) ... $2,400.00

Figure Set, Snow White & the Seven Dwarfs, pot metal, Britains, 1938-39, EX, A $235.00

Figure Set, Snow White and the Seven Dwarfs, stuffed felt with velvet outfits, fur beards, 16" Snow White and 10" dwarfs, Chad Valley, 1930s, NM, $1,200.00. (Photo courtesy James D. Julia Inc.)

Figure Set, Three Little Pigs, bisque, standing playing musical instruments, 3½", Borgfeldt, NM+IB, A $250.00

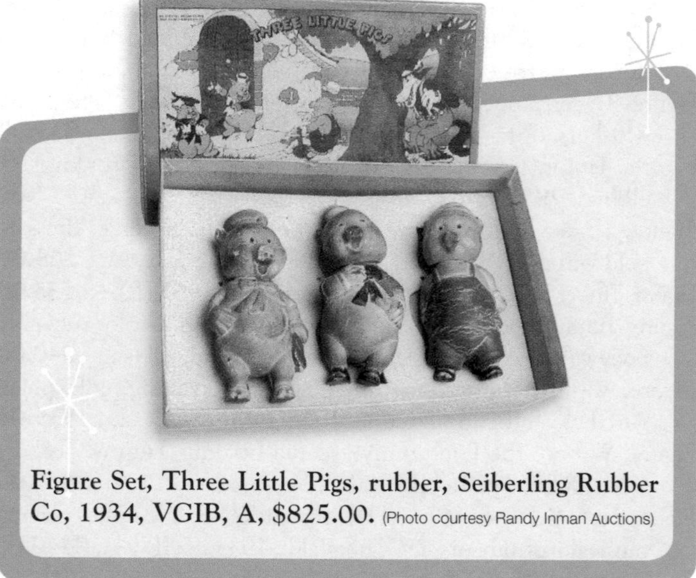

Figure Set, Three Little Pigs, rubber, Seiberling Rubber Co, 1934, VGIB, A, $825.00. (Photo courtesy Randy Inman Auctions)

Finger Puppet, Eeyore, vinyl, Gabriel, 1970s, NM $6.00

Finger Puppet, Pluto in begging pose, vinyl, 3", WDP, NM ... $6.00

Finger Puppet, Tigger (Winnie the Pooh), vinyl, Shelcore, NM $5.00

Finger Puppet, Winnie the Pooh, vinyl, Shelco, NM+ $5.00

Flashlight, Minnie chasing Mickey around tree on hdl, EX .. $150.00

Fun-E-Flex Toy, Mickey & Minnie on sled pulled by Pluto, wood, 10", EX, A $775.00

Fun-E-Flex Toy, Pluto in doghouse, wood, EX, A, $550.00. (Photo courtesy Randy Inman Auctions)

Funnee Movee, Donald Duck, Irwin/WDP, 1950s, unused, MIB, A $85.00

Game, Dopey's Bean Bag Game, Parker Bros, 1938, complete, VGIB, A $85.00

Game, Mickey Mouse Bagatelle, wood with large image of Mickey, Chad Valley, 1930s, NMIB, $400.00. (Photo courtesy Morphy Auctions)

Game, Mickey Mouse Bagatelle, 24", Marks Bros version, 1934, VG, A $250.00

Game, Mickey Mouse Soldier Set, 8 cb Mickey target figures, w/cork gun, VGIB, A $275.00

Game, Mickey Mouse Target Game, bull's-eye target w/lg image of Mickey, complete w/toy gun, VGIB, A $150.00

Game, Pin the Tail on Mickey, Marks Bros, 1935, complete, VGIB $65.00

Gift Set, Donald Duck Spoon & Fork Holder, pnt wood figure on wheels w/spoon & fork, 5½", William Rogers, 1936, VG+ $330.00

Hair Bows, Ferdinand the Bull, rayon w/gold metal center, Stark Prod/WDP, 1938, EXOC $50.00

Hand Puppet, Archimedes (Sword & the Stone), cloth body w/vinyl head, Gund, 1960s, M $95.00

Hand Puppet, Cinderella, full plush body w/vinyl head & slippers, Gund, 1950s, NM+ $75.00

Hand Puppet, Dachsie (Lady & the Tramp), cloth body w/vinyl head, Gund, 1950s, NM+ $75.00

Hand Puppet, Donald Duck, bl & wht checked cloth body w/red neck bow, vinyl head, Gund, 1950s, NM....................$50.00
Hand Puppet, Donald Duck, bl & wht checked cloth body w/red neck bow, vinyl head, Gund, 1950s, VG....................$20.00
Hand Puppet, Donald Duck, cloth body w/printed body image & anchor on water, molded vinyl head, Gund, 1950s, EX+..$40.00
Hand Puppet, Donald Duck, cloth w/printed body image & name, vinyl head, Walt Disney World, 1970s, EX......$20.00
Hand Puppet, Donald Duck, printed cloth body w/name on chest, vinyl head, Gund, 1960s, EX $25.00
Hand Puppet, Dopey, cloth body w/vinyl head, Gund, 1950s, NM...$50.00
Hand Puppet, Dumbo, printed cloth body w/name on chest, gray vinyl head w/red hat, Gund, 1960s, NM....................$50.00
Hand Puppet, Ferdinand the Bull, cloth body w/compo head, 1938, NM... $150.00
Hand Puppet, Flora or Fona (Sleeping Beauty), cloth bodies w/vinyl heads, Gund, 1950s, EX, ea $50.00
Hand Puppet, Gonzorgo (Babes in Toyland), cloth body w/vinyl head, Gund, 1960s, MIB...$95.00
Hand Puppet, Goofy, cloth body w/red neck bow, vinyl head w/red hat, open mouth, Gund, 1950s, NM...............$50.00
Hand Puppet, Grumpy, cloth body w/vinyl head, Gund, 1950s, NMIB..$75.00
Hand Puppet, Jiminy Cricket, cloth body w/vinyl head, Gund, 1960s, NM $50.00
Hand Puppet, King Stefen (Sleeping Beauty), cloth body w/vinyl head, NM+ $75.00
Hand Puppet, Lucky (101 Dalmatians), wht cloth body w/blk dots & red trim, vinyl head, Gund, 1960s, NM..........$50.00
Hand Puppet, Maleficent (Sleeping Beauty), cloth body w/vinyl head, Gund, 1950s, NM+....................................... $125.00
Hand Puppet, Mary Poppins, red & wht striped cloth body w/umbrella & name in red on wht apron, Gund, 1960s, NM+ $100.00
Hand Puppet, Merlin (Sword in the Stone), cloth body w/vinyl head, Gund, 1950s, NM+....................................... $110.00

Hand Puppet, Merryweather (Sleeping Beauty), cloth body with vinyl head, Gund, 1950s, NM+, $75.00. (Photo courtesy gasolinealleyantiques.com)

Hand Puppet, Mickey Mouse, print cloth body w/name across bottom, vinyl head, Korea, 1970s, EX+ $25.00
Hand Puppet, Minnie Mouse, cloth body w/vinyl head, Gund, 1950s, VG...$25.00
Hand Puppet, Mother Goose (Babes in Toyland), cloth body w/vinyl head, Gund, 1960s, NM+ $75.00
Hand Puppet, Peter Pan, Gund, 1950s, cloth body w/vinyl head, 1950s, EX $50.00
Hand Puppet, Pinocchio, cloth body w/vinyl head, Knickerbocker, 1962, MIP...$25.00
Hand Puppet, Pluto, cloth body w/vinyl head, Gund, 1950s, NM...$35.00
Hand Puppet, Pongo (101 Dalmatians), wht cloth body w/blk dots, red trim, vinyl head, Gund, 1960s, NM $75.00
Hand Puppet, Robin Hood, brn & gr cloth body w/wht collar, vinyl head w/gr felt hat, MPI Toys, 1960s, NM+..... $125.00

Hand Puppet, Shaggy Dog, cloth body with vinyl head, Gund, 1960s, NM+, $85.00. (Photo courtesy gasolinealleyantiques.com)

Hand Puppet, Sleeping Beauty, cloth body w/vinyl head, eyes closed, Gund, 1950s, NM $75.00
Hand Puppet, Soldier (Babes in Toyland), Gund, 1960s, MIB $125.00
Hand Puppet, Tinkerbell, cloth body w/vinyl head, Gund, 1950s, NM...$30.00
Hand Puppet, Wart (Sword in the Stone), cloth body w/vinyl head, Gund, 1960s, NM+....................................... $100.00
Hand Puppet, Wendy (Peter Pan), cloth body w/vinyl head, Gund, 1950s, NM $60.00
Handkerchief, Donald Duck about to set sail w/3 nephews, 8" sq, 1950s, unused, EX...$25.00
Handkerchief Set, Snow White & the Seven Dwarfs, 4 different prints, WDE, 1930s, unused, MIB.......................... $175.00
Jack-in-the-Box, Donald Duck, compo head w/cloth body, wood box w/push-button action, Spear, 1940s, NM, A..... $215.00
Jack-in-the-Box, Winnie the Pooh, litho tin, Carnival, 1960s, EX $65.00
Kaleidoscope, cb & plastic w/litho images of Disney characters, 7" L, Straco, EX+..$20.00
Lamp, Dopey, ceramic figure, airbrushed details, printed scene on shade, 12", NM, A $150.00

Lamp, Mickey Mouse, ceramic figure wearing serape and sombrero playing mandolin, Mickey figure inside lightbulb, glows pink when illuminated, 12", WWII era, G, A, $300.00. (Photo courtesy Randy Inman Auctions)

Lamp, Mickey Mouse, tin ball-shaped base w/Mickey decal, Mickey w/lantern & Pluto on shade, 11", 1935, VG+, A........ $275.00
Lamp, Snow White, pnt plaster figure, printed scene on shade, 13½", LaMode/WDE, EX+ $350.00

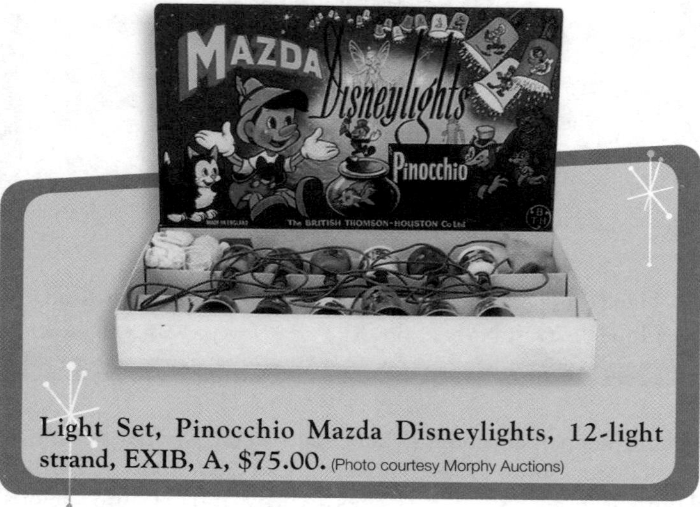

Light Set, Pinocchio Mazda Disneylights, 12-light strand, EXIB, A, $75.00. (Photo courtesy Morphy Auctions)

Light Set, Silly Symphony by Noma, Mazda lamps w/decals, 8-light strand, EXIB, A $150.00
Magic Slate, Winnie the Pooh, Western Publishing, 1965, unused, NM+ $50.00
Marionette, Alice in Wonderland, working mouth, Hazell, 14", NM.. $125.00
Marionette, Cinderella, pnt features, in evening gown, synthetic hair, Pelham, 1960s, NMIB $110.00
Marionette, Donald Duck, plastic, 7", 1960s or 1970s, EX+ .. $25.00
Marionette, Donald Duck, wood w/cloth jacket, open bill, 9", Pelham, 1976, MIB.. $125.00
Marionette, Dopey, working mouth, Peter Puppet Playthings, EX+ $225.00
Marionette, Goofy, compo w/cloth outfit, 10", Pelham, 1979, MIB... $150.00
Marionette, Jiminy Cricket, 9½", Pelham, EX+IB, A..... $175.00
Marionette, Mad Hatter, talker, cloth outfit, Peter Puppet Playthings, EX $100.00
Marionette, March Hair (Alice in Wonderland), talker, cloth outfit, Peter Puppet Playthings, EX+....................... $175.00
Marionette, Mickey Mouse, compo w/cloth outfit, 1940s, VG+ $95.00
Marionette, Mickey Mouse, fur-covered body w/pnt compo head & cb ears, 8", EX, A... $280.00

Marionette, Minnie Mouse, composition with cloth clothes, 1940s, EX, $150.00. (Photo courtesy gasolinealleyantiques.com)

Marionette, Peter Pan, Pelham, 1980s, ball-shaped head w/pnt features, dk hair, gr felt outfit, wht shoes, 11", MIB. $120.00
Marionette, Wendy (Peter Pan), talker, cloth outfit, Peter Puppet Playthings, NM... $125.00
Mechanical Toy, Climbing Mickey Mouse, cb figure climbs when string is pulled, 9", Dolly Toy Co, ca 1935, VGIB, A.. $280.00
Mechanical Toy, Mickey Mouse drummer figure, tin, toothy grin, when plunged he plays the drum, 6½", 1930s, EX... $1,345.00
Mechanical Toy, Mickey Mouse figure does jumping jacks when bellow is squeezed, pnt wood, 12", Nifty, 1930s, NM, A..$1,900.00
Mechanical Toy, Mickey Mouse sax player flat-sided squeeze figure, tin, jtd arms & legs, cymbals on feet, 6", EX.. $1,345.00
Mechanical Toy, Mickey Mouse Scooter-Jockey, w/up, plastic figure on 3-wheeled scooter, 6", Mavco, EXIB, A.... $150.00
Mechanical Toy, Pluto Twirly Tail Toy, w/up, plastic figure w/wire tail, 5½", EXIB, A $100.00
Mickey Mouse Bus Lines Bus w/Walt Disney Stars, pressed wood & tin, 20", Gong Bell Co, EXIB, A......................... $675.00
Mickey Mouse Explorers Outfit, complete & unused, NMIB, A...$250.00
Mickey Mouse Movie Projector, Keystone, 1934-35, NMIB. $1,050.00
Mickey's & Minnie's Merry Moments Stencil Outfit, Spear's, 1930s, complete, EXIB $150.00
Mini Winders, Donald Duck, plastic w/up, 3", Durham/WDP, 1970s, MOC $12.00
Movie Projector, Keystone, 1936, EXIB, A.................... $600.00
Mug, Dopey, ceramic w/emb full-figure image & name on banner, airbrushed pastel colors, glossy, 4", Enesco, 1950s, NM+..$30.00
Mystery Art Set, Mickey Mouse, Dixon/WDE, unused, MIB.. $400.00
Nodder, Donald Duck, standing w/hands on hips & winking, celluloid w/round tin base, rubber-band operated, 6", NM...$450.00
Paint Box, Snow White, litho tin, 4x1/2x9½" L, WD/MM Ltd, 1930s, unused, EX..$50.00

Parachutist, Donald Duck figure w/parachute, give a toss & he parachutes to the ground, 4", Durham, 1970s, unused, MOC $15.00
Party Favor, Donald Duck figure, celluloid upper body w/winking features, cloth bloomers, long red & wht cb legs, 6", NM $200.00
Pencil Case, Peter Pan, cb, snap front, sliding drawer, shows Peter looking in trunk full of pencils, 5x9", 1950s, EX, A $25.00
Pencil Holder, Dopey figure standing on 'Disneyland' base, ceramic, 4¼", EX+ $45.00
Pencil Holder, Sleepy (Snow White) figure on base marked 'Disneyland,' pnt ceramic, 4", NM $35.00
Pencil Holder, Winnie the Pooh & Rabbit holding onto 'Hunny' pot (holder) on grassy base, ceramic, 5", WDP, M $50.00
Pencil Set, Mickey Mouse, cb box w/snap closure, shows Mickey & friends, schoolhouse, 9" L, Japan, 1930s, EX+, A .. $260.00
Pencil Sharpener, Donald Duck, celluloid figure w/hands on hips, 3", EX+, A $165.00
Pencil Sharpener/Holder, 'Dopey's (or any dwarf) Storage Barrel,' ceramic, 4", Enesco/WDP, 1950s-60s, NM $55.00
Phonograph, Snow White & the Seven Dwarfs PortoFonic, litho tin, 14" dia, VG $175.00
Pillow Cover, Mickey w/flower, blk, gray & yel on wht cloth, 17x15", Vogue Needlecraft, 1930s, EX $50.00
Pip Squeek, Donald Duck figure w/an accordion-type body, plastic head, arms & feet, 4", Marx, 1970, MIB $20.00
Pip Squeek, Pinocchio figure w/accordion-type body, plastic, 4", Marx, 1970s, MIB $20.00
Plaque, Bambi, pnt image on wooden oval w/pnt rope-look border, 7x6", WDP, 1960s-70s, EX+ $8.00
Pop-Up Toy, Dumbo, plastic, 6", Kohner, 1960s, NM $30.00
Pull Toy, Donald Duck Ice Cream Wagon, paper litho on wood, 9", Marx, EXIB, A $200.00
Pull Toy, Donald Duck on Four Wheels, plastic, 4", US Plastics, 1950s, MIP (header reads 'Toy Time...25¢') $45.00

Pull Toy, Mickey Mouse in 'Express' cart pulled by Horace Horsecollar, wooden cart with painted bead-type wood figures, EX, A, $4,400.00. (Photo courtesy Bertoia Auctions)

Pull Toy, Mickey Mouse & Minnie on seesaw on 4-wheeled platform, wooden flex figures, PS base, 9½" L, EX, A .. $2,200.00
Pull Toy, Mickey Mouse pulling 2-wheeled bell, 13" L, N Hill Brass Co, 1936, VG+, A $385.00
Pull Toy, Mickey Standing on 3-wheeled scooter, celluloid figure, pnt-wood scooter, 4" H, Japan, EX+ $300.00
Pull Toy, Snow White on 2 lg wheels pulled by Doc & Dopey, paper-litho-on-wood figures, metal wheels, 14" L, EXIB, A $330.00
Push Puppet, Bambi, Kohner, 1960s, M $65.00
Push Puppet, Donald Duck, Gabriel, 1977, NM+ $35.00
Push Puppet, Donald Duck, Kohner, 1960s, M $50.00
Push Puppet, Donald Duck, Kohner, 1960s, Tricky Trapeze, NM+ $25.00

Push Puppet, Donald Duck, mini-puppet, Kohner, 1960s, M, $50.00. (Photo courtesy gasolinealleyantiques.com)

Push Puppet, Donald Duck, Maxi Puppet, Kohner, 1970s, NM $20.00
Push Puppet, Donald Duck's Nephew, Wara, 1960s, EX+ .. $45.00
Push Puppet, Goofy, Gabriel, Tricky Trapeze, NM $22.00
Push Puppet, Jiminy Cricket, Kohner, 1960s, NM $45.00
Push Puppet, Mickey Mouse, Gabriel, 1977, MOC $45.00
Push Puppet, Mickey Mouse, pnt wood bead figure standing on drum, yel, red, wht & blk, 5", EX, A $65.00
Push Puppet, Pinocchio, 'Mini-Pup 'Et' on label, 3", EX ... $20.00
Push Puppet, Pluto, 'Pluto Mini Puppet' on foil label, NM ... $20.00
Push Puppet, Pongo (101 Dalmatians), Kohner, 1960s, NM+ .. $35.00
Push-Button Puppet, Mickey Mouse, Kohner, 1960s, M ... $45.00
Push-Button Puppet, Pluto, 'Push-Up Puppet' on label, Gabriel, 1970s, NM $15.00
Ride-On Toy, Bambi, wood, natural wood Bambi figure on colorful rocker base, 29", Gong Bell Toy Co, 1956, EX $50.00
Ride-On Toy, Mickey Mouse figure on all fours, red & blk w/yel rockers & seat on Mickey's back, 34", Mengel Co, 1935, VG $225.00
Rubber Toy, Mickey Mouse Airmail Plane, Mickey in lt bl plane w/wht wheels, 6" L, Sun Rubber, EX+, A $88.00
Scrapbook, Disneyland, 'For Pictures & Clippings,' 8½x11", WDP, 1950s, unused, EX+ $50.00
Sled, Flexible Flyer No 80, 1935, natural wood w/Mickey's name & colorful Mickey & Minnie decal, metal runners, 32", VG $250.00

Slinky Figure, Pluto, litho tin head & rear w/Slinky center body, on wheels, 8", VG, A.. $200.00
Snap-Eeze, Figures, 12 different on 1 card, Marx, MIB... $100.00
Snow Dome, Goofey figure standing next to Christmas tree in clear plastic dome, red base, 3", Kurt Adler, NM+ $10.00
Snow Dome, Jiminey Cricket in glass globe on wooden base, New England Collector's Society, 1980s-90s, 4", NM+........$25.00
Soap Set, Aristocats, Marie, Toulouse & Berlioz soap figures, 2½", Avon, 1970s, unused, MIB.................................$25.00
Soap Set, Snow White, 7 bars ea w/incised image of dwarf & name, Kerk Guild/WDE, 1938, unused, NM+IB, A.. $135.00
Spinikin, Mickey Mouse, plastic, 4", Kohner, 1960s, NM.$40.00

Squeeze Toy, Baloo (Jungle Book), 7½", Holland Hall, 1960s, EX+, $38.00. (Photo courtesy whatacharacter.com)

Squeeze Toy, Donald Duck holding binoculars, 10½", Dell, 1960s, NM $50.00
Squeeze Toy, Donald Duck standing w/mouth open, hands together, 6½", Dell, 1950s-60s, EX+...........................$40.00
Squeeze Toy, Donald Duck standing w/mouth open, side-glance eyes, 10½", Sun Rubber, 1950s, VG+.........................$40.00
Squeeze Toy, Donald Duck standing w/mouth open, waving, 7½", Gabriel, 1978, NM $18.00
Squeeze Toy, Dopey (Snow White) standing looking coyly over his shoulder, 5", Lanco, 1965, M $10.00
Squeeze Toy, Dumbo, 3x4", Kohner Squeez-Mees, 1960s-70s, MIP.. $40.00
Squeeze Toy, Dumbo seated upright, bl & pk, 3", Gabriel/WDP, 1977, NM+ $15.00
Squeeze Toy, Dumbo seated upright w/trunk up, 5", Dell/WDP, 1950s, EX+...$32.00
Squeeze Toy, Eeyore seated upright, 8", Holland Hall, 1966, NM .. $55.00
Squeeze Toy, fork shape w/Mickey's head emb by tines & emb 'Mickey' on hdl, 8", Danara, 1970s, EX+ $10.00
Squeeze Toy, Grumpy (Snow White) standing w/arms crossed, pnt 2-tone bl outfit, 5½", Lanco, 1965, NM+ $10.00
Squeeze Toy, Huey, Louie & Dewey in a 'wooden' washtub, 5x6", Sun Rubber, 1950s, VG $35.00
Squeeze Toy, Kanga & Roo, vinyl, Roo emb in pouch, 8", Holland Hall, 1966, NM $50.00
Squeeze Toy, Lady (Lady & the Tramp) seated upright, vinyl, 2½", Lanco, 1960s-70s, M $12.00
Squeeze Toy, Mickey Mouse standing looking up w/arms behind back, 6", Dell, 1950s or 1960s, EX+ $50.00
Squeeze Toy, Mickey Mouse standing w/sack on stick thrown over shoulder, 10", Dell, EX+ $75.00
Squeeze Toy, Mowgli (Jungle Book) standing w/arms crossed on grassy base, 6½", Holland Hall, 1967, EX $40.00
Squeeze Toy, Peter Pan, 10", Sun Rubber, 1950s, EX.........$50.00
Squeeze Toy, Piglet (Winnie the Pooh) seated w/hands on tummy, 3½", Sears, 1970s, NM+ $10.00
Squeeze Toy, Pinocchio leaning on satchel admiring apple in hand, 7½", Dell, 1950s, EX+ $45.00
Squeeze Toy, Pluto sitting upright licking his chops, 6", Holland Hall/WDP, 1960s, EX $35.00
Squeeze Toy, Shaggy Dog seated in begging pose, 5½", Dell/WDP, 1960s, EX $45.00
Squeeze Toy, Sleeping Beauty on knees talking to squirrel & rabbit, name incised on base, 7", Dell, 1950s, EX............$55.00
Squeeze Toy, telephone w/Donald Duck's head on dial, 4", Danara/WDP, 1970s, unused, MIP (head card reads 'Squeek-A-Toy').. $20.00
Squeeze Toy, telephone w/Mickey's head on dial, yel, 4", Danara, 1970s, MIP (header card reads 'Squeek-A-Toy') $20.00

Squeeze Toy, Tigger seated upright, early characteristics, 8", Holland Hall, 1960s, EX, $40.00. (Photo courtesy whatacharacter.com)

Squeeze Toy, Tramp (Lady & the Tramp), seated upright w/head turned, wide-eyes, 4", Lanco, M $12.00
Squeeze Toy, Uncle Scrooge atop bank w/3 nephews looking on, 7", Dell, 1960s, NM+..$75.00
Squeeze Toy, Uncle Scrooge standing gestering w/finger up in air, 8", Dell, 1960s, NM $60.00
Squeeze Toy, Winnie the Pooh seated licking 'Hunny' pot, 6", Holland Hall, 1966, EX $35.00
Squeeze Toy, Winnie the Pooh seated w/'Hunny' pot & waving, 6", Shelco, 1978, VG+ $20.00
Squeeze Toy, 101 Dalmatians pup seated w/head turned looking up, 7", 1960s, NM..$25.00
Tableware, Snow White/Dwarfs dish set, wht ceramic w/decals, gr trim, 19-pc w/gravy boat, tureen, etc, Japan, 1930s, EX. $650.00

Tea Set, Donald Duck, wht china w/decals, red trim, 4 cups, saucers, teapot, sugar bowl & creamer, Occupied Japan, EXIB $200.00
Tea Set, Helpmates/Minnie & Mickey, litho tin, scenes w/orange trim, 6-pc, EX, A $135.00
Tea Set, litho tin w/various images of Mickey & friends, orange rims, 10-pc w/3 plates, cups & saucers, pot & lid, EXIB..... $1,035.00
Tea Set, Mickey & Minnie, ceramic, 8" teapot, 5" sugar bowl & 3" creamer, wht w/decals, gold trim, French, prewar, NM.. $400.00
Tea Set, Who's Afraid of the Big Bad Wolf/Three Little Pigs, litho tin, scenes w/gr trim, 13-pc, Ohio Art, EX...... $440.00
Telephone, Mickey Mouse on candlestick type phone, NN Hill Brass Co, 1930s, 9", EX, A $225.00

Toothbrush Holder, Two Donald Duck figures arm-in-arm, bisque, 4½", EX, A, $330.00. (Photo courtesy Randy Inman Auctions)

Toothbrush Holder, Mickey & Minnie standing side-by-side w/hands on hips, holder in back, pnt porc, 4½" H, EX $250.00
Toothbrush Holder, Mickey washing Pluto's face, bisque, 4½", EX, A $220.00
Top, Disney characters on parade, litho tin, Fretz Bueschel/WDE, 9" dia, EX, A $385.00
Toy Chest, Mickey Mouse, cb litho w/metal closure & corner support strips, bl, orange, yel & wht graphics, 12x28", VG, A $220.00
Train Set, Mickey Mouse Circus #1536, Lionel, 1935, litho tin set w/circular track, w/up, complete, EXIB, A $7,475.00
Train Set, Mickey Mouse Circus #306/2, litho tin set w/ciruclar track & circus tent, near complete, EXIB, A $4,880.00
Tray, Lady & the Tramp, litho tin w/illustrated 'spaghetti scene,' 13x17", EX $50.00
Tricky Trike, Mickey Mouse, Gabriel, 1977, NRFC $30.00
Wacky Heads (Puppet), Roger Rabbit, foam rubber head, fingers manipulate facial expressions, Applause, 1987, unused, MIP $10.00
Wall Walker, Donald Duck, plastic, 3½", Kenner/General Mills, 1972, unused, MOC $25.00
Weather Forecaster, plastic house labeled Mickey Mouse Weather House, 6", post WWII, EXIB, A $100.00

Dollhouse Furniture

Back in the 1940s and 1950s, little girls often spent hour after hour with their dollhouses, keeping house for their imaginary families, cooking on tiny stoves (that sometimes came with scaled-to-fit pots and pans), serving meals in lovely dining rooms, making beds, and rearranging furniture, most of which was plastic, much of which was made by Renwal, Ideal, Marx, Irwin, and Plasco. Jaydon made plastic furniture as well but sadly never marked it. Tootsietoy produced metal items, many in boxed sets.

Of all of these manufacturers, Renwal and Ideal are considered the most collectible. Renwal's furniture was usually detailed; some pieces had moving parts. Many were made in more than one color, often brightened with decals. Besides the furniture, they made accessory items as well as 'dollhouse' dolls of the whole family. Ideal's Petite Princess line was packaged in sets with wonderful detail, accessorized down to the perfume bottles on the top of the vanity. Ideal furniture and parts are numbered, always with an 'I' prefix. Most Renwal pieces are also numbered.

Advisor: Judith Mosholder

Acme/Thomas, carriage, any color combo, ea $6.00
Acme/Thomas, doll, baby; sucking thumb, hard plastic, pk, Thomas, 1¼" $3.00
Acme/Thomas, doll, baby; w/diaper, Thomas, 1⅛" to 2", any from $2 to $4.00
Acme/Thomas, doll, Dutch girl; flesh-colored, Thomas, 2⅜" .. $5.00
Acme/Thomas, doll, girl; hard plastic, yel dress, Thomas, 3½" .. $20.00
Acme/Thomas, doll, little brother; w/raised hand, Thomas... $3.00
Acme/Thomas, hammock, bl w/red supports $20.00
Acme/Thomas, rocker, yel w/gr or yel w/red, ea....... $4.00

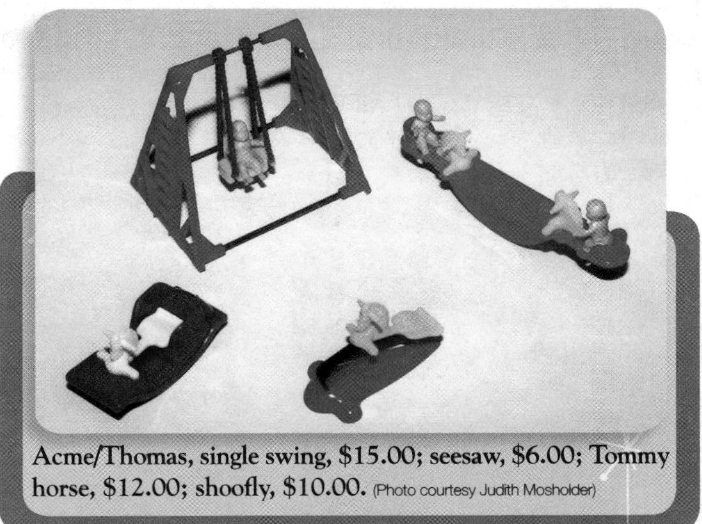

Acme/Thomas, single swing, $15.00; seesaw, $6.00; Tommy horse, $12.00; shoofly, $10.00. (Photo courtesy Judith Mosholder)

Acme/Thomas, stroller, any color combo....... $6.00
Allied/Pyro, bed, red w/wht spread....... $10.00
Allied/Pyro, chair, dining; pk, red or wht, ea $3.00
Allied/Pyro, chair, kitchen; gray, pk or red, unmk, ea....... $3.00
Allied/Pyro, cupboard, corner; aqua $8.00
Allied/Pyro, hutch, aqua or red $4.00
Allied/Pyro, night stand, yel....... $4.00
Allied/Pyro, piano, blk (unmk), or lt bl (Allied), ea $5.00
Allied/Pyro, radio, floor; yel....... $5.00

Allied/Pyro, sofa, aqua or lt bl, unmk....................................$5.00
Allied/Pyro, sofa, yel, unmk..$8.00
Allied/Pyro, stove, wht, unmk..$4.00
Allied/Pyro, table, kitchen; wht $4.00
Allied/Pyro, tub, lt bl..$4.00
Allied/Pyro, vanity, aqua, bl or pk, ea $4.00
Arcade, bath set (tub, sink, toilet), pnt CI, wht, VG pnt..$55.00
Arcade, bathtub, pnt CI, ivory $125.00
Arcade, breakfast nook set (Curtis), 3-pc (table & 2 benches), pnt CI, wht, G $100.00
Arcade, chair, bedroom; pnt CI, dk gr, VG pnt $95.00
Arcade, cupboard (Boone), pnt CI, wht, VG $90.00
Arcade, dresser, arched mirror, 4-drawer, 4-footed, gr, G .. $220.00
Arcade, icebox (Leonard), pnt CI, wht, VG.................. $185.00

Arcade, Karpen davenport and easy chair, removable cushions, rare, A, $300.00. (Photo courtesy Randy Inman Auctions)

Fisher-Price, barbecue grill & patio lounge chair, #272, 1983-84, MOC...$4.50
Fisher-Price, chair, kitchen; wht & yel...................................$2.00
Fisher-Price, chair, kitchen; wht w/marblized seat $1.00
Fisher-Price, chair dining; brn w/tan seat...........................$2.00
Fisher-Price, cradle, wht $5.00
Fisher-Price, doll family, any, MOC, ea...............................$3.00
Fisher-Price, dresser w/mirror, wht $5.00

Fisher-Price, kitchen set, #252, 1978 – 1984, M, $5.00 each. (Photo courtesy Brad Cassity)

Fisher-Price, refrigerator, wht w/yel...$5.00
Fisher-Price, sink, kitchen; yel, wht & orange $5.00
Fisher-Price, stove w/hood, yel $5.00
Fisher-Price, table, kitchen; wht w/red marbelized top $3.00
Fisher-Price, toilet/vanity, bright gr w/wht trim................$10.00

Ideal, two livingroom chairs, $15.00 each; tilt-top table, $45.00; floor lamp, $25.00; fireplace, $35.00; floor radio, $10.00; sofa, $22.00; coffee table, $10.00; end table/night stand, $6.00; table lamp, $20.00. (Photo courtesy Judith Mosholder)

Ideal, bench, lawn; bl...$18.00
Ideal, bird bath, marbleized ivory $18.00
Ideal, buffet, dk brn or dk marbelized brn, ea.....................$10.00
Ideal, buffet, red $15.00
Ideal, chair, dining room; brn w/bl seat, dk marbleized maroon w/bl or yel seat, ea..$10.00
Ideal, chair, kitchen; ivory w/various seat colors, ea $5.00
Ideal, chair, sq back, bl swirl, bright gr swirl or med gr swirl, all w/brn bases, ea $15.00
Ideal, chaise lounge, wht $18.00
Ideal, china closet, dk brn swirl or dk marbleized maroon, ea ...$15.00
Ideal, china closet, red...$20.00
Ideal, clothes washer, front load, wht..................................$22.00
Ideal, dishwasher, w/lettering $20.00
Ideal, doll, baby; pnt diaper $10.00
Ideal, hamper, bl $6.00
Ideal, hamper, ivory $4.00
Ideal, highboy, ivory w/bl..$18.00
Ideal, highchair, collapsible, bl or pk, ea $25.00
Ideal, iron, electric; wht w/blk...$18.00
Ideal, piano w/bench, caramel swirl $35.00
Ideal, playpen, bl w/pk bottom or pk w/bl bottom, ea........$25.00
Ideal, potty chair, pk, complete $15.00
Ideal, radiator..$25.00
Ideal, refrigerator, Deluxe, wht w/blk, opening door, cb backing...$30.00
Ideal, refrigerator, ivory w/blk...$15.00
Ideal, secretary, dk marbelized maroon, complete $40.00
Ideal, sewing machine, dk marbelized brn or dk marbelized maroon, ea $20.00
Ideal, shopping cart, bl w/wht baskets, wht w/red or bl baskets, ea $40.00
Ideal, sink, bathroom; bl w/yel or ivory w/blk, ea................$8.00
Ideal, sink, kitchen; ivory w/blk $15.00
Ideal, stool, vanity; ivory w/bl seat $6.00
Ideal, stove, ivory w/blk $15.00
Ideal, table, kitchen; ivory w/blk $6.00
Ideal, table, picnic, gr $20.00

Ideal, table, umbrella; yel w/red umbrella & red pole $25.00
Ideal, television, dog picture, yel detail $45.00
Ideal, toilet, bl w/yel hdl $10.00
Ideal, toilet, ivory w/blk hdl $20.00
Ideal, tub, corner; bl w/yel $18.00
Ideal, tub, ivory w/blk $10.00
Ideal, vacuum cleaner, no bag, bl w/red or yel or gr w/red-yel, ea $20.00
Ideal, vanity w/mirror, dk marbelized maroon, mirror wear...$12.00
Ideal, vanity w/mirror, ivory w/bl, mirror good $18.00
Ideal Petite Princess, bed, #4416-4, bl or pk, complete, w/orig box $30.00
Ideal Petite Princess, books & bookends, Heirloom #4428-9, ea $5.00
Ideal Petite Princess, boudoir chaise lounge, #4408-1, pk, MIB $25.00
Ideal Petite Princess, Buddha, #4437-0, metal $15.00
Ideal Petite Princess, buffet, Royal #4419-8, complete $4.00
Ideal Petite Princess, cabinet, Treasure Trove #4418-0......$10.00
Ideal Petite Princess, cabinet, Treasure Trove #4418-09, in orig box $12.00
Ideal Petite Princess, cabinet, Treasure Trove #4479-2, in orig box $12.00
Ideal Petite Princess, candelabra, Fantasia #4438-8, in org box $22.00
Ideal Petite Princess, candelabra, Royal #4439-6, in orig box.. $15.00
Ideal Petite Princess, chair, dining; Host #4413-1, w/orig box $17.00
Ideal Petite Princess, chair, drum; Salon #4411-5, gold or gr, w/orig box, ea $17.00
Ideal Petite Princess, chair, guest dining; #4414-9, in orig box..$17.00
Ideal Petite Princess, chair, host dining; #4474-3, in orig box ...$17.00
Ideal Petite Princess, chair, hostess dining; #4415-6...........$8.00
Ideal Petite Princess, chair, wing; Salon #4410-7, w/orig box . $15.00
Ideal Petite Princess, chair & ottoman, occasional; #4412-3, lt brn, w/orig box $22.00
Ideal Petite Princess, chest, Palace #4420-6.........................$5.00

Ideal Petite Princess, Salon Coffee Table Set, #4433-9, with accessories, in original box, $25.00.

Ideal Petite Princess, clock, grandfather; #4423-0 ....$10.00
Ideal Petite Princess, chest, Palace #4420-6, in orig box ...$17.00
Ideal Petite Princess, clock, grandfather; #4423-0, w/folding screen, in orig box $20.00
Ideal Petite Princess, doll family, father, mother, girl, boy, #9170-5, MIB $75.00
Ideal Petite Princess, dressing table, #4417-2, complete....$20.00
Ideal Petite Princess, hearthplace, Regency, #4422-2, complete, in orig box $18.00
Ideal Petite Princess, hearthplace, Regency #4422-2, complete ...$4.00
Ideal Petite Princess, lamp, table; Heirloom #4428-9 ....$5.00
Ideal Petite Princess, piano & bench, grand; Royal #4425-5 .. $25.00
Ideal Petite Princess, piano & bench, grand; Royal #4425-5, in orig box $30.00
Ideal Petite Princess, planter, Salon #4440-4 ....$15.00
Ideal Petite Princess, planter, Salon #9710-5, in orig box .$18.00
Ideal Petite Princess, sofa, #4407-3, beige/gold, in orig box ..$25.00
Ideal Petite Princess, table, coffee; Salon #4433-9, w/assorted accessories, in orig box $25.00
Ideal Petite Princess, table, dining room; #4421-4.............$15.00
Ideal Petite Princess, table, lyre; #4426-3............................$5.00
Ideal Petite Princess, table, occasional; #4437-0.................$5.00
Ideal Petite Princess, table, Palace #4431-3 ....$5.00
Ideal Petite Princess, table set, #4426-3, complete $15.00
Ideal Petite Princess, table set, Heirloom, #4428-99, complete in orig box $27.00
Ideal Petite Princess, table set, occasional; #4437-0, complete, in orig box $27.00
Ideal Petite Princess, table set, Palace #4431-3, complete.$20.00
Ideal Petite Princess, table set, pedestal; #4427-1, complete, in orig box $18.00
Ideal Petite Princess, table set, Salon #4433-9, complete, in orig box $27.00
Ideal Petite Princess, table set, tier; #4429-7, complete, in orig box $18.00
Ideal Petite Princess, tea cart, rolling, #4424-8, complete, in orig box $20.00
Ideal Petite Princess, telephone, Fantasy #4432-1 ....$8.00
Ideal Petite Princess, telephone set, Fantasy #4432-1, complete, in orig box $20.00
Ideal Young Decorator, bathtub, corner; bl w/yel..............$35.00
Ideal Young Decorator, carpet sweeper, 2 rollers, red w/bl hdl...$30.00
Ideal Young Decorator, chair, kitchen; wht.......................$10.00
Ideal Young Decorator, china closet, dk marbleized maroon.$25.00
Ideal Young Decorator, night stand, dk marbelized maroon..$15.00
Ideal Young Decorator, playpen, pk..................................$45.00
Ideal Young Decorator, sofa, right corner section, rose $12.00
Ideal Young Decorator, sofa, sm middle section, rose.........$12.00
Ideal Young Decorator, stove, wht.....................................$55.00
Ideal Young Decorator, table, coffee; dk marbelized maroon..$18.00
Ideal Young Decorator, table, kitchen; wht........................$10.00
Ideal Young Decorator, television, complete......................$45.00
Ideal Young Decorator, television, no cb backing..............$25.00
Irwin, broom, any color, ea $5.00
Irwin, clothes basket, bright yel, 3" across..........................$4.00
Irwin, dustpan, any color, ...$4.00
Irwin, hoe, orange $3.00
Irwin, pail, dk bl or gr $4.00

Irwin, shovel, gr or orange, ea....................$3.00
Irwin, spade, bright yel....................$3.00
Irwin, watering can, orange....................$10.00
Irwin Interior Decorator, bathtub, lt gr....................$5.00
Irwin Interior Decorator, plate, orange....................$3.00
Irwin Interior Decorator, refrigerator, under-the-counter; yel .. $3.00
Irwin Interior Decorator, refrigerator, yel....................$5.00
Irwin Interior Decorator, toilet, lt gr....................$5.00
Irwin Interior Decorator, yel w/chrome....................$5.00
Jaydon, bed w/spread, bl spread....................$15.00
Jaydon, chair, bedroom; bl or pk, ea....................$6.00
Jaydon, chair, living room; ivory w/brn base....................$8.00
Jaydon, chest w/2 opening drawers, reddish brn....................$5.00
Jaydon, cupboard, corner; red....................$5.00
Jaydon, hamper, red....................$5.00
Jaydon, lamp, table; ivory w/red shade or red shade, ea.....$15.00
Jaydon, night stand, pk....................$4.00
Jaydon, piano, reddish brn swirl....................$12.00
Jaydon, piano bench, reddish brn swirl....................$3.00
Jaydon, refrigerator, ivory w/blk....................$15.00
Jaydon, sink, bathroom; ivory....................$10.00
Jaydon, sink, kitchen; ivory w/blk....................$15.00
Jaydon, table, dining; reddish brn swirl....................$5.00
Jaydon, toilet, ivory w/red lid....................$10.00

Kahn Toy Co., Auto Trailer and Streamlined Car With 11 Pieces of Doll House Furniture, 14" L, EXIB, A, $200.00. (Photo courtesy Morphy Auctions)

Kilgore, lawnmower, reel-type, 3¾" L, EX+, A....................$525.00
Kilgore, Sally Ann Bathroom Set, w/tub, sink, toilet, stool, laundry basket & bisque baby, VG+IB, A....................$715.00
Kilgore, Sally Ann Dining Room Set, w/table & 4 chairs, sideboard & cabinet, pnt CI, EX+IB, A....................$1,045.00
Kilgore, Sally Ann Household (Laundry) Set, CI, NOS, A.. $715.00
Kilgore, Sally Ann Nursery Set, w/carriage, crib, highchair, potty chair & rocker, CI, VG+IB, A....................$990.00
Kilgore, Sally Ann Playground Set, 5-pc set, CI w/NP wheels, NOS, A....................$1,045.00
Lundby, bathroom set w/tub, sink & toilet, gr tile....................$30.00
Lundby, bed, bl & wht, no pillows....................$10.00
Lundby, chair, dining; wht w/gold-striped fabric seat....................$5.00
Lundby, chair, kitchen, red & wht checked seat....................$4.00
Lundby, chair, wht & gold striped fabric....................$8.00
Lundby, dishwasher, red-patterned back splash....................$8.00
Lundby, fireplace....................$15.00
Lundby, fireplace, corner; w/logs, wht....................$15.00
Lundby, garden table & 2 chairs, wood w/metal....................$20.00
Lundby, light, hanging; red w/gold trim....................$8.00
Lundby, living room set, Royal, MIP....................$40.00
Lundby, mirror, wht w/gold trim....................$5.00
Lundby, night table, 2 drawers, wht....................$5.00
Lundby, refrigerator, opening door, wht w/blk base....................$8.00
Lundby, sink, red-patterned back splash....................$8.00
Lundby, sofa, wht w/gold striped fabric....................$10.00
Lundby, stove, red-patterned back splash....................$8.00
Lundby, table, dining; wht top....................$8.00
Lundby, table, kitchen; red....................$6.00
Lundby, table, living room; walnut....................$12.00
Marklin, bed, brass w/spindle headboard & footboard, wire springs, cloth bedding, 8¼", VG, A....................$330.00
Marklin, fireplace, pnt & copper-plated tin, cherub decor, w/accessories, 5½", VG+, A....................$350.00
Marklin, settee, 2 chairs & 2 flower pots, ormolu w/rose satin upholstery, wht ceramic planters w/ormolu flowers, VG, A....................$650.00

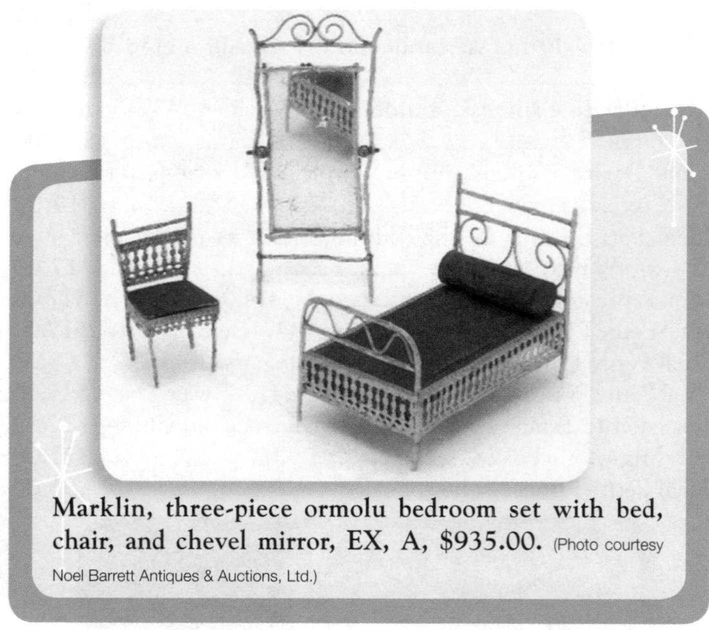

Marklin, three-piece ormolu bedroom set with bed, chair, and chevel mirror, EX, A, $935.00. (Photo courtesy Noel Barrett Antiques & Auctions, Ltd.)

Marx, hard plastic, ½" scale, any pc except barbecue, curved sofa, jukebox or milk bar, any color, ea from $3 to....................$5.00
Marx, hard plastic, ½" scale, curved sofa or milk bar, bright yel or red, ea from $15 to....................$18.00
Marx, hard plastic, ½" scale, juke box, bright yel or red, ea .$20.00
Marx, hard plastic, ¾" scale, any pc except iron, swimming pool or upright sweeper, ea from $3 to....................$6.00
Marx, hard plastic, ¾" scale, iron, wht....................$8.00
Marx, hard plastic, ¾" scale, swimming pool (red), upright sweeper (wht), ea....................$10.00
Marx, soft plastic, ¾" scale, any pc except floor lamp, ea from $3 to....................$4.00
Marx, soft plastic, ¾" scale, floor lamp, bright yel or lt yel, ea. $6.00
Marx Little Hostess, chair, bedroom occasional; ivory w/hot pk seat....................$8.00

Marx Little Hostess, chair, dining; brn w/red seats, armless, set of 6, boxed $25.00
Marx Little Hostess, chair, occasional; yel, boxed $10.00
Marx Little Hostess, chair, occasional; yel $8.00
Marx Little Hostess, chaise, ivory w/bright pk $12.00
Marx Little Hostess, chest, block front, rust or ivory, ea....$12.00
Marx Little Hostess, dresser, dbl; ivory $8.00
Marx Little Hostess, fireplace, ivory $20.00
Marx Little Hostess, lowboy, red $12.00
Marx Little Hostess, mirror, gilded, boxed $6.00
Marx Little Hostess, mirror, wall $5.00
Marx Little Hostess, refrigerator, avocado $25.00

Marx Little Hostess, rocking chair, $12.00; grandfather clock, $18.00; turquoise sofa, $8.00; wingback chair, $10.00. (Photo courtesy Judith Mosholder)

Marx Little Hostess, screen, folding; blk, boxed $10.00
Marx Little Hostess, sideboard, brn $12.00
Marx Little Hostess, sofa, turq, boxed $15.00
Marx Little Hostess, table, gate-leg; lt brn, boxed $8.00
Marx Little Hostess, table, gate-leg; rust $15.00
Marx Little Hostess, table, tilt-top; blk $12.00
Marx Little Hostess, table coffee; rnd, brn $8.00
Mattel Littles, armoire $8.00
Mattel Littles, doll, Belinda, w/4 chairs & pop-up room setting $25.00
Mattel Littles, doll, Hedy, w/sofa & pop-up room setting..$22.00
Mattel Littles, doll set, Littles Family (Mr & Mrs & baby)...$22.00
Mattel Littles, table, drop-leaf; w/4 plates & cups $15.00
Mattle Littles, sofa $5.00
Plasco, bathroom set, complete, in orig box w/insert & floor plan $50.00
Plasco, bathtub, any color, ea $4.00
Plasco, bed, brn headboard, yel spread $3.00
Plasco, bedspread, any color, ea $2.00
Plasco, buffet, any color, ea $4.00
Plasco, chair, dining; tan w/paper seat cover $4.00
Plasco, chair, kitchen; any color, ea $2.00
Plasco, chair, living room; no-base style, dk brn or yel, ea...$3.00
Plasco, chair, living room; w/base, bright gr, lt gr or mauve, ea .$15.00
Plasco, chair, patio; bl w/ivory legs $3.00
Plasco, chair dining (w/ or w/o arms); brn or marbelized brn, ea $3.00
Plasco, clock, grandfather; lt brn swirl or dk brn, cb face, ea..$15.00
Plasco, highboy, tan $8.00
Plasco, kitchen counter, no-base style, pk $3.00
Plasco, night stand, brn, med marbelized brn or tan, ea $3.00
Plasco, refrigerator, no-base style, pk or wht, ea $3.00
Plasco, refrigerator, wht w/bl base $5.00
Plasco, sink, kitchen; no-base style, lt gr w/rose trim, pk or wht, ea $3.00
Plasco, sofa, no-base style, any color, ea $3.00
Plasco, stove, no-base style, pk $3.00
Plasco, stove, wht w/bl base $5.00
Plasco, table, coffee; brn, med marbelized brn or tan, ea $3.00
Plasco, table, coffee; tan w/leather top $5.00
Plasco, table, dining room side; tan w/yel $4.00
Plasco, table, kitchen; pk $5.00
Plasco, table, patio (sm); bl w/ivory legs $4.00
Plasco, table, umbrella; bl w/ivory, complete $15.00
Plasco, toilet, turq w/wht $8.00
Plasco, vanity, w/ or w/o mirror, any color, ea $5.00
Plasco, vanity bench, any color, ea $5.00
Pyro, see Allied Pyro
Reliable, bathtub, ivory w/bl trim $15.00
Reliable, chair, dining; rust $5.00
Reliable, chair, kitchen; ivory w/bl seat $5.00
Reliable, chair, living room; bl w/rust base or red w/rust base, ea $15.00
Reliable, doll, baby; hard plastic, any, ea $10.00
Reliable, highboy, rust $8.00
Reliable, piano bench, brn $4.00
Reliable, piano bench, rust $25.00
Reliable, radio, floor; rust $15.00
Reliable, refrigerator, ivory w/bl trim $5.00
Reliable, stove, ivory w/bl trim $5.00
Reliable, table, dining; rust $20.00
Reliable, table, kitchen; ivory $12.00
Reliable, toilet, ivory w/bl seat $5.00

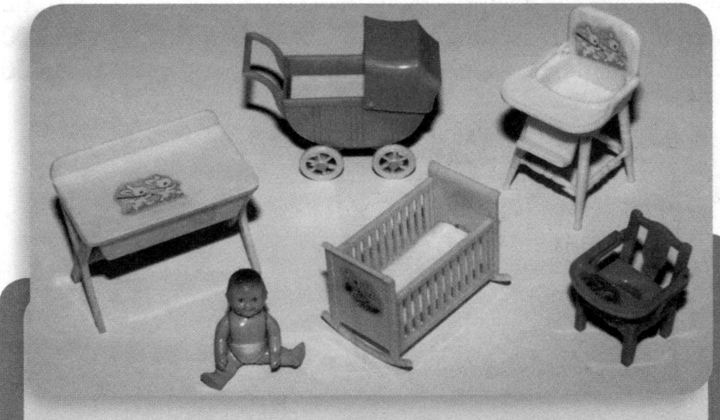

Renwal, pink baby bath with decal, $15.00; blue carriage with pink wheels, $25.00; pink highchair with decals, $25.00; blue potty chair with decals, $12.00; pink cradle with decals, $25.00; baby with white-painted diaper, $8.00. (Photo courtesy Judith Mosholder)

Renwal, bathroom tub/sink/toilet, med bl & turq w/blk....$35.00
Renwal, bed, brn w/ivory spread $8.00

Renwal, bench, piano/vanity; brn or lt gr, ea $2.00
Renwal, buffet, brn $6.00
Renwal, carriage, doll insert, pk w/pk wheels $30.00
Renwal, chair, barrel; bl w/red base $8.00
Renwal, chair, barrel; med bl w/metallic red base $9.00
Renwal, chair, club; bl w/brn base, pk w/red or metallic red base, ea $8.00
Renwal, chair, club; dk, bl w/brn base $15.00
Renwal, chair, folding; gold w/red seat $15.00
Renwal, chair, kitchen; brn w/ivory seats $2.00
Renwal, chair, kitchen; ivory w/blk $5.00
Renwal, chair, kitchen; ivory w/brn or red, red w/yel, ea $3.00
Renwal, chair, kitchen; lt gr w/blk seats, ea $5.00
Renwal, chair, teacher's; red $15.00
Renwal, china closet, brn, reddish brn or med maroon swirl, ea $5.00
Renwal, china closet, brn (stenciled) or ivory, ea $15.00
Renwal, china closet, reddish brn, stenciled $8.00
Renwal, clock, kitchen; ivory or red, ea $20.00
Renwal, clock, mantel; ivory or red, ea $10.00
Renwal, cradle, doll insert, lt bl, no decals $20.00
Renwal, desk, student's; any color, ea $12.00
Renwal, desk, teacher's; bl or red, ea $25.00
Renwal, doll, baby (chubby); pnt diaper $45.00
Renwal, doll, baby; flesh or pk, pnt diaper, ea $8.00
Renwal, doll, baby; plain $8.00
Renwal, doll, baby; pnt suit $10.00
Renwal, doll, brother; plastic rivets, all yel $20.00
Renwal, doll, father; metal rivets, dk brn suit $25.00
Renwal, doll, mother; metal rivets, rose dress $25.00
Renwal, doll, rubber nursery, ea $4.00
Renwal, doll, sister; metal rivets, yel dress $25.00
Renwal, dust pan, red or yel, ea $10.00
Renwal, garbage can, red w/yel, no decal $5.00
Renwal, garbage can, yel w/red, w/decal $8.00
Renwal, hamper, nonopening lid, ivory $2.00
Renwal, hamper, opening lid, lt gr $10.00
Renwal, hamper, opening lid, pk $5.00
Renwal, highboy, nonopening drawers, brn $6.00

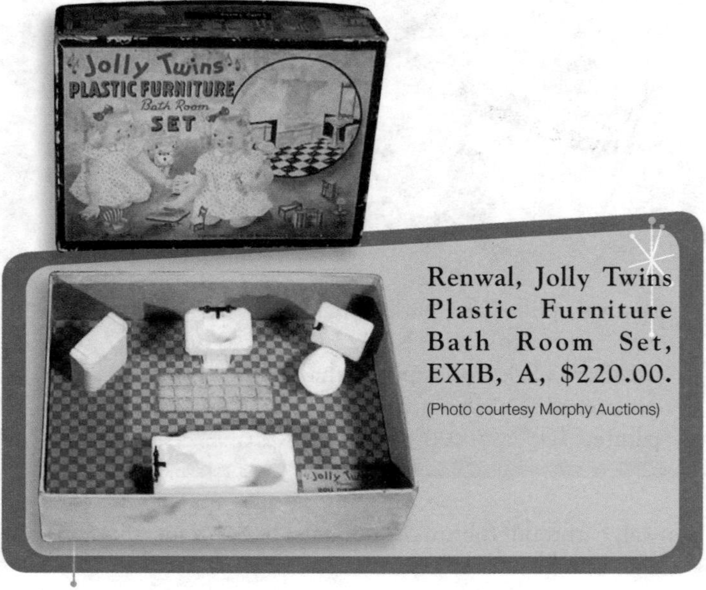

Renwal, Jolly Twins Plastic Furniture Bath Room Set, EXIB, A, $220.00.

(Photo courtesy Morphy Auctions)

Renwal, highboy, nonopening drawers, pk $12.00
Renwal, highboy, opening drawers, brn $8.00
Renwal, ironing board, bl or pk, ea $7.00
Renwal, ironing board & iron, pk w/bl & pk iron, ea $22.00
Renwal, Jolly Twins Kitchen Set, table & 4 chairs, sink, refrigerator & stove, EXIB, A $220.00
Renwal, kiddie car, red w/bl & yel $25.00
Renwal, lamp, floor; metallic red w/ivory shade $20.00
Renwal, lamp, floor; pk w/ivory shade $50.00
Renwal, lamp, table; brn w/ivory shade $6.00
Renwal, lamp, table; caramel w/ivory shade or metallic red ivory shade, ea $12.00
Renwal, lamp, table; red or metallic red, ea $10.00
Renwal, lamp, table; red w/ivory shade or yel w/ivory shade, ea $10.00
Renwal, nursery crib, any color & name, ea $10.00
Renwal, piano, marblized brn $35.00
Renwal, playground slide, any color, ea $22.00
Renwal, playpen, bl w/pk bottom or pk w/bl bottom, ea $15.00
Renwal, radio, floor; brn $8.00
Renwal, radio, table; brn $10.00
Renwal, radio, table; red or metallic red, ea $15.00
Renwal, radio/phonograph, brn or red, ea $20.00
Renwal, rocking chair, yel w/red $8.00
Renwal, scale, ivory or red, M7 .... $10.00
Renwal, seesaw, yel w/bl & red or bl w/yel & red, ea $25.00
Renwal, server, nonopening door, brn $6.00
Renwal, server, opening door, brn $8.00
Renwal, server, opening door, brn or reddish brn, stenciled $12.00
Renwal, server, opening drawer, red $15.00
Renwal, sewing machine, any color combo, ea $30.00
Renwal, sewing maching, tabletop; red w/bl base $85.00
Renwal, sink, bathroom; dk turq w/blk $8.00
Renwal, sink, bathroom; ivory w/blk, pk w/bl or lt bl, ea $5.00
Renwal, sink, kitchen; ivory w/blk $12.00
Renwal, sink, kitchen; opening door, ivory w/red $18.00
Renwal, smoking stand, ivory w/red or red w/ivory, ea $12.00
Renwal, sofa, bright pk w/metallic red base $18.00
Renwal, stool, ivory w/red seat or red w/ivory seat, ea $10.00
Renwal, stove, ivory w/blk $12.00
Renwal, stove, opening door, ivory w/red $18.00
Renwal, stove, wht w/blk $15.00
Renwal, table, cocktail; brn $6.00
Renwal, table, cocktail; reddish brn $8.00
Renwal, table, dining; orange $15.00
Renwal, table, end/night stand; brn, lt brn, reddish brn or dk maroon, ea $2.00
Renwal, table, end/night stand; caramel swirl or lt bl, ea $3.00
Renwal, table, end/night stand; pk or matte pk, ea $4.00
Renwal, table, folding; gold $20.00
Renwal, table, kitchen; brn or yel $8.00
Renwal, table, kitchen; ivory or very deep ivory, ea $5.00
Renwal, table & chairs set, folding; red & gold $120.00
Renwal, telephone, yel w/red $22.00
Renwal, toilet, ivory w/blk or pk w/bl hdl, ea $10.00
Renwal, toydee, bl, w/duck stencil $12.00
Renwal, toydee, bl or matte bl, pk or matte pk, ea $4.00
Renwal, toydee, pk, w/3 Bears decal $12.00

Renwal, tub, bathroom; ivory w/blk or pk w/bl, ea $7.00
Renwal, tub, bathroom; med bl & turq w/blk $12.00
Renwal, vacuum cleaner, red w/yel, no decal.....................$12.00
Renwal, vacuum cleaner, yel w/red, w/decal $25.00
Renwal, vanity, simplified style w/stenciled mirror, brn.....$12.00
Renwal, washing machine, bl w/pk or pk w/bl, bear decals, ea..$30.00
Renwall, Jolly Twins Bed Room Set, w/twin beds, 2 dressers w/mirrors, chest of drawers, bench & lamp, EXIB, A.......... $165.00
Sounds Like Home, bed w/night clothes...........................$12.00
Sounds Like Home, breakfront...$6.00
Sounds Like Home, chair $2.00
Sounds Like Home, dresser w/mirror....................................$6.00
Sounds Like Home, dresser w/music box..........................$12.00
Sounds Like Home, hair dryer, bl $5.00
Sounds Like Home, kitchen table $5.00
Sounds Like Home, night table w/electric alarm clock $8.00
Sounds Like Home, shower curtain rod $2.00
Sounds Like Home, sink, electronic.................................$12.00
Sounds Like Home, stove, electronic $12.00
Sounds Like Home, tissue box...$5.00
Strombecker, ¾" scale, bathtub, bl or ivory, ea $10.00
Strombecker, ¾" scale, bed, pk, 1940s.................................$8.00
Strombecker, ¾" scale, chair, bedroom/dining; unfinished, 1930s.. $6.00
Strombecker, ¾" scale, chair, living room; aqua, dk bl or red, 1940s-50s, ea...$10.00
Strombecker, ¾" scale, clock, grandfather; bl w/blk trim or dk peach w/blk trim, ea $15.00
Strombecker, ¾" scale, lamp, floor; unfinished..................$10.00
Strombecker, ¾" scale, night stand, lt gr or pk, ea $6.00
Strombecker, ¾" scale, scale, dk bl or gr, M7 ....$15.00
Strombecker, ¾" scale, sink, aqua or ivory $8.00
Strombecker, ¾" scale, sofa, gr flocking, 1940s $18.00
Strombecker, ¾" scale, stove, ivory, 1940s $8.00
Strombecker, ¾" scale, stove, lt gr, 1940s..........................$15.00
Strombecker, ¾" scale, stove, wht or wht w/blk, 1940s-50s, ea .$18.00
Strombecker, ¾" scale, stove, wht w/ivory trim, 1961 ....$15.00
Strombecker, ¾" scale, table & chairs set, dining; wood finish..$15.00
Strombecker, ¾" scale, television, paper screen, 1961 ....$20.00
Strombecker, 1" scale, living room set, 8-pc w/sofa, chair, foot stool, end & library tables, radio, clock & bench $135.00
Strombecker, 1" scale, sink, bathroom; gr w/gold swirl......$20.00
Strombecker, 1" scale, sofa, gr flocking............................$25.00
Strombecker, 1" scale, stove, ivory w/blk trim $20.00
Strombecker, 1" scale, table, dining; walnut $20.00
Tomy-Smaller Homes, armoire, no hangers $10.00
Tomy-Smaller Homes, armoire, w/hangers.......................$15.00
Tomy-Smaller Homes, bathtub..$15.00
Tomy-Smaller Homes, bed, canopy $15.00
Tomy-Smaller Homes, cabinet, bathroom; w/dbl sink bowls .. $20.00
Tomy-Smaller Homes, cabinet w/television, high $55.00
Tomy-Smaller Homes, cat $10.00
Tomy-Smaller Homes, chair, kitchen.................................$3.00
Tomy-Smaller Homes, checkerboard..................................$5.00
Tomy-Smaller Homes, diary $10.00
Tomy-Smaller Homes, dolls, father, sister or brother; ea $8.00
Tomy-Smaller Homes, lamp, table $15.00
Tomy-Smaller Homes, mirror, standing...........................$15.00
Tomy-Smaller Homes, night stand.......................................$8.00
Tomy-Smaller Homes, oven unit w/microwave & cherry pie ...$55.00
Tomy-Smaller Homes, place mat, yel & orange...................$5.00
Tomy-Smaller Homes, plant, tall..$8.00
Tomy-Smaller Homes, planter, bathroom; no towels.........$10.00
Tomy-Smaller Homes, refrigerator $15.00
Tomy-Smaller Homes, rocker $10.00
Tomy-Smaller Homes, rug, throw..$8.00
Tomy-Smaller Homes, scale...$15.00
Tomy-Smaller Homes, sink/dishwasher, no racks................$8.00
Tomy-Smaller Homes, sink/dishwasher w/2 racks.............$15.00
Tomy-Smaller Homes, sofa, 2-pc $12.00
Tomy-Smaller Homes, sofa, 3-pc $15.00
Tomy-Smaller Homes, speakers $3.00
Tomy-Smaller Homes, stereo cabinet...............................$15.00
Tomy-Smaller Homes, stove w/hood unit $15.00
Tomy-Smaller Homes, table, end $8.00
Tomy-Smaller Homes, table, kitchen $8.00
Tomy-Smaller Homes, television.......................................$50.00
Tomy-Smaller Homes, toilet...$10.00
Tomy-Smaller Homes, towel $5.00
Tomy-Smaller Homes, vanity $15.00
Tomy-Smaller Homes, vanity stool $6.00
Tootsietoy, bed w/headboard, footboard & slats, bl or pk, ea.. $20.00
Tootsietoy, buffet, opening drawer, cocoa brn $22.00
Tootsietoy, cabinet, medicine, ivory.................................$25.00
Tootsietoy, chair, bedroom; bl or pk, ea...............................$7.00
Tootsietoy, chair, club, bl $8.00
Tootsietoy, chair, kitchen; ivory $7.00
Tootsietoy, chair, simple back, no arms $7.00
Tootsietoy, chair, tufted look, dk red $20.00
Tootsietoy, chair, XX back, w/ or w/o arms, ea $7.00
Tootsietoy, cupboard, nonopening doors, ivory.................$20.00
Tootsietoy, icebox or stove, nonopening doors, ivory, ea $20.00
Tootsietoy, lamp, table; bl...$45.00
Tootsietoy, living room set, 5-pc w/2 chairs, floor lamp, foot stool & side table...$65.00
Tootsietoy, night stand, pk...$10.00
Tootsietoy, piano bench, yel w/tan seat $15.00
Tootsietoy, rocker, bedroom; bl..$12.00
Tootsietoy, rocker, wicker style w/cushion, gold or ivory ...$20.00
Tootsietoy, server, nonopening door, dk brn $22.00
Tootsietoy, simple back, w/arms, dk brn $8.00
Tootsietoy, table, long, gr crackle $22.00
Tootsietoy, table, rectangular, dk brn $22.00
Tootsietoy, tea cart, dk brn $22.00
Tootsietoy, vanity, blk...$18.00
Tootsietoy (Midget), bed, pk $18.00
Tootsietoy (Midget), dresser, pk $10.00
Tootsietoy (Midget), piano, ivory......................................$25.00
Tootsietoy (Midget), sofa, 2-pc, right side, red....................$6.00
Tootsietoy (Midget), vanity, pk $10.00
Tynietoy, bedroom set, 6-pc w/bed, night stand, dresser, highchair, straight-back chair & rug, yel, VG, A............ $275.00
Tynietoy, bedroom set, 6-pc w/4-poster bed, dresser, 2 straight-back chairs, cradle, rug, natural wood/cloth, VG, A........... $465.00
Tynietoy, dining-room set, 9-pc w/rnd table 4 Chippendale chairs, sideboard, grandfather clock, mirror, wood, VG, A .. $300.00

Tynietoy, parlor set, 9-pc w/Astro piano & stool, wingback chair, 2 shieldback chairs, banjo clock & Empire mirror, VG ...$660.00

Tynietoy, six-piece kitchen set, VG, A, $220.00. (Photo courtesy Noel Barrett Antiques & Auctions, Ltd.)

Dollhouses

Dollhouses were first made commercially in America in the late 1700s. A century later, Bliss and Schoenhut were making wonderful dollhouses that, even yet, occasionally turn up on the market, and many were being imported from Germany. During the 1940s and 1950s, American toy makers made a variety of cottages, which are also collectible.

Key:
PLW — paper lithograph on wood
PW — painted wood

American, Mt Vernon, 2-story, 10 rooms, PW, wht w/gr roof, 41x58", Chicago, ca 1890-1910, EX, A $12,000.00
American, Queen Ann Victorian, 2-story, 4 rooms plus attic, PW, lt/dk gray w/wht trim, accessories, 43x33x33" L, G+, A.. $1,980.00
Bliss, Adirondack Log Cabin, 4 rooms, PLW w/stained wood roof & base, 17½" H, VG, A.. $520.00
Bliss, fire station No 2, 2-story, PLW, w/steeple, portico over dbl doors, 13" H, G+, A $1,430.00
Bliss, Victorian, 2-story, 2 lg rooms, PLW, 1 lg & 2 sm attic dormers, porch w/steps, 27" H, VG, A $600.00
Bliss, 2 1/2-story, 4 rooms, PLW, porch w/steps, upper balcony, lattice foundation, PLW, 24x20x12", VG, A $1,650.00
Bliss, 2-story, PLW, full-length porch w/lattice work, sm top balcony, 2 top windows w/overhangs, 16" H, EX, A..... $500.00
Bliss, 2-story, PLW, stone/wood/decorative facade, front portico, arched windows, 2 chimneys, on platform, 12" H, EX, A............ $600.00
Bliss, 2-story, 2 rooms, PLW, 2 chimneys, dormers, wrap-around porch, steps, #575, 28x19x12", G, A.................... $3,300.00
Bliss, 2-story, 2-room, PLW, columned roof over front door, upper arched windows, 12½", G+, A................................ $600.00
Bliss, 2-story, 2-room, PLW, railed full-length front porch w/steps, upper balcony, 19" H, VG, A $715.00
Brumberger, colonial, 2-story, 5 rooms, wood compo, 20x24", 1970, EX $60.00
Converse, barn, PLW, weather vane/copula, arched doorway & windows, flat-sided animals, 20" L, EX, A............... $500.00
Converse, bungalow, PW, arched window above stone porch w/ribbed columns, 14" L, VG, A............................ $150.00
Converse, bungalow, PW, stone porch w/end columns, 3 steps, 10" L, EX, A... $120.00
Converse, cottage, stenciled wood, porch w/spool-turned pillars & planters, 13" W, EX+, A..................................... $400.00
Converse, 2-story, stained wood, simulated brick work, child & dog in upper window, 18" H, EX, A $250.00

Converse, two-story, two rooms, paper lithograph on wood, printed interior, 14" high, EX, A, $330.00. (Photo courtesy Noel Barrett Antiques & Auctions, Ltd.)

Deluxe Game Corp, Sunny Dell Acres, pressed board, 4 rooms, door marked 'Sparkle Plenty Lives Here,' 16x15x23", VG, A $475.00
Dunham, tall box w/4 shelf-like rooms, wood, stenciled brick facade, papered walls, 28x12x7", G, A.......................$85.00
England, Regency, 2-story, scored wood brickwork, 2 copper bays, 6 furnished rooms, 24" H, G+, A $4,675.00
England, Silber & Fleming type, 3-story, 9 rooms, PW, fully furnished, 54x48x20", VG, A $9,350.00
Fisher-Price, 3 story, 5 rooms, #280, b/o, 1981-84, M $30.00
Fisher-Price, 3-story, 5 rooms, #250, spiral staircase, 1978-80, M $40.00
Gottschalk, Deauville style, 2-story, PLW, electric, furnished, 34x17x15", 1905, Fair, A.....................................$1,325.00

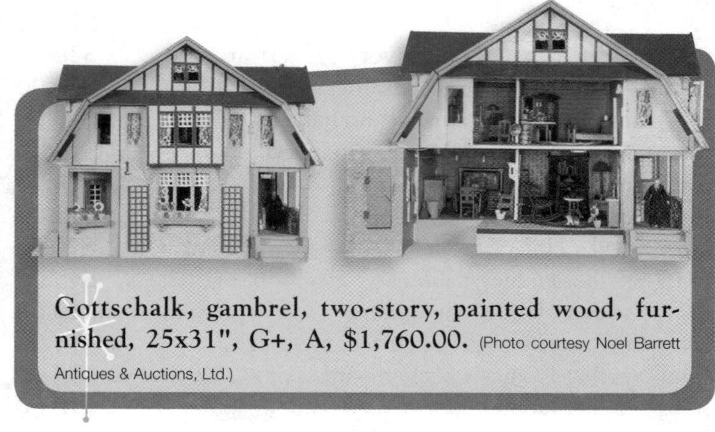

Gottschalk, gambrel, two-story, painted wood, furnished, 25x31", G+, A, $1,760.00. (Photo courtesy Noel Barrett Antiques & Auctions, Ltd.)

Gottschalk, mansion, 2-story, 4 rooms, PLW, brick facade w/bl roof, tower, 32x38x21", VG+, A $23,100.00

Jayline, 2 story, 5 rooms, litho tin, 14½x18½", 1949, VG..$50.00

Marx, Colonial, 2-story, litho tin, breezeway, clapboard over brick, 1960s, NM $75.00

Marx, split-level, litho tin, patio above garage, red w/gray roof, VG $65.00

Marx, 2 story w/2 side single rooms, litho tin, 15x43" L, EX..$40.00

Marx, 2-story w/flat-roofed side room, litho tin, bay window, 13x8x25" L, EX..$50.00

McLoughlin Bros, New Folding Dollhouse, 2-story, 2 rooms, cb, 16x17x12", G+IB, A $1,100.00

Meritoy, Cape Cod, litho tin w/plastic window inserts, 21x14", 1949, M.. $150.00

Reed, Gutter House, two-story, paper lithograph on wood, 18x9x10", VG, A, $1,065.00. (Photo courtesy James D. Julia, Inc.)

Rich, bungalow, cb, 32x21", 1930s, VG......................... $200.00

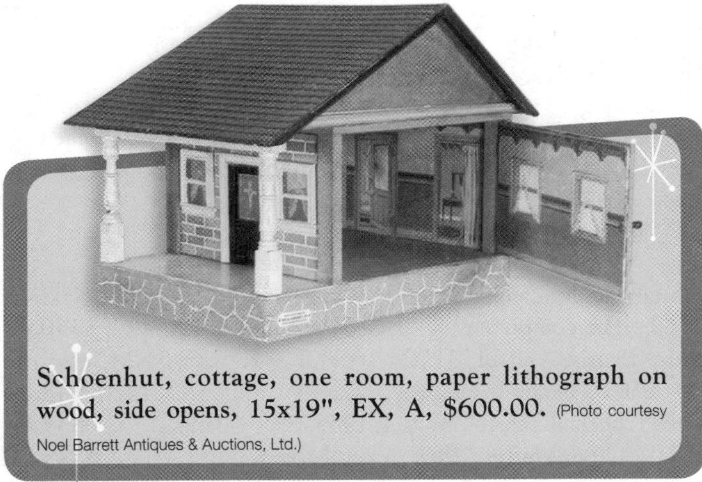

Schoenhut, cottage, one room, paper lithograph on wood, side opens, 15x19", EX, A, $600.00. (Photo courtesy Noel Barrett Antiques & Auctions, Ltd.)

Schoenhut, cottage, 1-story, wood/cb, long porch, door to left of window w/shutters & flower box, red roof, 17" L, EX, A $200.00

Schoenhut, 2-story, PW, full porch, 'brick' facade, curtained windows, metal furniture, 15", EX, A.....................$550.00

Stirn & Lyon, Combination Dollhouse construction set, 2-story, PW, box forms foundation, 18" W, EXIB, A $385.00

T. Cohn, two-story, six rooms, lithographed tin, 24x16x9", 1951, EX, $200.00.

Tootsietoy, Spanish-style mansion, 7 rooms, cb, simulated tile roof, 20x30x18", 1930s, EXIB, A $3,025.00

Tynietoy, New England townhouse ('A Model'), 2-story, 1-story side room, PW, 30x50x18", G+, A........................$3,025.00

Unknown, school house, 1 room, stucco w/red roof, PW, w/accessories, 27x23x20", VG, A.....................................$1,200.00

Wolverine, colonial mansion, no garage, ½" scale, EX......$50.00

Wolverine, country cottage, #800, ½" scale, 1986, EX $50.00

Shops and Single Rooms

Bathroom, Bing (?), 1880s, metal, 3-sided w/pk & wht decor, 12x7x6", EX, A... $670.00

Bathroom, Ernst Plank, metal, bl & wht pnt, toilet, tub & sink, pump for recycling water, 14" W, EX, A $1,760.00

Bathroom, Goso/Germany, metal, pk & wht pnt, flushable toilet, tub & sink, etc, 3 water reservoirs, 14" W, VG, A..$1,100.00

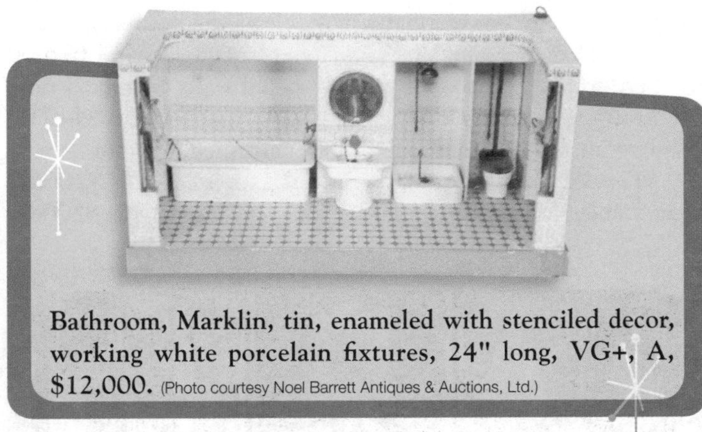

Bathroom, Marklin, tin, enameled with stenciled decor, working white porcelain fixtures, 24" long, VG+, A, $12,000. (Photo courtesy Noel Barrett Antiques & Auctions, Ltd.)

Bathroom, Wolverine #195 (Sunny Suzy), litho tin w/plastic furnishings & doll, 17" L, EX+IB, A....................... $200.00

Butcher Shop, Germany, PLW, 'tiled' walls, meat rack, w/counter & accessories, 13" W, VG+, A $360.00

Butcher Shop, Germany, PLW, back wall shelving, butcher table & accessories, 18½" L, G+, A................................. $715.00

Butcher Shop, Gottschalk, PW/PLW, 2-story, red brick w/bl roof, butcher & accessories, 13" L, EX, A.....................$2,750.00

Butcher Shop (M Osborn), wood shadow box frame w/paper interior, w/figure & accessories, 17x17x11", VG, A $6,050.00

Butcher Shop (Pet's), American, PLW, complete w/bisque figure, 12" H, VG, A....$500.00
Corner Grocer, Wolverine, 1930s, litho tin, complete w/counter & grocery items, 18x8x16", EX, A....$330.00
Dry Goods Store, Germany, late 19th C, PW, 3 wall cabinets, counter, storekeeper & goods, 10" H, G+, A....$385.00
Epicerie Parisienne, early 20th C, PLW, w/orig contents, 12", VG, A....$1,320.00
Gazebo, PLW, 8" H, red 'shingled' roof w/finial, wht table & 2 benches, VG+, A....$465.00
General Store, PW, spiral staircase, 16 drawers w/porcelain labels, figure & goods, 15x17", VG, A....$880.00
Kitchen, American, 1880s, metal, w/stove, table & accessories, 13" L, Fair+, A....$190.00
Kitchen, Germany, wood, lithoed walls, 1 side window, w/furnishings & figure, 16" L, VG, A....$600.00
Kitchen, Germany, wood, papered walls, many accessories, 17x22x21", VG+, A....$2,750.00

Kitchen, Hoge, cardboard trifold with paper floor, tin accessories, EX+IB, A, $1,540.00. (Photo courtesy Randy Inman Auctions)

Kitchen, Nuremburg Germany, PW, bisque figure, many accessories, VG, A....$4,675.00
Kitchen, wood, 3-sided, yel pnt w/papered walls & floor, 1 doll, furniture & accessories, 18" L, EX, A....$440.00
Livingroom, R Berbard, modern, fully furnished, 3 figures, 28" L, VG+, A....$200.00
Meat Market, Marx, litho tin, 5" W, complete, EX+IB, A...$200.00

Parlor, cardboard trifold, no floor, orante decor with wood furnishings, cloth drapes, 12x9x19", EX, A, $2,475.00. (Photo courtesy Noel Barrett Antiques & Auctions, Ltd.)

Pascall Parlour Stores, litho cb, front folds down, 6 glass jars & goods, 7½" H, VG+, A....$135.00
Roosevelt Stock Farm Barn, PW, 3 pnt compo & wood horses, 18" W, VG, A....$440.00
Toy Shop, Germany, 1910s, orante oak facade w/accordion wood blinds, accessories, 15x12x25" L, G+, A....$1,980.00

Dolls and Accessories

Obviously the field of dolls cannot be covered in a price guide such as this, but with the exception of Schoenhut and Shirley Temple, we wanted to touch upon some of the later dolls from the 1950s and 1960s, since a lot of collector interest is centered on those decades. For in-depth information on dolls of all types, we recommend those lovely doll books, all of which are available from Collector Books: *Doll Values* by Linda Edward; *Horsman Dolls, The Vinyl Era*, by Don Jensen; *Collector's Guide to Ideal Dolls* and *American Character Dolls* by Judith Izen; *Collector's Encyclopedia of Vogue Dolls* by Judith Izen and Carol Stover; *Collector's Encyclopedia of American Composition Dolls, 1900 – 1950*, by Ursula R. Mertz; and *Dolls of the 1960s and 1970s* by Cindy Sabulis. Other books are referenced in specific subcategories.

See also Action Figures; Barbie and Friends; Character, TV, and Movie Collectibles; Disney; GI Joe; and other specific categories.

Baby Dolls

Remnants of dolls have been found in the artifacts of most primitive digs. Some are just sticks or stuffed leather or animal skins.

Dolls teach our young nurturing and caring. Mothering instincts stay with us — and aren't we lucky as doll collectors that we can keep 'mothering' even after the young have 'left the nest.'

Baby dolls come in all sizes and mediums: vinyl, plastic, rubber, porcelain, cloth, etc. Almost everyone remembers some doll they had as a child. The return to childhood is such a great trip. Keep looking and you will find yours.

Advisor: Marcia Fanta

Annabelle, Madame Alexander, in sweater & skirt w/dbl rickrack border, complete w/comb & curlers in box, EX....$350.00
Baby Beans, Mattel, 1970s, several variations, NM, ea from $30.00 to....$45.00
Baby Cheerful Tearful, Mattel, 1966, 6½", MIB....$55.00
Baby Cheryl, Mattel, 1965, talker, MIB....$225.00
Baby Crawl-Along, Remco, 1967, 20", all orig, EX, from $25 to....$35.00
Baby Cuddles, Ideal, 1930-40, 22", redressed, EX....$150.00
Baby Drowsy, Mattel, 1969, talker, 15", MIB, from $175 to..$225.00
Baby First Step, Mattel, 1964, b/o, 18", M, from $40 to....$55.00
Baby First Step, Mattel, 1967, b/o, 18", longer hair than 1st issue, M, from $35 to....$45.00
Baby First Step, Mattel, 1967, talker, MIB....$175.00

Baby Flip-Flop, Mattel/JC Penney, 1970, talker, MIB........$85.00
Baby Fun, Mattel, 1968, 7", complete, EX........................$35.00
Baby Giggles, Ideal, 1967, 15", MIB.............................. $100.00
Baby Go Bye-Bye & Her Bumpety Buggy, Mattel, 1968, 10½", MIB.. $225.00
Baby Love Light, Mattel, 1971, NMIB..............................$55.00
Baby Pat-A-Burp, Mattel, 1963, 17", EX..........................$70.00
Baby Secret, Mattel, 1966, talker, 18", EX........................$55.00
Baby See 'N Say, Mattel, 1964, talker, MIB, from $175 to. $225.00
Baby Sing-A-Long, Mattel 1969, talker, 16½", MIB....... $150.00

Baby Small Talk, Mattel, 1968, talker, 10", MIB, $100.00. (Photo courtesy Cindy Sabulis)

Baby Snoozie, Ideal, 1965, 14", w/up knob, EX, from $50 to .. $75.00
Baby Teenietalk, Mattel, 1966, talker, 17", EX.................$75.00
Baby Tender Love (Brother), Mattel, NRFB................. $100.00
Baby Whisper, Mattel, 1968, talker, 17½", MIB $150.00
Belly Button Baby, Ideal, 1971, 9½", several variations, MIB, ea $85.00
Chatty Patty, Mattel, 1980s, MIB....................................$50.00
Cheerful-Tearful, Mattel, 1965, 13", orig outfit, NM.........$55.00
Cheerleader, Mattel, 1970, talker, several variations, MIB, ea..$75.00
Cynthia, Mattel, talker, M..$65.00
Dancerella, Mattel, 1972, 18", b/o, complete, M, from $35 to..$55.00
Dancerina, Mattel, 1968, 24", b/o, MIB, from $225 to... $275.00
Drink 'N Babe, Arranbee, unused, M (in case).............. $775.00
Drinkee Walker, Horsman, 1988, NM $50.00
Drowsy Sleeper Keeper, Mattel, 1966, talker, MIB......... $125.00
Gabbigale, Kenner, 1972, 18", MIB.................................$85.00
Ginny, Vogue Dolls #101, 1950s, 7½", hard plastic, walker, sleep eyes, several outfits, EXIB.. $450.00
Gramma & Grandpa, Mattel, 1968, talkers, MIB, ea $95.00
Hi Dottie, Mattel, 1972, talker, w/phone, blk, NM $75.00
Johnny Play Pal, Ideal, 1959, 24", NM.......................... $425.00
Kissy, Ideal, 1960s, 22", MIB, from $100 to.................... $125.00
Kissy (Tiny), Ideal, 1960s, 16", EX, from $25 to $40.00
Lil' Miss Fashion, Deluxe Reading, 1960, 20", MIB..........$75.00
Little Lost Baby, Ideal, 1968, 22", MIB $100.00
Little Miss Echo, American Character, b/o, 30", MIB, from $225 to $275.00
Little Miss Echo, American Character, b/o, 30", EX, from $125 to $150.00
Little Sister Look 'N Say, Mattel/Sears, talker, 18", M ... $150.00
Magic Baby Tender Love, Mattel, 1978, 14", MIB............$75.00

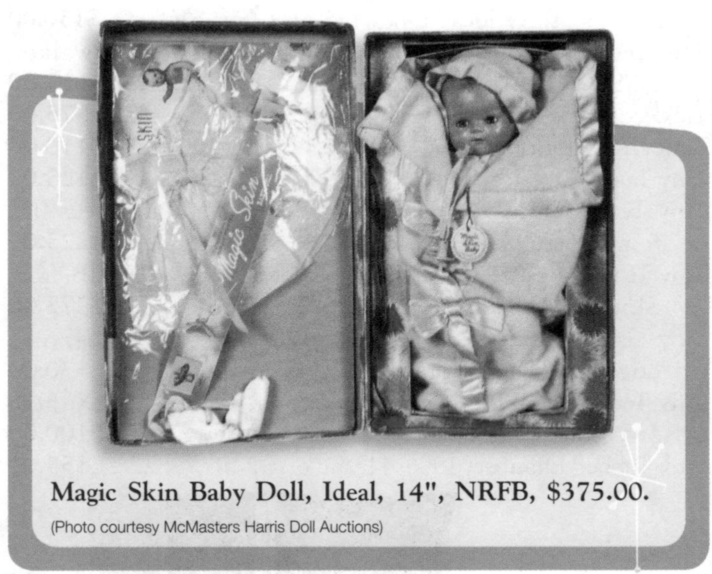

Magic Skin Baby Doll, Ideal, 14", NRFB, $375.00.
(Photo courtesy McMasters Harris Doll Auctions)

Marjorie, Belle Doll & Toy Co, vinyl, MIB $125.00
Matty the Talking Boy, Mattel, 1961, MIB $300.00
Miss Ideal the Photographer's Model, complete w/Playwave Kit, NMIB, from $250 to $300.00
Monique, Effanbee, 1978, 16", MIB, from $50 to $65.00
Nancy Nonsense, Kenner 1968, talker, 17", MIB $115.00
Nanette, Arranbee, 1949-59, 25", MIB.......................... $550.00
Patti Playful, Ideal, 1960s, nurse, 36", M........................ $350.00
Patti Playful, Ideal, 1970, 16", EX, from $45 to $65.00
Patti Prays, Ideal, 1957, NM..$55.00
Patty Play Pal, Ideal, 1981, reissue, MIB, from $200 to .. $250.00
Penny Play Pal, Ideal, 1959, 32", redressed, from $300 to .. $350.00
Pos'n Glamour Misty, Ideal, 1965, 11½", M.......................$45.00
Pretty Curls, Ideal, 1981-82, EX.....................................$25.00
Princess Mary, Ideal, 1950s, 19", M $175.00
Randi Reader, Mattel, 1968, talker, 20", MIB................ $175.00
Revlon Doll, Ideal, EXIB $300.00
Rub-A-Dub Dolly in Tugboat Shower, Ideal, 1974-78, 17", MIB...$100.00
Saucy Walker, Ideal, 17", EXIB $275.00
Sister Belle, Mattel, 1961, talker, MIB.......................... $300.00
Sister Small Talk, Mattel, 1968, talker, EX.......................$55.00
Small Talk Cinderella, Mattel, MIB, from $100 to......... $125.00
Somersalty, Mattel, 1970, talker, MIB........................... $200.00
Suzy Cute, Deluxe Reading, 1964, w/plastic crib, 7", MIB...$175.00
Sweet Cookie, Hasbro, 1972, w/accessories, 18", M, from $45 to $75.00
Talking Baby Alive, Kenner, 1992, MIB $100.00
Talkytot, Ideal, 1950s, stuffed body, vinyl face, hand-crank, 25", MIB $195.00
Taters, Mattel, M $125.00
Teachy Keen, Mattel/Sears, 1966, talker, 16", MIB $175.00
Teachy Keen, Mattel/Sears, 1966, talker, 16", NM............$95.00
Teachy Talk, Mattel, 1970, talker, MIB.......................... $145.00

Tearful Tender Love, Mattel, 1971, 16", VG+ $50.00
Tearie Dearie Twins, Ideal, 1963, 9", EX $40.00
Thumbelina, Ideal, 1960s, 18", NMIB, from $150 to $200.00
Thumbelina (Newborn), Ideal, 1960s, 9½", NM $95.00
Thumbelina (Tiny), Ideal, 1960s, 14", MIB $185.00
Thumbelina (Tiny), Ideal, 1960s, 21", NM, from $100 to ...$150.00
Thumbelina (Toddler), Ideal, 1960s, complete w/walker, NMIB $125.00
Tickles, Deluxe Reading, 1963, talker, MIB $75.00
Timey Tell, Mattel, talker, MIB $110.00
Tiny Tears, American Character, 1950s, 12", VG........... $125.00
Tiny Tears, American Character, 1960s, 17", complete, MIB, from $125 to $225.00
Tiny Tears (Lifesize), American Character, 1963, 21", MIB, from $150 to $275.00
Tiny Tears (Teenie Weenie), American Character, 1964, 8½", orig outfit, EX, from $25 to..$30.00
Tiny Tears (Teeny), American Character, 1960s, 12", EX, from $65 to $100.00
Tiny Tubber, Effanbee, 1976, 11", all orig, MIB $55.00

Tony Doll, Ideal, 'The Doll With Magic Nylon Hair,' unused, NMIB, A, $300.00. (Photo courtesy Morphy Auctions)

Upsy Dazy, Ideal, 1973, 15", EX $40.00
Winnie Walker, Advance, 1957, talker, 24", MIB $200.00

Betsy McCall

The tiny 8" Betsy McCall doll was manufactured by the American Character Doll Co. from 1957 through 1963. She was made from high-quality hard plastic with a bisque-like finish and hand-painted features. Betsy came in four hair colors — tosca, red, blond, and brunette. She had blue sleep eyes, molded lashes, a winsome smile, and a fully jointed body with bendable knees. On her back there is an identification circle which reads McCall Corp. The basic doll wore a sheer chemise, white taffeta panties, nylon socks, and Maryjane-style shoes and could be purchased for $2.25.

There were two different materials used for tiny Betsy's hair. The first was a soft mohair sewn into fine mesh. Later the rubber skullcap was rooted with saran which was more suitable for washing and combing.

Betsy McCall had an extensive wardrobe with nearly 100 outfits, each of which could be purchased separately. They were made from wonderful fabrics such as velvet, taffeta, felt, and even real mink. Each ensemble came with the appropriate footwear and was priced under $3.00. Since none of Betsy's clothing was tagged, it is often difficult to identify other than by its square snap closures (although these were used by other companies as well).

Betsy McCall is a highly collectible doll today but is still fairly easy to find at doll shows. Prices remain reasonable for this beautiful clothes horse and her many accessories.

Case, Betsy McCall's Pretty Pac, vinyl, NM+, $95.00. (Photo courtesy gasolinealleyantiques.com)

Doll, American Character, 8", hard plastic, rooted hair, 1957, EX... $350.00
Doll, American Character, 14", vinyl, jtd shoulders & hips, rooted hair, w/trunk & outfits, G, A $400.00
Doll, American Character, 14", vinyl w/swivel waist or 1-pc torso, rooted hair, 1958, EX, ea $500.00
Doll, American Character, 19" or 20", vinyl, rooted hair, 1-pc torso, 1959, EX, ea... $500.00
Doll, American Character, 22", vinyl w/jtd limbs & waist, 5 different colors of rooted hair, 1961, EX, ea...........$225.00
Doll, American Character, 29", vinyl w/jtd limbs & waist, 5 different colors of rooted hair, 1961, EX, ea $300.00
Doll, American Character, 36", Linda McCall (Betsy's cousin), vinyl w/Betsy face, rooted hair, 1959, EX................ $350.00
Doll, American Character, 36", vinyl w/Patti Play Pal style body, rooted hair, 1959, EX... $325.00
Doll, American Character, 39", Sandy McCall (Betsy's brother), vinyl w/molded hair, red blazer & navy shorts, 1959, EX $350.00
Doll, Amsco, 8", plastic, complete w/Pretty Pac accessories & booklet, G $325.00
Doll, Horsman, 12½", rigid body w/vinyl head, w/extra hair & accessories, 1974, EX $50.00
Doll, Horsman, 29", rigid plastic teen body w/vinyl head, rooted hair w/side part, orig clothing marked BMc, 1974, MIB.......$275.00
Doll, Ideal, 14", hard plastic body, rooted hair, EX $200.00

Doll, Uneeda, 11½", rigid vinyl body, rooted hair, wore 'hip' outfits, 1964, EX, minimum value $100.00

Outfit, rain coat, hat, umbrella, and vinyl boots, NM+, $75.00. (Photo courtesy gasolinealleyantiques.com)

Bride Dolls

Bride, Am Character, Sweet Sue, hard plastic, sleep eyes, wig, walker, orig complete outfit, 17", unused, NM (G box), A $125.00

Bride, Madame Alexander, Cissette, 1960s, hard plastic, blond wig, jointed, original lace-trimmed gown and veil with floral crown, 10", EX, A, $300.00. (Photo courtesy McMasters Harris Auction Co.)

Bride, M Alexander, Cissette, 1960s, hard plastic, jtd, dk brn wig, orig tulle-over-satin gown, 10½", EX, A........... $375.00
Bride, M Alexander, Godey, 1950s, hard plastic, sleep eyes, blond floss wig, orig satin gown & lacy veil, 14", EX, A . $3,700.00
Bride, M Alexander, Leslie, blk version, 1966-71, orig lacy gown, EXIB (incorrect box), A.. $150.00
Bride, M Alexander, Margaret, hard plastic, sleep eyes, blond wig, orig complete satin outfit, 14", unused, NM, A.......... $550.00
Bride, M Alexander, Mary Rose, 1950s, plastic, sleep eyes, floss wig, orig outfit, 17", EX, A $525.00
Bride, M Alexander, Yolanda, hard plastic w/vinyl head, red wig, orig tiered lacy gown, 1965, EXIB, A....................... $375.00
Bridesmaid, M Alexander, 1940s, compo, strung, sleep eyes, wig, orig pk gown w/foral hat & muff, 14", EX, A........... $250.00
Groom, M Alexander, 1948-49, Godey, hard plastic, wig w/mutton chops, sleep eyes, orig tux outfit, 14", rare, EX, A $3,600.00

Celebrity Dolls

Celebrity dolls have been widely collected for many years. Except for the rarer examples, most of these dolls are still fairly easy to find, and the majority are priced under $100.00.

Condition is a very important worth-assessing factor, and if the doll is still in the original box, so much the better! Should the box be unopened (NRFB), the value is further enhanced. Using mint as a standard, add 50% for the same doll mint in the box and 75% if it has never been taken out. On the other hand, dolls in only good or poorer condition drop at a rapid pace.

The dolls listed here are not character-related. For celebrity/character dolls see Action Figures; Character, TV, and Movie Collectibles; Rock 'N Roll.

Abbot & Costello, vinyl in cloth baseball uniforms, w/cassette of the comedy 'Who's on First?,' MIB, set $250.00
Alan Jackson (Country Music Stars), Exclusive Premiere, 1998, 9", MIB...$30.00
Andrew Jackson, Effanbee, 1990, military uniform, 16", MIB. $125.00
Andy Gibb, Ideal, 1979, 7½", MIB...................................$85.00
Ashley & Mary Kate Olsen, Mattel, 1st issue, Dance & Horseback Riding sets, 9½", MIB, ea..................................$30.00
Audrey Hepburn (Breakfast at Tiffany's), Mattel, 1998, 11½", MIB $50.00
Betty Grable, International Doll Co, 1940s, blond Dynel hair, w/tag, 19", NM, minimum value $400.00
Beverly Johnson (Real Model Collection), Matchbox, 1989, 11½", MIB...$50.00
Brooke Shields, LJN, 1982, pk & gray casual outfit, 11½", MIB $55.00
Brooke Shields, LJN, 1982, Prom Party, 11½", rare, MIB . $150.00
Brooke Shields, LJN, 1982, suntan doll, 11½", MIB..........$65.00
Captain & Tenille, Mego, 1977, 12½", MIB, ea $125.00
Charlie Chaplin (Little Tramp), Milton Bradley/Bubbles Inc, 1972, 19", MIB.. $100.00
Cher, Mego, 1976, Growing Hair, 12½", MIB $150.00
Cher, Mego, 1976, pk evening gown, 12½", MIB $125.00
Cher, Mego, 1981, swimsuit, 12", MIB..............................$50.00
Cheryl Ladd, Mattel 1978, 11½", MIB..............................$85.00
Cheryl Tiegs (Real Model Collection), Matchbox, 1989, 11½", MIB $50.00
Christy Lane, long red velvet skirt & wht blouse, 1965-70s, 14", M...$25.00
Chritsy Brinkley (Real Model Collection), Matchbox, 1989, 11½", MIB...$50.00

Danny Kaye (White Christmas), Exclusive Premiere, 1998, dressed as Santa, 9", MIB...$45.00

Deanna Durbin, Ideal, composition with synthetic hair, original outfit, unused, NMIB, A, $1,200.00. (Photo courtesy McMasters Harris Auction Co.)

Debbie Boone, Mattel, 1978, 11½", MIB...$100.00
Deidre Hall (Days of Our Lives), Mattel, 1999, 11½", MIB..$35.00
Dennis Rodman (Basketball Player), Street Players, 1990s, 12", MIB...$30.00
Diana Ross, Mego, 1977, 12½", MIB...$150.00
Diana Ross (of the Supremes), Ideal, 1969, 19", rare, MIB..$600.00
Dick Clark, Juro, 1958, 26½", MIB...$450.00
Dionne Quints, M Alexander, compo, molded hair, in diapers & bibs, 18" L pnt wood swing w/cloth canopy, VG, A... $990.00
Dionne Quints, M Alexander, compo, molded hair, sunsuits & bonnets, 7" dolls w/18" swing w/cloth canopy, EX+, A...$1,760.00
Dionne Quints, M Alexander, compo, molded hair, various colors of dresses & bonnets, 7½", G, A...$275.00
Dionne Quints, M Alexander, compo, wigged, orig wool snowsuits, homemade bench, 14", VG, A...$3,850.00
Dolly Parton, Goldberger, 1978, red & silver outfit, 11½", MIB...$100.00
Dolly Parton, Goldberger, 1990s, blk outfit w/silver boots, 12", MIB...$75.00
Donnie & Marie Osmond, Mattel, 1976, 12", MIB, ea...$85.00
Dorothy Hamill (Olympic Ice Skater), Ideal, 1977, 11½", MIB...$100.00
Dorothy Lamour, Film Star Creations, 1940s-50s, stuffed print cloth w/mohair wig, bathing suit, w/tag, 14", NM... $135.00
Ekaterina (Katia) Gordeeva (Olympic Ice Skater), Playmates, 1998, 11½", MIB...$25.00
Eleanor Roosevelt, Effanbee, 1985, brn dress, 14½", MIB.. $125.00
Elizabeth Taylor (Butterfield 8), Tri-Star, 1982, 11½", MIB.. $150.00
Elizabeth Taylor (National Velvet), Madame Alexander, 1990, 12", MIB...$100.00
Elvis Presley, Eugene, 1984, issued in 6 different outfits, 12", MIB...$75.00
Elvis Presley, Hasbro, 1993, Jailhouse Rock, Teen Idol or '68 Special, numbered edition, 12", MIB, ea...$50.00
Elvis Presley, World Doll, 1984, Burning Love, 21", MIB.. $125.00

Farrah Fawcett-Majors, see also Charlie's Angels in Character, TV & Movies category
Farrah Fawcett-Majors, Mego, 1977, wht jumpsuit, 12½", MIB...$125.00
Farrah Fawcett-Majors, Mego, 1981, swimsuit, 12", MIB..$50.00
Flip Wilson/Geraldine, Shindana, 1970, stuffed reversable talker, 15", MIB...$85.00

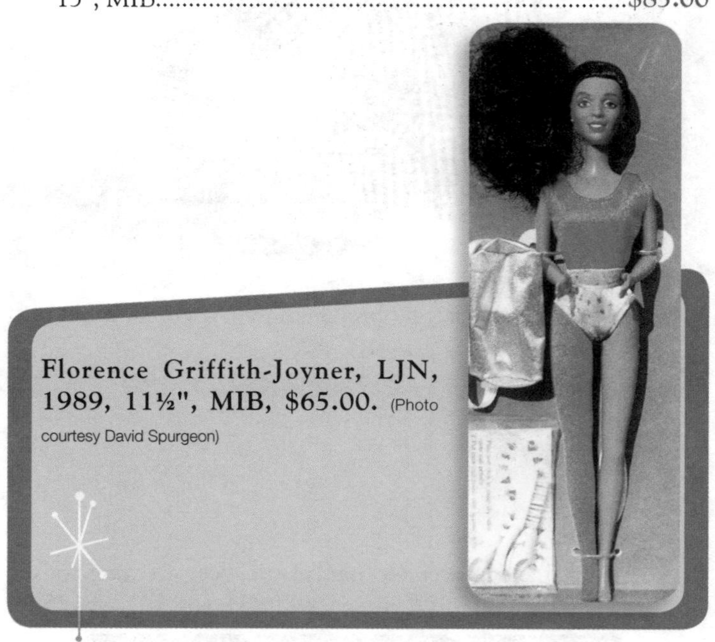

Florence Griffith-Joyner, LJN, 1989, 11½", MIB, $65.00. (Photo courtesy David Spurgeon)

George Burns, Effanbee, 1996, blk tuxedo holding cigar, 17", MIB...$150.00
George Burns, Exclusive Premiere, 1997, w/accessories, 9", MIB...$25.00
Ginger Rogers, World Doll, 1976, limited edition, MIB. $100.00
Gorbachev, Dreamworks, 1990, 11", MIB...$50.00
Grace Kelly (Swan or Mogambo), Tri-Star, 1982, 11½", MIB, ea...$100.00
Groucho Marx, Julius Henry/Effanbee, 1982, 18", MIB... $150.00
Harold Lloyd, 1920s, lithoed stuffed cloth, standing w/hands in pockets, 12", EX+...$100.00
Harry Truman, Effanbee, 1988, suit & har, red bow tie, 16", MIB...$125.00
Humphery Bogart (Casablanca), Effanbee, 1989, 16", MIB.. $150.00
Humphery Bogart & Ingrid Bergman (Casablanca), Exclusive Premiere, 1998, 9", MIB, ea...$30.00
Jacklyn Smith, Mego, 1977, 12½", MIB...$200.00
Jacklyn Smith, see also Charlie's Angels in Character, TV & Movies Collectibles category
James Cagney, Effanbee, 1987, pinstripe suit & hat, 16", MIB...$125.00
James Dean, DSI, 1994, sweater & pants, 12", MIB...$55.00
Jerry Springer, Street Players, 1998, 12", MIB...$50.00
Jimmy Olson, Mattel, 1978, 10", MIB...$125.00
John Travolta (On Stage...Super Star), Chemtoy, 1977, 12", MIB...$100.00
John Wayne (Great Legends), Effanbee, 1981, Symbol of the West (cowboy outfit), 17", MIB...$150.00
John Wayne (Great Legends), Effanbee, 1982, Guardian of the West (cavalry uniform), 18", MIB...$150.00

Kate Jackson, Mattel, 1978, 11½", MIB $85.00
Katerina Witt (Olympic Ice Skater), Playmates, 1998, 11½", MIB $25.00
KISS, Mego, 1978, any from group, 12½", MIB, ea $350.00
Kristi Yamaguchi, Playmates, 1998, 11½", MIB $25.00
Laurel & Hardy, Goldberger, 1986, bluejean overalls, 12", MIB $55.00
Laurel & Hardy, Hamilton Gifts, 1991, cloth suits, 16", MIB, ea $65.00
Laurel & Hardy, 1981, cloth bodies w/porcelain heads, cloth suits, 18" & 21", MIB, ea $75.00
Leann Rimes (Country Music Stars), Exclusive Premiere, 1998, 9", MIB....$30.00
Leslie Uggams, Madame Alexander, 1966, lt pk dress, 17", MIB....$350.00
Liberace, Effanbee, 1986, glittery blk & silver outfit w/cape, 16½", MIB.... $250.00
Louis 'Satchmo' Armstrong, Effanbee, 1984, bl & blk tuxedo, 15½", MIB.... $250.00

Lucille Ball, Effanbee, 1985, MIB, $175.00. (Photo courtesy David Spurgeon)

Lucille Ball (Hollywood Walk of Fame Collection), CAL-HASCO Inc, 1992, 20", MIB.... $350.00
Lyndon Johnson, Remco, 1964, plastic, 6", MIB $40.00
Mae West, Hamilton Gifts, 1991, 17", M $50.00
Mae West (Great Legends), Effanbee, 1982, 18", MIB... $125.00
Mandy Moore, Play Along, 2000, 11½", MIB....$20.00
Margaret O'Biren, Madame Alexander, 18", EX.... $675.00
Marie Osmond (Modeling Doll), Mattel, 1976, 30", MIB...$150.00
Marilyn Monroe, DSI, 1993, blk gown & wht fur stole, 11½", MIB....$50.00
Marilyn Monroe, Tri-Star, 1982, pk gown & gloves, 16½", MIB....$100.00
Marilyn Monroe, Tri-Star, 1982, 2nd issue (different face mold), 11½", MIB.... $150.00
Marlo Thomas (That Girl), Madame Alexander, 1967, 17", rare, MIB $800.00

Mary Martin, Madame Alexander, ca 1949, hard plastic, short curly wig, orig outfit, 14", EX, A $1,250.00
Marylin Monroe, Tri-Star, 1982, 1st issue (same face mold as 16½" doll), 11½", MIB....$75.00
Michael Jackson, LJN, 1984, bl & gold outfit holding microphone, 12", MIB $75.00
Muhammad Ali, Hasbro, 1997, 12", MIB $45.00
Muhammad Ali, Mego, 1976, 9", MOC $150.00
Nicole Boebeck (Olympic Ice Skater), Playmates 1998, 11½", MIB....$25.00
Patty Duke, Horsman, 1965, 12", rare, MIB.... $450.00
Penny Marshall or Cindy Williams, see Character, TV & Movie category under Laverne & Shirley
Prince Charles, Goldberg, 1983, dress uniform, 12", MIB.. $100.00

Prince Charles, Madame Alexander, 1957, walker, 8", G, $150.00. (Photo courtesy McMasters Harris Auction Co.)

Prince William, Goldberg, 1982, christening gown, 18", MIB ..$150.00
Prince William, House of Misbet, 1982, as baby, 18", MIB..$200.00
Princess Diana, Danbury Mint, 1988, pk satin gown, 14", MIB $125.00
Princess Diana, Effanbee (Fan Club), 1982, wedding dress, 16½", MIB $225.00
Princess Diana, Goldberg, 1983, wht gown w/wht boa, 11½", MIB $100.00
Princess Diana, Way Out Toys, 1990s, Royal Diana, pk dress, 11½", MIB....$20.00
Princess Maraget, Dean's Rag Book Co, 1920s, papier-maché over cloth, mohair wig, cloth coat & hat, 14", unused, M.. $350.00
Queen Elizabeth, Effanbee, 1980s, wht satin gown, 14", MIB...$75.00
Queen Elizabeth, Effanbee, 1989, red & wht satin gown, 14", MIB $125.00
Randy Travis (Country Music), Exclusive Premiere, 1998, 9", MIB $30.00
Red Foxx, Shindana, 1976, 2-sided stuffed print cloth talker, 16", MIB $150.00
Robert Crippen (Astronaut), Kenner, 1997, 12", MIB....$45.00
Ronald Reagan, Dots Okay, 1982, stuffed printed cloth (Reaganomics), 10", MIB....$25.00

Rosemary Clooney (White Christmas), Exclusive Premiere, 1998, red gown, 8", MIB....................................$45.00
Rosie O'Donnell, Mattel, 1999, red outfit, 11½", MIB......$30.00
Rosie O'Donnell, Tyco, 1997, The Rosie Doll, stuffed cloth, outfit, 14", MIB..$40.00
Selena, Arm Enterprise, 1996, red jumpsuit, 11½", MIB...$85.00
Shari Lewis, Direct International, 1994, rag doll holding Lamb-shop, 14", MIB..$30.00
Shari Lewis, Madame Alexander, 1959, yel sweater w/gr skirt & hat, 21", MIB.. $450.00
Sonny Bono, Mego, 1976, 12½", MIB........................... $150.00

Sonya Henie, Deans Rag Doll, 39", G, A, $550.00. (Photo courtesy James D. Julia, Inc.)

Soupy Sales, 1960s, yel sweater & red tie, 11½", MIB.... $250.00

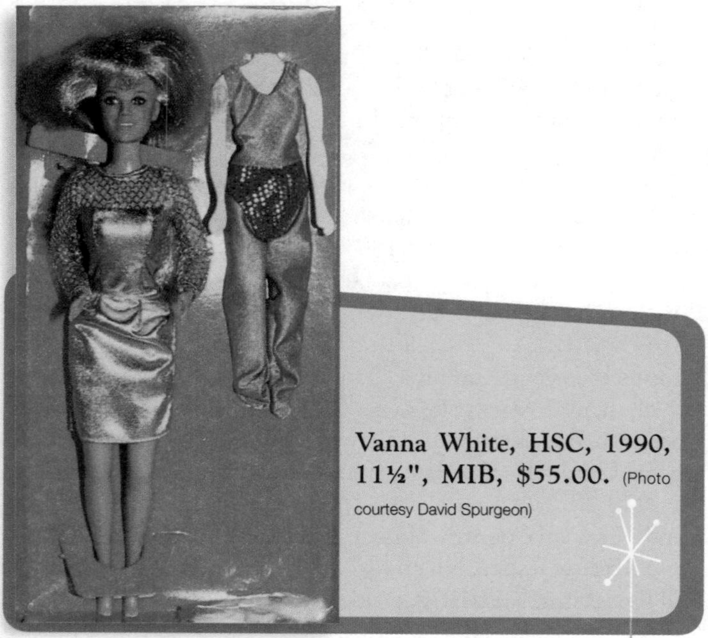

Vanna White, HSC, 1990, 11½", MIB, $55.00. (Photo courtesy David Spurgeon)

WC Fields, Effanbee, 1980, blk coat, checked pants & gray top hat, 15½", MIB $125.00
WC Fields, Knickerbocker, 1972, stuffed print cloth talker, 16", MIB..$75.00
Willie Nelson, Catena International Inc, 1989, stuffed cloth, yarn hair & head bandana, 16", M.............................$65.00
Winston Churchill, Madame Alexander, hard palstic, blk tuxedo & hat, 18", VG, A $375.00

Chatty Cathy

Chatty Cathy (made by Mattel) was introduced in the 1960s and came as either a blond or brunette. For five years, she sold very well. Much of her success can be attributed to the fact that Chatty Cathy talked. By pulling the string on her back, she could respond with many different phrases. During her five years of fame, Mattel added to the line with Chatty Baby, Tiny Chatty Baby and Tiny Chatty Brother (the twins), Charmin' Chatty, and finally Singin' Chatty. Charmin' Chatty had 16 interchang-able records. Her voice box was acitvated in the same manner as the above-mentioned dolls, by means of a pull string located at the base of her neck. The line was brought back in 1969, smaller and with a restyled face, but it was not well received.

Note: Prices given are for working dolls. Deduct half if doll is mute.

First Chatty Cathy Doll, red dress with white voile pinafore, red shoes with white socks, doll is not marked, MIB, $300.00. (Photo courtesy Cindy Sabulis)

Carrying Case, Chatty Baby, bl or pk, NM, ea..................$50.00
Carrying Case, Tiny Chatty Baby, bl or pk, NM, ea $40.00
Doll, Charmin' Chatty, EX, from $75 to $150.00
Doll, Chatty Baby, EX, from $65 to..................................$90.00
Doll, Chatty Cathy, any style except for unmarked 1st doll, EX, from $75 to $150.00
Doll, Chatty Cathy, 1970 reissue, MIB, from $35 to..........$50.00

Doll, Singin' Chatty, blond hair or brunette, M, from $40 to ...$75.00
Doll, Tiny Chatty Baby, blk, EX $150.00
Doll, Tiny Chatty Baby, brother, EX, from $45 to $65.00
Doll, Tiny Chatty Baby, EX, from $35 to $50.00
Outfit, Charmin' Chatty, Let's Go Shopping, MIP $75.00
Outfit, Charmin' Chatty, Let's Play Together, MIP $75.00
Outfit, Chatty Baby, Sleeper Set, MIP $50.00
Outfit, Chatty Cathy, Pink Peppermint Stick, MIP $125.00
Outfit, Chatty Cathy, Playtime, MIP $125.00
Outfit, Tiny Chatty Baby, Pink Frill, MIP $100.00
Outfit, Tiny Chatty Baby Bye-Bye, MIP $75.00

Crissy and Her Friends

Ideal's 18" Crissy doll with growing hair was very popular with little girls of the early 1970s. She was introduced in 1969 and continued to be sold throughout the 1970s, enjoying a relatively long market life for a doll. During the 1970s, many different versions of Crissy were made. Numerous friends followed her success, all with the growing hair feature like Crissy's. The other Ideal 'grow hair' dolls in the line included Velvet, Cinnamon, Tressy, Dina, Mia, Kerry, Brandi, and Cricket. Crissy is the easiest member in the line to find, followed by her cousin Velvet. The other members are not as common, but like Crissy and Velvet loose examples of these dolls frequently make their appearance at doll shows, flea markets, and even garage sales. Only those examples that are in excellent or better condition and wearing their original outfits and shoes should command book value. Values for the rare black versions of the dolls in the line are currently on the rise, as demand for them increases while the supply decreases.

Advisor: Cindy Sabulis, author of *Dolls of the 1960s and 1970s*

Crissy, Magic Hair, 1977, MIB, from $65.00 to $80.00. (Photo courtesy Cindy Sabulis and Marcia Fanta)

Baby Crissy, blk, 1973-76, pk dress, EX $80.00
Baby Crissy, 1973-76, pk dress, EX $65.00
Baby Crissy, 1973-77, redressed, from $35 to $45.00
Baby Crissy, 1976-76, pk dress, MIB $125.00
Brandi, blk, 1972-73, orange swimsuit, EX $125.00
Cinnamon, Curly Ribbons, blk, 1974, EX $75.00
Cinnamon, Curly Ribbons, 1974, EX $45.00
Cinnamon, Hairdoodler, blk, 1973, EX $75.00
Cinnamon, Hairdoodler, 1973, EX $40.00
Crissy, Beautiful, 1969, orange lace dress, EX $40.00
Crissy, Country Fashion, 1982-83, EX $20.00
Crissy, Country Fashion, 1982-83, MIB $45.00
Crissy, Look Around, 1972, EX $40.00
Crissy, Magic Hair, 1977, EX $30.00
Crissy, Magic Hair, 1977, NRFB $90.00
Crissy, Movin' Groovin', 1971, EX $40.00
Crissy, Movin' Grovin', blk, 1971, EX $100.00
Crissy, Swirla Curla, blk, 1973, EX $100.00
Crissy, Swirla Curla, 1973, EX $35.00
Crissy, Twirly Beads, 1974, MIB $65.00
Crissy Magic Hair, blk, 1977, EX $100.00
Dina, 1972-73, purple playsuit, EX $50.00
Kerry, 1971, gr romper, EX $55.00
Mia, 1971, turq romper, EX $50.00
Tara, blk, 1976, yel gingham outfit, MIB $200.00
Velvet, Beauty Braider, 1973, EX $35.00
Velvet, Look Around, 1972, EX $35.00
Velvet, Movin' Groovin', 1971, EX $35.00
Velvet, reissue, 1982, EX $30.00
Velvet, Swirly Daisies, 1974, EX $35.00
Velvet, Swirly Daisies, 1974, MIB $65.00
Velvet, 1st issue, purple dress, 1970, EX $35.00
Velvet Look Around, blk, 1972, EX $100.00

Dawn

Dawn and her friends were made by Deluxe Topper in the 1970s. They're becoming highly collectible, especially when mint in the box. Dawn was a 6" fashion doll, part of a series sold as the Dawn Model Agency. They were issued in boxes already dressed in clothes of the highest style, or you could buy additional outfits, many complete with matching shoes and accessories.

Advisor: Dawn Diaz

Accessory, Dawn's Apartment, complete $50.00
Doll, Dancing Angie, NRFB $50.00
Doll, Dancing Dale, NRFB $65.00
Doll, Dancing Dawn, NRFB $50.00
Doll, Dancing Gary, NRFB $50.00
Doll, Dancing Glori, NRFB $50.00
Doll, Dancing Jessica, NRFB $50.00
Doll, Dancing Ron, NRFB $50.00
Doll, Dancing Van, NRFB $80.00
Doll, Daphne Model Agency, gr & silver dress NRFB.... $100.00
Doll, Dawn Majorette, NRFB $100.00
Doll, Denise Model Agency, NRFB $100.00

Doll, Dinah Model Agency, NRFB $100.00
Doll, Gary, NRFB..$50.00
Doll, Jessica, NRFB...$50.00
Doll, Kip Majorette, NRFB $65.00
Doll, Longlocks, NRFB...$50.00
Doll, Maureen Model Agency, red & gold dress, NRFB .. $100.00
Doll, Ron, NRFB $50.00
Outfit, Bell Bottom Flounce, #0717, NRFB........................$25.00
Outfit, Green Slink, #0716, NRFB................................$25.00
Outfit, Sheer Delight, #8110, NRFB..............................$25.00

Dawn's Double Dance Party With Fancy Feet and Kevin, MIB, from $65.00 to $100.00. (Photo courtesy Cindy Sabulis and Nancy Jean Mong)

Dolly Darlings and Flower Darlings by Hasbro

Dolly Darlings by Hasbro are approximately 4" tall and have molded or rooted hair. The molded-hair dolls were sold in themed hatboxes with small accessories to match. The rooted-hair dolls were sold separately and came with a small brush and comb. There were four plastic playrooms that featured the rooted-hair dolls. Hasbro also produced the Flower Darling series which were dolls in flower corsages. The Dolly Darlings and Flower Darlings were available in the mid to late 1960s.

Advisor: Dawn Diaz

Dolly Darlings, John and His Pets, M (in case), from $35.00 to $55.00. (Photo courtesy Cindy Sabulis)

DD, Beth at the Supermarket, NRFB...............................$50.00
DD, Cathy Goes to a Party, M (EX case), from $35 to $45.00
DD, Daisy Darling, complete, EX.................................$15.00
DD, Flying Nun, MIB, from $50 to $75.00
DD, Go-Team-Go, dolly only, EX, from $25 to $35.00
DD, Hipster, doll only, EX, from $25 to $35.00
DD, Honey, NRFB...$50.00
DD, Lemon Drop, doll only, EX, from $30 to $50.00
DD, Powder Puff, doll only, EX, from $15 to $25.00
DD, School Days, doll only, EX, from $15 to.....................$25.00
DD, Shary Takes a Vacatiion, doll only, EX......................$10.00
DD, Slick Set, doll only, EX $25.00
DD, Slumber Party, doll only, EX $15.00
DD, Sunny Day, doll only, from $15 to $25.00
DD, Susie Goes to School, M (EX case), from $35 to $45.00
DD, Sweetheart, doll only EX, from $15 to $25.00
DD, Tea Time, NRFB $50.00
DD, Teeny Bikini, doll only, EX, from $15 to $25.00
DD, Violet Flower Darling, doll only, EX........................$10.00
FD, dolls, complete, M, ea from $15 to $25.00
FD, dolls, MIP, ea from $50 to $75.00
FD, dolls w/o flower pins, ea from $7 to $12.00

Fisher-Price

Though this company is more famous for their ruggedly durable, lithographed wooden toys, they made dolls as well. Many of the earlier dolls (circa mid-1970s) had stuffed cloth bodies and vinyl heads, hands, and feet. Some had battery-operated voice boxes. For company history, see the Fisher-Price category.

See also Advertising; Character, TV, and Movie Collectibles; Disney.

Doll, Mary, #200, 1974 – 1977, M, $30.00. (Photo courtesy Brad Cassity)

Doll, Audrey, #203, 1974-76, MIB....................................$50.00
Doll, Baby Ann, #204, 1974-76, MIB..............................$80.00
Doll, Baby Soft Sounds, #213, MIB.................................$65.00
Doll, Billie, #242, 1979-80, EX...$10.00
Doll, Elizabeth, #205, 1974-75, EX $25.00
Doll, Honey, #208, 1977-80, EX.......................................$20.00
Doll, Jenny, #201, 1974-76, MIB.......................................$55.00
Doll, Joey, #206, 1975-76, M...$40.00
Doll, Mandy, #4009, 1985, Happy Birthday, EX $50.00
Doll, Mary, #200, 1974-77, MIB.......................................$60.00
Doll, Mikey, #240, 1979-80, EXIB....................................$45.00
Doll, Muffy, #241, 1979-80, EX...................................... $100.00
Doll, My Baby Sleep, #207, 1979-80, EX...........................$25.00
Doll, My Friend Becky, #218, 1982-84, EX........................$20.00
Doll, My Friend Christie, #8120, 1990, EX, from $40 to...$75.00
Doll, My Friend Jenny, MIB $100.00
Doll, My Friend Jenny, 1978, with doll trunk, outfits & hangers, EX $65.00
Doll, My Friend Mandy, #216, 1984 only, EX....................$35.00
Doll, My Friend Mandy #210 (1977-78), #211 (1979-81), #215 (1982-83), EX, ea $25.00
Doll, My Friend Mikey, #205, 1982-84, EX........................$30.00

Doll, My Friend Nickey, #206, 1985, MIB, $95.00.

(Photo courtesy Brad Cassity)

Doll, Natalie, #202, 1974-76, MIB....................................$65.00
Doll, Rattle Rag Doll, #419, 1977, EX $30.00
Outfit, Aerobics, #4110, 1985, EX $10.00
Outfit, Let's Go Camping, #222, 1978-79, EX $10.00
Outfit, Miss Piggy's Sailor Outfit, #891, 1981-82, EX $12.00
Outfit, Party Dress Outfit & Pattern, #221, 1978-79, EX ..$10.00
Outfit, Rainy Day Slicker, #219, 1978-80, EX $10.00
Outfit, Springtime Tennis, #220, 1978-82, EX...................$10.00
Outfit, Sunshine Party Dress, #237, 1984, EX....................$10.00
Outfit, Valentine Party Dress, #238, 1984-85, EX.............$10.00

Flatsy

Flatsy dolls were a product of the Ideal Novelty and Toy Company. They were produced from 1968 until 1970 in 2", 5", and 8" sizes. There was only one boy in the 5" line; all were dressed in '70s fashions, and not only clothing but accessory items such as bicycles were made as well.

In 1994 Justoys reissued Mini Flatsys. They were sold alone or with accessories such as bikes, rollerblades, and jet skis.

Advisor: Dawn Diaz

Ali Fashion Flatsy NRFP, from $45 to..............................$65.00
Bonnie Flatsy, sailing, NRFP $55.00
Candy, Happy Birthday, complete, EX $25.00
Casey Flatsy, MIB...$55.00
Cory Flatsy, print mini-dress, NRFP, from $45 to..............$65.00
Dale Fashion Flatsy, hot pk maxi NRFP, from $45 to $65.00
Dewie Flatsy, NRFP $60.00
Dewie Flatsy Locket, NRFP, from $20 to...........................$40.00
Filly Flatsy, complete, EX...$25.00
Grandma Baker, Flatsyville series, complete, M, from $35 to . $50.00
Gwen Fashion Flatsy, NRFP, from $45 to..........................$65.00

Judy Flatsy, NRFB, from $55.00 to $70.00.

(Photo courtesy Cindy Sabulis and S. DeDivitis)

Kookie Flatsy, Flatsyville series, complete, M, from $35 to ..$50.00
Munch Time Flatsy, Mini Flatsy Collection, NRFP, from $50 to $85.00
Slumber Party Flatsy, Mini Flatsy Collection, NRFP, from $50 to $85.00
Spinderella Flatsy, complete, M, from $35 to.....................$40.00
Summer Mini Flatsy Collection, NRFP $65.00
Susie Flatsy complete, EX $25.00

Gerber Baby Dolls

The first Gerber Baby dolls were manufactured in 1936. These dolls were made of cloth and produced by an unknown manufacturer. Since that time, six different companies working with leading artists, craftsmen, and designers have attempted to capture the charm of the winsome baby in Dorothy Hope Smith's charcoal drawing of her friend's baby, Ann Turner (Cook). This drawing became known as the Gerber Baby and was adopted as the trademark of the Gerber Products Company, located in Fremont, Michigan. For further information see *Gerber Baby Dolls and Advertising Collectibles* by Joan S. Grubaugh.

Amsco, 10", pk & wht rosebud sleeper, vinyl, 1972-73, NM, from $45 to...$55.00
Amsco, 10", pk & wht rosebud sleeper, blk, vinyl, 1972-73, NM, from $60 to...$100.00
Amsco, 14", baby & feeding set, vinyl, 1972-73, complete, NMIB...$85.00
Arrow Rubber & Plastic Corp, 14", bib & diaper, 1965-67 Gerber premium, MIB, from $45 to...$60.00
Atlanta Novelty, 12", Baby Drink & Wet, blk, complete w/trunk & accessories, 1979-81, M...$100.00
Atlanta Novelty, 12", Bathtub Baby, 1985, MIB, from $70 to...$85.00
Atlanta Novelty, 12", porcelain, #D527, wht satin gown & bonnet, w/pillow & basket, 1982 limited edition, EX+...$50.00
Atlanta Novelty, 12", rag doll, pk or bl, EX...$20.00
Atlanta Novelty, 17", Baby Drink & Wet, complete w/trunk & accessories, 1979-81, M, from $75 to...$85.00
Atlanta Novelty, 17", goggly-eyed, wht or blk dolls, orig outfit, 1979, unused, MIB, from $45 to...$55.00
Atlanta Novelty, 17", 50th Anniversary, stuffed cloth & vinyl w/eyelet skirt & bib, 1978, NRFB...$75.00

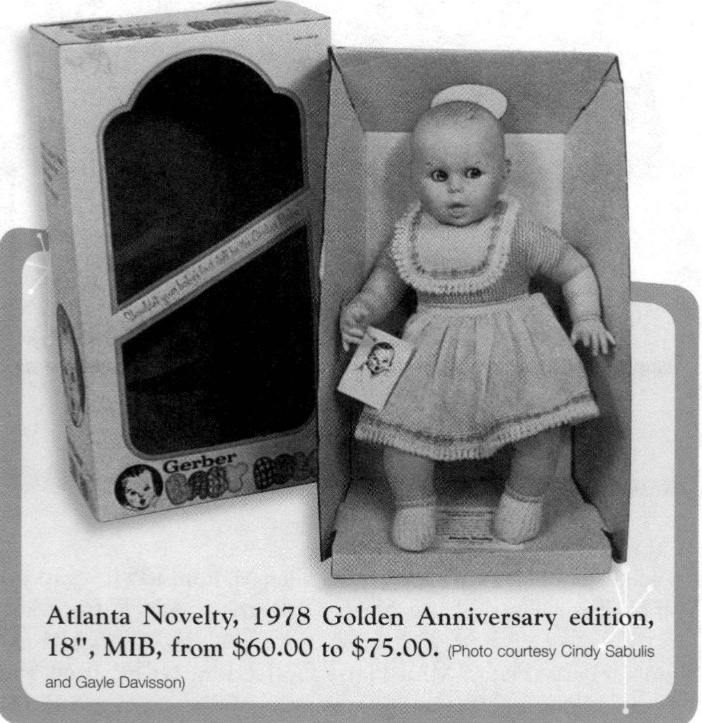

Atlanta Novelty, 1978 Golden Anniversary edition, 18", MIB, from $60.00 to $75.00. (Photo courtesy Cindy Sabulis and Gayle Davisson)

Lucky Ltd, 6", Birthday Party Twins, 1989, NRFB...$40.00
Lucky Ltd, 16", christening gown, 1989, EX...$40.00
Sun Rubber, 11", nude, 1956, EX...$50.00
Sun Rubber, 13", mouth open for bottle, in dress, matching panties & bonnet, 1955, NM...$175.00
Sun Rubber, 18", nude, EX...$75.00
Toy Biz, Baby Care Set, 1996, MIB...$25.00
Toy Biz, Food & Playtime Baby, 1995, MIB, from $25 to...$35.00
Toy Biz, Potty Time Baby, 1994-95, NRFB...$25.00

Holly Hobbie

Sometime around 1970 a young homemaker and mother, Holly Hobbie, approached the American Greeting Company with some charming country-styled drawings of children. Her concepts were well received by the company, and since that time over 400 Holly Hobbie items have been produced, nearly all marked HH, H. Hobbie, or Holly Hobbie.

See also Clubs, Newsletters, and Other Publications.

Bubble Bath Container, several figural variations, Benjamin Ansehl, 1980s, NM...$10.00
Doll, Country Fun Holly Hobbie, 16", 1989, NRFB...$20.00
Doll, Grandma Holly, 14", MIB...$20.00
Doll, Grandma Holly, 24", MIB...$25.00
Doll, HH, Amy or Carrie Dream Along, 12", MIB, ea...$15.00
Doll, HH, Bicentennial, 12", MIB...$25.00
Doll, HH, Day 'N Night, 14", MIB...$15.00
Doll, HH, Heather, Amy or Carrie, 09", MIB, ea...$10.00
Doll, HH, Heather, Amy or Carrie, 16", MIB, ea...$20.00
Doll, HH, Heather, Amy or Carrie, 27", MIB, ea...$25.00
Doll, HH, Heather, Amy or Carrie, 33", MIB, ea...$35.00
Doll, HH, Heather, Amy or Carrie, 6", MIB, ea...$5.00
Doll, HH, scented, clear ornament around neck, 18", 1988, NRFB...$30.00

Doll, Holly Hobby, 25th Anniversary Collector's Edition, 14", MIB, from $25.00 to $35.00; 26", MIB, from $45.00 to $55.00.

Doll, HH Dream Along, Amy or Carrie, 9", MIB, ea...$10.00
Doll, HH Talker, 4 sayings, 16", MIB...$25.00
Doll, Little Girl Holly, 15", 1980, MIB...$20.00

Doll, Robby, 9", MIB $15.00
Doll, Robby, 16", MIB $20.00

Doll, Sunbonnet Babies, May, Molly, and Mandy, 6½", MIB, from $20.00 to $25.00 each. (Photo courtesy Cindy Sabulis)

Dollhouse, M.. $200.00
Sand Pail, 6", Chein, 1974, EX $25.00
Sewing Machine, b/o, 5x9", Durham, 1975, EX $25.00

Jem

The glamorous life of Jem mesmerized little girls who watched her Saturday morning cartoons, and she was a natural as a fashion doll. Hasbro saw the potential in 1985 when they introduced the Jem line of 12" dolls representing her, the rock stars from Jem's musical group, the Holograms, and other members of the cast, including the only boy, Rio, Jem's road manager and Jerrica's boyfriend. Each doll was posable, jointed at the waist, head, and wrists, so that they could be positioned at will with their musical instruments and other accessory items. Their clothing, their makeup, and their hairdos were wonderfully exotic, and their faces were beautifully modeled. The Jem line was discontinued in 1987 after being on the market for only two years.

Doll, Clash of the Misfits, NRFB, $65.00; Flash 'n Sizzle Jem/Jerrica, NRFB, $85.00; Video, NRFB, $55.00.
(Photo courtesy James D. Julia Inc.)

Accessory, Video Madness, NRFB.....................................$75.00
Clock, rnd neon wall mount w/Jem in center, bl neon & background, 11" dia, unused, M..$55.00
Color, Activity and Paint Books, any, unused, M $50.00
Compact, oblong w/Jem image on lid, 3½x4½", M............$12.00
Doll, Aja, NRFB $245.00
Doll, Banee, NRFB $35.00
Doll, Glitter 'n Gold Jem/Jerrica, NRFB..........................$75.00
Doll, Glitter 'n Gold Rio, NRFB..$40.00
Doll, Jetta, MIB.. $100.00
Doll, Jetta, NRFB... $110.00
Doll, Kimber, complete, M $48.00
Doll, Kimber, MIB $70.00
Doll, Pizzazz, complete, M...$45.00
Doll, Pizzazz, 1st issue, MIB $85.00
Doll, Raya, NRFB $190.00
Doll, Rock 'N Curl, MIB $45.00
Doll, Rock 'n Curl Jem, NRFB...$40.00
Doll, Roxy, MIB.. $100.00
Doll, Shana, NRFB.. $100.00
Doll, Stormer, NRFB $95.00
Doll, Stormer, NRFB $110.00
Doll, Synergy, NRFB... $150.00
Eraser Set, Jem (star-shaped), Pizzazz (triangular), MOC..$90.00
Magic Slate, unused, M $20.00
Outfit, Glitter 'n Gold Midnight Magic, NRFP.................$20.00
Outfit, Glitter 'n Gold Purple Haze, NRFP........................$35.00
Outfit, How You Play the Game, MIP........................... $135.00
Outfit, Let's Rock This Town, NRFP..................................$70.00
Outfit, Like a Dream, NRFP $70.00
Outfit, Rock 'n Roses, NRFP $70.00
Outfit, Rock Country, NRFP $45.00
Outfit, Set Your Sails, MIP $100.00
Outfit, Sophisticated Lady, NRFP $50.00
Outfit, Splashes of Sound, NRFP $35.00
Outfit, You Can't Catch Me, complete, MIP $100.00
Paint w/Water Book, unused, M..$55.00

Liddle Kiddles

From 1966 to 1971, Mattel produced Liddle Kiddle dolls and accessories, typical of the 'little kid next door.' They were made in sizes ranging from a tiny ¾" up to 4". They were all posable and had rooted hair that could be restyled. Eventually there were Animiddles and Zoolery Jewelry Kiddles, which were of course animals, and two other series that represented storybook and nursery-rhyme characters. There was a set of extraterrestrials, and lastly in 1979, Sweet Treets dolls were added to the assortment.

In the mid-1970s Mattel reissued Lucky Locket Kiddles. The dolls had names identical to the earlier lockets but were not of the same high quality.

In 1994 – 1995 Tyco reissued Liddle Kiddles in strap-on, clip-on, Lovely Locket, Pretty Perfume, and baby bottle collections.

Loose dolls, if complete and with all their original accessories, are worth about 50% less than the same mint in the box. Dressed, loose dolls with no accessories are worth 75% less.

Advisor: Dawn Diaz

Alice in Wonderlittle, complete, M, $175.00. (Photo courtesy Cindy Sabulis)

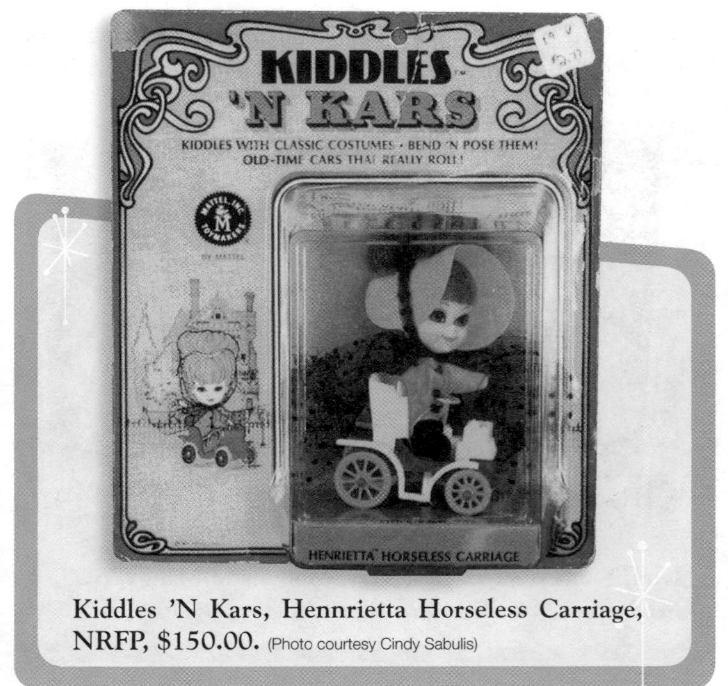

Kiddles 'N Kars, Hennrietta Horseless Carriage, NRFP, $150.00. (Photo courtesy Cindy Sabulis)

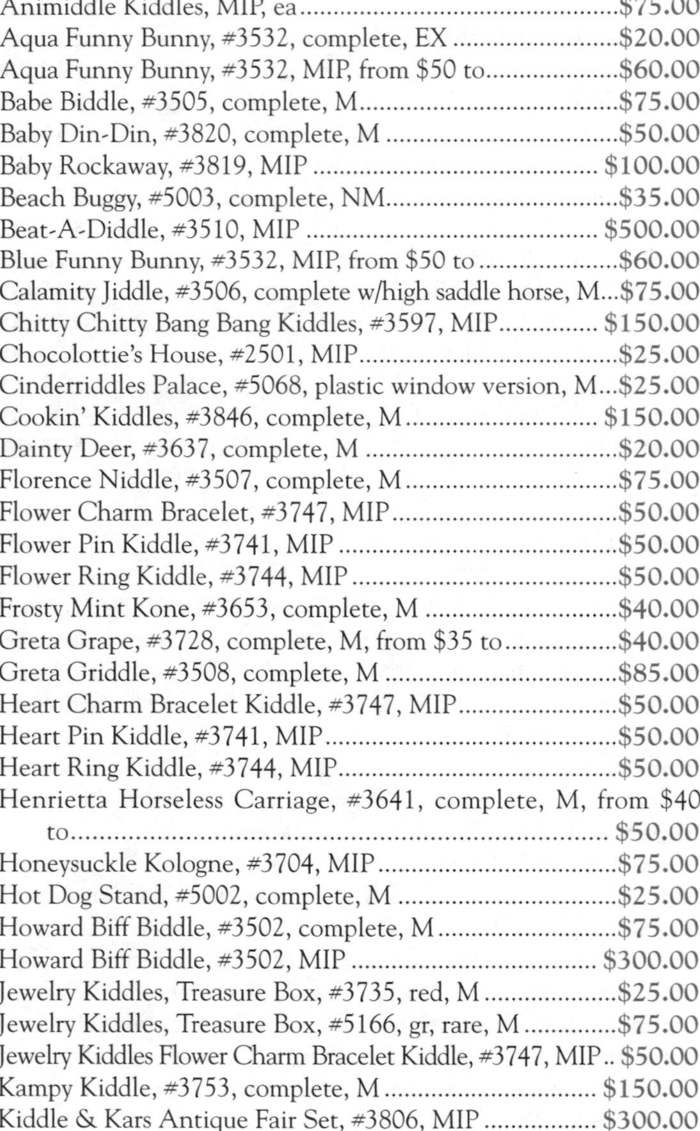

Animiddle Kiddles, MIP, ea...$75.00
Aqua Funny Bunny, #3532, complete, EX...$20.00
Aqua Funny Bunny, #3532, MIP, from $50 to...$60.00
Babe Biddle, #3505, complete, M...$75.00
Baby Din-Din, #3820, complete, M...$50.00
Baby Rockaway, #3819, MIP...$100.00
Beach Buggy, #5003, complete, NM...$35.00
Beat-A-Diddle, #3510, MIP...$500.00
Blue Funny Bunny, #3532, MIP, from $50 to...$60.00
Calamity Jiddle, #3506, complete w/high saddle horse, M...$75.00
Chitty Chitty Bang Bang Kiddles, #3597, MIP...$150.00
Chocolottie's House, #2501, MIP...$25.00
Cinderriddles Palace, #5068, plastic window version, M...$25.00
Cookin' Kiddles, #3846, complete, M...$150.00
Dainty Deer, #3637, complete, M...$20.00
Florence Niddle, #3507, complete, M...$75.00
Flower Charm Bracelet, #3747, MIP...$50.00
Flower Pin Kiddle, #3741, MIP...$50.00
Flower Ring Kiddle, #3744, MIP...$50.00
Frosty Mint Kone, #3653, complete, M...$40.00
Greta Grape, #3728, complete, M, from $35 to...$40.00
Greta Griddle, #3508, complete, M...$85.00
Heart Charm Bracelet Kiddle, #3747, MIP...$50.00
Heart Pin Kiddle, #3741, MIP...$50.00
Heart Ring Kiddle, #3744, MIP...$50.00
Henrietta Horseless Carriage, #3641, complete, M, from $40 to...$50.00
Honeysuckle Kologne, #3704, MIP...$75.00
Hot Dog Stand, #5002, complete, M...$25.00
Howard Biff Biddle, #3502, complete, M...$75.00
Howard Biff Biddle, #3502, MIP...$300.00
Jewelry Kiddles, Treasure Box, #3735, red, M...$25.00
Jewelry Kiddles, Treasure Box, #5166, gr, rare, M...$75.00
Jewelry Kiddles Flower Charm Bracelet Kiddle, #3747, MIP...$50.00
Kampy Kiddle, #3753, complete, M...$150.00
Kiddle & Kars Antique Fair Set, #3806, MIP...$300.00

Kiddle Komedy Theatre, #3592, EX...$35.00
Kiddles, Kolonge, #3705 Sweet Pea...$45.00
Kiddles Kologne, #3710 Gardinia, MIP...$75.00
Kiddles Sweet Shop, MIP...$300.00
King & Queen of Hearts, #3784, MIP...$150.00
Kleo Kola, #3729, complete, M, from $35 to...$40.00
Kola Kiddles Three-Pak, #3734, MIP...$300.00
Kosmic Kiddles, M, ea...$150.00
Lady Crimson, #A3840, MIP...$75.00
Lady Lavender, #A3840, MIP...$75.00
Laffy Lemon, ##732, MIP...$85.00
Larky Locket, #3539, complete, EX...$25.00
Lenore Limousine, #3743, complete, M, from $40 to...$50.00
Liddel Kiddles Kabin #3591, complete, EX...$25.00
Liddel Kiddles 3-Story House, complete, M...$35.00
Liddle Biddle Peep, #3544, complete, M...$150.00
Liddle Diddle, #3503, complete, M...$75.00
Liddle Kiddles Kastle, #3522, complete, M...$55.00
Liddle Kiddles Klub, #3301, M...$20.00
Liddle Kiddles Kolony, #3571, M...$25.00
Liddle Kiddles Kottage, #3534, complete, EX...$25.00
Liddle Kiddles Open House, #5167, MIP...$40.00
Liddle Kiddles Pop-Up Boutique, #5170, complete, M...$30.00
Liddle Kiddles Pop-Up Playhouse, #3574, complete, M...$30.00
Liddle Kiddles Talking Townhouse, #5154, MIB...$50.00
Liddle Lion Zolery, #3661, complete, M...$75.00
Liddle Red Riding Hiddle, #3546, complete, M...$175.00
Lilac Locket, #3540, MIP...$75.00
Limey Lou Spoonfuls, #2817, MIP...$25.00
Lois Locket, #3541, complete, M...$75.00
Lola Locket, #3536, MIP...$75.00
Lolli-Grape, #3656, complete, M...$60.00
Lolli-Lemon, #3657, MIP...$75.00
Lolli-Mint, #3658, MIP...$75.00
Lorelei Locket, #3717, MIP...$75.00
Lorelei Locket, #3717, 1976 version, MIP...$25.00

Lottie Locket, #3679, complete, M $25.00
Lou Locket, #3537, MIP $75.00
Luana Locket, #3680, complete, M $35.00
Luana Locket, #3680, Gold Rush version, MIP $85.00
Lucious Lime, #3733, complete, M, from $35 to...............$40.00
Lucky Lion, #3635, complete, M.......................................$20.00
Lucky Locket Jewel Case, #3542, M............................ $150.00
Lucky Locket Magic Paper Dolls, Whitman, 1968, EXIB..$30.00
Luscious Lime, #3733, glitter version, complete, M..........$50.00
Luvvy Duvvy Kiddle, #3596, MIP $50.00
Millie Middle, #3509, complete, M............................. $150.00
Miss Mouse, #3638, MIP $75.00
Nappytime Baby, #3818, complete, M $60.00
Nurse 'N Totsy Outfit, #LK7, MIP.....................................$25.00
Olivia Orange Kola Kiddle, #3730, MIP $80.00
Peter Pandiddle, #3532, MIP.. $300.00
Pink Funny Bunny, #3552, MIP, from $50 to.....................$60.00
Poisies 'N Pink Skediddle Outfit, #3585, MIP $30.00
Rah Rah Skediddle, #3788, complete, M....................... $125.00
Rapunzel & the Prince, #3783, MIP $150.00
Robin Hood & Maid Marion, #3785, MIP $150.00
Rolly Twiddle, #3519, complete, M.............................. $175.00
Romeo & Juliet, #3782, MIP.. $150.00
Santa Kiddle, #3595, MIP $40.00
Shirley Skediddle, #3766, MIP...$75.00
Shirley Strawberrie, #3727, complete, M, from $35 to......$40.00

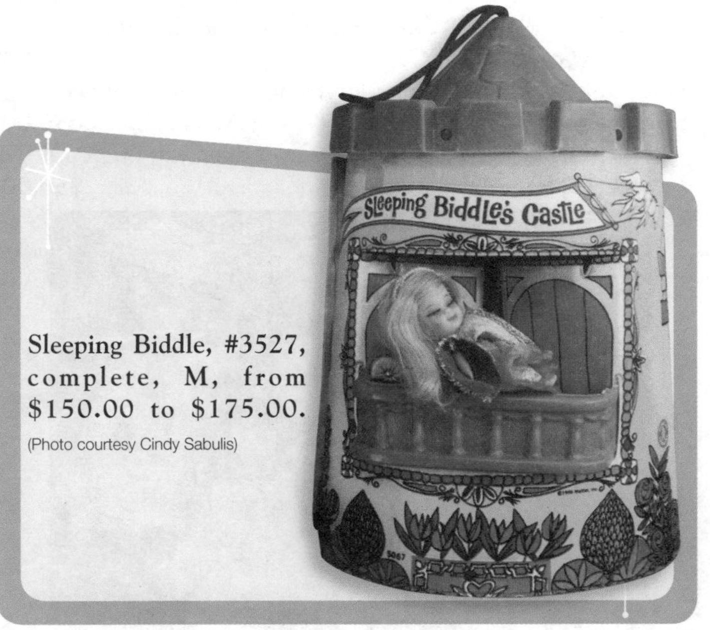

Sleeping Biddle, #3527, complete, M, from $150.00 to $175.00.
(Photo courtesy Cindy Sabulis)

Sizzly Friddle, #3513, complete, M.................................$75.00
Sizzly Friddle, MIP $300.00
Sleep 'N Totsy Outfit, #LK5, MIP $25.00
Sleeping Biddle, #3527, complete, M, from $150 to....... $175.00
Sleeping Biddle, #3527, MOC $300.00
Slipsy Sliddle, #3754, complete, M $125.00
Snap-Happy Bedroom, #5172, complete, M $15.00
Snap-Happy Living Room, #5173, NMIP..........................$20.00
Snap-Happy Patio Furniture, #5171, MIP, from $20 to $25.00
Snoopy Skediddleer & His Sopwith Camel, M.............. $150.00

Suki Skediddle, #3767, complete, M.................................$25.00
Surfy Skediddle, #3517, complete, M...............................$75.00
Swingy Skiddle, #3789, MIP $200.00
Teeter Time Baby, #3817, complete, M.............................$60.00
Teresa Touring Car, #3644, complete, M, from $40 to.......$50.00
Tessie Tractor, #3671, complete, NM............................ $150.00
Tiny Tiger, #3636, MIP...$75.00
Tracy Trikediddle, #3769, complete, M............................$50.00
Trikey Triddle, #3515, complete, M $75.00
Vanilla Lilly, #2819, MIP..$25.00
Violet Kologne, #3713, MIP..$60.00
Windy Fiddle, #3514, complete, M $85.00
World of the Kiddles Beauty Bazaar, #3586, NRFB $300.00

Littlechaps

In 1964, Remco Industries created a family of four fashion dolls that represented a typical American family. The Littlechaps family consisted of the father, Dr. John Littlechap, his wife, Lisa, and their two children, Judy and Libby. Their clothing and fashion accessories were made in Japan and are of the finest quality. Because these dolls are not as pretty as other fashion dolls of the era, and their size and placement of arms and legs made them awkward to dress, children had little interest in them at the time. This lack of interest during the 1960s has created shortages of them for collectors of today. Mint and complete outfits or outfits never-removed-from box are especially desirable to Littlechap collectors. Values listed for loose clothing are for ensembles complete with all their small accessoires. If only the main pieces of the outfit are available, then the value could go down significantly.

Carrying Case, EX..$40.00
Doll, Doctor John, MIB $65.00

Dolls, Libby Littlechap, MIB, $75.00; Judy Littlechap, MIB, $75.00.
(Photo courtesy James D. Julia, Inc.)

Doll, Lisa, MIB..$65.00
Family Room, Bedroom or Doctor John's Office, EX, ea.. $125.00
Outfit, Doctor John, complete, EX, from $15 to $30.00
Outfit, Doctor John, NRFB, from $40 to...........................$50.00

Outfit, Judy, complete, EX, from $25 to $40.00
Outfit, Judy, NRFB, from $35 to..$75.00
Outfit, Libby, complete, EX, from $20 to $35.00
Outfit, Libby, NRFB, from $35 to.......................................$50.00
Outfit, Lisa, complete, EX, from $20 to.............................$35.00
Outfit, Lisa, NRFB, from $35 to $75.00

Madame Alexander Character Dolls

In 1933, Beatrice Alexander took an interest in creating character and celebrity dolls by reissuing the 'Alice in Wonderland' doll, which was first sold in 1923. Acquiring the license to produce the Dion quintuplets dolls quicky gave recognition to the Alexander Doll Company. Many other character and celebrity dolls have since been produced, thus creating a good collector's market for such dolls.

For more information we recommend *Collector's Encyclopedia of Madame Alexander Dolls* and *Madame Alexander Collector's Dolls Price Guide*, both by Linda Crowsey (Collector Books).

Note: You will find the celebrity dolls listed in the Celebrity Dolls sub-category.

Alice in Wonderland, 1930s, felt mask face w/pnt features, blond yarn hair, orig dress & shoes, 16", rare, G+, A......... $250.00
Alice in Wonderland, 1950s, hard plastic, sleep eyes, blond wig, jtd, orig dress & shoes, 15", VG+IB, A $150.00
Alice in Wonderland, 1996, vinyl, sleep eyes, wig, jtd, 15", EX, A $200.00

Cinderella, 1949, 'poor' outfit, 14", unused, NM, A, $650.00. (Photo courtesy McMasters Harris Auction Co.)

Cinderella, 1960s, #1235, hard plastic, sleep eyes, blond synthetic wig, jtd, orig outfit, VGIB, A $150.00
Cinderella, 1960s, #1235, hard plastic, sleep eyes, wig, jtd, orig bl satin gown, w/tag, 12", NM+IB, A.......................... $600.00
David Copperfield, 1930s, felt mask face w/pnt features, blond mohair wig, blk & wht outfit & hat, 16", EX, A...... $400.00
Davy Crockett, 1950s, #446, hard plastic, sleep eyes, red caracul wig, orig outfit & hat, 8", EX, A............................. $125.00
Davy Crockett, 1950s, #446, hard plastic, sleep eyes, red caracul wig, orig outfit & hat, 8", NMIB, A $350.00
Little Men (Lissy), 1960s, hard plastic, wig, orig outfit, EX, A.$550.00
Little Men (Nat), 1950s, hard plastic, orig outfit w/gold felt jacket, 14", rare, EX, A..$2,100.00
Little Men (Stuffy), 1950s, hard plastic, sleep eyes, wig, orig outfit w/bl felt jacket & hat, 14", rare, EX, A............$2,450.00
Little Men (Tommy Bangs), 1950s, hard plastic, wig, orig outfit, 14", NM, A $875.00
Little Women (Amy), 1959-60, hard plastic, sleep eyes, wig, bent-knee walker, orig outfit, 8", EXIB, A $425.00
Little Women (Beth), 1949, hard plastic, wig, orig outfit, w/cloverleaf tag, EX+, A $625.00
Little Women (Jo), 1950s, hard plastic, wig, orig outfit, tagged, 14", EX+.. $375.00
Little Women (Marme), 1950s, hard plastic, wig, orig outfit, tagged, 14", EX, A $275.00
Little Women (Meg), 1950s, hard plastic, wig, orig outfit, tagged, 14", VG+ $275.00
Oliver Twist, 1930s, felt mask face w/pnt features, blond mohair wig, complete orig outfit, 16", rare, VG, A $275.00
Peter Pan, 1950s, #1505, hard plastic, wig, orig outfit, 15", EXIB, A $1,800.00
Prince Charming, 1950s, hard plastic, sleep eyes, caracul wig, orig outfit w/brocade jacket & hat, 18", NMIB, A... $550.00
Prince Charming, 1950s, hard plastic, strung, sleep eyes, caracul wig, orig outfit w/brocade jacket & hat, 14", EXIB, A..........$500.00
Scarlett O'Hara, 1940s, compo, sleep eyes, wig, orig lime gr organdy dress w/hat & leatherette shoes, 14", EX, A. $900.00
Snow White, 1939-42, compo, sleep eyes, blk mohair wig, orig outfit w/cape, 16", EX, A $525.00
Snow White, 1950s, hard plastic, strung, sleep eyes, blk wig, orig outfit w/gold lamè waistcoat, 18", EX, A................. $650.00
Snow White, 1970s, hard plastic, non-walker, jtd, orig outfit w/cape, 8", EX, A...$50.00

Sound of Music Doll Set, 1970s, Maria, Louisa, Brigitta, Liesl, Gretl, Friedrich, and Marta, 8" to 12", EX, A, $325.00. (Photo courtesy McMasters Harris Auction Co.)

Tiny Tim, mask face w/pnt features, blond wig, blk & wht checked pants & hat, blk jacket w/wht collar, 16", 1938, EX, A $300.00
Wendy (Peter Pan), 1950s, #1506, hard plastic, wig, orig dress, 14", EX, A...$1,350.00

Rockflowers

Rockflowers were introduced in the early 1970s as Mattel's answer to Topper's Dawn Dolls. Rockflowers are 6½" tall and have wire articulated bodies that came with mod sunglasses attached to their heads. There were four girls and one boy in the series with eighteen groovy outfits that could be purchased separately. Each doll came with their own 45 rpm record, and the clothing packages were also in the shape of a 45 rpm record.

Advisor: Dawn Diaz

Case, Rockflowers, #4991 (single doll), vinyl, NM............$10.00
Case, Rockflowers on Stage, #4993 (3 dolls), vinyl, NM...$15.00
Doll, Doug, #1177, NRFB, from $40 to.............................$50.00

Doll, Heather, NRFB, from $40.00 to $50.00. (Photo courtesy Cindy Sabulis)

Doll, Iris, NRFB, from $50 to $60.00
Doll, Lilac, #1167, NRFB, from $40 to $50.00
Doll, Rosemary, #1168, NRFB, from $50 to.......................$60.00
Gift Set, In Concert, Heather, Lilac & Rosemary, NRFB.. $150.00
Outfit, Flares 'N Lace, #4057, NRFP.................................$15.00
Outfit, Frontier Gingham, #4069, NRFP $15.00
Outfit, Jeans in Fringe, NRFP...$15.00
Outfit, Long in Fringe, #4050, NRFP $15.00
Outfit, Overall Green, #4067, NRFP $15.00
Outfit, Tie Dye Maxi, #4053, NRFP.................................$15.00
Outfit, Topped Lace, #4058, NRFP $15.00

Schoenhut

Schoenhut dolls are from the late nineteenth century to the early twentieth century. First came the all-wood dolls, then came the dolls with cloth bodies, and later the composition dolls. Their hair was carved or molded and painted or wigged. They had intaglio or sleep eyes and open or closed mouths.

Baby Boy, 12", wig, pnt eyes, closed mouth, redressed, EX, A.. $200.00
Boy Walker, 17", wig, intaglio eyes, closed mouth, re-dressed, EX, A $350.00
Character Boy, 14", wig, intaglio eyes, pouty mouth, re-dressed, G, A $355.00
Character Boy, 16", #309, wig, intaglio eyes, smiling mouth w/2 teeth, orig outfit, VG, A $3,025.00
Character Boy, 19", wig, intaglio eyes, re-dressed, G, A . $385.00
Character Girl, 14", #313, wig, intaglio eyes, re-dressed, VG, A $440.00
Character Girl, 16", #16/306, wig, intaglio eyes, closed mouth, orig outfit, EX, A $4,125.00
Character Girl, 16", #303, wig, intaglio eyes, smiling mouth w/6 teeth, orig outfit, VG, A $2,200.00
Girl, 14", wig, intaglio eyes, slightly open mouth, orig outfit, VG, A $700.00
Girl, 16", wig, intaglio eyes, redressed, VG, A................ $600.00
Girl Walker, 16", wig, intaglio eyes, closed mouth, orig outfit, VG, A $300.00
Miss Dolly, 16", #316, wig, pnt eyes, 4 bottom teeth, night clothes & slippers, VG, A $300.00

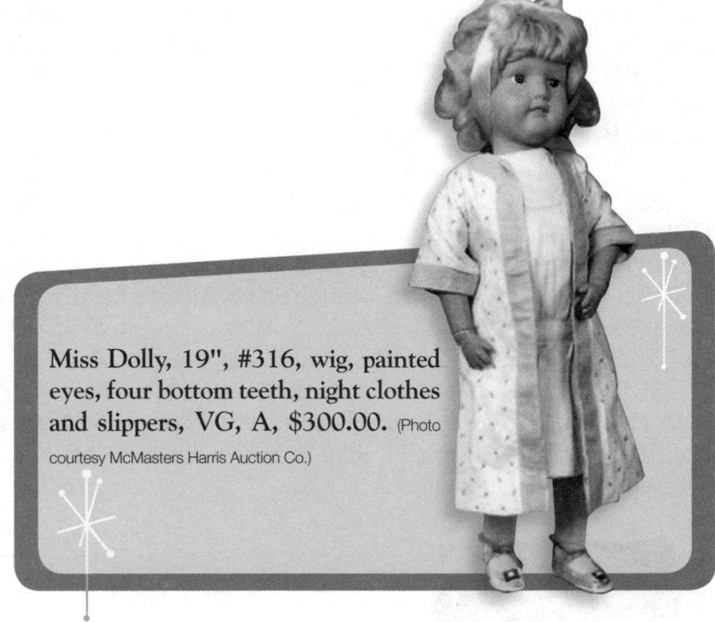

Miss Dolly, 19", #316, wig, painted eyes, four bottom teeth, night clothes and slippers, VG, A, $300.00. (Photo courtesy McMasters Harris Auction Co.)

Miss Dolly, 19½", wood, wig, pnt features, 4 upper teeth, orig outfit, VG, A.. $250.00
Nature Baby, 12½", pnt hair, spring-jtd, re-dressed, G, A . $110.00
Toddler Boy, 11", wig, pnt eyes, orig outfit w/hat, shoes & socks, VG, A $300.00
Toddler Boy, 11½", pnt hair, spring jtd, orig outfit, G, A .. $190.00
Toddler Girl, 16", wig, intaglio eyes, re-dressed, VG, A . $410.00

Shirley Temple

In 1957, the Ideal Toy Corporation reintroduced the Shirley Temple doll to a whole new generation of young fans who arose from watching her early movies on television along with her new TV show called *The Shirley Temple Storybook*. Shirley herself played a big part in the production of these new dolls, which were made of vinyl with rooted hair and sleep eyes.

For more information we recommend *The Complete Guide to Shirley Temple Dolls and Collectibles* by Tonya Bervaldi-Camaratta (Collector Books).

Note: The outfits on the dolls listed are original and complete with undergarments, shoes and socks, purses, and hang tags unless noted otherwise.

Doll, 12", dress, nylon (various colors), wht lacy trim, wht panties, #9717, 1960, MIB....$90.00
Doll, 12", dress, straw hat, wht socks & blk sandals (rare), blk signature purse, 1958, MIB (gold star box)....$350.00
Doll, 12", Heidi outfit w/gr felt headband, 1959, NM....$175.00
Doll, 12", ice skating outfit #9561, red shirt & tights w/blk skirt, matching stocking hat, wht shoes, 1959, NM....$300.00
Doll, 12", party dress, yel nylon w/wht lacy trim, straw hat, shoes w/snap closures, 1959, MIB....$250.00
Doll, 12", playsuit (1-pc) w/lacy trim, 1961-62, MIB....$225.00
Doll, 12", Scottie dog applique on red felt skirt, wht blouse, 1960, NM....$200.00
Doll, 12", slip (pk satin), pk hair bow, 1958, MIB....$200.00
Doll, 12", Wee Willie Winkie outfit, (rare red version), 1959, M (G box)....$250.00
Doll, 15", dress, bl w/wht nylon matador sleeves trimmed in red, 1963, NM....$300.00
Doll, 15", dress, lt bl w/wht lace & blk velvet trim, 1959-60, NMIB....$275.00
Doll, 15", dress, red w/wht & bl rickrack, red straw hat, 1961, NM....$200.00
Doll, 15", dress, yel w/wht lace trim, bl ribbon & flower accents, 1959-60, NM....$250.00
Doll, 15", Jr Prom dress, bl & wht checks w/lace & floral trim, 1961, MIB....$325.00
Doll, 15", jumper, red w/wht blouse, red hair bow, 1962, MIB....$350.00
Doll, 15", Little Red Riding Hood outfit, 1961, NM....$300.00
Doll, 17", Captain January, bl sailor dress w/red, wht & blk hat, 1960, MIB....$325.00

Doll, 17", cowgirl outfit, VG, A, $1,250.00. (Photo courtesy James D. Julia, Inc.)

Doll, 17", dress, bl nylon w/bl & wht trim, 1959-60, MIB....$325.00
Doll, 17", dress, red & wht flocking, 1958, NM....$250.00
Doll, 17", pinafore, wht nylon w/blk ribbon trim over pk dress, 1959-60, MIB....$325.00
Doll, 17", Stand Up & Cheer, wht nylon dress w/red polka-dots, red trim, 1960, NM....$225.00
Doll, 19", dress, taffeta w/bright floral design, 1960, NM..$250.00
Doll, 19", dress, wht nylon w/bl flower design, wht ribbon waist tie, #9532, 1959-60, NM....$225.00
Doll, 19", Wee Willie Winkie, red plaid dress w/bl short-sleeved jacket w/3 wht buttons, 1959, NM....$350.00

Doll, 22", Little Miss Marker, EX, $475.00. (Photo courtesy McMasters Harris Auction Co.)

Doll, 36", dress, bl nylon w/lace-trimmed collar, 2 lg pk roses on bodice, 1959, NM....$1,200.00
Doll, 36", Heidi dress (scarce) in wht w/gr vest & patterned trim around hemline, straw hat, 1960, NM....$2,000.00
Outfit, 12", coat, #9535, brn wool w/dk brn collar, hat & muff, rare, 1958, M....$90.00
Outfit, 12", dress, #9509, yel sleeveless V-neck w/bl embroidered floral trim, blk signature purse, 1958, M....$60.00
Outfit, 12", dress, #9757, sleeveless w/pear-&-leaf design on wht, red V-neck collar & skirt hem, purse, 1961, M....$45.00
Outfit, 12", pajama set, #9501, striped pants w/stripe & lace trim, red or bl, 1958, NM....$40.00
Outfit, 12", pajama set, #9541, red & wht 2-pc w/matching stocking cap, 1959, MIB....$75.00
Outfit, 12", playsuit, #9527, red 1-pc short-legged romper top w/red & wht striped skirt, w/signature purse, 1958, M....$50.00
Outfit, 12", raincoat, #9510, attached hood, matching belt, clear purse, various patterns, 1959, M....$60.00
Outfit, 12", sailor dress, #9543, bl w/red-trimmed wht collar & hat, 1959, M....$45.00
Outfit, 17", Rebecca of Sunnybrook Farm, bl denim jumper w/red & wht checked pockets & blouse, checked headband, 1960, M....$65.00
Shirley Temple's Treasure Board (Magic Slate), Saalfield #8806, 1959, unused, M....$25.00

STRAWBERRY SHORTCAKE

Berry Cycle, 1983, MIB, $38.00. (Photo courtesy whatacharacter.com)

Big Berry Trolley, 1982, EX.....$40.00
Birthday Candle, figural number w/Strawberry Shortcake figure, various numbers, American Greetings, 3½", unused, MOC.....$12.00
Candle, Raspberry Cream, figure, 4½", unused, M.....$10.00
Clock, Strawberry Shortcake w/berry basket on wht face of footed alarm clock, twin bells, 'Have a Berry Good Day!,' 6", NM.....$35.00

Doll, Café Olé with Burrito, MIB, $45.00; Mint Tulip with Marsh Mallard, MIB, $50.00; Almond Tea with Marza Panda, MIB, $30.00.

Doll, Angel Cake & Souffle, 6", NRFB.....$40.00
Doll, Apple Dumpling, 12", cloth w/yarn hair, EX+.....$25.00
Doll, Apple Dumpling & Tea Time Turtle, 6", MIB.....$75.00
Doll, Apricot, 15", NM.....$35.00
Doll, Baby Needs a Name, 15", NM.....$35.00
Doll, Berry Baby Orange Blossom, 6", MIB.....$35.00
Doll, Butter Cookie, 6", MIB.....$25.00
Doll, Cherry Cuddler, 6", NRFB.....$45.00
Doll, Huckleberry Pie, flat hands, 6", MIB.....$45.00
Doll, Lemon Meringue, 6", MIB.....$45.00
Doll, Lemon Meringue, 15", cloth w/yarn hair, EX.....$25.00
Doll, Lime Chiffon, 6", MIB.....$45.00
Doll, Orange Blossom & Marmalade, MIB.....$45.00
Doll, Peach Blush & Melonie Belle, 6", MIB.....$115.00
Doll, Purple Pieman w/Berry Bird, posable, MIB.....$35.00
Doll, Strawberry Shortcake & Strawberrykin, 6", NRFB. $300.00
Doll, Strawberry Shortcake & Custard, 6", NRFB.....$150.00
Dollhouse, no accessories, M.....$200.00

Dollhouse, NM, $150.00.

Figure, Almond Tea w/Marza Panda, PVC, 1", MOC.....$15.00
Figure, Butter Cookie w/Jelly Bear, PVL, 1", MOC.....$15.00
Figure, Cherry Cuddler w/Goosberry, Strawberryland Miniature, MIP, from $15 to.....$20.00
Figure, Lemon Meringue w/Frappo, PVC, 1", MOC.....$15.00
Figure, Lime Chiffon w/balloons, PVC, 1", MOC.....$15.00
Figure, Merry Berry Worm, MIB.....$35.00
Figure, Mint Tulip w/March Mallard, PVC, MOC.....$15.00
Figure, Raspberry Tart w/bowl of cherries, MOC.....$15.00
Figure, Sour Grapes w/Dregs, Strawberryland Miniatures, MIP, from $15 to.....$20.00
Figurine, Strawberry Shortcake, ceramic, 5", EX.....$8.00
Ice Skates, EX.....$35.00
Motorized Bicycle, NM.....$100.00
Musical Strawberry, w/happy-faced sun dial & moving scenery pictures, 1984, NM.....$18.00
Ornament, Raspberry Cream, pnt compo, 3¼", American Greetings, NM+.....$15.00
Ornament, Custard in Christmas stocking w/candy cane, compo, 4", American Greetings, 1981, NM+.....$15.00
Pillow Doll, Huckleberry Pie, 9", EX.....$100.00
Roller Skates, EX.....$35.00
Shoelaces, print on wht, American Greetings, 1981, MIP (pkg reads 'One Two...Tie My Shoe').....$10.00
Sleeping Bag, EX.....$25.00
Storybook Playcase, M.....$35.00
Stroller, Coleco, M.....$85.00
Telephone, Strawberry Shortcake figure, b/o, EX.....$85.00
Toothbrush Holder, lg berry & Strawberry Shortcake seated on grassy mound, plastic, 5½x7", 1981, NM+.....$25.00
Tray Table, American Greeting, 1981, tin, w/fold-down legs, 'Friends & Fun Go Together,' 13x18x7", NM+.....$15.00
Vase, wht porc, bulbous, 'Love Grows in Sweet Hearts,' gold trim, 4", WWA, 1980, M.....$25.00

Tammy

In 1962, the Ideal Novelty and Toy Company introduced their teenage Tammy doll. Slightly pudgy and not quite as sophisticated looking as some of the teen fashion dolls on the market at the time, Tammy's innocent charm captivated consumers. Her extensive wardrobe and numerous accessories added to her popularity with children. Tammy had a car, a house, and her own catamaran. In addition, a large number of companies obtained licenses to issue products using the 'Tammy' name. Everything from paper dolls to nurse's kits were made with Tammy's image on them. Her success was not confined to the United States; she was also successful in Canada and several other European countries.

Values have gone up and supply for quality mint-in-box items is going down. Loose, played-with dolls are still readily available and can be found for decent prices. Values are given for mint-in-box dolls.

Advisor: Cindy Sabulis

Accessory Pak, baseball bat, catcher's mask, mitt & ball, unknown #, NRFP....$35.00
Accessory Pak, electric skillet & frying pan w/lids, unknown #, NRFP....$50.00
Accessory Pak, luggage case, airline ticket & camera, #9183-9, NRFP....$25.00
Accessory Pak, Misty Hair Color Kit, #9828-5, MIB....$75.00
Accessory Pak, pizza princess phone, 'Tammy's Telephone Directory,' wht scandals, #9184-80, NRFP....$25.00
Accessory Pak, plate of crackers, juice, glasses, sandals & newspaper, #9179-3, NRFP....$30.00
Accessory Pak, poodle on leash, red vinyl purse & wht sneakers, #9186-80, NRFP....$30.00
Accessory Pak, tennis racket, score book & sneakers, #9188-8, NRFP....$20.00
Case, Dodi, gr background, EX....$30.00
Case, Misty, Dutch door-type, blk, EX....$30.00
Case, Misty, pk & wht, EX....$25.00
Case, Misty & Tammy, dbl telephone, gr or pk, ea....$25.00
Case, Misty & Tammy, hatbox style, EX....$30.00
Case, Paper & Patti, Montgomery Ward Exclusive, red, EX..$50.00
Case, Pepper, front snap closure, red or coral, EX....$15.00
Case, Pepper, hatbox style, turq, EX....$40.00
Case, Pepper, yel or gr, EX....$20.00
Case, Pepper & Dodi, front opening, bl, EX....$30.00
Case, Tammy, suitcase type w/doll compartment, closet & accessory compartment, red w/clear see-through front, EX..$50.00
Case, Tammy & Her Friends, pk or gr, EX....$30.00
Case, Tammy Beau & Arrow, hatbox style, bl or red, EX..$40.00
Case, Tammy Evening in Paris, blk, blk or red, EX....$20.00
Case, Tammy Model Miss, dbl trunk, red or blk, EX....$25.00
Case, Tammy Model Miss, hatbox style, bl or blk, EX....$30.00
Case, Tammy Model Miss, red or blk, EX....$25.00
Case, Tammy Traveller, red or gr, EX....$45.00
Doll, Bud, MIB, minimum value....$600.00
Doll, Dodi, MIB....$75.00
Doll, Glamour Misty the Miss Clairol Doll, MIB....$150.00
Doll, Grown Up Tammy, blk, MIB....$400.00
Doll, Grown Up Tammy, MIB....$85.00
Doll, Misty, blk, MIB, minimum value....$600.00

Doll, Misty, known as Tammy's best friend, this version is 'Glamour Misty the Miss Clairol Doll' featuring hair that can be colored, M, from $25.00 to $45.00. (Photo courtesy Cindy Sabulis)

Doll, Misty, MIB....$100.00
Doll, Patti, MIB....$200.00
Doll, Pepper, MIB....$65.00
Doll, Pepper (Canadian version), MIB....$75.00
Doll, Pepper (carrot-colored hair), MIB....$75.00
Doll, Pepper (trimmer body & smaller face), MIB....$75.00
Doll, Pos 'N Dodi, M (decorated box)....$100.00
Doll, Pos 'N Dodi, M (plain box)....$75.00
Doll, Pos 'N Misty & Her Telephone Booth, MIB....$125.00
Doll, Pos'n Pepper, MIB....$75.00
Doll, Pos'n Pete, MIB....$125.00
Doll, Pos'n Salty, MIB....$125.00
Doll, Pos'n Tammy & Her Telephone Booth, MIB....$100.00
Doll, Pos'n Ted, MIB....$100.00
Doll, Tammy, MIB....$100.00

Doll, Tammy, straight-legged version with 'Switchables' outfit, doll only from $25.00 to $40.00; outfit only, from $30.00 to $45.00. (Photo courtesy Cindy Sabulis)

Doll, Tammy's Dad, MIB $65.00
Doll, Tammy's Mom, MIB $85.00
Doll, Ted, MIB $50.00
Outfit, Dad & Ted, pajamas & slippers, #9456-5, MIB......$20.00
Outfit, Dad & Ted, sports car coat & cap, #9467-2, NRFP..$20.00
Outfit, Dad & Ted, sweater, shorts & socks, #9476-3, MIP $25.00
Outfit, Day & Ted, blazer & slacks, #9477-1, NRFP..........$20.00
Outfit, Pepper, After School, #9318-7, complete, M $30.00
Outfit, Pepper, Anchors Away, #9316-1, complete, M $35.00
Outfit, Pepper, Flower Girl, #9332-8, complete, M............$50.00
Outfit, Pepper, Happy Holiday, #9317-9, complete, M......$40.00
Outfit, Pepper, Miss Gadabout, #9331-0, MIP..................$50.00
Outfit, Pepper & Dodi, Light & Lacy, #9305-4, MIP.........$45.00
Outfit, Pepper & Dodi, Sun 'N Surf, #9321-1, MIP...........$75.00
Outfit, Tammy, Beach Party, #9056-3 or #99-6-9, complete, M..$45.00
Outfit, Tammy, Career Girl, #9945-7, complete, M...........$75.00
Outfit, Tammy, Cutie Coed, #9132-2 or #9932-5, complete, M..$45.00
Outfit, Tammy, Jet Set, #9155-3 or #9943-2, MIP $100.00
Outfit, Tammy, Knit Knack, #9094-4 or #9917-6, complete, M..$25.00
Outfit, Tammy, Opening Night, #9954-9, MIP.............. $100.00
Outfit, Tammy, Private Secretary, #9939-0, MIP $135.00
Outfit, Tammy's Mom, Evening in Paris, #9421-9, complete, M.. $40.00
Outfit, Tammy's Mom, Lazy Days, #9418-5, MIP..............$50.00
Pak Clothing, afternoon dress & shoes, #9345-2, NRFP..$45.00
Pak Clothing, nightgown, sandals & 3-pc fruit set, #9242-9, NRFP $30.00
Pak Clothing, pedal pushers, orange juice, newspaper & hanger, #9224-7, NRFP..$30.00
Pak Clothing, sheath dress, blk belt, shoes & hanger, #9243-7, NRFP $45.00
Pak Clothing, short-sleeved blouse, red glasses & hanger, #9231-2, NRFP..$20.00
Pak Clothing, skirt, belt, handkerchief, date book & hanger, #9220-5, MIP..$30.00
Pak Clothing, skirt & hanger, #9221-3, NRFP $25.00
Pak Clothing, sleeveless blouse, necklace & hanger, #9222-1, NRFP $25.00
Pak Clothing, sweater, scarf & hanger, #9244-5, NRFP $25.00
Pepper's Jukebox, M..$65.00
Pepper's Pony, MIB $250.00
Pepper's Treehouse, MIB.. $125.00
Tammy & Ted Catamaran, MIB.................................... $200.00
Tammy Bubble Bath Set, NRFB..$75.00
Tammy Dress-Up Kit, Colorforms, 1964, complete, MIB.. $30.00
Tammy Hair Dryer, sq or rnd case, NM...............................$50.00
Tammy's Bed, Dresser & Chair, MIB...............................$65.00
Tammy's Car, MIB $75.00
Tammy's Ideal House, M, minimum value $100.00
Tammy's Magic Mirror Fasion Show, NRFB $50.00
Tammy's Jukebox $50.00

Tressy

American Character's Tressy doll was produced in this country from 1963 to 1967. The unique feature of this 11½" fashion doll was that her hair 'grew' by pushing a button on her stomach. Tressy also had a little (9") sister named Cricket. Numerous fashions and accessories were produced for these two dolls. Never-removed-from-box Tressy and Cricket items are rare, so unless indicated, values listed are for loose, mint items. A never-removed-from-box item's worth is at least double its loose value.

Advisor: Cindy Sabulis

Apartment.. $350.00
Beauty Salon $250.00
Case, Cricket, M $30.00
Case, Tressy $30.00
Doll, American Character Tressy, MIB $100.00

Doll, Pre-Teen Tressy, $30.00. (Photo courtesy Cindy Sabulis)

Doll, Tressy, orig outfit, MIB... $100.00
Doll, Tressy & Her Hi-Fashion Cosmetics, MIB............. $145.00
Doll, Tressy in Miss America Character Outfit, NM $65.00
Doll, Tressy in orig dress $35.00
Doll, Tressy w/Magic Make-Up Face, M $25.00
Doll Clothes Pattern..$10.00
Gift Pak w/Doll Clothing, NRFB, minimum value......... $100.00
Hair Accessory Pak, NRFB..$20.00
Hair Dryer $25.00
Hair or Cosmetic Accessory Kits, ea minimum value........$50.00
Millinery $200.00
Outfits, MOC, ea $40.00
Outfits, NRFB, ea minimum value $65.00

Upsy Downsys

The Upsy Downsy dolls were made by Mattel during the late 1960s. They were small, 2½" to 3½", made of vinyl and plastic. Some of the group were 'Upsies' that walked on their feet, while others were 'Downsies' that walked or rode fantasy animals while upsidedown.

Advisor: Dawn Diaz

Baby-So-High, #3828, complete, M $50.00
Downy Dilly, #3832, complete, M $50.00
Downy Dilly, #3832, NRFB $90.00
Flossy Glossy, #3827, doll & playland, EX $25.00
Funny Feeder, #3834, Gooey Chooey only, EX $25.00
Hairy Hurry Downsy Wizzer, #3838, complete, EX $100.00

The Happy Go Round Playset, with Tingle Dingle and Foozie Woozie dolls, complete in original box, from $95.00 to $175.00. (Photo courtesy Cindy Sabulis)

Miss Information, #3832, NRFB $90.00
Mother What Now, #3829, complete, EX $50.00
Pocus Hocus, #3820, complete, M $50.00
Pudgy Fudgy, #3826, NRFB $90.00
Tickle Pinkle & Her Bugabout Car, MIB, from $75 to $100.00

Farm Toys

It's entirely probable that more toy tractors have been sold than real ones. They've been made to represent all makes and models, of plastic, cast iron, diecast metal, and even wood. They've been made in at least 1/16th scale, 1/32nd, 1/43rd, and 1/64th. If you buy a 1/16th-scale replica, that small piece of equipment would have to be 16 times larger to equal the size of the real item. Limited editions (meaning that a specific number will be made and no more) and commemorative editions (made for special events) are usually very popular with collectors. Listings are Ertl unless noted otherwise.

See also Cast Iron, Farm; Diecast.

Allis-Chalmers Tractor D-21 w/Duals, #13078, 1/16 scale, MIB $39.00
Allis-Chalmers Tractor Hi-Crop D-19, #13403, 1/64 scale, MIB $39.00
Allis-Chalmers Tractor WD-45, #13080, 1/16 scale, MIB ..$23.50
Allis-Chalmers Tractor WD-45 Precision #7, #13101, 1/16 scale, MIB $118.00
Allis-Chalmers Tractor 7060, w/cab, #13185, 1/16 scale, MIB $35.00
Case IH Combine 2388, #14176, 1/64 scale, MIB $11.00
Case IH Cotton Express Picker, #4300, 1/64 scale, MIB ...$11.00
Case IH Planter 12-Row 900, #656, 1/64 scale, MIB $4.50
Case IH Round Baler, #274, 1/64 scale, MIB $3.25
Case IH Tillage Plow, #14172, 1/64 scale, MIB $32.50
Case IH Tractor Maxxum MX120, #4487, 1997 Farm Show, 1/16 scale, MIB $45.00
Case IH Tractor MX135, #1458, 1/64 scale, MIB $5.00
Case IH Tractor MX270, #14134, 1/64 scale, MIB $5.00
Case IH Tractor STX Tracked, #14046, 1/64 scale, MIB $8.00
Case IH Tractor 6670 Row Crop, #229, 1/64 scale, MIB $3.00
Case IH Tractor 9260 w/4-Wheel Drive, #231, 1/64 scale, 1993 Farm Show, MIB $9.00
Case Skid Steer Loader 90XT, #4216, 1/64 scale, MIB $25.00
Case Tractor STX3754 w/4-Wheel Drive, #14005, 1/16 scale, MIB $70.00
Case Tractor 930 Precision #12, #4284, 1/16 scale, MIB .. $107.00
Case Tractor 1930 Western SP Precision #15, #14130, 1/64 scale, MIB $116.00
Caterpillar Flotation Liquid Fertilizer Spreader, #2324, 1/64 scale, MIB $4.75

Cockshutt Golden Arrow Tractor, 1/16 scale, MIB, $60.00.

Deutz Allis Tractor 7085, #1260, 1/64 scale, 1990 Farm Show, MIB $11.00
Deutz Allis Tractor 9150 Orlando Show, #1280, 1/16 scale, MIB $200.00
Farmall Crawler 340, #4734, 1/16 scale, MIB $25.00
Farmall Tractor B, #14113, 1/16 scale, MIB $23.50
Farmall Tractor H, #4441, 1/16 scale, MIB $25.00
Farmall Tractor Super M, #14270, 1/16 scale, MIB $22.00
Farmall Tractor 400 Precision, #14007, 1/16 scale, MIB... $110.00

Farmall Tractor 560 w/Mount Picker & Wagon, #14073, 1/64 scale, MIB $10.50
Ford Tractor F, #872, 1/16 scale, Collector's Ed, MIB $45.00
Ford Tractor 8N, #843, 1/16 scale, MIB $20.00
Ford Tractor 621, #13529, 1/16 scale, MIB $22.00
Ford Tractor 640, #3054, 1/16 scale, MIB $22.00
Ford Tractor 640 Precision 8, #13574, 1/16 scale, MIB .. $112.00
Ford Tractor 641 w/Precision Series Loader, #383, 1/16 scale, MIB $135.00
Ford Tractor 4000, #3024, 1/64 scale, MIB $3.00
Ford Tractor 5000 Precision, #13503, 1/64 scale, MIB ... $117.00
Ford Tractor 5640 w/Loader, #334, 1/64 scale, MIB............$5.00
Ford Tractor 7740 Row Crop, #973, 1/16 scale, Collector's Ed, MIB $50.00
Ford Tractor 7740 w/Loader, #387, 1/64 scale, MIB............$5.00
Ford Tractor 8340 w/Duals, #388, 1/64 scale, MIB $3.50
Ford Tractor 8340 w/4 Wheel Drive, #877, 1/16 scale, Collector's Ed, MIB $50.00

Fordson Super Major Tractor, Ertl, 1/16 scale, MIB, $30.00.

Fordson Tractor, #13573, 1/16 scale, MIB $27.00
Heston Skid Steer Loader SL-30, #2267, 1/64 scale, MIB ..$42.50
IH Combine 815, #4354, 1/64 scale, MIB....................$10.50
IH Tractor 460 Precision #11, #4355, 1/16 scale, MIB ... $110.00
IH Tractor 756 w/Cab, #14124, 1/16 scale, MIB...............$35.00
IH Tractor 756 WF, #2308, 1/16 scale, MIB....................$31.00
IH Tractor 1456 Diesel w/Cab, #2311, 1/16 scale, MIB.....$31.00
IH Tractor 1466 Precision, #14204, 1/16 scale, MIB $125.00

International 1066 Tractor, MIB, $30.00.

John Deere Combine 95, #5819, 1/64 scale, MIB..............$10.00
John Deere Cotton Picker 9986, #15440, 1/64 scale, MIB ..$10.50
John Deere Crawler 40, #5072, 1/16 scale, MIB $27.00
John Deere Field Cultivator 2200, #15081, 1/64 scale, MIB... $8.00
John Deere Forage Blower Model 150, #5728, 1/64 scale, MIB $3.35
John Deere Forage Harvester, #566, 1/64 scale, MIB...........$3.00
John Deere Mower Conditioner, #5657, 1/64 scale, MIB....$3.00
John Deere Skid Steer Loader, Ertl, #569, 1/16 scale, MIB..$18.50
John Deere Sprayer, #15180, MIB....................$8.00
John Deere Sprayer, #5752, 1/64 scale, MIB....................$9.00
John Deere Tractor D, #5179, 1/16 scale, MIB $26.00
John Deere Tractor G, #5104, 1/16 scale, MIB $20.00
John Deere Tractor 70, #5611, 1/16 scale, MIB $21.00
John Deere Tractor 630 w/Corn Picker & Wagon, #15086, 1/16 scale, MIB $10.50
John Deere Tractor 4010, #5716, 1/16 scale, MIB $25.00
John Deere Tractor 4040, #5133, 1/16 scale, MIB $30.00
John Deere Tractor 8200, #5064, 1/64 scale, MIB $3.50
John Deere Utility Tractor w/Loader, #517, 1/16 scale, MIB .. $22.00
John Deere Wing Disk, #5615, 1/64 scale, MIB...................$3.25
Massey-Ferguson Tractor 1155, #13170, 1/16 scale, MIB ..$43.00
Massey-Ferguson Tractor 3070 w/Front-Wheel Drive, #1107, 1/64 scale, MIB $3.50
Massey-Ferguson Tractor 3070 w/Loader, #1109, 1/64 scale, MIB $5.00
Massey-Ferguson Tractor 3140 w/Front-Wheel Drive, #1107, 1/64 scale, MIB $3.50
Massey-Ferguson Tractor 8280 w/Duals, #1352, 1/64 scale, MIB.................... $5.85
New Holand Box Spreader, #308, 1/64 scale, MIB $3.00
New Holland Combine CR960, #1395, 1/64 scale, MIB...$11.00
New Holland Hay Rake, #369, 1/64 scale, MIB...................$2.65
New Holland Skid Loader LS170, #13562, 1/64 scale, MIB..$4.00
New Holland Tractor TG-255, #13617, 1/64 scale, MIB.....$5.00
New Holland Tractor TM-150 w/4-Wheel Drive, #13560, 1/16 scale, MIB $40.00
New Holland Tractor 7840 w/Loader, #13588, 1/16 scale, MIB.. $48.00
New Holland Tractor 8560, #3032, 1/43 scale, MIB..........$11.00
New Holland Wing Disk, #3049, 1/64 scale, MIB $4.00
Oliver Crawler HG, #13079, 1/16 scale, MIB....................$22.00
Oliver Tractor 1655 w/Cab, #13186, 1/16 scale, MIB........$35.00
Oliver Tractor 88 w/Mounted Picker & Wagon, #13051, 1/64 scale, MIB $10.50

Oliver Tractor 77, Silk-Toy, aluminum, with driver, 8", EXIB, A, $575.00. (Photo courtesy Morphy Auctions)

Fisher-Price

Fisher-Price toys are becoming one of the hottest new trends in the collector's marketplace today. In 1930 Herman Fisher, backed by Irving Price, Elbert Hubbard, and Helen Schelle, formed one of the most successful toy companies ever to exist. Located in East Aurora, New York, the company has seen many changes since then, the most notable being the changes in ownership. From 1930 to 1968, it was owned by the individuals mentioned previously and a few stockholders. In 1969 it became an aquisition of Quaker Oats, and in June of 1991 it became independently owned. In November of 1993, one of the biggest sell-outs in the toy industry took place: Fisher-Price became a subdivision of Mattel.

There are a few things to keep in mind when collecting Fisher-Price toys. You should count on a little edge wear as well as some wear and fading to the paint. Pull toys found in mint condition are truly rare and command a much higher value, especially if you find one with its original box. This also applies to playsets, but to command higher prices, they must also be complete, with no chew/teeth marks or plastic fading. Another very important rule to remember is there are no standard colors for pieces that came with a playset. Fisher-Price often substituted a piece of a different color when they ran short. Please note that the dates on the toys indicate their copyright date and not the date they were manufactured.

The company put much time and thought into designing their toys. They took care to operate by their five-point creed: to make toys with (1) intrinsic play value, (2) ingenuity, (3) strong construction, (4) good value for the money, and (5) action. Some of the most sought-after pull toys are those bearing the Walt Disney logo. For more information, we reccomend *Fisher-Price, A Historical Rarity Value Guide*, by John J. Murray and Bruce R. Fox.

Additional information may be obtained through the Fisher-Price Collectors' Club who publish a quarterly newsletter; their address may be found in the Directory under Clubs, Newsletters, and Other Publications.

Note: With the ever increasing influence of the Internet it is becoming harder and harder to establish book value. A toy can sell for 100% more than the book value or 75% less on the Internet. The prices we have listed here are for toys in excellent condition unless noted otherwise.

See also Building Blocks and Construction Toys; Catalogs; Character, TV, and Movie Collectibles; Dollhouse Furniture; Dollhouses; Dolls; Optical Toys; other specific categories.

#5 Bunny Cart, 1948-49 .... $80.00
#6 Ducky Cart, 1948-49 .... $50.00
#7 Doggy Racer, 1942-43 .... $150.00
#7 Looky Fire Truck, 1950-53 & Easter 1954 .... $130.00
#8 Bouncy Racer, 1960-62 .... $45.00
#12 Bunny Truck, 1941-42 .... $65.00
#14 Ducky Daddles, 1941 .... $50.00
#20 Animal Cutouts, 1942-46, duck, elephant, pony or Scotty dog, ea $50.00
#28 Bunny Egg Cart, 1950 .... $75.00
#50 Bunny Chick Tandem Cart, 1953-54, no number on toy $50.00
#51 Ducky Cart, 1950 .... $50.00
#52 Rabbit Cart, 1950 .... $30.00
#100 Dr Doodle, 1931 .... $550.00
#100 Dr Doodle, 1995, Fisher-Price limited edition of 5,000, 1st in series $50.00
#100 Musical Sweeper, 1950-52, plays Whistle While You Work $60.00
#101 Granny Doodle & Family, 1931-32 .... $600.00

#101 Granny Doodle & Family, 1931 – 1932, NM, $1,800.00. (Photo courtesy Morphy Auctions)

#102 Drummer Bear, 1931 .... $500.00
#102 Drummer Bear, 1932-33, fatter & taller version $500.00
#103 Barky Puppy, 1931-33 .... $500.00
#104 Lookee Monk, 1931 .... $500.00

#104 Lookee Monk, 1931, VG, A, $400.00. (Photo courtesy Morphy Auctions)

#109 Lucky Monk, 1932-33 .... $400.00
#110 Chubby Chief, 1932-33 .... $500.00
#111 Play Family Merry-Go-Round, 1972-77, plays Skater's Waltz, w/4 figures $30.00
#112 Picture Disk Camera, 1968-71, w/5 picture disks $20.00
#114 Sesame Street Music Box TV, 1984-87, plays People in Your Neighborhood $1.00
#120 Cackling Hen, 1958-66, wht $35.00
#120 Gabby Goose, 1936-37 & Easter 1938 .... $350.00
#121 Happy Hopper, 1969-76 .... $10.00
#123 Cackling Hen, 1966-68, red litho $35.00

#123 Roller Chime, 1953-60 & Easter 1961 ....$30.00
#124 Roller Chime, 1961-62 & Easter 1963 ....$25.00
#125 Music Box Iron, 1966, aqua w/yel hdl $40.00
#125 Music Box Iron, 1966-69, wht w/red hdl..................$30.00
#125 Uncle Timmy Turtle, 1956-58 ....$50.00
#130 Wobbles, 1964-67, dog wobbles when pulled............$35.00
#131 Toy Wagon, 1951-54... $225.00
#135 Play Family Animal Circus, 1974-76, complete.........$60.00
#136 Play Family Lacing Shoe, 1965-69, complete $60.00
#138 Jack-in-the-Box Puppet, 1970-73 ....$20.00
#139 Tuggy Turtle, 1959-60 & Easter 1961 ....$75.00
#140 Katy Kackler, 1954-56 & Easter 1957 ....$75.00
#141 Snap-Quack, 1947-49 .... $200.00
#142 Three Men in a Tub, 1970-73, w/bell.........................$10.00
#142 Three Men in a Tub, 1974-75, w/flag $5.00
#145 Humpty Dump Truck, 1963-64 & Easter 1965 ....$35.00
#145 Husky Dump Truck, 1961-62 & Easter 1963.............$30.00
#145 Musical Elephant, 1948-50 .... $175.00
#146 Pull-A-Long Lacing Shoe, 1970-73, w/6 figures........$50.00
#148 Ducky Daddles, 1942 .... $200.00
#148 Jack & Jill TV Radio, 1959 & Easter 1960, wood & plastic $30.00
#149 Dog Cart Donald, 1936-37 .... $575.00
#150 Barky Buddy, 1934-35 .... $500.00

#150 Barky Buddy, 1934, NM, $1,000.00. (Photo courtesy Morphy Auctions)

#150 Pop-Up-Pal Chime Phone, 1968-78.........................$15.00
#150 Teddy Tooter, 1940-41 .... $225.00
#150 Timmy Turtle, 1953-55 & Easter 1956, gr shell, ... $75.00
#151 Goldilocks & the Three Bears Playhouse, 1967-71.....$40.00
#151 Happy Hippo, 1962-63 .... $100.00
#152 Road Roller, 1934-35 .... $525.00
#154 Frisky Frog, 1971-83, squeeze plastic bulb & frog jumps $10.00
#155 Moo-oo Cow, 1958-61 & Easter 1962 .... $130.00
#155 Skipper Sam, 1934... $850.00
#156 Baa-Baa Black Sheep TV-Radio, 1966-67, wood & plastic... $50.00
#156 Circus Wagon, 1942-44, band leader in wagon...... $500.00
#156 Jiffy Dump Truck, 1971-73, squeeze bulb & dump moves $15.00
#158 Katie Kangaroo, 1976-77, squeeze bulb & she hops....$15.00
#158 Little Boy Blue TV-Radio, 1967, wood & plastic......$50.00
#159 Ten Little Indians TV-Radio, 1961-65 & Easter 1966, wood & plastic...$20.00
#160 Donald & Donna Duck, 1937 .... $700.00
#161 Creative Block Wagon, 1961-64, 18 building blocks & 6 wooden dowels fit into pull-along wagon...................$60.00
#161 Looky Chug-Chug, 1949-52 .... $175.00
#161 Old Woman Who Lived in a Shoe TV-Radio, 1968-70, wood & plastic w/see-through window on back..........$30.00
#164 Mother Goose, 1964-66..$30.00
#166 Bucky Burro, 1955-57 .... $200.00
#166 Farmer in the Dell TV-Radio, 1963-66 ....$30.00
#166 Piggy Bank, 1981-82, pk plastic...............................$10.00

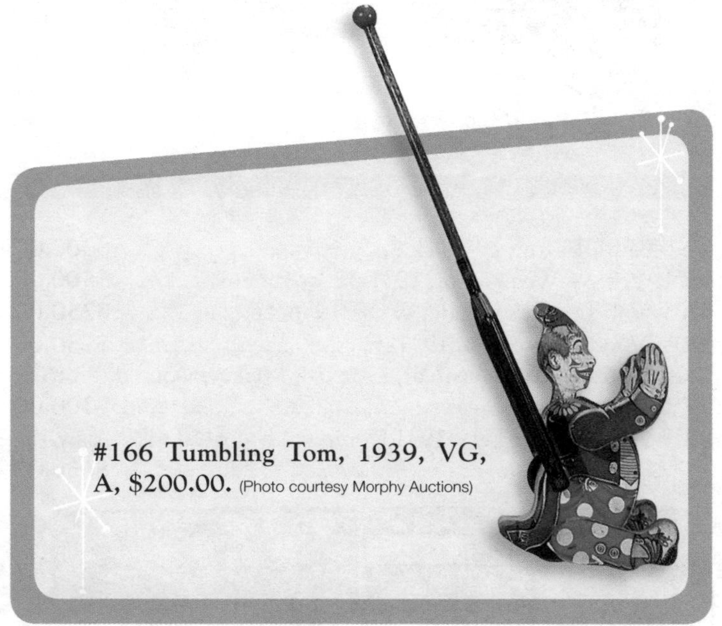
#166 Tumbling Tom, 1939, VG, A, $200.00. (Photo courtesy Morphy Auctions)

#168 Snorky Fire Engine, 1960 & Easter 1961, gr litho.... $175.00
#170 Change-A-Tune Carousel, 1981-83, music box w/crank hdl, 3 molded records & 3 figures $20.00
#171 Toy Wagon, 1942-47.. $250.00
#175 Gold Star Stagecoach, 1954-55 & Easter 1956...... $250.00
#175 Kicking Donkey, 1937-38 .... $425.00
#175 Winnie the Pooh TV-Radio, 1971-73, Sears only $35.00
#177 Donald Duck Xylophone, 1946-52, 2nd version w/'Donald Duck' on hat $325.00
#177 Oscar the Grouch, 1977-84 ....$10.00
#178 What's in My Pocket Cloth Book, 1972-74, boy's version...$20.00
#179 What's in My Pocket Cloth Book, 1972-74, girl's version...$20.00
#180 Snoopy Sniffer, 1938-55 .... $125.00
#183 Play Family Fun Jet, 1970, 1st version.......................$20.00
#185 Donald Duck Xylophone, 1938, mk WDE............ $500.00
#189 Looky Chug-Chug, 1958-60 .... $100.00
#190 Gabby Duck, 1939-40 & Easter 1941 .... $350.00
#190 Molly Moo-Moo, 1956 & Easter 1957 ....$75.00
#191 Golden Gulch Express, 1961 & Easter 1962............. $100.00
#192 Playland Express, 1962 & Easter 1963 .... $100.00
#192 School Bus, 1965 ....$50.00

#195 Peek-A-Boo Screen Music Box, 1965-68, plays 'Mary Had a Little Lamb'....................$25.00
#195 Teddy Bear Parade, 1938.................... $825.00

#195 Teddy Bear Parade, 1938, EX, A, $750.00. (Photo courtsey Morphy Auctions)

#198 Band Wagon, 1940-41.................... $300.00
#201 Woodsy-Wee Circus, 1931-32, complete.................... $500.00
#205 Walt Disney's Parade, WDE, 1936-41.................... $250.00
#205 Woodsy-Wee Zoo, 1931-32.................... $750.00
#207 Walt Disney's Carnival, 1936-38, Mickey, Donald, Pluto or Elmer, complete, ea.................... $300.00
#207 Woodsy-Wee Pets, 1931, complete w/goat, donkey, cow, pig & cart.................... $650.00

#207 Woodsy-Wee Pets, 1931, NMIB, A, $1,900.00. (Photo courtesy Morphy Auctions)

#208 Donald Duck, 1936-38.................... $175.00
#209 Woodsy-Wee Dog Show, 1932, complete w/5 dogs.....$500.00
#210 Pluto the Pup, 1936-38.................... $150.00
#211 Elmer Elephant, 1936-38.................... $175.00
#215 Fisher-Price Choo-Choo, 1955-57, engine w/3 cars..$75.00
#225 Wheel Horse, 1935 & Easter 1936.................... $500.00
#234 Nifty Station Wagon, 1960-62 & Easter 1963, removable roof.................... $250.00
#237 Riding Horse, 1936.................... $425.00
#250 Big Performing Circus, 1932-38.................... $500.00
#301 Bunny Basket Cart, 1957-59....................$35.00
#302 Chick Basket Cart, 1957-59....................$40.00
#302 Husky Dump Truck, 1978-84....................$15.00
#303 Adventure People Emergency Rescue Truck, 1975-78..$15.00
#303 Bunny Push Cart, 1957....................$50.00
#304 Adventure People Wild Safari Set, 1975-78....................$50.00
#304 Running Bunny Cart, 1957....................$50.00
#305 Adventure People Air-Sea Rescue Copter, 1975-80.$10.00
#305 Walking Duck Cart, 1957-64....................$40.00
#306 Bizzy Bunny Cart, 1957-59....................$40.00
#307 Adventure People Wilderness Patrol, 1975-79....................$30.00
#307 Bouncing Bunny Cart, 1961-63 & Easter 1964....................$35.00
#309 Adventure People TV Action Team, 1977-78....................$50.00
#310 Adventure People Sea Explorer, 1975-80....................$20.00
#310 Mickey Mouse Puddle Jumper, 1953-55 & Easter 1956....$115.00
#311 Bulldozer, 1976-77....................$15.00
#311 Husky Bulldozer, 1978-79....................$15.00
#312 Adventure People Northwoods Trail Blazer, 1977-82..$20.00
#312 Running Bunny Cart, 1960-64....................$40.00
#313 Husky Roller Grader, 1978-80....................$15.00
#314 Husky Boom Crane, 1978-82....................$25.00
#314 Queen Buzzy Bee, 1956-58....................$25.00
#315 Husky Cement Mixer, 1978-82....................$15.00
#316 Husky Tow Truck, 1978-80....................$15.00
#317 Husky Construction Crew, 1978-80....................$20.00
#318 Adventure People Daredevil Sports Van, 1978-82..$25.00
#319 Husky Hook & Ladder Truck, 1979-85....................$20.00
#320 Husky Race Car Rig, 1979-82....................$20.00
#322 Adventure People Dune Buster, 1979-82....................$10.00
#325 Adventure People Alpha Probe, 1980-84....................$20.00
#325 Buzzy Bee, 1950-56, 1st version, yel & blk litho, wooden wheels & antenna tips....................$25.00
#326 Adventure People Alpha Star, 1983-84....................$20.00
#327 Husky Load Master Dump, 1984....................$20.00
#328 Husky Highway Dump Truck, 1980-84....................$20.00
#329 Husky Dozer Loader, 1980-84....................$15.00

#331 Husky Farm Set, 1981 – 1983, EX, $20.00. (Photo courtesy Brad Cassity)

#332, Husky Police Patrol, 1981-84....................$15.00
#333 Butch the Pup, 1951-53 & Easter 1954....................$55.00
#334 Adventure People Sea Shark, 1981-84....................$20.00
#336 Husky Fire Pumper, 1983-84....................$15.00
#337 Husky Rescue Rig, 1982-83....................$20.00
#338 Husky Power Tow Truck, 1982-84....................$20.00
#339 Husky Power & Light Service Rig, 1983-84....................$30.00
#344 Copter Rig, 1981-84....................$10.00
#345 Boat Rig, 1981-84....................$10.00

#345 Penelope the Performing Penguin, 1935, w/up $800.00
#350 Adventure People Rescue Team, 1976-79................. $15.00
#350 Go 'N Back Mule, 1931-33, w/up.......................... $425.00
#351 Adventure People Mountain Climbers, 1976-79............. $15.00
#352 Adventure People Construction Workers, 1976-79.. $15.00
#353 Adventure People Scuba Divers, 1976-81................. $15.00
#354 Adventure People Daredevil Skydiver, 1977-81............ $10.00
#355 Adventure People White Water Kayak, 1977-80............ $10.00
#355 Go 'N Back Bruno, 1931 .... $425.00
#356 Adventure People Cycle Racing Team, 1977-81............. $10.00
#358 Adventure People Deep Sea Diver, 1980-84............. $10.00
#360 Adventure People Alpha Recon, 1982-84 .... $10.00
#360 Go 'N Back Jumbo, 1931-34, w/up......................... $425.00

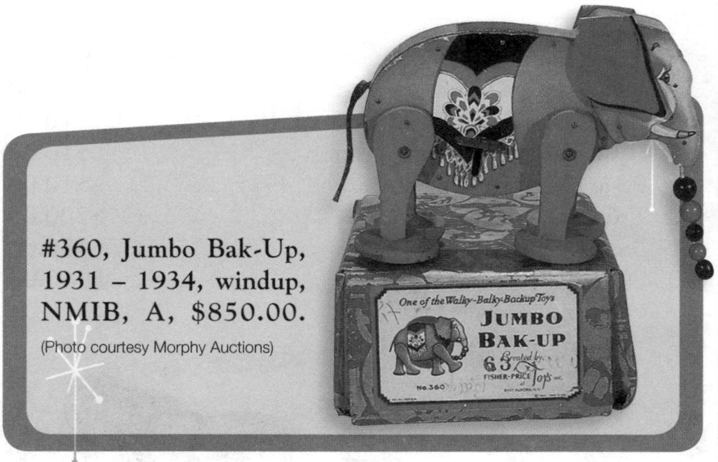

#360, Jumbo Bak-Up, 1931 – 1934, windup, NMIB, A, $850.00. (Photo courtesy Morphy Auctions)

#365 Puppy Back-up, 1932-36, w/up $800.00
#367 Adventure People Turbo Hawk, 1982-83.................. $10.00
#368 Adventure People Alpha Interceptor, 1982-83 .... $10.00
#369 Adventure People Ground Shaker, 1982-83 .... $10.00
#375 Adventure People Sky Surfer, 1978........................ $25.00
#375 Bruno Back-Up, 1932 .... $800.00
#377 Adventure People Astro Knight, 1979-80 .... $15.00
#400 Tailspin Tabby, 1931-38.. $200.00
#401 Push Bunny Cart, 1942... $200.00
#404 Bunny Egg Cart, 1949... $50.00
#405 Lofty Lizzy Pop-Up Kritter, 1931-33...................... $200.00
#407 Chick Cart, 1950-53.. $50.00
#407 Dizzy Dino Pop-Up Kritter, 1931-32 .... $225.00
#410 Stoopy Stork Pop-Up Kritter, 1931-32.................. $225.00

#415 Lop-Ear Looie Pop-Up Kritter, 1934, EX, $225.00. (Photo courtesy Brad Cassity)

#415 Super Jet, 1952 & Easter 1953.............................. $200.00
#420 Sunny Fish, 1955 .... $125.00
#422 Jumbo Jitterbug Pop-Up Kritter, 1940...................... $75.00
#425 Donald Duck Pop-Up, 1938 & Easter 1939 .... $350.00
#433 Dizzy Donkey Pop-Up Kritter, 1939 .... $100.00

#434 Ferdinand the Bull, 1939, EX, A, $950.00. (Photo courtesy Morphy Auctions)

#440 Goofy Gertie Pop-Up Kritter, 1935........................ $225.00
#440 Pluto Pop-Up, 1936, mk WDP $75.00
#444 Fuzzy Fido, 1941-42.. $225.00
#444 Puffy Engine, 1951-54... $50.00
#444 Queen Buzzy Bee, 1959, red litho............................ $30.00
#445 Hot Dog Wagon, 1940-41.. $200.00
#445 Nosey Pup, 1956-58 & Easter 1959........................... $30.00
#447 Woofy Wagger, 1947-48.. $50.00
#450 Donald Duck Choo-Choo, 1941 .... $325.00
#450 Donald Duck Choo-Choo, 1942-45 & Easter 1949 .... $100.00
#450 Kiltie Dog, 1936... $350.00
#454 Donald Duck Drummer, 1949-50 .... $275.00
#455 Tailspin Tabby Pop-Up Kritter, 1939-42 .... $225.00
#456 Bunny & Container, 1939-40................................. $225.00
#460 Dapper Donald Duck, 1936-37.............................. $200.00
#460 Suzie Seal, 1961-63 & Easter 1964........................... $20.00
#461 Duck Cart, 1938-39 .... $225.00
#462 Busy Bunny, 1937... $200.00
#465 Teddy Choo-Choo, 1937 .... $225.00
#466 Busy Bunny Cart, 1941-44.. $75.00
#469 Donald Duck Cart, 1940.. $225.00
#469 Rooster Cart, 1938-40 .... $100.00
#470 Tricky Tommy, 1936 .... $350.00
#472 Jingle Giraffe, 1956.. $175.00
#472 Peter Bunny Cart, 1939-40..................................... $125.00
#473 Merry Mutt, 1949-54 & Easter 1955 .... $75.00
#474 Bunny Racer, 1942.. $135.00
#476 Cookie Pig, 1966-70 .... $40.00
#476 Mickey Mouse Drummer, 1941-45 & Easter 1946..... $275.00
#476 Rooster Pop-Up Kritter, 1936.................................. $250.00
#477 Dr Doodle, 1940-41 .... $275.00
#478 Pudgy Pig, 1962-64 & Easter 1965 .... $40.00
#479 Donald Duck & Nephews, 1941-42 .... $400.00
#479 Peter Pig, 1959-61 & Easter 1962.............................. $40.00
#480 Leo the Drummer, 1952 & Easter 1953.................. $225.00

#480 Teddy Station Wagon, 1942 .... $200.00
#485 Mickey Mouse Choo-Choo, 1949-54, new litho version of #432 .... $100.00
#488 Popeye Spinach Eater, 1939-40 .... $625.00
#491 Boom-Boom Popeye $575.00

#491 Boom-Boom Popeye, 1937, NM, $950.00. (Photo courtesy Morphy Auctions)

#494 Pinocchio, 1939-40 .... $600.00
#495 Running Bunny Cart, 1941 .... $200.00
#495 Sleepy Sue Turtle, 1962-63 & Easter 1964 .... $40.00
#499 Kitty Bell, 1950-51 .... $100.00
#500 Donald Duck Cart, 1937, unpnt wheels $375.00
#500 Donald Duck Cart, 1951-53 .... $350.00
#500 Pick-Up & Peek Puzzle, 1972-86 .... $10.00
#500 Pushy Pig, 1932-35 .... $650.00

#500 Pushy Piggy, 1932, NMIB, A, $4,250.00. (Photo courtesy Morphy Auctions)

#502 Action Bunny Cart, 1949 .... $200.00
#503 Pick-Up & Peek Wood Puzzle, Occupations, 1972-76 . $10.00
#505 Bunny Drummer, 1946, bell on front $175.00
#507 Pushy Doodle, 1933 .... $575.00
#510 Pick-Up & Peek Wood Puzzle, Nursery Rhymes, 1972-81 .... $10.00
#510 Strutter Donald Duck, 1941 .... $150.00
#512 Bunny Drummer, 1942 .... $175.00
#515 Pushy Pat, 1933-35 .... $550.00
#517 Choo-Choo Local, 1936 .... $375.00
#517 Pick-Up & Piece Wood Puzzle, Animal Friends, 1977-84 .... $10.00
#520 Bunny Bell Cart, 1941 .... $150.00
#520 Pick-Up & Peek Puzzle, Three Little Pigs, 1979-84 .. $15.00
#525 Cotton Tail Cart, 1940 .... $175.00
#525 Pushy Elephant, 1934-35 .... $425.00
#530 Mickey Mouse Band, 1935-36 .... $775.00
#533 Thumper Bunny, 1942 .... $250.00
#544 Donald Duck Cart, 1942-44 .... $300.00
#549 Toy Lunch Kit, 1962-79, red w/barn litho, w/thermos . $25.00
#550 Toy Lunch Kit, 1957, red, wht & gr plastic barn shape, no litho $40.00
#552 Basic Hardboard Puzzle, Nature or any other, 1974-75, MIB, ea from $10 to $15.00
#563 Basic Hardboard Puzzle, Weather, 1975 .... $10.00
#568 Basic Hardboard Puzzle, bear on log $10.00
#569 Basic Hardboard Puzzle, Airport, 1975 .... $10.00
#600 Tailspin Tabby Pop-Up, 1947 .... $200.00
#604 Bunny Bell Cart, 1954-55 .... $50.00
#605 Donald Duck Cart, 1954-56 .... $150.00

#605 Horse and Wagon, 1933, NM, A, $950.00. (Photo courtesy Morphy Auctions)

#605 Woodsey Major Goodgrub Mole & Book, 1981-82, 32 pgs $15.00
#606 Woodsey Bramble Beaver & Book, 1981-82, 32 pgs .. $15.00
#607 Woodsey Very Blue Bird & Book, 1981-82, 32 pgs .. $15.00
#615 Tow Truck, 1960-61 & Easter 1962 .... $65.00
#616 Chuggy Pop-Up, 1955-56 .... $75.00
#616 Patch Pony, 1963-64 & Easter 1965 .... $25.00
#617 Prancy Pony, 1965-70 .... $25.00
#621 Suzie Seal, 1965-66, ball on nose $30.00
#623 Suzie Seal, 1964-65, umbrella on nose $30.00
#625 Playful Puppy, 1961-62 & Easter 1963, w/shoe $50.00
#629 Fisher-Price Tractor, 1962-68 .... $30.00
#630 Fire Truck, 1959-62 .... $45.00
#634 Drummer Boy, 1967-69 .... $60.00
#634 Tiny Teddy, 1955-57 .... $50.00
#637 Milk Carrier, 1966-85 .... $15.00
#640 Wiggily Woofer, 1957-58 & Easter 1958 .... $75.00
#641 Toot Toot Engine, 1962-63 & Easter 1964, bl litho .. $60.00
#642 Bob-Along Bear, 1979-84 .... $5.00
#642 Dinky Engine, 1959, blk litho $60.00

#642 Smokie Engine, 1960-61 & Easter 1962, blk litho............ $60.00
#649 Stake Truck, 1960-61 & Easter 1962........................$50.00
#653 Allie Gator, 1960-61 & Easter 1962.........................$75.00
#654 Tawny Tiger, 1962 & Easter 1963............................$75.00
#656 Bossy Bell, 1960 & Easter 1961, w/bonnet...............$50.00
#656 Bossy Bell, 1961-63, no bonnet, new litho design..$40.00
#657 Crazy Clown Fire Brigade, 1983-84..........................$45.00
#658 Lady Bug, 1961-62 & Easter 1963 ....$50.00
#662 Merry Mousewife, 1962-64 & Easter 1965 ....$45.00
#663 Play Family, 1966-70, tan dog, MIP....................... $170.00
#674 Sports Car, 1958-60 ....$75.00
#677 Picnic Basket, 1975-79 ....$20.00
#678 Kriss Kricket, 1955-57 ....$50.00
#679 Little People Garage Squad, 1984-90, MIP...............$15.00
#684 Little Lamb, 1964-65 ....$45.00
#685 Car & Boat, 1968-69, wood & plastic, 5 pcs............$50.00
#686 Car & Camper, 1968-70 ....$50.00
#686 Perky Pot, 1958-59 & Easter 1960 ....$50.00
#694 Suzie Seal, 1979-80...$10.00
#695 Pinky Pig, 1956-57, wooden eyes $75.00
#695 Pinky Pig, 1958, litho eyes...$75.00
#698 Talky Parrot, 1963 & Easter 1964.............................$50.00
#700 Cowboy Chime, 1951-53... $125.00

#700 Popeye, 1935, VG, A, $600.00. (Photo courtesy Morphy Auctions)

#700 Popeye, 1935 .... $700.00
#700 Woofy Wowser, 1940 & Easter 1941 .... $125.00
#703 Bunny Engine, 1954-56 ....$50.00
#703 Popeye the Sailor, 1936 .... $825.00
#705 Mini Snowmobile, 1971-73 ....$40.00
#705 Popeye Cowboy, 1937 .... $700.00
#710 Scotty Dog, 1933 .... $375.00
#711 Cry Baby Bear, 1967-69 ....$15.00
#711 Huckleberry Hound, 1961, Sears only.................... $200.00
#711 Raggedy Ann & Andy, 1941 ....$1,100.00
#711 Teddy Trucker, 1949-51 .... $125.00
#712 Fred Flintstone Xylophone, 1962, Sears only............ $250.00
#712 Johnny Jumbo, 1933-35 .... $525.00
#712 Teddy Tooter, 1957-58 & Easter 1959 .... $200.00
#714 Mickey Mouse Xylophone, 1963, Sears only.......... $175.00

#715 Ducky Flip Flap, 1964-65...$50.00

#717 Ducky Flip Flap, 1937, NM, $350.00. (Photo courtesy Morphy Auctions)

#718 Tow Truck & Car, 1969-70, wood & plastic $45.00
#719 Busy Bunny Cart, 1936-37..................................... $275.00
#720 Pinnochio Express, 1939-40 .... $625.00
#721 Peter Bunny Engine, 1949-51 .... $150.00
#722 Racing Bunny Cart, 1937 .... $175.00
#722 Running Bunny, 1938-40.. $225.00
#723 Bouncing Bunny Cart, 1936 .... $175.00
#724 Ding-Dong Ducky, 1949-50..................................... $200.00
#725 Musical Mutt, 1935-36 .... $375.00
#725 Play Family Bath/Utility Room Set, 1972................$10.00
#726 Play Family Patio Set, 1970-73...................................$10.00
#727 Bouncing Bunny Wheelbarrow, 1939.................... $425.00
#728 Buddy Bullfrog, 1959-60, yel body w/red coat $50.00
#728 Pound & Saw Bench, 1966-67 ....$30.00
#730 Racing Rowboat, 1952-53 .... $150.00
#732 Happy Hauler, 1968-70...$20.00
#733 Mickey Mouse Safety Patrol, 1956-57................... $250.00
#734 Teddy Zilo, 1964, no coat $40.00
#734 Teddy Zilo, 1965-66, w/coat $55.00
#735 Juggling Jumbo, 1958-59... $225.00
#737 Galloping Horse & Wagon, 1948-49...................... $175.00
#737 Ziggy Zilo, 1958-59 .... $550.00
#738 Shaggy Zilo, 1960-61 & Easter 1962 ....$75.00

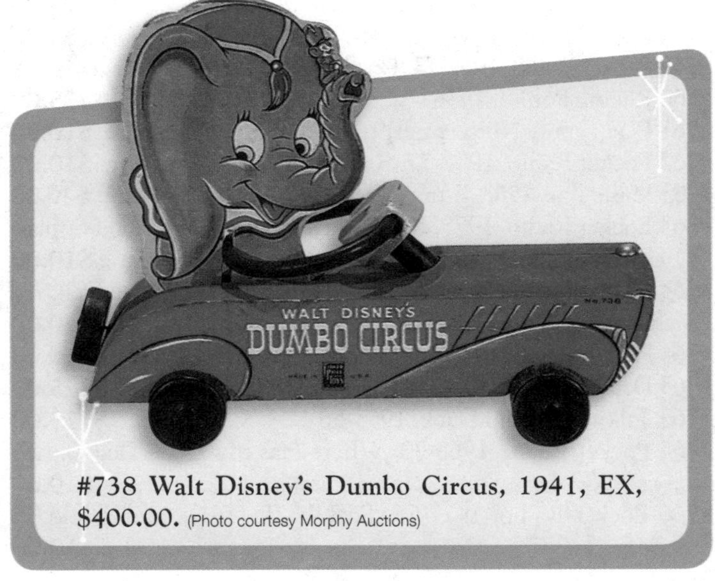

#738 Walt Disney's Dumbo Circus, 1941, EX, $400.00. (Photo courtesy Morphy Auctions)

#738 Walt Disney's Circus Racer, 1941 & Easter 1942 .... $400.00
#739 Poodle Zilo, 1962-63 & Easter 1964..........................$50.00
#741 Teddy Zilo, 1967 ....$35.00
#741 Trotting Donald Duck, 1937................................. $575.00
#742 Dashing Dobbin, 1938-40....................................... $425.00
#744 Doughboy Donald, 1942... $575.00
#745 Elsie's Dairy Truck, 1948-49, w/2 bottles................ $600.00

#745 Elsie's Dairy Truck, 1948 – 1949, with two bottles, VG, A, $450.00. (Photo courtesy Morphy Auctions)

#746 Pocket Radio, 1977-78, It's a Small World, wood & plastic $10.00
#747 Chatter Telephone, 1962-67, wooden wheels $25.00
#747 Talk-Back Telephone, 1961 & Easter 1962...............$75.00
#749 Egg Truck, 1947 .... $225.00
#750 Hot Dog Wagon, 1938.. $300.00
#750 Space Blazer, 1953-54 .... $175.00
#755 Jumbo Rolo, 1951-52 .... $225.00
#756 Pocket Radio, 1973, 12 Days of Christmas, wood & plastic $25.00
#757 Howdy Bunny, 1939-40 .... $325.00
#757 Humpty Dumpty, 1957 & Easter 1958 .... $250.00
#757 Snappy-Quacky, 1950.. $200.00
#758 Pocket Radio, 1970-72, Mulberry Bush, wood & plastic..$10.00
#758 Pony Chime, 1948-50.. $175.00
#758 Push-Along Clown, 1980-81 ....$5.00
#759 Pocket Radio, 1969-73, Do-Re-Me, wood & plastic ...$10.00
#760 Racing Ponies, 1936... $425.00
#761 Play Family Nursery Set, 1973.................................$10.00
#762 Pocket Radio, 1972-77, Raindrops, wood & plastic..$10.00
#763 Music Box, 1962, Farmer in the Dell, yel litho $40.00
#763 Pocket Radio, 1978, I Whistle a Happy Tune, wood & plastic $10.00
#764 Music Box, 1960-61 & Easter 1962, Farmer in the Dell, red litho...$40.00
#764 Pocket Radio, 1975-76, My Name Is Michael............$10.00
#765 Dandy Dobbin, 1941-44 .... $275.00
#765 Talking Donald Duck, 1955-58 .... $125.00
#766 Pocket Radio, 1968-70, Where Has My Little Dog Gone?, wood & plastic...$10.00
#766 Pocket Radio, 1977-78, I'd Like To Teach the World To Sing $10.00

#767 Pocket Radio, 1977, Twinkle Twinkle Little Star $25.00
#768 Pocket Radio, 1971-76, Happy Birthday, wood & plastic... $10.00
#770 Doc & Dopey Dwarfs, 1938................................. $850.00

#770 Dopey and Doc, 1938, G, $550.00. (Photo courtesy Morphy Auctions)

#772 Pocket Radio, 1974-76, Jack & Jill...........................$10.00
#775 Gabby Goofies, 1956-59 & Easter 1960 ....$25.00
#775 Pocket Radio, 1967-68, Sing a Song of Six Pence, wood & plastic $10.00
#775 Teddy Drummer, 1936 .... $325.00
#777 Squeaky the Clown, 1958-59 .... $225.00

#778 Ice-Cream Wagon, 1940, EX, $300.00. (Photo courtesy Morphy Auctions)

#779 Pocket Radio, 1976, Yankee Doodle, wood & plastic ..$15.00
#780 Jumbo Xylophone, 1937-38................................. $250.00
#780 Snoopy Sniffer, 1955-57 & Easter 1958 ....$50.00
#784 Mother Goose Music Chart, 1955-56 & Easter 1957..$50.00
#785 Blackie Drummer, 1939 .... $525.00
#788 Rock-A-Bye Bunny Cart, 1940-41 .... $200.00
#789 Lift & Load Road Builders, 1978-82.........................$15.00
#793 Jolly Jumper, 1963-64 & Easter 1965 ....$30.00
#794 Big Bill Pelican, 1961-63, w/cb fish $100.00
#795 Mickey Mouse Drummer, 1937............................ $300.00
#795 Musical Duck, 1952-54 & Easter 1955.......................$75.00
#798 Chatter Monk, 1957-58 & Easter 1959.......................$75.00
#798 Mickey Mouse Xylophone, 1939, w/hat $250.00
#798 Mickey Mouse Xylophone, 1942, no hat............... $350.00
#799 Quacky Family, 1940-42 ....$75.00

#800 Hot Diggety, 1934, w/up $625.00
#808 Pop'n Ring, 1956-58 & Easter 1959 ....$50.00
#810 Timber Toter, 1957 & Easter 1958 ....$75.00
#845 Farm Truck, 1954-55, w/booklet............................ $250.00
#870 Pull-A-Tune Xylophone, 1957-69, w/song book..............$25.00
#875, Looky Push Car, 1962-65 & Easter 1966..................$45.00
#900 Struttin' Donald Duck, 1939 & Easter 1940.......... $475.00
#900 This Little Pig, 1956-58 & Easter 1959.....................$25.00
#902 Junior Circus, 1963-70... $100.00
#904 Beginners Circus, 1965-68.......................................$50.00
#905 This Little Pig, 1959-62..$25.00
#909 Play Family Rooms, 1972, Sears only $175.00
#910 Change-A-Tune Piano, 1969-72, Pop Goes the Weasel, 'This Old Man' & 'The Muffin Man' $25.00
#915 Play Family Farm, 1968-79, 1st version w/masonite base.. $25.00
#919 Music Box Movie Camera, 1968-70, plays This Old Man, w/5 picture disks $35.00
#923 Play Family School, 1971-78, 1st version..................$20.00
#926 Concrete Mixer Truck, 1959-60 & Easter 1961..... $150.00
#928 Play Family Fire Station, 1980-82 ....$30.00
#929 Play Family Nursery School, 1978-79 ....$30.00
#931 Play Family Children's Hospital, 1976-78.................$75.00
#932 Amusement Park, 1963-65 .... $200.00

#932 Amusement Park, 1963, MIB, A, $600.00. (Photo courtesy Morphy Auctions)

#932 Ferry Boat, 1979-80 ....$25.00
#934 Play Family Western Town, 1982-84..........................$75.00
#935 Tool Box Work Bench, 1969-71 ....$20.00
#937 Play Family Sesame Street Clubhouse, 1977-79 ....$50.00
#938 Play Family Sesame Street House, 1975-76 ....$50.00
#942 Play Family Lift & Load Depot, 1977-79 ....$40.00
#943 Lift & Load Railroad, 1978-79 ....$40.00
#944 Lift & Load Lumber Yard, 1979-81 ....$40.00
#945 Offshore Cargo Base, 1979-80 ....$50.00
#960 Woodsey's Log House, 1979-81, complete $20.00
#961 Woodsey's Store, 1980-81, complete.........................$25.00
#962 Woodsey's Airport, 1980-81, complete $10.00
#969 Musical Ferris Wheel, 1966-72, 1st version w/4 wooden straight-body figures..$50.00
#972 Fisher-Price Cash Register, 1960-72 ....$20.00
#979 Dump Truckers Playset, 1965-67 ....$50.00

#982 Hot Rod Roadster, 1983-84, riding toy w/4-pc take-apart engine $40.00
#983 Safety School Bus, 1959, w/6 figures, Fisher-Price Club logo... $150.00
#985 Play Family Houseboat, 1972-76, complete $25.00
#987 Creative Coaster, 1964-82 ....$40.00
#990 Play Family A-Frame, 1974-76 ....$35.00
#991 Music Box Lacing Shoe, 1964-67 ....$50.00
#991 Play Family Circus Train, 1973-78, w/gondola car............ $15.00
#991 Play Family Circus Train, 1979-86, no gondola car ..$10.00
#992 Play Family Car & Camper, 1980-84 ....$25.00
#993 Play Family Castle, 1974-77, 1st version...................$75.00
#994 Play Family Camper, 1973-76....................................$25.00
#996 Play Family Airport, 1972-76, 1st version w/bl airport & clear look-out tower...$25.00
#997 Musical Tick-Tock Clock, 1962-63 ....$30.00
#997 Play Family Village, 1973-77 ....$40.00
#998 Music Box Teaching Clock, 1968-83 ....$10.00
#999 Huffy Puffy Train, 1958-62 .... $100.00
#2352 Little People Construction Set, 1985 ....$15.00
#2360 Little People Jetliner, 1986-88..................................$10.00
#2361 Little People Fire Truck, 1989-90..............................$10.00
#2453 Little People Beauty Salon, 1990 ....$15.00
#2454 Little People Drive-In Movie $15.00

#2454 Little People Drive-In Movie, 1990, MIB, $25.00. (Photo courtesy Brad Cassity)

#2455 Little People Gas Station, 1990...............................$15.00
#2500 Little People Main Street, 1986-90.............................$20.00
#2501 Little People Farm, 1986-89 ....$15.00
#2504 Little People Garage, 1986 ....$25.00
#2524 Little People Cruise Boat, 1989-90 ....$15.00
#2525 Little People Playground, 1986-90 ....$10.00
#2551 Little People Neighborhood, 1988-90........................$20.00
#2552 McDonald's Restaurant, 1990, 1st version $30.00
#2552 McDonald's Restaurant, 1991-92, 2nd version, same pcs as 1st version but lg-size figures..$25.00
#2580 Little People Little Mart, 1987-89.............................$15.00
#2581 Little People Express Train, 1987-90.........................$10.00
#2582 Little People Floating Marina, 1988-90 ....$15.00
#2712 Pick-Up & Peek Wood Puzzle, any, 1985-88, ea.....$10.00
#4500 Husky Helpers Workmen, 1985-86, 6 different, MOC, ea $10.00
#4520 Highway Dump Truck, 1985-86 ....$15.00
#4521 Dozer Loader, 1985-86 ....$15.00
#4523 Gravel Hauler, 1985-86 ....$15.00

Games

Early games (those from 1850 to 1910) are very often appreciated more for their wonderful lithographed boxes than their 'playability,' and you'll find collectors displaying them as they would any fine artwork. Many boxes and boards were designed by commercial artists of the day. The 'boomer' games are still highly sought after for their nostalgic quality.

Some game prices have come down a little since the last edition, with the Internet being an influencing factor.

When you buy a game, check to see that all pieces are there. The games listed below are complete unless noted otherwise. For further information we recommend *Board Games of the '50s, '60s and '70s* (L-W Book Sales).

See also Advertising; Black Americana; Halloween; other relevant categories.

A-Team, Parker Bros, 1984, EX+IB....$10.00
A-Team Grenade Toss, Placo Toys, 1983, NRFB (sealed)..$30.00
Addams Family, Ideal, 1960s, NMIB....$75.00
Addams Family (Cartoon Series), Milton Bradley, 1970s, NMIB....$25.00
Addams Family Card Game, Milton Bradley, 1965, NMIB..$20.00
Advance to Boardwalk, Parker Bros, 1985, NMIB....$15.00
Alfred Hitchcock Presents 'Why' Mystery Game, Milton Bradley, 1958, unused, MIB....$40.00
Alien, Kenner, 1979, EXIB....$15.00
All in the Family, Milton Bradley, 1972, NM+IB....$25.00
Alvin & the Chipmunks Acorn Hunt, Hasbro, 1960, EXIB.$20.00
Amazing Chan & the Chan Clan, Whitman, 1973, NMIB..$20.00
Amazing Spider-Man, Milton Bradley, 1966, EXIB....$25.00
American Boys Game, McLoughlin Bros, 1913, VGIB, A..$285.00
Annette's Secret Passage Game, Parker Bros, 1958, EX+IB...$15.00
Annie Oakley Game, Milton Bradley, 1950s, lg, NMIB....$45.00
Annie Oakley Game, Milton Bradley, 1950s, sm, NMIB..$35.00
Annie the Movie Game, Parker Bros, 1981, NMIB....$10.00
Apple's Way, Milton Bradley, 1974, NMIB....$18.00

Archie Bunker's Card Game, Milton Bradley #4239, 1972, NM+IB, $15.00. (Photo courtesy gasolinealleyantiques.com)

Archies, Whitman, 1969, NMIB....$25.00
Around the World in 80 Days, Transogram, NMIB....$25.00
As the World Turns, Parker Bros, 1966, NMIB....$25.00
Ask Popeye's Lucky Jeep/2 Games in 1, King Features, c 1929-36....$230.00
Atom Ant Saves the Day, Transogram, 1966, NMIB....$50.00

Babe Ruth's Baseball Game, Milton Bradley, 1920s, EX+IB, A, $500.00. (Photo courtesy Morphy Auctions)

Babes in Toyland, Whitman, 1961, EXIB....$20.00
Bamboozle, Milton Bradley, 1962, NMIB....$25.00
Barbie Queen of the Prom, Mattel, 1960s, NM+IB....$75.00
Baretta, Milton Bradley, 1976, NMIB....$45.00
Bargain Hunter, Milton Bradley, 1981, NMIB....$20.00
Barnabas Collins Dark Shadows Game, Milton Bradley, 1969, NMIB....$50.00
Barney Google & Spark Plug Game, Milton Bradley, 1923, EXIB....$100.00
Barney Miller, Parker Bros, 1977, NMIB....$35.00
Baseball Game, All-Fair, 1930, EX+IB....$150.00
Baseball Pitching Game, Marx, 1940s, NMIB....$225.00
Bash!, Milton Bradley, 1965, NMIB....$15.00
Bat Masterson, Lowell, 1958, NMIB....$45.00
Batman, Milton Bradley, 1966, NMIB....$35.00

Batman and Robin Game, Hasbro, 1965, NMIB, $50.00.

Batman & Robin, Hasbro, 1965, EXIB....$35.00
Batman & Robin Pinball Game, Marx, 1966, NM....$125.00
Batman Pinball Game, AHI, 1976, NMIB....$100.00
Battle Cry, Milton Bradley, 1962, EXIB....$30.00

Battle of the Planets, Milton Bradley, 1970s, NMIB..........$30.00
Battlestar Galactica, Parker Bros #58, 1978, NM+IB........$20.00
Beany & Cecil Match It, Mattel, 1960s, EXIB $35.00
Beany & Cecil Ring Toss, Pressman, 1961, EX+IB............$35.00
Beat the Clock, Lowell, 1954, NMIB...............................$35.00
Beat the Clock, Milton Bradley, 1960s, NMIB..................$15.00
Beatles Flip Your Wig Game, Milton Bradley, 1964, NM+IB..$175.00
Beetle Bailey The Old Army Game, Milton Bradley, 1963, EXIB $25.00
Ben Casey MD, Transogram, 1961, NMIB........................$20.00
Bermuda Triangle, Milton Bradley, 1976, EX+IB $15.00
Betsy Ross Flag Game, Transogram, 1960s, NM+IB..........$40.00
Beverly Hillbillies 'Set Back' Card Game, Milton Bradley, 1963, NMIB...$12.00
Beverly Hillbillies, Standard Toycraft, 1963, NM+IB $45.00
Bewitched, T Cohn Inc, 1965, NMIB...............................$65.00
Bewitched Card Game, Milton Bradley, 1965, EXIB.........$30.00
Big Game (Pinball), Marx, 1950s, NM $50.00
Big Maze, Marx, 1955, MIB...$50.00
Billionaire, Parker Bros, 1973, NMIB $12.00
Bionic Crisis, Parker Bros, 1975, NMIB...........................$12.00
Bionic Woman, Parker Bros, 1976, NMIB........................$12.00
Black Beauty, Transogram, 1957, NMIB $25.00
Blondie, Parker Bros, 1970s, NMIB.................................$12.00
Bo Bang & Hong Kong, Parker Bros, 1890s, EXIB $300.00
Bobbsey Twins, Milton Bradley, 1957, MIB $25.00
Bonanza Michigan Rummy, Parker Bros, 1960s, EXIB $25.00
Boots & Saddles, Chad Valley, 1960s, EX+IB...................$50.00
Boris Karloff's Monster Game, Gems, 1960s, EXIB $125.00

Bowling Game, Singer, EXIB, A, $1,035.00.
(Photo courtesy James D. Julia, Inc.)

Bozo Ed-U Cards, 1972, EXIB $15.00
Bozo the Clown in Circus Land, Transogram, 1960s, NMIB .$20.00
Brady Bunch, Whitman, 1973, MIB $75.00
Branded, Milton Bradley, 1966, EXIB $25.00
Buck Rogers & His Cosmic Rocket Wars, Lutz & Scheimkman, 1934, EXIB... $450.00
Buck Rogers Game, Milton Bradley, 1970, EXIB..............$15.00
Bugaloos, Milton Bradley, 1971, EXIB $20.00
Bullwinkle Hide 'N Seek Game, Milton Bradley, 1961, NMIB. $50.00
Bullwinkle's Supermarket Game, Whitman, 1970s, EXIB.$25.00
Buy & Sell, Whitman, 1953, EXIB $10.00
Candid Camera, Lowell, 1963, NM+IB $30.00
Candyland, Milton Bradley, 1955, EXIB..........................$20.00
Captain America, Milton Bradley, 1966, EXIB.................$30.00
Captain Gallant of the Foreign Legion Adventure Game, Transogram, 1950s, EXIB $25.00
Captain Kangaroo, Milton Bradley, 1956, NMIB $50.00
Captain Kangaroo TV Lotto, Ideal, 1961, EXIB...............$25.00
Captain Video, Milton Bradley, 1952, EXIB.....................$50.00
Car 54 Where Are You?, Allison, 1963, NMIB $75.00
Careers, Parker Bros, 1965, NMIB $20.00
Casey Jones, Saalfield, 1959, EXIB $25.00

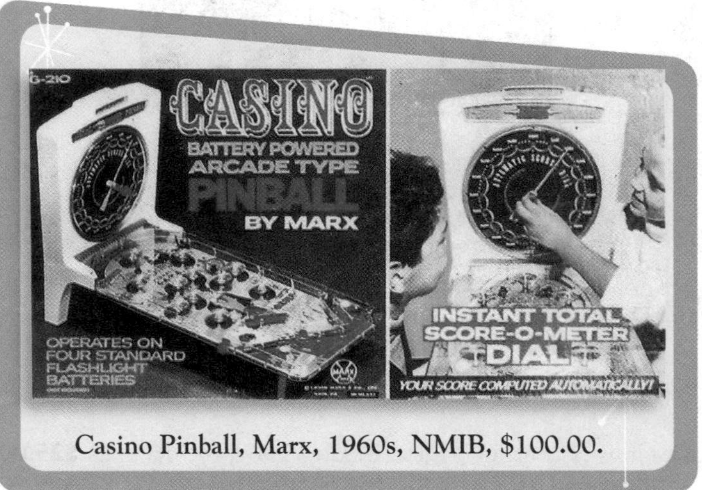

Casino Pinball, Marx, 1960s, NMIB, $100.00.

Casper the Friendly Ghost, Milton Bradley, 1959, NMIB .$15.00
Cat & Mouse Game, Parker Bros, 1964, EXIB..................$10.00
Charlette's Web, Hasbro, 1974, NMIB $30.00
Charlie McCarthy's Flying Hats, Whitman, 1930s, EXIB .$30.00
Charlie's Angels (Farrah on box), Milton Bradley, 1970s, NMIB $25.00
Cheyenne, Milton Bradley, 1950s, EXIB.........................$30.00
Chicken Lotto, Ideal, 1960s, EXIB..................................$15.00
CHiPs, Ideal, 1981, MIB...$15.00
CHiPs Game, Milton Bradley, 1977, NMIB $10.00
Chiromagica, McLoughlin Bros, early 1910s, VG+IB $300.00
Chug-A-Lug, Dynamic, 1969, NMIB...............................$15.00
Cinderella, Parker Bros, 1964, EXIB $25.00
Close Encounters of the Third Kind, Parker Bros, 1977, EXIB.$10.00
Clue, Parker Bros, 1970s, NMIB $10.00
Columbo, Milton Bradley, 1973, NMIB...........................$12.00
Combat, Ideal, 1963, NMIB..$50.00
Combat Card Game, Milton Bradley, 1960s, EXIB $12.00
Comical Tivoli Game, JW Spear, VGIB $100.00
Commercial Traveler, McLoughlin Bros, EXIB.............. $325.00
Conflict, Parker Bros, 1960, EXIB $20.00
Count Down Space Game, Transogram, 1960, NMIB.......$20.00
Countdown, Lowe, 1967, NMIB $35.00
Crazy Clock, Ideal, 1964, NMIB $30.00
Creature From the Black Lagoon, Hasbro, 1963, EX+IB. $175.00
Crusader Rabbit TV Game, Tryne 1960s, NMIB........... $125.00

Dallas, Marcus Industries, 1985, EXIB $20.00
Dangerous World of James Bond 007, Milton Bradley, 1965, NMIB $50.00
Daniel Boone Wilderness Trail Card Game, Transogram, 1960s, NMIB $45.00
Dark Crystal Game, Milton Bradley, 1980s, NM+IB.........$25.00
Dark Shadows, Whitman, 1968, NMIB $45.00
Dark Tower, Milton Bradley, 1981, NMIB $150.00

Dash for the North Pole, McLoughlin Brothers, 1890s, VG+IB, A, $2,760.00. (Photo courtesy James D. Julia, Inc.)

Dastardly & Muttley, Milton Bradley, 1969, EX+IB..........$25.00
Dating Game, Hasbro, 1967, EXIB $15.00
Davy Crockett Adventures, Gardner, 1950s, EXIB $50.00
Davy Crockett Radar Action, Ewing, 1950s, EX+IB.........$50.00
Davy Crockett Rescue Race, Gabriel, 1950s, EXIB $25.00
Daytona 500 Race Game, Milton Bradley, 1989, NMIB ...$30.00
Dennis the Menace Baseball Game, MTP, 1960, NMIB ...$45.00
Deputy (Starring Henry Fonda...), Bell, 1960s, EXIB........$25.00
Deputy Dawg TV Lotto, Ideal, 1960s, EXIB $20.00
Derby Day, Parker Bros, 1959, NMIB................................$40.00
Derby Steeple Chase, McLoughlin Bros, 1880s, EXIB.... $175.00
Detectives, Transogram, 1961, NMIB $35.00
Dick Tracy Card Game, Whitman, 1934, EXIB.................$35.00
Dick Tracy Crime Stopper Game, Ideal, 1963, EXIB.........$25.00
Dick Tracy the Master Detective, Selchow & Righter, 1960s, EX+IB $35.00
Dick Van Dyke Board Game, Standard Toykraft, 1960s, EX+IB $100.00
Dig, Parker Bros, 1930s, EXIB $25.00
Diner's Club Credit Card Game, Ideal, 1961, NMIB.........$25.00
Direct Hit, Northwestern Prod, 1950s, EX+IB $165.00
Disney's True Life Electric Quiz Game, 1952, VGIB $25.00
Disneyland Game, Transogram, 1954, EXIB.....................$30.00
District Messenger, McLoughlin Bros, 1880s, VGIB $250.00
Doc Holiday Wild West Game, Transogram, 1960, NMIB...$35.00
Dogfight, McLoughlin Bros, 1962, EXIB...........................$40.00
Don't Break the Ice, Schaper, 1960s, NMIB $15.00
Don't Have a Cow Dice Game (Simpsons), Milton Bradley 1990, NMIB $15.00

Donnie & Marie Osmond TV Game Show, Mattel, 1977, NMIB $30.00
Dr Kildare, Ideal, 1962, NMIB $30.00
Dracula Mystery Game, Hasbro, 1962, EXIB, A $75.00

Dragnet, Transogram, 1955, NMIB, A, $55.00.
(Photo courtesy serioustoyz.com)

Dream House, Milton Bradley, 1968, EXIB.......................$25.00
Dukes of Hazzard, Ideal, 1981, EXIB $10.00
Dynomutt, Milton Bradley, 1970s, NM+IB $20.00
Ed Wynn the Fire Chief, Selchow & Righter, 1930s, EXIB..$50.00

Election, Singer, VG+IB, A, $3,450.00.
(Photo courtesy James D. Julia, Inc.)

Eliot Ness and the Untouchables, Transogram, 1960s, EX+IB .$40.00
Emergency, Milton Bradley, 1970s, NMIB $30.00
Emily Post Popularity Game, Selchow & Righter, 1970s, NMIB $20.00
Ensign O'Toole USS Appleby Game, Hasbro, 1968, NMIB.$30.00
Escape From New York, TSR, 1980s, EX+IB $15.00
Escort Game of Guys & Gals, Parker Bros, 1955, unused, MIB. $30.00
Evel Knievel Stunt World, Ideal, 1975, self-contained suitcase unfolds to Coliseum & Snake River, NMIB $80.00
Excuse Me! A Game of Manners, Parker Bros, NMIB.......$25.00
Eye Guess, Milton Bradley, 1966, EXIB $15.00
F-Troop, Ideal, 1960s, VGIB...$35.00
Fall Guy, Milton Bradley, 1980s, NMIB $30.00
Family Affair, Whitman, 1960s, EX+IB $30.00
Family Feud, Milton Bradley, 1970s, NMIB.......................$15.00
Family Ties, Apple Street, 1986, EXIB.............................$15.00
Fantastic Voyage, Milton Bradley, 1968, NMIB.................$30.00
Fantasy Island, Ideal, 1978, NMIB, A $45.00

Farmer Jones Pigs, McLoughlin Bros, VGIB $125.00
FBI, Transogram, 1950s, EX+IB $45.00
Felix the Cat, Milton Bradley, 1960, 1st version, EXIB.....$35.00
Felix the Cat Dandy Candy Game, Built-Rite, 1950s, EX+IB..$10.00
Felix the Cat Target, Lido, 1960s, EXIB...........................$25.00
Ferdinand's Chinese Checkers w/the Bee!, Parker Bros, 1939, EXIB.. $150.00

Fess Parker Trail Blazers Game, Milton Bradley, 1964, NMIB, $40.00. (Photo courtesy serioustoyz.com)

Fish Pond, Milton Bradley, EX+IB $65.00
Flintstones, Milton Bradley, 1971, NMIB $20.00
Flintstones Brake Ball, Whitman, 1962, EXIB..................$85.00
Flintstones Stone Age Game Transogram, 1961, NMIB ...$55.00
Flipper Flips, Mattel, 1960s, EX+IB $35.00
Flying Nun Marble Maze Game, Milton Bradley, 1967, NMIB..$45.00
Fonz Hanging Out at Arnold's Card Game, Milton Bradley, 1976, MIB $30.00
Formula 1 Car Racing Game, Parker Bros, 1968, NMIB ...$55.00
4 Alarm Game, Milton Bradley, 1963, EXIB....................$20.00
Fox & the Hounds, Parker Bros, 1948, NM $25.00

Frankenstein Mystery Game, Hasbro, 1960s, EXIB, A, $75.00. (Photo courtesy serioustoyz.com)

Fu Manchu's Hidden Hoard, Ideal, 1960s, VGIB $15.00
Fugative, Ideal, 1964, NMIB $75.00
G-Men Clue Games, Whitman #3930, 1930s, VGIB........$75.00
Gambler, Parker Bros, 1970s, EX+IB................................$10.00
Game of A Dash for the North Pole, McLoughlin Bros, 1897, VG+IB, A $2,760.00
Game of Aladdin, Singer, ca 1890, VG+IB, A $4,312.50
Game of Boy Scouts, Parker Bros, 1920s, EXIB $250.00
Game of Famous Men, Parker Bros, VGIB.........................$50.00
Game of Flags, McLoughlin Bros, VGIB...........................$75.00
Game of Going to the Klondike, McLoughlin Bros, 1890s, EXIB, A $4,600.00
Game of Golf, Singer, VGIB $550.00
Game of International Spy, All-Fair, 1940s, EXIB............$50.00
Game of Life, Milton Bradley, 1960s, NM+IB...................$25.00
Game of Red Riding Hood, Parker Bros, 1895, VGIB.... $150.00
Game of Yuneek, McLoughlin Bros, 1880s, VGIB $200.00
Games People Play, Alpsco, 1967, NMIB $25.00
Games You Like to Play, Parker Bros, 1920s, EX+IB $50.00
Gang Way for Fun, Transogram, 1960s, VGIB..................$15.00
Garrison's Gorillas, Ideal, 1967, EXIB..............................$50.00
Gee-Wiz The Racing Game Sensation, Wolverine, 1920s, EX+ (VG box) $100.00

Gene Autry's Dude Ranch Game, Built-Rite, 1950s, EXIB, $25.00.

General Hospital, Parker Bros, 1970s, EX+IB....................$10.00
Gentle Ben Animal Hunt Game, Mattel, 1960s, EX+IB...$40.00
George of the Jungle, Parker Bros, 1968, NMIB $75.00
Get in That Tub, Hasbro, 1969, unused, NMIB $30.00
Get Smart, Ideal, 1966, NMIB..$35.00
Get Smart Card Game, Ideal, 1966, EXIB $20.00
GI Joe Adventure, Hasbro, 1980s, EX+IB $25.00
GI Joe Card Game, Whitman, 1960s, NM+IB $20.00
Gidget, Standard Toycraft, 1965, MIB $75.00
Gilligan's Island, Game Gems/T Cohn, 1965, EXIB....... $150.00
Gnip Gnop, Parker Bros, 1971, NMIB..............................$15.00
Godzilla, Mattel, 1978, EXIB $35.00

Going to the Klondike, McLoughlin Brothers, 1898, VG+IB, A, $4,600.00. (Photo courtesy James D. Julia, Inc.)

Gomer Pyle, Transogram, 1964, EXIB...$20.00
Goodbye Mr Chips, Parker Bros, 1969, EXIB...$10.00
Gray Ghost, Transogram, 1958, NMIB...$90.00
Great Charlie Chan Detective Game, Milton Bradley, 1930s, EXIB...$350.00
Great Escape, Ideal, 1967, EX+IB...$12.00
Great Grape Ape Game, Milton Bradley, 1975, EX+IB...$20.00
Green Acres, Standard Toykraft, 1960s, EXIB...$75.00
Green Ghost Game, Transogram, 1965, NMIB, A...$165.00
Green Hornet Quick Switch Game, Milton Bradley, 1960s, EX+IB...$100.00
Gremlins, International Games, 1980s, VGIB...$5.00
Groucho Marx TV Quiz, Pressman, 1950s, EXIB...$45.00
Gulliver's Travels, Milton Bradley, 1930s, EXIB...$135.00
Gumby & Pokey Playful Trails, 1968, NMIB...$25.00
Gunsmoke, Lowell, 1958, NMIB...$75.00
Hang on Harvey, Ideal, 1969, EXIB...$15.00
Happy Days, Parker Bros, 1976, NMIB...$20.00
Hardy Boys Mystery Game, Milton Bradley, 1968, EX+IB...$10.00
Hardy Boys Treasure Game, Parker Bros, 1957, NMIB, A.$35.00
Haunted House Game, Ideal, 1960s, EXIB...$125.00
Haunted Mansion, Lakeside, 1970s, EX+IB...$75.00
Hawaii Five-O, Remco, 1960s, EXIB...$25.00
Hawaiian Eye, Transogram, 1960s, EXIB...$50.00
Hen That Laid the Golden Egg, Parker Bros, 1900s, EXIB...$125.00
Hi-Way Henry Cross Country 'The Lizzy' Race, All-Fair, 1920s, EXIB, A...$895.00
Hide 'N Seek, Ideal, 1960s, EXIB...$25.00
Hogan's Heroes, Transogram, 1960s, VGIB...$25.00
Hollywood Squares, Ideal, 1970s, EX+IB...$10.00
Honey Bee Game, Milton Bradley, 1913, EX+IB...$60.00
Honey West, Ideal, 1960s, EXIB...$40.00

Hopalong Cassidy Game, Milton Bradley, 1950s, EXIB, $50.00.

Hopalong Cassidy, Milton Bradley, 1950, NMIB, A...$80.00
Hopalong Cassidy Game, Marx, 1950s, EXIB...$115.00
Hopalong Cassidy Lasso Game, Transogram, 1950, NMIB, A...$135.00
Hoppity Hooper Pinball Game, Lidu, 1965, NMIB...$85.00
Hot Wheels Wipe Out Race Game, Mattel, 1968, NMIB.$40.00
House Party, Whitman, 1968, EX+IB...$15.00
Howdy Doody Adventure Game, Milton Bradley, 1950s, VGIB...$25.00
Howdy Doody Bean Bag Game, Parker Bros, 1950s, EXIB...$75.00
Howdy Doody Card Game, Russell, 1950s, NMIB...$15.00
Howdy Doody's Own Game, Parker Bros, 1949, EXIB...$45.00
Howdy Doody's TV Game, Milton Bradley, 1950s, EXIB...$25.00
Huckleberry Hound Tiddly Winks, Milton Bradley, 1959, EXIB...$20.00
Huckleberry Hound Western Game, Milton Bradley, 1959, EXIB...$30.00
Hullabaloo, Remco, 1965, EXIB...$30.00
Humpty Dumpty Game, Lowell, 1950s, EXIB...$30.00
Hungry Ant, Milton Bradley, 1970s, NMIB...$15.00
Hurry Waiter!, Ideal, 1969, EXIB...$10.00
I Dream of Jeannie, Milton Bradley, 1965, NMIB, A...$60.00
I Spy, Ideal, 1965, EXIB...$40.00
I Wanna Be President, JR Mackey, 1983, NMIB...$15.00
Incredible Hulk, Milton Bradley, 1970s, NMIB...$10.00
Indiana Jones in Raiders of the Lost Ark, Kenner, 1981, NMIB...$15.00
Intercollegiate Football, Hustler, 1920s, EXIB...$200.00
International Automobile Race, Parker Bros, 1903, EXIB...$625.00
Intrigue, Milton Bradley, 1954, NMIB...$35.00
Ipcress File, Milton Bradley, 1966, MIB...$30.00
Ironside, Ideal, 1976, EXIB...$50.00
Jack & Jill, Milton Bradley, early 1900s, VGIB...$100.00
Jack & the Beanstalk Adventure Game, Transogram, 1957, EXIB...$30.00
Jackie Gleason & Away We Go! TV Fun Game, Transogram, 1956, EXIB...$50.00
James Bond Message From M, Ideal, 1966, EXIB...$150.00
James Bond Secret Agent 007, Milton Bradley, 1964, NMIB. $35.00
Jan Murray's Treasure Hunt, Gardner, 1950s, NMIB...$30.00
Jeopardy, Milton Bradley, 1964, NMIB...$20.00
Jerome Park Steeple Chase, McLoughlin Bros, EXIB...$400.00
Jetson's Fun Pad, Milton Bradley, 1963, NMIB...$75.00
Jetsons Game, Milton Bradley, 1985, NM+IB...$12.00

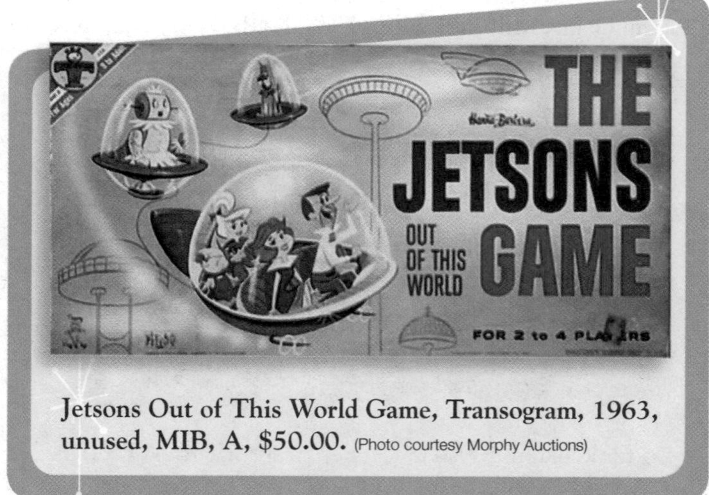

Jetsons Out of This World Game, Transogram, 1963, unused, MIB, A, $50.00. (Photo courtesy Morphy Auctions)

John Drake Secret Agent, Milton Bradley, 1966, EXIB...$18.00
Jolly Jungleers, Milton Bradley, VGIB...$100.00
Jonny Quest, Transogram, 1960s, EXIB...$225.00
Jungle Book, Parker Bros, 1966, NMIB...$35.00
Justice League of America, Hasbro, 1967, EXIB...$75.00
King Kong Game, Ideal, 1970s, EXIB...$50.00
King Kong Game, Milton Bradley, 1960s, NMIB...$25.00
King Leonardo & His Subjects, Milton Bradley, 1960, EXIB. $20.00
King of the Hill, Schaper, 1960s, EXIB...$30.00

KISS on Tour, Aucion, 1978, EXIB....$30.00
Knight Rider, Parker Bros, 1983, NMIB....$15.00

Kojak — The Stake Out Detective Game, Milton Bradley, 1975, MIB, A, $40.00. (Photo courtesy serioustoyz.com)

Kojak Stake Out Detective, Milton Bradley, 1975, EXIB...$15.00
Kooky Carnival, Milton Bradley, 1969, NMIB....$40.00
Kukla & Ollie — A Game, Parker Bros, 1962, NMIB....$30.00
Lame Duck, Parker Bros, 1928, VGIB....$125.00
Lancer, Remco, 1968, EX+IB....$50.00
Land of the Giants, Ideal, 1968, NMIB....$100.00

Land of the Lost, Milton Bradley, 1975, NMIB, $30.00. (Photo courtesy Greg Davis and Bill Morgan)

Laramie, Lowell, 1960, VGIB....$25.00
Lassie, Game Gems, 1965, EXIB....$25.00
Laugh-In's Squeeze Your Bippy, Hasbro, 1960s, VGIB....$25.00
Laverne & Shirley, Parker Bros, 1970s, EXIB....$10.00
Legend of Jessie James, Milton Bradley, 1965, EXIB....$35.00
Let's Make a Deal, Milton Bradley, 1960s, EX+IB....$15.00
Letter Carrier, McLoughlin Bros, VGIB....$275.00
Liberty Airport & Flying Airplanes, Liberty Playthings, EXIB, A....$880.00
Lie Detector, Mattel, 1961, NMIB....$50.00
Little Orphan Annie Game, Parker Bros, 1981, EXIB....$15.00
Little Rascals 'Our Gang' Clubhouse Bingo, Gabriel, 1958, EX+IB, A....$65.00
Little Red Riding Hood, McLoughlin Bros, 1900s, EXIB . $200.00

Little Red Riding Hood, circa 1900, VGIB, A, $125.00. (Photo courtesy James D. Julia, Inc.)

Lone Ranger, Milton Bradley, 1966, NMIB....$25.00
Lone Ranger Game, Milton Bradley, 1938, EXIB....$50.00
Lone Ranger Target Game, Marx, 1946, EXIB....$250.00
Looney Tunes, Milton Bradley, 1968, NMIB....$35.00
Lost in Space, Milton Bradley, 1965, NMIB....$75.00
Louisa, McLoughlin Bros, EXIB, A....$165.00
Lucy's Tea Party Game, Milton Bradley, 1971, EXIB....$20.00
M Squad, Bell Toys, 1950s, VGIB....$25.00
MAD Magazine, Parker Bros, 1979, NMIB....$10.00
MAD's Spy vs Spy, Milton Bradley, 1986, NMIB....$25.00
Magilla Gorilla, Ideal, 1960s, EX+IB....$50.00
Magnetic Fish Pond, McLoughlin Bros, 1890s, VGIB....$400.00
Magnetic Fish Pond, Milton Bradley, 1948, NMIB....$25.00
Man From UNCLE Target Game, Marx, 1965, NM....$250.00
Man From UNCLE the Pinball Game, 1966, EX....$100.00
Man From UNCLE Thrush Ray Gun Affair Game, Ideal, 1966, NMIB....$75.00
Manhunt, Milton Bradley, 1972, NMIB....$15.00
Markin Perkins' Zoo Parade, Cadaco-Ellis, 1960s, EXIB...$15.00
Marvel Comics Super-Heroes Card Game, Milton Bradley, 1970s, MIB (sealed)....$75.00
Mary Hartman Mary Hartman, Reiss Games, 1970s, EXIB..$15.00
Mary Poppins Carousel Game, Parker Bros, 1964, NMIB, A . $20.00
Masquerade Party, Bettye-B, 1955, EX+IB....$30.00
McHale's Navy, Transogram, 1962, NMIB....$35.00
Melvin Pervis' G-Men Detective Game, Parker Bros, 1936, EXIB....$100.00
Melvin the Moon Man, Remco, 1960s, NMIB....$75.00
Merry Go Round Game, Parker Bros, VG+IB, A....$355.00
Miami Vice, Pepper Lane, 1984, EXIB....$15.00
Mickey Mantle's Big League Baseball, Gardner, 1958, VGIB..$100.00
Mickey Mouse Circus Game, Marks Bros, 1930s, NMIB, A.$500.00
Mickey Mouse Club Card Games, Russell Mfg/WDP, die-cut cb club house display box w/3 boxed card games, NMIB, A....$65.00
Mickey Mouse Kiddy Keno, Jaymar, 1950s-60s, NMIB....$20.00
Mickey Mouse Picture Matching Game, Parker Bros, 1953, EX+IB, A....$25.00
Mickey Mouse Pop Up Game, Whitman, 1970s, MIB....$25.00
Mighty Comics Super Heroes, Transogram, 1966, NMIB..$75.00
Mighty Hercules Game, Hasbro, 1960s, NMIB....$325.00
Mighty Mouse Rescue Game, Harett-Gilmer, 1960s, NMIB.$55.00
Milton the Monster, Milton Bradley, 1966, EXIB....$15.00
Mini Golf, Technofix, 1960s, NMIB, A....$150.00
Mission Impossible, Ideal, 1967, EXIB....$50.00

Mister Ed, Parker Bros, 1962, EXIB....................................$25.00

Monday Night Football, Aurora, 1972, battery-operated, NMIB, A, $110.00. (Photo courtesy serioustoyz.com)

Monkees Game, Transogram, 1968, NMIB..................... $115.00
Monoply, Parker Bros, 1950s, NMIB..................................$65.00
Monster Old Maid Card Game, Milton Bradley, 1964, EXIB. $20.00
Monster Squad, Milton Bradley #4716, 1977, EXIB..........$15.00
Mork & Mindy, Milton Bradley, 1978, NMIB $20.00
Motor Carriage Game, Parker Bros, 1899, EX, A $550.00
Mr Knovak, Transogram, 1963, NMIB...............................$25.00
Munsters Card Game, Milton Bradley, 1964, NMIB, A $45.00
Munsters Masquerade Game, Hasbro, 1960s, VGIB....... $175.00
Munsters Picnic Game, Hasbro, 1960s, EXIB................ $250.00
Muppet Show, Parker Bros, 1977, EXIB............................$20.00
Murder on the Orient Express, Ideal, 1967, EXIB $25.00
Murder She Wrote, Warren, 1985, NMIB $8.00
Mushmouth & Pinkin Puss, Ideal, 1964, EXIB..................$50.00
My Favorite Martian, Transogram, 1963, EXIB $45.00

Mystery Date, Milton Bradley, 1965, NM+IB, $150.00.

Mystic Skull The Game of Voodoo, Ideal, 1964, NMIB....$35.00
Nancy & Sluggo Game, 1944, rare, NMIB $100.00
Nancy Drew Mystery Game, Parker Bros, 1950s, NMIB . $100.00
National Velvet, Transogram, 1950s, NMIB......................$30.00
Nebbs on the Air, Milton Bradley, 1930s, EXIB $100.00
New Game of Hunting, McLoughlin Bros, EXIB, A $990.00
Newlywed Game, Hasbro, 1st Edition, 1967, NMIB $20.00
Newport Yacht Race, McLoughlin Bros, VGIB $450.00
No Time for Sergeants, Ideal, 1964, EXIB $15.00
Nurses, Ideal, 1963, NMIB $45.00
Office Boy — The Good Old Days, Parker Bros, 1889, EXIB..$150.00
Oh Magoo, Warren, 1960s, NMIB $25.00
Orbit, Parker Bros, 1959, NMIB..$25.00

Outer Limits, Milton Bradley, 1964, NMIB, $175.00.

Overland Trail, Transogram, 1960, NMIB $60.00
Park & Shop, Milton Bradley, 1960, NMIB........................$45.00
Partridge Family, Milton Bradley, 1971, NMIB..................$25.00
Patty Duke Show, Milton Bradley, 1963, NMIB................$30.00
Peanuts The Game of Charlie Brown & His Pals, Selchow & Righter, 1959, EXIB..$25.00
Pebbles Flintstone Game, Transogram, 1962, NMIB.........$25.00
Perry Mason Case of the Missing Suspect, Transogram, NMIB $25.00
Peter Gunn Detective Game, Lowell, 1960, NMIB...........$30.00
Peter Pan, Selchow & Righter, 1920s, EX+IB $100.00
Peter Pan, Transogram, 1953, EXIB $12.00
Peter Potamus Game, Ideal, 1964, NMIB $45.00
Peter Rabbit Game, Milton Bradley, 1910s, EXIB $50.00
Petticoat Junction, Standard Toykraft, 1963, NMIB $75.00
Philip Marlow, Transogram, 1960, EXIB $15.00
Pink Panther, Warren, 1977, NMIB...................................$20.00
Pirate & Traveler, Milton Bradley, 1953, NMIB................$30.00
Pirate's Cove, Gabriel, 1950s, EX+IB................................$20.00
Pirates of the Caribbean, Parker Bros, 1967, NMIB $35.00
Planet of the Apes, Milton Bradley, 1974, EXIB................$25.00
Popeye Jet Pilot Target Game, Japan, NMIB $150.00
Popeye Menu Marble Game, Durable Toys & Novelty, c 1935, EX, A $440.00
Popeye Ring Toss Game, Rosebud Art Co, 1933, NMIB, A. $285.00
Popeye's Game, Parker Bros, 1948, unused, MIB $200.00
Price Is Right, Milton Bradley, 1958, 1st edition, EXIB $25.00
Prince Valiant, Transogram, 1950s, EXIB $25.00
PT 109, Ideal, 1963, VGIB...$45.00
Quick Draw McGraw Private Eye Game, Milton Bradley, 1960, EXIB...$10.00
Raggedy Ann & Andy Game, Milton Bradley, 1956, NMIB.. $15.00
Raise the Titanic, Hoyle, 1987, EXIB $15.00
Rat Patrol, Transogram, 1966, NMIB................................$75.00
Rebel, Ideal, 1961, NMIB, A...$80.00
Restless Gun, Milton Bradley, 1950s, EXIB $20.00

Rich Uncle — The Stock Market Game, Parker Bros, 1955, EXIB....$15.00
Ricochet Rabbit Game, Ideal 1965, EXIB....$50.00
Rifleman, Milton Bradley, 1959, NMIB....$50.00
Rin-Tin-Tin (Adventures of), Transogram, 1955, EXIB....$35.00

Risk! Parker Brothers, 1950s, EXIB, A, $40.00.
(Photo courtesy serioustoyz.com)

Road Runner, Milton Bradley, 1968, NMIB....$30.00
Road Runner Card Game, 1976, NMIB....$10.00
Robin Hood, Parker Bros, 1970s, EXIB....$10.00
Robin Hood (Adventures of), Bettye-B, 1956, EXIB....$25.00
Rocket Race to Saturn, Lido, 1950s, NM+IB....$25.00
Rocky & His Friends, Milton Bradley, 1960, EXIB....$50.00
Ruff & Reddy Spelling Game, Exclusive Playing Card Co, 1958, EXIB....$24.00
Run-Pig-Run Game, Schoenhut, EXIB....$500.00
Scooby Doo Where Are You?, Milton Bradley, 1973, NMIB..$25.00
Sealab 2020, Milton Bradley, 1973, NM+IB....$15.00
Secret Agent Man, Milton Bradley, 1966, EXIB....$30.00

77 Sunset Strip, Lowell, 1960, NMIB, $50.00.
(Photo courtesy gasolinealleyantiques.com)

Shenanigans, Milton Bradley, 1964, EXIB....$20.00
$64,000 Question, Lowell, 1955, EXIB....$15.00
Skeezix & the Air Mail, Milton Bradley, 1930s, EXIB....$60.00
Skippy, Milton Bradley, 1930s, EXIB....$80.00
Sleeping Beauty, see Walt Disney's Sleeping Beauty
Smitty, Milton Bradley, 1930s, EX+IB....$250.00
Snake's Alive, Ideal, 1967, NMIB....$25.00
Snoopy & the Red Baron, Milton Bradley, 1970, MIB....$40.00
Snoopy Card Game, Ideal, 1965, NMIB....$25.00
Snoopy Game, Selchow & Righter, 1960, VGIB....$15.00
Snoopy Snake Attack, Gabriel, 1980, MIB....$25.00
Snow White & Seven Dwarfs, Parker Bros, 1930s, EXIB.$150.00
Snow White & the Seven Dwarfs, Cadaco, 1970s, NMIB..$20.00
Snow White & the Seven Dwarfs, Milton Bradley, 1930s, EXIB....$100.00
Soldiers on Guard, McLoughlin Bros, VGIB....$125.00
Space Patrol Magnetic Target Game, American Toy, 1950s, EX....$50.00
Space: 1999, Milton Bradley, 1975, NMIB....$25.00
Sparky Marble Maze, Built-Rite, 1971, NMIB....$30.00
Spider-Man, see also Amazing Spider-Man
Spider-Man w/the Fantastic Four, Milton Bradley, 1977, NMIB....$35.00
Spot Shot Marble Game, Wolverine, 1930s, NM....$50.00
Spy Detector, Mattel, 1960, NMIB....$75.00
Stagecoach, Milton Bradley, 1958, NMIB....$25.00

Stanley Africa Game, Bliss, EXIB, A, $7,475.00. (Photo courtesy James D. Julia, Inc.)

Star Trek, Milton Bradley, 1979, EXIB....$45.00
Star Trek Adventure Game, West End Games, 1985, NMIB. $25.00
Star Trek: The Next Generation, Classics Games, 1990s, NM+IB....$35.00
Star Wars Escape From Death Star, Kenner, 1977, NMIB.$25.00
Star Wars Monopoly, Parker Bros, 1997, unused, MIB....$30.00
Starsky & Hutch Detective, Milton Bradley, 1977, NMIB..$25.00
Steeple Chase, Singer, 1890s, VGIB....$150.00
Steve Canyon Air Force Game, Lowell, 1950s, NM+IB...$50.00
Stop Thief, Parker Bros, 1979, NMIB....$30.00
Super Heroes Card Game, Milton Bradley, 1978, EXIB....$20.00
Superboy Game, Hasbro, 1960s, NMIB....$80.00
Superman (Adventures of), Milton Bradley, 1942, EXIB. $150.00
Superman Game, Hasbro, 1965, EXIB....$85.00
Superman III, Parker Bros, 1983, MIB....$25.00
Superstition, Milton Bradley, 1977, NMIB....$25.00
Surfside 6, Lowell, 1961, unused, EXIB....$35.00
Tales of Wells Fargo, Milton Bradley, 1959, EXIB....$45.00
$10,000 Pyramid, Milton Bradley, 1972, NMIB....$20.00
Tennessee Tuxedo, Transogram, 1963, EXIB....$100.00
That Girl, Remco, 1969, EXIB....$70.00
This Is Your Life, Lowell, 1954, EXIB....$25.00
Tic-Tac-Dough, Transogram, 1957, EXIB....$15.00

Tight Squeeze, Mattel, 1967, NMIB....................$25.00
Tim Holt Rodeo Dart Games, American Toys, unused, NMIB....................$100.00
Time Bomb, Milton Bradley, 1965, NMIB, A....................$88.00
Time Tunnel, Ideal, 1966, EXIB....................$100.00
Tiny Tim Game of Beautiful Things, Parker Bros, 1970, EXIB..$25.00
To Tell the Truth, Lowell, 1957, EXIB....................$20.00
Tom & Jerry, Milton Bradley, 1977, EXIB....................$10.00
Tom & Jerry Adventure in Blunderland, Transogram, EXIB..$20.00
Tom Sawyer & Huck Finn (Adventures of), Stoll & Edwards, VGIB....................$125.00

Tomorrowland Rocket to the Moon Game (Walt Disney's), Parker Brothers, 1956, NM+IB, A, $60.00. (Photo courtesy serioustoyz.com)

Top Cat, Cadaco-Ellis, 1961, NMIB....................$100.00
Town & Country Traffic, Ranger Steel, 1940s, NMIB.......$85.00
Town Hall, Milton Bradley, 1939, NMIB....................$20.00

Train for Boston, Parker Brothers, ca 1900, EXIB, A, $860.00. (Photo courtesy James D. Julia, Inc.)

Trip Round the World, McLoughlin Bros, VG+IB, A.... $275.00
Truth or Consequences, Gabriel, 1950s, NMIB....................$35.00
Turn Over, Milton Bradley, EXIB....................$75.00
Twelve O'Clock High, Ideal, 1965, VGIB....................$25.00
20,000 Leagues Under the Sea, Gardner, 1950s, EXIB. $30.00
20,000 Leagues Under the Sea Electric Quiz Game, Gardner, 1950s, NMIB, A....................$75.00
Twiggy, Milton Bradley, 1967, EXIB....................$65.00
Twilight Zone, Ideal, 1964, unused, NMIB, A....................$180.00
Uncle Remus Shooting Gallery, B&B Novelties, 1917 patent, VGIB, A....................$690.00

Uncle Sam's Mail, Milton Bradley, GIB....................$90.00
Uncle Wiggily, Parker Bros, 1979, NMIB....................$25.00
Untouchables, Marx, 1950s, NMIB....................$225.00
Untouchables Target Game, Marx, 1950s, NM....................$350.00
Virginian, Transogram, 1962, EXIB....................$100.00
Voodoo Doll Game, Schaper, 1967, EXIB....................$30.00

Voyage to the Bottom of the Sea, Milton Bradley, 1964, NMIB, A, $40.00. (Photo courtesy serioustoyz.com)

Voyage to the Bottom of the Sea Card Game, Milton Bradley, 1964, NMIB....................$50.00
Wagon Train, Milton Bradley, 1960, EXIB....................$50.00
Wally Gator Game, Transogram, 1963, NMIB....................$100.00
Walt Disney's Fantasyland, PB, 1950, MIB....................$50.00
Walt Disney's Sleeping Beauty, Whitman, 1958, EXIB.....$35.00
Wanted Dead or Alive, Lowell, 1959, EXIB....................$50.00
Wendy the Good Little Witch, Milton Bradley, 1966, VGIB...$25.00
Which Witch?, Milton Bradley, 1970, EXIB....................$50.00
Who Framed Roger Rabbit?, Milton Bradley, 1987, NMIB..$30.00
Wide World Travel Game, Parker Bros, 1957, NMIB........$30.00
Wild Bill Hickok's Cavalry & Indians Game, Built-Rite, NMIB....................$25.00

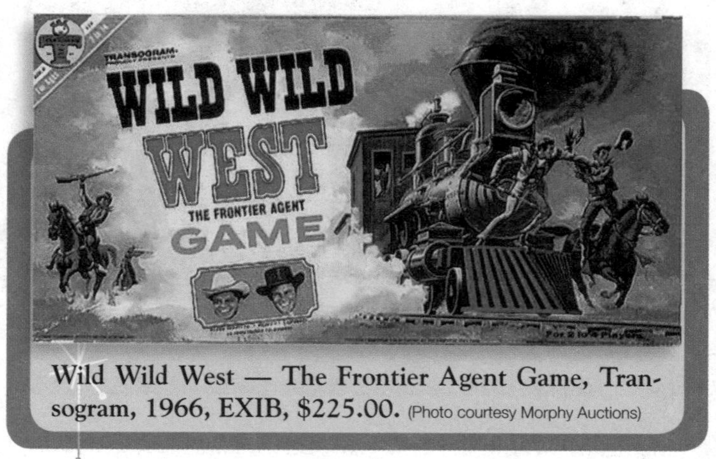

Wild Wild West — The Frontier Agent Game, Transogram, 1966, EXIB, $225.00. (Photo courtesy Morphy Auctions)

Wonder Woman, Hasbro, 1967, NMIB....................$30.00
Wonderful Game of Oz, Parker Bros, EXIB, A....................$200.00
Woody Woodpecker Game, Milton Bradley, 1959, NM+IB..$30.00
World's Fair Ed-U Cards, 1965, NMIB....................$15.00

Wyatt Earp, Transogram, 1958, EXIB................................$40.00
Yacht Race Game, McLoughlin Bros, GIB, A $140.00
Yachting, CM Co, 1890s, EXIB, A................................ $412.00
Yogi Bear Break a Plate Game, Transogram, 1960s, NMIB..$45.00
Yogi Bear Rummy Ed-U Cards, 1961, MIB (sealed) $15.00
You Don't Say, Milton Bradley, 1963, EXIB.......................$20.00
Zorro, Parker Bros, 1966, EXIB $30.00

Gasoline-Powered Toys

Two of the largest companies to manufacture gas-powered models are Cox and Wen-Mac. Since the late 1950s they have been making faithfully detailed models of airplanes as well as some automobiles and boats. Condition of used models will vary greatly because of the nature of the miniature gas engine and damage resulting from the fuel that has been used. Because of this, 'new in box' gas toys command a premium.

Advisor: Richard Trautwein

All-American Hot Rod, cast aluminum, 9", VG $250.00
Bremer Whirlwind #2, gr & wht, 18", 1939, NM $2,900.00

Bremer Whirlwind #8, 18", 1940, EX, $2,300.00.

Bremer Whirlwind #300, red, Brown Jr engine, 1939, VG . $1,250.00
Cameron Racer #4, red w/yel flames, 8", VG, from $200 to. $275.00
Cameron Rodzy Standard Racer, 1950s, 8", MIB............ $500.00
Cox AA Fuel Dragster, bl & red, 1968-70, M................. $125.00
Cox Acro-Cub, 1960s, MIB (sealed), from $60 to.............$85.00
Cox Baja Bug, yel & orange, 1968-73, M...........................$65.00
Cox Chopper, MIB, from $70 to $100.00
Cox Commanche, E-Z Flyer series, 1993-95, NMIB..........$35.00
Cox Delta F-15, Wing Series, gray, 1981-86, M.................$30.00
Cox E-Z Flyer Commanche, wht, NMIB $35.00
Cox Golden Bee, .49 engine, M $30.00
Cox Marine Helicopter, NM $35.00
Cox ME-109 Airplane, 1994, MIB (sealed), from $40 to ..$60.00
Cox Mercedes Benz W196 Racer, red, 1963-65, EX $85.00
Cox Navy Helldiver, 2-tone bl, 1963-66, EX, from $65 to .$80.00
Cox PT-19 Flight Trainer, yel & bl, EX..............................$45.00
Cox Sandblaster, brn & tan, 1968-72, M, from $45 to $65.00
Cox Shrike Bonneville Special, MIB, from $130 to $150.00
Cox Sky Rider, gray, EXIB $85.00
Cox Snowmobile, silver, 1968, M $100.00
Cox Stealth Bomber, blk, 1987-89, EX, from $30 to $50.00
Cox Super Stunter, 1874-79, EX, from $30 to $45.00
Cox Thimble Drom Racer #92, diecast, 8½", VG........... $150.00
Cox Thimble Drome Prop-Rod, yel & red, 12", EXIB.... $200.00
Cox Thimble Drome TD-1 Airplane, NMIB, from $95 to ..$125.00
Cox Thimble Drome TD-3 Airplane, 1950s, NMIB $85.00
Cox UFO Flying Saucer, Wings Series, wht, 1990-91, M..$25.00
Curtiss Jenny Airplane, WWI era, 65" WS, EX, from $250 to $300.00
Curtiss P-40D Tiger Shark, 13½", MIB, from $95 to $135.00

Dooling Flat Tail #1, 19", EX, $1,000.00; Dooling 1939 'Frog' Cabin Streamer, cast aluminum with 'Super Cyclone' ignition engine power, 16", EX, $3,200.00.

Dooling Knoxville Champ F Racer #3, red, 19", EX, from $1,000 to $1,400.00
Dooling Mercury Racer #59, Hornet engine, 1940s, 18½", from $1,800 to $2,300.00
Dooling Racer #4, orange, articulated front end, McCoy engine, EX rstr $1,500.00
Dooling Racer #5, red, 16", EX.................................... $1,200.00
Dooling Racer #6, bl, Super Cyclone engine, 1941, 18", EX . $2,300.00
Dooling Racer #8, Atwood .60 Champion engine, 1939, 19", EX, from $1,500 to $1,800.00
Dooling Sostilo Offy F Racer #54, from $2,000 to $2,450.00
Dooling Tether Racing Boat, red, .61 engine, 1955, 35", EX, from $500 to $700.00
Fairchild 22 Model Airplane, 47" WS, NM, from $250 to .. $350.00
Hiller Comet #5, red, 1942, 19", EX, from $1,200 to... $1,800.00

Hiller-Comet #18, circa 1940, 18", EX, $990.00.

Hiller T Racer #19, yel, Hiller .60 engine, 20", EX, from $1,400 to $1,800.00
Hot Rod Roadster, red, Hornet .60 engine, 15", EX $950.00
McCoy Invader #6, yel, McCoy .49 engine, 17", EX ... $1,400.00

McCoy Streamliner, gray, never drilled engine, 17", NM . $800.00
Melcraft Racer, ignition engine, 1940s, 16", EX, from $600 to $800.00
Ohlsson & Rice Racer #54, orig #29 engine, unused, NMIB, from $600 to $850.00
Railton Champion Racer #12, red & yel, 17", NM $2,700.00
Reuhl Racer #39, .49 McCoy engine, 1940, 17", EX, from $1,900 to $2,200.00
Roy Cox Thimble Drome Champion Racer, VGIB, from $400 to $600.00
Testors Avion Mustang Fighter Airplane, NMIB............ $100.00
Testors Cosmic Wind, Spirit of '76, M $60.00
Testors OD P-51 Mustang, VG........ $30.00

Testers 'Sprite' Racer, McCoy engine, 12½", 1960s, unused, NMIB, A, $125.00. (Photo courtesy serioustoyz.com)

Wen-Mac A-24 Army Attack Bomber, 1962-64, EX.........$45.00
Wen-Mac Albatross, Flying Wing Series, EX........ $40.00
Wen-Mac Boeing P-26 Pursuit Plane, 1960s, unused, MIB .$125.00
Wen-Mac Cutlass, bl, blk & yel, 1958-60, EX $50.00
Wen-Mac Marine Corsair, red, 1960s, EX........ $40.00
Wen-Mac P-63 King Cobra, chrome, 1962-64, EX............$50.00
Wen-Mac RAF Day Fighter, wht, 1963-64, EX $50.00
Wen-Mac Yellow Jacket Corsair, yel, 1959-64, EX $40.00

GI Joe

GI Joe, the most famous action figure of them all, has been made in hundreds of variations since Hasbro introduced him in 1964. The first of these jointed figures was 12" tall; they can be identified today by the mark each carried on his back: GI Joe T.M. (trademark), Copyright 1964. They came with four different hair colors: blond, auburn, black, and brown, each with a scar on his right cheek. They were sold in four basic packages: Action Soldier, Action Sailor, Action Marine, and Action Pilot. A Black figure was also included in the line, and there were representatives of many nations as well — France, Germany, Japan, Russia, etc. These figures did not have scars and are more valuable. Talking GI Joes were issued in 1967 when the only female (the nurse) was introduced. Besides the figures, uniforms, vehicles, guns, and accessories of many varieties were produced. The Adventure Team series, made from 1970 to 1976, included Black Adventurer, Air Adventurer, Talking Astronaut, Sea Adventurer, Talking Team Commander, Land Adventurer, and several variations. In 1974 Joe's hard plastic hands were replaced with kung fu grips, so that he could better grasp his weapons. Assorted playsets allowed young imaginations to run wild, and besides the doll-size items, there were wristwatches, foot lockers, toys, walkie-talkies, etc., made for the kids themselves. Due to increased production costs, the large GI Joe was discontinued in 1976.

In 1982, Hasbro brought out the smaller 3¾" GI Joe figures, each with its own descriptive name. Of the first series, some characters were produced with either a swivel or straight arm. Vehicles, weapons, and playsets were available, and some characters could only be had by redeeming flag points from the backs of packages. This small version proved to be the most successful action figure line ever made. Loose items are common; collectors value those still mint in the original packages at two to four times higher.

The 1990s through today has seen the exit and return of the 3¾" figures in various series along with the reintroduction of the 12" figure in a few different collections including the Classic Collection and the 30th Anniversay, among others. Joe is still going strong today.

For more information we recommend *Encyclopedia to GI Joe* and *The 30th Anniversary Salute to GI Joe* both by Vincent San Telmo; *Official Collector's Guide to Collecting and Completing, Official Guide to Completing 3¾" Series and Hall of Fame: Vol II*, and *Official Guide To GI Joe: '64 – '78*, all by James DeSimone. Note: All items are American issue unless indicated otherwise. (Action Man was made in England by Hasbro circa 1960 into the 1970s.) All listings are complete unless noted.

See also Games; Lunch Boxes; Puzzles.

12" GI Joe Figures and Figure Sets

Action Pilot, Talking, #7890, MIB, from $1,200.00 to $1,500.00. (Photo courtesy Cotswold Collectibles, Inc.)

Action Marine, #7700, EX to NM, from $100 to **$150.00**
Action Marine, #7700, MIB, from $375 to **$425.00**
Action Marine, Medic, #90711, EX to NM, from $300 to. **$400.00**
Action Marine, Medic, #90711 MIB, from $1,475 to.. **$1,525.00**

Action Marine, Talking, #7790, EX to NM, from $150 to...$200.00
Action Marine, Talking, #7790, MIB, from $775 to....... $825.00
Action Nurse, #8060, EX to NM, from $1,800 to........$2,100.00
Action Nurse, #8060, MIB, from $4,500 to $4,750.00
Action Pilot, #7800, EX to NM, from $150 to $175.00
Action Pilot, #7800, MIB, from $500 to........................ $600.00
Action Pilot, Talking, #7890, EX to NM from $200 to .. $250.00
Action Sailor, #7600, EX to NM, from $150 to............. $250.00
Action Sailor, #7600, MIB, from $375 to $425.00
Action Sailor, Talking, #7690, EX to NM, from $200 to. $325.00
Action Sailor, Talking, #7690, MIB, from $1,000 to ... $1,300.00
Action Soldier, #7500, EX to NM, from $100 to........... $200.00

Action Soldier, #7500, EXIB, A, $250.00. (Photo courtesy Morphy Auctions)

Action Soldier, #7500, MIB, from $400 to $450.00
Action Soldier, Black, #7900, EX to NM, from $475 to. $775.00
Action Soldier, Black, #7900, MIB, from $2,000 to $2,400.00
Action Soldier, Canadian Mountie, #5904, EX to NM, from $800 to...$1,600.00
Action Soldier, Canadian Mountie, #5904, MIB, from $3,500 to $4,000.00
Action Soldier, Forward Observer, #5969, EX to NM, from $225 to.. $350.00
Action Soldier, Forward Observer, #5969, MIB, from $700 to $800.00
Action Soldier, Green Beret, #7536, EX to NM, from $300 to .$500.00
Action Soldier, Green Beret, #7536, MIB, from $2,500 to . $3,000.00
Action Soldier, Talking, #7590, EX to NM, from $75 to. $125.00
Action Soldier, Talking, #7590, MIB, from $775 to $800.00
Adventures of GI Joe, Adventurer, Black, #7905, EX, from $425 to.. $475.00
Adventures of GI Joe, Adventurer, Black, #7905, EX to NM, from $400 to $800.00
Adventures of GI Joe, Adventurer, Black, #7905, MIP, from $2,500 to..$3,000.00
Adventures of GI Joe, Aquanaut, #7910, EX to NM, from $200 to.. $500.00
Adventures of GI Joe, Aquanaut, #7910, MIB, from $2,750 to..$3,250.00
Adventures of GI Joe, Astronaut, Talking, #7615, EX to NM, from $100 to $300.00

Adventures of GI Joe, Astronaut, Talking, #7915, MIB, from $1,000 to..$1,200.00
Adventures of GI Joe, Sharks Surprise Set w/Frogman, #7980, EX to NM, from $100 to $275.00
Adventures of GI Joe, Sharks Surprise Set w/Frogman, #7980, MIB, from $725 to $775.00
AT, Adventurer, Black, #7404, EX to NM, from $100 to . $175.00
AT, Adventurer, Black, #7404, MIB, from $350 to......... $400.00
AT, Adventurer, Black, Life-Like Hair, Kung Fu Grip, #7283, EX to NM, from $75 to $175.00

Adventure Team, Adventurer, Black, Life-Like Hair, Kung Fu Grip, #7283, MIB, from $225.00 to $275.00.

AT, Air Adventurer, Kung Fu Grip, #7282, EX to NM, from $100 to.. $175.00
AT, Air Adventurer, Kung Fu Grip, #7282, MIB, from $300 to... $350.00
AT, Air Adventurer, Kung Fu Grip, #7403, MIB, from $375 to... $425.00
AT, Air Adventurer, Life-Like Hair & Beard, #7282, EX to NM, from $75 to $125.00
AT, Air Adventurer, Life-Like Hair & Beard, #7282, MIB, from $175 to.. $225.00
AT, Astronaut, Talking, #7590, EX to NM, from $100 to.. $200.00
AT, Astronaut, Talking, #7590, MIB, from $400 to........ $450.00
AT, British Commando, #8104, EX to NM, from $275 to . $400.00
AT, Bullet Man, #8026, EX to NM, from $50 to............ $100.00
AT, Bullet Man, #8026, MIB, from $150 to $200.00
AT, Commander, Black, Talking, #7406, MIB, from $800 to .. $850.00
AT, Commander, Black, Talking, Kung Fu Grip, #7291, 1974, EX to NM, from $100 to $325.00
AT, Commander, Black, Talking, Kung Fu Grip, #7291, 1974, MIB, from $675 to $775.00
AT, Commander, Black, Talking, Kung Fu Grip, Life-Like Hair & Beard, #7291, 1976, MIB, from $575 to $650.00
AT, Commander, Talking, #7400, EX to NM, from $50 to ..$150.00
AT, Commander, Talking, #7400, MIB, from $375 to $400.00
AT, Commander, Talking, Kung Fu Grip, #7290, EX to NM, from $100 to.. $200.00
AT, Commander, Talking, Kung Fu Grip, #7290, MIB, from $450 to.. $550.00

AT, Commander, Talking, Life-Like Hair & Beard, #7400, EX to NM, from $75 .... $125.00
AT, Commander, Talking, Life-Like Hair & Beard, #7400, MIB, from $375 to $425.00
AT, Eagle Eye Commando, Black, #7278, EX to NM, from $75 to $150.00
AT, Eagle Eye Commando, Black, #7278, MIB, from $225 to $275.00
AT, Eagle Eye Land Commander, #7276, EX to NM, from $50 to $100.00
AT, Eagle Eye Land Commander, #7276, MIB, from $125 to.. $175.00
AT, Eagle Eye Man of Action, #7277, EX to NM, from $50 to $100.00
AT, Eagle Eye Man of Action, #7277, MIB, from $150 to . $175.00
AT, Intruder Commander, #8050, EX to NM, from $50 to. $75.00
AT, Intruder Commander, #8050, MIB, from $125 to $150.00
AT, Intruder Warrior, #8051, EX to NM, from $50 to $75.00
AT, Intruder Warrior, #8051, MIB, from $150 to.......... $200.00
AT, Land Adventurer, #7270, EX to NM, from $25 to...... $50.00
AT, Land Adventurer, #7270, MIB, from $150 to.......... $175.00
AT, Land Adventurer, #7401, EX to NM, from $50 to ... $100.00
AT, Land Adventurer, #7401, MIB, from $150 to.......... $175.00
AT, Land Adventurer, Life-Like Hair & Beard, Kung Fu Grip, #7280, EX to NM, from $25 to.......... $50.00

Adventure Team, Land Adventurer, Life-Like Hair and Beard, Kung Fu Grip, #7280, MIB, from $125.00 to $175.00. (Photo courtesy Morphy Auctions)

AT, Man of Action, #7274/#7284, EX to NM, from $25 to. $50.00
AT, Man of Action, #7274/#7284, MIB, from $150 to ... $200.00
AT, Man of Action, #7500, EX to NM, from $50 to....... $100.00
AT, Man of Action, #7500, MIB, from $200 to $250.00
AT, Man of Action, Life-Like Hair & Beard, Kung Fu Grip, #7284, EX to NM, from $50 to.......... $100.00
AT, Man of Action, Life-Like Hair & Beard, Kung Fu Grip, #7284, MIB, $175 to.......... $225.00
AT, Man of Action, Talking, #7292, EX to NM, from $100 to ... $200.00
AT, Man of Action, Talking, #7292, MIB, from $625 to . $675.00
AT, Man of Action, Talking, #7590, EX to NM, from $50 to.. $150.00
AT, Man of Action, Talking, #7590, MIB, from $325 to . $375.00

AT, Man of Action, Talking, Life-Like, Kung Fu Grip, #7292, EX to NM, from $100 to $200.00
AT, Man of Action, Talking, Life-Like, Kung Fu Grip, #7292, MIB, from $625 to $675.00
AT, Mike Powers Atomic Man, #8025, EX to NM, from $25 to.......... $50.00
AT, Mike Powers Atomic Man, #8025, MIB, from $100 to. $150.00
AT, Sea Adventurer, #7271, EX to NM, $50 to $100.00
AT, Sea Adventurer, #7271, MIB, from $225 to.......... $275.00
AT, Sea Adventurer, #7281, EX to NM, from $75 to $125.00
AT, Sea Adventurer, #7281, MIB, from $275 to.......... $325.00
AT, Sea Adventurer, #7402, MIB, from $225 to.......... $275.00
AT, Sea Adventurer, #7402, NM.......... $75.00
AT Commander, Black, Talking, #7406, EX to NM, from $125 to $450.00
Australian Jungle Fighter, #8105, EX to NM, from $225 to. $375.00
Australian Jungle Fighter, #8105, MIB, from $2,000 to . $2,750.00
Australian Jungle Fighter, #8205, MIB, from $1,000 to . $1,200.00
Australia Jungle Fighter, #8205, EX to NM, from $125 to. $250.00
British Commando, #8104, MIB, from $2,225 to $2,750.00
British Commando, #8204, EX to NM, from $125 to..... $250.00
British Commando, #8204, MIB, from $1,500 to $18.00
French Resistance Fighter, #8103, EX to NM, from $175 to. $225.00
French Resistance Fighter, #8103, MIB, from $2,000 to . $2,500.00
French Resistance Fighter, #8203, EX to NM, from $100 to. $200.00

French Resistance Fighter, #8203, MIB, from $1,000.00 to $1,500.00. (Photo courtesy Cotswold Collectibles, Inc.)

German Storm Trooper, #8100, EX to NM, from $250 to . $400.00
German Storm Trooper, #8100, MIB, from $2,250 to.. $2,400.00
German Storm Trooper, #8200, EX to NM, from $250 to . $350.00
German Storm Trooper, #8200, MIB, from $1,000 to.. $1,500.00
Japanese Imperial Soldier, #8101, EX to NM, from $400 to.. $650.00
Japanese Imperial Soldier, #8101, MIB, from $2,500 to. $2,800.00
Japanese Imperial Soldier, #8201, MIB, from $1,200 to. $1,500.00
Russian Infantry Man, #8102, EX to NM, from $250 to. $375.00
Russian Infantry Man, #8102, MIB, from $2,000 to $2,500.00
Russian Infantry Man, #8202, MIB, from $1,000 to $1,500.00

Accessories for 12" GI Joe

Action Marine Basics Set, #7722, EX, from $55 to $60.00
Action Marine Beachhead Assault Field Pack Set, #7713, EX, from $75 to $100.00
Action Marine Beachhead Flamethrower Set, #7718, NM, from $25 to...$35.00
Action Marine Communications Field Radio & Telephone, #7703, MIP, from $250 to.. $300.00
Action Marine Communications Poncho, #7702, NM, from $45 to...$55.00
Action Marine Demolition Set, #7730, NM, from $75 to.$85.00
Action Marine Dress Parade Set, #7710, MIP, from $425 to . $475.00
Action Marine Medic Set, #7720, MIP, from $100 to $150.00
Action Marine Paratrooper Helmet Set, #7707, MIP, from $80 to $90.00
Action Marine Tank Commander Set, #7731, MIP, from $1,200 to.. $1,500.00
Action Pilot Air Acadamy Cadet Set, #7822, MIP, from $900 to $1,200.00
Action Pilot Air Force Police Equipment, #7813, NM, from $100 to.. $125.00
Action Sailor Annapolis Cadet Outfit, #7624, MIP, from $1,200 to.. $1,500.00
Action Sailor Breeches Buoy, #7625, NM, from $400 to. $450.00
Action Sailor Deep Sea Diver Set, #7620, EX+, from $300 to.. $350.00
Action Sailor Frogman Scuba Tank Set, MIP, from $75 to..$125.00
Action Sailor MP Uniform Set, #7521, EX+ $500.00
Action Sailor Navy Attack Helmet Set, #7610, MIP, from $125 to... $175.00
Action Sailor Navy Basics Set, #7628, NM+, from $50 to.$60.00
Action Sailor Navy Machine Gun Set, #7618, NM $75.00
Action Sailor Shore Patrol Dress Jumper Set, #7613, MIP ..$200.00
Action Sailor Shore Patrol Dress Pant Set, #7614, EX+, from $35 to...$45.00
Action Soldier Bivouac Machine Gun Set, #7514, MIP, from $120 to.. $130.00
Action Soldier Bivouac Machine Gun Set, #7514, reissue, MIP, from $175 to $200.00
Action Soldier Combat Construction Set, #7572, EX+ . $350.00
Action Soldier Combat Fatigue Pants, #7504, NM, from $20 to... $30.00
Action Soldier Combat Field Jacket, #7505, EX, from $50 to..$60.00
Action Soldier Combat Field Pack Deluxe Set, #7502, MIP. $300.00
Action Soldier Combat Rifle Set, #7510, MIP, from $300 to .. $350.00
Action Soldier Green Beret & Small Arms Set, #7533, EX.$75.00
Action Soldier Heavy Weapons Set, #7538, EX+, from $150 to.. $200.00
Action Soldier Life Ring (USN), #7627C, MIP................$70.00
Action Soldier MP Ike Jacket, #7524, NM+, from $50 to.$60.00
Action Soldier Ski Patrol Deluxe Set, #7531, EX+, from $150 to $175.00
Action Soldier Snow Troop Set, #7529, MIP, from $150 to.. $200.00
Action Soldier Special Forces Bazooka Set, #7528, NM, from $40 to...$50.00
Action Soldier West Point Cadet Uniform Set, #7537, EX+, from $225 to $275.00

Adventures of GI Joe, Hidden Missile Discovery Set, #7952, EX, from $65 to $75.00
Adventures of GI Joe Adventure Locker, #7940, EX...... $175.00
Adventures of GI Joe Mysterious Explosion Set, #7921, MIP, from $400 to $450.00
Adventures of GI Joe Perilous Rescue Set, #7923, MIP, from $500 to $550.00
AT, Secret Mountain Outpost, #8040, EX, from $50 to $75.00
AT, Secret Mountain Outpost, #8040, MIB, from $125 to ..$175.00
AT Black Widow Rendezous Super Deluxe Set, #7414, EX+.. $150.00
AT Danger of the Depths, #7412, NM+ $200.00
AT Dangerous Climb Outfit, #7309E, MOC $70.00
AT Dangerous Climb Set, #7309-2, EX+ $25.00

Adventure Team Demolition Set, #7370, MIP, from $100.00 to $150.00. (Photo courtesy Cotswold Collectibles, Inc.)

Adventure Team Desert Explorer Action Outfit, #7309-5, MIP, from $75.00 to $85.00. (Photo courtesy Cotswold Collectibles, Inc.)

AT Desert Survival Set, #7308-6, NM+ $50.00
AT Diver's Distress, #7328-6, NM..................................$75.00
AT Emergency Rescue Set, #7374, EX+ $50.00
AT Fantastic Freefall Set, #7423, EX+ $150.00
AT Fight For Survival Set, #7308-2, NM+ $50.00
AT Fight For Survival Set, #7431, NM, from $525 to $575.00

Adventure Team Flying Rescue Set, #7361, MIB, from $75.00 to to $100.00.

AT Footlocker, #8000, NM+ $100.00
AT Headquarters, #7490CLN, NMIB $325.00
AT Hidden Treasure, #7308-1, MIP $50.00
AT Hurricane Spotter Set, #7343, NM $100.00
AT Jungle Ordeal Set, #7309-3, MIP, from $65 to $75.00

Adventure Team Jungle Survival Set, #7323, MIP, from $175.00 to $200.00. (Photo courtesy Cotswold Collectibles, Inc.)

AT Laser Rescue, #7311, MOC $65.00
AT Magnetic Flaw Detector Set, #7319-2, NM $25.00
AT Race For Recovery, #8028-1, EX $25.00
AT Radiation Detection Set, #7341, MIP $95.00
AT Rocket Pack Set, #7315, NM $25.00
AT Secret Agent Set, #7375, NM $60.00
AT Seismograph, #7319C, MIP $80.00
AT Signal Flasher Set, #7362, MIP $75.00
AT Special Assignment, #8028-3, EX $35.00
AT Training Center, #7495, MIB $250.00
AT Trouble at Vulture Pass, #59289, MIP, from $300 to .. $350.00
AT Underwater Demolitioin Set, #7310, MIP $50.00
AT Volcano Jumper Set, #7344, NM+ $200.00
AT White Tiger Hunt Set, #7436, NM+ $200.00

Australian Jungle Fighter Set, #8305, MIP $225.00
British Commando Set, #8304, MIP $335.00
French Resistance Fighter Set, #8303, NM+ $65.00
German Soldier Equipment Set, #8300, MOC $350.00
German Storm Trooper, #8300, EX+ $150.00
Japanese Imperial Soldier Set, #8301, NM+ $300.00
Russian Infantryman Equipment, #8302, MOC $350.00

Vehicles for 12" GI Joe

Action Pilot Official Space Capsule Set, #8020, MIB, from $325 to $375.00
Action Pilot Spacewalk Mystery, #7981, EXIB, from $125 to $150.00
Action Sailor Official Sea Sled & Frogman Set, #8050, NMIB, from $275 to $325.00
Action Soldier Armored Car, #5397, EXIB, from $150 to $175.00
Action Soldier Jet Fighter Plane, #5396, NMIB, from $450 to $500.00
Action Soldier Official Jeep Combat Set, #7000, w/ or w/o sound, EXIB, from $200 to $250.00

Action Soldier Official Combat Jeep Set, #7000, MIP, from $500.00 to $575.00.

Adventures of GI Joe Sharks Surprise Set, w/ or w/o figure, #7980 or #7980-83, NMIB, ea from $300 to $350.00
Adventures of GI Joe Spacewalk Mystery Set, w/ or w/o figure, #7981 or #7981-83, EXIB, ea from $100 to $150.00
AT Big Trapper, #7498, NMIB, from $100 to $125.00
AT Capture Copter, #7480, MIB, from $300 to $350.00
AT Chopper Cycle, #59114, EXIB, from $25 to $35.00
AT Combat Action Jeep, #59751, NMIB, from $60 to $75.00
AT Fantastic Sea Wolf Submarine, #7460, NMIB, from $75 to $125.00
AT Giant Air-Sea Helicopter, #59189, NMIB, from $100 to .. $150.00
AT Sandstorm Survival Adventure, #7493, NMIB, from $175 to $225.00
AT Sky Hawk, #7470, EXIB, from $50 to $75.00
AT Vehicle Set, #7005, NMIB, from $75 to $100.00

3¾" GI Joe Figures

Air Commandos, 1991, any character, MOC, ea from $25 to $35.00

Tripwire, Airborne, Doc, and Snow Job, 1983, MOC, each from $60.00 to $70.00. (Photo courtesy Morphy Auctions)

Airtight, 1985, MOC, from $55 to $65.00
Alley-Viper, 1989/1993/1994, MOC, ea from $10 to $18.00
Alpine, 1985, MOC, from $50 to $60.00
Ambush, 1990, MOC, from $12 to $18.00
Astro-Viper, 1988, MOC, from $20 to $30.00
Backblast, 1989, MOC, from $12 to $18.00

Flint, 1985, MOC, from $65.00 to $75.00; Barbecue, 1985, MOC, from $65.00 to $75.00; Quick Kick, 1985, MOC, from $65.00 to $75.00; Bazooka, 1985, MOC, from $60.00 to $70.00. (Photo courtesy Morphy Auctions)

Barbecue, 1992, MOC, from $8 to $12.00
BAT, 1986, MOC, from $30 to $40.00
BAT, 1991, MOC, from $12 to $18.00
Bazooka, 1993, MOC, from $12 to $18.00
Beach-Head, 1986, MOC, from $50 to $75.00
Beach-Head, 1993, MOC, from $12 to $18.00
Big Ben, 1991, MOC, from $12 to $18.00
Big Boa, 1987, MOC, from $15 to $25.00
Blizzard, 1988, MOC, from $15 to $25.00
Blow Torch, 1984, MOC, from $45 to $55.00
Breaker, 1983, MOC, from $50 to $60.00
Budo, 1988, MOC, from $15 to $25.00
Buzzer, 1985, MOC, from $55 to $65.00
Charbroil, 1988, MOC, from $15 to $25.00
Chuckles, 1987, MOC, from $20 to $30.00
Cobra, 1982, MOC, from $125 to $150.00
Cobra, 1983, MOC, from $75 to $100.00
Cobra Commander, 1982, mail-in, MOC, from $150 to . $200.00
Cobra Commander, 1983, MOC, from $75 to $100.00

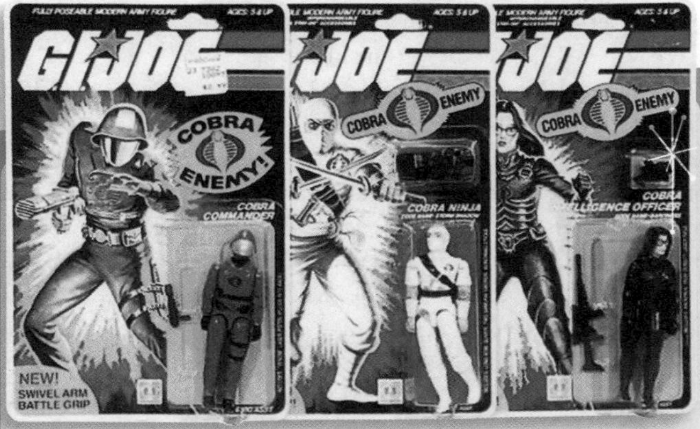

Cobra Commander, 1984, MOC, from $35.00 to $40.00; Storm Shadow, 1984, MOC, from $150.00 to $160.00; Baroness, 1984, MOC, from $175.00 to $185.00. (Photo courtesy Morphy Auctions)

Cobra Commander, 1987, MOC, from $25 to $35.00
Cobra Commander, 1991, w/eyebrows, MOC, from $45 to .. $55.00
Cobra Commander, 1991, w/o eyebrows, MOC, from $20 to ... $30.00
Cobra Commander, 1993, MOC, from $12 to $18.00
Cobra Officer, 1982, MOC, from $125 to $150.00
Cobra Officer, 1983, MOC, from $75 to $100.00
Cobra-La Team, 1987, set of 3, MOC, from $70 to $80.00
Crazy Legs, 1987, MOC, from $25 to $35.00
Crimson Guard, 1985, MOC, from $90 to $100.00
Crimson Guard Commander, 1993, MOC, from $12 to $18.00
Croc Master, 1987, MOC, from $25 to $35.00
Crystal Ball, 1987, MOC, from $15 to $25.00
Deep Six, 1989, MOC, from $15 to $25.00
DEF, 1992, any character, MOC, from $10 to $15.00
Destro, 1983, MOC, from $65 to $75.00
Dial-Tone, 1986, MOC, from $40 to $50.00
Downtown, 1989, MOC, from $15 to $25.00
Dr Mindbender, 1986, MOC, from $30 to $40.00
Dr Mindbender, 1993, MOC, from $10 to $15.00
Duke, 1983, MOC, from $85 to $95.00
Duke, 1984, MOC, from $70 to $80.00
Dusty, 1985, MOC, from $60 to $70.00
Eco Warriors, 1991, any character, MOC, ea from $10 to . $15.00
Eels, 1985, MOC, from $60 to $70.00
Eels, 1993, MOC, from $10 to $15.00
Falcon, 1987, MOC, from $25 to $35.00
Fast Draw, 1987, MOC, from $25 to $35.00
Firefly, 1984, MOC, from $165 to $185.00
Firefly, 1992/1993, MOC, ea from $12 to $18.00
Flak-Viper, 1993, MOC, from $12 to $18.00
Flash, 1982, MOC, from $80 to $90.00
Flash, 1983, MOC, from $65 to $75.00
Footloose, 1985, MOC, from $55 to $65.00

Grunt, 1982, MOC, from $80 to $90.00
Grunt, 1983, MOC, from $65 to $75.00
Gung-Ho, 1983, MOC, from $65 to $75.00
Gung-Ho, 1987, MOC, from $20 to $30.00
Hardball, 1988, MOC, from $12 to......................................$18.00
Hawk, 1986, MOC, from $45 to $55.00
Headhunter Stormtrooper, 1993, MOC, from $10 to........$15.00
HEAT Viper, 1993, MOC, from $10 to..............................$15.00
Hydro-Viper, 1988, MOC, from $20 to..............................$30.00
Ice Sabre, 1991, MOC, from $12 to $18.00
Iceberg, 1986, MOC, from $40 to $50.00
Iron Grenadier, 1988, MOC, from $15 to..........................$20.00
Iron Grenadiers Annihilator, 1989, MOC, from $18 to....$25.00
Iron Grenadiers Metal-Head, 1990, MOC, from $12 to....$18.00
Iron Grenadiers Underflow, 1990, MOC, from $12 to.......$18.00
Jinx, 1987, MOC, from $20 to $30.00
Lady Jaye, 1985, MOC, from $85 to..................................$95.00
Laser-Viper, 1990, MOC, from $12 to...............................$18.00
Law & Order, 1987, MOC, from $20 to.............................$30.00
Leatherneck, 1986, MOC, from $40 to..............................$50.00
Lifeline, 1986, MOC, from $40 to......................................$50.00
Low-Light, 1986, MOC, from $25 to $35.00
Low-Light, 1991, MOC, from $15 to $20.00
Mainframe, 1986, MOC, from $25 to $35.00
Major Bludd, 1982, MOC, from $100 to.......................... $125.00
Major Bludd, 1983, from $50 to $60.00
Major Bludd, 1994, MOC, from $12 to..............................$18.00
Monkeywrench, 1986, MOC, from $30 to..........................$40.00
Mutt, 1984, MOC, from $60 to..$70.00
Night Creeper, 1990, MOC, from $12 to............................$15.00
Night Creeper Leader, 1993, MOC, from $10 to...............$15.00
Night Force, 1988, any set of 2, MOC, ea from $65 to......$75.00
Ninja Force Dice or Slice, 1992, MOC, ea from $12 to $18.00
Ninja Force Dojo, Nunchuk, Storm Shadow or T'Jband, 1992, MOC, ea from $22 to $28.00
Outbreak, 1987, MOC, from $15 to...................................$25.00
Pathfinder, 1990, MOC, from $12 to $18.00
Psyche-Out, 1987, MOC, from $15 to $25.00
Python Patrol, 1989, any figure, MOC, from $20 to..........$30.00
Range-Viper, 1990, MOC, from $15 to...............................$20.00
Raptor, 1987, MOC, from $15 to $25.00
Recoil, 1989, MOC, from $12 to..$18.00
Recondo, 1984, MOC, from $55 to....................................$65.00
Repeater, 1988, MOC, from $15 to....................................$25.00
Rip Cord, 1983, MOC, from $50 to $60.00
Ripper, 1985, MOC, from $50 to $60.00
Road Pig, 1988, MOC, from $15 to $25.00
Roadblock, 1984, MOC, from $75 to..................................$85.00
Rock 'N Roll, 1982, MOC, from $85 to.......................... $100.00
Rock 'N Roll, 1983, MOC, from $75 to..............................$85.00
Rock 'N Roll, 1989, MOC, from $12 to..............................$18.00
Rock-Viper, 1990, MOC, from $15 to.................................$20.00
Sci-Fi, 1991, MOC, from $15 to $20.00
Scrap-Iron, 1984, MOC, from $45 to.................................$55.00
Sgt Slaughter's Renegades, 1987, set of 3, MOC, from $45 to $55.00
Shipwreck, 1985, MOC, from $65 to..................................$75.00
Short-Fuze, 1982 or 1983, MOC, from $55 to $65.00
Sky Patrol, 1990, any character, MOC, ea from $20 to.....$30.00
Slaughter's Maruaders, 1989, any figure, MOC, ea from $20 to $30.00

Zap, 1982, MOC, from $50.00 to $60.00; Snake Eyes, 1982, MOC, from $150.00 to $175.00; Breaker, 1982, MOC, from $65.00 to $75.00. (Photo courtesy Morphy Auctions)

Snake Eyes, 1985, MOC, from $140 to $150.00
Sneak Peek, 1987, MOC, from $25 to $35.00
Snow Serpent, 1985, MOC, from $65 to $75.00
Snow Serpent, 1991, MOC, from $12 to $18.00
Snow Storm, 1993, MOC, from $10 to..............................$15.00
Sonice Fighters, 1990, any character, MOC, ea from $15 to... $25.00
Spirit, 1984, MOC, from $70 to..$80.00

Stalker, 1982, MOC, from $100.00 to $125.00; Scarlett, 1982, MOC, from $165.00 to $185.00. (Photo courtesy Morphy Auctions)

Stalker, 1989, MOC, from $12 to......................................$18.00
Starduster, 1987, MOC, from $25 to.................................$35.00
Steel Brigade, 1987, MOC from $35 to.............................$45.00
Storm Shadow, 1988, MOC, from $35 to $45.00
Stretcher, 1990, MOC, from $12 to $18.00
Super Trooper, 1988, MOC, from $25 to $35.00
Talking Battle Commanders, 1991, any character MOC, ea from $12 to $18.00
Techno-Viper, 1987, MOC, from $15 to............................$25.00

Tele-Viper, 1985, MOC, from $40 to $50.00
Tiger Force, 1988, any character, MOC, from $40 to $50.00
Tomax & Xamot, 1985, MOC, from $175 to................. $200.00
Topside, 1990, MOC, from $12 to...................................$18.00
Torch, 1985, MOC, from $55 to $65.00
Torpedo, 1983, MOC, from $70 to...................................$80.00
Toxo-Viper, 1988, MOC, from $20 to...............................$30.00
Toxo-Zombie, 1992, MOC, from $10 to $15.00
Tracker, 1991, MOC, from $15 to $20.00
Tunnel Rat, 1987, MOC, from $25 to...............................$35.00
Viper, 1986, MOC, from $30 to $40.00
Viper, 1994, MOC, from $12 to $18.00
Voltar, 1988, MOC, from $15 to $25.00
Wild Bill, 1992, MOC, from $10 to $15.00
Wild Bill, 1993, MOC, from $10 to $15.00
Zandar, 1986, MOC, from $30 to $40.00
Zap, 1983, MOC, from $50 to $60.00
Zarana, 1985, MOC, from $30 to $40.00
Zarana, 1986, w/earrings, MOC, from $75 to $100.00

Vehicles and Accessories for 3¾" GI Joe

Air Defense, 1985, MIP, from $20 to................................$30.00
Anti-Aircraft Gun, 1987, MIP, from $10 to........................$20.00

Arctic Blast With Windchill, 1989, MIB, from $45.00 to $50.00.

Armadillo Mini Tank, 1985, MIP, from $30 to $40.00
Attack Cruiser, 1991, MIP, from $20 to $25.00
Avalanche, 1990, MIP, from $25 to.................................$35.00
Barracuda, 1992, MIP, from $15 to.................................$20.00
Battle Copter, 1991, MIP, from $20 to $30.00
Battle Copter w/Heli-Viper, 1992, MIP, from $20 to $25.00
Bomb Disposal, 1985, MIP, from $20 to $30.00
CAT, 1985, MIP, from $85 to $100.00
CLAW, 1984, MIP, from $40 to.......................................$60.00
Cobra Adder, 1988, MIP, from $20 to $25.00
Cobra Battle Barge, 1988, MIP, from $18 to $22.00
Cobra Glider, 1983, MIP, from $125 to $175.00

Cobra Ferret, 1985, MIB, from $40.00 to $50.00.

Cobra Hydro Sled, 1986, MIP, from $20 to........................$30.00
Cobra Rat, 1992, MIP, from $20 to $25.00
Cobra Rifle Range Unit, 1985, MIP, from $20 to..............$30.00
Condor Z25, 1989, from $50 to $60.00
Conquest X-30, MIP, from $20 to....................................$30.00
Crossfire-Alfa, 1987, MIP, from $75 to........................... $100.00
Devilfish, 1986, MIP, from $20 to....................................$30.00
Dominator Snow Tank, 1988, MIP, from $20 to $30.00
Dreadnok Air Skiff, 1987, MIP, from $25 to $35.00
Dreadnok Thunder Machine, 1986, MIP, from $30 to $40.00
Earth Borer, 1987, MIP, from $10 to................................$15.00
Eco Warriors Toxo-Lab, 1992, MIP, from $25 to...............$35.00
Falcon, 1983, MIP, from $125 to $175.00
FANG II, 1989, MIP, from $25 to $35.00
FLAK, 1982, MIP, from $75 to $85.00
Flight Pod, 1985, MIP, from $30 to $40.00
General, 1990, MIP, from $55 to $65.00
GI Joe Headquarters, 1992, MIP, from $50 to $75.00
Hammerhead, 1990, MIP, from $40 to $60.00
Headquarters Command Center, 1983, MIP, from $150 to $200.00
Headquarters Missile-Command Center, 1983, MIP, from $200 to $225.00
Hovercraft Killer WHALE, 1984, MIP, from $125 to..... $150.00
Ice Sabre, 1991, MIP, from $12 to $18.00
Iron Grenadiers DEMON, 1988, MIP, from $40 to............$50.00
Machine Gun Nest, 1988, MIP, from $10 to.....................$15.00
Mamba, 1987, MIP, from $25 to $35.00
Mean Dog, 1988, MIP, from $45 to $55.00
Mine Sweeper, 1988, MIP, from $10 to $15.00
MOBAT, 1982, MIP, from $125 to $150.00
Moray, 1985, MIP, from $75 to $85.00
Mountain Climber, 1987, MIP, from $10 to.......................$15.00
Movile Command Center, 1987, MIP, from $90 to $115.00
Night Raven S-3P, 1986, MIP, from $70 to........................$80.00
Outpost Defender, 1986, MIP, from $12 to $18.00
Overlord's Dictator, 1990, MIP, from $25 to $35.00
Patriot, 1992, MIP, from $30 to $35.00
Python Patrol ASP, 1989, MIP, from $25 to......................$35.00
Raider, 1989, MIP, from $55 to.......................................$65.00
Rattler, 1984, MIP, from $100 to $125.00
Rocket Sled, 1988, MIP, from $10 to $15.00

Rolling Thunder, 1988, MIP, from $100 to $115.00
Rope Crosser, 1987, MIP, from $12 to $18.00
Sky Hawk, 1984, MIP, from $40 to $50.00
Sky Patrol Hawk, 1990, MIP, from $30 to $35.00
Skystorm X-Wing Chopper, 1988, MIP, from $25 to $35.00
Slugger, 1984, MIP, from $50 to $75.00
Snow Cat, 1985, MIP, from $65 to $85.00
Storm Eagle Jet, 1992, MIP, from $20 to $30.00
Surveillance Port, 1986, MIP, from $20 to $30.00
Swamp Skier, 1984, MIP, from $140 to $150.00
Tiger Cat, 1988, MIP, from $45 to $55.00
Tiger Fish, 1989, MIP, from $20 to $30.00
Tiger Rat, 1988, MIP, from $100 to $125.00
Tomahawk, 1986, MIP, from $130 to $150.00
Transportable Tactical Battle Platform, 1985, MIP, from $50 to $75.00
USS Flagg, 1985, MIP, from $475 to $500.00
VAMP, 1982, MIP, from $80 to $100.00
VAMP Mark II, 1984, MIP, from $75 to $95.00
Weapon Transport, 1985, MIP, from $20 to $30.00
Whirlwind, 1983, MIP, from $40 to $50.00
Wolverine, 1983, MIP, from $100 to $125.00

Guns

Diecast guns were a popular toy for two decades, during which time the TV western was born. Kids were offered a dazzling array of these toy guns endorsed by stars like the Lone Ranger, Gene Autry, Roy Rogers, and Hopalong Cassidy. Space guns made popular by Flash Gordon and Tom Corbett, kept pace with the robots coming from Japan. Some of these early lithographed tin guns were fantastic futuristic styles that spat out rays of sparks when you pulled the trigger. But gradually the space race losts its fervor and westerns ran their course, being replaced with detective shows and sitcoms. Guns in disfavor is a recent phenomenon, not relevent before the mid-1980s.

Learn to be realistic when you assess condition; it's critical when evaluating the price of a toy gun. Advisor Bill Hamburg, tells us that 'Old toy gun values have stabilized after being negatively impacted for several years by the Internet auctions. Prices for relatively common toy guns have remained fairly constant over the last year with values for hard-to-find cap guns steadily increasing. I believe we can be fairly certain that most vintage toy guns from the late 1800s to the early 1960s, in excellent or better conition, will hold their value and continue to increase over the foreseeable future. In recent times, some pretty astounding prices have been paid at auctions for both relatively common and scarcer models, especially if they have their original boxes. We have reached a point where the boxes are almost worth as much as the toy they contained.'

Bill goes on to say that 'All vintage toy guns have become increasingly difficult to find at flea markets, antique shops, and toy shows. The exception being a few small regional shows specializing just in toy guns and related collectibles. EBay continues to be the best marketplace to buy and sell collectible toy guns. This is in spite of eBay's penchant for political correctness such as requiring sellers to insert orange plugs in the barrel of these vintage toy pistols. They also no longer allow the sales of toy caps (only the empty boxes) and restrict shipment of toy guns to within the United States. Failure to observe these requirements will result in the auction being cancelled by the eBay 'police.' Although eBay claims otherwise, these restrictions have nothing to do with federal or local law. It's just their rules. Other auction sites do not have these restrictions.'

Finally, Bill says 'Overall enthusiasm for vintage toy guns remains strong with the circle of collectors growing all the time. And why not, these great artifacts of simpler times are beautiful to behold. The quality of these toys will never be duplicated and the boxes that contain them are truly wonderful works of art. Even general collectors can add depth and interest to their collections by including those nostalgic toys of a time long past.'

Air Blaster Gun & Target Set, Wham-O, 1963, EX+IB, A .. $175.00
American Cap Pistol, Kilgore, 1940s, 1st version, flying eagle on ivory-colored grips, 9", EX $325.00

American Cap Pistol, Kilgore, with box of caps, NMIB, A, $700.00. (Photo courtesy Morphy Auctions)

Army .45 Cap Gun, Hubley, CI w/wht grips, EX $50.00
Atomic Buster Mystery Gun, Webb Electric Co, plastic, 11", MIB $250.00
Atomic Disintegrater Repeating Cap Pistol, Hubley, 1950s, MIB $350.00
Atomic Orbetor-X, Italy, plastic, MIB, A $75.00
Atomic Space Pistol, Rosko, b/o, tin, MIB, A $250.00
Automatic Repeater Cap Pistol No 50, Wyandotte, steel, 8", EX+IB, A $60.00
Baby Space Gun, Daiya, litho tin, friction, 6", NM+IB, A .. $150.00
Big Game Rifle, Marx, unused, MIB $125.00
Big Horn Cap Gun, Kilgore, 1940s, 2nd version, CI w/PS revolving cylinder, brn grips, 9", VG $250.00
Buck'n Bronc Cap Guns w/Cowboy Double Holster Set, Russell, NMIB $350.00
Civil War Centennial Sidearm Set, Marx, cap gun & holster, unused, complete, EXOC (NOS) $250.00
Combat Machine Gun #305 w/Automatic Bullet Action, TN, 1960s, tin, b/o, 20", MIB, A $150.00

Cork Shooting Submachine Gun, Marx, 1951, MIB...... $175.00
Cowboy Repeating Cap Pistol, Hubley, 1950s, NP, wht grips, 11½", unused, NMIB $200.00
Cowboy 6-Shooter Water Pistol, Irwin, MIB....................$75.00
Crack Shot Dart Pistol, Wyandotte, steel, w/2 darts, 7", NM (VG box)..$60.00
Darringer w/Dagger, Hubley, 1960s, NP w/red plastic push-out dagger, blk grips, 7", unused, NM $90.00

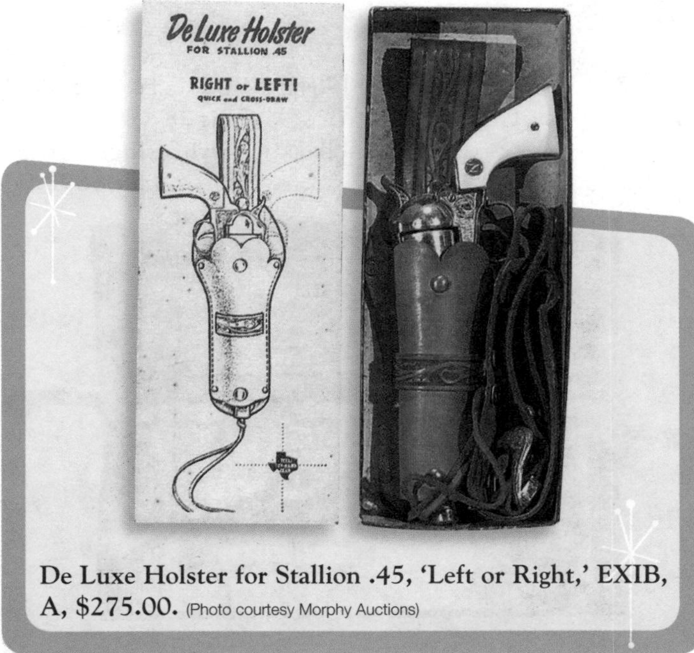

De Luxe Holster for Stallion .45, 'Left or Right,' EXIB, A, $275.00. (Photo courtesy Morphy Auctions)

Deputy Pistol, Hubley, NP, 10", unused, MIB, A $150.00
Detective Automatic Repeater Cap Gun, Roth American Inc, 1970s, MOC, A $60.00
Dixi Cap Pistol, Kenton, 1930s, NP, checked patterns on blk grips, red jewels, 6½", VG....................................... $100.00
Fanner-50 Smoking Cap Pistol, Mattel, revolving cylinder, 11", VGIB.. $200.00

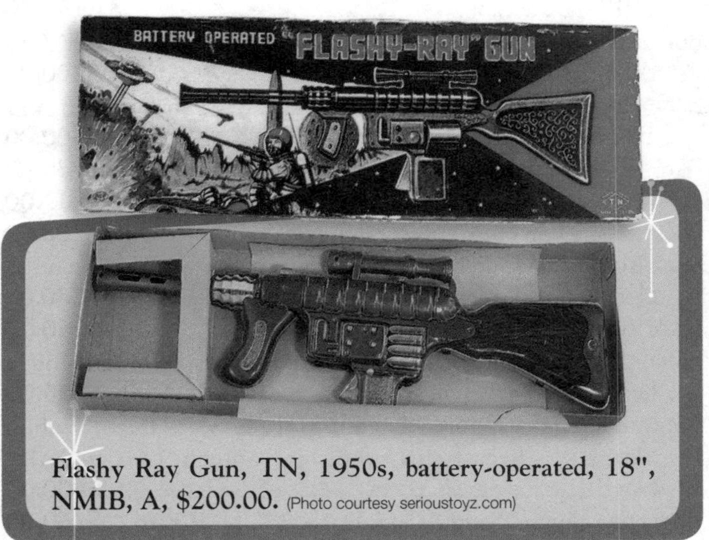

Flashy Ray Gun, TN, 1950s, battery-operated, 18", NMIB, A, $200.00. (Photo courtesy serioustoyz.com)

Frontier Smoker, PR Co, 1950s, 9", NMIB $150.00
Hide-A-Mite Secret Holster & Nicols Cap Pistol, Carnell, MOC...$45.00
Jet Jr 'S' Cap Gun, J&E Stevens, diecast, 6", MIB.......... $300.00
Johnny Seven OMA, Topper Toys, 1960s, Seven Guns in One, plastic, 38", NMIB... $250.00
Junior Rifle (Commando Auto Rifle), Nomura, tin, friction/sparkling shooting action, NMIB $100.00
Little Burp, Gurilla Machine Gun, Mattel, NMIB $100.00
Long Tom Six Shooter, Kilgore, NMIB.......................... $800.00
Mac Machine Gun (No 100), McDowell Mfg Co, 1920s, pump action, uses powderless paper caps, EX (Poor box) .. $100.00
Machine Gun (Cap-Firing), Mattel, 1960s, plastic & metal, 17", NM...$75.00
Marshall Revolving Cap Pistol, Leslie-Henry, 1950s, NP w/blk oval on wht grips, 10½", EX+ $150.00
Monster Space Gun, Horikawa, litho tin, b/o, 22", NM. $100.00
Mountie Repeating Cap Pistol, Hubley, 1950s, NP w/engraved grip, 7", MIB $50.00
Mustang 500, Nichols, NMIB $300.00
Padlock Cap Gun, Hubley, 1950s, NM+............................$75.00
Pioneer Repeating Cap Pistol, Stevens, 1950s, NP, blk grips, 7½", rare, NMIB.. $100.00
Pirate Pistol, Hubley, NM+IB... $200.00
Private Eye 50 Shot Repeater Cap Pistol #2038, Kilgore, 1960s, M (VG+ card) $30.00
Radar Raider (Cap Shooting Tommy Gun), Arliss/Premier Plastics, 18" L, unused, MIB, A $100.00
Ranger Cap Pistol, Kilgore, 1940s, NP w/dk reddish brn grip, 8", unused, EX+.. $225.00
Remmington .36 Cap Pistol, Hubley, NM+IB, A $200.00
Rex Mars Planet Patrol X-92 Sparkling Space Gun X-92, Marx, tin & plastic, w/up, 21½", NM+IB.......................... $300.00
Ric-O-Shay Jr, Hubley, NM+IB $200.00
Rocket-2 Sparkling Space Gun, Marx, tin & plastic, NMIB. $400.00
Rodeo Cap Gun, Hubley, 1950s, NP w/longhorn steer heads emb on wht grips, 8", MIB... $100.00

Scout Cap Rifle, Hubley, 1960s, 36", unused, M, A, $140.00. (Photo courtesy serioustoyz.com)

Sheriff Repeating Cap Pistol, J&E Stevens, 1940s, NP w/red jewels on blk horse-head grips, 8", unused, NMIB $200.00
Shootin' Shell Fanner Cap Pistol, Mattel, 6 Shootin' Shell cartridges, 12 bullet noses, built-in loader, NMIB, A ... $150.00
Shootin' Shell Scout Rifle, Mattel, unused, MIB........... $350.00
Sixfinger, Topper Toys (De Luxe Reading), 1965, plastic finger form shoots 6 different projectiles, MOC $150.00
Space Gun, Pery Nauta, plastic rifle type, blk barrel w/brn stock, 21", MIB, A $50.00

Space Gun, Y, litho tin, 5", unused, MIB $75.00

Space Gun S-68 (Space Rocket Pistol), Nomura, lithographed tin, battery-operated, 10", unused, NM+IB, A, $400.00. (Photo courtesy Smith House Toy and Auction Co.)

Space Jet (Space Super Jet Gun), Yoshiya, tin & plastic, friction, 9½", NM+IB $150.00
Space Machine Gun, SY, 1950s, tin, friction, 12½", NMIB.$150.00
Space Outlaw Atomic Pistol, BCM/England, chrome-plated diecast cap gun w/recoil barrel, 10", MIB................ $300.00
Space Pilot 3-Color Super-Sonic Gun, J&L Randall/England, ca 1953, plastic, b/o, 8½", NM (VG+ box) $150.00
Space Pistol, Rosko, b/o, litho tin, MIB $150.00
Space Pop Gun, Wyandotte, 1930s, PS, blk & red, 7", EX+, A $125.00
Spinner Rifle, Marx, NMOC.. $125.00
Stallion 32 Six Shooter, Nichols, NP, 8", NMIB $125.00
Stallion 38 Repeater Cap Pistol, Nichols, MIB $150.00
Stallion 41-40 Flip Out Six Shooter, Nichols, NM+IB .. $300.00
Stallion 45 Mark II Pistol, Nichols, complete w/blk or wht grips, bullets & caps, NM+IB.. $350.00

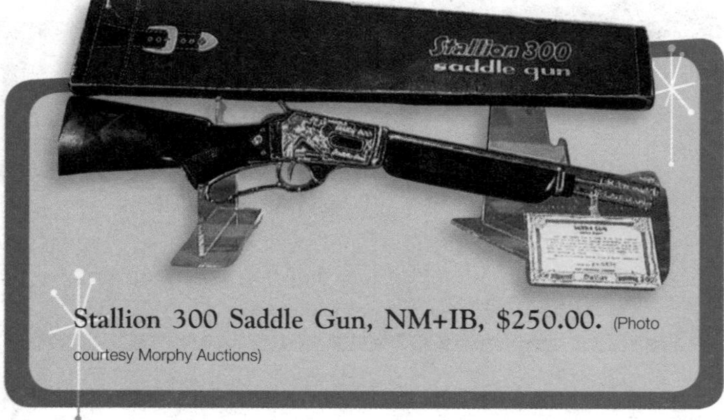

Stallion 300 Saddle Gun, NM+IB, $250.00. (Photo courtesy Morphy Auctions)

Texan .38 Cap Pistol, Hubley, 1960s, NP w/blk steer head emb on wht grips, 10½", MIB.. $250.00
Texan Double Gun & Holster Set, Halco, unused, MIB.. $400.00
Texan Gold De Luxe Pistol, Hubley, NM+IB, A $200.00
Texan Jr Double Gun & Holster Set, Hubley, 1950s, brn leather w/star medallions, stear heads emb on wht grips, NM ..$150.00
Texan Jr Gold Plated Pistol, Hubley, NM+IB, A........... $200.00
Texan Jr Repeating Cap Pistol, Hubley, NMIB, A.......... $100.00
Tiny Tommy Machine Gun, Hubley, 10", MIB.................$75.00
Tommy-Burp Mattel-O-Matic Cap Gun, Mattel, rapid-fire 50 shots, smoking barrel, 24", 1960s, unused, NM $175.00
X-Ray Gun, Nomura, litho tin, b/o, sits on tripod, 16½", NM+IB $325.00
2 Guns in 1 Cap Pistol, Hubley, 1960s, w/2 interchangable barrels, NP w/red star on wht grip, 8", NMIB $150.00

Character

Agent Zero Radio-Rifle, Mattel, 1964, NMIB $80.00
Annie Oakley Cowgirl Outfit, 2 9" guns in wht holsters w/blimages & trim, red & blk skirt w/wht fringe & trim, NMIB, A $690.00

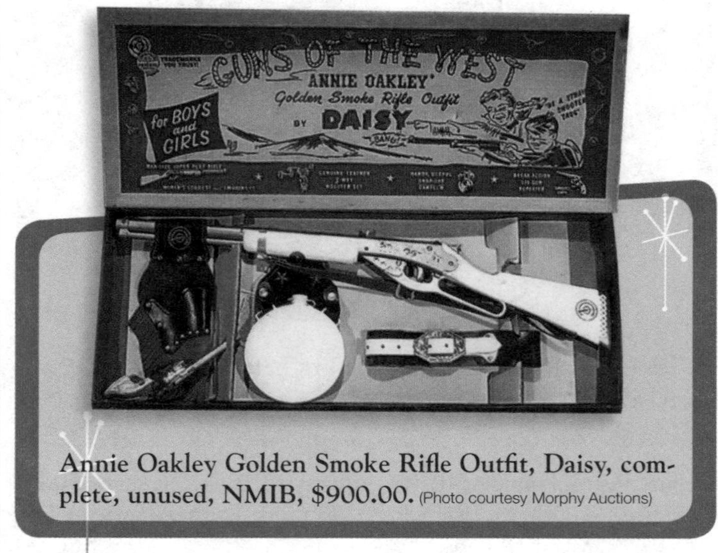

Annie Oakley Golden Smoke Rifle Outfit, Daisy, complete, unused, NMIB, $900.00. (Photo courtesy Morphy Auctions)

Annie Oakley Pistol, wht grips, 9", EX $250.00
Bonanza Double Holster Set, engraved tan leather, 2 9", NP CI Leslie-Henry guns w/blk grips, lever openings, EX+ . $250.00
Bonanza Genuine Leather Holster Set, 2 guns w/blk holsters, EXIB, A...$1,150.00
Bonanza Guns The Hoss Range Pistol, Marx, plastic, 12", EXOC, A $200.00
Buck Rogers Atomic Pistol, Daisy #U-235, 1936, metallic gold, 10", NMIB $500.00
Buck Rogers No U-235 Atomic Pistol, Daisy, PS, 9", VGIB, A $400.00
Buck Rogers Pop Gun, Daisy, PS, name on hdl, 10", EX . $200.00
Buck Rogers Pop Gun & Holster, 9" blk PS gun w/silver accents & cloth-type holster w/BR logos, metal rivets, VG, A... $280.00
Buck Rogers Rocket Pistol, 10", VGIB, A $250.00
Buffalo Bill Repeating Cap Pistol, J&E Stevens, NP w/emb horse heads & red jewels on wht grips, 8", NMIB $175.00
Captain Gallant Foreign Legion Holster Set, Halco, Hubley 'Army 45' diecast gun w/holster, canteen, handcuffs, ID, NMIB... $400.00
Cheyenne Singin' Saddle Gun, Daisy, 33", NMIB, A $260.00
Chuck Conners Cowboy in Africa Smoking Fanner-50 Pistol w/Holster, Mattel, NM+IB $350.00
Cowboy King Revolving Cap Pistol, J&E Stevens, 1940s, 2nd version, gold-tone, cowboy emb on wht grips, 9", VG..... $100.00

Dale Evans Shootin' Iron, Schmidt, crosshatched grips w/red 'jewel' & logo, unused, NM+IB $600.00
Dan Dare Planet Guns, Merit Toys, 1950s, complete, NMIB .. $150.00
Davy Crockett Cap Pistol, Marx, 1950s, pnt marblized plastic w/working metal 'flintlock' hammer & trigger, 10½", NM+ $75.00
Davy Crockett Cap Pistols, Schmidt, metal w/blk grips, 7½", EX, pr $250.00
Davy Crockett Double Gun & Holster Set, R&S Toys, tan & brn leather w/jeweled buckle, name & image on pockets, NMIB $200.00
Davy Crockett Frontier Rifle, Marx/WDP, metal, 34", NMIB. $175.00
Davy Crockett Pistol, Lacto, NP w/bronze-type floral grips, 10½", unused, NM+ $125.00
Dick Tracy Jr Click Pistol #78, Marx, 1930s, aluminum, EX+ $65.00

Dick Tracy 'Police' Siren Pistol, Marx, VGIB, A, $125.00. (Photo courtesy Morphy Auctions)

Dick Tracy Power Jet Squad Gun, Mattel, 1962, 29", EX+ ... $75.00
Dick Tracy Sub-Machine Gun, Tops Plastics, 1951, plastic water gun, 12", EX (VG box) $240.00
Dick Tracy Tommy Gun, Parker Jones Co, diecast, 20", EXIB, A $515.00
Dragnet Double-Barrel Cap Riot Gun, plastic, 33", EXIB, A .. $315.00

Dragnet Badge 714 Cap Gun, Knickerbocker, unused, EXOC, A, $150.00. (Photo courtesy Morphy Auctions)

Dragnet (Official) Police Holster Set, gun, holster, badge & handcuffs, EXIB, A $200.00
Flash Gordon Click Ray Gun, Marx, litho tin, 10", EXIB $350.00
Flash Gordon Signal Pistol, Marx, PS, 7", NMIB, A ... $2,875.00
G-Man Automatic, Marx, PS, w/up, 4", NM+IB $110.00
G-Man Gun, Marx, tin w/wood stock, w/up, 23", EX $175.00
G-Man Gun/Siren Alarm Pistol, Marx, 9", EXIB $225.00
G-Man Machine Gun, Japan, 1950s, 18", unused, MIB . $125.00
G-Man Sparkling Pop Pistol, Marx, steel, 8", NMIB $110.00
G-Man Sparkling Sub-Machine Gun, Marx, plastic, 26", VGIB, A $190.00
Gene Autry '44' Western Pistol, Leslie-Henry, 50-shot repeater, revolving barrel, auto release, side loader, NM+IB, A .. $350.00
Gene Autry Cap Pistol, Kenton, 1940s, 3rd version, NP, red grips, 8", VG $150.00
Gene Autry Cap Pistol, Leslie-Henry, 1950s, NP, transparent amber horse-head grips, 11", unused, EX $175.00
Gene Autry Double Gun & Holster Set, blk leather w/silver studs & yel jewels, 2 8½" Kenton guns w/wht grips, VG ... $325.00

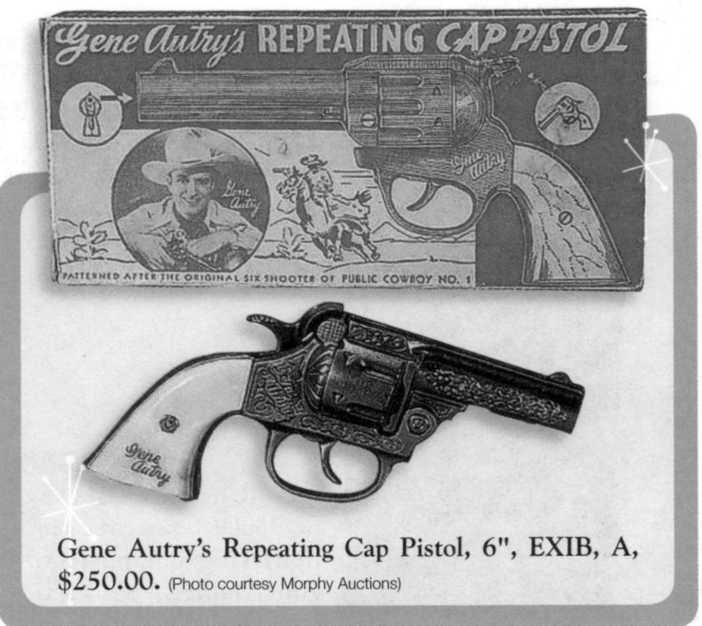

Gene Autry's Repeating Cap Pistol, 6", EXIB, A, $250.00. (Photo courtesy Morphy Auctions)

Gunsmoke Holster Set, Haldo, 2 8" diecast Pinto guns, leather holsters, GIB, A $300.00
Highway Patrol Official Dan Mathews Gun & Badge, EXOC, A $230.00
Hopalong Cassidy (Double) Holster Set, Schmidt, blk grips w/wht cameo busts, blk holsters w/silver studs, EX+IB, A . $1,100.00
Hopalong Cassidy Cap Pistol, Schmidt, blk grip w/wht cameo bust image, unused, 9½", NM+ $275.00
Hopalong Cassidy Cap Pistol, Wyandotte, 1950s, gold-plated w/blk grips, 7½", EXIB $400.00
Hopalong Cassidy Cap Pistol, Wyandotte, 1950s, NP w/blk outlined bust image of Hoppy & signature on wht grips, 8", EX $200.00
Hopalong Cassidy Double Holster Set, Wyandotte, 1950s, blk leather w/silver studs & red jewels, 8" guns w/wht grips, VG $500.00
Hopalong Cassidy Single Holster Set, Wyandotte, blk leather holster w/silver studs, NP pistol w/ivory grip, MIB .. $725.00
James Bond 007 Harpoon Gun, Lone Star, 1960s, EXIB . $100.00
James Bond 007 Hideaway Pistol, Coibel, 1985, NMIB $75.00

James Bond 007 Multi-Buster Machine Gun, plastic, complete, 19", EXIB $350.00

Johnny Ringo (Double) Gun & Holster Set, blk grips, blk holsters w/gold accents, NM+IB, A $800.00

Johnny Ringo Gun & Holster Set, 2 11" guns, brn holsters w/wht decor & line trim, NMIB, A $2,195.00

Johnny Ringo Lanyard Pull Action Gun & Holster, Marx, 10" gun, blk open holster w/staps to hold gun in place, EXIB, A $260.00

Jr-Ranger Cap Pistol, J&E Stevens, 1940s, single shot, NP w/horse heads & cowboys emb on wht grips, 7½", NMIB $125.00

Kit Carson Pistol, Kilgore, NP, lever opening, profile bust emb on blk grips, 9½", NMIB $250.00

Laramie Genuine Leather Holster Set, 2 8½" guns w/blk holsters, EXIB, A $690.00

Lawman Lever Gun (New Smoke/Bang Rifle), Daisy, 33", EXIB, A $230.00

Lone Ranger Carbine Rifle, Leslie-Henry, plastic, shoots caps, 26", NMIB $350.00

Lone Ranger Double Gun & Holster Set Esquire, 1947, blk leather, silver trim, red jewels, 2 Pony Boy cap guns, MIB (NOS) $300.00

Lone Ranger Hi-Yo Silver Pistol, Kilgore, 1938, NP w/brn plastic grips, 8", EX, A $200.00

Lone Ranger Official Outfit, double holster set with nonfiring composition guns, NMIB, $350.00. (Photo courtesy Morphy Auctions)

Lone Ranger Pistol, Kilgore, dk metal w/dk tan grips inscribed Hi-Yo Silver, 8½", EX $275.00

Lone Ranger Single Gun & Holster Set, Esquire, blk leather, silver trim, red jewels, Pony Boy cap gun, MIB $250.00

Lone Ranger Sparkling Pop Pistol, Marx, 1938, metal, 7½", EXIB $165.00

Lost in Space Helmet & Gun Set, Remco, 1966, NMIB. $500.00

Lost in Space Roto-Jet Gun, Mattel, 1966, 20", rare, EX, A. $250.00

Lost in Space Signal Ray Gun & Helmet, Remco, 11½", EXIB, A $630.00

Man From UNCLE Illya Kuryakin Gun Set, Ideal, 13" gun, EXIB, A $460.00

Man From UNCLE Illya Kuryakin Special Agent Secret Lighter Gun, Ideal, plastic, VGIP, A $200.00

Man From UNCLE Napoleon Solo Gun Set, Ideal, converts to rifle, complete, NMIB $500.00

Maverick (Double) Gun & Holster Set, Leslie Henry, 1958, unused, NM (EX box w/James Garner image) $900.00

Maverick Gun & Holster Set, Halco, 8½" diecast w/Maverick lettered in white on blk 'Genuine Leather' holster, EXIB $1,150.00

Maverick Gun & Holster Set, Halco, 10½" Leslie-Henry Gun w/Maverick name on brn holster, EXIB, A $1,370.00

Mickey Mouse Explorers Club Outfit, gun & holster, binocculars, & hat, NMIB, A $345.00

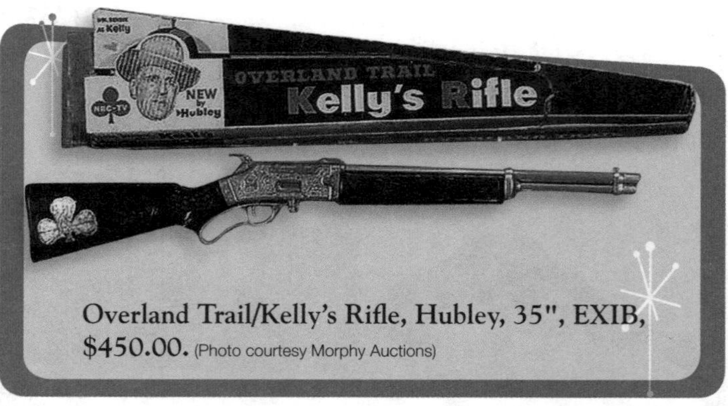

Overland Trail/Kelly's Rifle, Hubley, 35", EXIB, $450.00. (Photo courtesy Morphy Auctions)

Planet Patrol (Rocket-2) Sparkling Space Gun, Marx, tin & plastic, w/up, NMIB $400.00

Popeye Gun Set, Halco, 1961, dbl gun & holster set on 98¢ die-cut Popeye card, EX $300.00

Popeye Pirate Pistol, Marx, litho tin, NMIB, A $250.00

Red Ranger Jr Cap Pistol, Wyandotte, NP w/horse heads & star medallion on wht grips, 7½", NMIB $75.00

Restless Gun & Holster Set, 2 10" guns w/lt tan holsters VGIB, A $400.00

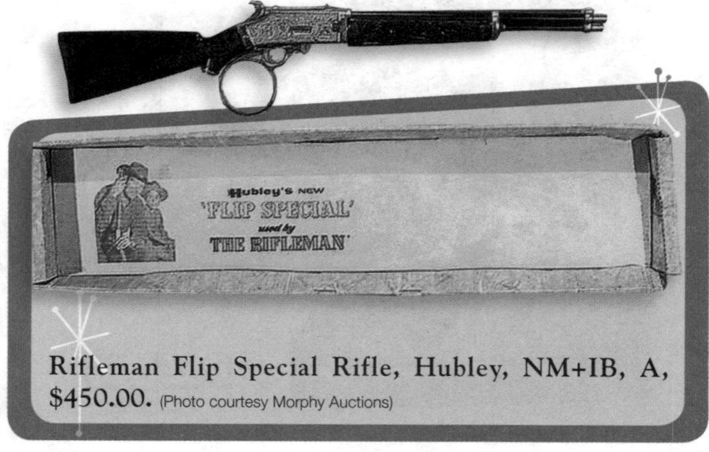

Rifleman Flip Special Rifle, Hubley, NM+IB, A, $450.00. (Photo courtesy Morphy Auctions)

Rin-Tin-Tin Cap Pistol, Actoy, copper-colored metal w/wht grips, 9", NM $125.00

Rin-Tin-Tin 101st Cavalry Outfit, w/single gun & holster, belt & telescope, EXIB, A $515.00

Roy Rogers & Trigger Official (Double) Holster Outfit, blk grips, tan tooled leather w/blk trim, silver studs, NM+IB. $900.00

Roy Rogers Cap Pistol, Kilgore, 1950s, gold-tone finish w/blk horse-head grips, 8", VG.. $175.00
Roy Rogers Cap Pistol, Leslie-Henry, 1950s, 2nd version, revolving, gold-tone w/blk grips, 9", EX+ $200.00
Roy Rogers Cap Pistol, Schmidt, emb Roy Rogers & RR, copper color metal grips w/red jewel, 9", EX....................... $250.00
Roy Rogers Cap Shooting Carbine Rifle, Marx, 25½", NM+IB, A $200.00
Roy Rogers Double Gun & Holster Set, Classy, brn & wht leather w/silver pockets, jewels, 10", Schmidt guns, EXIB $600.00
Roy Rogers Forty Niner Pistol & Spurs Set, Leslie Henry, diecast w/gold finish, blk grips, complete, NMIB................ $900.00
Roy Rogers Shootin' Iron, Kilgore, simulated pearl hdl, 9", MIB... $350.00
Roy Rogers Signal Gun, Langson, diecast, 5½", NM+IB, A . $125.00
Sally Starr Holster Set, 2 8" diecast Maverick Jr guns, wht leather holsters w/bl head images & star trim, EXIB, A........ $745.00
Sergeant Bilko Holster Outfit, Halco, Hubley 'Army 45' diecast gun w/hat & holster set, EXIB, A............................ $400.00
Shane Single Gun & Holster Set, marked Alan Ladd, EX gun/NM+ holster $900.00

Space-Outlaw Atomic Pistol, 10", NM+IB, A, $225.00. (Photo courtesy Morphy Auctions)

Tom Corbett Space Cadet Atomic Pistol Flashlite, Marx, plastic, 7½", NMIB.. $200.00
Tom Corbett Space Cadet Sparkling Space Gun, Marx, litho tin & plastic, 22½", NM+IB (NOS)............................ $400.00
Tom Corbett Space Cadet 1507-A Space Gun, Marx, plastic, 21", EXIB, A $515.00
Untouchables Tommy Gun, Marx, b/o, plastic, 24", EXOC, A $345.00
Wagon Train Complete Western Outfit, Leslie-Henry, w/50-Shot Repeater Rifle, 2 guns & holsters, Derringer, spurs, NMIB..$975.00
Wagon Train Gun & Holster Set, Halco, 2 10" diecast Fanner 50 guns, NM+IB, A $1,600.00
Wanted Dead or Alive Official Mare's Laig Rapid Fire Rifle Pistol, Marx, 19", NMIB, A $1,380.00
Wells Fargo Gun & Holster Set, 2 11" Wells Fargo diecast guns, lt tan holsters w/brn accents, EX+IB, A................$1,725.00
Western Heroes (Zorro) Holster Set, Daisy, Hubley Coyote diecast gun w/blk & wht Zorro holster set, NM+IB, A........... $190.00
Wild Bill Hickok & Jingles, Official Cowboy Outfit, Canadian, 2 9" guns, blk holsters w/wht fringe, NMIB, A $1,600.00
Wild Bill Hickok & Jingles Holsters, 1 10" gun, lg medallions on brn & wht single holster, NMIB, A $575.00
Wild Bill Hickok Cap Pistol, Leslie-Henry, Marshall... on grips, 9½", EX, pr.. $250.00
Wild Bill Hickok Double Gun & Holster Set, 2-tone leather w/name in relief, 11" .44 cap pistols, EX...................... $450.00
Wilma Deering's Gun & Holster (Buck Rogers), NM $500.00

Wyatt Earp Gun Belt (Gun and Holster Set), Esquire Novelty, NMIB, A, $850.00. (Photo courtesy Morphy Auctions)

Wyatt Earp (Double) Holster, Hubley, guns w/blk grips, tan & blk holsters, NM+IB, A.. $550.00
Zorro Cap Pistol, flintlock style, NM $100.00

Early Cast-Iron Cap Shooters

The early cap shooters listed are single shot and action unless noted otherwise.

Bomb, Lockwood, 1880, mk w/crescent moon, 4¼", G .. $200.00

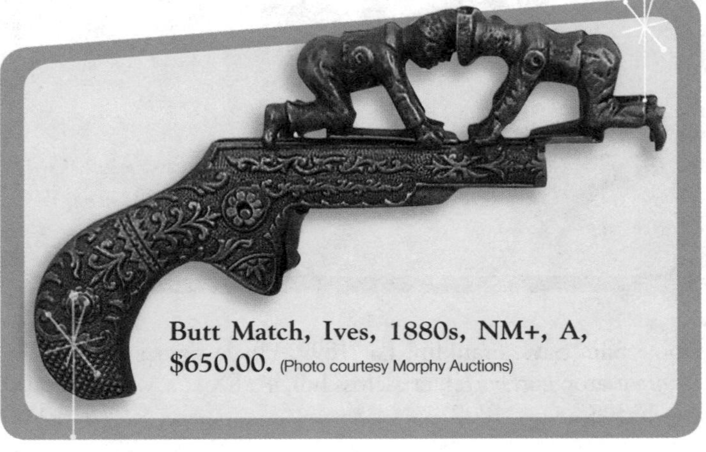

Butt Match, Ives, 1880s, NM+, A, $650.00. (Photo courtesy Morphy Auctions)

Chinese Must Go, Ives, 1880, 5", NM $2,200.00
Clown & Mule, Ives, 5", VG, A $750.00
Clown Seated on Keg, Ives, 4", VG+ $400.00
Frontier, Ives, ca 1890, blk pnt, 5½", VG $250.00
J&ES & Co, 1868, cut-out hdl, single rosette under emb name, VG $400.00
Just Out, Ives, 1884, yel enameled chick comes out of egg, 5¾", VG $2,500.00
Lion, Ives, 1887, lion's head on gun barrel, 5¼", EX $225.00

Mule, Ives, 5¼", VG, A, $750.00. (Photo courtesy James D. Julia, Inc.)

Man on Alligator, Ives, 1883, pnt mouth & hat, 5", EX .. $3,850.00
Pat Jun.10.81, Lockwood, 5", VG+, A $630.00
Punch & Judy, Ives, 1882, 5", EX, A $745.00
Sambo, Ives, 1883, 2 somersaulting figures, 6", VG $650.00
Snap Shot Camera, Ives, 1893, 3¼", NM $950.00

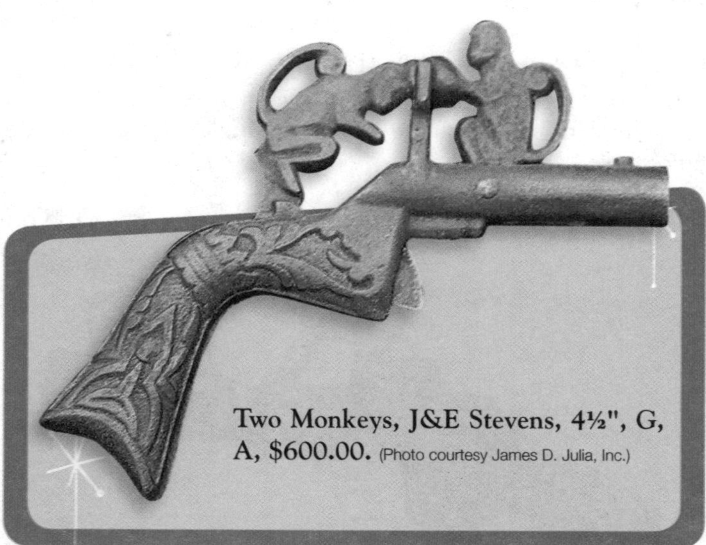
Two Monkeys, J&E Stevens, 4½", G, A, $600.00. (Photo courtesy James D. Julia, Inc.)

Uncle Sam Says, Franklin, Pat 1899, Uncle Sam kicks man in rear atop gun barrel, crisscross hdl, 4", EX $6,000.00
Zip, J&E Stevens, 1890, 4⅞", EX+ $150.00

Related Items and Accessories

Holster on Belt, Dale Evans, unmk, 1950s, tan leather w/blk trim & silver-tone studs, VG $150.00
Holster Set, Buck Rogers, 1930s, tan w/red images on yel rnd patches & stud & star trim on tan felt-type material, EX+ $250.00
Holster Set, Davy Crockett, Arrow Sales, wht leather w/emb medallion, MIB $150.00
Holster Set, Lone Ranger, Smallman & Sons, blk leather w/silver-tone studs & jewels, NMIB $300.00

Holster Set, Roy Rogers, brown leather, NM+IB, A, $500.00. (Photo courtesy Morphy Auctions)

Holster Set, Wild Bill Hickok, unmk, blk & tan leather w/silver-tone studs, diamond setail, VG, pr $200.00
Mechanical Shooting Gallery, Wyandotte, litho tin, w/up, complete w/plastic gun & accessories, 14" L, EXIB $125.00
Posse Shooting Gallery, Wyandotte, complete, EXIB..... $135.00
Shooting Gallery, Wolverine #151-A, litho tin, complete, NMIB $175.00

Tales of Wells Fargo Rifle Rack, wood, holds two rifles, 1959, NM, A, $75.00. (Photo courtesy Morphy Auctions)

Halloween

Halloween items are very collectible right now with old, new, and folk art items demanding great attention from collectors. Many items are being made 'new' in Germany and being sold as vintage items (pre-WWII), and collectors must beware of these items as they are creative and well designed and aged. The rising amount of important folk artists making Halloween-related items is very exciting as reflected in the difficulty of these artists to supply the demand. Haunted-house prop items are also being noticed by collectors. There is even the Castle Halloween Museum dedicated to the fun-loving 'kids' who embrace this most popular holiday. To learn more about the museum, see 'Categories of Special Interests' in the back of the book

For more information we recommend *Halloween Decorations and Games* and *Tastes and Smells of Halloween* by our advisor Pamela Apkarian-Russell, the 'Halloween Queen.'

See also Halloween Costumes.

Book, 'Ghosts What Ain't,' EX..$45.00
Book, Dennison's Boogie Book, 1924, hardcover, 36 pgs, EX..$175.00
Cake Decorations, 3 orange plastic figures w/blk accents, 1950s, 1½" to 1¾", EX+, set..$25.00

Candleholder, Casper the Friendly Ghost holding lid to smiling jack-o'-lantern on grassy base, bisque, United Silver & Cutlery, 1986, NM, $32.00. (Photo courtesy whatacharacter.com)

Candle Set, 5 orange J-O-L's w/wht candles, Gurley, 1950s, unused, NMIP (sealed)...$50.00
Candy Container, blk cat standing on all fours w/head turned, flock-covered compo, removable head, 3", VG+, A.. $100.00
Candy Container, blk cat w/carrot body, cucumber arms, hat & tie, EX.. $225.00
Candy Container, farmer w/orange J-O-L face, head removes to hold candy, pnt compo, 5", EX, A........................... $500.00
Candy Container, ghost, wht muslin-dressed figure w/cb tube body, wht-pnt compo hands, skull head, 6", VG+, A......... $330.00
Candy Container, girl nodder pulling pumpkin house on 2 wheels, pnt compo, 4", EX, A.................................. $385.00
Candy Container, girl nodder pulling pumpkin house w/2 molded wheels, pnt compo, 4", EX, A.................................. $350.00

Candy Container, jack-o'-lantern man riding on duck's back on round base, painted composition, 3½", Germany, NM, $800.00. (Photo courtesy Morphy Auctions)

Candy Container, J-O-L man w/body, pressed cb, orange w/blk top hat, gr vest, blk jacket, orange legs, 9", VG+, A $360.00
Candy Container, moon face, rnd pnt cb that separates to hold candy, detailed pnt features, 3½" dia, VG+, A $550.00
Candy Container, owl, pulp w/plastic eyes, orange & cream w/gr base, 10", US, VG+ $135.00
Candy Container, pear shape scowly face, bulging eyes, bobbing nose, pnt compo, 3½", NM, A $1,200.00
Candy Container, witch on rocket, plastic, blk w/orange wheels, 5½" L, EX... $150.00
Candy Pail, Buck Rogers head, molded plastic, wht w/red trim, 10", Renzi, 1979, NM+...$25.00

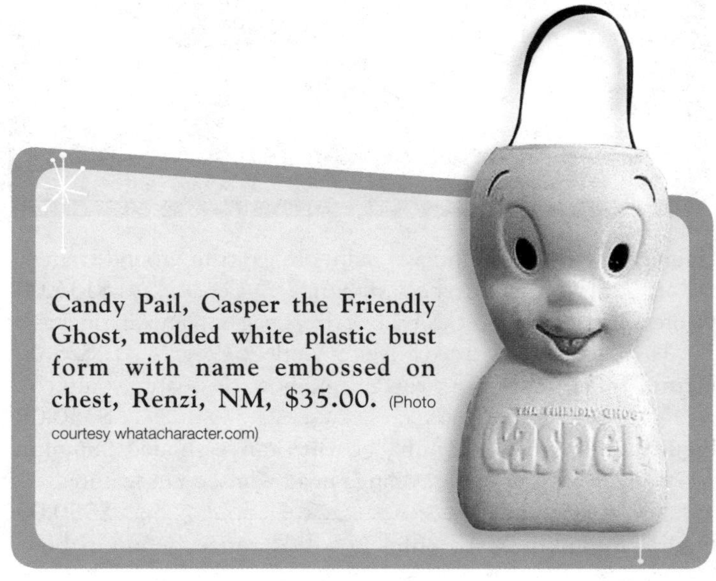

Candy Pail, Casper the Friendly Ghost, molded white plastic bust form with name embossed on chest, Renzi, NM, $35.00. (Photo courtesy whatacharacter.com)

Candy Pail, J-O-L, plastic, orange w/Treat imprinted above blk & wht triangle eyes/nose/toothy grin, blk hdl, 6", EX.... $125.00

Decoration, blk cat on J-O-L, die-cut cb, 12", US, 1930s, EX.. $125.00

Decoration, cat face w/snarling look, die-cut cb, 16x18", Dennison, 1920s, EX+ $75.00

Decoration, composition skeleton's head, wht w/blk eyes & nose, crossbones at chin, w/hanging string, Gremany, EX...$55.00

Decoration, jack-o'-lantern figure playing saxophone, die-cut cardboard stand-up, 27", EX, A, $250.00. (Photo courtesy Morphy Auctions)

Decoration, scarecrow w/J-O-L head, die-cut cb w/shredded tissue paper arms & legs, 28", Beistle, 1940s-50s, NM ...$40.00

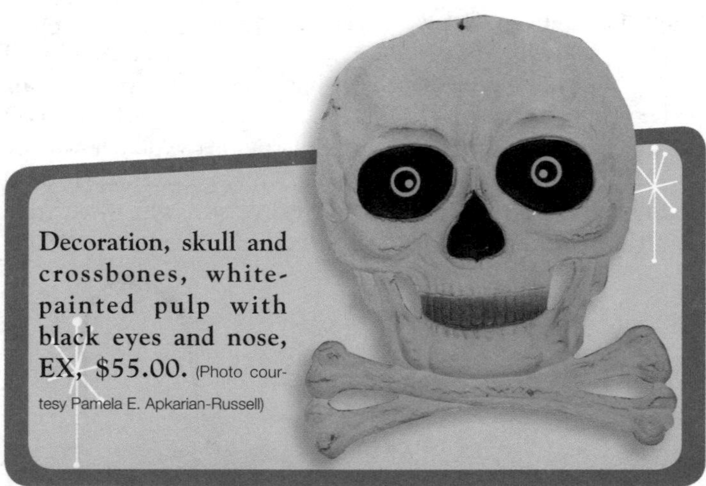

Decoration, skull and crossbones, white-painted pulp with black eyes and nose, EX, $55.00. (Photo courtesy Pamela E. Apkarian-Russell)

Figure, blk cat seated upright, pulp, orange trim around triangle eyes, nose & mouth, neck ribbon, 7", VG+ $135.00

Figure, Casper the Ghost w/Trick or Treat bag & pumpkin on grassy base, bisque, 5", United Silver & Cutlery, 1986, M $25.00

Figure, J-O-L man w/sm top hat & bow tie seated, pulp, 8", VG+ $350.00

Figure, Pumpkin Man, pulp, gr/wht/orange shaded pumpkin body w/arms & legs & orange head w/inserts in features, 8", NM+.. $550.00

Figure, Pumpkin Man, pulp, lg solid orange pumpkin body w/emb arms & feet & head w/cut-out features, 9½", NM, A $200.00

Game, Fortune Teller, Whitman, 1930s, complete, EXIB .$75.00

Game, Halloween Party, Saalfield #702, unused, NM $125.00

Halloween Party Decorations, 'Table Decorations for a Halloween Party,' complete, VGIB, A, $175.00. (Photo courtesy Morphy Auctions)

Lantern, blk cat's head, cb, blk w/gr insert eyes, red triangle insert nose & toothy smile, wire hdl, 4", Japan, EX........... $275.00

Lantern, blk cat's head (on fence), pulp, gr insert eyes, toothy scowl, 7½", EX $135.00

Lantern, cat's head, pnt compo, gray w/wht face & inner ears, inserted eyes & toothy mouth, bail hdl, 5", EX $1,540.00

Lantern, devil's bust, pulp, orange, paper inserts, wire hdl, 7", US, VG+, A $220.00

Lantern, devil's head (2-sided), cb, red w/blk detail, inserted eyebrows & mustache, wht eyes & teeth, 7", EX $150.00

Lantern, devil's head, red-painted composition with black detail, inserted eyes and teeth, 4", EX, A, $750.00. (Photo courtesy Morphy Auctions)

Lantern, devil's head w/scowl face, pulp, glossy orange, ribbed detailing on back, 5½", G+, A $55.00

Lantern, hexagonal top & bottom, emb cd w/various halloween images, wire hdl, 11" dia, VG+, A $55.00

Lantern, hexagonal top & bottom, emb cd w/various halloween images, wire hdl, 11" dia, VG+, A $55.00
Lantern, J-O-L, cb, orange, rnd paper insert eyes, red triangle nose, red around toothy insert smile, Germany, 5", EX, A......$75.00
Lantern, J-O-L, cb, orange (glossy), dbl-sided face w/rnd insert eyes, triangle nose, toothy mouth, 8", Germany, G+ . $600.00
Lantern, J-O-L, cb, orange w/pleated accordion-style shade top, rnd eyes, triangle nose, open mouth, 4", US, VG+, A..$55.00
Lantern, J-O-L, glass, orange pnt w/pk & blk-pnt eyes, triangle nose, toothy mouth, wire hdl, 4", US, G, A $220.00
Lantern, J-O-L, pressed cb, red (glittery), rnd insert eyes, triangle nose, toothy grin, wire hdl, 7", Germany, EX $525.00
Lantern, J-O-L, pressed cd, wht w/orange crepe inserts behind rnd eyes, triangle mouth, toothy smile, 3", Germany, EX, A...$55.00
Lantern, J-O-L, pulp, orange, cat-like cut-out features w/paper inserts, wire hdl, 5½", US, EX, A $65.00
Lantern, J-O-L, pulp, orange (glossy) human-like features, toothy grin, wire hdl, 7", US, VG...$75.00
Lantern, J-O-L, pulp, orange w/gr stem (on closed top), droopy eyes, triangle nose, wide open mouth, 6½", US, VG+, A $65.00
Lantern, J-O-L, tin, ball-shape, orange, rnd eyes, triangle nose, toothy smile, blk-pnt brows & mustache, 7", US, G, A............. $990.00

Lantern, Punch (Punch and Judy), painted composition with Dresden paper trim, inserted eyes and teeth, 4½", EX, A, $3,750.00. (Photo courtesy Morphy Auctions)

Lantern, skull, compo, realistic w/blk & orange fringed crepe collar, attached to pole for parade use, 41", Germany, VG+...$1,320.00
Lantern, skull, compo, wht w/orange crepe insert behind round eyes, triangle nose, toothy mouth, 2½", Germany, EX, A....... $330.00
Lantern, skull (2 flat sides), cd, inserted features, electric bulb socket, 7", EX...$50.00
Lantern, witch's head, pnt compo w/cb hat, inserted eyes & toothy mouth, blk hat, gray hair, orange collar, 5", VG+, A...$1,760.00
Lantern, witch's head (2 flat sides), cb, inserted features, wire hdl, 6½", NM+ $50.00

Light Bulb, with black ghost, NM, A, $250.00. (Photo courtesy Morphy Auctions)

Mechanical Toy, blk man in cloth costume on stick, when string is pulled prop turns & devil pops out of head, 14", EX, A $275.00

Mechanical Toy, 'goblin' man waddles when wound, composition head with wooden arms, metal feet, cloth outfit, 7", EX, A, $700.00. (Photo courtesy Morphy Auctions)

Mechanical Toy, witch w/tipping hat, orange figure w/blk witch's hat & blk cat pnt on front, lever action, 7", VG+... $135.00
Nightmare Before Christmas, watches, set of 4, Burger King, MIP $65.00
Nightmare Before Christmas Party Pack, MIP..................$55.00
Nodder, cat standing playing cello, pnt compo, spring neck, 10", EX, A $110.00
Noisemaker, ratchet, happy face lithoed on cb on wooden ratchet, 5", Germany, G+ $35.00
Noisemaker, ratchet, wht compo cat face on wire coil atop w/ wide flapper, 5½" L, VG..$25.00
Noisemaker, ratchet, wood w/carved wood cat straddling top, 8½x7", EX, A $100.00
Plastic Toy, cat pulling 4-wheeled J-O-L w/witch, blk & orange, 9" L, NM, A.. $1,400.00
Plastic Toy, cat w/J-O-L on 4-wheeled base, orange, gr, yel & blk, 7" L, rare, NM, A... $250.00
Plastic Toy, clown pirate marching w/drum, orange, gr, blk & yel, 7", very rare, EX, A.. $250.00

Plastic Toy, 'Pirates Auto,' 5", NM, A, $1,430.00. (Photo courtesy Morphy Auctions)

Plastic Toy, witch on motorcycle w/broom & J-O-L, orange & blk w/gr wheels, 7", EX, A $650.00
Plastic Toy, witch on rocket (2-wheeled), various colors, 5" L, EX, A $300.00
Plastic Toy, witch on rocket (4-wheeled), lt orange w/blk hat band & wheels, 7", rare, EX, A $300.00
Postcard, mechanical, J-O-L head moves over blk boy's head who is dressed in wht sheet, EX, A $275.00
Rattle, litho paper on cd, orange w/2-sided images of flying witch & devil w/pitchfork, 3" dia, Germany, EX, A $55.00
Rattle, round flat-sided J-O-L w/lithoed face, fringed crepe collar, on stick, 13", VG+, A $100.00

Roly Poly Figure, jack-o'-lantern, Schoenhut, NM, $5,000.00. (Photo courtesy Pamela E. Apkarian-Russell)

Saxophone, pressed cb, orange & blk pnt tiger-like stripes, wooden mouthpiece, 20", VG+ $200.00
Squeaker, orange dbl-faced accordion-style w/pnt smiley features, 2x3", VG, A $220.00

Halloween Costumes

During the '50s, '60s, and '70s, Ben Cooper and Collegeville made Halloween costumes representing the popular TV and movie characters of the day. If you can find one in excellent to mint condition and still in its original box, some of the better ones can go for over $100.00. MAD's Alfred E. Neuman (Collegeville, 1959 – 1960) usually carries an asking price of $150.00 to $175.00, and The Green Hornet (Ben Cooper, 1966), upwards of $200.00. Earlier handmade costumes are especially valuable if they are 'Dennison-Made.'

Advisor: Pamela E. Apkarian-Russell, 'The Halloween Queen'

Admiral Ackbar (Return of the Jedi), 1983, NMIB $25.00
Alf, Collegeville, MIB $35.00
Alfred E Neuman, mask only, Ben Cooper, 1960s, NM $50.00
Aquaman, Ben Cooper, 1967, NMIB $125.00
Archie, Collegeville, 1960, MIB $50.00

Barbarino, Collegville, 1976, MIB, $40.00. (Photo courtesy Greg Davis and Bill Morgan)

Barbie, TV-Comic/Collegeville, 1975, MIB $55.00
Barbie Super Star Bride, Collegeville, 1975, MIP $60.00
Baretta, NMIB (box reads 'TV Comic') $75.00
Batgirl, 1977, NMIB $35.00
Batman, Ben Cooper, 1969, NMIB $60.00
Batman (Super Heroes), Ben Cooper, 1973, EXIB $35.00
Beany & Cecil, Ben Cooper, 1950, NMIB $50.00
Beatles, any member, Ben Cooper, MIB, ea $450.00
Bewitched, Ben Cooper, 1965, MIB $45.00
Boss Hogg (Dukes of Hazzard), Ben Cooper, 1982, MIB $40.00
Brady Bunch, any character, Collegville, 1970s, MIB, ea from $25 to $35.00
C-3PO (Star Wars), Ben Cooper, 1977, MIB $45.00
Casper the Friendly Ghost, Collegeville, 1960s, EXIB $50.00
Charlie's Angels, any character, Collegeville, 1976, MIB $50.00
CHiPs, any character, Ben Cooper, 1978, MIB $25.00
Cookie Monster, Ben Cooper, 1989, MIB $30.00
Daffy Duck, Collegville, 1960s, EXIB $25.00
Darth Vader, Ben Cooper, 1977, MIP $25.00
Donny & Marie, Collegeville, 1977, MIB $35.00
Droopy Dog, Collegeville, 1952, EXIB $50.00

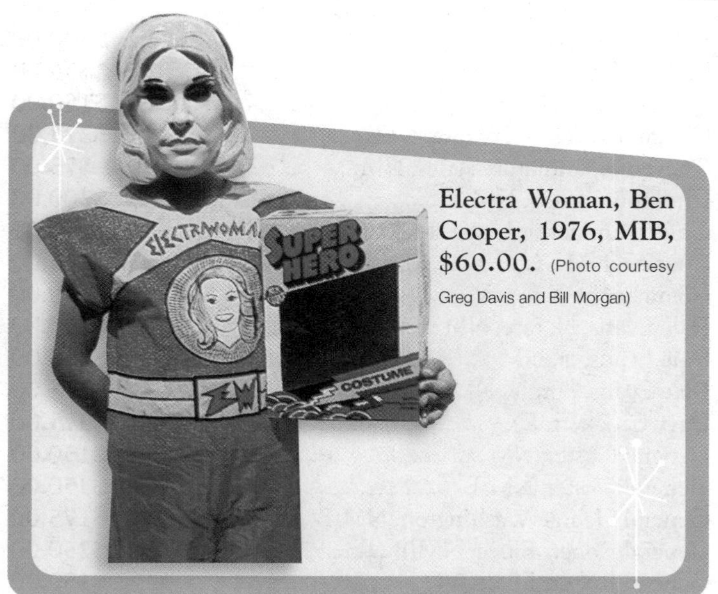

Electra Woman, Ben Cooper, 1976, MIB, $60.00. (Photo courtesy Greg Davis and Bill Morgan)

Flipper, Collegeville, 1964, MIB..$80.00
Fred Flintstone, Famous Faces, Ben Cooper, 1973, unused, MIB.. $65.00
GI Joe, Halco, 1960s, EXIB $65.00
Great Grape Ape, Ben Cooper, 1975, EXIB $50.00
Green Hornet, Ben Cooper, 1966, NMIB....................... $200.00

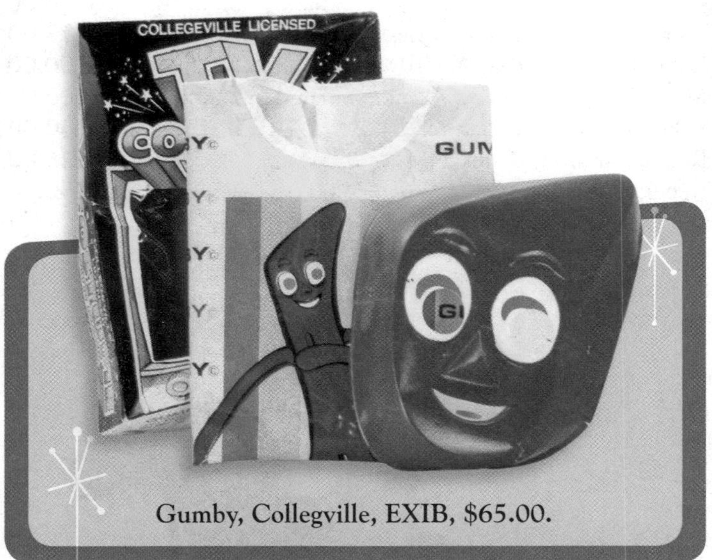

Gumby, Collegville, EXIB, $65.00.

Hardy Boys, Collegeville, 1978, MIB, ea...........................$45.00
He-Man, mask only, Mattel, M $10.00
Hong Kong Phooey, 1974, NMIB...$20.00
HR Pufnstuf, Collegeville, 1970s, MIB $80.00
Hush Puppy (Shari Lewis), Halco, 1961, EXIB.................$75.00
Impossibles, Ben Cooper, 1967, NMIB $50.00
Jeannie, TV-Comic/Ben Cooper, 1974, MIB $50.00
Jimmy Osmond, Collegeville, 1977, MIB $20.00
Joker, vinyl, 1989, MIB..$35.00
King Kong, Ben Cooper, 1976, MIB.............................. $100.00
KISS, Gene Simmons, Collegeville, 1978, MIB $100.00
Lambchop (Shari Lewis), mask only, Halco, 1962, NM $40.00
Land of the Giants, 1968, EX+ (no box) $50.00
Laugh-In, Ben Cooper, MIP $40.00
Laverne & Shirley, Collegeville, 1977, MIB, ea $30.00
Li'l Abner, Ben Cooper, 1957, NMIB $45.00
Li'l Tiger, 1960s, VGIB...$25.00
Little Audrey, Collegeville, 1959, MIB $50.00
Lost in Space, silver, Ben Cooper, EX (no box)................$60.00
Luke Skywalker (Return of the Jedi), Ben Cooper, EXIB . $125.00
Mandrake the Musician, Collegeville, 1950s, EXIB $85.00
Marie Osmond, 1977, NMIB...$35.00
Maverick, 1959, EX (no box) $50.00
Mickey Mouse, Ben Cooper, 1940s, VGIB........................$45.00
Miss Kitty (Gun Smoke), Halco, EXIB........................... $125.00
Monkees, any member, Blan Charnas, 1967, NMIB....... $200.00

Mork, Ben Cooper, 1978, NM (no box), $35.00. (Photo courtesy Greg Davis and Bill Morgan)

Morticia Addams, Ben Cooper, 1965, VG+IB..................$50.00
Morticia Addams, mask only, Ben Cooper, 1964, EX+......$35.00
Mr Spock (Star Trek), Ben Cooper, MIB..........................$50.00
Raggedy Andy, Ben Cooper, 1965, MIB...........................$30.00
Raggedy Ann, Ben Cooper, 1965, MIB $30.00
Rin-Tin-Tin, 1950s, NMIB...$50.00
Sabrina the Teenage Witch, Ben Cooper, 1971, NMIB $25.00
Samantha (Bewitched), Ben Cooper, 1965-67, VG (no box)..$35.00
Six Million Dollar Man, Ben Cooper, 1965, MIB.............$40.00
Space: 1999, Commander Koenig, 1975, EXIB.................$35.00
Spider-Man, Ben Cooper, 1972, NMIB.............................$50.00

Starsky and Hutch, Collegville, 1976, MIB, $50.00 each.

Steve Canyon, Halco, 1959, NMIB $50.00
Superman, Ben Cooper, early, EXIB....................$165.00
SWAT, Ben Cooper, 1975, NMIB $35.00
Tattoo (Fantasy Island), Ben Cooper, 1978, MIB $30.00
Top Cat, Ben Cooper, 1965, NMIB....................$75.00
Underdog, Collegeville, 1974, MIB $40.00
Winky Dink, Halco, 1950s, EX (no box) $65.00
Witchiepoo, Collegeville, 1971, MIB $50.00
Yoda (Empire Strikes Back), EXIB....................$35.00
Zorro, Ben Cooper #233, 1950s, deluxe edition, EXIB... $100.00

Hartland Plastics, Inc.

Originally known as the Electro Forming Co., Hartland Plastics Ind. was founded in 1941 by Ed and Iola Walters. They first produced heels for military shoes, birdhouses, and ornamental wall decor. It wasn't until the late 1940s that Hartland produced their first horse and rider. Figures were hand painted with an eye for detail. The Western and Historic Horsemen, Miniature Western Series, Authentic Scale Model Horses, Famous Gunfighter Series, and the Hartland Sports Series of Famous Baseball Stars were a symbol of the fine workmanship of the '40s, '50s, and '60s. The plastic used was a virgin acetate. Paint was formulated by Bee Chemical Co., Chicago, Illinois, and Wolverine Finishes Corp., Grand Rapids, Michigan. Hartland figures are best known for their uncanny resemblance to the TV Western stars who portrayed characters like the Lone Ranger, Matt Dillon, and Roy Rogers.

The prices listed are for figures that are complete with original accessories. For more inforamtion, we recommend *Hartland Horses and Riders* by Gail Fitch. See also Clubs, Newsletters, and Other Publications in the back of the book.

Alkine Ike, NM $150.00
Annie Oakley, NM $275.00
Bill Longley, NM....................$600.00
Brave Eagle, NM....................$200.00
Brave Eagle, NMIB....................$300.00
Bret Maverick, miniature series....................$75.00
Buffalo Bill, NM....................$300.00
Bullet, NM $35.00
Cactus Pete, NM....................$150.00
Champ Cowgirl, very rare, NM $275.00
Cheyenne, miniature series, NM....................$75.00
Cheyenne, w/tag, NM....................$200.00
Chief Thunderbird, rare shield, NM $150.00
Cochise, NM....................$225.00
Commanche Kid, NM $150.00
Dale Evans, bl, rare, NM $500.00
Dale Evans, gr, NM....................$250.00
Dale Evans, purple, NM....................$275.00
Davy Crockett, EX+ $375.00
General Custer, NM $150.00
General Custer, NMIB....................$350.00
General George Washington, NMIB $175.00
General Robert E Lee, NMIB....................$250.00
General Robert E Lee, VG $150.00
Gil Favor, prancing, very rare, M $1,100.00
Gil Favor, semi-rearing, NM+ $800.00
Hoby Gillman, NM $250.00
Jim Bowie, NM $250.00
Jim Hardy, NM....................$350.00
Jim Hardy, NMIB....................$300.00
Jockey, NM....................$150.00
Josh Randle, NM $650.00
Lone Ranger, miniature series, NM....................$75.00
Lone Ranger, rearing, NMIB $300.00
Matt Dillon, EX+....................$200.00
Paladin, NMIB....................$350.00
Rebel, miniature series, NM $125.00
Rebel, NM....................$250.00

Rebel, NMIB, $1,200.00; Brett Maverick, NMIB, $600.00. (Photo courtesy Kerry and Judy's Toys)

Rifleman, EX+, $275.00. (Photo courtesy Steve Humphries)

Rifleman, miniature series, EX....$75.00
Ronald MacKenzie, NM....$1,200.00
Roy Rogers, semi-rearing, NMIB....$600.00
Roy Rogers, walking, NM....$275.00
Seth Adams, EX....$275.00
Sgt Lance O'Rourke, NMIB....$300.00
Sgt Preston, EX....$425.00
Tom Jeffords, NM....$175.00
Tonto, EX....$200.00
Tonto, miniature series, NM....$75.00
Tonto, semi-rearing, rare, NM....$650.00
Wyatt Earp, EX+....$50.00

Standing Gunfighters

Bat Masterson, NMIB....$500.00
Bret Maverick, NM....$350.00

Brett Maverick, NMIB, $450.00. (Photo courtesy Morphy Auctions)

Chris Colt, NM....$150.00
Clay Holister, NM....$200.00
Dan Troop, NM....$600.00
Jim Hardy, NM....$150.00
Johnny M cKay, NM....$800.00
Paladin, NM....$400.00
Vint Bonner, NMIB....$850.00
Wyatt Earp, NM....$150.00

Horses

Horse riding being the order of the day, many children of the nineteenth century had their own horses to ride indoors; some were wooden while others were stuffed, and many had glass eyes and real horsehair tails. There were several ways to construct these horses so as to achieve a galloping action. The most common types had rocker bases or were mounted with a spring on each leg.

Gliding Horse, carved wood w/dapple finish, cloth & leather saddle, glass eyes, hair tail, 45", VG, A....$575.00
Horse on Wheels, dappled, glass eyes, w/saddle & trappings, pull string & horse whinnys, 13" L, VG, A....$240.00
Platform, pnt wood w/flat-sided legs & rump, pnt trappings, stenciled base, long stirrups, 35" L, G+, A....$355.00
Platform Rocker, dappled horse w/saddle bobbing up & down on lg coil spring, 41" L, Crandall, VG, A....$1,760.00
Rocking Horse, pnt wood, wht w/gr mottled look, gr-pnt rocker base, w/trappings, pnt eyes, 60" L, EX, A....$525.00

Rocking Horse, stuffed brown felt with light hair mane and tail, red leather saddle and harness, glass eyes, 37" wooden rockers, EX, $1,380.00. (Photo courtesy James D. Julia, Inc.)

Shoofly, oilcloth upholstered seat in pnt wood frame w/dbl horse heads on rockers, 35" L, VG, A....$1,320.00
Shoofly Rocking Horse, wood w/stenciled detail, cushioned seat, handlebar, 34" L, EX, A....$85.00

Wheeled Horse on Rocker Base, wheels fit in slots on wooden rocker base, fur-covered, with saddle and reins, German, EX, $175.00. (Photo courtesy Morphy Auctions)

Hot Wheels

When introduced in 1968, Hot Wheels vehicles were instantly successful. Sure, the racy style and flashy custom paint jobs were instant attention-getters, but what the kids loved most was the fact that the cars were fast! Fastest on the market! It's estimated that more than two billion Hot Wheels vehicles have been sold to date — every model with a little variation, keeping up with the big cars. The line has included futuristic vehicles, muscle cars, trucks, hot rods, racers, and some military vehicles. A lot of these can still be found for very little, but if you want to buy the older models (collectors call them 'red lines' because of their red sidewall tires), it's going to cost you a little more, though many can still be found for under $25.00. By 1977, black-wall tires had become the standard and by 1978, 'red lines' were no longer used.

A line of cars with Goodyear tires called Real Riders was made from 1983 until about 1987. (In 1983 the tires had gray hubs with white lettering; in 1984 the hubs were white.) California Customs were made in 1989 and 1990. These had the Real Rider tires, but they were not lettered 'Good Year' (and some had different wheels entirely).

Chopcycles are similar to Sizzlers in that they have rechargable batteries. The first series was issued in 1972 in these models: Mighty Zork, Blown Torch, Speed Steed, and Bruiser Cruiser. Generally speaking, these are valued at $35.00 (loose) to $75.00 (MIB). A second series issued in 1973 was made up of Ghost Rider, Rage Coach, Riptide, Sourkraut, and Triking Viking. This series is considerably harder to find and much more expensive today; expect to pay as much as $600.00 to $1,000.00 for a mint-in-package example.

Cars mint and in the original packages are holding their values and are still moving well. Near mint examples (no package) are worth about 50% to 60% less than those mint and still in their original package, excellent condition about 65% to 75% less.

Advisor: Steve Stephenson

'31 Doozie, 1986, maroon w/red-brn fenders, MIP............$12.00
'32 Ford Delivery, 1989, yel w/orange & magenta tampo, M.$15.00
'56 Flasher Pickup, 1990s, turq, MIP...................................$5.00
'57 T-Bird, 1990, Park 'n Plates, aqua, M...........................$10.00
'65 Mustang Convertible, 1980s, lt bl, MIP.......................$40.00
Air France Delivery Truck, 1990, wht, M (International box).$20.00
Alive '55 Chevy Station Wagon, 1974, lt bl, M............ $300.00
Alive '55 Chevy Station Wagon, 1976, Super Chromes, dk bl, lt gr & yel in tampo, M..$75.00

Ambulance, 1970, Heavyweights, green, MIP, $125.00. (Photo courtesy Jack Clark and Robert P. Wicker)

American Tipper, 1976, red, M...$60.00
American Victory, 1983, lt bl w/dk bl tampo, France, MIP.$70.00
AMX/2, 1971, purple, M.. $170.00
Assault Crawler, 1987, olive w/gr, tan & brn camp tampo, MIP... $25.00
Backwoods Bomb, 1975, lt bl, M.......................................$75.00
Backwoods Bomb, 1977, dk gr, blk-wall tires, M...............$35.00
Backwoods Bomb, 1977, dk gr, M.......................................$50.00
Battle Tank, 1984, tan, MIP...$25.00
Beach Patrol, 1983, Real Riders, wht, gray hubs, MIP.......$30.00
Beach Patrol, 1990, fluorescent gr, M...............................$15.00
Beatnik Bandit, 1968, aqua, US or Hong Kong, M $65.00
Beatnik Bandit, 1968, bl, US, M...$45.00
Beatnik Bandit, 1968, orange, US, M..................................$70.00

Beatnik Bandit, 1968, rose, US, M, $60.00. (Photo courtesy Jack Clark and Robert P. Wicker)

Big Bertha, 1988, tan, M..$10.00
Bronco Four-Wheeler, 1985, red, M...................................$10.00
Bugeye, 1971, gold, US, M... $225.00
Bugeye, 1971, gold, US, MIP... $425.00
Buzz Off, 1973, dk bl, M... $200.00

Buzz Off, 1973, fluorescent pink, M, $400.00. (Photo courtesy Jack Clark and Robert P. Wicker)

Buzz Off, 1973, red, M.. $250.00
Cadillac Seville, 1983, metal-flake gold, M..........................$8.00
Captain America Hot Bird, 1979, red, wht & bl, M..........$30.00
Carabo, 1970, hot pk, Hong Kong, M............................. $300.00
Carabo, 1970, lt gr, US, M..$75.00
Carabo, 1974, yel, M.. $1,000.00
Carabo, 1977, lt gr, M..$75.00
Cargoyle, 1986, orange, M..$7.00
Cement Mixer, 1970, Heavyweights, purple, MIP.......... $225.00
Chevy Monza 2+2, 1975, lt gr, Mexico, M $400.00
Chevy Monza 2+2, 1975, orange, M..................................$75.00

Choppin' Chariot, 1970, Rumblers, MOC, $175.00.
(Photo courtesy Jack Clark and Robert P. Wicker)

Classic '31 Ford Woody, 1969, creamy pk w/blk roof, M.. $400.00
Classic '31 Ford Woody, 1969, orange, M $75.00
Classic '32 Vicky, 1994, metal-flake pk, MIP $900.00
Classic '35 Caddy, 1989, silver w/beige interior, pk fenders, whtwalls, NM $25.00
Classic Nomad, 1970, magenta, M $150.00
Classic Nomad, 1970, red, MIP (unpunched) $225.00
Cockeny Cab, 1971, magenta, clear windows, US, M $160.00
Cockeny Cab, 1971, magenta, Hong Kong, M $200.00
Cockney Cab, 1971, bl, US, M $140.00
Combat Medic, 1988, gold & chrome, no horizontal lines, from 20th Anniversary set, M $45.00
Continental Mark III, 1969, hot pk, M $180.00
Custom AMX, 1969, bl, M $110.00
Custom Baracuda, 1968, lt bl, Hong Kong, M $500.00

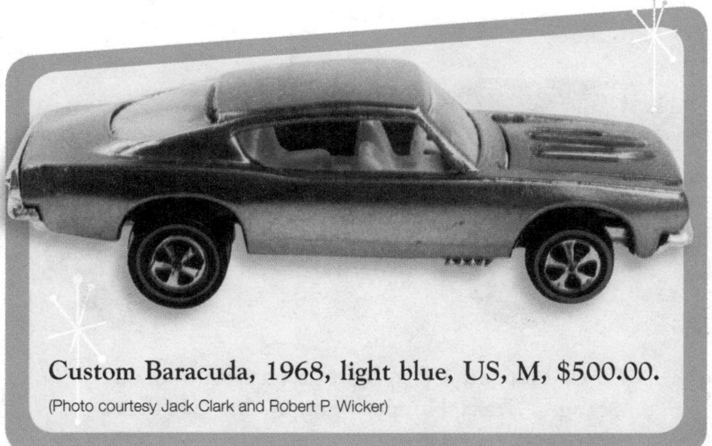
Custom Baracuda, 1968, light blue, US, M, $500.00.
(Photo courtesy Jack Clark and Robert P. Wicker)

Custom Camaro, 1968, lt bl, US, M $650.00
Custom Camaro, 1968, rose, US, M $900.00
Custom Corvette, 1968, Antifreeze, US, M $300.00
Custom Corvette, 1968, bl, Hong Kong, M $150.00
Custom Cougar, 1968, bl, pnt tooth, Hong Kong, M $250.00
Custom Cougar, 1968, bl, pnt tooth, US, M $500.00
Custom Cougar, 1968, orange, US, MIP $500.00

Custom Eldorado, 1968, bl, US, M $90.00
Custom Eldorado, 1968, olive, Hong Kong, M $125.00
Custom Firebird, 1968, red, Hong Kong, M $125.00
Custom Firebird, 1968, red, US, M $100.00
Custom Fleetside, 1968, purple, US, M $100.00

Custom Mustang, 1968, Antifreeze, smooth rear window, US, M, $350.00. (Photo courtesy Jack Clark and Robert P. Wicker)

Custom Mustang, 1968, purple, closed hood scoops, Hong Kong, M $450.00
Custom Mustang, 1968, purple, smooth rear window, US, M . $425.00
Custom Mustang, 1968, red w/red interior, Hong Kong, M .. $200.00
Custom Mustang, 1994, brn, MIP $10.00
Custom T-Bird, 1968, gold, all interiors except wht, US, M .. $325.00
Custom T-Bird, 1968, gold, blk roof, Hong Kong, M $125.00
Custom T-Bird, 1968, gold, blk roof, US, M $150.00
Custom T-Bird, 1968, gold, wht interior, US, M $500.00
Custom Volkswagen, 1968, bl, opening sunroof, Hong Kong, M $100.00
Custom Volkswagen, 1968, bl, US, M $75.00
Custom Volkswagen, 1968, hot pk, US, M $900.00
Demon, 1970, lt gr, M $150.00
Demon, 1994, metal-flake bl, Toy Fair Limited Edition, M... $150.00
Deora, 1968, Antifreeze, Hong Kong, MIP $250.00
Deora, 1968, Antifreeze, US, MIP $500.00
Deora, 1968, purple, Hong Kong, M $100.00
Deora, 1968, purple, US, M $150.00

Double Header, 1973, dark blue, M, $250.00.
(Photo courtesy Jack Clark and Robert P. Wicker)

Double Header, 1973, dk bl, MIP $700.00
Double Header, 1973, lt bl, M $300.00
Double Header, 1973, lt bl, MIP $650.00

Double Vision, 1973, dk bl, M.. $150.00

Double Vision, 1973, dark green, M, $250.00. (Photo courtesy Jack Clark and Robert P. Wicker)

Double Vision, 1973, fluorescent lime gr, engine exposed in back, M.. $300.00
Double Vision, 1973, fluorescent lime gr, engine exposed in back, MIP.. $600.00
Double Vision, 1973, lt bl or red, M, ea........................ $250.00
Double Vision, 1973, lt gr, M.. $250.00
Dump Truck, 1970, Heavyweights, orange, MIP............ $165.00
Dump Truck, 1970, Heavyweights, purple, MIP............ $175.00
Dump Truck, 1982, yel, MIP.. $10.00
Dumpin' A, 1983, gray w/chrome motor, M..................... $65.00
Dumpin' A, 1983, gray w/gray motor, M........................... $15.00
Dune Daddy, 1973, dk bl or red, M.............................. $100.00
Dune Daddy, 1973, fluorescent pk, M.......................... $375.00
Dune Daddy, 1973, lt gr, M.. $150.00
Dune Daddy, 1973, red, M.. $100.00
Dune Daddy, 1973, yel or lemon yel, M........................ $150.00
Dune Daddy, 1973, yel or lemon yel, MIP...................... $400.00
El Rey Special, 1974, dk bl, M.................................... $400.00
El Rey Special, 1974, dk bl, MIP.................................. $750.00
El Rey Special, 1974, dk gr, M..................................... $80.00
El Rey Special, 1974, dk gr, MIP.................................. $150.00
El Rey Special, 1974, gr, M.. $75.00
El Rey Special, 1974, gr, MIP...................................... $175.00

El Rey Special, 1974, light blue, M, $850.00. (Photo courtesy Jack Clark and Robert P. Wicker)

El Rey Special, 1974, lt bl, MIP.................................. $1,500.00
Emergency Squad, 1982, red, MIP................................. $50.00
Ferrari 512P, 1973, lt bl, M... $475.00
Ferrari 512S, 1972, red, M.. $200.00
Ferrari 512S, 1973, fluorescent pk, Shell promo, MIP.... $245.00
Fire Chief Cruiser, 1970, red, M................................... $50.00
Fire Chief Cruiser, 1970, red, MIP.............................. $125.00
Fire Eater, 1977, red w/yel & blk tampo, blk-wall tires, M..$20.00

Fire Eater, 1977, red with yellow and black tampo, black-wall tires, MIP, $50.00. (Photo courtesy Jack Clark and Robert P. Wicker)

Fire Eater, 1977, red w/yel & blk tampo, M....................... $45.00
Fire Eater, 1977, red w/yel & blk tampo, MIP................. $100.00
Firebird Funny Car, 1989, yel w/orange, blk & bl tampo, MIP..$5.00
Flame Stopper, 1988, red, MIP..................................... $10.00
Ford J-Car, 1968, Antifreeze, US, M............................. $250.00
Ford J-Car, 1968, red, US, M.. $50.00
Ford J-Car, 1968, wht enamel, Hong Kong, M................. $95.00
Formula Fever, 1983, yel, MIP...................................... $10.00
Formula PACK, 1976, blk, M... $75.00
Formula PACK, 1976, blk, MIP..................................... $135.00
Formula 5000, 1976, wht, M.. $40.00
Formula 5000, 1976, wht, MIP....................................... $80.00
Funny Money, 1977, gray, blk-wall tires, MIP.................. $50.00
Funny Money, 1977, gray, MIP....................................... $50.00
Grass Hopper, 1971, lt gr, M.. $100.00

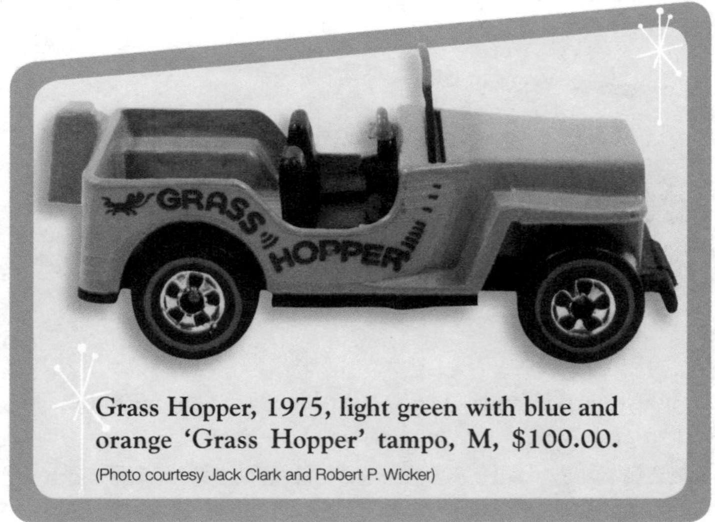

Grass Hopper, 1975, light green with blue and orange 'Grass Hopper' tampo, M, $100.00. (Photo courtesy Jack Clark and Robert P. Wicker)

Gremlin Grinder, 1975, dk gr, Herfy's logo on sides, M.. $350.00
Gremlin Grinder, 1975, dk gr, M.................................... $65.00
Gremlin Grinder, 1975, gr, M.. $45.00
Gulch Stepper, 1985, yel w/tan roof, mc tampo, MIP........ $10.00
Gulch Stepper, 1987, red, MIP....................................... $22.00
Gun Slinger, 1975, lt olive, M.. $40.00

Hairy Hauler, 1971, magenta, M $55.00
Hairy Hauler, 1971, salmon pk, M $165.00
Heavy Chevy, 1970, Spoilers, gr, M $125.00
Heavy Chevy, 1970, Spoilers, orange, M $175.00
Heavy Chevy, 1970, Spoilers, purple w/blk roof, M........ $850.00
Heavy Chevy, 1974, lt gr, M..$1,200.00
Heavy Chevy, 1974, yel, M.. $175.00
Hiway Robber, 1973, dk gr, M $250.00
Hiway Robber, 1973, dk gr, MIP.................................... $600.00
Hot Bird, 1980, bl w/orange & yel tampo, M....................$75.00
Hot Heap, 1968, orange, Hong Kong, M $80.00
Hot Heap, 1968, orange, Hong Kong, MIP..................... $175.00
Hot Heap, 1968, orange, US, M.......................................$50.00
Hot Heap, 1968, orange, US, MIP $150.00

Hummer, 1990s, beige camo, M, $8.00.
(Photo courtesy Dana Johnson)

Hummer, 1990s, beige camo, MIP...................................$10.00
Ice T, 1971, yel, M $60.00
Ice T, 1971, yel, MIP.. $200.00
Indy Eagle, 1969, aqua, M $40.00
Indy Eagle, 1969, olive, M..$90.00
Inferno, 1976, yel, M $60.00
Inside Story, 1979, gray w/red, yel & bl tampo, M............$15.00
Jack Rabbit Special, 1970, wht w/blk interior, clear windshield, US, M $40.00
Jet Threat, 1971, red, M $150.00
Jet Threat, 1971, yel, M..$90.00
Jet Threat, 1976, purple, M $200.00
King 'Kuda, 1970, bl, M... $125.00
King 'Kuda, 1970, bl, MIP $350.00
Large Charge, 1975, Super Chromes, blk, orange & yel in tampo, M $45.00
Letter Getter, 1977, wht, (red-line variation only available in the Truckin' Machines Gift Set), M........................ $550.00
Letter Getter, 1977, wht, blk-wall tires, M........................$25.00
Light-My-Firebird, 1970, Spoilers, red, MIP $225.00
Lola GT 70, 1969, Grand Prix, dk gr, Hong Kong, MIP....$80.00
Lola GT 70, 1969, Grand Prix, dk gr, US, MIP $75.00
Lotus Turbine, 1969, Grand Prix, copper, bl-tinted windows, Hong Kong only, MIP.. $125.00
Lotus Turbine, 1969, Grand Prix, olive, bl-tinted windows, Hong Kong only, M $65.00
Lowdown, 1977, gold chrome, blk-wall tires, M $35.00
Lowdown, 1977, gold chrome, red-line tires, M.................$50.00
Mantis, 1970, hot pk, Hong Kong, MIP.......................... $300.00
Mantis, 1970, hot pk, US, MIP $200.00
Maserati Mistral, 1969, gr, M.. $100.00
Maserati Mistral, 1969, gr w/blk roof, M $130.00
Maserati Mistral, 1969, red, MIP................................... $300.00
Maserati Mistral, 1969, red w/blk roof, MIP $300.00
Mazda MX-5 Miata, 1992, yel, M.......................................$5.00
Mean Machine, 1970, Rumblers, MOC.......................... $175.00
Mercedes-Benz C-11, 1972, lt gr, M $125.00
Mercedes-Benz SL, 1991, MIP...$10.00
Mighty Mantis, 1970, lime-yel, US, M $125.00
Mighty Maverick, 1970, aqua w/blk interior, US, M $125.00
Mighty Maverick, 1970, aqua w/blk interior & blk roof, Hong Kong, M $250.00
Mighty Maverick, 1970, orange w/brn interior, Hong Kong, M... $250.00
Minitrek 1983, wht, M $95.00
Mod Quad, 1970, magenta, Hong Kong, M.................... $125.00
Mod Quad, 1970, megenta, US, M $125.00
Mongoose (Funny Car), 1970, Mongoose vs Snake, red, M .$90.00

Mongoose (Funny Car), 1970, Mongoose vs Snake, red, MIP, $300.00. (Photo courtesy serioustoyz.com)

Monte Carlo Stocker, 1979, dk bl, M...............................$60.00
Moving Van, 1970, metallic gr w/blk interior & gray trailer, M.. $75.00
Mustang Stocker, 1976, Super Chromes, red, wht & bl tampo, M $100.00
Mustang Stocker, 1976, Super Chromes, red, wht & bl tampo, MIP $225.00
Mutt Mobile, 1971, aqua, M..$65.00
Mutt Mobile, 1971, bl, M $100.00
Mutt Mobile, 1994, metallic magenta, MIP......................$10.00
Neet Streeter, 1976, lt bl, MIP $100.00
Nitty Gritty Kitty, 1970, Spoilers, bl, MIP $300.00
Odd Job, 1973, lemon yel, M... $250.00
Odd Job, 1973, pk, M.. $450.00
Old Number 5 (Fire Engine), 1980, red, without louvers, M. $20.00
Olds 442, 1971, purple, M $4,000.00
Olds 442, 1971, yel, M.. $475.00
Omni 024, 1981, gray, unpnt base, MIP $10.00
Open Fire, 1972, bl, M.. $800.00
Open Fire, 1972, gold, M... $450.00
Open Fire, 1972, magenta, M $450.00

Open Fire, 1972, red, M..$750.00
P-911, 1988, blk, no tampo, M...$10.00
Packin' Pacer, 1980, orange, MIP..$10.00
Paddy Wagon (Police 3), 1973, dk bl, M $90.00

Peepin' Bomb, 1970, orange with chrome headlights, US, M, $75.00.

Peepin' Bomb, 1970, yel, US, M $50.00
Peppin' Bomb, 1970, aqua w/chrome headlights, Hong Kong, M $75.00
Peppin' Bomb, 1970, aqua w/chrome headlights, US, M...$50.00
Peppin' Bomb, 1970, orange w/orange headlights, US, M. $450.00
Peterbilt Dump Truck, 1983, yel, MIP $10.00
Peugeot 205 Rallye, 1989, wht w/#2 tampo MIP $15.00
Pit Crew Car, 1971, wht, M.. $150.00

Poison Pinto, 1976, light green, M, $50.00. (Photo courtesy Jack Clark and Robert P. Wicker)

Porsche Targa Christmas Car, 1996, red w/Santa & passenger, MIP $30.00
Porsche 911, 1976, Super Chromes, M $40.00
Porsche 959, 1991, yel, Getty promo, MIP $10.00
Power Plower Cabover, 1990, blk, tandem axle, M $10.00
Pro Circuit #2, 1993, wht w/Texaco logo, gray Pro Circut Indy wheels, NM+ $6.00
Prowler, 1978, Super Chrome, M $40.00
Python, 1968, brn, US, MIP... $300.00
Python, 1968, gold, Hong Kong, MIP $200.00
Python, 1968, purple, Hong Kong, M $75.00
Python, 1968, purple, US, M...$85.00

Quik Trik, 1984, metallic magenta, M $5.00
Ranger Rig (Dept of Agriculture/Forest Service), 1975, dk gr, MIP $100.00
Rapid Transit School Bus, 1984, yel, MIP..............................$7.00
Real Engine Snake, 1972, Mongoose vs Snake, yel, MIP ..$70.00
Rear Engine Snake, 1972, Mongoose vs Snake, yel, M .. $250.00
Red Baron, 1973, red, MIP $250.00
Renault 5 Turbo, 1991, bl w/yel, orange & wht tampo, MIP .$8.00
Revolution, Rumblers, 1970, MOC $125.00
Road Torch, 1987, red w/blk, wht & yel #9 tampo, MIP ...$10.00

Rock Buster, 1976, yellow, MIP, $25.00. (Photo courtesy Jack Clark and Robert P. Wicker)

Rock Buster, 1977, Super Chrome, M.....................................$20.00
Rocket-Bye-Baby, 1971, aqua, M...$80.00
Rocket-Bye-Baby, 1971, gold, M $160.00
S'Cool Bus, 1971, Heavyweights, yel, M.............................. $375.00
Sand Crab, 1970, red, Hong Kong, M................................... $125.00
Sand Crab, 1970, red, Hong Kong, MIP $250.00
Sand Crab, 1970, red, US, M $50.00
Sand Crab, 1970, red, US, MIP... $125.00
Second Wind, 1977, wht, blk-wall tires, MIP $65.00
Second Wind, 1977, wht, MIP $150.00
Sheriff Patrol, 1990, blk, MIP..$10.00
Short Order, 1971, gold w/blk interior, M.............................$80.00
Short Order, 1971, magenta, M.. $400.00
Show Hoss II, 1977, lemon yel, blk-wall tires, MIP $75.00
Show Hoss II, 1977, yel, blk-wall tires, MIP $75.00

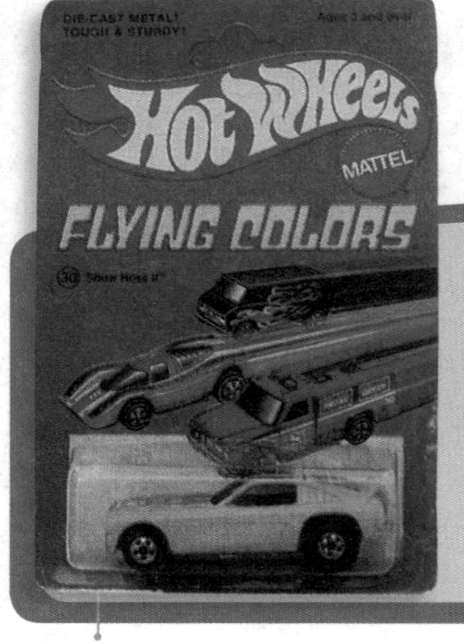

Show Hoss II, 1977, yellow, red line tires, MIP, $750.00. (Photo courtesy Jack Clark and Robert P. Wicker)

Silhouette, 1968, creamy pk, Hong Kong, M..................$150.00
Silhouette, 1968, creamy pk, US, M..............................$150.00
Silhouette, 1968, pk w/wht interior, M..........................$250.00

Six Shooter, 1971, aqua, M, $100.00.

Six Shooter, 1971, aqua, MIP..$225.00
Six Shooter, 1971, magenta, M.......................................$250.00
Snake, 1994, metal-flake gr, MIP.......................................$15.00
Snorkle, 1971, Heavyweights, purple, M.........................$250.00
Spider-Man, 1979, blk, M..$15.00
Splittin' Image, 1969, aqua or gold, MIP............................$95.00
Splittin' Image, 1969, bl, MIP..$100.00
Splittin' Image, 1969, gr or red, MIP.................................$90.00
Spoiler Sport, 1980, gr w/blk, yel & dk red tampo, 1 lg window, MIP...$15.00
State Police Cruiser, 1974, wht, metal base, M..............$100.00
State Police Cruiser, 1974, wht, metal base, MIP..........$200.00
Sting Rod, 1988, olive, MIP...$20.00
Straight Away, 1970, Rumblers, MOC..........................$100.00
Street Beast, 1991, red w/wht, MIP.....................................$25.00
Street Snorter, 1973, dk bl, M..$225.00
Street Snorter, 1973, lt bl, M..$275.00
Strip Teaser, 1971, gold, M...$150.00
Strip Teaser, 1971, magenta, M...$300.00

Sugar Caddy, 1971, Spoilers, red, MIP, $250.00. (Photo courtesy serioustoyz.com)

Super Van, 1976, Super Chromes, red & yel tampo, chrome plastic chassis, MIP..$75.00

Super Van, 1976, Super Chromes, yellow and red tampo, black plastic chassis, M, $45.00. (Photo courtesy Jack Clark and Robert P. Wicker)

Super Van, 1976, Super Chromes, yel & red tampo, blk plastic chassis, MIP...$75.00
Super Van, 1976, Super Chromes, yel & red tampo, chrome plastic chassis, M..$50.00
Superfine Turbine, 1973, dk bl or red, M........................$450.00
SWAT Van Scene, 1979, dk bl, M......................................$15.00
Sweet 16, 1973, fluorescent lime gr, M...........................$225.00
Sweet 16, 1973, red, M...$250.00
T-Bird Stocker, 1996, red & wht Bill Elliot car, Kellogg's promo, MIP..$15.00
T-4-2, 1971, bl, MIP...$215.00
T-4-2, 1971, lime yel, MIP..$175.00
Tall Rider, 1985, grape, MIP...$10.00
Team Trailer, 1971, Heavyweights, red, M......................$140.00
Thing, 1979, dk bl, M..$15.00
Thor Van, 1979, yel, M..$12.00
Thunderstreak, 1989, bl, Kraco, MIP..................................$10.00
Top Eliminator, 1974, dk bl, M..$90.00
Top Elininator, 1974, bl, M...$125.00
Torino Stocker, 1975, red, M...$75.00
Torino Stocker, 1975, red, MIP...$150.00
Torino Stocker, 1979, blk w/yel, orange & wht #3 tampo, M.$25.00
Tough Customer, 1975, olive, MIP......................................$75.00
Tow Truck, 1970, Heavyweights, aqua or bl, MIP...........$125.00
Tow Truck, 1970, Heavyweights, gr, M...............................$75.00

Tow Truck, 1970, Heavyweights, purple, M, $100.00. (Photo courtesy Jack Clark and Robert P. Wicker)

Tri-Baby, 1970, aqua, Hong Kong, M $100.00
Tri-Baby, 1970, aqua, US, M $125.00
Tri-Baby, 1970, rose, US, M $50.00
Tricar X8, 1988, yel, MIP $10.00
Turbo Heater, 1986, magenta, MIP $15.00
Turbo Streak, Real Riders, 1983, yel, gray hubs, MIP $25.00
Turbo Streak, 1988, wht, M $10.00
Turbo Streak, 1996, dk bl, Union 76 promo, M $6.00
Turbofire, 1969, rose, M $35.00
Turismo, 1981, red, MIP $10.00
Turismo, 1983, yel, MIP $10.00

Twin Mill, 1969, aqua, M, $40.00.

Twin Mill, 1969, olive, M $100.00
Twin Mill, 1969, yel, M $50.00
Vega Bomb, 1975, lt gr, M, minimum value $900.00
Vega Bomb, 1975, lt gr, MIP, minimum value $1,500.00
Vega Bomb, 1975, orange, MIP $200.00
Volkswagen, 1975, orange w/wht, yel & blk striped tampo on hood, roof & back, unpnt metal base, M $650.00
Volkswagen, 1975, orange w/wht, yel & blk striped tampo on hood, roof & back, unpnt metal base, MIP $1,000.00
Volkswagen Beach Bomb, 1969, bl, M $250.00
Volkswagen Beach Bomb, 1969, red, M $325.00
Waste Wagon, 1971, Heavyweights, bl, MIP $225.00
What-4, 1971, aqua or gr, M $100.00
Whip Creamer, 1970, purple, Hong Kong, M $150.00
Whip Creamer, 1994, dk metal-flake red, MIP $5.00
Xploder, 1973, lt bl or dk bl, M $150.00

Miscellaneous

Action City Playset, 1969, EX+, $50.00. (Photo courtesy Jack Clark and Robert P. Wicker)

Autorama, 1970, MIB $250.00
Bad to the Bone Watch, 1994, blk, MIB $15.00
Bug Bite Set, 1972, MIB $125.00
Button, Beatnik Bandit, metal, NM $8.00
Button, Cement Mixer, metal, NM+ $5.00
Button, Classi '31 Ford Woody, metal, NM $5.00
Button, Custom Barracuda, metal, NM $5.00
Button, Jet Threat, plastic, M $10.00
Button, Racer Ring, metal, NM+ $8.00
Button, S-Cool Bus, plastic, rare, NM $10.00
Button, Short Order, plastic, M $4.00
Button, Strip Tease, plastic, NM+ $4.00
Case, 12-car, 1969, yel w/red car on front, NM $20.00
Case, 12-car pop-up, 1968, orange w/name on front, cars on back, EX $35.00
Case, 24-car, 1969, yrl w/wht & bl cars on front, adjustable, EX $30.00
Case, 24-car, 1975, bl w/wht trays, Prosche 917, Super Van & Emergency Squad on front, NM $40.00

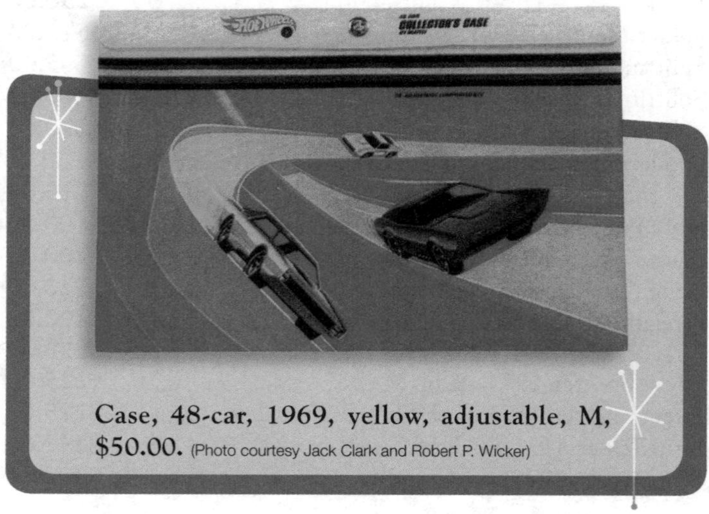

Case, 48-car, 1969, yellow, adjustable, M, $50.00. (Photo courtesy Jack Clark and Robert P. Wicker)

Case, 72-car, 1970, blk w/snake & Mongoose on front, EX $40.00
City Burger Stand, aqua mini truck, MIB $30.00
City Machines, 1982, set of 6, MIB $45.00
Club Kit, issued w/Boss Hoss, Heavy Chevy or King Kuda cars, unused, MIB (sealed), A $285.00
Competition Pak, 1968, MIB (sealed) $25.00

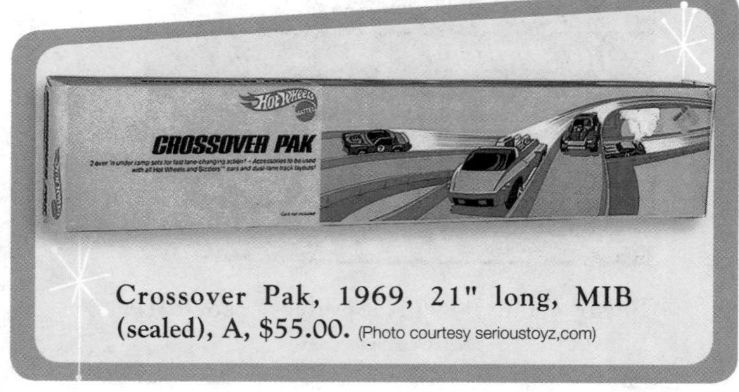

Crossover Pak, 1969, 21" long, MIB (sealed), A, $55.00. (Photo courtesy serioustoyz,com)

Cutoff Canyon Set, 1975, MIB $150.00
Dual-Lane Lap Counter, 1968, MIB $10.00

Dual-Lane Rod Runner Hand-Shift Power Booster, 1970, MIB $35.00

Flyin' Circus, 1971, EXIB, $450.00.

Funny Car Gift Pak, 1991, MIB $30.00
Gran Toros Match Race Set, 1970, complete, MIB........ $575.00
Gran Toros Chevy Astro 11, 1970, gray, complete, NM.. $125.00
Hazard Hill Race Set, 1970, MIB (no cars)..................... $550.00
Hot Curves Race Action Track Set, 1968, MIB (no cars) . $150.00
Hot Wheels Factory, 1970, MIB.. $200.00
Jigsaw Puzzle, Whitman, 1970s, 100 pcs, MIB $25.00
Pop-Up Service Station, 1968, MIB...................................$75.00
Pop-Up Speed Shop, 1968, MIB $75.00
Road King Highway Drive-Ins, 1974, MIB $250.00
Sizzlers Laguna Oval Set, complete, MIB........................ $250.00
Speed Stunter Set, 1974, MIB.. $125.00
Sto & Go Baywatch, MIB $25.00
Sto & Go Fix & Fill Center, MIB $25.00
Strip Action Set, 1969, MIB (sealed) $125.00
Super-Charger Double Action Set, 1969, MIB (no cars). $300.00

Super-Charger Rally 'N Freeway Set, 1968, EXIB, $450.00. (Photo courtesy Jack Clark and Robert P. Wicker)

Super-Charger Speed Test Set, 1970, MIB...................... $225.00
Talking Service Center, 1969, complete, scarce, NM..... $100.00
Tune-Up Tower, NMIB.. $125.00

Housewares

Little girls used to love to imulate their mothers and pretend to sew and bake, sweep, do laundry, and iron (gasp!). They imagined what fun it would be when *they* were big like mommy. Those little gadgets they played with are precious collectibles today, and any child-size houseware item is treasured, especially those from the 1940s and 1950s. If you're interested in learning more we recommend *Encyclopedia of Children's Sewing Collectibles* by Darlene J. Gengelbach and *Collector's Guide to Housekeeping Toys, 1870 – 1970*, by Margaret Wright.

Carriages and Strollers

Horse Stroller, dappled horse on wood 4-wheeled platform, oilcloth cushioned saddle, BRT, metal & wood handle, 23", VG+ $330.00
Horse-Drawn Stroller, lg front wheel on articulated horse, 2-wheeled wood sleigh w/hdl, 56", VG+, A............... $135.00
Tin pram w/Art Nouveau detail, storage compartment for diapers, 2 lg front wheels w/2 very sm back wheels, 7" L, G, A..$2,750.00

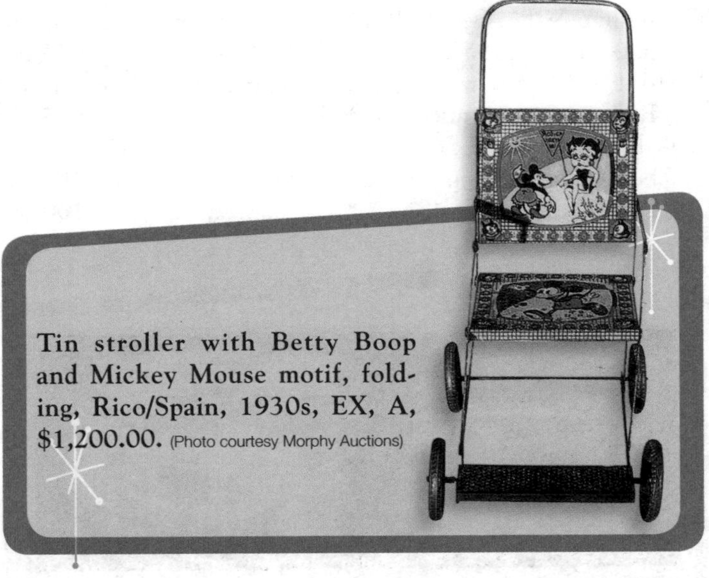
Tin stroller with Betty Boop and Mickey Mouse motif, folding, Rico/Spain, 1930s, EX, A, $1,200.00. (Photo courtesy Morphy Auctions)

Tin w/emb wicker design, folding top, 4 spoke wheels, 6", EX.$250.00
Wicker chair type w/scrolled arms, 2 lg wooden spoke wheels & 2 sm, curved hdl, 27", G $250.00
Wicker curved & stepped box body w/partially quilted interior, spoke wheels, 50" L, G... $150.00
Wicker sleigh type w/parasol canopy, wht w/bl spoke wheels & hdl, upholstered, 38" L, EX.................................... $100.00
Wicker sleigh type w/scroll design, 2 lg spoker wheels & 2 sm, curved hdl, 36" L, EX.. $500.00
Wood box frame w/upholstered bench seat, flat fringed top, wire supports, 27", EX.. $300.00
Wood pram w/leather top, 2 lg and 2 sm spoke wheels, 30" L, VG $200.00
Wood sleigh body w/blk leather fold-up hood, 3-wheeled, 29" L, Joel Ellis, VG $250.00
Wood sleigh body w/blk oilcloth fold-down hood (horse buggy type), pnt & stenciled, 25", EX $200.00

Wood sleigh body w/flat fringed top on wire supports, pnt & stenciled, 30" (to hadl), EX $325.00

Wood surry type w/rnd fringed top, upholstered seat, wooden spoke wheels, 24" L, VG.. $850.00

Wicker Victorian chair type w/scrolled arms, spoke wheels, 29" long, VG, A, $255.00. (Photo courtesy James D. Julia, Inc.)

CLEANING AND LAUNDRY

Clothes Drying Rack, wood fold-out type, 12", American, 1915, EX $35.00

Clothesline & Pin Set, Dolli-Pin, nylon line w/plastic clothespins, Hoflion, 1950s, unused, NMIB $25.00

Doll-E-Do Dish Set, w/dish pan & drainer, Ajax can, box of Vel, Brillo box, etc, Amsco, 1950s, EX+ $85.00

Doll-E-Housekeeper Set, 14-pc set w/sweeper, broom, mop, bucket & cleaning products in cb cabinet, Amsco, 1950s, EX+ $200.00

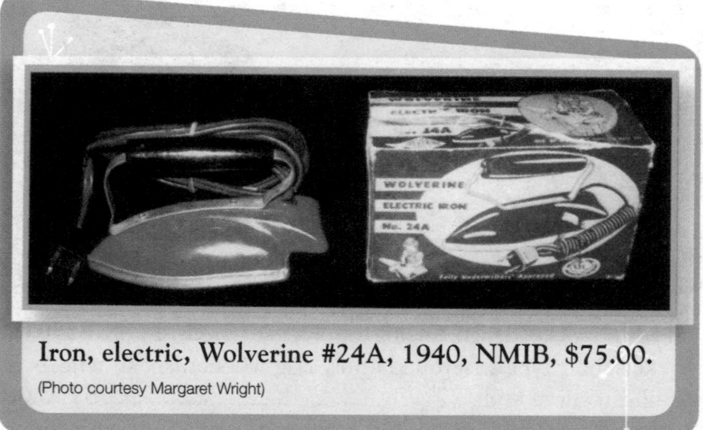

Iron, electric, Wolverine #24A, 1940, NMIB, $75.00. (Photo courtesy Margaret Wright)

Iron, Streamline Electric, Wolverine #25A, 1940s, NMIB..$75.00

Ironing Board and Iron, Sunny Suzy, litho tin, Wolverine-Spang, 1970s, EX...$50.00

Ironing Set, Little Sweetheart, w/iron, clothesline & 6 clothespins, Wolverine #295, unused, MIB (cut-out doll/clothes) $75.00

Kidd-E-Kitchen Set, w/dish pan, drainer, towel, dishes, apron, flateware, etc, Amsco, 1950s, complete, NMIB....... $175.00

Kitchen Cleaning Set, w/broom, dustpan, dust mop, & step-on wastebasket, Wolverine #268, unused, NM+IB....... $200.00

Laundry Set, Mickey Mouse, litho tin tub w/scrub board & clothesline stand, NMIB, A $450.00

Laundry Set, Mickey Mouse, litho tin tub w/scrub board & clothesline stand, VGIB, A $275.00

Laundry Set, New Eclipse, wooden tub w/free-standing 15" H wringer & 2 washboards, possible salesman's sample, VG+, A $525.00

Laundry Set, Three Little Pigs, washtub & washboard, litho tin, Ohio Art, 5½", VG, A... $150.00

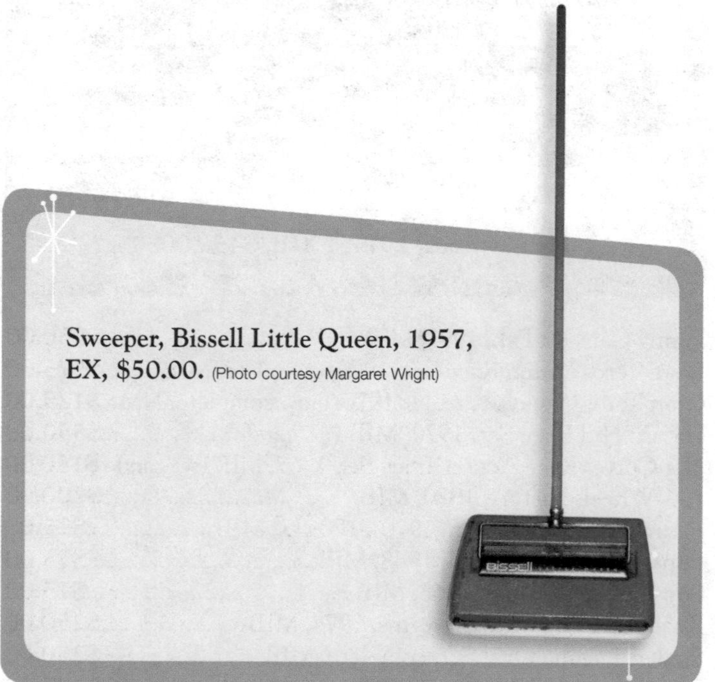

Sweeper, Bissell Little Queen, 1957, EX, $50.00. (Photo courtesy Margaret Wright)

Sweeper Set, Golden Girl Carpet Sweeper, w/sweeper, dustpan, apron & broom, Norstar, 1960s, NMIB $65.00

Wash Set, New Eclipse, wooden tub with 15" high free-standing wringer and two wash boards, possible salesman's sample, VG+, A, $525.00. (Photo courtesy Noel Barrett Antiques and Auctions, Ltd.)

Washer-Dryer, Sparkle Bright, PS, pk, 10" H, Structo, EX+IB, A...$130.00

Washing Machine, Dick Tracy, litho tin, Kalon Redro Corp, EXIB, A... $100.00

Washing Machine, Dolly's Washer, litho tin, crank-op, 9", Chein, EXIB, A $300.00
Washing Machine, Dolly's Washer, litho tin, crank-op, 9", Chien, VG, A $120.00
Washing Machine, glass drum (transparent gr) w/metal top & bottom, 10" Hoge, MIB, A $990.00
Washing Machine, glass drum w/metal top & legs, 10", Wolverine, NM, A $85.00

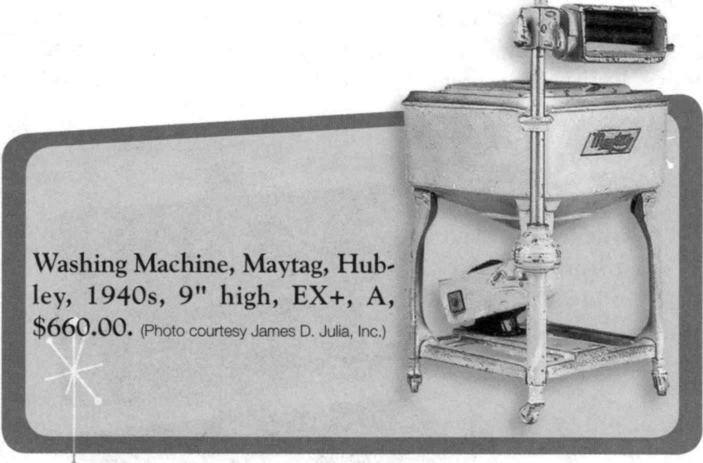

Washing Machine, Maytag, Hubley, 1940s, 9" high, EX+, A, $660.00. (Photo courtesy James D. Julia, Inc.)

Washing Machine, Mickey Mouse, litho tin, crank-op, Ohio Art, EX, A $385.00
Washing Machine, Three Little Pigs, litho tin, crank-op, 9", Chein, EX $450.00
Washing Machine, wooden 3-legged tub w/lid & wringer, American, late 19th C, VG+, A $660.00

COOKING AND KITCHENWARE

Automatic Dollee Blender, battery-operated, EXIB, A, $75.00. (Photo courtesy Randy Inman Auctions)

Baking Set, Betty Jane, 9-pc clear glass set w/covered casserole, 4 custards, pie plate, etc, Glasbake, 1940s, EXIB $150.00
Baking Set, Cake Box Set, litho tin, Blue Delph motif, Wolverine #260, 1940s, complete, EXIB $225.00
Baking Set, Cinderella Pastery Set, w/baking utensils & scale, Peerless Playthings, 1950s, complete, EXIB $90.00

Baking Set, Junior Chef Cake Mix Set, Argo Industries, 1956, complete and unused, NMIB, $100.00. (Photo courtesy Margaret Wright)

Baking Set, Kay Stanley's Dessert Set, w/real Pillsbury & Jell-O products & baking utensils, 1950s, complete, EXIB . $125.00
Baking Set, Sunny Suzy, 7-pc set marked Fire-King Oven Glass, Wolverine #260, complete, EXIB $140.00
Baking Set, Sunny Suzy Bake-A-Cake, w/hand beater, wooden board, measuring spoons, bowl, etc, Wolverine, complete, EXIB $100.00
Cabinet, litho tin w/Pennsylvania Dutch motif, 2 top shelves, drawer & 2 doors, 21x17x7", Ideal, 1950s, NM $65.00
Cabinet, Little Miss Structo Corner Cabinet, PS, pk, 12" H, EX+IB, A $110.00

Cabinet, Little Miss Structo Counter-Top, pressed steel, pink, 11", MIB, A, $85.00. (Photo courtesy Randy Inman Auctions)

Coffee Mill, Juvenile, Arcade, wood base w/drawer, crank top, 4" sq, VG+, A $165.00
Eggbeater, A&J (label reads Baby Bingo No 68...,) or Betty Taplin, EX, ea $25.00
Jar Beater, A&J (bowl marked 'Woolworth') or Betty Taplin (Glasbake footed bowl), 1920s-30s, EX+, ea $115.00
Kitchen Set, litho tin, 4 canisters, 'Pastery Board,' 'Cookie Sheet,' rolling pin, 3 bowls, 2 plates, Ohio Art, EX $200.00
Mini Serve-It Children's Serving Set, w/Tupperware pitcher, 4 cups, bowls & bowl lid, Dart Industries, 1979, NMIB .$65.00

Pan Set, aluminum, coffeepot, tube cake pan, roaster, skillet, 2 saucepans, dbl boiler, 1930s, EX+ $85.00

Pan Set, Revere Ware, 12-piece, 1950s, EX+, $150.00. (Photo courtesy Margaret Wright)

Percolator, metal w/emb motif such as Cinderella, Bo Peep or Three Little Kittens, Mirro, 1950s, EX, ea $20.00
Refrigerator, metal w/2 doors, food lithoed on inside of bottom door, wht w/red hdls, 13½" H, Wolverine, EX (no food) $50.00
Sink, lithoed tin, footed base, tall back w/lithoed glassware & shelves, red & cream, 10x11x6", Wolverine, 1930s, EX $65.00
Sink, pk metal w/'Running Water,' Wolverine #197, EXIB.$85.00
Stove, Detroit Stove Works in cut-out marquee, CI, ornate, footed, 17", EX, A $1,900.00
Stove, Eagle Gas Range, bl-pnt CI, cabriole legs, opening doors, 9" H, G, A $88.00
Stove, Favorite, gr-pnt & NP CI, w/4 accessories, 9" W, EX, A $600.00
Stove, Garland Stoves & Ranges logo on oven door, tin & CI, 12", VG, A $450.00
Stove, Globe, Kenton, CI, 18", EX, A $800.00
Stove, Jewel Range Jr, pnt CI w/NP doors & trim, 12½" H, VG, A $440.00
Stove, LA/Depose, French, pnt tin, high back splash w/shelf & hooks, w/7-pc wht enamel set, 22" H, G, A.................... $220.00
Stove, Little Chef, wht metal, 13x13x7", Ohio Art, 1950s, EX+ $150.00
Stove, Little Lady, wht metal w/red trim, 11x12x6", Metal Ware Corp, 1950, EX+ $75.00

Stove, Little Miss Structo, pressed steel, pink, 11½" long, MIB, A, $155.00. (Photo courtesy Randy Inman Auctions)

Stove, Little Orphan Annie, electric, 9x10x5½", Marx, 1930s, EX+ $125.00
Stove, Marx, wht metal w/blk & red trim, enclosed bottom, oven door w/window, 13x12x6½", 1950s, EX $60.00
Stove, Modern Play, wht metal w/red trim, Wolverine #188, 1950s, NMIB.................... $100.00
Stove, Novelty, pnt CI w/NP trim, warming oven & stove pipe, w/2 CI pots, 12½" H, Kenton, VG+, A.................... $220.00
Stove, Philadelphia Stove Works, pnt CI, 4-footed, w/stove pipe, coal shovel, 12" H, VG+, A $355.00
Stove, Royal Ester, CI, 16", VG, A $1,500.00
Stove, Ruth, NP CI, complete, 15" W, VG+, A $600.00

Waffle Iron, Arcade, cast iron, 5½", VG, A, $110.00. (Photo courtesy Randy Inman Auctions)

Waffle Iron, CI, rnd w/CI hdl & top/bottom wooden hdls, 8" L (w/hdl), Arcade, VG+, A.................... $130.00

Furniture

Armchair, Louis XVI style w/open arms, upholstered tops, back & 8½" dia seat, English, VG+, A $660.00
Armchair, Regency style, inlaid mahogany w/upholstered seat, 10½" H, VG, A.................... $190.00
Armchair, Victorian captain's style w/spindle back, turned legs, walnut, 17", English, 19th C, G+, A....................$55.00
Armchair, Windsor style w/saddle seat, wood, 26", stamped Selby, G+, A....................$65.00
Armoire, Louis XV style carved oak w/molded cornice, 2 doors, 3 interior shelves, 18" H, G, A.................... $300.00
Baby Sister Dolly Set, wood, wardrobe, baby bath, table tender, playpen & crib, FAO Schwartz, ca 1957, EX, A...... $150.00

Bed, Victorian, pine, hinged top, fold-down sides, brass trim, cloth bedding, 13", American, 1888, VG, A, $660.00. (Photo courtesy Noel Barrett Antiques and Auctions)

Bed, Victorian w/arched tester, mahogany, fish-net canopy w/tassels, 18", VG, A $330.00
Bed Steps, 2-step, mahogany w/leather inset, 4 turned feet, hinged, 5" W, VG, A $525.00
Chest, Jacobean style w/recessed panels carved foliage trim, hinged lid, oak, 11" W, VG, A $200.00
Chest, Victorain, flat top, 2 short & 2 long drawers, brass trim, 17" H, English, G, A $660.00
Chest of Drawers, Chippendale chest-on-chest type, 7 drawers, mahogany, 23½", G+, A $2,090.00
Chest of Drawers, Victorian, flat top, 2 short & 2 long drawers, mahogany w/brass trim, 7" H, English, G, A $660.00
Cradle, Victorian, straight sides, curved hood, turned finials, rockers, mahogany, 16", English, G+, A $135.00
Cupboard, Hoosier, gr-pnt wood complete w/flour bin & pullout wood board, 17" H, Schoenhut, EX, A $1,430.00
Cupboard, stepback w/top sliding glass doors, lt maple w/wht porc spice drawers, 10½" H, EX, A $660.00
Cupboard, stepback w/2 top glazed doors, 2 bottom doors, walnut, 26x20x8", American, late 19th C, VG, A $355.00
Desk, Biedermeier drop-front type w/top shelf, gold decor, 2 doors, porc knobs, 15" H, VG, A $600.00
Desk, Edwardian slant lid type w/single lg drawer, pnt satinwood & part ebonized, 14" H, G+, A $2,200.00
Dressing Chest, roll-top w/2 drawers, cheval mirror, fruitwood, 21", VG, A $700.00
Dressing Table, Edwardian style w/attached mirror, mahogany w/inlaid satinwood, porc knobs, 16", VG+, A $1,870.00
Dressing Table, empire style rnd ormolu mirror mounted on fruitwood table, 9½", French, VG, A $935.00
Garden Set, 2 side chairs/rnd 3-legged table w/feet curving out, CI a/ornate heart/flowers, 18", VG, A $55.00
Grandfather Clock, mahogany w/inlayed work, bottom drawer, 16", English, VG, A $525.00

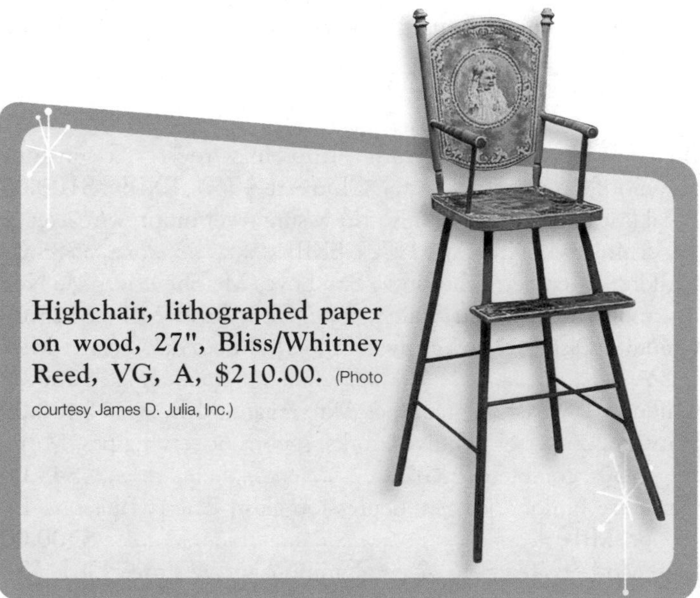

Highchair, lithographed paper on wood, 27", Bliss/Whitney Reed, VG, A, $210.00. (Photo courtesy James D. Julia, Inc.)

Side Cabinet, Victorian, upper arched glass door, 6-drawer bottom, mahogany, 33", American, G+, A $4,400.00
Side Chair, straight back w/2 slats, rush seat, turned legs, fauz rosewood w/gold trim, 10", G, A $1,760.00
Side Table, French Provincial drum style w/tall cabriole legs, 3 faux drawers, pnt wood, 9", VG+, A $415.00

Sideboard, solid oak with mirrored top, ornate trim, two opening drawers and doors, 22x15", EX, A, $4,125.00. (Photo courtesy James D. Julia, Inc.)

Table, Regency drop leaf, frieze drawer, pedestal w/4 down-swept legs, mahogany, 9" W, English, VG, A $440.00
Table, Victorian, rnd top, pedestal w/3-sided concave base, mahogany, 8½" dia top, J Bubb, VG+, A $660.00
Table, Victorian, tilt-top, pedestal w/angular cabriole legs, mahogany/beechwood, 13" H, English, G+, A $440.00
Table & Chairs, Mission-style 11" L table w/2 arm chairs & settee, stained pine, American, 20th C, G, ... $275.00
Wash Stand, Victorian, marble top, frieze drawer, rnd easel mirror, turned legs, wood, 14", French, G+, A $715.00

Writing Table, Victorian, rosewood with ebony trim, 14" high, England, 1870s, VG, A, $715.00. (Photo courtesy Noel Barrett Antiques and Auctions, Ltd)

Nursing Sets

Doll-E-Feeder Set, divided dish, sterilizer, tongs, funnel, juicer, box of Vel, 6 bottles in rack, etc, Amsco, 1950s, EX......... $100.00
Doll-E-Feedette, 12-pc w/Gerber's Oatmeal box, Evenflo cleanser, divided dish, etc, Amsco, 1950s, complete, NMIB.. $125.00

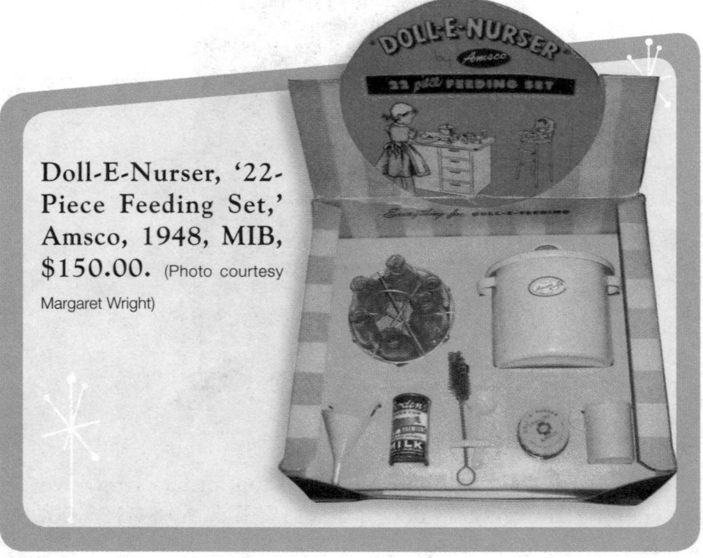

Doll-E-Nurser, '22-Piece Feeding Set,' Amsco, 1948, MIB, $150.00. (Photo courtesy Margaret Wright)

Sewing

Embriodery Set, Handkerchief Set, American Toy Works #5, 1940s, complete, unused, NMIB $35.00
Embroidery Set, Junior Miss, hatbox style case, Hassenfeld #1586, 1950s, complete, unused, NM $75.00
Embroidery Set, Shirley Temple Luncheon Embroidery Set, Gabriel #311, 1960s, complete, unused, NMIB $100.00

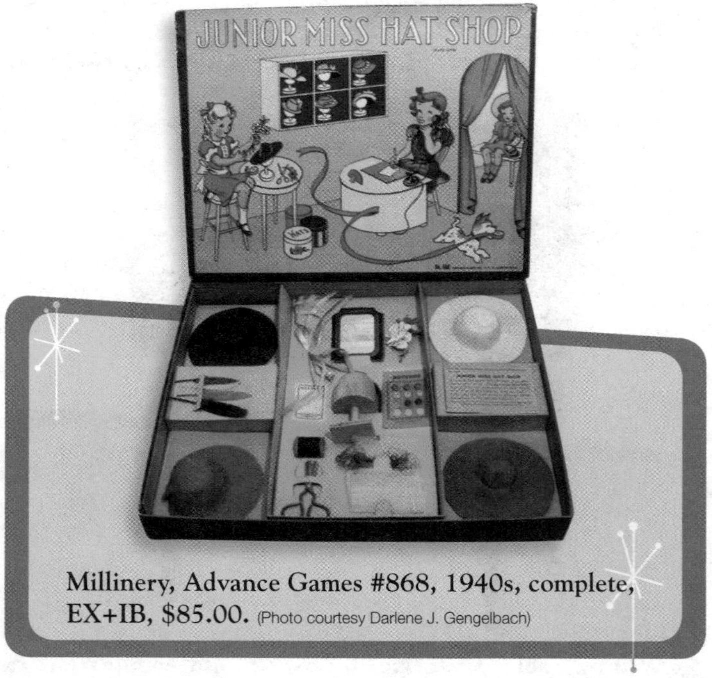

Millinery, Advance Games #868, 1940s, complete, EX+IB, $85.00. (Photo courtesy Darlene J. Gengelbach)

Millinary Set, La Velle #30, 1920s, complete, unused, NMIB . $100.00
Millinery Set, Junior Miss Hat Shop, Advance #868, 1940s, complete, unused, NMIB.. $100.00
Sewing Kit, Deb-U-Teen, vinyl hatbox style case complete w/sewing machine, doll & notions, Hassenfeld Bros #1546, NM $100.00
Sewing Kit, Doll House Dress Shop, Transogram #1515, 1930s, complete, unused, NMIB..$35.00
Sewing Kit, Junior Miss, suitcase style box complete w/ doll & sewing notions, Hassenfeld Bros #1535, unused, NMIB $75.00
Sewing Kit, Little Miss Model, plastic hatbox style case w/doll & sewing notions, Transogram #5385, 1950s, complete, EX.......$35.00
Sewing Kit, Little Miss Seamstress Set Featuring Toy Necchi Sewing Machine, w/doll & notions, Hasbro, 1950s, EXIB $100.00
Sewing Machine, Singer, early table model, complete, EXIB (box reads A Singer For The Girls), A............................ $200.00

Sewing Machine, Singer, 6", VG, A, $100.00. (Photo courtesy Morphy Auctions)

Sewing Machine Set, Take Along Sew-Rite, Hasbro #1543, 1969, complete, unused, NMIB (suitcase type) $75.00

Table Service

Breakfast Set, Good Morning, litho tin w/rooster-&-sunshine motif, 15-pc set w/toaster, Ohio Art, 1960s, EXIB .. $100.00
Breakfast Set, Sunshine, litho tin w/sunflower motif, w/toaster & fruit bowl, Ohio Art, 1970s, EXIB $85.00
Children's Tea Set, litho tin w/'She Loves Me She Loves Me Not' motif, artist signed 'Elaine,' 9-pc, Ohio Art, NMIB.. $125.00
Chiquita Dishes (My Carnival Colors), 8-pc, Akro Agate, MIB, A $220.00
Chiquita Toy Dishes, gr, 22-pc, Akro Agate, MIB, A..... $400.00
Flatware, 26-pc set w/knives, forks, spoons & serving pcs, Mirro, 1950s, complete, EXIB $45.00
Jeannette Junior Dish Set, depression glass, Cherry Blossom, 14-pc, MIB, A $300.00
Like Mothers Tea Set, 27-pc aluminum set w/'Three Little Kittens' emb images, Mirro, 1950s, 27-pc set, EXIB..... $165.00
Little American Maid Tea Set, depression glass, amber Interior Panel, 21-pc, Akro Agate, MIB, A $185.00
Little American Maid Tea Set, Lemonade & Oxblood, 17-pc, Akro Agate, MIB, A.. $465.00

Little American Maid Tea Set, Akro Agate, 29-piece set, unused, MIB, A, $360.00. (Photo courtesy Randy Inman Auctions)

Little American Maid Tea Set, wht & maroon marble, 21-pc, Akro Agate, MIB, A $550.00

Little American Maid Tea Set, wht w/decals, 11-pc, Akro Agate, MIB, A $110.00

Little Housekeeper Set, unfinished wood, complete set w/orig cookbook, VG+IB (wood box), A $465.00

Little Sweetheart Salad Set, litho tin, salad bowl w/4 serving bowls, tossing fork & spoon, Wolverine #253, EXIB..$75.00

Marx Plastic Tea Set #2093, 44-pc mc set w/4 clear goblets and 4 clear sherbets, w/napkins & flatware, complete, EXIB..$75.00

Play-Time Dish Set, bl, yel & gr, 19-pc, Akro Agate, MIB, A $385.00

Play-Time Glass Dishes, bl & wht marble, 8-pc, Akro Agate, MIB, A $300.00

Play-Time Glass Dishes, depression glass, gr Interior Panel Stacked Disc w/Darts, 16-pc, Akro Agate, MIB, A . $600.00

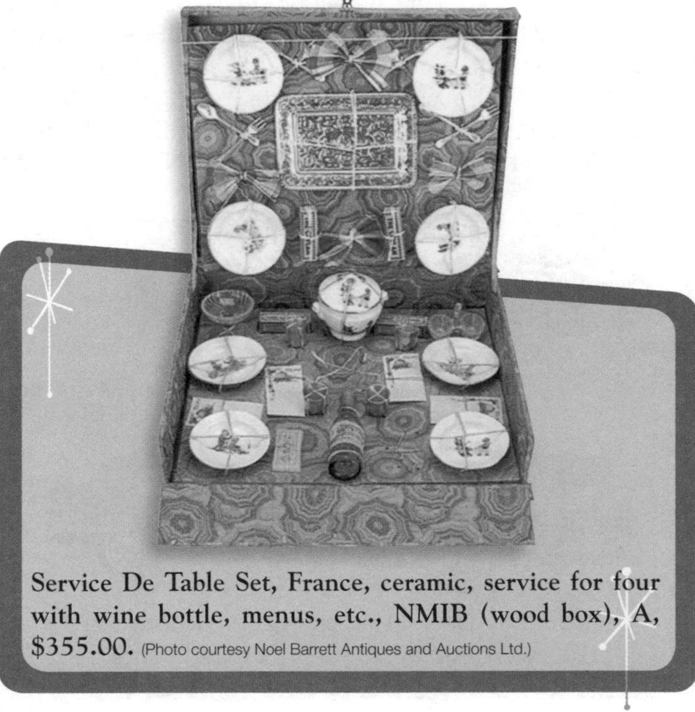
Service De Table Set, France, ceramic, service for four with wine bottle, menus, etc., NMIB (wood box), A, $355.00. (Photo courtesy Noel Barrett Antiques and Auctions Ltd.)

Play-Time Glass Dishes, transparent gr, 16-pc, Akro Agate, MIB, A $220.00

Play-Time Glass Water Set, gr pitcher w/6 yel glasses, ribbed pattern, Akro Agate, MIB, A $110.00

Play-Time Glass Water Set, pitcher & 6 glasses, octagonal, bl, yel, gr & wht, Akro Agate, MIB, A $145.00

Miscellaneous

Lawnmower, CI w/wooden hdl, Arcade, 1930s, 33", G+ . $130.00

Lawnmower, PS w/wooden hdl, rubber tires, Arcade, 1940s, 32", G+ $50.00

Little Deb Lemonade Server Set, Hazel-Atlas glass pitcher/4 glasses, 4-holed tray w/center hdl, Northwerstern Prod, NMIB $100.00

Little Yankee Carpenter & Joiner Set, Arcade, 1923, VG (wooden box), A $220.00

See 'em Pop Electric Pop Corn Popper & Vendor, complete w/bowls & instruction booklet, Two Rivers, 1950s-60s, EX+ $115.00

Sno-Cone Maker, plastic snowman shape, Hasenfeld Bros, 1960s, 9½", NM $75.00

Suzy Homemaker Sweet Shoppe Soda Fountain, Topper, 1960s, MIB $50.00

Swing, free-standing, facing seats, wire construstion, 18" H, G+, A $55.00

Swing, free-standing, straight wire construction, 12", G+, A. $120.00

Swing, free-standing, twisted wire construction, 28", Arcade, G+ $30.00

Tiny Tools Set, Arcade, 1941, 4-pc garden set, NP, MOC, A $120.00

Toy Carpenter Set, Arcade, 1941, 5-pc, NP, MOC, A $55.00

Toy Garage Set, Arcade, 1941, 5-pc, NP, MOC, A $220.00

Toy Garden Tools, Arcade, 1941, 5-pc, MOC, A $55.00

Typewriter, Berwin, 1940s, NMIB, A, $190.00. (Photo courtesy serioustoyz.com)

Typewriter, Dial/Junior Dial, litho tin, marx, EX, ea from $25 to $30.00

Wheelbarrow, Paris Mfg Co, wood w/red pinstripes & running squirrels, 34" L, EX, A $460.00

Japanese (and Other) Tin Vehicle Replicas

Listed here are the model vehicles (most of which were made in Japan during the 1950s and 1960s) that were designed to realistically represent the muscle cars, station wagons, convertibles, budget models, and luxury cars that were actually being made at the time. Most are tin and many are friction or battery-operated, some have remote control. In our descriptions, all are tin unless noted otherwise.

Austin Healey 100 SIX Convertible (1958), Bandai, friction, 8", EXIB, A, $500.00. (Photo courtesy Morphy Auctions)

Alfa Romeo Giuletta Sprint Veloce Coupe (1960s), Bandai, friction, 8", EX, A $275.00
Austin Healey 100 SIX Convertible (1958), Bandai, friction, 8", EX+, A $100.00
BMW Isetta B-588 (1950s), Bandai, friction, 6½", NM+IB .. $350.00
Buick (1950), Marusan, b/o, NM+IB, A $200.00

Buick (1959), TN, friction, 12", NMIB, A, $1,000.00. (Photo courtesy Morphy Auctions)

Buick Century (1958), Ichiko, friction, 14", VGIB, A... $1,800.00
Buick Sedan (1960s), TN, friction, 16", EXIB, A........ $1,700.00
Buick Sedan (1961), Ichiko, friction, 17", NMIB, A... $2,750.00
Buick Skylark (1966), Asakusa, b/o, 2 red & wht police lights on front fenders, 11½", NM+IB, A........ $350.00
Buick 2-Door, Cragstan, dashboard remote, 12", EXIB, A ... $275.00
Buick 2-Door (1959), MT, friction, 8", EXIB, A $275.00
Cadillac (1950), Normura, b/o, 8½", NMIB, A $175.00
Cadillac (1960), Marusan/IY Metal Toys, friction, 11½", NMIB, A $1,700.00
Cadillac (1960s), Yonezawa, friction, 14", NMIB, A... $1,000.00
Cadillac Convertible (1950), Nomura/Nikko, b/o, 13", NMIB, A $1,757.00
Cadillac Convertible (1950s), Alps, friction, 12", NM+IB, A........ $2,500.00
Cadillac Convertible (1959), Bandai, friction, 12", EX, A .. $150.00
Cadillac Convertible (1959), Bandai, friction, 12", NM+IB, A $325.00

Cadillac Convertible (1959), RS, friction, 11", NMIB, A $400.00. (Photo courtesy Morphy Auctions)

Cadillac Convertible (1961), SSS, b/o, 17", EXIB, A $750.00
Cadillac Fleetwood Eldorado, Ichiko, friction, rider, 28", NMIB, A $500.00
Cadillac Fleetwood Seventy-Five (1961), SSS, friction, 17", EXIB, A........ $1,400.00
Cadillac Fleetwood Sixty Special (1961), SSS, friction, NMIB $1,800.00
Cadillac Sedan (1954), Marusan, friction, 12", NMIB, A.. $1,900.00
Cadillac Sedan (1955), Bandai, friction, 17", NMIB...... $900.00
Cadillac Sedan (1960), Bandai, friction, 11½", NMIB, A ... $175.00
Cadillac Sedan (1960), Yonezawa, friction, 18", EXIB, A.. $1,300.00
Cadillac Sedan (1960), Yonezawa, friction, 18", NMIB, A.. $2,000.00
Cadillac Sedan (1963), Bandai, friction, 8", NM+IB, A... $155.00
Cadillac Sedan (1965), Yonezawa, friction, 22", NMIB . $900.00

Cadillac Two-Door (1960s), ATC, friction, 17", NMIB, A, $1,400.00. (Photo courtesy Morphy Auctions)

Celica Cobra GT, ATC, friction, 14", NMIB, A $225.00
Chevy (1960), IY, 11", EXIB, A $1,100.00

Chevy Bel Air Station Wagon, ATC, friction, 10", VGIB, A, $300.00. (Photo courtesy Morphy Auctions)

Chevy Camaro SS (1968), Nomura, friction, 11", NMIB, A..$375.00
Chevy Corvair (1960), Yonezawa, friction, 9", NM+IB, A..$300.00
Chevy Corvair (1961), Bandai, friction, 8", NM+IB, A.. $180.00
Chevy Corvair (1961), Ichiko, friction, 9", EX+IB, A ... $250.00

Chevy Corvair Compact Convertible, Yonezawa, friction, 9", EXIB, A, $350.00. (Photo courtesy Morphy Auctions)

Chevy Corvette (1958), Yonezawa, friction, 10", EX+IB, A.. $400.00
Chevy Corvette Sting Ray, Ichida, b/o, 12", EXIB, A $500.00
Chevy Impala, Bandai, b/o, 11", VGIB, A $400.00
Chevy Impala (1961), Bandai, friction, 11", NMIB, A .. $400.00
Chevy Pickup (1950s), Bandai, friction, 10", EX+IB, A... $350.00
Chevy Sedan (1954), Marusan, friction, 11", EX, A $750.00
Chevy Sedan (1959), TS, friction, 12", EXIB, A............ $850.00
Chevy 2-Door (1954), Linemar, friction, 11", EX, A $150.00
Chevy 2-door (1954), Marusan, b/o, electric headlights, 11", NMIB, A $2,750.00
Chevy 2-Door (1955), Marusan, r/c, doors open, celluloid driver, 11", EXIB, A $1,400.00
Chrysler Convertible (1952), Yonezawa/Sato, friction, 10", NMIB, A $575.00

Chrysler Imperial (1962), ATC, friciton, 15", NMIB, A.. $9,000.00
Chrysler New Yorker (1958), Alps, friction, 14", EX+, A ..$2,900.00

Citreon Convertible DS19, Bandai, friction, 8", EXIB, A, $600.00. (Photo courtesy Morphy Auctions)

Dodge Sedan, TN, friction, 11", EXIB, A $1,400.00
Edsel, KKS, friction, 8", EXIB, A $400.00
Edsel, TN, friction, 9", MIB, A $500.00
Edsel (1958), Nomura, friction, 9", NMIB, A................ $475.00
Edsel (1958), Yonezawa/Shinsei, friction, 10½", EX+IB, A.. $1,150.00
Edsel Station Wagon (1958), Nomura, friction, 10½", EX, A . $200.00
Ferrari, (1960s), Bandai, friction, 11", NMIB, A $450.00
Ferrari (1960s), Bandai, friction, 11", NM, A................ $175.00
Ferrari Berlinetta 250 LeMans #2, Asahi, b/o, 11", NMIB, A.. $150.00
Ferrari Convertible (1960s), Bandai, b/o, working lights, 11½", EXIB, A $250.00

Fiat 600, Bandai, friction, with sun roof, 7", NMIB, A, $350.00. (Photo courtesy Morphy Auctions)

Ford Capri GT (1970s), Ichiko, friction, 15", NM+IB, A.. $150.00
Ford Fairlane (1959), Masudaya, friction, 8½", NMIB, A.. $500.00
Ford Fairlane Convertible (1957), Bandai, friction, trunk opens, 12", NMIB, A $1,500.00
Ford Mustag GT, Nomura, friction, w/mirrors & antenna, 15½", EXIB, A... $450.00
Ford Mustang, Bandai, b/o, 'Slip Action,' 11", NM+IB, A ..$150.00

Ford Mustang Convertible, Bandai/Sears, b/o, w/gear shift, 11", EXIB, A $150.00
Ford Mustang Convertible, Yonezawa, b/o, see-thru hood w/visible engine, retractable roof, 13½", NMIB, A.......... $125.00
Ford Mustang Fastback, ATC, friction, 11", NMIB, A ... $700.00

Ford Pickup (1955), Bandai, friction, elephant decal, 12", EXIB, A, $800.00. (Photo courtesy Morphy Auctions)

Ford Ranchero (1957), Bandai, friction, 12", NM, A..... $255.00
Ford Skyliner Retractable (1958), Nomura, b/o, 9", NM+IB, A $250.00
Ford Station Wagon (Country Sedan), TN, friction, removable plastic roof, 10", EXIB, A $350.00
Ford Station Wagon (Custom Ranch), Bandai, friction, 12", MIB, A $550.00
Ford Station Wagon (1961), Ichimura, friction, 10", NMIB, A $130.00
Ford T-Bird, ATC, friction, 13", EXIB, A $400.00
Ford T-Bird, Bandai, friction, 11", EXIB, A $175.00

Ford T-Bird, Ichiko, friction, 11", EXIB, A, $300.00. (Photo courtesy Morphy Auctions)

Ford T-Bird, TN, electric lights, 11", NMIB, A $600.00
Ford T-Bird (1956), Nomura, b/o, 11", NMIB, A $400.00
Ford T-Bird (1956), Nomura, friction, w/snap-on clear plastic top, 11", NM, A $225.00

Ford T-Bird Convertible (1958), Bandai, friction, 8", MIB, A. $145.00
Ford T-Bird Convertible (1962), Haji, friction, 8", NMIB, A.. $210.00
Ford T-Bird Convertible (1964), Ichiko/Sears, friction, retractable roof, 15", NMIB, A $300.00
Ford 2-Door Hardtop, ATC, friction, 10", NMIB, A...... $500.00
Ford 2-Door Hardtop (1954), Marusan, friction, 10", EX, A ... $250.00
Ford 2-Door Hardtop (1956), Yonezawa, r/c, 12½", EX, A .. $1,120.00

Isetta, Bandai, friction, 7", EXIB, A, $400.00. (Photo courtesy Morphy Auctions)

Jaguar Convertible, Bandai, friction, 9", NMIB, A......... $400.00

Jaguar E.Type, TT, friction, 11", EXIB, A, $200.00. (Photo courtesy Morphy Auctions)

Jaguar XKE Coupe (1960s), Nomura, friction, 11½", NM, A $370.00
Jaguar XKE GTX-753 (1960s), Takatoku, r/c, 10½", NMIB, A $275.00
Jaguar 3.4 Sedan, Bandai, friciton, 8", EXIB $250.00
Lincoln Continental Mark III Sedan (1959), Bandai, friction, 12", EXIB, A $550.00
Lincoln Sedan (1950s), Ichiko, friction, 12", EX, A $750.00
Lincoln Sedan (1950s), Ichiko, friction, 12", NMIB, A.. $3,750.00
Lotus Elan (GT Car Series), Bandai, 1950s, friction, 8½", MIB, A $100.00
Mazda Delivery Cycle/Van (1950s), Bandai, friction, 3-wheeled, canvas cover, 8½", EX, A $950.00

Mercedes Convertible, Schuco #5503, 9", NMIB, A...... $450.00
Mercedes 219 Convertible (1950s), Bandai, friction, 8", EX, A $150.00
Mercedes 220, Bandai, b/o, 10", EXIB, A.......... $200.00
Mercedes 220S (1960s), Bandai, friction, 10", NM, A... $200.00
Mercedes 230 Taxi (1960s), Bandai, b/o, doors open, 10½", NMIB, A.......... $150.00
Mercedes 250S Sedan (1960s), Daiya, friction, 14", NM, A.. $150.00
Mercedes 300 Adenauer Limousine (1950s), Alps, b/o, 9½", NMIB, A.......... $1,300.00
Mercedes 300SE (1960s), Ichiko, rider, 24", unused, MIB, A.. $295.00
Mercedes 300SL Convertible Coupe, Bandai, 1950s, friction, 8", NMIB, A.......... $175.00
Mercedes 300SL Coupe (1950s), Bandai, friction, 8", MIB, A $225.00
Mercury Montclair Sedan (1958), Yonezawa, friction, 11½", EX, A $200.00
MG Magnette Mark III Sedan (1960s), Bandai, friction, 8", NM+IB, A $270.00
MG Midget, Bandai, friction, 8", EXIB, A.......... $300.00
MG Midget Convertible (1950s), Yoshiya, friction, 8½", EXIB, A $275.00
MG Midget Overland Racer #7 (1955), Bandai, friction, 8", VG, A $150.00
MGA 1600 Convertible (1950s), Bandai, b/o, 'International Gear Shift Series,' 8", NMIB, A.......... $175.00
MGA 1600 Coupe (1950s), Bandai, friction, 8", NM+IB, A.. $225.00
Nash Cross Country Station Wagon (1954), Marusan, friction, w/luggage rail on roof, 10", EX+IB, A.......... $1,850.00
Nash Rambler Station Wagon (1959), Bandai, friction, 11", EX, A $110.00
Nissan Gloria GL (1960s), Ichiko, friction, 16", MIB, A.. $175.00
Oldsmobile Sedan (1952), Yonezawa, friction, 10½", NMIB, A $175.00

Oldsmobile Sedan (1960s), Cragstan, friction, 12", EXIB, A, $450.00. (Photo courtesy Morphy Auctions)

Oldsmobile Toronado, ATC, friction, 16", NMIB, A..... $300.00
Oldsmobile Toronado, Ichiko, friction, 17", EXIB, A..... $400.00
Oldsmobile Toronado (1967), Bandai, b/o, 11", MIB, A .. $150.00
Oldsmobile 2-Door (1959), Ichiko, friction, 13", EXIB, A .. $365.00
Opel Olympia Rekord (1956), Yonezawa, b/o, 11½", EX+IB, A $575.00

Plymouth Belvedere, Alps, Friction, 8", EXIB, A, $500.00. (Photo courtesy Morphy Auctions)

Plymouth Fury (1956), Alps, b/o, 12", NM, A.......... $500.00
Plymouth Fury (1965), Bandai, friction, 8", NM, A.......... $85.00
Plymouth Fury Convertible (1958), Bandai, friction, 8", EX, A $110.00
Pontiac (1950s), KS, friction, 14", EX, A $750.00
Porsche Sportomatic, Takatoku, b/o, 11", NMIB, A....... $125.00
Rambler Classic Station Wagon, Bandai, friction, 11", EXIB, A.......... $225.00
Rambler Station Wagon w/Shasta Trailer, Bandai, friction, 21" overall, NM, A $1,100.00
Renault (1960), Yonezawa, friction, 7", NMIB, A....... $1,000.00
Renault Floride, ATC, friction, 9", VGIB, A.......... $225.00
Rolls Royce Silver Cloud (1960s), Yonezawa, friction, 8½", NM+IB, A $200.00

Rolls-Royce Silver Cloud, Bandai, friction, 12", NMIB, A, $400.00. (Photo courtesy Morphy Auctions)

Saab, Bandai, friction, 7", NMIB, A $400.00
Toyota 2000, Ichiko, 16", EXIB, A.......... $350.00
Toyota 2000 GT (1960s), Ichiko, friction, 14½", NM+IB, A.. $470.00
Triumph TR-3, Bandai, friction, 8", NMIB, A $750.00
Triumph TR-4, Bandai, r/c, 8", EXIB, A $150.00
Volkswagen Beetle (1960s), Masudaya, friction, has motor sound, license plate reads '1500,' 11", NM, A $300.00
Volkswagen Beetle Convertible, Showa, b/o, 9", NMIB, A.. $400.00

Volkswagen Beetle Convertible (1960s), Nomura, b/o, visible lighted engine w/working pistons, 10", EX, A $225.00
Volkswagen Bus, Bandai, b/o, 9½", NM+IB, A $575.00
Volkswagen Sedan (Kingsize), Bandai, b/o, 15", NMIB, A..$250.00

Volvo 1800ES, Ichiko, remote control, 9", NMIB, A, $350.00. (Photo courtesy Morphy Auctions)

Volvo 1800S, Ichiko, friction, 9", NMIB, A $550.00

Keystone

Though this Massachusetts company produced a variety of toys during their years of operation (ca 1920 – late 1950s), their pressed-steel vehicles are the most collectible, and that's what we've listed here. As a rule they were very large, with some of the riders being around 30" in length.

Air Mail Plane, 27" long, EX, A, $1,955.00. (Photo courtesy Morphy Auctions)

Airplane (Rapid Fire Motor), 24" WS, VG, A $2,640.00
Ambulance, #73, military vehicle w/open doors, cloth-covered sides, 27", EX+, A $2,400.00
American Railway Express, #43, 26", VG, A................. $950.00
Coast-to-Coast Bus, #84, 32", EX, A........................... $4,600.00
Coast-to-Coast Bus, #84, 32", VG, A.......................... $2,200.00
Delivery Truck, doorless cab, blk & red, 26", rpnt, A..... $355.00
Dump Truck, cabover, 25", G, A $450.00
Dump Truck, doorless cab, crank-op, 26", G, A............. $560.00
Dump Truck, doorless cab, crank-op, 26", VG, A........$1,092.00

Dump Truck, doorless cab, hydraulic-lift, 26", EX+, A $2,185.00. (Photo courtesy Morphy Auctions)

Dump Truck, doorless cab, hydraulic-lift, 26", G+, A..... $715.00
Fire Aerial Ladder Truck, #79, 31", G+, A...................... $935.00
Fire Aerial Ladder Truck, red w/yel ladders, 24", MIB, A... $400.00
Fire Chemical Pump Engine, #57, 28", EX, A $2,250.00
Fire Chemical Pump Engine, #57, 28", G, A $600.00

Fire Ladder Truck, #79, 31", EX+, A, $2,300.00. (Photo courtesy Morphy Auctions)

Fire Water Tower Truck, #56, 30", EX+, A $1,760.00
Golden Guernsey Milk Truck, 27", rstr, A $2,500.00
Greyhound Bus, 18", G+, A $385.00
Keystone Bus Terminal, pressed cb, wood & plastic, 1950s, complete, VG, A $280.00
Keystone Garage, cb w/plastic pump, 10" L, G+, A...........$75.00
Keystone Garage, wood, w/car, EXIB, A $250.00
Keystone Service Station, complete w/2 cars, 22" W, VG, A..$275.00
Koaster Truck, #54 , 25", VG, A $715.00
Moving Van, #58, doorless cab, 26", EX, A $2,500.00
Moving Van, #58, doorless cab, 26", G, A $1,345.00

Police Patrol, #51, 26", NM, A, $3,060.00. (Photo courtesy Morphy Auctions)

Police Patrol, #51, 26", VG, A $1,340.00
Pure Milk Co Delivery Truck, w/up, wht, 9", G+, A $330.00
Sprinkler Tank Truck, #53, 12", prof rstr, A $1,100.00
Steam Roller, #60, 21", EX, A $900.00
Steam Roller, #60, 21", G, A $275.00
Steam Shovel, #46, EX, A $185.00
Steam Shovel, #47, VG, A $250.00
Train Locomotive No 6400, 25", EX, A $675.00

Train Pullman Car No. 6800, 25", NM, A, $2,300.00.
(Photo courtesy Morphy Auctions)

Train Tender No 6500, 18", EX, A $725.00
Truck Loader, #44, 18", G, A $165.00
US Army Truck, #48, open seat, cloth cover, 27", VG+, A .. $990.00
US Mail Truck, #45, screened van, 26", EX, A $2,500.00
US Mail Truck, #45, screened van, 26", G+, A $1,650.00
Wrecker, #78, 26", EX, A $1,760.00
Wrecker, #78, 26", G, A $800.00

Lehmann

Lehmann toys were made in Germany as early as 1881. Early on they were sometimes animated by means of an inertia-generated flywheel; later, clockwork mechanisms were used. Some of their best-known turn-of-the-century toys were actually very racist and unflattering to certain ethnic groups. But the wonderful antics they perform and the imagination that went into their conception have made them and all the other Lehmann toys favorites with collectors today. Though the company faltered with the onset of WWI, they were quick to recover and during the war years produced some of their best toys, several of which were copied by their competitors. Business declined after WWI. Lehmann died in 1934, but the company continued for awhile under the direction of Lehmann's partner and cousin, Johannes Richter.

Advisor: Scott Smiles

Acrobat, VG $750.00
Adam the Porter, EX $600.00
Adam the Porter, NMIB $1,350.00
Africa Ostrich Cart, EX $550.00
Africa Ostrich Cart, G $300.00
AHA Deliver Truck, VG, A $475.00
Ajax, NM $1,400.00
Alabama Coon Jigger (Oh My), EX, A $500.00
Alabama Coon Jigger (Oh My), NM+IB $1,500.00
ALSO Auto, NM $550.00
AMPOL, EX $1,600.00

Anxious Bride, VG, $1,500.00.
(Photo courtesy courtesy Morphy Auctions)

Autin Pedal Car, 4", NM (w/American Boy box) $1,000.00
Auto Post Delivery Van, NMIB $1,400.00
Auto-Onkel, NMIB $1,400.00
Autobus No 590, EX $1,200.00
Autobus No 590, NMIB, A $2,750.00
Autohutte (Garage) w/Galop Racer #1 & Sedan, EX, A.. $850.00
Baker & Chimney Sweep, NMIB $3,250.00
Baker & Chimney Sweep, VG+ $1,250.00
Balky Mule, EXIB, A $650.00
Balky Mule, VG $275.00
Berolina Convertible, NM $3,500.00
Berolina Convertible, VG $2,000.00
Bird Flaps Wings, VG $400.00
Bucking Bronco, EXIB $1,200.00
Bucking Bronco, VG $650.00
Buster Brown in Auto, VG $800.00
Captain of Kopenick, NM $1,500.00
Climbing Miller, EXIB $500.00
Climbing Monkey (Kletter-Affe), EXIB $225.00
Coach w/Driver, VG+, A $700.00
Crawling Beetle, EXIB $450.00
Crawling Beetle, NM $250.00
Crocodile, NMIB $450.00
Dancing Sailor (Columbia), EX $600.00
Dancing Sailor (HMS Dreadnaught), EX+IB $1,300.00
Dancing Sailor (MARS), EXIB $900.00
Dare Devil, EX, A $500.00
DRGM Garage w/Racer & Sedan, EX, A $1,200.00
Duo, EX $935.00
Echo Cycle, EX $1,500.00
EHE & Co Truck, EX $500.00
EPL-I Zeppelin, EXIB $1,250.00
EPL-I Zeppelin, VG $400.00
EPL-II Zeppelin, EXIB $2,250.00
Express Porter, NM $650.00
Express Porter, VG $450.00
Futurus Peace Chime, VG $650.00
Gala Sedan, bl & wht, rare, VG $750.00
Galop Zebra Cart, 1954 issue, NMIB $525.00

Garage w/Galop Racer #1, EX $650.00
Garage w/Gnome (Series) Racer & Sedan, VG $550.00
Going to the Fair, G $900.00
Going to the Fair, NM $3,000.00
Gustav the Miller, EX $350.00
Gustav the Miller, NMIB $450.00
Halloh Motorcycle w/Rider, VG $1,400.00
Heavy Swell (Dapper Fella), EX $1,200.00
Icarus (Plane), VG+ $1,100.00
IHI Meat Van, EX $1,700.00
Ito Sedan & Driver, EX $750.00
Ito Town Car, VG $525.00
Jonny Lion, plastic, friction, MIB $50.00
Jonny Sailor Boy, EXIB $200.00

Kadi, EX, $1,000.00. (Photo courtesy Morphy Auctions)

Kadi, NMIB $2,400.00
Kamerun Ostrich Cart, EX $850.00
Kimbo Family, EX $1,700.00
Kutsche Motor Car, EX+IB $1,760.00
Lehmann's Auto Bus 590, see Auto Bus 590
Lexus Sedan, VG $2,300.00
Li La Hansom Cab, EX $1,000.00
Li La Hansom Cab, NMIB $2,000.00
Lo & Li, NM $7,500.00
Lo & Li, VG $3,500.00
Lo Lo, EX $5,000.00
Los Angeles Zeppelin, VG+ $475.00
Man Da Rin, EXIB $3,300.00
Man Da Rin, VG $1,800.00
Marke Coach, G+ $350.00

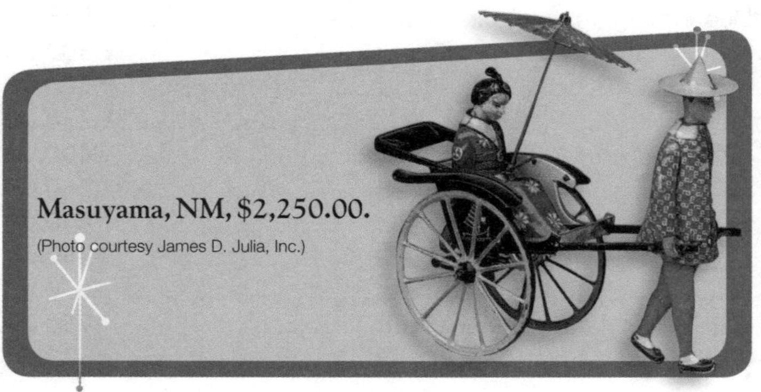

Masuyama, NM, $2,250.00. (Photo courtesy James D. Julia, Inc.)

May Beetle, EX $150.00
Mensa Delivery Van, EX $2,200.00
Mice on Spiral Rod, EX $250.00
Mikado Family, G+ $650.00
Minstrel Man, 1906, flat tin, scarce, NM $600.00
Miss Blondin (Tightrope Walker), EX $3,000.00

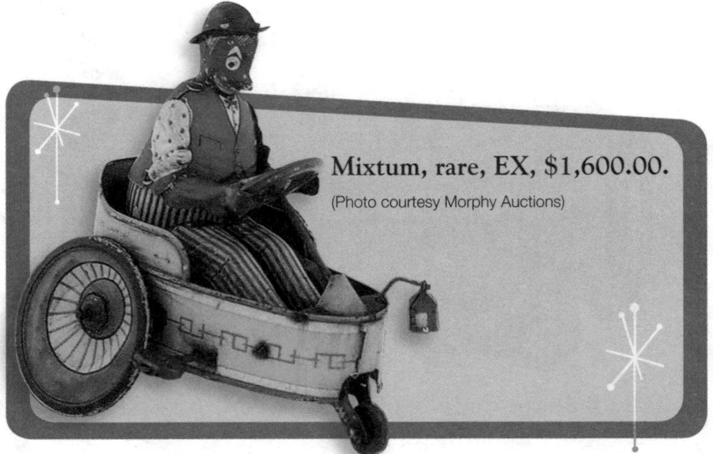

Mixtum, rare, EX, $1,600.00. (Photo courtesy Morphy Auctions)

Motor Car, EXIB $1,000.00
Motor Car, VG $300.00
NA-OB, EX+ $575.00
Nani Cart, plastic, friction, MIB $50.00
Naughty Boy, EXIB $1,000.00

Naughty Boy, VG, $525.00. (Photo courtesy Morphy Auctions)

New Century Cycle, NMIB $1,450.00
New Century Cycle, VG $475.00
Nu-Nu, VG $350.00
Oh My, see Alabama Coon Jigger
Paak-Paak Quack-Quack Duck Cart, EX $450.00
Paak-Paak Quack-Quack Duck Cart, NM+ $900.00
Paddy's Dancing Pig, NMIB $2,300.00
Paddy's Dancing Pig, VG $1,000.00
Performing Sea Lion, EXIB $600.00
Performing Sea Lion, VG $300.00
Pilot Motorcycle w/Driver, VG $3,500.00
Primus Roller Skater, rare, NM, from $6,500 to $7,000.00
Rad Cycle, NM $1,800.00

Rigi Cable Car, EX+IB $200.00
Roll Mops (Ball), VG $550.00
Royal Mail Van, NM $2,000.00
Sedan #756, VG $350.00
Shenandoah Zeppelin, NM $300.00
Ski Rolf, EX $2,700.00

Ski Rolf, NM+, $3,200.00.
(Photo courtesy Bertoia Auctions)

Snik-Snak, EXIB $5,000.00
Stiller Berlin Truck, rare, EX $900.00
Stubborn Donkey, NMIB $700.00
Susu (Realistic Turtle), NMIB $100.00
Tap-Tap, EX $700.00
Tap-Tap, NMIB $1,000.00
Terre Sedan, NM $1,250.00
Terre Sedan, VG $800.00
Titian Sedan, electric lights, G $600.00
Titian Sedan, electric lights, NM $2,300.00
Tom the Climbing Monkey, plain vest, pnt face, MIB.... $375.00
Tom the Climbing Monkey, polka-dot vest, litho face, MIB.... $400.00
Tut-Tut, EX $1,200.00
Tut-Tut, G $950.00
Tyrus the Walking Dog, NM $850.00
UHU Amphibious Car, EX $800.00
Velleda Touring Car, G $1,000.00
Vineta Monorail, EX $850.00
Waltzing Doll, NMIB, A $2,500.00
Wild West Bucking Bronco, see Bucking Bronco

Zig-Zag, EX, $1,000.00.
(Photo courtesy James D. Julia, Inc.)

Zig-Zag, NMIB $2,000.00
Zirka Dare Devil, G, A $475.00
Zirka Dare Devil, NM $1,200.00
Zulu Ostrich Cart 721, EX $700.00

Lunch Boxes

When the lunch box craze began in the mid-1980s, it was only the metal boxes that so quickly soared to sometimes astronomical prices. But today, even the plastic and vinyl ones are collectible. So pick a genre and have fun. There are literally hundreds to choose from, and just as is true in other areas of character-related collectibles, the more desirable lunch boxes are those with easily recognized, well-known subjects — western heroes, TV, Disney and other cartoon characters, and famous entertainers. Bottles are collectible as well.

The listings are ranged from excellent to near mint values. Bottles for metal boxes are listed under each lunch box, plastic and vinyl listings are complete with bottles.

If you would like to learn more, we recommend *A Pictorial Price Guide to Metal Lunch Boxes and Thermoses* and a companion book *A Pictorial Guide to Vinyl and Plastic Lunch and Plastic Lunch Boxes* by Larry Aikins.

Advisor: Terri Ivers

Metal Boxes with Bottles

18 Wheeler, 1970s, from $50 to $80.00
18 Wheeler, 1970s, plastic bottle, from $10 to $15.00
240 Robert, 1970s, from $2,500 to $3,500.00
240 Robert, 1970s, plastic bottle, from $350 to $450.00
A-Team, 1980s, from $25 to $40.00
A-Team, 1980s, plastic bottle, from $8 to $12.00
Action Jackson, 1970s, from $550 to $750.00
Action Jackson, 1970s, metal bottle, from $100 to $175.00
Adam-12, 1970s, from $50 to $100.00
Adam-12, 1970s, plastic bottle, from $20 to $30.00

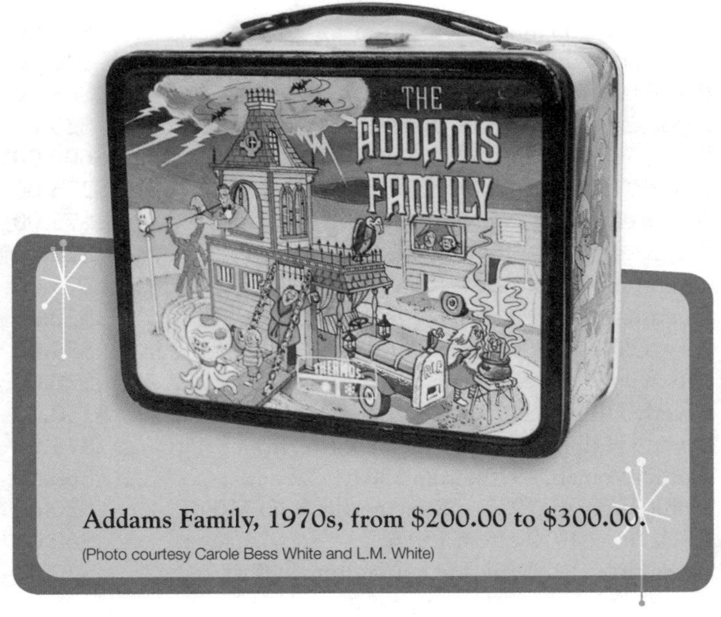

Addams Family, 1970s, from $200.00 to $300.00.
(Photo courtesy Carole Bess White and L.M. White)

Addams Family, 1970s, plastic bottle, from $25 to $50.00
America on Parade, 1970s, from $25 to $50.00
America on Parade, 1970s, plastic bottle, from $15 to $25.00
Animal Friends, 1970s, from $25 to $40.00
Annie, 1980s, from $30 to $40.00
Annie, 1980s, plastic bottle, from $5 to $10.00
Annie Oakley & Tag, 1950s, from $225 to $325.00
Annie Oakley & Tag, 1950s, metal bottle, from $50 to.. $100.00
Apple's Way, 1970s, from $50 to $75.00
Apple's Way, 1970s, plastic bottle, from $15 to $25.00
Archies, 1969, from $75 to $125.00
Archies, 1969, plastic bottle, from $20 to $40.00
Astronauts, 1960, dome, from $85 to $150.00
Astronauts, 1960, metal bottle, from $30 to $50.00
Astronauts, 1969, from $75 to $125.00
Astronauts, 1969, plastic bottle, from $20 to $50.00
Atom Ant, 1960s, from $75 to $175.00
Atom Ant, 1960s, metal bottle, from $35 to $65.00
Auto Race, 1960s, from $50 to $75.00
Auto Race, 1960s, metal bottle, from $15 to $25.00
Back in '76, 1970s, from $40 to $70.00
Back in '76, 1970s, plastic bottle, from $10 to $20.00
Batman & Robin, 1960s, from $150 to $200.00
Batman & Robin, 1960s, metal bottle, from $50 to............$75.00

Battle Kit, 1960s, from $100.00 to $175.00; metal bottle, from $50.00 to $75.00. (Photo courtesy serioustoyz.com)

Battle of the Planets, 1970s, from $50 to $75.00
Battle of the Planets, 1970s, plastic bottle, from $15 to $20.00
Battlestar Galactica, 1970s, from $35 to $65.00
Battlestar Galactica, 1970s, plastic bottle, from $15 to $25.00
Beatles, 1960s, from $450 to............ $600.00
Beatles, 1960s, metal bottle, from $125 to $225.00
Bee Gees, 1970s, from $50 to $75.00
Bee Gees, 1970s, plastic bottle, from $15 to $20.00
Berenstain Bears, 1980s, from $50 to $75.00
Berenstein Bears, 1980s, plastic bottle, from $10 to $20.00
Betsy Clark, 1970s, from $35 to............$55.00
Betsy Clark, 1970s, plastic bottle, from $10 to............$20.00
Beverly Hillbillies, 1960s, from $100 to $150.00
Beverly Hillbillies, 1960s, metal bottle, from $50 to $75.00
Bionic Woman, 1970s, from $30 to............$60.00
Bionic Woman, 1970s, plastic bottle, from $10 to............$20.00
Black Hole, 1970s, from $30 to $60.00
Black Hole, 1970s, plastic bottle, from $10 to $20.00

Bobby Sherman, 1970s, from $50 to $75.00
Bobby Sherman, 1970s, metal bottle, from $25 to............$35.00

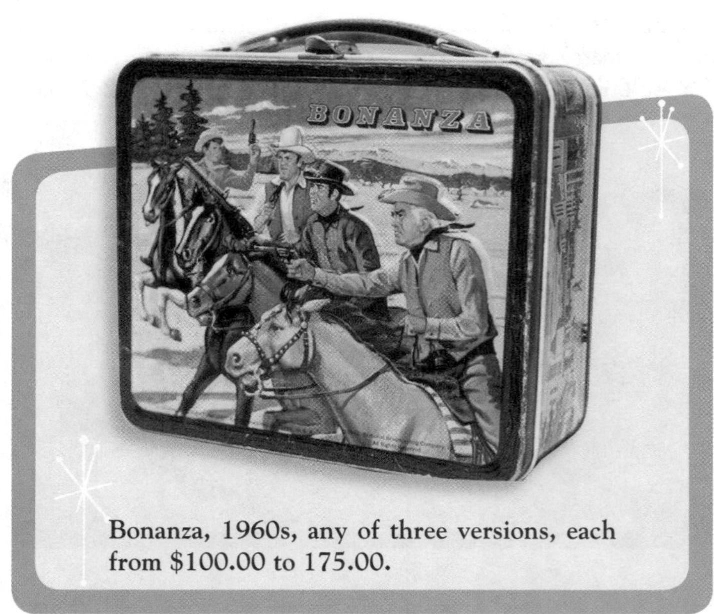

Bonanza, 1960s, any of three versions, each from $100.00 to 175.00.

Bonanza, 1960s, metal bottle, any 3 versions, ea from $50 to ...$75.00
Bozo the Clown, 1960s, dome, from $175 to $225.00
Bozo the Clown, 1960s, metal bottle, from $25 to............$50.00
Brady Bunch, 1970s, from $150 to $200.00
Brady Bunch, 1970s, metal bottle, from $25 to............$50.00
Brave Eagle, 1950s, from $150 to $200.00
Brave Eagle, 1950s, metal bottle, from $50 to............ $100.00
Buccaneer, 1950s, dome, from $150 to............ $225.00
Buccaneer, 1950s, metal bottle, from $75 to $120.00
Buck Rogers, 1970s, from $25 to $50.00
Buck Rogers, 1970s, plastic bottle, from $15 to $25.00
Bullwinkle & Rocky, 1960s, from $500 to............ $750.00
Bullwinkle & Rocky, 1960s, metal bottle, from $175 to. $275.00
Cabbage Patch Kids, 1980s, from $15 to $30.00
Cabbage Patch Kids, 1980s, plastic bottle, from $5 to.......$10.00
Campbell Kids, 1970s, from $125 to $175.00
Campbell Kids, 1970s, metal bottle, from $30 to............$60.00
Campus Queen, 1960s, from $50 to $75.00
Campus Queen, 1960s, metal bottle, from $10 to............$20.00
Captain Astro, 1960s, from $225 to $275.00
Care Bear Cousins, 1980s, from $25 to $50.00
Care Bear Cousins, 1980s, plastic, from $5 to............$10.00
Care Bears, 1980s, from $25 to............$50.00
Care Bears, 1980s, plastic bottle, from $5 to............$10.00
Carnival, 1950s, from $350 to $450.00
Carnival, 1950s, metal bottle, from $75 to $125.00
Cartoon Zoo Lunch Chest, 1960s, from $200 to............ $275.00
Cartoon Zoo Lunch Chest, 1960s, metal bottle, from $65 to .. $115.00
Casey Jones, 1960s, dome, from $400 to $550.00
Casey Jones, 1960s, metal bottle, from $100 to $150.00
Chan Clan, 1970s, from $60 to $115.00
Chan Clan, 1970s, plastic bottle, from $20 to $30.00
Charlie's Angels, 1970s, from $50 to............ $100.00
Charlie's Angels, 1970s, plastic bottle, from $10 to..........$20.00
Chavo, 1970s, from $40 to $90.00

Chavo, 1970s, plastic bottle, from $15 to $25.00
Chitty Chitty Bang Bang, 1960s, from $75 to................ $125.00
Chitty Chitty Bang Bang, 1960s, metal bottle, from $20 to...$40.00
Chuck Conners, 1960s, Cowboy in Africa, from $150 to .. $200.00
Chuck Conners, 1960s, Cowboy in Africa, metal bottle, from $75 to $100.00

Clash of Titans, 1980s, from $75.00 to $125.00. (Photo courtesy Carole Bess White and L.M. White)

Clash of the Titans, 1980s, plastic bottle, from $10 to $20.00
Close Encounters of the Third Kind, 1970s, from $50 to.. $100.00
Close Encounters of the Third Kind, 1970s, plastic bottle, from $10 to $20.00
Cracker Jack, 1970s, from $30 to.......................................$60.00
Cracker Jack, 1970s, plastic bottle, from $5 to...................$10.00
Cyclist, 1970s, from $25 to $50.00
Cyclist, 1970s, plastic bottle, from $10 to $20.00
Daniel Boone, Aladdin, 1950s, from $300 to................. $350.00
Daniel Boone, Aladdin, 1950s, metal bottle, from $50 to ..$75.00
Daniel Boone, Aladdin, 1960s, from $125 to................. $175.00
Daniel Boone, Aladdin, 1960s, metal bottle, from $55 to ..$70.00
Daniel Boone, KST, 1960s, Fess Parker, from $125 to $175.00
Daniel Boone, KST, 1960s, Fess Parker, metal bottle, from $60 to $80.00
Davy Crockett, 1955, At the Alamo, from $250 to........ $350.00
Davy Crockett, 1955, At the Alamo, metal bottle, from $400 to $600.00

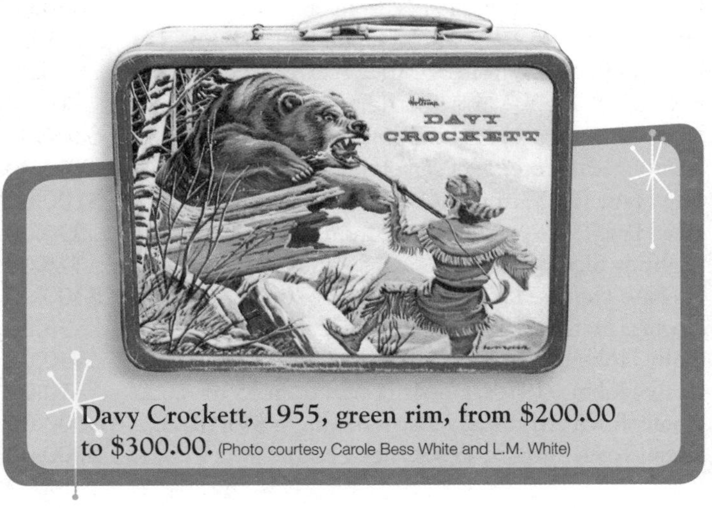

Davy Crockett, 1955, green rim, from $200.00 to $300.00. (Photo courtesy Carole Bess White and L.M. White)

Davy Crockett, 1955, gr rim, metal bottle, from $25 to $50.00
Davy Crockett, 1955, Official (Fess Parker), no bottle, from $200 to $300.00
Davy Crockett/Kit Carson, 1955, no bottle, from $150 to...$225.00
Dick Tracy, 1960s, from $125 to $175.00
Dick Tracy, 1960s, metal bottle, from $25 to $50.00
Disney Express, 1970s, from $25 to $50.00
Disney Express, 1970s, plastic bottle, from $5 to $15.00
Disney on Parade, 1970s, from $30 to $60.00
Disney on Parade, 1970s, plastic bottle, from $15 to $25.00
Disney's Magic Kingdom, 1970s, from $25 to $40.00
Disney's Magic Kingdom, 1970s, plastic bottle, from $10 to ..$15.00
Disney's Wonderful World, 1980s, from $15 to..................$30.00
Disney's Wonderful World, 1980s, plastic bottle, from $5 to... $15.00
Disney School Bus, 1960s-70s, dome, from $50 to.......... $100.00
Disney School Bus, 1960s-70s, metal bottle, from $20 to..$30.00
Disney World, 1970s, 50th Anniversary, from $30 to........$50.00
Disney World, 1970s, 50th Anniversary, plastic bottle, from $10 to $20.00
Disneyland, 1950s-60s, from $150 to $200.00
Disneyland, 1950s-60s, metal bottle, from $30 to.............$60.00
Doctor Dolittle, 1960s, from $75 to $125.00
Doctor Dolittle, 1960s, metal bottle, from $20 to..............$40.00
Double-Deckers, 1970s, from $50 to $75.00
Double-Deckers, 1970s, plastic bottle, from $15 to $30.00
Dr Seuss, 1970s, from $85 to $135.00
Dr Seuss, 1970s, plastic bottle, from $20 to $40.00
Dudley Do-Right, 1960s, from $500 to $800.00
Dudley Do-Right, 1960s, metal bottle, from $225 to...... $325.00
Dukes of Hazzard, 1980s, orig Duke boys, from $45 to.......$65.00
Dukes of Hazzard, 1980s, plastic bottle, from $10 to..........$20.00
Dyno Mutt, 1970s, from $35 to $55.00
Dyno Mutt, 1970s, plastic bottle, from $10 to $20.00
Early West, 1982-84, ea from $65 to $100.00
Emergency!, 1973, from $50 to...$75.00
Emergency!, 1973, plastic bottle, from $20 to....................$40.00
Emergency!, 1977, dome, from $150 to........................... $200.00
Emergency!, 1977, plastic bottle, from $20 to....................$40.00
Empire Strikes Back, 1980s, from $35 to............................$65.00
Empire Strikes Back, 1980s, plastic bottle, from $10 to.....$20.00

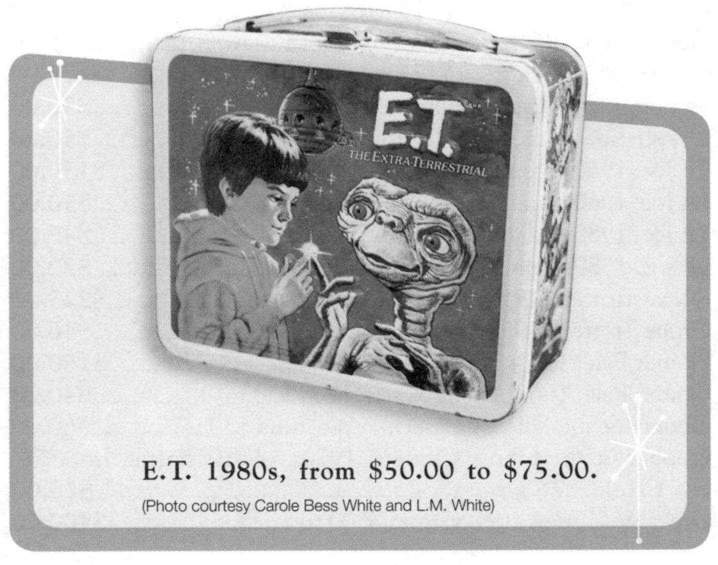

E.T. 1980s, from $50.00 to $75.00. (Photo courtesy Carole Bess White and L.M. White)

ET, 1980s, plastic bottle, from $10 to....$20.00
Evel Knievel, 1970s, from $50 to.... $100.00
Evel Knievel, 1970s, plastic bottle, from $15 to....$30.00
Fall Guy, 1980s, from $20 to....$40.00
Fall Guy, 1980s, plastic bottle, from $10 to....$20.00
Family Affair, 1960s, from $45 to....$90.00
Family Affair, 1960s, metal bottle, from $20 to....$40.00
Flintstones, 1960s, from $125 to.... $175.00
Flintstones, 1960s, metal bottle, from $30 to....$60.00
Flintstones, 1970s, from $100 to.... $150.00
Flintstones, 1970s, plastic bottle, from $20 to....$40.00
Flintstones & Dino, 1960s, from $125 to.... $175.00
Flintstones & Dino, 1960s, metal bottle, from $30 to....$60.00
Flipper, 1960s, from $100 to.... $150.00
Flipper, 1960s, metal bottle, from $20 to....$40.00
Flying Nun, 1960s, from $100 to.... $150.00
Flying Nun, 1960s, metal bottle, from $20 to....$40.00

Fraggle Rock, 1980s, from $50.00 to $75.00.
(Photo courtesy Carole Bess White and L.M. White)

Fraggle Rock, 1980s, plastic bottle, from $10 to....$20.00
Frontier Days, 1950s, from $125 to.... $175.00
Gene Autry Melody Ranch, 1950s, from $175 to.... $275.00
Gene Autry Melody Ranch, 1950s, metal bottle, from $50 to.... $100.00
Gentle Ben, 1960s, from $75 to.... $115.00
Gentle Ben, 1960s, metal bottle, from $20 to....$40.00
Get Smart, 1960s, from $125 to.... $175.00
Get Smart, 1960s, metal bottle, from $25 to....$50.00
Ghostland, 1970s, from $25 to....$50.00
GI Joe, 1960s, from $80 to.... $130.00
GI Joe, 1960s, metal bottle, from $25 to....$50.00
GI Joe, 1980s, from $25 to....$40.00
GI Joe, 1980s, plastic bottle, from $10 to....$20.00
Globe Trotters, 1950s, dome, from $175 to.... $225.00
Globe Trotters, 1950s, metal bottle, from $20 to....$40.00
Gomer Pyle, 1960s, from $100 to.... $150.00
Gomer Pyle, 1960s, metal bottle, from $20 to....$40.00
Goober & the Ghost Chasers, 1970s, from $30 to....$60.00
Goober & the Ghost Chasers, 1970s, plastic bottle, from $15 to....$25.00
Great Wild West, 1950s, from $300 to.... $400.00
Great Wild West, 1950s, metal bottle, from $65 to.... $115.00
Green Hornet, 1960s, from $200 to.... $300.00
Green Hornet, 1960s, metal bottle, from $50 to.... $100.00

Gremlins, 1980s, from $50.00 to $75.00; plastic bottle, from $15.00 to $25.00.
(Photo courtesy Carole Bess White and L.M. White)

Grizzly Adams, 1970s, dome, from $150 to.... $200.00
Grizzly Adams, 1970s, plastic bottle, from $20 to....$30.00
Guns of Will Sonnet, 1960s, from $100 to.... $150.00
Guns of Will Sonnet, 1960s, metal bottle, from $25 to....$50.00
Gunsmoke, 1959, from $100 to.... $200.00
Gunsmoke, 1959, Marshall, from $200 to.... $400.00
Gunsmoke, 1959, Marshall, metal bottle, from $50 to.... $100.00
Gunsmoke, 1959, metal bottle, from $50 to.... $100.00
Gunsmoke, 1962, from $175 to.... $225.00
Gunsmoke, 1962, metal bottle, from $40 to....$80.00
Gunsmoke, 1972, from $75 to.... $125.00
Gunsmoke, 1972, plastic bottle, from $30 to....$60.00
Gunsmoke, 1973, from $125 to.... $175.00
Gunsmoke, 1973, plastic bottle, from $25 to....$50.00
Hair Bear Bunch, 1970s, from $100 to.... $150.00
Hair Bear Bunch, 1970s, metal bottle, from $15 to....$30.00
Hansel & Gretel, 1980s, from $40 to....$60.00
Happy Days, 1970s, 2 versions, ea from $50 to....$75.00
Happy Days, 1970s, 2 versions, plastic bottle, ea from $10 to....$20.00
Hardy Boys Mysteries, 1970s, from $25 to....$50.00
Hardy Boys Mysteries, 1970s, plastic bottle, from $5 to....$15.00
Harlem Globetrotters, 1970s, from $30 to....$60.00
Harlem Globetrotters, 1970s, metal bottle, from $15 to....$25.00
Heathcliff, 1980s, from $20 to....$30.00
Heathcliff, 1980s, plastic bottle, from $5 to....$10.00
Hector Heathcote, 1960s, from $100 to.... $200.00
Hector Heathcote, 1960s, metal bottle, from $25 to....$50.00
Hee Haw, 1970s, from $50 to.... $100.00
Hee Haw, 1970s, metal bottle, from $15 to....$30.00
Highway Signs, 1960s or 1970s, 2 versions, ea from $30 to....$75.00
Hogan's Heroes, 1960s, dome, from $200 to.... $300.00
Hogan's Heroes, 1960s, metal bottle, from $30 to....$75.00
Holly Hobbie, 1970s, any version, from $30 to....$40.00
Holly Hobbie, 1970s, plastic bottle, from $5 to....$10.00
Home Town Airport, 1960s, dome, from $750 to.... $1,000.00
Home Town Airport, 1960s, metal bottle, from $150 to.... $200.00

Hopalong Cassidy, 1950-53, bl or red w/cloud or sq decal, ea from $175 to $250.00
Hopalong Cassidy, 1950-53, metal bottle, ea from $50 to ..$75.00
Hopalong Cassidy, 1954, from $275 to.......................... $350.00
Hopalong Cassidy, 1954, metal bottle, from $85 to $150.00
How the West Was Won, 1970s, from $30 to $50.00
How the West Was Won, 1970s, plastic bottle, from $10 to... $20.00
HR Pufnstuff, 1970s, from $100 to $150.00
HR Pufnstuff, 1970s, plastic bottle, from $20 to $40.00
Huckleberry Hound & Friends, 1960s, from $100 to...... $175.00
Huckleberry Hound & Friends, 1960s, metal bottle, from $20 to $40.00

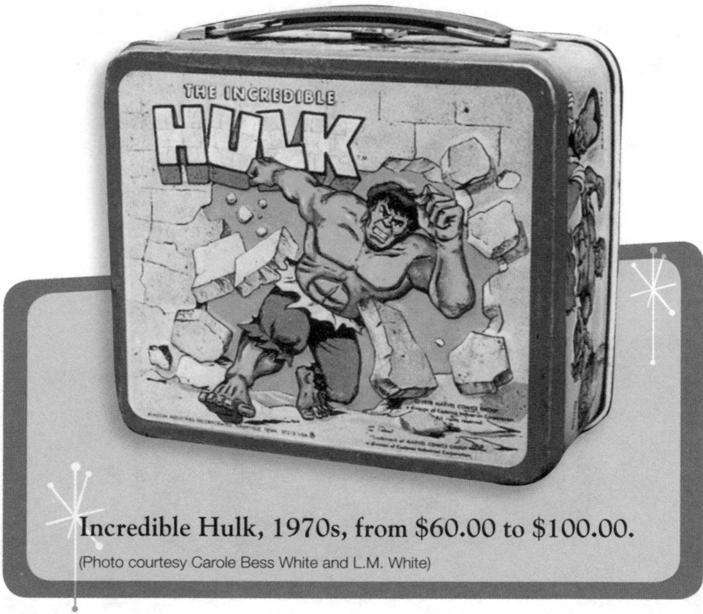

Incredible Hulk, 1970s, from $60.00 to $100.00.
(Photo courtesy Carole Bess White and L.M. White)

Incredible Hulk, 1970s, plastic bottle, from $10 to............$20.00
Indiana Jones, 1980s, from $20 to $40.00
Indiana Jones, 1980s, plastic bottle, from $5 to $15.00
James Bond 007, 1960s, from $150 to $225.00
James Bond 007, 1960s, metal bottle, from $25 to............$50.00
Jet Patrol, 1950s, from $200 to $300.00
Jet Patrol, 1950s, metal bottle, from $50 to $100.00

Jetsons, 1960s, dome top, from $1,000.00 to $1,800.00; metal bottle, from $200.00 to $300.00.
(Photo courtesy Carole Bess White and L.M. White)

Johnny Lightning, 1970s, from $40 to.............................$50.00
Johnny Lightning, 1970s, plastic bottle, from $15 to.........$20.00

Jr Miss, 1956, from $30 to..$65.00
Jr Miss, 1956, metal bottle, from $20 to $30.00
Jr Miss, 1960, from $25 to..$50.00
Jr Miss, 1960, metal bottle, from $15 to $20.00
Jr Miss, 1962, from $25 to..$50.00
Jr Miss, 1962, metal bottle, from $15 to $20.00
Jr Miss, 1966, from $25 to..$45.00
Jr Miss, 1966, metal bottle, from $15 to $20.00
Jr Miss, 1970, from $20 to..$40.00
Jr Miss, 1970, plastic bottle, from $5 to............................$15.00
Jr Miss, 1973, from $15 to..$30.00
Jr Miss, 1973, plastic bottle, from $5 to............................$15.00
Julia, 1960s, from $50 to $100.00
Julia, 1960s, metal bottle, from $15 to $40.00
Jungle Book, 1960s, from $45 to...$90.00
Jungle Book, 1960s, metal bottle, from $15 to $30.00
Knight Rider, 1980s, from $20 to $40.00
Knight Rider, 1980s, plastic bottle, from $5 to $15.00
Korg, 1970s, from $35 to...$65.00
Korg, 1970s, plastic, from $10 to $20.00
Krofft Supershow, 1970s, from $50 to............................ $100.00
Krofft Supershow, 1970s, plastic bottle, from $15 to..........$25.00
Kung Fu, 1970s, from $40 to...$80.00
Kung Fu, 1970s, plastic bottle, from $5 to.........................$15.00
Lance Link Secret Chimp, 1970s, from $75 to $125.00
Lance Link Secret Chimp, 1970s, metal bottle, from $15 to .. $30.00
Land of the Giants, 1960s, from $100 to........................ $160.00
Land of the Giants, 1960s, plastic bottle, from $20 to.......$40.00
Land of the Lost, 1970s, from $75 to $125.00
Land of the Lost, 1970s, plastic bottle, from $15 to...........$30.00
Lassie, 1970s, from $35 to $55.00
Laugh-In, 1968, from $75 to... $125.00
Laugh-In, 1968, plastic bottle, ea from $15 to $30.00
Laugh-In, 1971, from $75 to... $150.00
Laugh-In, 1971, plastic bottle, from $15 to.......................$30.00
Lawman, 1960s, from $75 to... $150.00
Lawman, 1960s, metal bottle, from $20 to $40.00
Legend of the Lone Ranger, 1980s, from $45 to.................$75.00
Legend of the Lone Ranger, 1980s, plastic bottle, from $15 to $30.00
Little Dutch Miss, 1959, from $50 to $100.00
Little Dutch Miss, 1959, metal bottle, from $20 to............$40.00
Little Friends, 1980s, from $350 to................................ $475.00
Little Friends, 1980s, plastic bottle, from $75 to............. $150.00
Little House on the Prairie, 1970s, from $50 to $100.00
Little House on the Prairie, 1970s, plastic bottle, from $20 to ... $40.00
Little Orphan Annie, 1980s, from $25 to $50.00
Lone Ranger, 1950s, from $300 to.................................. $450.00
Looney Tunes, 1959, from $175 to $250.00
Looney Tunes, 1959, metal bottle, from $30 to $60.00
Lost in Space, repro, dome, from $20 to...........................$40.00
Lost in Space, 1960s, dome, from $750 to.................... $1,000.00
Lost in Space, 1960s, metal bottle, from $50 to $75.00
Ludwig Von Drake in Disneyland, 1960s, $125 to $175.00
Ludwig Von Drake in Disneyland, 1960s, metal bottle, from $20 to $40.00
Magic of Lassie, 1970s, from $45 to..................................$75.00
Magic of Lassie, 1970s, plastic bottle, from $15 to............$30.00

Man From UNCLE, 1960s, from $100 to $150.00
Man From UNCLE, 1960s, metal bottle, from $20 to $40.00
Marvel Super Heroes, 1970s, from $25 to $50.00
Mary Poppins, 1960s, from $50 to $100.00
Mary Poppins, 1960s, metal bottle, from $15 to $30.00
Masters of the Universe, 1980s, from $30 to......................$60.00
Masters of the Universe, 1980s, plastic bottle, from $5 to ..$10.00
Mickey Mouse & Donald Duck, 1950s, from $250 to..... $350.00
Mickey Mouse & Donald Duck, 1950s, metal bottle, from $75 to $150.00
Mickey Mouse Club, 1960s, from $65 to........................ $100.00
Mickey Mouse Club, 1960s, metal bottle, from $15 to $30.00
Mickey Mouse Club, 1970s, from $30 to...........................$60.00
Mickey Mouse Club, 1970s, plastic bottle, from $5 to.......$15.00
Miss America, 1970s, from $50 to $100.00
Miss America, 1970s, plastic bottle, from $15 to $30.00
Monroes, 1960s, from $75 to $150.00
Monroes, 1960s, metal bottle, from $25 to $50.00
Mork & Mindy, 1970s, from $25 to..................................$50.00
Mork & Mindy, 1970s, plastic bottle, from $5 to..............$15.00
Mr Merlin, 1980s, from $20 to $35.00
Mr Merlin, 1980s, plastic bottle, from $5 to $15.00

Munsters, 1960s, from $450.00 to $650.00; metal bottle, from $75.00 to $125.00. (Photo courtesy Carole Bess White and L.M. White)

Muppet Babies, 1980s, from $20 to $40.00
Muppet Babies, 1980s, plastic bottle, from $5 to $10.00
Muppets, 1970s, any, ea from $20 to $50.00
Muppets, 1970s, plastic bottle, from $5 to $10.00
Nancy Drew Mysteries, 1970s, from $30 to.......................$60.00
Nancy Drew Mysteries, 1970s, plastic, from $10 to $20.00
Orbit, 1950s, from $50 to $125.00
Orbit, 1960s, metal bottle, from $25 to............................$50.00
Osmonds, 1970s, from $50 to $75.00
Osmonds, 1970s, plastic bottle, from $15 to $25.00
Our Friends, 1980s, from $200 to $400.00
Our Friends, 1980s, metal bottle, from $50 to $75.00
Pac Man, 1980s, from $20 to $35.00
Pac-Man, 1980s, plastic bottle, from $5 to........................$10.00
Paladin, 1960s, from $150 to $225.00
Paladin, 1960s, metal bottle, from $40 to $80.00
Partridge Family, 1970s, from $40 to $80.00
Partridge Family, 1970s, metal bottle, from $15 to $30.00
Pathfinder, 1959, from $300 to $400.00
Pathfinder, 1959, metal bottle, from $75 to $150.00
Peanuts, 1960, from $30 to $60.00
Peanuts, 1960, metal bottle, from $10 to $20.00
Peanuts, 1973, from $25 to $50.00
Peanuts, 1973, plastic bottle, from $5 to $15.00
Peanuts, 1976, from $20 to $35.00
Peanuts, 1976, plastic bottle, from $5 to $15.00
Peanuts, 1980, from $15 to $30.00
Peanuts, 1980, plastic bottle, from $6 to $12.00
Pebbles & Bamm Bamm, 1970s, from $40 to $80.00
Pebbles & Bamm Bamm, 1970s, plastic bottle, from $15 to .. $30.00
Pele, 1970s, from $50 to $100.00
Pele, 1970s, plastic bottle, from $15 to $30.00

Pete's Dragon, 1970s, from $50.00 to $100.00. (Photo courtesy Carol Bess White and L.M. White)

Pete's Dragon, 1970s, plastic bottle, from $15 to $25.00
Peter Pan, 1960s, from $50 to.. $100.00
Peter Pan, 1960s, plastic bottle, from $20 to......................$40.00
Pigs in Space, 1970s, from $35 to $50.00
Pigs in Space, 1970s, plastic bottle, from $5 to $15.00
Pink Panther & Sons, 1980s, from $20 to.........................$40.00
Pink Panther & Sons, 1980s, plastic bottle, from $5 to.....$15.00
Pinocchio, 1970s, from $50 to....................................... $100.00
Pinocchio, 1970s, plastic bottle, from $15 to.....................$30.00
Pit Stop, 1960s, from $50 to $100.00
Planet of the Apes, 1970s, from $75 to $125.00
Planet of the Apes, 1970s, plastic bottle, from $15 to $25.00
Play Ball, 1960s, from $40 to $80.00
Play Ball, 1960s, metal bottle, from $15 to $30.00
Police Patrol, 1970s, from $125 to................................ $175.00
Police Patrol, 1970s, plastic bottle, from $15 to................$25.00
Polly Pal, 1970s, from $20 to $35.00
Polly Pal, 1970s, plastic bottle, from $5 to $10.00
Pony Express, 1950s, from $225 to $275.00
Popeye, 1962, from $350 to $550.00
Popeye, 1962, metal bottle, from $175 to $250.00
Popeye, 1964, from $100 to $150.00
Popeye, 1964, metal bottle, from $40 to $80.00

Popeye, 1980, from $40 to $80.00
Popeye, 1980, plastic bottle, from $10 to $20.00
Popples, 1980s, from $15 to $25.00
Popples, 1980s, plastic bottle, from $5 to $10.00

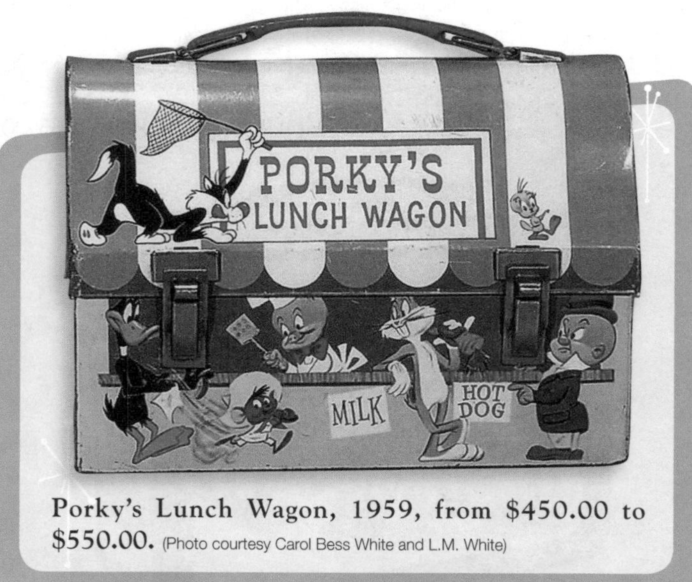

Porky's Lunch Wagon, 1959, from $450.00 to $550.00. (Photo courtesy Carol Bess White and L.M. White)

Porky's Lunch Wagon, 1959, metal bottle, from $50 to.....$75.00
Raggedy Ann & Andy, 1970s, from $20 to $40.00
Raggedy Ann & Andy, 1970s, plastic bottle, from $10 to ..$20.00
Rambo, 1980s, from $20 to $30.00
Rambo, 1980s, plastic bottle, from $5 to $10.00
Rat Patrol, 1960s, from $75 to $125.00
Rat Patrol, 1960s, metal bottle, from $20 to $40.00
Rescuers, from $25 to $50.00
Rescuers, 1970s, plastic bottle, from $15 to $25.00
Return of the Jedi, 1980s, from $30 to $60.00
Return of the Jedi, 1980s, plastic bottle, from $10 to $20.00
Rifleman, 1960s, from $275 to $350.00
Rifleman, 1960s, metal bottle, from $50 to $90.00
Road Runner, 1970s, from $40 to $80.00
Road Runner, 1970s, metal bottle, from $15 to $30.00

Robin Hood, 1950s, from $200.00 to $275.00; metal bottle, from $50.00 to $100.00. (Photo courtesy Carole Bess White and L.M. White)

Robin Hood, 1970s, from $30 to $60.00
Robin Hood, 1970s, plastic bottle, from $8 to $18.00
Ronald McDonald, 1980s, from $15 to $30.00
Ronald McDonald, 1980s, plastic bottle, from $6 to $12.00
Rose Petal Place, 1980s, from $20 to $40.00
Rose Petal Place, 1980s, plastic bottle, from $5 to.............$15.00
Rough Rider, 1970s, from $50 to $75.00
Rough Rider, 1970s, plastic bottle, from $18 to $28.00

Roy Rogers and Dale Evans, 1950s, many variations, each from $250.00 to $350.00. (Photo courtesy Carole Bess White and L.M. White)

Roy Rogers & Dale Evans, 1950s, metal bottle, ea from $45 to $75.00
Satellite, 1950s, from $80 to $120.00
Satellite, 1950s, metal bottle, from $20 to $40.00
Satellite, 1960s, from $50 to $75.00
Satellite, 1960s, metal bottle, from $15 to $30.00
School Days, 1980s, from $350 to $450.00
School Days, 1980s, plastic bottle, from $65 to $125.00
Scooby Doo, 1970s, any, ea from $50 to........................ $100.00
Scooby Doo, 1970s, plastic bottle, from $22 to.................$38.00
Secret Agent T, 1960s, from $50 to............................... $100.00
Secret Agent T, 1960s, metal bottle, from $25 to $50.00
Secret of NIMH, 1980s, from $15 to $30.00
Secret of NIMH, 1980s, plastic bottle, from $5 to $10.00
Secret Wars, 1980s, from $50 to $75.00
Secret Wars, 1980s, plastic bottle, from $18 to $28.00
Sesame Street, 1970s, from $25 to $50.00
Sesame Street, 1970s, plastic bottle, from $5 to................$10.00
Sesame Street, 1980s, from $20 to $40.00
Sesame Street, 1980s, plastic bottle, from $5 to................$10.00
Sigmund & the Sea Monsters, 1970s, from $65 to.......... $125.00
Sigmund & the Sea Monsters, 1970s, plastic bottle, from $25 to $45.00
Six Million Dollar Man, 1970s, any, ea from $35 to..........$55.00
Six Million Dollar Man, 1970s, plastic bottle, ea from $18 to ..$28.00
Skateboarder, 1970s, from $35 to $65.00
Skateboarder, 1970s, plastic bottle, from $15 to $25.00
Smokey Bear, 1970s, from $225 to $300.00
Smokey Bear, 1970s, metal bottle, from $75 to............... $150.00
Smurfs, 1980s, from $100 to $150.00

Smurfs, 1980s, plastic bottle, from $5 to $15.00
Snoopy, 1969, dome, from $50 to.................................... $100.00
Snoopy, 1969, metal bottle, from $15 to $25.00
Snow White, 1975, from $35 to...$70.00
Snow White, 1975, plastic bottle, from $10 to $20.00
Snow White, 1977 or 1980, ea from $25 to $50.00
Space Shuttle Orbiter Enterprise, 1970s, from $45 to $85.00
Space Shuttle Oribter Enterprise, 1970s, plastic bottle, from $15 to $25.00
Space: 1999, 1970s, from $50 to.......................................$75.00
Space: 1999, 1970s, plastic bottle, from $15 to.................$25.00
Spider-Man & The Hulk, 1980s, from $75 to................ $125.00
Spider-Man & The Hulk, 1980s, plastic bottle, from $10 to... $20.00
Sport Goofy, 1980s, from $20 to.......................................$40.00
Sport Goofy, 1980s, plastic bottle, from $5 to...................$15.00

Star Trek, 1960s, dome top, from $750.00 to $950.00; metal bottle, from $300.00 to $400.00.
(Photo courtesy Morphy Auctions)

Star Trek: The Motion Picture, 1980, from $50 to $100.00
Star Trek: The Motion Picture, 1980, plastic bottle, from $20 to $30.00
Star Wars, 1970s, any, ea from $50 to $100.00
Star Wars, 1970s, plastic bottle, any, ea from $10 to $20.00
Steve Canyon, 1959, from $150 to............................... $250.00
Steve Canyon, 1959, metal bottle, from $55 to................$85.00
Strawberry Shortcake, 1980s, from $20 to $40.00
Strawberry Shortcake, 1980s, plastic bottle, from $5 to $10.00
Street Hawk, 1980s, from $70 to $135.00
Street Hawk, 1980s, plastic bottle, from $20 to................$40.00
Submarine, 1960, from $50 to $100.00
Submarine, 1960, metal bottle, from $15 to $30.00
Super Friends, 1970s, from $40 to $80.00
Super Friends, 1970s, plastic bottle, from $10 to $20.00
Super Heroes, 1970s, from $35 to.....................................$70.00
Super Heroes, 1970s, plastic bottle, from $10 to...............$20.00
Super Powers, 1980s, from $45 to.....................................$85.00
Super Powers, 1980s, plastic bottle, 1980s, from $10 to $20.00
Superman, 1954, from $750 to $1,000.00
Superman, 1960s, from $100 to...................................... $175.00
Superman, 1960s, metal bottle, from $50 to $75.00
Superman, 1970s, from $40 to...$80.00
Superman, 1970s, plastic bottle, from $15 to.....................$25.00

Tarzan, 1960s, from $100 to... $150.00
Tarzan, 1960s, metal bottle, from $20 to $40.00
Three Little Pigs, 1980s, from $40 to $80.00
Thundercats, 1980s, from $25 to $50.00
Thundercats, 1980s, plastic bottle, from $5 to $10.00
Tom Corbett Space Cadet, 1952, from $100 to $200.00
Tom Corbett Space Cadet, 1952, metal bottle, from $30 to .. $55.00
Tom Corbett Space Cadet, 1954, from $125 to $275.00
Tom Corbett Space Cadet, 1954, metal bottle, from $35 to .. $65.00

Track King, 1970s, from $300.00 to $500.00.
(Photo Carole Bess White and L.M. White)

Track King, 1970s, metal bottle, from $150 to............... $200.00
Transformers, 1980s, from $25 to $50.00
Transformers, 1980s, plastic bottle, from $5 to $15.00
Treasure Chest, 1960s, dome, from $175 to $275.00
Treasure Chest, 1960s, metal bottle, from $75 to........... $125.00
UFO, 1970s, from $50 to $85.00
UFO, 1970s, plastic bottle, from $15 to $30.00
Underdog, 1970s, from $350 to $750.00
Underdog, 1970s, metal bottle, from $150 to $250.00
US Mail/Zippy, 1969, dome, from $35 to $65.00
US Mail/Zippy, 1969, plastic bottle, from $15 to...............$30.00
V, 1980s, from $75 to $125.00
V, 1980s, plastic bottle, from $20 to $40.00
Voyage to the Bottom of the Sea, 1960s, from $175 to... $250.00
Voyage to the Bottom of the Sea, 1960s, metal bottle, from $50 to $75.00
Wagon Train, 1960s, from $100 to $200.00
Wagon Train, 1960s, metal bottle, from $25 to $50.00
Waltons, 1970s, from $50 to..$75.00
Waltons, 1970s, plastic bottle, from $15 to........................$30.00
Welcome Back Kotter, 1970s, from $50 to..........................$75.00
Welcome Back Kotter, 1970s, plastic bottle, from $10 to..$20.00
Wild Bill Hickok & Jingles, 1950s, from $150 to $200.00
Wild Bill Hickok & Jingles, 1950s, metal bottle, from $40 to $80.00
Wild Wild West, 1960s, from $175 to $250.00
Wild Wild West, 1960s, plastic bottle, from $35 to $65.00
Winnie the Pooh, 1970s, from $150 to $200.00
Winnie the Pooh, 1970s, plastic bottle, from $25 to $50.00

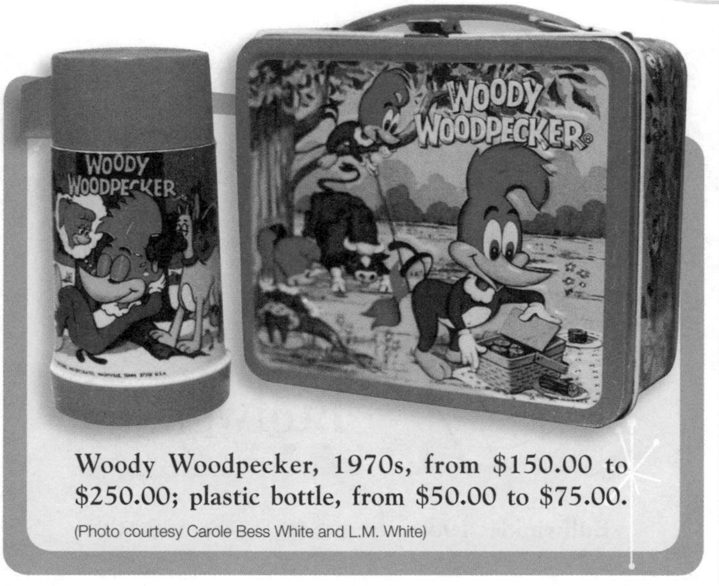

Woody Woodpecker, 1970s, from $150.00 to $250.00; plastic bottle, from $50.00 to $75.00. (Photo courtesy Carole Bess White and L.M. White)

Yankee Doodle, 1970s, from $25 to....................$50.00
Yellow Submarine, 1968, from $500 to....................$800.00
Yellow Submarine, 1968, metal bottle, from $100 to....................$200.00
Yogi Bear, 1970s, from $75 to....................$125.00
Yogi Bear, 1970s, plastic bottle, from $25 to....................$50.00
Yogi Bear & Friends, 1960s, from $85 to....................$135.00
Yogi Bear & Friends, 1960s, metal bottle, from, $20 to....................$40.00
Zorro, 1950s or 1960s, ea from $100 to....................$200.00
Zorro, 1950s or 1960s, metal bottle, ea from $40 to....................$75.00

Plastic Boxes Complete with Bottles

A-Team, 1980s, from $15 to....................$20.00
Astrokids, 1980s, from $15 to....................$25.00
Barbie, 1990s, from $10 to....................$15.00
Barney Baby Bop, 1990s, from $5 to....................$10.00

Batman, 1989, dark blue, from $15.00 to $25.00. (Photo courtesy Carole Bess White and L.M. White)

Batman, 1989, lt bl, from $40 to....................$40.00
Batman Returns, 1991, from $15 to....................$20.00
Benji, 1970s, from $20 to....................$30.00
Cabbage Patch Kids, from $15 to....................$20.00
Care Bears, 1980s, from $10 to....................$15.00
Casper the Friendly Ghost, 1990s, from $8 to....................$15.00
CB Bears, 1970s, from $15 to....................$20.00
Chip 'n Dale, 1980s, from $5 to....................$10.00
Chuck E Cheese, 1990s, from $25 to....................$35.00
Crest Toothpast, 1980s, tubular, from $50 to....................$75.00
Dick Tracy, 1990s, red, from $10 to....................$15.00
Disney School Bus, 1990s, from $20 to....................$30.00
Dr Seuss, 1990s, from $20 to....................$25.00
Fat Albert, 1970s, from $20 to....................$30.00
Flintstones, 1981, dome, from $50 to....................$75.00
Flintstones (A Day at the Zoo), 1989, Denny's logo, from $20 to....................$30.00
Garfield, 1980s, from $15 to....................$20.00
Holly Hobby, 1989, from $20 to....................$25.00
Hot Wheels, 1990s, from $15 to....................$20.00
Incredible Hulk, 1980s, dome, from $40 to....................$50.00
Jabber Jaw, 1970s, from $30 to....................$40.00
Jem, 1980s, from $8 to....................$15.00
Jurassic Park, 1990s, w/recalled bottle, from $25 to....................$30.00
Keebler Cookies, 1980s, from $30 to....................$50.00
Kermit the Frog, 1980s, dome top, from $30 to....................$40.00
Little Orphan Annie, 1970s, dome, from $35 to....................$45.00
Looney Tunes, 1970s, from $15 to....................$25.00
Lucy Luncheonette, 1980s, dome, from $20 to....................$30.00

Mickey Mouse, boarding school bus, yellow, from $40.00 to $60.00. (Photo courtesy Carole Bess White and L.M. White)

Mickey Mouse, 1980s, head form, from $25 to....................$35.00
Mickey Mouse & Donald Duck, 1980s, from $10 to....................$15.00
Mighty Mouse, 1970s, from $25 to....................$35.00
Minnie Mouse, 1980s, head form, from $30 to....................$40.00
Muppet Babies, 1980s, from $15 to....................$25.00
Muppets, 1990s, from $10 to....................$18.00
Nestlè's Quik, 1980s, from $25 to....................$30.00
New Kids on the Block, 1990s, from $15 to....................$25.00
Nosey Bears, 1990s, from $10 to....................$20.00
Pee Wee Herman, 1980s, from $20 to....................$30.00
Pepsi, 1980s, from $30 to....................$40.00
Pink Panther, 1980s, from $25 to....................$30.00

Pink Panther and Sons, 1980s, from $25.00 to $30.00.

Bullwinkle, 1960s, from $400.00 to $500.00. (Photo courtesy Morphy Auctions)

Popeye, 1979, dome, from $30 to $40.00
Rap It Up, 1990s, from $20 to $25.00
Robot Man, 1980s, from $20 to $30.00
Rocky Roughneck, 1970s, from $25 to $35.00
Rover Dangerfield, 1990s, from $20 to $30.00
Shadow, 1990s, from $10 to $20.00
Smurfs, 1980s, dome, from $20 to $30.00
Snoopy & Woodstock, 1970s, dome, from $20 to $30.00
Snoopy as Joe Cool, 1970s, from $15 to $25.00
Star Trek (TNG), 1970s, from $10 to $20.00
Star Wars Ewoks, 1980s, from $20 to $30.00
Sunnie Miss, 1970s, from $50 to $75.00
Superman, 1980s, phone booth scene, from $30 to $40.00
SWAT, 1970s, dome, from $30 to $40.00
The Tick, 1990s, from $25 to $50.00
Tom & Jerry, 1990s, from $10 to $20.00
Train Engine #7, 1990s, from $15 to $25.00
Winnie the Pooh, 1990s, from $15 to $25.00
Yogi Bear, 1990s, from $15 to $25.00
Young Astronauts, 1980s, from $20 to $30.00

Vinyl Boxes Complete with Bottles

Alice in Wonderland, 1970s, from $150 to $200.00
All Dressed Up, 1970s, from $50 to $75.00
Alvin and the Chipmunks, 1960s, from $200 to $300.00
Annie, 1980s, from $50 to $75.00
Banana Splits, 1969, from $425 to $475.00
Barbarino, 1970s, brunch bag, from $225 to $275.00
Barbie, 1970s, from $65 to $85.00
Barbie & Midge, 1960s, dome, from $425 to $475.00
Barbie and Francie, 1960s, from $125 to $175.00
Barbie and Midge, 1960s, from $125 to $175.00
Barbie Lunch Kit, 1960s, from $300 to $400.00
Batman, 1990s, from $15 to $25.00
Beany and Cecil, from $750 to $850.00
Beatles, 1960s, no bottle, from $750 to $850.00

Captain Kangaroo, 1960s, from $350.00 to $450.00. (Photo courtesy Morphy Auctions)

Casper the Friendly Ghost, 1960s, from $365 to $425.00
Charlie's Angels, 1970s, brunch bag, from $150 to $200.00
Denim, 1970s, from $45 to $65.00
Deputy Dawg, 1960s, from $325 to $375.00

Donnie and Marie, 1970s, long or short hair versions, from $75.00 to $125.00. (Photo courtesy Carole Bess White and L.M. White)

Donnie and Marie, 1970s, brunch bag, from $75 to $125.00
Dr Seuss (World of), 1970, from $30 to $60.00
Fire Station Engine Co #1, 1970s, from $115 to............ $135.00
Holly Hobbie, 1970s, from $50 to $75.00
Jr Deb, 1960s, from $100 to $150.00
Li'l Jodie, 1980s, from $50 to...$75.00

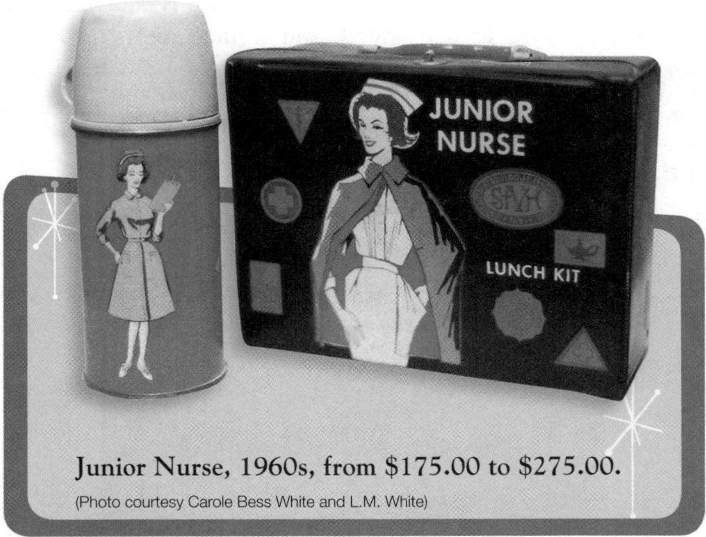

Junior Nurse, 1960s, from $175.00 to $275.00.
(Photo courtesy Carole Bess White and L.M. White)

Lion in the Van, 1970s, from $50 to.................................$75.00
Little Old Schoolhouse, 1970s, from $50 to.......................$75.00
Mardi Gras, 1970s, from $50 to $110.00
Mary Poppins, 1970s, from $75 to $100.00
Monkees, 1960s, from $300 to... $350.00
Pac Man, 1980s, from $40 to $60.00
Pepsi-Cola, 1980s, yel, from $50 to $75.00
Pink Panther, 1980s, from $75 to $100.00
Psychedelic Blue, 1970s, from $40 to $60.00
Ringling Bros & Barnum & Bailey Circus, 1970s, from $125 to.. $175.00

Smokey, 1960s, from $425.00 to $475.00.
(Photo courtesy Carole Bess White and L.M. White)

Ronald McDonald, 1980s, lunch bag, from $15 to $25.00
Snoopy, 1970s, brunch bag, from $75 to $125.00
Snoopy at Mailbox, 1969, red, from $65 to.........................$85.00
Soupy Sales, 1960s, from $300 to $375.00
Speedy Turtle, 1970s, drawstring bag, from $15 to.............$25.00
The Sophisticate, 1970s, drawstring bag, from $50 to $75.00
Tic-Tac-Toe, 1970s, from $50 to..$75.00
Wonder Woman, 1970s, from $100 to $150.00
World of Barbie, 1971, from $50 to...................................$75.00
Ziggy, 1979, from $50 to $75.00

Marbles

Antique marbles are divided into several classifications: 1) Transparent Swirl (Solid Core, Latticinio Core, Divided Core, Ribbon Core, Lobed Core, and Coreless); 2) Lutz or Lutz-type (with bands having copper flecks which alternate with colored or clear bands; 3) Peppermint Swirl (made of red, white, and blue opaque glass); 4) Indian Swirl (black with multicolored surface swirls); 5) Banded Swirl (wide swirling bands on opaque or transparent glass); 6) Onionskin (having an overall mottled appearance due to its spotted, swirling lines or lobes; 7) End-of-Day (single pontil, allover spots, either two-colored or multicolored); 8) Clambroth (evenly spaced, swirled lines on opaque glass); 9) Mica (transparent color with mica flakes added); 10) Sulfide (nearly always clear, colored examples are rare, containing figures). Besides glass marbles, some were made of clay, pottery, china, steel, and even semiprecious stones.

Most machine-made marbles are still very reasonable, but some of the better examples may sell for $50.00 and up, depending on the colors that were used and how they are defined. Guineas (Christensen agates with small multicolored specks instead of swirls) sometimes go for as much as $200.00. Mt. Peltier comic character marbles often bring prices of $100.00 and more with Betty Boop, Moon Mullins, and Kayo being the rarest and most valuable.

From the nature of their use, mint-condition marbles are extremely rare and may be worth as much as three to five times more than one that is near-mint, while chipped and cracked marbles may be worth half or less. The same is true of one that has been polished, regardless of how successful the polishing was. If you'd like to learn more, Everett Grist has written two books on the subject that you will find helpful: *Antique and Collectible Marbles* and *Everett Grist's Big Book of Marbles*. Also refer to MCSA's *Marble Identification and Price Guide*, recently re-written by Robert Block (Schiffer Publishing). See Clubs, Newsletters, and other Publications for club information.

Artist-Made, end-of-day w/lutz or mica, Mark Matthews ⅝" to ¾", M, ea $50.00
Artist-Made, swirl w/lutz or mica, Bill Burchfield, 1½", M...$75.00
Artist-Made, swirls & ribbons, Harry Boyer, 1⅝", M $50.00
Artist-Made, 1 flower or 3 flowers, Harry Boyer, 1½", M, ea .. $75.00
Banded Opaque Swirl, wht w/red & bl swirls from top to bottom, ⅝", M $150.00
China, hand-pnt bull's-eye pattern in mc on wht, 1¾"... $900.00
China, hand-pnt circles w/lines surrounding them giving them 'eye-like' appearance on wht, 1¾" $375.00
China, hand-pnt flower on creamy wht, 2 hairline stripes running from pole to pole, ⅝", M $275.00

Clambroth, opaque white with pink and green swirls, 19/32", NM, A, $315.00. (Photo courtesy Morphy Auctions)

China, hand-pnt overlapping mc flowers on creamy wht, ⅝" .. $350.00
Clambroth Swirl, bl w/wht swirls, ⅝", rare $400.00
Clambroth Swirl, opaque wht w/mc swirls, ⅝" $225.00
Clay, commonly found, dyed or natural, 1¾", ea $5.00
Cloud, wht, red & yel w/bl bits in clear, 1¾" $2,000.00
Cloud, wht, red & yel w/bl bits in clear, ⅝" (rare size) ... $150.00
Comic, 1920s-30s, Andy Gump, Bimbo, Sandy or Emma, ea from $85 to $90.00
Comic, 1920s-30s, Annie, Herbie, Ko Ko or Skeezix, ea .. $100.00
Comic, 1920s-30s, Betty Boop or Moon Mullins, ea $275.00
Comic, 1920s-30s, Kayo $375.00
Comic, 1920s-30s, Smitty $110.00
Divided Core Swirl, peewee, any variation, ⅜" to ½", M, ea. $25.00
Divided Core Swirl, 4 yel outer bands w/3 mc inner bands, 11/16", NM $100.00
End-of-Day, cobalt w/silver mica in clear, 1⅝" $2,000.00

End-of-Day, multicolored onionskin, 1¾", NM+, A, $850.00. (Photo courtesy Morphy Auctions)

End-of-Day, single pontil cloud w/mica, mc, 1⅝", NM $55.00
End-of-Day, wht w/bl & red specks, dashes of yel w/deep bl at base, 1¾" $2,500.00
End-of-Day, 1 red & 1 wht feathery wing-like sections on clear, 11/16" $2,500.00

Indian Swirl, any color variation, ½" to ⅞", ea $125.00
Indian Swirl, Colonial Blue, 1¾" $1,750.00
Joseph's Coat, transparent bl base w/mc swirl, 15/16" $75.00
Lutz Ribbon Core, blood red w/single wht-bordered gold swirl, ⅝" $300.00
Lutz Type 1, clear swirl, bright bl & wht bordered gold surface swirls, ⅝" $125.00
Lutz Type 2, wht & gold surface swirls on amber, ⅝" $225.00
Lutz Type 3, wht & wht-edged gold surface swirls on aqua, ⅝" $350.00

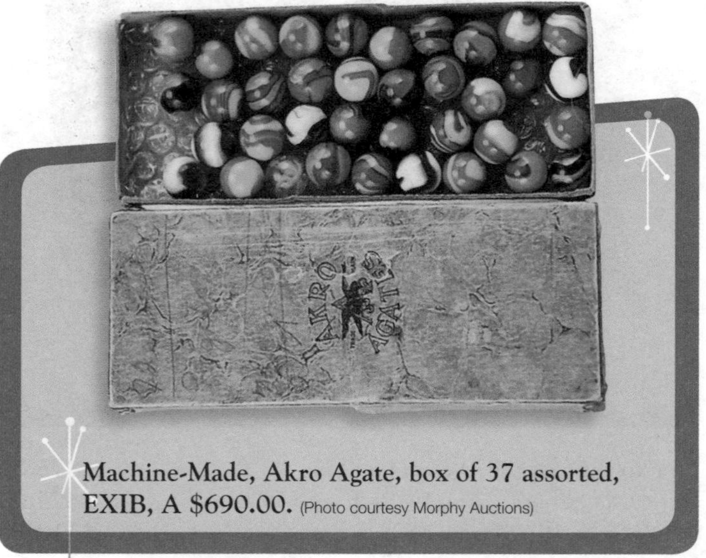

Machine-Made, Akro Agate, box of 37 assorted, EXIB, A $690.00. (Photo courtesy Morphy Auctions)

Machine-Made, Akro Agate, corkscrew, red w/wht swirl $7.00
Machine-Made, Akro Agate, lemonade oxblood, 9/16"-11/16", ea $130.00
Machine-Made, Akro Agate, limeade corkscrew or swirl, 9/16"-11/16", ea $30.00
Machine-Made, Carnelian Agate containing oxblood, 9⅙"-11/16", ea $100.00

Machine-Made, Christensen Agate, box of 12 assorted, ⅝", NMIB, A, $1,400.00. (Photo courtesy Morphy Auctions)

Machine-Made, clear or transparent w/ribbon corkscrew, 9/16"-11/16", ea from $15 to $25.00
Machine-Made, corkscrew, 3-color, 9/16"-11/16", ea $40.00
Machine-Made, Orange Peel, opaque blk base w/orange & yel triangular patch, rare $250.00
Machine-Made, Rocket, blk & orange translucent swirls, 11/16" $250.00

Onionskin, mica flecks overlaid on red, gr & wht, slight swirling of colors, 1¾" $2,500.00

Onionskin, red/yellow and blue/white swirls, single pontil, 1⅞", NM+, A, $690.00. (Photo courtesy Morphy Auctions)

Onionskin, red, yel & gr swirls, 1¾" $1,200.00
Onionskin, 4-lobed, red & wht w/hints of pk, touch of bl, very misty & blended, 1¾" $2,750.00
Onionskin, 4-lobed, 1 yel swirl w/red flecks & 1 swirl of wht w/gr flecks, spattered w/blk flecks & some mica, 1¾" $750.00
Peppermint Swirl, opaque w/red, wht & bl swirls, 1¾" ..$3,500.00
Peppermint Swirl, opaque w/red, wht & bl swirls, ⅝" $100.00
Solid Opaque, set of 60 for Chinese checkers game, 10 ea red, yel, bl, gr, blk, wht, #00, Berry Pink, 1930s, M (VG+ box) $75.00
Sulfide, ape man standing, 2⅜", EX, A $110.00
Sulfide, baby crawling, 2$\frac{7}{16}$", EX, A $55.00
Sulfide, bear standing, 1¾" $200.00
Sulfide, child in highchair, 1¾" $650.00
Sulfide, child in long dress, 1¾" $650.00
Sulfide, clown standing in pointed hat, 1½", EX+ $285.00
Sulfide, Crucifix, crudely made, 1¾" $650.00
Sulfide, dog, spaniel standing, 1$\frac{9}{16}$", EX, A $55.00
Sulfide, fish, 1¾" $300.00
Sulfide, girl seated in chair, 2⅜", EX, A $165.00
Sulfide, girl seated reading book, 1½", NM $250.00
Sulfide, girl w/doll seated, 1$\frac{13}{16}$", EX, A $55.00

Sulphide, hen, tricolor, 1$\frac{5}{32}$", NM+, $2,265.00. (Photo courtesy Morphy Auctions)

Sulfide, horse standing 1¾" $175.00
Sulfide, lion standing, 1$\frac{11}{16}$", NM, A $88.00
Sulfide, Little Boy Blue seated, 1$\frac{11}{16}$", VG, A $110.00
Sulfide, owl, 1¾" $200.00
Sulfide, peacock in gr grass, 1¾", rare $8,000.00
Sulfide, pocket watch, 2$\frac{7}{16}$", EX, A $660.00
Sulfide, rabbit crouching, 1¾" $250.00
Transparent Swirl, divided core (red, wht & bl), 5 yel & 5 wht alternating lines w/1 gr & yel line, 1¾" $325.00
Transparent Swirls, divided core (red & yel), red, wht & bl outer bands w/yel & wht alternating inner bands, ⅝" $45.00
Transparent Swirl, divided core (red & yel), red, wht & bl outer lines w/yel & wht alternating inner lines, 1¾" $475.00

Transparent Swirl, divided core, 2½", NM+, A, $2,250.00. (Photo courtesy Morphy Auctions)

Transparent Swirl, latticinio core (wht), bl & orange outer bands, 1¾" $275.00
Transparent Swirl, latticinio core (wht), bl & wht outer bands, ⅝" $20.00
Transparent Swirl, latticinio core (wht), red, wht & bl outer bands w/inner lines of yel, ⅝" $30.00
Transparent Swirl, latticinio core (wht), red, wht & bl outer bands w/yel inner lines, 1¾" $425.00
Transparent Swirl, latticinio core (yel), red & wht, ⅝" $25.00
Transparent Swirl, latticinio core (yel), red & wht outer bands, 1¾" $325.00
Transparent Swirl, latticino core (orange & wht), 1$\frac{13}{16}$" .. $220.00
Transparent Swirl, latticino core (yel), 2$\frac{3}{16}$" $110.00
Transparent Swirl, lobed core (blk, red, yel & wht w/sm amount of gr), 3 groups of 4 wht lines near outer surface, ⅝" $100.00
Transparent Swirl, lobed core (blk/red/yel/wht w/sm amount of gr), 3 groups of 4 wht lines near outer surface, 1¾" $1,500.00
Transparent Swirl, ribbon core (8 red stripes alternating w/wht & edged w/bl stripe), 2 swirls of 9 yel lines, ⅝" $60.00
Transparent Swirl, ribbon core (8 red stripes alternating w/wht edged w/bl stripe), 2 swirls of 9 yel lines, 1¾" $1,500.00
Transparent Swirl, solid core (red & wht surrounded by yel), bl & wht outer bands, 1¾" $450.00
Transparent Swirl, solid core (red & wht surrounded by yel), bl & wht outer bands, ⅝" $60.00
Transparent Swirl, solid core (wht, gr & yel), red w/outer bands of wht, ⅝" $60.00
Transparent Swirl, solid core (wht, gr & yel), red w/wht outer bands, 1¾" $450.00
Transparent Swirl, solid core (3-stage), 1 $\frac{15}{16}$", EX, A.... $193.00

Marx

Louis Marx founded his company in New York in the 1920s. He was a genius not only at designing toys but also marketing them. His business grew until it became one of the largest toy companies ever to exist, eventually expanding to include several factories in the United States as well as other countries. Marx sold his company in the early 1970s, and died in 1982. Although toys of every description were produced, collectors today admire his mechanical toys above all others.

Advisors: Tom Lastrapes, battery-operated; Scott Smiles, windups

See also Advertising; Banks; Character, TV, and Movie Collectibles; Dollhouse Furniture; Games; Guns; Plastic Figures; Playsets; and other categories. For toys made by Linemar (Marx's subsidiary in Japan), see Battery-Operated Toys; Windup, Friction, and Other Mechanical Toys.

Battery-Operated

Alley the Roaring Stalking Alligator, 18", NMIB........... $275.00
Barking Terrior Dog, plush, w/collar, 8", EXIB............... $100.00
Baseball Pitching Game, EXIB.......................................$75.00

Bengali Tiger, remote control, 13", 1960s, MIB, $275.00. (Photo courtesy Don Hultzman)

Big Parade (Drill Team), plastic, 1963, unused, MIB, A.. $220.00
Brewster the Rooster, plus, 10", EXIB $75.00
Buttons the Puppy w/a Brain, plush & tin, 12", EX, A......$75.00
Chief Big Mouth Ball Blowing Target Game, unused, NMIB, A $250.00
Colonel Hap Hazzard, litho tin, 12", NMIB.................. $975.00
Fred Flintstone on Dino, plush, 1961, NM $325.00
Fred Flintstone on Dino, plush, 1961, NMIB $600.00
Giant Sonic Robot, Masudaya, b/o, tin, 15½", EXIB, A... $2,000.00
Great Garloo, r/c, 24", EXIB, A $550.00
Great Garloo, r/c, 24", VG $225.00
Hootin' Hollow Haunted House, 11", EX $550.00
Hootin' Hollow Haunted House, 11", NMIB.............. $1,450.00
Locomotive, r/c, 6", EXIB...$85.00
Mighty Kong, r/c, plush, 11", EXIB $500.00
Mr Mercury, r/c, plastic, 13", EXIB, A $575.00
Mr Mercury, r/c, tin, gold version, 13", NMIB, A........ $1,150.00
Nutty Mad Car, 9½", EX.. $150.00
Nutty Mad Indian, EX $100.00

Nutty Mad Indian, MIB, $225.00. (Photo courtesy Don Hultzman)

Peppy Puppy, Y, plush, r/c, 7", EXIB...............................$40.00
Ride-Er Convertible, 32", NRFB (sealed), A................. $550.00
Scootin'-Tootin' Hot Rod, 13", GIB $175.00
Walking Tiger, r/c, plush, 12", EXIB.............................. $325.00

Whistling Spooky Kooky Tree, dark brown and light brown versions, 14", NMIB, $1,500.00 each. (Photo courtesy Don Hultzman)

Whistling Spooky Kooky Tree, lt brn & dk brn versions, 14", VG, ea $600.00
Yeti the Abominable Snowman, r/c, 11", NMIB, A $750.00

Vehicles (Pressed Steel, Tin, and Plastic)

A&P Super Markets Delivery Truck Van, tin, red & silver, 19½", NM, A.. $575.00
ACE Hauler & Van Trailer, tin, 21", NMIB, A $450.00
Ambulance (Military), PS, gr w/MD War Dept emblem on doors, CC S8061/Co 1367-8 on hood, BRT, 14" L, G, A .. $400.00
Army Transport Truck, tin, gr w/canvas cover, 13", NM+IB ... $350.00
Army Transport Truck (marked RA) w/Mobile Field Cannon, tin w/canvas cover, gr, 13", NMIB, A $325.00
Bulldozer, litho tin, blk rubber treads, w/driver, 11", G+, A..$85.00
Cannonball Keller Roadster w/Racer on Trailer, tin/plastic, w/up, 17" overall, NMIB, A $725.00
Caterpillar Heavy Duty Bulldog Tractor w/Road Grader, tin, w/up, 10", EXIB, A $125.00
Cities Service Tow Truck, tin, gr & wht, 21", NM, A $225.00

Cities Service Tow Truck, tin, gr & wht, 21", VG, A..... $150.00
City Coal Co Truck, tin, w/up, 13", VG, A $350.00
Coast-to-Coast Double-Decker Bus, litho tin, w/up, 10", VG...$525.00
Contractor's Truck, front loader, spring-loaded dumping action, 20", EX.. $200.00
Coupe, long streamline hood, low roof, covered wheels, w/up bump-&-go action, 16", EX..................................... $500.00
Delivery Truck/Van, plastic, doorless sides, rear doors open, 2-tone, 10", NM+IB, A... $100.00
Deluxe Auto Transport, PS, w/2 plastic cars, 24", unused, NMIB, A $400.00
Deluxe Delivery Ride-On Truck, PS, 26", unused, NM, A... $350.00
Dump Truck, PS, yel cab w/red dump bed, 18", unused, NMIB, A $400.00
Emergency Searchlight Unit Truck, tin & PS, b/o light, wht, 19", NM, A.. $175.00
Emergency Service Tow Truck, tin, friction, b/o roof light & siren, 14", EX, A $125.00

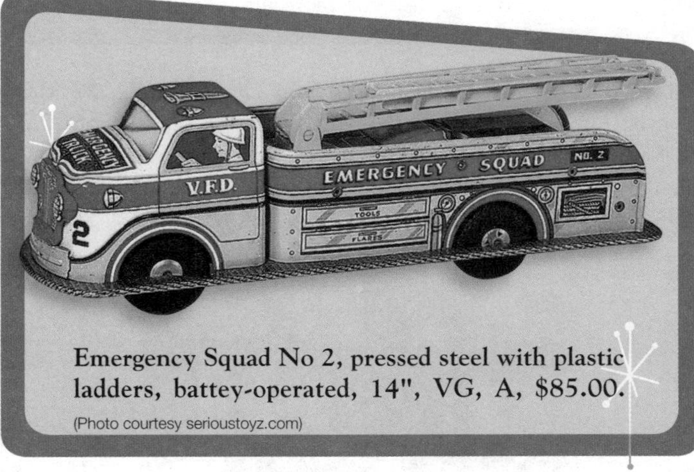

Emergency Squad No 2, pressed steel with plastic ladders, battey-operated, 14", VG, A, $85.00. (Photo courtesy serioustoyz.com)

Fill-Up w/Billups Semi, #3632-B, PS, 26", NMIB, A .. $1,400.00
Fire Dept Car, tin, friction, b/o lights, red, BRT, 15", EX+ ...$450.00
Fire Ladder Truck, PS, w/up, open, red w/yel ladders, BRT, 14", VG, A $260.00

Fire Ladder Truck, rider, pressed steel, 31", M (NOS), A, $2,000.00. (Photo courtesy Morphy Auctions)

Fire Pumper Truck (VFD 9), PS, 22", unused, M, A....... $500.00
Fire Truck w/Automatic Flashing Light, Aerial Ladders & Siren, plastic, red, wht & yel, NM+IB, A.......................... $150.00

G-Man Pursuit Car, pressed steel, 14", NM (VG box), A, $3,750.00. (Photo courtesy Morphy Auctions)

G-Man Pursuit Car, tin, w/up, red, wht & bl, 15", VG... $525.00
Gas Truck, PS, BRT, 11", VG, A.................................. $120.00
Hess Fire Hose Truck, 11", 1970, M, A $585.00
Hess Tanker, plastic, B-Mack cab, 13", 1964, NM+IB.... $750.00
Home Dairy (Dairy Delivery Truck), tin, w/single milk container, 11", NM+IB, A... $625.00
HQ Staff Car, litho tin, w/up, gr, BRT, 15", EX, A $2,310.00
Inter-City Delivery Service Truck, tin, 16½", NMIB, A.. $400.00
Lazy Day Farms Stake Truck, tin, 18", EX+, A $100.00
Livestock Transport Co (Cattle Van Trailer), tin, 15½", EX+IB, A $150.00
Lumar Contractors Dump Truck, PS w/litho tin wheels, hand-op bed, 17", EX, A $100.00
Lumar Dump Truck w/Front Loader, tin, red, wht & bl, 15", EX, A $125.00
Lumar Wrecker Service Truck, 16", NM, A.................... $650.00

Merchants Transfer Truck, 10½", G, A, $300.00. (Photo courtesy Morphy Auctions)

Motor Market Stake Truck, PS, 14", EX+, A................. $150.00
Mystery Car, PS, red w/NP grille, bumper & headlights, covered wheel wells, 10", EX, A $800.00
North American Van Lines Tractor-Trailer, PS, rear gate opens, 13½", EX+, A.. $225.00
Police 1 Car, tin, w/up, b/o lights, gr, BRT, 15", EX, A...$1,100.00
Powerhouse Transit Mix Cement Mixer, PS, 21", unused, NRFB (sealed), A $300.00
Racer #410, litho tin, w/up, w/driver, 11", EX, A $275.00
Railway Express Agency Van, tin, 20", EX+, A $450.00

Reversible Coupe, tin, 16½" L, NMIB, A $1,325.00
Royal Bus Line Bus, litho tin, w/up, roof rack, rear trunk, w/driver, 11", VG, A $385.00
Safety Highway Express Set, #5 Comet, #6 White, truck, w/up, MIB, A....................$100.00
Sand & Gravel Dump Truck, PS & tin, 16", NM, A...... $125.00

Sanitation Truck, pressed steel, 13", unused, NM+IB, A, $800.00. (Photo courtesy Morphy Auctions)

Siren Fire Chief Car, PS, w/up, 14", VG $300.00
Siren Fire Chief Car, tin, friction, 8", EX, A....................$200.00
Siren Police Car, PS, w/up, rear spare, 13", G, A........... $135.00
Sparkling Highboy Tractor, PS w/plastic driver, 10" L, MIB .. $145.00
Stake Truck, litho tin, wht w/blk & orange detail, 13½", GIB, A....................$30.00
Stake Truck, litho tin cab w/PS stake bed, plastic wheels, red & yel, 12½", EX+IB $200.00
Sunshine Fruit Growers Deluxe Trailer Truck, plastic cab w/metal trailer, 14", NMIB, A....................$200.00
Tractor w/Scoop Loader, PS, 13", unused, MIB, A $250.00
US Mail Truck #3, litho tin, 10", VG $400.00
US Mobile Guided Missile Squadron Truck, 18", VG.... $150.00
Van Truck, plastic, red cab w/clear see-through box van, 10", NMIB....................$50.00
Western Auto Tractor-Trailer, PS, red cab w/silver trailer, 25", NM+IB, A $500.00

Willys Jeep and Trailer, pressed steel, complete, 23" overall, MIB, A, $350.00. (Photo courtesy Randy Inman Auctions)

Yellow Taxi, plastic, 1930s, 4", NM, A....................$55.00
24 Hour Towing Service Truck, PS, wht & bl w/red trim, 31", NM+IB, A $1,000.00

WINDUP, FRICTION, AND OTHER MECHANICAL TOYS

Amos 'N' Andy Fresh Air Taxi, 8", EX, A $600.00
Amos 'N' Andy Fresh Air Taxi, 8", NMIB....................$1,500.00
Amos 'N' Andy Walkers, 11", EXIB (1 box)....................$1,500.00
Amos 'N' Andy Walkers, 11", VG, ea....................$400.00

Balky Mule, 8½", NM+, $175.00. (Photo courtesy Scott Smiles)

Balky Mule, 8½", NM+IB....................$200.00
Beat It! The Komikal Kop, 7" L, NMIB....................$800.00
Beat It! The Komikal Kop, 7" L, VG, A $400.00
Big Parade, 24" L, EX....................$650.00
Big Parade, 24" L, VG....................$450.00

Big Show Circus Truck, 9", VG+, A, $500.00. (Photo courtesy Noel Barrett Antiques and Auctions, Ltd.)

Blondie's Jalopy, 16", EXIB, A....................$3,250.00
BO Plenty, 9", EXIB....................$275.00
BO Plenty, 9", G $150.00
Buck Rogers Police Patrol, 11½", EX $1,400.00
Buck Rogers 25th Century Rocket Ship, 12", EXIB, A..$2,000.00
Busy Bridge, 24" L, EX, A....................$650.00
Caterpillar Heavy Duty Sparkling Climbing Bulldozer Tractor, 10½", NMIB, A $200.00
Charleston Trio, 9", EX+ $850.00
Charleston Trio, 9", NMIB....................$1,800.00
Charlie McCarthy & Mortimer Snerd Private Car, 16", VG, A....................$1,500.00
Charlie McCarthy Benzine Mobil, 8", EXIB, A............. $725.00
Charlie McCarthy the Drummer Boy (Strike Up the Band/Here Comes Charlie), 9", NMIB....................$1,500.00

Charlie McCarthy Benzine Mobile, 8", G+, A, $375.00; Charlie McCarthy Walker, 8", VG, A, $275.00. (Photo courtesy James D. Julia, Inc.)

Chompy the Beetle, 5½", EXIB, A $150.00
Climbing Fireman, 22" (extended), EXIB $325.00
Clown on Tricycle, 9" H, EX $1,200.00
Coast Defense, 9" dia, NM $975.00
College Jalopey, 6", VG, A $275.00
Coo Coo Car, 8", VG, A $250.00
Coo-Coo Car, 8", EX $450.00
Dagwood's Solo Flight (Aeroplane), 8", G+, A $550.00

Dagwood the Driver, 8", EX+IB, A, $1,350.00. (Photo courtesy Scott Smiles)

Dapper Dan, box only, VG, A $275.00
Dapper Dan, 10", EXIB, A $1,275.00
Dare Devil Flyer, 13", G $350.00
Dare Devil Flyer, 13", NMIB $1,650.00
Dept of Police Car, friction, 8½", VG $175.00
Dick Tracy Police Station, w/car, 9" L, EXIB $500.00
Dick Tracy's Bonnie Braids, 11", EX (VG box) $150.00
Dick Tracy Squad Car, camo graphics, gunner on knees, 5", NMIB, A $225.00
Dick Tracy Squad Car, 11", VG $150.00
Dippy Dumper (Bluto), 9", VG, A $300.00
Dippy Dumper (Brutus), 9", EXIB, A $1,760.00
Dippy Dumper (Popeye), 9", EX $650.00
Disney Kart (Donald Duck), friction, 6", VG $300.00
Disney Parade Roadster, 11", NMIB $750.00
Disney Train, engine mk 376, 15", VG $250.00
Donald (Duck) the Driver, 7", EX+IB $600.00
Donald Duck (Twirling Tail), 6½", NM+IB, A $325.00
Donald Duck Duet, 10", EX, A $550.00
Donald Duck Duet, 10", NM+IB $1,200.00
Donald Duck on Tractor, plastic, friction, 4" L, EX $75.00
Donald Duck the Drummer, plastic w/tin drum, 10", EX $200.00
Donald Duck the Skier, plastic w/tin skis & poles, 10", EX $300.00
Dopey Walker, 8", EX $425.00
Dottie Driver, celluloid nodder figure, 8" L, EXIB $100.00
Doughboy Tank, 9", VG+IB, A $250.00
Drive-Ur-Self Car, 14", EX $200.00
Driver Training Car, 7", EXIB, A $175.00

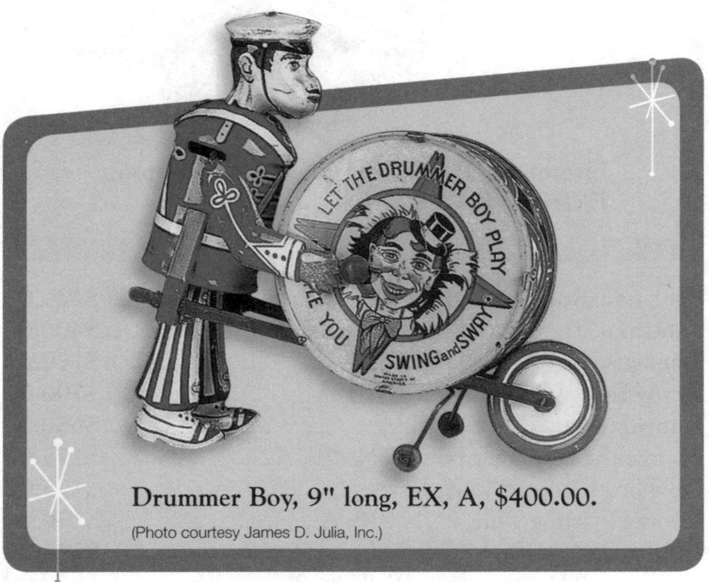
Drummer Boy, 9" long, EX, A, $400.00. (Photo courtesy James D. Julia, Inc.)

Drummer Boy, 9" L, EXIB, A $600.00
Dumbo the Acrobatic Elephant, 4", EXIB, A $650.00

Dumpy Dipper (Bluto), 9", VG, A, $300.00. (Photo courtesy Morphy Auctions)

Ferdinand the Bull, 6", EXIB $325.00
Figaro, 5", NMIB, A $350.00
Fireman Joe, 2 firemen on ladder, 9½", G+, A $375.00
Flash Gordon Rocket Fighter #5, 12", EX $600.00
Flash Gordon Rocket Fighter #5, 12", NMIB $3,000.00
Flintstone Car (Barney), friction, 4", NM $200.00
Flintstone Flivver, 7", EX+, A $175.00
Flintstone Log Car, friction, 1977, MIB $250.00
Flintstone Pals (Barney on Dino), 8" L, EXIB $375.00

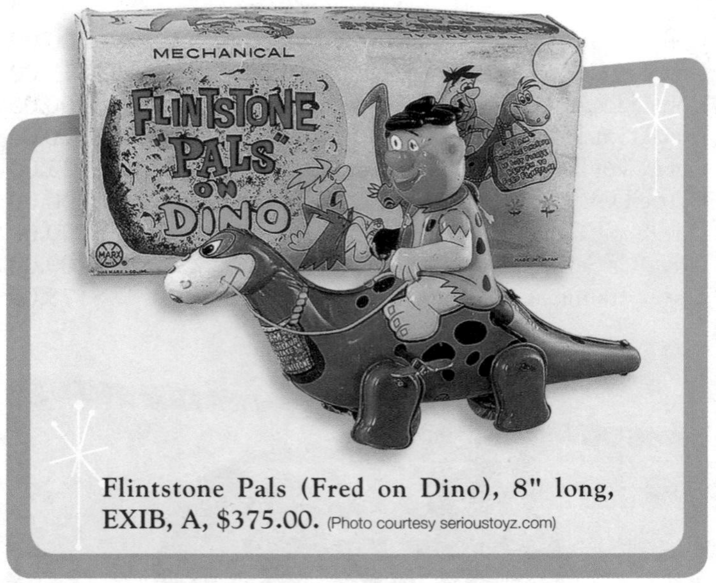

Flintstone Pals (Fred on Dino), 8" long, EXIB, A, $375.00. (Photo courtesy serioustoyz.com)

Flintstone Rollover Tank, 4", EX $225.00
Flintstone Tricycle (Wilma), 4", EX+IB.......................... $400.00
Frankenstein (Walker), VGIB, A.................................. $750.00
Funny Face Walker, 10½", VGIB, A $700.00
Funny Flivver, 7" L, EX+IB, A $650.00
George the Drummer Boy, 9", NMIB, A......................... $175.00
Gobbling Goose, 8", EX+IB, A $75.00
Goofy (Twirling Tail), 8", NMIB, A............................... $250.00
Gorilla, 7½", MIB, A $225.00
Harold Lloyd 'Funny Face' Walker, 10½", VGIB, A $800.00
Hey! Hey! Chicken Snatcher, 9", G, A $650.00

Hey! Hey! Chicken Snatcher, 9", NM, A, $1,500.00. (Photo courtesy Morphy Auctions)

Hi-Yo Silver the Lone Ranger, no base, scarce chrome version, 8", EXIB, A $650.00
Hi-Yo Silver the Lone Ranger, rocker base, 9", EXIB $675.00
Honeymoon Express, 9½" dia, EX+IB, A $275.00
Honeymoon Special, 6" dia, EX $225.00
Hopalong Cassidy, rocker base, 10", EXIB, ... $475.00
Huckleberry Hound Car (Huckleberry Hound), friction, 4", NMIB, A.. $200.00
Huckleberry Hound Car (Quick Draw McGraw), friction, 4", NMIB, A.. $250.00
Huckleberry Hound Car (Yogi Bear), friction, 4", NMIB, A ... $150.00

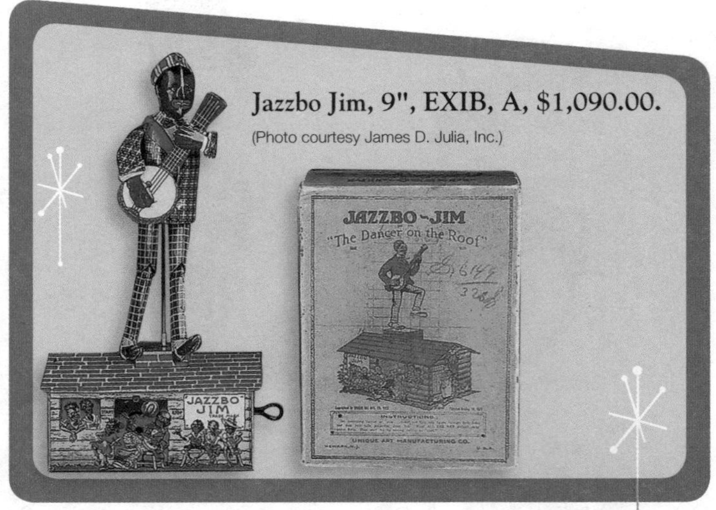

Jazzbo Jim, 9", EXIB, A, $1,090.00. (Photo courtesy James D. Julia, Inc.)

Jazzbo Jim, 9", EX.. $350.00
Jetson Express/Jetson Choo Choo Train, 12", 1960s, NM+ .. $350.00
Joe Penner & His Duck, 8", EX $425.00
Jolly Joe Jeep, 6", VG (partial box), A $275.00
Joy Rider, 7½", EX.. $400.00
Jumpin' Jeep, 6", EXIB, A... $200.00
King Racer, 9", NMIB... $1,550.00

Knockout Champs, 7" long, EXIB, $850.00.

Knockout Champs, 7" L, VG... $400.00
Komikal Kop, see Beat It! the Komikal Kop
Limping Lizzie, 4", EX+IB, A $450.00
Little Orphan Annie, 5½", EXIB..................................... $450.00
Looping Plane, 7½" WS, EXIB $400.00
Lucky Stunt Flyer, 6½", VG+, A $400.00
Machine Gun, 5", EX+IB, A $250.00
Main Street, 24" L, NMIB, A.. $650.00
Main Street, 24" L, VGIB... $400.00
Mammy's Boy, 1929, 10½", EX+IB, A......................... $1,500.00
Matador & Ferdinand the Bull, VG $325.00
Merry Makers, conductor on piano, no marquee, EX $900.00
Merry Makers, conductor on piano, w/marquee, EXIB, A .. $1,200.00
Merry Makers, violinist on piano, no marquee, EXIB, A...... $1,200.00
Mickey Mouse, see also Whirling Tail Mickey Mouse
Mickey Mouse Dipsy Car, 6", VGIB............................... $500.00
Mickey Mouse Express, 10" dia, NMIB, A $850.00
Mickey Mouse Meteor Train, 5-pc, 43" overall, NMIB .. $650.00

Mickey the Driver, 7", NMIB.. $600.00
Midget Racer, plastic, NMIB, A....................................... $150.00
Military Motorcyclist, 8", VG... $300.00
Milton Berle Car, 6", EXIB... $400.00
Monkey on Tricycle, lever-op, 6", EX............................... $100.00
Monkey Tumbling w/Two Chairs, 5", EX......................... $275.00
Moon Mullins & Kayo Handcar, 6", VG........................... $400.00
Moon Mullins & Kayo Handcar, 6", VGIB, A................ $500.00
Mortimer Snerd's Home Town Band (Mortimer Snerd the Drummer Boy), ca 1936, 8½", EXIB................................ $1,450.00
Mortimer Snerd Tricky Auto, 7" L, NM+IB, A............. $775.00
Mortimer Snerd Walker, 8", NM+IB, A........................... $575.00
Mortimer Snerd Walker, 8", VG, A................................. $275.00
Motorcycle Cop, 8", EX, A.. $400.00
Motorcycle Delivery, see Speed Boy 4 (Motorcycle Delivery)

Mystic Motorcycle, first version, 1936, EXIB, $300.00.

Mysterious Pluto, 10" L, EX+IB, A................................ $550.00
New York City, 9½" H, NM+IB................................. $1,250.00
Noddy & His Car, friction, 4" L, MIB, A........................ $150.00
Parade Drummer, in uniform & hat, side-glance eyes, 9", EX, A... $100.00
PD (Police) Motorcycle, 8", EX, A................................ $550.00
Pinocchio the Acrobat, 16", VG+.................................. $350.00
Pinocchio Walker, 8", EX+IB, A.................................... $725.00
Planet Patrol X-1 Space Tank, 10" L, EX........................ $225.00
Planet Patrol X-1 Space Tank, 10" L, EXIB, A.............. $350.00
Pluto, see also Mysterious Pluto, Roll-Over Pluto, or Wise Pluto
Pluto (Spinning Tail), plastic, 6", 1950s, VG................ $125.00
Pluto the Drum Major, 7", EX.. $250.00
Police Squad Motorcycle #3 w/Sidecar, 9", EX+IB......... $350.00
Police Squad Motorcycle #3 w/Sidecar, 9", VG+, A....... $250.00
Police Tipover Motorcycle, 8½" L, EX, A....................... $250.00
Popeye, see also Dippy Dumper (Popeye)
Popeye & Olive Oyl Jiggers, 9", VG.............................. $600.00
Popeye & Olive Oyl Jiggers, 9", VGIB........................... $825.00
Popeye Express, 2 planes circle train & tunnels on rnd base, 9" dia, EX+IB, A.. $1,425.00
Popeye Express (Fliers), 2 planes circle tower, 9", EX.. $1,000.00
Popeye Express (Parrot on Trunk), 9" H, EX, A............ $625.00
Popeye Handcar, 7½", NMIB...................................... $1,550.00
Popeye in Horse Cart (Mechanical Horse & Cart w/Driver), 7½", NMIB.. $110.00
Popeye Jigger, 9", EXIB.. $750.00
Popeye the Champ, 7x7", EXIB................................ $3,000.00
Popeye the Pilot, 9" L, EX.. $600.00
Popeye the Pilot, 9" L, NM.. $900.00
Popeye Walker, 8", NMIB.. $1,300.00
Popeye Walker w/2 Parrot Cages, 8", EX+..................... $575.00
Porky Pig w/Lasso, 8", EXIB, A.................................... $500.00
Porky Pig w/Umbrella, 8", EX+..................................... $350.00
Porter, see Walking Porter
Racer, multicolored w/all wht driver, 16", G, A................ $75.00
Ranger Rider (Cowboy), 10" H, EXIB, A........................ $400.00

Ranger Rider (Cowboy w/ Lasso), 10", 1941, NM, A, $190.00. (Photo courtesy serioustoyz.com)

Ranger Rider (Lone Ranger), 10" H, NMIB..................... $525.00
Red Cap Porter, see Walking Porter
Ride 'Em Cowboy, 8", NMIB.. $225.00

Ring-A-Ling Circus, 8" dia, EX, $1,200.00. (Photo courtesy Bertoia Auctions)

Ring-A-Ling Circus, 8" dia, NMIB.............................. $2,200.00
Rocket Fighter, 12", EXIB... $1,300.00

Rocket Fighter, 12", VG, A $300.00
Rocket Racer, 16", EX.......... $750.00
Roll-Over Airplane, 6" WS, EX $100.00
Roll-Over Cat, 6", EXIB $125.00
Roll-Over Pluto, 8" L, EXIB $350.00
Roll-Over Tank, 8", EX $150.00
Rookie Cop, 8½" , NMIB, A $475.00
Rookie Pilot, 8" WS, EXIB $600.00
Royal Bus Lines, 10", G $325.00
Sam the City Gardener, 8", EX, A $275.00
Sandy (Orphan Annie) & Sandy's Dog House, 3-wheeled Sandy, 8", w/cb Dog House box, EX, A $335.00
Scottie the Guid-A-Dog, EX $150.00
Sheriff Sam & His Whoopie Car, 6", NMIB $250.00
Skybird Flyer, 9", NMIB, A $375.00
Skyhawk, 8", EX+, A $125.00
Smitty Skooter, 6" H, EX, A $1,500.00
Smokey Sam the Wild Fireman, 6½" L, NMIB, A $175.00

Snoopy and Gus Hook and Ladder Truck, 8", EX, A, $1,150.00. (Photo courtesy James D. Julia, Inc.)

Snoopy & Gus Hook & Ladder Truck, 9", VG, A $825.00
Sparkling Climbing Fighting Tank, 10", NMIB $250.00
Sparkling Hot Rod Racer, friction, 7½", NM+IB, A $125.00
Sparkling Soldier, soldier on camp motorcycle, 8", EXIB... $525.00
Speed Boy 4 (Motorcycle Delivery), 10", EX $375.00

Speed Boy 4 (Motorcycle Delivery), 10", NM+IB, A, $550.00.

Speedway Racer #2, 4", EXIB $100.00
Spic & Span, 10", NMIB $2,500.00
Spinning Tail Pluto, see Pluto (Spinning Tail)

Streamline Speedway, complete, 18", NM $175.00
Super Hero Express, 12", 1968, EX $825.00

Superman Rollover Plane, 6½", EX, A, $1,200.00. (Photo courtesy James D. Julia, Inc.)

Thor (Marvel Comics) on Tricycle, 1960s, NM $325.00
Tick & Tack the Tumbling Two, 11", VGIB $175.00
Tidy Tim, 9" L, VG+, A $275.00
Tiger Cart, friction, 6" L, NMIB, A $100.00
Tom Corbett Space Cadet #2 Spaceship, 12", EX $550.00
Tom Corbett Space Cadet #2 Spaceship, 12", NM+IB, A...$975.00
Tom Tom Jungle Boy, 1967, 7", NMIB, A $125.00
Toyland's Milk & Cream Wagon, 10" L, EX, A $150.00
Toytown Dairy Wagon, 10", EX, A $150.00
Tricky Motorcycle, 4", EX+IB, A $225.00
Turnover Tank, 4", EXIB $150.00
Uncle Wiggily Car, 8", EXIB $825.00

Uncle Wiggily Car, 8", VG+, $550.00. (Photo James D. Julia, Inc.)

Walking Porter (Carrying Luggage), 8", EXIB $750.00
Walking Porter (Carrying Luggage), 8", VG $350.00
Walking Porter (Pushing Cart w/Trunk), 8", EXIB $775.00
Walking Porter (Pushing Cart w/Trunk), 8", VG $375.00
Walking Tiger, plush, 8", NMIB, A $125.00
Wee (Running) Scottie, 5", NMIB $200.00
Whirling Tail Mickey Mouse, 7½", EX+IB $200.00
Whoopee Car (College Student), 8", EX $325.00
Whoopee Car (Cowboy), 8", EX $375.00
Whoopee Car (Cowboy), 8", NMIB, A $750.00
Wise Pluto, 1939, 8" L, EXIB $425.00
Wonder Cyclist, boy on tricycle, 9" T, NMIB $600.00
Wonder Cyclist, boy on tricycle, 9" T, VG $350.00

Miscellaneous

Airport (Universal), litho tin, complete, EXIB $400.00

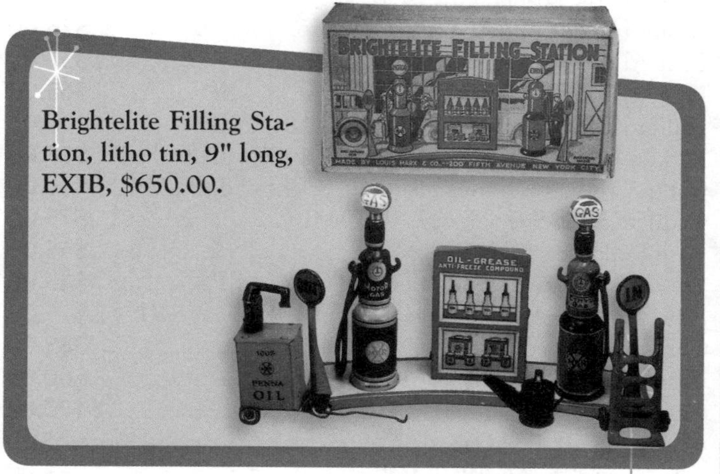

Brightelite Filling Station, litho tin, 9" long, EXIB, $650.00.

Bus (Universal) Terminal, w/2 Wyandotte vehicles scaled for station, EXIB, A $650.00

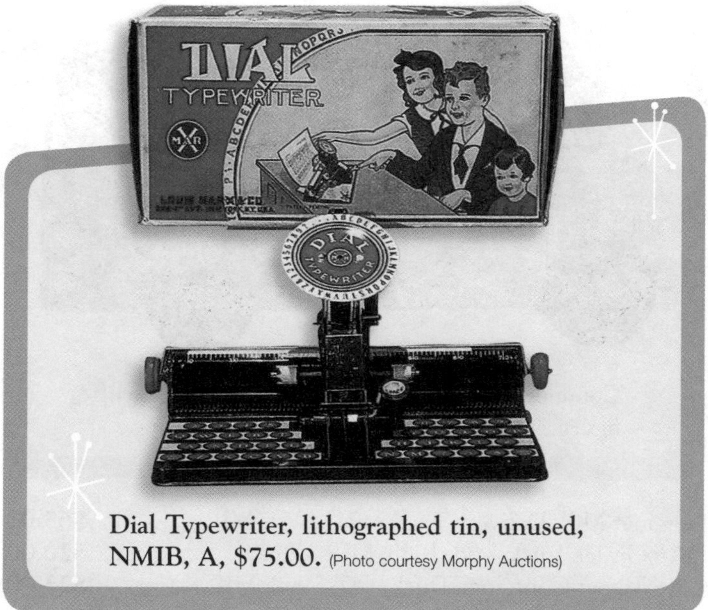

Dial Typewriter, lithographed tin, unused, NMIB, A, $75.00. (Photo courtesy Morphy Auctions)

City (Universal) Airport, 12" L, EXIB, A $330.00
Fire Dept Headquarters, litho tin, complete, EXIB......... $500.00
Freight (Universal) Station, litho tin, NMIB $650.00
Garage, litho tin barn shape w/opening door, 10", EX.......$50.00
Gas Station Island, litho tin, b/o, w/gas pump, oil case & air pump, 9" L, G $100.00
General Alarm Firehouse w/Firechief Car & Patrol Truck, litho tin, 11x17" base, postwar, VG+IB.......................... $575.00
Glendale Depot, litho tin, complete w/accessories, VG... $250.00
Glendale Depot, litho tin, complete w/accessories, VGIB ...$400.00
Grand Central Station, litho tin, EXIB.......................... $600.00
Grand Central Station, litho tin, VG $200.00
Gull Service, litho tin, 17", complete, EX+ $200.00
Home Town Fire House, #186, litho tin, complete, 3x5x2½", NMIB.. $650.00
Main Street Airport, PS, 11x16", VG, A $150.00

Main Street Airport (Sky Way Station), litho tin, b/o lights, 17" L, EX $225.00

Midtown Service Station, complete and unused, MIB, $450.00. (Photo courtesy Randy Inman Auctions)

Oil Tank, litho tin, 100% Penna Oil, 3½", G $125.00
Roadside Rest Service Station, complete, 10x14", VG, A...$550.00

Roadside Rest Service Station (Electric Lighted Filling Station), 14" long, EXIB, $700.00. (Photo courtesy Morphy Auctions)

Sears Service Center, 15x23", complete, NMIB (NOS)....$75.00
Service Island, tin, gas pump, Oil/Grease rack, Free Air pump, In/Out signs & Motor Oil dolly, VG, A.................. $200.00
Service Station w/Take-A-Part Car, plastic, complete, NMIB.. $175.00
Sunny Side Service Station, complete, EX $250.00
Tractor Sales & Service Farm Machinary Set, litho tin tractor w/driver & 2 implements, 13" L tractor, EXIB......... $375.00
Tractor Sales & Service Farm Machinery Set, 1950s, unused, NMIB.. $350.00
Traffic Light, 8", EX+IB $50.00
TV & Radio Station, tin & plastic, NMIB $300.00
Two-Car Garage Complete w/Convertible & Hot Rod, litho tin garage never assembled, EXIB $550.00

Matchbox

The Matchbox series of English and American-made autos, trucks, taxis, Pepsi-Cola trucks, steamrollers, Greyhound buses, etc., was very extensive. By the late 1970s, the company was cranking out more than five million cars every week, and while those days may be over, Matchbox still produces about seventy-five million vehicles on a yearly basis.

Introduced in 1953, the Matchbox Miniatures series has always been the mainstay of the company. There were 75 models in all but with enough variations to make collecting them a real challenge. Larger, more detailed models were introduced in 1957; this series, called Major Pack, was replaced a few years later by a similar line called King Size. To compete with Hot Wheels, Matchbox converted most models over to a line called SuperFast that sported thinner, low-friction axles and wheels. (These are much more readily available than the original 'regular wheels,' the last of which were made in 1969.) At about the same time, the King Size series became known as Speed Kings; in 1977 the line was reintroduced under the name Super Kings.

In the early 1970s, Lesney started to put dates on the baseplates of their toy cars. The name 'Lesney' was coined from the first names of the company's founders, Leslie and Rodney Smith. The last Matchbox toys that carried the Lesney mark were made in 1982. Today many models can be bought for less than $10.00, though a few are priced much much higher.

In 1988, to celebrate the company's fortieth anniversary, Matchbox issued a limited set of five models that, except for minor variations, were exact replicas of the originals. These five were repackaged in 1991 and sold under the name Matchbox Originals. In 1993, a second series expanded the line of reproductions.

Another line that's become very popular is their Models of Yesteryear. These are slightly larger replicas of antique and vintage vehicles.

The Matchbox brand has changed hands several times, first to David Yeh and Universal Toy Company in 1982, then to Tyco Toys in 1992, and finally by Mattel, who purchased Tyco, and along with it, Matchbox, Dinky, and several other Tyco subsidiaries, such as Fisher-Price, Milton-Bradley, and View Master.

To learn more, we recommend *Matchbox Toys 1947 to 2003 Fourth Edition* and *The Other Matchbox Toys 1847 – 2004* by Dana Johnson.

To determine values of examples in conditions other than given in our listings, based on MIP prices, deduct a minimum of 10% if the original container is missing, 30% if the condition is excellent, and as much as 70% for a toy graded only very good.

Regular Wheels

AEC Ergomatic 8-Wheel Tipper, #51, 1969, MIP $30.00
Alvis Stalwart BP Exploration, #61, 1966, MIP $35.00
Army Ambulance, #63, 1959, Ford 3-Ton truck, MIP.......$50.00
Army Half Track Mark III, #49, 1958, MIP $60.00
Aston Martin Racer, #19, 1961, MIP $10.00
Austin Mk 2 Radio Truck, #68, 1959, olive, MIP.............$60.00
Aveling Barford Tractor Shovel, #43, 1962, yel w/yel base & driver, red shovel, MIP $60.00
Aveling Bradford Diesel Road Roller, #1, 1953, dk gr, MIP ..$125.00
Bedford Dunlop 12CWT Van, #25, 1956, MIP $75.00
Bedford Lomas Ambulance, #14, 1962, MIP $50.00
Bedford Low Loader, #27, 1958, MIP $135.00
Bedford Milk Delivery Van, #29, 1956, MIP.....................$75.00
Bedford Petrol Tanker, #25, 1964, MIP.............................$30.00
Bedford Ton Tipper, #3, 1961, blk wheels, MIP $65.00
Bedford Ton Tipper, #3, 1961, gray wheels, MIP $100.00
Berkley Cavalier Travel Trailer, #23, 1956, pale bl, MIP ...$75.00
Cabin Cruiser & Trailer, #9, 1966, bright bl deck, MIP $30.00
Cadillac Sixty Special, #27, 1960, MIP.............................$75.00
Case Bulldozer, #16, 1969, MIP...$35.00
Caterpillar Crawler Bulldozer, #18, 1964, MIP $45.00
Caterpillar DB Bulldozer, #18, 1956, MIP..........................$75.00
Caterpillar Tractor, #8, 1959, MIP $85.00
Caterpillar Tractor, #8, 1961, MIP $60.00
Cement Mixer, #3, 1953, MIP....................................... $100.00
Chevy Impala Taxi Cab, #20, 1965, MIP $25.00
Citroen DS19, #66, 1959, MIP..$55.00
Claas Combine Harvester, #65, 1967, MIP $30.00
Commer Ice Cream Canteen, #47, 1963, w/figure, MIP....$70.00

Commer Ice Cream Canteen, #47, 1962, with figure, NM, $45.00. (Photo Courtesy Dana Johnson)

Commer Milk Delivery Truck, #21, 1961, MIP $65.00
DAF Girder Truck, #58, 1968, MIP $20.00
DAF Tipper Container Truck, #47, 1968, MIP $25.00
Daimler Ambulance, #14, 1956, MIP $100.00
Daimler Bus, #74, 1966, cream, 'Esso Extra Petrol' decals, MIP $30.00
Dennis Fire Escape, #9, 1955, MIP...................................$50.00
Dennis Refuse Truck, #15, 1963, MIP...............................$35.00
Dodge BP Wreck Truck, #13, 1965, MIP $30.00
Dodge Crane Truck, #63, 1968, red hook, MIP $20.00
Dodge Stake Truck, #4, 1967, MIP....................................$30.00
Drott Excavator, #58, 1962, MIP......................................$65.00
Dumper, #2, 1953, MIP.. $100.00
Dumper, #2, 1957, MIP..$85.00
Dumper, #2, 1961, 'Laing' decal, MIP $28.00
Dumper, #2, 1961, MIP..$35.00
Eight-Wheel Crane Truck, #30, 1965, MIP $30.00
Euclid Quarry Truck, #6, 1964, MIP.................................$30.00
Ferret Scout Car, #61 1959, MIP $25.00
Field Car, #18, 1969, MIP...$20.00
Foden Concrete Truck, #21, 1968, MIP $20.00

Foden Concrete Truck, #21, 1968, NM, $10.00. (Photo courtesy Dana Johnson)

Ford Cortina, #25, 1968, MIP $15.00
Ford Fairlane Station Wagon, #31, 1960, MIP $75.00
Ford Galaxie Police Car, #55, 1966, MIP....................$65.00
Ford Mustang Fastback, #8, 1966, MIP $40.00
Ford Pickup, #6, 1969, w/camper, MIP....................$25.00
Ford Thames Trader Compressor Truck, #28, 1959, yel, MIP...$80.00
Ford Thames Trader Wreck Truck, #13, 1961, MIP........ $100.00
Ford Tractor #39, 1967, MIP $28.00
Ford Zephyr 6 MKIII, #33, 1963, MIP....................$28.00
Fordson Tractor, #72, 1959, MIP $75.00
GMC Tipper Truck, #26, 1968, MIP $18.00
Greyhound Bus, #66, 1967, MIP $35.00
Grit Spreading Truck, #70, 1966, MIP $20.00
Hay Trailer, #40, 1967, MIP $18.00

Honda Motorcycle and Trailer, #38, 1968, MIP, $45.00. (Photo courtesy serioustoyz.com)

Jaguar (Mark Ten), #28, 1964, MIP $34.00
Jaguar XK140 Coupe, #32, 1962, MIP $65.00
John Deere-Lanz Tractor, #50, 1964, blk wheels, MIP.......$39.00
Jumbo Crane, #11, 1965, MIP....................$35.00
Land Rover, #12, 1957, left-side steering, w/driver, MIP...$80.00
Land Rover, #12, 1960, right-side steering, no driver, MIP...$70.00
London Bus, #5, 1965, 'Longlife' decals, MIP $28.00
Long Distance Bus, #40, 1961, MIP $35.00
Lyons Maid Ice Cream Mobile Shop, #47, 1963, MIP.... $125.00
Mercedes Lorry, #1, 1968, MIP....................$25.00
Mercedes Trailer, #2, 1968, MIP....................$18.00
Mercedes Unimog, #49, 1967, MIP....................$22.00
Mercedes 220SE, #53, 1963, MIP....................$50.00
Merryweather Marquis Fire Engine, #9, 1959, MIP $43.00
MG 1100 Sedan, #64, 1966, w/driver and dog, MIP..........$18.00

MG 1100, #64, 1966, NM, $12.00. (Photo courtesy Dana Johnson)

MGA Sports Car, #19, 1958, MIP.................... $130.00
Pipe Truck, #10, 1966, MIP $30.00

Pony Trailer, #43, 1968, MIP, $40.00. (Photo courtesy serioustoyz.com)

Ready Mix Concrete Truck, #26, 1961, blk wheels, MIP ..$35.00
Ready Mix Concrete Truck, #26, 1961, gray wheels, MIP..$80.00
Refrigerator Truck, #44, 1967, red wheels, MIP................$23.00
Road Tanker, #11, 1955, MIP.................... $100.00
Scammell Breakdown Lorry, #64, 1959, MIP....................$80.00
Studebaker Lark Station Wagon, #42, 1965, MIP $60.00
Sugar Container Truck, #10, 1961, Tate & Lyle, MIP $83.00
Taylor Jumbo Crane, #11, 1965, MIP....................$25.00
TV Service Van, #62, 1963, 'Rentaset' decals, MIP........ $110.00
Vauxhall Cresta, #22, 1956, MIP $75.00
Vauxhall Cresta, #22, 1958, MIP $150.00
Vauxhall Victor Estate Car, #38, 1963, MIP $55.00
Volkswagen Camper, #34, 1968, silver, MIP $68.00
Volkswagen 1200 Sedan, #25, 1960, MIP $75.00
Volkswagen 1600 TL, #67, 1967, red, no roof rack, MIP...$25.00
Weatherhill Hydraulic Excavator, #24, 1959, blk wheels, MIP... $39.00

Superfast

Airport Coach, #65, 1979, various tampos, MIP $10.00
Ambulance/Emergency Medical Service, #41, MIP...........$10.00
Armored Jeep, #38, 1977, MIP....................$8.00

Badger Exploration Truck, #16, 1974, NM, $8.00. (Photo courtesy Dana Johnson)

Baja Dune Buggy, #13, 1971, flower tampo, MIP..............$15.00
Beach Hopper, #47, 1973, MIP..$10.00
Big Banger, #26, 1973, MIP..$20.00
Big Foot 4x4, #22, 1982, MIP..$15.00
Blaze Buster, #22, 1976, MIP..$8.00
BMW 3.0 CSL, #45, 1975, MIP..$12.00
Car Transport, #11, 1978, MIP..$10.00
CAT Bulldozer, #64, 1981, MIP..$8.00
Cement Truck, #19, 1977, MIP..$5.00
Chevy ('57), #4, 1981, MIP...$6.00
Chevy Corvette, #62, MIP..$10.00
Citroen Station Wagon, #66, 1980, MIP.............................$8.00
Datsun 260Z, #75, 1979, MIP...$10.00
De Tomasa Pantera, #8, 1975, MIP.....................................$8.00
Dodge Challenger, #1, 1976, bl or red, MIP.......................$20.00

Dodge Challenger Hot Rod, #1, 1983, NM, $5.00. (Photo courtesy Dana Johnson)

Dodge Challenger, #1, 1982, yel, MIP...............................$10.00
Dodge Charger Funny Car Dragster, #70, 1972, MIP........$18.00
Dodge Charger Mark III, #52, 1970, MIP...........................$20.00
Fire Pumper, #29, 1970, MIP..$65.00
Flying Bug, #11, 1973, MIP..$15.00
Ford Capri, #54, 1971, MIP...$10.00
Ford Escort RS2000, #9, 1978, MIP...................................$10.00
Ford GT, #41, 1970, MIP...$25.00
Ford Mustang Fastback, #8, 1970, MIP.........................$100.00
Ford Mustang GT-350, #23, 1981, MIP..............................$18.00
Ford Pickup, #6, 1970, w/camper, MIP.............................$20.00
Ford Refuse Truck, #7, 1970, MIP.....................................$10.00
Ford Tractor, #39, 1970, MIP..$22.00
Formula 5000 Racer, #36, 1977, MIP................................$10.00
Freeman Inter-City Commuter Coach, #22, 1970, MIP....$10.00

GMC Tipper Truck, #26, 1970, NM, $10.00. (Photo courtesy Dana Johnson)

Greyhound Bus, #66, 1971, MIP..$25.00
Gruesome Twosome, #4, 1971, MIP....................................$15.00
Hairy Hustler, #7, MIP..$12.00
Hi-Lift Fork Lift Truck, #15, 1973, MIP..............................$10.00

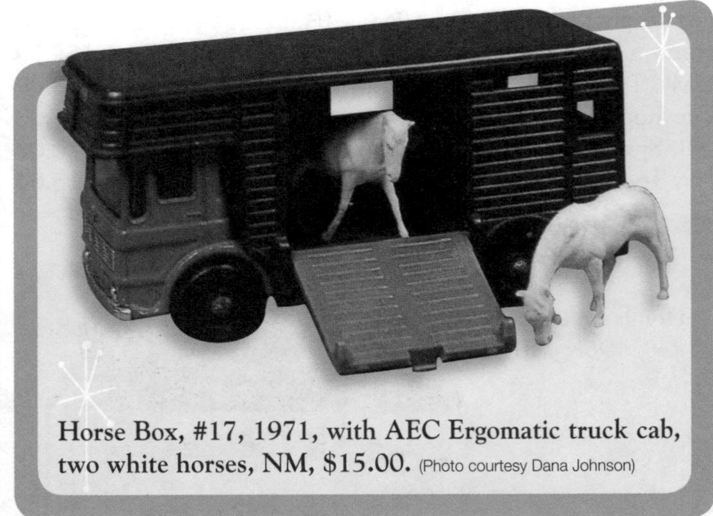
Horse Box, #17, 1971, with AEC Ergomatic truck cab, two white horses, NM, $15.00. (Photo courtesy Dana Johnson)

Horse Box, #40, 1978, MIP..$12.00
Hot Rocker, #67, 1973, MIP...$10.00
Hovercraft, #2, 1976, MIP..$10.00
Iso Grifo, #14, 1970, MIP..$22.00
Javelin AMX, #9, 1972, MIP..$8.00
Jeep CJ6, #53, 1978, MIP..$10.00
Jeep Hot Rod, #2, 1972, MIP...$15.00
Lamborghini Countach, #27, 1973, MIP.............................$15.00
Lamborghini Marzai, #20, 1970, MIP..................................$22.00
Leyland Tanker, #32, 1970, MIP..$20.00
Lincoln Continental, #28, 1979, MIP.................................$10.00
Lincoln Continental, #31, 1970, MIP.................................$35.00
Lotus Europa, #5, 1979, MIP...$12.00
Mack Dump Truck, #28, 1970, MIP....................................$20.00
Maserati Bora, #32, 1973, MIP..$15.00
Mercedes Ambulance, #3, 1970, MIP................................$22.00

Mercedes Lorry, #1, 1970, MIP....................$20.00
Mercedes Trailer, #2, 1970, MIP....................$18.00
Mercedes 230SL, #27, 1970, MIP....................$22.00
Mercury Cougar, #62, 1970, MIP....................$28.00
Mod Rod, #1, 1971, wildcat head decal, MIP....................$25.00
Mod Tractor, #25, 1972, MIP....................$8.00
Monteverdi Hai, #3, 1973, MIP....................$15.00
Piston Popper, #10, 1974, MIP....................$12.00
Piston Popper, #60, 1982, MIP....................$5.00
Plymouth Grand Fury, #10, 1979, Police tampos, MIP......$10.00
Pontiac Firebird, #4, 1975, MIP....................$8.00
Pontiac Grand Prix, #22, 1970, MIP....................$50.00
Porsche 911 Turbo, #3, 1979, MIP....................$6.00
Ranger Wild Life Truck, #57, 1973, MIP....................$15.00
Refrigerator Truck, #44, 1970, MIP....................$18.00
Renault 5TL, #21, 1979, MIP....................$10.00
Road Dragster, #19, 1971, MIP....................$8.00
Rolls-Royce Convertible Coupe, #69, 1970, MIP....................$20.00
Rolss-Royce Silver Shadow, #24, 1970, MIP....................$18.00
Saab Sonnet, #65, MIP....................$12.00
Safari Land Rover, #12, 1970, gold, MIP....................$22.00
Scoop Coopa, #37, 1973, MIP....................$10.00
Seafire, #5, 1976, MIP....................$6.00
Seasprite Rescue Helicopter, #75, 1977, MIP....................$10.00
Site Dumper, #26, 1976, MIP....................$35.00
Site Engineer Vehicle, #20, 1977, MIP....................$15.00
Snorkel Fire Engine, #13, 1977, MIP....................$10.00
Stake Truck, #4, 1970, MIP....................$18.00
Swamp Rats Patrol Boat, #30, 1977, MIP....................$10.00
T-Bird Convertible ('57), #42, 1981 or 1982, MIP....................$8.00
Tanzara, #53, 1973, MIP....................$8.00
Tyre Fryer, #42, 1973, MIP....................$10.00
Vantastic, #34, 1976, MIP....................$10.00
Volkswagen Beetle (Dagon Wheels), #43, 1973, MIP.......$15.00
Volkswagen Beetle (Hi Ho Silver), #15, 1981, MIP..........$10.00
Volkswagen Beetle (Hot Chocolate), #46, 1982, MIP.......$10.00
Volkswagen Golf, #7, 1977, MIP....................$10.00
Volkswagen 1600TL, #67, 1970, MIP....................$30.00
Wells Fargo Truck, #69, 1979, MIP....................$15.00
Wildcat Dragster, #8, 1971, MIP....................$10.00

King Size, Speed Kings, and Super Kings

Citroen SM, #K-33, 1972, NM, $6.00. (Photo courtesy Dana Johnson)

Bazooka Custom Street Rod, #K-44, 1973, MIP....................$15.00
Bertone Runabout, #K-31, 1972, MIP....................$15.00
Blaze Trailer Fire Chief's Car, #K-40, 1973, MIP....................$15.00
Bridge Transporter, #K-44, 1981, MIP....................$15.00
Cambuster Custom Street Rod, #K-43, 1973, MIP....................$15.00
Cement Truck, #K-26, 1980, red, 'McAlpine' decal, MIP...$20.00
Cement Truck, #K-26, 1980, yel, MIP....................$12.00
Corvette Caper Cart, #K-55, 1975, bronze & dk bl, MIP..$15.00
Corvette Caper Cart, #K-55, 1975, lt bl, MIP....................$20.00
Datsun 260Z Rally Car, #K-52, 1975, MIP....................$15.00
Dodge Ambulance, #K-38, 1980, MIP....................$15.00
Dodge Articulated Horse Box, #K-18, 1966, MIP....................$80.00
Dodge Dragster, #K-22, 1969, dk bl, MIP....................$75.00
Dodge Monaco Fire Chief, #K-67, 1978, yel, 'Hackensack' decal, MIP, from $15 to....................$20.00
Dodge Tractor w/Twin Tippers, #K-16, 1966, MIP......... $150.00
Easy Rider Motorcycle, #K-47, 1973, lt brn or orange driver, MIP....................$15.00
Easy Rider Motorcycle, #K-47, 1973, wht driver, MIP......$40.00
Ford Mustang Cobra, #K-60, 1978, red or metallic red, MIP.. $25.00
Ford Mustang Cobra, #K-60, 1978, wht, MIP....................$15.00
Ford Tractor w/Dyson Low Loader & Case Tractor, #K-11, 1966, MIP....................$75.00
Gran Fury Fire Chief Car, #K-78, 1990, orange or wht, MIP.. $8.00
Gran Fury Fire Chief Car, #K-78, 1990, red, IAAFC, MIP...$15.00
Gran Fury Police Car, #K-78, 1979, blk & wht w/City Police decal or plain wht, MIP....................$10.00
Gran Fury Police Car, #K-78, 1979, blk w/bl interior, MIP...$30.00
Gran Fury Taxi, #K-79, 1979, MIP....................$15.00
Helicopter Transporter, #K-92, 1982, MIP....................$20.00
Hot Fire Engine, #K-53, 1975, MIP....................$15.00
Hydraulic Shovel, #K-1, 1960, MIP....................$80.00
JCB Excavator, #K-41, 1981, MIP....................$20.00
Leyland Tipper Truck, #K-37, 1979, MIP....................$15.00

Londoner Double-Decker Bus, #K-15, 1973, MIP, $60.00. (Photo courtesy Dana Johnson)

Maserati Bora, #K-56, 1975, metallic gold, MIP....................$50.00
Maserati Bora, #K-56, 1975, metallic gray, MIP....................$15.00
Maserati Bora, #K-56, 1975, red, MIP....................$20.00
Matra Rancho, #K-90, 1982, MIP....................$15.00
Mercedes-Benz Ambulance, #K-63, 1977, MIP....................$15.00

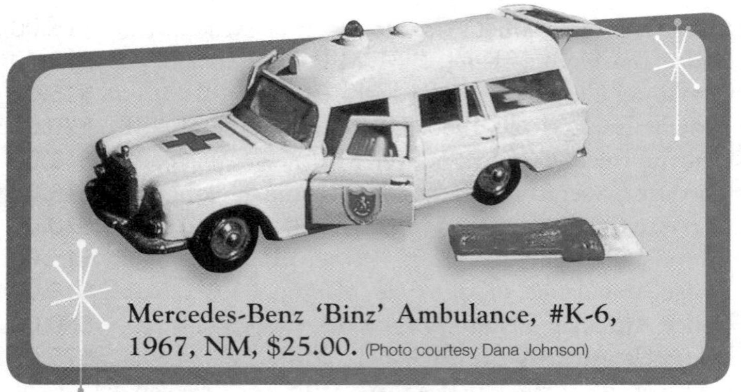
Mercedes-Benz 'Binz' Ambulance, #K-6, 1967, NM, $25.00. (Photo courtesy Dana Johnson)

Mercury Cougar Dragster, #K-21, 1968, MIP....................$50.00
Peterbilt Wreck Truck, #K-20, 1979, dk gr, MIP $15.00
Peterbilt Wreck Truck, #K-20, 1979, lt gr, MIP.................$20.00
Peterbilt Wreck Truck, #K-20, 1979, wht, MIP.................$50.00
Petrol Tanker, #K-16, 1974, gr, Texaco decal, MIP............$75.00
Petrol Tanker, #K-16, 1974, red, Texaco decal, MIP $25.00
Plymouth Trail Duster Rescue Vehicle, #K-65, 1978, red, MIP...$15.00

Tractor Transporter, #K-20, 1968, EX, $75.00. (Photo courtesy Dana Johnson)

Tractor Transporter, #K-20, 1968, MIP $125.00
Tractor Transporter, #K-21, 1974, MIP $50.00
Volvo Ambulance, #K-96, 1984, MIP...............................$15.00
Wheel Tipper Truck, #K-1, 1964, MIP..............................$50.00

Models of Yesteryear

AEC Y-Type Lorry (1916), #Y-6, 1958, MIP.................. $100.00
Auburn 851 Boattail Speedster (1933), #Y-19, 1980, MIP..$30.00

Crossley (1918) Ambulance Truck, #Y-13, 1973, RAF decal, MIP, $75.00. (Photo courtesy Dana Johnson)

Daimler (1911), #Y-13, 1966, MIP.....................................$60.00
Daimler (1922), 1966, #Y-13, 1966, MIP...........................$40.00
Diddle Trolley Bus (1931), #Y-10, 1988, MIP....................$35.00
Ford Model A Breakdown Truck (1930), #Y-7, 1984, MIP...$25.00
Ford Model T Tanker (1912), #Y-3, MIP...........................$50.00
Ford Pickup Truck (1930), #Y-35, 1990, MIP $20.00
GMC Van (1937), #Y-12, 1988, various ads, MIP.............$20.00
Grand Prix Mercedes, #Y-10, 1958, wht, MIP $150.00
Jaguar SS100 (1936), #Y-1, 1977, MIP $15.00
Lagonda Drophead Coupe (1938), #Y-11, 1973, gold & red, MIP...$450.00
Lemans Bently (1929), #Y-5, 1958, MIP......................... $175.00
Leyland Van (4-Ton), #Y-7, 1957, cream roof, blk plastic wheels, 3 lines of text, MIP $1,500.00
Leyland Van (4-ton), #Y-7, 1957, wht or cream roof, metal wheels, 3 lines of text, MIP $100.00
London E Class Tram Car (1907), #Y-3, 1956, Dewars, MIP...$500.00

Mack Model AC Truck (1920), #Y-30, 1985, 'Acorn Storage Co.' advertising, MIP, $25.00. (Photo courtesy Dana Johnson)

Mercedes Truck Stuttgarter (1913), 1988, MIP.................$20.00
Mercedes-Benz 36/220 (1928), #Y-10, 1963, wht, MIP.. $140.00
Mercer Raceabout (1913), #Y-7, 1961, lilac w/blk tires, MIP...$50.00
Mercer Raceabout (1913), #Y-7, 1961, lilac w/gray tires, MIP.. $125.00
Model A Ford Van (1930), #Y-22, 1982, MIP $15.00

Packard Lanaulet (1912), #Y-11, 1964, MIP, $40.00. (Photo courtesy Dana Johnson)

Peugeot (1907), #Y-5, 1969, MIP $25.00
Prince Henry Vauxhall (1914), #Y-2, MIP $25.00
Renault Type AG (1910), #Y-25, 1983, MIP $25.00
Rolls Royce (1912), #Y-7, 1968, silver w/gray roof, MIP... $200.00
Rolls Royce (1912), #Y-7, 1968, silver w/red roof, MIP..... $40.00
Rolls Royce Fire Engine (1920), #Y-6, 1977, MIP $25.00
Rolls Royce Silver Ghost (1906), #Y-10, 1969, MIP $25.00
Sentinel Steam Wagon, #Y-4, 1956, blk wheels, MIP $225.00
Sentinel Steam Wagon, #Y-4, 1956, unpnt metal wheels, MIP $60.00
Spyker (1904), #Y-16, 1961, lt gr w/blk tires, MIP $2,000.00
Spyker (1904), #Y-16, 1961, maroon w/blk tires, MIP.. $1,200.00
Spyker (1904), #Y-16, 1961, yel w/blk tires, MIP $35.00
Spyker (1904), #Y-16, 1961, yel w/gray tires, MIP.......... $100.00
Stutz Bearcat (1931), #Y-14, 1974, lime or cream, MIP $20.00
Stutz Bearcat (1931), #Y-15, 1974, bl w/chrome wheels, MIP... $25.00
Walker Electric Van, #Y-29, 1985, any ad, MIP $20.00
4.5 Litre Supercharged Bently, #Y-2, 1984, purple, MIP.... $20.00

Model Kits

ATM/Ertl, Star Trek the Undiscovered Country, USS Enterprise, #8617, MIB, $35.00.

Though model kits were popular with kids of the '50s, who enjoyed the challenge of assembling a classic car or two or a Musketeer figure now and then, when the monster series hit in the early 1960s, sales shot through the ceiling. Made popular by all the monster movies of that decade, ghouls like Vampirella, Frankenstein, and the Wolfman were eagerly assembled by kids everywhere. They could (if their parents didn't object too strongly) even construct an actual working guillotine. Aurora had other successful series of figure kits, too, based on characters from comic strips and TV shows as well as a line of sports stars.

But the vast majority of model kits were vehicles. They varied in complexity, some requiring much more dexterity on the part of the model builder than others, and they came in several scales, from 1/8 (which might be as large as 20" to 24") down to 1/43 (generally about 3" to 4"), but the most popular scale was 1/25 (usually between 6" to 8"). Some of the largest producers of vehicle kits were AMT, MPC, and IMC. Though production obviously waned during the late 1970s and early 1980s, with the intensity of today's collector market, companies like Ertl (who now is producing 1/25 scale vehicles using some of the old AMT dies) are proving that model kits still sell very well.

As a rule of thumb, assembled kits (built-ups) are priced at about 25% to 50% of the price range for a boxed kit, but this is not always true on the higher-priced kits. One mint in the box with the factory seal intact will often sell for up to 15% more than if the seal were broken, though depending on the kit, a sealed perfect box may add as much $100.00. Condition of the box is crucial. Last but not least, one must factor in Internet sales, which could cause some values to vary considerably.

For more information, we recommend *Collectible Figure Kits of the '50s, '60s, and '70s* by Gordy Dutt.

See also Plasticville.

Addar, Evel Knievel, 1974, #152, MIB $50.00
Addar, Jaws, 1975, MIB $100.00
Addar, Planet of the Apes, Caesar or Gen Aldo, 1974, MIB, ea $50.00
Addar, Planet of the Apes, Cornelius, 1974, MIB $50.00
Addar, Planet of the Apes, Dr Zaius, 1974, MIB $40.00
Addar, Planet of the Apes, Dr Zira, 1974, MIB $40.00
Addar, Planet of the Apes, Gen Ursus 1973-74, MIB........ $45.00
Addar, Planet of the Apes, Jail Wagon, 1975, NMIB $45.00
Addar, Planet of the Apes, Stallion & Soldier, 1974, MIB .. $100.00
Addar, Planet of the Apes, Tree House, 1975, NMIB........ $45.00
Addar, Super Scenes, Jaws in a Bottle, 1975, MIB............ $75.00
Addar, Super Scenes, Spirit in a Bottle, 1975, MIB........... $50.00
Airfix, Bigfoot, 1978, MIB $75.00
Airfix, Boy Scout, 1965, MIB $30.00
Airfix, Flying Saucer, 1981, MIB $35.00
Airfix, James Bond & Odd Job, 1966, MIB $200.00
Airfix, James Bond's Aston Martin, 1965, MIB $250.00
Airfix, Julius Caesar, 1973, MIB $40.00
Airfix, Napoleon, 1978, MIB $25.00
Airfix, Royal Sovereign, #F901S, 1950s, EXIB $15.00
Airfix, 2001: A Space Odyssey, Orion, 1970, #701, MIB.. $100.00
AMT, Farrah's Foxy Vet, 1977, MIB $65.00
AMT, Flintstones Rock Crusher, 1974, MIB $75.00
AMT, Flintstones Sports Car, 1974, MIB........................... $75.00
AMT, Ford Pinto, 1974, MIB (sealed) $55.00
AMT, Get Smart Sunbeam Car, 1967, MIB $75.00
AMT, Girl From UNCLE, 1974, MIB............................. $350.00
AMT, KISS Custom Chevy Van, 1977, MIB $100.00
AMT, Laurel & Hardy '27 Touring Car, 1976, MIB $65.00
AMT, Man from UNCLE Car, MIB $225.00
AMT, My Mother the Car, 1965, MIB $45.00
AMT, Sonny & Cher Mustang, 1960s, MIB $325.00
AMT, Star Trek, Klingon Cruiser, #S952-802, 1968, MIB... $225.00
AMT, Star Trek, Spock, 1973, NMIB (sm box)............. $150.00
AMT, Star Trek, USS Enterprise Command Bridge, 1975, MIB $75.00
AMT/Ertl, A-Team Van, 1983, MIB $30.00
AMT/Ertl, Back to the Future Delorian, 1991, MIB (sealed) ... $35.00
AMT/Ertl, Batman (movie), Batman Cocoon, 1989, MIB... $20.00

AMT/Ertl, Batman (movie), Batwing, 1990, MIB (sealed) ..$30.00
AMT/Ertl, Monkeemobile, 1990, MIB (sealed) $100.00
AMT/Ertl, Robocop 2, Robo 1 Police Car, 1990, MIB......$25.00
AMT/Ertl, Star Trek, USS Enterprise, Chrome Set, Special Edition #6005, MIB $35.00
AMT/Ertl, Star Trek (TV), Kirk, 1994, MIB (sealed) $25.00
AMT/Ertl Star Trek: TNG, USS Enterprise, 1988, MIB...$30.00
Anubis, Jonny Quest, Robot Spy, 1992, MIB....................$60.00
Anubis, Jonny Quest, Turu the Terrible, 1992, MIB..........$60.00
Aurora, Addams Family Haunted House, 1964, MIB..... $850.00
Aurora, Alfred E Neuman, 1965, MIB $175.00
Aurora, Anzio Beach, 1968, MIB.....................................$80.00
Aurora, Archie's Car, 1969, MIB.................................. $100.00
Aurora, Banana Splits Banana Buggy, 1969, MIB........... $525.00
Aurora, Batman, 1964, MIB (sealed) $250.00

Aurora, Batman, Comic Scenes, 1974, MIB (sealed), $125.00. (Photo courtesy Morphy Auctions)

Aurora, Batmobile, 1966, MIB $450.00
Aurora, Big Frankie, see Frankenstein
Aurora, Bloodthirsty Pirates, Blackbeard, 1965, MIB..... $225.00
Aurora, Bride of Frankenstein, 1965, MIB..................... $300.00
Aurora, Captain Action, 1966, MIB............................... $325.00
Aurora, Captain America, 1966, MIB............................ $325.00
Aurora, Captain Kid, 1965, MIB................................... $125.00
Aurora, Castle Creatures, Vampire, 1966, MIB $225.00
Aurora, Creature From the Black Lagoon, 1963, MIB.... $450.00
Aurora, Creature From the Black Lagoon, glow-in-the-dark, 1969, MIB $200.00
Aurora, Cro-Magnon Man or Woman, see Pre-Historic Scenes
Aurora, Dick Tracy in Action, 1968, MIB $350.00
Aurora, Dr Jekyll as Mr Hyde, 1964, MIB...................... $375.00
Aurora, Dr Jekyll as Mr Hyde, glow-in-the dark, 1969, MIB ... $200.00
Aurora, Dracula, 1967, MIB $300.00
Aurora, Dracula, Monsters of the Movies, 1975, MIB.... $350.00
Aurora, Fantastic Voyage, Voyager, 1969, MIB............. $500.00
Aurora, Flying Sub, 1968, MIB $235.00
Aurora, Flying Sub, 1975, MIB $100.00
Aurora, Forgotten Prisoner, Frightning Lightning, glow-in-the-dark, 1969, MIB... $200.00
Aurora, Forgotten Prisoner, Frightning Lightning, 1969, MIB $475.00
Aurora, Forgotten Prisoner, 1966, MIB.......................... $425.00
Aurora, Frankenstein, 1961, MIB.................................. $350.00
Aurora, Frankenstein, glow-in-the-dark, 1971, MIB $150.00
Aurora, Frankenstein, Monster Scenes, 1971, MIB........ $125.00
Aurora, Frankenstein, Monsters of the Movies, 1975 MIB..$325.00
Aurora, Frankenstein (Big Frankie), #470, 1964, 19", EX....$275.00
Aurora, Frankenstein (Big Frankie), #470, 1964, 19", MIB...$1,200.00
Aurora, George Washington, 1965, MIB (sealed) $100.00
Aurora, Ghidrah, Monsters of the Movies, 1975, MIB... $325.00
Aurora, Gladiator w/Trident, Famous Fighters, 1959, MIB... $175.00
Aurora, Godzilla, 1964, MIB $550.00
Aurora, Godzilla, glow-in-the-dark, 1964, MIB............. $350.00
Aurora, Godzilla, glow-in-the-dark, 1972, MIB............. $225.00
Aurora, Godzilla's Go-Cart, 1966, assembled, NM...... $1,000.00
Aurora, Godzilla's Go-Cart, 1966, MIB $3,500.00
Aurora, Gold Knight of Nice, 1957, MIB $325.00
Aurora, Gold Knight of Nice, 1965, MIB $275.00

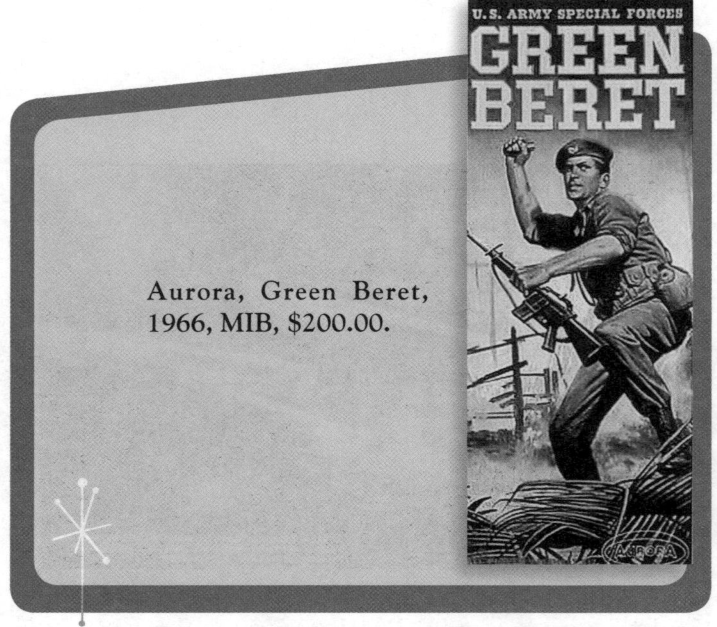

Aurora, Green Beret, 1966, MIB, $200.00.

Aurora, Green Hornet Black Beauty, 1966, MIB........... $525.00
Aurora, Gruesome Goodies, Monster Scenes, 1971, MIB.. $100.00
Aurora, Hunchback of Notre Dame, Anthony Quinn, 1964, MIB $300.00
Aurora, Hunchback of Notre Dame, glow-in-the-dark, 1969, MIB $150.00
Aurora, Incredible Hulk, 1966, MIB $325.00
Aurora, Incredible Hulk, Comic Scenes, 1974, MIB...... $100.00
Aurora, Invaders, UFO, 1968, MIB............................... $100.00
Aurora, Invaders, UFO, 1975, MIB.................................$75.00
Aurora, James Bond 007, 1966, MIB............................ $350.00
Aurora, Jesse James, 1966, MIB.................................. $200.00
Aurora, John F Kennedy, 1965, MIB............................. $150.00
Aurora, King Kong, 1964, MIB $475.00
Aurora, King Kong, glow-in-the-dark, 1969, MIB.......... $300.00
Aurora, King Kong, glow-in-the-dark, 1972, MIB.......... $200.00
Aurora, Land of the Giants, Diorama, 1968, MIB $450.00
Aurora, Land of the Giants, Space Ship, 1968, MIB...... $425.00
Aurora, Lone Ranger, 1967, MIB $200.00
Aurora, Lone Ranger, Comic Scenes, 1974, MIB (sealed)...$75.00

Aurora, Lost in Space, Robot, 1968, MIB....................... $875.00
Aurora, Man From UNCLE, Illy Kuryakin, 1966, MIB.. $275.00
Aurora, Man From UNCLE, Napoleon Solo, 1966, MIB.. $275.00

Aurora, Mexican Caballero, 1957, MIB, $150.00.

Aurora, Mummy, 1963, MIB, $375.00.

Aurora, Mummy, Frightning Lightning, 1969, MIB $425.00
Aurora, Mummy, glow-in-the-dark, 1969, MIB............. $200.00
Aurora, Mummy's Chariot, 1965, MIB $575.00
Aurora, Munster's Living Room, 1964, MIB............... $1,500.00
Aurora, Odd Job, Gold Finger, 1966, MIB...................... $475.00
Aurora, Pendulum, Monster Scenes, 1971, MIB............ $100.00
Aurora, Phantom of the Opera, 1963, MIB $325.00
Aurora, Phantom of the Opera, Frightning Lightning, 1969, MIB $375.00
Aurora, Phantom of the Opera, glow-in-the-dark, 1969, MIB $175.00
Aurora, Phantom of the Opera, glow-in-the-dark, 1972, MIB $100.00
Aurora, Prehistoric Scenes, Cave Bear, MIB $50.00
Aurora, Prehistoric Scenes, Cro-Magnon Man, 1971, MIB..$50.00
Aurora, Prehistoric Scenes, Cro-Magnon Woman, 1971, MIB... $50.00
Aurora, Prehistoric Scenes, Neanderthal Man, 1971, MIB ..$75.00
Aurora, Prehistoric Scenes, Tar Pit, 1972, MIB............. $150.00
Aurora, Rat Patrol, 1967, MIB $115.00
Aurora, Robin, 1966, MIB.. $175.00
Aurora, Robin, Comic Scenes, 1974, MIB...................... $100.00
Aurora, Robin the Boy Wonder, 1966, MIB $125.00
Aurora, Robin the Boy Wonder, Comic Scenes, 1974, MIB ..$125.00
Aurora, Rodan, Monsters of the Movies, 1975, rare, MIB ...$425.00
Aurora, Spider-Man, 1966, MIB $300.00
Aurora, Spider-Man, Comic Scenes, 1974, MIB $125.00
Aurora, Steve Canyon, Famous Fighters, 1958, MIB...... $200.00
Aurora, Superboy, Comic Scenes, 1974, MIB................ $100.00
Aurora, Superboy, 1964, MIB.. $250.00

Aurora, Superman, 1963, MIB, $400.00.

Aurora, Superman, 1975, MIB (sealed) $165.00
Aurora, Tarzan, 1967, MIB.. $200.00
Aurora, Tarzan, Comic Scenes, 1974, MIB.................... $100.00

Aurora, Tonto, 1967, MIB, $250.00. (Photo courtesy gasolinealleyantiques.com)

Aurora, Tonto, Comic Scenes, 1974, MIB.........................$75.00
Aurora, Viking, Famous Fighters, 1959, MIB................. $250.00

Aurora, Voyage to the Bottom of the Sea, Seaview, 1966, MIB $325.00
Aurora, Voyage to the Bottom of the Sea, Seaview, 1975, MIB $200.00
Aurora, Whoozis, Alfalfa, 1966, MIB........ $85.00
Aurora, Whoozis, Kitty, 1966, MIB........ $75.00
Aurora, Whoozis, Snuffy, 1966, MIB........ $75.00
Aurora, Witch, 1965, MIB $325.00
Aurora, Witch, glow-in-the-dark, 1969, MIB $200.00
Aurora, Wolf Man, #425, Toys R Us reissue, MIB (sealed)...$30.00
Aurora, Wolfman, 1962, MIB........ $300.00
Aurora, Wolfman, Frightning Lightning, 1969, MIB $425.00
Aurora, Wolfman, glow-in-the-dark, 1969, MIB $175.00
Aurora, Wolfman, glow-in-the-dark, 1972, MIB $75.00
Aurora, Wolfman, Monsters of the Movies, 1975, MIB... $250.00
Aurora, Wolfman's Wagon, 1965, MIB $450.00
Aurora, Wonder Woman, 1965, MIB........ $550.00
Bandai, Armoured Car (Bogey Wheeled Puma), #K-108, 1970s, MIB $100.00
Bandai, Godzilla, 1984, MIB $50.00
Bandai, Jeep, #PA1, 1970s, MIB........ $35.00
Bandai, Pzkw-IV Heuschrecke (German Army Tank IV Grasshopper), #4254H, 1970s, MIB........ $40.00
Billiken, Batman, type A, 1989, MIB........ $125.00
Billiken, Batman, type B, 1989, MIB $150.00
Billiken, Bride of Frankenstein, 1984, MIB $225.00
Billiken, Creature From the Black Lagoon, 1991, MIB .. $150.00
Billiken, Cyclops, 1984, MIB $225.00
Billiken, Dracula, 1989, MIB........ $175.00
Billiken, Frankenstein, 1988, MIB $150.00
Billiken, Joker, 1989, MIB $150.00
Billiken, Mummy, 1990, MIB $175.00
Billiken, Phantom of the Opera, 1980s, MIB........ $300.00
Billiken, Predator, 1991, MIB........ $80.00
Billiken, She-Creature, 1989, MIB........ $75.00
Billiken, The Thing, 1984, MIP $325.00
Billiken, Ultraman, 1987, MIB........ $65.00
Dark Horse, King Kong, 1992, vinyl, MIB........ $75.00
Dark Horse, Mummy, 1995, MIB $150.00
Dark Horse, Predator II, 1994, MIB $175.00
Eldon, Pink Panther, 1970s, MIB $75.00
Hawk, Bobcat Roadster, 1962, MIB $50.00
Hawk, Cobra II, 1950s, MIB........ $100.00
Hawk, Digger & Dragster, 1963, MIB $125.00
Hawk, Endsville Eddie, 1963, MIP $125.00
Hawk, Frantic Banana, 1965, MIB........ $150.00
Hawk, Freddie Flame Out, 1963, MIP........ $135.00
Hawk, Hidad Silly Surfer, 1964, MIP $125.00
Hawk, Killer McBash, 1963, MIB $175.00
Hawk, Leaky Boat Louie, 1963, MIB $150.00
Hawk, Sling Rave Curvette, 1964, MIB........ $100.00
Hawk, Steel Pluckers, 1965, MIB........ $125.00
Hawk, Thunderbird, Indian Totem Poles, 1966, MIB $50.00
Hawk, Woodie on a Surfari, 1964, MIB $125.00
Horizon, Bride of Frankenstein, 1990s, MIB........ $80.00
Horizon, Dr Doom, Marvel Universe, 1991, MIB........ $65.00
Horizon, Frankenstein, 1990s, MIB........ $75.00
Horizon, Incredible Hulk, Marvel Universe, 1990, MIB ...$50.00
Horizon, Invisible Man, 1990s, MIB $75.00
Horizon, Mole People, Mole Man #2, 1988, MIB........ $75.00
Horizon, Punisher, Marvel Universe, 1988, MIB........ $50.00
Horizon, Robocop, ED-209, MIB $75.00
Horizon, Robocop, Robocop #30, 1992, MIB $75.00
Horizon, Spider-Man, Marvel Universe, 1988, MIB........ $50.00
Horizon, The Thing, Marvel Universe, 1991, MIB $50.00

Hubley, 1932 Chevrolet Coupe, Metal Kit, MIB, $50.00.

Imai, Captain Blue, 1982, MIB $15.00
Imai, Missile Tank BB-1 (Motorized), #524, 1960s, MIB... $400.00
Imai, Orguss, Cable, 1994, MIB $40.00
Imai, Orguss, Incredible Hulk, 1990, MIB $45.00
Imai, Orguss, Spider-Man (new pose), 1994, MIB........ $30.00
ITC, USS Oregon Battleship (Motorized), #H-3680, 1950s, VGIB........ $75.00
Lindberg, Big Wheeler, 1965, MIB........ $100.00
Lindberg, Creeping Crusher, 1965, MIB $50.00
Lindberg, Flintstone's Flintmobile, 1994, MIB $25.00
Lindberg, Flying Saucer, 1952, MIB $200.00
Lindberg, Satan's Crate, 1964, MIB $150.00
Monogram, Bad Machine, 1970s, MIB $60.00
Monogram, Bathtub Buggy, 1960s, MIB (sealed)........ $100.00
Monogram, Battlestar Galactica, Colonial Viper, 1979, MIB...$55.00
Monogram, Battlestar Galactica, Cylon Raider, 1979, MIB .. $55.00
Monogram, Buck Rogers, Marauder, 1970, MIB........ $75.00
Monogram, Dracula, 1983, MIB........ $45.00
Monogram, Elvria Macabre Mobile, 1988, MIB $35.00
Monogram, Godzilla, 1978, MIB........ $100.00

Monogram, Miami Vice Daytona Spider, 1986, MIB, $28.00. (Photo courtesy whatacharacter.com)

Monogram, Model Missile Paket, #MP6, 1950s, MIP........$35.00
Monogram, Sand Crab, 1969, MIB..................................$50.00
Monogram, Snoopy as Joe Cool, 1971, MIB.................. $100.00
Monogram, TV Orbiter, 1959, MIB.............................. $150.00
Monogram, Voyage to the Bottom of the Sea, Flying Sub, 1979, MIB..$50.00
Monogram, Wolfman, 1983, MIB.................................$50.00
MPC, Alien, 1979, MIB (sealed)................................. $100.00
MPC, Barnabas, Dark Shadows, 1968, MIB................... $425.00
MPC, Barnabas Vampire Van, Dark Shadows, 1969, MIB...$275.00
MPC, Batman, Super Powers, 1984, MIB.........................$65.00
MPC, Beverly Hillbillies Truck, 1968, MIB................... $200.00
MPC, Bionic Woman, Bionic Repair, 1976, MIB.............$80.00
MPC, Black Hole, Cygnus, 1979, MIB.......................... $175.00
MPC, Black Hole, Maximillian, 1979, MIB.................. $100.00
MPC, Darth Vader, glow-in-the-dark light saber, 1979, MIB...$50.00
MPC, Dukes of Hazzard, Cooter's Tow Truck, 1981, MIB..$30.00
MPC, Dukes of Hazzard, Daisy's Jeep CJ, 1980, MIB.........$40.00
MPC, Dukes of Hazzard, General Lee, #661, 1979, MIB...$45.00
MPC, Dukes of Hazzard, Sheriff Rosco's Police Car, 1982, MIB.. $30.00
MPC, Empire Strikes Back, Luke Skywalker's Snow Speeder, 1980, MIB...$45.00
MPC, Empire Strikes Back, Snow Destroyer, 1980, MIB..$80.00
MPC, Fonzie & Motorcycle, 1976, MIB...........................$50.00

MPC, Hemi-Cuda Barracuda Street Machine, 1980, MIB (sealed), $45.00. (Photo courtesy serioustoyz.com)

MPC, Hogan's Heroes Jeep, 1968, MIB......................... $125.00
MPC, Incredible Hulk, 1978, MIB (sealed).......................$50.00
MPC, Incredible Hulk Van, 1977, MIB............................$25.00
MPC, Knight Rider, KITT 2000, 1982, MIB.....................$25.00
MPC, Mannix Roadster, 1968, MIB...............................$50.00
MPC, Pirates of the Carribean, Dead Men Tell No Lies, 1972, MIB.. $100.00
MPC, Raiders of the Lost Ark Chase Scene, 1982, MIB...$50.00
MPC, Return of the Jedi, C-3PO, 1983, MIB...................$50.00
MPC, Return of the Jedi, R2-D2, MIB...........................$40.00
MPC, Road Runner & the Beep-Beep T, 1972, MIB.........$75.00
MPC, Six Million Dollar Man, Jaws of Doom, 1975, MIB..$50.00
MPC, Space, 1999, Hawk Spaceship, 1977, MIB.............$55.00
MPC, Space: 1999, Alien Creature & Vehicle, 1976, MIB..$60.00
MPC, Space: 1999, Eagle I Transporter, 1976, MIB....... $130.00

MPC, Star Wars, AT-AT, 1981, MIB..................................$35.00
MPC, Star Wars, Boba Fett's Slave I, 1982, MIB...............$35.00
MPC, Star Wars, Darth Vader TIE Fighter, 1978, MIB.....$35.00
MPC, Star Wars, R2-D2, 1979, MIB................................$35.00
MPC, Strange Changing Time Machine, 1974, MIB........$75.00
MPC, Strange Changing Vampire, 1974, MIB..................$75.00
MPC, Stroker McGurk & Surf Rod, 1960s, MIB........... $150.00
MPC, Sweathogs 'Dream Machine,' 1976, MIB................$45.00
Polar Lights, Jetson Spaceship, #6810, 2001, NRFB..........$50.00

Polar Lights, Lost in Space, The Jupiter 2, 2000, MIB (sealed), $50.00.

Pyro, Design-A-Car, 1950s, MIB, $75.00.
(Photo courtesy serioustoyz.com)

Pyro, Gladiator Show Cycle, 1970, MIB............................$65.00
Pyro, Indian Warrior, 1960s, MIB.....................................$75.00
Pyro, Prehistoric Monsters Gift Set, 1950s, MIB............ $125.00

Pyro, Rawhide, Gil Favor, 1956, MIB $125.00
Pyro, Restless Gun, Deputy, 1959, MIB $65.00
Pyro, Surf's Up !, 1970, MIB $40.00
Renwal, General Patton II Medium Tank, Series M, 1960s, MIB (Sealed) $40.00
Renwal, Visible Man, 1959, 1st issue, unused, M (NM box), A $80.00
Renwal, Visible V8 Engine, 1960s, MIB (sealed) $200.00
Renwal, Visible Woman, 1960, 1st issue, unused, M (NM box), A $165.00
Revell, Alien Invader, w/lights, 1979, MIB (sealed) $50.00
Revell, Amazing Moon Mixer, 1970, MIB $35.00
Revell, Apollo Astronaut on Moon, 1970, MIB $125.00
Revell, Apollo Columbia/Eagle, 1969, MIB (sealed) $100.00
Revell, Ariane 4 Rocket, 1985, MIB $35.00
Revell, Baja Humbug, 1971, MIB $85.00
Revell, Beatles, any member, 1965, MIB, ea $250.00

Revell, Bed Bug Panel Pad, MIB, $45.00.

(Photo courtesy gasolinealleyantiques.com)

Revell, CHiPs, any kit, 1980s, MIB, ea $35.00
Revell, Code Red, Fire Chief's Car, 1981, MIB $25.00
Revell, Disney's Love Bug Rides Again, 1974, MIB $100.00
Revell, Disney's Robin Hood Set #1, 1974, MIB $100.00
Revell, Dr Seuss Horton the Elephant, 1960, MIB $425.00
Revell, Dr Seuss Zoo, Kit #1, 1959, MIB $400.00
Revell, Dr Seuss Zoo, Kit #2, 1960, MIB $525.00
Revell, Dune, Ornithopter, 1985, MIB (sealed) $60.00
Revell, Dune, 1985, Sand Worm, MIB (sealed) $75.00

Revell, Ed 'Big Daddy' Roth, Road Agent, 1960, MIB, $80.00.

Revell, Ed 'Big Daddy' Roth, Angel Fink, 1965, MIB $180.00
Revell, Ed 'Big Daddy' Roth, Drag Nut #1303, 1963, MIB (sealed), A $170.00
Revell, Ed 'Big Daddy' Roth, Fink-Eliminator, 1965, MIB $125.00
Revell, Ed 'Big Daddy' Roth, Mr Grasser, 1964, MIB $100.00
Revell, Flash Gordon & the Martian, 1965, MIB $150.00
Revell, Flipper, 1965, MIB $150.00
Revell, Hardy Boys Van, 1977, MIB $35.00
Revell, Love Bug, 1970s, MIB $50.00
Revell, Magnum PI, any kit, 1980s, MIB, ea $50.00
Revell, McHale's Navy PT-73, 1965, MIB $75.00
Revell, Moon Ship, 1957, MIB $225.00
Revell, Moonraker Space Shuttle, 1979, MIB $25.00
Revell, Penny Pincher VW Bug, 1980, MIB $35.00
Revell, Peter Pan Pirate Ship, 1960, MIB $100.00
Revell, Red October Submarine, 1990, MIB $65.00
Revell, Rif Raf & Hid Spitfire, 1971, MIB $50.00
Revell, Robotech, Commando, 1984, MIB (sealed) $50.00
Revell, Robotech, Condar, 1984, MIB (sealed) $35.00
Revell, Robotech, Defenders Thoren, 1984, MIB (sealed) $35.00
Revell, Space Explorer Solaris, 1969, MIB $125.00

Revell, Superior Bakery, MIB, $35.00.

(Photo courtesy gasolinealleyantiques.com)

Revell, Terrier Missile, 1958, MIB $200.00
Revell, US Army Nike Hercules, 1958, MIB $60.00
Screamin', Friday the 13th's Jason, MIB $125.00
Screamin', Star Wars, Stormtrooper, 1993, MIB $45.00
Screamin', Werewolf, MIB $100.00
Screamin' Contemplating Conquest, 1995, MIB (sealed) $50.00
Strombecker, Disneyland Stagecoach, 1950s, MIB $200.00
Strombecker, Walt Disney's Spaceship, 1958, MIB $300.00
Toy Biz, Ghost Rider, 1996, MIB $30.00
Toy Biz, Hulk, 1996, MIB $25.00
Toy Biz, Spider-Man, w/ or w/o wall, 1996, MIB, ea $25.00
Toy Biz, Storm, 1996, MIB $20.00
Toy Biz, Thing, 1996, MIB $20.00
Toy Biz, Wolverine, 1996, MIB $25.00
Tsukada, Ghostbusters, Stay Puft Man (sm), 1984, MIB $40.00
Tsukuda, Creature From the Black Lagoon, MIB $150.00
Tsukuda, Frankenstein, 1985, MIB $100.00
Tsukuda, Ghostbusters Terror Dog, MIB $125.00
Tsukuda, Metaluna Mutant, MIB $100.00
Tsukuda, Mummy, MIB $100.00
Tsukuda, Wolfman, MIB $100.00

Movie Posters and Lobby Cards

This field is a natural extension of the interest in character collectibles, and one where there is a great deal of activity. Listed here are posters relating to the great monster classics, Disney, westerns, adventure movies, and cartoons.

Davy Crockett, set of eight lobby cards, Walt Disney, 1955, 11x14", EX, $400.00. (Photo courtesy Morphy Auctions)

Abbott & Costello Meet Dr Jekyll & Mr Hyde, 1-sheet, 1953 reprint, 39x25", rolled, EX....$15.00
Aladdin, 1-sheet, Disney, 40x27", NM+....$200.00
Aladdin & His Magic Lamp, 1-sheet, 1975, 41x27", NM ..$60.00
Alice in Wonderland, lobby card, Disney characters on yel, 1942, NM....$45.00
Alien, 1-sheet, title above Alien egg-like image on blk w/gr & yel blaze of light, 1979, 41x27", NM....$350.00
American Graffiti, lobby card, 1973, VG+....$45.00
An American Tail, 1-sheet, 1986, 41x27", NM....$75.00
Back to the Future, 1-sheet, Michael J Fox, 1985, 41x27", NM+....$175.00
Bambi, 1-sheet, 1975, 41x27", EX+....$60.00
Batman, lobby card, Adam West, Burt Ward, Cesar Romero, 1966, EX+....$75.00
Batman, 1-sheet, image of Batman symbol on blk, 1989, 40x27", NM....$75.00
Beauty & the Beast, 1-sheet, dbl-sided, glowing silhouette image on red, Disney, 1992, 40x27", rolled, EX....$250.00
Beetlejuice, 1-sheet, 41x27", NM....$75.00
Beneath the Planet of the Apes, lobby card, astronauts, ape, wrecked ship in blue stairway scene, 1970, 11x14", EX....$20.00
Boy & the Pirates, 3-sheet, 1960, EX....$125.00
Boy Who Cried Werewolf, lobby card, #2, closeup of Werewolf's face, Universal Studios, 1973, NM....$15.00
Bride of Frankenstein, lobby card, 1956, EX+....$150.00
Captain Midnight in Ambushed Ambulance, 1-sheet, 'Chapter 5 in Columbia's Chapter Play,' 1942, EX, A....$575.00
Cassidy of Bar 20, 3-sheet, 'William Boyd as Hopalong Cassidy,' 1938, NM....$1,500.00
Charlotte's Web, 1-sheet, Hanna-Barbera, 1973, EX+....$45.00
Charro, 1-sheet, Elvis, 1969, 41x27", NM....$65.00
Cinderella, lobby card, 1950, VG....$175.00
Cinderella, 1-sheet, 1950, 41x27", NM+....$900.00
Clash of the Titans, ½-sheet, 1981, 22x28", NM....$225.00
Close Encounters of the Third Kind, 1-sheet, Steven Spielberg movie, 41x27", NM+....$100.00
Conan the Destroyer, 1-sheet, looming image of Conan (Schwazenagger) over cast members & horse riders, 1984, 41x27", NM....$90.00
Creature From the Black Lagoon, 6-sheet, Creature holding up man to throw before Golden Gate bridge, 81x81", EX+...$5,000.00
Dangerous When Wet, lobby card, Ester Williams swimming w/Tom & Jerry, NM....$250.00

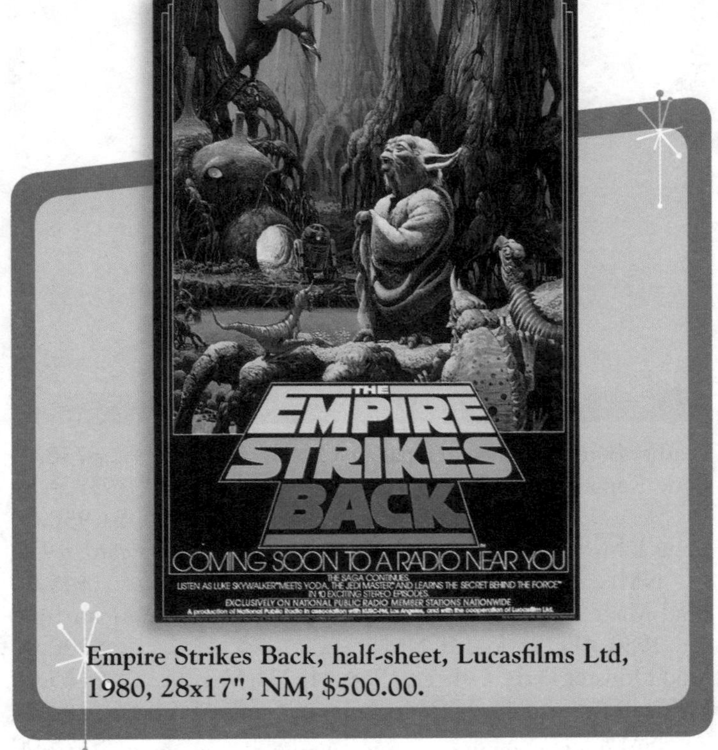

Empire Strikes Back, half-sheet, Lucasfilms Ltd, 1980, 28x17", NM, $500.00.

Dumbo, lobby card, Walt Disney, 1941, 11x14", VG+, A ...$260.00
Empire Strikes Back, 1-sheet, towering image of Darth Vader w/ cast below on lt bl, 1980, 41x27", NM+....$250.00
ET, 1-sheet, fingers touching, 1982, 41x27", NM....$175.00
Forbidden Planet, 1-sheet, Robby the robot holding damsel, Walter Pidgeon & Anne Francis, MGM, 1956 reprint, 40x27", NM....$20.00
Frankenstein, 1-sheet, Boris Karloff, blk & wht on gr background, 1962 reissue, 41x27", EX+....$1,200.00
Ghostbusters, lobby card, 1984, NM....$45.00
Gulliver's Travels, lobby card, 1957 reissue, EX+....$60.00
Harry Potter & the Prisoner of Azkaban, 1-sheet, dbl-sided, closeup of 3 cast member's faces, 2004, 40x27", NM+....$45.00
Heart of the Golden West, 1-sheet, Roy Rogers, Gabby Hayes & Smiley Burnette, 1942, NM+....$600.00

Hey There It's Yogi Bear, lobby card, 1964, EX+ $45.00
In Search of the Castaways (Walt Disney's), lobby card, 1962, NM+ $45.00
Indiana Jones & the Last Crusade, door panel, 'The Man With the Hat Is Back...,' 1989, 60x20", NM $300.00
James & the Giant Peach, 1-sheet, dbl-sided, 1996, NM.. $175.00
Jungle Book (Walt Disney), 1/2 sheet, 1967, 22x28", EX .. $300.00

Laurel and Hardy in Pardon Us, one-sheet, 1931, 41x27", NM, $3,000.00.

Leather Burners, 1-sheet, Hopalong Cassidy, 1943, NM+....$750.00
Lone Ranger Rides Again, 1-sheet, Republic Serial, 1939, NM, A $1,950.00
Long John Silver's Return to Treasure Island, lobby card, 1954, NM..............$45.00
Mad Max, 1-sheet, Mel Gibson w/gun drawn, American Int'l, 1980, 41x27", folded, NM $300.00
Mad Monster Party, 1-sheet, 1968, 41x27", VG $125.00
Mexicali Rose, 1-sheet, Gene Autry & Smiley Burnette, 41x27", NM.............. $275.00
Munster Go Home, lobby card, 1966, 21x28", NM........ $250.00
On Top of Old Smokey, 1-sheet, Gene Autry & Champion, lg image of Gene w/gun drawn against mountain, 41x27", EX, A $300.00
Peter Pan, insert, Disney, 1953, 36x14", NM.............. $475.00
Peter Pan, 3-sheet, 1969 reissue, 81x41", NM $125.00
Pinocchio, lobby card, Walt Disney, 1940, Coachman, Foulfellow & Gideon gathered around table, 11x14", EX, A $58.00
Return of the Jedi, 1-sheet, style A, 1983, 41x27", NM .. $125.00
Robin Hood of Texas, 1-sheet, Gene Aurty, 1947, 41x27", EX.............. $375.00
Robin Hood of the Pecos, 1-sheet, Roy Rogers & Gabby Hayes, 1941, 41x27", EX $500.00
Roll On Texas Moon, 6-sheet, Roy Rogers, Dale Evans, Gabby Hayes & Sons of the Pioneers, 81x81", NM+.......... $750.00
Rootin' Tootin' Rhythm, 1-sheet, Gene Autry & Smiley Burnette, 41x27", NM.............. $375.00

Saludos Amigos (Hello Friends), window card, 'Introducing Joe Carioca...,' Walt Disney, 1942, 22 x 14", VG+, $115.00.

Satan's Satellites, 1-sheet, Commando Cody, Republic 1958, 41x27", NM $100.00
Snow White & the Seven Dwarfs, lobby card, Disney, 1951, VG+ $125.00
Speedway, 1-sheet, Elvis Presley & Nancy Sinatra, 1968, 44x27", VG $85.00
Star Wars, 1-sheet (style-A), looming head image of D Vader in back of Princess Leia & Luke Skywalker, 1977, 41x27", NM+ $600.00
Stardust on the Sage, lobby card, Gene Autry, 1942, NM+..$100.00
Tarzan's Magic Fountain, 3-sheet, Lex Barker, Brenda Joyce, 1949, 81x41", EX.............. $375.00
Tarzan the Ape Man, 1/2-sheet, Johnny Weissmuller, Maureen O'Sullivan, 1954 reissue, 22x28", EX+ $175.00
Texas Bad Man, lobby card, Tom Mix, 1932, NM $300.00
Three Worlds of Gulliver, 3-sheet, Kerwin Mathews, 1960, 81x41", NM $175.00
Time Machine (HG Wells'), insert, Rod Taylor & Yvette Mimieux, linen-backed, 1960, EX.............. $450.00
Tom Mix the Miracle Rider in Chapter 5 'Double Barrelled Doom,' 1-sheet, Mascot Serials, 1935, 41x27", NM, A.............$460.00
Winnie the Pooh & Tigger Too, 1/2-sheet, 1974, 22x28", EX+ $125.00
Young Frankenstin, 1-sheet, Mel Brooks Film, 1974, 41x27", VG..............$85.00
101 Dalmatians, 1-sheet, dbl-sided, Glenn Close & dogs against imge of moon, Disney, 1986, 40x27", rolled, NM+ $10.00
2001: A Space Odyssey, window card, exterior image of space station, Stanley Kubrick Production, 1968, 22x14", EX+ $500.00

Musical Toys

Whether meant to soothe, entertain, or inspire, musical toys were part of our growing-up years. Some were as simple as a wind-up music box, others as elaborate as a lacquered French baby grand piano.

See also Character, TV, and Movie Collectibles; Disney; Rock 'n Roll; Western.

Bingophone II, 12" high, Bing, ca 1909, EX, A, $250.00. (Photo courtesy serioustoyz.com)

Accordion, 2-octave, leatherette case, 10", Horner, NM.. $250.00
Church Organ, litho tin, hand crank, 10", Chein, EXIB .. $150.00
Drum, emb tin & wood w/pigskin top & bottom, leather snare straps on 1 side, 7½" dia, EX, A............................... $140.00
Drum, litho tin side w/Uncle Wiggily's Parade scene, wooden bands w/paper top, w/1 drumstick, 1920s, VG+, A... $460.00

Drum, lithographed tin with Boy Scout scenes, black wooden bands, 8" diameter, 1920s, VG, A, $200.00. (Photo courtesy James D. Julia, Inc.)

Drum, litho tin w/circus graphics, paper heads, spring tension body, wooden sticks, 11" dia, Chein, EX+ $100.00
Drum, litho tin w/Noah's Ark grapics, Ohio Art, NM ... $150.00
Drum, litho tin w/scenes of children on parade, decorative wooden bands w/zigzag string, 9" dia, 1920s, EX...... $500.00
Electric Player Piano, Chein, NM.. $300.00
Farmer in the Dell Music Maker, litho tin, crank-op, Mattel, 1950s, EX $125.00
Golden Banjo, Emenee, 1960s, NMIB $125.00
Golden Piano Accordion, Emenee, EX+IB........................$75.00
Harmonica, detachable horn, Strauss, 1925, EXIB $150.00
Kiddyphone Record Player, litho tin, w/up, 7½" dia, VG... $300.00
Piano, grand style w/internal xylophone, 16", Bliss, EX... $115.00
Piano, Little Bo Peep, wood, 10" H, Marks Bros, VG, A .. $275.00
Piano, pnt wood w/decal trim, wooden stool, 24x23", Schoenhut, EX, A $550.00
Piano, upright, Schoenhut, EX+ $400.00
Play-Away Piano, songbook w/16 tunes to play, Marx, 10x9", EXIB.. $100.00
Showboat Band Set #50, plastic, Spec-Toy-Culars Inc, 1952, EXIB..$35.00

Noah's Ark

What Bible story is more delightful to children than the story of Noah's Ark? What fun it was for children from 'way back when' to spend hours playing with their arks and animals. Some of those wonderful arks have survived the years to become highly sought after by collectors. Most arks with accessories were made of wood and produced in Germany.

Barge, 12" L, wood, pitched hinged roof w/lithoed animal in lithoed window, flat-sided stamped animals, Converse, VG+, A $150.00
Barge, 18" L, wood w/cb pitched roof, flat-sided stamped animals & figures on bases, Converse, G+, A $155.00
Barge, 19" H, wood (pnt), pitched roof, arched windows, 17 prs of animals, 2 figures, G+, A $1,870.00
Barge, 20" L, wood, hinged roof, cream, gr & red detail, 12 prs of carved wood & pnt animals, 6 chicks & Noah, VG, A. $515.00
Barge, 23" L, wood, opening hull/roof/side panel, brn hull, yel simulated log walls, many prs of animals, Noah/wife, EX . $1,980.00
Barge, 23" L, wood, pitched hinged roof, flat-sided stamped animals & figures on bases, Converse, VG, A.............. $225.00

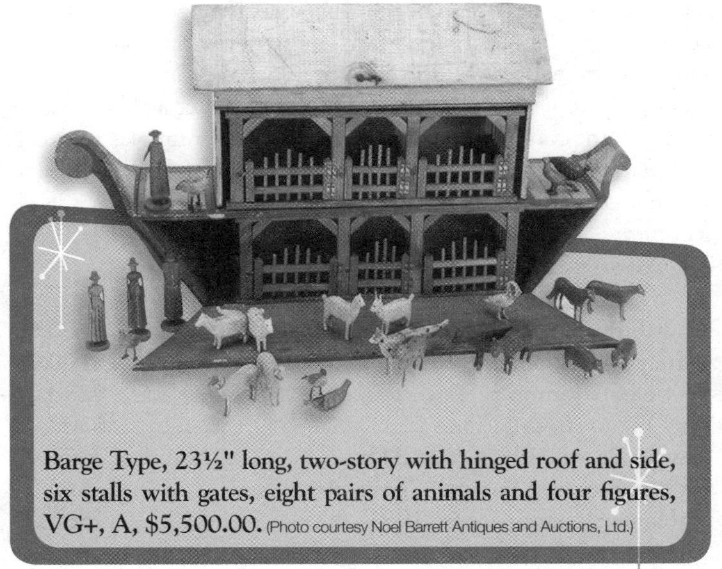

Barge Type, 23½" long, two-story with hinged roof and side, six stalls with gates, eight pairs of animals and four figures, VG+, A, $5,500.00. (Photo courtesy Noel Barrett Antiques and Auctions, Ltd.)

Barge, 26" L, wood (stained), sliding side, 23 prs unpnt wood animals, 4 figures, EX, A.. $1,045.00
Barge, 36" L, wood (pnt & stenciled), 3 hinged compartments, 11 prs of animals, 5 singles, VG+, A.................... $6,050.00
Flat Bottom, 10" L, wood (pnt), hinged roof, 15 prs of animals, 5 singles, 3 figures, VG+, A.................................. $1,760.00
Flat Bottom, 12" L, wood, pitched hinged roof, no animals or figures, Converse, VG+, A..$75.00

Flat Bottom, 17" long, paper lithograph on wood, hinged roof, 28 animals, two figures, G.H. Ireland, Pat. 1878, EX, A, $4,125.00. (Photo courtesy Noel Barrett Antiques and Auctions, Ltd.)

Flat Bottom, 18½" L, wood (paper litho), hinged roof, 7 prs of animals, 15 singles, VG+, A.................................. $550.00
Flat Bottom, 18½" L, wood (pnt), hinged roof, 99 pnt animals & 68 birds, German, VG+, A................................. $1,760.00
Flat Bottom, 23" L, wood (paper litho), slide side, 26 prs of animals, 8 singles, 4 figures, German, VG+, A $2,750.00
Sled Base, 22" L, The Wonder, wood, pitched roof, wood figures, VG+, A.. $440.00

Nodders

Most of the nodders listed are papier-maché or ceramic and made in Japan in the 1960s and 1970s. Some are earlier bisque and ceramic figures made in Germany around the 1930s. They reflect accurate likenesses of the characters they portray and have become popular collectibles. Many of the newer ones were sold as souvenirs from Disney, Universal Studios, and Six Flags amusement parks as well as roadside concessions. Values are for nodders in near mint condition. To calculate prices for examples in excellent or very good condition reduce these prices by 25% to 40%.

For other nodders see also Character, TV, and Movie Collectibles; Santa; other specific categories.

Advisors: Matt and Lisa Adams

Andy Griffith, ceramic, 1992, from $75 to..................... $100.00
Barney Fife, ceramic, 1992, from $75 to......................... $100.00
Beetle Bailey, from $150 to... $250.00
Bugs Bunny, from $175 to... $300.00
Charlie Brown, 1970s, from $45 to $75.00
Charlie Brown as Baseball Player, ceramic.........................$60.00
Chinaman, compo, Japan, 1960s.......................................$65.00
Chinese Boy & Girl, 5½", pr $65.00
Colonal Sanders, 2 different, ea from $150 to................ $250.00
Dagwood, compo, 'Kiss Me' on gr base, 1950s, from $150 to. $200.00
Danny Kaye & Girl Kissing, pr from $150 to.................. $200.00
Dobie Gillis, from $300 to $400.00
Donald Duck, 'Walt Disney World,' sq wht base, from $75 to. $100.00
Donald Duck, Irwin/WDP, from $100 to......................... $125.00
Donald Duck, rnd gr base, 1970s, from $75 to $100.00
Donny Osmond, wht jumpsuit w/microphone, from $100 to.. $150.00
Dr Ben Casey, from $150 to.. $250.00
Dr Kildare, compo, rnd wht base, 1960s, from $150 to... $250.00
Dumbo, rnd red base, from $100 to $150.00
Elmer Fudd, from $200 to $300.00
Foghorn Leghorn, from $200 to....................................... $300.00
Goofy, arms at side, from $100 to $125.00
Goofy, arms folded, from $100 to $125.00
Hobo, compo, Japan, 1960s $60.00
Linus, sq blk base, from $100 to $150.00
Linus as Baseball Catcher, ceramic, Japan..........................$60.00
Little Audrey, from $150 to $200.00
Lt Fuzz (Beetle Bailey), from $150 to $250.00
Lucy, no base, sm, 1970s, from $75 to $100.00

Lucy, Snoopy, and Charlie Brown, each from $75.00 to $125.00.

Lucy as Baseball Player, ceramic, from $75 to................ $100.00
Mammy (Dogpatch USA), from $75 to.......................... $125.00
Mary Poppins, wood, Disneyland, 1960s, from $150 to.. $200.00
Maynard G Krebs Holding Bongos, (Dobie Gillis), from $300 to $400.00
Mickey Mouse, red, wht & bl outfit, Disney World, from $75 to $125.00
Mickey Mouse, red, wht & bl outfit, Disneyland, sq wht base, from $100 to $150.00
Mickey Mouse, yel & red outfit, rnd gr base, from $100 to ..$125.00
Mr Peanut, moves at waist, from $150 to....................... $200.00
NY World's Fair Boy & Girl Kissing, from $100 to......... $125.00
Oodles the Duck (Bozo the Clown), from $200 to $250.00
Peppermint Patti as Baseball Player, ceramic, Japan, from $45 to $60.00
Phantom of the Opera, gr face, from $150 to................. $200.00
Pig Pen, Lego, 1960s, from $100 to $150.00
Pluto, rnd gr base, 1970s, NM, from $100 to $125.00
Porky Pig, from $200 to $300.00

Raggedy Andy, bank, 'A Penny Earned,' from $75 to..... $100.00
Raggedy Ann, bank, 'A Penny Saved,' from $75 to........ $100.00
Roy Rogers, compo, sq gr base, Japan, 1960s, from $150 to... $200.00
Schroeder, sq blk base, Lego, from $100 to $150.00
Sgt Snorkel (Beetle Bailey), from $150 to $250.00
Smokey the Bear, rnd base, from $150 to....................... $200.00
Smokey the Bear, sq base, from $150 to $200.00
Snoopy as Baseball Player, ceramic, Japan, from $45 to $60.00
Snoopy as Flying Ace, 1970s, from $60 to $75.00
Snoopy as Joe Cool, no base, sm, 1970s, from $60 to $75.00
Snoopy as Santa, 1970s, from $60 to.................................$75.00
Space Boy, blk spacesuit & helmet.....................................$75.00
Speedy Gonzoles, from $200 to $300.00
Three Little Pigs, red rnd base, ea from $150 to $200.00
Three Stooges, bisque, set of 3, MIB, from $150 to $175.00
Topo Gigio, w/fruit or w/o fruit, ea from $60 to $75.00
Topo Gigio, 9", Rossini/Japan, 1960s, from $60 to $75.00
Tweety Bird, from $200 to $300.00
Wile E Coyote, from $200 to... $300.00
Winnie the Pooh, rnd gr base, 1970s, from $100 to........ $150.00

Phantom of the Opera and Wolfman, rare, each from $300.00 to $500.00.

Woodstock, no base, sm, 1970s, from $45 to......................$60.00
Woodstock, 1970s, from $45 to $60.00
Woodstock as Baseball Player, ceramic, Japan, from $45 to ..$60.00
Yosemite Sam, from $200 to $300.00
Zero (Beetle Bailey), from $150 to $250.00

Optical Toys

Compared to the bulky viewers of years ago, contrary to the usual course of advancement, optical toys of more recent years have tended to become more simplified in concept.

See also Character, TV, and Movie Collectibles; Disney; View-Master and Tru-View; Western.

Automatic Space Viewer, Stephens, 1950s, EX $175.00
Cinderella Pixie Viewer, Stori-Views, 1950s, complete, NMIB $20.00
Cini Vue, 1939 Golden Gate International/100 Movie Views & Pathegrams, complete, EXIB, A $55.00
Comicscope Viewer, Remington Moris, 1900s, comic strip viewer w/3 comic strips, EX $50.00
Easy Show Motorized Movie Projector, Kenner, 1960s, b/o, MIB $110.00
Flashy Flickers Magic Picture Gun, Marx, 1960s, NMIB, A..$77.00
Give-A-Show Projector, Kenner, 1971-73, features various cartoon characters, MIB $75.00

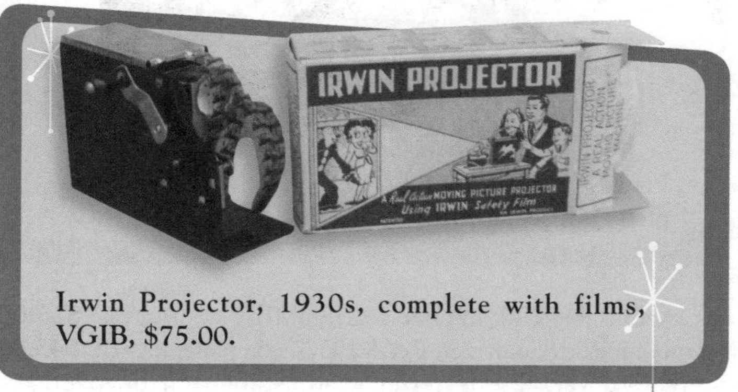

Irwin Projector, 1930s, complete with films, VGIB, $75.00.

Kaleidoscope, Du-All Products, 1940s, leatherette camera shape w/interior glass stems, VG+ $250.00
Kaleidoscope Wonder Wheel, Steven Mfg, 1975, NM......$20.00
Kiddie Kamera, Allied, 1934, features various comic characters, EXIB...$75.00
Komic Kamera, Allied, 1934, features various comic characters, EXIB...$75.00
Magic Lantern, Bing, tin, w/orig glass sliders & instructions, 6½", EX (in cb box) $80.00
Magic Lantern, JS, tin w/CI feet, kerosene lamp w/glass chimney, lens & slides, 9", EXIB.. $150.00
Magic Lantern, Plank, pnt tin, complete w/lamp w/glass chimney, 13 lg format slides, EXIB, A $165.00
Magic Mirror, McLoughlin Bros, paper litho images appears on mercury glass tube, EX (in wooden box).............. $1,500.00
Mickey Mouse Safe-Toy Cinema, Pathescope/England, b/o crank projector w/2 films, 9", EXIB, A $150.00
Movie Viewer Theater, Fisher-Price, 1977-86, #463, MIB...$25.00

Ombro-Cinema, France, early 1900s, features Charlie Chaplin, EX+, $600.00.

Optical Illusions Science Kit, Remco, 1961, NM (orig can)..$25.00

Play N' Show Phono Projector, Kenner, 1969, complete, unused, NMIB, $50.00.

See-Action Football, Kenner, 1973, NMIB $25.00
Starmaster Astronomy Set, Reed, 1950s, complete, EX+IB..$45.00
Stereo Viewer, wood viewer w/adjustable mirror, over 100 various views of mostly European subjects, EX (in divided box) $500.00

Paper Dolls

Turn-of-the-century paper dolls are seldom found today and when they are, they're very expensive. Advertising companies used them to promote their products, and some were printed on the pages of leading ladies' magazines. By the late 1920s, most paper dolls were being made in book form — the doll on the cover, the clothes on the inside pages. Because they were so inexpensive, paper dolls survived the Depression and went on to peak in the 1940s. Although the advent of television caused sales to decline, paper doll companies were able to hang on by making paper dolls representing Hollywood celebrities and TV stars. These are some of the most collectible today. Even celebrity dolls from more recent years like the Brady Bunch or the Waltons are popular. Remember, condition is very important; if they've been cut out, even when they're still in fine condition and have all their original accessories, they're worth only about half as much as an uncut book or box set. Our values are for mint and uncut dolls unless noted otherwise.

For more information, refer to *Price Guide to Lowe and Whitman Paper Dolls, Price Guide to Saalfield and Merrill Paper Dolls* and *20th Century Paper Dolls* by Mary Young, our advisor for this category.

Alice in Wonderland Dolls, Milton Bradley #4100..........$35.00
Angel Face, Gabriel #293 ....$20.00
Animated Cinderella Doll, Milton Bradley #4030..........$30.00
Animated Goldilocks With the Three Bears, Milton Bradley #4101 ....$35.00
Ballerina Dolls, Gabriel #D115, 1956 ....$35.00
Barbie Christie Stacey, Whitman #1976, 1968, from $35 to... $55.00
Bedknobs & Broomsticks, Whitman #1999, 1971, from $35 to.. $55.00
Betsy McCall, Whitman #1969, 1971, from $15 to..........$25.00
Betty Boop Goes to Hollywood, Betty's Store LTD/Trina Robins, 1984, from $20 to $35.00
Betty Grable, Whitman #962, 1946 ....$200.00
Betty Grable, Whitman #989, 1941 ....$300.00
Bewitched, Magic Wand #114, 1965, boxed set $75.00
Blondie, Saalfield #4434, 1968 ....$65.00
Bob Hope & Dorothy Lamour, Whitman #976, 1942 .... $300.00
Brady Bunch, Whitman #4784, 1972..........$45.00
Brenda Lee, Lowe #2785, 1961, from $50 to..........$75.00
Bronco Bess, Milton Bradley #4043, 1950 ....$35.00

Brownie Scout Paper Doll, De Journette Mfg Co, #11-947, EXIB, $30.00.

Buffy, Whitman #1995, 1968, from $35 to..........$45.00
Career Girls, Lowe #1045, 1942..........$75.00
Carol Lynley, Whitman #2089, 1960 ....$70.00
Children in the Shoe, Merrill #1562, 1949..........$40.00
Chitty Chitty Bang Bang, Whitman #1982, 1968, from $30 to..........$45.00
Cinderella, Golden #1545, 1989, from $5 to $10.00
Cindy & Mindy, Whitman #1974, 1960, from $20 to $35.00
Connie Darling & Her Dolly, Saalfield #6092, 1964, from $20 to $30.00
Cute Quintuplets, Western #1818-5, 1964, from $15 to ...$30.00
Cutie Cut Ups, Transogram #4101, 1964..........$35.00
Cyd Charisse, Whitman #2084, 1956 ....$150.00
Daisy & Donald, Whitman, #1990-21, 1978, from $10 to...$20.00
Daisy Dolly, Goldsmith #2005, 1930..........$30.00
Date Time, Saalfield #1754, 1969..........$15.00
Deanna Durbin, Merrill #3480, 1940..........$175.00
Debbie Reynolds, Whitman #1178, 1953 ....$125.00
Dinah Shore, Whitman #977, 1943, from $100 to $200.00
Dionne Quints, Whitman #998, 1935 ....$125.00

Dolls of Other Lands, Whitman #2074, 1963....................$25.00
Dolly Rosycheeks With Her Pretty Dresses & Hats, JW Spears..$150.00
Doris Day Doll, Whitman #1977, 1957..........................$125.00
Dorothy Provine, Whitman #1964, 1962..........................$70.00
Dottie Dress-Up, Dot & Peg Productions, 1950................$35.00
Dr Kildare Play Book, Lowe #955, ca 1963.......................$30.00

Elizabeth Taylor, Whitman #968, 1949, $200.00.

Elly May, Watkins Strathmore #1819A, 1963, from $60.00 to $75.00. (Photo courtesy Greg Davis and Bill Morgan)

Family Affair Dolls (5), Whitman #4767, 1968................$40.00
Farmer Fred, Lowe #523, 1943 ....$25.00
Fay Emmerson, Saalfield #2722, 1952............................$125.00
Flatsy, Whitman #1994, 1970, from $20 to........................$35.00
Flatsy, Whitman #4756, 1969, from $15 to........................$25.00
Flying Nun, Saalfield #5121, 1968 ....$75.00

Flying Nun, Saalfield #6069, 1968, from $75.00 to $100.00. (Photo courtesy Greg Davis and Bill Morgan)

Fonzie, Toy Factory #105, 1976...$25.00
Funny Bunnie Cut-Out Book, McLoughlin Bros #553, 1938..$100.00
Gabby Hayes, Lowe #4171, 1954 ....$60.00
Gene Autry's Melody Ranch, Whitman #990, 1950 ...... $150.00
Gene Tiereny, Whitman #992, 1947.............................. $225.00
Giget Magic Paper Doll, Standard Toycraft #601, 1965 ....$75.00
Gigi Perreau, Saalfield #2605, 1951 ....$75.00
Goldilocks & the Three Bears, Lowe #2561, 1955 ....$35.00
Goldilocks & the Three Bears, Peck-Gandrè, 1988, from $5 to...$10.00
Green Acres, Whitman #4773, 1968 ....$65.00
Gulliver's Travels, Saalfield #1261, 1939........................ $125.00
Hayley Mills Summer Magic Cutouts, Whitman #1966, 1963 . $50.00
Hedy Lamar, Saalfield #2600, 1951 .... $150.00
Heidi, Whitman #1954, 1966...$35.00
Here Comes the Bride, Saalfield #1320, 1967, from $55 to ..$75.00
Holly With Magic Fabric Fashions, Janex #2000, 1971.....$15.00
Ivy With Magic Fabric Fashions, Janex #2001, 1971.........$15.00
Jane Russell, Saalfield #4328, 1955 ....$95.00
Jet Airline Stewardess, Jaymar #913.................................$40.00
Julia, Saalfield #6055, 1970 ....$60.00
Julie Andrews, Saalfield #4424, 1958............................. $125.00
June Allyson, Whitman #970, 1950................................ $175.00
Junior Fashions, Gabriel #D117 ....$70.00
Kewpie Dolls, Saalfield-Artcraft #6088, 1963, from $50 to...$80.00
Lacey Daisy, Kits Inc #1050, 1949....................................$25.00
Laugh In, Saalfield #1324, 1969 ....$40.00
Lennon Sisters, Whitman #1979, 1958.......................... $100.00
Let's Play Paper Dolls, McLoughlin Bros #551, 1938.........$60.00
Li'L Holly, Janex #0130, 1973 ....$15.00
Liddle Kiddles, Whitman #1981, 1967...............................$60.00
Little Audrey, Gabriel #250...$50.00
Little Lulu & Tubby, Whitman #1987, 1974 ....$25.00
Little Miss Christmas & Holly Belle, Merrill #2968, 1965, from $65 to $85.00
Little Miss Muffet, Lowe #2787, 1969, from $15 to...........$25.00
Little Red Riding Hood, Peck-Grandrè, 1988, from $5 to.$10.00

Little Women, Artcraft #5127, from $30 to $40.00
Lucille Ball/Desi Arnaz w/Little Ricky, Whitman #2116, 1953 .... $150.00
Magic Mary, Milton Bradley #4010-1, 1966.......................$30.00

Magic Mary Ann, Milton Bradley #4010-2, $35.00.

Malibu Francie, Whitman #1955, 1973 ....$30.00

Mary and her Little Lamb, J. Ottman, circa 1900, complete in original box, from $200.00 to $300.00.

(Photo courtesy Skinner, Inc.)

Mary Ann Goes to Mexico, Reuben H Lilja #912.............$20.00
Mary Poppins, Whitman #1977, 1973, from $30 to...........$45.00
Mod Fashions Featuring Jane Fonda, Saalfield/Artcraft #4469, 1966, from $45 to $65.00
Mother Goose Village Cut Outs, Harter #H-164, 1935.....$30.00
Mouseketeers, Whitman #1974, 1963..............................$85.00
Munsters, Whitman #1959, 1966................................. $125.00
Muppet Babies Paper Doll Book, Random House, 1984....$10.00
My Best Friend, Whitman #1978-23, 1980.......................$10.00
My Doll Jack/Jill, Gabriel #D78/#D79, ea.........................$40.00
Nancy, Whitman #1971, 1971 ....$30.00
National Velvet, Whitman #1948, 1962..........................$65.00
National Velvet, Whitman #1958, 1961..........................$65.00
Nurses, Whitman #1975, 1963, from $40 to $65.00

Ozzie & Harriet, Saalfield #4319, 1954 .... $125.00

Partridge Family, Saalfield #6050, 1971, $75.00.

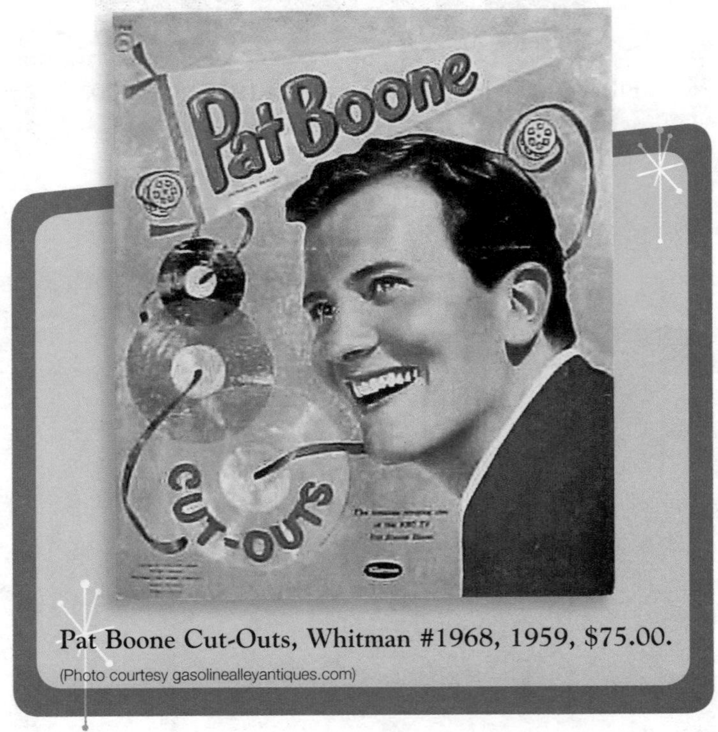

Pat Boone Cut-Outs, Whitman #1968, 1959, $75.00.

(Photo courtesy gasolinealleyantiques.com)

Patty Duke, Whitman #4775, 1965.................................$45.00
Patty Duke Fashion Dolls, Milton Bradley, #4441, 1963...$50.00
Pebbles, Wonder Books #6685, 1974, from $15 to............$25.00
Pebbles Flintstone, Whitman #1997, 1963, from $40 to ...$50.00
Petticoat Junction, Whitman #1954, 1964 .... $100.00
Pollyanna, Whitman #995, 1941...................................... $100.00
Raggedy Ann & Andy, Whitman #1979, 1966..................$30.00
Raggedy Ann & Andy, Whitman #1987-32, 1980 ....$15.00
Raggedy Ann Cutout Dolls, Milton Bradley #4106/Johnny Gruelle, 1941... $100.00

Robin Hood and Maid Marian, Saalfield #2748, 1956, $75.00. (Photo courtesy Mary Young)

Rock Hudson, Whitman #2087, 1957..............................$65.00
Round About Dolls on Parade, McLoughlin Bros #2992, 1941.. $80.00
Sandra Dee, Saalfield #4417, 1959...................................$75.00
Sandy, Western #1805D, 1964, from $8 to.........................$12.00
School Days, Gabriel, #D118 ....$50.00
Sheree North, Saalfield #4420, 1957............................ $100.00
Shirley Temple, Whitman #1986, 1976 ....$20.00
Snap-On Paper Dolls, Gabriel #118, 1958.........................$25.00
Sonja Henie, Merrill #3418, 1941 .... $250.00
Strawberry Shortcake Playhouse, Random House, 1980 ...$15.00
Sunshine Family, Whitman #1980, 1977 ....$12.00
Suzie Sweet, Grinnell #N2009, 1940 ....$40.00
Tammy & Her Family, Whitman #1997, 1964...................$75.00

Sweathogs (Welcome Back Kotter), Toy Factory #108, 1976, $30.00.

That Girl, Saalfield #1351, 1967, from $45 to $75.00
This Is the House That Jack Built, Harter #H-169, 1935..$85.00
Tiny Chatty Twins, Whitman #1985, 1963.......................$45.00
Tuesday Weld, Saalfield #4432, 1960 ....$70.00
Tuesday Weld, Saalfield #5112, 1960 ....$60.00
Two-Gun Pete, Milton Bradley #4042, 1950 ....$35.00
Velva Doll (Jill), Kingston #D21, 1932............................$30.00
Vera Miles, Whitman #2086, 1957 .... $150.00
Waltons, Whitman #4334, 1974, boxed set.......................$30.00
Wedding Belles, Dot & Peg Productions, 1945.................$50.00
White House Party Dresses, Merrill #1550, 1961, from $35 to.. $55.00
Wide Awake & Fast Asleep Doll, Samuel Gabriel & Sons #D114...$100.00
Winking Winky, Whitman #4754, 1969...........................$18.00
Winnie the Pooh & Friends, Whitman #1977-24, 1980, from $15 to $25.00
Wishnik, Whitman #1965, 1965, from $30 to $40.00

Paper-Lithographed Toys

Following the development of color lithography, early toy makers soon recognized the possibility of using this technology in their own field. By the 1800s, both here and abroad, toys ranging from soldiers to involved dioramas of entire villages were being produced of wood with colorful and well detailed paper lithographed surfaces. Some of the best known manufactures were Crandell, Bliss, Reed, and McLoughlin. This style of toy remained popular until well after the turn of the century.

Advisors: Mark and Lynda Suozzi

See also Black Americana; Dollhouses; Games; Puzzles; Santa; Schoenhut.

Block Set, Alphies ABC Blocks, Schoenhut, ca 1916, VGIB...$165.00
Block Set, Baby's ABC Blocks, 12 blocks w/jungle & farm animals, 3½x2½x1½" ea, EXIB (box lid w/Santa & child)..... $2,475.00
Block Set, Circus Menagerie, McLoughlin Bros, 1898, 6-pc, EX+, A $1,200.00

Block Set, Mother Goose, Singer, set of 27 with six different themes, VG+IB, A, $1,980.00. (Photo courtesy Morphy Auctions)

Block Set (Double), German, circus scenes, 2 sets of 6 ea w/12 guide sheets, VG+IB (12x16" box), A $660.00
Boat, Admiral Battleship, 20", EX, A $1,760.00
Boat, Cass Battleship, 15½", EX, A $715.00
Boat, City of Chicago Sidewheeler, 12½", EX, A $1,540.00

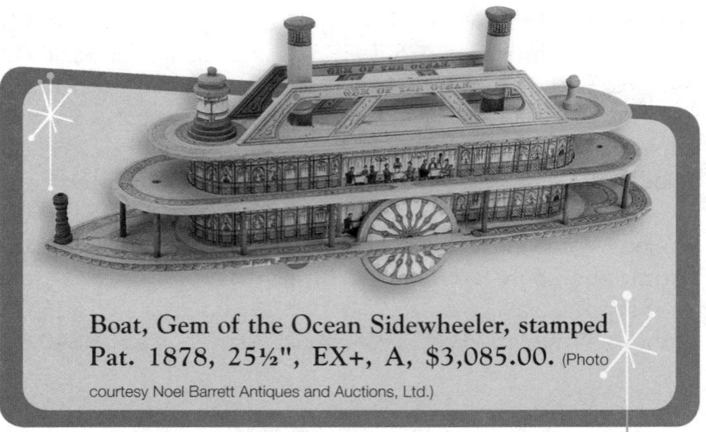

Boat, Gem of the Ocean Sidewheeler, stamped Pat. 1878, 25½", EX+, A, $3,085.00. (Photo courtesy Noel Barrett Antiques and Auctions, Ltd.)

Boat, Japanese Battleship, 15", EX, A $935.00
Boat, Philadelphia Battleship, Bliss, 1880s, 30", EX $1,400.00
Boat, Pilgrim Side-Wheeler, Reed, ca 1895, 28", EX ... $3,500.00
Boat, Texas Battleship, 17½", EX $1,150.00
Boat, US Columbia Battleship, Bliss, 25½", some rstr, A ... $1,200.00
Boat, Volunteer Fishing Ship, Reed, ca 1883, 3 masts, 2 figures on deck, 32" L, rstr, A $1,050.00
Game, Brownie Band (Ten Pin), Reed, complete, EXIB, A .. $1,760.00

Firehouse and Horse-Drawn Fire Pumper, Bliss, circa 1895, EX+, $2,500.00. (Photo courtesy McMasters Harris Auctions)

Game, Buster Brown Bean Bag, Bliss, 1910s, 10x24", EX .. $575.00
Game, Dude (Marble Toss), EXIB $525.00
Game, Humpty Dumpty Marble Game, Reed, 25" L, VG ... $750.00
Game, Jolly Marble Game, Bliss, ca 1892, 19" L, EX+, A $975.00
Game, Mother Goose Pop-Up, Bliss, when lever is pulled different MG characters pop up, 11x18x6", VG, A $515.00
Game, Nine Pins, McLoughlin Bros, nursery rhyme characters lithoed on board on wood bases, 10" (tallest), VG+, A $440.00
Game, Reed's Game of Baseball, EXIB, A $1,320.00
Game, Ring a Sailor, Parker Bros, EXIB $175.00
Game, Rubber Ball Shooting Gallery, Schoenhut, w/gun, VG $675.00
Game, Shuttle Battledorf, Bliss, 15" W, G, A $440.00
Game, Windmill, w/up, target figure standing in archway, no accessories, 17" H, VG+ $100.00
Game, World's Educator, Reed, EXIB $450.00
Horse-Drawn Chariot, Bliss, 23" L, EX, A $3,575.00
Marble Toy, Christopher Columbus Tower, Reed, ca 1892, 58" H, VG+, A $5,500.00
Marble Toy, Jack & Jill, Reed, 14" L, EX, A $660.00
Marble Toy, Joker Marble Drop, Reed, 23" W, VG+ $500.00
Marble Toy, Marble Arch, Reed, 15" W, EX $250.00
Marble Toy, Maypole, spring wire coiled around pole w/4 children attached by ribbon, Bliss, 13½" H, G+, A $525.00
Marble Toy, Tip I Marble Game, Reed, 17" H, VG+, A .. $275.00
Nesting Blocks, Fabrication Francaise, alphabet & pictures, 7-pc, lg is 7½x6", EX+, A $525.00
Nesting Blocks, Gabriel, ca 1919, 7-pc, alphabet, numbers & graphics, VG, A $220.00
Nesting Blocks, Germany, alphabet, kids & dogs, 7-pc, 20" H overall, EX, A $385.00
Nesting Blocks, The Circus Nested Blocks, w/SBCs & circus scenes, 6-pc, 6" lg, EX, A $715.00
New Pretty Village, McLoughlin Bros, cb, complete, EXIB .. $325.00
Noah's Ark, Bliss, 12 cb litho animals on wooden bases illustrating ABC's, 9" L, VG+, A $1,430.00

Pansy Stage Coach, Bliss, 1890, 30" long, EX+, $4,500.00. (Photo courtesy Bertoia Auctions)

Pony Circus Horse-Drawn Wagon, Gibbs, ca 1910, 2 horses w/articulated legs, MSW, 19", EX+ $450.00
Punch & Judy Musical Roly Stage, lithoed characters, ca 1884, 8½" H, VG $400.00
Punch & Judy Rocker Toy, litho cb & wood w/puppet show & audience scene, plays chimes, 8½" H, VG+, A $330.00
Puzzle, Santa Claus Cube Puzzle/The Night Before Christmas, shows Santa w/toys at fireplace, 20-pc, 14x11", EXIB, A $1,650.00
Train, Boston & Albany RR Coach, Mason & Converse, flanged wheels, 11" L, EX, A $440.00
Train, Golden Gate Special, Bliss, ca 1889, US Grant locomotive, tender & American Palace Car, 37", EX....... $7,150.00
Train/Block Set, New York Central Rail Road, Bliss, 2-pc train w/complete set of ABC blocks, 12" L, EX, A $975.00

Pedal Cars and Other Wheeled Vehicles

Just like Daddy, all little boys (and girls as well) are thrilled and happy to drive a brand new, shiny car. Today both generations search through flea markets and auto swap meets for cars, boats, fire engines, tractors, and trains that run not on gas but pedal power. Some of the largest manufacturers of wheeled goods were AMF (American Machine and Foundry Company), Murray, and Garton. Values depend to a very large extent on condition, and those that have been restored may sell for $1,000.00 or more, depending on the year and mode. The following listings are in original condition unless noted otherwise.

Advisor: Nate Stoller

Airplane (Air Mail CN 67), Steelcraft, top-wing, 3-wheeled, gold w/orange trim, 46" L, EX, A $1,980.00

Airplane (Air Mail No 5), top-wing, 3-wheeled (wood), red w/yel pinstripe detail, 63", G, A $2,585.00

Airplane (Little Jim), Steelcraft/J.C. Penney, 49", EX, A, $11,000.00. (Photo courtesy Noel Barrett Antiques and Auctions, Ltd.)

Airplane (Navy Patrol), Murray, 3-wheeled, silver w/bl & red trim, 48", EX, A $1,540.00

Airplane (Pursuit), Murray, silver w/red detail, 3 BRT w/red disk wheels, chrome hubs, 47", EX rstr $165.00

Buick, Steelcraft, V-shaped windshield, chrome-like bumper, lights, hood trim & hubs, disk wheels, 35", EX rstr $2,100.00

Car (6-638 on License Plate), Gendren, 3-pc windshield, ballon tires w/rubber slip-ons, spoke wheels, 56" L, VG, A.. $9,200.00

Casey Jones/Cannon Ball Express Train Engine No 9, BRT w/4 perforated spoke wheels, red & blk w/yel trim, 40" L, EX $1,550.00

Chevrolet, 1930, NP mascot windshield, curved seat, fenders & running boards, rubber tires, disk wheels, 36", rstr .. $2,500.00

Chrysler (1941), Steelcraft, 37", rstr, A $4,125.00

Dolphin Boat, Murray, 40", VG $550.00

Earth Mover w/Payload Dump, yel w/blk & wht trim, wht-wall tires, 47", VG $800.00

Fire Chief Car, ADF license plate, 2 ladders, wht-wall tires w/spokes, bell on radiator, 64" L, EX rstr, A........................ $2,575.00

Fire Chief Car (Deluxe), Toldeo, 57", EX rstr, A......... $2,185.00

Fire Chief/Jet Flow Drive, Murray, red w/yel trim, bell on hood, VG, A $600.00

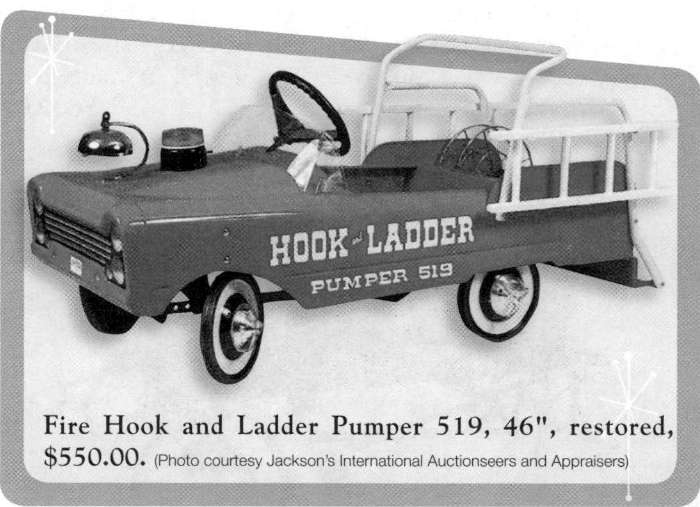

Fire Hook and Ladder Pumper 519, 46", restored, $550.00. (Photo courtesy Jackson's International Auctioneers and Appraisers)

Gilmore Tank Truck, C-style cab, wht & blk w/ad decals, BRT w/red disk wheels & chrome hubs, 54", EX rstr, A .. $575.00

Gulf 24-hr Service Wrecker, orange w/blk wench, blk wheels w/NP hubs, flip-down windshield, 49", EX rstr, A....... $780.00

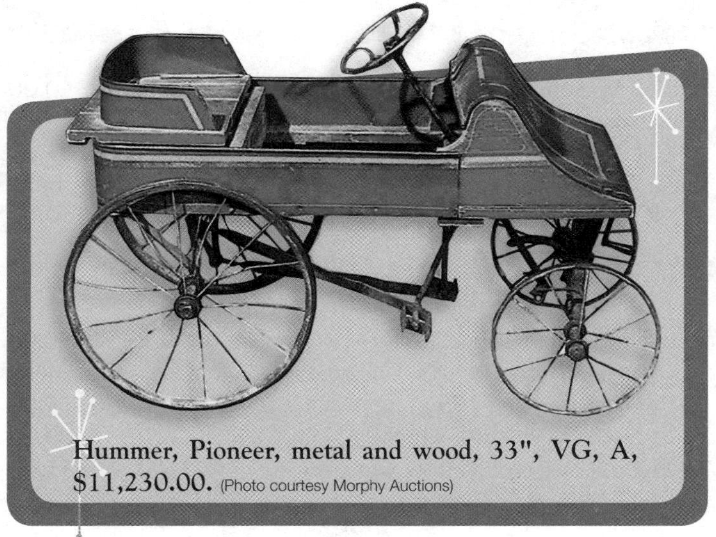

Hummer, Pioneer, metal and wood, 33", VG, A, $11,230.00. (Photo courtesy Morphy Auctions)

Kidillac, Garton, 1960s, chain drive, working headlights & horn, complete, NM rstr $2,000.00

Mogul Pedal Car, American National, early model w/bench seat, wood spoke wheels, red & blk, gold trim, 48" L, VG, A $2,750.00

Packard, American National, w/roof, side spare & running boards, BRT, 28", EX, A $16,500.00

Packard, Gendron, open w/bench seat, fold-down windshield, rear luggage trunk, disk wheels, gr w/red trim, 54", G+, A $7,700.00

Police Sergeant Car, Murray, 36", rstr $350.00

Pontiac Station Wagon, Murray, 1949, maroon & tan w/wht windshield & rear railing, chrome hubs, 47", G, A... $600.00

Racer #8, Irwin, plastic, red w/silver trim, blk rubber tires w/wht trim, 55", VG $350.00

Ranch Wagon, Garton, chain drive, electric lights, antenna, 45", rstr, A $250.00

Ranch Wagon, Murray, 1940s, Ball Bearing Drive on sides, chrome windshield & hubs, 48", prof rstr, A............ $200.00
Sand & Gravel Dump Truck, Murray, working dump bed, yel, mk Jet Flow Drive, wht-line tires w/chrome hubs, 45", G+....... $950.00
Speedway Pace Car 500, Murray, 1958, wht w/blk & orange trim, 35", rstr, A.. $600.00

Star Pedal Car, American National, octagonal steering wheels, spoke wheels, 32", restored, $350.00.
(Photo courtesy Randy Inman Auctions)

Station Wagon, Murray, 1940s, 36", G+, A.................... $350.00
Studebaker, Murray, dk bl w/wht detail, BRT w/wht disk wheels, 34", EX rstr.. $285.00
Super Sport, Murray, 1953, orange, wht-wall tires, silver hubs, EX, A $2,250.00

WAGONS

Aero-Flite, 1930s, electric lights, red w/wht trim, 47", EX...$2,350.00
Auto-Wheel Coaster, wood w/stenciled name on sides, metal spoke wheels, 42", G... $375.00
Flyer, Fisher, wood, disk wheels, 45" G........................... $100.00
Jet Flyer, 1950s, red w/blk & wht trim, w/'wings,' NM, A .$55.00

Lindy Flyer, 1933 World's Fair, electric lights, VG, A, $1,035.00. (Photo courtesy Morphy Auctions)

Skippy Airflow, 1930s, electric lights, 48", rstr $1,500.00

MISCELLANEOUS

Good Humor Cycle, 3-wheeled, chain-drive, w/bell, wht w/lt bl, orig decals, 36", VG+ $1,400.00

Jet Mobile, 1950s, 36", G, $1,250.00.
(Photo courtesy Randy Inman Auctions)

Pioneer Handcar, Gendron, 2 sm front & 2 lg back disk wheels, wood seat w/decal, 30" L, VG, A $390.00
Scooter, red w/yel pinstripe detail, wht grips, 42", EX rstr, A .. $90.00

Scooter (Henley Roll About), wood with four spoke wheels, 28", EX, A, $400.00.
(Photo courtesy Morphy Auctions)

Soap Box Derby Car, wood, w/red, wht & bl Soap Box Derby shield, disk wheels, VG, A $440.00
Wonder Bread Sit-N-Ride Rocket, no pedals, gear shift w/knob, 26", M, A $2,185.00

Penny Toys

Penny toys were around as early as the late 1800s and as late as the 1920s. Many were made in Germany, but some were made in France as well. With few exceptions, they ranged in size from 5" on down; some had moving parts, and a few had clockwork mechanisms. Although many were unmarked, you'll sometimes find them signed 'Kellermann,' 'Meier,' 'Fischer,' or 'Distler,' or carrying an embossed company logo such as the 'dog and cart' emblem. They were made of lithographed tin with exquisite detailing — imagine an entire carousel less than 2½" tall. Because of a recent surge in collector interest, many have been crossing the auction block of some of the country's large galleries. Most of our values are prices realized from some of these auctions.

Child in Carriage Playing With Doll, marked Gesch, 3", NM, $750.00. (Photo courtesy Morphy Auctions)

Aeroplane w/Pilot, Meier, pilot seated on top wing, 4 props & wheels, 3" L, G, A.................. $570.00
Air Plane Spinning Toy, Einfalt, 2 planes on rod, 7" H, EX.. $825.00
Alligator on Wheels, Germany, articulated head & tail, 4¾" L, VG, A.................. $65.00
Alter w/Crucifix, Meier, alter opens to reveal compartment, 3¾" H, EX, A.................. $330.00
Bird Cage, Meier, bird on perch, opening door, 3¼", VG, A ... $165.00
Boar on 4-Wheeled Platform, Germany, 2½" L, VG+, A . $220.00
Boat (Gunboat), Meier, w/'smoke' coming out of stack, 4¼", VG, A.................. $250.00
Boat (Launch), Fischer, railed, w/flag, 3-wheeled, 4½", EX, A.................. $825.00
Boat (Ocean Liner), Fischer, 2 stacks, 3-wheeled, inertia drive, 4¼", EX, A.................. $220.00
Boat (Ocean Liner), Meier, 2 stacks, wht w/lt bl & red trim, 4½", EX, A.................. $385.00
Boat (Sailboat), w/paper sail, inertia drive, 3¾", NM, A .. $715.00
Boat (Sailor on Deck), Meier, 4½", VG, A.................. $250.00
Boat (Side-Wheeler), Meier, 3¼", EX, A.................. $300.00
Boat w/driver & #5 flag, Germany, 6½", VG, A.................. $250.00
Boy Seated on Sled, Levy, marked UTCC Chicago Ill & Made in Germany, 2½" L, VG+, A.................. $225.00
Boy Waving Sausage at Dog on 4-Footed Platform, Meier, 4" L, G, A.................. $415.00
Camel w/Backpack, Meier, non-wheeled version, 2¾" L, VG+, A.................. $360.00
Carousel w/Horses & Riders, Meier, 2½" H, EX, A.................. $450.00
Chinaman w/Parasol Seated on 4-Wheeled Platform, Distler, 2¾" L, VG+, A.................. $300.00
Clock w/Clown Marquee, Germany, w/up, w/pendulum, 4¼", EX, A.................. $825.00
Clown & Donkey on 4-Footed Platform, Meier, lever action, 3¾" L, VG+, A.................. $525.00
Clown in Rolling Barrel, marked DC Kenny Co, 2½", VG, A.................. $200.00
Clowns (2) on Bar Hitting Ball Back & Forth, 4½", EX, A .. $275.00
Dog & Monkey (3-Wheeled), Germany, dog in dress w/fan being assisted by dressed monkey, 3¼", EX, A.................. $1,540.00
Dog House Bank, 2½" L, EX, A.................. $300.00
Dog on 4-Wheeled Platform, Distler, head turned, wide-eyed, neck scarf, 2½", VG+, A.................. $440.00

Dog Walking Dog on Four-Wheeled Platform, marked Gesch KICO Germany, 4", VG, A, $550.00. (Photo courtesy Morphy Auctions)

Dray Wagon, Germany, w/driver, simulated spoke wheels, chain drive, 3", VG, A.................. $195.00
Elephant Cart, Fischer, nodding head, 5" L, VG, A.................. $220.00
Elephant House Bank, 2¾" H, G+, A.................. $330.00
Elephant on 4-Wheeled Platform, Distler, w/spring trunk, 2½" L, VG+, A.................. $220.00
Elephant w/Howdah on 4-Wheeled Platform, Meier, 3" L, EX.................. $525.00
Elves (2) Sawing Log on 4-Wheeled Platform, Germany, 4" L, EX, A.................. $400.00
Field Kitchen Auto, Meier, w/cast-metal driver, cooker w/opening lid, 4", EX, A.................. $600.00
Fieldpost Cycle, Distler, w/driver, 4½" L, EX+.................. $660.00
Fieldpost Truck, Distler, w/driver, 3¼" L, NM, A.................. $715.00
Fire Engine, Germany, open, w/driver & rear figure facing backwards, 3" L, EX, A.................. $500.00
Garage w/Limousine, 2-door opening, 3½", VG, A.................. $110.00
Garage w/Limousine & Roadster, Kellerman, 3½x3½", VG+ . $300.00
Garage w/Racer, Germany, 'brick' garage, yel racer w/bl & red trim, flat driver, disk wheels, 4", EX+, A.................. $250.00
General Bus #NS293, Germany, 4" L, VG, A.................. $225.00

Girl in Hat in Swing, Distler, 2¾" H, EX, A $200.00
Girl Playing w/Doll in Baby Carriage, 3", NM $825.00
Girls (2) in Double Swing, Meier, 3¼" H, VG+, A $275.00
Goat Cart, Germany, female rider w/hands in a muff, 3¾", G+, A $275.00
Goat on 4-Wheeled Platform, German, articulated, 4" L, EX, A $1,000.00
Highchair w/Child, Fischer, transforms from a highchair to a play table, 4" H, VG, A $165.00
Horn (Ferris Wheel), 3¾", VG+ $100.00
Horn (Horse Race), 4½", VG+ $100.00
Horn (Merry-Go-Round), 4", EX, A $135.00
Horn (Performing Dog), 4" L, EX+, A $165.00
Horse w/Rider on 4-Wheeled Platform, German, 3", VG, A .. $400.00

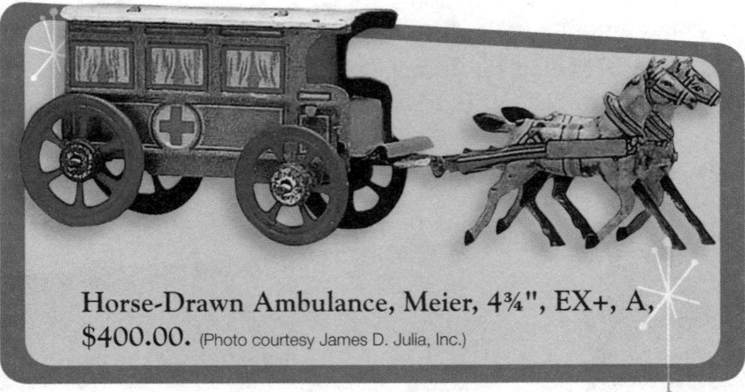

Horse-Drawn Ambulance, Meier, 4¾", EX+, A, $400.00. (Photo courtesy James D. Julia, Inc.)

Horse-Drawn Cab, Fischer, single horse, driver seated on high open seat, enclosed cab, 4½" L, EX, A $300.00
Horse-Drawn Cab, Meier, single horse, family lithoed in windows, spoke wheels, no driver, 4¾", VG, A $140.00
Horse-Drawn Open 4-Wheeled Carriage, Meier, single horse, w/driver on high open seat, 4¾", EX, A $288.00
Horse-Drawn Trolley, Germany, 3 curtained windows ea side, front & back platforms, 4½", VG, A $400.00
Hot Air Balloons/Zeppelin Gondola Ride, 4", EX, A .. $3,300.00
Jigger on Footed Box, Distler, hand-crank, 3¾" H, EX, A .. $465.00

Jockey on Horse on Four-Wheeled Platform, Fischer, 3" long, EX+, A, $720.00. (Photo courtesy James D. Julia, Inc.)

Jockey on Horse on 4-Wheeled Platform, Germany, 4" L, A ... $200.00
Jockey on Rocking Horse, Meier, 3¾", VG, A $300.00
Jockey on Rocking Horse, Meier, 3¾", NM, A $900.00
Limousine, Germany, doorless cab w/driver, lady passenger lithoed in rear window, 3", EX, A $350.00
Limousine, Germany, lady & boy lithoed in windows, w/driver, 3", EX, A $350.00
Limousine w/Driver, Germany, open car w/spoke wheels, 5", VG, A $165.00
Lion on 4-Wheeled Platform, Meier, 3" L, EX, A $465.00
Locomotive, Germany, 'steam' coming from stack, red w/bl, blk & yel trim, 4", VG, A $200.00
Man Feeding Dog on Platform, Germany, lever-action, 4" L, EX, A $450.00
Monkey on All Fours on 4-Wheeled Platform, Germany, 2½", G+, A $275.00
Monkey on Ladder, Distler, w/counter weight, 7" H, EX, A .. $200.00
Motorcyclist, Germany, prewar, driver w/orange & wht outfit, turq cycle, 4" L, NM, A $1,300.00
Mule on 4-Wheeled Platform, Germany, 3" L, EX, A $550.00

Noah's Ark, Germany, 4¾", EX, $650.00.
(Photo courtesy Bertoia Auctions)

Omnibus, Fischer, 4½" L, VG+, A $200.00
Omnibus (Electric), Meier, passengers atop & lithoed in windows, 3¼" L, G, A $250.00
Ostrich Cart w/Jockey, Meier, marked Ges Gesch, 4" L, VG+, A $720.00
Pool Player, Germany, prewar, man at end of pool table, 4" L, VG, A $75.00
Punch & Judy Theater, Meier, 2 figures interacting, lever action, 3½" H, EX, A $770.00
Punch & Judy Theater Bank, lithoed scene, 3" H, VG+, A .. $275.00
Punch on 4-Wheeled Platform, marked HA Depose on base, 4" H, VG+, A $75.00
Rabbit in Stake Wagon, Fischer, rabbit in lithoed clothes steering wagon, 3" L, EX, A $900.00
Racer, Fischer, flat rear end curves up, spoke wheels, w/driver, 4¾", VG+, A $245.00
Racer, Germany, flat upswept back, w/driver, blk & bl w/yel trim & spoke wheels, 5" L, VG, A $150.00
Racer #32, German, w/driver, 5", EX $550.00
Red Cross Touring Car, Meier, open w/red cross on hood & flag, w/driver & 2 passengers, 5¼", EX, A $600.00
Sailboat w/Sailor on 4-Wheeled Base, Gesch, 4", VG .. $2,200.00

Santa (Father Christmas) Pulling Sled With Box, 3½", EX, A, $6,050.00.
(Photo courtesy Morphy Auctions)

Slide Viewer, paper roll depicting soldiers & battle scenes, 1¾" L, VG, A $330.00
Soldiers (2) Squaring Off w/Rifles, Gesch, 4", NM, A.... $385.00

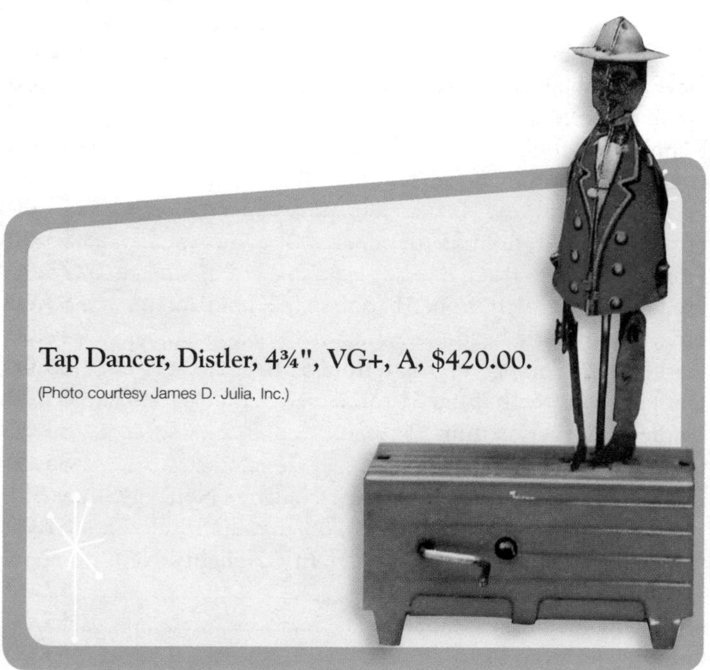
Tap Dancer, Distler, 4¾", VG+, A, $420.00.
(Photo courtesy James D. Julia, Inc.)

Taxi Cab, Distler, open w/convertible top, spoke wheels, w/driver, 3" L, A.......... $415.00
Telefon 946, German, 4½", EX, A.......... $200.00
Tiger on 4-Wheeled Platform, 3½" L, VG+, A $385.00
Touring Car, Fischer, open, wht w/red & gold trim, driver & passenger, spoke wheels, 4" L, VG+ $415.00
Touring Car, Germany, open w/driver, working headlights, 4½", NM, A.......... $800.00
Train Set, Hess, 04-pc, locomotive/tender combo & 3 passenger cars, NMIB, A.......... $450.00
Train Set, Hess, 7-pc set w/2 #575 passenger cars, NMIB, A $700.00
Train Set, Hess, 8-pc, locomotive #575/tender combo, 1 boxcar/2 #575 passenger cars/3 open cars, EXIB, A.......... $550.00
Train Set, Hess, 10-pc set w/#575 locomotive/tender combo, EXIB, A.......... $225.00
Truck #245, Germany, van roof covers open seat w/driver, 4", VG, A $350.00
Whistle (Airplane), France, 4¼" L, VG+, A $165.00
Whistle (Squirrel in Cage), marked France EC Depose, 4½", VG, A $200.00
Wild Boar on 4-Wheeled Platform, Germany, 3" L, EX, A..$250.00

PEZ Dispensers

PEZ was originally designed as a breath mint for smokers, but by the 1950s, kids were the target market, and the candies were packaged in the dispensers that we all know and love today. There are several hundred variations to collect with more arriving on the store shelves everyday. Although early on collectors seemed to prefer the dispensers without feet, that attitude has changed, and now it's the character head on which they concentrate. Feet were added in 1987, so if you were to limit yourself to only 'feetless' dispensers, your collection would be far from complete. Some dispensers have variations in color and design that can influence their values. Don't buy any that are damaged, incomplete, or that have been tampered with in any way; those are nearly worthless. For more information refer to *A Pictorial Guide to Plastic Candy Dispensers Featuring PEZ* by David Welch and *Collector's Guide to PEZ* by Shawn Peterson.

Advisor: Richard Belyski

Aardvark, w/ft.......... $5.00
Angel, no ft.......... $65.00
Arlene, w/ft, pk, from $3 to $5.00
Asterix Line, Asterix, Obelix, Roman or Getafix $5.00
Baloo, w/ft.......... $30.00
Bambi, no ft $50.00
Barney Bear, no ft $40.00
Barney Bear, w/ft.......... $30.00
Baseball Glove, no ft.......... $150.00
Batgirl, no ft, soft head $160.00
Batman, no ft $15.00
Batman, no ft, w/cape $125.00
Batman, w/ft, bl or blk, ea from $3 to.......... $5.00

Betsy Ross, no feet, $150.00.

Bouncer Beagle, w/ft $5.00
Boy, w/ft, brn hair $3.00
Bozo, no ft, die-cut $150.00
Bubble Man, w/ft $3.00
Bubble Man, w/ft, neon hat $3.00
Bugs Bunny, no ft $15.00
Bugs Bunny, w/ft, from $1 to $3.00
Bullwinkle, no ft $200.00
Candy Shooter, red & wht, w/candy & gun license, unused .. $125.00
Captain America, no ft $90.00
Captain Hook, no ft $75.00

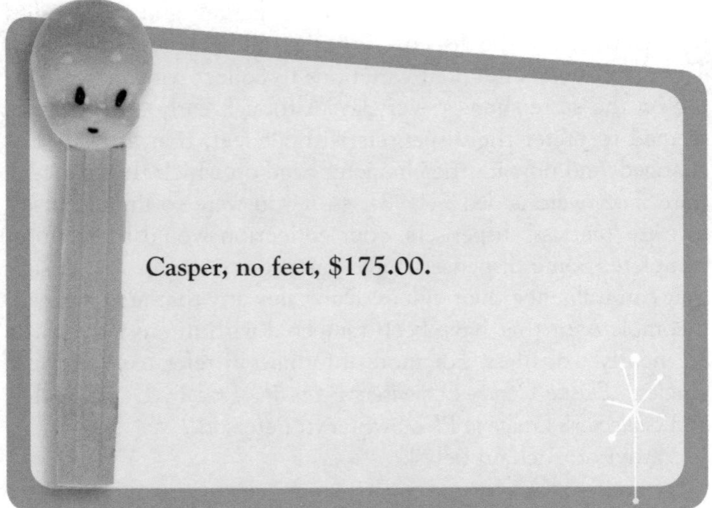

Casper, no feet, $175.00.

Charlie Brown, w/ft, from $1 to $3.00
Charlie Brown, w/ft & tongue $20.00
Chicago Cubs 2000, Charlie Brown in pkg w/commerative card $30.00
Chick, w/ft, from $1 to $3.00
Chick in Egg, no ft $15.00
Chick in Egg, no ft, w/hair $125.00
Chip, w/ft $45.00
Clown, w/ft, whistle head $6.00
Clown w/Collar, no ft $60.00
Cockatoo, no ft, bl face, red beak $50.00
Cool Cat, w/ft $65.00
Cow (A or B), no ft, bl, ea, from $80 to $90.00
Creature From the Black Lagoon, no ft $300.00
Crocodile, no ft $95.00
Crystal Hearts, eBay, limited edition $10.00
Daffy Duck, no ft $15.00
Daffy Duck, w/ft, from $1 to $3.00
Dalmatian Pup, w/ft $50.00
Daniel Boone, no ft $175.00
Dino, w/ft, purple, from $1 to $3.00
Dinosaur, w/ft, 4 different, ea from $1 to $3.00
Donald Duck, no ft, die-cut $150.00
Donald Duck, no ft, from $10 to $15.00
Donald Duck's Nephew, no ft $30.00
Donald Duck's Nephew, w/ft, gr, bl or red hat, ea $10.00
Donkey, w/ft, whistle head $6.00
Droopy Dog (A), no ft, plastic swivel ears $25.00
Droopy Dog (B), w/ft, pnt ears, MIP $6.00
Duck Tales, any character, w/ft, ea $6.00
Dumbo, w/ft, bl head $25.00
Eerie Spectres, Air Spirit, Diabolic or Zombie (no ft), ea .. $185.00

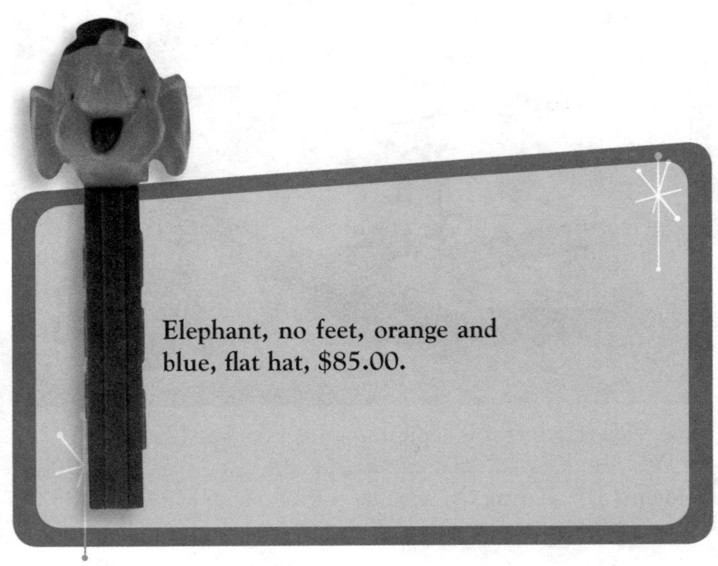

Elephant, no feet, orange and blue, flat hat, $85.00.

Fat-Ears Rabbit, no ft, pk head $20.00
Fat-Ears Rabbit, no ft, yel head $15.00
Fireman, no ft $80.00
Fishman, no ft, gr $185.00
Foghorn Leghorn, w/ft $65.00
Football Player $175.00
Fozzie Bear, w/ft, from $1 to $3.00
Frankenstein, no ft $225.00
Fred Flintstone, w/ft, from $1 to $3.00
Frog, w/ft, whistle head $40.00
Garfield, w/ft, orange w/gr hat, from $1 to $3.00
Garfield, w/ft, teeth, from $1 to $3.00
Garfield, w/ft, visor, from $1 to $3.00
Gargamel, w/ft $5.00
Ghosts (Glowing), Happy Henry, Naughty Neil, or Slimy Sid, ea $1.00
Ghosts (Non-Glowing), Happy Henry, Naughty Neil, or Slimy Sid, ea $2.00
Girl, w/ft, yel hair $3.00
Gonzo, w/ft, from $1 to $3.00
Goofy, no ft, ea $15.00
Gorilla, no ft, blk head $80.00
Green Hornet, 1960s, from $200 to $250.00
Gyro Gearloose, w/ft $6.00
Henry Hawk, no ft $75.00
Hulk, no ft, dk gr $40.00
Hulk, no ft, lt gr, remake $3.00
Indian, w/ft, whistle head $20.00
Indian Brave, no ft, reddish $100.00
Indian Chief, no ft, yel headdress $90.00
Indian Maiden, no ft $150.00
Inspector Clouseau, w/ft $5.00
Jerry Mouse, w/ft, plastic face $15.00
Jerry Mouse, w/ft, pnt face $6.00
Jiminy Cricket, no ft $175.00
Joker (Batman), no ft, soft head $175.00

Jungle Mission, interactive dispenser $3.00
Kermit the Frog, w/ft, red, from $1 to....................$3.00
Knight, no ft....................$250.00
Koala, w/ft, whistle head....................$40.00
Krazy Animals, Blinky Bill, Lion, Hippo, Elephant or Gator, ea, from $4 to $6.00
Lamb, no ft....................$15.00
Lamb, w/ft, from $1 to $3.00
Lamb, w/ft, whistle head....................$20.00
Lazy Garfield, w/ft $5.00
Li'l Bad Wolf, w/ft....................$25.00
Lion's Club Lion, minimum value $1,500.00
Lion w/Crown, no ft $100.00
Lucy, w/ft, from $1 to....................$3.00
Make-A-Face, works like Mr Potato Head....................$2,000.00
Mary Poppins, no ft....................$500.00
Merlin Mouse, w/ft....................$15.00
Merry Melody Makers, rhino, donkey, panda, parrot, clown, tiger or penguin, w/ft, MOC, ea $6.00
Mexican, no ft....................$200.00
Mickey Mouse, no ft, removable nose or cast nose, ea from $10 to $15.00
Mickey Mouse, w/ft, from $1 to....................$3.00
Mimic Monkey (monkey w/ball cap), no ft, several colors, ea $50.00
Miss Piggy, w/ft, ea from $1 to $3.00
Miss Piggy, w/ft, eyelashes....................$15.00
Monkey Sailor, no ft, w/wht cap....................$50.00
Mowgli, no ft....................$30.00
Mr Ugly, no ft....................$45.00
Muscle Mouse (gray Jerry), w/ft, plastic nose $15.00
NASCAR Helmets, various numbers, from $1 to....................$3.00
Nermal, w/ft, gray $3.00
Nintendo, Diddy Dong, Koopa Trooper, Mario, Yoshi, ea from $4 to $6.00

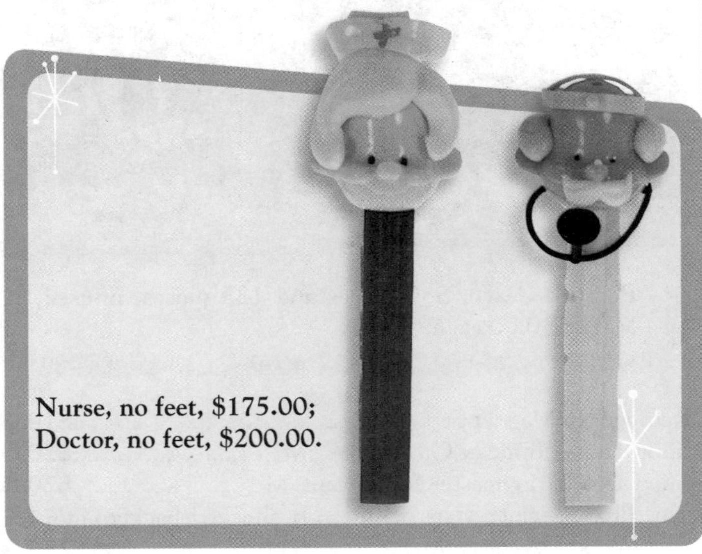
Nurse, no feet, $175.00; Doctor, no feet, $200.00.

Octopus, no ft, blk $85.00
Odie, w/ft $5.00
Olive Oyl, no ft....................$200.00
Panda, no ft, diecut eyes $20.00
Panda, w/ft, remake, from $1 to....................$3.00
Panda, w/ft, whistle head....................$6.00
Papa Smurf, w/ft, red....................$6.00
Parrot, w/ft, whistle head....................$6.00
Pebbles Flintstone, w/ft, from $1 to....................$3.00
Penguin, w/ft, whistle head....................$6.00
Penguin (Batman), no ft, soft head $175.00
Peter Pez (A), no ft....................$50.00
Peter Pez (B & C), w/ft, from $1 to....................$3.00
Pilgrim, no ft $125.00

Pinocchio, no feet, $125.00; Snow White, no feet, $225.00.

Pink Panther, w/ft $5.00
Pirate, no ft $65.00
Pluto, no ft $15.00
Pluto, no ft, red $15.00
Pluto, w/ft, from $1 to....................$3.00
Pokemon (non-US), Kottins, Meowith, Mew, Pikachu, or Psyduck, ea from $5 to $10.00
Policeman, no ft....................$60.00
Popeye (B), no ft....................$90.00
Popeye (C), no ft, w/removable pipe....................$110.00
Practical Pig (B), no ft....................$30.00
Psychedelic Eye, no ft $350.00
Psychedelic Eye, remake, blk or pk, MOC, ea $20.00
Psychedelic Flower, no ft $300.00
Pumpkin (A), no ft, from $10 to $15.00
Pumpkin (B), w/ft, from $1 to $3.00
Raven, no ft, yel beak $70.00
Rhino, w/ft, whistle head....................$6.00
Ringmaster, no ft....................$300.00
Road Runner, no ft $25.00
Road Runner, w/ft....................$15.00
Rooster, w/ft, whistle head....................$35.00
Rooster, w/ft, wht or yel head, ea....................$30.00
Rudolph, no ft....................$50.00
Santa Claus, w/ft, from $1 to $3.00
Santa Claus (A), no ft, steel pin....................$125.00
Santa Claus (B), no ft....................$125.00
Santa Claus (C), no ft, from $5 to....................$15.00
Santa Claus (C), w/ft, B1, from $1 to....................$3.00
Scrooge McDuck (A), no ft....................$35.00

Scrooge McDuck (B), w/ft $6.00
Sheik, no ft $55.00
Skull (A), no ft, from $10 to $15.00
Skull (B), w/ft, from $1 to $3.00
Smurf, w/ft $5.00
Smurfette, w/ft $5.00
Snoopy, w/ft, from $1 to $3.00
Snowman (A), no ft $15.00
Snowman (B), w/ft, from $1 to $5.00
Space Trooper Robot, no ft, full body $300.00
Spaceman, no ft $125.00
Speedy Gonzales (A), w/ft $15.00
Speedy Gonzales (B), no ft, from $1 to $3.00
Spider-Man, no ft, from $10 to $15.00
Spider-Man, w/ft, from $1 to $3.00
Spike, w/ft, B1 .... $6.00
Star Wars, Boba Fet, Ewok, Luke Skywalker, or Princess Leia, ea from $1 to $3.00
Star Wars, C3PO, Chewbacca, Darth Vader, or Storm Trooper, ea from $1 to $3.00
Sylvester (A), w/ft, cream or wht whiskers, ea $5.00
Sylvester (B), w/ft, from $1 to $3.00
Teenage Mutant Ninja Turtles, 8 different, w/ft, ea from $1 to .. $3.00
Thor, no ft $300.00
Thumper, w/ft, no copyright $50.00
Tiger, w/ft, whistle head $6.00
Tinkerbell, no ft $225.00
Tom, no ft $35.00
Tom, w/ft, plastic face $15.00
Tom, w/ft, pnt face $6.00
Truck, many variations, ea, minimum value $1.00
Tweety Bird, no ft $15.00
Tweety Bird, w/ft, from $1 to $3.00
Tyke, w/ft $15.00

Uncle Sam, no feet, $175.00.

Valentine Heart, from $1 to $3.00
Wal-Mart Smiley Pez, ea from $1 to $2.00
Whistle, w/ft, from $1 to $3.00
Wile E Coyote, w/ft $50.00
Winnie the Pooh (A), w/ft $75.00
Winnie the Pooh (B), Eeore, Piglet, Pooh, or Tigger, ea from $1 to $2.00
Witch, 3-pc, no ft $15.00
Wolfman, no ft $275.00
Wonder Woman, no ft, soft head $175.00
Wonder Woman, w/ft, from $1 to $3.00
Woodstock, w/ft, from $1 to $3.00
Woodstock, w/ft, pnt feathers $15.00
Yappy Dog, no ft, orange or gr, ea $75.00
Yosemite Sam, w/ft, from $1 to $3.00
Zorro $65.00

Miscellaneous

Bank, truck #1, metal $200.00
Bank, truck #2, metal $40.00
Body Parts, fit over stem of dispenser & make it look like a person, many variations, ea $1.00
Bracelet, pk $5.00
Bubble Wand $3.00
Clicker, US Zone Germany, 1950, litho tin, 3½", NM ... $150.00
Clicker, 1960s, metal, 2", EX, N2 .... $45.00
Coin Plate $15.00
Coloring Book, Safety #2, non-English, B1 .... $15.00
Giant PEZ Dispenser, various, 12", ea from $10 to $25.00
Mini PEZ Sets, various sets, Japan, ea set from $10 to $25.00
Power PEZ, rnd mechanical dispenser, B1 .... $3.00
Puzzle, Springbok/Hallmark, 500 pcs $15.00

Puzzles, Ceaco, 550 pieces and 125 pieces, unused, MIB, $30.00 each.

Refrigerator Magnet Set $10.00
Snow Dome, Bride & Groom, 4½", M $20.00
Snow Dome, ringmaster & elephant, M $20.00
Tin, PEZ Specials, stars & lines on checked background, gold colors, 2½x4½", rare, EX $225.00
Toy Car, Johnny Lightning Psychedelic Eye racer $20.00
Toy Car, Johnny Lightning Racing Dreams PEZ racer $10.00
Watch, pk face w/yel band or yel face w/bl band, ea $5.00
Watch, Psychedelic Hand $10.00
Yo-Yo, 1950s, litho metal w/peppermint pkg, rare, NM .. $300.00

Pin-Back Buttons

Pin-back buttons, produced up to the early 1920s, were made with a celluloid covering. After that time, a large number of buttons were lithographed on tin; these are referred to as tin 'lithos.'

Character and toy-related buttons represent a popular collecting field. There are countless categories on which to base a collection. Buttons were given out at stores and theatres, offered as premiums, attached to dolls or received with a club membership.

In the late 1940s and into the 1950s, some cereal companies packed one in each box of their product. Quaker Puffed Oats offered a series of movie star pin-backs, but probably the best known are Kellogg's Pep Pins. There were 86 in all, so theoretically if you wanted the whole series as Kellogg hoped you would, you'd have to buy at least that many boxes of their cereal. Pep Pins came in five sets, the first in 1945, three more in 1946, and the last in 1947. They were printed with full-color lithographs of comic characters licensed by King Features and Famous Artists — Maggie and Jiggs, the Winkles, and Dagwood and Blondie, for instance. Superman, the only D.C. Comics character, was included in each set. Most Pep Pins range in value from $10.00 to $15.00 in NM/M condition, but some sell for much more.

Nearly all pin-backs are collectible. Be sure that you buy only buttons with well-centered designs, well-alligned colors, no fading or yellowing, no spots or stains, and no cracks, splits, or dents. In the listings that follow, sizes are approximate.

Advisors: Michael and Polly McQuillen

America's FOIST Family/The Bunkers, 3½" diameter, 1972, NM, $25.00. (Photo courtesy gasolinealleyantiques.com)

Annie Oakley, head image on bl, 1" dia, Green Duck, 1950s, M $25.00

Bat Kids Fan Club, bl head image on gold-tone, 2½" dia, 1960s, M....................$20.00

Batman & Robin, image of Batman & Robin crashing through red & yel background, no lettering, 6" dia, 1982, M ..$15.00

Batman Club, see Ron Riley's Batman Club

Batman or Robin, head images w/names on side, red, wht, bl & blk, ⅞" dia, 1966, NM, ea....................$15.00

Brave Eagle, 1", Green Duck, 1950s, M $25.00

Bruce Springsteen on Tour, blk & wht lettering & image of Bruce w/microphone, 2" sq, 1970s, NM+....................$15.00

Bruce Springsteen/Born to Run, blk lettering & blk pr of sneakers on wht, 1¾" dia, M....................$14.00

Bullet, profile head image & name, ¾" dia, Post's Grape-Nuts/Canadian issue, EX $40.00

Buttermilk, color head image & name on wht, 1" dia, Post's Grape-Nuts, 1953, EX $20.00

Cheyenne, head image of Clint Walker on orange, 1" dia, Green Duck, 1950s, M....................$25.00

Creature (The), wht name & blk & wht image on orange background, 1" dia, Universal Pictures, 1960s, EX....................$22.00

Daisy Air Rifle World-Wide Safety League on bl border around Shoot Safe Buddy in center on wht, ⅞" dia, 1930s-40s, EX $18.00

Dale Evans, color portrait & name, ¾" dia, Post's Grape-Nuts/Canadian issue, very scarce, EX $40.00

Dale Evans, color portrait & name on wht, 1" dia, Post's Grape-Nuts, 1953, EX....................$20.00

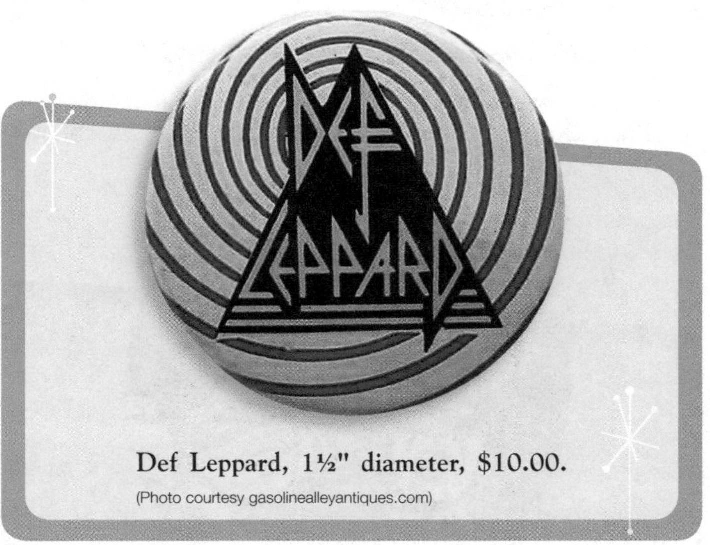

Def Leppard, 1½" diameter, $10.00. (Photo courtesy gasolinealleyantiques.com)

Elvis Presley, blk & wht profile image & wht faux signature on red, 1" dia, EPE, 1950s, NM+.................... $100.00

Green Hornet Club/WCMU/FM, blk lettering around head image in mask on gr, 2" Bastian Bros, EX....................$55.00

Ha-Ha-Ha-Haaa-Ha!/Win With Our Woody/U.S.C.-Rose Bowl-1974, 3½" diameter, NM, $200.00. (Photo courtesy serioustoyz.com)

Help Smokey Prevent Forest Fires on wht band around head image on gr, 3" dia, 1980s, M $7.50

Hopalong Cassidy, portrait image of Hoppy & horse, 6" dia, 1950s, NM, A $32.00

Howdy Doody Safety Club CBC, 1¼" diameter, M, $200.00. (Photo courtesy gasolinealleyantiques.com)

I Love the Beatles, blk lettering on wht w/red-line border, 3½", 1964, EX, A $24.00

I'm A Batman Crime Fighter, 1½" diameter, NM+, $12.50. (Photo courtesy gasolinealleyantiques.com)

I'm Smokey's Helper, cartoon image of Smokey in forest w/wht bird perched on hdl, brn, gr, blk & wht, 3" dia, 1970s, M....... $7.50

I Saw Buck Rogers 25th Century Did You?/A Century of Progress 1934, orange & wht on aqua bl, 1⅛", NM, A.......... $460.00

Jim Bowie, head image on bl, 1", Green Duck, 1950s, M ..$25.00

Join Smokey's Campaign/Prevent Forest Fires!, head image, brn & yel, 1½" dia, 1950s, M $24.00

Junior G-Men Club/12 Action-Packed Chapters/It's A Universal Chapter Film, blk & gold, rnd, 1930s, M................ $195.00

KZOK Welcomes the Beach Boys/Summer Sunday '78 in Seattle, blk lettering on red w/yel star burst, 1¾", NM+..........$20.00

Leo Sayer Silverbird on Warner Bros, bl eyes & nose, red cheeks & lips on wht w/red lettering around rim, 3" dia, M...$25.00

Lone Ranger (The), Lone Ranger on Silver in orange cloud of dust w/bl sky, w/yel ribbon & boots adornment, 1¼", EX+ ..$70.00

Mackenzie's Raiders Starring Richard Carlson/Fiery TV Action, red, wht & bl w/head image, 3½" dia, 1960s, NM $50.00

Madonna, closeup head image covers entire background w/name, 1½" dia, 1988, M..$7.00

Marilyn Monroe Fan Club, blk & wht bust image & wht lettering on lt bl background, 3" dia, NM, A $60.00

Matt Dillon's Favorite/All Star Dairies encircled photo on red, wht & bl shield on wht, 1¼" dia, 1960s, EX $35.00

Monkees, blk & wht group photo image w/Monkees in red guitar shape on wht, 3½" dia, 1966, scarce, EX....................$45.00

Monkees, name in red guitar shape on yel, 2¼" dia, 1967, NM+ $48.00

My Friend Umbriago/Jimmy Durante, photo image of Jimmy & Umbriago hand puppet on yel, 1¼" dia, 1945, EX......$35.00

New Kids on the Block/Official Fan Club Member, group in blk tuxes w/orange 'Member' above on wht, 2¼" dia, 1989, NM+ $8.00

Pat Brady, color portrait & name on on wht, ¾" dia, Post's Grape-Nuts/Canadian issue, EX+ $40.00

Pat Brady, color portrait & name on wht, 1" dia, Post's Grape-Nuts, 1953, EX...$20.00

Patty (Peanuts Gang), blk outline image of head & name below on wht, 1950s, 1" dia, NM..$8.00

PI Copper Calhoon, lady's head image & name on wht w/thin red border, 2" dia, 1940s, M.................................... $125.00

Pink Floyd, name lettered in blk on wht 'brick' background, blk rim, 2" sq, M $10.00

Poor Peter Pillow Who Never Gets a Bath! on yel around mad-looking wht duck in center, 1" dia, 1930s-40s, EX+ ...$18.00

Red Goose Shoes in yel lettering on Red Goose on yel w/'Half the Fun of Having Feet' in blk at bottom, 1" dia, 1936, NM $15.00

Remember...Only You Can Prevent Forest Fires!, head image of Smokey on gr, 1½" dia, 1980s, M $5.00

Renfrew of the Mounted, rnd portrait image above phrase on red, 1¼" dia, Wonder Bread premium, 1936, NM, A $13.00

Rex Allen, blk & wht portrait photo & name on red, 1¼" dia, 1940s, M $25.00

Ron Riley's Batman Club/WLS/WBKB-TV, 2¼" dia, 1966, M.. $7.00

Roy Roger's saddle pictured on yel background, 1" dia, Post's Grape-Nuts Flakes, 1953, VG $16.50

Roy Rogers, blk & wht bust image on deep yel w/red, wht & bl ribbon, 1¼", 1940s, EX+...$50.00

Roy Rogers, color portrait w/red name on yel, ¾" dia, Post's Grape-Nuts/Canadian issue, 1953, very scarce, EX $45.00

Roy Rogers & Trigger, blk & wht head images on yel w/names on bottom rim, w/ribbon & horseshoe medal, 1¾", 1950s, NM $150.00

Roy Rogers & Trigger, 1¾" diameter, 1953, NM, $35.00. (Photo courtesy serioustoyz.com)

Roy Rogers King of the Cowboys, color portrait, name & phrase on wht, 1¾" dia, Post's Grape-Nuts, 1953, EX............$30.00
Roy Rogers Sheriff, yel star & name on red, 1" dia, Post's Grape-Nuts Flakes, VG............$16.50
Roy's Brand, red & blk brand symbol on yel sun burst on red background, 1" dia, Post's Grape-Nuts Flakes, VG.....$16.50
Roy's Ranch, pictures gateway to Double R Bar Ranch, ¾" dia, Post's Grape-Nuts/Canadian issure, 1953, VG............$25.00
Santa Claus Club/Have You Read It?, lettering around head image of Santa on bl, 1¼" dia, Whitehead & Hoag, 1910s, EX............$85.00
The Boss (referring to Bruce Springsteen), wht lettering on royal bl, 1¼" dia, M............$7.00

The Flash/Fastest Man Alive, 1942, rare, EX+, A, $550.00. (Photo courtesy Morphy Auctions)

The Police, group image on bl, 1¼" dia, NM............$8.00
Trigger, head image & name against sky, 1" dia, Post's Grape-Nuts Flakes, 1953, EX............$20.00
Violet (Peanuts), blk outlined head image w/name below on wht, 1" dia, 1950s (?), NM............$8.00
Walt Disney World, lg bust image of Donald Duck on bl background w/silhouette of a castle, 3"dia, WDP, 1970s-80s, EX............$5.00

Kellogg's Pep Pins

Andy Gump, EX............$10.00
BO Plenty, NM............$30.00
Cindy, EX............$15.00
Corky, EX............$10.00
Dagwood, NM............$30.00
Dick Tacy, G............$12.00
Dick Tracy, NM............$30.00
Don Winslow, EX............$20.00
Emmy, VG............$10.00
Fat Stuff, NM............$15.00
Felix the Cat, NM............$60.00
Flash Gordon, NM............$25.00
Flat Top, NM............$23.00
Fritz, VG............$12.00
Goofy, NM............$10.00
Gravel Gerttie, NM............$15.00

Harold Teen, NM, $15.00. (Photo courtesy gasolinealleyantiques.com)

Harold Teen, VG............$8.00
Herby, VG............$12.00
Inspector, NM............$12.50
Jiggs, NM............$25.00
Judy, NM............$10.00
Junior Tracy, VG............$12.00
Kayo, NM............$12.00
Lillums, EX............$8.00
Little King, NM............$15.00
Little Moose, NM............$15.00
Maggie, NM............$25.00

Maggie, VG, $12.00. (Photo courtesy gasolinealleyantiques.com)

Mama De Stross, NM............$30.00
Mama Katzenzammer, NM............$25.00
Mamie, NM............$15.00
Moon Mullins, EX............$10.00
Nina, VG............$10.00
Olive Oyle, NM............$18.00
Orphan Annie, NM............$25.00
Pat Patton, NM............$15.00
Perry Winkle, NM............$15.00
Phantom, NM............$60.00
Pop Jenks, NM............$15.00
Popeye, NM............$30.00
Punjab, VG............$15.00
Rip Winkle, NM............$20.00
Sandy, VG............$12.00
Shadow, VG............$10.00
Skeezix, NM............$15.00
Smilin' Jack, EX............$12.00

Smokey Stover, VG, $20.00. (Photo courtesy gasolinealleyantiques.com)

Spud, VG $12.00
Superman, EX $20.00
Superman, NM $25.00
Toots, NM $15.00
Uncle Walt, NM $20.00
Uncle Walt, VG $10.00
Uncle Willie, NM $12.50
Winkle Twins, NM $25.00
Winnie Winkle, EX $12.00
Winnie Winkle, NM $15.00

Plastic Figures

Plastic figures were made by many toy companies. They were first boxed with playsets, but in the early 1950s, some became available individually. Marx was the first company to offer single figures (at 10¢ each), and even some cereal companies included one in boxes of their product. (Kellogg offered a series of 16 54mm Historic Warriors and Nabisco had a line of 10 dinosaurs in marbleized, primary colors.) Virtually every type of man and beast has been modeled in plastic; today some have become very collectible and expensive. There are lots of factors you'll need to be aware of to be a wise buyer. For instance, Marx made cowboys during the mid-1960s in a flat finish, and these are much harder to find and more valuable than the later figures with a waxy finish. Marvel Super Heroes in the fluorescent hues are worth about half as much as the earlier, light gray issue. Beware that Internet sales may cause values to change greatly.

Because of limited space, it isn't possible to evaluate more than a representative few of these plastic figures in a general price guide, so if you would like to learn more about them, we recommend *Geppert's Guide* by Tim Geppert.

See also Clubs, Newsletters, and Other Publications for information concerning *Prehistoric Times* magazine for dinosaur figure collectors, published by Mike Fredericks, and *Playset Magazine* published six times a year by Rusty and Kathy Kern.

Note: All listings are figures by Marx unless noted otherwise.

See also Playsets.

Size Conversion:

20mm — ¾"	60mm — 2½"
54mm — 2⅛"	50mm — 2"
45mm — 1¾"	70mm — 2¾"

Action and Adventure

Apollo Astronaut, 6", w/American Flag, wht, NM $14.50
Apollo Astronaut Explorers, 54mm, set of 8 in 7 poses, orange, NM $33.00
Apollo Astronaut Moon Walker, 6", lt bl, EX $6.50

Arctic — Dew Line, Eskimos, any pose, bl, $3.00 each. (Photo courtesy gasolinealleyantiques.com)

Arctic — Dew Line, scientists, any, bl, NM, ea $4.00
Ben Hur, 54mm, set of 16, NM $70.00
Captain Video, 2", any, various colors, Lido, 1950s, M, ea...$25.00
Deep Sea Diver, 3", Ideal $35.00
Fox Hunt, 60mm, fox running, NM $10.00
Fox Hunt, 60mm, hound sniffing, NM $10.00
Man From UNCLE, 6", Alexander Waverly, Illya Kuryakin or Napoleon Solo, steel bl, NM, ea from $12 to $20.00
Man From UNCLE, 6", Illya Kuryakin or Napoleon Solo, lt gray, NM (Watch for Mexican copies in near exact gray), ea.. $25.00
Royal Canadian Police, Dulcop, NM $5.00
Space Patrol, 45mm, driver seated, tan & orange, NM, ea ..$15.00

Space People, Space Men, Space Women, Space Children, set of 11, Archer, EXIB, A, $345.00. (Photo courtesy Morphy Auctions)

Spaceman, 3", various poses & colors, Premier, ea..............$5.00
Spaceman, 45mm, metallic bl or yel, NM, ea $5.00
Sports, 60mm, bowler, boxer, figure skater, golfer or runner, wht, NM, ea from $2.50 to $3.00
Sports, 60mm, hockey player, lt bl, NM...........................$12.00
Super Heroes, Captain America, 7", gr, 1967, NM...........$22.00
Super Heroes, Dare Devil, 7", red, NM...........................$20.00
Super Heroes, Incredible Hulk, 5½", orange, 1967, NM ...$20.00
Super Heroes, Iron Man, 7", red, 1967, NM $22.00
Super Heroes, Thor, 7½", gr, 1967, NM $30.00

Untouchables, 54mm, NM, $15.00 each.
(Photo courtesy Martin and Carolyn Berens)

Animals

Arctic Animals, any, cream, ea...$4.00
Champion Dogs, 84mm, any, NM, ea $6.50
Circus Animals, elephant w/howdah, NM........................$10.00
Circus Animals, giraffe, tan, NM $10.00
Circus Animals, gorilla, NM $3.00
Farm Stock, 60mm, any, NM, ea from $2 to $5.00
Farm Stock, 60mm, any from 2nd issue, NM, ea $2.00
Ice-Age Mammals, any, NM, from $10 to.........................$20.00
Prehistoric Dinosaurs, any color, NM, ea from $8 to $12.00
Ranch & Rodeo, 54mm, Indian pony running, various colors, EX..$3.50
Ranch & Rodeo, 60mm, bucking bronco, reddish brn, NM..$5.00
Ranch & Rodeo, 60mm, longhorn steer haulting, reddish brn, NM..$8.00

Campus Cuties and American Beauties

Dinner for Two and Nighty Night, $8.00 each.

American Beauties, ballerina, 1955, NM..........................$20.00
American Beauties, hula dancer, NM $20.00
American Beauties, reclining nude, M..............................$40.00
Campus Cuties, any, ea..$8.00

Comic, Disney, and Nursery Characters

Disneykin Play Sets, 19 figures in 3 complete sets in 1 box, Snow White, Pinocchio & assorted, Marx, 1961, NRFB, A ..$220.00

Disneykings, Goofy and Donald Duck, MIB, $20.00 each.

Fairykins, any, MIB (individual window boxes), ea $20.00
Fairykins, book-shaped box set of 21 different plastic figures, 1962 issue, M (VG box) $300.00
Fairykins, various characters, MIB, ea $20.00
Nursery Rhymes, 60mm to 70mm, any, NM, ea from $5 to..$10.00
Oz-Kins, set of 10, Aurora/MGM, 1967, unused, NMOC ...$100.00
Rolykins, any, NM, ea from $10 to...................................$15.00
Rolykins, 6 different figures on 1 card, Marx, M (G card).. $100.00
Tinykins, any character, NM, ea from $15 to.....................$20.00
Tinykins, any character, NMIB, ea from $25 to................$30.00

Famous People and Civilians

Civilians & Workmen, cameraman, 2½", NM..................$15.00
Civilians & Workmen, racetrack pit crew, 54mm, cream, NM...$100.00
Civilians & Workmen, railroad station people, 45mm, cream, set of 5, NM...$20.00
International VIPs, Queen Elizabeth, 60mm, wht, NM $30.00
International VIPs, Royal Family, any except Queen Elizabeth II, 60mm, wht, NM $20.00
Politicians, Adlai Stevenson, NM.....................................$50.00
Religious Leaders, Cardinal Spellman, NM $20.00
US Presidents, Eisenhower, 60mm, NM $20.00
US Presidents, Lincoln, 60mm, NM $6.50
US PResidents, Nixon, 60mm, NM $12.50
US Presidents, Washington, 60mm, NM $8.00

Military and Warriors

American Heroes, Gen Arnold, 60mm, wht......................$20.00
American Heroes, Gen Bradley, 60mm, wht.....................$20.00
American Heroes, Gen Eisenhower, 60mm, wht $20.00
American Heroes, Gen Grant, 60mm, wht, NM $30.00
American Heroes, Gen Gruenther, 60mm, wht, NM........$15.00
American Heroes, Gen Jackson, 60mm, wht, NM $40.00

American Heroes, Gen Lee, 60mm, wht, NM $40.00
American Heroes, Gen Lemay, 60mm, wht, NM $15.00
American Heroes, Gen MacArthur, 60mm, wht, NM.......$20.00
American Heroes, Gen Pershing, 60mm, wht, NM..........$40.00
American Heroes, Gen Pickett, 60mm, wht......................$50.00
American Heroes, Gen Ridgeway, 60mm, wht, NM.........$25.00
American Heroes, Gen Sheridan, 60mm, wht, NM $40.00
American Heroes, Gen Spaatz, 60mm, wht, NM $20.00
American Heroes, Gen Taylor, 60mm, wht, NM..............$40.00
American Heroes, Gen Washington, 60mm, wht, NM $40.00
Civil War, Confederate soldiers, any, Andy Guard, ea from $3 to $4.00
Civil War, Union officers or soldiers, any, Andy Guard, ea from $6 to..$8.00
Plastic Toys, soldiers, EX to NM, ea from $6 to $8.00
Warriors of the World, Cadets, set of 6, NMIB.............. $125.00
Warriors of the World, Knights, 6", any, silver, ea $8.00
Warriors of the World, US Combat Soldiers, set of 6, NMIB..$125.00
Warriors of the World, Vikings, 6", any, NM, ea $18.00

WWII Soldier taking aim with rifle, 5½", $4.00.

NUTTY MADS

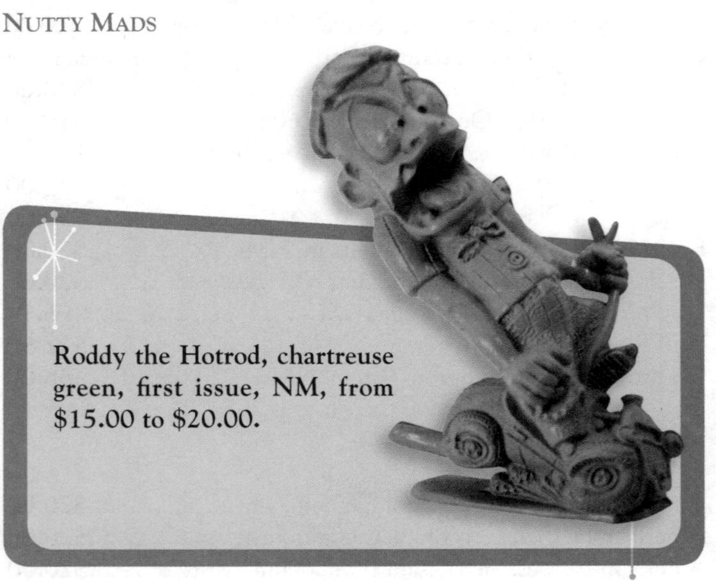

Roddy the Hotrod, chartreuse green, first issue, NM, from $15.00 to $20.00.

All Heart Hogan, pk w/cream swirl, NM $20.00
Bullpen Boo Boo, dk gr, NM $30.00
Dippy the Sea Diver, cobalt, 1st issue, EX........................$10.00
End Zone Football Player, dk gr, 1st issue, NM, from $15 to..$20.00
Lost Teepee, fluorescent red, NM, from $15 to $20.00
Manny of the Wreckless Mariner, lt gr, 1st issue, NM $35.00
Manny of Wreckless Mariner, lime gr, NM $20.00
Rocko the Champ, lime gr, 1st issue, NM, from $15 to.....$20.00
Rocko the Champ, pk, NM $16.50
Suburban Sidney, maroon, 1st issue, NM..........................$35.00
The Thinker, dk gr, NM $35.00
Waldo the Weight Lifter, pk, 1st issue, NM $25.00

WESTERN AND FRONTIER HEROES

Buffalo Bill, Atlantic #1202, MIP (sealed) $50.00
Buffalo Bill, 60mm, beige, EX...$5.00
Cavalery (7th), 60mm, mounted, ea $18.00
Cowboy, 45mm, mounted w/rope, NM $36.00
Cowboy, 54mm, mounted w/rifle, NM $27.00
Cowboy, 6", any, Crescent, NM, ea.................................$10.00

Cowboys, 6", standing with rifle and standing with rope, Marx, NM, $10.00 each.

Dale Evans, 60mm, cream, NM..$22.00
Davy Crockett, 50mm, cream, NM $25.00
Gunsmoke, Chester, NM... $375.00
Gunsmoke, cowboys, bl, NM, ea from $75 to $100.00
Gunsmoke, cowboys, tan, NM, ea.......................................$3.00
Gunsmoke, Doc, NM.. $375.00
Gunsmoke, driver seated, bl, NM.................................. $100.00
Gunsmoke, Marshall Dillon, NM, minimum value $700.00
Gunsmoke, Miss Kitty, NM $375.00
High Chaparral, ½", 42-pc set, Airfix, unused, MIB..........$25.00
Indian Chief, 54mm, w/club, NM $10.00
Lone Ranger & Tonto, 54mm, NM...................................$65.00
Pioneer, 60mm, clubbing, NM $5.00
Ranch Hand, 60mm, walking, NM $60.00
Rough Rider, 60mm, mounted, NM..................................$18.00
Roy Rogers, hands on hips, NM $27.00
Roy Rogers on Trigger, 5", Ideal, M $150.00
Sky King or Sheriff, NM, ea $18.00
Tonto, 60mm, cream, NM $110.00
Wagon Driver, 6", cream, NM...$5.00
Zorro w/Horse, Tornado, NM $60.00

Plastic Toys

During the 1940s and into the 1960s, plastic was often the material of choice for consumer goods ranging from dinnerware and kitchenware items to jewelry and even high-heel shoes. Toy companies used brightly colored plastic to produce cars, dolls, pull toys, banks, games, and thousands of other types of products. Of the more imaginative toys, those that have survived in good collectible condition are beginning to attract a considerable amount of interest, especially items made by major companies.

Atomic Cannon Truck, Ideal, 1960s, 43", complete, unused, NMIB, A ... $225.00
Barney's Auto Factory, Remco #730, complete, 22" L, NMIB, A ... $200.00
Car Wash, Ideal, #3031, NMIB, A ... $125.00
Carnival Caravan Set, Banner Plastics, MIB, A ... $200.00
Cement Mixer Truck, Renwal, 1948, mixer revolves, red w/yel & bl trim, door opens to reveal bl driver, 7", NM, A ... $180.00
Cop-Cycle, Nosco, police motorcycle w/sidecar & 2 policemen, 3-color, friction, 5½", NMIB ... $175.00

Fire Truck, Renwal, 15", NMIB, $150.00. (Photo courtesy Morphy Auctions)

Fix-It Car of Tomorrow, Ideal #XP-600, working horn & headlights, EXIP, A ... $125.00
Fix-It Convertible, Ideal #3058, 1952, complete, NMIB, A .. $130.00
Gilmark's Service & Hi-Way Fleet, 10-pc, EXIB ... $75.00
Golden Arrow Land Speed Record Car, marked Made in USA, 1930s (?), cream w/bl wheels, 2¾", NM, A ... $25.00
Hardy County Fair, unused, MIB ... $100.00
Hardy Farm, unused, MIB ... $100.00
Hot Dog Wagon, Ideal, 7", NM+IB, A ... $85.00
International Tractor Truck, Product Miniature Co, 1950s, 9", EXIB, A ... $175.00
Jet Bomber Escort Squadron, Payton Prod, 7-pc set w/6 fighter jets & 1 bomber, unused, MIB, A ... $125.00
Maxwell Auto Pull Toy, Revell, 1951, red & blk w/driver in wht, complete, 7", NMIB, A ... $60.00
MC Sports Car ('With Real Life 3-Speed Gear Shift'), Ideal, 9", NMIB ... $220.00
Modern Toys — The Kilgore Line, 1930s, 2 planes w/sedan, coupe & truck, 5" to 12", EXIB, A ... $350.00

Race Car #5 w/Motor, Rite Spot Plastic Prod, w/up, 10", NMIB, A ... $100.00
Racing Car (Plastic Mechanical Super...), Irwin, 12", EXIB, A ... $150.00

Road Building Set, Hubley, four-piece, VGIB, $175.00. (Photo courtesy Morphy Auctions)

Satellite Launcher, EXIB, A ... $275.00
Steer-O Car (The Convertible That Steers by Tilting), 12", EXIB, A ... $100.00
Super-X Gasoline Truck, Renwal, 1950, tank holds warer, doors open to reveal driver, bl & yel w/wht tires, 7", NM, A ... $140.00
Tillicum Toys Harbor Master Set (Little Boats for Little Folks), Milton Bradley, NMIB, A ... $50.00
Trailer Fleet, Banner, 3½" truck cab w/3 different 4½" trailers, NMIB, A ... $425.00

U.S. Army Mobile Units (6 All Plastic), Pyro, EXIB, A, $165.00. (Photo courtesy Morphy Auctions)

US Army Set (21 Piece), Pyro, NMIB, A ... $220.00

Plasticville

From the 1940s through the 1960s, Bachmann Brothers produced plastic accessories for train layouts such as buildings, fences, trees, and animals. Buildings often included several smaller pieces — for instance, ladders, railings, windsocks, etc. — everything you could ever need to play out just about any scenario. Beware of reissues.

Advisor: Gary Mosholder, Gary's Trains

Airport Administration Building, #AD-4, EXIB $55.00
Bank, #BK-1, EXIB $18.00
Bank, #1801, EXIB $28.00
Barbeque, EX $3.00
Barn, #BN-1, wht w/red roof, chrome silo top, EXIB $18.00
Barn, #BN-1, wht w/red roof, EXIB $15.00
Barnyard Animals, EX, ea $1.25
Bridge (Trestle), #BR-2, EXIB $18.00
Bridge & Pond, #BL-2, EXIB $6.00
Cape Cod House, #HP-9, dk gray roof, red trim, EXIB $10.00
Chruch, #113, Littletown, EXIB $20.00
Church, #CC9, EXIB $12.00
Church, #1600, EXIB $16.00
Church, #1818, EXIB (sm box) $12.00
Colonial (2-Story), #LH-4, EXIB $18.00
Colonial (2-Story), #LH-4, MIB $29.00
Colonial Mansion, #1703, Littletown, EX $29.00
Corner Store, #1626, gray w/wht roof, VGIB $65.00
Covered Bridge, #1920, MIB $25.00

Diner, #DE-7, MIB, $25.00. (Photo courtesy gasolinealleyantiques.com)

Diner, #DE-7, yel roof & trim, EXIB $15.00
Figure Set, #953, Lionel, VGIB $65.00
Fire House, #FH-4, w/hollow siren, EXIB $25.00
Fire House, #FH-4, w/lg base siren, EXIB $16.00
Fire House, #FH-4, w/sm base siren, EXIB $15.00
Five & Ten Cent Store, #CS-5, EXIB $15.00
Frosty Store, #FB-1, yel w/chrome bar, EXIB $18.00
Gas Station, #1800, w/auto, EXIB $18.00
Hardware-Pharmacy, #DH-1, EXIB $18.00

Highway Motel, #5402, complete, MIB, $25.00.
(Photo courtesy gasolinealleyantiques.com)

Hospital, #HS-6, w/furniture, EXIB $35.00
Hospital, #HS-6, w/o furniture, EXIB $22.00
House & Yard Set, #HY-6, VGIB $18.00
House Under Construction, #1624, lt gray, complete, VGIB ... $60.00
Loading Platform, #1817, MIB $16.00
Log Cabin, #LC-2, w/chimney & rustic fence, EXIB $18.00
Log Cabin, #LC-2, w/rustic fence & tree, VGIB $18.00
Motel, #1621, EXIB $15.00
Pine Trees, #2410, set of 8, VGIB (HO box) $18.00
Plasticville Hall, #PH-1, EXIB $35.00
Platform Fence & Gate Unit, #3F, VGIB $20.00
Playground, #1406, EXIB $30.00
Police Dept, #PD-3, dk gray, EXIB $25.00
Police Dept, #PD-3, lt gray, EXIB $20.00
Ranch House, #RH-1, EXIB $15.00
Ranch House, #1603, turq sides, wht roof, GIB $18.00
Ranch House, #1603, wht sides, lt bl roof, EXIB $16.00
Ranch House, EX $10.00
School, #SC-4, EX $10.00
School, #SC-4, VGIB $15.00
Split-Level, #1908, EXIB $22.00
Street Signs, EX, G1 .... $1.00
Suburban Station, #RS-8, GIB $10.00
Switch Tower, #1814, EXIB $12.00
Telephone Booth, EX $15.00
Union Station, #1901, EXIB $25.00
Watchman's Chanty, #1407, EXIB $12.00

Play Sets

Louis Marx is given credit for developing the modern-age play set. During the 1950s and 1960s Marx produced hundreds of boxed sets, each with the buildings, figures, and accessories that when combined with a child's imagination could bring any scenario alive, from the days of Ben Hur to medieval battles, through the cowboy and Indian era, and on up to Cape Canaveral. Marx's prices were kept low by mass marketing (through retail giants such as Sears and Montgomery Wards) and overseas production. But on today's market, playsets are anything but low-priced; some mint-in-box examples sell for upwards of $1,000.00 or more. Remember that a set that shows wear or has even a few minor pieces missing quickly drops in value. The listings below are for complete examples unless noted otherwise.

See the Clubs, Newsletters, and Other Publications section for information on how to order *Prehistoric Times*, by Mike and Kurt Fereicks, and *Playset Magazine* published six times a year by Rusty and Kathy Kern.

Alamo, Marx #3534, NMIB $350.00

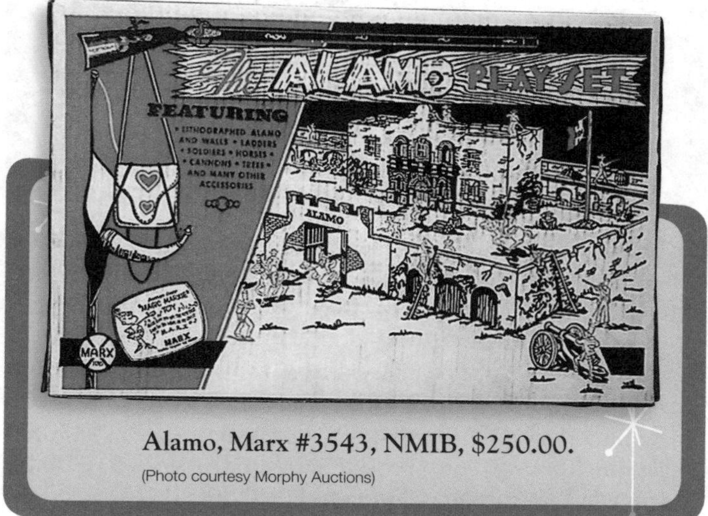

Alamo, Marx #3543, NMIB, $250.00. (Photo courtesy Morphy Auctions)

Alamo, Marx #3546, NMIB $400.00
Alaska, Marx #2755-6, EX+IB $350.00
Alaska, Marx #3707-8, NMIB $800.00
American Airlines Astrojet Airport Set, Marx, GIB $135.00
American Airlines International Jetport, Marx #4812, Series 2000, NMIB $450.00
Anzio Beach, Aurora, HO scale, VGIB $50.00
Arctic Explorer, Marx #3702, EXIB $300.00
Army Combat Training Center, Marx #4153, NMIB $75.00
Battle of Iwo Jima, Marx #4147, NMIB $300.00

Battle of Little Big Horn, Marx #4679MO, MIB, $500.00. (Photo courtesy Morphy Auctions)

Battle of the Blue & Gray, Marx #4744, NMIB $800.00
Battle of the Blue & Gray, Marx #4745-6, Series 2000, EXIB .. $150.00
Battle of the Blue & Gray, Marx #4758, Series 2000, EX+IB .. $350.00
Battleground, Marx #4749-50, NMIB $450.00
Battleground, Marx #4752, EXIB $150.00
Battleground, Marx #4756, EXIB $75.00
Ben Hur, Marx #4696, EXIB $250.00
Ben Hur, Marx #4701, Series 5000, rare, NMIB $1,200.00
Ben Hur, Marx #4702, Series 2000, NMIB $850.00
Beyond Tomorrow Lunar Station, Multiple Toys, EXIB .. $125.00
Big Top Circus, Marx #4310, NMIB $375.00
Big Top Circus, Marx #4310, EXIB $150.00

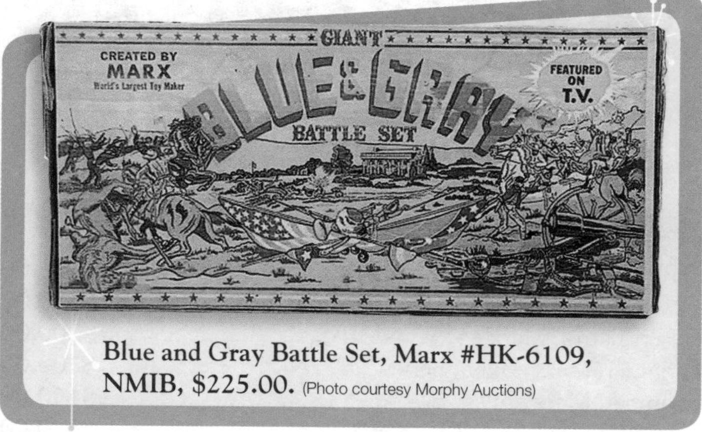

Blue and Gray Battle Set, Marx #HK-6109, NMIB, $225.00. (Photo courtesy Morphy Auctions)

Cape Canaveral Missile Base, Marx, #5963, NMIB $375.00
Cape Canaveral Missile Base, Marx #4526, NMIB $250.00
Captain Gallant, Marx #4729, NMIB $750.00
Captain Gallant, Marx #4729, unused, MIB $6,500.00
Captain Space Solar Port, Marx #7018, NMIB $275.00
Castle, Elastolin #9756, EXIB $300.00
Cattle Drive, Marx #3983, NMIB $275.00
Civil War Centennial 1861/1865 (Happi-Time), Marx #5927, MIB $550.00

Combat!, Cohn, NMIB, $600.00. (Photo courtesy Morphy Auctions)

Construction Camp, Marx #4439, NMIB $300.00
Cowboy & Indian Camp, Marx #3950, EXIB $125.00
Custer's Last Stand, Marx #4670, NMIB $1,500.00
Custer's Last Stand, Marx #4779, Series 500, NMIB $400.00
D-Day Army Set, Marx #6027, NMIB $300.00
Daktari, Marx #3717, NMIB $325.00
Daktari, Marx #3718, NMIB $375.00
Daktari, Marx #3720, NMIB $450.00

Daniel Boone Frontier, Marx #1393, NMIB $250.00
Daniel Boone Wilderness Scout, Marx #0670, NMIB $250.00
Daniel Boone Wilderness Scout, Marx #3442, NMIB $400.00

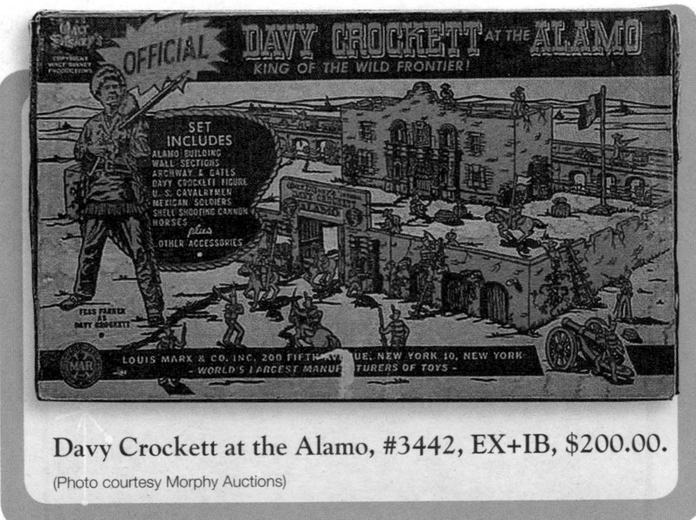

Davy Crockett at the Alamo, #3442, EX+IB, $200.00.
(Photo courtesy Morphy Auctions)

Davy Crockett at the Alamo, Marx #3530, NMIB $300.00
Desert Fox, Marx #4178, NMIB $350.00
Desert Patrol, Marx #4174, NMIB $200.00
Farm Set, Marx #3948, Series 2000, NMIB $300.00
Farm Set, Marx #3953, EXIB $150.00
Fire House, Marx #4820, EX+IB $800.00
Fireball XL5 Space City, Multiple Prod, VGIB $650.00
Flintstones, Marx #4672, NMIB $350.00

Flintstones, Marx #5948, EXIB, A, $165.00.
(Photo courtesy Morphy Auctions)

Flintstones, Marx #5948, NMIB $350.00
Fort Apache, Marx #3609, NMIB $300.00
Fort Apache, Marx #3680, unused, MIB (sealed) $3,025.00
Fort Apache, Marx #3685, EXIB $200.00
Fort Apache Stockade, Marx #3660, Series 2000, NMIB .. $250.00
Fort Boone, Multiple NMIB $275.00
Fort Dearborn, Marx #3510, NMIB $300.00
Fort Dearborn, Marx #3514, NMIB $150.00
Fort Dearborn, Marx #3688, NMIB $275.00
Fort Laramie (Giant), Ideal, NMIB $550.00
Fort Liberty, Hong Kong, 1970s, MIB $100.00
Fort Mohawk, Marx #3751-2, EXIB $150.00
Fort Pitt, Marx #3741, Series 750, EX+IB $125.00

Gallant Men, Marx #4634, NMIB $300.00
Gunsmoke, MPC #1117, EXIB $250.00
Gunsmoke Dodge City, Marx #4268, Series 2000, EXIB .. $800.00
Home Farm Set, Blue Box #6042, EXIB $40.00

Indian Warfare Set, Marx #4778, NMIB, $400.00.
(Photo courtesy Morphy Auctions)

Invasion Day, Marx, miniature, NMIB $500.00
Johnny Apollo Moon Launcher Center, Marx #4630, EXIB .. $75.00
Johnny Service Mechanic's Garage w/Motorized Car, Topper, EXIB $40.00
Johnny Tremain Revolutionary War Set, Marx #3402, EXIB .. $925.00
Jungle, Marx/Sears #3716, NMIB $100.00
Jungle Jim, Marx #3705-6, Series 1000, EXIB $350.00
Jungle Jim, Marx #3706-6, Series 1000, MIB (sealed) .. $1,500.00
Keystone Fire Department, Keystone, 1940, EX+IB $200.00
Knights & Vikings, Marx #4733, 1973, NMIB $175.00
Legend of the Lone Ranger, MPC, later issue, MIB (sealed) .. $75.00
Lone Ranger Ranch, Marx #3969, Series 500, NMIB $300.00
McDonaldland Remco, 1976, unused, MIB $135.00

Medieval Castle, Marx #4700, unused, MIB (sealed), $550.00. (Photo courtesy Morphy Auctions)

Medieval Castle, Marx #4733, EXIB $100.00
Medievel Castle, Marx #4704, NMIB $250.00
Medievel Castle, Marx #4709-10, NMIB $175.00
Midtown Service Station, Marx #3420, EXIB $75.00
Midtown Shopping Center, Marx #2644, NMIB $125.00
Mobile Army Battlefront, MPC #3501, EXIB $150.00
Modern Farm Set, Marx #3931, NMIB $175.00
Modern Farm Set, Marx #3932, EX+IB $100.00
Modern Service Station, Marx #6044, EXIB $50.00
Mountain Assault, Atlantic #202, unused, MIB $175.00
Navarone Mountain Battleground, Marx #3412, MIB ... $250.00

Noah's Ark, Marx, miniature, EX+IB $100.00
One Million BC, Marx #59842, EXIB.......... $125.00
Operation Moon Base, Marx #4653-1, MIB $500.00
Operation Moon Base, Marx #4653-4, EXIB $150.00

Outdoor Swimming Pool and Patio Set, Marx, EXIB, $300.00. (Photo courtesy Morphy Auctions)

Pet Shop, Marx #4209-10, EXIB.......... $125.00
Pirate's Canoe, Multiple Toys, 1950s, MIP.......... $100.00
Planet of the Apes, MPC, unused, MIB.......... $125.00
Prehistoric Dinosaur Set, Marx #4208, EXIB.......... $125.00
Prehistoric Times, Marx #3389, Series 500, NMIB.......... $200.00
Prehistoric Times, Marx #3390, Series 1000, NMIB.......... $250.00
Prince Valiant Castle, Marx #4705, EXIB.......... $150.00
Project Apollo Moon Landing, Marx #4646, NMIB $175.00
Project Mercury Cape Canaveral, Marx #4524, EXIB.......... $150.00
Ready Gang Action-Town Set, Marx, 1970s, unused, NMIB...$200.00
Revolutionary War Set, Marx #3401, Series 500, unused, MIB (sealed) $1,500.00

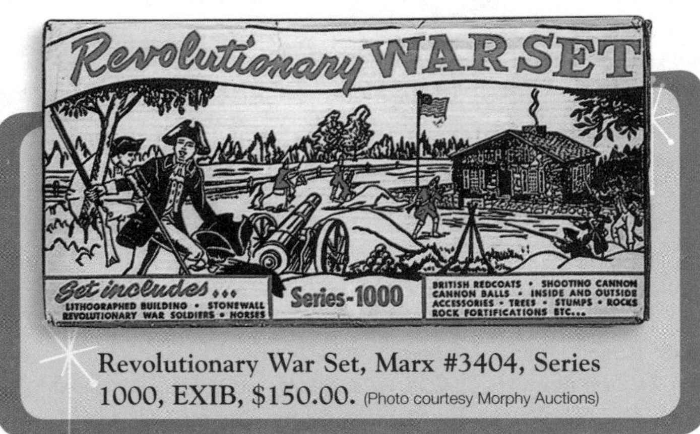

Revolutionary War Set, Marx #3404, Series 1000, EXIB, $150.00. (Photo courtesy Morphy Auctions)

Rifleman Ranch, Marx #3997-8, EX+IB.......... $300.00
Rin Tin Tin Fort Apache, Marx #3628, NMIB.......... $550.00
Rin Tin Tin Fort Apache, Marx #3628, unused, MIB (sealed).......... $1,000.00
Robin Hood Castle, Marx #4717, NMIB.......... $400.00
Robin Hood Castle, Marx #4718, EXIB.......... $200.00
Robin Hood Castle, Marx #4723, EXIB.......... $150.00
Roman Warship (Motorized), Ideal, unused, NM (EX box), A $300.00
Roy Rogers Double R Bar Ranch, Marx #3982, EXIB.... $150.00
Roy Rogers Mineral City, Marx #4227, NMIB $350.00
Roy Rogers Rodeo Ranch, Marx #3985, NMIB.......... $275.00
Roy Rogers Rodeo Ranch, Marx #3992, NMIB.......... $300.00
Roy Rogers Rodeo Ranch, Marx #3996, NMIB.......... $425.00
Roy Rogers Western Town, Marx #4216, NMIB $275.00
Sands of Iwo Jima (296-Pc), Marx, miniature, EXIB...... $175.00
Sears Store, Marx #5490, EXIB.......... $400.00
See & Play Disney Castle, Marx #48-24388, miniature, EXIB..$225.00
Service Station, Marx #3485, NMIB $400.00
Service Station, Marx #3501, MIB.......... $275.00
Service Station (Steel), T Cohn, 1960s, unused, NMIB... $225.00
Silver City Western Town, Marx #4220, NMIB.......... $175.00
Sons of Liberty (Sears Heritage), Marx #59147C, NMIB.. $325.00
Super Circus, Marx #4320, EXIB $200.00
Tactical Air Command, Marx #4106, NMIB..........$50.00
Tales of Wells Fargo, Marx #4262, NMIB.......... $525.00
Tales of Wells Fargo, Marx #4263, NMIB.......... $300.00
Tales of Wells Fargo Train Set, Marx #54752, NMIB..... $700.00
Tank Battle, Marx/Sears #6056, NMIB.......... $125.00

Television Playhouse, Marx #4350 or #4352, NMIB, $500.00 each. (Photo courtesy Morphy Auctions)

Tom Corbett Space Academy Set, Marx #7010, EXIB... $250.00
Tom Corbett Space Academy Set, Marx #7012, NMIB .. $825.00
Torpedoes Away Sea Battle, Kentline, 1940s, EX+IB........$75.00
Treasure Cove Pirate Set, Marx #4597-8, NMIB.......... $250.00
Undersea Attack, Atlantic #206, EXIB $100.00
Untouchables, Marx #4676, EXIB.......... $600.00
US Armed Forces Training Center, Marx #4158, NMIB.. $375.00
US Army Mobile Set, Marx #3655, NMIB..........$75.00
US Army Training Center, Marx #4123, NMIB.......... $100.00
Viking Ship, Eldon, 1960s, 18" L, unused, MIP (sealed)... $125.00
Voice Control Kennedy Airport, Remco, 1960s, unused, NRFB $250.00
Voyage to the Bottom of the Sea Submarine Explorer Set, Remco, 1967, NMIB.......... $400.00
Wagon Train, Marx #4788, Series 2000, NMIB.......... $400.00
Wagon Train, Marx #4805, Series 1000, NMIB.......... $500.00
Wagon Train, Marx #4888, Series 5000, NMIB..........$1,000.00
Ward's Service Station, Marx #3488, 1959, NMIB.......... $275.00
Western Frontier Town, Ideal #3298, EXIB.......... $150.00
Western Ranch Set, Marx #3980, NMIB.......... $100.00
Wild West, Multiple, NMIB.......... $250.00
Wyatt Earp Dodge City Western Town, Marx #4228, Series 1000, NMIB.......... $475.00
Yogi Bear at Jellystone National Park, Marx #4363-4, EXIB.. $400.00
Yogi Bear at Jellystone National Park, Marx #4363-4, MIB... $1,200.00

Zoo Set, Blue Box #6002, 1960s, EXIB $40.00
Zorro, Marx #3554, Series 1000, unused, MIB (sealed)... $1,500.00
Zorro, Marx #3753, Series 1000, NMIB........................ $800.00
Zorro, Marx #3754, Series 1000, EXIB.......................... $500.00

Zorro, Marx #3754, unused, MIB (sealed), $1,500.00.
(Photo courtesy Morphy Auctions)

Premiums

Those from the 'pre-boomer' and 'boomer' eras remember waiting in anticipation for that silver bullet ring, secret membership kit, decoder pin, coloring book, or whatever other wonderful item they'd seen advertised in their favorite comic book or heard about on the Tom Mix show. Tom wasn't the only one to have these exciting premiums. Just about any top character-oriented show from the 1930s through the 1940s made similar offers, and even through the 1950s some were still being distributed. Often they could be had free for a cereal boxtop or an Ovaltine inner seal, and if any money was involved, it was usually only a dime. Not especially durable and often made in somewhat limited amounts, few have survived to the present. Today some of these are bringing fantastic prices, but the market at present is very volatile. Note: Those trademark/logo characters created to specifically represent a cereal product or company (for example Cap'n Crunch) are listed in the Advertising category.

Condition is very important in assessing value; items in pristine condition bring premium prices.

Advisor: Bill Campbell

See also Advertising; Character, TV, and Movie Collectibles; Pin-Back Buttons.

Ace Williams, badge, ...Holsum Observer, brass-tone metal w/bl lettering, 1930s, EX $45.00
Amos & Andy, map, Eagles View of Weber City, Pepsodent, 1935, NM+ (w/mailer) $95.00
Andy Pafko, ring, baseball scorekeeper, EX $215.00
Annie, badge, SG Captain, plastic glow-in-the-dark wht eagle shape w/bl lettering, from Secret Guard Club, NM, A............. $85.00
Annie, book, Radio Orphan Annie's Book About Dogs, Ovaltine, 1936, VG...$65.00
Annie, cup, plastic, Beetleware, EX $215.00
Annie, decoder, 1935, EX...$35.00
Annie, decoder, 1936, EX...$40.00
Annie, decoder, 1937 or 1938, EX, ea................................$50.00
Annie, decoder, 1938, EX...$50.00
Annie, decoder, 1939, EX...$55.00
Annie, decoder, 1940, EX...$75.00
Annie, game, Treasure Island, Ovaltine, 1933, framed, 12x17", complete, EX...$75.00
Annie, manual & badge, Secret Society, EX (orig mailer)...$75.00
Annie, map of Simmons Corner, NM, A........................ $125.00
Annie, mask, die-cut paper, Ovaltine, 1933, EX+ $40.00
Annie, mug, Shake-Up, 1931, ivory w/orange top, EX.......$50.00
Annie, mug, Shake-Up, 1935, beige w/orange top, EX $75.00
Annie, mug, Shake-Up, 1938, aqua w/orange top, EX ... $175.00
Annie, mug, Shake-Up, 1939, brn w/orange top, EX $150.00
Annie, mug, Shake-Up, 1940, gr w/red top, EX............. $150.00
Annie, mug, 50th Anniversary, ceramic, EX $25.00
Annie, Orphan Annie Circus, Ovaltine, 1930s, NM+ (w/mailer) $600.00
Annie, ring, face, EX $65.00
Annie, ring, face, NM+ $100.00
Annie, ring, initial, EX.. $125.00
Annie, ring, Mystic Eye, w/instructions, EX $200.00
Annie, ring, Secret Guard Magnifying, 1940s, EX....... $2,500.00
Annie, ring, secret message, EX....................................... $250.00
Annie, ring, silver star, EX.. $350.00
Annie, sheet music, Little Orphan Annie's Song, Ovaltine, 1931, M...$65.00
Annie, stationery, 5 sheets w/images of gang, NM (w/orig mailer)...$15.00
Annie, watch, Miracle Compass, NM+ $60.00
Babe Ruth, ring, Baseball Club, EX............................. $165.00
Batman, ring, Nestlé, M $90.00
Bobby Benson, cereal bowl, red glass w/blk graphics in center (name/Howdy Pard/H-O Ranger/cowboy on horse), 6½", NM+ $75.00
Buck Rogers, badge, Solar Scouts Chief Explorer, burgundy, EX $360.00
Buck Rogers, badge/whistle, Space Commander, NM $325.00
Buck Rogers, book, City of Floating Globes, Big Little Books, Cocomalt, EX+ $175.00
Buck Rogers, coloring book, 25th Century, Kellogg's, 1933, EX $65.00
Buck Rogers, Cut-Out Adventure Book, Cocomalt, 1933, unused, VG $375.00
Buck Rogers, Flying Saucer, heavy cb disk w/steel rim, 1939, 6¼" dia, NM.. $100.00
Buck Rogers, manual, Solar Scouts, Cream of Wheat, 1936, EX (w/orig mailer).. $300.00
Buck Rogers, Penny Card, American Amoco Gas, 3x3", any number, ea.. $275.00
Buck Rogers, pocket knife, Cream of Wheat/Camillus Cutlery, 1935, 3", EX.. $975.00
Buck Rogers, pop gun, XZ-31, Cocomalt, 1934, EX $350.00
Buck Rogers, ring, birthstone, EX $565.00
Buck Rogers, ring, birthstone/initial, Cocomalt & Popcicle premium, 1934, EX+, A.. $150.00
Buck Rogers, ring, Buck Rogers Solar Scouts, rare, NM, A.. $3,160.00
Buck Rogers, ring, Saturn, NM+ $600.00
Buck Rogers, Satellite Pioneers Confidential Bulletin, EX+... $75.00

Buck Rogers, Space Ranger Kit, Sylvania TV, 1952, unused, NM+ (in sealed envelope) $150.00
Buck Rogers, tab pin, Member of ...Rocket Rangers, red, wht & bl litho tin, very scarce, EX+ $225.00
Buck Rogers, tab pin, Satellite Pioneers, red, wht & blk litho tin, unbent tab/unused, NM.. $125.00
Bulldog Drummond, bomber airplane, cb punchout, w/4 cut-out battleships, Horton's Ice Cream, 1930s, 9½", EX..... $150.00
Bullwinkle, Electric Quiz Fun Game, General Mills, 1961, EX. $50.00
Buster Brown, bandana, Buster & Tige & pals' images around Smilin' Ed McConnel, MC, 1940s, 23 x20", VG........$50.00

Captain America, badge, Sentinels of Liberty, EX+, A, $700.00. (Photo courtesy Morphy Auctions)

Capt Frank Hawks, manual, Sky Patrol Pilot's..., NM $75.00
Capt Marvel, key ring, Capt Marvel Club, EX..................$75.00
Capt Marvel, Magic Flute, MOC $100.00
Capt Marvel, Magic Whistle, EX $50.00
Capt Marvel, patch, Capt Marvel Club, rectangular, red, wht & bl, EX $225.00

Captain Marvel, ring, compass, 1946, EX, A, $350.00. (Photo courtesy Morphy Auctions)

Capt Midnight, badge, Mysto-Magic Weather Forecasting Wings, w/litmus paper, Skelly Oil, 1939, EX..........................$50.00
Capt Midnight, badge, pilot's wings, 24k gold-finished brass, 1943, EX $225.00
Capt Midnight, badge, Secret Squadron Decoder, brass-plated tin, 2¼", EX $125.00
Capt Midnight, cup, red plastic w/decal, EX.....................$35.00

Capt Midnight, decoder, SQ plane puzzle, chrome-plated badge, 1955-56, NM+ $350.00
Capt Midnight, decoder, 1941, Code-O-Graph, EX....... $100.00
Capt Midnight, decoder, 1945, EX $125.00
Capt Midnight, decoder, 1946, EX $100.00
Capt Midnight, decoder, 1948, EX $70.00
Capt Midnight, decoder, 1949, EX+ $110.00
Capt Midnight, decoder, 1949, Key-O-Matic, w/key, EX.. $225.00

Captain Midnight, decoder, 1949, VG, $75.00. (Photo courtesy gasolinealleyantiques.com)

Capt Midnight, decoder, 1955, EX................................ $175.00
Capt Midnight, decoder, 1955, w/membership card & manual, EX $300.00
Capt Midnight, decoder, 1957, badge w/tailfin, EX $200.00
Capt Midnight, manual, 1942, NM+ $100.00
Capt Midnight, manual, 1945, EX $75.00
Capt Midnight, manual, 1946, NM+ $90.00
Capt Midnight, manual, 1947, EX $75.00
Capt Midnight, manual, 1948, NM................................ $100.00
Capt Midnight, manual, 1955-56, w/code book, EX....... $200.00
Capt Midnight, manual, 1957, EX (w/mailer) $100.00
Capt Midnight, manual, 1957, w/letter, EX (w/mailer).. $150.00
Capt Midnight, manual, 1957, 1957, G $75.00
Capt Midnight, membership kit, 1957, complete, EX $575.00
Capt Midnight, patch, Secret Squadron, stick-on type, 1956, MIP $75.00
Capt Midnight, plane detector tube, 1942, no accessories o/w NM.. $250.00
Capt Midnight, Spy Scope, w/instructions, M (w/mailer)....$500.00
Capt Midnight, whistle, 1947, EX...................................$75.00
Davy Crockett, ring, TV screen flicker action, Karo Syrup, 1955, NM, A... $125.00
Detectives Black & Blue, badge, metal, Iodent Toothpaste, 1930s, NM+ $120.00
Dick Track, book, Secret Service Patrol Secret Code Book, 1938, VG+ (w/mailer).. $175.00
Dick Tracy, badge, Inspector General/Secret Service Patrol, emb star w/eagle & leaf swag, Quaker, 1938, 2½", NM, A $1,035.00
Dick Tracy, badge, metal wreath w/emb star & Captain on ribbon banner, EX $500.00

Don Winslow, badge, Lt Commander/Squadron of Peace, silvered brass, Kellogg's, 1939, VG+ $175.00
Flyer Soucoupe (Shreddies/Freddie & Eddie), plastic disk, 5", various, NM+, ea $10.00
Helen Trent, broach, metal arched TV shape w/blk & wht photo & red ruby-like stone, 1949, very scarce, NM $120.00
Hop Harrigan, wings badge, All American Flying Club, brass, EX..$95.00
Howdy Doody/Poll Parrot, ring, plastic w/raised image of Howdy's head, Poll Parrot incised on sides, open band, EX+ ... $150.00
Jack Armstrong, badge, JA/Lieutenant/Listening Squad, 1940s, EX+, A $100.00

Jack Armstrong, Hike-O-Meter, Wheaties, 1938, NM

Jack Armstrong, ring, Dragon's Eye, glow-in-the-dark, plastic, 1940, G, A $350.00
Jack Armstrong, Stamp Set, Wheaties, 1935, M (w/mailer)..$50.00
Jimmy Allen, membership club kit, NM (w/mailer)... $275.00
Little Orpahn Annie, see Annie
Lone Ranger, coloring book, Lone Ranger Health & Safety Club, 5x7", Merita Bread, 1955, unused, NM.......................$50.00
Lone Ranger, Flashlight Pistol, b/o, plastic, secret compartment in hdl, w/instructions, 6", General Mills, 1949, NMIB ... $275.00

Lone Ranger, National Defenders Danger Warning Siren, 1941, EX (with original mailer), $115.00.
(Photo courtesy Morphy Auctions)

Lone Ranger, pedometer, w/ankle strap, EX.......................$25.00
Lone Ranger, ring, atomic bomb, EX $215.00
Lone Ranger, ring, flashlight, w/instructions, EX............ $150.00
Lone Ranger, ring, gold ore/meteorite, EX..................$2,000.00
Lone Ranger, ring, Six Shooter, 1947, EX....................... $150.00
Lone Ranger, Western Tattoos, Fritos, 1959, unused, EX+ ..$45.00
Mandrake the Magician, pin, profile bust image in top hat, enamel on brass, Tastee Bread, 1934, 1", scarce, EX $125.00
Maverick, spinner coin, silver-dollar size w/emb images of the Maverick brothers, Kaiser Aluminum, NM+.............$20.00
Melvin Pervis, manual, Secret Operator's, Post Toasties, 1937, NM+ (w/mailer) $100.00
Melvin Pervis, ring, Jr G-Men Corps, EX $85.00
Mickey Mouse, book, Merry Christmas From Mickey Mouse, 1939 store premium, VG, A $200.00
Mickey Mouse, Globe Trotters, w/map & 12 pictures from MM Globe Trotter weekly publications, EX (VG mailer), A............ $100.00
Mighty Mouse, Merry Pack punchouts, Post Cereal/CBS-TV Ent, 1956, unused, EX $75.00
Orphan Annie, see Annie
Our Gang, comic book, March of Comics Featuring MGM Our Gang, Poll-Parrot, 1947, EX+ $50.00
Our Gang, Fun Kit, 12 die-cut pgs featuring the gang & different activities, Morton Salt, 1930s, NM......................... $175.00
Phantom, Pilot Patrol, membership kit, complete, Langendorf Bread, 1930s, extremely rare, NM+ $2,000.00
Phantom, ring, skull, brass w/red eyes, 1950s, EX $800.00
Philip H Lord's Gang Busters, badge, brass w/enameled detail, 1930s, EX $100.00
Red Ryder, badge, Victory Patrol, V-shaped w/name & Red Rider on horse, glow-in-the-dark fiberboard version, NM+.........$500.00
Red Ryder, postcard, Victory Patrol application, unused, M .. $100.00
Rin Tin Tin, dexterity (B-B) puzzle, rnd w/image of Rinny, Nabisco cereal premium, 1950s, EX+.........................$18.00

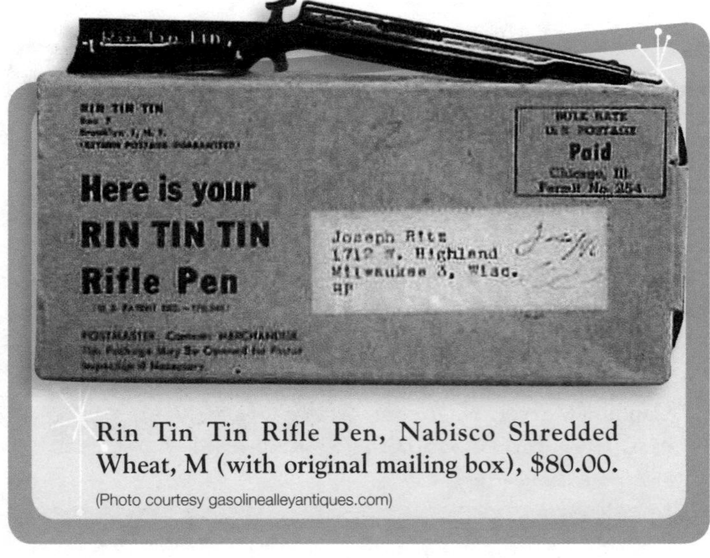

Rin Tin Tin Rifle Pen, Nabisco Shredded Wheat, M (with original mailing box), $80.00.
(Photo courtesy gasolinealleyantiques.com)

Roy Rogers, Double-R-Bar Ranch, cut-out on paper, Post Cereal, 1955, unused, M $150.00
Roy Rogers, harmonica, Cowboy Band, chrome top w/etched name & head image, offered as premium only, 4", NM+.........$75.00
Roy Rogers, Hobby Art Plaque Set, paint-by-number plastic plaque, Collector's Brand/Nestlé's Quik, 1959, unused, NMIB, A.. $200.00

Roy Rogers, lantern, litho tin, 8" (w/hdl up), EX $50.00
Roy Rogers, paint-by-number set, RRE Set C/Post Sugar Crisp, 1954, unused, MIB...$75.00
Roy Rogers, ring, microscope, EX.................................. $125.00
Roy Rogers, ring, saddle, silver, EX $350.00
Scoop Ward, badge & brochure, How to Become a Member of Scoop Ward's Press Club, NM+ $125.00
Sgt Preston, Ore Detector, NM (w/orig mailer box)....... $200.00
Sgt Preston, pedometer, 1952, EX $25.00
Sgt Preston, 10-in-1 Trail Kit, complete, 1958, EX, A $75.00

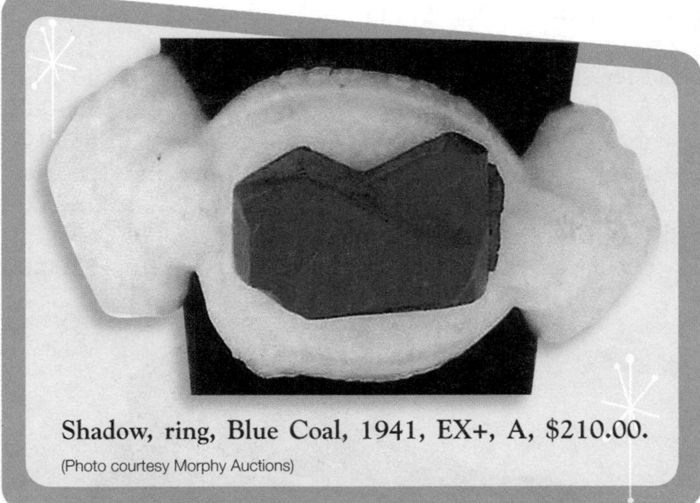

Shadow, ring, Blue Coal, 1941, EX+, A, $210.00. (Photo courtesy Morphy Auctions)

Shadow, ring, bust, EX.. $150.00
Shadow, ring, Magic, plastic, Carey Salt, 1941, EX, A ... $450.00
Sky King, Detecto-Microscope, 1950s, NM (EX mailer) .. $225.00
Sky King, Detecto-Writer, aluminum or brass, EX, ea $125.00
Sky King, ring, Aztec, EX $800.00
Sky King, ring, MagniGlo Writing, EX $115.00
Sky King, ring, radar, EX $125.00
Sky King, ring, Telebinger, EX.. $255.00
Sky King, Stamping Kit, Your Personal Name & Address..., litho tin, 1953, complete, EX..$50.00
Smokey the Bear, badge, Jr Forest Ranger, 1960s, 2", NM..$25.00
Smokey the Bear, Jr Forest Ranger Kit, USDA, 1956-57, complete, EX+ (w/mailer) $65.00
Snow White & the Seven Dwarfs, game board, Tek Toothbrush, WDE, 1930s, EX $60.00
Space Patrol, badge, red, wht & bl under plastic, EX $350.00
Space Patrol, binoculars, Ralston, 1953, NM $150.00
Space Patrol, decoder belt buckle, brass & aluminum, Ralston, 1950s, EX $175.00
Space Patrol, ring, Hydrogen Ray Gun, Wheat Chex, 1950s, EX...$250.00
Space Patrol, Space-O-Phone, plastic, Ralston Purina Wheat or Rice Chex, complete w/instruction sheet & mailer, NM, A $85.00
Straight Arrow, ring, face, EX...$70.00
Straight Arrow, ring, Nugget Cave w/photo, EX $275.00
Straight Arrow, War Drum, complete, scarce, MIB........ $450.00
Superman, airplane, Kellogg's Pep, EX.......................... $200.00
Superman, ring, Crusader, EX... $235.00
Superman, ring, S logo, gold finish, Nestlé, 1978, EX+ $25.00

Superman, ring, Secret Chamber, Defense Milk Club Program, 1941, VG, A, $3,500.00. (Photo courtesy Morphy Auctions)

Superman, Stereo Pix, Kellogg's 1954, 8", NM, ea from $10 to. $15.00
Terry & the Pirates, ring, gold detector, EX $125.00
Tom Corbett, patch (from membership kit), bl, gold & red stitched fabric, Kellogg's, 1951, NM+ $50.00
Tom Corbett, ring, face, EX.. $125.00
Tom Corbett, ring, rocket, w/expansion band, unused, M ...$475.00
Tom Mix, badge, Deputy Sheriff of Dobie County whistler, w/papers, EX... $75.00
Tom Mix, badge, Straight Shooter, EX..............................$72.00
Tom Mix, badge, Straight Shooter, MOC (w/catalog & mailer) $150.00
Tom Mix, belt buckle, brass w/emb portrait image & name on checkerboard background, EX................................ $100.00
Tom Mix, belt buckle, brass w/rope design encircling diagonal red, wht & bl Straight Shooters emblem, EX $75.00
Tom Mix, book, 'The Life of Tom Mix & Secret Manual of the Tom Mix Ralston Straight Shooters,' M (w/mailer) .. $125.00
Tom Mix, comic book, 'Ralston Straight Shooters #3,' EX..$50.00
Tom Mix, compass, brass w/western symbols & rope border, EX $85.00
Tom Mix, compass, Ralston Straight Shooters, ca 1936, EX+ ..$35.00
Tom Mix, Golden Bullet Telescope, 1949, NM $35.00
Tom Mix, ID bracelet, 1947, NM+ $50.00
Tom Mix, periscope, Straight Shooters, cb w/tin cap ends, Ralston, 1939, EX $50.00
Tom Mix, Postal Telegraph Signal Set/International System, 1927, MIB (mailer)... $175.00
Tom Mix, postcard promoting premiums to Ralston dealers, reads 'Check your stock...build Ralstan displays!,' 1940s, NM.. $50.00
Tom Mix, puzzle, 125-pc jigsaw, Rexall, 1920s, complete, NM (w/envelope).. $150.00
Tom Mix, ring, Look Around, EX $125.00
Tom Mix, ring, Straight Shooter, EX $100.00
Tom Mix, ring, target, Marlin Guns, 1937 (also issued in the 1950s), EX+, A $125.00
Tom Mix, Telegraph Set, Ralston Straight Shooters, EX+...$150.00
Wild Bill Hickok, Colt 6-Shooter Pistol, Sugar Pops, 1958, 10", MIB $300.00
Wild Bill Hickok, Treasure Map & Secret Treasure Guide, Kellogg's Sugar Pops, 1950s, M (w/mailer) $125.00
Wonder Woman, ring, Nestlè, 1977, EX........................ $110.00
Woody Woodpecker, ring, Club Stamp, EX.................... $150.00
Zorro, ring, silver plastic w/logo on blk top, EX................$60.00

Pressed Steel

Many companies were involved in the manufacture of pressed-steel automotive toys which were often faithfully modeled after actual vehicles in production at the time they were made. Because they were so sturdy, some from as early as the 1920s have survived to the present, and those that are still in good condition are bringing very respectable prices at toy auctions around the country. Some of the better-known manufacturers are listed in other sections or their own categories.

See also Aeronautical; Buddy L; Keystone; Marx; Pedal Cars and Other Wheeled Vehicles; Smith- Miller; Structo; Tonka; Wyandotte.

Automobiles

Airflow, Kingsbury, w/up, electric lights, WRT, red, 13½", G, A $250.00
Chrysler Airflow, Kingsbury, 1930s, w/up, electric lights, open rear wheel wells, WRT, 14", VG+, A $400.00
Convertible Coupe, Kingsbury, w/up, electric lights, red & tan, gr hubs, rumble seat, WRT, 12", VG, A $875.00

Coupe, Kingsbury, electric lights, 12", EX+, A, $1,650.00. (Photo courtesy Morphy Auctions)

DeSoto Airflow, Cor-Cor, w/up, electric lights, BRT, rstr, A.. $650.00
DeSoto Sedan, Kingsbury, w/up, sunroof, BRT, orange, 14", EX, A $450.00
Graham Paige Sedan, Cor-Cor, BRT, 20", G, A $900.00
Graham Paige Sedan, Cor-Cor, BRT, 20", rstr, A $650.00
Jaguar Convertible Coupe, Doepke, lt bl, BRT, 18", VG, A .. $400.00
Lincoln Zephyr Coupe w/Boat on Trailer, Kingsbury, 1937, gr w/red boat trailer, BRT, 22½", G, A $550.00
Lincoln Zephyr Pulling Travel Trailer, Kingsbury, 1930s, BRT, 23", NM $1,500.00
Mercury Sedan, Doepke, 1950s, yel w/blk top, BRT, 14", rstr, A $385.00
MG Convertible Coupe, Doepke, red w/blk interior, chrome trim, BRT, perforated hubs, 15", EX+, A $385.00
Packard Roadster, Turner, simulated cloth top, BRT, 26", EX, A $1,265.00
Phaeton, Wilkins, w/up, open, spoke wheels, lady driver, 9", rpnt, A $400.00
Pierce Arrow (1934), Girard, w/up, lt gr w/off-wht top & radiator, orange frame, BRT, 14", EX, A $450.00
Pontiac Roadster, early 1930s, w/up, electric lights, 16", EX, A $450.00
Racer, Lionel, electric track racer w/driver, WRT, spoke wheels, rear spare, brass trim, 8", VG, A $525.00
Roadster, Dayton, 1914, w/up, high open seat w/driver at steer stick, gr w/red trim, gold MSW, 12", VG, A $500.00
Roadster, Dayton, 1920s, friction, open high seat w/CI driver, luggage on back, MSW, 8", G $150.00
Roadster, Girard, w/up, b/o lights, rstr, A $325.00
Roadster, Republic, open rumble seat, 2 windshields, MDW, yel, red & gr, driver, 18", VG, A $1,430.00
Roadster, Schieble, flat top, BRT w/perforated disk wheels, rear spare, 18", VG+, A $500.00
Roadster, Turner, friction, bl w/blk hardtop, MSW, 13", EX, A $550.00
Scarab, Ny-Lint, w/up, 14", VG+, A $130.00
Sedan, electric lights, covered wheel wells, red, WRT, 9", rstr, A $75.00
Sedan, gr w/red roof, silver 2-window windshield, silver-pnt grille & bumpers, disk wheels, 11", G, A $200.00

Sedan, Kingbury, windup, steerable front end, 13", restored, A, $650.00. (Photo courtesy Bertoia Auctions)

Sedan, Schieble, 1920s, MSW, 17½", G, A $325.00
Sedan, Turner, early, long-nose, flat roof w/visor, BRT w/disk wheels, 29", rstr, A $1,980.00
Sedan Pulling Trailer, Kingsbury, 1930s, long nose w/wheel covers, WRT, 26", VG, A $500.00
Touring Car, high bench seat, 6-sided radiator, red w/gold trim, gold-pnt MSW, marked April 27 1909, 11", VG, A .. $130.00

Buses and Trolleys

Intercity Bus, Boycroft, 24", restored, A, $550.00. (Photo courtesy Randy Inman Auctions)

City Hall Park 175 Trolley, Converse, ca 1910, w/up, open sides, 16", EX (EX wood box), A $1,320.00
City Hall Park 175 Trolley, Converse, ca 1910, w/up, open sides, 16", G+, A $275.00
Greyhound Bus, Kingsbury, 1930s, 18", EX+, A $600.00
Greyhound Bus, Kingsbury, 1930s, 18", VG........ $350.00
Inter-City Bus, Cor-Cor, 24", G, A $520.00
Inter-City Bus, Steelcraft, 23", VG, A $750.00
Overland Stage Lines, cream & red w/2 wht-wall side spares, 32", MIB, A........ $1,540.00
Pickwick Stages System Double-Decker, newer model, blk, red & yel, chrome grille, BRT, MIB, A........ $650.00
Trolley No 783, Kingsbury, w/up, 14" L, EX........ $350.00
Trolley No 782, Kingsbury, yel, 9", G........ $200.00

Construction

Barber-Greene Bucket Loader, Doepke, track version, metal treads, 19", EX, A $330.00
Barber-Greene Bucket Loader, Doepke, vehicle version w/steering wheel, BRT, 24", EX, A $300.00
Big Boy Coal Pocket Chain Bucket, #508, EX, A........ $720.00
Big Boy Steam Shovel, Kelmet, #502, EX+, A $385.00
Big Boy Steam Shovel Truck, Kelmet #507, blk & red, spoke wheels w/BRT, rstr, A $3,600.00
Cari-Car, w/9-pc lumber set, 12", A $175.00
Caterpiller Bulldozer, Doepke, yel w/blk 'upholstered' seat, blk treads, 15", EX, A $385.00
Construction Co Truck, Sturditoy, doorless cab, open dump bed, disk wheels, 27½", G........ $750.00
Crane, Doepke, orange & blk, BRT, 28", G+, A........ $300.00

Crane, Doepke, 1948, 19½" (with boom), EX, $210.00. (Photo courtesy serioustoyz.com)

Euclid, Doepke, 27", NM, A........ $330.00
Heiliner Earth Mover, Doepke, BRT, 28", EX+, A $300.00
Jaeger Mixer, Doepke, yel w/4 sm BRT, 15", VG, A $225.00
Lumar Rocker Dump, 18", VG+, A........ $125.00
Road Grader, Doepke, 26", NMIB, A........ $330.00
Steam Roller, Steelcraft, blk & red, 17" L, EX, A........ $300.00
Steam Shovel, Sturditoy, gr, 26" L, G, A $185.00
Steam Shovel, Turner, 20", NM, A $385.00
Steam Shovel Truck, Lumar, working shovel, 20", Fair+, A .. $75.00

Turnpike 28-Wheeled Hydraulic Dump Truck, SSS, 1960, friction, 20", EX, $50.00. (Photo courtesy serioustoyz.com)

Woolridge Bottom Dump, Doepke, 1950s, 25", G, A..... $130.00
Woolridge Loader, Doepke, yel w/4 BRT, 24", EX $150.00

Firefighting

Aerial Ladder Truck, Dayton, flywheel-op, horse-drawn (no horses, wooden ladders, driver, 4 MSP, 20", G, A.... $285.00
Aerial Ladder Truck, Doepke, 1950s, open cab, red w/aluminum ladders, BRT, 34", EX........ $200.00
Aerial Ladder Truck, early, open seat & sides, red w/gold trim & ladders, gold-pnt MSW, 20", G+, A........ $225.00
Aerial Ladder Truck, Kingsbury, w/crank extension ladder & 2 side ladders, WRT, 33" L, EX, A $1,850.00
Aerial Ladder Truck Bo 80, Hill Climber, w/driver & figure on ladder, MSW, 22" L, VG, A $1,500.00

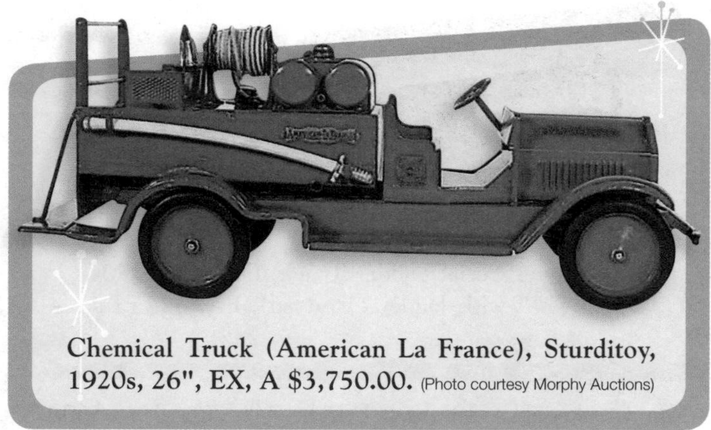

Chemical Truck (American La France), Sturditoy, 1920s, 26", EX, A $3,750.00. (Photo courtesy Morphy Auctions)

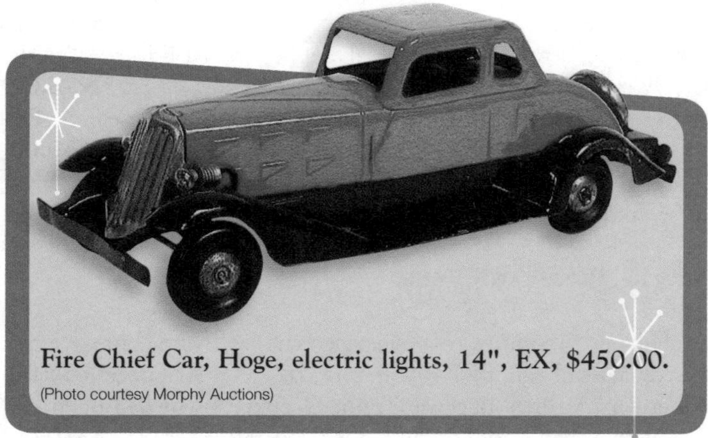

Fire Chief Car, Hoge, electric lights, 14", EX, $450.00. (Photo courtesy Morphy Auctions)

Fire Station & Ladder Cart, Kingsbury, w/up, 13" cart w/front & rear figures, 20" station, EX $2,875.00

Hook & Ladder Truck, Turner, 1930s, long-nose w/ladders on sides of bed w/curved open back, BRT, rstr, A $150.00
Ladder Truck, Converse, open w/2 portholes ea side of bed, driver, 4 MSW, red w/yel ladders, 13", NM........... $2,875.00
Ladder Truck, Hill Climber, open framed, cream & red, 3 ladders, driver, MSW, 22", Fair, A $125.00
Ladder Truck, Kelmet, open cab, WRT, disk wheels, 29", VG, A..$1,100.00
Ladder Truck, Kingsbury, open cab w/curved nose, red w/yel ladders, BRT, 24", VG+, A.. $150.00
Ladder Truck, Kingsbury, open frame, 4 spoke wheels, driver on open seat, wood ladder, 18", VG, A $275.00
Ladder Truck, Schieble, CI inertia drive, all open, w/driver, 3 wood ladders, center steering, 19", VG $650.00
Little Jim Aerial Ladder Truck, Kingsbury/JC Penney, w/up, open seat, WRT, 35", EX, A $5,500.00
Pumper Cart, Kingsbury, w/up, driver on open seat, yel w/2 lg red & 2 sm MSW, 11", EX... $500.00
Pumper No 7, Sturditoy, 1930s, 25", EX, A $1,725.00
Pumper Truck, Kingsbury, w/up, cab pulls pumper trailer, red, gold trim, wood accessories, 18", EX, A $250.00
Pumper Truck, Kingsbury, w/up, early 'wagon' type w/2 sm & 2 lg spoke wheels, CI driver, 11½", G, A $425.00
Pumper Truck, Schieble, open w/driver, 2 lg rear/2 sm front MSW, yel brass-look boiler & trim, 15", EX $1,725.00
Pumper Truck, Turner, open, long front end, red w/brass-pnt boiler, 4 blk wheels w/red hubs, 26", VG, A $225.00

Rossmoyne Aerial Ladder Truck, Doepke, 1950s, 28½" (34" with ladder extended), EX, $225.00.
(Photo courtesy serioustoyz.com)

Rossmoyne Aerial Ladder Truck, Doepke, 34", VG+IB, A..$600.00
Rossmoyne Fire Truck, newer open cab w/windshield, BRT, 19", VG+, A... $350.00
Rossmoyne Searchlight Truck, Doepke, wht, BRT, 19", VG+, A..$2,970.00
Water Tower Truck, Sturditoy, open front & rear seats, BRT w/red hubs, 34", EX+, A.................................... $2,530.00
Water Tower Truck, Sturditoy, open front & rear seats, BRT w/red hubs, 34", VG, A $1,800.00

Trucks, Buses, and Vans

Ambulance, Sturditoy, roof over open cab, wht w/red cross symbol on sides of van, BET w/wht hubs, 26", VG, A $8,050.00
American Airlines Baggage Train, Doepke, 4-wheeled open car w/open box trailer & flatbed, 27" overall, EX, A..... $330.00
American Emergency Unit No 6000, Nylint, 1963, red & wht, 11", MIB, A $375.00
American Railway Express Van Truck, Sturditoy, roof over open seat, screened van, BRT, 27", EX, A.....................$1,750.00
Army Truck, see also US Army Truck
Army Truck, Steelcraft, Mack C-style cab, yel w/red hubs, 'Army Truck' stamped sides of bed, MDW, 25", G, A......... $450.00
Army Truck, Steelcraft, Mack cab w/doors, 'Army Truck' stamped on cloth canopy, gold w/gr hubs, 23", EXIB, A......$2,000.00
Army Truck (Little Jim), Steelcraft/JC Penney, 1927, open Mack cab, 22", VG, A $325.00
Army Truck & Searchlight, Lumar, army gr w/tan canvas cover, 19" truck & 12½" searchlight, EX, A $200.00
Boycraft Dump Truck, red w/gr dump bed, BRT, 23", G .. $250.00
City Dairy Co Truck, Steelcraft, open cab, bl & gr, 24", prof rstr $250.00
City Delivery Box Truck, Steelcraft, BRT, disk wheels, 2-tone tan, 18½", G.. $400.00
City Delivery Stake Truck, Steelcraft, 22", NM............. $700.00
City Ice Co Truck, Steelcraft, Mack cab, wht w/red hubs, BRT, 24", complete rstr, A... $600.00
Coal Truck, Sturditoy, doorless cab, deep box bed w/3 parts, BRT, disk wheels, orange, 25", G, A $900.00
Delivery Panel Truck, Republic, friction, doorless, yel/gr trim, MDW, driver, G, A.. $275.00
Delivery Truck, American National, Mack cab w/screened van, 25", rstr, A..$1,100.00
Delivery Truck, Metalcraft, 1930s, 'Plee-Zing Quality Products' on gr box van, blk cab, MDW, 11", G+, A $275.00

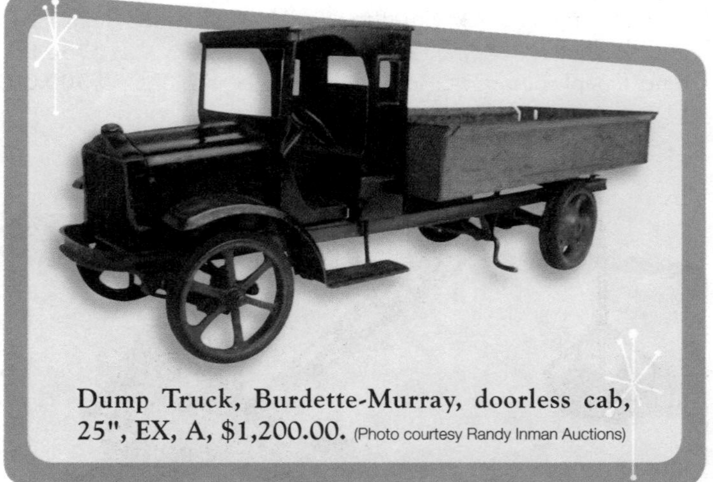
Dump Truck, Burdette-Murray, doorless cab, 25", EX, A, $1,200.00. (Photo courtesy Randy Inman Auctions)

Dump truck, Cor-Cor, 1930s, straight-sided bed, gr & blk w/red lights & hubs, 24" old rpnt, ... $300.00
Dump Truck, Girard, 1930s, slanted bed, 4-wheeled, electric lights, 10", EX, A $125.00
Dump Truck, Kingsbury, 1920s, blk cab w/orange bed & hubs, WRT, 11", G, A $175.00
Dump Truck, Son-ny, open cab, disk wheels, 26", old rstr, A... $250.00
Dump Truck, Steelcraft, Mack cab, gr w/red hubs, 26½", prof rstr, A $375.00
Dump Truck, Steelcraft, open bench seat, blk w/red hubs, w/orig pull cord, 27", VG, A $550.00
Dump Truck, Steelcraft, open cab, 26", rpnt, A............. $100.00
Dump Truck, Steelcraft, 1920s, C-shaped windows, MDW, red & blk, 24", VG, A.. $150.00

Dump Truck, Sturditoy, doorless cab, 25", VG+, A, $3,300.00. (Photo courtesy Randy Inman Auctions)

Dump Truck, Turner, Dodge cab, railed bed, BRT, 6-wheeled, 28", prof rstr, A $500.00
Dump Truck, Turner, enclosed cab, crank-op bed, electric lights, 18½", G+, A $250.00
Dump Truck, Turner, Mack cab, blk w/red roof & hubs, gold-trimmed grille, BRT, 20½", VG, A $350.00
Dump Truck, Turner, Mack cab, red & gr, 23", early rpnt, A . $175.00
Dump Truck, Turner, 1930s, orange & bl, BRT, 27", rstr, A... $250.00
Dump Truck (Oh Boy), Kiddie Metal Toys #100, 1926, ratcheting dump mechanism, 4-wheeled, 19", VG, A $250.00
Electronic Cannon Truck, Ny-Lint, BRT, 22", G, A $110.00

Gilmore Red Lion Tank Truck, Mack cab, 27", restored, A, $2,090.00. (Photo courtesy Randy Inman Auctions)

Ice Truck, American National, open cab w/bench seat, railed bed labeled Pure Ice, BRT, rstr, A $775.00
Ice Truck, Cor-Cor, 1920s, blk w/orange bed, orange hubs, 23½", EX, A $550.00
Kroger Food Express Box Truck, Metalcraft, orange, disk wheels, 12", G, A.. $500.00
Little Jim Dump Truck, Steelcraft, 1920s, MDW, 24", VG, A $500.00
Lumar Utility Service Truck, w/accessories, 20", EX, A... $300.00
Moving Van, Son-ny, 1930s, van roof over open cab, blk & orange, MDW, 26", G+, A $880.00
Parcel Delivery Truck, Kingsbury, w/up, doorless milk truck type, orange, 9½", VG, A $225.00
Parcel Post Truck, Son-ny, 1930s, roof over open cab, blk w/gr screened van, NPDW, 26", G+, A $1,200.00
Pickup Truck, Schieble, inertia driver, bl w/red top yel hubs, WRT, EX+, A $950.00
Play Boy Trucking Co Wrecker, Steelcraft, Mack cab, BRT, wht w/red hubs, 18½", G, A $450.00

Police Department Van, Sturditoy, 25", restored, A, $1,980.00. (Photo courtesy Randy Inman Auctions)

Pure Oil Co Tank Truck, Metalcraft, bl w/wht lettering, rear wheels covered, NP grille, BRT, electric lights, 15", EX, A .. $1,430.00
Pure Oil Co Tank Truck, Metalcraft, bl w/wht lettering, rear wheels covered, NP grille, BRT, no electric lights, VG, A .. $1,230.00
Railway Express Van, Steelcraft, 1920s, open Mack cab, screened van, MDW, 24", G, A.. $1,100.00

Railway Express Van, Steelcraft, open Mack cab, 1920s, 24", EX, A, $4,500.00. (Photo courtesy Morphy Auctions)

Richfield Tandem Tank Truck, open Mack cab, WWT w/spoke wheels, 51", rstr, A.. $2,750.00
Sand & gravel Truck, Dayton, yel & red, MDE, 17", VG .. $650.00
Sheffield Farms Sealed Dairy Products, Mack-type cab w/running boards, red w/yel hubs, BRT, 21", VG, A $400.00
Stake Truck, Dayton, friction, open bench seat w/CI driver on right side, bl, MSW, 15", VG, A $300.00
Stake Truck, Gama, 1950s, w/up, tin/PS, orange w/bl undercarriage, rear duals, hand-op lift gate, 2 cb boxes, 12", NMIB $400.00
Stake Truck, Metalcraft, 1930s, 'White King Express,' dk bl, MDW, 12", Fair, A..$85.00
Stake Truck, Schiebles, counter-weight driven, early boxy type, high stake bed, MSW, driver, 13", VG $400.00
Stake Truck, Steelcraft, blk & orange w/orange MDW, 21", VG, A $500.00
Stake Truck, Turner, C-style cab, yel w/red roof & front fenders, no back fenders, BRT, 17", G, A $200.00
Sturditoy Coal Co Truck, doorless cab, blk w/red hubs, 27", VG, A $1,300.00

Sturditoy Construction Co Dump Truck, blk w/gr bed, red hubs, 27", VG+, A $2,300.00
Tanker Truck, Sturditoy, doorless cab, steerable wheels, BRT, red, 35", VG, A $3,000.00
Transport (Dump) Truck, Tri-ang, lever action, cream & turq, BRT, 14½", VG+, A $85.00
US Army Truck, Sturditoy, 1920s, open cab, gr w/'US Army' on on canvas top, USA in blk on bed sides, BRT, 27", EX, A $3,735.00
US Army Truck, 1920s, open Mack cab, army gr w/'US Army' on canvas top, USA 1120 on hood, 26½", VG, A $1,840.00
USA Defense Truck, Kingsbury, w/up, olive gr w/tan canvas cover, 14", EX, A $200.00
USA 1120 Anti-Aircraft Truck, Son-ny, 1930s, olive gr, BRT, 24", VG+, A $1,760.00
USA 1120 Army Truck, Son-ny, open C-cab style w/cloth cover, MDW, 26", prof rstr, A $650.00
White Army Truck, Kelmet #523, blk w/red undercarriage, 'Army Truck' stamped on canvas cover, WRT, red hubs, rstr, A $1,200.00
White Big Boy Army Truck, Kelmet, 1920s, open seat, blk, red undercarriage, tan canvas canopy, WRT, 25½", VG, A $1,090.00

White Big Boy Tank Truck, Kelmet, restorted, $1,800.00. (Photo courtesy Leslie Hindman Auctioneers)

White Dump Truck, Kelmet, #501, blk w/red undercarriage, WRT w/red hubs, 25", NM, A............................. $3,360.00
Wrecker, Schieble, inertia driver, bl w/red top, yel hubs, WRT, 19", EX... $875.00
Wrecker, Sturditoy, doorless cab, 'Sturditoy Trucking Company' on sides of bed, BRT, rstr, A $1,650.00

Promotional Vehicles

Miniature Model T Fords were made by Tootsietoy during the 1920s, and a few of these were handed out by Ford dealers to promote the new models. In 1932 Tootsietoy was contacted by Graham-Paige to produce a model of their car. These 4" Grahams were sold in boxes as sales promotions by car dealerships, and some were sold through the toy company's catalog. But it wasn't until after WWII that distribution of 1/25 scale promotional models and kits became commonplace. Early models were of cast metal, but during the 1950s, manufacturers turned to plastic. Not only was the material less costly to use, but it could be molded in the color desired, thereby saving the time and expense previously involved in painting the metal. Though the early plastic cars were prone to warp easily, by the early '60s they had become more durable. Some were friction powered, and others battery-operated. Advertising extolling some of the model's features was often embossed on the underside. Among the toy manufacturers involved in making promotionals were National Products, Product Miniature, AMT, MPC, and Jo-Han. Interest in '50s and '60s models is intense, and the muscle cars from the '60s and early '70s are especially collectible. The more popularity the life-size models attain, the more popular the promotional is with collectors.

Check the model for damage, warping, and amateur alterations. The original box can increase the value by as much as 100%. Jo-Han has reissued some of their 1950s and 1960s Mopar and Cadillac models as well as Chrysler's Turbine Car.

Nothing controls values of promos more than color. Thus, the difference can be substantial.

If you'd like more information we recommend *The Little Ones Sell the Big Ones!*, by Larry Blodget.

Cadillac de Ville 2-Door Hardtop (1964), Jo-Han, silver w/blk top, M $110.00
Cadillac Eldorado 2-Door Hardtop (1973), Jo-Han, NM (NM box)...$77.00
Cadillac Fleetwood 'Sixty Special' 4-Door Hardtop (1958), Jo-Han, wht w/pk interior, MIB................................. $365.00
Cadillac Fleetwood 4-Door Hardtop (1959), Jo-Han, blk, wht-wall tires, M $120.00

Chevy Corvett (1974), orange with orange interior, M (EX box), $155.00.

Chevy Corvette (1976), Classic White, 7½", M (EX box)..$75.00
Chevy Corvette (1978 Anniversay Edition), MPC, 2-tone, MIB $53.00
Chevy Corvette (1992 Special Edition 1 Millionth Corvette), AMT, M (M box) $53.00
Ford Crestline Sedan 91953), AMT, EX.............................$50.00
Ford Fairlane GT (1966), 390 engine, dk red, EX+........ $100.00
Ford Galaxie Convertible w/Top Up (1962), lt bl w/wht tip, EX $200.00
Ford Galaxie 500XL 2-Door Hardtop (1964), AMT, deep red, M $90.00
Ford Galaxie 500XL 2-Door Hardtop (1965), AMT, bl, NM...$68.00
Ford Mustang Coupe (1965), aqua, VG+ $50.00
Ford Mustang Fastback (1967), yel, NM....................... $100.00
Ford Thunderbird Convertible (1955), mint gr, VG+.... $150.00

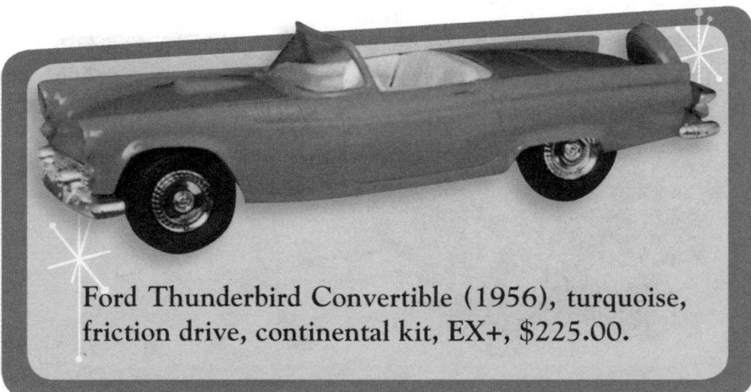

Ford Thunderbird Convertible (1956), turquoise, friction drive, continental kit, EX+, $225.00.

Ford Thunderbird Convertible (1962), lt bl, EX+ $250.00
Ford Thunderbird 2-Door Hardtop (1963), AMT, NM.....$55.00
Ford Thunderbird 2-Door Hardtop (1964), AMT, NM.....$55.00
Ford 4-Door Sedan (1950), maroon, NM, A $125.00
Hudson, 13", EX, A $550.00
Lincoln Continental Mark III 2-Door Hardtop (1958), AMT, missing hood ornament o/w M $125.00
Oldsmobile Cutless (1964), cream w/dk gr interior, M... $130.00
Oldsmobile Starfire Convertible (1963), Jo-Han, metallic fleck pnt, M $95.00
Oldsmobile Starfire 2-Door Hardtop (1963), Jo-Han, red, M. $95.00
Oldsmobile Toronado (1970), metallic Gold Nugget w/blk interior, M (EX+ box)...$85.00
Oldsmobile 442 2-Door Hardtop (1970), Jo-Han, metallic orange, M.. $100.00
Pontiac Bonneville 2-Door Hardtop (1958), AMT, M... $200.00
Pontiac Chieftain Sedan (1951), AMT, NM.................. $150.00
Pontiac V-8 2-Door Hardtop (1955), Jo-Han, 2-tone gr, M... $75.00
Rambler Crosscountry Station Wagon (1959), Jo-Han, metallic, M.. $100.00

Pull and Push Toys

Pull and push toys from the 1800s often were hide- and cloth-covered animals with glass or shoe-button eyes on wheels or wheeled platforms. Many were also made of tin or wood. The cast-iron bell toys of that era can be found in the Cast Iron category under Bell Toys.

See also Character, TV, and Movie Collectibles; Disney; Fisher-Price.

Beauty Pacers Wagon, 2 litho-on-wood horses w/articulated tin legs, MSW, 19", Gibbs, EXIB, A $880.00
Boat, tin, flat bottom w/sides turned up, barrel (side wheels) w/stack, Fallows, 11", G, A....................................$550.00
Buffalo on 4-Wheeled Platform, lt-colored hide covering w/wht curly mane, wooded platform, 5", EX, A................. $250.00
Bull Dog on Wheels, molded pnt & flocked papier-maché, glass eyes, nodding head, 23" L, VG+, A $1,100.00
Bull on 4-Wheeled Platform, cloth-covered, brn & tan spotted, belly chain & collar, 11", EX.................................. $880.00
Camel on 4-Wheeled Platform, pnt tin, 9" L, Adolph Bergman, EX $500.00
Circus Band Truck w/Elephant, tin, parade band lithoed on sides, 12", Courtland, VG, A $100.00
Circus Cage Wagon, litho tin, 11" L, Harrison, EX........ $450.00
Circus Parade (Elephant) Truck, tin, lion cage lithoed on sides, 12" L, Courtland, VG... $175.00
Clowns (2) w/1 Beating Drum on 4-Wheeled Platform, Gong Bell, paper-litho-on-wood figures, tin base, 13x13", EX..... $165.00

Couple on Horses on Four-Wheeled Platform, painted tin, 8x9" long, Hull and Stafford, VG, A, $5,980.00.

(Photo courtesy James. D. Julia, Inc.)

Cow on 4-Wheeled Platform, pnt brn & wht papier-maché cow, wood platform, 5½", EX, A.................................... $325.00
Dog on 4-Wheeled Platform, lt poodle-like cloth over papier-maché body, wood platform, 8", G $150.00

Duck, lithographed tin, head moves and quacks when pulled, T. Cohn, 9" long, NMIB, A, $300.00.

(Photo courtesy Randy Inman Auctions)

Easter Bunny Truck, tin, lithoed bunny pulling trailer w/Easter scene, pk, gr & wht, 12" L, Courtland, EX, A $150.00
Goat Cart, tin, 2-wheeled cart emb w/branches & leaves, 11", Hull & Stafford, VG, A... $600.00

Goat on 4-Wheeled Platform, long furry hide, glass eyes, red wood base, 6", EX, A $138.00
Goat on 4-Wheeled Platform, realistic, off-wht & gray long-haired plush, red bell collar & back blanket, 10x12", EX, A $1,540.00
Goat on 4-Wheeled Platform, shorter fur, glass eyes, wooden horns, wood platform, 11", G, A $360.00
Grasshopper, pnt CI w/aluminum legs, 2 sm front wheels, 9", Hubley, VG, A $660.00
Horse Cart, tin, 2-wheeled cart emb w/branches & leaves, 8", Hull & Stafford, 1880s, VG, A $300.00
Horse on 4-Wheeled Platform, carved wood w/pnt saddle, braided mane/tail, wood handle, 20" L, VG+, A $200.00
Horse on 4-Wheeled Platform, CI, articulated legs, 10", Ives, EX, A $350.00
Horse on 4-Wheeled Platform, papier-maché w/mohair fabric covering, metal eyes/leather ears, 14", EX, A $150.00
Horse on 4-Wheeled Platform, pnt tin, 8x12" L, George Brown, G, A $1,090.00
Horse on 4-Wheeled Platform, wht, hair mane & tail, glass eyes, w/trappings, wood base, 12", VG+, A $330.00
Horse on 4-Wheeled Platform, wht-pnt tin horse w/blk mane, red-pnt saddle, gr base w/blk wheels, VG, A $300.00
Horse on 4-Wheeled Platform, wood, blk w/wht spots, hair mane & tail, w/saddle, wood platform, 12", EX, A $2,475.00

Horse-Drawn Alderney Milk Wagon, mostly wood, with deliveryman and bottles, 25½" long, Schoenhut, EX+, A, $7,150.00. (Photo courtesy Bertoia Auctions)

Horse-Drawn Barrel Wagon, pnt wood, horse on 4-wheeled platform, MSW on flatbed wagon w/ramp, 26", EX, A .. $110.00
Horse-Drawn Bell Toy, pnt tin, bell between 2 heart-shaped spoke wheels, 9", EX, A $500.00
Horse-Drawn Bell Toy, tin, horse w/bell between 2 CI wheels, 7½" L, Gong Bell, VG, A $200.00
Horse-Drawn City Hall & 51st St Trolley, pnt tin, 2 wht horses, 12½", EX, A $1,320.00
Horse-Drawn Dray Wagon, pnt tin, 5x12" L, Althof Bergmann, G, A $400.00
Horse-Drawn DSC New York City Cart, litho tin, no driver, 13", G, A $55.00
Horse-Drawn Express Wagon, litho tin, bl & wht w/'Express' on both sides, wht horse, 11" L, G, A $430.00

Horse-Drawn Express Wagon, painted tin, 7x14" long, Merriam, VG, A, $1,265.00. (Photo courtesy James. D. Julia, Inc.)

Horse-Drawn Fine Groceries Wagon, litho tin, 1 horse, 12" L, ca 1900, VG, A $430.00
Horse-Drawn Fine Groceries/Special Delivery Huckster Wagon, wood w/MSW, 2 horses, 14", ca 1900, EX, A $935.00
Horse-Drawn Fire 'Hose No 3' Wagon, pnt wood, 2 blk horses, 24½", Germany, EX, A $525.00
Horse-Drawn Fire Ladder Wagon, pnt wood, open frame 6-wheeled wagon w/2 blk horses, 37", Germany, EX, A $1,200.00
Horse-Drawn Gravel Cart, paper-litho-on-wood horse, 2-wheeled wood cart stamped Gravel, MSW, 12", VG, A $110.00
Horse-Drawn Grocery Delivery Wagon, pnt tin, roof extends over seat, 12" L, Althog Bergmann, VG, A $1,150.00
Horse-Drawn Gypsy Wagon, 2 litho-on-wood horses w/articulated legs, Conastoga-like cover, 18", Gibbs, NM, A $275.00
Horse-Drawn Hillside Farm Milk Wagon, pnt & stenciled wood, horse on 4-wheeled platform, 23", EX, A $300.00
Horse-Drawn Ice Wagon #15, litho tin & wood, 12" L, VG, A $225.00
Horse-Drawn Klondike Ice Company Wagon, litho tin, 2 horses, 17" L, ca 1900, G, A $460.00
Horse-Drawn Menagerie Wagon, litho tin & wood, 13" L, Converse, EX, A $300.00
Horse-Drawn Milk Wagon, litho tin, covered wagon w/bench seat, 2 horses, yel, 17", Converse, G, A $250.00
Horse-Drawn National Dairy Wagon No 200, pnt wood, MSW, 15", EX+, A $825.00
Horse-Drawn National Express Wagon, litho tin, 2 articulated horses, 20", Converse, 1898, EX, A $440.00
Horse-Drawn Platform Toy, 2 rnd rotating bases on 4-wheeled platform w/kids on donkey/horse, 20", Gropper & Sons, EX, A $500.00
Horse-Drawn Sulky w/Driver, pnt tin, 7" L, George Brown, G, A $400.00
Horse-Drawn US Mail Cart, litho-on-wood horse w/articulated tin legs, 12", Gibbs, VG+, A $275.00
Horse-Drawn Wicker Cart w/Musical Girl Doll, cloth-covered horse, tin spoke wheels, 15", Germany, VG $1,100.00
Horse-Drawn Yankee Dump Cart, litho-on-wood horse w/articulated tin legs, 19", Gibbs, EX, A $220.00
Horse-Drawn 2-Wheeled Cart, 2 sm spoke wheels, 14" L, Merriam, G, A $255.00
Hustler Twist, pnt wood, 2 figures dance around on 4-wheeled paddle-shaped platform, 9", EX+IB, A $75.00

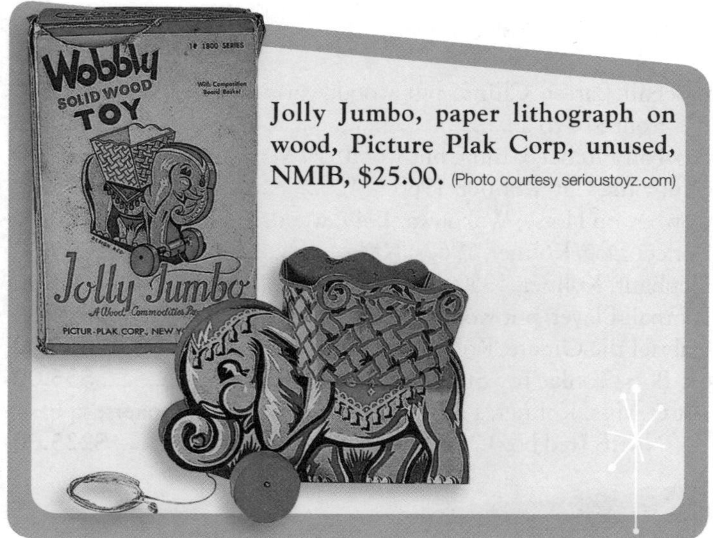

Jolly Jumbo, paper lithograph on wood, Picture Plak Corp, unused, NMIB, $25.00. (Photo courtesy serioustoyz.com)

Leopard on Pole & Horse Trainer on 4-Wheeled Platform, tin, articulated, 10", Bergmann, 1870, VG, A............$2,750.00
Lion on 4-Wheeled Platform, hide-covered, furry mane, wood base w/CI insert wheels, 26" L, VG, A.................... $355.00
Locomotive & Tender, Fallows, pnt tin, pitched roof over cab, spoke wheels, 9" L, EXIB, A.................................. $975.00
Ox Cart, pnt tin, 2 oxen pulling 2-wheeled cart w/open back, 10" L, George Brown, VG, A....................................... $515.00
Performer w/Pigs on 4-Wheeled Platform, figure w/bisque head, cloth outfit, 3 pigs, 19", Germany, VG, A............$2,475.00
Racing Skull, wooden 4 bead-type figures, yel w/4 red wheels, pull string, 14", Hustler, VG, A.................................$55.00

Sheep on Four-Wheeled Platform, wooly coat with papier-maché face, 12", EX, A, $1,955.00. (Photo courtesy James D. Julia, Inc.)

Teddy Bear on 4 Wheels, dk brn mohair, 8x11½", Germany, 1920s, G, A... $220.00
Train Engine, pnt tin, 2 sm & 2 lg spoke wheels, w/bell, 8" L, American Metal Toys, VG, A $450.00
Train Set, pnt wood, engine/tender w/metal boiler, baggage & passenger cars, 59", Toddler Toys, VG, A $225.00
Train Set, Union Pacific, pnt tin, locomotive, tender, coach & caboose, 25", Hull & Stafford, EX, A...................$1,760.00
Train Set, Victory engine, Express US Mail car, Union Railroad car, coal tender, 30", G, A $485.00
Trolley #59 (All Cars Transfer to Bloomingdale's), pnt wood & litho tin, conductor, 13", Rich Toy, EX, A.............. $600.00

Puppets

Puppet theaters have been a long-lasting form of entertainment for kids and adults alike. What child has not had a puppet or two of their own that they have brought to life? Here we have listed the noncharacter-related hand puppets, marionettes, and push-button puppets. You will find the character-related puppets listed in the Character, TV, and Movie Collectibles and Western categories.

See also Advertising; Black Americana.

Hand Puppets

Chimp, Hazelle, 1960s, MIP, $45.00. (Photo courtesy gasolinealleyantiques.com)

Chinese Girl, Scripture Press, 1968, cloth body w/vinyl face, blk-pnt hair, NM+ $50.00
Chipmunk, Hazelle #100A, 1960s, brn cloth body w/brn vinyl head, MIB $45.00
Clown (Ringling Bros Barnum & Bailey Circus), cloth body w/vinyl head, EX $75.00
Dog, Hazelle, 1960s, blk & wht checked cloth body w/blk & wht vinyl head, blk-pnt eyes, brows & nose, MIP.............$45.00
Dog, 1950s, cloth body w/wht polka-dots, vinyl head w/sm red hat cocked to side & bow tie, wht/blk ears, NM.........$50.00
Elephant (Ringling Bros Barnum & Bailey Circus), cloth body w/logo, brn vinyl head, EX $75.00
Elf, Zany, 1950s, silky cloth body w/vinyl head, mouth open, lg plastic eyes, molded pointy hat, EX............................$50.00
Leopard, Hazelle, 1960s, blk, wht & brn spotted cloth body w/vinyl head, mouth w/fangs, MIP.................................$45.00
Policeman, Hazelle, plain bl cloth body w/vinyl head & hat, glancing eyed, 9", EX...$45.00
Prince Phillip, Gund, 1950s, cloth body w/vinyl head, NM ..$75.00
Ralph, Hazelle, 1960s, wht cloth body w/bl polka-dots, vinyl head w/yel hair, pnt-on brn-dotted 'wiskers,' MIP......$65.00
Red the Clown, Hazelle, 1960s, red cloth body w/wht polka-dots, vinyl head & hat, MIP..$55.00
Wise Owl, Hazelle, 1960s, wht cloth body w/vinyl head, MIP .$45.00

MARIONETTES

Ballet Dancer, Pelham, wht satiny dress w/silver pointed shoes, MIB $100.00

Bimbo the Clown, Pelham, 1960s, NM+IB, $120.00. (Photo courtesy gasolinealleyantiques.com)

Bobby (Policeman), Pelham, working mouth, dk bl uniform, about 14", MIB $175.00
Cat, Pelham, wood, beaded legs & tail, blk & wht, red ribbon neck bow, 5½" L, NM+ $100.00
Clown, Hazelle, wht cloth body w/red, bl & yel polka-dots, vinyl head w/yel hair, red vinyl hat & shoes, 12½", VG $75.00
Clown, Hazelle, wht face/hands/shoes, blk brows/eyes, red cheeks/lips, red costume w/wht dots, red hat/collar, 15", EX $75.00
Clown, Hazelle's Hobby Kit #101, wht face & hands, blk shoes, colorfull outfit, 15", NMIB $125.00
Girl w/Yo-Yo, Pelham, ball-shaped head w/dk hair, yo-yo in hand, NMIB $100.00
Hillbilly, Hazelle #881, 1949-50, nonmovable mouth w/pipe, 13½", NMIB $150.00
Lady, Hazelle, nonmovable mouth, blond hair, print house dress w/long sleeves, wht shoes, 14", NM $85.00
Lady, Hazelle, nonmovable mouth, dk hair, long print skirt w/wht blouse, red ribbon neck bow & sash, wht shoes, NM $85.00
Lady, Hazelle, working mouth, blond hair, bl skirt w/red & wht checked blouse, wht apron, blk-pnt shoes, 14", NM+ $100.00
Lady in Long Gown, Pelham, yel blond hair, satiny gown, NM $75.00
Minstrel, Pelham, wood, dk brn skin w/red lips, lt bl pants, wht striped jacket, w/banjo, NRFB $175.00
Prince Charming, Hazelle #916, working mouth, NMIB $175.00
Sailor, Hazelle, working mouth, US Navy uniform, 14", NM+ $100.00
Skeleton, Pelham, boney structure w/lg red-rimmed bug-eyes, very scarce, NM $275.00
Small Fry Club Girl, Peter Puppet Playthings, working mouth, NM+ $125.00
Witch, Hazelle, nonmovable mouth, blk w/red belt, buggy eyes outlined in blk w/blk facial markings, wht hair, EX+ $125.00
Witch, Hazelle, working mouth, blk outfit, holding broom, 15", NM+ $150.00

PUSH-BUTTON PUPPETS

Baseball Batter, China, pnt wood, various styles, about 5", M, from $15 to $20.00
Baseball Pitcher, China, pnt wood, 5", M $18.00
Candy the Cat, Kohner, 1960s, M $75.00
Cowboy on Horse, Wakouwa, 1949, wood, sq base, EX+ $150.00
Dancer Dog, Kohner, 1960s, NM $65.00
Elephant, Kohner, 1950s, NM+ $125.00
Football Player, pnt wood, 5¼", M $15.00
Gabriel the Giraffe, Kohner, 1960s, EX+ $65.00
Go Bots, Tonka/Toy Store Ltd, 1986, M $35.00
Hit & Miss, Kohner, 1940s, pnt wood, wht & blk boxers, sq base, NMIB (red box) $225.00

Hit and Miss (Boxers), Kohner, 1950s, painted wood boxers on round plastic base, MIB, $225.00. (Photo courtesy gasolinealleyantiques.com)

Hit & Miss, Kohner, 1960s, 2 boxers, pnt plastic, silver foil label on rnd base, NM $75.00
Horse, wood, brn w/blk ears & hooves, sq base, 3", M (Poor box) $65.00
Huba Huba, dog on sq base, wood w/leather ears, EX $75.00
I'm Robot, Kohner, 1960s, EX $35.00
Lion, TM, 1970s, sq base, NM+ $30.00
Lucky the Lion, Kohner, 1960s, M $85.00
Robot, TM, 1970s, M $65.00
Skateboarder, China, pnt wood bead type on rnd base, M $20.00
Terry the Tiger, Kohner, 1960s, M $65.00
Tiger, TM, 1970s, orange on sq blk base, EX $40.00

Puzzles

Jigsaw puzzles have been around almost as long as games. The first examples were handcrafted from wood, and they are extremely difficult to find. Most of the early examples featured moral subjects and offered insight into the social atmosphere of their time. By the 1900s, jigsaw puzzles had become a major form of home entertainment. Cube puzzles or blocks were often made by the same companies as board games. Early examples display lithography of the finest quality. While all subjects are collectible, some (such as Santa blocks) often command prices higher than games of the same period.

Because TV and personality-related puzzles have become so popular, they're now regarded as a field all their own apart from character collectibles in general, and these are listed here as well, under the subtitle 'Character.'

Note: All puzzles are complete unless indicated otherwise.

See also Advertising; Black Americana; Paper-Lithographed Toys; Santa.

A Peep at the Circus Puzzle (Dissected), McLoughlin Bros, 1887, 12x10", VGIB $175.00
Ann Hathaway's Cottage, 1930s, plywood, 566 pcs, 16x20", orig box $75.00
Autumn Along the Seine, Joseph Sterns, 1930s, plywood, 300 pcs, orig box $40.00
Battle of Lake Erie (War of 1812), JLG Ferris, 1930s, plywood, 204 pcs, 16x11", EXIB $50.00
Birth of Old Glory, Madmar/Interlox, 1930s, plywood, 210 pcs, 12x10", EXIB $50.00
Blooms & Blossoms (house & garden), 1930s, pressed board, 505 pcs, 18x26", rpl box $150.00

Boy Eating Apples, 1930s, plywood, 135 pieces, 11½x9", EXIB, $20.00. (Photo courtesy Bob Armstrong)

Cattle in Pasture (farming), Julien Dupre (artist), 1930s, plywood, 188 pcs, 10x14", rpl box $45.00
Children & Swan, Red Seal Jig, 1930s, plywood, 545 pcs, 16x20", EX+IB $200.00
Circus Picture Puzzles, McLoughlin Bros, paper litho on fiber board, set of 3 w/guide sheets, EX (in 12x10" wood box), A $825.00
Cottage of Mary Arden, Parker Bros/Pastime, 1920-30, plywood, 71 pcs, 8x6", EXIB $35.00
Day Break & the Hunt Is On, Busy Bee/Novelty, 1930s, plywood, 523 pcs, 20x16", EXIB $150.00
Deer in Mountain Valley, Edward Leggett Clark (maker), 1930s, plywood, 850 pcs, 16x22", orig box $250.00
Dutch Scene, H Cassiers, 1909, wood, 224 pcs, 10x13", EX (rpl box) $90.00
Fire Department Puzzle Box, Milton Bradley, paper litho, set of 3, 10x16", VGIB $350.00

First Steps, 1909, wood, 15x10", EXIB, $50.00. (Photo courtesy Bob Armstrong)

George Washington's Ancestral Home (garden), Lloyd Clift/Miloy, 1930s, plywood, 607 pcs, 16x20", orig box ... $175.00
Gleaners (farming scene), Jean Francois Miller (artist), cb, 325 pcs, 12x16", orig box $10.00
Gloucester Harbor Massachusetts, Charles Russell, 1940-50, plywood, 358 pcs, 13x10", EXIB $125.00
Happy Family (home scene w/peasants), F Zampighi (artist), 1930s, 12x16", rpl box $100.00
Hide & Seek, 1909, wood, 106 pcs, 7x8", VGIB $40.00
Household Cavalry (horse/humor), Thomson (artist), 1909, 200 pcs, 12x18", orig box $225.00
In the Gloaming (countryside at sunset), Qualitee Jig Saw Puzzles, 1930s, plywood, 334 pcs, 12x16", orig box $80.00
Jewel Case (woman), Parker Bros/Pastime, 1926, plywood, 257 pcs, 10x13", orig box $110.00
King of the Desert (Lion), 1920s, plywood, 288 pcs, 12x16", EXIB $80.00
King's Cavalier, Joseph Straus/Regal/Doheny (artist), 1940-50, plywood, 1000 pcs, 22x28", orig box $200.00
Lanterns (female pirate), Pressler (artist), 1930s, plywood, 321 pcs, 11x14", rpl box $75.00
Mountain Train, Parker Bros/Kohler's Puzzles, 1930s, plywood, 412 pcs, 16x19", orig boxes $150.00
News of Peace (Civil War/town), Clyde O Deland (artist), 1910s, wood, 321 pcs, 12x16", orig box $140.00
Old Fort Antigua, Lowell, 1920-30, plywood, 116 pcs, 9x8", EXIB $35.00
Old Mill (stream), Macy's, 1930s, plywood, 200 pcs, 9x12", orig box $70.00
Oriental Travelers in Venice (harbor), Milton Bradley, 1930s, plywood, 1009 pcs, orig box $330.00

People's Advocate (Lincoln addressing court), Griswald Fang (artist ?), 1920s, wood, 540 pcs, 16x21", rpl box...... $150.00
Philadelphia Centennial Expo Puzzle Set, paper on wood, 5 scroll-cut puzzles of various buildings, G (12x22" wood box) $165.00
Restful Moments, Parker Bros/Pastime, 1920-30, EXIB.. $300.00
Rounding the Capes (clipper ship), Joseph Straus, 1930s, plywood, 300 pcs, 12x16", orig box.................................$40.00
Setters on Point, GB Fox, 1930s, plywood, 805 pcs, 22x16", EXIB.. $220.00
Springtime (woman), Parker Bros/Pastime, 1917, plywood, 81 pcs, EXIB..$35.00
Summer on the Riviera (sailing scene), Parker Bros/Pastime, G Roger (artist), 1930s, plywood, 1000 pcs, 24x35", rpl box $450.00
Taj Mahal, Chad Valley, 1930s, plywood, 535 pcs, 20x15", VGIB... $110.00
Three Graces (closeup of girl by water w/swans), attributed to Chad Valley, 1930s, plywood, 727 pcs, 20x16", rpl box $175.00
Tranquil Mountain Waters, Fairchild Corp/Fairco E, 1930-40, cb, 350 pcs, 13x19", EXIB $80.00

Unconquered Places, 1920s, plywood, 324 pieces, 12x16", VG, $25.00. (Photo courtesy Bob Armstrong)

Union w/Scotland (historical), Hayter/Victory/Artistic, plywood, 1000 pcs, 21x22", orig box.. $175.00
Untitled (ships at sea), Joseph Straus, 1930s, plywood, 750 pcs, 18x23½", rpl box...$85.00
Welcome Guest (camp scene w/bear), Zig-Zag Puzzle Co, 1930s, plywood, 500 pcs, 16x20", orig box........................ $135.00
White Squadron, McLoughlin Bros, ca 1892, interlocking, 9½x9½", EX+IB, A $412.00
Wild West Picture Puzzle, McLoughlin Bros, 1890, paper on wood, EX (framed & w/box), A $350.00
Winter on the Spreewald (winter countryside), 1910, plywood, 631 pcs, 24x18", EXIB $300.00
Yacht Puzzle, Bradley, litho on cb, sq-cut pcs, 5x6½" wood box w/hinged lid & paper litho label, EX, A $300.00
York Coach (coaching scene), Victor Venner (English artist), 1909, wood, 14x24", orig box $250.00

Character

Annie Oakley, fr-tray, Milton Bradley, Annie on rearing horse, EX $35.00
Banana Splits, fr-tray, Whitman, boxed set of 4, NM..... $100.00
Banana Splits, fr-tray, Whitman #4534, 1969, EX.............$50.00

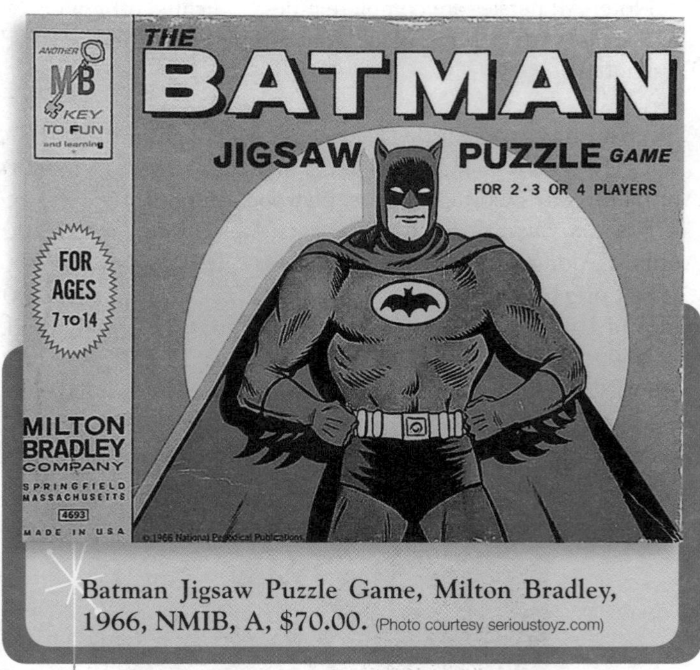

Batman Jigsaw Puzzle Game, Milton Bradley, 1966, NMIB, A, $70.00. (Photo courtesy serioustoyz.com)

Ben Casey, jigsaw, Milton Bradley, #43, 'The Ordeal is Over,' EXIB..$45.00
Broken Arrow, fr-tray, Built-Rite #1229, 1957, NM $55.00
Buffalo Bill Jr, fr-tray, Built-Rite #1229, 1956, EX $40.00
Bugs Bunny, fr-tray, Whitman, 1979, Bugs w/lg Carrot & Porky Pig mountain climbing, mountain goat on peak, EX+.........$6.00
Captain Kangaroo, fr-tray, Whitman #4446, 1960, EX......$38.00
Circus Boy, fr-tray, Whitman #4428, 1958, NM+..............$65.00
Dennis the Menace, fr-tray, Whitman, 1960, 'Ice Cold Lemonade 2¢ A Glass,' NM $45.00
Dennis the Menace, fr-tray, Whitman, 1960, painting a chair, NM..$45.00
Dennis the Menace, fr-tray, Whitman, 1961, washing his dog in the birdbath, M (sealed)..$60.00
Ding Dong School, fr-tray, Whitman, 1953, boat, blk & wht photo of Miss Francis upper right corner, VG+ $20.00
Ding Dong School, fr-tray, Whitman, 1953, train, blk & wht photo inset of Miss Francis upper right, VG+.............$20.00
Ding Dong School, fr-tray, Whitman, 1955, jungle animals, VG+ $20.00
Dr Kildare, jigsaw, Milton Bradley #4318, 1960s, Emergency, EXIB..$45.00
Felix the Cat, Bilt-Rite #1229, 1959, fishing scene, NM...$65.00
Flintstones, fr-tray, unknown maker, 1961, Dino in apron vacuuming and talking on phone, EX $38.00
Flintstones, fr-tray, Warren, 1974, Splat, Dino slips in soapy puddle as Fred tries to give him a bath, NM+.............$35.00
Flintstones, fr-tray, Whitman #4428, 1960, NM................$40.00
Flintstones, fr-tray, Whitman #4434, 1960s, EX $35.00
Flintstones, fr-tray, Whitman #4434, 1963, EX..................$38.00

Flip the Frog, jigsaw, Saalfield/Celebrity Prod, 1932, boxed set of 4, EXIB....$75.00
Gene Autry, fr-tray, Whitman #2962, 1950, VG+....$65.00
Green Hornet, fr-tray, Whitman, 1966, boxed set of 4, NMIB....$125.00
Gunsmoke, fr-tray, Whitman #4427, 1960, VG....$15.00
Gunsmoke, jigsaw, Whitman #4609, 1969, NMIB....$25.00
Hippty Hooper, fr-tray, Whitman #4523, 1965, EX+....$45.00
Howdy Doody, fr-tray, Whitman #4428, 1953, VG+....$40.00

It's Howdy Doody Time, jigsaw, Kagran, 1950s, 9x12", NM, $100.00. (Photo courtesy serioustoyz.com)

Lassie, frame-tray, Whitman, 1957, NM, $45.00. (Photo courtesy gasolinealleyantiques.com)

Little Beaver, fr-tray, Whitman #4428, 1950s, EX+....$25.00

Lone Ranger Picture Puzzles, Whitman #3902, set of 2, NMIB, A....$125.00
Munsters, Whitman, 1965, 'painterly' image of cast watching grandpa mix a potion, NMIB, A....$50.00
Rin Tin Tin, fr-tray, Whitman #4128, 1950s, EX+....$45.00
Rocky & Bullwinkle, fr-tray, Whitman #4792, 1961, set of 4, M (VG+ box)....$100.00
Rocky the Flying Squirrel, fr-tray, Whitman, 1960, Bullwinkle balancing Rocky & aliens Gidney & Cloyd on feet, NM...$50.00
Rootie Kazootie Wins the Soap-Box Race..., fr-tray, Fairchild, 1940s, 10x14", EX....$28.00
Roy Rogers, fr-tray, Artcraft Series 1004, photo image of Marx Double Bar ranch playset w/figures, horses & dogs, EX..$35.00
Roy Rogers, fr-tray, ROHR Co, dated 1950, seated by bush w/Trigger or leaning on saddle w/chaps hanging from post, EX, ea . $55.00
Roy Rogers, fr-tray, Whitman #4427, VG+....$40.00
Sgt Preston, fr-tray, Milton Bradley, Sgt Preston on horseback in stream looking down at his dog King, EX....$45.00
Sgt Preston, jigsaw, Milton Bradley #4828, NMIB....$35.00
Smokey the Bear, fr-tray, NFRS #94015, unused, NM....$18.00
Snow White, picture cubes, paper on wood, 20 cubes, complete picture measures 7½x6", VG+IB (wood box), A..... $125.00
Spider-Man, Poster-Puzzle, 'Giant 9 Sq Feet,' Aurora, 1974, complete, NMIB, A....$30.00
Tales of Wells Fargo, fr-tray, Whitman #4427, 1958, EX...$40.00
Top Cat, fr-tray, Whitman #4457, 1961, scarce, G....$20.00
Wagon Train, fr-tray, Whitman, 1958, Seth Adams & Flint McCulloch w/guns drawn behind corral fence, EX+ ..$35.00
Wagon Train, fr-tray, Whitman, 1961, 2 riders chasing buffalo w/wagon train in the distance, EX+....$35.00
Wyatt Earp, fr-tray, Whitman #4427, 1958, NM....$45.00

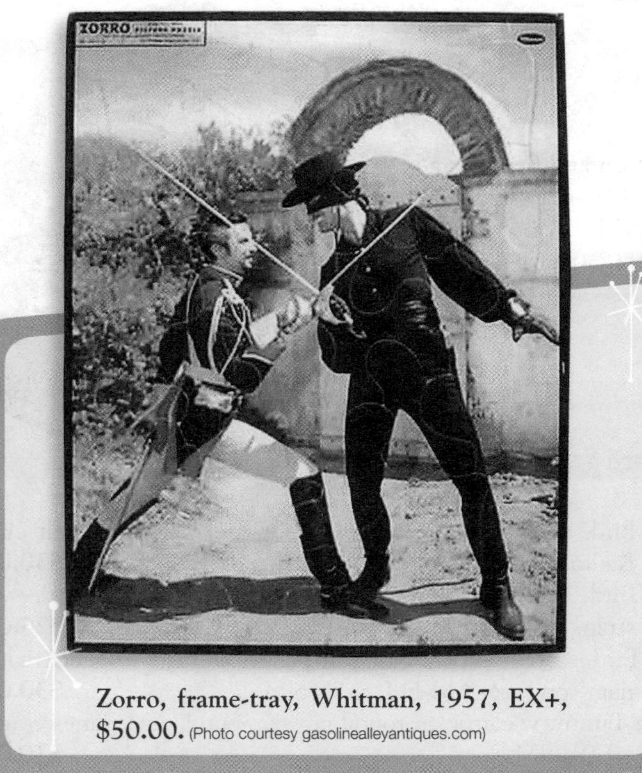

Zorro, frame-tray, Whitman, 1957, EX+, $50.00. (Photo courtesy gasolinealleyantiques.com)

Zorro, jigsaw, Jaymar #2311 or #2710, 1950S, NM+, ea....$45.00

Radios

Many novelty radios are made to resemble a commercial product box or can, and with the crossover interest into the advertising field, some of the more collectible, even though of recent vintage, are often seen carrying very respectible price tags. Likenesses of famous personalities such as Elvis or characters like Charlie Tuna house transistors in cases made of plastic that scarcely hint at their actual function. Others represent items ranging from baseball caps to Cadillacs.

BA Baracus (Mr T), plastic keyhole shape w/photo insert image of BA flexing muscles on red ground, w/strap, EX......$55.00

Batman, two-dimensional half-figure, Hong Kong, 1973, EX+, $65.00. (Photo courtesy gasolinealleyantiques.com)

Bert & Ernie, half-figures on figure-8 base w/Sesame Street label, AM, 7", NM......$25.00

Bert and Ernie, vaudville act on stage, AM, 7", NM+, $28.00. (Photo courtesy gasolinealleyantiques.com)

Big Bird, head form w/red & wht bow tie, w/strap & belt clip, Radio Shack, 1990, MIB......$30.00

Big Bird, in nest w/Sesame Street street sign emb on side, yel strap, AM, 8", NM......$25.00

Big Bird, seated on oval base leaning on vintage 'wooden' radio, name on base, AM-FM, 8x7", NM......$30.00

Bugs Bunny, w/carrot on round grassy mound, AM, Janex/Sears, 1970s, NM......$30.00

Charlie Brown, Snoopy & Woodstock, flat decaled plastic figures w/strap, AM, 7", Determined, 1970s, NM+......$35.00

Cheeseburger, w/strap, 5" dia, 1970s, NM+......$22.00

Coca-Cola Bottle, 8", EX, $60.00. (Photo courtesy gasolinealleyantiques.com)

Comet Transistor Radio, red, wht & bl oblong case w/antenna, bl vinyl strap, rocket emblem, Japan, 1960s, NM+......$60.00

Elvis, doll figure singing into micorphone on blk base w/name & birth/death dates, 8½", UNIC, M, A......$50.00

Evel Knievel, triangular w/photo decal, w/strap, Krypton Electronics, 1970s, scare, EX......$85.00

Golden State Warriors/Coca-Cola Classic, basketball form, orange w/blk lettering, 3½" dia, 1980s, NM......$45.00

Mickey Mouse, Emerson/FAO Schwarz, 1930s, EX, $950.00. (Photo courtesy Morphy Auctions)

Nestlé Crunch Candy Bar, w/strap, EX+......$55.00

Oscar the Grouch, Oscar pops up from garbage can w/lid on head, Concept 2000, 1976, NMIB......$60.00

Pac-Man, w/headphones, NM......$50.00

Pig in Overalls, standing upright looking up, 2 red hearts on overalls, AM, Hong Kong, 1970s, MIB (NOS)......$25.00

Planters Cocktail Peanuts Can, NM......$85.00

Rabbit, gray w/wht hair tuft, cheeks & tummy, red ears, nose & mouth, seated upright, AM, Hong Kong, 1970s, MIB (NOS)......$25.00

San Francisco Giants, blk & red baseball cap form w/orange SF logo, Pro Sports, 1976, NM.......................................$65.00
Sesame Street, characters in gr stage box draped w/yel swag, oblong dial on front, vinyl & plastic, electric, 1970s, EX...........$30.00
Smurfs, head form, bl & wht w/blk outline detail, w/strap, 1982, EX $45.00
Smurfs, singing Smurf, 2-D, bl & wht w/blk outline detail, wht dial w/blk musical note, 5x3", Nasta, 1980s, NM+.....$15.00
Snoopy, seated, 2-D, wht w/blk outline detail, AM, w/earplugs, 7", 1970s, NM (VG box)..$50.00
Snorky, yel w/lg wht & blk eyes, Wallace Berrie, 1984, M...$40.00
Star Explorer Space Ship AM Band Radio, Hong Kong, AM-FM, NMIB..$75.00
Texas Rangers, wht baseball form w/strap, Gatorade promo, EX+ $45.00
Tony the Tiger, standing, 2-D, orange & wht w/blk outline details, the name Tony at bottom, Kellogg's, 1980, MIB...........$85.00
Welch's Frozen Concentrated Sweetened Grape Juice Can, AM-FM, pull-up antenna, NM $55.00

Ramp Walkers

Ramp walkers date back to at least 1873 when Ives produced two versions of a cast-iron elephant walker. Wood and composition ramp walkers were made in Czechoslovakia and the U.S.A. from the 1930s through the 1950s. The most common were made by John Wilson of Pennsylvania and were sold worldwide. These became known as 'Wilson Walkies.' Most are two-legged and stand approximately 4½" tall. While some of the Wilson Walkies were made of a composite material with wood legs (for instance, Donald, Wimpy, Popeye, and Olive Oyl), most are made with cardboard thread-cone bodies with wood legs and head. The walkers made in Czechoslovakia are similar but they are generally made of wood.

Plastic ramp walkers were primarily manufactured by the Louis Marx Co. and were made from the early 1950s through the mid-1960s. The majority were produced in Hong Kong, but some were made in the United States and sold under the Marx logo or by the Charmore Co., which was a subsidiary of the Marx Co. Some walkers are still being produced today as fast-food premiums.

The three common sizes are small, about 1½" x 2"; medium, about 2¾" x 3"; and large, about 4"x 5". Most of the small walkers are unpainted while the medium or large sizes were either spray painted or painted by hand. Several of the walking toys were sold with wooden plastic or colorful lithographed tin ramps.

Unless another manufacturer is noted within the descriptions, all of the following Disney ramp walkers were made by the Marx company.

Advertising

Captain Flint, Long John Silvers, 1989, w/plastic coin weight.$15.00
Choo-Choo Cherry, Funny Face Kool-Aid, w/plastic coin weight..$60.00
Flash Turtle, Long John Silvers, 1989, w/plastic coin weight.$15.00
Goofy Grape, Funny Face Kool-Aid, w/plastic coin weight...$60.00
Jolly Ollie Orange, Funny Face Kool-Aid, w/plastic coin weight...$60.00
Quinn Penguin, Long John Silvers, 1989, w/plastic coin weight...$15.00
Root'n Toot'n Raspberry, Funny Face Kool-Aid, w/plastic coin weight $60.00
Sydney Dinosaur, Long John Silvers, 1989, yel & purple, w/plastic coin weight...$15.00
Sylvia Dinosaur, Long John Silvers, 1989, lavender & pk, w/plastic coin weight...$15.00

Czechoslovakian

Bird $35.00
Bird (lg, store display).. $200.00
Chicago World's Fair (1933), wood, G, T1 .... $100.00
Cow...$35.00
Dog $30.00
Dutch Girl...$60.00

Man With Carved Wood Hat, $45.00; Policeman, $60.00. (Photo courtesy gasolinealleyantiques.com)

Monkey $45.00
Pig $30.00

Disney Characters

Big Bad Wolf & Mason Pig...$50.00
Big Bad Wolf & Three Little Pigs.................................. $150.00
Donald Duck & Goofy Riding Go-Cart.............................$40.00
Donald Duck Pulling Nephews in Wagon..........................$35.00
Donald Duck Pushing Wheelbarrow, all plastic.................$25.00
Donald Duck Pushing Wheelbarrow, plastic w/metal legs, sm..$25.00
Donald's Trio, France, Huey, Louie & Dewey dressed as Indian Chief, cowboy & 1 carrying flowers, NMOC, A...... $150.00
Fiddler & Fifer Pigs $50.00
Figaro the Cat w/Ball...$30.00
Goofy, riding hippo..$45.00
Jiminy Cricket, w/cello $30.00
Mad Hatter w/March Hare $50.00

Mickey Mouse and Donald Duck Riding Alligator, $40.00. (Photo courtesy Randy Welch)

Mickey Mouse & Minnie, plastic w/metal legs, sm............$40.00
Mickey Mouse & Pluto Hunting..$40.00
Mickey Mouse Pushing Lawn Roller.................................$35.00
Minnie Mouse Pushing Baby Stroller................................$35.00
Pluto, plastic w/metal legs, sm...$35.00

Hanna-Barbera, King Features & Other Characters by Marx

Astro..$150.00
Astro & George Jetson..$75.00
Astro & Rosey...$75.00
Bonnie Braids' Nursemaid..$50.00
Chilly Willy, penguin on sled pulled by parent.................$25.00
Fred & Wilma Flintstone on Dino......................................$60.00

Fred Flintstone and Barney Rubble, $40.00. (Photo courtesy Randy Welch)

Fred Flintstone on Dino...$75.00
Hap & Hop Soldiers..$25.00
Little King & Guard..$60.00
Pebbles on Dino..$75.00
Popeye, Irwin, celluloid, lg...$60.00
Popeye & Wimpy, heads on springs, MIB..........................$85.00
Popeye Pushing Spinach Can Wheelbarrow.......................$30.00
Santa, w/gold sack..$45.00
Santa, w/wht sack...$40.00
Santa, w/yel sack..$40.00
Santa & Mrs Claus, faces on both sides.............................$50.00
Santa & Snowman, faces on both sides..............................$50.00
Spark Plug..$200.00
Top Cat & Benny..$65.00
Yogi Bear & Huckleberry Hound..$50.00

Marx Animals With Riders Series

Ankylosaurus w/Clown...$40.00
Bison w/Native..$40.00
Brontosaurus w/Monkey...$40.00
Hippo w/Native...$40.00
Lion w/Clown..$40.00
Stegosaurus w/Black Caveman...$40.00
Triceratops w/Native..$40.00
Zebra w/Native...$40.00

Plastic (Boxes Complete With Bottles)

Baby Walk-A-Way, lg...$40.00
Bear..$20.00
Boy & Girl Dancing...$45.00
Bull...$20.00
Bunnies Carrying Carrot...$35.00
Bunny on Back of Dog...$50.00
Bunny Pushing Cart...$60.00
Camel w/2 Humps, head bobs..$20.00
Chicks Carrying Easter Egg...$35.00
Chinese Men w/Duck in Basket..$30.00
Chipmunks Carrying Acorns...$35.00
Chipmunks Marching Band w/Drum & Horn....................$35.00
Cow, w/metal legs, sm..$20.00
Cowboy on Horse, w/metal legs, sm...................................$30.00
Dachshund..$20.00
Dairy Cow...$20.00
Dog, Pluto look-alike w/metal legs, sm..............................$20.00
Double Walking Doll, boy behind girl, lg...........................$60.00
Duck..$20.00
Dutch Boy & Girl..$40.00
Elephant..$20.00
Elephant, w/metal legs, sm...$30.00

Farmer Pushing Wheelbarrow, $30.00; Pig, $20.00. (Photo courtesy Randy Welch)

Firemen ...$35.00
Frontiersman w/Dog...$95.00
Goat ...$20.00
Horse, circus style ...$20.00
Horse, lg ...$30.00
Horse, yel w/rubber ears & string tail, lg ...$30.00
Horse w/English Rider, lg...$50.00
Indian Woman Pulling Baby on Travois ...$95.00
Kangaroo w/Baby in Pouch...$30.00
Mama Duck w/3 Ducklings...$35.00
Marty's Market Lady Pushing Shopping Cart ...$65.00
Mexican Cowboy on Horse, w/metal legs, sm...$30.00
Milking Cow, lg...$40.00
Monkeys Carrying Bananas ...$60.00
Mother Goose ...$45.00
Nursemaid Pushing Baby Stroller...$20.00
Pigs, 2 carrying 1 in basket ...$40.00
Pumpkin Head Man & Woman, faces both sides... $100.00
Reindeer...$45.00
Sailors SS Shoreleave ...$25.00
Sheriff Facing Outlaw ...$65.00
Slugger the Walking Bat Boy, w/ramp & box... $250.00
Teeny Toddler, walking baby girl, Dolls Inc, lg ...$40.00
Tin Man Robot Pushing Cart ... $150.00
Walking Baby, in Canadian Mountie uniform, lg ...$50.00
Walking Baby, w/moving eyes & cloth dress, lg...$40.00
Wiz Walker Milking Cow, Charmore, lg ...$40.00

WILSON

Clown...$30.00
Donald Duck ... $175.00
Elephant...$30.00
Eskimo... $100.00
Indian Chief...$70.00
Little Red Riding Hood ...$40.00
Mammy ...$40.00

Nurse, $30.00; Soldier, $30.00.
(Photo courtesy gasolinealleyantiques.com)

Olive Oyl ... $175.00
Penguin ...$25.00
Pig ...$40.00
Pinocchio ... $200.00
Popeye ... $200.00
Rabbit...$75.00
Sailor ...$30.00
Santa Claus ...$90.00
Wimpy... $175.00

Records

Most of the records listed here are related to TV shows, cartoons, and movies, and are specifically geared toward children. The more successful the show, the more collectible the record. But condition is critical as well, and unless the record is excellent or better, its value is lowered very dramatically. The presence of the original sleeve or cover is crucial to establishing collectibility.

33⅓ RPM RECORDS

Alice in Wonderland, Disneyland #ST3909, 1962, w/10-pg story book, EX (EX sleeve)...$15.00
Alice in Wonderland Starring Magilla Gorilla, Columbia, 1977, M (EX sleeve) ...$60.00
Archies, Post Cereals premium, cb picture disc, Archies characters shown on bl background, yel label, EX+ ...$25.00
Babes in Toyland, Disneyland #ST3910, 1961, w/10-pg story book, VG+ (EX sleeve) ...$15.00
Bambi, Disneyland #ST3903, 1962, w/1-pg story book, EX (EX sleeve) ...$15.00

Batman — Exclusive Original Television Soundtrack Album, Mercury, 1966, EX+ (EX+ sleeve), $75.00.
(Photo courtesy gasolinealleyantiques.com)

Batman/The Catwoman's Revenge, Power Records 2306, 1975, 7", M (sealed sleeve)...$55.00
Big Bird's Bedtime Stories, Sesame Street #CTW22093, 1980, G+ (VG sleeve) ...$5.00

Bonanza/Ponderosa Party Time!, RCA Victor #LPM2583, 1962, EX (EX sleeve)....$40.00
Bugs Bunny Songfest, Giant Golden #LP71, sleeve only, EX..$8.00
Charlie Brown's All-Stars, #2602, 1978, NM (EX+ sleeve)...$30.00
Christmas with the Chipmunks, Mistletoe Records, 1970s, VG (VG sleeve)....$8.00
Cinderella, Disneyland #ST3908, 1962, w/10-pg story book, VG+, (EX sleeve)....$15.00
Dark Shadows/Quentin's Theme, w/poster, 1969, NM (NM sleeve)....$75.00
David & Goliath/Little Golden Book & Record, Disneyland #218, 1976, NM (NM sleeve)....$18.00
Don Adams Get Smart, United Artist, 1960s, very scare, EX (NM sleeve)....$75.00

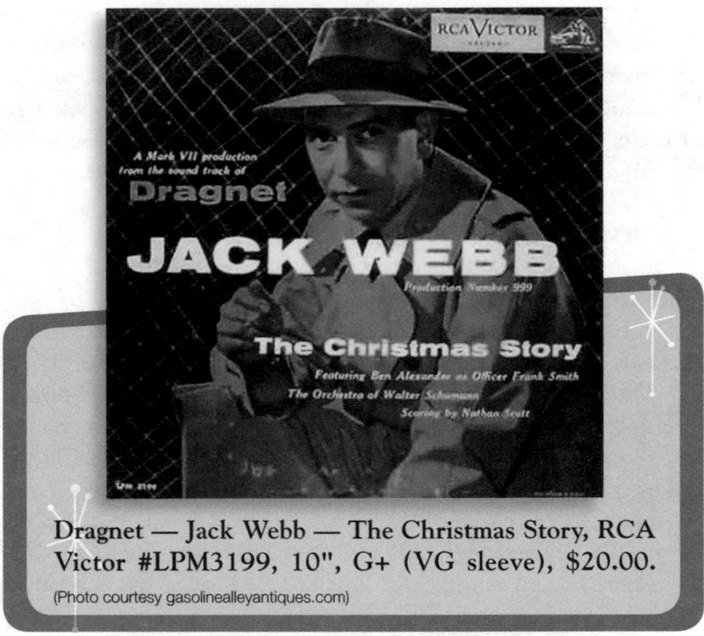

Dragnet — Jack Webb — The Christmas Story, RCA Victor #LPM3199, 10", G+ (VG sleeve), $20.00.

(Photo courtesy gasolinealleyantiques.com)

Ewoks Join the Fight, Buena Vista Book & Record Set #460, 1983, w/26-pg illus book, NM....$15.00
Fat Albert & the Cosby Kids Creativity, Kid Stuff #KS201, 1980, M (NM sleeve)....$75.00
Fat Albert & the Cosby Kids Halloween, Kid Stuff #KSO29, 1980, M (sealed)....$95.00
Fonzie Favorites, Precision Records #TVLP177602R, 1976, Canadian issue only, EX+ (EX+ sleeve)....$35.00
Gizmo & the Gremlins/Story #2, Warner, 1984, w/16-pg story book, M (NM sleeve)....$18.00
Groovie Goolies, RCA Victor #LSP4420, 1970, scarce, EX+ (VG sleeve)....$175.00
Halloween Staring Fat Albert & the Cosby Kids, Kid Stuff #KS029, 1980, unused, M (sealed)....$100.00
Jackson Five, Post cereals premium, cb picture disc w/5 songs including 'ABC,' EX+....$25.00
Jesus Loves Me/Roy Rogers Dale Evans & Their Family, RCA Victor #CAL1022, 1960, Canadian issue, EX+ (NM sleeve)....$30.00
Jetsons First Family on the Moon, Columbia, 1977, M (EX sleeve)....$65.00
John Denver & the Muppets A Christmas Together, RCA #AFL3451, 1979, VG (EX+ sleeve)....$6.00

Large & Growly Bear/Little Golden Book & Record, Disneyland #210, 1976, NM (NM sleeve)....$18.00
Let's All Sing With the Chipmunks, Liberty #LRP3132, 1959, VG+ (VG sleeve)....$8.00
Little Marcy Visits Smokey Bear, Word Label #K707, Canadian issue, EX+ (M sleeve)....$75.00
Man From UNCLE, RCA Victor #LPM3475, 1965, EX (NM sleeve)....$35.00
Mary Poppins, RCA Victor #CSO111, 1964, orig soundtrack, VG+ (EX jacket)....$10.00
Merry Christmas From the Brady Bunch, EX+ (EX+ sleeve)...$60.00
Merry Merry Merry Merry Merry Christmas From Captain Kangaroo, NM (NM sleeve)....$75.00

Nancy — Listen, Laugh & Learn, Kid Stuff #KSS5020, 1982, NM (EX+ sleeve), $45.00.

(Photo courtesy gasolinealleyantiques.com)

Noah's Ark/Little Golden Book & Record, Disneyland #222, 1976, NM (NM sleeve)....$18.00
Nutcracker Suite From Walt Disney's 'Fantasia,' EX (EX sleeve)....$45.00
Oh Good Grief!/Vince Guaraldi, Warner Bros #1747, 1968, NM (NM sleeve)....$20.00
Peter Pan, Disneyland #ST3910, 1962, w/10-pg story book, EX (EX sleeve)....$15.00
Pinocchio, Disneyland #ST3903, 1962, w/10-pg story book, EX (EX sleeve)....$15.00
Precious Pup & Granny Sweet in Hot Rod Granny, HBR #HLP2039, 1965, VG (G sleeve)....$25.00
Puss in Boots/Little Golden Book & Record, Disneyland #208, 1976, NM (NM sleeve)....$18.00
Reluctant Dragon Starring Touchè Turtle & Dum-Dum, 1965, EX (EX sleeve)....$100.00
Rocky & His Friends, Golden #LP64, 1961, EX (EX sleeve)..$75.00
Route 66 Theme, Capitol #T1771, 1960s, w/various TV-show theme songs, EX+ (VG sleeve)....$18.00
Rumpelstiltskin/Little Golden Book & Record, Disneyland #204, 1976, NM+ (NM+ sleeve)....$18.00
Saggy Baggy Elephant, Little Golden Book & Record #201, NM+....$18.00

Scuffy the Tugboat/Little Golden Book & Record, Disneyland #205, 1976, NM (NM sleeve) $18.00

Sesame Street Featuring Rubber Duckie, Wonderland #LP256, 1974, VG+ (VG sleeve) $10.00

Seven Little Postmen/Little Golden Book & Record, Disneyland #222, NM (NM sleeve) $18.00

Snoopy & His Friends the Royal Guardsmen, Laurie #SLP2042, Canadian, EX (EX+ sleeve) $20.00

Snow White & the Seven Dwarfs, Disneyland #ST3906, 1962, w/10-pg story book, EX (EX sleeve) $15.00

Songs From Annette/Walt Disney Serials, Disneyland #MM24, NM (EX sleeve) $65.00

Songs of the Pogo, AA Records #AR2, 1956, 12", EX+ (EX sleeve), $150.00. (Photo courtesy gasolinealleyantiques.com)

Sugar Bears, Post Cereals premium, cb picture disc, w/5 songs, EX+ $22.00

Superman, Power #8156, NM (EX+ sleeve) $20.00

Tammy's Big Parade, Little World Records/Ideal #LW904, 1965, G (VG sleeve) $35.00

Tammy's Sing-A-Long Party, Little World Records/Ideal, 1965, EX (VG sleeve)..$35.00

Tawny Scrawny Lion/Little Golden Book & Record, 1976, NM+..$18.00

Theme From Ben Casey, Carlton #LP143, Valjean at piano, w/various other TV show theme songs, NM (EX sleeve).........$20.00

Thumbelina/Little Golden Book & Record, Disneyland #206, 1976, NM (NM sleeve) $18.00

Top Cat Original Soundtrack, Colpix #CP212, G (EX sleeve)... $25.00

Toucan Sam Workout, Kellogg's premium, 1983, picture disc w/5 different images of TS exercising on yel ground, NM+ .. $20.00

Treasure Island Starring Sinbad Jr, HBR #HLP2039, 1965, VG (VG sleeve) $25.00

Twelve Days of Christmas With the Chipmunks, Pickwick Records, 1980, VG (w/sleeve).......................................$8.00

Wonderful World of Disneyland Music Vol 1 or Vol 2, unused, M (M sleeves), ea $75.00

You're a Good Man Charlie Brown, MGM #A1E90C, EX (VG sleeve) $18.00

45 RPM Records

A Hap-Hap-Happy Christmas From Yogi Bear, Golden #R50, EX (EX sleeve)..$40.00

Bambi, Disnyland #DNR-27, NM (EX+ sleeve)................$18.00

Banana Splits — Doin' the Banana Split, Kellogg's premium #347, 1969, NM+ (NM sleeve), $30.00. (Photo courtesy gasolinealleyantiques.com)

Bibbidi Bobbidi Boo/Oh Sing Sweet Nightingale, Disneyland #LG771, 1963, NM (NM sleeve)...............................$15.00

Bimbo & Punchy the Clown, Cricket #C754, VG (VG sleeve) $10.00

Bozo & the Birds, Capitol #EAXF3033, 38-pg illus story, EX (EX sleeve) $55.00

Bozo New Songs/I Like People & Wowee!, Golden #681, EX (NM sleeve)...$34.00

Bozo Under the Sea, Capitol #EAXF3031, w/38-pg illus story, VG+ (EX+ sleeve)..$35.00

Brave Engineer, RCA Victor #WY400, Jerry Colonna, VG+ (VG+ 2-pg sleeve)...$40.00

Campaign Songs of...Magilla Gorilla & Yogi Bear, Golden #768, 1964, VG+ (EX sleeve) $35.00

Captain Kangaroo/In the Good Old Summertime, Golden #2033, NM+ (EX+ sleeve) $35.00

Captain Kangaroo — The Horse in Striped Pajamas and Happy Hands, Golden #578, 1959, G (VG+ sleeve), $30.00. (Photo courtesy gasolinealleyantiques.com)

Captain Kangaroo/Victor Herbert's Toyland & March of the Topys, Golden #FF471, 1958, NM (EX+ sleeve)........$35.00

Casper the Friendly Ghost, Peter Pan #PP1081, 1960s, worn record (EX sleeve)...$12.00

Chipmunk Fun With Chip 'N Dale, Disneyland #LG-704, EX (EX sleeve)...$20.00

Chipmunk Song/Almost Good, Liberty #F55168, NM (EX plain sleeve)..$10.00

Doggie Daddy & Augie Doggie in Songs From Pinocchio, HBR #7041, very scarce, EX+ (EX+ sleeve).......................$55.00

Flintstones Goldi Rocks & the Three Bearosauruses, HBR #7021, scarce, EX+ (EX+ sleeve).....................................$50.00

Frosty the Snowman, Golden #69, EX (VG sleeve)..........$10.00

Grassopper & the Ants/The World Owes Me a Living, Disneyland #LG760, 1962, unused, M (NM sleeve).............$15.00

Here Come the Dukes of Hazzard, Kid Stuff #KSR954, 1983, w/16-pg storybook, unused, scarce, M (NM+ sleeve).$40.00

Higitus Figitus (Sword & the Stone), Disneyland #LG767, 1963, NM+ (NM+ sleeve)...$15.00

Huck, Yogi & Quick Draw Safety Song, Golden #674, 1961, M (NM+ sleeve)...$38.00

Huckleberry Hound & Yogi Bear, Golden #550, 1960, NM (EX+ sleeve)...$35.00

Huckleberry Hound Presents Hokey Wolf/Ding-A-Ling A Wolf's Work Is Never Done, Golden #660, 1961, VG (EX sleeve)...$40.00

Huckleberry Hound Tells the Stories of Uncle Remus, HBR #7030, scarce, EX+ (EX+ sleeve)...............................$50.00

Jetsons, Golden, #EP742, 1960s, NM (NM sleeve)...........$45.00

Johnny Appleseed, RCA Victor #EYA6, 1949, Dennis Day, G+ (VG+ sleeve)...$22.00

Jungle Book I Wan'na Be Like You/That's What Friends Are For, Disneyland #LG796, 1967, NM (NM sleeve).............$20.00

Lady & the Tramp, Peggy Lee, Decca #ED728, 2-record set, NM+ (EX+ sleeve)...$30.00

Lady & the Tramp/Lady & He's a Tramp, Golden #D190, EX (EX sleeve)...$32.00

Lenonard Nimoy (Mr Spock) A Visit to a Sad Planet/Theme From 'Star Trek,' Dot #17038, NM (EX sleeve).........$25.00

Little Engine That Could, Golden #682, EX+ (EX sleeve).$7.00

Lone Ranger Theme/Hi-Yo Silver Hi-Yo, Golden #Ff521, 1958, EX (EX sleeve)...$45.00

Maverick, Golden #498, 1958, NM (NM sleeve), $45.00. (Photo courtesy gasolinealleyantiques.com)

Mary Poppins Chim Chim Cheree/Let's Go Fly a Kite, Disneyland #LG783, unused, M (NM+ sleeve).....................$15.00

Merry Christmas From Hank Ketcham's Dennis the Menace, Golden #A22, 1961, EX (EX sleeve)..........................$35.00

Mickey Mouse Club Merry Mouseketeers/Talent Round Up, Golden #D235, 1962, VG+ (NM sleeve)..................$32.00

Mickey Mouse Club Pledge, Golden #D223, 1962, VG+ (NM sleeve)..$32.00

Mickey Mouse Club/You the Human Animal & The Mickey Mouse Club Book Song, Golden #D224, 1962, VG+ (NM sleeve)..$32.00

Mitch Miller's Little Sir Echo/Bobby Shaftoe Hickory-Dickory Dock, Golden #588, VG+ (NM sleeve).....................$12.00

101 Dalmatians Song From 'Cruella De Ville,' Golden #D626, 1960, VG (VG sleeve)..$24.00

Peter Rabbit/Rumpelstiltskin, RCA Victor #WBY37, Paul Wing, EX (EX sleeve)..$15.00

Planet of the Apes Book & Record Set, Power #PR18, 1974, EX+ (NM sleeve)..$15.00

Quick Draw's A-Comin' (And Baba Looey Too) to Clean Up Your Town, Golden #646, 1961, VG+ (EX sleeve)....$35.00

Ruff and Reddy and Professor Gizmo, Golden #558, EX+ (EX+ sleeve), $38.00. (Photo courtesy gasolinealleyantiques.com)

Seven Dwarfs Washing Song (Bluddle-Uddle-Um-Dum)/Story From Snow White, Disneyland #LG742, 1962, NM+ (NM+ sleeve)..$15.00

Sing Along With the Chipmunks, Liberty #LSX1008, 1961, NM (NM sleeve)...$35.00

Sleeping Beauty Once Upon a Dream, Golden #480, EX (EX sleeve)..$30.00

Smokey the Bear, Peter Pan #543, 1950s, VG+ (VG+ sleeve).$12.00

Songs From Robin Hood Starring Top Cat, HBR #7038, EX+ (EX+ sleeve)...$55.00

Songs From Walt Disney's 101 Dalamtians, Disneyland #LG714, unused, M (NM+ sleeve).......................................$15.00

Songs of the Flintstones The Original TV Voices, Golden #680, 1961, VG (EX+ sleeve)..$38.00

Songs of the Jetsons/Push Button Blues & Rama Rama Zoom, Golden #755, VG+ (VG+ sleeve)...............................$45.00

Spin & Marty/The Triple-R Song, Am-Par #DBR-58, EX (EX sleeve)..$40.00

Stardust Lullaby/Wake-Up Song, Cricket #C7103, VG (VG sleeve) $10.00
There Goes Robin/The Wonderful Boy Wonder, Batman #BT96, 1966, NM (NM die-cut sleeve) $15.00
Three Little Pigs Sing Polly Wolly Doodle & Alouette, Disneyland #LG710, 1962, NM (NM sleeve) $15.00

Tweety's Puddy Tat Twouble, Capitol #CBXF-3102, two-record set with 20-page story book, EX+ (EX sleeve), $85.00. (Photo courtesy gasolinealleyantiques.com)

Three Stooges, Golden #586, 1960s, VG (EX sleeve) $38.00
Tom & Jerry & the Fire Engine, MGM #SK19, M (EX+ sleeve) $40.00
Tonka the Theme Song/Tomahawk War Dance, Golden #531, 1959, EX+ (EX+ sleeve) $38.00
Tramp Tramp Tramp the Boys Are Marching/Hail Hail the Gang's All Here, Golden #590, VG (NM sleeve) $12.00
Tweety's Puddy Tat Twouble, Capitol #CBXF-3102, 2-record set w/20-pg story book, EX (EX+ sleeve) $85.00
Ugly Duckling, Golden #697, EX+ (EX sleeve) $7.00
Westward Ho the Wagons!/Jimmie Dodd & the Mousketeers, Am-Par #DBR-67, EX+ (EX sleeve) $35.00
Woody Woodpecker & His Friends Andy Panda & Chilly Willy, Golden #EP620, 1960, M (EX+ sleeve) $38.00
Yogi Bear Introduces Loopy de Loop/Let's Have a Song Yogi Bear, Golden #592, 1960, VG (EX sleeve) $45.00
Yogi Bears Friends, Golden #EP654, 1961, EX+ (EX+ sleeve) .. $45.00

78 RPM Picture and Non-Picture Records

A Ha-Hap Happy Christmas From Yogi Bear, Golden #650, 1961, NM+ (NM+ sleeve) $38.00
Absent Minded Professor, Golden #648, EX (EX sleeve) ..$28.00
Adventures of The Lone Ranger, Decca #K29, 1951, G+ (worn sleeve) $15.00
Alice in Wonderland Musical Story, Peter Pan #565, VG (VG sleeve) $12.00
Alice in Wonderland Title Song/In a World of My Own, Golden #RD18, EX (VG+ sleeve) $25.00
Animal Supermarket/It's Fun to Go Shopping, CRG #9004, EX+ (EX sleeve) $10.00
Anyone for Exploring/The Mickey Mouse Newsreel Music, Golden #D234, EX (VG+ sleeve) $26.00
At the County Fair, Golden #D188, EX (EX sleeve) $35.00
Babes in Toy Land 'March of the Toys,' Golden #662, NM (M sleeve) $35.00
Ballad of Davy Crockett, Golden #D197, NM (NM sleeve) .. $40.00
Ballad of Davy Crockett, RCA Victor #BY25, Sons of the Pioners, EX+ (EX sleeve) $35.00
Big Rock Candy Mountain, CRD #509, Tom Glazer, VG+ (EX sleeve) $8.00
Blue Tail Fly/Billy Boy, Columbia Playtime #347-PV, 1950s, EX (EX sleeve) $14.00
Bozo & His Magic Whistle & Belinda's Rainy Day, Golden #698, 1962, M (EX+ sleeve) $34.00
Brave Little Sambo, Peter Pan #L11, red vinyl, VG (EX sleeve) $20.00
Bugs Bunny & the Grow-Small Juice, Capitol, 1950s, NM ..$75.00
Bugs Bunny in Storyland, Capitol #DBX3021, 1949, 36-pg illus story, VG (VG album) $75.00

Bugs Bunny Railroad Engineer and Yosemite Sam Hold-Up Man, Golden #R249, EX (EX sleeve), $38.00. (Photo courtesy gasolinealleyantiques.com)

Captain Kangaroo When a Bunny Wants a Carrot/The Treasure House Band on Parade, Peter Pan #590, VG (VG sleeve) $15.00
Cinderella Work Song, Golden #D281, EX+ (EX sleeve) ..$30.00
Cinderella Work Song (As Sung in the Movie), Golden #RD10, M (NM sleeve) $35.00
Cinderella/A Dream Is a Wish Your Heart Makes Starring The Mice, Golden #RD11, M (NM sleeve) $35.00
Cowabonga & Big Chief (Howdy Doody), Little Golden Record #R221, EX (w/sleeve) $45.00
Daffy Duck Song, Golden #R186, EX+ (EX sleeve) $38.00
Davy Crockett Be Sure You're Right (Davy's Motto), Golden #D213, EX (EX sleeve) $30.00
Dennis the Menace, Golden #534, 1959, EX+ (EX sleeve) ..$32.00
Dennis the Menace Songs/The Dennis the Menace Theme & Ka-pow! Ka-pow! Ka-pow!, Golden #603, 1960, M (NM sleeve) $35.00
Disneyland & When You Wish Upon a Star, Golden #D194, EX (VG+ sleeve) $30.00

Donald Duck Presents Quack Quack Quack, Golden #D251, NM (NM sleeve) $28.00
Elmer Fudd, Golden #R189, EX (EX sleeve) $38.00
Flintstones Dino the Dino, Golden #739, 1963, EX....................$36.00

Flipper the Fabulous Dolphin, Golden #1105, EX+ (EX+ sleeve), $35.00. (Photo courtesy gasolinealleyantiques.com)

Fury Theme Song/What Did You Do Before You Had TV?, Golden #R440, 1957, EX+ (VG+ sleeve)....................$35.00
Goofy the Toreador, Golden #D151:25, VG+ (EX+ sleeve)..$36.00
Huck, Yogi & Quick Draw Safety Song, Golden #674, 1961, EX (VG+ sleeve)....................$30.00
Huckleberry Hound & Yogi Bear, Golden #550, 1959, NM (EX sleeve)....................$35.00
Huckleberry Hound Presents Pixie & Dixie & Iddy Biddy Buddy, Golden #610, 1960, M (M sleeve)....................$40.00
Huckleberry Hound Presents Pixie & Dixie/Iddy Biddy Buddy, Golden #610, 1960, EX (VG sleeve)....................$30.00
Huckleyberry Hound Presents Hokey Wolf & Ding-A-Ling/A Wolf's Work Is Never Done, Golden #660, 1961, NM (NM sleeve)....................$38.00
I Taut I Taw a Puddy Tat/Yosemite Sam, Capitol #CAS3104, 1950s, EX (EX sleeve)....................$50.00
Irving Berlin's White Christmas, Golden #R103, NM+ (NM sleeve)....................$14.00
Johnny Tremain Title Song, Golden #D340, NM (NM sleeve)....................$35.00
Lassie Song/We're Good Pals Together, Cricket #C-769, EX (EX sleeve)....................$32.00
Little Sir Echo/Pony Boy Buffalo Gals, Peter Pan #404, EX (EX+ sleeve)....................$35.00
Little Space Girl/Roly-Poly on the Moon, Golden #546, VG (EX+ sleeve)....................$30.00
March From Peter & the Wolf/Jing-A-Ling, Golden #R65A, EX (EX sleeve)....................$25.00
Maverick, Golden #498, VG (EX sleeve)....................$34.00
Most Befuddling Thing (The Sword & the Stone)/Blue Oak Tree, Disney #LG-769, M (NM sleeve)....................$15.00
Mr Chip 'N Dale/Goofy's Song, Golden #RD46, NM (NM sleeve)....................$35.00
Mr Jinks & Boo Boo Bear, Golden #591, 1959, NM (NM sleeve)....................$35.00
Mr Mickey Mouse/Mickey's New Car, Golden #RD7:25, VG (EX sleeve)....................$28.00
Mr Toad, Capitol #EAS 3048, 1949, VG+ (w/sleeve)....................$35.00
Old Yeller Title Song, Golden #D390, NM (NM sleeve)..$25.00
Peter Pan A Pirates Life/The Elegant Captain Hook, Golden #RD38, 1952, NM (NM sleeve)....................$35.00
Peter Pan The Second Star to the Right/March of the Lost Boys, Golden #RD36, 1952, EX (EX+ sleeve)....................$32.00

Pinocchio 'hi-diddle-dee-dee...,' Golden #671, EX (EX sleeve), $30.00. (Photo courtesy gasolinealleyantiques.com)

Pinocchio When You Wish Upon a Star, Golden #675, EX (NM sleeve)....................$25.00
Popeye Launches His New Hit Song, Peter Pan #474, 1958, EX (EX+ sleeve)....................$35.00
Popeye the Sailor Man & Blow Me Down, Golden #R60, G+ (VG sleeve)....................$20.00
Quick Draw McGraw! & Baba Looey, Golden #589, 1960, EX (EX+sleeve)....................$42.00
Raggedy Ann & the Magic Book, Decca #K55, 1952, very scarce, EX (NM sleeve)....................$100.00
Rescue in Space With Tom Corbett Space Cadet, RCA Victor #Y450, 1952, NM (EX sleeve)....................$100.00
Robin Hood Riddle-De-Diddle-De-Day/The Robin Hood Ballad, Golden #D247, NM (EX+ sleeve)....................$35.00
Rootie Kazootie & Polka Dottie Polka, Golden #R98, 1952, EX+ (EX sleeve)....................$50.00
Ruff & Reddy & Professor Gizmo, Golden #558, 1959, EX (EX sleeve)....................$36.00
77 Sunset Strip, Golden #580, NM (NM sleeve)....................$45.00
Shari Lewis Sings Aren't You Glad You're You?/Tiki-Tiki-Timbo, Golden #555, EX (EX+ sleeve)....................$35.00
Siamese Cat Song From Walt Disney's Lady & the Tramp, Golden #D214, EX (EX sleeve)....................$38.00
Sleeping Beauty 'Skumps' (The Two Kings Plan a Wedding), Golden #483, NM (NM sleeve)....................$32.00
Sleeping Beauty I Wonder, Golden #489, EX+ (EX+ sleeve)...$30.00
Sleeping Beauty Sing a Smiling Song, Golden #D482, EX+ (EX+ Sleeve)....................$25.00
Three Little Pigs, Capitol #DBX3013, 1949, Don Wilson, EX (EX album)....................$75.00
Toot & a Whistle a Plunk & a Boom, Golden #D162, EX (EX sleeve)....................$34.00

Top Cat Theme Song, Golden #689, 1962, EX (VG+ sleeve).. $36.00
20,000 Leagues Under the Sea/Whale of a Tale & Snoopy the Seal, Golden #D174, VG+ (EX+ sleeve) $38.00
Wagon Train & Square Dance, Golden #R495, NM (EX sleeve) $40.00

Walt Disney's Song of Fantasyland, Golden #D300, EX+ (EX+ sleeve), $35.00. (Photo courtesy gasolinealleyantiques.com)

Walt Disney's Song of Frontierland, Golden #D300, EX+ (EX+ sleeve) $35.00
Wild Bill Hickok, Peter Pan #480, unused, M (M sleeve).$24.00
Wizard of Oz, Golden #R50, EX (EX sleeve) $38.00
Woody Woodpecker March, Golden #699, VG (VG sleeve) ..$25.00
Woody Woodpecker Song/Woodpecker Dance, Golden #R58, EX (EX sleeve)..$28.00
Yogi Bear Introduces Loopy de Loop/Let's Have a Song Yogi Bear!, Golden #592, 1961, M (NM sleeve) $38.00

Kiddie Picture Disks

Listed here is a representative sampling of kiddie picture disks that were produced through the 1940s. Most are 6" to 7" in diameter and are made of cardboard with plastic-laminated grooves. They are very colorful and seldom seen with original sleeves. Ultimately, the value of any collectible is what a buyer is willing to pay, and prices tend to fluctuate. Our values are for records only (no sleeves except where noted). Unlike other records, the value of a picture disk is not diminished if there is no original sleeve.

A Birthday Song to You, Voco #35215, 5" sq, NM $20.00
Alice in Wonderland, Toy Toon Records, 1952, NM $15.00
Bible Storytime, Standard Publishing, 78 rpm, 1948, 7", NM ..$10.00
Bunny Easter Party, Voco #EB-1, 1948, EX.......................$15.00
Cinderella Toy Toon Records, 1952, NM $15.00
Disneyland Main Street Electrical Parade, 1973, 7", VG+ ..$60.00
Flash Gordon 'City of the Sea Caves' Part 1, Record Guild of America/King Features, 1948, EX $50.00
Gilbert & Sullivan Series, Picture Tone Record Co, 1948, 78 rpm, rare, 6½", EX $40.00
Greetings & Here's Good Wishes for a 14 Carrot Christmas, features Bugs Bunny dressed as Santa, Capitol, 1948, 8", NM $125.00
Jack in the Beanstalk, Toy Toon Records, 1952, NM.......$15.00
Kitty Cat, Voco, ca 1948, 7", EX $8.00
Kitty Cat, Voco 'Pic Disc,' ca 1948, 6" (rare size), EX $15.00
Lionel Train Sound Effects, 1951, NM.............................$60.00

Little White Duck, Red Raven Movie Records, VG, $15.00. (Photo courtesy Peter Muldavin)

Red River Valley, Record Guild of America #2002P, 1949, EX (EX rare sleeve) $25.00
Red Ryder, Record Guild of America, 1948, NM....... $45.00
Round & 'Round the Village,' Voco 'Pic Disc,' 1948, 78 rpm, 6" (rare size), EX...$15.00
Round & 'Round the Village,' Voco 'Pic Disc,' 1948, 78 rpm, 7", EX $6.00
Rover the Strongman, Voco, 1948, EX $25.00
Shepherd Boy, Bible Storytime, 1948, NM.......................$10.00
Songs From Mother Goose, Toy Toon Records, 1952, NM ..$15.00
Swing Your Partner, Picture Play Records #PR11A/Record Guild of America, 1948, NM.. $100.00
Ten Little Indians, Voco, 1948, 7", NM $8.00
Ten Little Indians, Voco, 1948, 16", NM $25.00
Terry & the Pirates, Record Guild of America, F501, 1949, 6½", NM..$45.00
The Fox, Talking Book Corp, 1917, 78 rpm, very rare, EX..$90.00
Three Bears With Uncle Henry, Kidisks, KD-77A, 1948, rare, NM..$75.00
Trial of 'Bumble' the Bee Part 1, Vogue #R-745, 1947, 10", EX... $60.00
Winnie the Pooh & Christopher Robin Songs, RCA Victor, 1933, very rare, NM... $500.00

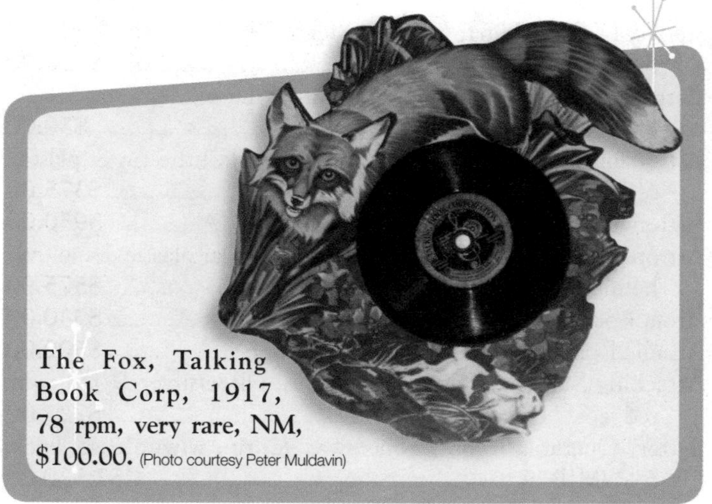
The Fox, Talking Book Corp, 1917, 78 rpm, very rare, NM, $100.00. (Photo courtesy Peter Muldavin)

Robots and Space Toys

Space is a genre that anyone who grew up in the '50s and '60s can relate to, but whether you're from that generation or not, chances are the fantastic robots, space vehicles, and rocket launchers from that era are fascinating to you as well. Some emitted beams of colored light and eerie sounds and suggested technology the secrets of which were still locked away in the future. To a collector, the stranger, the better. Some were made of lithographed tin, but even plastic toys (Atom Robot, for example) are high on the want list of many serious buyers. Condition is extremely important, both in general appearance and internal workings. Mint-in-box examples may be worth twice as much as one mint-no-box, since the package art was often just as awesome as the toy itself.

Because of the high prices these toys now command, many have been reproduced. Beware!

See also Marx; Guns.

Action Planet Robot, Yoshia, 1950s, w/up, tin, 9", NM+IB, A $250.00
Apollo Spacecraft, MT, 1960s, b/o, tin, 10", MIB, A...... $310.00
Apollo-Z Moon Traveler, Nomura, b/o, tin, 12", NMIB.. $150.00

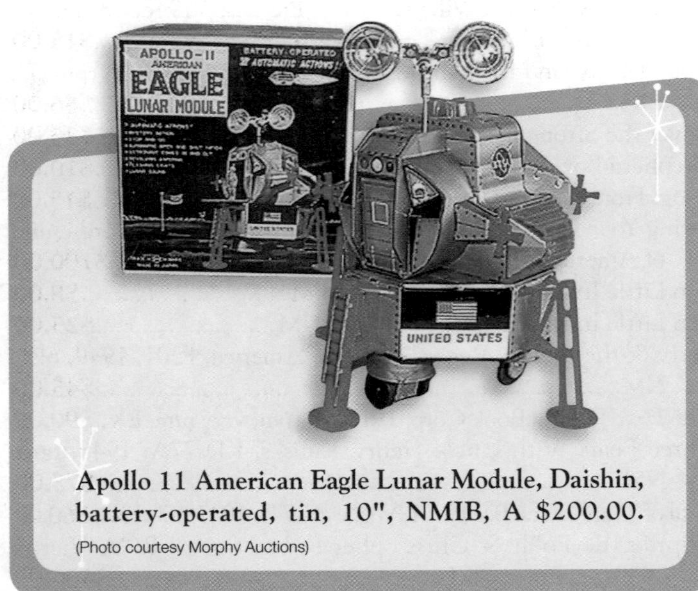

Apollo 11 American Eagle Lunar Module, Daishin, battery-operated, tin, 10", NMIB, A $200.00. (Photo courtesy Morphy Auctions)

Apollo-11 Eagle Lunar Module, Mego, 1960s, b/o, tin & plastic, NMIB, A........ $320.00
Astro Fleet 4-Manned Space Craft w/Launcher Gun, Parks #5055, 1950s, MIB, A........ $30.00
Astronaut, Ahi, friction, w/up crank in back, litho tin & plastic, 6½", NM+IB, A........ $375.00
Astronaut Robot, Shudo, w/up, tin, 6", MIB, A $950.00
Astronaut w/Laser Gun, Daiya, b/o, tin w/clear plastic dome over helmeted head, 14", VG+ (repro box), A........ $575.00
Atom Rocket 7, MT, b/o, litho tin, 9" L, EXIB, A........ $330.00
Atomic Robot Man, Japan, w/up, tin, 5", EX, A $500.00
Attacking Martian, Horikawa, b/o, tin, blk w/silver & red trim, red feet, 11", NMIB, A........ $225.00
Battery-Operated Robot, Yonezawa, r/c, tin, w/wire easel back, 6", NMIB, A $2,520.00
Bump 'N Go Space Explorer, Yoshiya, crank-op, tin & plastic, 6" L, NMIB, A........ $350.00

Busy Cart Robot, Horikawa, battery-operated, plastic, 11½", NM, A, $560.00. (Photo courtesy Morphy Auctions)

Capsule Mercury, Horikawa, friction, tin, 9", NM+, A .. $390.00
Chief Robotman, Yoshiya, b/o, tin & plastic, 12", NMIB, A...$1,250.00

Chief Smoky Robot, Oshiya, battery-operated, tin with plastic cap, 11½", MIB, A, $3,640.00. (Photo courtesy Morphy Auctions)

Commander (Spaceship), Yoshiya, friction, tin w/plastic nose, 10" L, NMIB, A........ $500.00
Cragstan Astronaut, Daiya, b/o, tin, 14", NMIB, A..... $2,100.00
Cragstan Astronaut, Yonezawa, friction, tin, 9", EX, A.. $560.00
Cragstan Great Astronaut, Alps, b/o, tin & plastic, NMIB, A $2,650.00
Cragstan Mr Robot, Yonezawa, b/o, tin w/plastic dome head, wht w/red version, 11", VG+, A........ $428.00
Cragstan Satellite (Mystery Action), b/o, tin, complete w/2 astronauts, 8" W, NMIB, A $250.00
Cragstan Space Mobile (Lunar Patrol), b/o, tin, 10", NMIB, A $900.00

Dino Robot, Horikawa, b/o, tin & plastic, 11", NM+IB, A .. $525.00
Docking Rocket, Daiya, b/o, 16", MIB, A $165.00

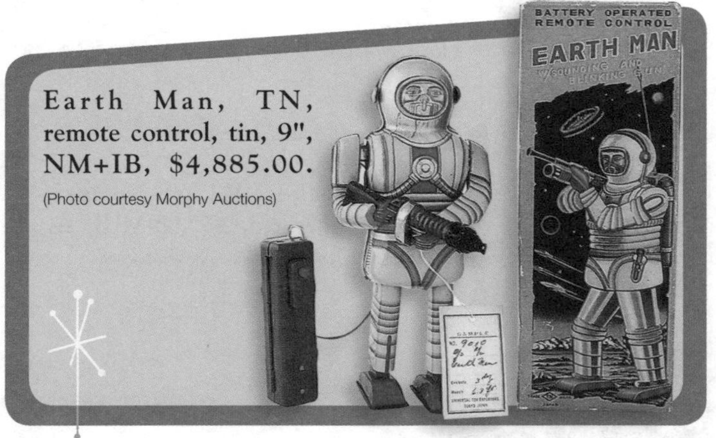

Earth Man, TN, remote control, tin, 9", NM+IB, $4,885.00. (Photo courtesy Morphy Auctions)

Electric Robot & Son, Marx, 1950s, plastic, w/son & tools for 'tool chest,' nonworking o/w NMIB, A $200.00
Flash Gordon Rocket Fighter, see Marx category
Florida Air Boat, see Regulus
Flying Air Car, TPS, b/o, aluminum, NMIB, A $275.00
Flying Saucer, Cragstan, b/o, litho tin w/clear plastic dome over cockpit, 7½" dia, EXIB, A $300.00
Flying Saucer, Haji, friction, tin, 7", MIB, A $280.00
Friendship 7 Capsule 'Mercury,' Horikawa, friction, tin, 9", NMIB, A $260.00

Giant Sonic (Train) Robot, Masudaya, battery-operated, tin, 15", EX, A, $2,800.00. (Photo courtesy Morphy Auctions)

Golden Robot, see Robot (Golden Robot)
Gyro Space Car, Japan, friction, tin, EX, A $200.00
High-Wheeled Robot, Yoshiya, w/up, tin, 10", MIB, A.. $560.00
ICBM Launching Station, Horikawa, friction/crank-op, tin, 18½", NMIB, A $475.00
Interplanetary Rocket, Yonezawa, b/o, tin & plastic, 14", MIB, A $200.00
Juniper Robot, Yoshiya, w/up, tin & plastic, MIB, A...... $310.00
Jupiter Spacecraft (Flying Saucer), K Co/Frankonia import, 1950s, w/up, tin, 5" dia, MIB, A.............................. $100.00
King Flying Saucer, KO, 1960s, b/o, tin, unused, MIB, A .. $100.00
Lantern Robot (Powder Robot), Linemar, r/c, tin, 8", EX, A .. $1,500.00
Lost in Space Robot, AHI, 1977, b/o, 10", unused, MIB, A.. $235.00
Luna Expedition, Technofix, w/up, plastic, NM, A $125.00
Lunik 2000, Tibidabo/Italy, b/o, plastic, 11" L, NMIB, A . $225.00
Man Made Satellite S-2, Yonezawa, friction, tin, 4" dia, NMIB, A $275.00
Mars Patrol No 17 (Cragstan Space Tank), Yanoman, friction, 6" L, NMIB, A... $575.00
Martian, see Walking Martian
Marvelous Mike Tractor, Saunders-Swadar Toy Co #1000, tin & plastic, 13" L, VGIB, A $350.00
Mechanical Robot, Yonezawa, w/up, tin, 6", EXIB, A .. $1,350.00
Mighty Robot, Yonezawa, w/up, tin & plastic, 10", EX, A ...$625.00

Mobile Space T.V. Unit With Trailer, Rosco, battery-operated, tin, 10½" long, EXIB, A, $3,300.00. (Photo courtesy Bertoia Auctions)

Moon Explorer, Alps, b/o, tin & plastic, 18", EXIB, A .. $2,000.00
Moon Explorer (Astronaut), Yoshiya, crank-op, tin, 7", EX, A $150.00
Moon Explorer M-27, Yonezawa, r/c, tin & plastic, 8" L, NM+IB, A $3,070.00
Moon Express (Magic Color), TPS, b/o, tin & plastic, NMIB, A...$250.00
Moon Man 001, Hong Kong, b/o, plastic, 6", NM+IB, A.. $175.00
Moon Rocket, Masudaya, b/o, tin, 9½" L, NMIB, A $275.00
Moon Scout Helicopter, Marx, b/o, tin & plastic, 16" L, NMIB, A $100.00

Mr. Atom the Electronic Walking Robot, battery-operated, plastic, 18", EXIB, A, $300.00. (Photo courtesy Morphy Auctions)

Mr LEM, Hong Kong, b/o, plastic, 13", scarce, EX, A $150.00
Mr Mercury, Linemar, r/c, tin & plastic, 13", EXIB, A ... $750.00
Mr Robot, see Cragstan Mr Robot
Musical Drummer Robot, Nomura, r/c, tin, 8", EXIB, A.. $2,400.00
Non Stop Robot (Lavender Robot), Masudaya, b/o, litho tin, 15", EXIB, A $4,051.00
Orbit Explorer w/Airborne Satellite, Yoshiya, w/up, tin & plastic, 8½" L, EX+IB, A $225.00
Piston-Action Robot ('Pug Robby Robot'), Nomura, r/c, tin & plastic, 9", EX+, A $600.00
Planet Explorer, Alps, b/o, tin, 11½" L, scarce, NMIB, A ..$1,225.00
Planet Patrol Tank, Yanoman, friction, tin & plastic, 6" L, NMIB, A $500.00
Planet Robot, Yoshiya, w/up, tin, 9", MIB, A $400.00
Porthole Spaceman Robot, Linemar, r/c, tin, 8", EX, A .. $3,360.00
Powder Robot, see Lantern Robot (Powder Robot)
Radar-Scope Space Scout Robot, Horikawa, b/o, tin, MIB, A $225.00

Ranger Robot, Daiya, battery-operated, plastic, NMIB, A, $3,080.00. (Photo courtesy Morphy Auctions)

Regulus (Florida Air Boat), ATC, b/o, tin, 8", NMIB, A.. $250.00
Rex Mars Planet Patrol Sparkling Space Tank, w/up, tin, 10" L, EXIB, A $500.00
Road Construction Roller (w/Robby-type Robot Driver), Daiya, b/o, tin, 9" L, VGIB, A $2,500.00
Robby Robot Bulldozer, Marusan, friction, tin, 7", EX, A.. $225.00
Robby Space Patrol, Nomura, b/o, tin, 13", EXIB, A.... $6,750.00
Robert the Robot (on Bulldozer), Ideal, r/c, plastic w/rubber treads, 9½" L, NMIB, A $725.00
Robot ('Robot' printed on chest), Japan, r/c, tin, 8", EXIB, A $480.00
Robot (Golden), Linemar, r/c, tin, 6½", EX, A $1,000.00
Robot (Golden), Linemar, r/c, tin, 6½", EXIB, A $1,600.00
Robot Car, ATC, friction, litho tin, 8", EXIB, A $900.00
Robot Cosmic Raider Force, Taiwan, 1970s, b/o, plastic, 14½", MIB, A $138.00
Robot R-35, Linemar, b/o, tin, 7½", NMIB, A $610.00
Roby Robot, Yonezawa, w/up, tin, 8", EXIB, A $1,900.00
Rocket Man, Alps, r/c, tin & plastic, 16", EX+IB, A ... $2,500.00
Rocket 7 (Space Rocket), Yoshiya, friction, tin, robot driving rocket, 5½", MIB, A $1,000.00
Rotate-O-Matic Super Astronaut, Horikawa, 1960s, b/o, tin, NMIB, A $225.00
Satellite X-12 (Space Surveyor), Masudaya, tin, 8" dia, NMIB, A $950.00

See-Thru Robot, Hong Kong, b/o, plastic, chest gears turn & light flashes, 12", NMIB, A $1,100.00
Sky Patrol (w/Blinking Jet Engines), Japan, b/o, tin & plastic, 13" L, NMIB, A $700.00
Sky Patrol Flying Saucer, Horikawa, b/o, tin, 8" dia, MIB, A... $200.00

Solar-X 7 Space Rocket, Nomura, battery-operated, 15", NMIB, A, $175.00. (Photo courtesy Morphy Auctions)

Sonicon Sonic Control Space Ship, Masudaya, b/o, tin, 13" L, NMIB, A $900.00
Space Astronaut Robot, Horikawa/SH, 1960s, b/o, tin, human face in helmet, 12", nonworking o/w NM, A.............. $75.00
Space Car, Yonezawa, b/o, tin, 9½" L, NMIB, A $4,500.00
Space Commando, Nomura, 1956, w/up, tin & plastic, 8", EX, A $285.00
Space Conqueror (Robot), Daiya, b/o, tin, 12", EX, A... $600.00
Space Dog, Yoshiya, b/o, tin, EX+, A $675.00
Space Dog, Yoshiya, friction, tin, 7½" L, EX+, A $275.00
Space Dog, Yoshiya, w/up, tin, 7½" L, EX, A $250.00
Space Drome, Superior, tin & plastic, complete w/accessories, EXIB, A $460.00
Space Explorer S-61, Normura, friction, tin, resembles modern train engine, 12½" L, NMIB, A $350.00
Space Explorer 11 (Moon Explorer), Takatoku, w/up, tin & plastic, NMIB, A $175.00
Space Man, Noguchi, w/up, tin, 5½", NMIB, A $125.00
Space Man Robot, Nomura, b/o, tin, MIB, A $1,120.00
Space Man Robot, Yoneya, w/up, tin, 8", EXIB, A $1,000.00
Space Patrol (Snoopy), Japan, b/o, tin & plastic Snoopy-type figure, 11", NMIB, A $390.00
Space Patrol Tank, Ichimura, friction, tin, 5" L, NM+IB, A.. $475.00
Space Patrol 3 (Space Pilot Flying Saucer), Yoshiya, b/o, tin, 7½" dia, NMIB, A $175.00
Space Patrol/NASA, Masudaya, friction, tin w/plastic astronaut under clear plastic dome, 7" L, NMIB, A $175.00
Space Pioneer, Masudaya, b/o, tin, space vehicle w/driver under clear plastic shield, 12", NM, A $390.00
Space Radar Scout Pioneer, Masudaya, friction, plastic, 7" L, NMIB, A $300.00
Space Robot RX-008, Noguchi, w/up, tin & plastic, 6", EXIB, A $350.00
Space Robot X-70 (Tulip Head), Nomura, b/o, tin & plastic, 12", NMIB, A $2,200.00

Space Robot X-70 (Tulip Head), Nomura, b/o, tin & plastic, 12", EX, A $895.00

Space Scooter, Masudaya, b/o, tin & plastic, 'Snoopy'-like dog on scooter, 8" L, EX+IB, A $720.00

Space Scooter, Masudaya, b/o, tin & plastic, astronaut figure on scooter, 8" L, NMIB, A... $150.00

Space Ship (Cragstan Flying Saucer), IY Metal Toys, b/o, tin, 9½" dia, NMIB, A... $325.00

Space Ship (Magic Color Dome Mercury Explorer), TPS, b/o, tin & plastic, 8" L, NMIB, A $225.00

Space Station NASA, Horikawa, battery-operated, tin, 11" wide, NMIB, A, $5,800.00. (Photo courtesy Smith House Toy and Auction Company)

Space Surveillant X-07, Masudaya, b/o, tin, 8½" L, NMIB..$175.00

Space Tank, MT, b/o, litho tin, 8" L, EX+IB, A............. $410.00

Space Tank, Takatoku, windup, tin, 5" long, NMIB, A, $250.00. (Photo courtesy Smith House Toy and Auction Company)

Space Tank, Vohra Toys/India, friction, tin, 6" L, EX+IB, A ... $175.00

Space Tank M-41, Masudaya, b/o, tin & plastic, 8½" L, NMIB, A $275.00

Space Tricycle w/Robot Rider, Frankonia, 1960, w/up, hollow vinyl robot on litho tin trike w/bell, 4", EX, A........ $315.00

Space Trip, Masudaya, b/o, tin, 19" L, NMIB, A $775.00

Space Trooper w/Rifle, Haji, b/o, tin, 6", EX, A.............. $725.00

Space Vehicle (Lighted) #28905, Masydaya, b/o, tin, w/'Foating Satellite,' 8½", NMIB, A $300.00

Spaceman Robot, Modern Toys, b/o, tin, 7", NM, A...$1,790.00

Sparking Robot, Noguchi, w/up, tin, 6", MIB, A........... $250.00

Sparkling Space Ranger, SI, friction, tin, 7", MIB, A..$2,200.00

Sparkling Space Ranger, SI, friction, tin, 7", VGIB, A... $575.00

Sparky Robot, Yoshiya, 1950s, tin, w/up, 8", unused, EXIB, A ..$345.00

Sputnik-X Super Rocket, West Germany, friction, tin, 18", EXIB, A $1,792.00

Stratoliner 10-3 (Huki), Germany, 8", MIB, A, $850.00. (Photo courtesy Morphy Auctions)

Super Hero Flying (Tetsuwan) Atom Boy, 1960s, w/up, tin, EXIB, A $3,080.00

Super Hero Flying Par Man, 1960s, w/up, tin, wearing helmet w/eyes & wings, EXIB, A.......................................$5,040.00

Super Hero Flying Tetsujin 28-Go (aka Ironman or Gigantor), 1960s, w/up, tin, EXIB, A.....................................$3,640.00

Super Hero Flying 8 Man, 1960s, w/up, tin, ring hanger on back, EXIB, A...$3,360.00

Super Moon Patroller, Japan, b/o, tin w/plastic wheels & tinted windshield, 9" L, VGIB, A $100.00

Super Robot, Noguchi, w/up, tin, 5", MIB, A................. $195.00

Super Space Capsule, Horikawa, b/o, tin & plastic, 9" L, NMIB, A $150.00

Swinging Baby Robot, Yone, w/up, litho tin, 6½", NMIB, A... $400.00

Talking Robot (Cragstan), Yonezawa, battery-operated talking function, friction, tin, 11", EX+IB, A, $800.00. (Photo courtesy Morphy Auctions)

Target Robot, Masudaya, b/o, tin, 15", EX+, A........... $4,900.00

Television Space Robot, Alps, 1959, b/o, tin, 14", NM, A...$300.00

Television Spaceman, Alps, 1965, b/o, tin, 7", MIB, A.. $670.00

Tobotank-Z, Nomura, b/o, tin & plastic, 11", NMIB, A... $375.00

Tractor (Robot-Driven) w/Visible Lighted Piston Movement, Nomura, b/o, tin, 10", EXIB, A $425.00
Tulip Head Robot, see Space Robot

T.V. Space Patrol, Asahim, friction, tin with driver under clear plastic dome, 9" long, NM+IB, A, $8,500.00. (Photo courtesy Smith House Toy and Auction Company)

Two-Stage Rocket Launching Pad, Nomura, b/o, tin, 8", MIB, A...$560.00
United States Space Capsule, Horikawa, 1960s, litho tin, b/o, plastic astronaut rotates above, NMIB, A............... $230.00
Universe Reconnaissonce Boat, China, b/o, tin & plastic, 12", NMIB, A.. $100.00
V-2 Space Tank (aka Robby Tank), Yoshiya, b/o, scarce lt bl version, NMIB, A $875.00
Video Robot, Horikawa, b/o, tin, 9", MIB, A................. $195.00
Walking Martian, Hishimo, w/up, tin, rnd red head w/'veins' & mask-like eyes, octopus-like legs, 8", EX, A.......... $5,000.00
X-07 Space Surveillant, Modern Toys, b/o, litho tin, 8", EX+, A..$250.00
XB-115 Rocket, Horikawa, friction, 11", NMIB, A........ $550.00
XT-978 (Moon Patrol), TPS, b/o, tin, 8" L, NMIB, A ... $580.00
XX-3 Atomic Spaceship With Sparks, Nomura, friction, tin, 10", MIB, A... $390.00

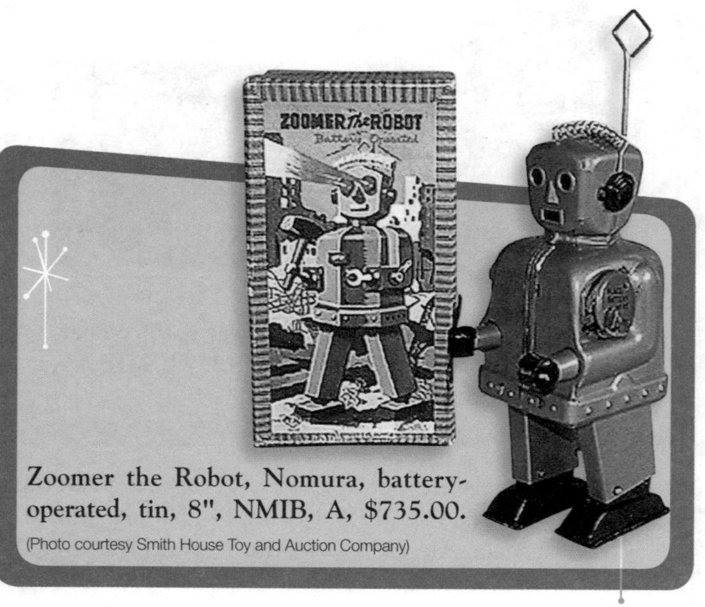

Zoomer the Robot, Nomura, battery-operated, tin, 8", NMIB, A, $735.00. (Photo courtesy Smith House Toy and Auction Company)

MISCELLANEOUS

Apollo Staging Rockets, Parks Plastics, 1960s, unused, MIB (sealed), A $65.00
Astro Ray Flashlight Target Gun, shoots darts at target board, EXIB, A.. $110.00

Astronaut Space Helmet With RCA Built-in Speaker, complete, 1960s, plays set of 45 rpm records, NMIB, A, $160.00. (Photo courtesy serioustoyz.com)

Bank, Guided Missile, Astro Mfg, 12", NMIB $125.00
Bank, Mr Robot, Wolverine, 1950s, 10½", NM................$50.00
Bank, Space Scout Bubble Gum Bank, red cb dispenser w/space graphics, 5", unopened, EX, A................................ $110.00
Jet Morgan Space Suit, England, complete, EXIB, A $500.00
Pencil Case, marbleized plastic rocket shape w/4 crayons, pencil & sharpener, 8½" L, 1950s, EX.................................$35.00
Rocket Patrol Magnetic Target Game, American Toy Prod, 1950s, complete, EX $50.00

Rocket Patrol Magnetic Target Game, American Toy Products, 1950s, complete, NM, A, $40.00. (Photo courtesy serioustoyz.com)

Satellite Explorer Helmet, Mirro, aluminum, NM+IB, A.. $335.00
Space Fleet Set, Handi-Craft, casting & coloring set, complete, VGIB, A $25.00
Space Globe, tin, 10", NM, A $450.00

Space Lantern, light-up globe featuring solar system, 5½", NMIB $250.00

Space Target, Superior Toy Co, 1952, EX, $170.00. (Photo courtesy serioustoyz.com)

Spaceman Toy Sparkler, Arnold, tin, 5", NM, A $112.00
Walkie Talkies, Remco, plastic electronic phones w/wired & magnetic power, NMIB $125.00

Rock 'n Roll

From the 1950s on, rock 'n roll music has been an enjoyable part of many of our lives, and the performers themselves have often been venerated as icons. Today artists such as Elvis, the Beatles, KISS, and the Monkees, have fans that not only continue to appreciate their music but actively search for the ticket stubs, concert posters, photographs, and autographs of their favorites. More easily found, though, are the items that sold through retail stores at the height of their careers — dolls, games, toys, books, magazines, etc. In recent years, some of the larger auction galleries have sold personal items such as guitars, jewelry, costumes, automobiles, contracts, and other one-of-a-kind items that realized astronomical prices. If you're an Elvis fan, we recommend *Elvis Collectibles* and *Best of Elvis Collectibles* by Rosalind Cranor (Overmountain Press).

See also Coloring, Activity, and Paint Books; Lunch Boxes; Paper Dolls; Pin-Back Buttons.

Andy Gibb, Wireless FM Microphone, LJN, 1978, MIB ... $50.00
Beatles, banjo, Mastro, 22", EXIB $3,000.00
Beatles, bank, Ringo half-figure, ceramic, orange shirt w/red tie, red & bl striped sweater, 8", 1968, EX, A $105.00
Beatles, Beatles Colouring Set, Kitfix, 1964, complete, MIB ... $2,000.00
Beatles, Bobbin' Head Beatles set, pnt compo figures playing instruments, 7½", Car Mascots Inc, 1960s, MIB, A $1,265.00
Beatles, brooch, group photo set in plastic, MOC $60.00
Beatles, bubble bath container, any band member, Colgate-Palmolive, 1960s, NM+, ea $50.00
Beatles, bulletin board, Yellow Submarine, 24x24", Unicorn Creations, MIP $900.00
Beatles, chair, Yellow Submarine, inflatable vinyl, NM $50.00
Beatles, charms, set of 4 mc plastic ovals w/head images, 1½", 1960s, M, A $45.00
Beatles, Dimensionals Wild Wall Hang-Ups, Craft Master, 1968, unused, MOC, A $295.00
Beatles, dolls, any member, plastic w/lifelike hair, w/instruments, about 4½", Remco, 1964, EX, ea $65.00
Beatles, dolls, soft bodies, set of 4, Remco, NM $375.00
Beatles, guitar, Four Pop, head images of group & name, NM ... $650.00
Beatles, guitar, Junior by Selcol, red plastic w/group photos, paper label, 14", rare, EX $1,500.00
Beatles, light-switch plate, 'mod' image of group standing against orange background, 10½", 1968, VG, A $15.00
Beatles, nodder bank, figure w/guitar on base w/'Yeah Yeah Yeah,' 10½", Japan, NM $350.00
Beatles, nodders, plastic, set of 4, 4", EX $40.00
Beatles, pennant, 'I love the Beatles,' felt, 29", EX $200.00
Beatles, pin, rnd John Lennon photo on guitar shape, 4¼", 1960s, NM $55.00
Beatles, record player, inside lid displays group w/instruments, 1964, VG $4,700.00
Beatles, rug, colorful head images w/music notes & instruments on background, 22x34", 1960s, EX $230.00
Beatles, scrapbook, 'The Beatles Scrap Book,' 4 head images, Whitman/Nems, 1964, EX $75.00
Beatles, spatter toy, 16", rare, MIP $300.00
Beatles, throw rug, head images w/musical instruments & notes on colorful background, 22x34", 1960s, VG+, A $230.00
Beatles, wallet, red vinyl w/portrait & signatures, w/coin slots, comb & nail file, zipper closure, VG $50.00
Beatles, watercolor set, 'Yellow Submarine,' Craftmaster, complete, MIB $150.00
Bee Gees, record case, for 45 rpms, photo image on wht, Vanity Fair, 1979, EX+ $50.00
Bobby Sherman, ring, 'Love & Peace,' 1971, M $25.00
Boy George, doll, LJN, 1984, 11½", rare, MIB $150.00
Boy George, puffy stickers, set of 6, 1984, M $15.00

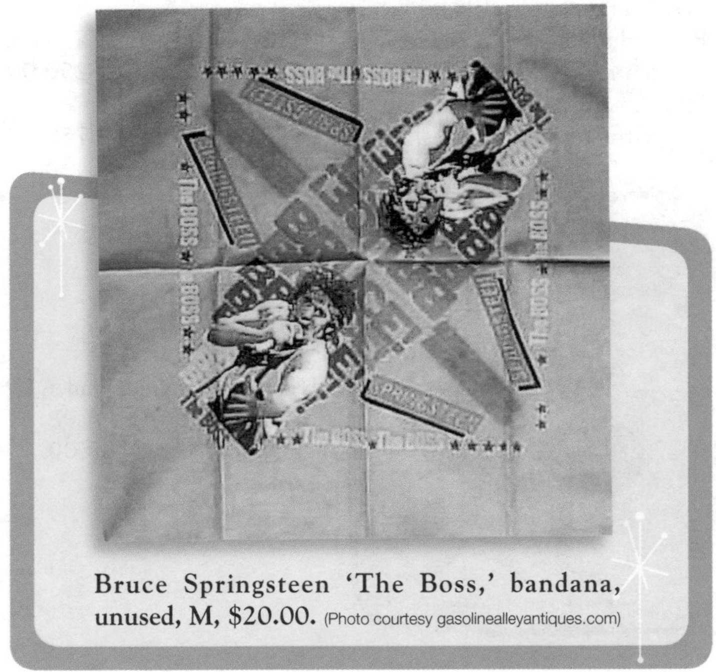

Bruce Springsteen 'The Boss,' bandana, unused, M, $20.00. (Photo courtesy gasolinealleyantiques.com)

Chicago, patch, red name embroidered on wht sq w/bl stars, red stitched border, 3x3", unused, M $15.00
Chubby Checker, Twister set, complete w/45 rpm 'practice' record, Empire Plastic Corp, 1960s, EXIB $75.00
David Cassidy, Dress-Up Set, 1972, MIP $30.00

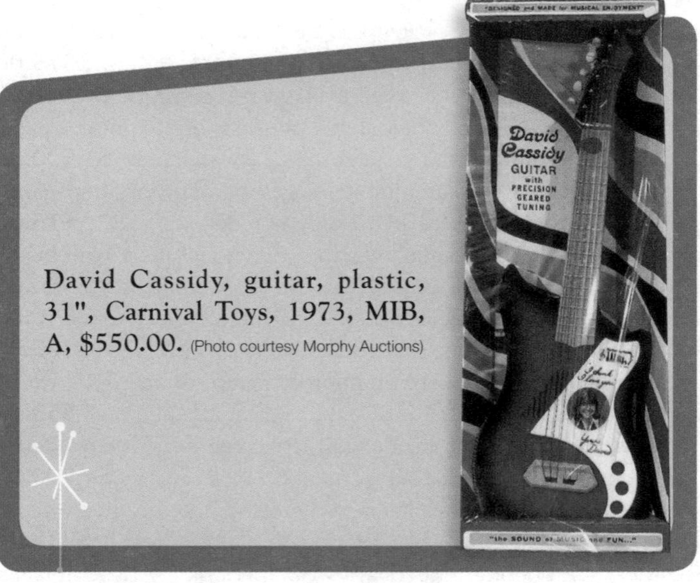

David Cassidy, guitar, plastic, 31", Carnival Toys, 1973, MIB, A, $550.00. (Photo courtesy Morphy Auctions)

David Cassidy, slide-tile puzzle, 1970s, M $35.00
Dick Clark, autograph doll, cloth body w/vinyl head, 26", 1950s, EX, A $75.00
Dick Clark, doll, 27", Juro, 1960, NM, A $235.00
Donny & Marie, marionettes, in bl show outfits, 12", Osbro Prod, 1978, MIB, ea $100.00
Donny & Marie, Poster Pen Set, Craft House, 1971, unused, MIP $20.00
Donny & Marie, tambourine, Lapin, 1977, M $35.00
Elvis, autograph book, EP Enterprises, 1950s, unused, EX+ $550.00
Elvis, earrings, 'Loving You...,' gold-framed protraits w/pierced backs, MIP $225.00
Elvis, flasher ring, 1957, EX $100.00
Elvis, guitar, Lapin, 1984, MOC (sealed) $75.00
Elvis, Hound Dog, plush w/'Elvis' lettered on wht neck ribbon, Smile Toy Co, NM $250.00
Elvis, overnight case, simulated leather w/images of Elvis & signature, EP Enterprises, 1956, EX $750.00

Elvis Presley, school binder, three-ring, Penn State/EPE, 1950s, EX, A, $285.00. (Photo courtesy Morphy Auctions)

Herman's Hermits, doll, Peter Noone, Show Biz Babies, NMIB $250.00
Jackson Five, banner, 'I Love Jackson 5,' blk felt w/wht lettering & red trim, 29", NM $25.00
KISS, backpack, photo on red canvas, Thermos, 1979, EX $100.00
KISS, Colorforms, 1979, complete, MIB $85.00
KISS, necklace, ½x1" 'KISS' logo on chain, 1977, MIB $45.00

KISS, poster, 21x30", Rock Steady #2260, dated 1979, NM, $35.00. (Photo courtesy gasolinealleyantiques.com)

KISS, Your Face Makeup, Remco, 1978, MIB (sealed) $200.00
Led Zeppelin, blimp, inflatable vinyl, distributed to music stores for record promo, M $100.00
Mamas & Papas, Show Biz Babies, Remco, MOC, ea $200.00
Marie Osmond, Hair Care Set, Gordy, 1976, MOC $25.00
Monkees, charm bracelet, gold-tone chain w/4 rnd picture charms, Raybert Prod, 1967, MOC, A $60.00
Monkees, finger puppets, 1970, EX, ea $35.00
Monkees, flasher rings, various, Vari-Vue, 1967, NM, ea $18.00

Monkees, hand puppet, Mattel talker, 1966, NM, $100.00. (Photo courtesy serioustoyz.com)

Monkees, Flip Movies, Topps, 1967, NM (EX+ wrapper) $25.00
Monkees, Show Biz Babies, vinyl, 4¼", set of 4, NMOC $515.00
New Kids on the Block, Colorforms Deluxe Playset, 1991, MIB $15.00

New Kids on the Block, dolls, In Concert, 5 different, 12", Hasbro, MIB, ea $50.00
New Kids on the Block, dolls, Show Time Kids Rag Dolls, 5 different, 19", Hasbro, 1990, MIB, ea $65.00
New Kids on the Block, Fashion Plates, Hasbro, 1990, unused, MIB $35.00

Pat Boone, pendant, metal heart shape, NM, $25.00. (Photo courtesy gasolinealleyantiques.com)

Pink Floyd, patch, name embroidered in pk on blk, 2x5", M.. $15.00

Rick Nelson, fan magazine, 1958, EX+, $48.00. (Photo courtesy gasolinealleyantiques.com)

Rick Nelson, Picture Patch, 1950s, MOC....................$20.00
Rolling Stones, doll, Keith Richards, vinyl w/synthetic hair & cloth outfit, Eegee, 1964, NM $150.00
Rolling Stones, doll, Mick Jagger, vinyl w/synthetic hair & cloth outfit, 5", Play Pal, 1963, NM.................... $150.00
Rolling Stones, sticker album, Stanley, 1983, NM+ $20.00
Shawn Cassidy, record case, cb, Vanity Fair, 1978, EX $35.00
Van Halen, binoculars, plastic w/'VH' logo, EX....................$20.00
Village People, guitar, 36", Carnival Toys, 1976, MIP.... $150.00
ZZ Top, mirror, 6x6", 1980s, M $10.00

Roly Polys

Popular toys with children around the turn of the century, roly polys were designed with a weighted base that caused the toy to automatically right itself after being kicked or knocked over. Their popularity faded to some extent, but they continued to be produced until WWI and beyond. Most were made of papier maché (composition), although later on, some were made of celluloid and tin. Schoenhut made some in a variety of sizes — up to almost a foot in height. They represented clowns, animals, and children, as well as some well known story book characters.

The following listings are composition unless noted otherwise.

See also Black Americana; Chein; Character, TV, and Movie Collectibles; Disney; Santa.

Clown, 7", sm hat cocked, yel w/wht fluted collar, wht face w/minimal red/blk detail, Schoenhut, EX, A $110.00
Clown, 10", orange hair, yel jacket, pk vest, bl bottom, blk bow tie, internal bells, VG+, A $440.00
Clown, 11", blk top hat cocked, blk bow tie, orange striped jacket, lt bl bottom, Germany, VG+, A.................... $275.00
Clown, 11", sm blk top hat cocked, red hair/jacket, gr bottom, blk arched brows, Germany, VG+, A.................... $300.00
Clown, 14", orange & cream w/blk & bl line trim, decals of news hawk, etc, Schoenhut, EX, A $715.00

Clown, 15", Germany, VG, A, $350.00. (Photo courtesy Morphy Auctions)

Clown, 15", yel jacket & vest w/orange & gr plaid stripes, bl bottom, blk bow tie & trim, chimes, VG, A $275.00
Clown, 15", 2-pc w/separate head, cone hat, red-pnt collar w/points, bl jacket/yel vest/gr bottom, VG, A..... $360.00
Clown, 16", cone hat, concerned look, gr cheeks, orange/yel, gr collar/bottom, 2 buttons, Germany, VG, A $330.00
Drummer Boy, 4½", holding drum sticks, long hair, bl uniform, wht hat, VG.................... $100.00
Felix the Cat, 7", closed-mouth smile, blk & wht, Germany, 1920s, VG, A $1,455.00
Foxy Grandpa, 11", hands on belly, Schoenhut, ca 1915, EX, A $600.00

Happy Hooligan, 4", hands in pockets, exaggerated face w/arched eyebrows & lg eyes, gr & red, EX $200.00
Indian Baby, 4", pnt markings on face, yel outfit w/red trim, wht hood, Schoenhut, G $85.00
Keystone Cop, 5", hands on belly, bl single-breasted jacket & hat, detailed face w/mustache, EX........................... $125.00
Keystone Cop, 10", musical, hands on belly, bl single-breasted jacket, lg buttons, mustache, VG $165.00
Man, 16", compo, hands on belly, yel jacket, bl bow tie & bottom, sm red hat, rosey cheeks, red lips, EX, A $220.00
Mother Goose, 8½", holding goose, bl & wht w/red trim, Schoenhut, EX.. $165.00

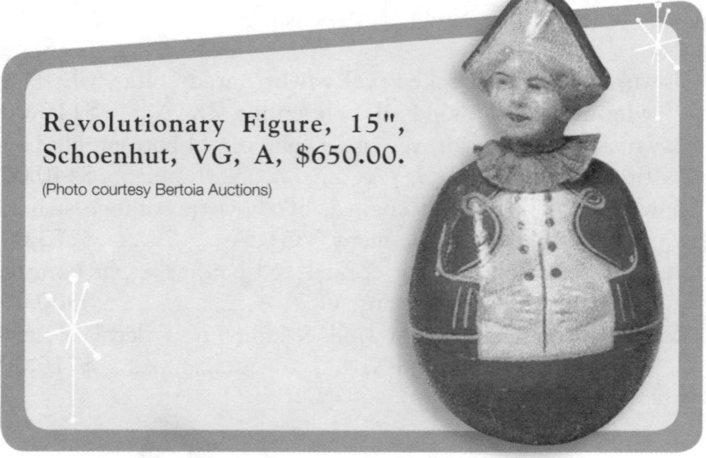
Revolutionary Figure, 15", Schoenhut, VG, A, $650.00. (Photo courtesy Bertoia Auctions)

Uncle Sam, 3", VG, A, $225.00. (Photo courtesy Morphy Auctions)

Sand Toys and Pails

By 1900, companies were developing all sorts of sand toys, free-standing models. The Sand Toy Company of Pittsburgh patented and made 'Sandy Andy' from 1909 onward. The company was later bought by the Wolverine Supply & Manufacturing Co. and continued to produce variations of the toy until the 1970s.

Today if you mention sand toys, people think of pails, spades, sifters, and molds.

We have a rich heritage of lithographed tin pails with such wonderful manufacturers as J. Chein & Co., T. Cohn Inc., Morton Converse, Kirchoff Patent Co., Marx Toy Co., Ohio Art Co., etc, plus the small jobbing companies who neglected to sign their wares. Sand pails have really come into their own and are now recognized for their beautiful graphics and designs. The following listings are lithographed or painted tin. For more information we recommend *Pails by Comparison, Sand Pails and Other Sand Toys, A Study and Price Guide*, by Carole and Richard Smyth.

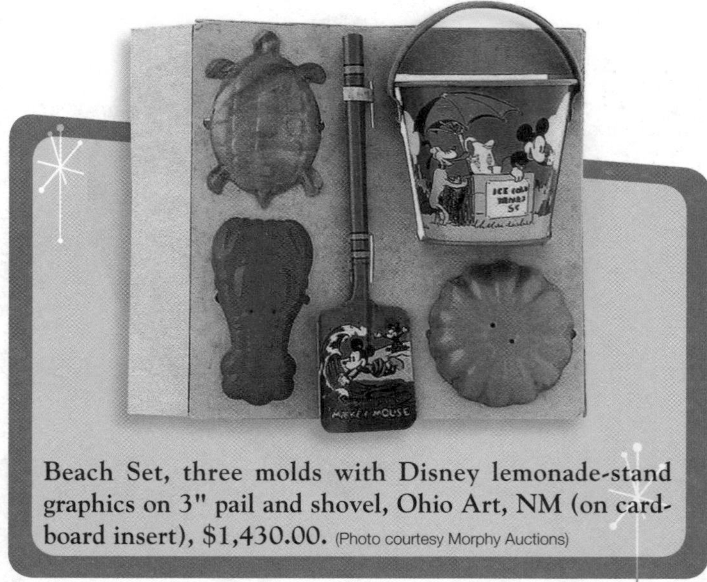
Beach Set, three molds with Disney lemonade-stand graphics on 3" pail and shovel, Ohio Art, NM (on cardboard insert), $1,430.00. (Photo courtesy Morphy Auctions)

Beach Set, 5 molds w/screen & scoop, litho tin, Wolverine, VG+IB, A $275.00
Bowler Andy Mill, Wolverine #57A, 20", NMIB........... $400.00
Captain Sandy Andy, Wolverine #63C, 13½", MIB....... $375.00
Coal Loader, Wolverine, 11", MIB................................ $400.00
Crane, 17½", Wolverine #020, MIB.............................. $375.00
Dandy Sandy Andy, 11", Wolverine, G $75.00
Dutch Mill, 12", Mac #26 (McDonell), 1930s, EX......... $100.00
Dutch Mill, 12", Mac #26 (McDowell), 1930s, NMIB... $200.00

Pail, half-moon shape, WWI battleship scene, 4½x9x4", marked Stock Package Co., very rare shape, EX, A, $785.00. (Photo courtesy Morphy Auctions)

Pail, rnd, Asbury Park, royal bl, bail hdl, 6", G, A.......... $300.00
Pail, rnd, Asbury Park on red, wht & bl patriotic graphics, bail hdl w/wood grip, 5½", VG+, A $1,100.00
Pail, rnd, Atlantic City, red, wht & bl patriotic graphics, bail hdl w/wood grip, 6½", VG+, A..................................... $825.00
Pail, rnd, beach scene w/kids, orange band top & bottom, elephant graphics on shovel bowl w/wooden hdl, 6", G+, A.... $220.00

Pail, rnd, beach scene w/kids, w/zeppelin & airplane overhead, red, bl & yel, 6", USA, 1930s, EX, A $390.00
Pail, rnd, beach scene w/kids in water gathering shells, catching fish, digging clams, bail hdl, wood grip, 6", T Bros, EX, A....$140.00
Pail, rnd, beach scene w/kids in goat cart, bail hdl, 6", marked Germany & emb w/horse & MO2O, 1910s, EX, A .. $165.00
Pail, rnd, beach scene w/kids playing on lg ball & playing under lg umbrella, lt bl interior, bail hdl, 5", VG+, A $275.00
Pail, rnd, beach scene w/sailor & his girl, fancy floral & vine border, bail hdl, 6", VG+, A $330.00
Pail, rnd, beach scene w/Victorian kids on path, girl picking flowers & child on donkey, 6", Germany, 1910s, EX+, A $600.00
Pail, rnd, circus scene on yel w/lt bl interior, rimmed foot, 7", G+, A...$75.00
Pail, rnd, clown heads in metallic gold circles on wht, red trim, bail hdl w/wood grip, shovel, 6½", Converse, VG, A......... $550.00

Pail, round, Disney, Atlantic City, Mickey and Minnie, 8", Ohio Art, EX+, A, $2,000.00. (Photo courtesy Morphy Auctions)

Pail, rnd, Disney, Atlantic City, Pluto pulling Donald Duck in wagon on red background, 8" Ohio Art, VG, A...$1,100.00
Pail, rnd, Disney, Donald Duck appears to be in a dither on beach, red footed base & shovel, 5½", Ohio Art, EX, A $495.00
Pail, rnd, Disney, Donald Duck as captain of the ship looking in spyglass backwards, bl shovel, 4½", Ohio Art, EX, A.. $385.00
Pail, rnd, Disney, Donald Duck in beach scene w/nephews, red shovel, 4¼", Ohio Art, 1939, EX, A $275.00
Pail, rnd, Disney, Donald Duck's nephews on merry-go-round & other amusement themes, 5¼", Chein, EX, A $110.00
Pail, rnd, Disney, Mickey & friends in rowboat w/Mickey pointing, wht clouds in bl-gray sky, 3", Ohio Art, NM, A......$1,100.00
Pail, rnd, Disney, Mickey & Minnie standing in front of fenced cottage w/Pluto, 11", Ohio Art/WDE, 1938, VG, A........ $200.00
Pail, rnd, Disney, Mickey Mouse, Donald Duck & Goofy on golf outing, 6", Ohio Art, 1938, EX+, A........................ $425.00
Pail, rnd, Disney, Mickey Mouse & Donald Duck on yel w/bl & red stars, bl hdl, Happynak #706, EX, A $250.00
Pail, rnd, Disney, Mickey Mouse & Minnie on 'pirate's' raft w/yel fenced beach scene & sky behind, 6", Ohio Art, NM, A.$300.00
Pail, rnd, Disney, Mickey's Band, w/shovel marked 'Mickey Mouse' & graphics, 10", Ohio Art, EX+, A $770.00
Pail, rnd, Disney, Snow White & the Seven Dwarfs, w/shovel, 6", Ohio Art, EX (inside worn), A $140.00
Pail, rnd, Disney, Three Little Pigs lettered at bottom, pigs in front of houses, bl footed base, 5½", EX $385.00
Pail, rnd, Disney, Three Little Pigs lettered at bottom, pigs on lt gr background, 3½", WDE, EX $360.00
Pail, rnd, Disney, Treasure Island, Mickey & friends on beach seeking treasure, 4½", NM, A...............................$1,200.00
Pail, rnd, Disney, Who's Afraid.../Three Little Pigs lettered top/bottom, brick wall/gr & yel, gr shovel, 4½", VG, A... $385.00
Pail, rnd, Disney, Who's Afraid.../Three Little Pigs lettered top/bottom, yel sky & footed base, shovel, 7", WDE, NM, A.......... $1,540.00
Pail, rnd, eagle on rock/kids at the beach doing various activities, 6", AMSCO, 1920s, EX, A...................................... $450.00
Pail, rnd, For a Good Child, red, wht & bl patriotic graphics on wht, bail hdl w/wood grip, 6", VG, A $715.00
Pail, rnd, From Wildwood Beach, metallic gold, bail hdl, 3¼", G, A $300.00
Pail, rnd, Funny Face, 3¼", Ohio Art, EX, A................. $200.00
Pail, rnd, kids playing cowboys & Indians in yel desert scene w/ wht mountins & bl sky, 5", Chein, NM, A $110.00
Pail, rnd, Mary Had a Little Lamb, emb images, 6", Germany, 1910s, EX, A $165.00
Pail, rnd, Popeye the Sailor, Popeye diving into water, yel sky, 3⅓", KFS, 1929-33, NM, A $1,045.00
Pail, rnd, Sea Side & fancy floral graphics emb in silver on bl, bail hdl w/wood grip, 5", G+, A $550.00
Pail, rnd, Sea Side in red, wht & bl w/crossed flags & eagle on metallic gold, bail hdl w/wood grip, 6½", T Bros, VG $550.00
Pail, rnd, straight sides, Jumbo Sea Side on orange, bail hdl, 3x4½" dia, VG+, A.. $465.00

Pail, round, Teddy Roosevelt riding on bear's back, 3½", VG, A, $850.00. (Photo courtesy James D. Julia, Inc.)

Pail, rnd, Young America, beach scene w/kids, fancy floral & vine border, bail hdl, 7", G+, A.............................. $525.00
Pail, sq, Disney, bail hdl, 6", Willow Prod, 1940s-50s, NM, A $225.00
Sand Lift, 11", Ohio Art, VGIB.. $100.00
Sand Loader, 11", Wolverine, MIB $400.00
Sand Sifter, tin w/Disney characters & Krazy Kat lithoed on sides, Chein, 1930s, VG $200.00
Sand Sifter/Watering Can, Donald Duck/donkey graphics, Ohio Art/WDE, 1938, VG+, A.. $150.00

Sandy Andy Merry Miller Mill, 12", Wolverine, VG $100.00
Sandy Andy No 75, Wolverine, 14", EX+ (VG box), A... $120.00
Sandy Andy Sand Loader, Wolverine #50, EX $30.00
Shovel, Mickey, Minnie & Donald Duck in snowball fight on wide fluted tin shovel pan, wooden hdl, 27", Ohio Art, VG, A $385.00
Tub, Three Little Pigs singing & dancing as they work, yel sky, no hdl, 3", EX, A $250.00
Water Pump, metal w/lithoed children & elephant, 20", Ohio Art, EX... $100.00
Watering Can, Disney, cylindrical w/blk & wht images on bl, red rim, yel & red spout, side hdl, 3", EX $385.00

Watering Can, Disney, Mickey Mouse, 6", EX, A, $495.00. (Photo courtesy Morphy Auctions)

Watering Can, Disney, Mickey Mouse watering flowers by fence, yel sky & spout, high loop hdl, 8", VG, A $385.00
Watering Can, Disney, Who's Afraid.../Three Little Pigs lettered top & bottom, w/graphics, 4½", G, A $330.00
Watering Can, flying gulls/2 mallards in flight over water, 6½" (w/hdl up), Germany 1910s, EX, A.......................... $200.00
Watering Can, kids playing war in military garb, various flag imagery, 8", French, VG+, A.................................... $470.00
Watering Can, mallard in flight over pond/egret flying over water, 7½" (w/hdl up), AMSCO, 1920s, EX, A....... $390.00

Santa Claus

Christmas is a magical time for young children; visions of Santa and his sleigh are mirrored in their faces, and their eyes are wide with the wonder of the Santa fantasy. There are many who collect ornaments, bulbs, trees, etc., but the focus of our listings is Santa himself.

Among the more valuable Santas are the German-made papier-maché figures and candy containers, especially the larger examples and those wearing costumes in colors other than the traditional red.

See also other specific categories.

Bank, Animated Santa Bank, b/o, Santa seated atop house, 12", VGIB, A $75.00
Candy Container, Santa in chimney, litho die-cut face w/tall pointy red crepe-paper hat, 'brick' chimney, 6", EX, A........... $385.00
Candy Container, Santa seated on rocket ship, cloth-dressed Santa holding tree, bl pants, blk shoes, 5x6", EX, A $770.00
Candy Container, Santa standing holding tree, red cloth jacket & bl pants, blk belt & boots, wht fur beard, 10", VG+ .. $500.00
Candy Container, Santa w/bisque head & red crepe-paper suite w/fur trim & beard standing on rnd red crepe box, 6", EX, A...$275.00
Doll, holding tree, bisque w/pnt eyes, wool beard & trim on red suit, blk belt & pnt boots, 5", Germany, 1900, EX, A...........$700.00
Game of Merry Christmas, Parker Bros, dated 1898, EXIB, A $6,600.00
Game of the Christmas Jewel, McLoughlin Bros, EXIB (box lid shows Santa at chimney on roof), A $880.00

Jack-in-the-box, Santa pops up in wooden box w/paper lithograph covering, 5", Germany, VG+, A, $950.00. (Photo courtesy Morphy Auctions)

Lantern, Santa head w/open mouth, inserted eyed, bail hdl, red hat covered w/mica, wht beard, 6", Germany, NM, A ... $1,150.00
Marble Game, wood back & sides w/paper litho game board showing Santa w/tree in early auto & kids w/toys, 16", VG+ $1,760.00
Mechanical Toy, Santa Claus #M-70 (Eyes Light Up/Sitting on House), b/o, plush, HTC, 1950s, EXIB $65.00
Mechanical Toy, Santa Claus w/Bell, Santa on sled w/single reindeer, litho tin, rubber antlers, Japan, 7" L, NMIB.... $250.00
Mechanical Toy, Santa in plush suit, wht fur beard & boots w/toy sack, rings bell, b/o, 10", Alps, 1950s, EXIB................$65.00
Mechanical Toy, Santa on Rocking Horse, w/up, Santa in red robe w/wht trim, wht fur beard, wooden rockers, 7x8", EX, A $1,980.00
Mechanical Toy, Santa on Scooter, b/o, fur beard, cloth hat & toy bag, 9" L, MT, 1950s, EXIB $125.00
Mechanical Toy, Santa ringing bell, b/o, red cloth suit w/wht plastic belt & fur trim, wht fur beard, 12", VGIB $75.00

Night Before Christmas Puzzle Box, complete with three puzzles, Milton Bradley, NMIB, A, $2,750.00.

(Photo courtesy Morphy Auctions)

Ornament, yel plastic Santa figure w/wht beard & cuffs, red belt, bl base, E Rosen, 1950s, EX+, A $25.00
Puppet, paper litho on flat cb figure, pull string to activate arms & legs, 12", VG+, A $220.00
Push-button puppet, Kohner, 1960s, EX $75.00
Puzzle Blocks, paper litho on wood, 35-pc set showing Santa & kids in snow against dark bl sky, VG+IB, A....$1,760.00
Roly Poly, 4½", pnt compo & papier-machè, red suit & hat, blk-outlined wht cuffs, yel bottom, wht-pnt beard, VG, A..$83.00
Roly Poly, 6", pnt compo & papier machè, red suit w/pointy hat, blk-trimmed cuffs & belt, wht beard, VG, A $83.00
Roly Poly, 11½", pnt compo, holding tree & horse, red, wht & gr outlined w/blk trim, toothy smile, Schoenhut, EX, A....$1,980.00
Santa on Donkey w/Nodding Head, papier-machè w/fur-type covering, Santa in red jacket & bl pants, 8" H, VG, A ... $175.00

Schoenhut

Albert Schoenhut & Co. was located in Philadelphia, Pennsylvania. From as early as 1872 they produced toys of many types including dolls, pianos and other musical instruments, games, and a good assortment of roly polys (which they called Rolly Dollys). In 1902 –'03 they were granted patents that were the basis for toy animals and performers that Schoenhut designated the 'Humpty Dumpty Circus.' It was made up of circus animals, ringmasters, acrobats, lion tamers, and the like, and the concept proved to be so successful that it continued in production until the company closed in 1935. During the nearly 35 years they were made, the figures were continually altered either in size or by construction methods, and these variations can greatly affect their values today. Besides the figures themselves, many accessories were produced to go along with the circus theme — tents, cages, tubs, ladders, and wagons, just to mention a few. Teddy Roosevelt's 1909 African safari adventures inspired the company to design a line that included not only Teddy and the animals he was apt to encounter in Africa but native tribesmen as well. A third line in the 1920s featured comic characters of the day, all with the same type of jointed wood construction, many dressed in cotton and felt clothing. There were several, among them were Felix the Cat, Maggie and Jiggs, Barney Google and Spark Plug, and Happy Hooligan. (See Character, TV, and Movie Collectibles.)

Several factors come into play when evaluating Schoenhut figures. Foremost is condition. Since most found on the market today show signs of heavy wear, anything above a very good rating commands a premium price. Missing parts and retouched paint sharply reduce a figure's value, though a well-done restoration is usually acceptable. The earlier examples had glass eyes; by 1920 eyes were painted. In the early 1920s the company began to make their animals in a reduced size. While some of the earlier figures had bisque heads or carved wooden heads, by the '20s, pressed wood heads were the norm. Full-size examples with glass eyes and bisque or carved heads are generally more desirable and more valuable, though rarity must be considered as well.

During the 1950s, some of the figures and animals were produced by the Delvan Company, who had purchased the manufacturing rights.

For more information we recommend *Schoenhut Toy Price Guide* in full color by Keith Kaonis and Andrew Yaffee. Mr. Kaonis is listed in the Directory under Schoenhut.

Advisors: Keith and Donna Kaonis

See also Character, TV, and Movie Collectibles; Pull and Push Toys; Roly Polys; Santa.

Humpty Dumpty Circus Animals

Humpty Dumpty Circus animals with glass eyes, circa 1903 – 1914, are more desirable and can demand much higher prices than the later painted-eye versions. As a general rule, a glass-eye version is 30% to 40% more than a painted-eye version. (There are exceptions.) The following list suggests values for both glass eye and painted eye versions and reflects a low painted eye price to a high glass eye price.

There are other variations and nuances of certain figures: Bulldog — white with black spots or brindle (brown); open-and closed-mouth zebras and giraffes; ball necks and hemispherical necks on some animals such as the pig, leopard, and tiger, to name a few. These points can affect the price and should be judged individually.

Alligator, PE/GE, from $250 to $750.00
Arabian camel, 1 hump, PE/GE, from $250 to....$750.00
Bactrain camel, 2 humps, PE/GE, from $200 to....$1,200.00
Brown Bear, PE/GE, from $200 to....$800.00
Buffalo, carved mane, PE/GE, from $200 to....$1,200.00
Bulldog, PE/GE, from $400 to $1,500.00
Burro, farm set, PE/GE, no harness/no belly hole for chariot, from $300 to....$800.00
Burro, made to go w/chariot & clown, w/leather track, PE/GE, from $200 to $800.00
Cat, PE/GE, rare, from $500 to....$3,000.00
Cow, PE/GE, from $300 to $1,200.00
Deer, PE/GE, from $300 to $1,500.00
Donkey, PE/GE, from $75 to $300.00
Donkey w/Blanket, PE/GE, from $100 to....$600.00
Elephant, PE/GE, from $75 to....$300.00
Gazelle, PE/GE, rare, from $500 to....$3,000.00

Giraffe, PE/GE, from $200 to $900.00
Goose, PE only, from $200 to $750.00
Gorilla, PE only, from $1,500 to.................................. $4,000.00
Hippo, PE/GE, from $200 to... $900.00
Horse, brn, saddle & stirrups, PE/GE, from $250 to........ $500.00

Horse, dappled paint, platform, painted or glass eyes, from $250.00 to $700.00. (Photo courtesy McMasters Harris Auctions)

Hyena, PE/GE, very rare, from $1,000 to..................... $6,000.00
Kangaroo, PE/GE, from $200 to $1,500.00
Lion, carved mane, PE/GE, from $200 to..................... $1,400.00
Monkey, 1-part head, PE only, from $200 to.................. $600.00
Monkey, 2-part head, wht face, from $300 to $1,000.00
Ostrich, PE/GE, from $200 to... $900.00
Pig, 5 versions, PE/GE, from $200 to............................. $800.00
Polar Bear, PE/GE, from $200 to $2,000.00
Poodle, PE/GE, from $100 to... $300.00
Rabbit, PE/GE, very rare, from $500 to........................ $3,500.00
Rhino, PE/GE, from $250 to.. $800.00
Sea Lion, PE/GE, from $400 to $1,500.00
Sheep (Lamb), w/bell, PE/GE, from $200 to.................. $800.00

Tiger, painted or glass eyes, from $250.00 to $1,200.00. (Photo courtesy Bertoia Auctions)

Wolf, PE/GE, very rare, from $500 to.......................... $5,000.00
Zebra, PE/GE, rare, from $500 to $3,000.00

Humpty Dumpty Circus Clowns and Other Personnel

Clowns with two-part heads (a cast face applied to a wooden head) were made from 1903 to 1916 and are most desirable — condition is always important. There have been nine distinct styles in 14 different costumes recorded. Only eight costume styles apply to the two-part headed clowns. The later clowns, ca. 1920, had one-part heads whose features were pressed, and the costumes were no longer tied at the wrists and ankles.

Note: Use the low end of the value range for items in only fair condition. Those in good to very good condition (having very minor scratches and wear, good original finish, no splits or chips, no excessive paint wear or cracked eyes and, of course, complete) may be evaluated by the high end.

Black Dude, 1-part head, purple coat, from $250 to $750.00
Black Dude, 2-part head, blk coat, from $400 to $1,000.00
Chinese Acrobat, 1-part head, from $200 to $900.00
Chinese Acrobat, 2-part head, rare, from $400 to $1,600.00
Clown, reduced size, from $75 to.................................. $125.00
Hobo, reduced size, from $200 to $400.00
Hobo, 1-part head, from $200 to.................................... $400.00
Hobo, 2-part head, curved-up toes, blk coat, from $500 to .. $1,200.00

Lady and Gent Acrobats, bisque heads, each from $300.00 to $800.00. (Photo courtesy Noel Barrett Antiques and Auctions, Ltd.)

Lady Acrobat, 1-part head, from $150 to $400.00
Lady Rider, bisque head, from $250 to $550.00
Lady Rider, 2-part head, very rare, from $500 to............ $100.00
Lion Tamer, 1-part head, from $150 to........................... $700.00
Lion Tamer, 2-part head, early, very rare, from $700 to $1,600.00
Ringmaster, bisque, from $300 to $800.00
Ringmaster, 1-part head, from $200 to........................... $450.00
Ringmaster, 2-part head, blk coat, very rare, from $800 to.. $1,800.00
Ringmaster, 2-part head, red coat, very rare, from $700 to.. $1,600.00

Humpty Dumpty Circus Accessories

There are many accessories: wagons, tents, ladders, chairs, pedestals, tight ropes, weights, and various other items.

Band Wagon With Musicians, 40" overall, EX, A, $44,000.00. (Photo courtesy Bertoia Auctions)

Cage Wagon, 10", VG, A $1,200.00
Cage Wagon, 12", G, A $1,050.00
Circus Set, w/clown, donkey, elephant, chair, tub & ladder, EX+IB, A $300.00
Humpty Dumpty Circus Toys Set No 21-21, 10-pc w/2 clowns, 2 chairs, elephant, donkey & 2 ladders, VG+IB, A.... $475.00
Tent, 24x18" wood & paperboard box-type base, w/orig pennants & trapeze, G, A $2,200.00

Tent, 32" wide, EX+IB, A, $4,950.00. (Photo courtesy Noel Barrett Antiques and Auctions, Ltd.)

Tent, 35x56" L, w/rare tightrope ring, VG, A............. $8,250.00

Schuco

A German company noted for both mechanical toys as well as the teddy bears and stuffed animals we've listed here, Schuco operated from the 1930s well into the 1950s. Items were either marked Germany or US Zone, Germany.

See also Aeronautical; Battery-Operated; Character, TV, and Movie Collectibles; Diecast; Disney; Windup, Friction, and Other Mechanical Toys.

Bear, 2½", blk, shoe-button eyes, felt pads, VG $200.00
Bear, 2½", cream, tan nose & mouth, metal eyes, 1920s, VG..$150.00
Bear, 2½", pale gold, metal eyes, paper label, 1950s, NM.. $225.00
Bear, 3½", cinnamon, orig ribbon, 1950s, M.................. $250.00
Bear, 4", lt gold, 1940s-50s, EX....................................... $125.00
Bear, 12", yel, metal eyes, 1920s, VG $350.00
Bear Tumbler, 9", furry head w/jtd felt body, w/wire tumbling support, VG, A.. $660.00
Bingo-Bello Dog, 14", orig clothes, NM........................ $150.00
Black Scottie, 3", Noah's Ark, 1950s, MIB $225.00
Blackbird, 3", Noah's Ark, 1950s, MIB $200.00
Dalmatian, 2½", Noah's Ark, 1950s, rare, M $375.00
Elephant, 2½", Noah's Ark, 1950s, NM.......................... $125.00
Monkey, 8", brn & wht shaggy mohair, glass eyes, posable fingers & toes, EX... $650.00

Monkey on Roller Skates, 7½", dressed in overalls and shirt, G, A, $390.00. (Photo courtesy James D. Julia, Inc.)

Mouse, 6", mc dress w/gr shoes, EX+ $200.00
Orangutan, 3", Noah's Ark, 1950s, rare, MIB................ $300.00
Owl, 3", Noah's Ark, 1950s, M..$75.00
Penguin, 3", Noah's Ark, 1950s, EX.............................. $150.00
Perfume Bear, 3½", gold, 1920s, no bottle o/w VG......... $150.00
Perfume Monkey, 5", cinnamon, G, A $255.00
Perfume Monkey, 5", long bottle neck, EX, A $330.00
Two-Faced Bear, 3½", brn, blk shoe-button eyes, 1950s, EX .. $250.00
Yes/No Bear, 5", caramel, glass eyes, 1950s, NM............ $450.00

Yes/No Bear, 12", caramel, glass eyes, G, A, $285.00. (Photo courtesy James D. Julia, Inc.)

Yes/No Bear, 13", caramel, pre-WWI, G, A $275.00
Yes/No Bear, 17", caramel, amber glass eyes, VG $1,000.00
Yes/No Bear, 19", caramel, amber glass eyes, 1920s-30s, EX, A $440.00
Yes/No Bellboy Bear w/Cello, 15", VG $1,150.00
Yes/No Bellboy Monkey, 9", 1920s-30s, EX $350.00
Yes/No Bellboy Monkey, 14", 1920s-30s, G $125.00
Yes/No Bulldog, 7", cream & brn, glass eyes, 1930s, NM ...$1,200.00
Yes/No Cat, 5", M $650.00
Yes/No Donkey, 5", 1950s, NM $475.00
Yes/No Elephant, 5", 1948, EX $400.00
Yes/No Panda, 3½", 1950s, NM $1,000.00
Yes/No Panda, 8", 1940-50, rare, EX $850.00
Yes/No Trickey Monkey, 14", NM $450.00
Yes/No Tricky Bear, 8", 1950, NM $950.00
Yes/No Tricky Bear, 13", 1948, M $1,200.00
Yes/No Tricky Monkey, 10", orig tag, 1940s-50s, EX $350.00
Yes/No Tricky Orangutan, 8", EX $375.00
Yes/No Tricky Orangutan, 14", NM $950.00

Slot Cars

Slot cars first became popular in the early 1960s. Electric raceways set up in retail storefront windows were commonplace. Huge commercial tracks with eight and ten lanes were located in hobby store and raceways throughout the United States. Large corporations such as Aurora, Revell, Monogram, and Cox, many of which were already manufacturing toys and hobby items, jumped on the bandwagon to produce slot cars and race sets. By the end of the early 1970s, people were loosing interest in slot racing, and its popularity diminished. Today the same baby boomers that raced slot cars in earlier days are revitalizing the sport. The popularity of the Internet has stabilized the pricing of collectible slots. It can confirm prices of common items, while escalating the price of the 'rare' item to new levels. As the Internet grows in popularity, the accessibility of information on slots also grows. This should make the once hard-to-find slot cars more readily available for all to enjoy. Slot cars were generally well used, so finding vintage cars and race sets in like-new or mint condition is difficult. Slot cars replicating the muscle cars from the '60s and '70s are extremely sought after, and clubs and organizations devoted to these collectibles are becoming more and more commonplace. Large toy companies such as Tomy and Tyco still produce some slots today, but not in the quality, quantity, or variety of years past.

Aurora produced several types of slots: Screachers (5700 and 5800 number series, valued at $5.00 to $20.00); the AC-powered Vibrators (1500 number series, valued at $20.00 to $150.00); DC-powered Thunderjets (1300 and 1400 number series, valued at $20.00 to $150.00); and the last-made AFX SP1000 (1900 number series, valued at $15.00 to $75.00).

Complete Sets

AMT, Cobra Racing Set, NMIB $185.00
Arnold, Minimobil, 1960s, unused, NMIB, A $30.00
Atlas, Racing Set #1000, HO scale, GIB $100.00
Aurora, Ford Street Van, #1943, lt bl & brn, NM $15.00
Aurora, Home Raceway by Sears, #79N9513C, VG....... $225.00
Aurora AFX, Blazer, #1917, bl & wht, VG $12.00
Aurora AFX, Chevy Nomad, #1760, chrome, EX $25.00
Aurora AFX, Chevy Nomad, #1760, orange, EX...............$20.00
Aurora AFX, Devil's Ditch Set, EX.................................$40.00
Aurora AFX, Dodge Rescue Van, #1937, red, gr & wht, EX... $15.00
Aurora AFX, Furious Fueler Dragster, #1774, wht & yel, EX.. $15.00
Aurora AFX, Peterbilt Shell Rig, #1155, yel, red & wht, EX.. $25.00
Aurora AFX, Porsche 917-10, #1747, wht, red & bl, EX...$12.00
Aurora AFX, Shadow Cam Racer, blk, EX $20.00
Aurora AFX, Speed Banner #11, red, wht & bl, NM $15.00
Aurora AFX, Ultra 5, EXIB..$75.00
Aurora Cigarbox, Ford Lola GT, red w/wht stripe, G+......$10.00
Aurora G-Plus, Ferrari F1, #1734, red & wht, EX..............$25.00
Aurora G-Plus, Indy Valvoline, blk, VG...........................$12.00
Cox, Baja Raceway, Super Scale, NMIB $150.00
Cox, Ontario 8 #3070 w/Eagle & McLaren, GIB $75.00
Eldon, Dodge Charger Road Race Set, NMIB $75.00
Eldon, Gold Cup Road Race, 1962, 1/32 scale, EXIB..... $150.00
Eldon, Raceway Set #24, 1/24th scale, VG $75.00
Gilbert, Miniature Race Set #19041, VGIB $95.00
Ideal, Alcan Highway Torture Track, 1968, MIB...............$50.00
Ideal, Dukes of Hazzard Racing Set, MIB...........................$85.00
Ideal, Mini-Motorific Set, #4939-5, EX.............................$85.00
Ideal, Motorific Alcan Highway Torture Track, 1966, missing vehicles o/w complete, NMIB, A $60.00
Ideal, Motorific GTO Torture Track, lg, EXIB $100.00

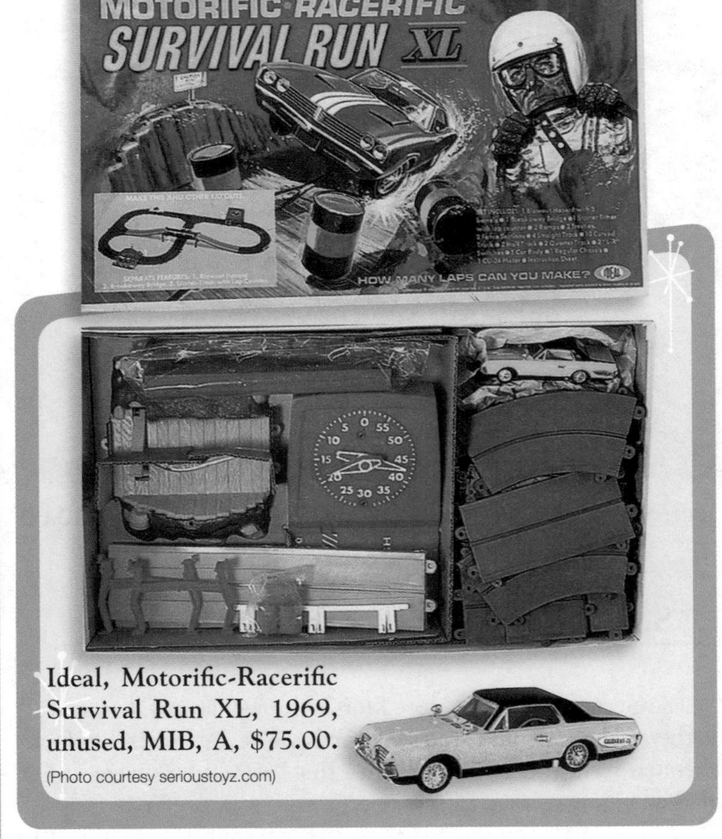

Ideal, Motorific-Racerific Survival Run XL, 1969, unused, MIB, A, $75.00.
(Photo courtesy serioustoyz.com)

Jouef, Circuit Geant, 1960s, unused, NMIB $140.00
Marklin, Sprint, West Germany, 1960s, unused, MIB $225.00

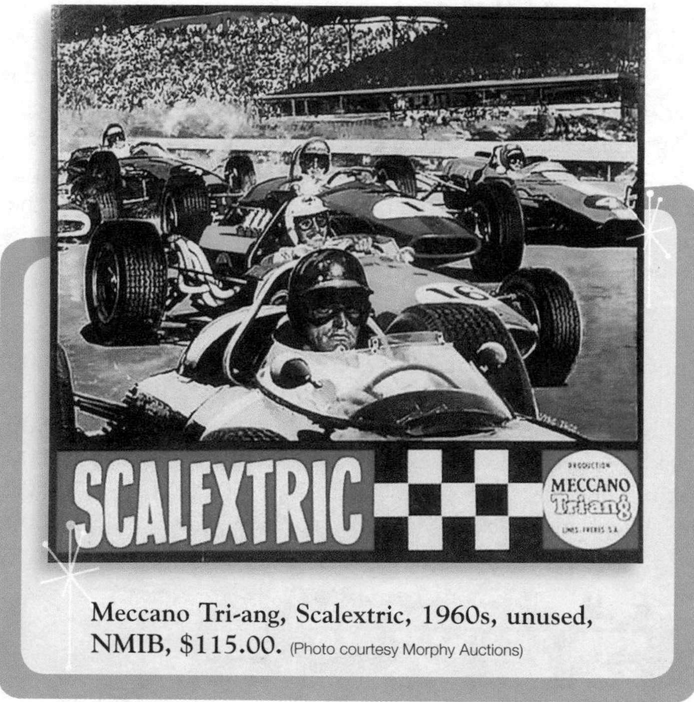

Meccano Tri-ang, Scalextric, 1960s, unused, NMIB, $115.00. (Photo courtesy Morphy Auctions)

Remco, Mighty Mike Action Track, NMIB........................$50.00
Strombecker, Plymouth Barracuda, 1/32 scale set........... $150.00
Strombecker, Thunderbolt Monza, Montgomery Ward, VGIB..$150.00
Strombecker, 4 Lane Mark IV Race Set, VGIB.............. $250.00
Tyco, '57 Chevy, red & orange w/yel stripes, EX................$20.00
Tyco, Autoworld Carrera, wht & red w/bl stripe, G $10.00
Tyco, Blazer, red & blk, VG..$10.00
Tyco, Chaparral 2G #66, #8504, VG $14.00
Tyco, Firebird Turbo #12, blk & gold, EX $10.00
Tyco, Lighted Porsche #2, silver w/red nose, EX................$20.00
Tyco, Pinto Funny Car Goodyear, red & yel, EX..............$20.00
Tyco, Racing Bandits, EX $30.00

Slot Cars Only

Aurora, Ford Baja Bronco, #1909, red, EX........................$15.00
Aurora, Model Motoring, Thunderbird, #1544, bl w/wht top, NMIB, A.. $182.00
Aurora, Snowmobile, #1485-400, yel w/bl figure, MIB......$55.00
Aurora AFX, Autoworld Porsche #5, wht w/bl stripes, EX..$12.00
Aurora AFX, BMW 3201 Turbo, #1980, yel & orange, EX..$20.00
Aurora AFX, Camaro Z-28, #1901, red, wht & bl, EX......$20.00
Aurora AFX, Chevy Nomad, #1760, orange, EX..............$20.00
Aurora AFX, Dodge Challenger, #1773, lime & bl, NM...$35.00
Aurora AFX, Dodge Fever Dragster, wht & yel, EX $15.00
Aurora AFX, Ferrari 612, #1751, yel & blk, EX................$10.00
Aurora AFX, Ford Thunderbird Stock Car, NMIB............$25.00
Aurora AFX, Mario Andretti NGK Indy Car, blk, M........$35.00
Aurora AFX, Monza GT, #1948, wht & gr, EX.................$15.00
Aurora AFX, Pontiac Firebird #9, wht, bl & blk, EX $25.00
Aurora AFX, Porsche Carrera #3, 1933, wht, red & blk, NM..$12.00
Aurora AFX, Rallye Ford Escort, #1737, gr & bl, EX $15.00
Aurora AFX, Speed Beamer, red, wht & bl stripe, VG......$10.00
Aurora Cigarbox, Cobra GT, #6113, chromed w/dbl blk stripe, M (EX+ box)...$45.00
Aurora Cigarbox, Dino Ferrari, red, EX $20.00
Aurora Cigarbox, Ford GT, wht w/blk stripe, NM+ $20.00
Aurora Cigarbox, Ford J, #6104, yel & bl w/bl stripe, M (EX+ box)..$25.00
Aurora Cigarbox, Mako Shark, #6103, bl, MIB................$25.00
Aurora G-Plus, Corvette, #1011, red, orange & wht, EX..$15.00
Aurora G-Plus, Indy Valvoline, blk, VG...........................$12.00
Aurora G-Plus, Rallye Ford Escort, #1737, gr & bl, EX.....$15.00

Aurora, Snowmobile, #1485-400, MIB, $55.00. (Photo courtesy Gary Pollastro)

Aurora Thunderjet, Chaparral 2F #7, #1410, lime & bl, EX .. $25.00
Aurora Thunderjet, Cobra, #1375, yel w/blk stripe, VG+ ...$30.00
Aurora Thunderjet, Cougar, #1389, wht, EX.....................$40.00
Aurora Thunderjet, Dune Buggy, wht w/red striped roof, EX ...$30.00
Aurora Thunderjet, Ford Car, #1382, wht & bl, VG.........$25.00
Aurora Thunderjet, Ford GT 40, #1374, red w/blk stripe, EX..$25.00
Aurora Thunderjet, Mangusta Mongoose, #1400, yel, EX..$45.00
Aurora Vibator, Mercedes, #1542, yel, EX $50.00

Ideal, Jaguar XK-E, #1, Motorific Custom Cars, 1968, MIB, $40.00. (Photo courtesy serioustoyz.com)

Strombecker, Pontiac Bonneville, EX...............................$40.00
TCR, Maintenance Van, red & whtm, EX.........................$15.00
Tyco, '40 Ford Coupe, #88534, blk w/flames, EX..............$20.00
Tyco, '83 Corvette Challenger #33, silver & yel, EX..........$25.00
Tyco, Bandit Pickup, blk & red, EX $12.00
Tyco, Caterpillar #96, blk & yel, EX $20.00
Tyco, Corvette #12, wht & red w/bl stripes, EX................$12.00

Tyco, Firebird, #6914, cream & red, VG....$12.00
Tyco, Funny Mustang, orange w/yel flame, EX....$25.00
Tyco, Jam Car, yel & blk, EX....$10.00
Tyco, Lamborghini, red, VG....$12.00
Tyco, Military Police #45, wht & bl, EX....$30.00
Tyco, Pinto Funny Cargotcha, dk red w/gold stripe, VG...$20.00
Tyco, Rokar 240-Z, #7, blk, EX....$10.00
Tyco, Superbird, #8533, red, wht & bl, VG+....$15.00
Tyco, Turbo Hopper #27, red, EX....$12.00
Tyco, Volvo 850 #3, wht & bl, EX....$20.00

Miscellaneous

AMT Service Parts Kit, #2000, VG....$65.00
Aurora AFX Billboard Retaining Walls, set of 8, EXIB....$15.00
Aurora AFX Pit Kit, G....$15.00
Aurora AFX Terminal Track, plug-in or wire-type, EX, ea..$5.00
Aurora AFX 45 OHM Hand Controller w/Brakes, EXIB..$15.00
Aurora Model Motoring Hill Track, 9", EX....$8.00
Aurora Model Motoring Thumb-Style Controller, EX....$6.00
Aurora Model Motoring Y Turn-Off Track w/Switch, EX..$20.00
Aurora Model Motoring 4-Way Stop Track, 9", EX....$15.00
Aurora Thunderjet Country Bridge Roadway, EXIB....$20.00
Eldon Power Track, MOC....$10.00

Gilbert Autorama Grand Stand #19340, MIB, $25.00. (Photo courtesy Gary Pollastro)

Gilbert Automatic Fly Over Chicane Kit, #19342, MIB...$40.00
Gilbert Automatic Lap Counter, #19339, MIB....$35.00
Monogram Lane Change Track, MIB....$20.00
Monogram Tapered Chicane Track, MIB....$20.00
Strombecker Scale Lap Counter, 1/32 scale, MIB....$25.00
Tyco HO Scale 1973-74 Handbook, EX....$10.00
Tyoc Trigger Controller, orange, EX....$8.00

Smith-Miller

Smith-Miller (Los Angeles, California) made toy trucks from 1944 until 1955. During that time they used four basic cab designs, and most of their trucks sold for about $15.00 each. Over the past several years, these toys have become very popular, especially the Mack trucks which today sell at premium prices. The company made a few other types of toys as well, such as the train toy box and the 'Long, Long Trailer.'

See also Advertising.

Army Materials Truck, L Mack, 20", 1950s, EX+....$400.00
Bank of America Armored Truck, GMC, 14", 1940s, unused, NM+IB....$950.00
Bank of America Box Truck, GMC, 14", 1950s, VG....$500.00
Bekins Van Lines Co Semi, L Mack, 25", 1950s, NM....$1,700.00
Bell Telephone Truck, L Mack, dk gr, 1950s, VG+....$375.00

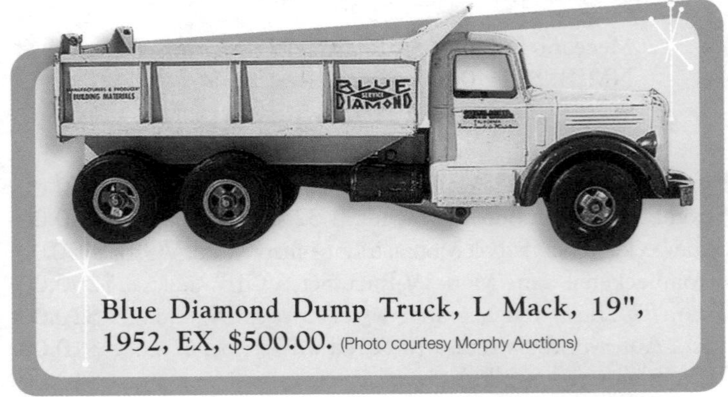

Blue Diamond Dump Truck, L Mack, 19", 1952, EX, $500.00. (Photo courtesy Morphy Auctions)

Blue Diamond Hydraulic Dump Truck, B Mack, wht, 1954, EX+....$650.00
Crane Truck, L Mack, yel, 10-wheeled, rstr....$715.00
Drive-O Dumo Truck, GMC, 1940s, EX....$250.00
Dump Truck, B Mack, orange, hydraulic, 1950s, VG+...$500.00
Dump Truck, GMC, crank action, 7½", 1950s, rstr....$175.00
Dump Truck, GMC, crank action, 12", 1950s, NM....$275.00
Dump Truck w/Front Scoop, GMC, 14", G+....$650.00
Fire Aerial Ladder Truck (LAFD), open Mack cab, 24", NMIB, A....$1,100.00
Fire Aerial Ladder Truck No 3 (SMFD), L Mack, 36", 1950s, NM, A....$1,330.00
Flatbed Semi, Chevy, wood trailer, 1940s, EX+....$275.00
Fruehauf Lowboy, GMC, 26", rstr....$275.00
GMC Cab Only, 10", 1950s, VG....$175.00
Lincoln 2-Door Hardtop Pulling House Trailer, bl & wht, w/ accessories, 40" overall, EX....$875.00
Lumber Truck w/Pup Trailer, L Mack, orig wood & chains, 36", EX+....$600.00
Lyon Van Lines, L Mack, 20½", 1950s, VG+, A....$385.00
Material's Truck, GMC, wooden bed w/side holes & curved open back, 14", 1940s, EX....$250.00
MIC Barrel Stake Truck, w/2 barrels, 18", EX+....$600.00
MIC Dump Truck, yel, BRT, 10-wheeled, 17", NM....$750.00
MIC Wrecker, 17", 1950s, EX....$525.00
Mobiloil Gas Tanker, GMC, 22", G....$225.00
Mobiloil Tanker, GMC, all red, 22", EX....$375.00

P*I*E Semi, L Mack, 27", 1950, EX, $375.00. (Photo courtesy serioustoyz.com)

Searchlight Truck, B Mack, b/o, 1950s, EX+ $600.00
Silver Streak Semi, GMC, U-shaped aluminum trailer, 28", 1950, unused, NM $1,500.00

Smith-Miller Moving Van With Pup Trailer, 36" long overall, NM, A, $975.00. (Photo courtesy Morphy Auctions)

Stake Truck, Chevy, yel, EX+.. $200.00
Terrible Herbst Oil Co...Tandem Tanker, wht cab w/silver van top, BRT, 36" overall, EX $950.00
Utility Truck, GMC, aluminum bed w/chained openings, 14½", 1950s, EX, A... $250.00

Soldiers and Accessories

'Dimestore' soldiers were made from the 1920s until sometime in the 1960s. Some of the better-known companies who made these small-scale figures and vehicles were Barclay, Manoil, and American Metal Toys, formerly known as Jones (hollow cast lead); Grey Iron (cast iron); and Auburn Rubber. They are 3" to 3½" high and were sold in Woolworth's, Kresge's, and other five-and-dime stores for a nickel or a dime, hence the name 'Dimestore.' Marx made tin soldiers for use in target gun games; these sell for about $10.00 to $25.00. Condition is most important as these soldiers saw a lot of action. They are most often found with much of the paint worn off and with some serious 'battle wounds' such as missing arms or rifle tips. Nearly 2,000 different figures and vehicles were made by the major manufacturers, plus a number of others by minor makers such as Tommy Toy and All-Nu.

Another very popular line of toy soldiers has been made by Britains of England since 1893. They are smaller and usually more detailed than 'Dimestores,' and variants number in the thousands. Serious collectors should refer to *Collecting American Made Toy Soldiers* for 'Dimestore' soldiers, and *Collecting Foreign-Made Toy Soldiers* for Britains and others not made in America. Both books are by Richard O'Brien (1997).

You'll notice that in addition to the soldiers, many of our descriptions and values are for vehicles, cannons, planes, animals, and cowboys and Indians made and sold by the same manufacturers. Note: Percentages in the 'Dimestore' description lines refer to the amount of original paint remaining, a most important evaluation factor.

The following 'Dimestore' listings were provided by our advisors, Stan and Sally Alekna. To contact them, see Categories of Special Interest in the back of the book under Soldiers.

See also Dinky; Plastic Figures.

Key:
A — Animals
AFB — American Family on the Beach
AFF — American Family on the Farm
AFH — American Family at Home
AFR — American Family on the Ranch
AFT — American Family Travels
AMT — American Metal Toys
C — Civilians
C&I — Cowboys & Indians
CH — cast helmet
EV — early version
GK — Greyklip
HF — Happy Farm
LS — long stride
M — military
Med — medieval
MRC — My Ranch Corral
PF — pod foot
PH — pot helmet
PW — postwar
SS — short stride
TH — tin helmet
unpnt — unpainted
USD — Uncle Sam's Defenders
V — Vehicles

Dimestore

AMT, A, calf, 95% $15.00
AMT, A, cow standing, any color, 98% $18.00
AMT, A, horse, blk, 97% $17.00
AMT, A, horse, blk & wht, 99%..$19.00
AMT, A, sheep, 98%..$18.00
AMT, C, farmer, 99% $20.00
AMT, C, farmer's wife, 96% $17.00
AMT, C, hobo, 99% $40.00
AMT, C&I, cowboy kneeling w/raised gun, no base, rare, 95% $90.00
AMT, C&I, Indian on rearing horse w/rifle, rare, 98%... $325.00

AMT, M, AA gun, silver, rare, NM....................................$50.00
AMT, M, AA gunner, gray, rare, 97%........................... $165.00
AMT, M, AA gunner, khaki, rare, 97%......................... $120.00
AMT, M, ammo carrier, khaki, very rare, 96% $375.00
AMT, M, anti-tank gunner kneeling, khaki, rare, 97%.. $125.00
AMT, M, flagbearer, khaki, 97% $275.00
AMT, M, German soldier kneeling firing long rifle, very rare, 99%... $225.00
AMT, M, grenade thrower, 97%..................................... $170.00
AMT, M, howitzer, rubber tires, 7", rare, 99% $95.00
AMT, M, machine (dbl) gunner prone, khaki, rare, 96%.. $133.00
AMT, M, machine gunner firing on stump, gray, rare, 98%.. $135.00
AMT, M, observer, khaki, sm, rare, 98%........................ $100.00
AMT, M, officer in greatcoat pointing gun, khaki, rare, 99%.. $325.00
AMT, M, soldier kneeling at searchlight, khaki, rare, 99%... $110.00
AMT, M, soldier kneeling firing long rifle, khaki, rare, 95%.... $125.00
AMT, M, soldier prone w/rifle, rare, 95%....................... $180.00
AMT, M, soldier standing firing rifle, khaki, rare, 99% .. $140.00
AMT, M, wire cutter, khaki, very rare, 93%-95%.......... $400.00

AMT, V, tank, 98%, $150.00. (Photo courtesy Stan and Sally Alekna)

Auburn, A, calf, 98%...$12.00
Auburn, A, collie dog, lg, NM..$25.00
Auburn, A, hen, 99% $12.00
Auburn, A, pig, NM $13.00
Auburn, A, sheep, 99% $13.00
Auburn, C, football lineman, red, rare, 97%......................$57.00
Auburn, M, bugler, khaki, 95% $20.00
Auburn, M, bugler, wht tunic & bl pants, EV, rare, 98%...$28.00
Auburn, M, doctor, wht, rare, 93%-95%...........................$44.00
Auburn, M, infantry officer, M $35.00
Auburn, M, infantry private, wht, NM $25.00
Auburn, M, observer w/binocculars, khaki, 97% $25.00
Auburn, M, officer, M $35.00
Auburn, M, soldier marching at port arms, khaki, NM $25.00
Auburn, M, tommy gunner charging, 98% $27.00
Auburn, M, White Guard officer, 92%-94%......................$18.00
Auburn, V, Marmon-Harrington tank, 3¼", 98% $37.00
Auburn, V, US Army open bed truck, 4½", 97% $42.00
Auburn, V, 1917 International truck, red, 4¼", 98%.........$38.00
Auburn, V, 1937 International cabover stake truck mk USA, khaki, 97%...$3.50
Barclay, A, cow grazing, tan & wht, M..............................$20.00
Barclay, A, cow standing, tan & wht, M $20.00
Barclay, A, horse grazing, wht w/blk mane & tail, M.........$20.00
Barclay, A, ram, M $20.00
Barclay, A, reindeer for pulling Santa's sleigh, very scarce, 98%..$100.00
Barclay, A, sheep resting, M $20.00
Barclay, C, boy in gray or tan, NM, ea $18.00
Barclay, C, Boy Scout hiking, NM $65.00
Barclay, C, Boy Scout saluting, 98% $61.00
Barclay, C, Boy Scout signaling, NM $65.00
Barclay, C, boy skater, M $21.00
Barclay, C, bride or groom, 98%, ea $27.00
Barclay, C, burgler (masked), rare, 97%......................... $178.00
Barclay, C, couple in horse-drawn sleigh, 98% $102.00
Barclay, C, couple on park bench (summer), M.................$45.00
Barclay, C, couple on park bench (winter), M...................$45.00
Barclay, C, elderly man w/cane, NM $22.00
Barclay, C, elderly woman in lavender, 99% $21.00
Barclay, C, fireman w/axe, 98% $42.00
Barclay, C, fireman w/hose, 99% $45.00
Barclay, C, girl figure skater, M..$23.00
Barclay, C, girl in lt gr or red, NM, ea $21.00
Barclay, C, girl in rocker, lime gr dress, rare, 97%.............$25.00
Barclay, C, girl in rocker, red dress, M...............................$26.00
Barclay, C, girl on sled, M...$29.00
Barclay, C, girl skater, M...$22.00
Barclay, C, girl skier, M...$30.00
Barclay, C, jockey in bl & gold silks on gold horse w/#5, NM...$44.00
Barclay, C, jockey in red silks on silver horse w/#6, 98%...$42.00
Barclay, C, mailman, NM $22.00
Barclay, C, man on sled, NM...$28.00
Barclay, C, man skier, NM $29.00
Barclay, C, man speed skater, 98% $20.00
Barclay, C, minister holding hat, M $30.00
Barclay, C, minister walking, scarce, 97% $81.00
Barclay, C, Mountie, very scarce, 92% $70.00
Barclay, C, newsboy in yel shirt & brn pants, 99% $21.00
Barclay, C, policeman, figure-8 base, NM $25.00
Barclay, C, policeman, 99%...$24.00
Barclay, C, Santa (sm) on sled, NM $56.00
Barclay, C, Santa on skis, 97% $68.00
Barclay, C, Santa's sleigh, NM...$40.00
Barclay, C, Santa seated on holly sprig, very scarce, 98% .. $175.00
Barclay, C, Santa seated w/bag of toys, very scarce, 99% .. $325.00
Barclay, C, shoeshine boy, scarce, 95% $39.00
Barclay, C, train conductor, M $22.00
Barclay, C, train passenger (man), 99% $22.00
Barclay, C, train passenger (woman) bl or yel, 98%, ea.....$24.00
Barclay, C, train porter w/wisk broom, 99%.......................$27.00
Barclay, C, train redcap w/bags, 99%.................................$31.00
Barclay, C&I, cowboy rider (masked), red & blk, gray horse, 97% $52.00
Barclay, C&I, cowboy rider (masked) w/gun drawn, blk & wht, 99% $54.00
Barclay, C&I, cowboy rider w/lasso, lasso missing, 99% $68.00
Barclay, C&I, cowboy w/lasso standing, gray, NM $29.00
Barclay, C&I, cowboy w/raised gun, 98%...........................$22.00
Barclay, C&I, Indian chief w/arm across chest, 95% $20.00
Barclay, C&I, Indian chief w/rifle, PF, rare, 98% $40.00

Barclay, C&I, Indian chief w/tomahawk & shield, 94%....$19.00
Barclay, C&I, Indian rider w/rifle, 98%....$48.00
Barclay, C&I, Indian w/bow & arrow, 98%....$19.00
Barclay, C&I, Indian w/bow & arrow kneeling, unmarked, 99%....$24.00
Barclay, C&I, Indian w/hatchet & shield, 97%....$16.00
Barclay, HO, brakeman, NM....$12.00
Barclay, HO, bride, NM....$26.00
Barclay, HO, bridesmaid, gr or pk, very scarce, NM....$45.00
Barclay, HO, conductor, M....$13.00
Barclay, HO, dining steward, 99%....$11.00
Barclay, HO, engineer, dk bl, NM....$12.00
Barclay, HO, fireman, NM....$19.00
Barclay, HO, gateman w/pegleg, scarce, 99%....$24.00
Barclay, HO, groom, wht carnation, scarce, 98%....$24.00
Barclay, HO, hobo, 98%....$10.00
Barclay, HO, little boy, 99%....$20.00
Barclay, HO, little girl, NM....$21.00
Barclay, HO, mailman, 99%....$11.00
Barclay, HO, man, bl or gray, 99%, ea....$11.00
Barclay, HO, newsboy, M....$13.00
Barclay, HO, oiler, NM....$12.00
Barclay, HO, policeman, NM....$12.00
Barclay, HO, porter, brn face, tan coat, 99%....$11.00
Barclay, HO, redcap, M....$13.00
Barclay, HO, woman carrying baby, 99%....$20.00
Barclay, HO, woman in red, no dog, 99%....$11.00
Barclay, M, AA gun crew (2), bl barrel, 97%....$41.00
Barclay, M, ammo carrier, silver boxes, 99%....$29.00
Barclay, M, anti-aircraft gunner, gr, 96%....$21.00
Barclay, M, anti-aircraft gunner, khaki, 98%....$22.00
Barclay, M, aviator, gr, M....$34.00
Barclay, M, aviator, khaki, 99%....$25.00
Barclay, M, aviator, PF, khaki, 98%....$24.00
Barclay, M, bazooka gunner, khaki w/tan bazooka, 99%....$21.00
Barclay, M, bomb thrower, gr, M....$29.00
Barclay, M, bomb thrower, khaki, M....$27.00
Barclay, M, bomb thrower, rifle off ground, TH, M....$40.00
Barclay, M, bugler, midi PF, very rare, 95%....$100.00
Barclay, M, cadet officer w/sword, SS, wht, 98%....$30.00
Barclay, M, cadet w/rifle, SS, 95%....$26.00
Barclay, M, cannon (field), closed hitch, unmk, sm, NM..$27.00
Barclay, M, cannon (long range), ruber tires, mk Made in USA on barrel, 96%....$20.00
Barclay, M, cannon crew (2) working mobile cannon, PF, 99%....$42.00
Barclay, M, cavalryman, 2¼", 1930s, 97%....$35.00
Barclay, M, doctor in wht coat w/red cross on arm, flat base, unmk, 95%....$27.00
Barclay, M, drummer, LS, TH, 97%....$38.00
Barclay, M, field phone operator leaning out, CH, rare, 93%....$79.00
Barclay, M, flag bearer, LS, TH, 97%....$28.00
Barclay, M, grenade thrower, tall, very scarce, 98%....$525.00
Barclay, M, Japanese soldier advancing w/rifle, scarce, 95%..$45.00
Barclay, M, Japanese soldier marching w/rifle, scarce, 95%....$45.00
Barclay, M, machine gun car (2-man), scarce, 99%....$75.00
Barclay, M, machine gunner charging, 96%....$44.00
Barclay, M, machine gunner prone, gr, 96%....$26.00
Barclay, M, machine gunner prone, khaki, 97%....$20.00
Barclay, M, marine, SS, 94%....$32.00
Barclay, M, marine, 98%....$28.00
Barclay, M, marine officer, CH, bl, 88%....$86.00
Barclay, M, marine officer, LS, wht cap, rare, 99%....$55.00

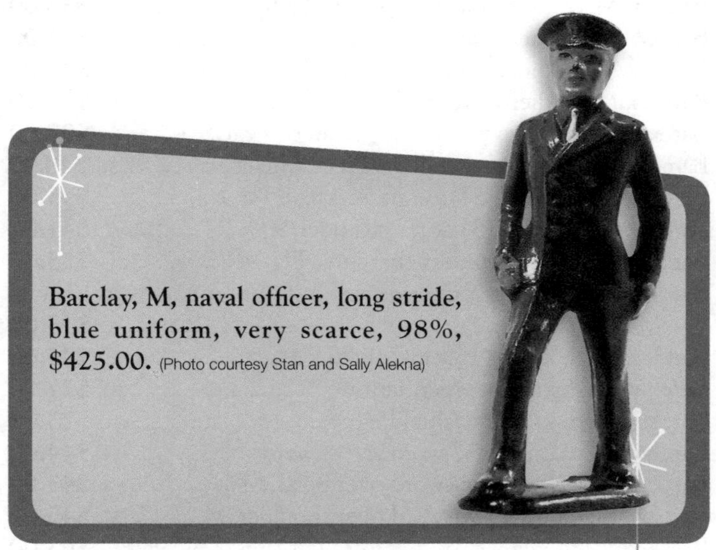
Barclay, M, naval officer, long stride, blue uniform, very scarce, 98%, $425.00. (Photo courtesy Stan and Sally Alekna)

Barclay, M, naval officer, LS, wht uniform, 99%....$27.00
Barclay, M, naval officer, LS, 95%....$28.00
Barclay, M, nurse, blk hair, rare, 99%....$46.00
Barclay, M, nurse w/bag, 94%....$26.00
Barclay, M, officer, gr PH, 98%....$31.00
Barclay, M, officer, khaki, M....$21.00
Barclay, M, officer, PF, bl w/wht helmet, very scarce, 98%....$175.00
Barclay, M, officer in helmet mounted, rare, 98%....$125.00
Barclay, M, officer w/gas mask & pistol, M....$34.00
Barclay, M, officer w/sword, LS, TH, 98%....$31.00
Barclay, M, officer w/sword drawn on cantering horse, rare, 98%....$85.00
Barclay, M, radio operator, separate antenna, 94%....$55.00
Barclay, M, sailor, bl, 99%....$27.00
Barclay, M, sailor, wht, 96%....$24.00
Barclay, M, searchlight operator, smooth lense, very scarce, 90%....$225.00
Barclay, M, sentry in overcoat, 95%....$95.00
Barclay, M, shell loader, 94%....$21.00
Barclay, M, shell loader, 99%....$28.00
Barclay, M, soldier at order arms, gr PH, no space between right leg & rifle butt, M....$32.00
Barclay, M, soldier charging, gr, 99%....$23.00
Barclay, M, soldier charging, SS, TH, 95%....$28.00
Barclay, M, soldier charging w/rifle across waist, 94%....$21.00
Barclay, M, soldier clubbing w/rifle, TH, rare, 95%....$65.00
Barclay, M, soldier eating & sitting, rare, 95%....$40.00
Barclay, M, soldier kneeling firing, khaki, 98%....$25.00
Barclay, M, soldier kneeling firing, LS, TH, 96%....$26.00
Barclay, M, soldier kneeling firing, red, very rare, 96%....$142.00
Barclay, M, soldier marching, khaki, 99%....$21.00
Barclay, M, soldier marching, sling arms, CH, M....$45.00
Barclay, M, soldier marching, SS, TH, early, 96%....$26.00
Barclay, M, soldier marching w/pack & rifle, CH, rare, 95%..$40.00
Barclay, M, soldier marching w/pack & rifle, TH, 95%....$28.00

Barclay, M, soldier marching w/right shoulder arms, gr PH, 98%........$28.00
Barclay, M, soldier prone firing rifle, TH, 98%........$32.00
Barclay, M, soldier running looking up, gr, M........$23.00
Barclay, M, soldier running looking up, khaki, NM........$21.00
Barclay, M, soldier running w/rifle, CH, 93%........$36.00
Barclay, M, soldier standing at searchlight, 97%........$51.00
Barclay, M, soldier standing firing, 99%........$23.00
Barclay, M, soldier w/french horn, 98%........$31.00
Barclay, M, soldier w/sentry dog, scarce, 99%........$97.00
Barclay, M, soldier w/wounded head & arm, gr, scarce, 97%..$48.00
Barclay, M, soldiers (2) on raft, scarce, 95%........$95.00
Barclay, M, soldiers (3) at range finder, 97%........$41.00
Barclay, M, tommy gunner charging, TH, 96%........$23.00
Barclay, M, wireless operator, separate antenna, rusty helmet, M........$95.00
Barclay, Med, knight (blk) w/shield, M........$45.00
Barclay, Med, knight w/pennant, 99%........$27.00
Barclay, Med, knight w/shield, 98%........$23.00
Barclay, Med, knight w/sword across waist, NM........$44.00
Barclay, Med, knight w/sword over head, M........$45.00
Barclay, Med, knight w/sword over shoulder, M........$45.00
Barclay, V, ambulance, sm bl cross, wht tires, 3½", 98%....$63.00
Barclay, V, armoured truck, khaki, WRT, 98%........$27.00
Barclay, V, Austin coupe, metal wheels, ca 1931, scarce, 99%..$43.00
Barclay, V, auto carrier, 1st version, 1930s, very scarce, 98%.. $575.00
Barclay, V, cannon (costal defense), rarest Barclay cannon, NM........$185.00

Barclay, V, cannon truck, movable cannon, scarce, M, $180.00. (Photo courtesy Stan and Sally Alekna)

Barclay, V, circus wagon, horse w/plumes, ca 1930, very scarce, 99%........$325.00
Barclay, V, coupe, blk metal wheels, 2¼", 97%........$45.00
Barclay, V, delivery truck, open bed, w/4 milk cans, red w/blk tires, 99%........$41.00
Barclay, V, dirigible, 1930s, very scarce, 95%........ $225.00
Barclay, V, fire engine, hook & ladder, scarce, NM........ $185.00
Barclay, V, milk wagon, 1 horse, very scarce, 90%........ $225.00
Barclay, V, Renault tank, wht tired, ca 1937, 4", 98%........$59.00
Barclay, V, streamline coupe, orange, 3¼", 97%........$55.00
Barclay, V, taxi, w/ or w/o Taxi stencil on hoold, 99%........$60.00
Barclay, V, US Army truck, rare, 98%........$42.00
Barclay, V, wrecker, orig wire hook, ca 1931, 3½", 96%.....$80.00
Barclay, V, zephyr train, very scarce, 99%........$475.00
Grey Iron, AFB, bench, 99%........$15.00
Grey Iron, AFB, boy w/life preserver, very rare, M........$76.00
Grey Iron, AFB, girl catching ball, very rare, 95%........$68.00
Grey Iron, AFB, girl in slacks, very rare, 97%........$70.00
Grey Iron, AFF, calf, 99%........$18.00
Grey Iron, AFF, collie dog, 95%........$14.00
Grey Iron, AFF, cow, 99%........$19.00
Grey Iron, AFF, fence posts & rails, set of 3 posts w/9" rails, rare, 99%........$80.00
Grey Iron, AFF, girl holding cat, 96%........$18.00
Grey Iron, AFF, goat, 98%........$17.00
Grey Iron, AFF, goose, 98%........$17.00
Grey Iron, AFF, horse, 99%........$18.00
Grey Iron, AFF, pig, M........$20.00
Grey Iron, AFF, sheep, 99%........$18.00
Grey Iron, AFH, bench, M........$17.00
Grey Iron, AFH, blk cook, rare, 96%........$35.00
Grey Iron, AFH, boy flying kite, no kite, 98%........$25.00
Grey Iron, AFH, boy flying kite, w/orig kite, NM........$35.00
Grey Iron, AFH, delivery boy, 95%........$23.00
Grey Iron, AFH, girl skipping rope, w/orig rope, M........$36.00
Grey Iron, AFH, milkman, 98%........$26.00
Grey Iron, AFH, old man sitting, 99%........$16.00
Grey Iron, AFH, old woman sitting, NM........$17.00
Grey Iron, AFH, woman w/basket, 95%........$16.00
Grey Iron, AFR, calf w/head turned, very rare, 97%........$69.00
Grey Iron, AFR, colt, blk, very rare, 93%-95%........$67.00
Grey Iron, AFR, stallion for girl rider, very scarce, 98%....$71.00
Grey Iron, AFT, bench, M........$17.00
Grey Iron, AFT, boy in traveling suit, NM........$18.00
Grey Iron, AFT, girl in traveling suit, 96%........$14.00
Grey Iron, AFT, man in traveling suit, aluminum, rare, M..$20.00
Grey Iron, AFT, newsboy, 97%........$16.00
Grey Iron, AFT, old blk man sitting, 97%........$32.00
Grey Iron, AFT, policeman, aluminum, rare, M........$20.00
Grey Iron, AFT, policeman, NM........$18.00
Grey Iron, AFT, postman, gray or bl, 97%, ea........$15.00
Grey Iron, AFT, preacher, 98%........$16.00
Grey Iron, AFT, train conductor, aluminum, rare, M........$20.00
Grey Iron, AFT, train conductor, 99%........$17.00
Grey Iron, AFT, train engineer, aluminum, rare, NM........$19.00
Grey Iron, AFT, train engineer, 98%........$16.00
Grey Iron, AFT, train porter, aluminum, rare, M........$20.00
Grey Iron, AFT, train porter, 96%........$17.00

Grey Iron, C, baseball fielder, baseball batter, baseball pitcher, NM, $150.00 each. (Photo courtesy Stan and Sally Alekna)

Grey Iron, C, Boy Scout walking, orange neckerchief (rare color), 98% $40.00
Grey Iron, C, pirate (Jim from Treasure Island), rare, 95% .. $39.00
Grey Iron, C&I, cowboy (masked) on wht horse, very rare, 96% $475.00
Grey Iron, C&I, cowboy in blk (aka Hoppy), M $51.00
Grey Iron, C&I, cowboy on bucking bronc, rare, 96% $73.00
Grey Iron, C&I, cowboy standing w/legs apart & hands on hips, 97% $26.00
Grey Iron, C&I, cowboy w/lasso, no lasso, rare, 99% $47.00
Grey Iron, GK, drummer charging, EX $7.00
Grey Iron, GK, officer charging, EX $7.00
Grey Iron, GK, soldier marching w/rifle, EX $4.00
Grey Iron, M, cadet, EV, 96% $33.00
Grey Iron, M, cadet marching, 97% $36.00
Grey Iron, M, cadet officer marching, 96% $36.00

Grey Iron, M, cavalryman on brown horse, 97%, $46.00.
(Photo courtesy Bertoia Auctions)

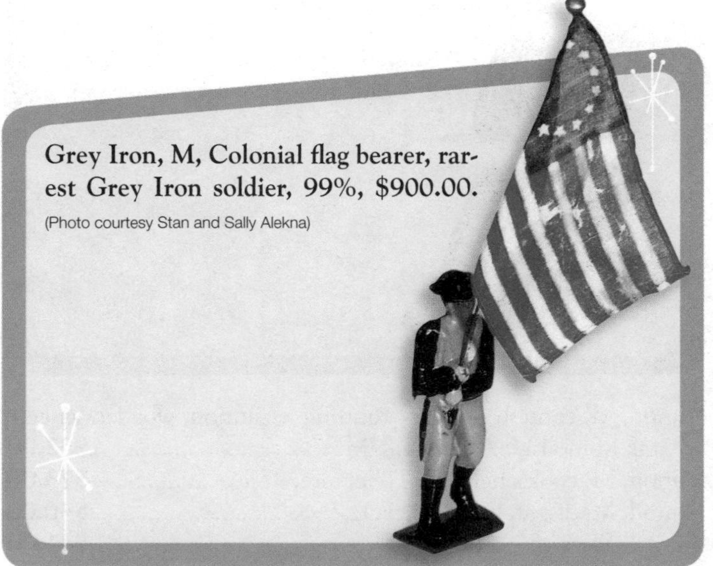
Grey Iron, M, Colonial flag bearer, rarest Grey Iron soldier, 99%, $900.00.
(Photo courtesy Stan and Sally Alekna)

Grey Iron, M, colonial officer, 96% $28.00
Grey Iron, M, colonial officer (Geo Washington) mounted, 99% $72.00
Grey Iron, M, Ethiopian chief, ca 1936, rare, 94% $73.00
Grey Iron, M, Ethiopian officer, ca 1936, scarce, 95% $80.00
Grey Iron, M, Ethiopian tribesman, ca 1936, rare, 96% $75.00
Grey Iron, M, gattling gun, cap, 1930s, very scarce, 95% ... $575.00
Grey Iron, M, Legion bugler, 98% $30.00
Grey Iron, M, Legion drum major, EV, rare, 97% $52.00
Grey Iron, M, Legion drum major, 95% $27.00
Grey Iron, M, Legion drummer, EV, 99% $33.00
Grey Iron, M, machine gunner kneeling, 97% $21.00
Grey Iron, M, machine gunner prone, PW, 94% $29.00
Grey Iron, M, naval officer, EV or PW, 98%, ea $28.00
Grey Iron, M, officer marching w/sword, EX $7.00
Grey Iron, M, Red Cross doctor, 95% $46.00
Grey Iron, M, Red Cross nurse, 95% $29.00
Grey Iron, M, sailor, bl, EV, 95% $25.00
Grey Iron, M, sailor, bl, 96% $25.00
Grey Iron, M, sailor signalman, rare, 92%-94% $42.00
Grey Iron, M, ski trooper w/rifle, w/skis, rare, 97% $73.00
Grey Iron, M, US doughboy, port arms, EV, 93%-95% $20.00
Grey Iron, M, US doughboy charging, bl or olive (rare colors), 80%-85%, ea $30.00
Grey Iron, M, US doughboy charging, desert tan (rare color), 65% $20.00
Grey Iron, M, US doughboy charging, PW, 95% $21.00
Grey Iron, M, US doughboy combat trooper, PW, 97% $56.00
Grey Iron, M, US doughboy officer, EV, 95% $21.00
Grey Iron, M, US doughboy officer w/field glasses, 95% $40.00
Grey Iron, M, US doughboy signaling, 95% $41.00
Grey Iron, M, US infantry officer, EV, 97% $25.00
Grey Iron, M, US infantry port arms, EV, NM $21.00
Grey Iron, M, US infantry port arms, olive (rare color), EV, 94% $25.00
Grey Iron, M, wounded soldier on crutches, rare, 98% $77.00
Grey Iron, M, wounded soldier on stretcher (Stretcher w/ Patient), 95% $45.00
Grey Iron, Med, knight in armor, NM $45.00
Jones, Annapolis cadet port arms, bl, M $35.00
Jones, British Marine firing upward, bayonet intact, red & wht uniform, 96% $30.00
Jones, Kings Royal Rifle Corps, 99% $32.00
Jones, Marines of 1809, #5436, set of 7, very rare, MIB.. $250.00
Jones, Midshipmen of 1928, #544, set of 8, very rare, MIB .. $250.00
Jones, Pilot of the 17th Pursuit Squadron, 1937, 99% $25.00
Jones, Scot Highlander Of 1814, 98% $29.00

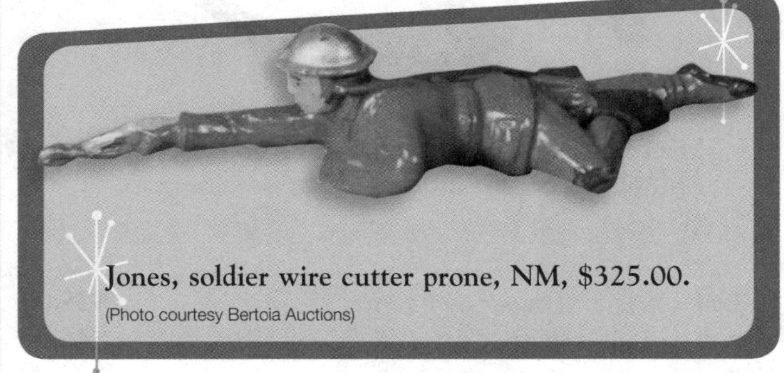
Jones, soldier wire cutter prone, NM, $325.00.
(Photo courtesy Bertoia Auctions)

Jones, US Infantry, #5413, set of 8, very rare, MIB......... $250.00
Jones, US infantry, 1940 (?), 96% $30.00
Jones, US marine, 1809, no pigtail, rare, 96% $35.00
Jones, Waynes Legion soldier on guard w/bayonet, M $34.00
Lincoln Log, C&I, cowboy w/lasso, 98% $17.00
Lincoln Log, C&I, cowboy w/pistol, 99% $20.00
Lincoln Log, C&I, Indian brave (1 feather) standing w/bow & arrow), rare, 88%-90% $19.00
Lincoln Log, C&I, Indian rider (1 feather) w/rifle, rare, 97% ... $48.00

Lincoln Log, C&I, Indian w/war bonnet & rifle, 98%.......$18.00
Lincoln Log, C&I, pioneer, thick arm, M.........................$22.00
Lincoln Log, caveman (Og), rare, 99%.............................$71.00
Lincoln Log, cavewoman (Nada), wht, rare, 97%.............$71.00
Lincoln Log, farmer, 99%..$22.00
Lincoln Log, M, foot soldier of 1812, rare, M....................$30.00
Lincoln Log, M, foot soldier of 1918 charging, 99%..........$25.00
Lincoln Log, M, foot soldier of 1918 marching, 99%........$25.00
Lincoln Log, M, machine gunner of 1918 prone, concave base, 98%...$21.00
Lincoln Log, M, machine gunner of 1918 prone, flat base, 98%... $21.00
Lincoln Log, M, officer of 1918 mounted, 95%.................$36.00
Lincoln Log, policeman, NM..$20.00
Lincoln Log, telegraph messenger, tan, NM......................$20.00
Lincoln Log, train conductor, 97%....................................$17.00
Lincoln Log, train endineer, 98%......................................$18.00
Lincoln Log, train redcap, 98%...$18.00
Lincoln Log, traveling man, M...$21.00
Manoil, C, couple on bench, 98%......................................$46.00
Manoil, C, man in olive suit, 95%.....................................$16.00
Manoil, C, policeman w/nightstick, NM............................$32.00
Manoil, C, shepherd playing flute, scarce, 97%.................$74.00

Manoil, C&I, cowboy on galloping horse pointing gun, scarce, M, $76.00. (Photo courtesy Stan and Sally Alekna)

Manoil, C&I, cowboy w/raised pistol, 97%........................$28.00
Manoil, HF, blacksmith w/wheel, 97%...............................$28.00
Manoil, HF, boy carrying wood, 98%.................................$29.00
Manoil, HF, cobbler making shoes, rare, 98%....................$42.00
Manoil, HF, farmer carrying sheaves, 97%.........................$28.00
Manoil, HF, farmer cutting corn, 99%................................$30.00
Manoil, HF, farmer cutting grain, 98%...............................$29.00
Manoil, HF, farmer sharpening scythe, 98%.......................$29.00
Manoil, HF, hound, 96%...$27.00
Manoil, HF, man at water pump, 99%.................................$30.00
Manoil, HF, man blowing out lantern, 97%.........................$30.00
Manoil, HF, man carrying door, rare, M.............................$75.00
Manoil, HF, man carrying pumpkin, 99%............................$30.00
Manoil, HF, man chopping wood, 94%................................$15.00
Manoil, HF, man cutting w/scythe, NM...............................$31.00
Manoil, HF, man dumping wheelbarrow, cream, EV, 98%..$44.00
Manoil, HF, man planting tree, dk bl (rare), 99%...............$66.00
Manoil, HF, man planting tree, gray, 98%...........................$65.00
Manoil, HF, man sawing lumber, NM...................................$31.00
Manoil, HF, man w/barrel of apples, rare, 96%...................$73.00
Manoil, HF, scarecrow in straw hat, 99%.............................$30.00
Manoil, HF, scarecrow in top hat, 99%................................$30.00
Manoil, HF, school teacher, 98%...$60.00
Manoil, HF, woman laying out wash, NM.............................$33.00
Manoil, HF, woman sweeping w/broom, 95%.......................$26.00
Manoil, HF, woman working butter churn, NM.....................$31.00
Manoil, M, AA gunner, composition material, rare, 95%..$70.00
Manoil, M, AA gunner, gun barrel ends & gunner's arm, 97%...$33.00
Manoil, M, AA gunner w/ranger finder, 97%.......................$33.00
Manoil, M, aviation mechanic w/orange prop against head, rare, 95%...$180.00
Manoil, M, banjo player, very rare, 98%............................$155.00
Manoil, M, bazooka soldier kneeling, 97%..........................$41.00
Manoil, M, blacksmith making horseshoes, 98%..................$29.00
Manoil, M, boxer, very rare, 98%......................................$125.00
Manoil, M, bulger, 2nd version, NM...................................$36.00
Manoil, M, cadet marching, dk bl, very scarce, 95%......$175.00
Manoil, M, cadet marching, lt bl, M...................................$32.00

Manoil, M, cannon loader, 97%, $30.00. (Photo courtesy Bertoia Auctions)

Manoil, M, cannon operator running w/cannon, wooden wheels, mk Manoil USA 2, rare, NM..$82.00
Manoil, M, cook's helper w/ladle, rare, 97%.......................$73.00
Manoil, M, dispatcher on bicycle, 99%...............................$40.00
Manoil, M, doctor in wht, M...$41.00
Manoil, M, drummer, stocky version, 99%..........................$47.00
Manoil, M, flag bearer, 2nd version, NM.............................$36.00
Manoil, M, flag bearer, 3rd version, 97%............................$38.00
Manoil, M, flagbearer, wht helmet, 93%..............................$49.00
Manoil, M, General (Patton) standing on podium saluting, khaki helmet, very rare, 97%...$185.00
Manoil, M, grenade thrower, 99%..$56.00
Manoil, M, machine gunner prone, flat base, no grass, NM..$39.00
Manoil, M, machine gunner prone, thin, scarce, 96%....$111.00
Manoil, M, mine detector kneeling, 96%.............................$43.00
Manoil, M, nurse w/bowl, NM...$34.00

Manoil, M, observer kneeling w/binoculars, 95%.............$37.00
Manoil, M, observer w/periscope, scarce, 99%..................$58.00
Manoil, M, parade soldier, stocky version, 98%................$29.00
Manoil, M, parade soldier, thin, 99%...............................$48.00
Manoil, M, parade soldier, 5th version, 99% $29.00
Manoil, M, parade soldier, 97%..$54.00
Manoil, M, radio operator standing, scarce, NM $95.00
Manoil, M, sailor, bl uniform, 2nd version, very scarce, 95%...$225.00
Manoil, M, sailor, wht uniform, 2nd version, M $36.00
Manoil, M, shell loader, 97%..$30.00
Manoil, M, signalman, hollow base, 93-95% $67.00
Manoil, M, sniper firing carbine at angle, 98%.................$45.00
Manoil, M, sniper prone, camouflaged, 98%......................$41.00
Manoil, M, soldier at map table w/phone, no buttons, 94% ..$62.00
Manoil, M, soldier firing rifle in air, 95% $51.00
Manoil, M, soldier in gas mask w/rifle, 95%......................$32.00
Manoil, M, soldier marching w/rifle & pack, 97%............$36.00
Manoil, M, soldier marching w/right shoulder arms, 98% ..$29.00
Manoil, M, soldier standing at attention, present arms, wht helmet, 99%...$44.00
Manoil, M, soldier standing looking & pointing gun to left, 93% $44.00
Manoil, M, soldier w/camera, thick arm, rare, 94%...........$85.00
Manoil, M, soldier wounded, 94%......................................$20.00

Manoil, M, soldiers boxing, NM, $350.00 for the pair. (Photo courtesy Skinner Auctions)

Manoil, M, stretcher bearer, gr cross on pouch, NM $15.00
Manoil, M, stretcher bearer, no medical kit, 98%.............$35.00
Manoil, M, tommy gunner charging, 96% $48.00
Manoil, M, tommy gunner standing sideways pointing gun, 97% $41.00
Manoil, MRC, blanket over fence section, scarce, 95%....$58.00
Manoil, MRC, bull w/head turned, 99%...........................$26.00
Manoil, MRC, calf bawling, 99%.....................................$19.00
Manoil, MRC, colt, maroon or tan, scarce, 99%, ea..........$30.00
Manoil, MRC, cow feeding, 99% $26.00
Manoil, V, fire engine, red & silver, 96% $43.00
Manoil, V, Gasoline truck, 99% $35.00
Manoil, V, oil tanker, red, 95%..$42.00
Manoil, V, submarine, silver, 98% $58.00
Manoil, V, tank, silver, 95% $32.00
Manoil, V, tow truck, 2-pc, red w/silver chassis, scarce, NM.. $103.00
Manoil, V, tractor w/plain front, NM.................................$30.00
Manoil, V, tractor w/tow loop in front, M..........................$32.00
Manoil, V, water wagon (no number), 98%.......................$31.00
Manoil, V, water wagon #72, 97%......................................$35.00
Marx, C&I, cowboy rider, PW, rare, EX+ $23.00
Marx, C&I, cowboy w/gun drawn, rare, M.........................$26.00
Marx, C&I, cowboy w/rifle, rare, EX.................................$20.00
Marx, C&I, Indian chief w/spear, rare, EX+ $23.00
Marx, C&I, Indian w/hatchet & bow, rare, NM...............$23.00
Marx, Gordon Highlander, tin, NM....................................$8.00
Marx, Indian Sikh, VG...$8.00
Marx, M, howitzer, NM $14.00
Marx, M, infantry private at attention, tin, M...................$10.00
Marx, M, nurse in cape, tin, very rare, EX+ $125.00
Marx, M, Soldiers of Fortune Set, 8 tin figures from armies of the world, 4" ea, NMIB, A.. $105.00

Foreign-Made

Britains, American Cowboys #183, 7-pc, 1950s, VGIB, A ..$165.00
Britains, Arabs of the Desert #164, 5-pc, NMIB, A........ $250.00
Britains, Argentine Infantry #216, 8-pc, NMIB, A $335.00
Britains, Army Service Corps #146, wagon, 2 horses w/driver & mounted soldier, prewar, EX, A............................... $390.00
Britains, Australian Infantry #1544, 8-pc, 1930s, NMIB, A... $385.00
Britains, Austrian Dragoons (Mounted) #176, 5-pc, VGIB, A ..$500.00
Britains, Austrian-Hungarian Army #177, 8-pc, prewar, NMIB, A $1,008.00
Britains, Band of the Royal Marines #1291, 12-pc, 1930s, NMIB, A $950.00
Britains, Belgian Infantry #189, 8-pc, 1930s, EXIB, A ... $400.00
Britains, Bengal Cavalry (1st) #47, 5-pc mounted, ca 1900, rare brn tunics, NMIB, A $880.00
Britains, Bikanir Camel Corps #123, 6-pc, prewar, VGIB, A...$560.00
Britains, Bluejackets of the Royal Navy #78, 10-pc, ca 1900, EXIB, A... $400.00
Britains, Body Guard of the Emperor of Abyssinia #1424, 8-pc, prewar, EXIB, A... $336.00
Britains, Bombay Lancers (Mounted) #66, 5-pc, ca 1900, EXIB, A $250.00

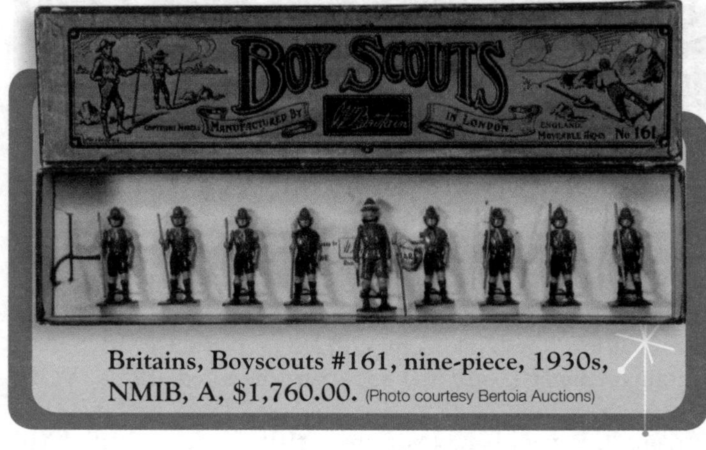

Britains, Boyscouts #161, nine-piece, 1930s, NMIB, A, $1,760.00. (Photo courtesy Bertoia Auctions)

Britains, British Infantry & Cavalry #310A, EXIB, A.... $385.00
Britains, British Infantry #1260, firing, 9-pc, prewar, NMIB, A.$112.00

Britains, British Machine Gunners Set #1318, 7-pc, NMIB, A.$110.00
Britains, Cape Town Highlands #1901, 8-pc, 1938, NMIB, A..$660.00
Britains, Cavalry (Service Dress) #229, 5-pc mounted, 1930s, VGIB, A $385.00
Britains, Civilians #168, 1st version, 8-pc, 1910s, VGIB, A...$1,200.00
Britains, Coldstream Guards (Kneeling & Firing) #120, 10-pc, 1901, NMIB $550.00
Britains, Coldstream Guards #120, 10-pc, (Kneeling & Firing) VGIB........ $165.00
Britains, Cuirassiers (Mounted) #138, 5-pc, EXIB, A..... $150.00
Britains, Devonshire Regiment #1260, dugaree w/sq base at the trail, 8-pc, prewar, NMIB, A $336.00
Britains, Dragoons (6th Inniskilling) #108, 5-pc, 1930s, EXIB, A $500.00
Britains, Drums & Bugles #30, 6-pc, EXIB, A........ $150.00
Britains, Drums & Bugles of the Line #30, 1950s, NMIB, A ... $138.00
Britains, Duke of Cambridge's Own Middlesex Regiment #76, ca 1905, EXIB, A........ $600.00
Britains, Duke of Cornwall's Light Infantry #2088, 8-pc, postwar, EXIB, A........ $112.00
Britains, Egyptain Cavalry #115, 5-pc, 1st version, ca 1901, EXIB, A........ $615.00
Britains, Fifth (5th) Dragoon Guards #35, 5-pc, prewar, VGIB, A $140.00
Britains, First (1st) King George's Own Gurkha Rifles #197, 8-pc, prewar, NMIB, A $85.00
Britains, Foreign Legion Set #1711, 7-pc, NMIB, A....... $250.00
Britains, Gordon Highlanders #118, legs together, 10-pc, 1st version, EX, A........ $196.00
Britains, Highlanders #114, 8-pc, 1936, NMIB, A $175.00
Britains, Historical Series #9401, state coach w/8 horses & 3 riders & figure in coach, NMIB, A $300.00
Britains, Howitzer #2107, 18", postwar, EXIB, A........... $112.00
Britains, Infantry of the Line (Austro-Hungarian Army) #177, 8-pc, 1930s, EXIB, A $600.00

Britains, Japanese Infantry #134, eight-piece, 1930s, EXIB, A, $600.00. (Photo courtesy Bertoia Auctions)

Britains, King African Rifles #225, 8-pc, prewar, EXIB, A....$112.00
Britains, Kings Royal Rifle Corps #2072, 8-pc, postwar, EXIB..$56.00
Britains, Lancer (16th/5th) #33, 5-pc mounted, 1950s, VGIB, A........$300.00
Britains, Lifeguard Band (Mounted) #101, 12-pc, ca 1919, EXIB, A $175.00
Britains, Limberd Wagon #1330, rare version, NMIB, A.. $300.00
Britains, Machine Gun Section (Sitting Position) #198, rare butterscotch uniforms, 4-pc, VGIB, A $300.00
Britains, Machine Gun Section #194, 6-pc, prewar, EXIB, A..$195.00
Britains, Marines #228, 8-pc, 1930s, NMIB, A.............. $225.00
Britains, Mexican Ruoles #186, 8-pc, NMIB, A $500.00
Britains, Mono Plane #435, 1st version, ca 1931, VG, A... $950.00
Britains, North American Indians #208, mounted & dismounted, 13-pc, ca 1935, EXIB, A $500.00
Britains, Princess Louise's Argyle & Sutherland Highlanders #15, 8-pc, rnd base, ca 1910, EXIB, A $550.00
Britains, Queens Own Hussars (4th) #8, EXIB, A.......... $250.00
Britains, Railway Station Staff #1256, O gauge, 1930s, EXIB, A $715.00
Britains, Royal Canadian Mounted Police #1349, 5-pc mounted, 1950s, EXIB, A $200.00
Britains, Royal Company Archers #2079, 13-pc, 1950s, EXIB, A........$330.00
Britains, Royal Gunners #1730, 8-pc, 1950s, EXIB, A ... $275.00
Britains, Royal Horse Artillery #39, 1930s, NMIB, A $800.00

Britains, Royal Scots Greys/Second Dragoons #32, 1930s, NMIB, $400.00. (Photo courtesy Morphy Auctions)

Britains, Seaforth Highlanders #112, 8-pc, 1930s, VGIB, A.... $140.00
Britains, Seaforth Highlanders #112, 8-pc, 1930s, EXIB, A..... $193.00
Britains, Seaforth Highlanders Set #2062, 17-pc, NMIB, A.... $465.00
Britains, Second Lifeguards (Mounted) #43, 5-pc, EXIB, A.... $250.00
Britains, Seven Regiment Display (9407) #73, ca 1962, NMIB, A $4,200.00
Britains, Seventh (7th) Rajput #1342, 8-pc, prewar, NMIB, A $140.00
Britains, Somerset Infantry #17, 8-pc, 1950s, NMIB, A .. $193.00
Britains, Spanish Infantry #92, 8-pc, prewar, NMIB, A.. $560.00
Britains, Territorial Infantry (Service Dress) #160, 8-pc, ca 1920, EXIB, A........ $125.00
Britains, Third Light Infantry (Mounted) #45, 5-pc, 1920s, EXIB, A $175.00
Britains, Turcos #191, 8-pc, prewar, EXIB, A.................. $140.00
Britains, Turkish Infantry #167, 8-pc, 1930s, EX (no box), A.. $100.00
Britains, Twenty-First Lancers Mounted (Steel Helmets) #94, 5-pc, ca 1916, EXIB, A $225.00
Britains, United Nations Infantry #2155, 8-pc, 1957-60 production only, EXIB, A $195.00
Britains, Uruguayan Cavalary #220, 5-pc, NMIB, A $275.00
Britains, USA Infantry #227, 8-pc, prewar, NMIB, A $112.00
Britains, West India Regiment #19, 9-pc, 1st version, ca 1901, EXIB, A........ $450.00

Britains, West Point Cadets #1208, 10-pc, 1940s, VGIB, A.. $330.00
Britains, Wild West #179, 1958, EXIB, A....................... $330.00
Britains, Yorkshire Regiment #113, 8-pc, 1937, NMIB, A...$500.00
Britains, Zulus (Africa's Savage Warriors) #147, 8-pc, 1930s, EXIB, A.. $500.00

Elastolin, Hansel and Gretel, house with fenced base and background panel and figures, NM, A, $2,880.00.
(Photo courtesy James D. Julia, Inc.)

Mignot, Dutch Grenadiers of the Imperial Guard, 31-pc, postwar, G, A $425.00
Mignot, English Line Infantry Advancing (1812), 4-pc, MIB, A... $40.00
Mignot, French Colonial Infantry Marching (1890-1914), 8-pc, postwar, MIB, A..$70.00
Mignot, French Napoleonic Infantry Marching (1890-1914), 8-pc, postwar, VG, A $180.00
Mignot, French North African Goumiers, 5-pc, postwar, NMIB, A $140.00
Mignot, Prussian Infantry Marching (1810), 4-pc, postwar, MIB, A $60.00
Mignot, Standard Bearer, wooden bases, 4-pc, G, A $300.00

Star Trek

The Star Trek concept was introduced to the public in the mid-1960s via a TV series which continued for many years in syndication. The impact it had on American culture has spanned two generations of loyal fans through its animated TV cartoon series (1977), six major motion pictures, Fox network's 1987 TV show, 'Star Trek, The Next Generation,' and two other television series, 'Deep Space 9,' and 'Voyager.' As a result of its success, vast amounts of merchandise (both licensed and unlicensed) has been marketed in a wide variety of items including jewelry, clothing, calendars, collector plates, comics, costumes, games, greeting and gum cards, party goods, magazines, model kits, posters, puzzles, records and tapes, school supplies, and toys. Packaging is very important; an item mint and in its original box is generally worth 75% to 100% more than one rated excellent.

See also Character and Promotional Drinking Glasses; Comic Books; Halloween Costumes; Lunch Boxes; Model Kits.

Figures

Galoob, ST V, 7", any character, 1989, M, ea from $10 to...$12.00
Galoob, ST V, 7", any character, 1989, MIP, ea from $20 to..$25.00
Galoob, STNG, Antican, Ferengi, Q, or Selay, M, ea.......$30.00
Galoob, STNG, Antican, Ferengi, Q, or Selay, MOC, ea..$60.00
Galoob, STNG, Data, bl face, M...$25.00
Galoob, STNG, Data, bl face, MOC $55.00
Galoob, STNG, Data, brn face, M $18.00
Galoob, STNG, Data, brn face, MOC..................................$35.00
Galoob, STNG, Data, flesh face, M $10.00

Galoob, Star Trek: The Next Generation, Data, flesh face, MOC, $22.00.
(Photo courtesy whatacharacter.com)

Galoob, STNG, Data, spotted face, M $8.00
Galoob, STNG, Data, spotted face, MOC.........................$15.00
Galoob, STNG, LaForge, Lt Worf, Picard, or Riker, M, ea...$8.00
Galoob, STNG, LaForge, Lt Worf, Picard, or Riker, MOC, ea ...$15.00
Galoob, STNG, Tasha Yar, M $10.00
Galoob, STNG, Tasha Yar, MOC $22.00
Mego, 3¾", Acturian, Betelgeusian, Klingon, Megarite, Rigelluian, or Zatanite, Series 2, M, ea.................................$80.00
Mego, 3¾", Acturian, Betelgeusian, Klingon, Megarite, Rigelluian, or Zatanite, Series 2, MOC, ea......................... $160.00
Mego, 3¾", Capt Kirk, Decker, Dr McCoy, Illia, Mr Spock, or Mr Scott, Series 1, M, ea $15.00
Mego, 3¾", Capt Kirk, Decker, Dr McCoy, Illia, Mr Spock, or Mr Scott, Series 1, MOC, ea $40.00
Mego, 8", Andorian, 1970s, M $350.00

Mego, 8", Andorian, 1970s, MOC, $650.00.

Mego, 8", Capt Kirk, 1970s, M $30.00
Mego, 8", Capt Kirk, 1970s, MOC $60.00
Mego, 8", Cheron, 1970s, M $90.00
Mego, 8", Cheron, 1970s, MOC $175.00
Mego, 8", Dr McCoy, 1970s, M $45.00
Mego, 8", Dr McCoy, 1970s, MOC $85.00
Mego, 8", Gorn, 1970s, M $95.00
Mego, 8", Gorn, 1970s, MOC $175.00
Mego, 8", Klingon, 1970s, M $30.00
Mego, 8", Klingon, 1970s, MOC $55.00
Mego, 8", Lt Uhura, 1970s, M $65.00
Mego, 8", Lt Uhura, 1970s, MOC $135.00
Mego, 8", Mr Scott, 1970s, M $40.00
Mego, 8", Mr Scott, 1970s, MOC $90.00
Mego, 8", Mr Spock, 1970s, M $30.00
Mego, 8", Mr Spock, 1970s, MOC $60.00
Mego, 8", Mugato, 1970s, M $300.00
Mego, 8", Mugato, 1970s, MOC $550.00
Mego, 8", Neptunian, 1970s, M $125.00
Mego, 8", Neptunian, 1970s, MOC $230.00
Mego, 8", Romulan, 1970s, M $800.00
Mego, 8", Romulan, 1970s, MOC $1,200.00
Mego, 8", Talos, 1970s, M $300.00
Mego, 8", Talos, 1970s, MOC $525.00
Mego, 8", The Keeper, 1970s, M $80.00
Mego, 8", The Keeper, 1970s, MOC $180.00
Mego, 12½", Arcturian, 1979, M $65.00
Mego, 12½", Arcturian, 1979, MIP $130.00
Mego, 12½", Capt Kirk, 1979, M $40.00

Mego, 12½", Captain Kirk, 1979, MIP, $80.00.

Mego, 12½", Decker, 1979, M $60.00
Mego, 12½", Decker, 1979, MIP $120.00
Mego, 12½", Ilia, 1979, M $40.00
Mego, 12½", Ilia, 1979, MIP $80.00
Mego, 12½", Klingon, 1979, M $60.00
Mego, 12½", Klingon, 1979, MIP $120.00
Mego, 12½", Mr Spock, 1979, M $40.00
Mego, 12½", Mr Spock, 1979, MIP $80.00
Playmates, DS9, Chief Miles O'Brien, Commander Sisko, Major Kira Nerys, Morn, Odo, or Quark, 1994, M, ea $8.00
Playmates, DS9, Chief Miles O'Brien, Commander Sisko, Major Kira Nerys, Morn, Odo, or Quark, 1994, MIP, ea $12.00
Playmates, DS9, Dr Julian Bashir, 1994, M $12.00
Playmates, DS9, Dr Julian Bashir, 1994, MIP $22.00
Playmates, DS9, Lt Jadzia Dax, 1994, M $8.00
Playmates, DS9, Lt Jadzia Dax, 1994, MIP $18.00
Playmates, First Contact, 5", Borg, Dr Beverly Crusher, Capt Picard, or Lily, 1996, M, ea $10.00
Playmates, First Contact, 5", Borg, Dr Beverly Crusher, Capt Picard, or Lily, 1996, MOC, ea $16.00
Playmates, First Contact, 5", Data, Deanna Troi, La Farge, Cpat Piccard, Riker, Worf, or Cochrane, 1996, M, ea $8.00
Playmates, First Contact, 5", Data, Deanna Troi, La Forge, Capt Piccard, Riker, Worf, or Cochrane, 1996, MOC, ea $14.00
Playmates, First Contact, 9", Capt Picard in 21st C outfit or Cochrane, 1996, M, ea $20.00
Playmates, First Contact, 9", Capt Picard in 21st C outfit or Cochrane, 1996, MIP $26.00
Playmates, First Contact, 9", Data, Capt Picard, or Riker, 1996, M $15.00
Playmates, First Contact, 9", Data, Capt Picard, or Riker, 1996, MIP, ea $20.00
Playmates, Insurrection, 9", any character, 1998, M, ea from $6 to $8.00
Playmates, Insurrection, 9", any character, 1998, MIP, ea from $10 to $15.00
Playmates, Insurrection, 12", any character, 1998, M, ea $8.00
Playmates, Insurrection, 12", any character, 1998, MIP, ea from $12 to $16.00
Playmates, STNG, 1st Series, Borg, Capt Picard, Commander Riker, Lt Commander Data, or Lt Worf, 1992, MOC, ea $22.00
Playmates, STNG, 1st Series, Deanna Troi or Romulan, 1992, M, ea $20.00
Playmates, STNG, 1st Series, Deanna Troi or Romulan, 1992, MOC, ea $35.00
Playmates, STNG, 1st Series, Ferengi, Gowron, or Lt Commander La Forge, M, ea $15.00
Playmates, STNG, 1st Series, Ferengi, Gowron, or Lt Commander La Forge, 1992, MOC, ea $30.00
Playmates, STNG, 2nd Series, any character, 1993, M, ea from $5 to $10.00
Playmates, STNG, 2nd Series, any character, 1993, MOC, ea from $12 to $18.00
Playmates, STNG, 3rd Series, any character accept Esoqq or Data in red Redemption outfit, 1994, M, ea from $6 to $12.00
Playmates, STNG, 3rd Series, any character except Esoqq or Data in red Redemption outfit, 1994, MOC, ea from $16 to $22.00
Playmates, STNG, 3rd Series, Data in red Redemption outfit, 1994, M $125.00
Playmates, STNG, 3rd Series, Data in red Redemption outfit, 1994, MOC $325.00
Playmates, STNG, 3rd Series, Esoqq, 1994, M $40.00

Playmates, STNG, 3rd Series, Esoqq, 1994, MOC $80.00
Playmates, STNG, 4th Series or 5th Series, any character, 1995, M, from $8 to $12.00
Playmates, STNG, 4th Series or 5th Series, any character, 1995, MOC, ea from $12 to $22.00
Playmates, Voyager, Capt Janeway or Lt B'Elanna Torres, 5", M, ea $18.00
Playmates, Voyager, Capt Janeway or Lt B'Elanna Torres, 5", MOC, ea $30.00
Playmates, Voyager, Chakotay, Kazon, Lt Carey, Meelix, Seska, Tom Paris, Torres as Klingon, Tuvok, or Vidian, 5", M, ea $10.00
Playmates, Voyager, Chakotay, Kazon, Lt Carey, Neelix, Seska, Tom Paris, Torres as Klingon, Tuvok or Vidian, 5", MIP, ea $12.00
Playmates, Voyager, Chakotay the Maquis, Doctor or Harry Kim, 1995-96, 5", M, ea $10.00
Playmates, Voyager, Chakotay the Maquis, Doctor or Harry Kim, 5", MIP, ea $18.00

Playsets and Accessories

Command Communications Console, Mego, 1976, MIB, from $125 to $150.00
Communications Set, Mego, 1974, MIB $150.00
Engineering, Generations Movie, Playmates, MIB $35.00
Mission to Gamma VI, Mego, 1975, rare, MIB $400.00
Telescreen Console, Mego, 1975, MIB $125.00
Transporter Room, Mego, 1975, MIB $125.00
USS Enterprise Bridge, Mego, 1975, complete w/3 figures, EX.. $80.00
USS Enterprise Bridge, Mego, 1975, MIB $130.00
USS Enterprise Bridge, STNG, Playmates, 1991, MIB $50.00

Vehicles

Borg Ship (sphere), Playmates, MIB $60.00
Ferengi Fighter, STNG, Galoob, 1989, NRFB $75.00
Klingon Bird of Prey, TNG, Playmates, 1995, MIB $80.00
Klingon Cruiser, Mego, 1980, 8" L, MIB $70.00
Klingon Warship, Star Trek II, Corgi #149, MOC $30.00
Romulan Warbird, Playmates, MIB $50.00
USS Enterprise, Star Trek II, Corgi, 1982, MOC, from $25 to.. $30.00
USS Enterprise B, Motion Picture, Playmates, M $65.00
USS Enterprise E, Motion Picture, Playmates, NMIB.... $135.00

Miscellaneous

Action Toy Book, Motion Picture, 1976, unpunched, EX..$30.00
Bank, Spock, plastic, Play Pal, 1975, 12", MIB $60.00
Belt Buckle, marked 200th Anniversary USS Enterprise on back, 3½", M $15.00
Book, Star Trek Pop-Up, Motion Picture, 1977, EX $25.00
Book, Where No One Has Gone Before, a History in Pictures, Dillard, M (sealed) $25.00
Bop Bag, Spock, 1975, MIB $80.00
Classic Science Tricorder, Playmates, MIB $65.00
Colorforms Adventure Set, MIB (sealed) $35.00
Coloring Book, Adventure, Wanderer Books, 1986, unused, NM+ $8.00
Comic Book, Gold Key #1, 1967, EX $75.00
Comic Book, Gold Key #1, 1967, M $215.00
Decanter, Mr Spock bust, ceramic, M $40.00
Flashlight Gun, plastic, 1968, NM $50.00
Gum Cards, complete set of 88 w/22 sitckers & display box, Topps, 1976, M cards/VG display box, A $150.00

Inter-Space Communicator, Lone Star, 1974, MIB, $55.00.

Kite, Spock, Hi-Flyer, 1975, unused, MIP $35.00
Metal Detector, Jetco, 1976, EX $150.00
Mix 'n Mold Casting Set, Kirk, Spock, or McCoy, MIB, ea..$65.00
Model Kit, Romulan Scoutship, resin, Amaquest, MIB.....$50.00
Patch, America 1977 Convention, M $40.00
Patch, command insignia, w/instructions for uniform, M..$25.00
Patch, Motion Picture, Kirk or Spock, M $35.00
Pennant, Spock Lives, blk, red & yel on wht, Image Products, 1982, 30", M $15.00
Phaser Battle, Mego, 1976, NMIB $200.00
Phaser Ray Gun, clicking flashlight effect, 1976, MOC....$75.00
Phaser Water Gun, Motion Picture, 1976, MOC $55.00
Puzzle Book, Wanderer Books, 1986, unused, NM+ $8.00
Starfleet Phaser, Motion Picture, Playmates, MIB $150.00
Trading Cards, 25th Anniversary, Series I, Impel, 1991, complete set of 160 different cards, NM+ $15.00
Tricorder, Mego, 1976, tape recorder, EXIB $125.00
Utility Belt, Remco, 1975, M $55.00
Wastebasket, Motion Picture, M $35.00
Water Gun, Motion Picture, Azrak Hamway Int'l, 1976, MOC $50.00

Star Wars

The original 'Star Wars' movie was a phenomenal box office hit of the late 1970s, no doubt due to its ever-popular space travel theme and fantastic special effects. A sequel called 'Empire Strikes Back' (1980) and a third hit called 'Return of the Jedi' (1983) did just as well. Interest has been sustained through the release of three more films: 'Episode I, The Phantom Menace'; 'Episode II, Attack of the Clones'; and 'Episode III, The Revenge of the Sith.' As result, an enormous amount of related merchandise was released — most of which was made by the Kenner Company. Palitoy of London supplied England and other overseas countries with Kenner's products and also made some toys that were never distributed in America. Until 1980 the logo of the 20th Century Fox studios (under whom the toys were licensed) appeared on each item; just before the second movie, 'Star Wars' creator, George Lucas, regained control of the merchandise rights, and items inspired by the last films can be identified by his own Lucasfilm logo. Since 1987 Lucasfilm, Ltd., has operated shops in conjunction with the Star Tours at Disneyland theme parks.

The first action figures to be introduced were Luke Skywalker, Princess Leia, R2-D2, and Chewbacca. Because of delays in production that prevented Kenner from getting them on the market in time for Christmas, the company issued 'early bird' certificates so that they could be ordered by mail when they became available. In all, more than 90 action figures were designed. The 'Power of the Force' figures came with a collector coin on each card.

Original packaging is very important in assessing a toy's worth. As each movie was released, packaging was updated, making approximate dating relatively simple. A figure on an original 'Star Wars' card is worth more than the same character on an 'Empire Strikes Back' card, etc.; and the same 'Star Wars' figure valued at $50.00 in mint-on-card condition might be worth as little as $5.00 'loose.'

Especially prized are the original 12-back Star Wars cards (meaning 12 figures were shown on the back). Second issue cards showed eight more, and so on. Unpunched cards tend to be valued at about 15% to 20% more than punched cards, and naturally if the proof of purchase has been removed, the value of the card is less. (These could be mailed in to receive newly introduced figures before they appeared on the market. Remember, pricing is not a science — it hinges on many factors.

The following 'MOC' and 'MIB' listings are for mint items in mint packaging. Loose items are complete unless noted otherwise.

Because of the vast amount of Star Wars collectibles, listings are of vintage Kenner items only, including 'Power of the Force.'

For more information we recommend *Star Wars Super Collector's Wish Book Identification & Values, Fourth Edition,* by Geoffrey T. Carlton.

See also Character and Promotional Drinking Glasses; Halloween Costumes; Lunch Boxes; Model Kits.

Key:
ESB — Empire Strikes Back POTF — Power of the Force
ROTJ — Return of the Jedi SW — Star Wars

Figures

A-Wing Pilot, Droids, M $50.00
A-Wing Pilot, Droids, MOC $150.00
A-Wing Pilot, POTF, M $50.00
A-Wing Pilot, POTF, MOC $100.00
Admiral Ackbar, ROTJ, M $10.00
Admiral Ackbar, ROTJ, MOC $50.00
Amanaman, POTF, M $135.00
Amanaman, POTF, MOC $260.00
Anakin Skywalker, M (in sealed mailer bag) $40.00
Anakin Skywalker, POTF, M $40.00

Anakin Skywalker, POTF, MOC, $2,250.00.
(Photo courtesy Morphy Auctions)

AT-AT Commander, ESB, MOC $90.00
AT-AT Commander, ROTJ, M $10.00
AT-AT Commander, ROTJ, MOC $60.00
AT-AT Driver, ESB, MOC $115.00
AT-AT Driver, ROTJ, M $10.00
AT-AT Driver, ROTJ, MOC $70.00
AT-ST Driver, POTF, M $15.00
AT-ST Driver, POTF, MOC $85.00
AT-ST Driver, ROTJ, M $10.00
AT-ST Driver, ROTJ, MOC $40.00
B-Wing Pilot, POTF, M $10.00
B-Wing Pilot, POTF, MOC $45.00
B-Wing Pilot, ROTJ, M $10.00
B-Wing Pilot, ROTJ, MOC $45.00
Barada, POTF, M $60.00
Barada, POTF, MOC $120.00
Ben (Obi-Wan) Kenobi, ESB, gray or wht hair, M $15.00
Ben (Obi-Wan) Kenobi, ESB, gray or wht hair, MOC, ea $125.00
Ben (Obi-Wan) Kenobi, POTF, M $30.00
Ben (Obi-Wan) Kenobi, POTF, MOC $200.00
Ben (Obi-Wan) Kenobi, ROTJ, gray or wht hair, M, ea $10.00
Ben (Obi-Wan) Kenobi, ROTJ, gray or wht hair, MOC, ea $60.00
Ben (Obi-Wan) Kenobi, ROTJ, gray or wht hair, MOC (tri-logo), ea $200.00
Ben (Obi-Wan) Kenobi, SW, gray hair, MOC (12-back) $750.00
Ben (Obi-Wan) Kenobi, SW, 12", MIB $450.00
Bespin Security Guard, ESB, blk or wht, M $15.00
Bespin Security Guard, ESB, blk or wht, MOC $65.00
Bespin Security Guard, ROTJ, blk or wht, M, ea $15.00
Bespin Security Guard, ROTJ, blk or wht, MOC $55.00
Bib Fortuna, ROTJ, M $15.00
Bib Fortuna, ROTJ, MOC $45.00
Biker Scout, POTF, M $15.00
Biker Scout, POTF, MOC $110.00
Biker Scout, ROTJ, M $15.00
Biker Scout, ROTJ, MOC $85.00
Boba Fett, Droids, MOC $1,085.00
Boba Fett, ESB, M $35.00
Boba Fett, ESB, MOC $500.00
Boba Fett, ESB, 12", MIB $625.00

Boba Fett, ROTJ, MOC (desert scene) $400.00
Boba Fett, ROTJ, MOC (fireball) $425.00

Boba Fett, ROTJ, MOC (tri-logo), $635.00.
(Photo courtesy Morphy Auctions)

Boba Fett, SW, MOC $1,650.00
Boba Fett, SW, 12", MIB $1,225.00
Bobba Fett, Droids, M $25.00
Bossk, ESB, M $15.00

Bossk, ESB, MOC, $140.00.
(Photo courtesy serioustoyz.com)

Bossk, ROTJ, M $10.00
Bossk, ROTJ, MOC $100.00
C-3PO, Droids, MOC $95.00
C-3PO, ESB, removable limbs, M $10.00
C-3PO, ESB, removable limbs, MOC $100.00
C-3PO, POTF, removable limbs, M $15.00
C-3PO, POTF, removable limbs, MOC $120.00
C-3PO, ROTJ, M $8.00
C-3PO, ROTJ, removable limbs, MOC $75.00
C-3PO, SW, MOC (12-back) $350.00
C-3PO, SW, MOC (21-back) $125.00
C-3PO, SW, 12", MIB $425.00
Chewbacca, ESB, MOC $215.00
Chewbacca, POTF, MOC $150.00
Chewbacca, ROTJ, MOC $125.00

Chewbacca, ROTJ, MOC (Endor photo), $50.00.
(Photo courtesy serioustoyz.com)

Chewbacca, SW, M $15.00
Chewbacca, SW, 12", MIB $235.00
Chief Chirpa, ROTJ, M $15.00
Chief Chirpa, ROTJ, MOC $50.00
Cloud Car Pilot, ESB, M $22.00
Cloud Car Pilot, ESB, MOC $130.00
Cloud Car Pilot, ROTJ, MOC $60.00
Darth Vader, ESB, MOC $125.00
Darth Vader, POTF, MOC $160.00
Darth Vader, ROTJ, MOC (light saber drawn) $65.00
Darth Vader, ROTJ, MOC (pointing) $55.00
Darth Vader, ROTJ, MOC (tri-logo) $125.00
Darth Vader, SW, MOC $300.00

Darth Vader, SW, MOC (12-back), $625.00; Chewbacca, SW, MOC (12-back), $375.00.
(Photo courtesy Morphy Auctions)

Darth Vader, SW, 12", MIB $270.00
Death Squad Commander, ESB, MOC $125.00
Death Squad Commander, SW, M $15.00
Death Squad Commander, SW, MOC $160.00
Death Squad Commander, SW, MOC (12-back) $330.00
Death Star Droid, ESB, MOC $160.00
Death Star Droid, ROTJ, MOC $75.00

Death Star Droid, SW, MOC $230.00
Dengar, ESB, M.......... $10.00
Dengar, ESB, MOC $95.00
Dengar, ROTJ, MOC.......... $45.00
Dulok Scout, Ewoks, M $10.00
Dulok Scout, Ewoks, MOC $35.00
Dulok Shaman, Ewoks, M $16.00
Dulok Shaman, Ewoks, MOC $35.00
Emperor, POTF, MOC.......... $85.00
Emperor, ROTJ, M.......... $14.00
Emperor, ROTJ, MOC.......... $65.00
Emperor's Royal Guard, ROTJ, M.......... $15.00
Emperor's Royal Guard, ROTJ, MOC.......... $55.00
EV-9D9, POTF, M.......... $90.00
EV-909, POTF, MOC $245.00
FX-7, ESB, MOC $95.00
FX-7, ESB or ROTJ, M $10.00
FX-7, ROTJ, MOC $75.00
Gammorrean Guard, ROTJ, M $8.00
Gammorrean Guard, ROTJ, MOC $45.00
General Madine, ROTJ, M.......... $8.00
General Madine, ROTJ, MOC.......... $40.00
General Madine, SW, MOC.......... $295.00
Greedo, ESB, MOC $155.00
Greedo, ROTJ, MOC $80.00
Greedo, SW, M $15.00

Greedo, SW, MOC, $295.00; R5-D4, SW, MOC, $350.00. (Photo courtesy Morphy Auctions)

Hammerhead, ESB, MOC $120.00
Hammerhead, ROTJ, MOC $75.00
Hammerhead, SW, M $10.00
Hammerhead, SW, MOC $270.00
Han Solo, ESB, Bespin outfit, M $15.00
Han Solo, ESB, Bespin outfit, MOC $145.00
Han Solo, ESB, Hoth gear, MOC $95.00
Han Solo, POTF, Carbonite Chamber, M.......... $125.00
Han Solo, POTF, Carbonite Chamber, MOC.......... $275.00
Han Solo, POTF, trench coat, M.......... $20.00
Han Solo, POTF, trench coat, MOC $500.00
Han Solo, ROTJ, Bespin outfit, MOC $75.00
Han Solo, ROTJ, Hoth gear, M.......... $15.00
Han Solo, ROTJ, Hoth gear, MOC.......... $75.00
Han Solo, ROTJ, MOC (Death Star) $165.00
Han Solo, ROTJ, MOC (Mos Eisley) $185.00
Han Solo, ROTJ, MOC (tri-logo).......... $125.00
Han Solo, ROTJ, trench coat, MOC $50.00
Han Solo, SW, lg head, MOC $650.00
Han Solo, SW, lg head, MOC (12-back) $1,000.00
Han Solo, SW, sm head, M.......... $35.00
Han Solo, SW, sm head, MOC $540.00
Han Solo, SW, sm head, MOC (12-back) $775.00
IG-88, ESB, MOC $190.00
IG-88, ESB, 12", MIB $1,200.00
IG-88, ROTJ, MOC $80.00
Imperial Commander, ESB, MOC $85.00
Imperial Commander, M $10.00
Imperial Commander, ROTJ, MOC.......... $50.00
Imperial Dignitary, POTF, M $35.00
Imperial Dignitary, POTF, MOC.......... $155.00
Imperial Gunner, M $85.00
Imperial Gunner, POTF, MOC $165.00
Imperial Storm Trooper, ESB, Hoth weather gear, MOC... $145.00
Imperial Storm Trooper, ROTJ, Hoth weather gear, MOC .. $60.00
Jann Tosh, Droids, M $25.00
Jann Tosh, Droids, MOC.......... $65.00
Jawa, ESB, MOC $125.00
Jawa, POTF, MOC.......... $160.00
Jawa, ROTJ, MOC.......... $50.00
Jawa, SW, cloth cape, MOC (12-back) $290.00
Jawa, SW, plastic cape, M $280.00
Jawa, SW, plastic cape, MOC (12-back) $3,500.00

Jawa, SW, plastic cape, MOC (12-back/unpunched), A, $4,500.00. (Photo courtesy Morphy Auctions)

Jawa, SW, 12", M $95.00
Jawa, SW, 12", MIB $315.00
Jord Dusat, Droids, M $22.00
Jord Dusat, Droids, MOC $65.00
Kea Moll, Droids, M $26.00
Kea Moll, Droids, MOC $65.00
Kez-Iban, Droids, M $16.00
Kez-Iban, Droids, MOC $75.00
King Gorneesh, Ewoks, MOC $35.00
Klaatu, ROTJ, Palace outfit, M $10.00

Klaatu, ROTJ, Palace outfit, MOC $50.00
Klaatu, ROTJ, Skiff outfit, M $10.00
Klaatu, ROTJ, Skiff outfit, MOC $50.00
Lady Ugrah Gorneesh, Ewoks, M $10.00
Lady Ugrah Gorneesh, Ewoks, MOC $35.00
Lando Cairissian, ESB, MOC $80.00
Lando Cairissian, ESB, no teeth, M $15.00
Lando Cairissian, ESB, no teeth, MOC $175.00
Lando Cairissian, ROTJ, MOC $45.00
Lando Cairissian, ROTJ, Skiff outfit, M $15.00
Lando Cairissian, ROTJ, Skiff outfit, MOC $45.00
Lando Cairissian General, POTF, M $95.00
Lando Cairissian General, POTF, MOC $145.00
Leia, see Princess Leia
Lobot, ESB, M $10.00
Lobot, ESB, MOC $85.00
Lobot, ROTJ, M $10.00
Lobot, ROTJ, MOC $45.00
Logray, Ewoks, M $10.00
Logray, Ewoks, MOC $35.00
Logray, ROTJ, M $18.00
Logray, ROTJ, MOC $60.00
Luke Skywalker, ESB, Bespin fatigues, blond hair, M $20.00

Luke Skywalker, ESB, Bespin fatigues, blond hair, MOC (looking), $150.00. (Photo courtesy Morphy Auctions)

Luke Skywalker, ESB, Bespin fatigues, blond hair, MOC (walking) $250.00
Luke Skywalker, ESB, Bespin fatigues, brn hair, M $25.00
Luke Skywalker, ESB, Bespin fatigues, brn hair, MOC (looking) $200.00
Luke Skywalker, ESB, Bespin fatigues, brn hair, MOC (walking) $250.00
Luke Skywalker, ESB, blond hair, MOC $250.00
Luke Skywalker, ESB, brn hair, MOC $285.00
Luke Skywalker, ESB, Hoth battle gear, MOC $125.00
Luke Skywalker, ESB, X-Wing Pilot, MOC $150.00
Luke Skywalker, POTF, battle poncho, M $85.00
Luke Skywalker, POTF, battle poncho, MOC $170.00
Luke Skywalker, POTF, Stormtrooper outfit, M $165.00
Luke Skywalker, POTF, Stormtrooper outfit, MOC $365.00
Luke Skywalker, POTF, X-Wing Pilot, MOC $165.00
Luke Skywalker, ROTJ, Bespin fatigues, blond hair, MOC (looking) $150.00
Luke Skywalker, ROTJ, blond hair, MOC (Falcon Gunwell)...$180.00
Luke Skywalker, ROTJ, blond hair, MOC (Tatoonie).... $240.00
Luke Skywalker, ROTJ, brn hair, M $40.00
Luke Skywalker, ROTJ, brn hair, MOC $300.00
Luke Skywalker, ROTJ, Hoth battle gear, M $18.00
Luke Skywalker, ROTJ, Hoth battle gear, MOC $80.00
Luke Skywalker, ROTJ, X-Wing Pilot, M $15.00
Luke Skywalker, ROTJ, X-Wing Pilot, MOC $65.00
Luke Skywalker, ROTJ, X-Wing Pilot outfit, MOC (tri-logo) ..$200.00
Luke Skywalker, SW, blond hair, MOC $265.00
Luke Skywalker, SW, dbl telescoping saber, MOC (12-back)...$4,800.00
Luke Skywalker, SW, MOC (12-back) $850.00
Luke Skywalker, SW, X-Wing Pilot, MOC $250.00

Luke Skywalker, SW, 12", MIB, $435.00; Han Solo, SW, 12", MIB, $595.00. (Photo courtesy Morphy Auctions)

Luke Skywalker Jedi, POTF, MOC $270.00
Luke Skywalker Jedi, ROTJ, bl light saber, M $65.00
Luke Skywalker Jedi, ROTJ, bl light saber, MOC $175.00
Luke Skywalker Jedi, ROTJ, gr light saber, M $40.00
Luke Skywalker Jedi, ROTJ, gr light saber, MOC $95.00
Lumat, POTF, MOC $75.00
Lumat, ROTJ, MOC $60.00
Nien Nunb, M (in sealed mailer bag) $30.00
Nien Nunb, ROTJ, M $10.00
Nien Nunb, ROTJ, MOC $75.00
Nikto, ROTJ, M $20.00
Nikto, ROTJ, MOC $40.00
Paploo, POTF, M $34.00
Paploo, POTF, MOC $80.00
Paploo, ROTJ, M $10.00
Paploo, ROTJ, MOC $55.00
Power Droid, ESB, MOC $130.00
Power Droid, ROTJ, MOC $50.00
Power Droid, SW, MOC $200.00
Princess Leia, ROTJ, Boushh outfit, MOC $85.00
Princess Leia, ESB, Bespin crew neck, MOC (front view)...$185.00
Princess Leia, ESB, Bespin crew neck, MOC (profile) ... $200.00
Princess Leia, ESB, Hoth outfit, M $28.00

Princess Leia, ESB, Hoth outfit, MOC........................... $160.00

Princess Leia, ESB, Hoth outfit, MOC (unpunched), $225.00. (Photo courtesy Morphy Auctions)

Princess Leia, ESB, MOC... $295.00
Princess Leia, POTF, combat poncho, M $35.00
Princess Leia, POTF, combat poncho, MOC................. $115.00
Princess Leia, ROTJ, Bespin turtleneck, MOC.............. $125.00
Princess Leia, ROTJ, Boushh outfit, M $20.00
Princess Leia, ROTJ, Boushh outfit, M (sealed mailer bag) ..$35.00
Princess Leia, ROTJ, Boushh outfit, MOC $60.00
Princess Leia, ROTJ, combat poncho, MOC......................$50.00
Princess Leia, ROTJ, Hoth outfit, MOC.......................... $100.00
Princess Leia, ROTJ, MOC $390.00
Princess Leia, ROTJ, MOC (tri-logo) $200.00
Princess Leia, SW, MOC $240.00
Princess Leia, SW, MOC (12-back) $175.00
Princess Leia, SW, 12", MIB.. $285.00
Pruneface, ROTJ, M $14.00
Pruneface, ROTJ, M (sealed mailer bag)..........................$20.00
Pruneface, ROTJ, MOC...$40.00
Rancor Keeper, ROTJ, M $10.00
Rancor Keeper, ROTJ, MOC $55.00
Rebel Commander, ESB, MOC....................................... $140.00
Rebel Commander, ROTJ, MOC.......................................$50.00
Rebel Commando, ROTJ, M...$10.00
Rebel Commando, ROTJ, MOC...$50.00
Rebel Soldier, ESB, MOC $75.00
Rebel Soldier, ROTJ, MOC $40.00
Ree-Yees, ROTJ, M..$10.00
Ree-Yees, ROTJ, MOC...$40.00
Romba, POTF, M...$50.00
Romba, POTF, MOC.. $100.00
R2-D2, Droids, M $55.00
R2-D2, Droids, MOC $150.00
R2-D2, EDB, M..$35.00
R2-D2, ESB, MOC $140.00
R2-D2, ESB, w/sensorscope, M...$25.00
R2-D2, ESB, w/sensorscope, MOC $120.00
R2-D2, POTF, w/pop-up light saber, M........................... $120.00
R2-D2, POTF, w/pop-up light saber, MOC...................... $175.00
R2-D2, ROTJ, w/pop-up light saber, MOC (tri-logo) $200.00
R2-D2, ROTJ, w/sensorscope, MOC..................................$65.00
R2-D2, SW, MOC $280.00
R2-D2, SW, MOC (12-back) $425.00
R2-D2, SW, 12", MIB... $425.00
R5-D4, ESB, MOC $120.00
R5-D4, ROTJ, MOC $60.00
Sandpeople, ESB, MOC $120.00
Sandpeople, SW, MOC (12-back) $390.00
Snaggletooth, ESB, MOC $160.00
Snaggletooth, ROTJ, MOC..$65.00

Snaggletooth, SW, MOC, $200.00. (Photo courtesy Morphy Auctions)

Squidhead, ROTJ, M $15.00
Squidhead, ROTJ, MOC...$45.00
Star Destroyer Commander, ESB, MOC......................... $125.00
Star Destroyer Commander, ROTJ, MOC..........................$80.00
Stormtrooper, ESB, MOC $125.00
Stormtrooper, POTF, MOC... $260.00
Stormtrooper, ROTJ, MOC..$65.00
Stormtrooper, SW, MOC (12-back)................................ $425.00

Stormtrooper, SW, 12", M, $145.00.

Stormtrooper, SW, 12", MIB $225.00
Teebo, POTF, MOC $200.00

Teebo, ROTJ, MOC, $55.00; Wicket Warrick, ROTJ, MOC, $75.00. (Photo courtesy Morphy Auctions)

Thall Joben, Droids, MOC $65.00
TIE Fighter Pilot, ROTJ, M $18.00
TIE Fighter Pilot, ROTJ, MOC $65.00
Tig Fromm, Droids, M $60.00
Tig Fromm, Droids, MOC $165.00
Tusken Raider, ROTJ, MOC $75.00
Ugnaught, ESB, MOC $100.00
Ugnaught, ROTJ, MOC $40.00
Uncle Gundy, Droids, M $18.00
Uncle Gundy, Droids, MOC $55.00
Walrus Man, ESB, MOC $135.00
Walrus Man, ROTJ, MOC $65.00
Walrus Man, SW, MOC $280.00
Warok, POTF, M $75.00
Warok, POTF, MOC $125.00
Weequay, ROTJ, M $10.00
Weequay, ROTJ, MOC $40.00
Wicket, Ewoks, M $28.00
Wicket, Ewoks, MOC $50.00
Wicket Warrick, POTF, MOC $200.00
Yak Face, POTF, no weapon, MOC $2,000.00
Yak Face, POTF, w/weapon, MOC $2,200.00
Yak Face, POTH, M $225.00
Yoda, ESB, brn snake, MOC $350.00
Yoda, ESB, orange snake, MOC $275.00
Yoda, POTF, MOC $585.00
Yoda, ROTJ, MOC $175.00
Zuckuss, ESB, MOC $125.00
Zuckuss, ROTJ, MOC $60.00

Playsets and Accessories

Cantina Adventure Set, SW, complete, EX $175.00
Cantina Adventure Set, SW, MIB $700.00
Cloud City, ESB, complete, EX $135.00
Cloud City, ESB, MIB $475.00
Creature Cantina, SW, complete, EX $75.00
Creature Cantina, SW, MIB $360.00
Dagobah, Darth Vadar & Luke Battle, ESB, MIB $150.00
Dagobah, Darth Vader & Luke Battle, ESB, complete, EX ... $25.00
Darth Vader's Star Destroyer, ESB, MIB $245.00
Death Star Space Station, SW, complete, EX $115.00
Death Star Space Station, SW, MIB $295.00
Droid Factory, ESB, complete, EX $60.00
Droid Factory, ESB, MIB $170.00
Droid Factory, SW, MIB $145.00
Ewok Village, ROTJ, complete, EX $35.00
Ewok Village, ROTJ, MIB $225.00
Hoth Ice Planet, ESB, complete, EX $60.00
Hoth Ice Planet, ESB, MIB $335.00
Imperial Attack Base, ESB, complete, EX $40.00
Imperial Attack Base, ESB, MIB $145.00
Jabba the Hut, ROTJ, complete, EX $20.00
Jabba the Hut, ROTJ, MIB (Sears) $75.00
Jabba the Hut Dungeon w/Amanaman, ROTJ, complete, EX .. $135.00
Jabba the Hut Dungeon w/Amanaman, ROTJ, MIB $335.00
Jabba the Hutt Dungeon w/8D8, ROTJ, complete, EX $55.00
Jabba the Hutt Dungeon w/8D8, RTOJ, MIB $145.00
Land of the Jawas, SW, complete, EX $55.00
Land of the Jawas, SW, MIB $185.00
Rebel Command Center, ESB, complete, EX $80.00
Rebel Command Center, ESB, MIB $350.00
Turret & Probot, ESB, complete, EX $35.00
Turret & Probot, ESB, MIB $160.00

Vehicles

Ewok Battle Wagon, POTF, MIB, $325.00. (Photo courtesy Morphy Auctions)

A-Wing Fighter, Droids, complete, EX $175.00
A-Wing Fighter, Droids, MIB $550.00
All Terrain Attack Transport, complete, EX $90.00
All Terrain Attack Transport (AT-AT), ESB, MIB $350.00
All Terrain Attack Transport (AT-AT), ROTJ, MIB $285.00
Armored Sentinel Transport (AST-5), ROTJ, complete, EX .. $6.00
Armored Sentinel Transport (AST-5), ROTJ, mini-rig, MIB ... $45.00
ATL Interceptor, Droids, complete, EX $25.00
ATL Interceptor, Droids, MIB $125.00
B-Wing Fighter, ROTJ, complete, EX $65.00

B-Wing Fighter, ROTJ, MIB $250.00
Captivator (CAP-2), ESB, mini-rig, MIB $35.00
Captivator (CAP-2), mini-rig, complete, EX $10.00
Captivator (CAP-2), ROTJ, mini-rig, MIB $20.00
Darth Vader's TIE Fighter, SW, complete, EX $55.00
Darth Vader's TIE Fighter, SW, MIB $140.00
Darth Vader's TIE Fighter, SW, MIB (w/collector series sticker) $225.00
Desert Sail Skiff, ROTJ, complete, M $12.00
Desert Sail Skiff, ROTJ, mini-rig, MIB $45.00
Endor Forest Ranger, ROTJ, complete, EX $12.00
Endor Forest Ranger, ROTJ, mini-rig, MIB $75.00
Ewok Battle Wagon, POTF, complete, EX $60.00
Imperial Cruiser, ESB, complete, EX $50.00
Imperial Cruiser, ESB, MIB $150.00
Imperial Shuttle, ROTJ, complete, EX $100.00
Imperial Shuttle, ROTJ, MIB $650.00
Imperial Shuttle Pod (ISP-6), ROTJ, complete, EX $10.00
Imperial Shuttle Pod (ISP-6), ROTJ, mini-rig, MIB $25.00
Imperial Sniper, POTF, complete, EX $30.00
Imperial Sniper, POTF, MIB $110.00
Imperial Troop Transport, complete, EX $48.00
Imperial Troop Transport, ESB, MIB $128.00
Imperial Troop Transport, SW, MIB $135.00
Interceptor (INT-4), complete, EX $10.00
Interceptor (INT-4), ESB, mini-rig, MIB $30.00
Interceptor (INT-4), ROTJ, mini-rig, MIB $45.00
Landspeeder, Sonic, SW, complete, EX $185.00
Landspeeder, Sonic, SW, MIB $620.00
Landspeeder, SW, complette, EX $20.00
Landspeeder, SW, MIB $85.00
Millennium Falcon, complete, EX $100.00
Millennium Falcon, ESB, MIB $255.00
Millennium Falcon, ROTJ, MIB $285.00
Millennium Falcon, SW, MIB $375.00
Mobile Laser Cannon (MLC-3), ESB, mini-rig, MIB $40.00
Mobile Laser Cannon (MLC-3), mini-rig, M $10.00
Mobile Laser Cannon (MLC-3), ROTJ, mini-rig, MIB $30.00
Multi-Terrain Vehicle (MTV-7), complete, EX $10.00
Multi-Terrain Vehicle (MTV-7), ESB, mini-rig, MIB $35.00
Multi-Terrain Vehicle (MTV-7), ROTJ, mini-rig, MIB $25.00
One-Man Sand Skimmer, POTF, complete, EX $38.00
One-Man Sand Skimmer, POTF, MIB $100.00
Personnel Deployment Transport (PDT-8), complete, EX .. $10.00
Personnel Deployment Transport (PDT-8), ESB, mini-rig, MIB $30.00
Personnel Deployment Transport (PDT-8), ROTJ, mini-rig, MIB $20.00
Rebel Armored Snowspeeder, ESB, bl background, MIB .. $185.00
Rebel Armored Snowspeeder, ESB, pk background, MIB .. $195.00
Rebel Transport, ESB, bl background, MIB $190.00
Rebel Transport, ESB, yel background, MIB $175.00
Sandcrawler, radio controlled, ESB, MIB $500.00
Sandcrawler, radio-controlled, complete, EX $175.00
Sandcrawler, radio-controlled, SW, MIB $665.00
Scout Walker (AT-ST), complete, EX $35.00
Scout Walker (AT-ST), ESB, MIB $175.00
Scout Walker (AT-ST), ROTJ, MIB $150.00

Security Scout, POTF, complete, EX $25.00
Security Scout, POTF, MIB $115.00
Side Gunner, Droids, complete, EX $25.00
Side Gunner, Droids, MIB $85.00
Slave I, ESB, complete, EX $60.00
Slave I, ESB, MIB $185.00
Speeder Bike, ROTJ, complete, EX $15.00
Speeder Bike, ROTJ, MIB $50.00
Tatooine Skiff, POTF, complete, EX $250.00

Tatooine Skiff, POTF, MIB, $670.00.

(Photo courtesy Morphy Auctions)

TIE Fighter, complete, EX $75.00
TIE Fighter, ESB, MIB $265.00
TIE Fighter, SW, MIB $150.00
TIE Fighter, SW, MIB (Free Figures Inside) $950.00
TIE Fighter (Battle Damage), ESB, MIB $195.00
TIE Fighter (Battle Damage), ROTJ, complete, EX $45.00
TIE Fighter (Battle Damage), ROTJ, MIB $135.00
TIE Interceptor, ROTJ, complete, EX $55.00
TIE Interceptor, ROTJ, MIB $250.00
Twin-Pod Cloud Car, ESB, complete, EX $45.00
Twin-Pod Cloud Car, ESB, MIB $130.00
X-Wing Fighter, complete, EX $65.00
X-Wing Fighter, ESB, MIB $495.00
X-Wing Fighter, SW, MIB $425.00
X-Wing Fighter (Battle Damage), complete, EX $40.00
X-Wing Fighter (Battle Damage), ESB, MIB $295.00
X-Wing Fighter (Battle Damage), ROTJ, MIB $165.00
Y-Wing Fighter, ROTJ, complete, EX $60.00
Y-Wing Fighter, ROTJ, MIB $225.00

Miscellaneous

Bank, Chewbacca (kneeling), Sigma, M $45.00
Bank, C3-PO, Roman Ceramics, M $75.00
Bank, Princess Kneesaa figure playing tambourine, vinyl, 7", Adam Joseph Industries, 1983, MIB $28.00
Bank, R2-D2, Roman Ceramics, M $50.00
Bank, Yoda, SW, Sigma, M $90.00
Bath Soap, blk bar w/emb Darth Vader image, 2½x4", Omni Cosmetics Corp, 1981, unused, NMIB $10.00
Book, Empire Strikes Back, pop-up, Random House, M.... $16.00

Book, Return of the Jedi — Things to Do & Make, Random House, 1983, paperback, EX+ $5.00
Book, Return of the Jedi Pop-Up Book, Random House, 1983, hardback, MIB $18.00
Book, Splinter of the Mind's Eye, by A Foster, Del Ray Books, 1978, hardback, NM+ $12.00
Bop Bag, Darth Vader, Kenner, MIB $125.00
Bop Bag, Jawa, Kenner, MIB $225.00
Bubble Bath Container, Darth Vader figure, Omni, 1981, NM $15.00
Bubble Bath Container, Yoda, Omni, 1981, NM..............$15.00
Card Game, Return of the Jedi-Play for Power, Parker Bros, 1983, MIB $15.00
Case, Darth Vader, EX $15.00
Chewbacca Bandolier Strap, ROTJ, EXIB........................$25.00
Chewbacca Bandolier Strap, ROTJ, MIB $40.00

Collector's Cases, C-3PO, MIB, Jedi Laser Rifle, MIB, Darth Vader, MIB, $50.00 each. (Photo courtesy Morphy Auctions)

Color 'N Clean Machine, Craftmaster, M.........................$50.00
Coloring Book, Ewoks, Kenner #18240, 1985, unused, NM+ ..$12.00
Doll, Chewbacca, Kenner, 1978-79, synthetic fur w/plastic eyes & nose, 20", EX $25.00
Doll, Latara the Ewok, plush, 1984, 16", MIB...................$50.00
Doll, Paploo the Ewok, ROTJ, plush, MIB $135.00
Doll, R2-D2, Kenner, 1978-79, stuffed cloth, w/speaker, 10", EX..$25.00
Doll, Wicket the Ewok, plush, w/cape, Kenner, 1983, 15", EX+ $30.00
Eraser & Sharpener, Ewok, 1983, MOC $15.00
Erasers, ROTJ, 3-pc, 1983, MOC......................................$10.00
Game, Destroy Death Star, Kenner, MIB..........................$55.00
Game, ESB Yoda Jedi Master, Kenner, 1981, NMIB..........$75.00
Game, Escape From Death Star, Kenner, 1977, NMIB......$40.00
Game, Laser Battle, SW, Kenner, MIB..............................$85.00
Give-A-Show Projector, ESB, Kenner, complete, MIB $95.00
Gum Wrapper, 1977, 5x6", VG+.......................................$10.00
Hand Puppet, Yoda, vinyl w/wht silky hair, Kenner, 1980, MIB.. $85.00
Laser Pistol, SW, Kenner, 1978-83, plastic, battery-op, 18½", EX...$40.00
Laser Rifle, ESB, Kenner, 1980, plastic, battery-op, 18½", EX ..$75.00
Magnets, ROTJ, set of 4, MOC, B5 ....$25.00
Movie Viewer, SW, Kenner, 1978-79, plastic w/snap-in cartridge, 7", EX...$35.00
Night Light, Yoda (Return of the Jedi), 1980s, MOC $12.00
Paint Kit, Craftmaster, Luke Skywalker or Han Solo, MOC, ea...$16.00
Pencil, ROTJ, Butterfly Originals, 4-pack, 1983, 7½", MOC .. $5.00
Poster Set, Craftmaster, 1979, w/2 posters, MIB (sealed) ..$30.00
Puppet, Yoda, Kenner, 1981, hollow vinyl, 10", EX..........$25.00
Puzzle, Return of the Jedi Match Blocks, fr-tray, Craft Master, 1983, MIP (sealed) $12.00
Radio Watch, Lucasfilm/Bradley, 1982, R2-D2 & C-3PO on face, MIB...$50.00
Ruler, ROTJ, shows 8 characters, 1983, 12", EX...............$10.00
Scissors, ROTJ, MOC...$10.00
Sew 'N Show Cards, Wicket & Friends, MIB $18.00
Sit 'N Spin, Ewoks, MIB...$80.00
Soap, Princess Leia emb on wht soap bar, 3¾x2½", Omni Cosmetics, 1981, unused, MIB $10.00
Speaker Phone, Darth Vader, MIB $95.00
Stick Pin, Darth Vader's mask, diecast metal, 1977, MOC...$25.00
Stickers, ROTJ, 12-pc, 1983, MOC $10.00
Talking Telephone, Ewoks, MIB.......................................$50.00
Yo-Yo, Darth Vader, Dairy Queen promo, Humphrey, 1970s, rare, NM...$25.00
Yo-Yo, Stormtrooper, Spectra Star, sculpted plastic, MIP....$6.00

Steam-Powered Toys

During the early part of the century until about 1930, though not employed to any great extent, live steam power was used to activate toys such as large boats, novelty toys, and model engines.

See also Boats; Trains.

Castle w/Two Swans in Moat, Fleischmann, tin, swans rotate on rod around 'moat,' 6¼" dia, VG, A $440.00
Ferris Wheel, Germany, 6 gondolas w//compo figures facing each other on ornate metal framwork, 29" H, EX, A $9,350.00
Fountain, Doll (?), painted metal, 10" sq base w/4 decorative railed corners, VG, A $115.00
Gondola Runabout, Germany, pnt tin, 3 gondola seats w/figures rotate on upright open frame, 13", G, A........$275.00

Merry-Go-Round, M&K, tin, 8", VG, A, $300.00. (Photo courtesy Morphy Auctions)

Sawmill, Doll, pnt & litho tin, 16" L, EX $390.00

Steam Engine, Ernst Plank, tall stack, 12x11x6", EX, A, $1,000.00. (Photo courtesy Morphy Auctions)

Steam Engine, Faulk, vertical, 6½", VG+, A $360.00
Steam Engine, Germany, verticle, rnd flared base, 8½", EX .. $440.00
Steam Engine, Germany, verticle, sq footed base, 14", EX, A .. $360.00
Steam Engine, Jensen, No 90 Atomic Plant, 11x10x9", NM, A $210.00
Steam Engine, Stuart, CI & PS, 8½", restored, A..... $185.00
Steam Engine, Weeden, dual fly-wheel single piston engine & steam plant, CI footed base, 10x7", VG, A $230.00
Steam Engine Kit, Stewart, vertical, complete, 12x9½", MIB, A (Est: $100-$125) $100.00
Steam Launch, Weeden, PS, brass boiler, 12", VG+, A... $250.00
Steam Launch, Weeden, PS, brass boiler, 14", EX, A..... $275.00
Windmill, Doll, 9", VG, A $175.00
Zeppelin Roundabout, Germany, tin, 3 zeppelins rotate around tower w/flag, 12", rpnt, A $660.00

Steiff

Margaret Steiff made the first of her felt toys in 1880, stuffing them with lamb's wool. Later followed toys of velvet, plush, and wool, and in addition to the lamb's wool stuffing, she used felt scraps, excelsior, and kapok as well. In 1897 and 1898 her trademark was a paper label printed with an elephant; from 1900 to 1905 her toys carried a circular tag with an elephant logo that was different than the one she had previously used. The most famous 'button in ear' trademark was registered on December 20, 1904. The button with an elephant (extremely rare) and the blank button (which is also rare) saw use in 1904 and 1905. The button with Steiff and the underscored or trailing 'F' was used until 1948, and the raised script button is from the 1950s.

Steiff teddy bears, perhaps the favorite of collectors everywhere, are characterized by their long thin arms with curved wrists and paws that extend below their hips. Buyer beware: The Steiff company is now making many replicas of their old bears. For more information about Steiff's buttons, chest tags, and stock tags as well as the inspirational life of Margaret Steiff and the fascinating history of Steiff toys, we recommend *Button in Ear Book* and *The Steiff Book of Teddy Bears*, both by Jurgen and Marianne Cieslik; *4th Teddy Bear and Friends Price Guide* by Linda Mullins; *Collectible German Animals Value Guide* by Dee Hockenberry; and *Steiff Sortiment 1947 – 1995* by Gunther Pefiffer. (This book is in German; however, the reader can discern the size of the item, year of production, and price estimation.)

See also Character, TV, and Movie Collectibles; Disney.

Ali the Alligator, 25", VG, A $125.00
Baboon (Coco), 8", beige fure w/felt face, ears & paws, jtd at neck, rpl ear, G, A $50.00
Bear, hand puppet, brn w/lt tan muzzle & paws, brn glass eyes, ear button, 1950s, NM $100.00
Bear, 3", champaign mohair, blk bead eyes, swivel head, bendable limbs, no tags, NM... $100.00
Bear, 7", very early, brn w/blk shoe-button eyes, blk-stitched nose & mouth, leather collar, button, EX, A $600.00
Bear, 9", lt brn, darker brn-stitched nose, glass eyes, fuzzy pads, no tags, 1950s, EX $150.00
Bear, 9", 1970s, beige, glass eyes, brn-stitched nose, yel neck ribbon, ear button, EX, A $20.00
Bear, 10", pre-WWI, silver, shoe-button eyes, blk-stitching, lt felt pads, blank button, G, A $770.00
Bear, 11½", 1918-22, golden, glass eyes, stitched nose & claws, G, A $1,210.00
Bear, 12", lt blond short plush, brn-stitched nose & mouth, lt beige felt pads, glass eyes, ear button, 1980s, NM+... $175.00
Bear, 12½", pre-WWI, shoe-button eyes, blk-stitched nose, mouth & claws, lt felt pads, G, A......................... $1,540.00
Bear, 13", beige, shoe-button eyes, felt pads, w/underscored button, G, A.. $935.00
Bear, 13", Golden, 1905, shoe-button eyes, stitched nose & claws, shaved muzzle, no ear button, EX, A $1,760.00

Bear, 13", light beige, shoe-button eyes, reddish brown stitched nose and mouth, blank ear button, VG, A, $5,400.00. (Photo courtesy James D. Julia, Inc.)

Bear, 16", apricot mohair, shoe-button eyes, blk stitching, lt felt pads, VG, A $4,950.00
Bear, 16", 1905, brn, blk shoe-button eyes, brn-stitched nose & mouth, lt tan felt pads, G, A $3,525.00

Bear, 16½", 1905, lt beige, shoe-button eyes, brn-stitched nose/mouth, tan felt pads, bl gingham shirt, G, A $2,935.00
Bear, 18", honey-colored mohair, blk shoe-button eyes, stitched nose & mouth, felt pads, G, A $1,955.00
Bear, 19", 1905, golden, shoe-button eyes, stitched nose & claws, shaved muzzle, ear button, EX+, A $6,050.00
Bear, 23", golden tan, shoe-button eyes, stitched nose, felt hands, blank button, VG, A $8,800.00
Bear, 24", cinnamon, long-haired, shoe-button eyes, brn-stitched nose, orig ear button, VG, A $4,485.00
Bear, 24", 1905, golden, shoe-button eyes, stiched nose/claws, shaved muzzle, no ear button, EX, A.................... $4,675.00
Bear Couple Dancing, 13"/14", 1920s, golden mohair boy & wht mohair girls in cloth outfits, VG, A $20,900.00
Bear in Wheels, 10½" L, brn grizzly type on all 4s, shoe-button eyes, stitched nose & mouth, VG, A $940.00
Bear on All Fours on Wheeled Base, 14x20", med brn w/dk brn collar, mouth open looking down, G, A $250.00

Boy Scout Doll, 8½", original button and tag on ear, NM, A, $3,360.00. (Photo courtesy Morphy Auctions)

Brosos Dinosaur, 30" L, EX, A $200.00
Buffalo, 10x12" L, EX, A $200.00
Bulldog, hand puppet, ca 1955, lt alabaster w/blk ears, nose & head markings, glass eyes, EX+...................................$85.00
Camel on Wheeled Base, 12x17", 2 humps, brn felt w/plush trim, red felt back blanket, CI wheels, EX $300.00
Camel on Wheeled Base, 8x12", 2 humps, grap plusy, red felt back blanket, CI wheels, EX, A $300.00
Captain (Katzenjammer Kids), 15", ca 1910, felt & cloth, head & arms swivel, 15", EX+, A................................. $3,500.00
Cat, hand puppet, 1950s, blk mohair, red-stitched nose, gr glass eyes, ear button, EX+...$85.00
Dog on Wheeled Base, 12x16", wht curly plush w/lg brn side spots, brn ears & eye area, wht snout, CI wheels, VG, A .. $3,575.00
Elephant Head Wall Mount, 22" L, 1950s, G, A $350.00
Elephant on Wheeled Base, 14x19", alabster fur w/red back blanket, VG, A $385.00
Eric the Bat, 7", 1960s, EX+, A $380.00
Flossy Fish, 27", EX, A $125.00

French Poodle, 8½" H, 1950s, mohair & velvety plush, red collar, ear button, jtd legs, EX+..$38.00
Frog, 4¼" L, 1950s, 2-tone gr velvety plush, EX $25.00
Giraffe, 18" H, orig button & tags, EX, A $175.00
Giraffe, 56", EX, A... $800.00
Giraffe on Wheels, 20", curved neck looking up, beige w/brn spots, EX, A $385.00

Happy Hooligan, 15", ca 1915, EX, A, $2,750.00. (Photo courtesy Morphy Auctions)

Hedgehog, 30", EX, A...$25.00
Hockey Camel, 5½", paper chest tag, gold ear button w/yel tag, M...$80.00
Hoppel-Dackel the Dog on Wheeled Cart, 7x10" L, 1950s, EX, A $450.00
Jocko the Monkey, 4½", paper label on chest, ear button w/yel tag, M...$90.00
Kangaroo, 20" H, EX, A $225.00
Lamb on Wheeled Base, 9x14", wht wooly plush w/sheered legs, CI wheels, EX, A $825.00
Lamb on Wheels, 10" L, early, wooly w/felt ears, snout & lower legs, shoe-button eyes, VG, A $1,645.00
Lamb on Wheels, 12" L, wht, shoe-button eyes, orig underscore ear button, Fair+, A... $750.00
Lamby Lamb, 4x5" L, wht, gr glass eyes, no buttons or tags, NM $75.00
Llama, 7" H, 1950s, lt plush w/velveteen face & legs, dk spot on back & rump, ear button w/yel tag, EX $65.00
Mama Katzenjammer Tea Cozy Doll, 14½", ca 1915, felt & cloth, head & arms swivel, EX+, A $2,250.00
Mongo Monkey Seated on 4-Wheeled Cart, 8", 1930s, chest tag, G, A $1,500.00
Moose, 9" H, button & stock tag, EX, A........................ $175.00
Mopsy Dog, 5¼", sitting upright, paper chest tag, ear button w/yel tag, M $100.00
Peggy Penguin, 21", EX, A $450.00
Poodle, 11", gray, w/tag, EX, A $28.00
Poodles (4) in a Basket, 4" to 6", FAO Schwarz Exclusive, 1950s-60s, EX, A $500.00
Possy Squirrel, 4", no tags, NM+ $45.00

Rabbit (Manni), 23", 1930s, light tan, glass eyes, jointed at neck only, underscored 'FF' ear button, EX, A, $900.00. (Photo courtesy McMasters Harris Auction Co.)

Rabbit Seated on 4-Wheeled Cart, 9" L, wht mohair, stitched nose, Germany (US-Zone), VG, A $200.00
Rabbit Sitting Upright, 13" H, 1930s-40s, w/squeaker, 'FF' button, EX, A $275.00
Rabbit Sitting Upright, 27" H, EX, A $500.00
Rabbit Standing Upright, 11" H, 1950s, wht, glass eyes, pk-stitched nose, skirt w/felt top & shoes, VG, A $175.00
Robby Seal, 6x12" L, chest tag, metal & cloth tag on foot, NM+ $50.00
Slo Turtle, 5¼" L, plush w/rubber-like shell, felt toes, NM+ .. $45.00
Snuffy Kitty Cat, 5" H, 1970s, bl eyes, chest tag, NM $22.00
St Bernard Lying Down, 50", brn & wht, EX, A $125.00
Starfish Stool, 14x18" dia, EX, A $350.00
Stork, 22", wht & blk w/orange beak & legs, EX, A $150.00
Turtle Stool, 17x20" L, EX, A $300.00
Typos Dinosaur, 17" H, 1954, EX, A $400.00
Tysus T-Rex Dinosaur, 18", 1960s, airbrushed plush w/gr felt backbone scale, goggle-eyed, EX, A $700.00
Zotty Bear, 6½", beige, open mouth, bl neck ribbon, paper chest tag, silver ear button w/yel tag, M $300.00
Zotty Fox, 4¼x7", silver ear tag, EX+ $85.00

Strauss

Imaginative, high-quality, tin windup toys were made by Ferdinand Strauss (New York, later New Jersey) from the onset of World War I until the 1940s. For about 15 years prior to his becoming a toymaker, he was a distributor of toys he imported from Germany. Though hard to find in good working order, his toys are highly prized by today's collectors, and when found in even very good to excellent condition, many are in the $500.00 and up range.

Advisor: Scott Smiles

Air Devil, w/pilot, EX $550.00
Alabama Coon Jigger, EX $525.00
Alabama Coon Jigger, EX+IB $1,100.00
Alabama Coon Jigger, VG $400.00
Auto Dump Cart, EX $350.00
Big Show Circus Truck, EX $875.00
Boob McNutt, EXIB $900.00
Boob McNutt, VG $400.00
Bus De Luxe, EX $675.00
Bus De Luxe, G $375.00
Circus Cage Truck, VG $825.00
Dandy Jim, EXIB $1,100.00
Dandy Jim, VG $700.00
Dizzy Lizzy, NMIB $500.00
Emergency Tow Car #54, VG $1,200.00
Flying Airship, VGIB $400.00
Ham & Sam, EX+IB $1,100.00
Ham & Sam, G $450.00
Ham & Sam, VG $750.00
Hott & Tott, VG $600.00
Inter-State Bus, EX $625.00
Inter-State Bus, G+ $375.00
Inter-State Bus, NMIB $1,250.00
Jackee the Hornpipe Dancer, EXIB $900.00
Jackee the Hornpipe Dancer, G $425.00
Jazzbo Jim (Banjo Player), EX $450.00
Jazzbo Jim (Jigger), NMIB $650.00
Jazzbo Jim (Jigger), VG $399.99
Jenny the Balking Mule, VG $350.00
Jitney Bus, EX $425.00
Knock-Out Prize Fighters, 1920s, EXIB $600.00
Krazy Car, VG+ $500.00
Leaping Lena Car, EX $500.00
Locomotive & Tender, VG $150.00

Long Haulage Truck, VG+, $500.00.
(Photo courtesy James D. Julia, Inc.)

Lumber Tractor-Trailer, G $375.00
Miami Sea Sled #38, VG $200.00
Parcel Post Truck, NM $1,000.00
Play Golf, EXIB $500.00
Play Golf, NMIB $700.00
Red Flash Racer #31, EX $725.00
Red Flash Racer #31, G+ $350.00
Santee Claus Sleigh, VG $1,100.00
Speed Boat 28, w/figure, EX $300.00
Spirit of St Louis, 7" W, VG $350.00
Standard Oil Truck #73, VG $400.00
Thrifty Tom's Jigger Bank, EX $2,100.00
Timber Truck, VG $500.00

Tip Top Dump Truck, EX.. $750.00
Tip Top Porter, EXIB.. $350.00
Tombo, see Alabama Coon Jigger
Trackless Trolley/Twin Trolleys, VG.. $250.00
Travelchiks Boxcar, EX.. $500.00
Trik Auto, EX.. $350.00

Water Sprinkler Truck #72, EX, $450.00. (Photo courtesy James D. Julia, Inc.)

What's It?, NMIB.. $900.00
Wildfire, EXIB.. $350.00
Yell-O-Taxi No 59, VG.. $450.00

Structo

Pressed steel vehicles were made by Structo (Illinois) as early as 1920. They continued in business well into the 1960s, producing several army toys, trucks of all types, and firefighting and construction equipment.

Airport Mail Truck, gr w/airplane decals on sides of screened van, red hubs, wht MDW, 24", VG, A.. $880.00
Army Truck, snub-nosed cab w/high cloth-covered bed, 4-wheeled, 13", VG, A.. $50.00
Auto Builder Roadster, open seat, MDW, w/up, 16", VG .. $350.00

Auto Haul, 20", NMIB, A, $500.00. (Photo courtesy Morphy Auctions)

Communications Center Truck, 1960s, 21", EX+.......... $250.00
Concrete Mixer, 1950s, 10-wheeled, red w/yel drum, 21", VG.. $125.00
Diamond T Semi, 1940s, 26", EX, A.. $300.00
Diamond T Transport, 1940s, 26" w/15" extra trailer, VG, A.. $155.00
Dump Truck, cabover, bl & red, 15", unused, NMIB, A .. $225.00
Dump Truck, open cab, MDW, 18", G, A.. $165.00
Dump Truck, open cab, MSW, red & blk, w/up, 18", EX, A.. $1,200.00
Dump Truck, 1930s, blk & orange, 23", old rpnt, A....... $165.00
Fire Aerial Ladder Truck, red & silver, 30", NMIB, A.... $550.00
Fire Pumper, open bench seat, red w/orange water tank & wheel hubs, 21", G, A.. $275.00

Fire (S.F.D.) Pumper Truck, 20", NM+IB, A, $650.00. (Photo courtesy Morphy Auctions)

Guided Missile Launcher Truck, 1960s, 14", EXIB......... $200.00
Hydraulic Dump Truck, orange & gr, 10-wheeled, 22", VG, A.. $400.00
Kennel Truck, 1968, w/6 dogs, 9", NM, A.. $190.00
Motor Dispatch Truck, bl w/airplane decals on sides of van, MDW, red hubs, 24", EX, A.. $1,980.00
Racer, 2 seater, MSW, 'Structo' decal on radiator, w/up, 12½", EX+.. $550.00
Ready Mix Concrete Truck, 20", VG+, A.. $150.00
Ride-Er-Dumper, 1960s, 20", EX+, A.. $75.00
Roadster, open, spoke wheels, w/up, 16", G, A.............. $550.00
Sanitation Dept Truck, 1960s, 16", VG+.. $125.00
Steam Shovel, 4-wheeled, med bl, 21", EX, A............... $100.00
Structo 66 Tank Truck, 13", VGIB, A.. $275.00
Tank, gr w/red turret & wheels, w/treads, 11½", VG+.... $450.00
Tractor, 1920s, open seat w/vertical steer wheel, blk treads, clockwork motor, 12", EX+.. $750.00
Wrecker, 1930s, blk w/orange hubs, 22", G, A............... $300.00
Wrecker, 1940s, 24", G, A.. $225.00
24-Hour Towing Service Truck, wht cabover, 8-wheeled, 11½", missing boom, G, A.. $30.00

Teddy Bears

The history of teddy bears goes way back to about 1902 – 1903. Today's collectors often find it difficult to determine exactly what company produced many of these early bears, but fortunately for them, there are many excellent books now available that contain a wealth of information on those early makers.

Because most teddies were cherished childhood toys and were usually very well loved, many that survived are well worn, so an early bear in mint condition can be very valuable.

We would like to direct your attention to the books on the market that are the most helpful on the detailed history and identification of teddies. *A Collector's History of the Teddy Bear* by Patricia Schoonmaker; *Teddy Bears Past and Present, Vols 1* and *II*; and *American Teddy Bear Encyclopedia* by Linda Mullins; *Teddy Bears — A Complete Guide to History, Collecting, and Care*, by Sue Pearson and Dottie Ayers; *Teddy Bear Encyclopedia* and *Ultimate Teddy Bear Book* by Pauline Cockrill; and *Big Bear Book* by Dee Hockenberry. The reader can easily see that a wealth of information exists and that it is impossible in a short column such as this to give any kind of a definitive background. If you intend to be a knowledgeable teddy bear collector, it is essential that you spend time in study. Many of these books will be available at your local library or through dealers who specialize in bears.

See also Schuco; Steiff.

10", silver-beige mohair, glass eyes, blk stitching, dressed in coat, Germany, 1920s, G, A....$525.00
11", lt beige, glass eyes, stitched nose, rnd cupped ears, jtd, ca 1910, much mohair loss, G, A....$85.00
11", lt beige mohair, glass eyes, brn stitched nose, mouth & claws, lt felt pads, Germany, 1920s, G, A....$550.00
13", beige mohair, shoe-button eyes, blk-stitched nose, mouth & claws, felt pads, long jtd arms, VG, A....$510.00

13", gold, wearing sunsuit, VG, A, $150.00. (Photo courtesy McMasters Harris Auction Co.)

13", golden beige mohair, blk shoe-button eyes, blk stitching, lt felt pads, 'Ideal' face, EX, A....$1,870.00
13", lt beige mohair, shoe-button eyes, stitched nose, mouth & claws, lt pads, Germany, pre-WII, VG, A....$1,210.00
13½", brn mohair, brn glass eyes, jtd, long arms, humped back, pointed snout, red neck ribbon, G, A....$450.00
14", lt brn mohair, shoe-button eyes, blk stitched nose, mouth & claws, lt felt pads, Germany, G, A....$1,320.00
14", lt cotton plush, celluloid goggly eyes, pnt nose w/blk stitched mouth & claws 1930s, G, A....$300.00
15", gold, shoe-button eyes, stitched nose & claws, rnd head & ears, jtd football body, American, 1915, VG, A....$250.00
16", beige mohair, glass eyes, blk stitching, left feet pads, lg hump, Ideal (?), G, A....$1,320.00
18", gold, long mohair, shoe-button eyes, stitched pointy nose, jtd, ca 1935, VG, A....$70.00

21", beige mohair, hump back, pointed snout, suede pads, VG, A, $390.00. (Photo courtesy James D. Julia, Inc.)

24", American, jtd, gold, brn glass eyes, felt pads, straw stuffed, VG+, A....$440.00
25", Panda, blk & wht w/red tongue, blk eyes, short stubby arms, long legs, 1940s-50s, G....$50.00
26", Super Bear, brn, brn plastic eyes, long wht snout w/blk felt nose, beige ears & paws, Commonwealth Toy Co, VG....$125.00

Telephones

Novelty phones representing a well-known advertising or cartoon character are proving to be the focus of a lot of collector activity — the more recognizable the character the better. Telephones modeled after a product container are collectible too, and with the intense interest currently being shown in anything advertising related, competition is sometimes stiff and values are rising.

AC Spark Plug, figural, blk, gr & wht, NM....$75.00

Alf, NM, $75.00.

Bart Simpson, Columbia, 1990s, MIB....$40.00
Batmobile, Columbia, 1990, MIB, from $25 to....$35.00
Bugs Bunny in 'Tux' Standing w/Leg Crossed on Base, number keys on bottom of base, 12", 1980s, EX....$40.00

Buzz Lightyear, conventional phone on stand next to Buzz Lightyear figure, unused, MIB (sealed) $125.00
Charlie Tuna, standing upright w/hands on hips, mouth open, 10", MIB..$60.00
Crest Sparkle, figural, MIB, from $50 to $75.00
Garfield, figural, lying down, Tyco, 1980s, NM+ $45.00
Heinz Ketchup, realistic ketchup bottle, 8½", NM+ $55.00
Keebler Elf, 'Elf Phone' emb on base, 1980s, NM+............$65.00
Kermit the Frog, receiver rests on Kermits leg while seated in chair atop push-button base, American Telecommunications, 1983 .... $125.00
Little Sprout, figure on base w/hand on hip & receiver in other, various gr tones, 12", 1984, NM+ $65.00
Mickey Mouse, Western ELectric, 1976, EX.................. $175.00
Power Rangers, MIP..$30.00
Strawberry Shortcake, MIB $75.00
Tetley, mascot figure standing in wht coat on bl base w/'Tetley' lettered in wht, Canadian issue, scarce, NM+ $75.00
Ziggy, 1989, MIB...$75.00

Tin Vehicles

There is such a huge variety of tin vehicles, that to do them justice, we decided to list some of them in their own category. You will find old painted tin limousines with their intricate details to the newer lithographed tin models. Many are friction, battery-operated, or windups, with a few being just the plain ol' push-pull type. Most of the listings are from recent auctions, and they are bringing very good prices.

See also Aeronautical; Battery-Operated; Boats; Japanese (and Other) Tin Vehicle Replicas; Lehmann; Marx; Strauss; Windups, Friction, and Other Mechanicals.

Automobiles

Limousine, Carette, 15", windup, glass windows and headlamps with driver, VG+, A, $6,325.00.
(Photo courtesy James D. Julia, Inc.)

American Yellow Cab Co Lenox 530, Bing, 7", w/up, blk & orange w/yel hubs, MDW, G, A $285.00
Beauty Car, 6", friction, NMIB, A.....................................$80.00
Buick Electricmobile (1950), Mizuno/Alps, 8", b/o, hood ornament controls steering, 8", NMIB, A $125.00
Cadillac (1950s), 10", friction, lithoed trunk emblem & taillights, EXIB, A... $200.00
Cadillac DeVille (1959) Pulling Boat & Trailer, Lang Crafts, plastic & wood b/o speedboat, EXIB, A $410.00
Car & House Trailer (House Trailor No 3), Naito, 6" w/7" trailer, friction, NM+IB, A $400.00
Car & Trailcraft (Skipper M-333 boat), MT, 1950s, 13" overall, friction, crank-op boat, MIB, A $325.00
Caravan Car, Joustra/France, 18", friction, red & wht convertible w/2 figures pulling trailer, NMIB, A....................... $935.00
Chevy Impala 4-Door (1963), IY, 13", b/o, bump & go action, EX+, A $175.00
Chrysler Airflow, Kosuge/Kuramochi, 8½", w/up, VG, A .. $425.00
Chrysler Convertible, Yonezawa, 10", friction, red w/plaid litho seat, EXIB, A $700.00
Concept Car (1960s), Linemar, 8", friction, 2-tone station wagon type w/clear plastic front shield, NM, A $250.00
Continental Super Special Convertible, Cragstan, 14", friction, working wipers, G, A... $140.00
Convertible Car, Alps, friction, maroon Buick style w/driver, BRT, 10", NMIB, A $650.00
Corvair Bertone (1960s Concept Car), Bandai, b/o, vinyl driver, NM+IB, A $300.00
Coupe, Distler, 9½", w/up, cream w/red open seat, red fenders w/NP headlights, EX+IB, A $660.00
Cunningham Sports Car, Asahi, friction, 2-tone w/chrome trim, BRT, 8", EXIB, A.. $275.00
Cunningham Sports Car (1960s), Irco, friction, 2-door coupe, 7½", NMIB, A $125.00
Datsun Fairlady Z, Ichiko, 11½", friction, NM+IB, A $125.00
De Dion, Bing, 1904, 8", pnt tin, early open auto w/'tuffted' curved-back seat, center steering, EX, A $1,955.00
Edsel (New), Japan, friction, 8", NMIB, A $500.00
Electrical Emergency Service Car (1963), Yonezawa, 11", b/o, NMIB, A.. $350.00
Electro Car, TN, 1950s, 7", b/o, MIB, A $150.00
Electromatic 7500 Convertible, Distler, b/o, w/ignition key, EX, A $350.00
Flivver Roadster, Bing, 6½", w/up, blk, simulated cloth top, MSW, lithoed driver, EX, A $345.00
Ford (1957) Convertible Pulling Boat & Trailer (Friction Boat & Trailer), Haji, 16", EX+IB, A $350.00
Ford Falcon (1961), Marusan, friction, plastic windshield wipers, 9", EX, A.. $110.00
Ford Model T Roadster, Bing, w/up, blk, 6½", VG, A $175.00
Ford Thunderbird (1968), Ichiko, friction, 11", MIB, A... $175.00
Ford 2-Door Convertible (1946), Marchesini/Italy, 10", w/up, b/o headlights, w/built-in music box, VG+, A.............. $325.00
Ford-Gyron, Ichida, 11", r/c, EXIB, A........................... $350.00
Ford-Type Sedan, Bing, 6", w/up, blk, flat roof, spoke wheels w/driver, VGIB, A $350.00
Hansom Cab, Converse, 10½", w/up, tiller steering, 2 sm/2 lg MSW, blk w/gold trim, VG, A $2,530.00
Honk-Along Lincoln (1957), Ichiko, 7", friction, NM+IB, A $100.00
James Bond's Aston-Martin, Gilbert, 11", r/c, NMIB, A .. $500.00

Jeep w/Boat-Trailer, SSS, 5½" Jeep, 7½" trailer & 8" crank-op boat, friction, NM+IB, A $375.00

Limousine, Bing, 1920s, 15", w/up, electric lights, 4 door, flat roof, bl & blk, MDW w/orange hubs, driver, EX, A $1,650.00

Limousine, Burnett/England, 13½", w/up, open front seat, opening doors, bl & blk, MDW, right-side driver, EX, A.. $990.00

Limousine, Carette, 10", w/up, roof extends over front seat, w/ driver & passenger, VG, A $1,840.00

Limousine, Carette, 12½", w/up, open front, railed top, headlamps, lithoed driver, G, A $1,550.00

Limousine, Distler, 10", w/up, electric lights, '603' on grille, blk & yel w/red trim, MSW, EX+, A $1,430.00

Limousine, Eberl, 10", w/up, lithoed, driver helps lady out of auto, EX, A $5,500.00

Limousine, Eberl, 14", w/up, rack on flat roof over open front seat, opening rear doors, right-sided driver, VG, A $1,540.00

Limousine, Fischer, 7", w/up, lithoed, roof extends over seat, no windshields, w/driver, G, A $250.00

Limousine, Gunthermann, 8", w/up, railed top, 4 opening doors, lamps at open windshield, MSW, G, A $575.00

Limousine, Karl Bub, 14", w/up, flat roof over open front seat, NP headlamps, red & blk, MSW, driver, EX, A $1,430.00

Limousine, Marklin, 17", w/up, roof opens, doorless front, WRT, spoke wheels, right steering & brake, VG+, A ...$35,650.00

Limousine, Marklin, 18", w/up, railed top w/spare tire over open front, glass windows, WRT w/spokes, prof rstr, A...$24,200.00

Limousine, Richter, 6", w/up, lithoed, lady driver, spoke wheels, EX, A $375.00

Limousine, Tipp, 15", w/up, electric lights, long pointy nose, metal Dunlop Cord Balloon tires, bl & cream, EX, A....... $1,050.00

Lincoln (1957), Masudaya/Ichiko, 7", b/o, passengers lithoed on all windows, 7", EX (VG+ box), A $300.00

Lincoln Futura, 11", friction, plastic windshield, EX, A $200.00

Luxury 40 CV Coupe, JEP, 18", w/up, open front seat, enclosed rear w/viewing window, metal ballon tires, bl/cream, rstr...$3,850.00

Mercedes Benz 220 Convertible (1960s), M, 8", friction, plastic hood ornament, lithoed interior, NM+IB, A........... $150.00

Model T Coup, Bing, 6½", w/up, blk, w/driver, EX......... $390.00

Model T Roadster, Bing, 6", w/up, blk, WRT, spoke wheels, EX, A $550.00

Model T Sedan, Orobr, w/up, blk over aqua, WRT, spoke wheels, 6", NMIB, A $615.00

Model T Sedan, Orobr, 6", w/up, blk, WRT, spoke wheels, VG $300.00

New Sports Car (1962), ATC, friction, 10", NMIB, A .. $700.00

Old Fashion Car, SH, 1950s, 9", jalopy w/driver, EXIB $65.00

Open Car No 6 (1957 Chevy Convertible), Masudaya, friction, lithoed driver & details, NM+IB, A $575.00

Packard Convertible, Distler, w/up, NM (VG box), A... $500.00

Pontiac Firebird III Concept Car (1950s), Alps, 11½", b/o, 2 clear plastic domes w/drivers, EX, A $225.00

Renault K2 Torpedo Convertible, JEP, 1920s, 13", w/up, celluloid windshield, MDW, blk w/red interior, EX, A........ $1,650.00

Roadster, Converse, 13", fly-wheel action, NPSW, full-figure driver, VG, A $280.00

Saloon, Richter, 6", w/up, roof w/luggage rack extends over seat w/driver, MSW, red, tan & gold, EX+, A............. $2,200.00

Sedan, C Rossignol, 14", w/up, electric lights, opening trunk, MDW, rear spare, gr, tan & red, right-side driver, VG, A $1,320.00

Sonic Car (1966 Dodge Charger Sonic Car), Nomura, 16", b/o, NM+IB, A $275.00

Sports Car (Jaguar XK 120 Convertible), Masudaya, friction, 7½", NM+IB, A $250.00

Sunliner, Nomura, 8", b/o, fat convertible w/removable interior for battery access, BRT, NMIB, A $175.00

Taxi, Fischer, 8", w/up, doorless front, rear convertible top, working rear windows, driver, VG+, A $1,760.00

Taxi (1950 Buick), Mizuno, 8", b/o, working headlights & roof light, NM+IB (box marked 'Electro-Toy'), A $325.00

Touring Car, Bing, 10", open, gr w/orange 'tuffted' seats, brass-look cowl, headlamps & trim, MSW, compo driver, EX, A $3,160.00

Touring Car, Bing, 15", w/up, open, high front/back seats, glass windshield, NP headlamps, rubber tires, driver, VG, A $5,500.00

Touring Car, Fischer, 9", w/up, open seat w/driver, 2 lady passengers, rear top down, MSW, VG+, A..................... $1,760.00

Touring Car, German, 10", crank-wind, lithoed, open w/driver on right side, MSW, 10", VG+ $850.00

Touring Car, H Yamada, 11", open high seats w/driver on right side, 4 doors, headlamps, MSW, EX, A $3,025.00

Touring Car, Karl Bub, w/up, simulated cloth top down, bl w/blk trim, MDW, lithoed driver on right side, 5½", EX, A ...$440.00

Touring Car (1911), Wilkins, 8", w/up, open, yel, MSW, CI driver, VG, A $345.00

Tourneau 203, Richter, 7", w/up, open, wht w/red & wood-grain trim, goggled driver in yel coat, VG, A............... $1,140.00

United Air Lines Jeep, Yoshiya, friction, EX+IB, A................ $80.00

Venus Ford, Nomura, 8", friction, b/o lighted visible piston action, NMIB, A.. $235.00

Volkswagen Beetle, Germany, 4", w/up, bl w/lithoed driver & passengers, EX, A... $525.00

Volkswagen Beetle Convertible (1960s), Bandai, 7", r/c, NM+IB, A $150.00

Yellow Taxi, Gunthermann, 8½", blk & orange-yel w/orange-yel hubs, right-sided driver, VG, A $465.00

Pierce Arrow Open Car, Converse, 16", windup, tin with wooden side lamps and headlights, rear doors open, G, A, $3,160.00. (Photo James D. Julia, Inc.)

Buses and Trolleys

All State Express Bus (See America First), MT, 1950s, 8½", friction, NM+IB $150.00
Bluebird National Park Excursion Bus, Daiya, 14", friction, EX+IB, A $140.00
Broadway/Lexington Ave Trolley, Morton & Converse, 12", w/up, passengers lithoed in windows, VG, A $1,540.00
Camping Bus (Volkswagen), Yonezawa, friction, b/o music & twittering bird sound, 9", NMIB, A $325.00
Cragstan Siren Greyhound Bus, NGS, 1950s, 20", friction, door opens & stewardess appears, NMIB, A $300.00

Double-Decker Bus, Gunthermann, 10", windup, 'Ford's Automobile' and 'Cailler's Chocolates' advertising, driver seated to the right of the hood, VG+, A, $2,475.00. (Photo courtesy Bertoia Auctions)

Double-Decker Bus, Orobr, ca 1915, w/up, rear stairs, spoke wheels, w/driver, 6", EX $670.00
Double-Decker Trolley, Gunthermann, 12", w/up, yel w/orange stripes, w/guide pole, VG, A $275.00
Dream (Avenue) Bus, Daiya, 9½", friction, EX+ (VG+ box), A $100.00
Giant Bus, Normura, friction, 23", G+, A $125.00
GM Coach (Passenger Bus), Yonezawa/Rosho Toy, 16", b/o, passengers lithoed on windows, NMIB, A $175.00
Greyhound, NGS/Cragstan, 1960s, 9", friction, skyline view, MIB, A $100.00
Greyhound, Y/Cragstan, 1950s, 12", friction, moving passengers, MIB, A $435.00
Greyhound Highway Traveler, Ichimura, 10½", friction, NM+IB, A $65.00
Greyhound Red Ribbon, Marusan, 12½", friction, VG, A...$225.00
Greyhound Scenicruiser, Daiya/Cragstan, 1950s, 8½", friction, MIB, A $150.00
Greyhound Scenicruiser, Germany, pre-war (?), 5½", w/up, driver & 2 top passengers move in & out, NM, A $200.00
Greyhound Scenicruiser, Japan, 1960s, 11½", friction, 'Travel USA' & 3 landmark scenes on roof, MIB, A $400.00
Greyhound Scenicruiser, KK, 1950s, 7", b/o, MIB, A $140.00
Greyhound Scenicruiser, KK, 16", friction, EXIB, A $150.00

Greyhound Scenicruiser, Marusan, 1950s, 12½", EX+, A $125.00. (Photo courtesy serioustoys.com)

Greyhound Scenicruiser, NGS/Cragstan, 11½", friction, door opens & conductor appears, MIB, A $335.00
Greyhound Scenicruiser, SN/Cragstan, 1950s, 9", friction, NMIB, A $83.00
Greyhound Scenicruiser, Stone, 11", r/c, 'Realistic Roof Illumination,' unused, MIB, A $170.00
Infants Bus, Nishimura, 9", friction, animals lithoed below passengers in windows, EX+IB, A $135.00
Nifty (Double-Decker) Bus #1100, w/up, orange & bl w/wht trim, rear stairs w/ticket taker, driver, 9½", VG+, A $700.00
Old Fashioned Bus, MT, 13", NMIB $85.00
Panoramic Overland Bus, Hayashi, friction, lithoed driver & passengers w/blk porter in rear of bus, 13", EX+, A $600.00
San Francisco Lines AR 7510 (American Sight Seeing Bus), dated 1956, 10", friction, VG+, A $250.00
Sight-Seeing Bus, IY Metal Toys, 16", friction, celluloid roof windows, wht, blk & yel, 16", EX, A $55.00
Sight-Seeing Bus, Masydaya, 14", friction, passengers lithoed in windows, NMIB, A $150.00
Super Coach (GM Scenicruiser), Nomura, 21", friction, silver, wht & red w/bl-tinted windshield, roof lights, EX+, A $175.00
Trolley, Converse, 16", City Hall Park 175, VG, A $390.00
Trolley, Gunthermann, 8", w/up, yel w/orange & gr stripe, windows, w/guide pole, VG+, A $200.00
World Lines Bus #501, Nomura, friction, 10½", EX, A .. $150.00

Construction

Courtland Excavating 51 Mechanical Operating Crane, 13", windup, tin and plastic, EX+, A, $100.00. (Photo courtesy serioustoyz.com)

Auto-Shovel Bulldozer, Yoshiya, 14" L, b/o, blk rubber treads w/driver, NM+IB, A $150.00

Cement Mixer, Sears/Japan, 15", friction, 3 axels, lever-controlled dump action, EX+IB, A $125.00

Cement Mixer/Tools Truck, Japan, 1950s, 10½", orange & yel w/silver-tone cement drum, EX, A $100.00

Forklift, KY, w/some plastic, yel w/blk treads, runs back & forth w/engine light, w/driver, 12½" L, MIB, A $100.00

Lion Tractor 38 & Canyon 56/8 Platform (Electro Toy), Nomura, 6½" & 9", b/o, NM+IB, A $175.00

Magnetic Crane Truck (Electromagne), Excelo, 13", friction, magnetic boom, w/driver, NMIB, A $1,150.00

P&H Mamouth Crane (Super Mobile Clam), Asahi, 16", friction, NM+IB, A $350.00

Power Shovel in Diesel Truck, SSS, 13½", lever & push-button control, NMIB, A $125.00

Road Grader, Yamaichi, 1950s, 12½", red w/blk grader, BRT, MIB, A $75.00

Turnpike 28-Wheeled Hydraulic Dump Truck, SSS, 1960, 20", engine growls as dump rises, EX, A $50.00

Emergency and Service Vehicles

Fire Ladder Engine, TKK, 19", friction, NMIB, $300.00. (Photo courtesy Morphy Auctions)

Allstate 24 Hour Emergency Service, 1950s, 5", friction, NMIB, A $182.00

Ambulance No 62 (1966 Buick Skylark Superior Ambulance), Asakusa, b/o, 11½", NMIB, A $125.00

Checker Cab #416, w/up, passengers lithoed in windows, red button-type disk wheels, 6", VG, A $180.00

Electrical Emergency Service Car (1963), Yonezawa, 11", b/o, NMIB, A $350.00

Emergency Car, K, 1950s, 5", friction, wht 'fat-bodied' car w/'Emergency' lettered in red w/red crosses, BRT, EXIB, A $65.00

Fire Aerial Ladder Truck, appears 1950s, 5", friction, lithoed detail, EX, A $135.00

Fire Aerial Ladder Truck, San/Japan, 15", friction, 4 seated firemen, VG, A $350.00

Fire Aerial Ladder Truck (MFD Super Fire Engine), K, 1950s, 15", friction, w/4 lithoed firemen figures, NMIB, A..... $75.00

Fire Chief Car (Ford Falcon Station Wagon), Alps, 9", friction, figures lithoed in windows, NM+IB, A $100.00

Fire Command Car, Nomura, 11", b/o, bump-&-go action, driver & passenger, NMIB, A $150.00

Fire Dept Car (1952 Ford), Marusan, 10", b/o, red siren on roof, 2 lithoed figures in front seat, NM, A $200.00

Fire Engine, Cragstan, 14", friction, red w/gray extension ladder atop, 6-wheeled, VGIB, A $200.00

Fire Engine, Gunthermann, 14", w/up, 4 firemen, crank-op top-ladders, lever-op water pump, EX, A $1,980.00

Fire Engine, TKK, 19", friction, open w/top ladder, w/driver, NMIB, A $300.00

Fire Extension Ladder Truck, Gunthermann, 12", w/up, open w/overhead appartus, WRT/spokes, EX, A $4,125.00

Fire Ladder Truck, Tipp, 9", open, right driver, 2 rear seated figures, overhead ladder, EX, A $880.00

Fire Pumper, Gunthermann, 10", w/up, open, red/brass, right steering, WRT/spokes, back not railed, 2 compo figures, VG, A.. $1,760.00

Fire Pumper, Gunthermann, 13", w/up, open, red/brass, right steering, WRT/spokes, railed back, 3 compo figures, EX, A $3,575.00

Fire Truck w/2-Wheeled Hose Real, Gunthermann, 12", w/up, open w/flat canopy roof, WRT/spokes, 5 compo figures, VG, A $2,200.00

Flag Fire Engine, TN, 1950s, 7", friction, fireman waves flag, NMIB, A $150.00

G-Men Car, Electro Toy, 8", battery-operated, NM+IB, $385.00. (Photo courtesy Morphy Auctions)

Highway Patrol (Police Convertible), Daiya, 14", b/o, 1963, 2 vinyl figures, NMIB, A $150.00

Highway Patrol (Ford Falcon Station Wagon), Alps, 9", friction, blk & wht, figures lithoed in windows, roof siren, NMIB $85.00

Highway Patrol Jeep, Daiya, 1960s, 10", b/o, NMIB, A.. $100.00

Jeep Wreck Truck (1960s), Nomura, 12", friction, NMIB, A .. $125.00

NYC High Way (Police) Patrol #54 Car, 1950s, 7", friction, gr & wht w/red & wht lithoed interior, VG, A $45.00

PAA Air Port Set, SSS, friction, fork lift, cargo trailer & accessories, NM+IB, A $250.00

Police Car, Niedemeir, 1950s, friction, 13", bl body w/Police on sides, lithoed figures & tires, gun on hood, EX+, A .. $200.00

Police Car, Nomura, 7", friction, moving gun on hood, gr & cream, chrome-looking grille & bumper, NM+IB, A $125.00

Police Car, Nomura, 7", friction, moving gun on hood, 2-tone gr, EXIB, A $100.00

Police Car (1954 Lincoln), Mizuno, 9", b/o, working lights, NM+IB (box marked 'Electromobile'), A $250.00

Police Car Patrol NO-1 (1957 Dodge), China, 10", b/o, working light, NMIB, A $150.00

Police M38 Turn-O-Matic Jeep, Nomura, 10", b/o, w/driver, NMIB, A $100.00

Police Patrol Car No 1 (1952 Ford), Marusan, 10", b/o, siren on roof, 2 lithoed figures in front seat, NM, A $275.00
Police Patrol Jeep, Nomura, 11", b/o, bump-&-go action, driver & passenger, NMIB, A $125.00
Police Patrol Motorcycle, Mettoy, 1936, 8", w/up, integral driver, EX, A $460.00
Police Pressmobile Car, Alps, 6", w/up, NM+IB, A........ $107.00
Polizei Wagen (Mercedes 250S Convertible), Daiya, 14", b/o, police figures in front seat, NMIB, A $150.00
School Picnic Bus (Volkswagen), Daiya, 9", friction, NMIB, A $225.00
Secret Agents Car (007/Unmarked), Spesco, b/o, bl w/red lights on roof & sirens on fenders, 14", NMIB, A $350.00
Taxi, Carette, 12½", w/up, open front seat, right-sided driver, blk top, G $1,750.00
Wreck Truck, SSS, 6½", friction, NM+IB, A................. $160.00

Military and Warriors

Air Defense Pom Pom Guns, Linemar, 14", friction, b/o guns, w/gun operator, NMIB, A.. $125.00

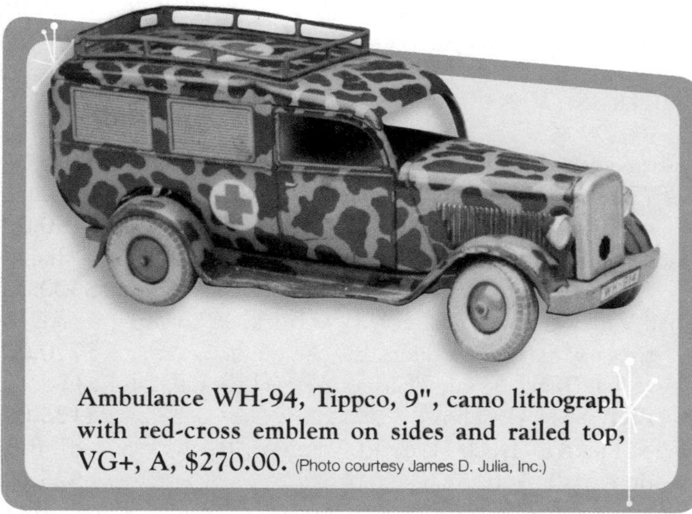

Ambulance WH-94, Tippco, 9", camo lithograph with red-cross emblem on sides and railed top, VG+, A, $270.00. (Photo courtesy James D. Julia, Inc.)

Armored Car (WWII), Germany, 10", golden camo w/red hubs, MDW, German soldier at window, VG, A............... $345.00
Army M-75 Anti-Aircraft Tank (Firing Cannons), Okuma, 9", b/o, gunner in turret, NMIB, A.................................$85.00
Cannon, Bing, 14", w/elevation adjustment, detailed carriage, VG, A $110.00
Dump Truck w/Gravel Loader, Alps, 12½" w/8" loader, b/o, red w/orange bed, NM+IB, A.. $275.00
Gama Tank, West Germany, 1950s, 5½", w/up, pop-up driver, wht rubber treads, NM, A $150.00
German Mercedes Benz Staff Car w/Fuhrer, Tipp, 9", w/up, top down, 4 compo figures, EX, A $1,500.00
German Staff Car, Schuco, 10", b/o, top down, 4 compo figured, EX, A $460.00
German Transport Truck w/Soldiers, Lionel, 9", open chain treads, 9 compo figures, VG+, A $460.00
Guided Missile Launcher, Yonezawa, swivels into position, pull lever & missiles fire, w/8 missiles, NMIB, A $250.00
Jeep, Minic #2, 1950s, 6", w/up, army gr w/wht star & 2068315-S on hood, w/spare wheel & plastic jerrycan, NMIB, A........$115.00

MP Military Jeep, K, 1950s, 7½", red w/yel seats, wht top w/stenciling, BRT, EX, A $35.00
M38 (Turn-O-Matic) Military Jeep (1960s), Nomura, b/o, w/2 figures, EXIB, A $100.00
M38 Radio Jeep (1960s), Nomura, b/o, w/2 figures, phone rings & soldier picks up, NMIB, A.................................. $150.00
No 1 Army Combat Patrol Jeep, Nomura, 13½", b/o, w/2 figures, EXIB, Abox), A $400.00
Radar Jeep, Nomura, 11", b/o, w/driver & rear radar operator, NMIB, A $150.00
Rocket Launcher, Nomura, 8½", friction, army gr, spring-launcher, 2 plastic rockets, EXIB, A...........................$85.00

Searchlight Truck, Tippco, 10", windup with battery-operated light, two composition German soldiers, NM, A, $285.00. (Photo courtesy James D. Julia, Inc.)

Super Control AntiCraft Jeep, Suzuki & Edwards, 9", b/o, w/rear gunner, NMIB, A... $100.00
Tank (M), Nomura, 9", b/o, camo detail, rubber treads, advances w/moving turret, makes sounds, lights blink, NMIB, A $85.00
Tank Carrier w/Net, Toymaster, 1950s, 8", complete, MIB, A..$95.00
Tunderbolt Cap Firing Tank, Japan, 1950s, 6", friction, unused, MIB, A+ box), A...$92.00
USAF Radio Jeep (1960s), Momoya, 9", friction, w/3 figures, NMIB, A...$85.00

Motorcycles

Motorcycliste, Fischer, windup, 7", EXIB, A, $21,275.00. (Photo courtesy James D. Julia, Inc.)

Civilian Motorcycle, Arnold/Germany (US Zone), 7½", w/up, w/driver, NMIB, A... $525.00
Condor Motorcycle w/Civilian Driver, 1950s, 11½", friction, spoke wheels, integral lithoed driver, EX, A $1,440.00

Harley-Davidson, Japan, 1959, 8", friction, EX, A $250.00
Harley-Davidson (Auto Cycle), Nomura, 8½", friction/piston action, litho detail, no driver, GIB, A..................... $230.00
Motorcycle w/Sidecar, Marusan, 9", friction, wht, blk trim, spoke wheels, gr litho sidecar interior, VG, A $275.00
Motorcyclist, Gunthermann, 8", w/up, early bicycle type, spoke wheels, lithoed civilian driver, EX, A $1,345.00
Silver Pigeon Scooter, Bandai, 9½", friction, blk leather seat & BRT, EX $150.00
Traffic Delivery Cycle-Car, Hoge, 10" L, w/up, 3-wheeled, van roof extends over driver, A $4,950.00

Race Cars

Agajanian Racer #98, Yonezawa, 19", w/up, driver in goggles & helmet, BRT, VG+IB, A...................................... $2,760.00
Champion #8 (Cragstan Stock Car) 380 MP, Cragstan/NGS, 12", b/o, NM+IB, A.. $300.00
Champion #8 Midget Racer, Y, 18½", friction, BRT, w/driver, VG, A $1,760.00
Champion Racer #8, ATC, 8½", friction, BRT, w/driver, EX+IB, A $250.00

Champion's Racer #98, 1950s, 18½", VG+, A, $1,780.00. (Photo courtesy James. D. Julia, Inc.)

Electro #21 Midget Racer, Y, 1950s, 10", bl (scarce), w/driver, NMIB.. $4,400.00
Electro #21 Midget Racer, Y, 1950s, 10", red, w/driver, VG+.. $1,375.00
Emmets Racer #7, 1931, 23", orange & yel, VG, A........ $250.00
Ferrari Berlietta 250 LeMans #2, ATC, 11", b/o, marked '24 Heurs Le Mans,' NMIB, A $125.00
Ferrari 813 #2 Racer (1960s), Bandai/Cragstan, 8", friction, MIB, A $400.00
Ford Hot Rod (1930s) #7, Bandai, 8", friction, exposed engine w/ lithoed detail, lithoed open interior, BRT, EX, A $310.00
Gordon Bennet Racer, Gunthermann, early 1900s, 12", w/up, driver, VG, A...$26,450.00
Indianapolis 500 Racer, TN #4247/Sears, 1960s, 15", r/c, unused but not working o/w MIB, A $275.00
Jet Racer, Tanaguchi/Cragstan, 1950s, 12", friction, driver under clear dome, NMIB, A $1,100.00
Jet Racer #7, Masuya, 8", friction, BRT, w/driver, NMIB, A .. $150.00
Jumping Racer, Marusan, 24½", friction, racers marked 'Jaguar' & 'Tiger,' w/cb ramp, NM+IB, A.............................. $550.00
Lotus Formula Racing Car, Daishin, 16", b/o, vinyl-headed driver, lighted engine w/moving pistons, NM+IB, A $175.00
Lotus Hi-Speed Racer, Okuma, 12", b/o, MIB, A $100.00
Lotus 49 Ford F-1 Racer, Asahi/Junior, 16", b/o, blinking engine, NM+IB, A $370.00
Lotus 49B Formula Racing Car, J Toy, 11", lighted vibrating engine, vinyl-headed driver, NMIB, A $150.00
MG Midget Overland Race Winner 7 (1955), Bandai, 8", EX+, A $225.00
MGA 1600 Race Car (1960s), Bandai, 8", friction, EX+IB, A $350.00
Porsche 914 (1960s #55 2-Door Rally Car), Daiya, b/o, NM+IB, A $275.00
Racer #7, Kosuge, 7", w/up, w/driver, 7", EX, A............. $600.00
Racer #8, Lupor, 12", w/up, red, gr & yel w/blk disk wheels, lithoed driver, EX+, A $275.00
Red Devil Racer, 8", w/up, EXIB, A $100.00
Rocket Racer #54, Bandai, 7", friction, BRT, w/driver, G+, A..$75.00
Shooting Star Jet Racer #9, Ichimura, 9", friction, NMIB, A ..$750.00
Silver Dash Racer, Buffalo Toys, 12", pull mechanism, w/2 figures, VG, A $390.00
Speed Demon 385 HP #11 Stock Car (1960s Jaguar XKE), Bandai/NGS, 8", friction, EX+IB, A $250.00
Stock Race Car #15 375 HP, 1960s, 13", red, wht & bl, various advertising logos, NM, A..$60.00

Trucks and Vans

Assorted 4-in-1 Trailers Set, SSS, friction, MIB, A........ $100.00
Auto Transport w/4 Cars, Linemar, 11½", friction, 2 rear loading ramps, NMIB, A $150.00
Black Diamond Coal Co, Courtland, w/up, tin & plastic, hand-op scissor dump action, NM+IB, A......................... $300.00
Chad Valley Co LDT Delivery Box Truck, 10", w/up, roof advertises toy maker's products, EX, A............................. $770.00
Chevrolet Truck, Asahi, 7", friction, low bed, red, 2-tone bl & gr, BRT, NM+ (VG box), A $125.00
Chevy Pick-Up Truck (1967 El Camino), Japan, 1960s, 8", friction, MIB, A $25.00
Corvair AAA Highway Truck, Tatsuya, 8", friction, wht, BRT w/wht-walls, 8", EXIB, A.. $160.00
Corvair Panel Truck, Tatsuya, 8", friction, NM+IB, A ... $250.00
Corvair Pickup Truck, Tatsuya, 8", friction, NM+IB, A ... $125.00
Corvair Sports Wagon, Tatsuya, 8", friction, NM+IB, A .. $125.00

Courtland Dump Truck, 1940s, 12", windup, EX, A, $75.00. (Photo courtesy serioustoyz.com)

Courtland Express & Hauling Stake Truck, #900, 1946, 8½", plastic wheels, driver lithoed in window, EX, A $55.00

Courtland Moving Truck #1300, Courtland, 8½", w/up, yel, plastic wheels, lithoed driver, NMIB, A $85.00
Disneyland Van Trailer, Linemar, friction, 12", trailer lithoed w/ Disney characters, EXIB, A $920.00
Dugan's (Bakery) Delivery Truck, HTC, 7", friction, wht w/blk hood, bl lettering on sides, BRT, EX, A $200.00
Dump Truck, Daiya, 1950s, 5½", friction, red & wht, BRT, NMIB, A...$30.00
Dump Truck (Heavy Duty), Yonezawa, 15", b/o, top light flashes, dump bed dumps w/sound, NMIB, A $150.00
Dump Truck w/Gravel Loader (ADT), Alps, 12½" truck & 8" H gravel loader, b/o, NM+IB, A................................ $300.00
Dump Truck w/Side Tipper Bed, Courtland, 1940s, 12", w/up, BRT, 6-wheeled, EX, A...$75.00
Farm Truck, Alps, 11", b/o, cow moos, EXIB, A $125.00
Ferris Wheel Truck, Nomura, 8", friction, Ferris wheel w/3 gongolas in truck bed, EX+IB, A.................................. $400.00
Ferris Wheel Truck, Nomura, 8", friction, w/3 gondolas marked 'Mars', 'Earth' & 'Star,' NMIB, A............................ $300.00
Flat Bed Truck 8330, Bandai, 13", friction, EXIB $135.00
Ford Motor Transport (Turbine Experimental Semi), Meiwa Kogyo, 18" overall, scarce, EX, A............................ $975.00
Fork Truck No 200, Masudaya, friction, NMIB, A $95.00
Gasoline - Motor Oil Tanker Truck, Courtland, 1940s, 13", w/up, red, wht & bl, EX, A... $150.00

G.B.C. Pickup Truck, Asahi, 7", battery-operated, NMIB, A, $225.00. (Photo courtesy Morphy Auctions)

Jeep Forward Control Truck, Bandai, 8", friction, NM+IB, A...$125.00
Jeep Stake Truck (1960s), Bandai, 7½", friction, NMIB, A .. $125.00
JYT Trucking Co Dump Truck, Yonezawa, 1950s, 14", friction, EX+, A $125.00
Livestock Tailer (Truck), Yamaichi, 1950s, 7", friction, red & wht, BRT, NMIB, A $40.00
Merry Go-Round Truck, Nomura, 8", friction, merry-go-round on truck bed w/3 horses & riders, NMIB, A $350.00
Mickey's Mousemovers Moving Van, Linemar, 1950s, 12½", friction, VG+, A $265.00
Mobil Gas Tank Car, Daiya, 1950s, 6", friction, unused, MIB, A.. $160.00
Mobilgas Tanker, Cragstan/Yonezawa, 10", friction, Ford cab, opening side door, NMIB, A $425.00
Modern Bakery Delivery Panel Truck, Courtland, 7", w/up, lithoed driver, EX+IB, A $200.00
NAR Television Truck, Japan, b/o, 11" L, EX, A............ $650.00
Oven-Fresh Bread & Cake Truck, 1950s, 6", canopy over open bench seat, advertising on sides, NM, A....................$70.00
REA Air Express Corvair Van, Tatsuya, 8", friction, gr, silver top, BRT w/wht-walls, NM+IB, A $150.00
Stake Truck, Bing, 8", w/up, open bench seat, simulated wood bed, MSW, blk & yel w/red trim, EX, A $660.00
Stake Truck, Gama, w/up w/crank-op rear gate, NM+, A.. $175.00
Stake Truck, Linemar, 15", friction, b/o headlights, gr, yel trim, NM+IB, A $200.00
Stake Truck (1954 GMC), Yonezawa, 10", friction, lithoed interioir & bed, EX, A $225.00
Studebaker Mogilgas Tank/Condor Stake Truck, Marusan, 1950s, 14", friction, has interchangable tank & stake bed, EX+, A $375.00
US Mail, AC Gilbert, w/up, roof extends over open seat w/driver, MSW, blk & yel w/red MSW, VG, A....................... $510.00
Volkswagen Micro Bus Ice-Cream Truck, Taiyo, 9", friction, wht, bl trim, NM, A... $225.00

Sets

Drive Set, Masudaya, friction, Ford Fairlane convertible w/gas pump & 6 street signs in English/Japanese, EX+IB, A............$325.00
Fleet of 3 Haulers Set, Linemar, 1950s, Allied Van Lines/Sinclair/Diamond T Pacific Log Co, 15" ea, friction, NMIB, A $750.00
Hi Way Transport Set, Harusame, set of 3 trucks, 15" ea, friction, NM.. $275.00
Lindstrom's Trailer Trucks Set, w/up, w/6 tractor cabs & 8 trailers, EX+IB, A..$8,800.00
Military Set (10-pc), Hayashi, from 6" helicopter to 11" transport, friction, NMIB, A $300.00

Miscellaneous

Gibbs Service Station, EX, A, $175.00.
(Photo courtesy Morphy Auctions)

Auto-Laundry, crank-op car wash, 5½x14" L, EX..............$85.00
Auto-Road 1001, MS/Germany (US Zone), electric, steering wheel navigates car around 'town,' 15x18", EXIB, A $225.00
Distler Electromatic Power Filling Station w/1955 Studebaker Coupe, VGIB, A.. $200.00
Garage w/2 Autos, TCO, w/up, litho tin, 1 car w/electric spotlight & 1 w/headlights, disk wheels, dbl doors, EX, A....$2,970.00
Gibbs Gas Station, paper litho on tin, pump island under portico, simulated tile roof, 8x15" L, VG, A $240.00
Service Station w/Car, Ichimura, 4" L station, 3" friction car, EX+ (EX car), A... $150.00
Toygas Station, Hurco, tin & cb, EX, A......................... $500.00

Tonka

Since the mid-'40s, the Tonka Company (Minnesota) has produced an extensive variety of high-quality painted metal trucks, heavy equipment, tractors, and vans.

Air Force Ambulance, #402, 1965-66, 14", NM............ $100.00
Airport Service Set, #2100, 1962, NM $250.00
Auto Transport, #840, 1962, EX................................... $100.00
Backhoe Truck, #422, 1960s, 17", NM.............................$75.00
Big Mike Hydraulic Dump Truck w/Snow Plow, #45, 1950s, 17", EX+ $350.00
Bulldozer, #10, 1960, 9", EX $100.00
Camper Pickup, #530, 1960s, NM..................................$85.00

Cement Mixer, Mini-Tonka #77, 1963, NMIB, A, $135.00. (Photo courtesy serioustoyz.com)

Cement Truck, #620, 1960s, EX.................................... $100.00
Crater Crawler, #2546, 1970, 12" L, NM..........................$20.00
Dozer Packer, #524, 1960s, EX $225.00
Dump Truck, #180, 1949, 12", EXIB $125.00
Dump Truck, #315, 1964, 14", NMIB $75.00
Dump Truck, #2315, 1970, 14", NMIB $25.00
Fire Aerial Ladder Truck, #700, 1950s, 33" L, EX........... $200.00
Horse Van, #2430, 1960s-70, NM $35.00
Hydraulic Dump Truck, #520, 1962, EX+ $100.00
Hydraulic Dump Truck, #3902, 1970s, Mighty Tonka, 19", EX+ . $100.00
Jeep Pumper, #425, 1960s, 11", EX................................ $125.00
Jeepster Convertible Sedan, #2245, 1969, 13", NM $25.00
Life Guard Jeep, #2309, 1969, 10", complete w/rescue raft on top, EX $25.00
Livestock Hauler, #500, 1950s, 22", EX $150.00
Loadmaster, #4002, 1970s, Mighty Tonka, NM $25.00
Lumber Truck, #850-6, 1950s, 19", EX.......................... $150.00
Military Jeep & Box Trailer, #384, 1960s, 20", EX............$65.00
Pickup Truck, #880-5, 1950s, 13", EX $100.00
Power Boom Loader Truck, #115, 1960s, 19", EX........... $325.00
Ramp Hoist Truck, #640, 1960s, 19", VG $150.00
Rescue Squad, #105, 1960s, 14", EX+ $150.00
Road Grader, #12, 1960s, 17", EX+..................................$85.00

Sand Loader, 1960s, NM, $45.00.

Sanitary Truck, #140, 1960s, 20", EX+.......................... $450.00
Sportsman Pickup, #5, 1959, VG $65.00
Stake Truck, #860-5, 1955, 17", VG+ $150.00
State Hi-Way Dept Dump Truck, #980-6, 1950s, 13", EX+ .. $150.00

State Hi-Way Department Steam Shovel Truck, M, $450.00.

Steam Shovel, #100, 1947, 21", EX+ $150.00
Steel Carrier, #145, 1950s, 23", EX $130.00
Tanker, #145, 1960s, 28" L, EX+ $150.00
Thunderbird Express, #34, 1957, 24" L, EX+, A............. $175.00
Tonka Toy Transport Semi, #140, 1940s, 22", VG+ $150.00
Trencher, #534, 1960s, 18", NM+ $100.00
Utility Truck, #3, 1950s, EX+.. $125.00
Volkswagen, #150, 1960s, 9", NM+ $20.00
Wrecker, #18, 1950s-60s, EX+...................................... $100.00
Wrecker, #3915, 1970s, Mighty Tonka, 17", EX+.............$30.00

Tootsietoy

The first diecast Tootsietoys were made by the Samuel Dowst Company in 1906 when they reproduced the Model T Ford in miniature. Dowst merged with Cosmo Manufacturing in 1926 to form the Dowst Manufacturing Company and continued to turn out replicas of the full-scale vehicles in actual use at the time. After another merger in 1961, the company became known as the Stombecker Corporation. Over the years, many types of wheels and hubs were utilized, varying in both style and material. The last all-metal car was made in 1969; recent Tootsietoy mix plastic components with the metal and have soft plastic wheels. Early prewar mint-in-box toys are scarce and now command high prices on today's market.

Auto Transport w/3 cars, 8", NMIB, A........................$1,080.00
Auto Transport w/4 Cars, 10½", EX.............................. $350.00
Buck Rogers 25th Century Destroyer (Sub), #1032, 5", NMIB, A $550.00
Combination Set #9130A, w/fire ladder truck, US Airmail truck, stake truck & auto, 3" ea, NMIB, A.....................$1,840.00
Fire Department Set, #5211, 1940s, 4-pc, EX+ to NM (Fair box), A $275.00
Greyhound Bus, #3571, 1948, 6", EX, A...........................$20.00
Greyhound Deluxe Bus, #1045, 1937, 6", NM, A.......... $145.00
Greyhound Scenicruiser Bus, 1955, 7", M, A $40.00
Insurance Patrol Fire Engine, #237, 1930s, 3", NM, A......$22.00
Interchangable Truck, w/tank, stake & dump trailers, 3x4", NMIB, A... $800.00
Little Toughs Ladder Truck, #1249, 1971, 4", MOC, A $22.00
Mack Fire Truck 4 Series, #1040, 1937, 5½", NM, A $20.00
Motors Set, 8 vehicles & 1 airplane, EX+IB, A............. $410.00

Oil Tanker, #669, 1954, MIB, A, $160.00.
(Photo courtesy serioustoyz.com)

Pick-Up Truck, 1930s, WRT rubber tires, 5¾", early rpnt o/w NM, A...$28.00
Playtime Set #05050, plane, wrecker & 3 autos, VG+IB, A.. $1,650.00
Road Construction Assortment Set, 2 trucks, grader & dozer, w/6 signs, EXIB, A... $275.00
Set #5031, 10 vehicles/1 airplane, EXIB, A.................... $800.00
Set #7005, 8 vehicles/2 airplanes, NMIB, A.................. $750.00
Shell Tanker Truck, 1946, orange, 6", EX+, A..................$40.00
Sky Fleet, set of 5 airplanes, 1950s, NMOC $135.00
Tootsietoy Dairy (Milk Trailers), truck pulling 3 tank trailers, yel & wht, 13" overall, VGIB, A $450.00
Tootsietoy Fleet, complete w/12 ships, EXIB, A $390.00
Tootsietoy Funnies, Andy Gump Car 348, 3", NM, A ... $575.00
Tootsietoy Funnies, Keystone Cops Police Patrol, 3", NM, A ...$345.00
Tootsietoy Funnies, Mamie in boat, 3", EX, A................ $200.00
Tootsietoy Funnies, Smitty on Motorcycle w/Sidecar, 3", NM, A...$620.00
Tootsietoy Funnies, Uncle Walt in open car, 3", EX, A... $400.00

Tootsietoy Funnies Set, six vehicles with comic character drivers, EXIB, A, $10,080.00. (Photo courtesy Morphy Auctions)

Tootsietoy Service Island, Car Lift w/car, red, EX, A...... $130.00

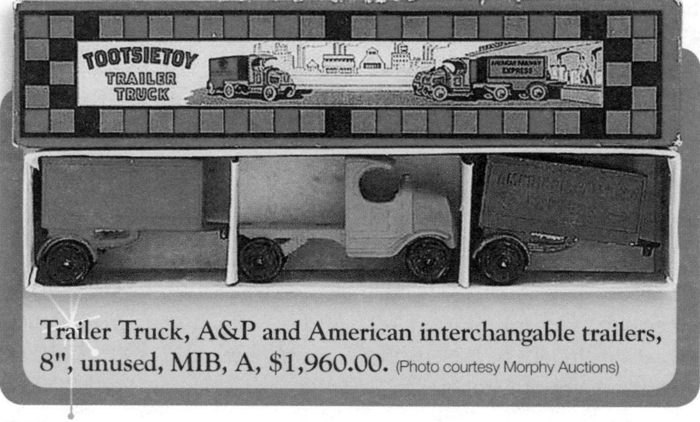

Trailer Truck, A&P and American interchangable trailers, 8", unused, MIB, A, $1,960.00. (Photo courtesy Morphy Auctions)

Wrigley Spearmint Chewing Gum Truck, yel, 4½", G, A..$50.00

Trains

Some of the earliest trains (from ca 1860) were made of tin or cast iron, smaller versions of the full-scale steam-powered trains that transversed America from the East to the West. Most were made to simply be pushed or pulled along, though some had clockwork motors. Electric trains were produced as early as the late nineteenth century. Three of the largest manufacturers were Lionel, Ives, and American Flyer.

Lionel trains have been made since 1900. Until 1915 they produced only standard gauge models (measuring 2½" between the rails). The smaller O gauge (1¼") they introduced at that time proved to be highly successful, and the company grew until by 1955 it had become the largest producer of toys in the world. Until discontinued in 1940, standard gauge trains were produced on a limited scale, but O and 027 gauge models dominated the market. Production dwindled and nearly stopped in the mid-1960s, but the company was purchased by General Mills in 1969, and they continue to produce a very limited number of trains today.

The Ives company had been a major producer of toys since 1896. They were the first to initiate manufacture of the O gauge train and at first used only clockwork motors to propel them. Their first electric trains (in both O and #1 gauge) were made in 1910, but because electricity was not yet a common commodity in many areas, clockwork production continued for several years. By 1920, #1 gauge was phased out in favor of standard gauge. The company continued to prosper until the late 1920s when it floundered and was bought jointly by American Flyer and Lionel. American Flyer soon turned their interest over to Lionel, who continued to make Ives trains until 1933.

The American Flyer company had produced trains for several years, but it wasn't until it was bought by AC Gilbert in 1937 that it became successful enough to be considered a competitor of Lionel. They're best noted for their conversion from the standard (wide gauge) three-rail system to the two-rail S gauge (⅞") and the high-quality locomotives, passenger, and freight cars they produced in the 1950s. Interest in toy trains waned during the space-age decade of the 1960s. As a result, sales declined, and in 1966 the company was purchased by Lionel. Today both American Flyer and Lionel trains are being made from the original dies by Lionel Trains Inc., privately owned.

For more information we recommend *Collecting Toy Trains, An Identification and Value Guide*, by Richard O'Brien.

See also Buddy L (for that company's Outdoor Railroad); Cast Iron, Trains; Paper-Lithographed Toys; Pull and Push Toys.

American Flyer

Accessory, barn, #164, red w/blk roof, inset windows, EX, A...$250.00
Accessory, Central Station, #97, VG $230.00
Accessory, freight & passenger station w/crane, #612, EX....$200.00
Accessory, freight station, #91 or #95, EX, ea $200.00

Accessory, station figure set #578, S gauge, complete, VG, $200.00. (Photo courtesy Stout Auctions)

Accessory, Switch Tower, #108, EX+, A $925.00
Accessory, Switch Tower, #108, G, A $180.00
Accessory, Talking Station #799, S gauge, complete, VGIB, A $400.00
Accessory, Trainorama #790, scenic cb background pc for S gauge, complete, VGIB, A $180.00
Accessory, Union Station #110, prewar, VG, A $3,600.00
Accessory, Water Tower #23772, EX, A.......................... $150.00
Boxcar, 24106, MKT, VG $550.00
Boxcar, 24409, Northern Pacific, EX+IB $1,250.00
Caboose, 484, 10th Anniversary, NM............................. $100.00
Caboose, 4011, yel & brn, VGIB $275.00

Car, Golden State Wide Lines Coach, VG+, $500.00. (Photo courtesy Stout Auctions)

Flatcar w/2 'American Flyer' trailers, 24536, Monon, EX...$1,300.00

Flying Colonial Set #4686, standard gauge, blue, EX, A, $4,140.00. (Photo courtesy James D. Julia, Inc.)

Hopper, Western Maryland 24219, S gauge, NM, A $80.00
Hopper, 632, Lehigh, gray, EX..$40.00
Hopper, 4006, red, EXIB.. $450.00
Loco, 499, New Haven EP-5, EX $375.00
Loco, 3020, gr w/yel-trimmed windows, VG, A............. $130.00
Loco & Tender, early w/up loco w/cow catcher & 328 tender, VG & EX, A $900.00
Loco & Tender, 302A, EX $175.00
Loco & Tender, 332, DC Northern, G.............................. $250.00
Loco & Tender, 336, Union Pacific steam engine, VG, A. $275.00
Loco & Tender, 343, VG $350.00

Locomotive and Tender, 4680 steam engine and 4671 tender, prewar, G (with boxes), $450.00. (Photo courtesy Stout Auctions)

Loco & Tender, 4692 Annapolis loco, 4693 tender, EX, A. $1,345.00
Loco & Tender, 4694 Golden State Tender, VG $400.00
Loco & Tender, 4696, prewar, rstr $1,100.00
Loco & Tender, 21166 4-4-0 Burlington, M $100.00
Lumber Loader, 751, VGIB $175.00
Piggy Back Unloader & Car 23830, complete, unused, NMIB, A... $120.00
Tank Car, 910, Gilbert Chemicals, EXIB $325.00
Tank Car, 24309, Gulf, EX $75.00
Track Maintenance Car 23743, yel w/key and worker, VG, A.. $70.00

American Flyer Sets

Burlington Zephyr, loco 9900 & 4 cars, litho tin, silver & blk, VG $225.00
Butcher Bros Special #F3222, 3-pc complete w/track, O gauge, VGIB, A $325.00
Chicago Passenger, loco, tender & 2 coaches, prewar, G, A .. $2,100.00
Comet, loco & 3 cars, VG $450.00
Empire Express, #700, O gauge, w/up, prewar, complete w/tracks, EX+IB, A $525.00
Empire Express, 3-pc, EX, A $350.00
Freight Set, loco & tender 420, 2 boxcars, gondola, searchlight car & caboose, G to VG (w/boxes), A $270.00
Golden State, loco 3115 & 3 cars, VGIB....................... $575.00
Hamiltonian Passenger, loco 4678, baggage car 4341, Pullman 4341 & observation car 4342, NMIB, A.............. $5,600.00
Macy's Electric Speed Special, red, NMIB $1,300.00
Minnie Ha Ha, loco & 3 cars, VG $300.00
Passenger, unnumbered, loco (w/up bell), tender, observation car 513, 2 coaches 515, complete w/track, prewar, VGIB, A... $275.00
Pocahontas, 4-pc, standard gauge, EX, A $3,335.00
President Special, loco 4687, United States Mail car, West Point Pullman & Annapolis observation car, NM, A $2,520.00
Reliable Freight, #30705, w/loco & 3 cars, EXIB $150.00
Steel Mogul Freight, #1349, loco 3198, tender, flatbed w/lumber 3216, gondola 3207, boxcar 3208, caboose 3211, VGIB $675.00
Warrior, loco w/tender 4693, Hancock combine 4380, coach 4381, observation car 4382, VG.......................... $4,600.00

Lionel

Accessory, Billboard Set, #310, EXIB............................... $20.00

Accessory, Control Tower #192, NMIB, A, $475.00. (Photo courtesy Stout Auctions)

Accessory, Crossing Signal, #87, EX, A $90.00
Accessory, High Tension Line Standard, #92, EXIB, A.. $225.00

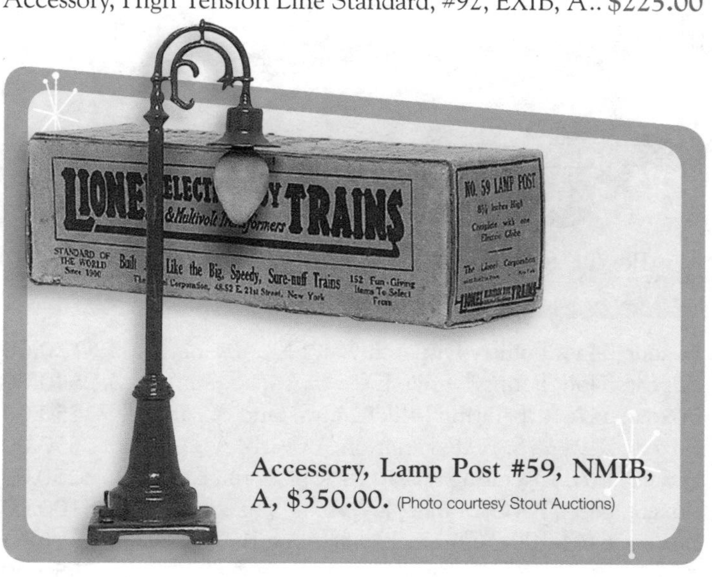

Accessory, Lamp Post #59, NMIB, A, $350.00. (Photo courtesy Stout Auctions)

Accessory, Lamp Post, #61, prewar, VG+IB, A.............. $200.00
Accessory, Platform w/Truck & Trailer, #461, VGIB, A. $120.00
Accessory, Power Station, #435, VG, A......................... $250.00
Accessory, Signal, #154, EXIB.. $35.00
Accessory, Signal, #69, VG $55.00
Accessory, Signal, #69, VG+IB, A $80.00
Accessory, Signal Bridge, #440, NMIB, A $700.00
Accessory, Signal Tower, #438, G, A $300.00

Accessory, Station, #114 (Illuminated), VGIB, A, $3,200.00. (Photo courtesy Stout Auctions)

Accessory, Station, #121, EX (worn box), A $180.00
Accessory, Station, #127, tin, G, A.................................. $60.00
Accessory, Switch Tower, #437, VG, A $500.00
Accessory, Transformer, #1033, EX $65.00
Accessory, Transformer, #1073, EX $30.00
Accessory, Transformer, type Z, marble-like base, EX, A.. $1,150.00
Accessory, Trestle, #110, EXIB $22.00
Accessory, villa, #191, VG+, A $250.00
Accessory, Water Tank, #93, VGIB.................................. $55.00
Baggage Car, 2530, EX+, A $140.00
Barrel Car, 3562-75, orange, NMIB, A $180.00
Boxcar, 814, cream w/wht roof, VG $75.00

Boxcar, 814, EXIB, A, $500.00. (Photo courtesy Stout Auctions)

Boxcar, 3434, Poultry Dispatch Car, EX $120.00
Boxcar, 3458, Pennsylvania, EX $40.00
Boxcar, 3472, Operating Milk Car, w/stand & cans, EX $50.00
Boxcar, 3494-275, BAR variation, VG+IB, A $50.00
Boxcar, 3672, Operating Bosco Car w/platform, EXIB, A $250.00
Boxcar, 6454, NYC, orange, EX, A $100.00
Boxcar, 6464-100, Western Pacific, type IIa body, orange, VGIB, A $550.00
Boxcar, 6464-250, Western Pacific w/IV body, gold door commemorates the Baltimore MD 1967 TCA convention, NM+, A $250.00
Boxcar, 6464-325, Baltimore & Ohio Sentinel, EX+, A $350.00
Boxcar, 6464-400, Baltimore & Ohio Type IIb, EXIB, A $90.00
Boxcar, 9205, Norfolk & Western, EXIB $20.00
Boxcar, 9413, Napierville Junction, MIB $20.00
Caboose, 2472, Pennsylvania, EX $30.00
Caboose, 4357, EX, A $225.00
Caboose, 6517-60, TCA, bay window, MIB, A $475.00

Caboose, 6557, VG, A, $140.00. (Photo courtesy Stout Auctions)

Caboose, 6571, Erie C301, bay window, NM, A $400.00

Coal Car, 816, scarce dark red color, VG+, A, $425.00. (Photo courtesy Stout Auctions)

Dining Car, 7203, Norfolk & Western, MIB, A $90.00
Dome Car, 2412, Santa Fe, VG+, A $60.00
Flatcar, 6414, auto loader w/4 autos, VG $55.00
Flatcar, 6500, w/orig Beech Bonanza airplane, NMIB $425.00
Flatcar, 6531, w/Express Mail trailers, EXIB $25.00
Flatcar, 6809, w/2 USMC Trucks, G $75.00
Flatcar, 6817, w/earth scraper, EX+IB, A $625.00
Flatcar, 9157, C&O, w/construction kit, EXIB $59.00
Flatcar, 9351, auto carrier, EXIB $29.00
Flatcar, 16371, Burlington I-Beam, EXIB $39.00
F3B, 8059, Pennsylvania, gr, MIB $250.00
F3B, 8062, Burlington, chrome, unused, NMIB $350.00
Gondola, 6142, gr, EX $8.00
Gondola, 17404, EXIB $25.00
Hopper, 784, LRRC, 1984, MIB $45.00
Hopper, 6446, N&W, unused, NM+ $550.00
Hopper, 6446-60, Lehigh Valley, EXIB, A $350.00
Hopper, 9338, Pennsylvania Power & Light, VGIB $75.00
Loco, 56, M&ST L Mine Transport, G $265.00
Loco, 235, plastic, scarce, EX $165.00
Loco, 2328, Burlington GP7 Diesel, G+ $180.00
Loco, 2332, Pennsylvania GG1, gr, VG+, A $400.00
Loco, 2338, Milwaukee Road, blk & orange, EX+IB, A $1,000.00
Loco, 2350, New Haven Electric, blk, orange & wht, VGIB, A $1,050.00

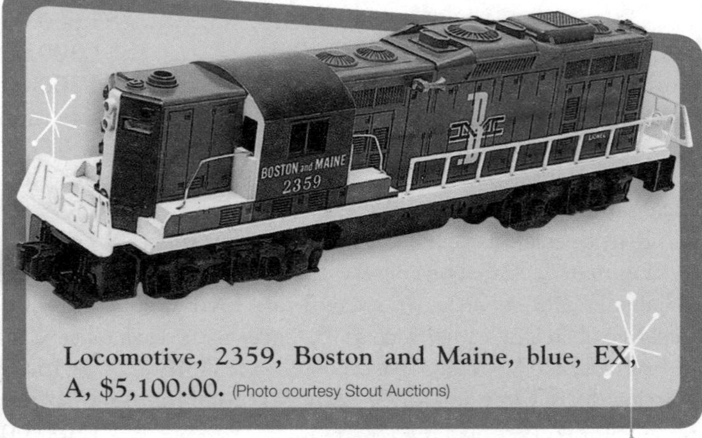

Locomotive, 2359, Boston and Maine, blue, EX, A, $5,100.00. (Photo courtesy Stout Auctions)

Loco, 8056, Chicago North Western Train Master Diesel, NMIB, A $200.00
Loco, 8300, Pennsylvania Mint Series GG1, MIB, A $190.00
Loco, 8376, Union Pacific SD40 Diesel, unused, NMIB $130.00
Loco, 8687, Jersey Central Train Master Diesel, MIB, A $170.00
Loco, 8850, Penn Central GG1, MIB, A $200.00
Loco, 8872/8873, Santa Fe SD18, MIB $180.00
Loco, 8951, Southern Pacific Train Master Diesel, MIB, A $300.00
Loco, 18303, Amtrak GG1, MIB $300.00
Loco, 18311, Disney EP-5 electic, MIB, A $150.00
Loco, 18818, Railroad Club GP-38 Deisel, 1992 Edition, NM+IB, A $70.00
Loco, 18823, Chicago and Midland SD9 Diesel, MIB, A .. $110.00
Loco, 33000, GP9 GA Railscope, MIB $125.00
Loco & Tender, 225 2-6-2 loco/2235W tender, EX+, A $300.00
Loco & Tender, 225E 2-6-6 loco/2225TX tender, VG+, A .. $200.00
Loco & Tender, 226E 2-6-4 loco/2226WX tender, VG+, A . $425.00
Loco & Tender, 229 2-4-2 loco/2666W tender, EX+, A $250.00

Locomotive and Tender, 238E Pennsylvania steam engine and 238E tender, VG, A, $300.00.
(Photo courtesy Stout Auctions)

Loco & Tender, 671 loco/2671 Pennsylvania, EX, A........ $200.00
Loco & Tender, 681 6-8-6 loco/2046W-50 tender, EXIB......... $195.00
Loco & Tender, 736 Berksire 2-8-4 loco/2671WX tender (sm letter), EXIB, A... $500.00
Loco & Tender, 2020 loco w/TCA 1972 front/2671-1968 TCA tender, VG+, A... $170.00
Loco & Tender, 700E Hudson 5299 loco/5299 tender, Fair, A $750.00
Loco & Tender, 8406, 783 4-6-4 loco/New York Central tender, MIB, A.. $375.00
Loco Set, 205, Missouri Pacific Alco A-A, EX+, A........ $225.00
Loco Set, 8054/8054, Burlington F3 A-A, silver, unused, NM (NM boxes), A $3,250.00
Loco Set, 8357/8358, Pennsylvania GP9, MIB, A.......... $200.00
Loco Set, 8359/8463, B&O GM50 GP7/B&O GP 20 Chessie System, MIB, A $160.00
Loco Set, 8454/8455, Rio Grande GP7, MIB, A $150.00
Loco Set, 8470/8560, C&O Chessie System, NM+IB, A $100.00
Loco Set, 8571/8572, Frisco U36B, NMIB, A $120.00
Loco Set, 8650/8651, Burlington Northern U36B, NMIB, A.....$180.00
Loco Set, 8758/8774, Southern GP7, NMIB, A $160.00
Loco Set, 8759/8760, Erie Lackawanna GP9, MIB, A.... $180.00
Loco Set, 8872/8873, Santa Fe SD18, MIB, A $180.00
Passenger Car, 400, B&O RDC Budd, EX...................... $165.00
Searchlight Car, 6520, w/on-off switch, EX $40.00
Searchlight Car, 16803, LRRC, 1990, MIB $29.00
Switcher, 51, Navy Yard New York, EX+IB, A $160.00
Switcher, 65, Union Pacific NW2, yel w/red trim, NM+, A. $200.00
Switcher, 602, Seaboard NW2, EX+, A......................... $140.00
Switcher, 610, Erie NW2, blk, EX, A............................ $100.00
Switcher, 624, EXIB, A... $350.00
Switcher, 625, Lehigh Valley 44-ton, red & blk, EX+, A...... $275.00
Tank Car, 783, LRRC, 1995, M, G1 ....$25.00
Tank Car, 6315, Gulf, orange, BLT 1-56 under ladders, unused, NMIB, A.. $275.00
Tank Car, 6463, Rocket Fuel, wht w/red lettering, EX, A.....$50.00
Tank Car, 9152, Shell Oil, EXIB $25.00
Tank Car, 9347, TTOS, New York, 1979, EXIB $35.00
Tender, 2426W, Lionel Lines, diecast, EX, A................. $180.00
Trolley Car, 60, EX+IB, A $150.00

Lionel Sets

B&O, 1980s, unused, MIB (sealed), A........................... $150.00
Black Cave Flyer Set, 1982, unused, MIB (sealed), A.......$50.00
Blue Comet, #400, loco 400E, tender 400, Faye coach 420, Westpal coach 421 & Tempel observation car 422, VG, A...$6,720.00
Chesapeake Flyer, 1980s, unused, MIB (sealed)............. $100.00
Commando Assault Train, 1982, unused, MIB (sealed) .. $125.00
Freight, #X533NA, EXIB, A $950.00

Freight, #1186, Cross Country Express, complete, NMIB, A, $225.00.
(Photo courtesy Stout Auctions)

Freight, #1516WS, EXIB (boxes), A.............................. $424.00
Freight, #1562, Sears 1985 Chessie, NMIB, A................ $100.00
Freight, #1586W, w/Santa Fe Alco, EX+IB, A $900.00
Freight, #1629, w/225 Chesapeake & Ohio GP, EX+IB, A $325.00
Freight, #1637W, w/218 Santa Fe AA Alcos, EXIB, A..... $525.00
Freight, #2281, w/2243 Santa Fe F3 AB units, EXIB, A.....$1,400.00
Freight, #2547WS, w/637 steam loco, EX+IB, A............ $275.00
Freight, #400E, loco 400E, tender 400T, crane car 219, gondola 212, searchlight 220 & caboose 217, NM, A........$3,080.00
Freight, #9651, EXIB, A $575.00
Freight, #11500, steam, NMIB, A $150.00
Freight, #11590, EXIB, A $425.00
Freight, #19519, NMIB to MIB, A................................. $400.00
Illinois Central Freight, 1970s, unused, MIB (sealed) $225.00
Land, Sea & Air Marines Set, #1805, NMIB, A..........$2,700.00
LASER Train, 1981, unused, MIB (sealed), A................ $125.00
Milwaukee Special, #1387, MIB, A................................ $140.00
Passenger, #1612, NMIB, A... $225.00
Passenger, loco 408, baggage car 419, parlor car 418, dining car 431, observation car 490, gr, EX, A.......................$3,080.00
Union Pacific, #751E, loco 52E, coach 753, vestibule coach 754, complete w/accessories & track, EXIB (boxes) $1,230.00

Miscellaneous

Beggs, locomotive, live steam, cow catcher, 12", G, A... $500.00
Bing, overhead crane, pnt tin w/corrugated roof, dbl hand-crank, 11x10", G, A...$1,200.00
Bing, platform, pnt metal, center pc w/bench & roof w/8 posts, 2 railed side pcs, gr w/red trim, 10x25" L, G, A $1,650.00
Bing, set, New York Central Lines, 5-pc train w/1-pc oval track, EX+IB, A $385.00

Bing, station, country look w/emb pitched roof & siding, hand-op signal, 12x19" L, VG+, A $1,650.00

Bing, station, pnt emb tin, 2-story w/center passage, w/up bell, candlelit, 10x14", G+, A $550.00

Bing, station, tin w/lithoed windows & door frames, center pass-through flanked by telegraph/telephone windows, 15x8", G $360.00

Bing, tower for Spirit of St Louis set, tin, 10", VG, A $125.00

Boucher, set, Blue Comet, 6-pc w/#2500 American outline 4-6 2 electric loco, VG (rstr), A $17,600.00

Carette, Loco (4-4-0 & Tender), w/up, 15½", VG, A..... $220.00

Carlisle & Finch, Buffalo Ticket Office, paper litho on tin w/ wood frame, pnt tin roof, 5x11" L, G+, A............ $1,870.00

Carlisle and Finch, Electric Railway Trolly, 1 gauge, brass, 19", EX, $5,750.00. (Photo courtesy James D. Julia, Inc.)

Carlisle & Finch, Depot, litho paper on ti w/wood frame, 7x13" L, G, A $3,025.00

Carlisle & Finch, freight set, 0-4-4 loco 131, tender, PRR bl gondola 131, box car 1141, caboose, electric, VG to NM, A.. $2,750.00

Carlisle & Finch, loco 683 & tender, tin & wood, blk w/red & gold trim, VG, A $1,000.00

Dorfan, bell signal, cut-out diamond shape warning signal above bell pole, VG+, A $1,250.00

Dorfan, Freight Set, O gauge, six-piece, G to VG, A, $600.00. (Photo courtesy Stout Auctions)

General Trains, Union Pacific engine & coach, PS, 1930s, 24", G, A $1,230.00

General Trains, Union Pacific Zephyr Set, PS, 4-pc w/12-pc tracks, 1933 give away, VG, A $1,565.00

Gunthermann, loco, litho tin, w/up, blk & red w/gold trim, 1 stack, bell, 2 sets lg/2 sets sm spoke wheels, 11", G, A $275.00

Hafner Overland Flyer, set, Sunshine Special, w/up loco, 5-pc, VG, A $625.00

Hornby, Flying Scotsman Passenger Set, 4-4-2 electric loco 4472, LNER tender, Arcadia & Iolanthe Pullmans, G to VG, A.. $770.00

Hornby, station, litho & pnt tin, lithoed center passage 2 side ramps w/fencing, electric lighting, 16" L, VG, A..... $220.00

Howard, loco, 4-2-0 Steam Profile, electric, 10½", EX, A ..$6,050.00

Ives, passenger set, w/up, loco & tender 17, 2 baggage cars 50, chair car 51, 28" L, G+, A $250.00

Ives, passenger set, w/up, steam loco 11, tender 328, baggage car 50, Brooklyn coach 51, Buffalo coach 52, 24", VG........ $1,100.00

Ives, Power Station #201, standard gauge, VG, A, $525.00. (Photo courtesy Stout Auctions)

Ives, water tower, The Ives Railway Lines on orange tank w/blk 4-legged tower base, VG, A.................................... $140.00

Ives, Yankee set, O guage, 4-pc, w/transformer, 26" L, VGIB, A $330.00

Ives/Dorfan, passenger set, bl steam engine (1134) & 4 passenger cars, contemporary version, EX $950.00

Kibri, station, pnt tin w/glass window panels, 2 removable tower roofs, electric lighting, 15x28", VG+, A $275.00

Marklin, Caboose, PRR 90309, O gauge, prewar, VG, A, $1,200.00. (Photo courtesy Stout Auctions)

Marklin, caboose PRR 90309, w/orig stove, table & bench, VG+, A $3,025.00
Marklin, Central Station, pnt tin, Turkish dome, wide center passage, 13x14", Fair, A $1,000.00
Marklin, coach/baggage combine, Royal Blue Limited, II gauge, hinged roof, VG+, A $4,125.00
Marklin, Electric Tramway, 2-pc, enameled metal, 9" L, EX, A $25,300.00
Marklin, engine house, I gauge, tin, corrugated curved roof, dbl doors, 12x14", VG, A $440.00
Marklin, engine house, O gauge, tin, corrugated curved roof, dbl doors, 9x11", VG, A $440.00
Marklin, freight station, enameled tin, w/tin awning, complete w/accessories, sliding doors, 20x12", VG+, A $23,100.00
Marklin, Grand Central Station, litho tin, 10x15", EX, A... $18,700.00
Marklin, hospital car, II gauge, hinged roof, EX, A...... $8,800.00
Marklin, loco & tender, blk w/red & chrome trim, 15", VG, A $700.00
Marklin, overhead crane, enameled tin, hand-crank, 9x13", VG, A $3,850.00
Marklin, passenger coach PRR, II gauge, hinged roof, VG, A... $4,950.00
Marklin, round house & turn table, 6-track shed w/3 rear opeing dbl doors, 35" W, Fair+, A $220.00
Marklin, roundhouse, O gauge, pnt tin, cream w/gray cross-hatched roof, arched doors & windows, EX, A........ $600.00
Marklin, set, freight, w/up, 4-pc, incomplete, Fair to G . $1,045.00
Marklin, set, Rhienuferbahn, 3-pc, I gauge, ca 1929, 50" overall, EX to NM, A $33,000.00
Marklin, sleeping car, II gauge, hinged roof, G+, A..... $3,025.00
Marklin, snow plow St E V 22, II gauge, EX, A $3,025.00
Marklin, station, Gare, pnt tin, 2 story w/emb removable roof, 9x11", VG, A $225.00
Marklin, station, Gepack, pnt tin, electric w/operating doors, German signage, 7x19", VG+, A $165.00
Marklin, station, lithoed & pnt tin, center passage flanked by awnings over doorways, 2 chimneys, 10x13", VG+, A........ $1,320.00
Marklin, station, pnt tin, w/dining balcony, removable roof & clock tower, 12x27", VG, A $385.00
Marklin, track inspection car w/3 figures, w/up, tin, 9½" L, EX, A $17,600.00
Marklin, train house, 0-gauge, 2 sets of opening dbl doors, arched roof, 'brick' facade, 14x12", EX, A $850.00
Marklin, tunnel, enameled tin w/emb & lithoed archways, 10x10x14" L, VG+, A $135.00
Marx, crossing gate, #438, all metal, EX, G1 .... $15.00
Marx, signal, #464, manual block, EX, G1........ $15.00
Schoenhut, Railroad Station, paper litho tin wood & cb, red roof, 14" W, VG+, A $300.00
Schuco, Disneyland Alweg-Monorail Set, 1959, complete, NM+IB, A $550.00
Smith-Miller, boxcar, AT & SF 63132, orange, blk rubber wheels, 33", VG, A........ $390.00
Tyco, Petticoat Junction HO Scale Electric Train Set, complete, 1966, EX+IB, A $400.00
Tyco, Walt Disney's Santa Fe & Disneyland RR Set, 1955, EX+IB, A $385.00
Voltamp, freight set, steeple-cab loco 2130, hopper 2112, stock car 2114, oil tank 2113, caboose 2110, VG, A ... $10,450.00
Voltamp, interurban trolley, electric, 16½", some rstr, A ... $12,100.00
Voltamp, loco, 0-4-4-0 Suburban, red w/blk roof, electric, 15", some minor rstr, A $6,050.00
Voltamp, trolley, United Electric tandem set, red & wht, 24" overall, some rpnt, A $9,350.00

MTH, Rail King #30-4140 Freight Set, MIB (sealed), A, $275.00. (Photo courtesy Stout Auctions)

Transformers

Made by the Hasbro Company, Transformers were introduced in the United States in 1984. Originally there were 28 figures — 18 cars known as Autobots and 10 Decepticons, evil robots capable of becoming such things as a jet or a handgun. Eventually the line was expanded to more than 200 different models. Some were remakes of earlier Japanese robots that had been produced by Takara in the 1970s. (These can be identified through color differences and in the case of the Diaclone series, the absence of the small driver or pilot figures.)

The story of the Transformers and their epic adventures were told through several different comic books and animated series as well as a highly successful movie. Their popularity was reflected internationally and eventually made its way back to Japan. There the American Transformer animated series was translated into Japanese and soon inspired several parallel series of the toys which were again produced by Takara. These new Transformers were sold in the U.S. until the line was discontinued in 1990.

In 1993, Hasbro reintroduced the line with Transformers: Generation 2. Transformers once again had their own comic book, and the old animated series was brought back in revamped format. In 1996, Hasbro reinvented the series by introducing Beast Wars that change from robot to animal. Now, Transformers has returned to its roots with the Armada series that transforms from robot to vehicle. Sustained interest in them has spawned a number of fan clubs with chapters worldwide.

Because Transformers came in a number of sizes, you'll find a wide range of pricing. Our values are for Transformers that are mint in mint or nearly mint original boxes. One that has been used is worth much less — about 25% to 75%, depending on whether it has all its parts (weapons, instruction book, tech specks, etc.), and what its condition is — whether decals are well applied or if it is worn. A loose Transformer complete and in near-mint condition is worth only about half as much as one mint in the box.

Series 1, 1984

Autobot Car, Bluestreak (Datsun), bl $350.00
Autobot Car, Bluestreak (Datsun), silver $300.00
Autobot Car, Camshaft (car), silver, mail-in $40.00
Autobot Car, Downshaft (car), wht, mail-in $40.00
Autobot Car, Hound (jeep), MIB $250.00
Autobot Car, Jazz (Porsche) $275.00
Autobot Car, Mirage (Indy car) $235.00
Autobot Car, Overdrive (car), red, mail-in $40.00
Autobot Car, Powerdasher #1 (jet), mail-in $20.00
Autobot Car, Powerdasher #2 (car), mail-in $20.00
Autobot Car, Powerdasher #3 (drill), mail-in $40.00
Autobot Car, Prowl (police car) $300.00
Autobot Car, Rachet (ambulance) $150.00
Autobot Car, Sunstreak (Countach), yel $300.00
Autobot Car, Trailbreaker (camper) $150.00
Autobot Car, Wheeljack (Mazzerati) $275.00
Autobot Commander, Optimus Primus w/Roller (semi) ... $175.00
Cassette, Frenzy & Lazerbreak $50.00
Cassette, Ravage & Rumble $50.00
Collector's Case $15.00
Collector's Case, red 3-D version $25.00
Collector's Showcase $15.00
Decepticon Jet, Skywrap, blk $150.00
Decepticon Jet, Starcream, gray $200.00
Decepticon Jet, Thundercracker, bl $150.00
Decepticon Leader, Megatron, Walther P-38 .... $175.00
Minicar, Brawn (jeep) $65.00
Minicar, Bumblebee (VW Bug), red or yel $100.00
Minicar, Cliffjumper (race car), gr, red or yel $75.00
Minicar, Gears (truck) $65.00
Minicar, Huffer (semi), orange cab $55.00
Minicar, Windcharger (Firebird) $60.00

Series 2, 1985

Decepticon, Ramjet, $110.00.

Autobot, Red Alert (fire chief) $150.00
Autobot Air Guardian, Jetfire (F-14 jet) $325.00
Autobot Car, Grapple (crane) $150.00
Autobot Car, Hoist (tow truck) $150.00
Autobot Car, Inferno (fire engine) $150.00
Autobot Car, Skids (Le Car) $225.00
Autobot Car, Smokescreen (Datsun), red, wht & bl $200.00
Autobot Car, Tracks (Corvette) $200.00
Autobot Commander, Blaster (radio/tapeplayer) $125.00
Autobot Scientist, Perceptor (microscope) $100.00
Constructicon, Bonecrusher $60.00
Constructicon, Hook $50.00
Constructicon, Long Haul $50.00
Constructicon, Mixmaster $50.00
Constructicon, Scavenger $50.00
Constructicon, Scrapper $50.00
Decepticon, Dirge $110.00
Decepticon, Thrust, maroon $120.00
Deluxe Insecticon, Chop Chop $70.00
Deluxe Insecticon, Ransack $65.00
Deluxe Vehicle, Roadbuster $175.00
Deluxe Vehicle, Whirl (helicopter) $150.00
Dinobot, Grimlock (Tynnosaurus) $200.00
Dinobot, Slag (Triceratops) $125.00
Dinobot, Sludge (Brontosaurus) $150.00
Dinobot, Snarl (Stegosaurus) $150.00
Insecticon, Bombshell $50.00
Insecticon, Kickback $50.00
Insecticon, Sharpnel $50.00
Insecticon, Venom $50.00

Jumpstarter, Topspin, $45.00.

Minicar, Beachcomber (dune buggy) $30.00
Minicar, Brawn (jeep) $65.00
Minicar, Bumblebee (VW Bug), w/ or w/o minispy $100.00
Minicar, Cliffjumper (race car), red or yel, ea $45.00
Minicar, Cliffjumper (race car), w/minispy $100.00
Minicar, Cosmos (spaceship) $30.00
Minicar, Gears (truck), bl $60.00
Minicar, Gears (truck), w/minispy $75.00
Minicar, Huffer (semi) $50.00
Minicar, Huffer (semi), w/minispy $50.00
Minicar, Powerglide (plane) $35.00
Minicar, Seaspray (hovercraft) $30.00
Minicar, Warpath (tank) $50.00
Minicar, Windcharger (Firebird) $50.00
Minicar, Windcharger (Firebird), w/minispy $75.00
Motorized Autobit Defense Base, Omega Supreme $300.00
Triple Charger, Astrotrain (shuttle/train) $100.00
Triple Charger, Blitzwing (tank/plane) $100.00

Series 3, 1986

Aerialbot, Air Raid	$50.00
Aerialbot, Fireflight	$50.00
Aerialbot, Silverbot	$100.00
Aerialbot, Skydive	$60.00
Autobot Car, Blurr (futuristic car)	$100.00
Autobot Car, Hot Rod (race car)	$200.00
Autobot Car, Kup (pickup truck)	$100.00
Autobot City Commander, Ultra Magnus (car carrier)	$135.00
Battlecharger, Runabout (Trans Am)	$30.00
Battlecharger, Runamuck (Corvette)	$35.00
Combaticon, Blast Off	$60.00
Combaticon, Brawl	$50.00

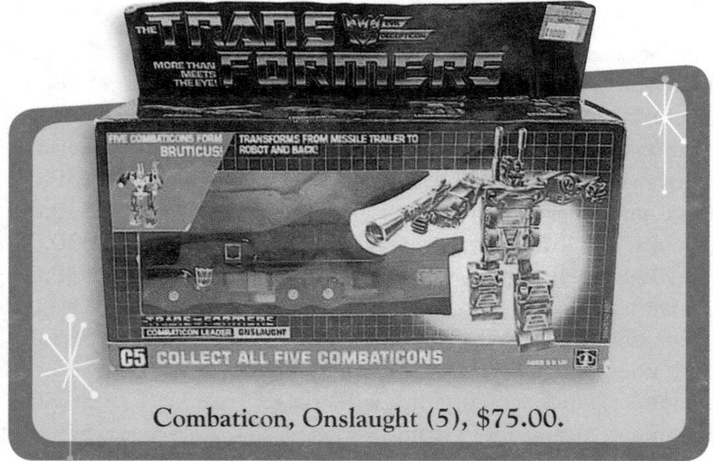

Combaticon, Onslaught (5), $75.00.

Combaticon, Swindle	$50.00
Combaticon, Vortex	$60.00
Decepticon City Commander, Galvatron	$150.00
Heroes, Rodimus Prime (futuristic RV)	$150.00
Heroes, Wreck-Car (futuristic motorcycle)	$100.00
Jet, Cyclous Space Jet	$125.00
Jet, Scrouge (hovercraft)	$125.00
Minicar, Hubcap (race car)	$35.00
Minicar, Outback (jeep)	$50.00
Minicar, Pipes (semi)	$50.00
Minicar, Swerve (truck)	$40.00
Minicar, Tailgate (Firebird)	$40.00
Minicar, Wheelie (futuristic car)	$35.00
Predacon, Gnaw (futuristic shark)	$100.00
Predacon, Headstrong	$75.00
Predacon, Rampage	$85.00
Predacon, Razorclaw	$85.00
Predacon, Tantrum	$85.00
Predocon, Divebomb	$85.00
Stunticon, Breakdown	$50.00
Stunticon, Dead End	$50.00
Stunticon, Drag Strip	$50.00
Stunticon, Motormaster (semi)	$75.00
Stunticon, Wildrider (Ferrari)	$50.00
Triple Charger, Broadside (aircraft carrier/plane)	$75.00
Triple Charger, Octane (tanker truck/jumbo jet)	$100.00
Triple Charger, Sandstorm (dune buggy/helicopter)	$100.00
Triple Charger, Springer (armored car/copter)	$125.00

Series 4, 1987

Clone, Fastlane & Cloudraker (dragster & spaceship)	$65.00
Clone, Pounce & Wingspan (puma & eagle)	$45.00
Double Spy, Punch-Counterpunch (Fiero)	$75.00
Duocon, Battlestap (jeep/copter)	$40.00
Duocon, Flywheels (jet/tank)	$30.00
Headmaster Autobot, Brainstorm w/Arcana (jet)	$100.00
Headmaster Autobot, Chromedome w/Stylor (futuristic car)	$10.00
Headmaster Autobot, Hardhead w/Duros (tank)	$100.00
Headmaster Autobot, Highbrow w/Gort (copter)	$100.00
Headmaster Decepticon, Mindwipe w/Vorath (bat)	$100.00
Headmaster Decepticon, Skullrunner w/Grax (alligator)	$100.00
Headmaster Decepticon, Weirdwolf w/Monzo (wolf)	$100.00
Headmaster Horrorcon, Apeface w/Spasma (jet/ape)	$100.00
Headmaster Horrorcon, Snapdragon w/Krunk (jet/dinosaur)	$100.00
Monsterbot, Doublecross (2-headed dragon)	$75.00
Monsterbot, Grotusque (tiger)	$75.00
Monsterbot, Repugnus (insect)	$75.00
Targetmaster Autobot, Blurr w/Haywire (futuristic car & gun)	$150.00
Targetmaster Autobot, Crosshairs w/Pinpointer (truck & gun)	$100.00
Targetmaster Autobot, Hot Rod & Firebolt (race car & gun)	$300.00
Targetmaster Autobot, Kup & Recoil (pickup truck & gun)	$150.00
Targetmaster Autobot, Pointblank w/Peacemaker (race car w/ gun)	$100.00
Targetmaster Autobot, Sureshot w/Spoilsport (off-road buggy & gun)	$75.00
Targetmaster Decepticon, Misfire w/Aimless (spaceship & gun)	$135.00
Targetmaster Decepticon, Scrouge w/Fracas (hovercraft & gun)	$375.00
Targetmaster Decepticon, Slugslinger w/Caliburts (twin jet & gun)	$100.00
Technobot, Afterburner	$45.00
Technobot, Afterburner, w/decoy	$55.00
Technobot, Lightspeed	$45.00
Technobot, Lightspeed, w/decoy	$50.00
Technobot, Nosecone	$40.00
Technobot, Nosecone, w/decoy	$45.00
Technobot, Scrouge	$40.00
Technobot, Starfe, w/decoy	$55.00
Technobot, Starfe	$50.00
Terrocon, Blot	$40.00
Terrocon, Blot (moster), w/decoy	$50.00
Terrocon, Cutthroat (Vulture), w/decoy	$50.00
Terrocon, Cutthroat	$40.00
Terrocon, Hun-gr	$40.00
Terrocon, Rippersapper, w/decoy	$50.00
Terrocon, Ripperspapper	$40.00
Terrocon, Sinnertwin	$40.00
Terrocon, Sinnertwin, w/decoy	$50.00
Throttlebot, Chase (Ferrari)	$35.00
Throttlebot, Chase (Ferrari), w/decoy	$40.00
Throttlebot, Freeway (Corvette)	$35.00
Throttlebot, Freeway (Corvette), w/decoy	$40.00
Throttlebot, Goldbug (VW bug)	$50.00
Throttlebot, Rollbar (jeep)	$20.00
Throttlebot, Rollbar (jeep), w/decoy	$35.00

Throttlebot, Searchlight (race car) $30.00
Throttlebot, Shearchlight (race car), w/decoy..................$35.00
Throttlebot, Wideload (dump truck) $30.00
Throttlebot, Wideload (dump truck), w/decoy.................$35.00

SERIES 5, 1988

Firecon, Cindersaur (dinosaur)..$35.00
Firecon, Flamefeather (monster bird)..............................$35.00
Firecon, Sparkstalker (monster) $45.00
Headmaster Autobot, Hosehead w/Lug (fire engine).........$85.00
Headmaster Autobot, Nightbeat w/Muzzle (race car) $85.00
Headmaster Autobot, Siren w/Quig (fire chief car)...........$85.00
Headmaster Decepticon, Fangry w/Brisko (winged wolf) ..$85.00
Headmaster Decepticon, Horri-Bull w/Kreb (bull)...........$85.00
Headmaster Decepticon, Squeezeplay w/Lokos (crab).......$85.00
Powermaster Autobot, Getaway w/Rev (Mr2)..................$75.00
Powermaster Autobot, Joyride w/Hotwire (off-road buggy) ..$75.00
Powermaster Autobot, Slapdash w/Lube (Indy car)...........$75.00
Powermaster Autobot Leader, Optimus Prime w/HiQ (semi) .$200.00
Pretender, Bomb-burst (spaceship), w/shell $65.00
Pretender, Cloudburst (jet), w/shell $65.00
Pretender, Finback (sea skimmer), w/shell.........................$65.00
Pretender, Groundbreaker (race car), w/shell $150.00
Pretender, Iguanus (motorcycle), w/shell $65.00
Pretender, Landmine (race car), w/shell............................$65.00
Pretender, Skullgrin (tank), w/shell $65.00
Pretender, Sky High (jet), w/shell $75.00
Pretender, Submarauder (submarine), w/shell...................$75.00
Pretender, Waverider (submarine), w/shell $65.00
Pretender Beast, Carnivac (wolf), w/shell..........................$65.00
Pretender Beast, Catilla (sabertooth tiger), w/shell $65.00
Pretender Beast, Chainclaw (bear), w/shell $65.00
Pretender Beast, Snarler (boar), w/shell............................$65.00
Pretender Vehicle, Gunrunner (jet) w/vehicle shell, red...$65.00
Pretender Vehicle, Roadgrabber (jet) w/vehicle shell, purple $85.00
Seacon, Nautilator...$60.00
Seacon, Overbite $60.00
Seacon, Seawing $50.00
Seacon, Skalor $60.00
Seacon, Tenakil..$60.00
Sparkbot, Fizzle (off-road buggy) $30.00
Sparkbot, Guzzle (tank)..$30.00
Sparkbot, Sizzle (funny car)...$35.00
Targetmaster Autobot, Landfill w/Flintlock & Silencer (dump truck & 2 guns)..$65.00
Targetmaster Autobot, Quickmix w/Boomer & Ricochet (cemet mixer & 2 guns)..$65.00
Targetmaster Autobot, Scoop w/Tracer & Holepunch (front-end loader & 2 guns) $65.00
Targetmaster Decepitcon, Needlenose w/Sunbeam & Zigzag (jet & 2 guns) $100.00
Targetmaster Decepticon, Spinster & Singe & Hairsplitter (heli-copter & 2 guns)..$85.00
Tiggerbot, Backstreet (race car)...$30.00
Tiggerbot, Override (motorcycle)..$30.00
Triggercon, Crankcase (jeep)...$30.00
Triggercon, Rucus (dune buggy) $35.00
Triggercon, Windsweeper (B-1 bomber) $35.00

SERIES 6, 1989

Legends (K-Mart Exclusive), Bumblebee (VW bug) $35.00
Legends (K-Mart Exclusive), Grimlock (dinosaur)............$35.00
Legends (K-Mart Exclusive), Jazz (Porsche) $35.00
Legends (K-Mart Exclusive), Starscream (jet)...................$40.00
Mega Pretender, Crossblades (copter w/shell)................ $115.00
Mega Pretender, Thunderwing (jet w/shell) $165.00
Mega Pretender, Vroom (dragster w/shell)...................... $150.00
Micromaster Base, Skyhopper w/Micromaster (copter & F-15)..$55.00
Micromaster Base, Skystalker (Space Shuttle Base & Micromaster Porsche)..$55.00
Micromaster Patrol, Battle Patrol Series, 4 different, ea....$30.00
Micromaster Patrol, Off-Road Series, 4 different, ea $30.00
Micromaster Patrol, Sports Car Patrol Series, 4 different, ea... $30.00
Micromaster Station, Greasepit, pickup w/gas station.......$30.00
Micromaster Station, Ironworks (semi w/construction site) ..$30.00
Micromaster Transport, Flattop (aircraft carrier)..............$30.00
Micromaster Transport, Overload (car carrier)..................$30.00
Micromaster Transport, Roughstuff (military transport)....$30.00
Pretender, Bludgeon (tank), w/shell................................ $150.00
Pretender, Doubleheader (twin jet), w/shell $85.00
Pretender, Longtooth (hovercraft), w/shell.......................$85.00
Pretender, Pincher (scorpion), w/shell $85.00
Pretender, Stranglehold (rhino), w/shell...........................$75.00
Pretender Monster, Icepick..$12.00
Pretender Monster, Wildfly..$65.00
Ultra Pretender, Roadblock (tank w/figure & vehicle)......$85.00
Ultra Pretender, Skyhammer (race car w/figure & vehicle) ..$65.00

SERIES 7, 1990

Action Masters, Blaster With Flight Pack, $30.00.

Action Masters, Devastator $30.00
Action Masters, Grimlock $30.00
Action Masters, Gutcruncher...$50.00
Action Masters, Inferno...$30.00

Action Masters, Over-Run $40.00
Action Masters, Prowl $60.00
Action Masters, Rad $15.00
Action Masters, Shockwave $30.00
Action Masters, Skyfall $30.00
Action Masters, Soundwave $30.00
Action Masters, Wheeljack $70.00
Micromaster Patrol, Air Patrol: Thread Bolt, Eagle Eye, Sky High & Blaze Master $30.00
Micromaster Patrol, Hot Rod Patrol: Big Daddy Trip-Up, Greaser & Hubs....................................$40.00
Micromaster Patrol, Military Patrol: Bombshock, Tracer, Dropshot 7 Growl $45.00
Micromaster Patrol, Race Track Patrol: Barricade, Roller Force, Ground Hog Motorhead....................................$15.00

Beast Wars

Maximal, Airrazor, M $25.00
Maximal, Blackarachina, 1996, MOC $85.00
Maximal, Cheeter, MOC....................................$18.00
Maximal, Depth Charge, MIB....................................$20.00
Maximal, Optimus Primal (Gorilla), MIB $110.00
Maximal, Polar Claw, 1995, MIB $15.00
Maximal, Rattrap, MOC $100.00
Predacon, Dinobot, 1995, MOC $110.00
Predacon, Inferno, 1996, MIB $35.00
Predacon, Megatron (Dragon), Transmetal II, MIB..........$20.00
Predacon, Megatron (T-Rex), MIB $110.00
Predacon, Scorponok, dk purple/bl, MIB (Japanese) $85.00
Predacon, Shokaract, BotCon 2000 exclusive, MIB..........$70.00
Predacon, Terroraur, MOC....................................$90.00
Predacon, Tripedacus, w/instructions, loose, M $60.00
Predacon, Waspinator, rare, MOC $110.00

Generation 2, Series 1, 1992 – 1993

Autobot Car, Inferno (fire truck) $30.00
Autobot Car, Jazz (Porsche) $35.00
Autobot Leader, Optimus Prime w/Roller (semi w/electronic sound effect box) $150.00
Autobot Minicar, Bumble (VW bug), metallic.................$30.00
Autobot Minicar, Hubcap, metallic $20.00
Autobot Minicar, Seaspray (hovercraft), metallic $15.00
Autobot Obliterator (Europe only), Spark........................$45.00
Color Change Transformer, Deluge....................................$20.00
Color Change Transformer, Gobots $20.00
Constructicon, Bonecrusher, orange $12.00
Constructicon, Bonecrusher, yel....................................$10.00
Constructicon, Long Haul, orange $12.00
Constructicon, Long Haul, yel $10.00
Constructicon, Scrapper, orange $12.00
Constructicon, Scrapper, yel....................................$10.00
Decepticon, Mixmaster, MOC $15.00
Decepticon Jet, Starscream (jet w/electronic light & sound effect box), gray $30.00
Decepticon Leader, Megatron (tank w/electonic sound-effect treads) $45.00

Decepticon Obliterators (Europe Only), Colossus, $75.00.

Dinobot, Grimlock (Tyrannosaurus), bl....................................$25.00
Dinobot, Grimlock (Tyrannosaurus), turq $90.00
Dinobot, Snarl (Stegosaurus), gray or bl, ea.......................$50.00
Small Autobot Car, Skram $15.00
Small Autobot Car, Turbofire $15.00
Small Decepticon Jet, Afterburner....................................$15.00
Small Decepticon Jet, Terredive....................................$15.00
Small Decepticon Jet, Windrazor $15.00
Small Decpeticon Jet, Eagle Eye....................................$15.00

Generation 2, Series 2, 1994

Aerialbot, Fireflight $10.00
Aerialbot, Silverbot $25.00
Aerialbot, Skydive $15.00
Aerialbot, Superion $225.00
Combaticon, Blast Off....................................$10.00
Combaticon, Brawl $10.00
Combaticon, Onslaught $25.00
Heroes, Autobot Hero Optimus Prime....................................$20.00
Heroes, Autobot Hero Optimus Prime, Japanese box........$35.00
Heroes, Decepticon Hero Megatron....................................$20.00
Laser Rod Transformer, Electro....................................$15.00
Laser Rod Transformer, Electro, Japanese box...................$20.00
Laser Rod Transformer, Jolt $15.00
Laser Rod Transformer, Jolt, Japanese box $20.00
Lead Force, Leadfoot, Manta Ray, or Ransack, ea...............$7.00
Rotor Force, Leadfoot $7.00
Stunticon, Breakdown, BotCon '94 Exclusive $100.00
Watch, Superion, Ultra Magnus, or Scorpia, ea................$12.00

Japanese Remakes

Blot, MIB $70.00
GodGinrai, MIB (sealed)....................................$70.00
Hot Rod, MIB $60.00
Jazz, MIB (sealed)....................................$35.00
Optimus Prime, New Year's edition.............................. $150.00
Prowl, MIB (sealed) $35.00
Ratchet, MIB (sealed) $50.00

Red Alert, MIB (sealed) $90.00
Rodimus Prime, MIB (sealed)....................$60.00
Sixshot, MIB (sealed) $60.00
Skids, MIB (sealed)....................$35.00
Skywrap, MIB (sealed).................... $120.00
Tracks, MIB (sealed)....................$35.00
Ultra Magnus, NRFB....................$80.00

Megatron, $90.00.

Trolls

The first trolls to come to the United States were modeled after a 1952 design by Marti and Helena Kuuskoski of Tampere, Finland. The first trolls to be mass produced in America were molded from wood carvings made by Thomas Dam of Denmark. They were made of vinyl, and the original issue was marked 'Dam Things Originals copyright 1964 – 1965 Dam Things Est.; m.f.g. by Royalty Designs of Fla. Inc.' (Other marks were used as well; look on the troll's back or on the bottom of his feet for the Dam trademark.) As the demand for these trolls increased, several US manufacturers were licensed to produce them. The most noteworthy of these were Uneeda Doll Company's Wishnik line and Inga Scandia House True Trolls. Thomas Dam continued to import his Dam Things line.

The troll craze from the 1960s spawned many items other than dolls such as wall plaques, salt and pepper shakers, pins, squirt guns, rings, clay trolls, lamps, Halloween costumes, animals, lawn ornaments, coat racks, notebooks, folders, and even a car.

In the 1970s, 1980s, and 1990s, new trolls were produced. While these trolls are collectible, the avid troll collector still prefers those produced in the 1960s.

Condition is a very important worth-assessing factor.

Baby Boy, Dam, 10", yel diaper, yel spikey hair, amber eyes, VG....................$22.00
Baseball Player, Dam, 1977, 9", striped outfit, cap & felt glove, NM....................$20.00
Batman, 5½", complete silscreened costume, EX....................$18.00

Bat-Nik, MIP, $25.00. (Photo courtesy serioustoyz.com)

Black Nurse, Russ, 5", wht uniform & hat w/red cross, pk hair, M....................$55.00
Boy, Dam, 1982, 10½", felt outfit w/cap & neck scarf, wht hair, M....................$22.00
Boy, Dam, 1984, 6", purple pants & yel shirt, wht hair, EX...$35.00
Boy, Dam/Norfin, 1990, 8", bl jeans, red & gr T-shirt, yel hair, NM+ $20.00
Boy, Dam/Norfin #604, 9", orange & gr outfit, orange hair, EX. $28.00
Bride & Groom, Ace/Dam, 1986, 4½" ea, M, pr....................$18.00
Caveman, Dam, 8", orange hair, leopard outfit, brn fuzzy slippers, EX $15.00
Chef Norfini, Dam/Norfin, 1977, 9", all wht, M....................$18.00
Clown, Norfin/Dam, 1977, 9½", mc outfit & hat, EX........$20.00
Clown Bank, Dam, 1988, 7", red outfit, wht balding hair, red nose, EX....................$20.00
Donkey, Dam, 9", pk skin tone w/blond mane & tail, gold glass eyes, EX.................... $100.00
Dr Olav, Dam/Norfin #6058, 1977, 9½", gr surgeon's outfit, EX $30.00
Elephant, Dam, 6½", 'wrinkled' skin tone, purple hair, amber eyes, EX.................... $100.00
Fire Chief, Dam/Norfin, 1980s, 10", yel slicker, red felt hat, VG.................... $25.00
Giraffe Seated Looking Up, Dam, 12", wht hair, amber eyes, VG+....................$75.00
Girl, Dam, 1960s, 2½", bl swimsuit & hat w/fish, blond hair, amber eyes, EX....................$45.00
Girl, Dam, 1960s, 2½", cat on outfit, pearls, pk hair, NM .. $100.00
Girl, Dam, 1979, 17½", gr dress, orange hair, amber eyes, EX ... $85.00
Girl, Dam/Norfin #520, 5", felt outfit, wht hair, amber eyes, EX $45.00
Girl, Dam/Peachy, 3", Luna Creations outfit, yel hair & eyes, NM....................$30.00
Girl, Scandia, 1960s, 2½", purple outfit w/lace, red hair & eyes, NM....................$28.00
Girl, Scandia, 1960s, 2¾", tutu outfit, lavender hair, gr spiral eyes, EX.................... $110.00
Grandma/Grandpa, Norfin, 14", felt outfit, wht hair, amber eyes, EX $75.00
Hanna Elf, Norfin, 1980, bl & yel felt outfit, wht hair, EX ..$35.00

Happy-Go-Lucky Nodder, Dam, papier-maché, 1960s, NM, $120.00. (Photo courtesy gasolinealleyantiques.com)

Ice Skater, Scandia, 3", felt outfit, bl hair, purple spiral eyes, EX $75.00
Iggy, Dam, 11", street clothes, blond hair, gr eyes (rare), EX . $125.00
Iggy, Dam, 11", Tartan Boy overalls, blk hair, amber eyes, G .. $32.00
Iggy, Dam, 12", clown outfit, blk hair, orange eyes, EX... $125.00
Monk, Dam/Norfin, 1972, 10", brn felt outfit, brn hair & eyes, EX $30.00
Mouse, Dam/Norfin, 1986, 3", lime hair, gray & pk mouse, EX .. $12.00
Prisoner #51538, Dam/Norfin, 1977, 9", prison outfit, purple hair, EX $22.00
Scuba diver, unmarked, 4", yel hair, bl suit, gr mask & fins, EX $22.00
Stressed Out, Dam, 1986, 4½", gray sweater, hot pk hair, EX.. $18.00
Ye Ye, Dam, 12", yel hair & bl eyes, felt outfit, EX $100.00

View-Master and Tru-Vue

View-Master, the invention of William Gruber, was introduced to the public at the 1939 – 1940 New York World's Fair and the Golden Gate Exposition in California. Since then, View-Master reels, packets, and viewers have been produced by five different companies — the original Sawyers Company, G.A.F (1966), View-Master International (1981), Ideal Toys, and Tyco Toys (the present owners). Because none of the non-cartoon single reels and three-reel packets have been made since 1980, these have become collectors' items. Also highly sought after are the three-reel sets featuring popular TV and cartoon characters. The market is divided between those who simply collect View-Master as a field all its own and collectors of character-related memorabilia who will often pay much higher prices for reels about Barbie, Batman, The Addams Family, etc. Our values tend to follow the more conservative approach.

The first single reels were dark blue with a gold sticker and came in attractive gold-colored envelopes. They appeared to have handwritten letters. These were followed by tan reels with a blue circular stamp. Because these were produced for the most part after 1945 and paper supplies were short during WWII, they came in a variety of front and back color combinations, tan with blue, tan with white, and some were marbleized. Since print runs were low during the war, these early singles are much more desirable than the printed white ones that were produced by the millions from 1946 until 1957. Three-reel packets, many containing story books, were introduced in 1955, and single reels were phased out. Nearly all viewers are very common and have little value except for the very early ones, such as the Model A and Model B. Blue and brown versions of the Model B are especially rare. Another desirable viewer, unique in that it is the only focusing model ever made, is the Model D. For more information we recommend *View-Master Single Reels, Volume I*, by Roger Nazeley.

Note: Unless noted otherwise, the following values are for complete, mint in package (MIP) reels with cover and book.

Adam & the Ants, BD199 .... $20.00
Addams Family, B486 .... $115.00
Annie Oakley, B470 .... $22.00
Apollo Moon Landing July 20th 1969, B663 .... $25.00
Aristocats, B365 .... $8.00
Bambi, B400 .... $10.00
Barbie & the Rockers, 4071 .... $12.00
Batman, B492 .... $12.00
Black Beauty, D135 .... $12.00
Bonanza, BB487 .... $22.00
Captain Kangaroo, 755abc $18.00
Casper the Friendly Ghost, B533 .... $8.00

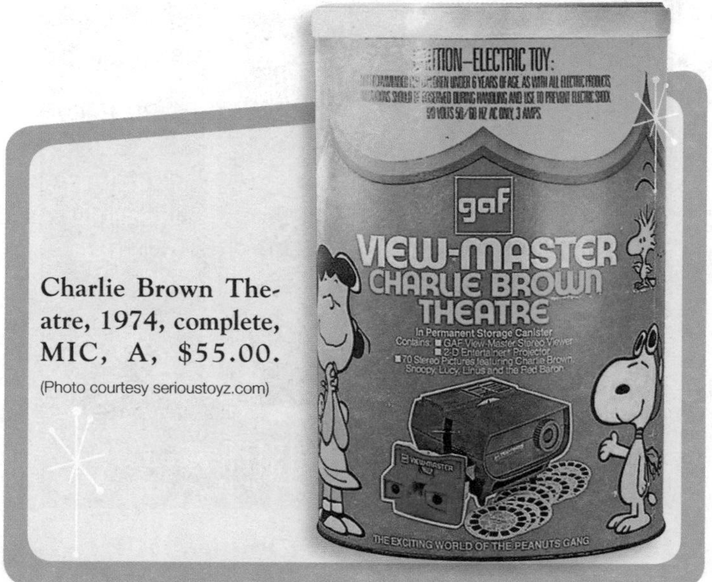

Charlie Brown Theatre, 1974, complete, MIC, A, $55.00. (Photo courtesy serioustoyz.com)

Chip 'n Dale Rescue Rangers, 3075 .... $8.00
CHiPs, L14 .... $18.00
City Beneath the Sea, B496 .... $28.00
Curious George, 2015 .... $15.00
Daniel Boone, B479 .... $25.00
Dick Tracy, 4105 .... $10.00
Dracula, B324 .... $18.00
Dune, 4058 .... $15.00
Eight Is Enough, K76 .... $15.00
ET The Extra-Terrestrial, N7 .... $18.00
Family Matters, 4118 .... $10.00
Fantastic Four, K36 .... $15.00
Fat Albert & the Cosby Kids, B554 .... $8.00
Flipper, BB480 .... $15.00

Flying Nun, B495 .... $30.00
Fraggle Rock, 4053 .... $8.00
Ghostbusters, 1062 .... $10.00
Godzilla, J23 .... $18.00
Goldilocks, B317 .... $12.00
Green Hornet, B488 .... $65.00
Happy Days, J13 .... $10.00
Heidi, B425 .... $12.00
Hopalong Cassidy, 956 .... $5.00
Howard the Duck, 4073 .... $12.00
Huckleberry Hound & Yogi Bear, B512 .... $6.00
Inspector Gadget, BD232 .... $15.00
Ironman, H44 .... $8.00
James Bond (Moonraker), K68 .... $18.00
Jem, 1059 .... $8.00
Knight Rider, 4054 .... $8.00
Land of the Giants, B494 .... $35.00
Lassie & Timmy, B472 .... $12.00
Last Star Fighter, 4057 .... $15.00
Little Mermaid, 3078 .... $5.00

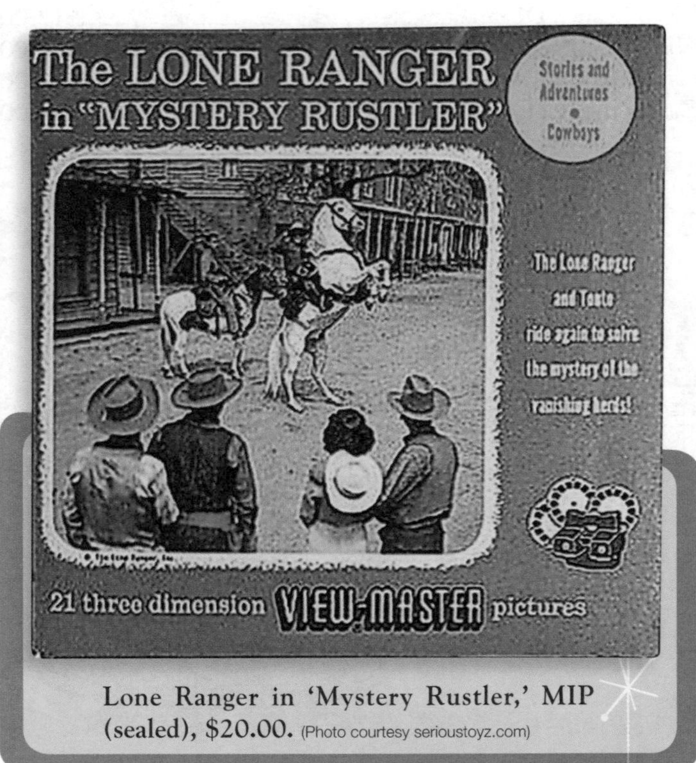

Lone Ranger in 'Mystery Rustler,' MIP (sealed), $20.00. (Photo courtesy serioustoyz.com)

Little Red Riding Hood, B310 .... $10.00
Mannix, BB450 .... $30.00
Monkees, B493 .... $30.00
Munsters, B481 .... $100.00
Muppets, BK026 .... $10.00
Nanny & the Professor, B573 .... $30.00
Noah's Ark, B851 .... $12.00
Pete's Dragon, H38 .... $10.00
Pink Panther, J12 .... $8.00
Planet of the Apes, B507 or BB507, ea $40.00
Popeye, B516 .... $8.00
Poseidon Adventure, B301 .... $28.00
Power Rangers, 36870 .... $6.00
Rescuers, BH026 .... $8.00
Return to Witch Mountain, J25 .... $8.00
Rin-Tin-Tin, B467 .... $20.00
Rocketeer, 4115 .... $12.00
Rookies, BB452 .... $18.00
Roy Rogers, N475 .... $30.00
Run Joe Run, B594 .... $18.00
Scooby Doo, B553 .... $8.00
Sebastian, D101 .... $35.00
Secret Squirrel & Atom Ant, B535 .... $15.00
Sesame Street Goes on Vacation, 4077 .... $6.00
Shaggy DA, B368 .... $15.00
Six Million Dollar Man, B556 .... $18.00
Sleeping Beauty, B308 .... $6.00
Smokey Bear, B404 .... $18.00
Snoopy & the Red Baron, B544 .... $8.00
Snowman, BD262 .... $10.00
Spider-Man, H11 .... $15.00
Superman, 1064 .... $6.00
Superstar Barbie, J070 .... $18.00
Teenage Mutant Ninja Turtles (Movie), 4114 .... $8.00
Terrahawks, BD230 .... $18.00
Thor, H39 .... $6.00
Thunderbirds, B453 .... $45.00
Tom Corbett Space Cadet, 970abc $28.00
Top Cat, BB513 .... $18.00
Treasure Island, B432 .... $25.00
Tron, M37 .... $12.00
Tweety & Sylvester, BD1161 .... $10.00
Welcome Back Kotter, J19 .... $15.00
Wind in the Willows, 4084 .... $12.00
Wiz, J14 .... $22.00
Woody Woodpecker, B522 .... $18.00

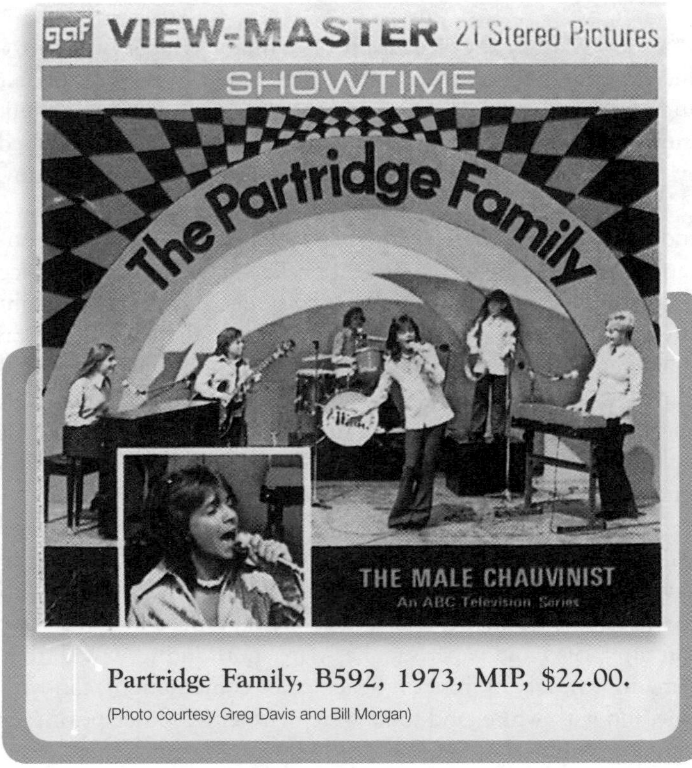

Partridge Family, B592, 1973, MIP, $22.00.
(Photo courtesy Greg Davis and Bill Morgan)

Western

No friend was ever more true, no brother more faithful, no acquaintance more real to us than our favorite cowboys of radio, TV, and the silver screen. They were upright, strictly moral, extremely polite, and tireless in their pursuit of law and order in the American West. How unfortunate that such role models are practically extinct nowadays.

For more information and some wonderful pictures, we recommend *Guide to Cowboy Character Collectibles* by Ted Hake.

See also Advertising Signs, Ads, and Displays; Books; Character and Promotional Drinking Glasses; Character Clocks and Watches; Coloring, Activity, and Paint Books; Guns; Lunch Boxes; Premiums; Puzzles, Windup, Friction, and Other Mechanicals.

Annie Oakley, belt, blk & wht leather emb w/'Annie Oakly' & 'Tag' names, silver-tone buckle, 1950s, NMOC, A.....$60.00

Annie Oakley, belt, brn tooled leather w/cast metal buckle reads Annie Oakley & Tagg, 1950s, MOC $75.00

Bat Masterson, cane, chrome-covered plastic hdl w/name emb across top, 1958, EX+ $35.00

Bat Masterson, outfit w/shirt, pants & tie, Gene Barry labels, Kaynee, MIB $160.00

Buffalo Bill, gloves, Wells Lamont, 1950s, EX+, $35.00. (Photo courtesy serioustoyz.com)

Cisco Kid, belt, blk leather w/brn embellishments & name tags, 1950s, NM $55.00

Cisco Kid, stick horse, vinyl head w/fur-like mane & name, 32" L wooden stick, 1950s, VG...$35.00

Cisco Kid and Poncho, cereal bowl, 1950s, 5" diameter, NM+, $45.00. (Photo courtesy serioustoyz.com)

Dale Evans, lamp, plaster figure of Dale on rearing horse, printed shade, 8", EX, A.. $150.00

Dale Evans, Western Dress-Up Kit, Colorforms/Roy Rogers Ent, 1959, EXIB..$50.00

Daniel Boone, coonskin cap, Fess Parker as Daniel Boone, Arlington/American Tradition, 1964, EX...................$50.00

Daniel Boone, figure, pnt plastic w/soft vinyl head, fur cap & powder horn, 5½", American Tradition Co, 1964, NM.......$50.00

Davy Crockett, Auto Magic Picture Gun, 1950s, complete, EX+IB $175.00

Davy Crockett, binoculars, plastic, Harrison, MIB......... $175.00

Davy Crockett, Dart Gun Target, Knickerbocker, unused, MIB $80.00

Davy Crockett, doll, hard plastic walker in cloth costume, hat & musket, red wig, 8", Madame Alexander, 1955, EXIB, A...... $120.00

Davy Crockett, doll, pnt hard plastic w/realistic outfit & hat, plastic rifle, 7", Fortune Toy/WDP, 1950s, EX+IB ... $100.00

Davy Crockett, Frontier Wagon/Stage, Linemar, 2-pc set, friction, ea 3x5" L, NMIB... $650.00

Davy Crockett, guitar, plastic w/yarn strap, mc paper litho label on front, w/up mechanisim plays music, Mattel, 14", EX $50.00

Davy Crockett, horse, Pied Piper Toys, MIB.................. $125.00

Davy Crockett, lamp, chalkware figural base w/mountain scene pnt on shade, 18", VG $100.00

Davy Crockett, mariontte, talker, 15", Hazelle's, MIB.... $350.00

Davy Crockett, outfit, shirt & pants, brn cloth w/plastic fringe, Davy & Alamo scene on shirt, WDP, 1950s, EX $65.00

Davy Crockett, pencil case, 'Frontierland...,' brn vinyl holster w/gun-shaped pencil case, 8", 1950s, VG...................$50.00

Davy Crockett, pencil case, 'Walt Disney's Official...' 'Fronterland...,' slide-out box, 5x8", Hassenfeld, 1950s, EX....$50.00

Davy Crockett, tent, brn & wht Davy graphics on tan canvas, Empire Mfg/WDP, 1950s, complete, NM................ $135.00

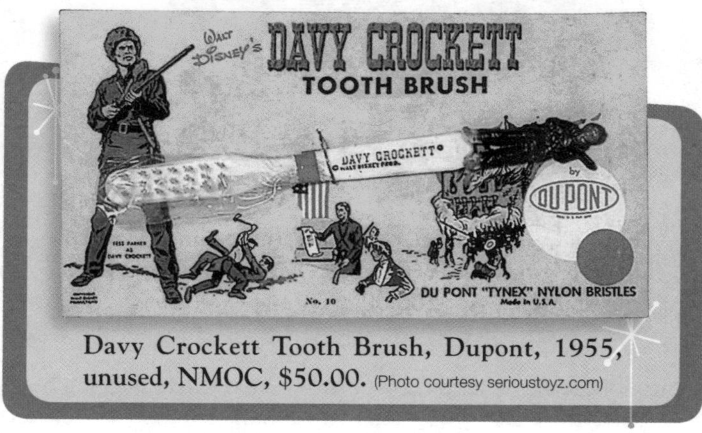

Davy Crockett Tooth Brush, Dupont, 1955, unused, NMOC, $50.00. (Photo courtesy serioustoyz.com)

Davy Crockett, wallet, brn vinyl w/profile of Davy in furry coonskin cap, 5x4", WDP, 1955, EX+IB $75.00

Davy Crockett, woodburning set, Frontier..., ATF/USA, MIB $175.00

Gabby Hayes, Champion Shooting Target, Haccker/Ind, 1950s, NMIB.. $225.00

Gabby Hayes, doll, stuffed cloth w/fur beard & felt hat, name on belt, 13", 1960s, M..$40.00

Gabby Hayes, Fishing Outfit, steel 2-part rod & reel, VG (in litho tin cylindrical container)................................ $175.00

Gabby Hayes, hand puppet, cloth body w/rubber head, JVZ, 1949, EX $175.00
Gene Autry, doll (Terry Lee), compo, cloth outfit & felt hat, 16", NM+ $500.00
Gene Autry, flashlight, Cowboy Lariat, EXIB $100.00
Gene Autry, guitar, w/automatic cord player, plastic, 33", Emenee, 1950s, NMIB, A $315.00
Gene Autry, inflatable horse, 'Champion,' 23" H, 1950s, NM, A $75.00
Gene Autry, Official Ranch Outfit, G+IB, A $75.00
Gene Autry, spurs, NP w/red Autry signature on wht leather boot straps, 1940s, EX, pr $115.00
Gene Autry, wallet, leather w/zipper closure, image of Gene & Champion, Aristocrat, 1950s, VGIB $75.00
Gene Autry, wrist cuffs, lt brn leather w/silver studs & red rhinestones, VG, A $150.00
Gene Autry, writing tablet, cover shows Gene seated w/leg over knee playing guitar, 8x10", 1940s, unused, NM, A $45.00
Gunsmoke, cowboy hat, brn felt w/Gunsmoke & Marshal Matt Dillon emblem on front, vinyl trim, tie string, 1950s, EX $65.00
Gunsmoke, slippers, blk vinyl w/yel & red image of Matt, Chester & Doc, Columbia, 1959, unused, NM+IB $200.00

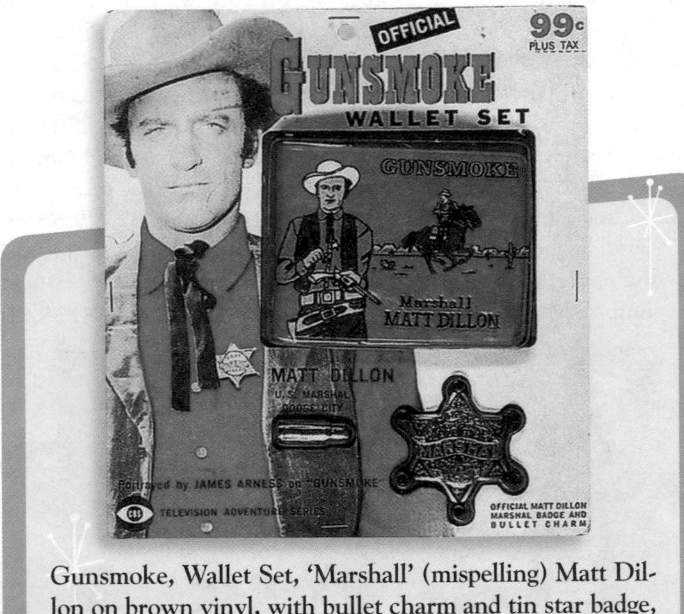

Gunsmoke, Wallet Set, 'Marshall' (mispelling) Matt Dillon on brown vinyl, with bullet charm and tin star badge, unused, MOC, A, $200.00. (Photo courtesy Morphy Auctions)

Gunsmoke, writing tablet, cover shows Miss Kittie hugging horse head, unused, NM+ $45.00
Hopalong Cassidy, bank, 'Hoppy Savings Club,' plastic bust figure w/removable hat, copper color, 4", 1950s, EX $50.00
Hopalong Cassidy, bank, copper plastic bust figure w/removable hat, Savings Club, Ohio S&L, 4", 1950s, EX $50.00
Hopalong Cassidy, Coloring Outfit, Transogram, 1950s, slight use, NM+IB, A $85.00
Hopalong Cassidy, cowboy boots, 3-color leather, Acme, EXIB (box pictures Hoppy on Topper in landscape) $800.00
Hopalong Cassidy, Cowboy Outfit, complete, G+IB, A $90.00
Hopalong Cassidy, Cowboy Soap, 4" bar, Colgate-Palmolive, 1940s, unused, MIP (sealed) $55.00
Hopalong Cassidy, Crayon & Stencil Set, Transogram, 1950s, complete, some use, EXIB $50.00
Hopalong Cassidy, doll, rubber head, cloth outfit, w/gun & holster, 21", 1950s, NM $300.00
Hopalong Cassidy, Dudin-Up Kit, w/shampoo, Hair Trainer, comb & 2 trading cards, Fuller Brush, 1950s, unused, MIB, A $315.00
Hopalong Cassidy, Figure & Paint Set, Laurel Ann, complete, used, EXIB $250.00
Hopalong Cassidy, hand puppet, cloth body w/vinyl head, 1950s, scarce, NM $200.00
Hopalong Cassidy, handkerchief, wht w/Hoppy & Topper embroidery in blk on wht, 11½x11½", EX+ $50.00
Hopalong Cassidy, hat, blk w/name & steer head in wht on band, Bailey of Hollywood, adult size, EX, A $460.00
Hopalong Cassidy, Junior Chow Set, knife, fork & spoon w/emb name & image on handles, Imperial, 1950, NMIB, A $83.00

Hopalong Cassidy, lamp, Econolite, 10", NM+, $500.00.

Hopalong Cassidy, motion lamp, plastic, Roto-Vue/AB Leech, 1950, NM, A $400.00
Hopalong Cassidy, motion lamp, scene w/Hoppy & Indian chief at campfire w/waterfall, red top & bottom, 9½", NM, A $400.00
Hopalong Cassidy, night light, figural glass gun in holster w/image of Hoppy, Aladdin, 1950s, NM $350.00
Hopalong Cassidy, night light set, decaled milk glass wall-mount guns & holsters w/free-standing footed cylinder, 9", EX $750.00
Hopalong Cassidy, pants, blk cloth chaps-like w/2 images of Hoppy & Topper, covered wagons & steer heads, 1950s, VG $50.00
Hopalong Cassidy, pencil case, vinyl w/zipper opening, blk/wht image of Toppy w/name & 'Pencil Case,' 5x8", EX+, A $95.00
Hopalong Cassidy, playhouse, 4 lithoed panels, William Boyd/Charcook, 1950, EX+ $650.00
Hopalong Cassidy, potato chip can, close-up image of Hoppy & Topper on cream, slip lid, 11", 1950s, EX, A $175.00
Hopalong Cassidy, rocking chair, image on tan vinyl back w/black seat, chrome tubing-like frame w/flat rockers, 24", EX $225.00

Hopalong Cassidy, scrapbook, tan vinyl hard cover w/emb image of Hoppy on Topper, string-bound pgs, 1950s, unsued, NM $125.00
Hopalong Cassidy, shoe caddy, red vinyl w/8 shoe pockets showing various yel & blk scenes, 1950s, EX $125.00
Hopalong Cassidy, Shooting Gallery, w/up, litho tin, spring-loaded gun fires steel balls at moving target, NMIB, A.............$35.00
Hopalong Cassidy, spurs, silver-tone & brass w/blk leather straps, NM.. $200.00
Hopalong Cassidy, Stagecoach Toss beanbag target, litho tin & masonite, 24x18", Transogram, 1950s, EX $75.00
Hopalong Cassidy, sweater, tan w/color images showing Hoppy & name, child-size, 1950s, EX $100.00
Hopalong Cassidy, TV set, plastic w/pull-out knob, filmstrips revolve inside TV, 5x5", Automatic Toy, EXIB $250.00
Hopalong Cassidy, wallet, brn leather w/cloth litho head images of Hoppy & Topper, zippered closure, 4x5", 1950s, EX......$50.00
Hopalong Cassidy, wallet, vinyl w/colorful images of stagecoach & Hoppy on Topper, 3x7½", 1950s, EX $60.00
Hopalong Cassidy, wallet, vinyl w/full-color litho front & back, 3x7¼" (unfolded), 1950s, uncommon, EX.................$50.00
Hopalong Cassidy, waste basket, tan metal w/mc image of Hoppy on Topper surrounded other images/name in script, 12", EX $150.00
Hopalong Cassidy, Western Frontier Set, Milton Bradley, 1950s, complete, NMIB... $300.00
Hopalong Cassidy, Woodburning Set, American Toy, 1950s, unsued, EXIB $100.00
Hopalong Cassidy, wrist cuffs, 'Hoppy' on blk w/silver stud trim, EX+ $200.00
Kit Carson, 3-Powered Binocular, 1950s, EXIB $125.00
Lone Ranger, binoculars, plastic, Harrison, EX+IB......... $135.00
Lone Ranger, De Luxe Movie Views, Acme Plastics, NM+IB, A... $150.00

Lone Ranger, deputy badge, 2¼", NM, $45.00. (Photo courtesy serioustoyz.com))

Lone Ranger, doll, stuffed body w/compo head, cloth outfit w/gun & holster, hat, 15", Dollcraft Novelty, EX+............ $600.00
Lone Ranger, guitar, heavy cb w/wooden neck, 28½", Jefferson, 1950s, EX $100.00
Lone Ranger, hand puppet, printed vinyl body w/guns drawn & name, vinyl head, 1966, NM+ $125.00
Lone Ranger, horseshoe set, rubber, Gardner, NMIB.........$85.00
Lone Ranger, neck scarf & concho slide, purple silk-type material w/images of Lone Ranger & Silver, 1940s-50s, EX........$50.00
Lone Ranger, Official Outfit, leather holster w/compo gun, blk mask & red scarf, Feinburg-Henry, 1938, EXIB $200.00
Lone Ranger, Official outfit, w/chaps, shirt, vest, hat, wrist cuffs, neckerchief & lasso, Henry, 1940s, NMIB.............. $475.00
Lone Ranger, Punch-Out Set, Lone Ranger, Tonto & Silver w/accessory punch-outs, DeJornette, 1940s, unused, EXIB, A... $85.00
Lone Ranger, push-button puppet, Lone Ranger on Silver, Press Action Toys, 1939, NMIB...................................... $150.00
Lone Ranger, record player, molded plastic image of the Lone Ranger on Silver on front panel, Mercury, 1950s, VG+, A $85.00
Lone Ranger, record player, wood case, 10x12", Decca/Lone Ranger Inc, EX... $350.00

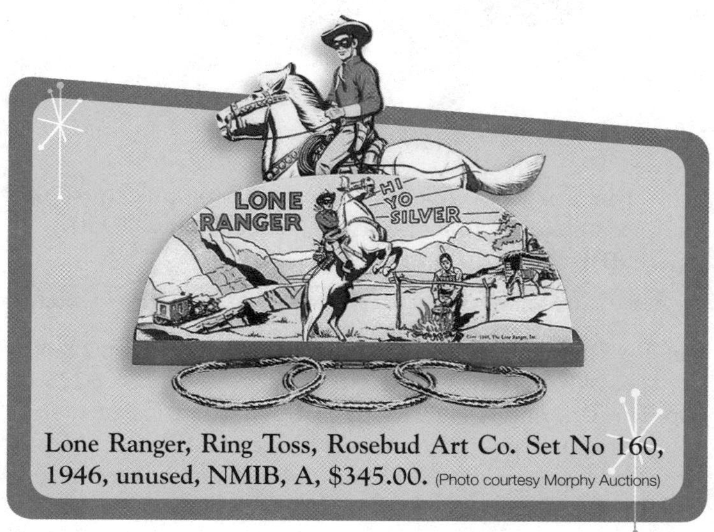

Lone Ranger, Ring Toss, Rosebud Art Co. Set No 160, 1946, unused, NMIB, A, $345.00. (Photo courtesy Morphy Auctions)

Lone Ranger, school bag, canvas w/plastic hdl, image of Lone Ranger on side pocket, 1950s, EX $100.00
Lone Ranger, soap figure, 4½", Kerk Guild, unsued, EXIB..$65.00
Lone Ranger, target, litho tin w/metal support, Marx, 9½" sq, TLR, Inc, 1930s, EX $50.00
Lone Ranger, target game, Hi-Yo Silver..., Marx, EXIB.....$65.00
Maverick, belt, tooled leather w/names & images, Maverick emb on brass-tone cast-metal rectangular buckle, EX+ $65.00
Maverick, Eras-O-Picture Book, Hasbro, 1958, complete, EX... $40.00
Maverick, paint-by-number set, Hasbro, 1958, complete, EXIB $75.00

Rawhide, Official Canteen, Carnell Mfg., 1959, unused, MOC, A, $90.00. (Photo courtesy serioustoyz.com)

Red Rider, gloves, Playmates, brn, red & bl cloth, tag w/premium offers, Wells Lamont Corp & SS, 1950s, NM............$30.00

Rin Tin Tin, canteen, 'Official Rin Tin Tin 101st Cavalry' on front, Nabisco premium, 1957, EX, A........................$20.00

Rin Tin Tin, Official Corporal Rusty and Horse, complete with accessories, plastic, Marx, 1950s, MIB, A, $200.00. (Photo courtesy serioustoyz.com)

Rin Tin Tin, outfit, Corporal Rusty 101st Cavalry, w/gun & holster, Iskin/Screen Gems, EXIB............................... $225.00

Rin Tin Tin, outfit, Fighting Blue Devil 101st Cavalry, shirt, leather belt, pouch w/bullets & holster, NMIB........ $175.00

Rin Tin Tin, scrapbook, bl spiralbound cover w/picture of Rusty & Rinty seated on log by creek bed, 1950s, unused, EX, A $25.00

Roy Rogers, archery set, Ben Pearson, scarce, unused, MOC ..$175.00

Roy Rogers, bank, metal boot form w/copper finish, 5½", Almar Metal Arts Co, 1950s, EX...$75.00

Roy Rogers, Branding Set/Ink Pad, tin container, 2" dia, 1950s, unused, EX $65.00

Roy Rogers, Camera w/Telescopic Sight, Herbert George Co, NMIB... $225.00

Roy Rogers, Crayon Set w/Roy Rogers Pictures & Stencils, Standard Toycraft, 1950s, complete & unused, MIB, A.. $400.00

Roy Rogers, Fix-It Chuck Wagon & Jeep Set, 24", Ideal, 1950s, complete, NMIB, A.. $360.00

Roy Rogers, flashlight, 'Signal Siren,' tin, 7", Usalite, unused, MIB $150.00

Roy Rogers, fountain pen, name on blk plastic barrel, gold trim, 5", 1950s, VG...$50.00

Roy Rogers, game, Lucky Horseshoe, Ohio Art, 1950s, complete, EX $50.00

Roy Rogers, gloves, 2-tone brn suede w/name in wht, studded horseshoe & image of Roy on Trigger on cuffs w/fringe, VG.. $75.00

Roy Rogers, guitar, wood & pressed wood w/red & wht silhouette images, 31", Range Rhythm/Rich Toys, NMIB........ $200.00

Roy Rogers, hand puppet, cloth w/vinyl head & hat, 1950s, EX $75.00

Roy Rogers, hat, taupe felt w/Roy Rogers band, wht whipstitching around hat rim, NM+, A.................................. $100.00

Roy Rogers, Hauler & Van Trailer & Nelly Belle Jeep, w/2 horses, 3 figures & Bullet the dog, Marx, no jeep o/w NM+IB, A $525.00

Roy Rogers, modeling clay set, complete, unused, NM (in box w/image of Roy on Trigger) $150.00

Roy Rogers, paint-by-number set, various sets, Roy Rogers Ent, 1954, unused, EXIB, ea...$75.00

Roy Rogers, pencil case, vinyl w/wht stitching, name & image of Roy & Trigger on front, snap closure, 8", EX $50.00

Roy Rogers, pull toy, horse-drawn covered wagon, paper litho on wood, removable cloth cover, 20", NN Hill, EX...... $250.00

Roy Rogers, school bag, brn textured vinyl w/brn leather strap, badge above graphics on front pocket flap, 1950s, G+..$100.00

Roy Rogers, Signal Siren Flashlight, Usalite, NMIB, A . $175.00

Roy Rogers, telescope, plastic, H George, 9", MIB $200.00

Roy Rogers, tent, yel canvas w/red litho image of Roy on Trigger, EX, A $200.00

Roy Rogers, Trick Lasso, Classy, 1950s, EXIP $75.00

Roy Rogers, wagon train w/up toy, plastic stagecoach w/driver & horse leading 3 litho tin wagons, 14" L, VG $135.00

Roy Rogers, woodburning set, Burn-Rite, complete, EXIB ..$175.00

Roy Rogers & Dale Evans, school tablets, 8x10", Frontiers Inc, 1950s, unused, EX, ea $25.00

Roy Rogers and Dale Evans, Western Dinner Set, Ideal, complete, NM+IB, A, $150.00. (Photo courtesy Morphy Auctions)

Tales of Wells Fargo, paint-by-number set, 1959, complete, unused, NMIB..$65.00

The Texan (Rory Calhoun), hand puppet, full body in wht shirt w/blk vest & pants, holster, Tops in Toys, 1960s, NM ..$175.00

Tom Mix, School Tablet, salesman's sample w/4 different photo covers attached, M... $450.00

Tom Mix, Shooting Gallery, Parker Bros, c 1930, complete, EXIB, A.. $230.00

Tonto, doll, stuffed body w/compo head, cloth outfit, guns & holster, headband w/feather, EX $500.00

Tonto, hand puppet, printed body & name on gr vinyl w/vinyl head, 1966, NM+ $125.00

Tonto, soap figure, 4", Kerk Guild, 1939, EXIB (unopened) .. $50.00

Virginian, Movie Viewer, Chemtoy, 1966, MIB.................$40.00

Wild Bill Hickok, wallet, fastens w/western buckle, NM+ ..$75.00

Zorro, accessory set w/mask, whip, lariat & ring, Shimmel/WDP, M (w/24" L card picturing Guy Williams) $150.00

Zorro, bolo tie, metal medallion w/plastic insert featuring Zorro portrait in red logo, NM $50.00

Zorro, bookends, ceramic, figural w/red 'Z' on wht base, glossy w/red cold pnt, Enesco, 1960s, NM $225.00
Zorro, bowl & plate set, 5" dia/7" dia, Sun-Valley Melmac, EX $40.00
Zorro, hand puppet, Don Diego, cloth body w/vinyl head, Gund, 1950s, NM $85.00
Zorro, hand puppet, tag reads 'Zorro' but looks like Don Diego, Canadian issue, Reliable, 1950s, EX+ $100.00
Zorro, hand puppet, vinyl head w/cloth body, felt hat, Gund/WDP, 1950s, EX+ $75.00
Zorro, key chain/flashlight, c WDP, 1950s, EX+ $75.00
Zorro, magic slate, Watkins/Strathmore/WDP, 1950s-60s, EX .$75.00
Zorro, magic slate, Whitman, 1965, unused, NM $50.00
Zorro, Official 'Secret Sight' Scarf Mask 49¢, Disney, 1959, NRFC..$75.00
Zorro, oil-paint-by-number set, Hassenfeld Bros, 1960s, complete, VGIB...$65.00
Zorro, ring, blk plastic w/Zorro lettered in gold tone on blk stone, M...$75.00
Zorro, target board, litho tin w/cb stand-up back, 15x23", T Cohn/WDP, 1950s-60s, EX $75.00
Zorro, Target Shoot, Lido/WDP, MIB $225.00
Zorro, tote bag, red vinyl, EX $275.00

Windup, Friction, and Other Mechanical Toys

Windup toys represent a fun and exciting field of collecting — our fascination with them stems from their simplistic but exciting actions and brightly colored lithography, and especially the comic character or personality-related examples are greatly in demand by collectors today. Though most were made through the years of the 1930s to the 1950s, they carry their own weight against much earlier toys and are considered very worthwhile investments. Various types of mechanisms were used — some are key wound while others depend on lever action to tighten the mainspring and release the action of the toy. Tin and celluloid were used in their production, and although it is sometimes possible to repair a tin windup, experts advise against investing in a celluloid toy whose mechanism is not working, since the material is usually too fragile to withstand the repair.

Many of the boxes that these toys came in are almost as attractive as the toys themselves and can add considerably to their value.

Advisor: Scott Smiles

See also Aeronautical; Boats; Chein; Japanese and Other Replica Vehicles; Lehmann; Marx; Robots and Space Toys; Strauss; Tin Vehicles.

Acrobatic Monkeys, Wyandotte, w/up, litho tin, 10" dia, VG.. $225.00
Acrocycle, Alps, w/up, litho tin, clown performs tricks on motorcycle, 6", EXIB... $400.00
Air Carousel (Kiddie City Amusement Park), AHI, w/up, litho tin, 7", NM+IB $175.00
Airport, Ohio Art, w/up, litho tin, 2 airplanes spiral down center rod atop rnd 2-tiered building, 9" T, EXIB.............. $275.00
Alpine Express, Techno Fix, w/up, litho tin, 20", MIB, A....$200.00
American Circus, Japan, w/up, 6", NM, A...................... $275.00
Amos (Amos & Andy) Sparkler, die-cut litho tin face w/Taxi lettered on hat band, 6", EX, A $450.00
Animal Train, Masuya, friction, litho tin, 15" L, NMIB. $125.00

Artie the Clown in Crazy Car, Unique Art, windup, lithographed tin, 7" long, VG, A, $350.00. (Photo courtesy serioustoyz.com)

Artie the Clown Crazy Car, Unique Art, w/up, litho tin, 7½", G...$250.00
Atlantic City (Riding on the Boardwalk) Rollo-Chair, Germany, w/up, litho tin, 8" L, EX, A $1,400.00
Automatic Dockyard Crane, Linemar, w/up, litho tin, 8½" L, NMIB, A.. $250.00
Babes in Toyland Marching Soldier, Linemar, 6", EXIB, A... $250.00
Balloon & Toy Vendor, Distler, 1930s, w/up, litho tin, w/Mickey Mouse & other lithoed toys on string, 6½", NM $725.00
Balloon & Toy Vendor, Distler, 1930s, w/up, litho tin, w/Mickey Mouse & other lithoed toys on string, 6½", VG $350.00
Banana Man, Distler, w/up, litho tin blk figure carrying bunches of bananas, 7½", NMIB, A $3,450.00
Bar-X Cowboy (Cowboy on Horse w/Lasso), Alps, w/up, litho tin, 5", NMIB, A.. $225.00
Barber (Mouse ?) Shaving Rabbit, TPS, w/up, litho tin, 5", EX, A $290.00
Barnacle Bill Rowboat, Emmert-Hammes & Co, rubber-band activated, litho tin, 10" L, EX+IB $500.00
Barnie Google on Spark Plug, Germany, w/up, litho tin, 7", VG, A $500.00

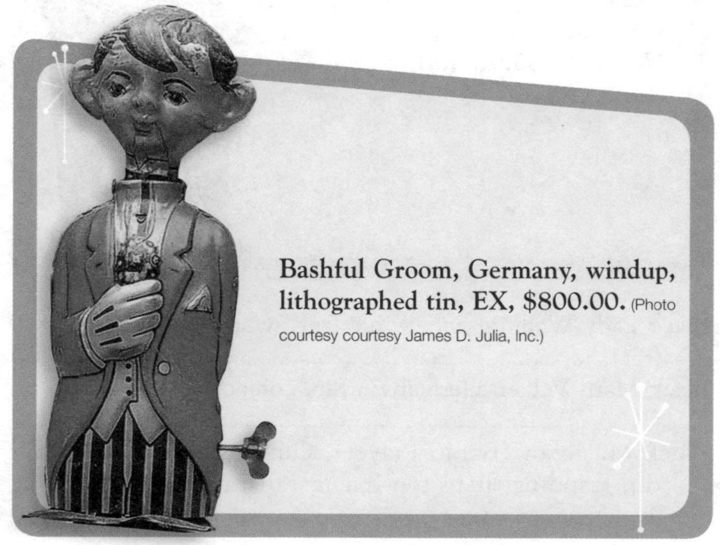

Bashful Groom, Germany, windup, lithographed tin, EX, $800.00. (Photo courtesy courtesy James D. Julia, Inc.)

Bear (Circus Performer), w/up, litho tin, 4⅓" L, EX+ $350.00
Bear Performing, Martin, w/up, brn plush bear standing upright holding bar across back of neck, red muzzle, 8", EX, A.......... $550.00
Begging Rollover Pluto, see Pluto (Begging Rollover)

Betty's (Boop) Acrobat, Japan, prewar, windup, celluloid figure on wire apparatus, 9", NMIB, $1,225.00. (Photo courtesy Morphy Auctions)

Betty's (Boop) Acrobat, Japan, prewar, w/up, celluloid figure on wire apparatus 9", EX... $500.00
Bird in Cage, Germany, ca 1900, w/up, pnt tin sq shape w/gold-footed base, 8" H, EX, A.. $600.00
Black Boy Riding Turtle, Germany, w/up, litho tin, 5", EX+.. $450.00
Black Boy w/Dog Biting Seat of Pants, Germany, w/up, litho tin, red ball cap, bl pants, articulated limbs, 7", G $400.00
Black Couple Dancing, w/up, pnt tin, w/squeaking bellows, 6½", VG $1,000.00

Black Deep Sea Diver, Germany, windup, lithographed tin, 7½", VG+, A, $3,960.00. (Photo courtesy James D. Julia, Inc.)

Black Lady Walking w/Serving Tray, w/up, pnt tin, 6½", VG (rpt).. $425.00
Black Man Walker, Germany, w/up, compo head, cloth outfit, 5½", VG $450.00
Black Musician (Banjo Player), Gunthermann, w/up, pnt tin, standing, lt bl top hat & tails, plink-plunk music, 9", EX $2,500.00
Black Musician (Banjo Player), Gunthermann, w/up, tin, in chair, articulated arms & legs, plink-plunk music, 7", EX.. $950.00
Black Musician (Drummer w/Cymbal), Gunthermann, w/up, pnt tin, standing wearing top hat, articulated arms, 9", EX (rstr) $900.00
Black Musician (Ringing Bells w/Cymbals on Feet), w/up, pnt tin, seated in chair, articulated arms & legs, 7", rpnt........ $600.00
Black Musicians (Banjo & Cymbal Players), Gunthermann, w/up, pnt tin, seated facing on base, plink-plunk music, 9" L, VG $1,750.00
Black Musicians (Horn & Accordion Players), Gunthermann, w/up, tin/cloth, barrel/ball on base, plink-plunk music, 9", VG...$2,500.00
Black Musicians (Horn & Cymbal Players), w/up, tin/cloth, seated on barrel & ball on base, plink-plunk music, 9", VG, A $1,200.00
Black Musicians (Violinist & Tambourine Player), w/up, tin/cloth, in chairs on base, plink-plunk music, 9", EX (rstr)... $1,100.00
Boat Ride, Unique Art, w/up, litho tin, 3 boats w/passengers on rods swing from tower, 9", EX.................................. $200.00
Bonzo on 3-Wheeled Scooter, Germany, 1920s, w/up, tin, 8", EX..$1,550.00
Boxers, Germany, w/up, litho tin, wht & blk figures on 4-wheeled platform, 7", EX $450.00

Boxers, Germany, windup, lithographed tin, VG, A, $1,200.00. (Photo courtesy Morphy Auctions)

Boy Juggler, Germany, w/up, pnt tin w/wooden clubs, boy in nickers, 9", EX $475.00
Boy Lying on Sled, Hess, friction, litho & pnt tin, 6½", EX.. $550.00
Boy Lying on Sled, Japan, w/up, litho tin w/cloth outfit 6½", VG+ $175.00
Boy on Bicycle, Gunthermann, w/up, enameled figure, tin bike, 8" H, VG, A... $975.00
Boy on Scooter, Germany, litho tin, red & wht striped jacket, bl nickers, 7½", EX, A $600.00
Boy on Tricycle (Wonder Cyclist), Unique Art, w/up, litho tin, spoke wheels, 8" L, VG... $275.00
Boy Twirling Ball in Each Hand, Gunthermann, w/up, pnt tin w/celluloid balls, 9½", VG $450.00
Boy w/Balloon In Each Hand, Germany, w/up, pnt tin, 7½", EX..$500.00
Bozo (Playing Drum), Alps, w/up, litho tin, 8", NMIB, A ...$350.00

Bubble Blowing Bear, Alps, w/up, litho tin, plush & plastic, 8", EX+ $150.00
Bull Dog, see Descamps Bull Dog
Bump Car w/Pop-Up Clown, Wakasuto, friction, litho tin, 6½", NMIB, A $200.00
Bunny Bell Tricycle, Sato, w/up, litho tin, 6", EX, A $150.00
Buster Brown & Tige on Rocker Base, w/up, pnt tin, Buster & Tige lift beam & ball rolls back & forth, 9½" L, VG, A... $1,200.00
Busy Betty, Lindstrom, w/up, litho tin, 8", VG $150.00

Busy Lizzy Sweeper, Fischer, windup, lihtographed tin, 7", VG, A, $400.00. (Photo courtesy James D. Julia, Inc.)

Buttercup (Crawling Baby), Germany, 1920s, w/up, tin, 8", EXIB $1,000.00
Capitol Hill Racer, Unique Art, w/up, litho tin, 11" L, EX+IB $175.00
Carnival, Wyandotte, 1930s, lever action, litho tin/steel/paper, various rides & activities on lg base, 16x12", EX+, A $450.00
Carousel, Bing, w/up, pnt tin, 4 children riding horses, perforated base, flag atop, musical, 11", VG, A $550.00
Carousel, Germany, w/up, pnt tin, hot-air ballons, planes & dirigables, flag atop canopy, 11½", G+, A $5,500.00
Carousel, Germany, w/up, pnt tin, open 2-tier cylinder form w/ figures on pigs & teacups, 10" H, EX, A.................. $775.00
Carousel, Muller & Kadeler, w/up, pnt tin, riders in 4 boats w/ paper props, flags at top, EX+, A $1,750.00
Casper the Friendly Ghost, Linemar, w/up, litho tin figure w/bobbing head, 4½", VG $175.00
Casper the Friendly Ghost Rollover Tank, Linemar, w/up, litho tin, 4" L, EX $225.00
Cat in Car, Ingap/Italy, w/up, litho tin, mice & cats graphics on car body & wheels, 6", EX, A $3,750.00
Cat Knitting, TN, w/up, wht plush, 6", EX..................... $125.00
Cat Musicians (2) Standing on Base, w/up, pnt tin, upright in sweaters playing instruments, plink-plunk music, 9", VG+ $1,250.00
Celloist, Gunthermann, w/up, pnt tin, in top hat standing on base, 10", rpnt, A $600.00
Charlie Chaplin, see also Zig-Zag Chap
Charlie Chaplin, B&R Co, w/up, tin w/CI feet, lithoed face, 8½", VG $950.00
Charlie Chaplin Cymbol Player, Distler, 1920s, plunger activated, tin figure holding cat, 6", EX $725.00
Charlie Chaplin Dancer, KW, 1920s, crank-op, flat tin figure jtd at knees holding cane, tin base, 6½", EX $1,000.00
Charlie Chaplin Tumbler, Gee, 1920s, w/up arms, cloth-stiffed body w/compo head & hands, 13", VG.................... $250.00

Charlie Chaplin Walker, Germany, wind-up, lithographed tin with cast-iron shoes, 8½", VG, A, $650.00. (Photo courtesy James D. Julia, Inc.)

Charlie Chaplin Walker, Gunthermann, w/up, litho tin w/CI feet, 10", VG+ $700.00
Charlie Chaplin Walker, Schuco, w/up, felt-covered w/cloth outfit & cane, 6½", NMIB $900.00
Chef on Roller Skates, TPS, w/up, litho tin blk figure w/articulated arms, 6", G $300.00
Child Clock, see Time Is Money Clock/Bank

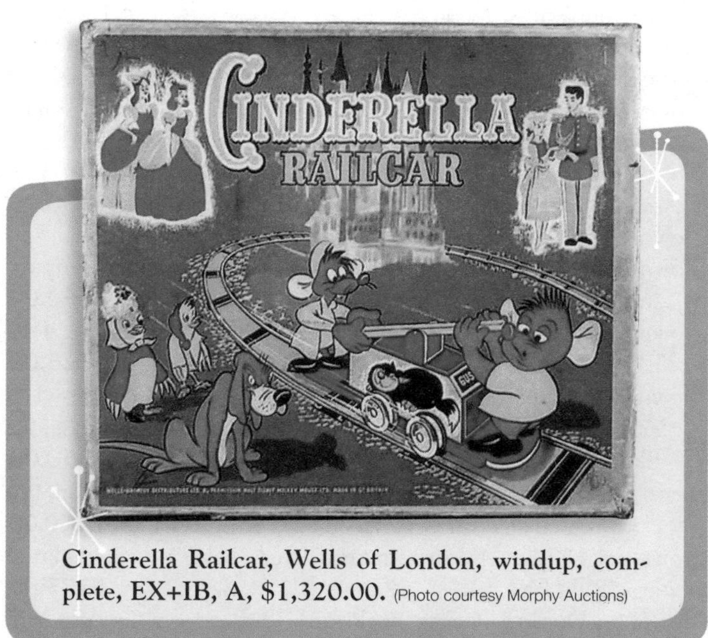

Cinderella Railcar, Wells of London, windup, complete, EX+IB, A, $1,320.00. (Photo courtesy Morphy Auctions)

Circus Boy, France, w/up, litho tin, colorful boy ringing bell & waving Circus sign, 6½", EX+IB $200.00
Circus Bugler, TPS, w/up, tin long-legged clown figure in cloth outfit, 9", MIB, A $425.00
Circus Car, KO, w/up, litho tin, blows ball into air, 4½" L, EXIB $75.00
Circus Clown, Cragstan, cloth suit w/litho tin head & limbs, celluloid feet, clown climbs along string, 9", EXIB...... $150.00

Circus Cyclist (Clown), TPS, w/up, litho tin w/cloth outfit, w/ bell, 6½", NMIB, A $600.00
Circus Henry, Japan, prewar, celluloid, Porter on elephant's back w/Henry riding on trunk, 8", EXIB........................ $2,000.00
Circus Hoop, MT, w/up, litho tin, clown inside 6" dia hoop, EXIB.. $300.00
Circus Parade, TPS, w/up, litho tin, elephant leads 3 performing clowns, 11" L, EXIB.. $175.00
Clown & Trick Dog on 3-Wheeled Apparatus, w/up, pnt tin, 6" L, EX (rstr).. $325.00
Clown Acrobat, Gunthermann, w/up, pnt tin, articulated, 8", some rpnt, A $825.00
Clown Acrobat Doing Handstands, Distler, w/up, litho tin, 7", VG $335.00
Clown Artist Seated at Easel on Stepped Base, Vielmetter, 1885, hand-crank, pnt tin, EX.. $3,000.00
Clown Carousel w/2 Whales & 2 Boats, Carette, w/up, pnt tin, whales & boats rotate around clown, 11", VG, A.. $2,750.00
Clown Circus Cyclist, TPS, w/up, litho tin figure in cloth costume on lg-wheeled cycle w/sm back wheel, 6½", EX $325.00
Clown in Hoop, Germany, w/up, pnt tin, twirls over & over on 4-wheeled wire apparatus, 5", G.............................. $400.00
Clown Jack-in-the-Box, w/up, pnt compo head w/crepe paper collar, paper litho on wood box, 6", EX+, A $220.00
Clown Juggler, Alps, w/up, cloth outfit, manipulates 3 rods w/ plates & balls, 11", EX+IB.. $350.00
Clown Juggler w/Monkey, TPS, w/up, litho tin, clown balancing monkey seated in chair, 9", VGIB, A........................ $475.00
Clown Juggling Balls, Germany, w/up, pnt tin, celluloid balls on wire apparatus, 14" H, VG+ $1,000.00
Clown Musician (Banjo Player), Gunthermann, w/up, pnt tin, seated on rnd base, 6½", rpnt, A $500.00
Clown Musician (Bell Player), Germany, w/up, litho tin, standing on rnd flat base, articulated arms, 5½", EX $400.00
Clown Musician (Cello Player), w/up, pnt tin w/cloth costume, seated in chair, plink-plunk music, 8", VG, A $600.00
Clown Musician (Drummer), see also Bozo (Playing Drum)
Clown Musician (Guitarist), Distler, w/up, litho tin, standing on striped rnd base, 8½", EX+IB.. $650.00
Clown Musician (Violinist), Schuco, w/up, tin w/felt outfit, 4½", EX, A $225.00
Clown Musicians (Drummer & Cymbal Player), Germany/US Zone/EHN, w/up (on-off switch), tin, seated on rnd base, 9", EX $350.00
Clown Musicians (Violinist & Bell Player), Gunthermann, w/up, tin/cloth, seated on chair & barrel on base, 9" L, VG........ $1,750.00
Clown on Donkey, Gunthermann, w/up, litho tin, articulated legs, 5" L, EX.. $275.00
Clown on Donkey Facing Backward, Germany, w/up, pnt tin, clown pulls the donkey's tail, 6" L, VG+ $1,000.00
Clown on Horse on 4-Wheeled Platform, Germany, w/up, litho tin, dapple gray horse rears back & forth, 7" L, EX, A.... $1,200.00
Clown on Horse w/4 Wheels, w/up, pnt tin, 8" H, EX (rstr), A $275.00
Clown on Horseback (Standing w/Trinket on Stick), Germany, w/up, litho tin w/cloth pants, 8" H, VG, A.............. $550.00
Clown on Round Circus Drum & Girl on Horseback, H Yamada, pre-WW II, w/up, litho tin, 7", G $500.00
Clown on Scooter, Tipp, w/up, litho tin, 6" H, EX......... $525.00
Clown on 3 Wheels w/Clown Facing Backwards on His Back, Germany, w/up, litho tin, 6" L, EX+ $1,000.00

Clown Roller Skater, TPS, windup, lithographed tin with cloth pants, 6", EX, A, $225.00. (Photo courtesy serioustoyz.com)

Clown Standing w/Hands in Pockets, Fischer, w/up, litho tin, vibrates & turns head w/big nose, 8½", G+.............. $775.00
Clown Strong Man, Distler, w/up, litho tin, bends over to pick up weight, 5½" L, EX, A $2,750.00
Clown Tightrope Walker, Germany, w/up, pnt tin, articulated, 8x16", EX+.. $1,650.00
Clown Trainer & His Acrobatic Dog, TPS, w/up, litho tin, dog jumps through ring of 'fire,' 5½", NM+IB $275.00
Clown Trainer w/Dog, Gunthermann, w/up, tin litho, clown holding dogs front paws, 6½", G.............................. $500.00
Clown Trainer w/Dog Ready to Jump Through Hoop, Gunthermann, pnt tin, plink-plunk music, 6", EX (rstr), A.... $550.00
Clown Trainer w/Pig Performing on Stepped Platform, w/up, litho tin, 6", VG $750.00
Clown w/Parasol Seated, Germany, w/up, pnt tin, spins on half-ball base marked 'Gesenia,' articulated limbs, 7", G, A $500.00
Clown w/Spinning Star, Germany, w/up, pnt tin, 5", VG.. $400.00
Clown w/Umbrella, Germany, w/up, litho tin w/pnt umbrella that spins the clown around, 6", VG+ $725.00
Clown w/Umbrella Hat Standing w/Hands in Pockets, Germany, w/up, litho tin, 8", VG.. $400.00
Clown Walking, w/up, pnt tin w/flocked hat, articulated arms, fixed legs, 9", VG, A $600.00
Clown Walking in 2-Wheel Apparatus, w/up, pnt tin, 7" dia, G+ $375.00
Clowns (2) Handstanding on Round Base, hand-turned, pnt tin, 7", some rpnt, A.. $775.00
Clowns (2) on Rocker Base, Gunthermann, w/up, pnt tin, clowns lift beam & ball rolls back & forth, 7½" L, G+ $900.00
Clowns (2) on See-Saw w/Rings, Gunthermann, w/up, pnt tin, plays plink-plunk music, 8½x8", EX, A................ $1,650.00
Clowns (2) on Tricycle, Fischer, w/up, litho tin, sm clown playing horn facing rear, 8" L, VG+........................... $4,000.00
Clowns (2) Performing on Beveled Base, Gunthermann, w/up, tin, 1 rolling barrel in feet & 1 playing banjo, 9" L, rpnt, A.. $2,200.00

Clowns (2) Tumbling in 2-Wheel Apparatus, w/up, pnt tin, 9" dia, G+ $400.00
Coney Island, Technofix, w/up, plastic & tin, cars travel around roller coaster, 21x15", NMIB, A $200.00
Convertible Coupe, Bing, w/up, litho tin, 'tin lizzy'-type woman driver, 7", EX, A $950.00
Couple Waltzing, Gunthermann, w/up, pnt tin, 8", G, A .. $600.00
Covered Wagon, Occupied Japan, w/up, tin Conastoga wagon w/wht cloth top, celluloid mule, 9" L, NMIB $150.00
Cowboy on Horse w/Lasso, see Bar-X Cowboy
Cowboy on Rocking Horse, Cragstan, w/up, litho tin, wht horse w/red rocker, 7" L, EXIB $250.00
Crawling Mickey Mouse, see Mickey Mouse (Crawling)
Cubby the Reading Bear, Alps, w/up, plush w/cloth overalls, 7", EXIB $200.00
Cycling Quacky, Alps, w/up, litho tin duck on tricycle, 6", NMIB, A $150.00
Dalli w/Driver, Schuco #1001, w/up, litho tin, celluloid driver w/hat & glasses, 6", NMIB, A $400.00
Dancer on Beaded Carousel, Japan, prewar, celluloid, 3-step platform, 5½", EX $650.00
Dancing Sam, S&E, w/up, litho tin figure w/cane on drum base, 8½", EX $425.00
Dandy, Mikuni, w/up, litho tin, man tips his hat, 6", EX+IB . $150.00
Dandy Jim w/Clown Violinist Atop Roof, Unique Art, w/up, litho tin, 10½" H, EX, A $725.00

Davy Crockett Stagecoach and Frontier Wagon, Linemar, 1950s, windup, lithographed tin, each 4" long, NMIB, $700.00. (Photo courtesy whatacharacter.com)

Deep Sea Diver, Germany, w/up, litho tin, 8", NM $3,500.00
Delivery Cycle, Japan, prewar, w/up, litho tin, rider on 3-wheeled motor cart, 5½", VG, A $770.00
Descamps Bull Dog, w/up, cloth covered, glass eyes, w/leash, walks & moves head, 9" L, VG+, A $500.00
Descamps Elephant, w/up, cloth covered, glass eyes, red back blanket, lumbering walking motion, 13" L, VG+, A $400.00
Descamps Lion, w/up, hide-covered, glass eyes, head moves, crouches, growls, leaps forward, 17" L, EX, A $600.00
Descamps Tiger, w/up, cloth covered, glass eyes, moves head & growls, crouches back & leaps, 15" L, EX, A $650.00
Disneyland Skating Rink, England, plunger action, litho tin, Mickey & Donald move around rink, 5" L, EXIB, A $1,350.00
Dodgem Car, w/up, litho tin, 4½" L, EXIB $85.00

Dog Chariot w/Poodle Driver, Gunthermann, w/up, emb litho & pnt tin, 8½" L, EX, A $2,750.00
Doin' the Howdy Doody, Unique Art, w/up, litho tin, Buffalo Bob plays the piano while Howdy dances, 8x7", EXIB, A..$1,500.00
Doin' the Howdy Doody, Unique Art, w/up, litho tin, Buffalo Bob plays the piano while Howdy dances, 8x7", NMIB .. $2,000.00
Donald Duck, Japan, 1950s, w/up, celluloid, jtd arms & legs, eyes wide open, mouth shows red tongue, head bobs, 6", EX $675.00
Donald Duck, Schuco, 1930s, tin w/cloth jacket & hat, jtd arms & legs, makes quacking sound, w/ID tag, 6", EXIB...... $2,250.00
Donald Duck, w/up, celluloid figure w/long bill, articulated arms, 3", EX+IB $600.00
Donald Duck & Nephews Hunting, Linemar, w/up, litho tin Donald & 3 nephews w/guns on a string, 11" L, EX $475.00
Donald Duck Carousel, Borgfeldt, prewar, w/up, celluloid figure under beaded umbrella w/figures, tin platform, 9", EXIB $7,500.00
Donald Duck Climbing Fireman, Linemar, litho tin, 14", EX, A $400.00

Donald Duck Climbing Fireman, Linemar, 1950s, windup, lithographed tin, NM, $500.00. (Photo courtesy serioustoyz.com)

Donald Duck Crawler, Japan, prewar, windup, celluloid, 9", NMIB, A, $6,725.00. (Photo courtesy Morphy Auctions)

Donald Duck Drummer, Linemar, w/up, litho tin, 6", VG+.. $250.00
Donald Duck Hopper, Linemar, w/up, litho tin figure, 5", EX.. $350.00
Donald Duck in Fire Chief Car, Linemar, w/up, tin, 5½" L, VG+, A $775.00
Donald Duck in Pluto Cart, Borgfeldt/Japan, prewar, w/up, celluloid figures, tin cart, 9" L, EX $1,800.00
Donald Duck in Pluto Cart, Borgfeldt/Japan, prewar, w/up, celluloid figures, tin cart, 9" L, G+, A $900.00

Donald Duck in Pluto Cart, Borgfeldt/Japan, prewar, w/up, celluloid figures, tin cart, 9" L, NM+IB, A $3,000.00
Donald Duck on Rocking Horse, Japan, w/up, celluloid Donald on pnt wood horse, 7½" L $2,500.00
Donald Duck on Trike w/Bell, Japan, w/up, early long-billed celluloid figure, bl trike w/red wheels, 4", no flag, EX... $475.00
Donald Duck on Trike w/Bell, Linemar, w/up, newer celluloid figure, mc trike, 3½" L, EX+IB $175.00
Donald Duck Pulling Huey in Three-Wheeled Car, Linemar, tin, Donald walks & quacks, 6", VGIB $450.00
Donald Duck Race Car, Occupied Japan, w/up, celluloid Donald in tin race car, 3", NMIB $350.00
Donald Duck Rail Car, Lionel, w/up, compo Donald at controls w/Pluto protruding from doghouse, EXIB $1,100.00
Donald Duck the Straight Shooter, Mauco Prod, 1950, plastic, articulated arms hold 2 6-shooters, 6", EXIB $525.00
Donald Duck w/Huey & Voice, Linemar, friction, litho tin, Donald pulls Huey & quacks, 5", NMIB $1,100.00
Donald Duck Waddler, Borgfeldt, prewar, w/up, celluloid, jtd arms & legs, winking, 5½", EX $600.00
Donald Duck Waddler, Borgfeldt, prewar, w/up, celluloid, jtd arms & legs, winking, 5½", EXIB $1,000.00
Donald Duck Waddler, Linemar, w/up, tin & plush, 6", NMIB, A $450.00

Donald Duck Walker, Schuco, 1930s, windup, tin with cloth jacket and hat, articulated arms and legs, makes quacking sound, 6", EXIB, A, $2,200.00.
(Photo courtesy Morphy Auctions)

Donald Duck Washing Machine w/Comic Action, MT, w/up, litho tin, 7½", EXIB (box reads 'Wind-Up Washing Machine...') $375.00
Donald Duck Whirling Tail, Linemar, w/up, litho tin, 5", NMIB, A $775.00
Donkey, Marusan, w/up, standing upright smoking pipe, plush w/cloth outfit, 10", EXIB $125.00
Drum Major, Wolverine #27, w/up, litho tin, 14", NMIB.. $450.00
Drummer (The), Japan, 1930s, w/up, celluloid figure standing on wooden base, cloth outfit, beats drum, 11½", EXIB .. $250.00
Drunkard, Martin/France, w/up, cloth-clothed figure in top hat, hold wooden bottle & lead cup, 8", EX+, A $750.00

Duck the Mailman w/2 Cases Carrying Geese, TPS, w/up, litho tin, 4", scarce, EX, A $275.00
Ducky Ducklings, Wyandotte, w/up, litho tin, mama duck pulling 2 ducklings, EXIB, A $100.00
Ducky the Early Bird, K Co, 1950s, w/up, litho tin, 4", MIB, A $75.00
Elephant, see also Descamps Elephant
Elephant Barker, Japan, w/up, celluloid stand-up figure in pnt circus uniform, waves arms & moves head, 9", VG+ $450.00
Elephant in Dapper Outfit w/Cane & Eye Glasses, Gunthermann, w/up, pnt tin w/cast metal feet, 6", EX, A $4,400.00
Elephant on 3-Wheeled Scooter, Gunthermann, w/up, litho tin, 6½" H, VG+, A $300.00
Elephant Performing on Ball w/Bell at End of Trunk, Gunthermann, flocked tin elephant w/pnt tin ball, 6" H, VG+, A $525.00
Elephant w/Arab in Howdah, w/up, pnt tin, 5" L, EX (rstr).. $425.00
Elf Pushing Wheelbarrow, w/up, pnt tin, 7", VG+, A $500.00
Erco Clown Barrel Walker, US Zone, w/up, litho tin, 8", NMIB $650.00
Exposition Universelle, Martin, flywheel mechanism, pnt tin, Asian pulling lady passenger in rickshaw, 8" L, EX+, A......... $3,300.00
Express Bellboy, Gescha, Germany/US Zone, 1940s, compo figure w/tin arms & legs, runs w/Express steamer trunk, 3" H, EX $200.00

Felix on Wheeled Platform, Nifty, 1926, windup, lithographed tin, 11x14" long, EX, A, $29,120.00.
(Photo courtesy Morphy Auctions)

Felix Scooter, Nifty, ca 1930, w/up, litho tin, Felix on 3-wheeled scooter, 8", NMIB, A $6,150.00
Felix the Cat, Germany, w/up, pnt tin figure seated w/head turned sideways, darts out & circles, 5½", VG, A $1,100.00
Felix the Cat Dancing Toy, 1920s, w/up, plush figure w/tin feet, 10" (12" w/ears extended), EXIB, A $725.00
Felix the Cat in Race Car, Nifty/Borgfeldt, pnt wood, articulated axle allows Felix to jump up & down, 12" L, VG, A . $330.00
Felix the Cat on 3-Wheeled Scooter, INGAP/Italy, w/up, litho tin, 5" H, VG, A $1,650.00

Felix the Cat on 3-Wheeled Scooter, Nifty, litho tin, 7½" H, VG........ $525.00

Felix the Cat Walker, Germany, w/up, pnt tin, balances on long tail, flat-sided legs, 6½", VG, A........ $450.00

Felix the Moving Cat Sparkler, Nifty/Borgfeldt, plunger-activated, 5", EX........ $300.00

Ferris Wheel & Tower on Beveled Platform, Doll et Cie, hand-crank, pnt tin w/compo figures, 20" H, G, A........ $1,800.00

Ferry Boat, Yonezawa, w/up, litho tin, boat shuttles back & forth w/bus, EXIB, A........ $250.00

Finnegan In Again Out Again, Unique Art, w/up, litho tin, 13½" L, EXIB, A........ $300.00

Fishing Monkey on Whales, TPS, w/up, litho tin, 9", NMIB, A........ $300.00

Flirt Open Auto w/Driver, Hess, flywheel action, litho tin, 2-seat open auto w/driver on right side, 5", VG+, A........ $1,200.00

Flying Circus, Unique Art, w/up, litho tin, complete, 13" H, NMIB, A........ $1,700.00

Flying Trapeze, Wolverine, w/up, litho tin, 9", VG+IB, A........ $125.00

Flying Trapeze Aparatus, Gunthermann, w/up, pnt & litho tin w/paper prop at rear, w/figure, 7" L, VG+........ $3,575.00

Fox the Magician, TN, w/up, plush & tin, 6", EXIB........ $225.00

Foxy Grandpa, Germany, squeeze his belly and he tips his hat, composition head with wooden hands and feet, cloth outfit, EX, A, $350.00. (Photo courtesy Morphy Auctions)

Foxy Grandpa, Germany, 1910s, w/up, compo head & hands, lead feet, cloth outfit, 6", EX, A........ $550.00

Foxy Grandpa, Germany, 1910s, w/up, pnt tin figure w/wire-rimmed eye glasses, 8½" T, EX+, A........ $550.00

Frankenstein Mechanical Monster, Linemar, w/up, plastic, 6", MIB........ $725.00

Fred Flintstone on Dino, Linemar, 1960s, w/up, litho tin w/vinyl head, 8" L, EX, A........ $125.00

Friendly Motorcycle, IY/Japan, friction, litho tin, man & woman riders, 12", NMIB, A........ $8,000.00

Frog, Kellerman, w/up, pnt tin, stands upright & chases fly, gr & yel w/red bow tie, 4½" H, NM........ $1,150.00

Frog Standing Upright Singing, Gunthermann, w/up, pnt tin, holding songbook, 7½", EX (rstr), A........ $650.00

Fruit Vendor, Martin, windup, lithographed tin, 4x7½" long, EX, A, $1,035.00. (Photo courtesy James D. Julia, Inc.)

Futurmatic Airport, Automatic Toy Co, 1950s, w/up, litho tin, 15x15", NMIB........ $150.00

Gely, German, w/up, litho tin, 6", VG, A........ $450.00

General Butler Walker, Ives, clockwork, cloth outfit, pnt features, NM, A........ $3,350.00

George Washington Bridge, Fritz Bueschel, w/up, litho tin, w/Greyhound bus, 25" L, EX........ $500.00

GI Joe & his Jouncing Jeep, 7½", EX, $200.00. (Photo courtesy Morphy Auctions)

GI Joe & His Jouncing Jeep, Unique Art, w/up, litho tin, 7½", EX+IB, A........ $350.00

GI Joe & His K-9 Pups, Unique Art, w/up, litho tin, 9", EX........ $200.00

GI Joe & His K-9 Pups, Unique Art, w/up, litho tin, 9", EXIB, A........ $350.00

Giant Train, SSS, friction, litho tin train engine, EXIB, A........ $75.00

Girl Feeding Parrot, Germany, w/up, pnt tin, girl standing next to table w/parrot cage, 6½" H, G, A........ $4,025.00

Go Stop/Safety First, Japan, w/up, celluloid traffic cop standing next to Go/Stop sign on 'brick' base, NM+ $1,200.00
Good Time Charlie, Alps, w/up, clown w/cloth outfit & paper hat blows on party whistle, 13", NMIB, A.............. $200.00
Goofy Cyclist, Linemar, w/up, litho tin, Goofy on tricycle w/bell, 7½", EX+IB, A.. $1,750.00

Goofy Windups, Linemar, Whirl-tail Goofy, 5"; Goofy on unicycle, VG, 1835, $250.00 each. (Photo courtesy Morphy Auctions)

Groggy, Occupied Japan, w/up, celluloid man in litho tin car, 4½" H, NMIB, A.. $375.00
Gym-Toys Acrobat, see Pluto Acrobat
Gyro Cycle, Tri-Ang, litho tin, VGIB............................ $450.00
Ham 'N Sam, Linemar, w/up, litho tin, 5½" H, EX......... $650.00
Happy Bunny (Drummer), Nomura, w/up, litho tin, standing, 8", EX+IB $525.00
Happy Bunny (Piano Player), Japan, w/up, plush & litho tin, 8" H, EXIB.. $225.00
Happy Clown, Germany, w/up, litho tin, bl jacket, red & wht striped pants, raises neck & blinks, 6", NMIB $250.00
Happy Easter Hand Car, Wyandotte, 1940s, w/up, litho tin, bunny steering 4-wheeled car w/basket, 6½", VG+, A.......... $250.00
Happy Hippo, TPS, w/up, litho tin, native on hippo's back dangles bananas as hippo opens mouth, 6", NM+IB $475.00
Happy Hooligan, see Let's Go! Happy (Hooligan)
Happy Jack Dancer, Kellerman, crank-op, litho tin, blk man in top hat w/hands on hips, 6", VG, A........................ $325.00
Happy Life, Alps/Occupied Japan, w/up, bobble-head girl rocks in chair under spinning parasol w/balls on base, 9", EXIB.. $600.00
Happy Penguin, Marusan, w/up, litho tin, 6", NMIB, A.. $200.00
Happy the Violinist (Clown), TPS, w/up, litho tin w/red & wht striped cloth pants, 8½", NMIB.............................. $150.00
Harold Lloyd Bumper Car, Germany, ca 1925, w/up, litho tin, 5", EX, A $3,850.00
Harold Lloyd Sparkler, Germany, litho tin, head only, 5½", EX, A .$225.00
Harold Lloyd Sparkler, Isla, 1920s, litho tin, full articulated figure, 9", EX.. $1,750.00
Harold Lloyd Waddler, Germany, 1920s, w/up, litho tin, 7", EX $1,450.00

Hen in Basket, Baldwin, 1939, hand-crank, lithographed tin, clucks and lays wooden eggs, EX, A, $550.00.

Hen Pulling Chick on 2-Wheeled Box, Hans Eberl/Germany, w/up, litho tin, 9½" L, VG.. $350.00
Henry, see also Circus Henry
Henry & Henrietta Running Away, Japan, 1930s, celluloid, Henry w/suitcase attached to wire walking apparatus, 8", EX, A $1,900.00
Henry & His Brother, Japan, prewar, w/up, celluloid figures on separate wheeled platforms attached w/string, 7", EX, A.....$775.00

Henry and His Brother, Japan, prewar, windup, celluloid figures, 7", NMIB, A, $2,000.00. (Photo courtesy Morphy Auctions)

Henry & His Swan, Japan/Borgfeldt, 1930s, w/up, celluloid w/tin cart, 6x9", NMIB, A $1,800.00
Henry & Porter on Elephant, Borgfeldt, prewar, w/up, celluloid, Henry on elephant's trunk & porter on back, 8" L, EXIB $1,350.00
Henry & Porter on Elephant, Borgfeldt, prewar, w/up, celluloid, Henry on elephant's trunk & Porter on back, 8" L, VG............ $775.00
Henry & Porter on 4-Wheeled Platform, Borgfeldt, prewar, w/up, celluloid figures, tin base, VGIB........................... $1,350.00
Henry Eating Candy, Linemar, 1950s, w/up, litho tin, 5½", EX $400.00
Henry Motoring (w/Porter in 3-Wheeled Cycle Cart), Borgfeldt, prewar, celluloid figures, tin cycle, 6", NMIB........ $2,250.00

Henry Motoring (w/Porter on 3-Wheeled Cycle Cart), Borgfeldt, prewar, celluloid figure, tin cycle, 6", VG $675.00

Henry on Swan Cart, Japan, prewar, w/up, celluloid figures, 4-weeled cart, 8", EX+ $825.00

Henry the Acrobat, w/up, celluloid figure on metal trapeze apparatus, 6", EX+IB $300.00

Henry Trapeze, Japan, prewar, w/up, 3 celluloid figures on wire apparatus, 10", EXIB.. $950.00

Henry w/Suitcase, CK/Japan, 1930s, w/up, celluloid figure w/litho tin suitcase on wire walking apparatus, 5", EX, A..$1,200.00

Hi-Way Henry, Nifty, w/up, litho tin jalopy w/figures, 10", EX, A $3,250.00

Hi-Way Henry, Nifty, windup, lithographed tin jalopy, 10", NM, A, $760.00. (Photo courtesy Morphy Auctions)

Hi-Way Henry, Nifty, w/up, litho tin jalopy w/figures, 10", VG, A $2,100.00

Hoky & Poky Handcar, Wyandotte, w/up, litho tin, 7" L, EXIB, ... $225.00

Home Run King, Selrite, w/up, litho tin, 6" L, VG $450.00

Home Town Laundry Van, IY Metal Toys, 1960s, friction, tin, blk & orange w/wht roof, celluloid driver, 12½", VG+, A $325.00

Honk-Along Roadster, Kanto, friction, tin, w/driver, 7", NM+IB, A $125.00

Hot Rod, Masuya, friction, litho tin w/BRT, Hot Rod lettered on sides, dog driver makes barking sound, 8" L, NM+IB, A $400.00

Hott 'an' Tott, Unique Art, w/up, litho tin, 8", EX+ $775.00

Hott 'an' Tott, Unique Art, windup, lithographed tin, 8", VG, $475.00. (Photo courtesy James D. Julia, Inc.)

Howdy Doody Acrobat, Arnold, lever-activated, figure w/plastic head & cloth body, tin base, 14", EX, A $100.00

Howdy Doody Cart, Ny-Lint, w/up, litho tin, 9", VG $300.00

Huckleberry Hound Hopper, Linemar, 1962, w/up, litho tin hopping figure, 4", EX+... $175.00

Humphery Mobile, Wyandotte, windup, lithographed tin, 8", EXIB, $500.00. (Photo courtesy serioustoyz.com)

Humphrey Mobile, Wyandotte, w/up, litho tin, 8", NMIB..$650.00

Ice Cream (5¢) Scooter, Courtland, w/up, litho tin, driver rings bell, 6½", EX, A $225.00

Ice Cream (5¢) Scooter, Courtland, w/up, litho tin, driver rings bell, 6½", EX+IB, A $325.00

Ice Cream Vendor (Monkey), Yone, w/up, tin & plastic, monkey pushes cart as umbrella spins, 5", NMIB, A $150.00

Indian Rowing in Canoe, Arnold, w/up, tin, 8", NM, A . $875.00

Indian w/Bow & Arrow Walking, w/up, pnt tin, 7", EX. $450.00

Injun Chief, Ohio Art, w/up, EX+IB $175.00

Jacko the Organ Grinder, Distler, w/up, litho tin, man playing 2-wheeled street organ w/monkey atop, 6½" L, EX+, A $3,025.00

Jazzbo Jim, Unique Art, w/up, litho tin, 10", NMIB, A.. $775.00

Jazzbo Jim, Unique Art, w/up, litho tin, 10", VGIB, A... $350.00

JFK Rocking Chair, Kamar/Japan, 1963, w/up, JFK reading newspaper in rocking chair, musical, vinyl & wood, 12", NMIB $450.00

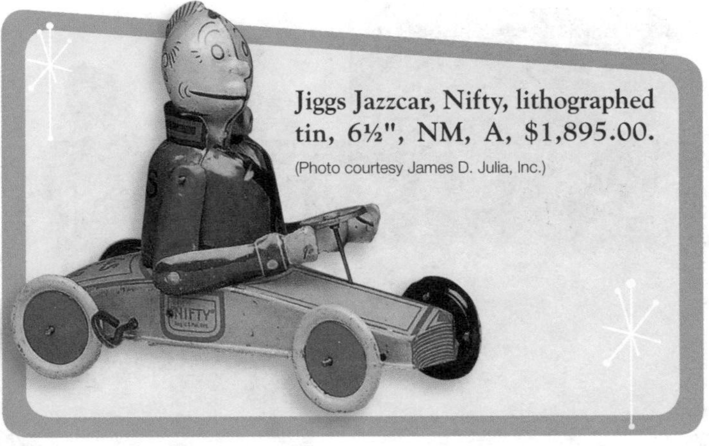

Jiggs Jazzcar, Nifty, lithographed tin, 6½", NM, A, $1,895.00. (Photo courtesy James D. Julia, Inc.)

Joe's Kitchen Wagon, H, friction, litho tin, side of van opens to reveal Joe in his kitchen, 10", EX........................... $225.00

Johnny the Clown, Lindstrom, w/up, litho tin, 8", EX ... $175.00

Johnny the Clown, Lindstrom, w/up, litho tin, 8", NM+.. $275.00

Judo Man, Japan, w/up, tin w/cloth judo outfit, 9½", NMIB.. $575.00
Juggler, see Boy Juggler
Juggling Clown (Alps), see Clown Juggler
Juke Box, Haji, w/up, 5", litho tin, NM+IB, A $300.00
Jumbo (the Elephant w/Rider Under Umbrella), Germany/US Zone, litho tin, 4" L, NM+IB $1,050.00

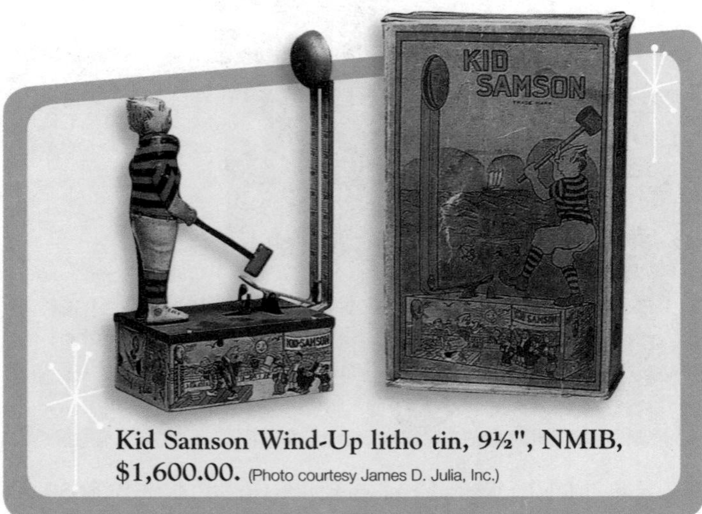

Kid Samson Wind-Up litho tin, 9½", NMIB, $1,600.00. (Photo courtesy James D. Julia, Inc.)

Kiddie Kampers, Wolverine, 1930s, w/up, litho tin, 14" L, EXIB $450.00
Kiddy Cyclist, Unique Art, w/up, litho tin, 9", EX+IB... $375.00
Kiddy Cyclist, Unique Art, w/up, litho tin, 9", VG $225.00
Koko the Clown, Germany, 1920s, w/up, papier-maché w/lead feet, cloth outfit/hat, yel pom-pon buttons, wht trim, 9", EX.. $1,250.00
Krazy Kar, Unique Art, w/up, litho tin, 8" L, EXIB $675.00
Le Champion (Buffalo Bill), France (?), lever action, pnt tin, man w/gun on 'grassy' mound, 9", EX $1,450.00
Le Petit Livreur (Boy Pushing Handcart w/Box), Martin, w/up, pnt & litho tin w/cloth outfit, 8" L, EX+IB, A $1,875.00
Lester the Jester, Alps, w/up, celluloid & tin clown figure in cloth costume twirls cane, 9½", NMIB........................... $250.00
Let's Go! Happy (Hooligan), Kiddies Metal Toys, w/up, litho tin, 10", NMIB, A $1,500.00

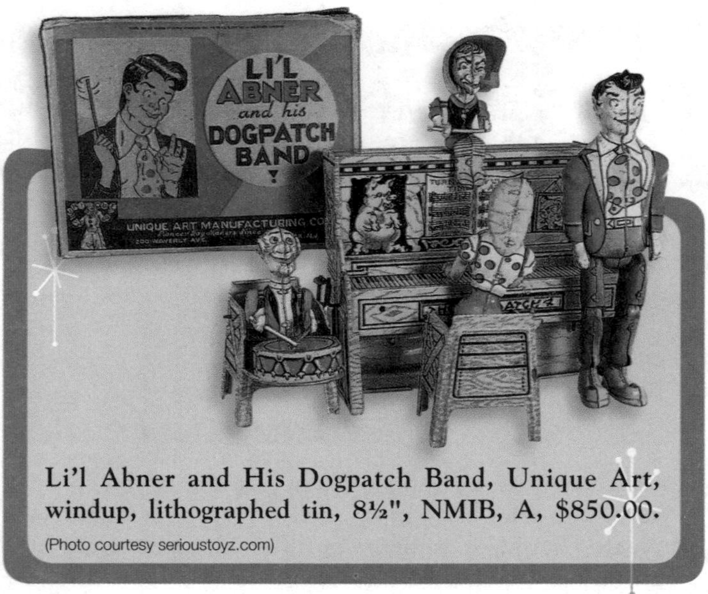

Li'l Abner and His Dogpatch Band, Unique Art, windup, lithographed tin, 8½", NMIB, A, $850.00. (Photo courtesy serioustoyz.com)

Li'l Abner & His Dogpatch Band, Unique Art, w/up, litho tin, 8½", EX+, A... $475.00
Lil'l Abner & Lonesome Polecat Canoe, Ideal, w/up, plastic, 11½", MIB.. $225.00
Lincoln Tunnel, Unique Art, w/up, litho tin, 24" L, NMIB, A $375.00
Lion, see Descamps Lion
Little Monkey Artist, TN, plush, w/cloth jacket & hat, seated w/artist's palette, 7", EXIB $200.00
Little Monkey Shiner, TN, w/up, plush figure w/vinyl face, 6", EXIB.. $100.00
Little Orphan Annie & Sandy, Japan, w/up, celluloid figures on tin platforms, wind Annie & she pulls Sandy, 6½", EX... $700.00
Little Shoemaker, Japan, w/up, litho tin figure w/realistic wht hair, cloth jacket, EXIB $175.00
Loop the Loop, McDowell, w/up, litho tin, 13" L, VGIB.. $250.00
Lucky #7 Scooter, Yoshiya, crank-op, litho tin w/vinyl-headed driver, 5½", EXIB, A $85.00
Lucky Monkey Playing Billiards, TPS, w/up, litho tin, 4", NMIB $350.00
Mad Hatter's Sky View Taxi, Linemar, friction, litho tin, 5", EX+IB, A $550.00
Maggie & Jiggs, Nifty, w/up, litho tin, ea figure on 2-wheeled platform connected by steel spring, 6" H, EX+..... $1,000.00

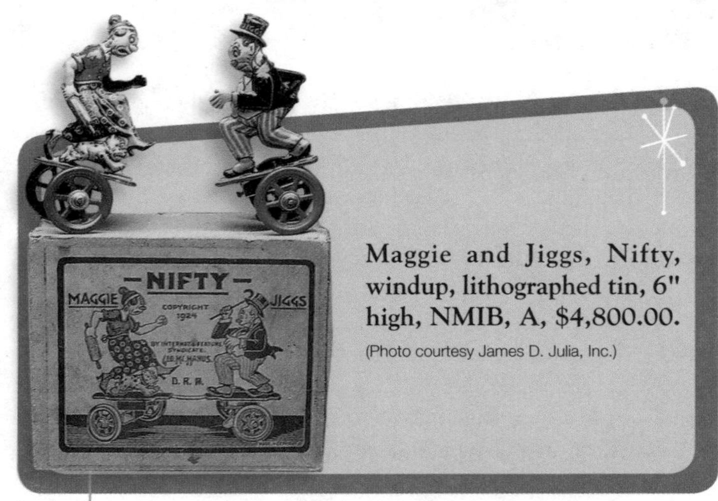

Maggie and Jiggs, Nifty, windup, lithographed tin, 6" high, NMIB, A, $4,800.00. (Photo courtesy James D. Julia, Inc.)

Maggie & Jiggs, Nifty, w/up, litho tin figures facing off on 4-wheeled base, 7" L, EXIB, A................................. $1,500.00
Magic Boat, Yoshiya, crank-op, litho tin speedboat w/driver & outboard motor advances w/mystery action, 8", NMIB.... $300.00
Magic Car No 2, Masudaya, friction, litho tin, 6", EX+IB, A .. $175.00
Mama Kanagroo w/Playful Baby, TPS, w/up, litho tin, 6½", EX+IB, A $100.00
Mammy, Lindstrom, w/up, litho tin, red, 8", VG, A....... $225.00
Mammy, Lindstrom, w/up, litho tin, scarce gr version, 8", VG..$425.00
Man Carrying Suitcases, Distler, w/up, litho tin, red hat & pants, plaid jacket, 7½", VG+... $1,100.00
Man fishing on Octagonal Base, Gely/Germany, w/up, litho tin, 4x4", EX $250.00
Man in Runabout, Paya/Spain, w/up, litho tin, driver seated in 2-wheeled vehicle w/sm front wheel, lg horn, 5", EX+, A $1,750.00

Man on the Flying Trapeze, Wyandotte, w/up, litho tin, 9", VG+IB, A $100.00
Man Pushing Wheelbarrow, Girard, w/up, tin, 6", EX.... $175.00

Marionette Theatre, Japan, windup, two celluloid figures, 11", VG, A, $250.00. (Photo courtesy Morphy Auctions)

Mary & Her Little Lamb, Japan, w/up, celluloid figures on separate wheeled bases attached w/string, 6½", EX......... $250.00
Mechanical Playground, Lee MFG, w/up, litho tin, 14x9½", NM+IB, A $175.00
Mercury Special #21 Racer, Asahitoy, 1960s, w/up, driver raises arms to signal a turn, 7½", EX, A $150.00
Merry Cockyolly See-Saw, Yoneya, w/up, litho tin, 6" L, NMIB $175.00
Merry Tourist Land, K, w/up, litho tin, 6" sq, NMIB...... $100.00
Merry Xmas Santa Car S-1, Epoch, friction, litho tin, 5½", NM, A $125.00
Merry-Go-Round, Alps, w/up, litho tin, cars w/riders move around 3 balls on rods in center, 9½" dia, NMIB, A.............. $225.00
Merry-Go-Round, Wolverine #31A, w/up, tin, 11", EX+IB, A $300.00

Merry-Go-Round, Wyandotte, lever action, lithographed tin, 5" high, NM+IB, A, $400.00. (Photo courtesy Smith House Toy and Auction Co.)

Mickey Mouse (Crawling), Japan, prewar, w/up, cloth-covered body w/celluloid head & limbs, 5", NMIB, A.......$8,400.00
Mickey Mouse (Tumbling), Schuco, w/up, cloth covered, 4½", EX, A $300.00
Mickey Mouse (Twirling Tail), Linemar, w/up, litho tin figure, 5", VG $250.00
Mickey Mouse & Donald Duck on Seesaw, Japan, rubber-band action w/lead weight pendulum, center gear, celluloid, 5" H, VG $500.00
Mickey Mouse & Donald Duck on Trapeze, Borgfeldt/WD, w/up, celluloid figures on wire apparatus, 7" H, A..........$2,750.00
Mickey Mouse & Donald Duck Race Car, WDP, w/up, tin, ea figure in own car, 3" L, EXIB (1 box), A................. $450.00
Mickey Mouse & Felix the Cat (Cigar-Smoking) Sparkler, Rogelio, Sanchez/Spain (mk La Isla RS), litho tin, 6", EX, A $12,100.00
Mickey Mouse & Minnie Acrobat, Japan, w/up, celluloid figures on wire apparatus, 8", EXIB, A............................$2,520.00

Mickey Mouse and Minnie on Elephant, Japan, windup, celluloid, 9½", EX, A, $4,400.00. (Photo courtesy Morphy Auctions)

Mickey Mouse Carousel, Borgfeldt, w/up, celluloid & tin, under beaded umbrella w/Minnie, Donald & Pluto, 10", NMIB, A $6,700.00
Mickey Mouse Carousel, Japan, prewar, w/up, celluloid & tin, under beaded umbrella, no figures, 7", EX, A........... $575.00
Mickey Mouse Circus (Lionel) Train, Wells & Co Ltd/England, complete w/accessories, EX+IB, A $6,050.00
Mickey Mouse Circus Train, Lionel/WDE, w/up, litho tin w/tent & truck, compo Mickey figure, EXIB, A $5,500.00
Mickey Mouse Crazy Car, Occupied Japan, w/up, celluloid Mickey in tin car, 4", NMIB, A............................$2,125.00
Mickey Mouse Cyclist, Linemar, w/up, litho tin, Mickey riding tricycle w/bell, 7", EXIB, A $1,650.00
Mickey Mouse Cyclist, Linemar, w/up, litho tin, Mickey riding tricylce w/bell, 7" H, EX, A $775.00
Mickey Mouse Cyclist (Walt Disney's Mechanical Tricycle), Linemar, w/up, celluloid figure on litho tin trike, 4" L, EXIB $6,600.00
Mickey Mouse Drummer, Nifty, litho tin, flat figure plays drums w/articulated arms, 8", VG, A $1,050.00
Mickey Mouse Drummer, Nifty, litho tin, flat figure plays drums w/articulated arms, 8", EXIB, A $4,600.00

Mickey Mouse Handcar, Wells of London, 1930s, w/up, pnt compo Mickey & Minnie figures, w/track & 2 buildings, EX+IB, A $2,000.00

Mickey Mouse Handcar, Wells of London, 1940s, w/up, compo Mickey & Donald Duck figures, w/track & 2 buildings, EXIB, A $1,500.00

Mickey Mouse Hurdy Gurdy, Germany, 1930s, windup, lithographed tin, 8", EX, A, $7,275.00. (Photo courtesy Morphy Auctions)

Mickey Mouse in Convertible, Japan, friction, litho tin w/allover images of friends, 5", EX+, A $225.00

Mickey Mouse in Open Auto, Germany/US Zone, w/up, cotton-spun Mickey figure in tin auto w/clown graphics, 4" L, EX+, A $750.00

Mickey Mouse Nodder, Borgfeldt, w/up, celluloid figure standing w/hand on hip & mandolin, 7", EX, A $525.00

Mickey Mouse on Motorcycle, Linemar, friction, litho tin, 4" L, EX $600.00

Mickey Mouse on Rocking Horse, Borgfeldt, prewar, w/up, celluloid Mickey w/wooden horse, 8", NMIB $8,400.00

Mickey Mouse on Rocking Pluto, Borgfeldt, prewar, w/up, celluloid, 6½", VG, A $1,100.00

Mickey Mouse on Rocking Pluto, Linemar, litho tin, 7" L, VGIB, A $1,775.00

Mickey Mouse on 3-Wheeled Scooter, Linemar, w/up, litho tin, 5" H, EX+, A $375.00

Mickey Mouse Roller Skater, Linemar, w/up, litho tin w/cloth pants, 6" H, VG $600.00

Mickey Mouse Silver Streak Train #2509, Wells, w/up, tin, w/the Mickey Stoker, Band & Circus cars, 22" L, VG $500.00

Mickey Mouse Sparkler, Nifty, lever-activated, litho tin head figure w/name in wht on blk bow tie, 5", EX, A $325.00

Mickey Mouse Sparkler, Spain, 1930s, plunger action, litho tin, Mickey waits for cat to pop out of basket, VG+, A .. $5,000.00

Mickey Mouse the Magician, Linemar, w/up, litho tin, 6", EX, A $1,100.00

Mickey Mouse Unicyclist, Linemar, w/up, litho tin w/cloth pants, 5½", EX+, A $1,325.00

Mickey Mouse Walker, Borgfeldt/WDE, 1930s, w/up, string-jtd celluloid figure, 7", EX, A $1,750.00

Mickey Mouse Walker, Borgfeldt/WDE, 1930s, w/up, string-jtd celluloid figure, 7", G, A $550.00

Mickey Mouse Walker, Germany, w/up, compo w/felt head & glass eyes, cloth outfit, early unauthorized version, 8", EX, A $825.00

Mickey Mouse Whirligig, STS/Japan, prewar, celluloid Mickey standing on tin base under beaded parasol, 12", EXIB, A, $8,950.00. (Photo courtesy Morphy Auctions)

Mickey Mouse Xylophone, Linemar, w/up, 7", VG, A ... $225.00

Mike Mallard Climbing Fireman, Linemar, w/up, litho tin, 13½", EX $250.00

Minnie Mouse (Nannie) Pushing Felix the Cat in Pram, Rogelio Sanchez/Spain, 1930s, w/up, litho tin, 8x7" L, EX .. $20,900.00

Minnie Mouse Carousel, Japan, prewar, w/up, celluloid figure under beaded umbrella on platform, 12", EX, A ... $2,240.00

Minnie Mouse Carrying Cages w/Felix the Cat, Rogelio Sanchez/Spain, w/up, litho tin, 8", EX, A $775.00

Minnie Mouse Cart Pulled By Pluto, Japan, prewar, tin cart w/celluloid figures, 7", EX $450.00

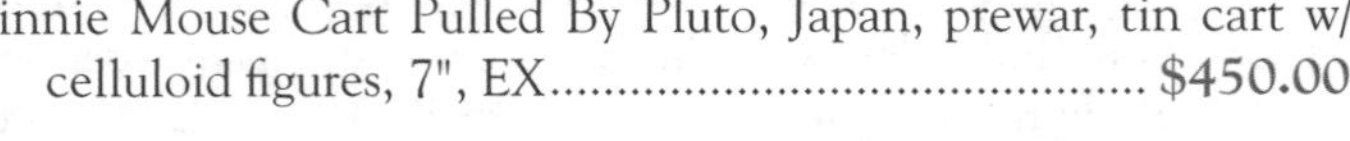

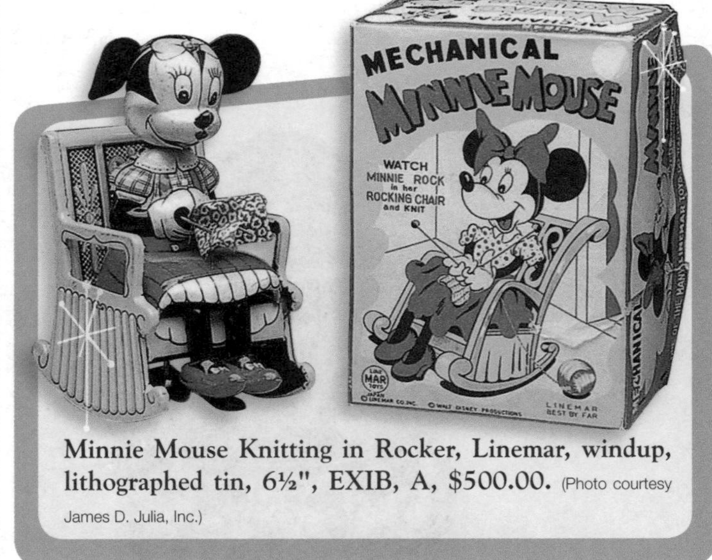

Minnie Mouse Knitting in Rocker, Linemar, windup, lithographed tin, 6½", EXIB, A, $500.00. (Photo courtesy James D. Julia, Inc.)

Minnie Mouse Knitting in Rocker, Linemar, w/up, litho tin, 6½" H, NMIB, A $825.00

Mobile Duck (Who Plays the Xylophone), Sankei, w/up, litho tin, 5½", NMIB, A $350.00

Monkey Batter (Baseball), Sankei, w/up, litho tin w/rubber tail, 7½", EX+IB, A $325.00

Monkey Car, Distler, windup, lithographed tin, 6", NM, $1,300.00. (Photo courtesy James D. Julia, Inc.)

Monkey Car, Distler, w/up, litho tin, dapper monkey w/top hat driving open car, 6", VG, A $550.00
Monkey Drummer, Schuco, w/up, tin w/felt outfit, 4½", EX, A $110.00
Monkey Drummer w/Bell, Gunthermann, w/up, pnt tin, plink-plunk music, 9", EX $1,000.00
Monkey on Whale Fishing, see Fishing Monkey on Whale
Monkey Riding Bull & Playing Violin, w/up, pnt tin, 6½", EX (rstr), A $675.00
Monkey Walking Upright, Gunthermann, w/up, pnt tin, yel jacket, red pants & bl hat, 7", EX (rstr), A $275.00
Motodrill Clown, Schuco, w/up, litho tin w/felt hat & jacket, 5" L, EX, A $250.00
Motorcycle, see also Friendly Motorcycle
Motorcycle Racer, Schuco #1012, w/up, litho tin, 5" L, VG.. $150.00
Mounted Cavalryman w/Cannon, TPS, w/up, litho tin w/2 wooden wheels, 5", NM+IB, A $300.00
Mr Cragstan (Cragstan's The Man), Daiya, w/up, tin & plastic, 6½", NMIB $225.00
Mr Dan the Hot Dog Eating Man, TN, 1960s, w/up, litho tin w/vinyl head, 7", NM+IB $150.00
Mr Lucky, Marusan, w/up, figure in cloth outfit & vinyl head standing at gaming table sipping martini, 10", NMIB $200.00
Mr Machine, Ideal, w/up, mc plastic, VGIB $200.00

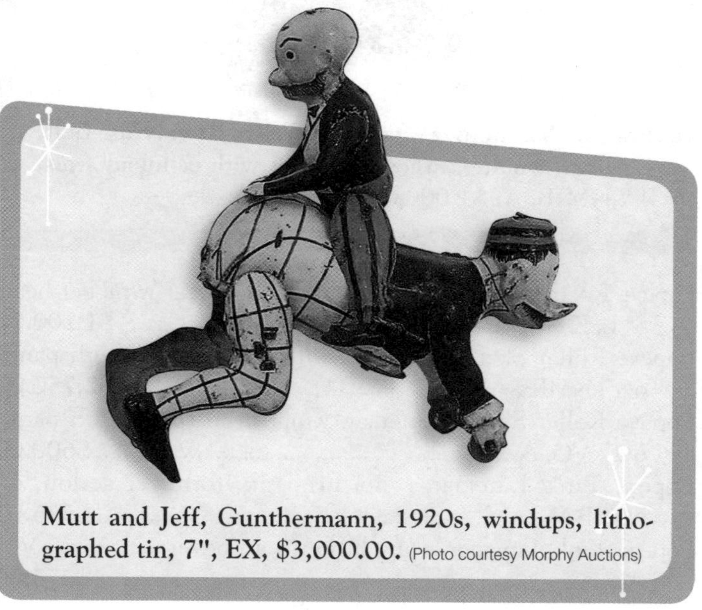
Mutt and Jeff, Gunthermann, 1920s, windups, lithographed tin, 7", EX, $3,000.00. (Photo courtesy Morphy Auctions)

Musical Chimp, Alps, w/up, plush, 6", EXIB $50.00
Musician (Violinist), Gunthermann, w/up, pnt tin, street performer in top hat standing on beveled base, 8½", rpnt, A $700.00
Musician (Violinist), Martin/France, w/up, cloth-dressed figure in top hat standing playing violin, no base, 8", EX+..... $450.00
Musician & Dancer on Base, Gunthermann, 1880s, w/up, musical, pnt tin, 8½" L, VG, A $1,000.00
Musicians, see also Black Musicians or Clown Musicians
Musicians (2) & Ballerina, Gunthermann, w/up, pnt tin, beveled base, plink-plunk music, 9" L, rpnt, A $1,045.00
Mutt & Jeff, Gunthermann, ca 1925, w/up, tin, Mutt riding backwards on Jeff's back while he crawls, 7", EX.. $3,000.00
Mysterious Ball, Martin, pull-string activated w/up, girl in ball atop spiral on base, 13½", VG+, A $1,375.00
Olive Oyl Ballet Dancer, Linemar, friction, litho tin, 5½", EX+ (VG box), A $900.00
Olive Oyl Pop-Up w/Squeaker, Linemar, push down & she squeaks, standing w/parasol, cloth dress, 7", NMIB, A $1,335.00
Olive Oyl Roadster, Linemar, friction, litho tin, 8" L, EX+, A ..$925.00

Oliver Hardy Sparkler, Isla, 1920s, lithographed tin, articulated, 9", very rare, VG, A, $1,100.00. (Photo courtesy Morphy Auctions)

Operation Air Lift, Automatic Toy Co, w/up, tin & plastic, 10" H, NMIB, A $150.00
Orange Vendor, Martin, w/up, litho & pnt tin, cloth-clothed blk vendor at front of 4-wheeled cart, 7½" L, EX, A .. $1,050.00
Organ Grinder, French, w/up, litho tin w/pnt compo head, metal hands/feet, cloth outfit, plink-plink music, 10", EX .. $1,650.00
Panama Pile Driver, Wolverine, 1905, marble weights cause pile driver to raise or lower, tin, 17", EX $200.00
Peacock, Ebo/Germany, w/up, litho tin, 9" L, EX, A $350.00
Percy Penguin, Nomura, friction, litho tin, 5", NMIB, A .. $250.00
Peter Rabbit Chick Mobile, Lionel, prewar, #1107, track variation w/flanges, VG, A $325.00
Peter Rabbit Chick Mobile, Lionel, prewar, 9" L, VGIB, A.. $725.00
Piano Player, Martin, w/up, cloth-dressed figure w/wig seated at piano on base, EX, A $1,200.00
Pig Violinist, Borgfeldt, w/up, celluloid, 4", VG, A $150.00

Pigeon Scooter, Marusan, friction, litho tin w/celluloid windshield, 6", EX+IB $950.00
Pinocchio (Walking Walt Disney's), Linemar, w/up, litho tin, 6", NM+IB, A $725.00
Pinocchio Musical Carousel, French, w/up, tin carousel w/swings on chains above compo figure on wood base, 14", VG....... $350.00
Pioneer Spirit, Alps, friction, litho tin, 11", EX+IB, A .. $150.00
Pirate w/Pegleg, Japan, 1950s, w/up, tin w/plastic arms, raises telescope & opens eye, 7", NM, A $125.00

Playland Sky Bus Ride, Yone, 1950s, windup, lithographed tin, 6½", NMIB, A, $135.00.

Pluto (Begging Rollover), Linemar, w/up, flocked tin w/rubber nose, 7" L, EXIB........ $225.00
Pluto (Playful), Linemar, w/up, litho tin, jtd legs, 6" L, NMIB, A........ $750.00
Pluto (Playful), Linemar, w/up, litho tin, jtd legs, 6" L, VG+, A........ $300.00
Pluto Acrobat, Linemar, w/up, celluloid figure on wire apparatus, 9", EXIB (box reads 'Gym-Toys Acrobat') $400.00
Pluto Convertible, Linemar, friction, tin, 6" L, EX, A.... $275.00
Pluto Drum Major, Linemar, w/up, litho tin, w/whistle in mouth, bell & cane in hands, 6½", EX $400.00
Pluto on Tricycle w/Revolving Bell, Linemar, w/up, tin & celluloid, 4" H, NMIB, A $475.00

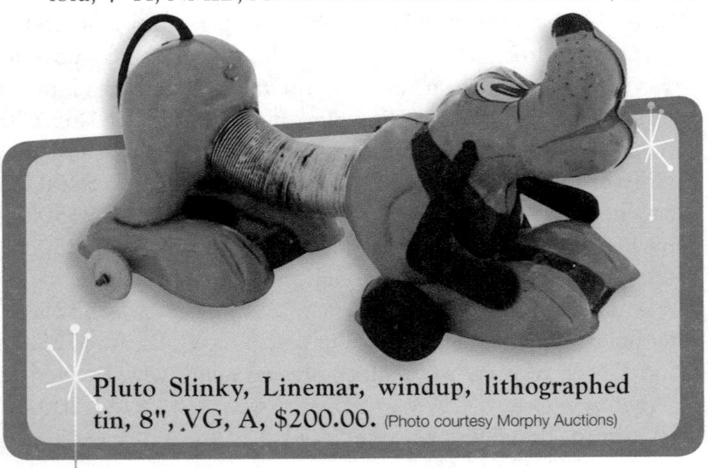
Pluto Slinky, Linemar, windup, lithographed tin, 8", VG, A, $200.00. (Photo courtesy Morphy Auctions)

Police Man, Japan, w/up, litho tin, directs traffic w/whistle in mouth, 6½", EX $225.00
Police Motocycle, Gunthermann, w/up, tin litho, 7", EX+, A $2,280.00
Pool Player, Gunthermann, w/up, litho/pnt tin, figure w/que at end of table, 7½" L, EX, A........ $715.00
Pool Players, American, w/up, litho tin, 2 players at ea end of table, 14" L, VG+, A $300.00
Popeye, Japan/KFS, w/up, celluloid, head w/pipe in mouth lifts when activated, articulated arms, 9", EXIB, A $825.00
Popeye & Mean Man, Linemar, w/up, celluloid figures on wheeled apparatus, 6", NMIB, A........ $3,000.00
Popeye & Olive Oyle Nodders, Linemar, w/up, litho tin figures, hopping & nodding action, 4½" ea, EX, A, pr...... $2,090.00
Popeye Cyclist, Linemar, w/up, litho tin, cloth pants, 7", EX+IB, A $1,450.00
Popeye Cyclist, Linemar, w/up, litho tin, cloth pants, 7", VG, A........ $450.00
Popeye in Airplane #7, Linemar, w/up, litho tin, Popeye's head in helmet w/pipe in mouth, 8", EX, A........ $1,430.00
Popeye in Rowboat, Hoge, w/up, PS, VG, A $2,200.00

Popeye Mechanical Tricycle With Revolving Bell, Linemar, windup, lithographed tin with celluloid arms, 4", NMIB, A, $1,000.00. (Photo courtesy Morphy Auctions)

Popeye Roadster, Linemar, friction, litho tin car w/rubber head, 8" L, EX+ $1,200.00
Popeye Roller Skater, Linemar, w/up, litho tin w/cloth pants, 6½", NMIB, A $2,750.00
Popeye Roller Skater, Linemar, w/up, litho tin w/cloth pants, 6½", VG, A $600.00
Popeye Tank, Linemar, w/up, litho tin, turnover action, 4", NMIB, A........ $525.00
Popeye Tank, Linemar, w/up, litho tin, turnover action, 4", VG, A $275.00

Popeye the Basketball Player, Linemar, windup, lithographed tin, 9", NMIB, A, $1,550.00. (Photo courtesy James D. Julia, Inc.)

Popeye Tumbler, Linemar, w/up, litho tin, 4", EX........... $525.00
Popeye Unicyclist, Linemar, w/up, litho tin w/cloth pants, 5½", EX $1,200.00

Powerful Katrinkar Holding Jimmy, Nifty, windup, lithographed tin, 6", EX, A, $1,900.00. (Photo courtesy Morphy Auctions)

Powerful Katrinka Holding Jimmy, Nifty, w/up, litho tin, 6", G, A $900.00
Powerful Katrinka Pushing Jimmy in Wheelbarrow, Nifty, w/up, litho tin, 6", EX.. $1,780.00
Punch (Punch & Judy) Walking Figure, Gunthermann, w/up, pnt w/cloth costume, lead feet, bell on hat, 9", VG+, A $3,850.00
P51 Airplane, Yoshiya, friction, litho tin w/dog chasing rabbit graphics, NMIB, A $250.00
Quick Draw McGraw (In His Friciton Car), Linemar, litho tin, 9", EXIB, A $1,600.00
Quick Draw McGraw/Huckleberry Aeroplane w/Yogi Bear Pilot, Linemar, friction, litho tin, 9" WS, EXIB, A........ $1,500.00
Rabbit & Bear Playing Ball, Japan, w/up, litho tin, 18½" L, EXIB $225.00
Range Rider, Yonezawa, w/up, litho tin, cowboy on rocking horse, 6", NMIB, A... $250.00
Rap & Tap in a Friendly Scrap, Unique Art, w/up, litho tin, 2 boxers in ring, 5½" H, EX.. $400.00
Rioter, Modern Toy Laboratory/Japan, w/up, tin & celluloid Popeye-type figure w/cloth sailor outfit, EXIB, A........... $660.00
Riverboat w/2 Circling Airplanes, Paya, w/up, litho tin, VG, A $525.00
Rocky (Fred Flintstone Look-Alike), Japan, w/up, litho tin, 4", EXIB.. $150.00
Rodeo Joe Crazy Car, Unique Art, w/up, litho tin, 7½" L, EXIB, A $400.00
Rodeo Joe Crazy Car, Unique Art, w/up, litho tin, 7½" L, NM, A $175.00
Rollin Rufus, Germany, w/up, blk porter atop split barrel, 7½", EX+IB, A $1,750.00
Rollover Pluto, see Pluto (Begging Rollover)

Roosters Fighting, Nifty, windup, lithographed tin, 10", EX, $500.00. (Photo courtesy Morphy Auctions)

Roulette Man, JF, 1950s, w/up, tin, 10", unused, MIB $200.00
Roundabout, Doll, w/up, pnt tin, hexagonal base supports 6 gondolas & riders, flag atop, 13", EX, A....................... $825.00
Rubber-Neck Willie the Clown, w/up, celluloid figure w/hands in pockets, stretches neck as he wobbles, 8", VG+ $55.00
Rudy the Ostrich, Nifty, w/up, litho tin, 9", EX............. $450.00
Run Horse, T, w/up, pnt wood Kobe toy, cowyboy on wheeled horse, 8", EX+IB, A $175.00
Safety First, Distler, w/up, litho tin beveled base w/traffic & figures around gas station, 8½" sq, G+IB, A................ $500.00
Sail Away, Unique Art, lever action, litho tin, 9", VG, A ...$115.00
Sambo (Monkey Playing Ukulele on Stump), Alps, w/up, 9½", NM+IB, A $225.00
Santa Fe Stage Coach, Frankonia, friction, litho tin stage coach w/plastic horses, 11½", MIB, A $150.00
School Master, Kellerman, w/up, teacher at blackboard & students at desks on sq base, 6" sq, VG+, A............ $1,850.00
Sea Lion, German, w/up, litho tin, w/ruffled clown hat, 6" L, EX...$450.00
Seal & Monkey w/Fish, TPS/Cragstan, w/up, litho tin, monkey on back of seal dangles fish, 8", NMIB, A................ $300.00
See America First Bus, see All State Express Bus

Sharpshooter, Alps, w/up, celluloid soldier figure w/rifle on belly, 8½" L, NM+IB, A $175.00
Shy-Anne Indian (Indian Chief), Linemar/WDP, w/up, litho tin w/ rubber hands, nose & arrowhead, cloth outfit, 6", EX..... $300.00
Silver Streak (Super Electric Locomotive), Masudaya, friction, litho tin, 17½", NM+IB........ $325.00
Singing Warbler, Japan, w/up, litho tin bird w/realistic detail, 5", EXIB........ $175.00
Skiing Duck, Linemar, w/up, litho tin, 4", NMIB, A...... $275.00
Skip Rope Animals, TPS, w/up, litho tin, 8½" L, NMIB, A. $200.00
Sky Rangers, Unique Art, w/up, litho tin, 10" H, EXIB, A... $350.00
Sli Slope, Wolverine, litho tin & paperboard, skier on 4 wheels goes down slope, G $125.00
Smiling Sam the Carnival Man, Alps, w/up, litho tin w/cloth outfit, 9", EX $125.00
Smiling Sam the Carnival Man, Alps, w/up, litho tin w/cloth outfit, 9", NM+IB $300.00
Snapping Alligator (w/Leaping Fish in His Mouth), Cragstan, w/up, litho tin, 12" L, VG+IB $100.00
Snookums, Germany, w/up, pnt tin figure, 6½", EXIB, A .. $825.00
Spiral Speedway, Automatic Toy, w/up, 2 4" buses travel speedway, NMIB $200.00

Spirit of Saint Louis With Pilot, Schuco, friction, lithographed tin, 4", EX, A, $850.00. (Photo courtesy Morphy Auctions)

Strolling Traveler, West German, w/up, litho tin w/litho paper legs, man carrying suitcase, 4½", VG+ $600.00
Strutting Parade, Alps, rabbit taking pictures, w/up, plush w/ cloth outfit, plastic camera, 8", EXIB $125.00
Sumo Wrestlers in Ring, Japan, air-bulb activated, celluloid & cb, 5½" H, NM+ $275.00
Sunny Andy Kiddie Campers, Wolverine, 1920s, litho tin, Scout camping scene w/marbles rolling down shoot, 14" L, EXIB $350.00
Sunny Andy Merry-Go-Round, Wolverine, spring-loaded action, litho tin, chrome center tower, 12x11" dia, EX+IB .. $300.00
Super Electric Locomotive, see Silver Streak
Superman M-25 Rollover Tank, Linemar, w/up, litho tin, 4" L, EX $450.00
Sweeping Mammy, see Black Americana category
Swimmer 'B,' Kuramochi, w/up, tin/celluloid, NMIB, A .. $100.00

Ta-Ra-Ra-Bumm Clown Car, Eberl, w/up, litho tin, car w/driver & 2 passengers, 7" L, VG, A........ $3,300.00
Taxi, Bing, w/up, early flat top 4-door, yel w/blk top, hood & running boards, 8", NM, A $2,500.00
Thirsty Monkey, TN, w/up, plush w/vinyl face, 6", EXIB... $100.00
Thirsty Rabbit, Alps, w/up, plush w/cloth outfit, 8", VGIB ..$75.00
Three Little Pigs Acrobat, Japan, prewar, w/up, 3 celluloid figures on wire apparatus, 10", MIB $600.00
Three Little Pigs Bank, Schuco, w/up, felt-covered pig standing beating on tin drum, NM, A $500.00
Tiger, Descamps Tiger
Time Is Money Clock/Bank (Child Clock), Marusan, w/up, tin tower clock w/2 celluloid birds, 8", EX+IB, A $225.00
Tom (Tom & Jerry) Twirling Figure, Ahi, 1967, w/up, vinyl, NMIB........ $75.00

Tom and Dick Hand Car, Excelo, windup, lithographed tin, 5", NMIB, A, $85.00. (Photo courtesy serioustoyz.com)

Toonerville Trolley, Dent, w/up, litho tin, 7" L, NMIB, A .. $1,430.00
Toonerville Trolley, Nifty, w/up, litho tin, 7", EX, A...... $800.00
Toonerville Trolley, Nifty, w/up, tin, 7", NM+IB......... $1,250.00
Topsy Turvy Clown Car #13, Eberl, w/up, litho tin, 10", VG, A $1,100.00
Topsy Turvy Clown Car #13, Eberl, w/up, litho tin, 10" L, NMIB, A $3,850.00
Touchdown Chimp, Technofix, w/up, litho tin chimp w/celluloid ball, 4½" H, NMIB, A $350.00
Touchdown Pete, Linemar, w/up, litho tin, football player bends up & down at waist in running motion, 5½", EX, A....... $275.00
Traffic Cop, TN, w/up, litho tin figure in bl uniform w/wht gloves, whistle in mouth, 6½", EX, A $100.00
Trans-World Flyer, West Germany, w/up, litho tin, 6x12", EX+IB, A $330.00
Trapeze Artist, Germany, w/up, pnt tin, 10½" H, G, A .. $330.00
Traveller, Alps, w/up, plush monkey in cloth outfit w/camera, 6", EXIB........ $175.00
Twirling Tail Mickey Mouse, see Mickey Mouse (Twirling Tail)
Typist, Kanto, w/up, litho tin, 5½", EX $100.00

Uncle Wiggily's Crazy Car, Germany, 1920s, windup, lithographed tin, 9½", EX, A, $2,500.00. (Photo courtesy Morphy Auctions)

Unique Artie, Unique Art, w/up, litho tin, clown in crazy car, 7" L, EX+ $325.00
Unique Artie, Unique Art, w/up, litho tin, clown in crazy car, 7" L, EXIB $450.00
Uran (Astro Boy's Sister), Tada/TPS, w/up, tin & vinyl w/cloth dress, bounces ball, 5½", very scarce, NMIB, A $2,230.00
Vacationland Express, Linemar, w/up, litho tin, 5½" sq, NM+IB, A $185.00
Violinist, see Musician (Violinist)
Wagon 'Fantasyland,' TPS, w/up, litho tin, Beetle pulls leaf w/2 squirrels & monkey driver, 12" L, NM+IB, A $230.00
Walt Disney's Mechanical Tricycle w/Revolving Bell, see specific character
Wandering Chimpanzee, Japan, w/up, plush w/vinyl face, hands & feet, 5", EXIB $125.00
Western Ranger, Kokyu, w/up, litho tin w/rubber tail, ranger on horse w/gun drawn, 5", EXIB, A $150.00
Whip (The), Germany, w/up, litho tin amusement ride toy on 9" sq beveled base, EX+IB $2,800.00
Whoopie Plane, w/up, litho tin, wht w/red & bl details, 9½" WS, VG $250.00
Willie the Clown, see Rubber-Neck Willie the Clown
Wimpy's Mechanical Tricycle, Linemar, w/up, litho tin, 4" L, EXIB, A $1,430.00
Woman (Elderly) w/Basket & Folded Umbrella, Gunthermann, w/up, pnt tin, rocks back & forth, 6", EX+ $500.00
Wonder Cyclist, see Boy on Tricycle
Wonder MG Car, Marusan, w/up, litho tin, w/driver & passenger under umbrella, runs back & forth across bridge, 12", EXIB $375.00
Xylophone Player, Linemar, w/up, hefty clown w/articulated arms, 5", G $325.00
Yogi Bear Go-Kart, Linemar, 1961, friciton, tin w/vinyl head, 6", EX+ $175.00
Zig-Zag Chap, Ferguson Novelty, 1920s, cloth-dressed figure w/ como head & hands, lead feet, 9½", NMIB $1,350.00
Zilotone Player, Wolverine, w/up, litho tin, complete w/disks, 7½" L, EX, A $750.00
Zilotone Player, Wolverine, w/up, litho tin, complete w/disks, 7½" L, G+ $475.00

Wyandotte

Wyandotte produced toys mostly of heavy gauge steel with a few being tin or plastic. The following listings are of vehicles and related toys from the 1920s to the 1960s. All are steel unless noted otherwise.

See also Aeronautical; Boats; Character, TV, and Movie Collectibles; Guns; Windup, Friction, and Other Mechanical Toys.

Airflow Coupe, 1930s, 5½", friction, G+ $100.00
Allied Van Lines, 1950s, 24", 14-wheeled, Chiefton Lines on door, aluminum trailer w/advertising, VG $75.00
Ambulance, 1930s, 6", streamline styling w/'Ambulance' imprinted on top, EX+ $375.00
Ambulance, 1940s, 11", wht w/red decals, NP grille, blk-pnt wooden wheels, rear door opens, EX $200.00
Ambulance, 1950s, 9", plastic w/friction motor, wht w/red lettering & cross symbol, VG $25.00
Amusement Park, 12x16", VG, A $275.00
Army Supply Corps No 42 Truck, 1940s, 18", 4-wheeled, w/cloth cover, EX+ $125.00

Army Supply Corps No 42 Truck, 1940s, 18", EX, A, $130.00. (Photo courtesy Randy Inman Auctions)

Auto Pulling Leisure Trailer, 1930s, 24" overall, VG, A .. $850.00
Auto Transport, 1950s, 09", 6-wheeled, #455, VG+ $65.00
Auto Transport, 1950s, 23", 8-wheeled, sq-nose cab, EXIB .. $150.00
Automatic Loading Dump Truck, 1950s, 15", 4-wheeled, front loader, NM+ $225.00
Automobile Society Tow Truck, 1950s, 10", 4-wheeled, blk & yel checked band, VG $150.00
Car-A-Van Automobile Transport, 1950s, 22", 8-wheeled, EX $125.00
Cargo Lines Motor Transport Fleet Semi, 1950s, 26", 6-wheeled, EX $150.00
Circus Cage Truck, 10½", VG $400.00

Circus Cage Truck Pulling Cage Trailer, Greatest Show on Earth, two paper animals, 20" overall, EX, A, $880.00. (Photo courtesy Noel Barrett Antiques and Auctions, Ltd.)

City Airport, 1940s, litho tin, 2 hangars & runway on sq base, b/o light tower, 4 PS airplanes, EX, A $660.00
Coal Truck, 1950s, 11", 4-wheeled, whole truck slants forward, VG $65.00
Construction Endloader & Dump Trailer, 1950s, 21", 4-wheeled, EX+ $50.00
Construction Set, 1940s, dump truck, sand hopper & steam shovel, about 10" ea, EX $110.00
Construction Supply Co Stake Truck, 1950s, 23", 14-wheeled, EX $175.00
Cord Convertible, 1930s, 13", NP hood trim, BRT, EX, A ..$935.00
Cord Coupe, 13", w/up, BRT, wooden hubs, VG $275.00
Coupe, 8", electric lights, gr w/blk running boards, WRT w/tread, EX, A $440.00
Delivery Truck, 1930s, 6", 4-wheeled, slanted bed sides, EX .. $175.00
Dept of Streets Cleaning Truck, 1930s, 11", 4-wheeled, silver tone, blk wooden wheels w/red hubs, EX+, A $390.00
Ducky Waddles, 1950s, 9" L, litho tin, EX $75.00
Dump Truck, 1930s, 7", 4-wheeled, WRT, slanted bed sides, VG $60.00
Dump Truck, 1930s, 12", 4-wheeled, MDW, slanted bed sides, EX+ $200.00
Dump Truck, 1930s, 15", 4-wheeled, WRT, slanted bed sides, EX+ $300.00
Dump Truck, 1930s, 15", 4-wheeled, WRT, slanted bed sides, G $165.00
Dump Truck, 1930s, 15", 6-wheeled, MDW, slanted bed sides, EX+ $275.00
Dump Truck, 1940s, 11", 6-wheeled, V-shaped side-dump bed, EX $125.00
Dump Truck, 1940s, 12", 4-wheeled, cab slants forward, slanted bed sides, cab wheels covered, EX $125.00
Dump Truck, 1950s, 10", 4-wheeled, open back, front wheels covered, blk & yel check, EX $125.00
Dump Truck, 1950s, 11", 4-wheeled, high dump bed w/tailgate, front wheeles covered, blk & yel check, EX $125.00
Dump Truck, 1950s, 11", 4-wheeled, snub-nose plastic cab, DUMP on side of bed, EX $100.00
Dump Truck, 1950s, 12", 4-wheeled, cab slants forward w/covered wheels, slanted bed sides, VG+ $65.00
Dump Truck, 1950s, 12", 4-wheeled, front loader, slanted open back, G $30.00
Dump Truck, 1950s, 13", front loader, straight-sided bed w/tailgate, front wheels covered, EX $150.00
Dump Truck, 1950s, 13", 4-wheeled, sq nose, straight-sided bed w/tailgate, all wheels covered, G $65.00
Dump Truck, 1950s, 17", 4-wheeled, short-nose w/grille & bumper, straight sides w/tailgate, EX $85.00
Dump Truck, 1950s, 17", 6-wheeled, rnd-nose cab w/covered wheels, oblong bed w/side dump, NM $175.00
Dump Truck, 1950s, 20", 6-wheeled, short nose cab w/grille & bumper, V-shaped bed w/side dump action, NM...... $175.00
Dump Truck, 1960s, 22", 4-wheeled, long-nosed sq cab, straight-sided bed w/tailgate, EX $75.00
Dump Truck, 1960s, 22", 6-wheeled, hydraulic, long-nosed sq cab, straight-sided bed w/tailgate, VG $65.00
Easter Bunny Delivery, 9½", litho tin, bunny on cycle w/3-wheeled sidecart, EX+, A $300.00
Emergency Auto Service Tow Truck, 1950s, 15", 4-wheeled, plastic cab, boom w/2 wheels, NM $200.00
Express Co Stake Truck, 1940s, 22", 6-wheeled, U-shaped stake trailer, EX $85.00
Express Service Delivery Truck, 1950s, 10", 4-wheeled, snub-nose cab w/covered wheels, EXIB $300.00
Express Service Delivery Truck, 1950s, 10", 4-wheeled, snub-nose cab w/covered wheels, VG $100.00
Express Service Delivery Truck, 1950s, 10", 4-wheeled, snub-nose cab w/covered wheels, VG+ $100.00
Fire Dept #5 Truck, 1950s, 10", 4-wheeled, EX $100.00
Fire Engine Co No 1, 1950s, 24", 6-wheeled, NM $250.00
Fire Engine Co No 4, 1940s, 12", 4-wheeled, long nose, red w/yel & gr trim, EX $150.00
Fire Engine Co No 4, 1950s, 12", 4-wheeled, cab slants forward, red w/yel trim, EX $100.00
Fire Engine Co No 10, 1940s, 18", 4-wheeled, EX.......... $125.00
Fire Hook & Ladder No 1, 20", 6-wheeled, plastic cab, EX ... $100.00
Fire Hook & Ladder No 10, 23", crank-op ladder, VG+, A ... $350.00
Flash Strat-O-Wagon, 6", litho tin, EXIB $175.00
Flatbed Truck, 1950s, 13", 4-wheeled, all wheels covered, EX ..$75.00

Garage (two car), 4x5", EX, A, $200.00. (Photo courtesy Randy Inman Auctions)

Garage w/Auto, 5½", gr w/red lithoed roof, VG, A $110.00
Gardner's Truck No 121, 10", 4-wheeled, NM+IB.......... $510.00
Gas Pumps, 1930s, 9", steel & glass, crank-op, 1 w/dome top & 1 w/ribbed flat top, NM, ea $450.00
Giant Construction Co Dump Truck, 1950s, 19", 6-wheeled, VG+ $125.00
Grader (Power Charger), 1950s, 18", enclosed cab, orange, EX $30.00
Great Plains Cattle Ranch Stake Truck, 1950s, 23", 6-wheeled, NM $150.00
Green Valley Stock Ranch Stake Truck, 1950s, 17", 6-wheeled, NM $150.00
Grey Van Lines Semi, 1950s, 24½", 14-wheeled, VG..... $150.00
High-Lift Loader, 1950s, 15", orange, VG $25.00
Igloo Ice Co Truck, 1950s, 10", 4-wheeled, EX+ $150.00
Jiffy Painting/Decorating Truck, 1950s, 10", 4-wheeled, w/ladders, EX $125.00
Log Truck, 1950s, 10", 4-wheeled, yel & blk checks, EX+ ...$125.00
Log Truck, 1950s, 26", 14-wheeled, open-framed trailer w/logs, VG $75.00
Lowboy Machinery Re-Hauler, 1940s, 22", 6-wheeled, 4 cab wheels covered, open trailer wheels, G+ $75.00

Mobile Artillery Flatbed Truck, 1950s, 13", 4-wheeled, mk 'USA 5' on door, all wheels covered, EX+ $75.00
Moto-Fix Towcar, 1950s, 15", 4-wheeled, VG, A $125.00
Motor Bus, 1930s, 6", 4-wheeled, all wheels covered, chrome grille & bumper, NM $425.00
Motor Fleet Hauling Service Dump Truck, 1950s, 17", 6-wheeled, side-dump, VG $100.00
Motor Freight Lines Semi, 1950s, 23", 14-wheeled, U-shaped trailer w/open back, EX+ $225.00
Nation-Wide Air Rail Service Delivery Van, 1950s, 11", 4-wheeled, plastic cab, G+ $100.00
North American Van Lines Semi, 14", 6-wheeled, long-nose cab w/covered wheels, red, yel & blk, NM $175.00
Official Service Car Tow Truck, 1940s, 13", cab slants forward, front wheels covered, G+ $55.00
Parcel Service (Anywhere Anytime), 1950s, 9½", 4-wheeled, cab wheels covered, G+ $35.00
Pickway Projects Building Co Dump Truck, 1950s, 17", 6-wheeled, side dump action, G $55.00
Racer, 8½", 'World's Fair' decal, b/o lights, pontoon wheel covers, WRT, EX.... $425.00
Railway Express Agency Delivery Truck, 1940s, 12", 4-wheeled, 'Wyandotte Toys Good & Safe,' VG+ $125.00
Railway Express Agency Delivery Truck, 1950s, 6½", 4-wheeled, 'Wyandotte For Boys & Girls,' EX $100.00
Roadster, 9", Deco style w/fin-like covered wheels, b/o lights, WRT, VG+ $150.00
Roadster, 13", wht top w/lt bl body, NP trim, BRT, red hubs, Fair+.... $300.00
Sand Truck #443, 1950s, 13", 4-wheeled, whole truck slants forward, front loader, VG.... $110.00
Sedan, 9", litho tin tires, NM, A $500.00
Semi, 1950s, 17", 6-wheeled, rnd nose cab, front wheels covered, streamlined trailer, EX.... $130.00
Shady Glenn Stock Ranch Cattle Truck, 1950s, 6-wheeled, 17", EX+ $150.00
Sit & Ride Truck, 16", flatbed truck w/high seat & steer stick, EX.... $375.00
Soap Box Derby #226 Racer, 6", tin w/wooden wheels, EX, A. $225.00
Stake Truck, 1930s, 6", 4-wheeled, straight nose w/chrome grille & bumper, front wheeles covered, EX....$90.00
Stake Truck, 1950s, 16", 4-wheeled, cab wheels covered, VG.... $100.00
Stake Truck (All Purpose), 1950s, 9", 8-wheeled, U-shaped trailer w/tailgate, cab wheels covered, EX....$35.00
Sunshine Dairy Wagon (Early Bird Milk Wagon & Horse), 1950s, 8", plastic, NMIB....$30.00
Super Service Garage, 9x9", litho tin, EX.... $250.00
Tank Truck, 17", 4-wheeled, early long nose w/covered streamline wheels, VG, A $390.00
Tank Truck, 1930s, 9", 4-wheeled, chrome grille & bumper, covered wheels, NM+ $375.00
Tow Truck, 1950s, 10", 4-wheeled, snub-nose cab w/lithoed grille & bumper, front wheels covered, VG $55.00
Tow Truck, 1950s, 14", 4-wheeled, rnd-nose cab, cab wheels covered, NM.... $250.00
Tow Truck, 1950s, 15", 4-wheeled, short-nosed cab w/grille & bumper, open wheels, rstr $65.00
Towing Service Nite/Day Tow Truck, 1950s, 9½", 4-wheeled, cab wheels covered, NM $250.00
Towing Service Tow Truck, 1950s, 15", 4-wheeled, 2-wheeled boom, NM.... $425.00

Toy Town Delivery Wagon, doors open, 21", EX, A, $300.00. (Photo courtesy Randy Inman Auctions)

Toy Town Fire Dept, 6½x8", litho tin, w/plastic fire truck, VG+.... $50.00
Toy Town Ice Co Truck, 1940s, 12", 4-wheeled, cab slants forward, cab wheels covered, G+ $75.00
Transmobile Jr, 1950s, 13", 6-wheeled, complete, VG....$75.00
Truck w/3 Trailers, 1930w, 24" overall, box van, tanker & side dumper, VG $175.00
Turn Pike Semi, 1950s, 15", 6-wheeled, rnd-nose cab w/streamline trailer, EX.... $150.00
Valley Farms Livestock Produce Stake Truck, 1950s, 8½", 6-wheeled, plastic cab, EX $75.00
Wagon, 1940s, 12", U-shaped back, streamline wheel covers, wooden pull hdl, EX $65.00
Wagon, 1940s, 5½", gr w/pk wheel covers, EX....$75.00
Woody Convertible, 12½", top goes up & down, lithoed detail, VG+ $250.00
Wrecker & Service Truck, 1950s, 6", 4-wheeled, all wheels covered, VG $110.00
Wrecker Car, 1950s, 13", 4-wheeled, cab slants forward, wooden wheels, G+ $75.00
Wyandotte #7 Racer, 8", lithoed detail, G $25.00
Wyandotte Construction Co Dump Truck, 1940s, 21", 4-wheeled, G $100.00
Wyandotte Construction Co Dump Truck, 1950s, 17", 6-wheeled, side-dump action, NM.... $325.00
Wyandotte Construction Co Hopper, 1950s, 10" H, EX ...$50.00
Wyandotte Construction Co Semi & Steam Shovel, 1950s, 23", 6-wheeled, VG+ $150.00
Wyandotte Construction Co Semi & Steam Shovel, 1950s, 25", 12-wheeled, rstr $100.00
Wyandotte Construction Co Stake Truck, 1950s, 23", 14-wheeled, NM+.... $375.00
Wyandotte Express Co Stake Truck, 1950s, 17", 6-wheeled, curved trailer, EX.... $175.00
Wyandotte Truck Lines/Construction Semi, 1950s, 23", 6-wheeled, VG $75.00
Wyandotte Van Lines, 1940s, 6-wheeled, whole truck slants forward, VG.... $125.00
Wyandotte Van Lines, 1950s, 15", plastic cab, EX+ $200.00
Wyandotte Van Lines Coast to Coast Truck, 1940s, 8", 6-wheeled, cab wheels covered, NM $225.00
Wyndot (sic) Package Delivery Truck, 1950s, 12", 4-wheeled, all wheels covered, G....$50.00

Directory of Advisors and Contributors

In this section we have listed dealers, authors, specialists, and collectors who have contributed photographs, served as our advisors, or in any other way assisted us in preparing this guide. (See also Clubs, Newsletters, and Other Publications, as some of our advisors who represent a club or a publication are listed in that section.) This is a complimentary service; none of these people are under any obligation to answer questions. Some may have the time to respond to you; others may not. If you write to them, please include an SASE. Your phone number and/or your e-mail address may expedite a response as well.

Matt and Lisa Adams
Tatonka Toys
8155 Brooks Dr.
Jacksonville, FL 32244
904-772-6911
matadams@bellsouth.net
Bubble bath containers including foreign issues, nodders, character collectibles, character bobbin' head nodders, and Dr. Dolittle

Stan and Sally Alekna
732 Aspen Lane
Lebanon, PA 17042-9073
717-228-2361
fax: 717-228-2362
Soldiers: Barclay, Manoil, Grey Iron, other Dimestore soldiers and accessories, also Syroco figures

Bob Armstrong
Worcester, MA 01609
508-799-0644
raahna@oldpuzzles.com
www.oldpuzzles.com
Puzzles: wood jigsaw type, from before 1950

Richard Belyski
P.O. Box 14956
Surfside Beach, SC 29587
peznews@juno.com
www.pezcollectorsnews.com
Pez candy dispensers

Bojo
P.O. Box 1403
Cranberry Township, PA 16066-0403
phone/fax: 724-776-0621
bojo@zbzoom.net
Buying and selling old and new Beatles memorabilia; one piece or collection; also dolls, rock 'n roll personalities

Felicia Browell
123 Hooks Lane
Cannonsburg, PA 15317
fbrowell@nauticom.net
Breyer horses and other animals; author of book, order direct

Bill Campbell
Kirschner Medical Corp.
1221 Littlebrook Lane
Birmingham, AL 35235
205-853-8227
fax: 205-853-9951
acamp10720@aol.com
Character clocks and watches, also radio premiums and decoders, P-38 airplane-related items from World War II, Captain Marvel and Hoppy items, Lone Ranger books with jackets, selected old comic books, toys, and cap guns; buys and sells Hoppy and Roy items

Joel J. Cohen
Cohen Books and Collectibles
P.O. Box 810310
Boca Raton, FL 33481-0403
561-487-7888
fax: 561-487-3117
disneyana@disneycohen.com
www.disneycohen.com
Disney, books, animation art

Cotswold Collectibles
P.O. Box 716
Freeland, WA 98249
877-404-5637 (toll free)
fax: 360-331-5344
www.elitebrigade.com
GI Joe, also diecast and Star Wars

Marl Davidson
Marl & B Inc.
10301 Braden Run
Bradenton, FL 34202
941-751-6275
fax: 941-751-5463
www.marlbe.com
Barbie dolls; wanted: Bob Mackie dolls as well as vintage Barbie dolls; buying and selling circa 1959 dolls to present issues

Dawn Diaz
20460 Samual Dr.
Saugus, CA 91350-3812
661-263-TOYS (8697)
jamdiaz99@earthlink.net
Liddle Kiddles and other small dolls from the late 1960s and early 1970s

Ron and Donna Donnell
Saturday Heroes
15847 Edwardian Dr.
Northport, AL 35475
Early Disney, Gone With the Wind, Western heroes, premiums, and other related collectibles

Marcia Fanta
Marcia's Fantasy
4275 33rd St. SE
Tappen, ND 58487-9411
701-327-4441
tofantas@bektel.com
Ad dolls, Barbie and other Mattel dolls, premiums, character memorabilia, modern dolls, related items

Mike and Kurt Fredericks
145 Bayline Circle
Folsom, CA 95630-8077
916-985-7986
Plastic figures and playsets, also GI Joe, Star Trek, and dinosaurs

Gary's Trains
186 Pine Springs Camp Road
Boswell, PA 15531
814-629-9277
gtrains@floodcity.net
Trains: Lionel, American Flyer, and Plasticville

Gasoline Alley Antiques
Keith Schneider, Proprietor
Liz Cormier, Manager
6501 20th NE
Seattle, WA 98115
206-524-1606
fax: 206-524-6343
www.gasolinealleyantiques.com
Model kits, diecast scale models, character collectibles, sports memorabilia, nostalgia

Bill Hamburg
Happy Memories Collectibles
P.O. Box 536
6023 Lubao Ave.
Woodland Hills, CA 91367
818-346-0251
WHamburg@aol.com

Guns, especially cap guns
George Hardy
Charlottesville, VA 22901
804-295-4863
fax: 804-295-4898
georgeh@comet.net
www.comet.net/personal/georgeh/
Building blocks and construction toys, especially Anchor Stone Building Blocks by Richter

Dan Iannotti
212 W. Hickory Grove Rd.
Bloomfield Hills, MI 48302-1127S
248-335-5042
modernbanks@prodigy.net
Modern mechanical banks: Reynolds, Sandman Designs, James Capron, Book of Knowledge, Richards, Wilton; sales lists available

Terri Ivers
Terri's Toys & Nostalgia
114 Whitworth Ave.
Ponca City, OK 74601
580-762-8697
toylady@cableone.net
Lunch boxes, Halloween, also any and all character collectibles, and Hartland figures

David Kolodny-Nagy
Toy Hell
P.O. Box 75271
Los Angeles, CA 90075
toyhell@yahoo.com
www.toyhell.com
Specializing in Transformers, Robotech, Shogun Warriors, Gadaikins, and any other robot; want to buy these MIP — also selling

Tom Lastrapes
6050 86th Ave.
Pinellas Park, FL 33782
727-230-0801
tomlas1@fastmail.fm
Battery-operated toys

Michael and Polly McQuillen
McQuillen's Collectibles
P.O. Box 50022
Indianapolis, IN 46250-0022
317-845-1721
michael@politicalparade.com
www.politicalparade.com
Political toys, also pin-back buttons

Judith A. Mosholder
186 Pine Springs Camp Road
Boswell, PA 15531
814-629-9277
jlytwins@floodcity.net
Dollhouse furniture: Renwal, Ideal, Marx, etc.

Peter Muldavin
173 W 78th St., Apt. 5-F
New York, NY 10024
212-362-9606
kiddie78s@aol.com
http://members.aol.com/kiddie78s/
Records: 78 rpm children's records and picture disks; buys, sells, and trades records as well as makes cassette recordings for a small fee

Gary Pollastro
5160 Mercer Way
Mercer Island, WA, 89040-5128
206-232-3199
Slot cars and model racing from the '60s – '70s, especially complete sets in original boxes

Judy Posner
P.O. Box 2194
Englewood, FL 34295
judyposner@yahoo.com
judyposner.com
Character-related pottery, china, ceramics, salt and pepper shakers, cookie jars, tea sets, and children's china with special interest in Black Americana and Disneyana

John Rammacher
Son's a Poppin' Ranch
1610 Park Ave.
Orange City, FL 32763-8869
386-775-2891
sonsapoppin@earthlink.net
www.sonsapoppin.com
Ertl banks, farm toys, trucks, and construction toys

Cindy Sabulis
P.O. Box 642
Shelton, CT 06484
203-926-0176
toys4two@snet.net
www.dollsntoys.com
Author of *Collector's Guide to Dolls of the 1960s and 1970s* (Collector Books); co-author of *Collector's Guide to Tammy, the Ideal Teen,* (Collector Books); specializes in dolls from the 1960s – 1970s, including Liddle Kiddles, Barbie, Tammy, Tressy, etc

Scott Smiles
157 Yacht Club Way, Apt. #112
Hypoluxo, FL 33462-6048
561-582-6016
stsmiles@bellsouth.net
Windups, also friction and battery-operated; fast food displays
Antique Toy Information Service: Send SASE, good photos (35mm preferred), and $9.95 per toy

Steve Stephenson
11117 NE 164th Pl.
Bothell, WA 98011-4003
425-488-2603
fax: 425-488-2841
Hot Wheels

Nate Stoller
960 Reynolds Ave.
Ripon, CA 95366
209-599-5933
multimotor@aol.com
www.maytagclub.com
Pedal cars, also specializing in Maytag collectibles

Stout Auctions
Greg Stout
11 West Third Street
Williamsport, IN 47993-1119
765-764-6901
fax: 765-764-1516
Trains of all types; holds cataloged auctions, seeking quality collections for consignment

Mark and Lynda Suozzi
P.O. Box 102
Ashfield, MA 01330
phone/fax: 413-628-3241 (9am to 5pm)
marklyn@valinet.com
www.marklynantiques.com
Paper lithograph toys, antique McLoughlin games, Bliss and Reed boats, toy wagons, Ten Pin sets, cube blocks, puzzles and Victorian doll houses. Buy and sell; lists available upon request. Mail order and shows only

Richard Trautwein
437 Dawson St.
Sault Ste. Marie, MI 49783
906-635-0356
rtraut@up.com
Character collectibles, especially tinplate toys and cars, battery-operated toys and toy trains, boats, and bicycles

Marci Van Ausdall
4532 Fertile Valley Road
Newport, WA 99156
509-292-1311
betsymcallfanclub@hotmail.com
Betsy McCall

Randy Welch
Raven'tiques
27965 Peach Orchard Rd.
Easton, MD 21601-8203
410-822-5441
Ramp walking figures, also mechanical sparklers and other plunger-type toys

whatacharacter.com
hugh@whatacharacter.com or
bazuin32@aol.com
Comic & cartoon character, television series

Larry White
108 Central St.
Rowley, MA 01969-1317
978-948-8187
larrydw@erols.com
Cracker Jack; author of *Cracker Jack Toys* and *Cracker Jack, The Unauthorized Guide to Advertising Collectibles*

Phoenix Toy Soldier Co.
Bob Wilson
8912 E. Pinnacle Peak Rd.
PMB 552
Scottsdale, AZ 85255
480-699-5005
877-269-6074 (toll free)
Plastic figures and playsets, especially Marx, but also figures from about 100 other old manufactuers; buying parts of playsets as well

Mary Young
Box 9244
Dayton, OH 45409
937-298-4838
Paper dolls; author of books

Clubs, Newsletters, and Other Publications

There are hundreds of clubs, newsletters, and magazines available to toy collectors today. Listed here are some devoted to specific areas of interest. You can obtain a copy of many newsletters simply by requesting a sample.

We will list other organizations and publications upon request. Please send your information to us by June 1.

A.C. Gilbert Heritage Society
1440 Whalley Ave. PMP 252
New Haven, CT 06515
www.acghs.org

Antique Advertising Association of America
Pastimes newsletter
P.O. Box 1121
Morton Grove, IL 60053
aaa@aol.com
subscription: $35

Antique Doll Collector
Keith and Donna Kaonis
6 Woodside Ave., Suite 300
Northport, NY 11768
631-261-4100 (daytime)
631-361-0982 (evenings)

Antique Trader
700 East State Street
Iola, WI 54990-001
robyn.austin@fwpubs.com
www.antiquetrader.com
subscription: $35 (52 issues)

Association of Game and Puzzle Collectors
197M Boston Post Road W.
Marlborough, MA 01752
membership: $35 per year (US); $45 (Canada and overseas)
www.agca.com

Barbie Bazaar
5711 Eighth Ave.
Kenosha, WI 53140
262-658-1004
fax: 262-658-0433
www.barbiebazzar.com
subscription: $25.95 (US); $38.95 (Canada); $58.95 (foreign) for 6 issues per year

Betsy's Fan Club (Betsy McCall)
P.O. Box 946
Quincy, CA 95971-0946
916-283-2770
dreams@psln.com
subscription: $16 per year (quarterly)

Beyond the Rainbow Collector's Exchange Exchange
P.O. Box 31672
St. Louis, MO 63131
314-217-2727
www.jgdb.com/mfaq4.htm

Beatlefan
PO Box 33515
Decatur, GA 30033
subscription: $25 (US) 6 issues; $32 (Canada/Mexico)
770-492-0444 (credit card order)
www.beatlefan.com

Big Little Times
Big Little Book Collectors Club of America
Larry Lowery
P.O. Box 1242
Danville, CA 94526
925-837-2086
www.biglittlebooks.com

Bojo
P.O. Box 1403
Cranberry Township, PA 16066-0403
724-776-0621 (9 am to 8 pm EST, phone or fax)
bojo@zbzoom.net
Issues fixed price catalog containing Beatles and Rock 'n Roll memorabilia; catalog: $3

Buckeye Marble Collectors Club
Brian Estepp (membership or shows)
2206 Mardi Court
Grove City, OH 43125
bthomas0725@woway.com
www.buckeymarble.com

Candy Container Collectors of America
The Candy Gram newsletter
Jim Olean, Membership Chairperson
115 Mac Beth Dr.
Lower Burrel, PA 15068-2628
lostincandyland2004@yahoo.com
or
Jeff Bradfield
90 Main St.
Dayton, VA 22821
www.candycontainer.org
membership: $25

Collector's Life
The world's foremost publication for Steiff enthusiasts
Beth Savino
P.O. Box 798
Holland, OH 43528
800-862-8697 (toll free)
fax: 419-531-2730
www.toystorenet.com

Cracker Jack Collectors Association and *Prize Insider Newsletter*
Deb Gunnerson (membership chairperson)
3225 Edward St. NE
St. Anthony, MN 55418
raegun@comcast.net
www.collectoronline.com/CJCA/
subscription/membership: $20 per year (single); $24 (family)

Doll Castle News
P.O. Box 247
Washington, NJ 07882
1-800-572-6607
fax: 908-689-6320
www.dollcastlenewsmagazine.com

Doll News
United Federation of Doll Clubs
10900 N. Pomona Ave.
Kansas City, MO 65153
816-891-7040
undcinfo@ufdc.org

The Fisher-Price Collector's Club
The Gabby Goose newsletter
Jacquie Hamblin
38 Main St.
Oneonta, NY 13820-2519 or
Donna Devaney
668 Mac Young Drive
Kincardine, ON, Canada N2Z1T1
gasper_b@bellsouth.net
www.fpclub.org
membership: $20 ($30 for first class mailing); $25 (international)

Friends of Hoppy club and *Hoppy Talk* newsletter
Laura Bates
6310 Friendship Dr.
New Concord, OH 43762-9708
LBates1205@cs.com
www.hopalong.com/home.asp
membership: $20 (4 newsletters and *free* ads)

Game Times
Gene Autry Star Telegram
Gene Autry Museum
P.O. Box 67
Gene Autry, OK 73436
580-294-3047 (museum information)
www.autry-museum.org

Hopalong Cassidy Fan Club International
Laura Bates
6310 Friendship Dr.
New Concord, OH 43762
LBates1250Acs.com
www.hopalong.com/home/asp
subscription: $20 (US) or $25 (overseas); includes quarterly newsletter and information on annual Cambridge, Ohio, festival

John's Collectible Toys and Gifts catalog
John DeCicco
14 Lodge St..
Worcester, MA 01604
800-505-8697

www.johns-toys-store.com/store
Order free catalog online

Little Kiddle Konvention
Paris Langford
415 Dodge Ave.
Jefferson, LA 70121
bbean415@aol.com
liddlekiddlenewsletter@yahoo.com
Or send SASE for information about Konvention; additional SASE for *Liddle Kiddle Newsletter* information

Lone Ranger Fan Club
P.O. Box 9561
Amarillo, TX 79105
806-373-3969
lonerangerfanclub@sbcglobal.net
www.lonerangerfanclub.com
Silver Bullet newsletter available with membership

Marble Mania
Marble Collectors Society of America (MCSA)
Stanley A. Block, Chairman
P.O. Box 222
Trumbull, CT 06611
blockglss@aol.com

Marl & B catalog (Barbie dolls)
Marl Davidson
10301 Braden Run
Bradenton, FL 34202
941-751-6275
fax: 941-751-5463
marlbe@aol.com
www.marlbe.com

McDonald's Collector Club
Joyce and Terry Losonsky
7506 Summer Leave Ln.
Columbia, MD 21046-2455
JoyceUSA@aol.com
Authors of several books on McDonald's Happy Meal collectibles

McDonald's Collector's Club (Florida Sunshine Chapter)
Bill and Pat Poe
220 Dominica Circle E.
Niceville, FL 32578-4085
850-897-4163
fax: 580-897-2606
BPOE220@Cox.net
membership: $15 (individual); $20 (family/couple); $25 (international)

Model and Toy Collector Magazine
P.O. Box 347240
Cleveland, OH 44134-9998
216-843-9522
fax: 216-843-9523
subscription: $20 (4 issues)

Promotional Collectors Glass Association
Marilyn Johnston, Treasurer
528 Oakley
Central Point, OR 97502
www.pgcablassclub.com
membership: $20 (1 year); $35 (2 years)

Toy Scouts, Inc.
137 Casterton Ave.
Akron, OH 44303
330-836-0668
fax: 330-869-8668
info@toyscouts.com
www.toyscouts.com

National Fantasy Fan Club (Disney)
Box 19212
Irvine, CA 92623-9212
Attention: CHAPTERS
714-731-4705
www.nffc.org
membership: $24 (US); $30 (Canada); $40 (foreign)
Includes newsletters, free ads, chapters, conventions, etc.

Paper Dolls
Golden Opportunities
Nan Moorehead
P.O. Box 252
Golden CO 80402
subscription: 4 issues for $24 US (sample copy $7); $26 Canada; $32 foreign

Pez Collector's News
Richard Belyski
P.O. Box 14956
Surfside Beach, SC 29587
info@pezcollectorsnews.com
www.pezcollectorsnews.com
www.MySpace4PezHeads.com

Playset Magazine
1240 Marlstone Place
Colorado Springs, CO, 80904
719-634-7430
playsetmagazine@aol.com
www.playsetmagazine.com
subscripton: $48.90 (first class); $38.90 (bulk rate)

The Prehistoric Times
Mike and Kurt Fredericks
145 Bayline Circle
Folsom, CA 95630-8077
916-985-7986 (before 5pm PST)
pretimes@comcast.net
www.prehistorictimes.com
subscription: $25 (4 issues; 3rd class); $30 (first class)

The Prize Insider Newsletter for Cracker Jack collectors
Deb Gunnerson, Membership Chairman
3325 Edward St. NE
St. Anthony, MN 55418
raegun@comcast.net
www.tias.com/mags/cjca
subscription: $20 (single); $24 (family)

The Puppet Collector's Newsletter
Steven Meltzer
1255 2nd St.
Santa Monica, CA 90401
310-656-0483
smpuppets@aol.com
www.puppetmagic.com

The Replica
Craig Purcell, Editor
Hwys 136 & 20
Dyersville, IA 52040
319-875-2000
www.toytractorshow.com/the_replica.htm
Free on-line newsletter
Marketing tool that previews upcoming diecast releases and articles of interest to collectors; included are Wm Britain pewter figures, Ertl diecast automotive replicas, and John Deere kits (Pre-School)

Schoenhut Collectors Club
Patricia J. Girbach
1003 W Huron St.
Ann Arbor, MI 48103-4217
734-662-6676 (phone and fax)
aawestie@provide.net
membership: $20 (single); $30 (family)

Snow Biz newsletter
Nancy McMichael
P.O. Box 53262
Washington, DC 20009
subscription; $10 (3 times a year)
Club has annual meeting and swap meet

Star Wars online guide
Geoffrey T. Carlton
www.StarWarsGuide.net
info@starWarsGuide.net
Author of *Star Wars Super Collector's Wish Book* (Collector Books)
Star Wars online newsletter

Brian's Toys, Inc.
W730 Hwy 35
Fountain City, WI 54629
608-687-7574
fax: 608-687-7573
sales@brianstoys.com
www.brianstoys.com (sign up for newsletter)

Still Bank Collectors Club of America
SBCCA Membership Chairman
440 Homestead Ave.
Metairie, LAl 70005
contact@stillbankclub.com
www.stillbankclub.com
membership: $35

Toynutz.com (online catalog)
Dana Johnson Enterprises
P.O. Box 1824
Bend, OR 97709-1824
541-318-7176 (24 hour message line)
toynutz@earthlink.net
www.toynutz.com

Toy Collector Club of America (SpecCast toys)
P.O. Box 368
Dyersville, IA 52040-0368
563-875-8706
fax: 563-875-8056
www.speccast.com

Toy Shop
P.O. Box 420235
Palm Coast, FL 32142
877-300-0245 (subscriptions)
715-445-2214 (editorial)
www.toyshopmag.com
subscription: $24.99 (12 issues)

Toy Soldier Collectors of America
Charles L. DuVal
P.O. Box 179
New Ellenton, SC 29809-0179
toysoldiercollectorsamerica@yahoo.com
www.toysoldiercollectors.homestead.com
membership: $10 (US and Canada)

Train Collectors Association/National Toy Museum
300 Paradise Lane or
P.O.Box 248
Strasburg, PA 17579-0248
717-687-8623 (business office)
717-687-8976 (Toy Museum)
fax: 717-687-0742
tca-office@traincollectors.org
www.traincollectors.org

Trick or Treat Trader
Pamela E. Apkarian-Russell & C.J. Russell
Halloween Queen Antiques
577 Boggs Run Road
Benwood, WV 26031-1002
304-233-1031
halloweenqueen@castlehalloween.com
subscription: $15 (4 issues); $20 (International)

Auction Houses

We would like to thank the following auction houses for letting us use their catalogs, online sources, and photographs in this guide. They have been an invaluable source for all 11 editions.

Bertoia Auction Gallery
2141 DeMarco Dr.
Vineland, NJ 08360
856-692-1881
fax: 856-692-8697
toys@bertoiaauctions.com
bertoiaauctions.com

James D. Julia, Inc.
P.O. Box 830
Rt. 201, Skowhagen Rd.
Fairfield, ME 04937
207-453-7125
fax: 207-453-2502
info@jamesdjulia.com
juliaauctions.com

LiveAuctioneers
liveauctioneers.com

McMasters Harris Auction Co.
P.O.Box 1755
5855 John Glenn Hwy
Cambridge, OH 43725
740-432-7400
800-842-3526
fax: 740-432-3191
info@mcmastersharris.com
mcmastersharris.com

Morphy Auctions
2000 N. Reading Rd.
Denver, PA 17517
717-335-3435
fax: 717-336-7115
morphyauctions.com

Noel Barrett Antiques and Auctions, Ltd.
P.O. Box 300
Carversville, PA 18913
215-297-5109
fax: 215-297-0457
toys@noelbarrett.com
noelbarrett.com

Randy Inman Auctions
P.O. Box 726
Waterville, ME 04903
207-872-6900
207-872-6966
info@inmanauctions.com
inmanauctions.com

Serious Toyz
82 Main Street
Cold Spring, NY 10516
866-OLD-TOYZ (653-8699)
fax: 914-827-9366
auctions@serioustoyz.com
serioustoyz.com

Smith House Toy & Auction Company
P.O. Box 129
Telford, PA 18969
215-721-1389
fax: 215-721-1503
auctions@smithhousetoys.com
smithhousetoys.com

Stout Auctions
529 State Route 28 East
Williamsport, IN 47932
765-764-6901
fax: 765-764-1515
info@stoutauctions.com
stoutauctions.com

Index